Skip·Beat!

Everybody, long time no see. I sincerely thank you from the bottom of my heart for picking up volume 31.
And I apologize that there are sections where my drawing ability just was not adequate enough.
—Yoshiki Nakamura

Skip·Beat!

Volume 31

CONTENTS

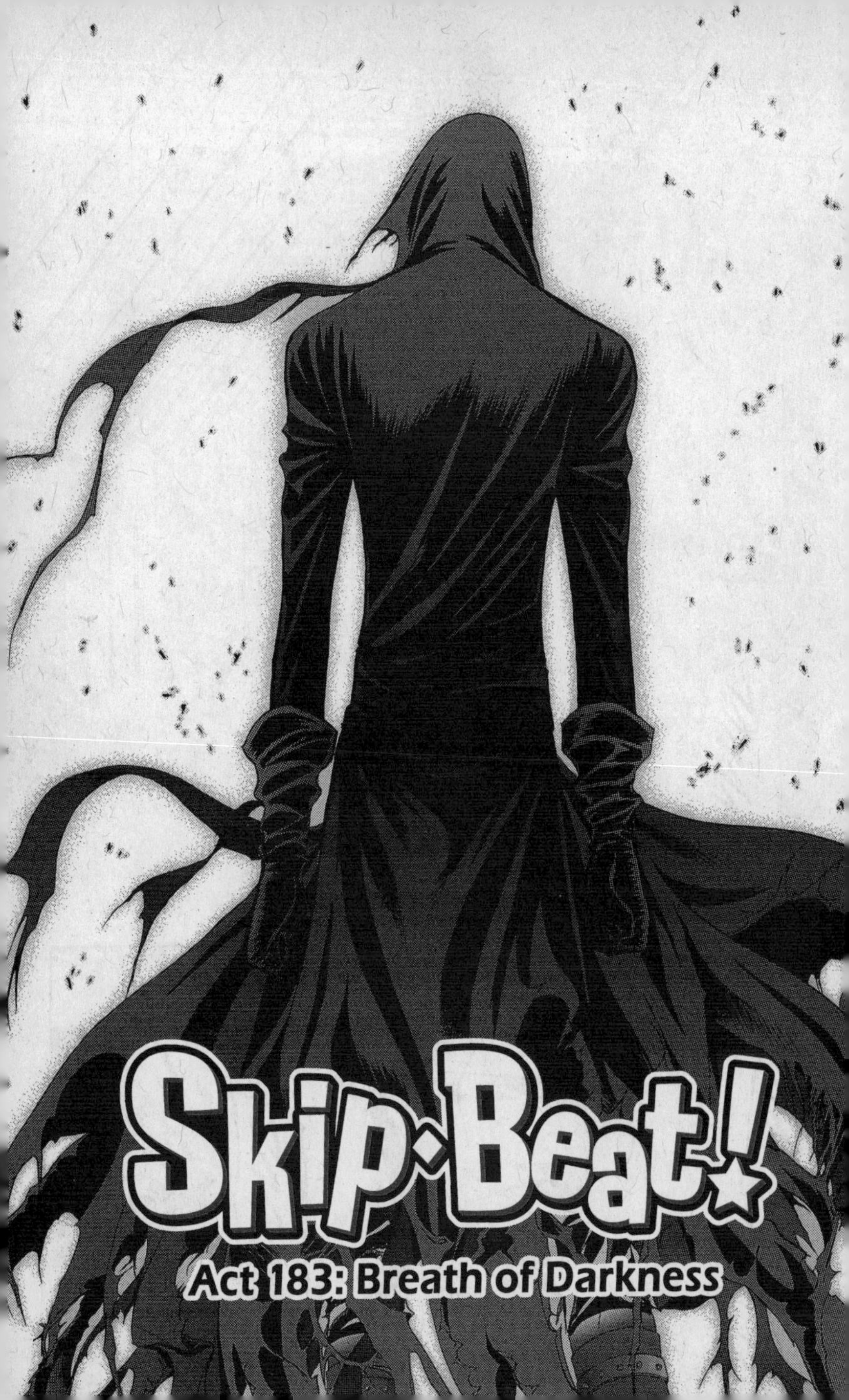
Skip·Beat!
Act 183: Breath of Darkness

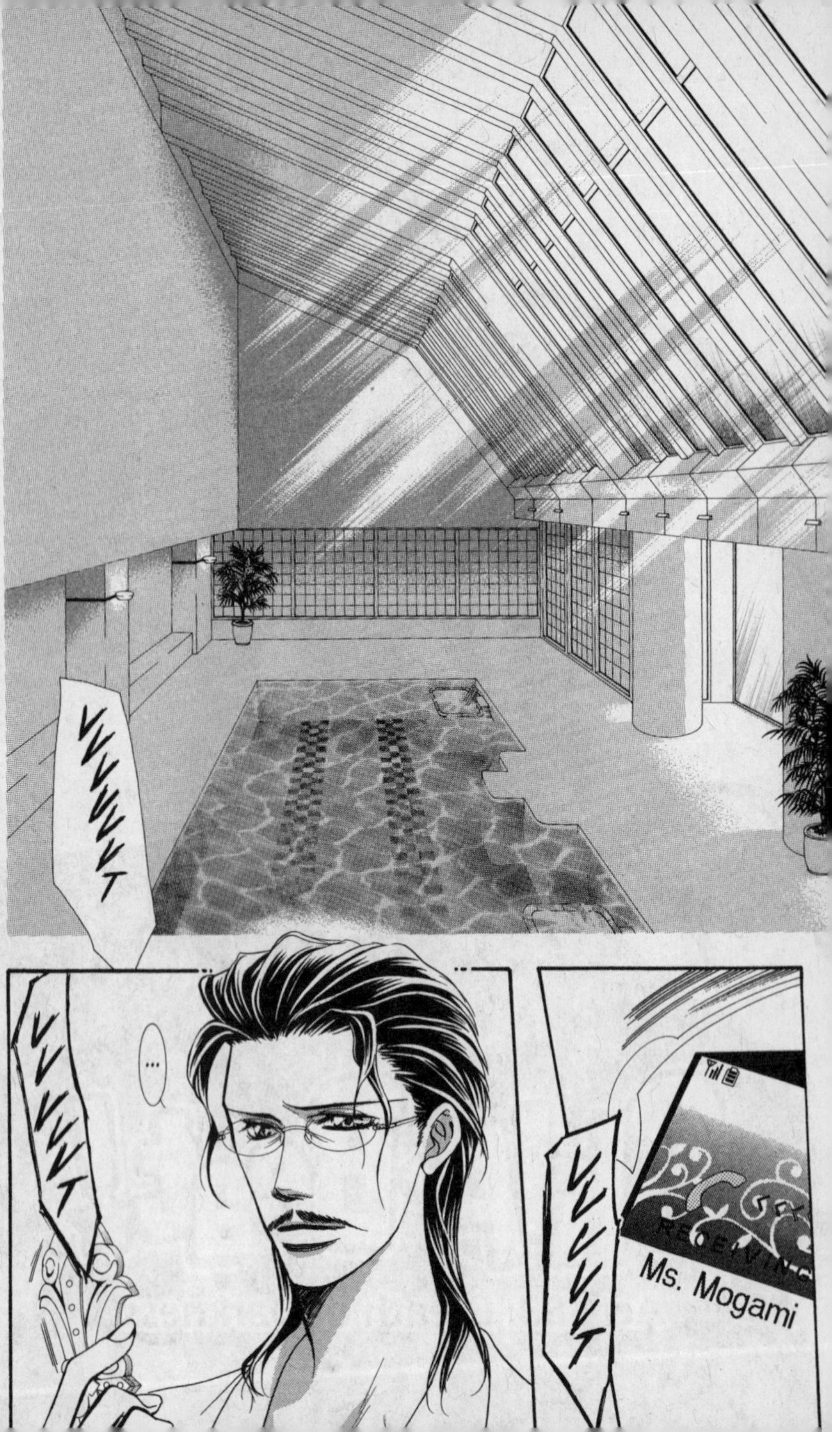
VVVVVVT
VVVVVT
RECEIVING
Ms. Mogami
VVVVVT
...

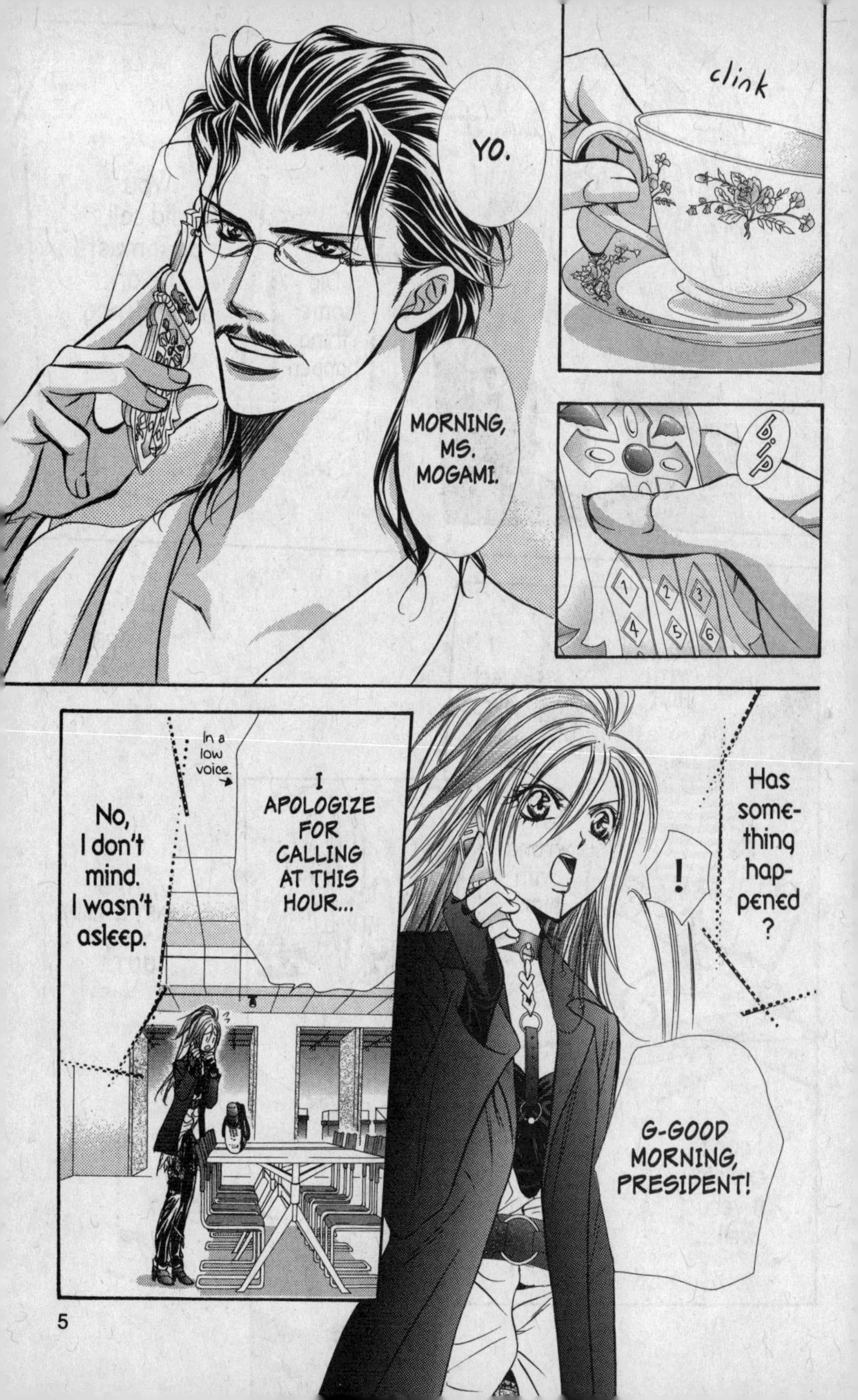
clink
bip
YO.
MORNING, MS. MOGAMI.
Has something happened?
!
G-GOOD MORNING, PRESIDENT!
I APOLOGIZE FOR CALLING AT THIS HOUR...
In a low voice.
No, I don't mind. I wasn't asleep.

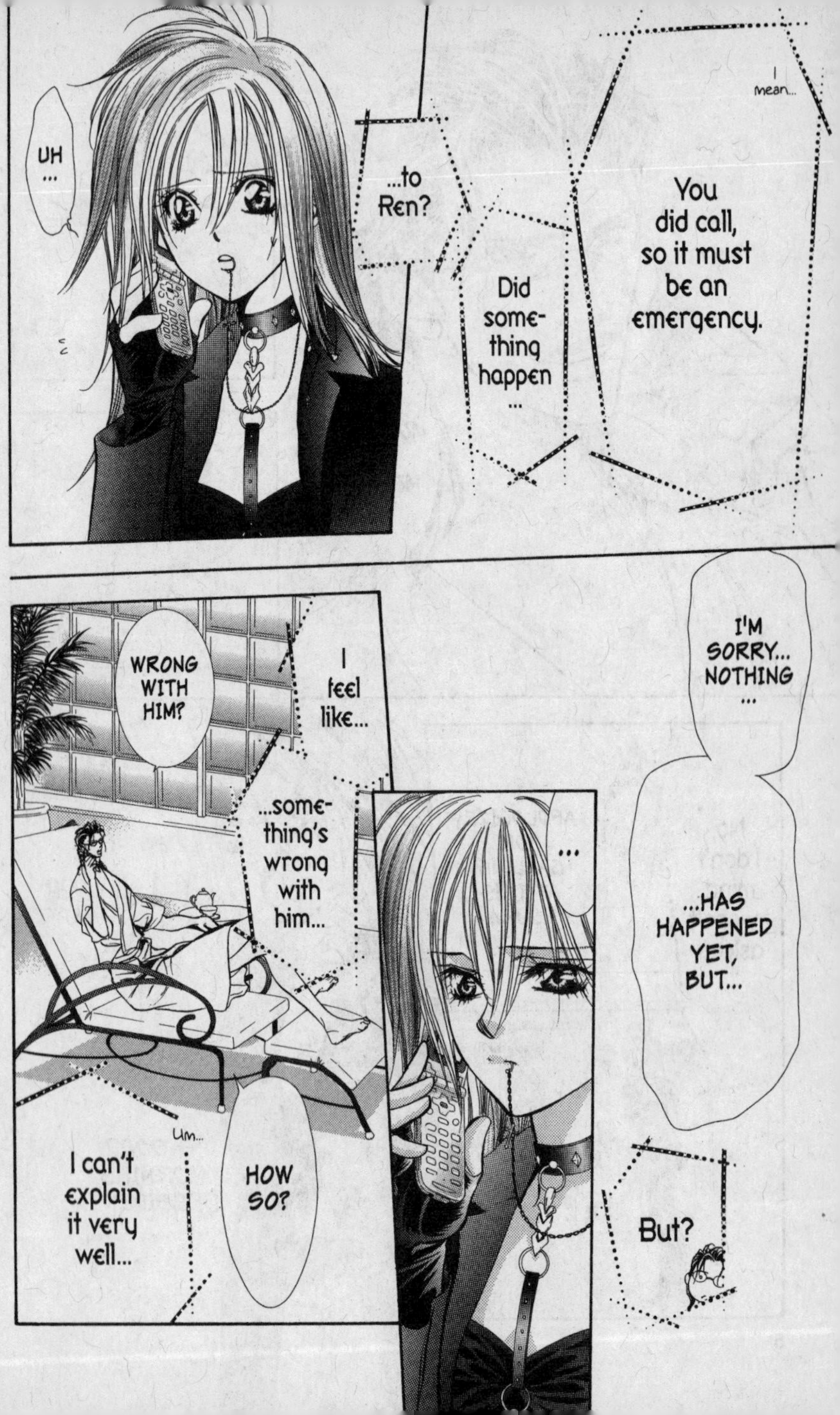

I mean...
You did call, so it must be an emergency.
Did some-thing happen...
...to Ren?
UH...
I'M SORRY... NOTHING...
...HAS HAPPENED YET, BUT...
But?
...
I feel like...
...some-thing's wrong with him...
WRONG WITH HIM?
HOW SO?
Um...
I can't explain it very well...

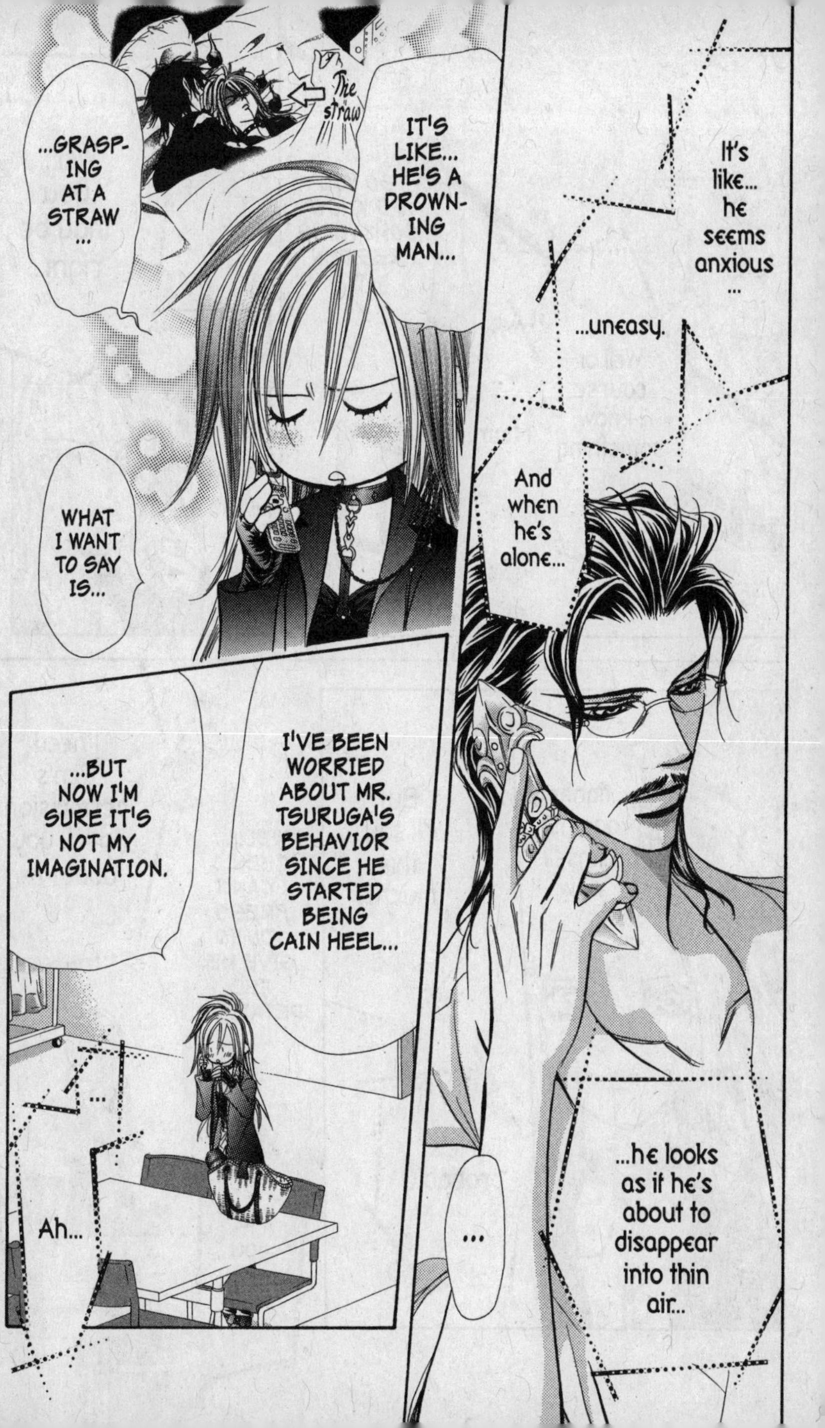
It's like... he seems anxious...
...uneasy.
And when he's alone...
...he looks as if he's about to disappear into thin air...
...
IT'S LIKE... HE'S A DROWNING MAN...
...GRASPING AT A STRAW...
The straw
WHAT I WANT TO SAY IS...
I'VE BEEN WORRIED ABOUT MR. TSURUGA'S BEHAVIOR SINCE HE STARTED BEING CAIN HEEL...
...BUT NOW I'M SURE IT'S NOT MY IMAGINATION.
...
Ah...

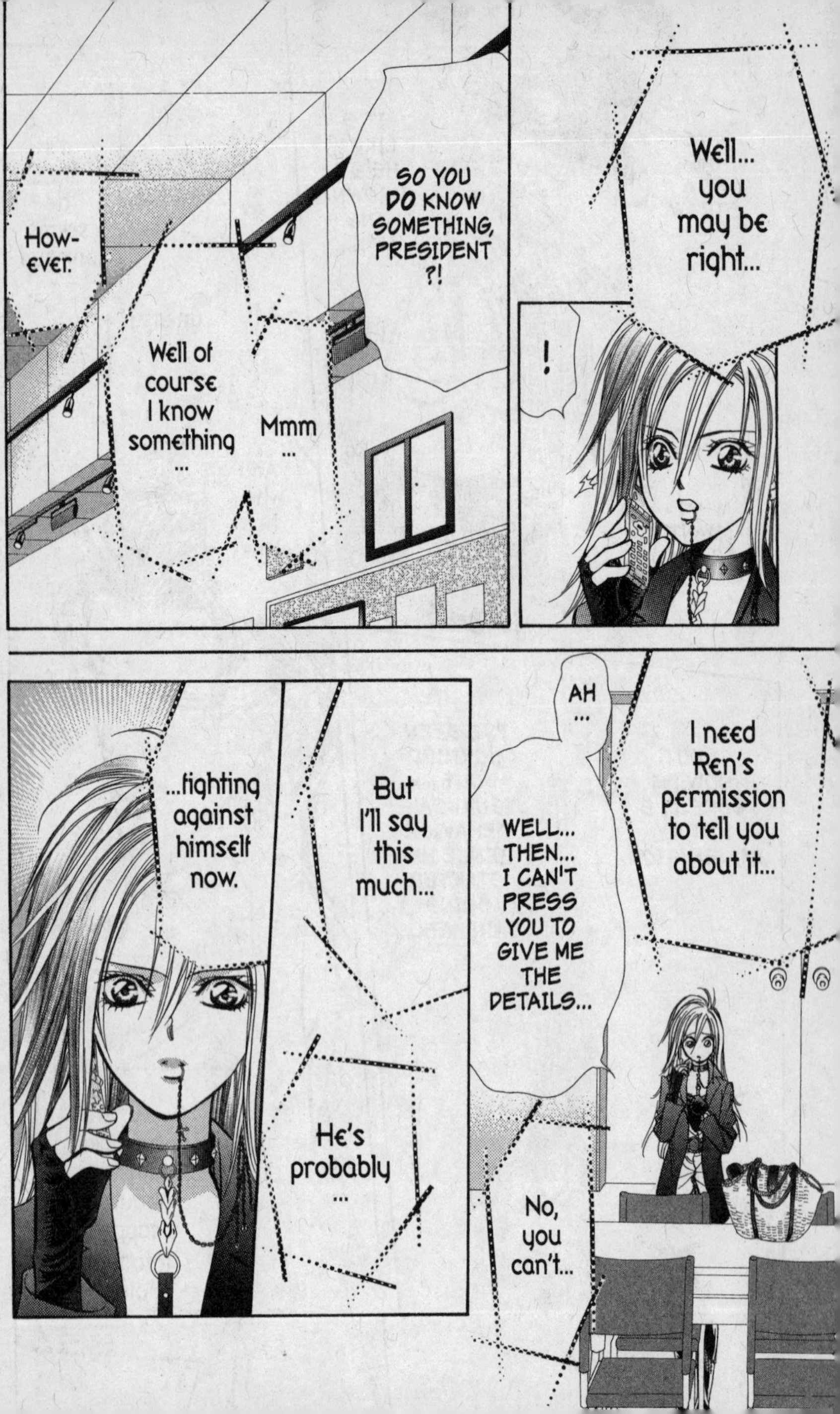
Well... you may be right...
!
SO YOU DO KNOW SOMETHING, PRESIDENT?!
Mmm...
Well of course I know something...
How-ever.
I need Ren's permission to tell you about it...
AH...
WELL... THEN... I CAN'T PRESS YOU TO GIVE ME THE DETAILS...
No, you can't...
But I'll say this much...
He's probably...
...fighting against himself now.

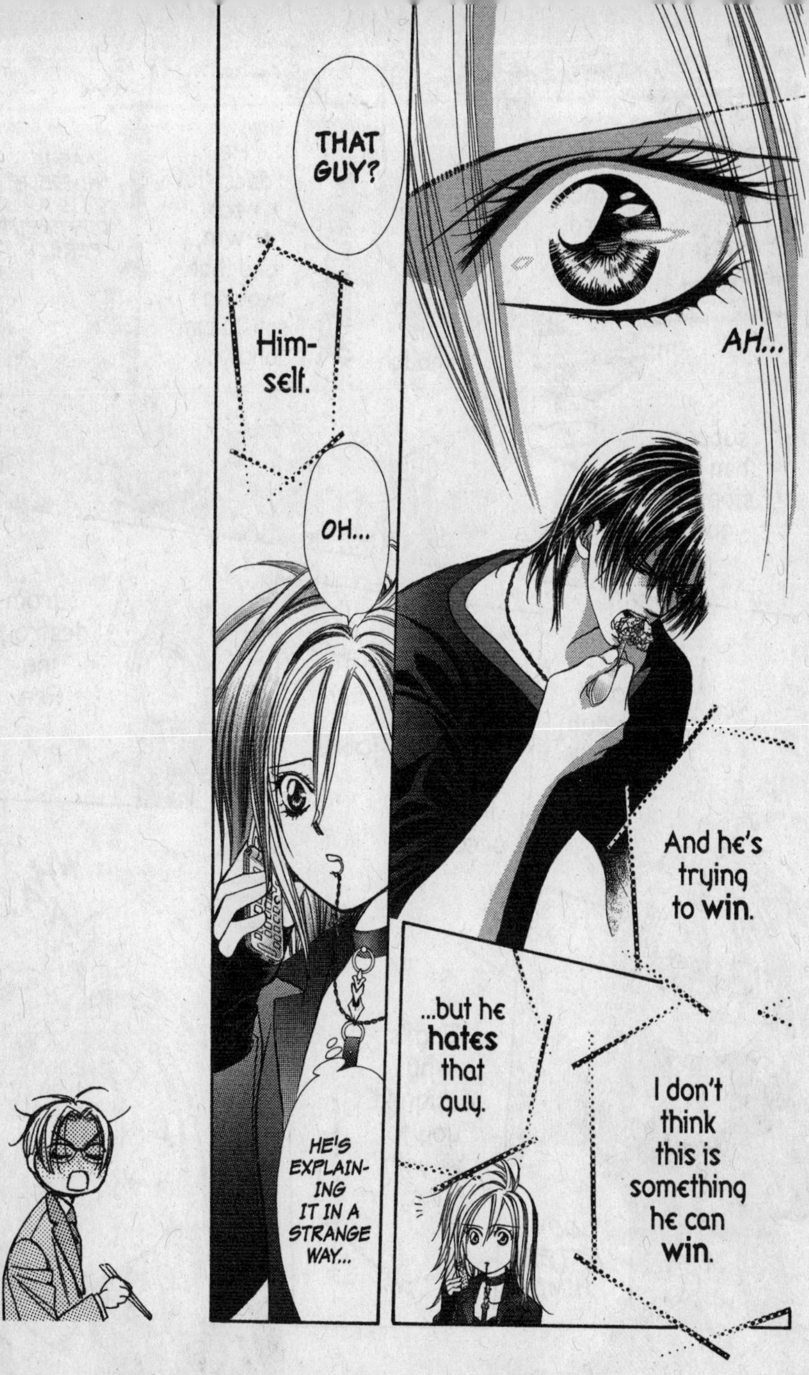
AH...
And he's trying to win.
I don't think this is something he can win.
...but he hates that guy.
THAT GUY?
Him-self.
OH...
HE'S EXPLAIN-ING IT IN A STRANGE WAY...

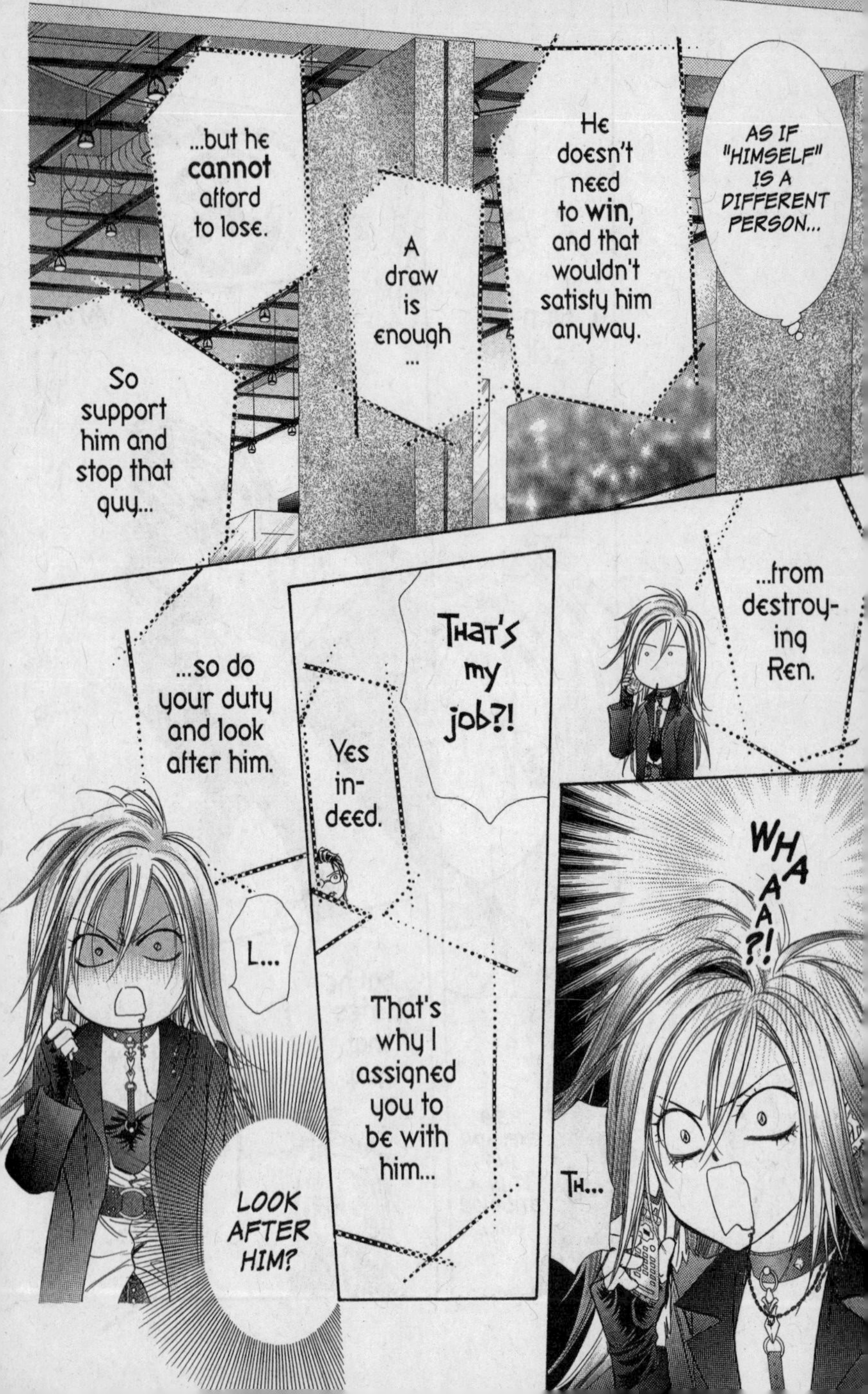
AS IF "HIMSELF" IS A DIFFERENT PERSON...
He doesn't need to win, and that wouldn't satisfy him anyway.
A draw is enough...
...but he cannot afford to lose.
So support him and stop that guy...
...from destroying Ren.
...so do your duty and look after him.
L...
LOOK AFTER HIM?
That's why I assigned you to be with him...
That's my job?!
Yes indeed.
Th...
WHAAAA?!

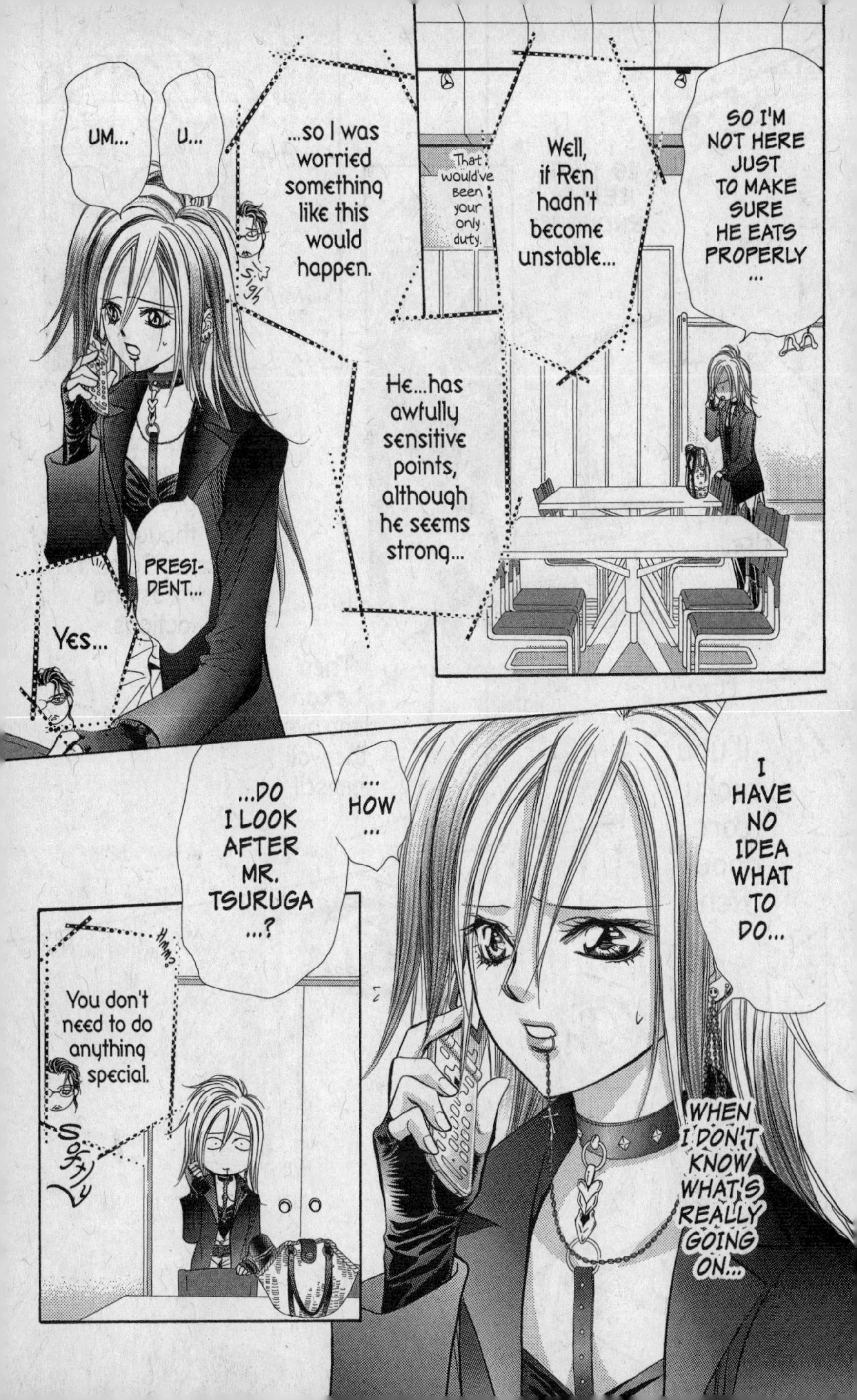
SO I'M NOT HERE JUST TO MAKE SURE HE EATS PROPERLY ...
Well, if Ren hadn't become unstable...
That would've Been your only duty.
...so I was worried something like this would happen.
U...
UM...
Sigh
He...has awfully sensitive points, although he seems strong...
PRESIDENT...
Yes...
I HAVE NO IDEA WHAT TO DO...
... HOW ...
...DO I LOOK AFTER MR. TSURUGA ...?
WHEN I DON'T KNOW WHAT'S REALLY GOING ON...
Hmm?
You don't need to do anything special.
Softly

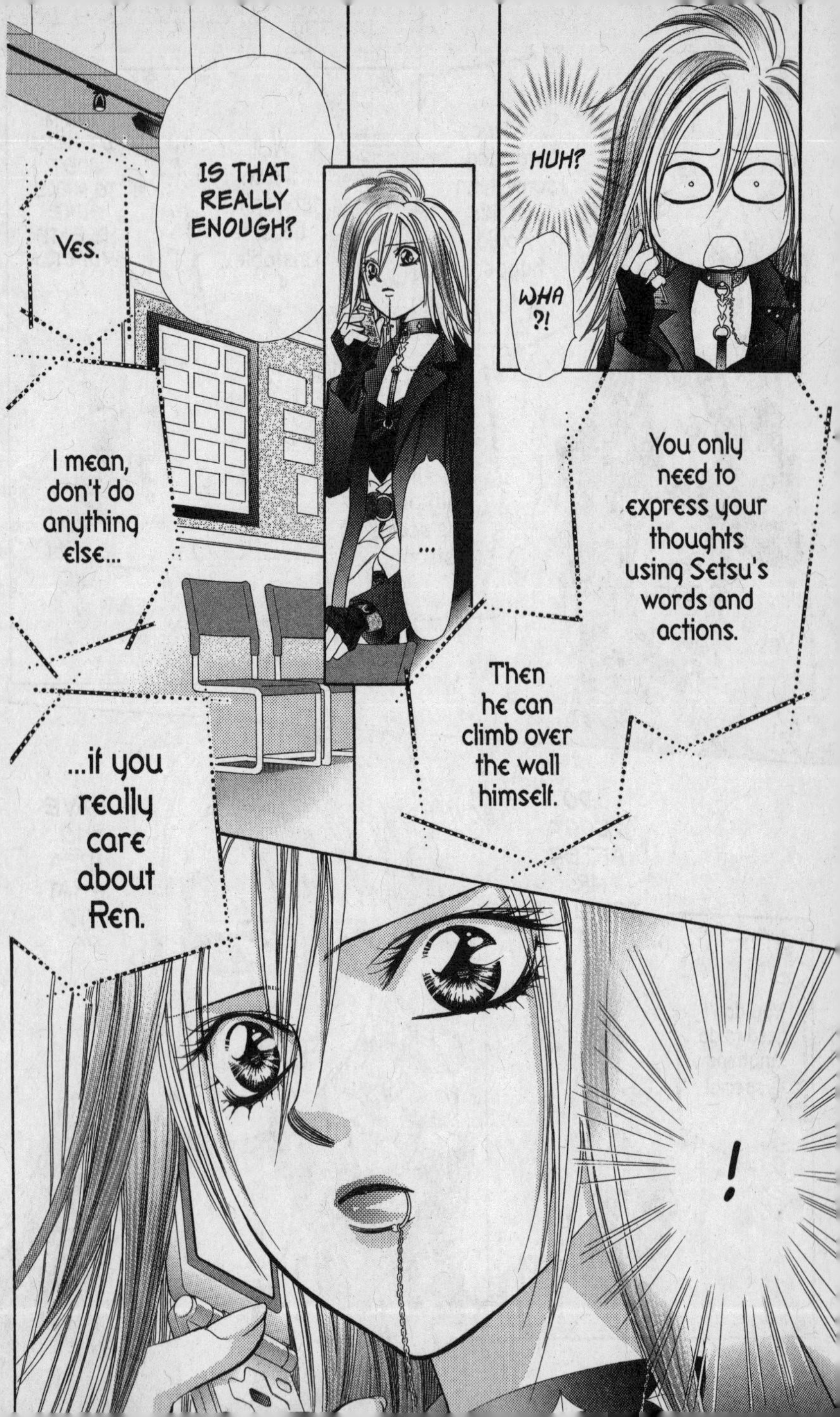
HUH?
WHA ?!
You only need to express your thoughts using Setsu's words and actions.
Then he can climb over the wall himself.
...
IS THAT REALLY ENOUGH?
Yes.
I mean, don't do anything else...
...if you really care about Ren.
!

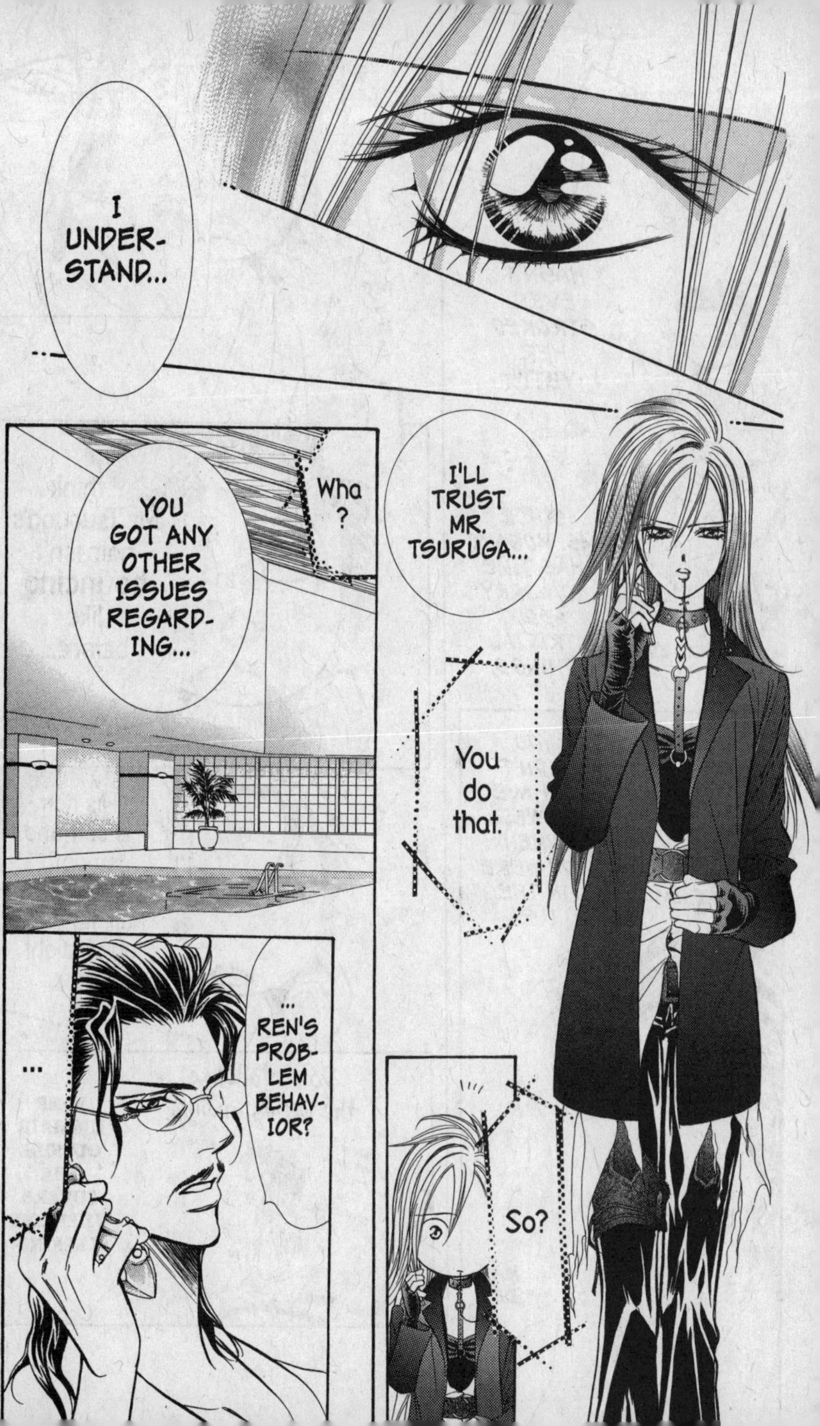
I UNDER-STAND...
I'LL TRUST MR. TSURUGA...
You do that.
Wha?
YOU GOT ANY OTHER ISSUES REGARD-ING...
...REN'S PROB-LEM BEHAV-IOR?
...
So?

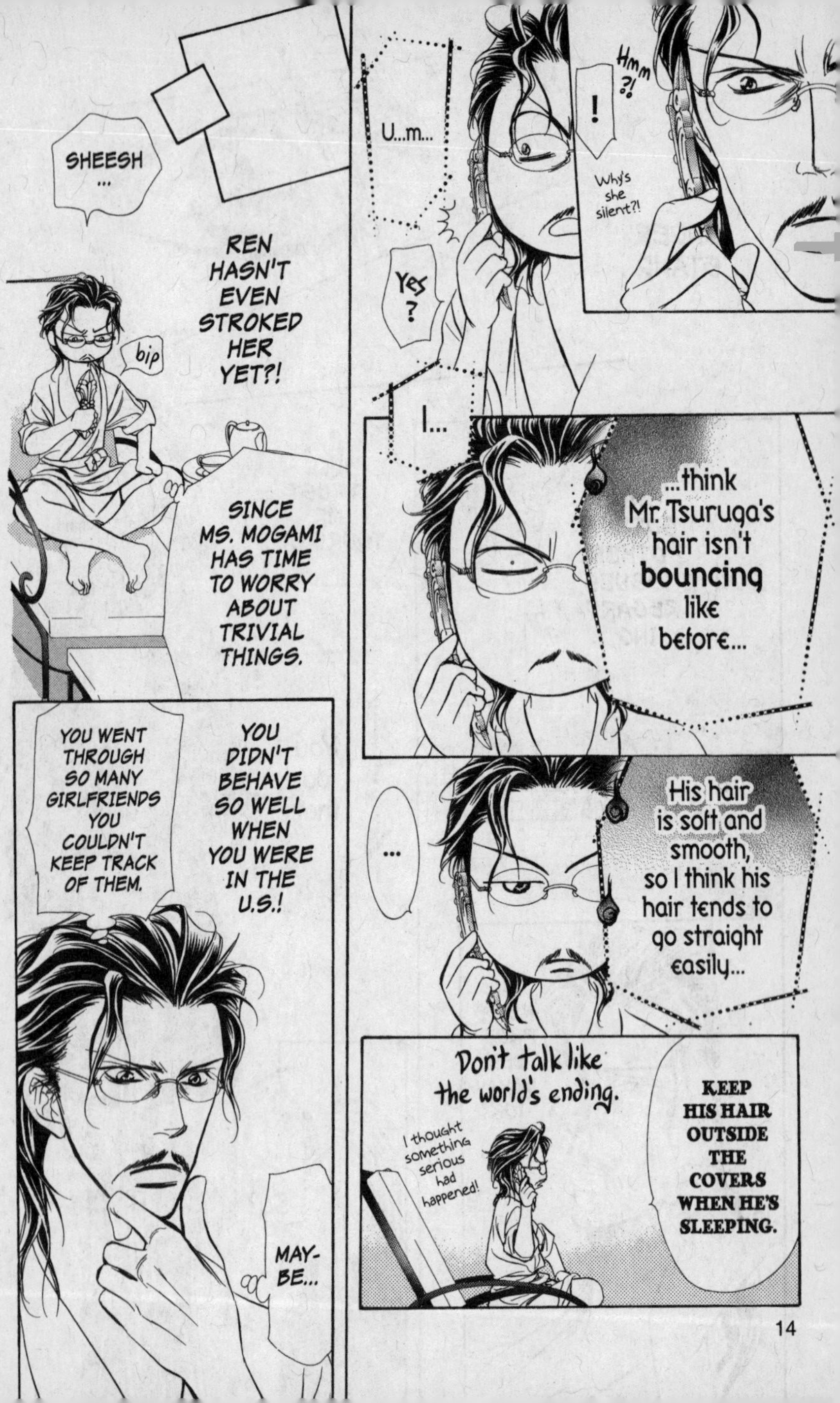

Hmm ?!
!
Why's she silent?!
U...m...
Yes?
I...
...think Mr. Tsuruga's hair isn't **bouncing** like before...
...
His hair is soft and smooth, so I think his hair tends to go straight easily...
KEEP HIS HAIR OUTSIDE THE COVERS WHEN HE'S SLEEPING.
Don't talk like the world's ending.
I thought something serious had happened!
SHEESH ...
REN HASN'T EVEN STROKED HER YET?!
bip
SINCE MS. MOGAMI HAS TIME TO WORRY ABOUT TRIVIAL THINGS.
YOU DIDN'T BEHAVE SO WELL WHEN YOU WERE IN THE U.S.!
YOU WENT THROUGH SO MANY GIRLFRIENDS YOU COULDN'T KEEP TRACK OF THEM.
MAY-BE...

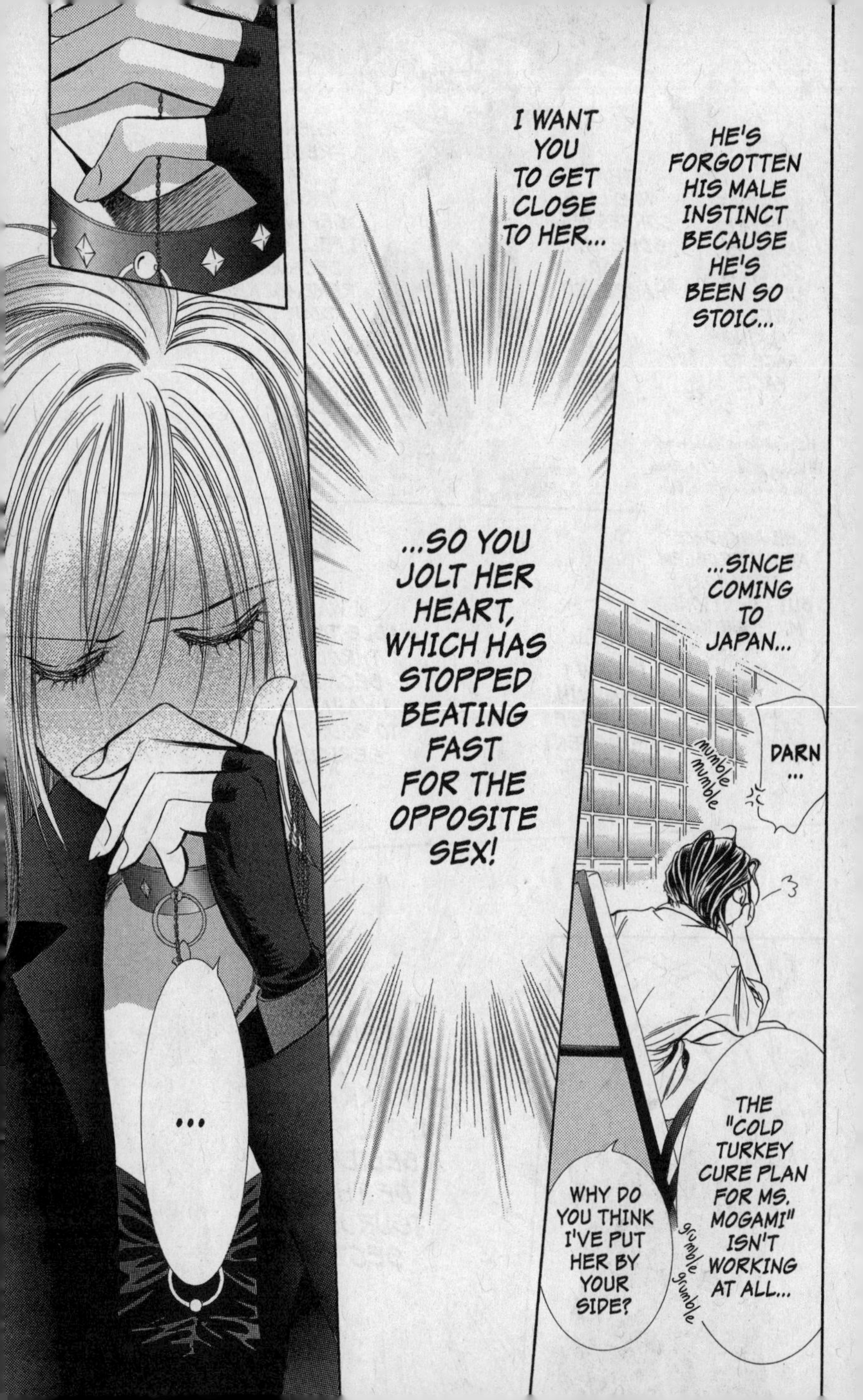
HE'S FORGOTTEN HIS MALE INSTINCT BECAUSE HE'S BEEN SO STOIC...
...SINCE COMING TO JAPAN...
DARN ...
mumble mumble
THE "COLD TURKEY CURE PLAN FOR MS. MOGAMI" ISN'T WORKING AT ALL...
grumble grumble
WHY DO YOU THINK I'VE PUT HER BY YOUR SIDE?
I WANT YOU TO GET CLOSE TO HER...
...SO YOU JOLT HER HEART, WHICH HAS STOPPED BEATING FAST FOR THE OPPOSITE SEX!
...

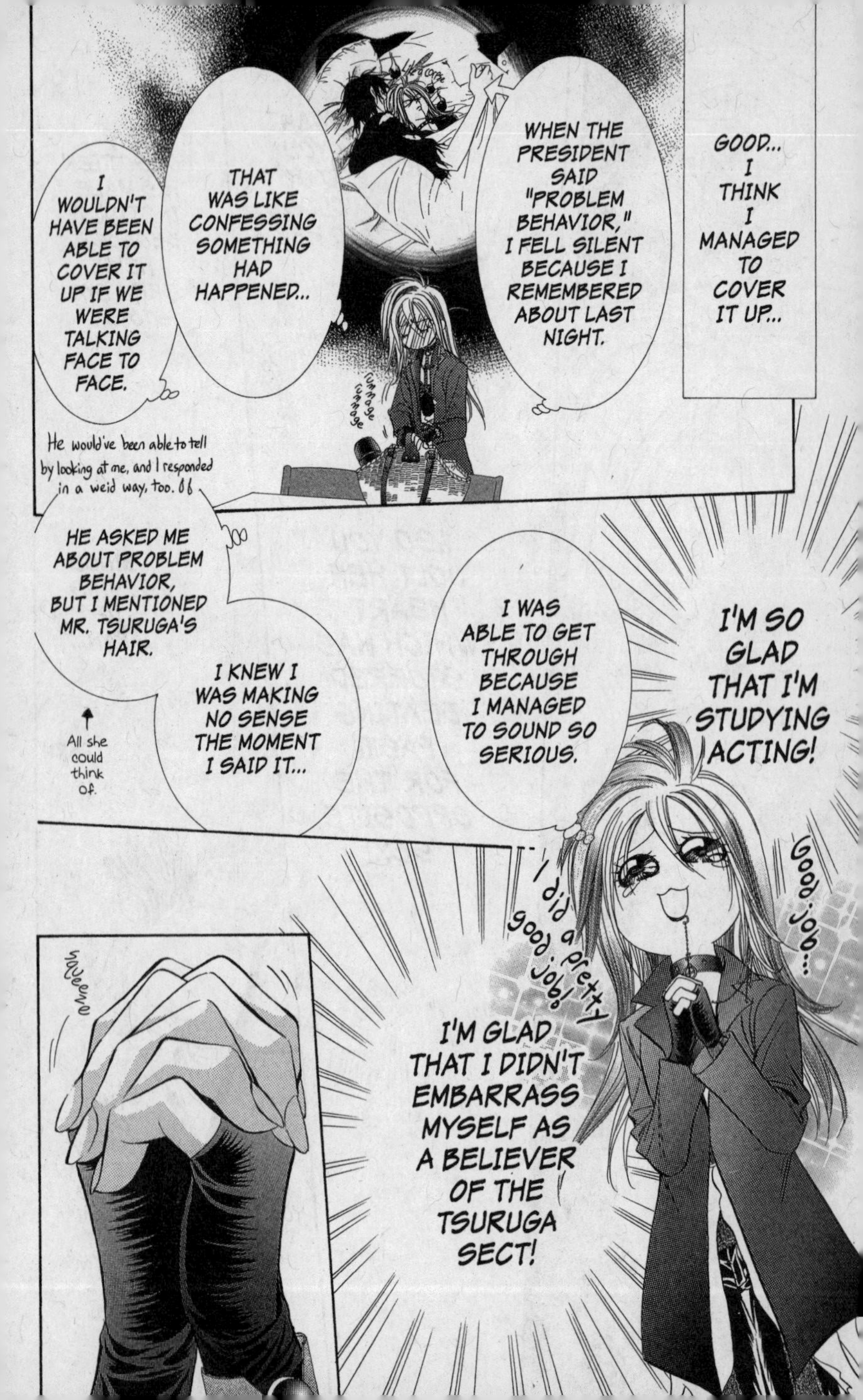
GOOD... I THINK I MANAGED TO COVER IT UP...
WHEN THE PRESIDENT SAID "PROBLEM BEHAVIOR," I FELL SILENT BECAUSE I REMEMBERED ABOUT LAST NIGHT.
THAT WAS LIKE CONFESSING SOMETHING HAD HAPPENED...
I WOULDN'T HAVE BEEN ABLE TO COVER IT UP IF WE WERE TALKING FACE TO FACE.
rummage rummage rummage
He would've been able to tell by looking at me, and I responded in a weid way, too.
HE ASKED ME ABOUT PROBLEM BEHAVIOR, BUT I MENTIONED MR. TSURUGA'S HAIR.
I KNEW I WAS MAKING NO SENSE THE MOMENT I SAID IT...
All she could think of.
I'M SO GLAD THAT I'M STUDYING ACTING!
I WAS ABLE TO GET THROUGH BECAUSE I MANAGED TO SOUND SO SERIOUS.
Good job...
I did a pretty good job!
I'M GLAD THAT I DIDN'T EMBARRASS MYSELF AS A BELIEVER OF THE TSURUGA SECT!
squeeze

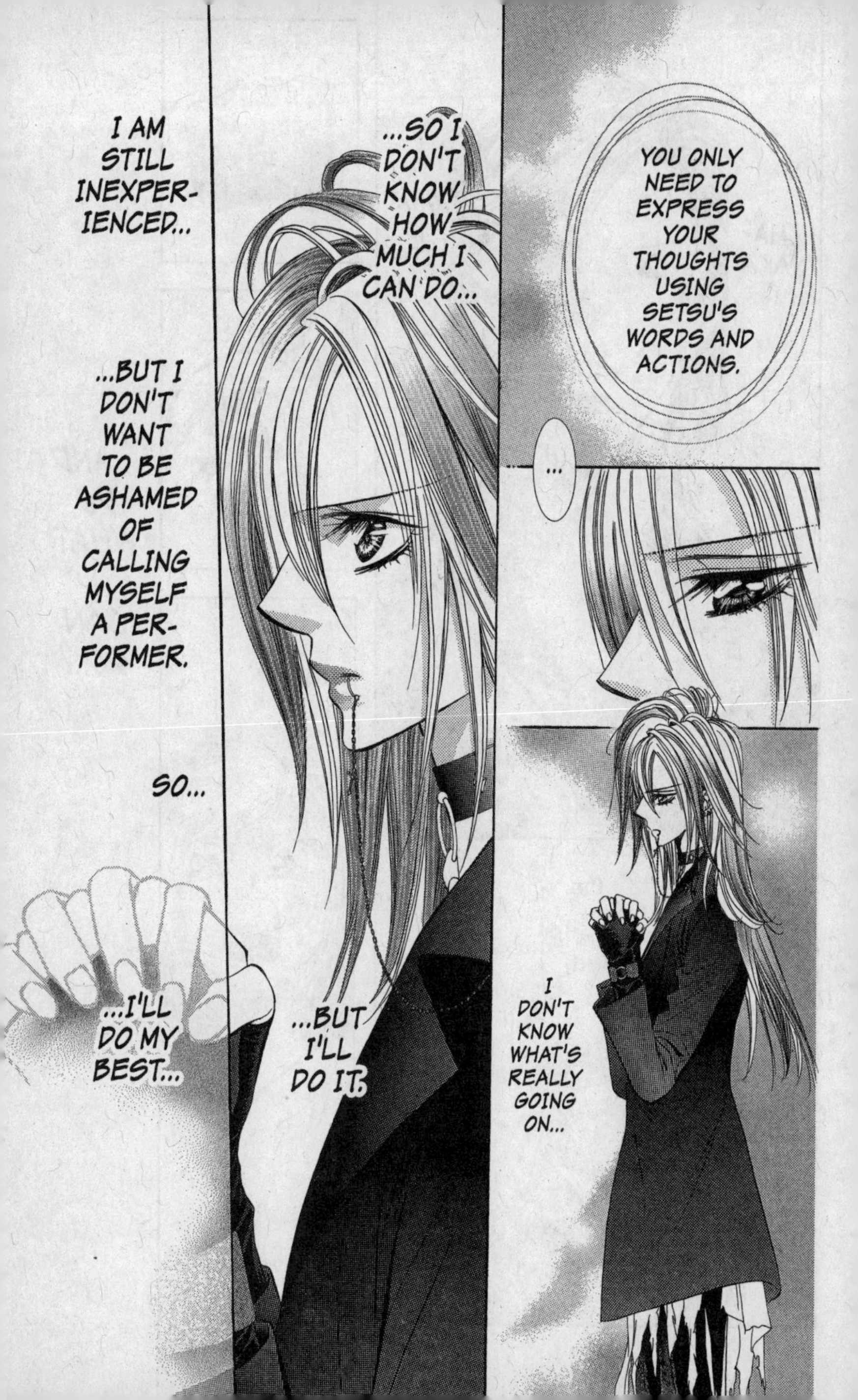
YOU ONLY NEED TO EXPRESS YOUR THOUGHTS USING SETSU'S WORDS AND ACTIONS.
...
I DON'T KNOW WHAT'S REALLY GOING ON...
...SO I DON'T KNOW HOW MUCH I CAN DO...
...BUT I'LL DO IT.
I AM STILL INEXPER-IENCED...
...BUT I DON'T WANT TO BE ASHAMED OF CALLING MYSELF A PER-FORMER.
SO...
...I'LL DO MY BEST...

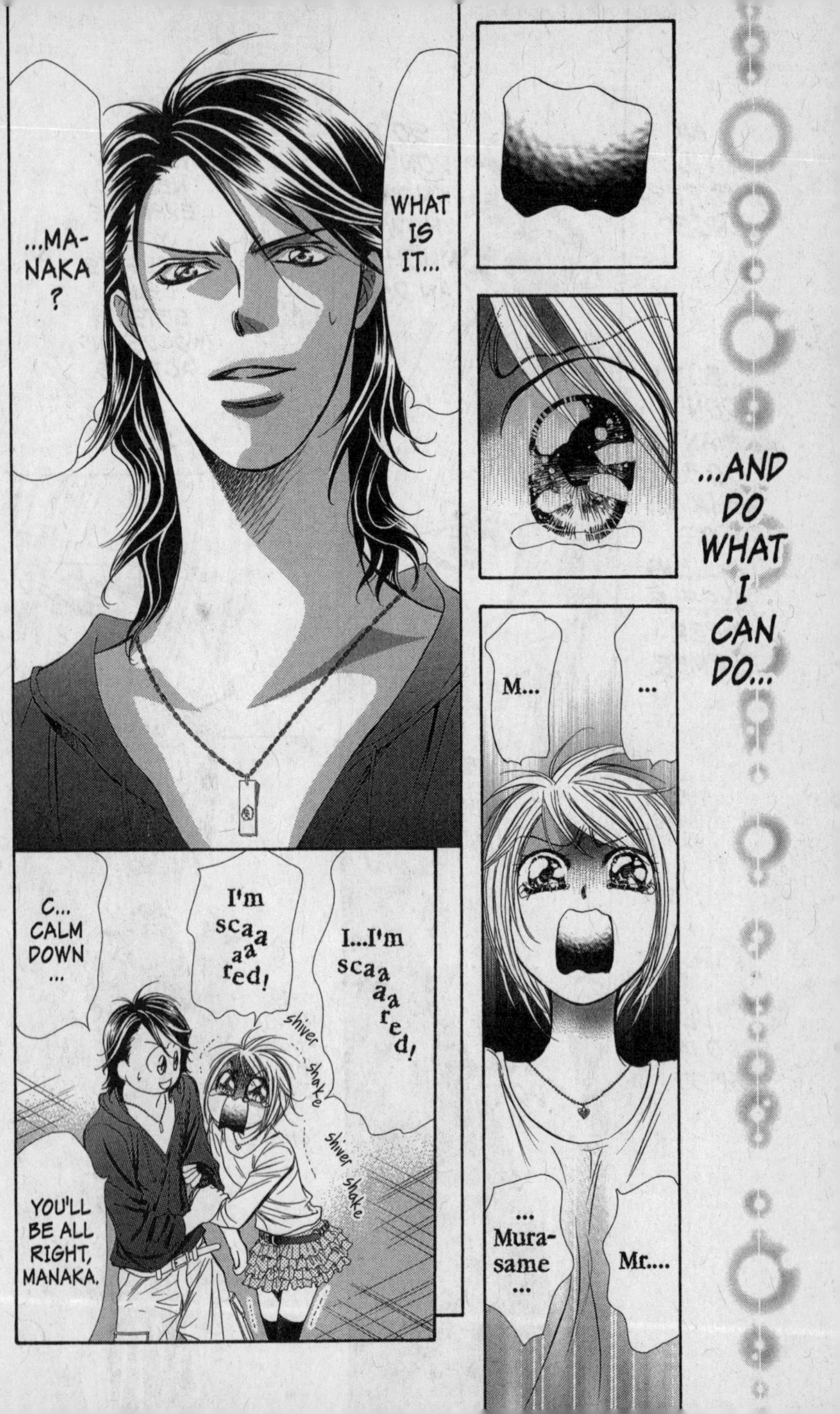

...AND DO WHAT I CAN DO...
...
M...
Mr....
...Mura-same...
WHAT IS IT...
...MA-NAKA?
I...I'm scaaaaared!
shiver shake
shiver shake
I'm scaaaaared!
C... CALM DOWN...
YOU'LL BE ALL RIGHT, MANAKA.

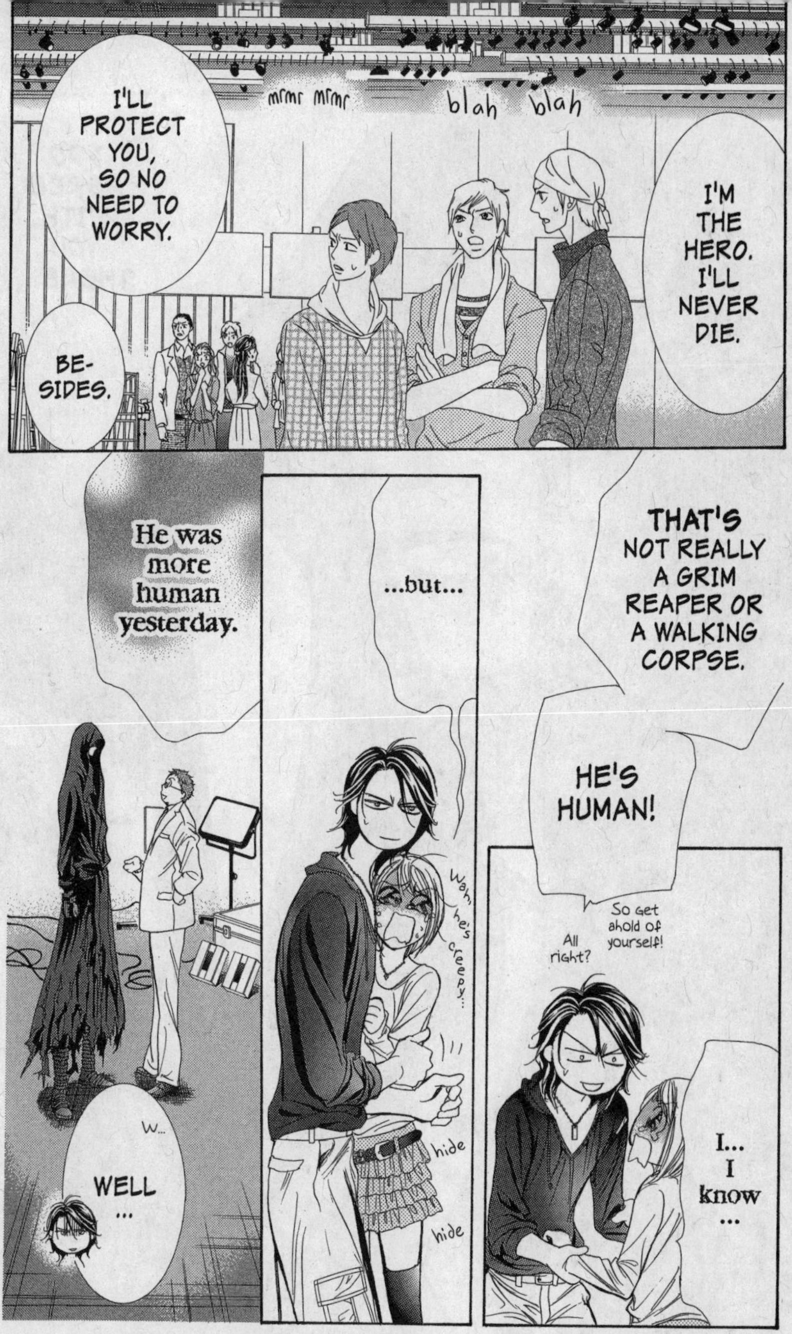
I'M THE HERO. I'LL NEVER DIE.
blah blah
mrmr mrmr
I'LL PROTECT YOU, SO NO NEED TO WORRY.
BE-SIDES.
THAT'S NOT REALLY A GRIM REAPER OR A WALKING CORPSE.
HE'S HUMAN!
So get ahold of yourself!
All right?
I... I know...
...but...
Wah, he's creepy...
hide
hide
He was more human yesterday.
W...
WELL...

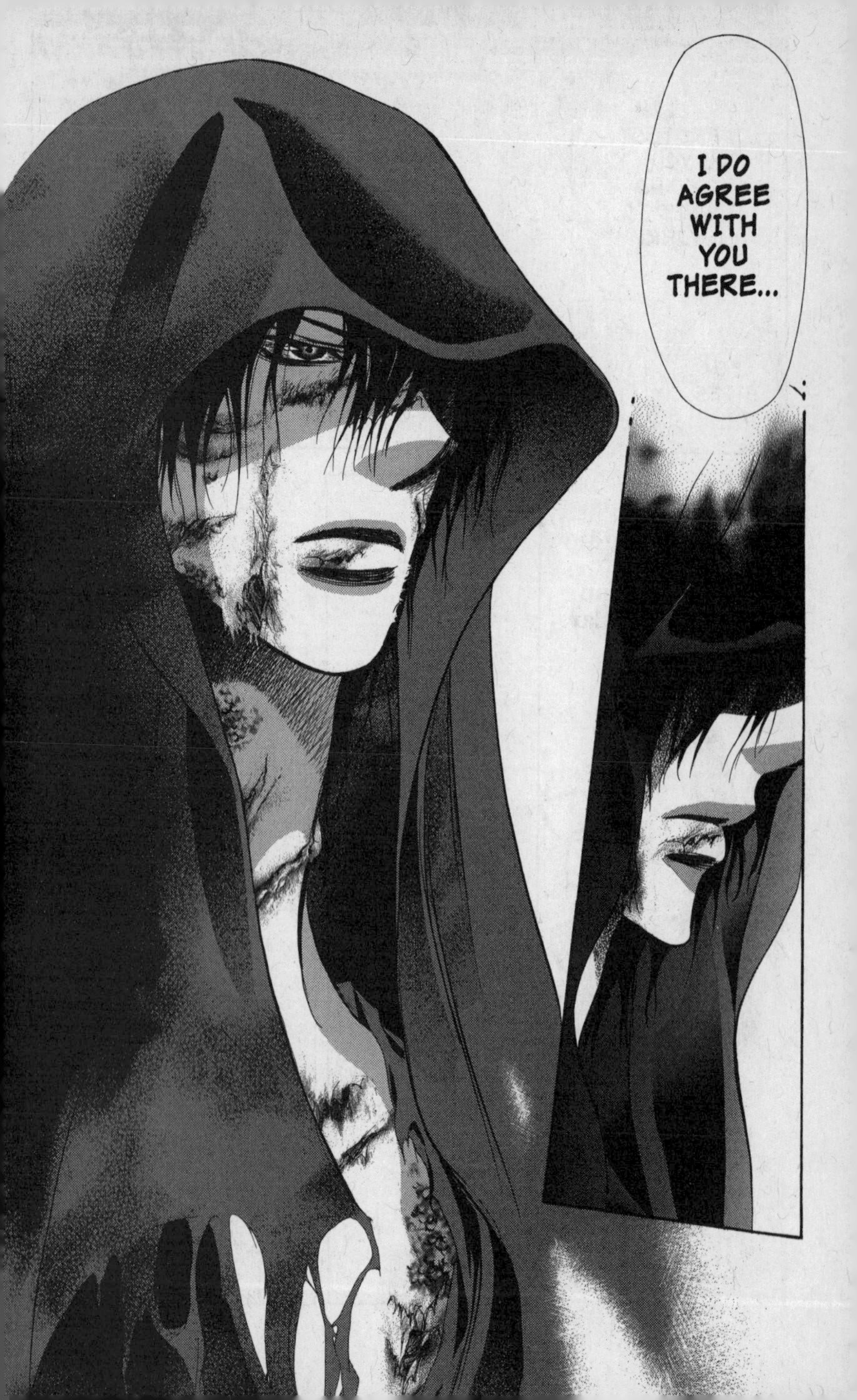
I DO AGREE WITH YOU THERE...

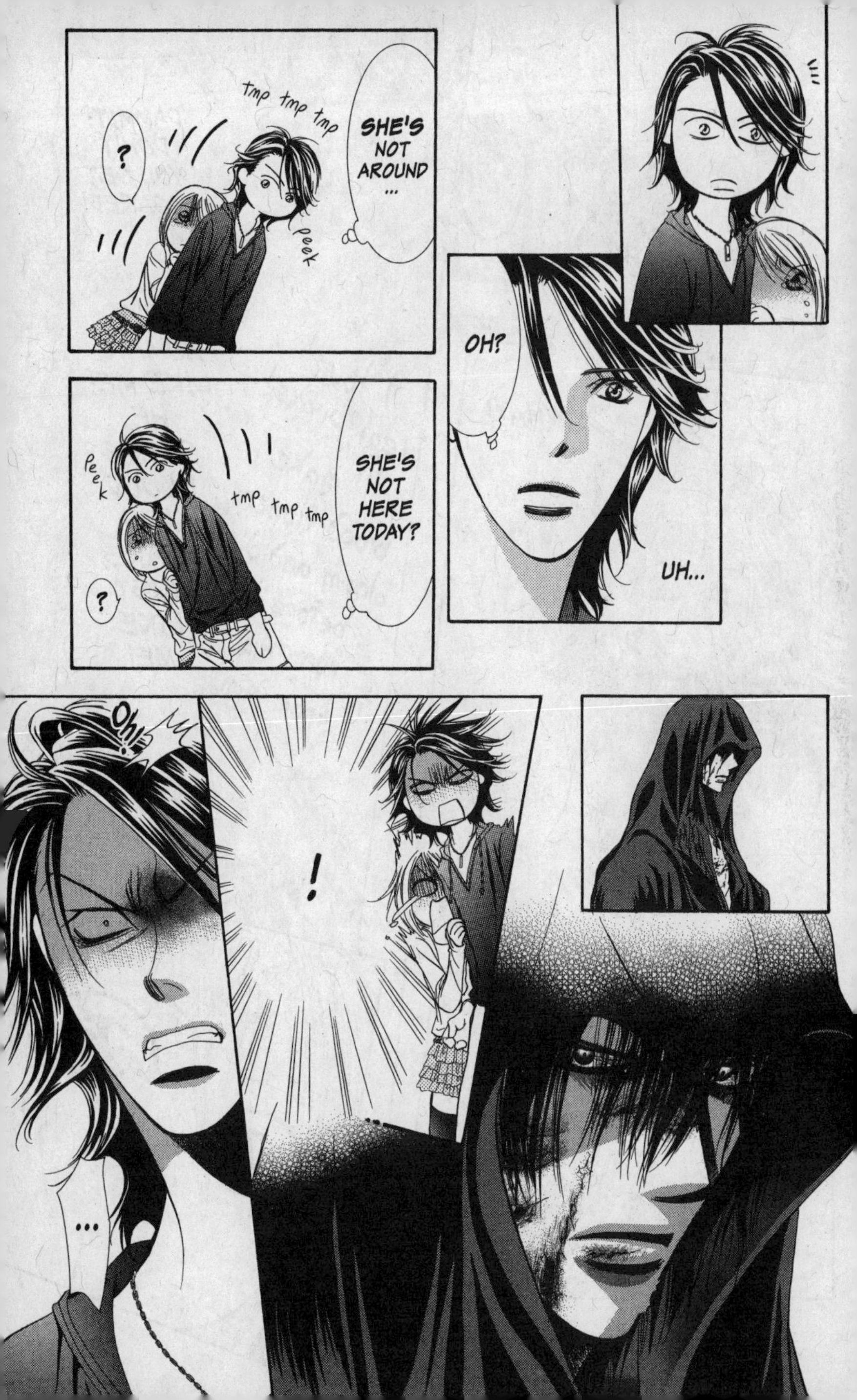
SHE'S NOT AROUND ...
tmp tmp tmp
peek
?
OH?
UH...
SHE'S NOT HERE TODAY?
tmp tmp tmp
Peek
?
!
Oh!
...

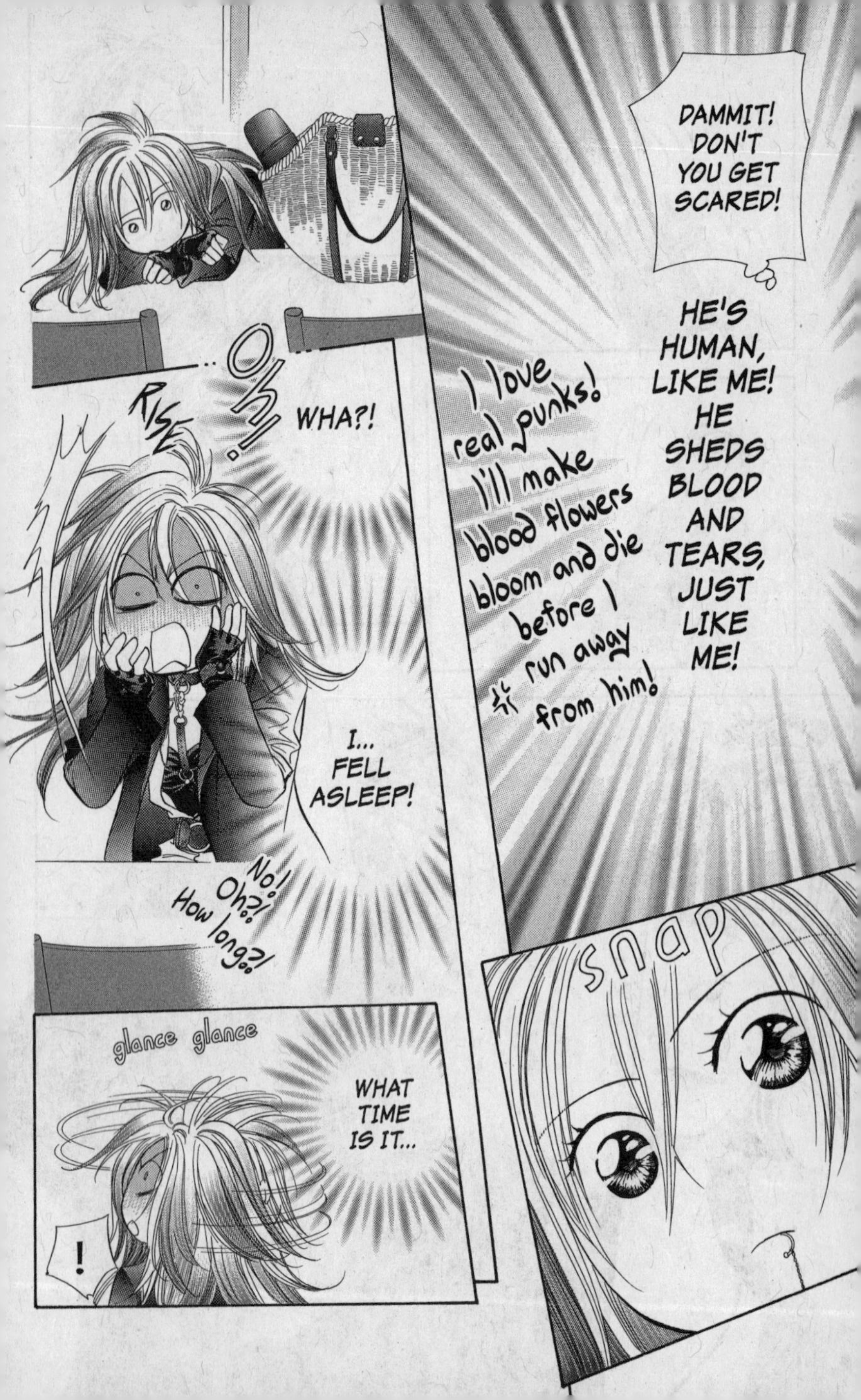
DAMMIT! DON'T YOU GET SCARED!
HE'S HUMAN, LIKE ME! HE SHEDS BLOOD AND TEARS, JUST LIKE ME!
I love real punks! I'll make blood flowers bloom and die before I run away from him!
snap
...Oh!
RISE
WHA?!
I... FELL ASLEEP!
No! Oh?! How long?!
glance glance
WHAT TIME IS IT...
!

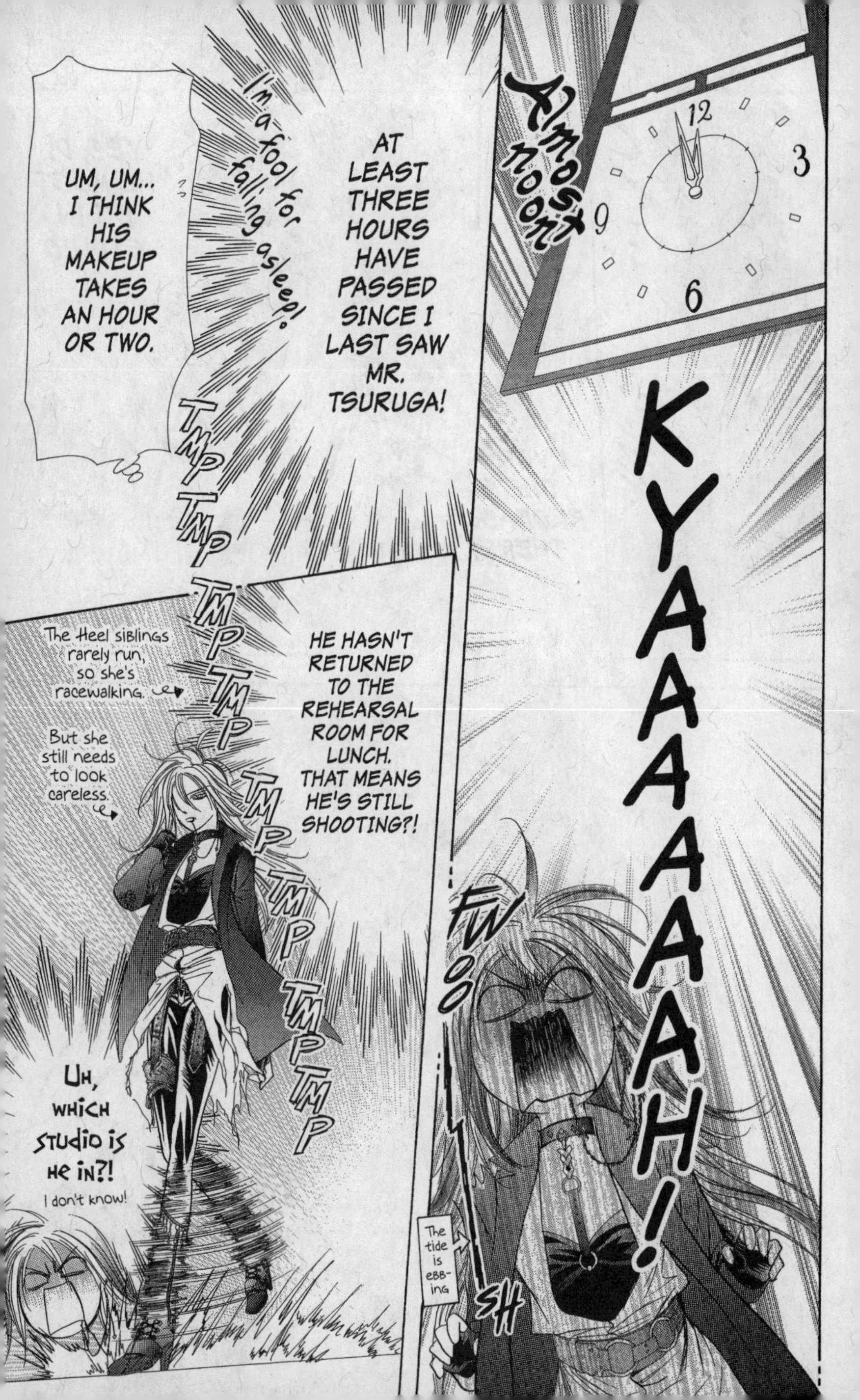

Almost noon!
KYAAAAAH!
FWOOSH
The tide is ebbing
AT LEAST THREE HOURS HAVE PASSED SINCE I LAST SAW MR. TSURUGA!
I'm a fool for falling asleep!
UM, UM... I THINK HIS MAKEUP TAKES AN HOUR OR TWO.
TMP TMP
HE HASN'T RETURNED TO THE REHEARSAL ROOM FOR LUNCH. THAT MEANS HE'S STILL SHOOTING?!
TMP TMP TMP TMP TMP TMP
The Heel siblings rarely run, so she's racewalking.
But she still needs to look careless.
Uh, which studio is he in?!
I don't know!

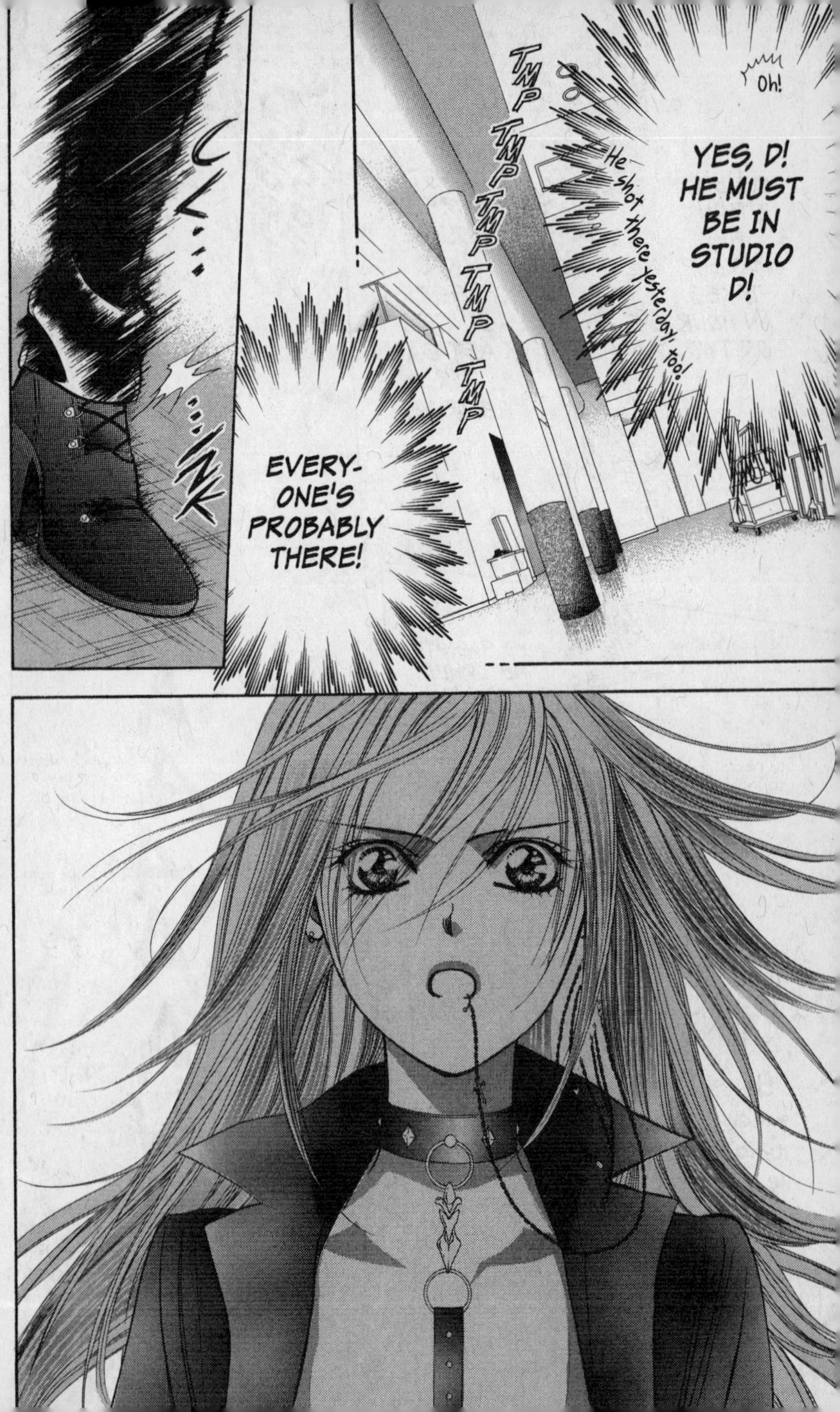
Oh!
YES, D! HE MUST BE IN STUDIO D!
He shot there yesterday, too!
TMP TMP TMP TMP TMP TMP
EVERY-ONE'S PROBABLY THERE!
...INK

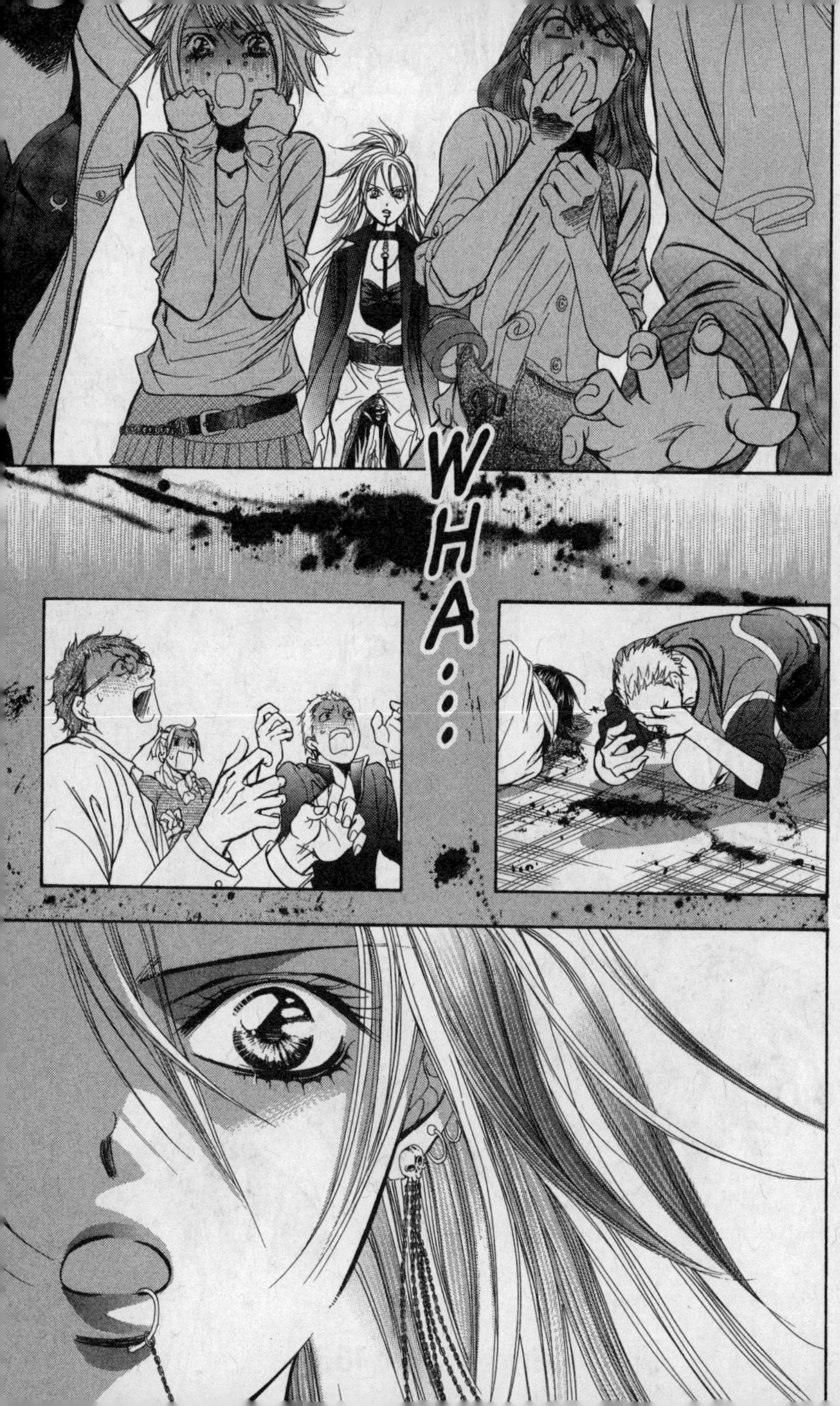
WHA...

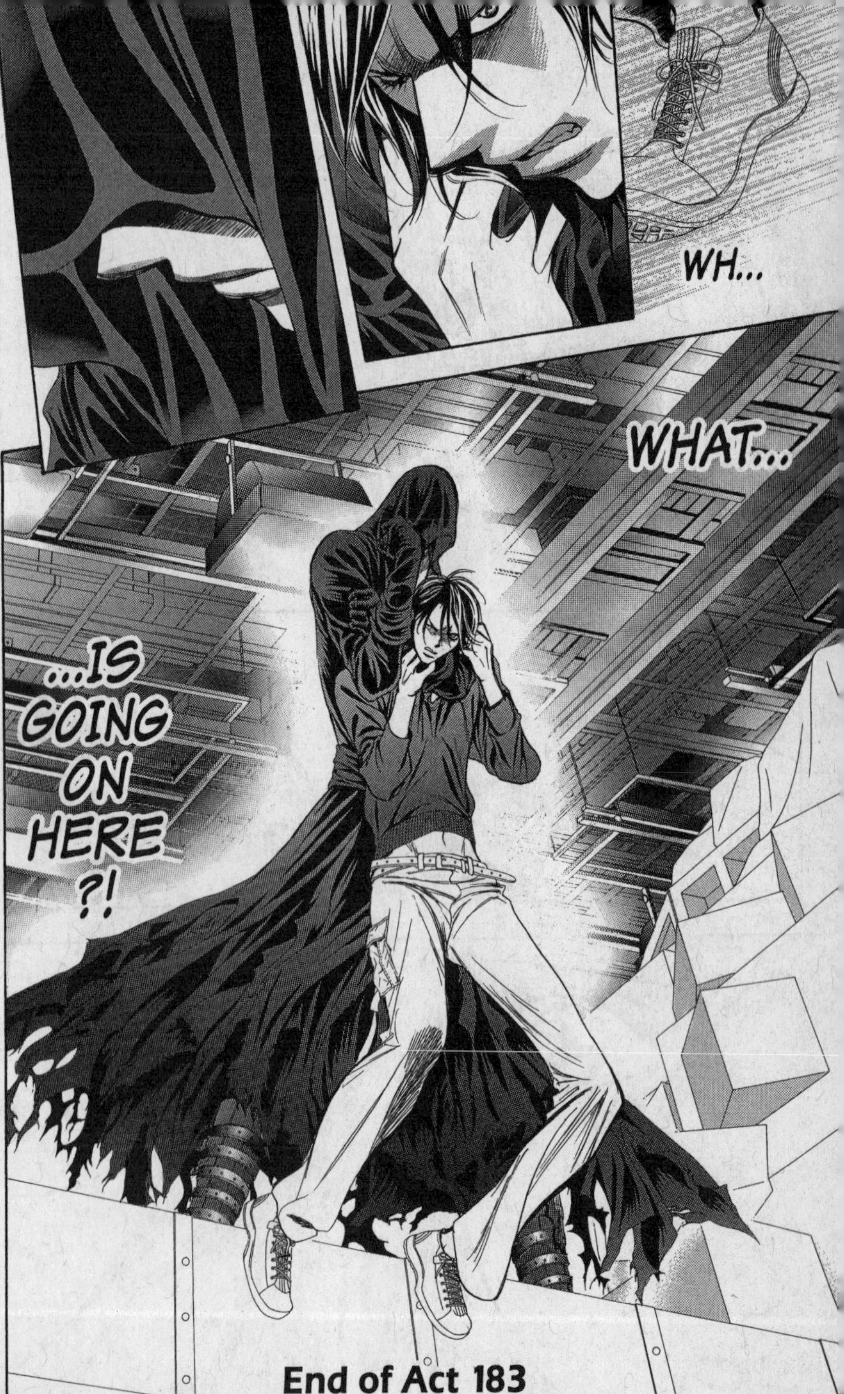
WH...
WHAT...
...IS GOING ON HERE ?!

End of Act 183

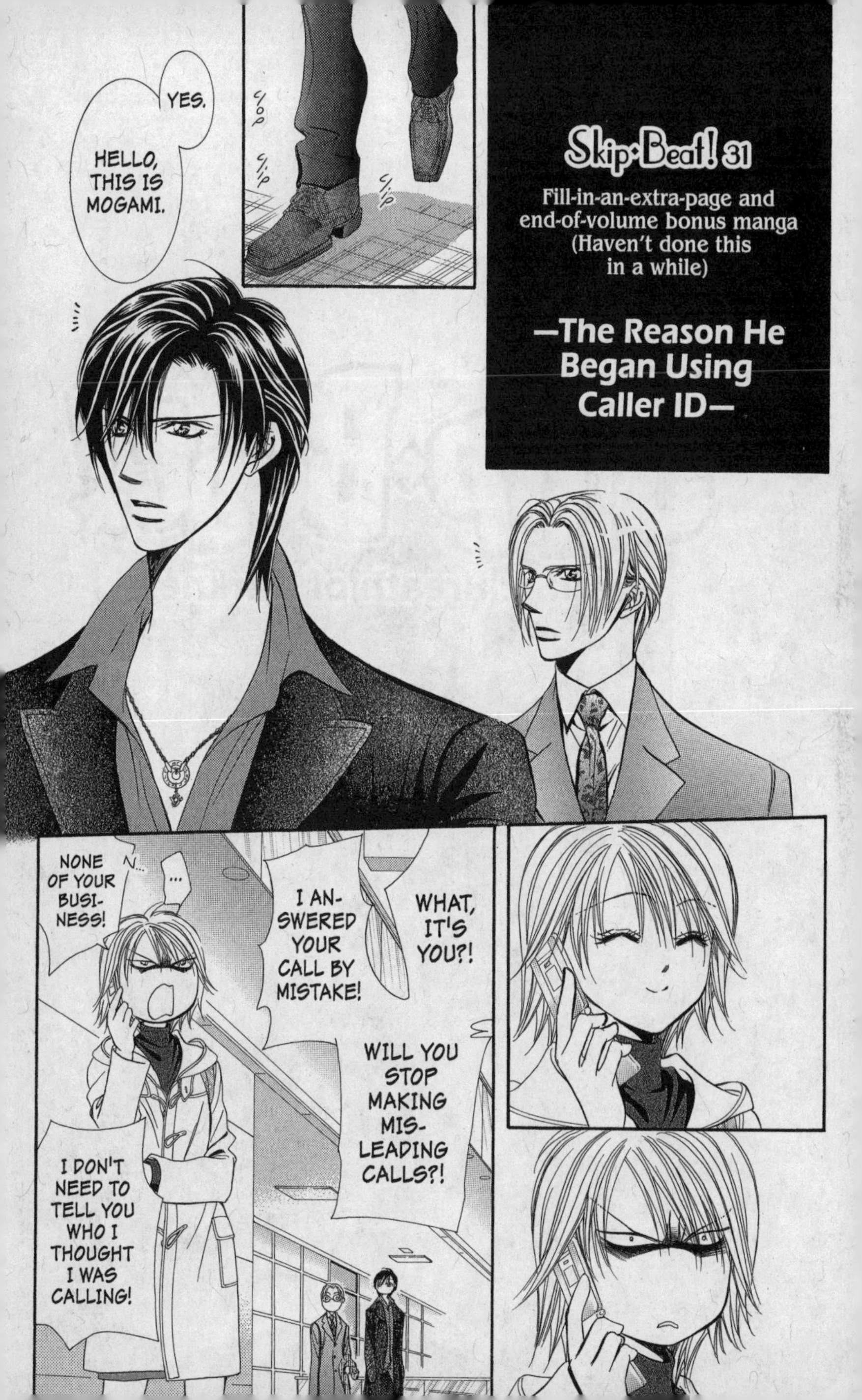
Skip·Beat! 31
Fill-in-an-extra-page and end-of-volume bonus manga (Haven't done this in a while)
—The Reason He Began Using Caller ID—
YES.
HELLO, THIS IS MOGAMI.
WHAT, IT'S YOU?!
I ANSWERED YOUR CALL BY MISTAKE!
...
N...
NONE OF YOUR BUSINESS!
WILL YOU STOP MAKING MISLEADING CALLS?!
I DON'T NEED TO TELL YOU WHO I THOUGHT I WAS CALLING!

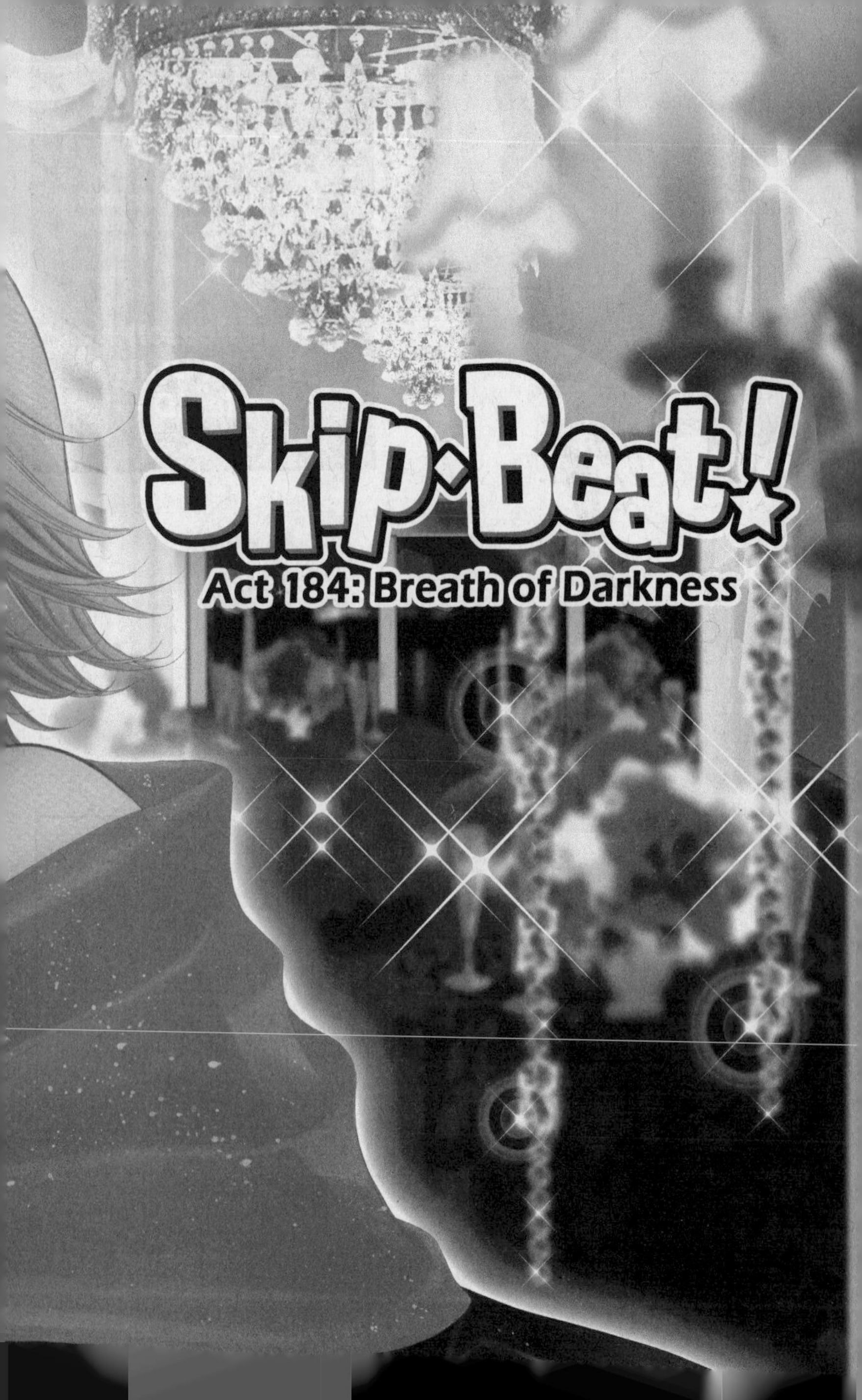
Skip·Beat!
Act 184: Breath of Darkness

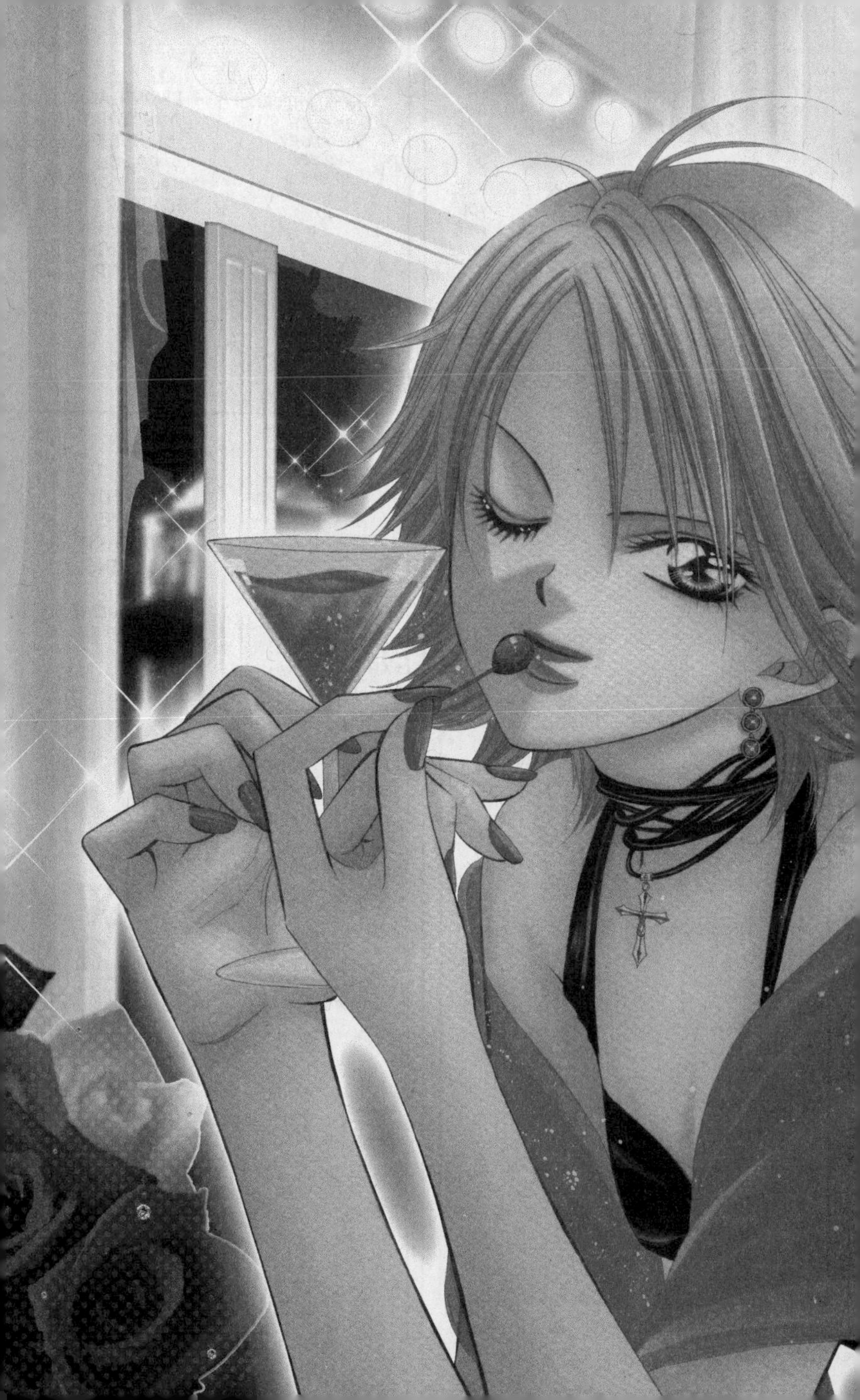

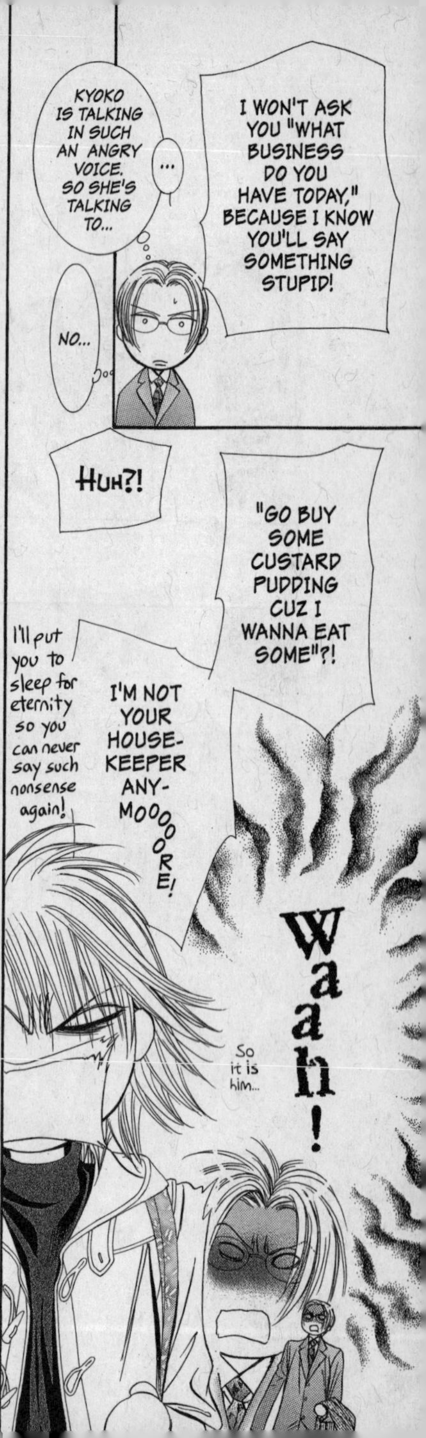
I WON'T ASK YOU "WHAT BUSINESS DO YOU HAVE TODAY," BECAUSE I KNOW YOU'LL SAY SOMETHING STUPID!
KYOKO IS TALKING IN SUCH AN ANGRY VOICE. SO SHE'S TALKING TO...
...
NO...
HUH?!
"GO BUY SOME CUSTARD PUDDING CUZ I WANNA EAT SOME"?!
I'M NOT YOUR HOUSE-KEEPER ANY-MOOOOORE!
I'll put you to sleep for eternity so you can never say such nonsense again!
Waah!
So it is him...

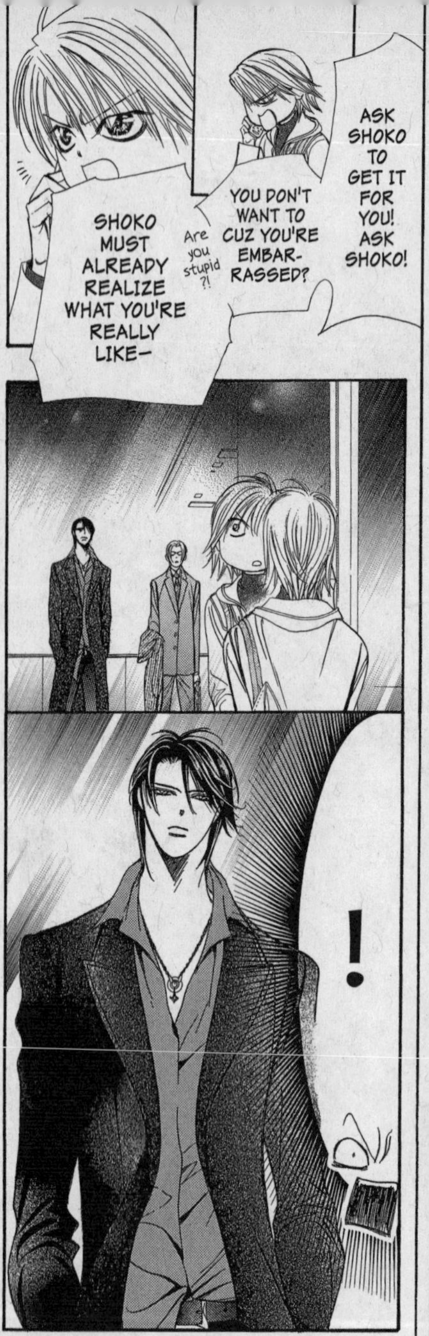
ASK SHOKO TO GET IT FOR YOU! ASK SHOKO!
YOU DON'T WANT TO CUZ YOU'RE EMBARRASSED?
Are you stupid ?!
SHOKO MUST ALREADY REALIZE WHAT YOU'RE REALLY LIKE—
!

←Continued at the end of this volume

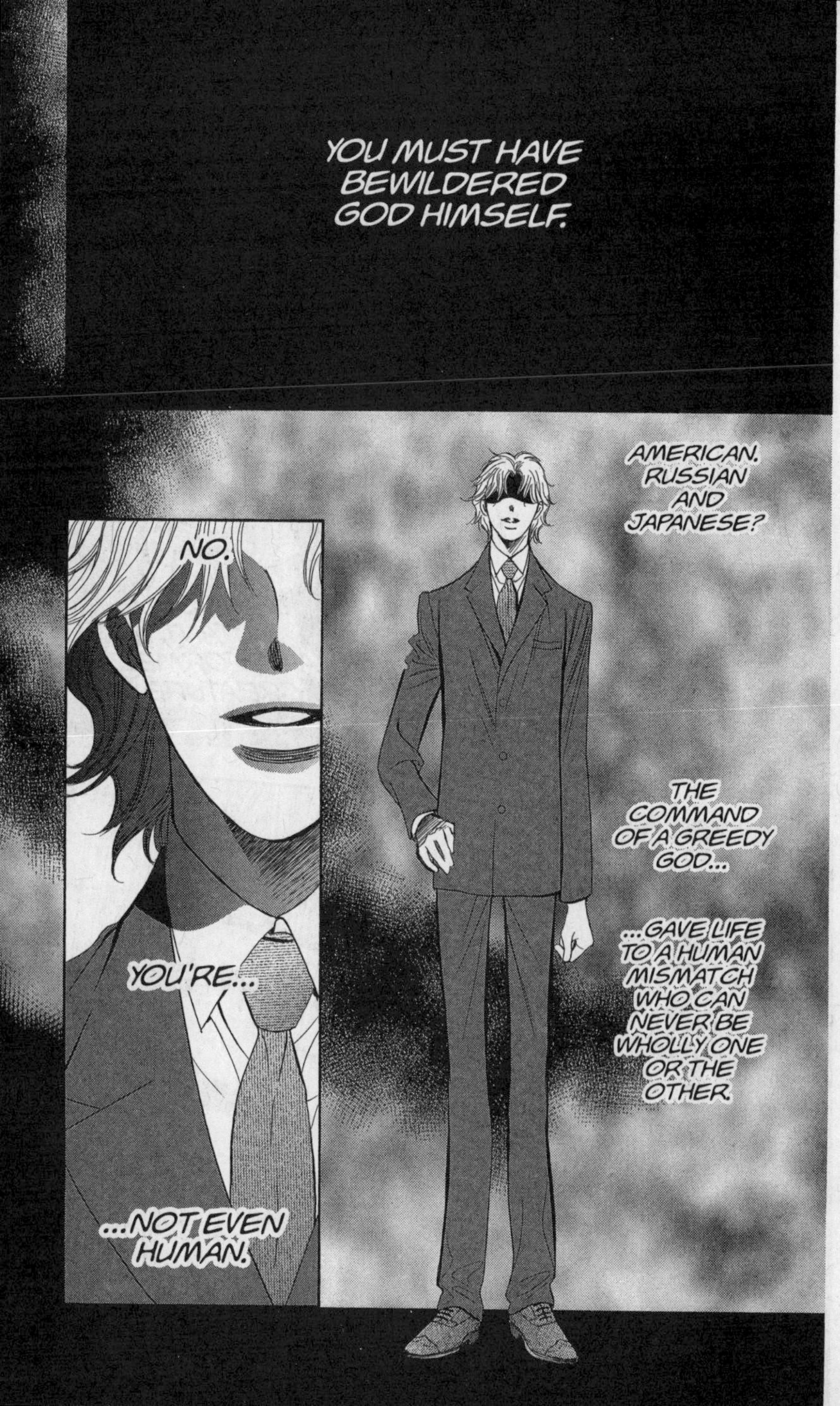
YOU MUST HAVE BEWILDERED GOD HIMSELF.
AMERICAN. RUSSIAN AND JAPANESE?
THE COMMAND OF A GREEDY GOD...
...GAVE LIFE TO A HUMAN MISMATCH WHO CAN NEVER BE WHOLLY ONE OR THE OTHER.
NO.
YOU'RE...
...NOT EVEN HUMAN.

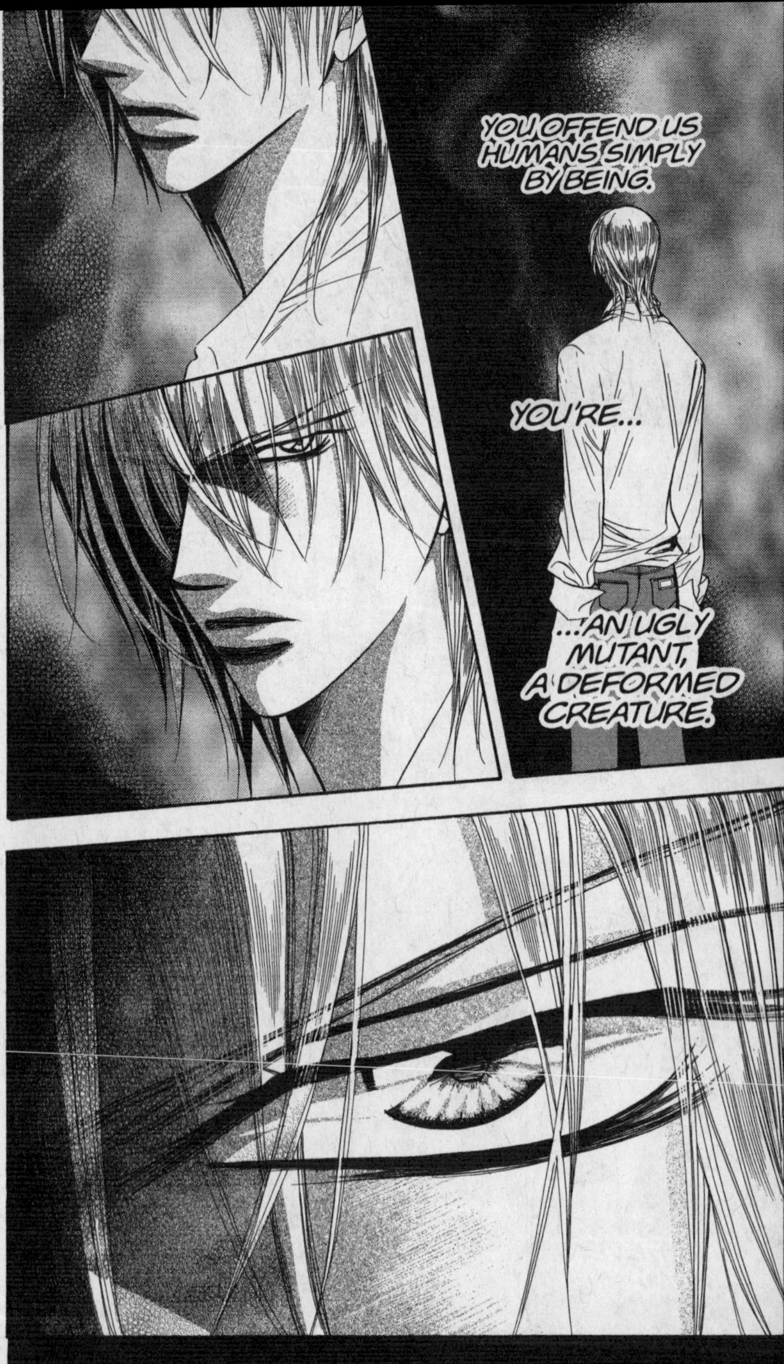
YOU OFFEND US HUMANS SIMPLY BY BEING.
YOU'RE...
...AN UGLY MUTANT, A DEFORMED CREATURE.

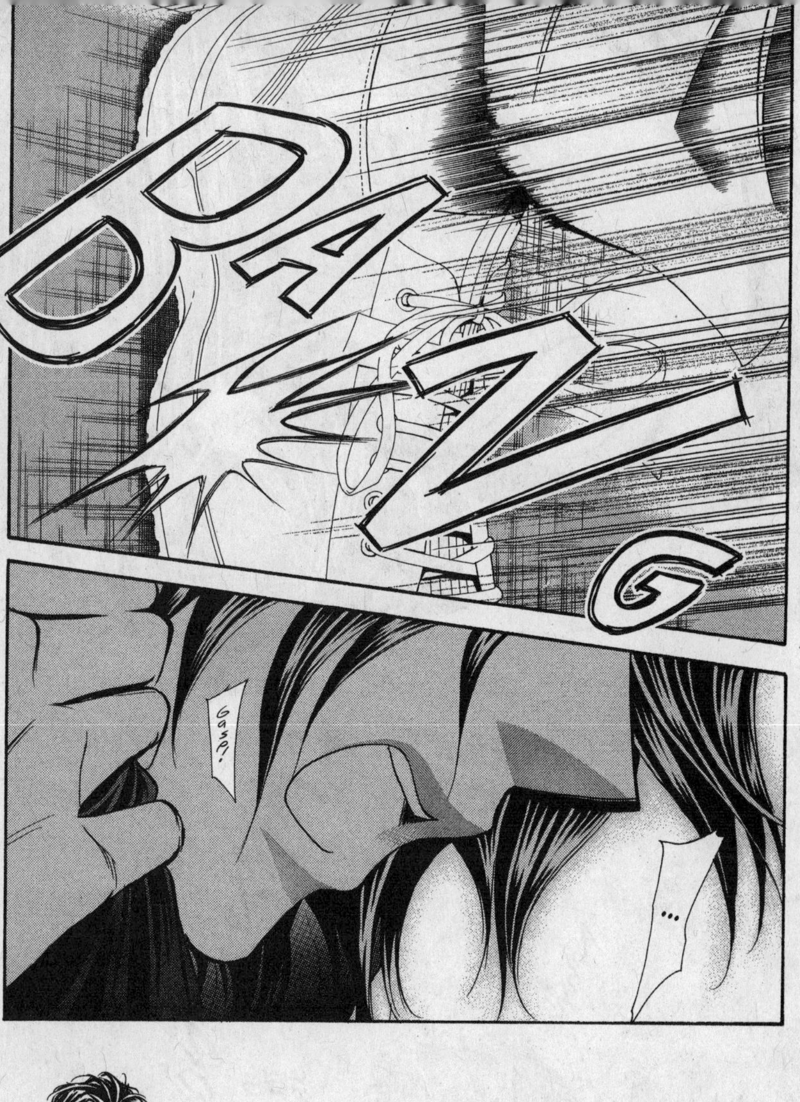
BANG
...
Gasp!

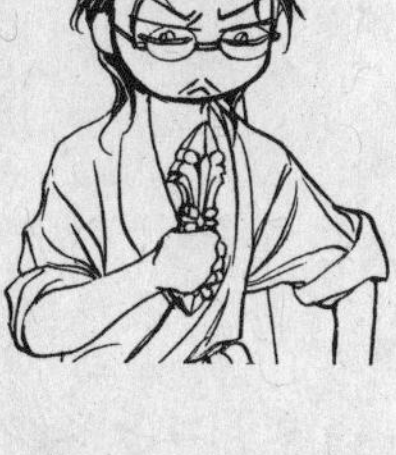

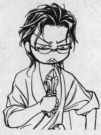

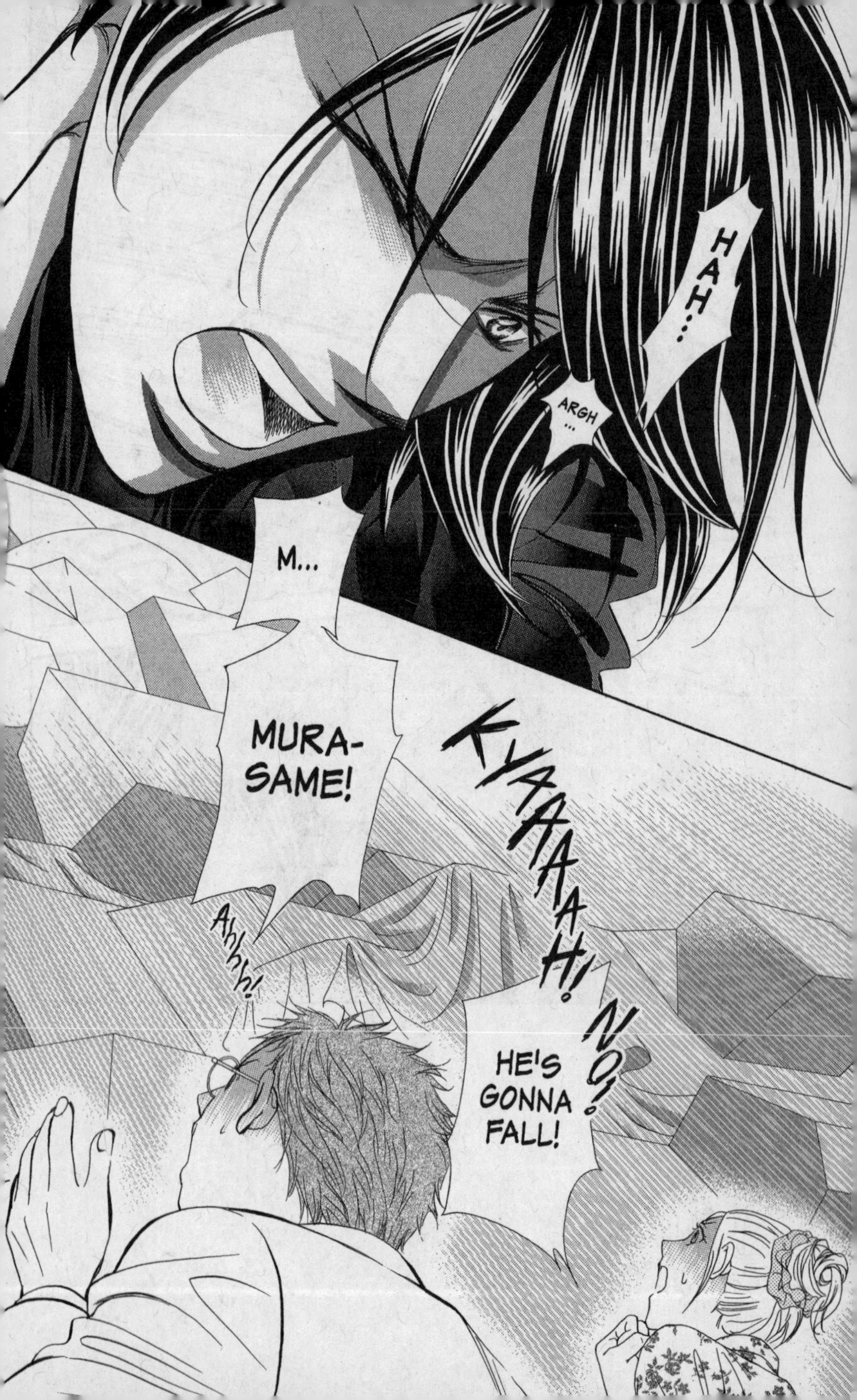
HAH...
ARGH...
M...
MURA-SAME!
KYAAAAH!
NO!
HE'S GONNA FALL!
Ahhh!

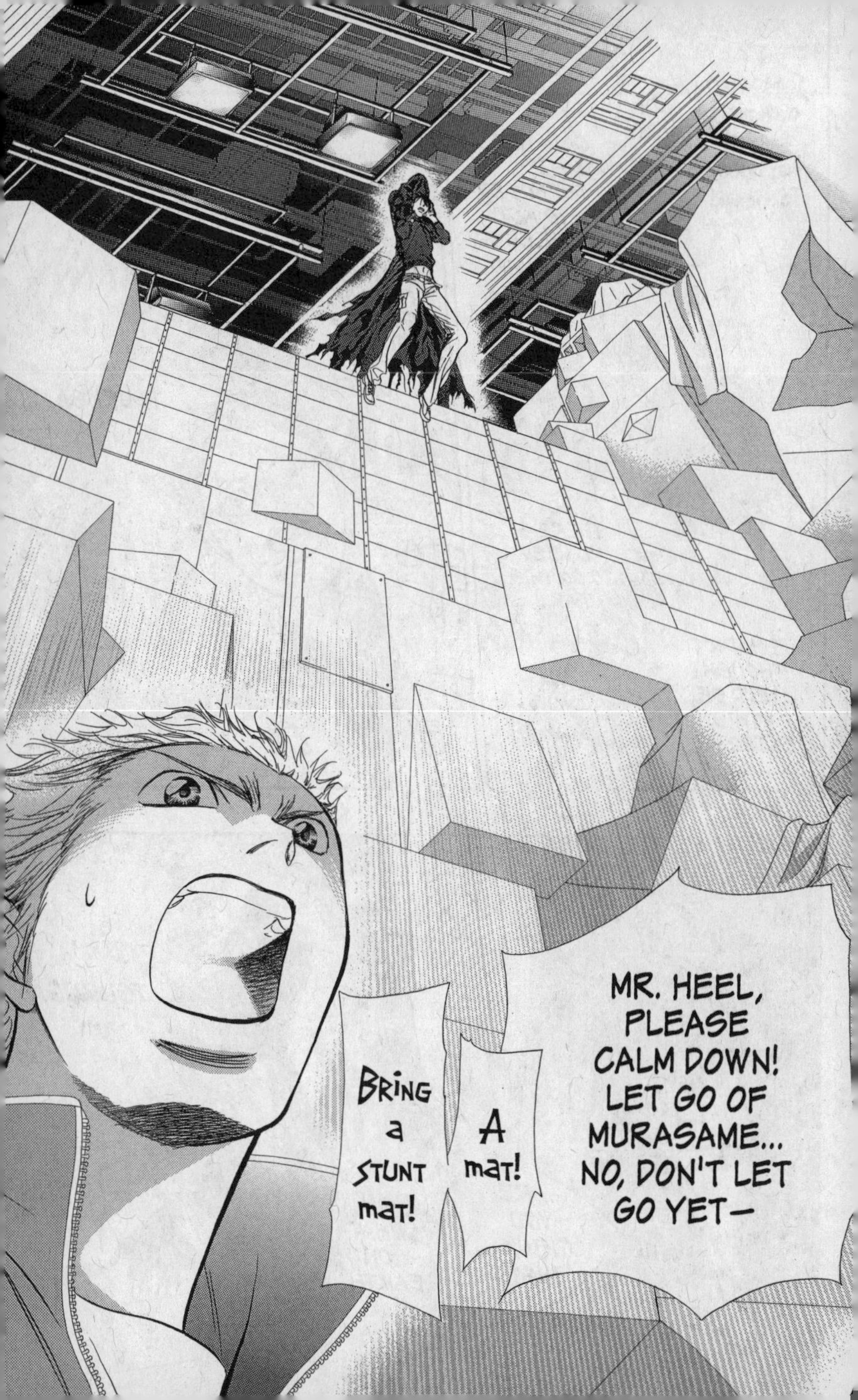
MR. HEEL, PLEASE CALM DOWN! LET GO OF MURASAME... NO, DON'T LET GO YET—
A mat!
Bring a stunt mat!

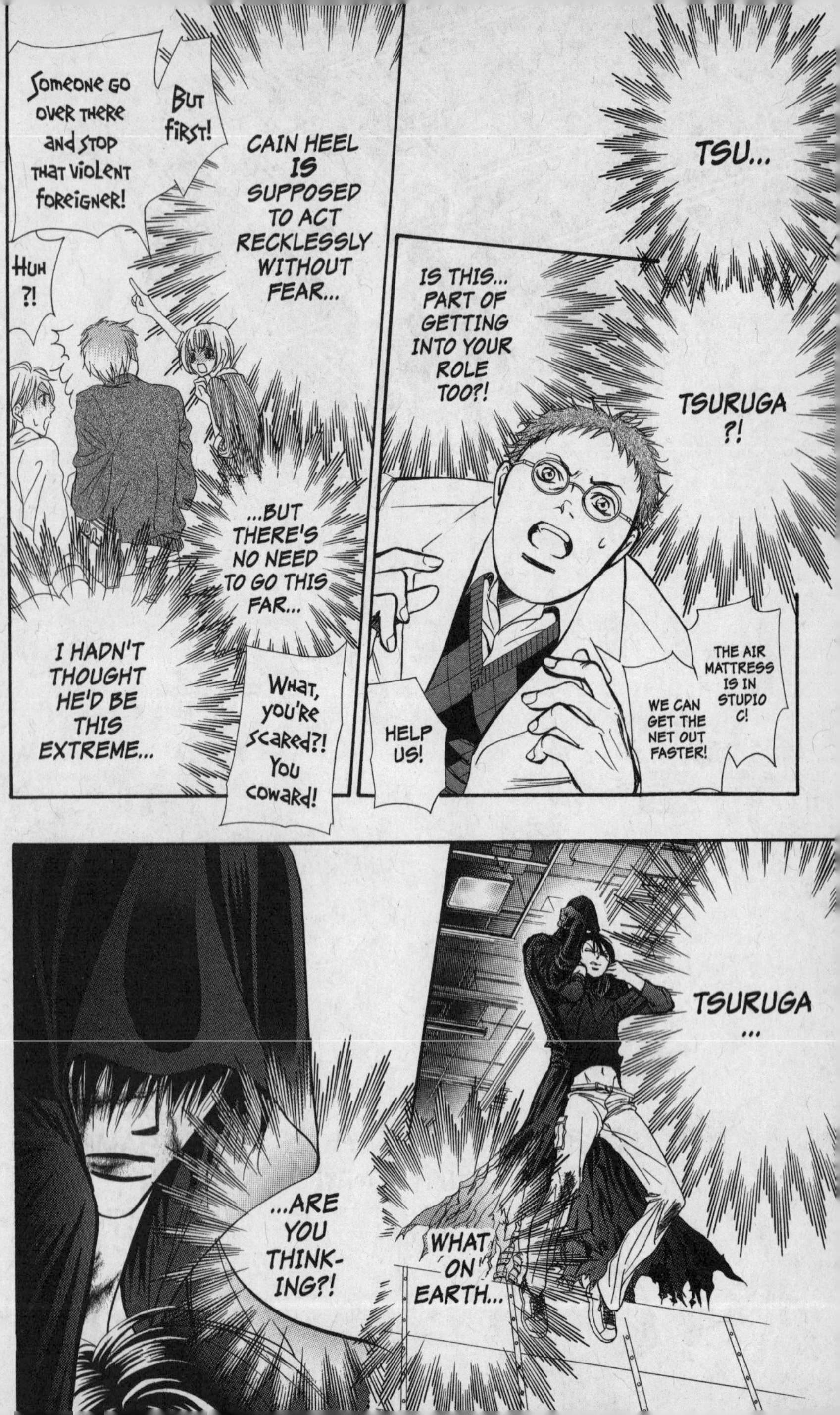
TSU...
IS THIS... PART OF GETTING INTO YOUR ROLE TOO?!
TSURUGA ?!
THE AIR MATTRESS IS IN STUDIO C!
WE CAN GET THE NET OUT FASTER!
HELP US!
CAIN HEEL IS SUPPOSED TO ACT RECKLESSLY WITHOUT FEAR...
But first!
Someone go over there and stop that violent foreigner!
Huh ?!
...BUT THERE'S NO NEED TO GO THIS FAR...
What, you're scared?! You coward!
I HADN'T THOUGHT HE'D BE THIS EXTREME...
TSURUGA ...
WHAT ON EARTH...
...ARE YOU THINKING?!

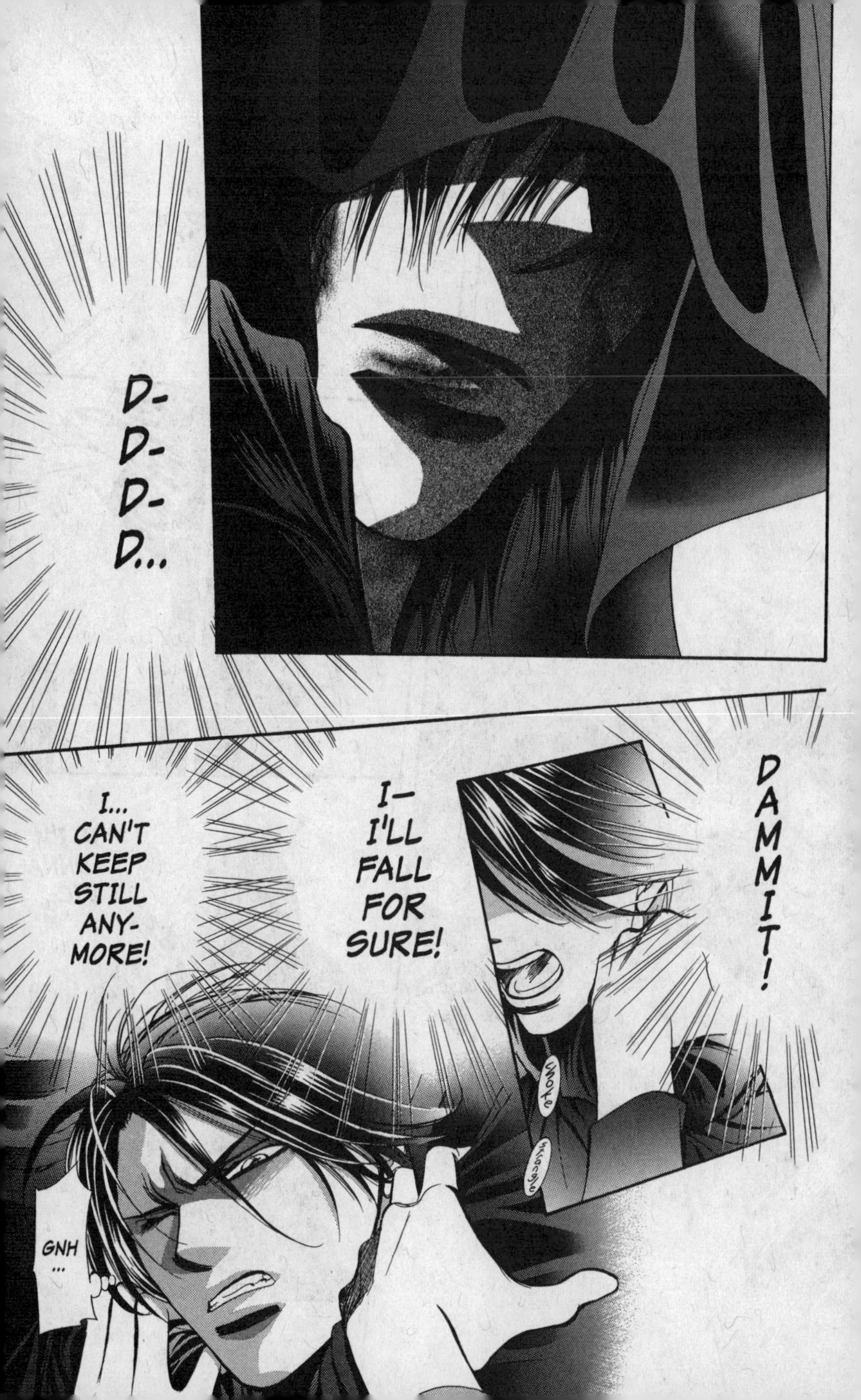
D-
D-
D-
D...
DAMMIT!
choke
struggle
I—
I'LL
FALL
FOR
SURE!
I...
CAN'T
KEEP
STILL
ANY-
MORE!
GNH
...

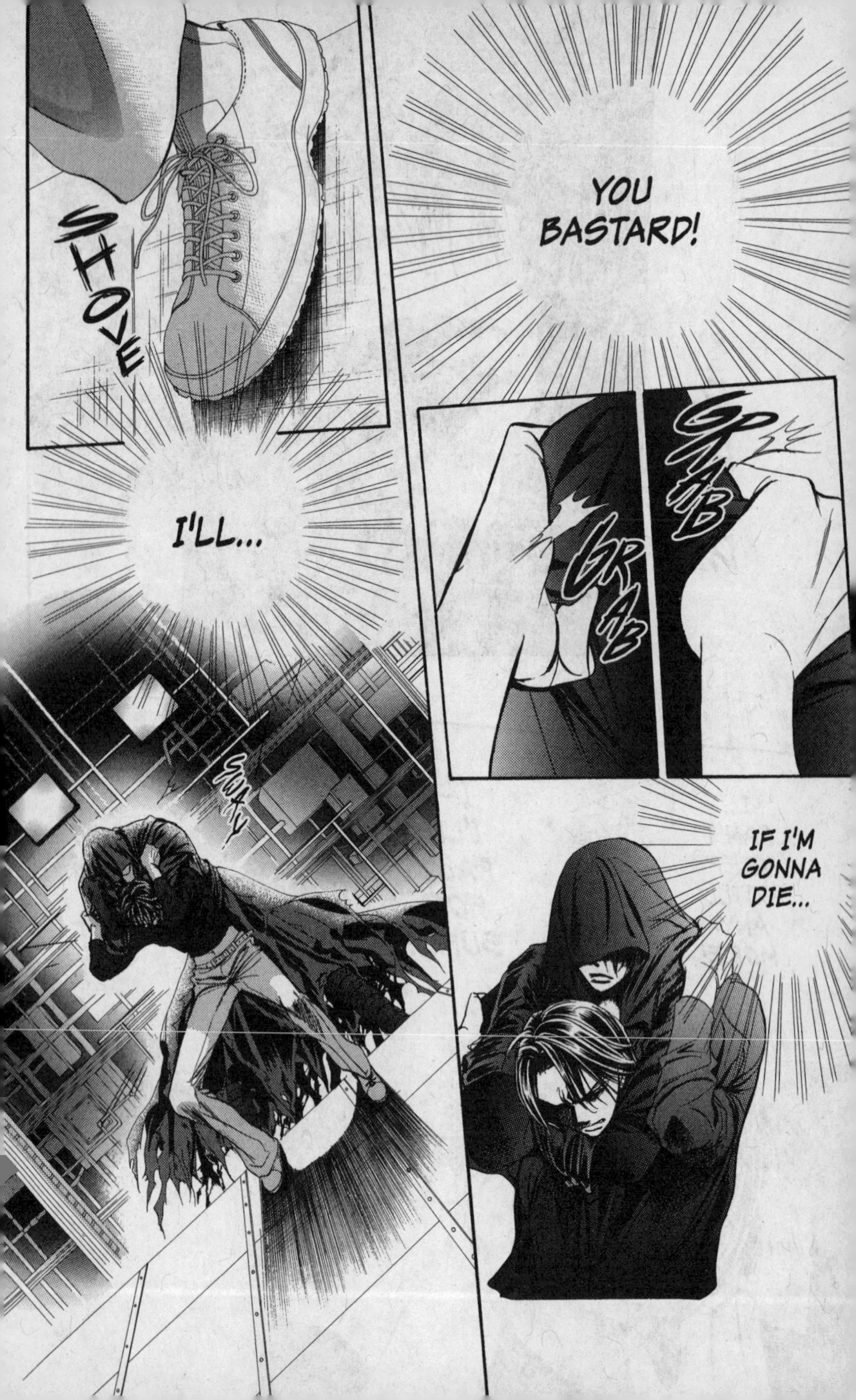
YOU BASTARD!
SHOVE
GRAB
GRAB
I'LL...
SWAY
IF I'M GONNA DIE...

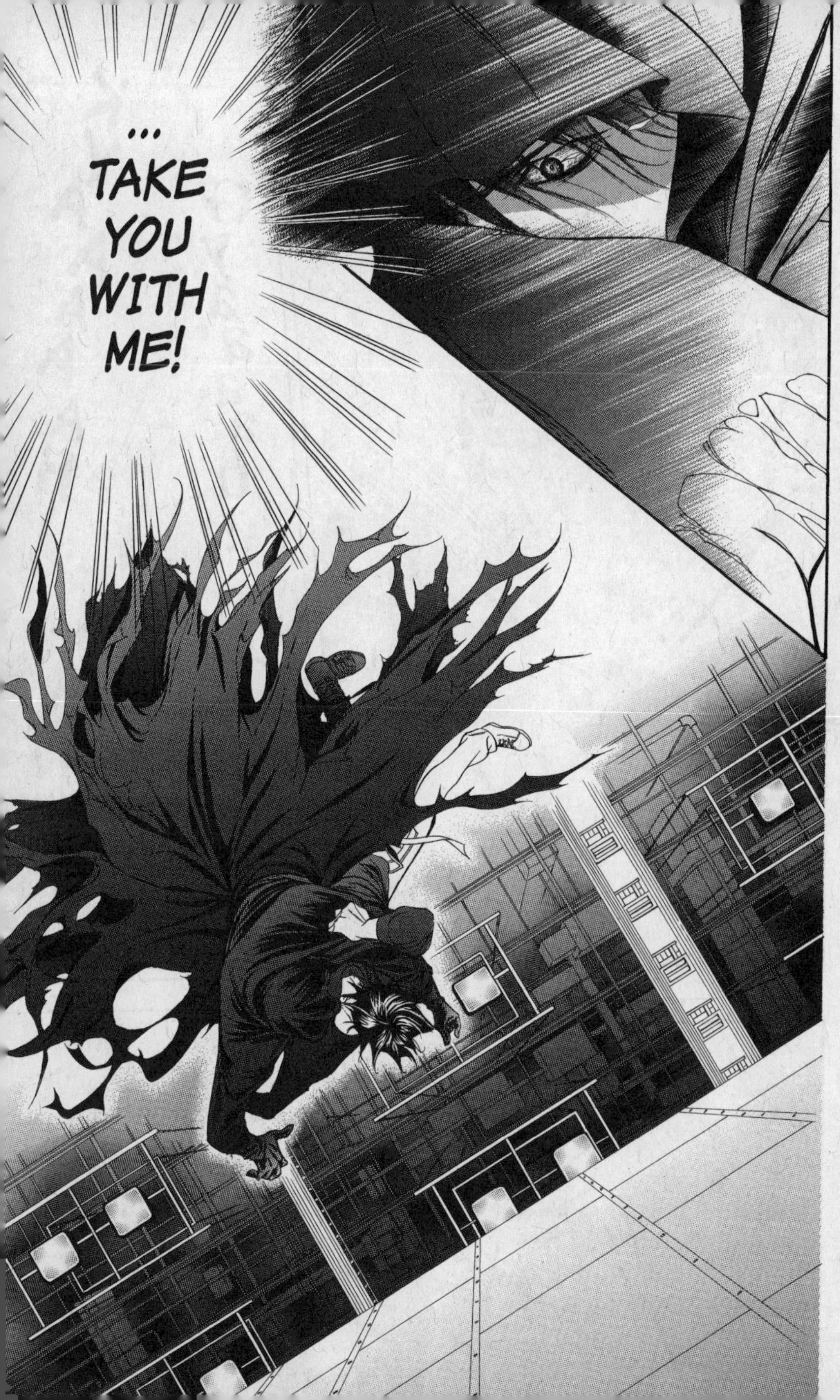
... TAKE YOU WITH ME!

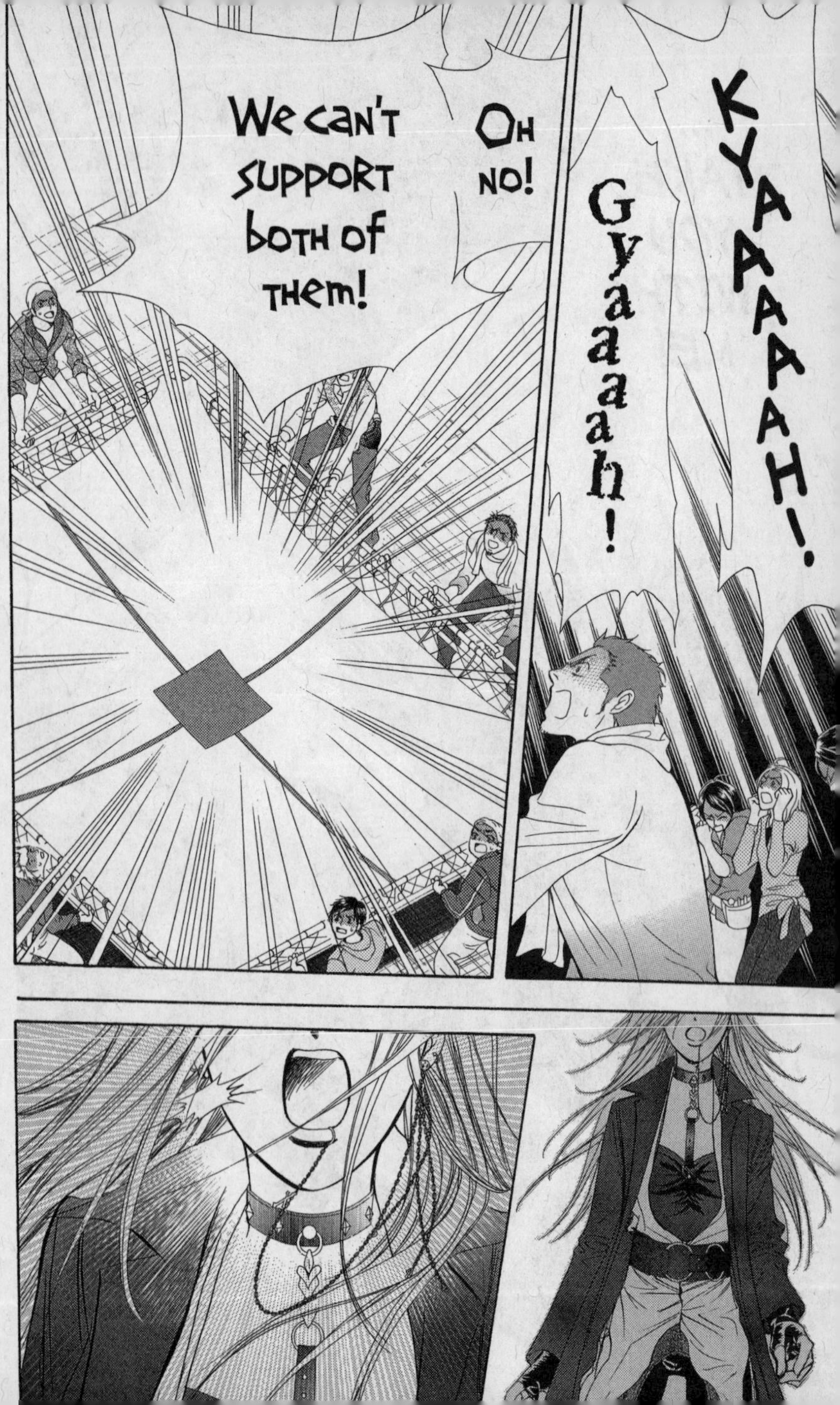
KYAAAAH!
Gyaaaah!
OH NO!
We can't support both of them!

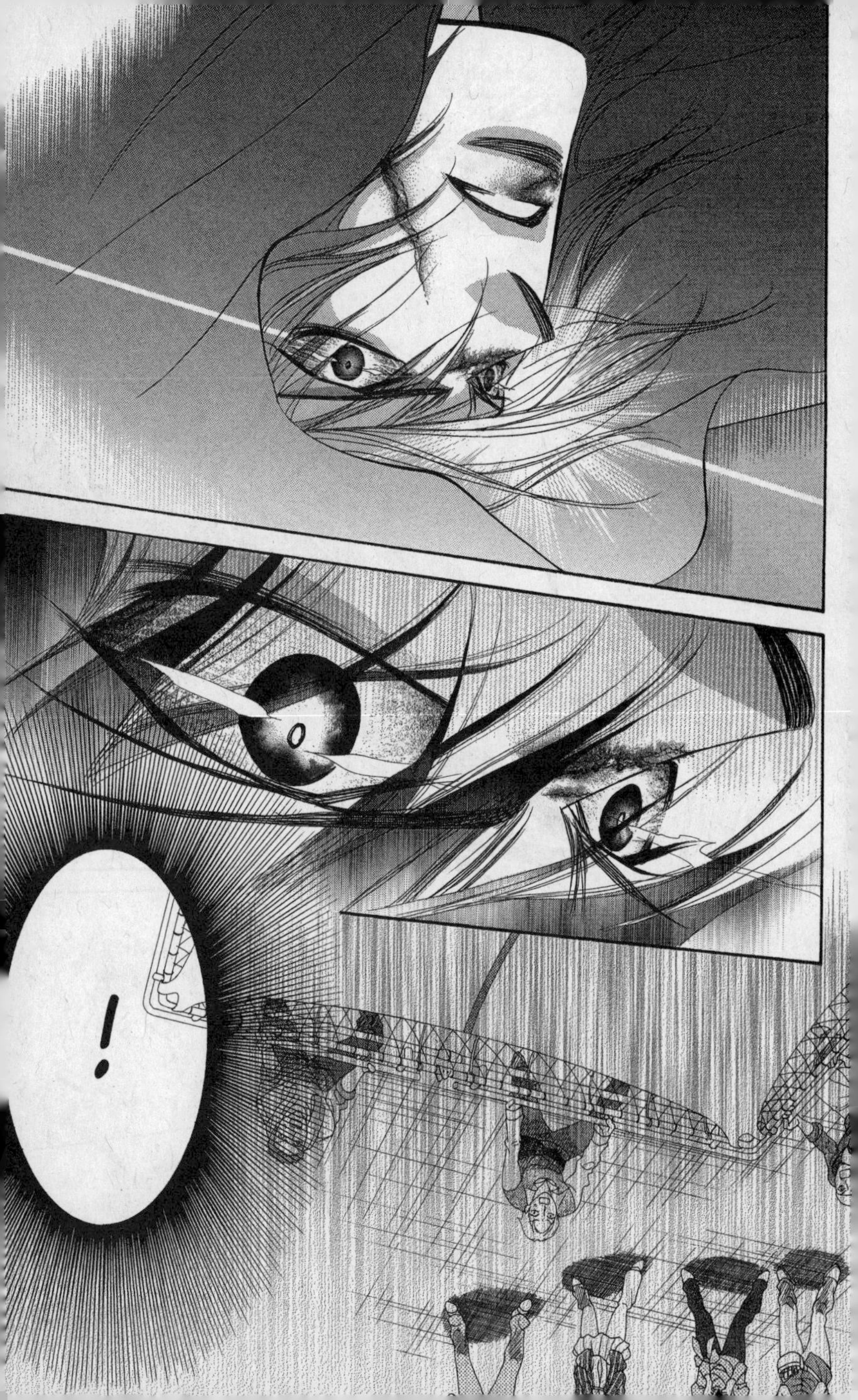
!

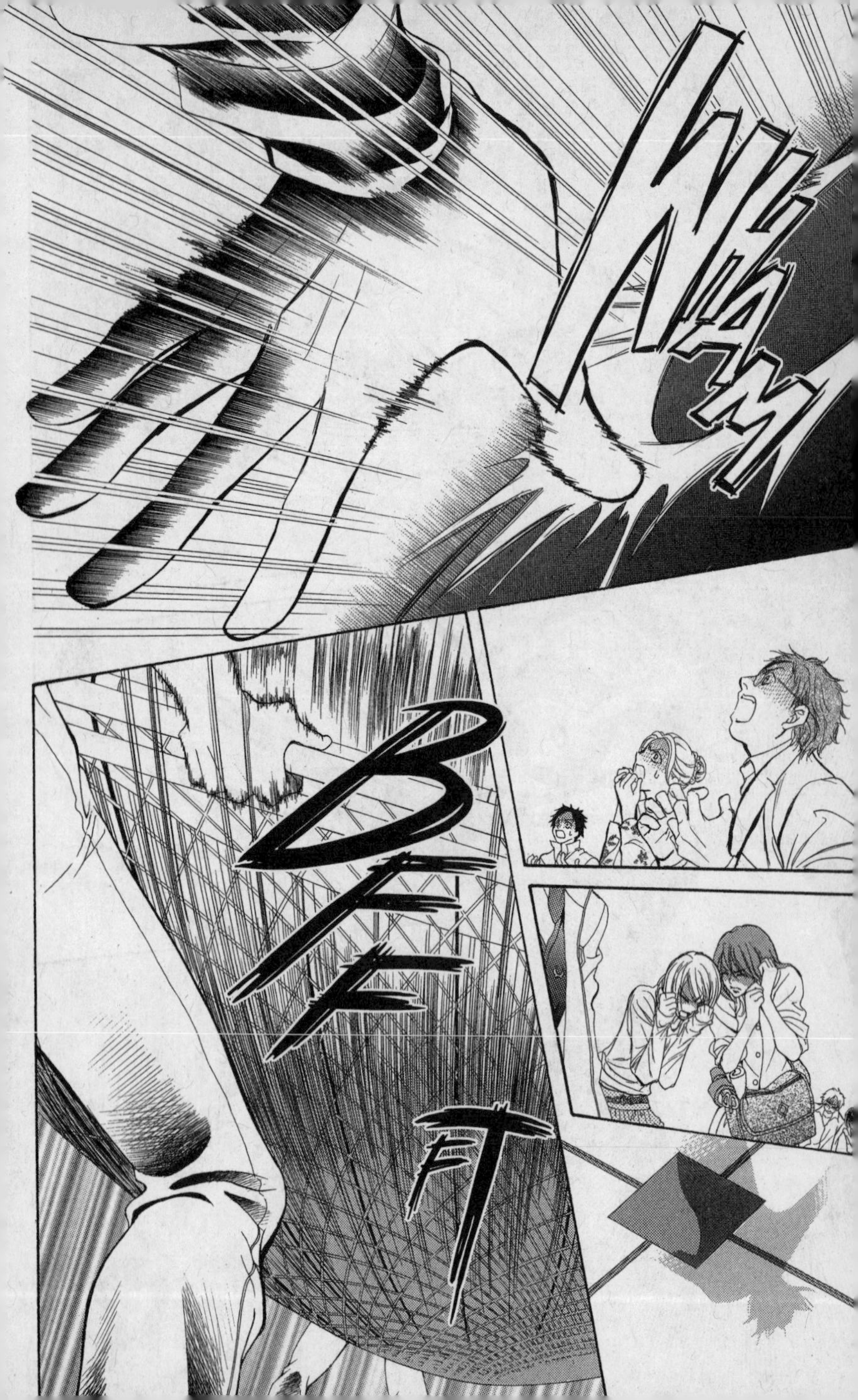
WHAAM
BEFFT

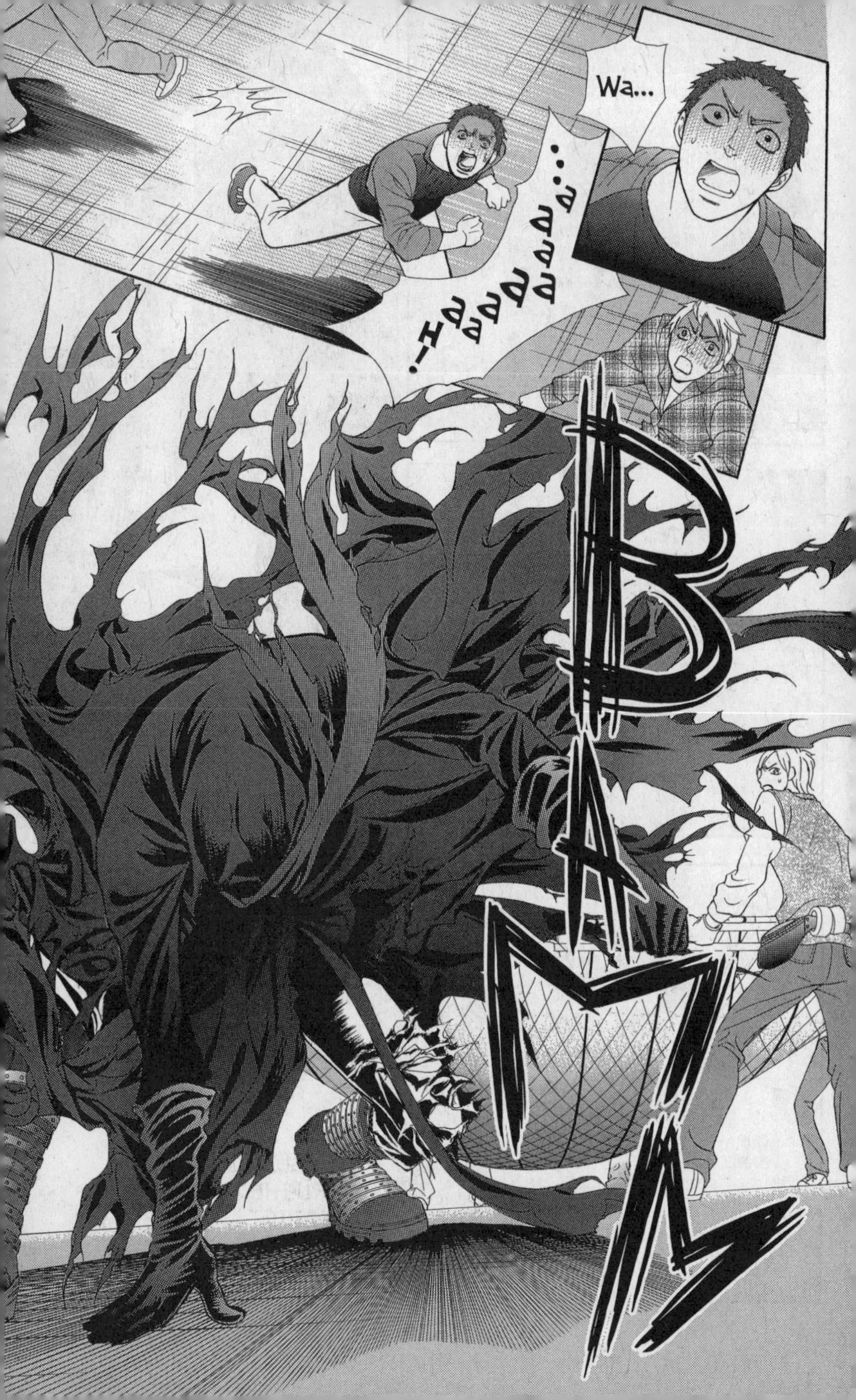
Wa...
...aaaaaaaaaH!
BAM

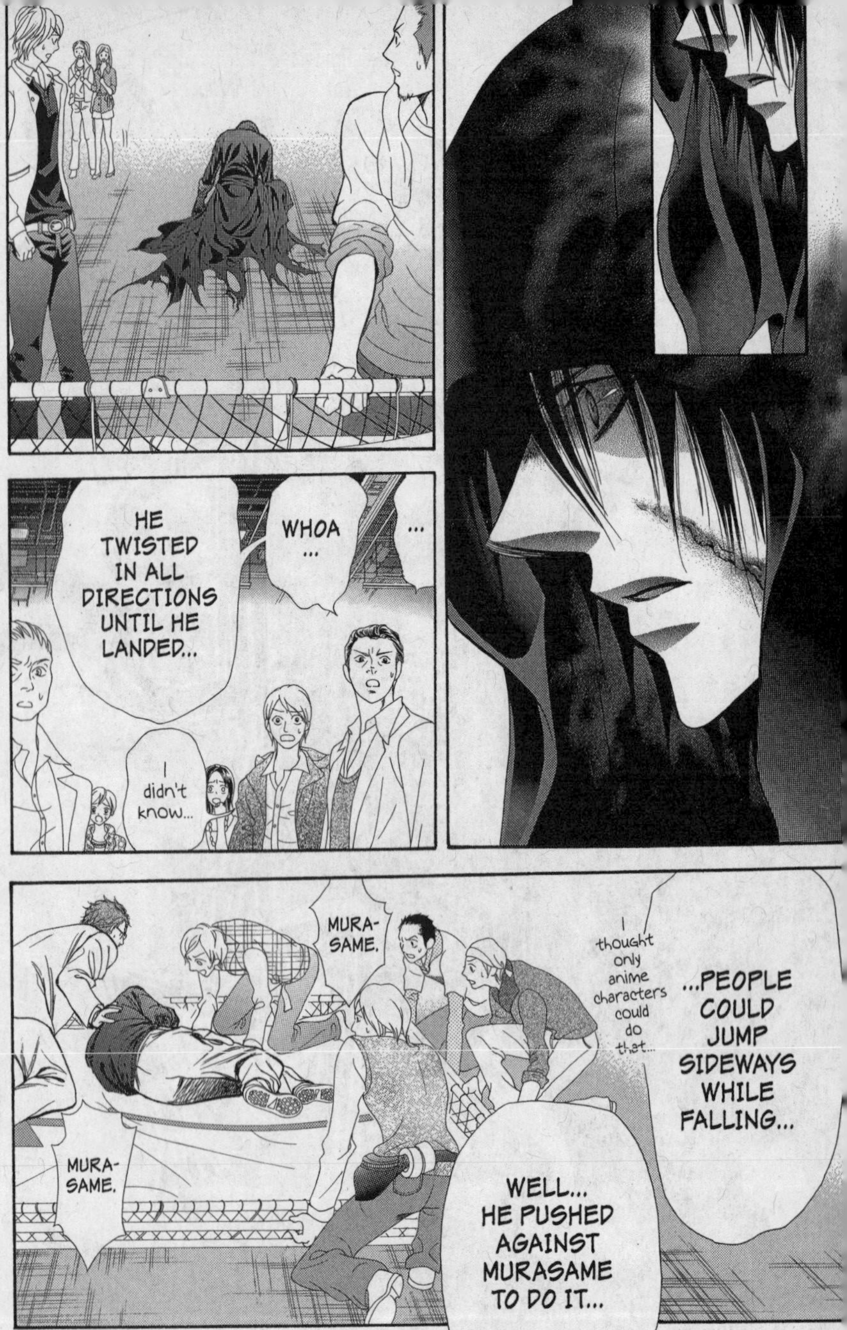
...
WHOA...
HE TWISTED IN ALL DIRECTIONS UNTIL HE LANDED...
I didn't know...
...PEOPLE COULD JUMP SIDEWAYS WHILE FALLING...
I thought only anime characters could do that...
WELL... HE PUSHED AGAINST MURASAME TO DO IT...
MURA-SAME.
MURA-SAME.

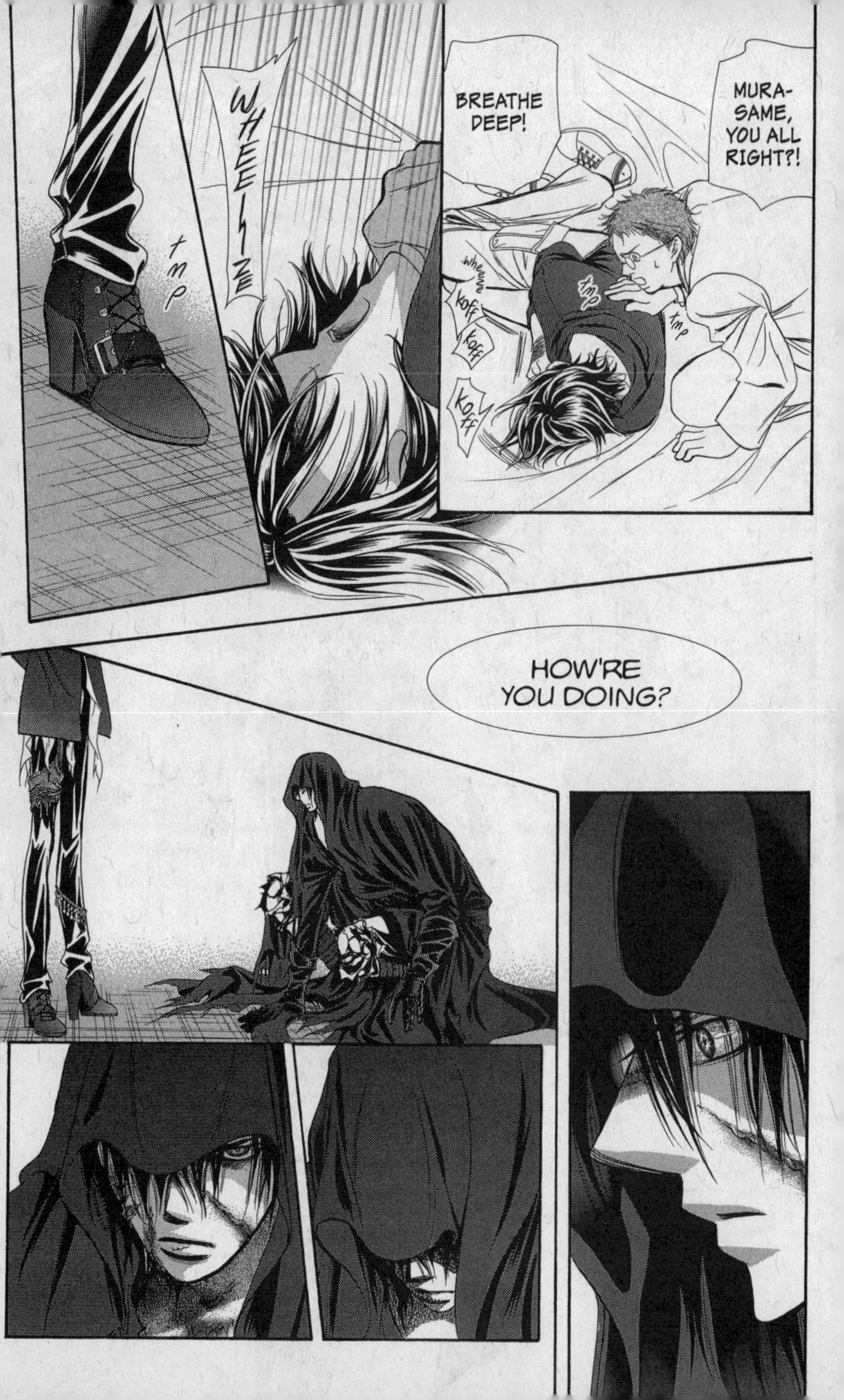
MURA-
SAME,
YOU ALL
RIGHT?!
BREATHE
DEEP!
wheeze
koff
koff
koff
xmp
xmp
WHEEEZE
xmp
HOW'RE
YOU DOING?

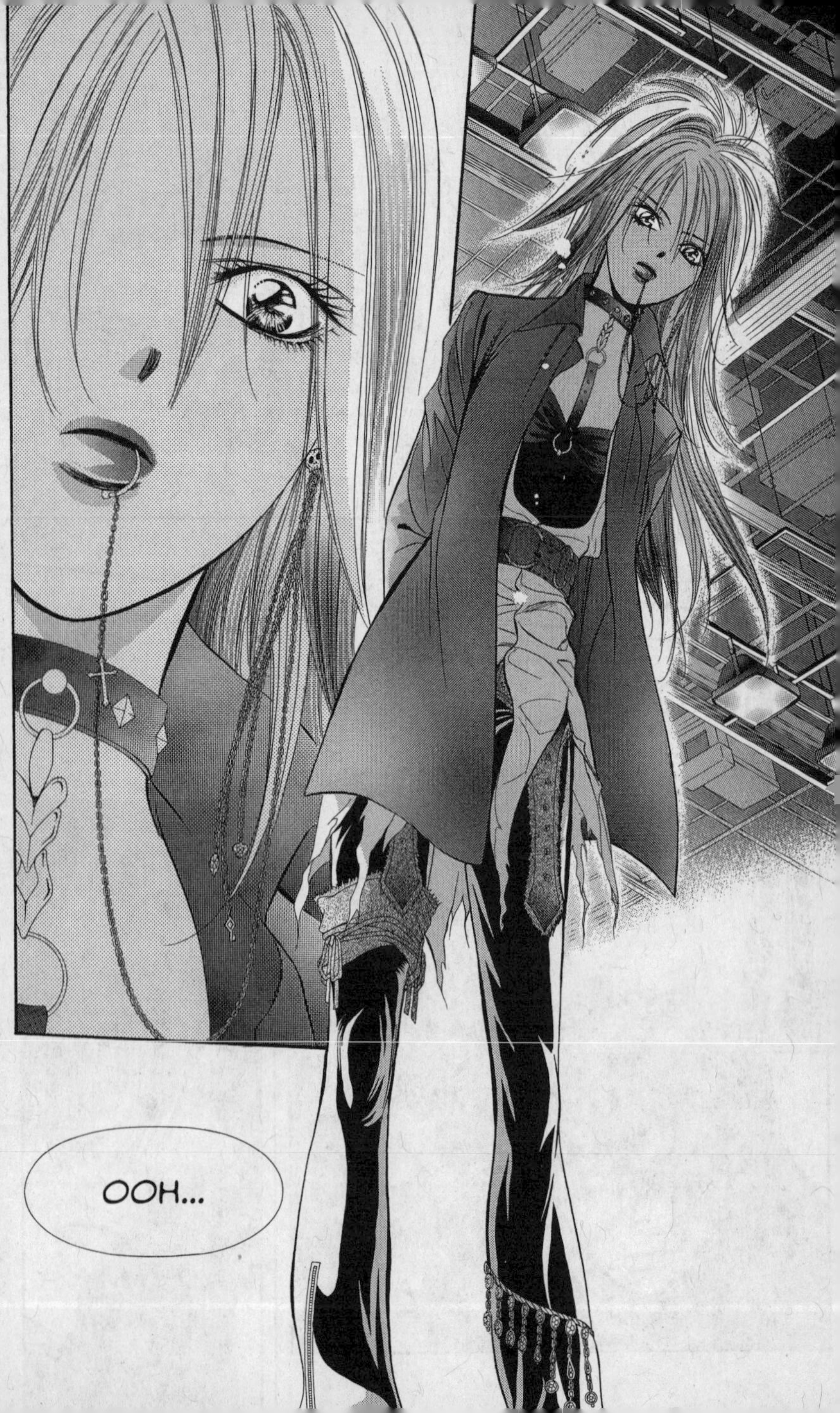
OOH...

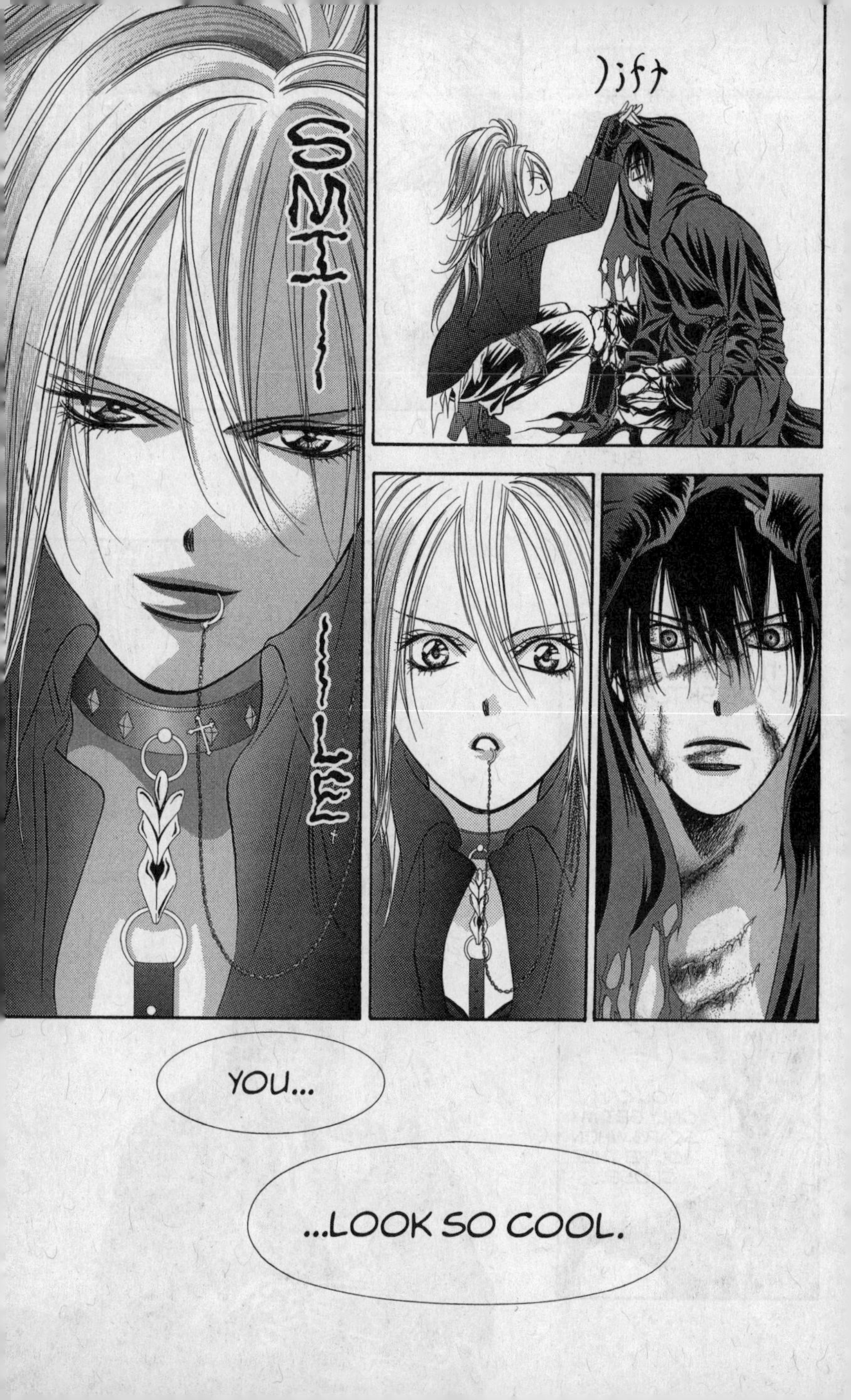
lift
SMI—LE
YOU...
...LOOK SO COOL.

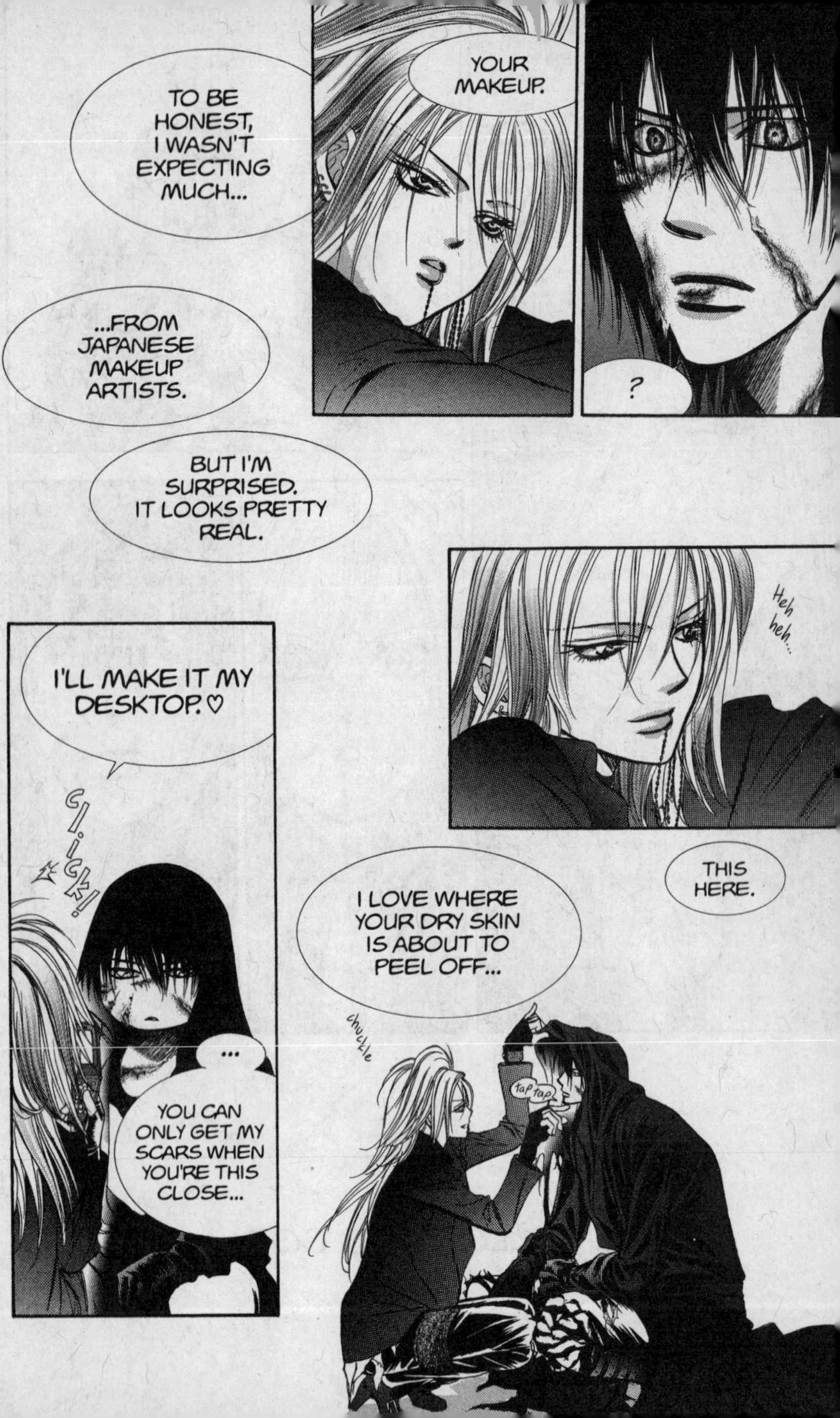
YOUR MAKEUP.
?
TO BE HONEST, I WASN'T EXPECTING MUCH...
...FROM JAPANESE MAKEUP ARTISTS.
BUT I'M SURPRISED. IT LOOKS PRETTY REAL.
Heh heh...
THIS HERE.
I LOVE WHERE YOUR DRY SKIN IS ABOUT TO PEEL OFF...
chuckle
tap tap
I'LL MAKE IT MY DESKTOP. ♡
Click!
...
YOU CAN ONLY GET MY SCARS WHEN YOU'RE THIS CLOSE...

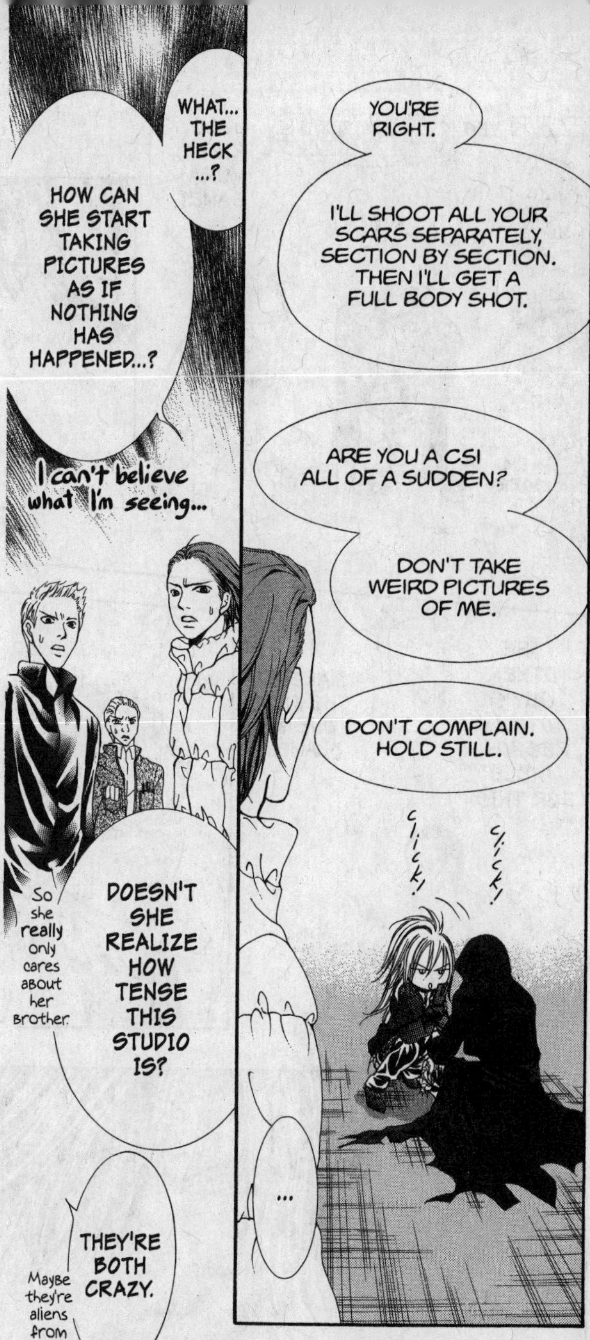
YOU'RE RIGHT.
I'LL SHOOT ALL YOUR SCARS SEPARATELY, SECTION BY SECTION. THEN I'LL GET A FULL BODY SHOT.
ARE YOU A CSI ALL OF A SUDDEN?
DON'T TAKE WEIRD PICTURES OF ME.
DON'T COMPLAIN. HOLD STILL.
CLICK!
CLICK!
...
WHAT... THE HECK ...?
HOW CAN SHE START TAKING PICTURES AS IF NOTHING HAS HAPPENED...?
I can't believe what I'm seeing...
DOESN'T SHE REALIZE HOW TENSE THIS STUDIO IS?
So she really only cares about her brother.
THEY'RE BOTH CRAZY.
Maybe they're aliens from outer space...
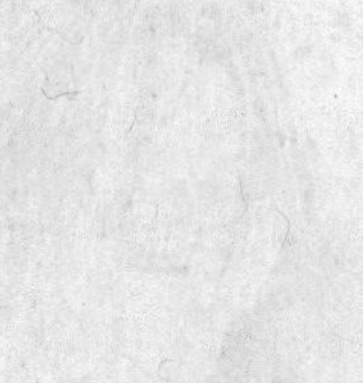

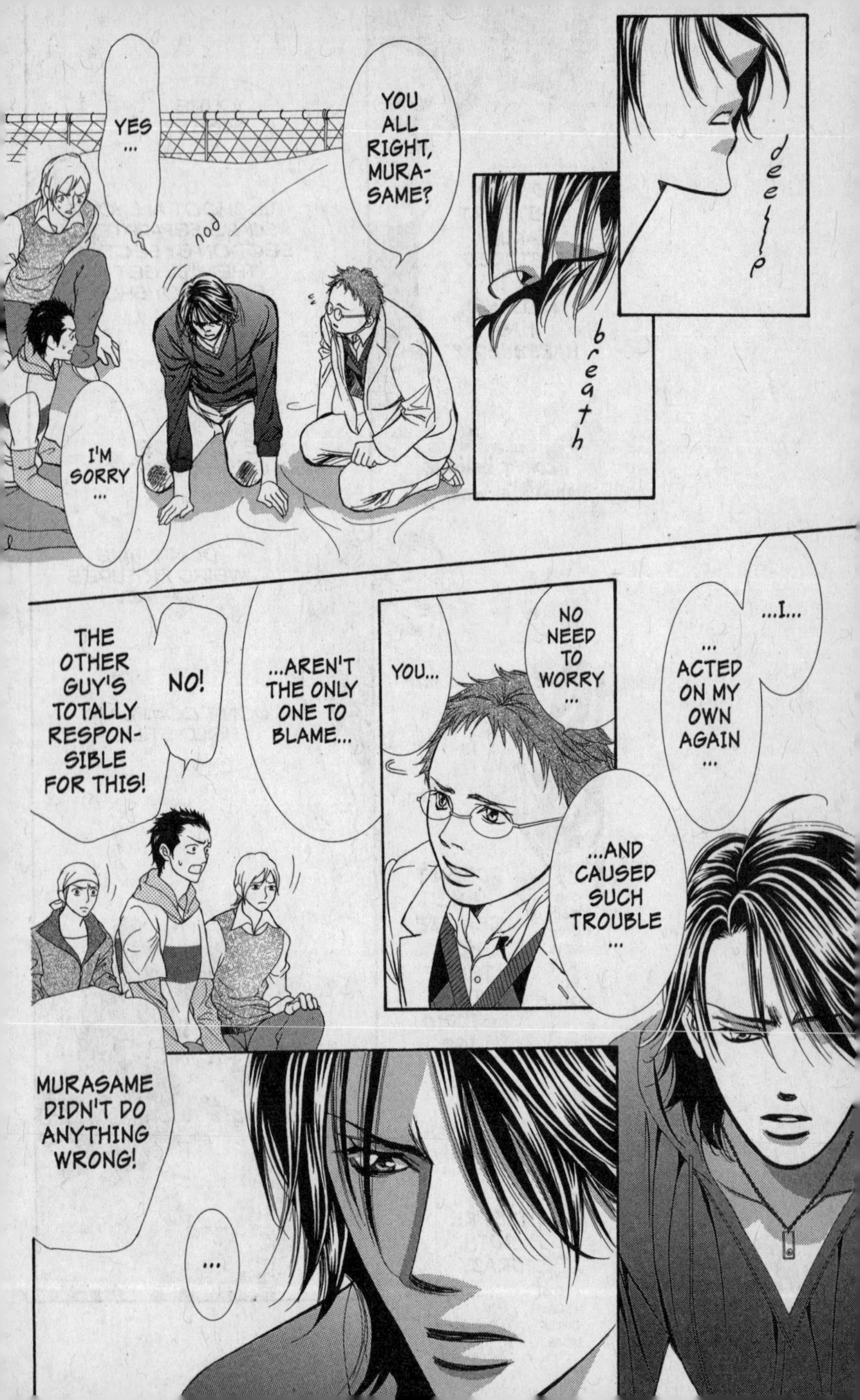
deeep
breath
YOU ALL RIGHT, MURA-SAME?
nod
YES ...
I'M SORRY ...
...I...
... ACTED ON MY OWN AGAIN ...
...AND CAUSED SUCH TROUBLE ...
NO NEED TO WORRY ...
YOU...
...AREN'T THE ONLY ONE TO BLAME...
NO!
THE OTHER GUY'S TOTALLY RESPON-SIBLE FOR THIS!
MURASAME DIDN'T DO ANYTHING WRONG!
...

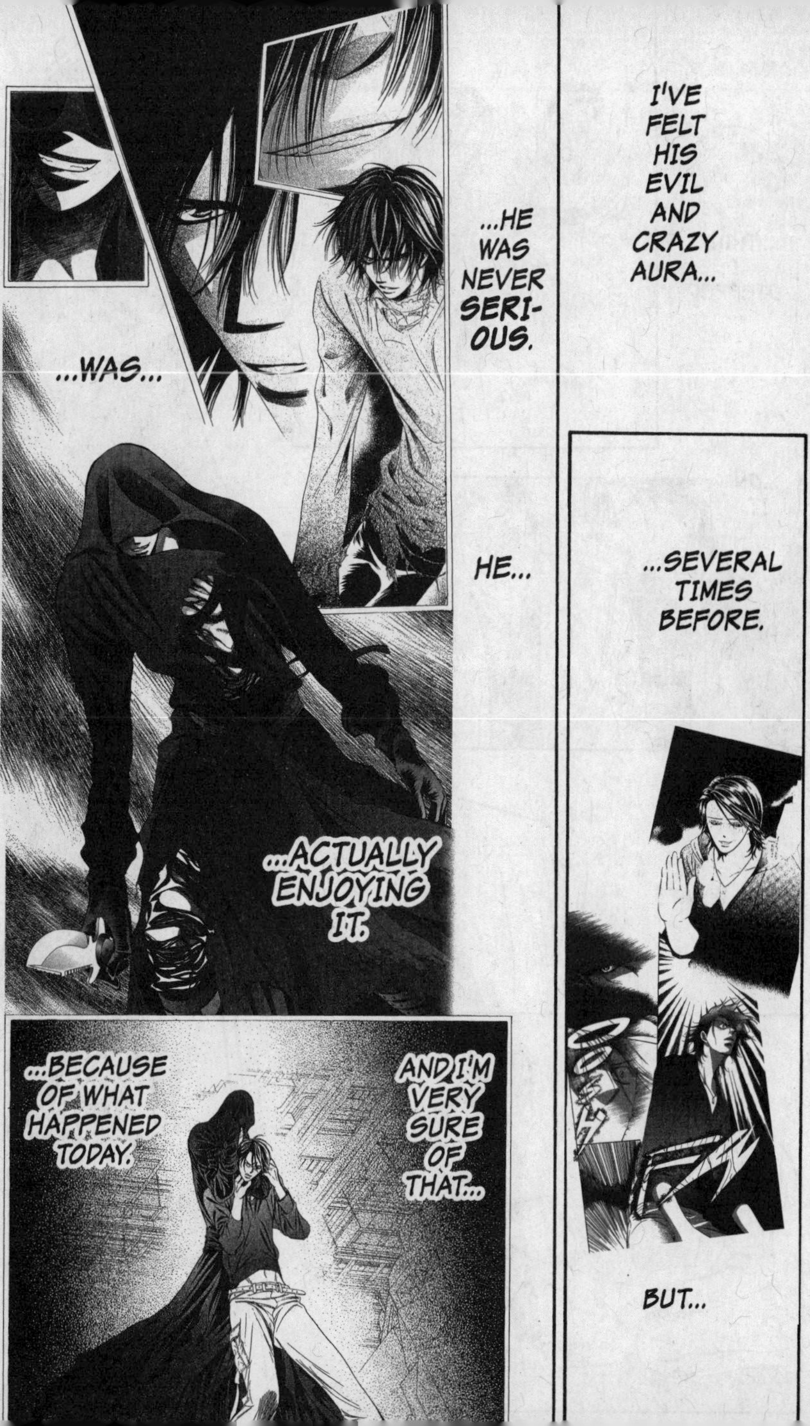
I'VE FELT HIS EVIL AND CRAZY AURA...
...SEVERAL TIMES BEFORE.
BUT...
...HE WAS NEVER SERIOUS.
HE...
...WAS...
...ACTUALLY ENJOYING IT.
AND I'M VERY SURE OF THAT...
...BECAUSE OF WHAT HAPPENED TODAY.

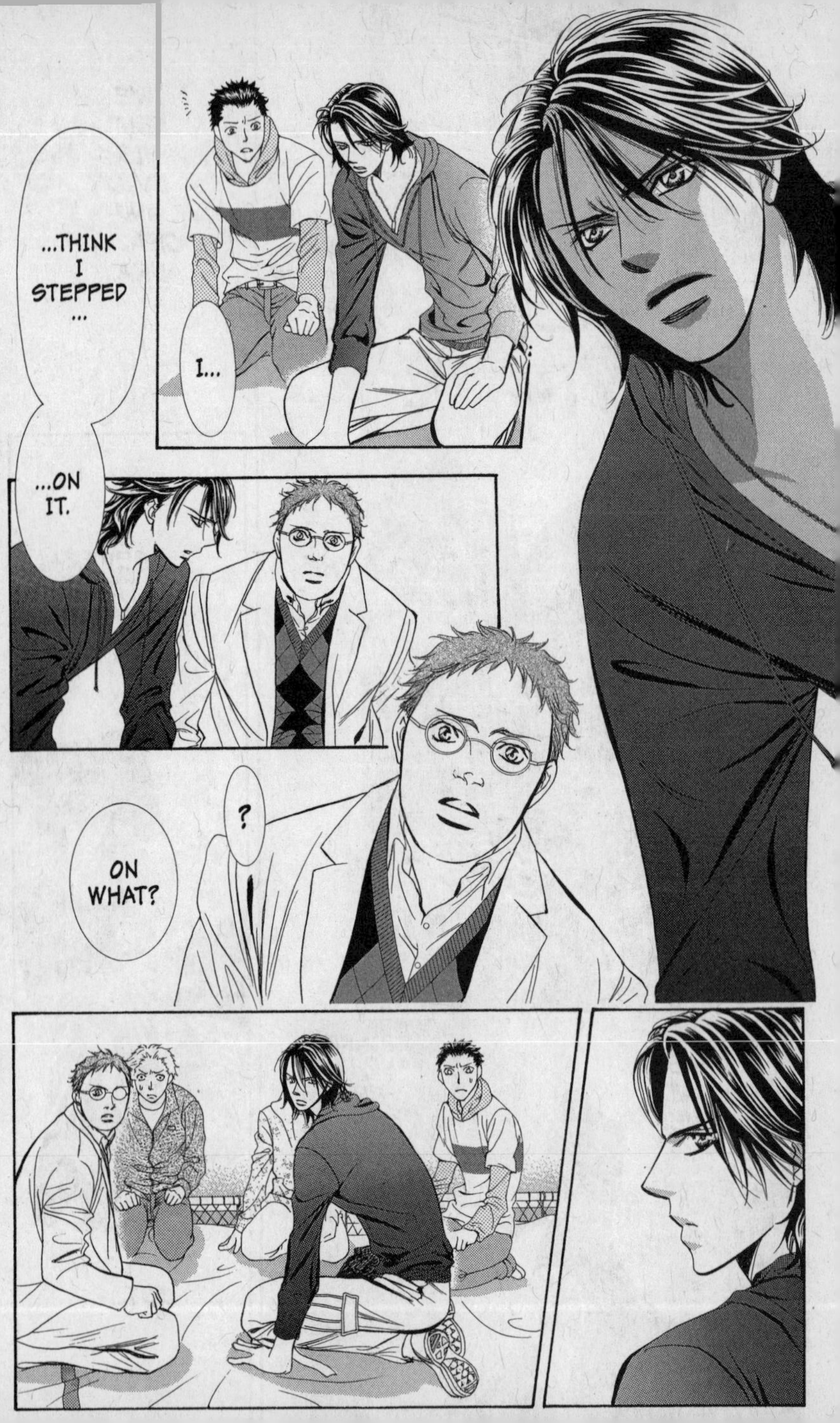
I...
...THINK I STEPPED ...
...ON IT.
?
ON WHAT?

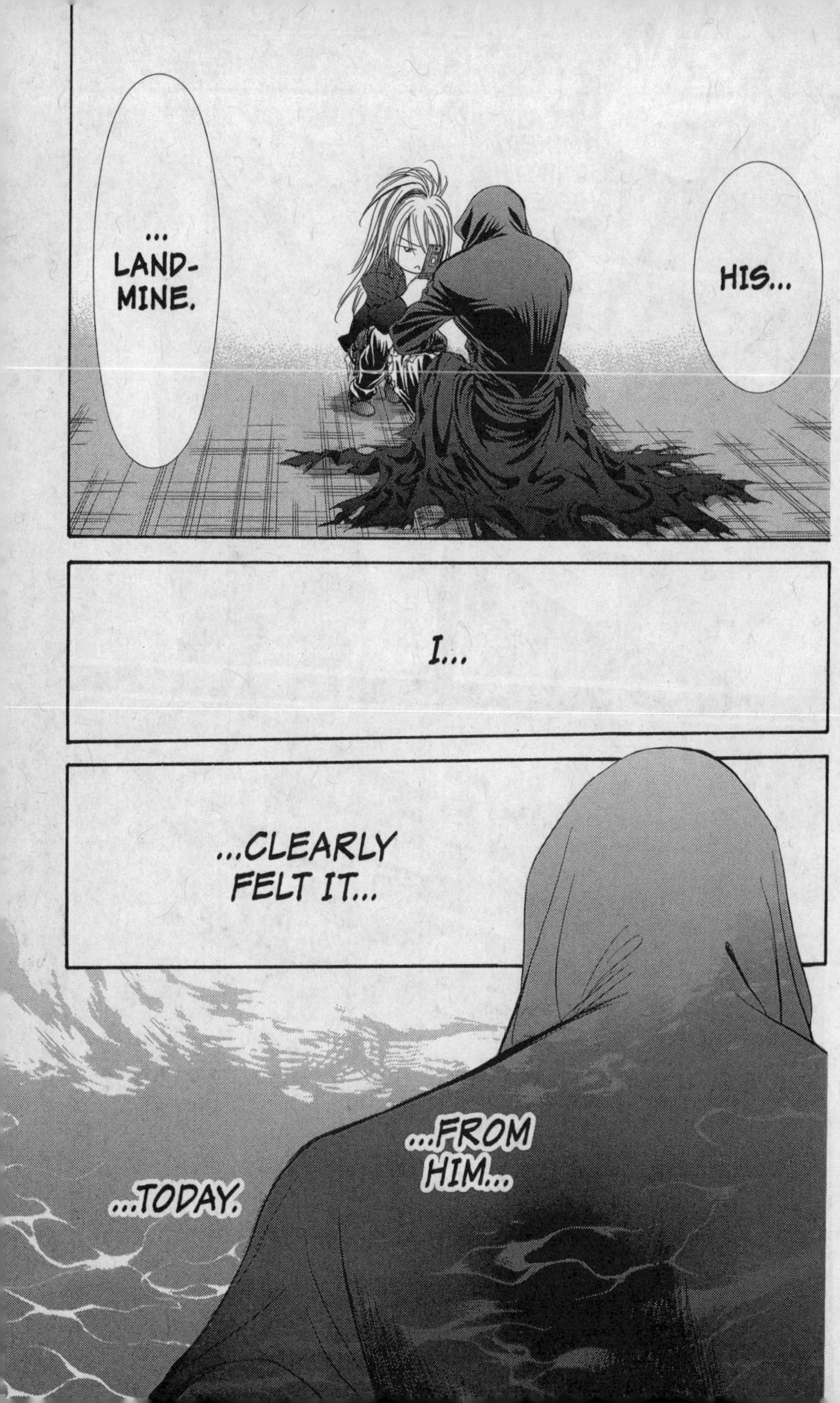
HIS...
...LAND-MINE.
I...
...CLEARLY FELT IT...
...FROM HIM...
...TODAY.

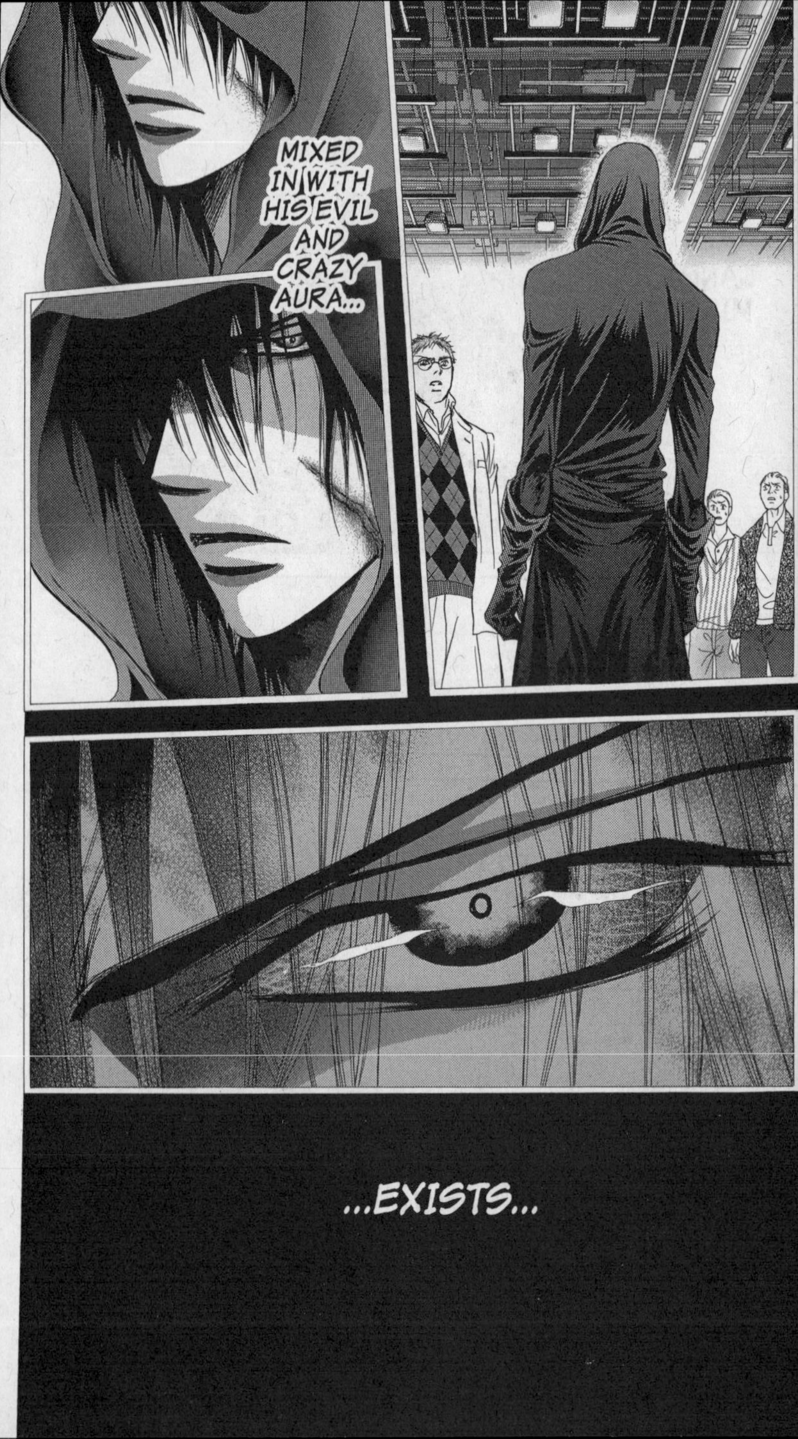
MIXED IN WITH HIS EVIL AND CRAZY AURA...
...EXISTS...

...A FIERCE INTENT TO KILL.

glub

glub glub

AREN'T YOU GOING TO ASK ME?

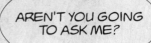

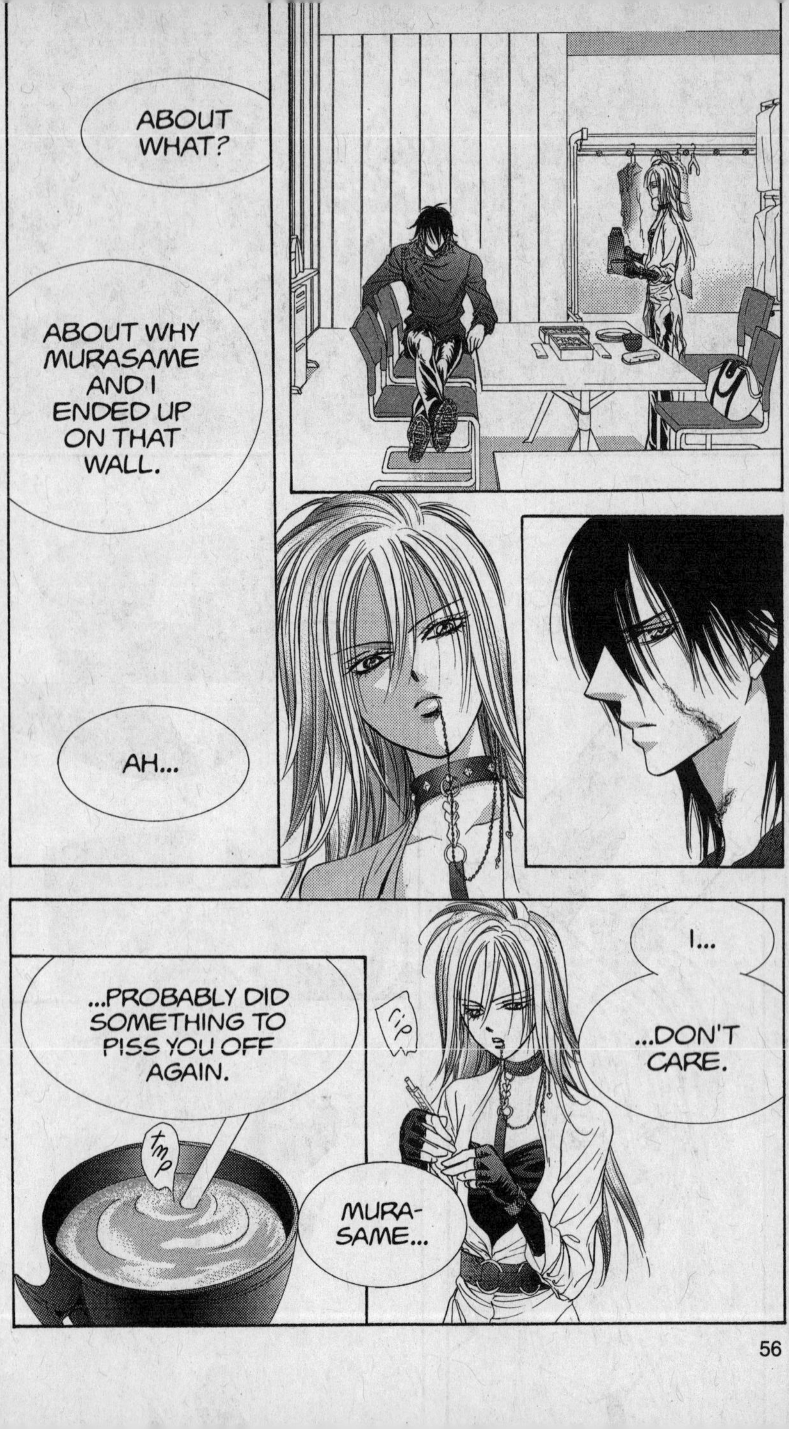
ABOUT WHAT?
ABOUT WHY MURASAME AND I ENDED UP ON THAT WALL.
AH...
I...
...DON'T CARE.
rip
MURA-SAME...
...PROBABLY DID SOMETHING TO PISS YOU OFF AGAIN.
tmp

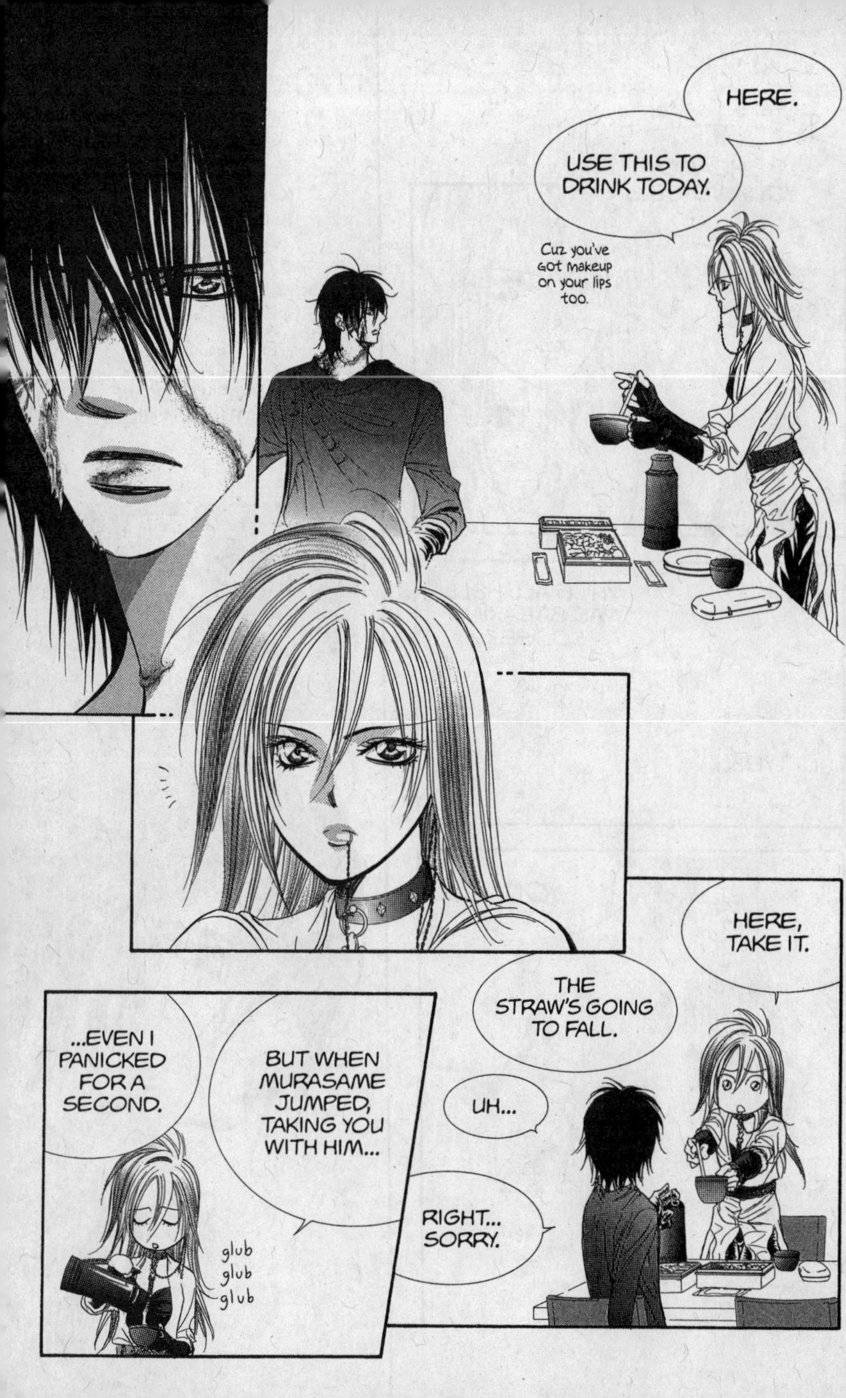
HERE.
USE THIS TO DRINK TODAY.
Cuz you've got makeup on your lips too.
HERE, TAKE IT.
THE STRAW'S GOING TO FALL.
UH...
RIGHT... SORRY.
BUT WHEN MURASAME JUMPED, TAKING YOU WITH HIM...
...EVEN I PANICKED FOR A SECOND.
glub glub glub

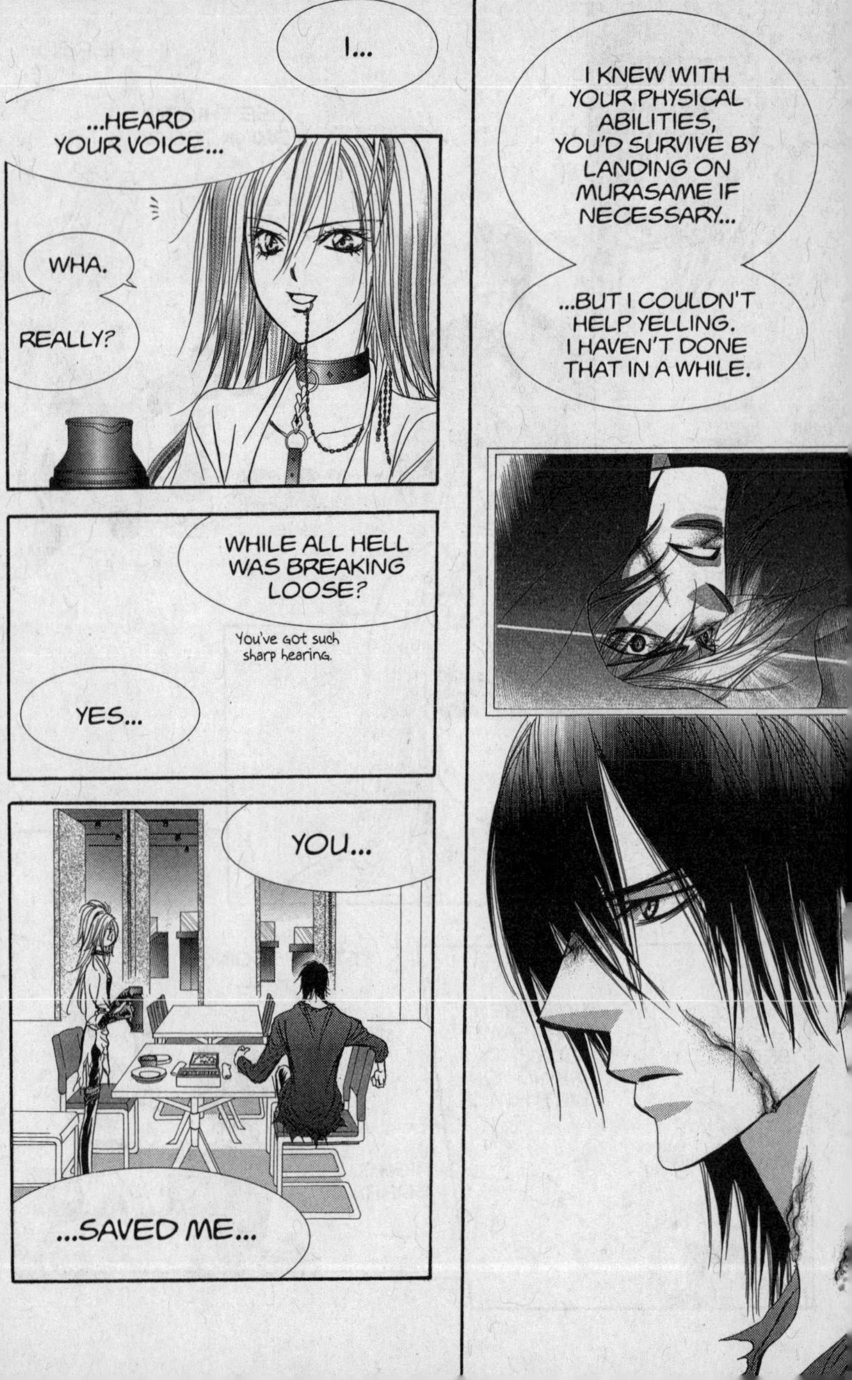
I KNEW WITH YOUR PHYSICAL ABILITIES, YOU'D SURVIVE BY LANDING ON MURASAME IF NECESSARY...
...BUT I COULDN'T HELP YELLING. I HAVEN'T DONE THAT IN A WHILE.
I...
...HEARD YOUR VOICE...
WHA.
REALLY?
WHILE ALL HELL WAS BREAKING LOOSE?
You've got such sharp hearing.
YES...
YOU...
...SAVED ME...

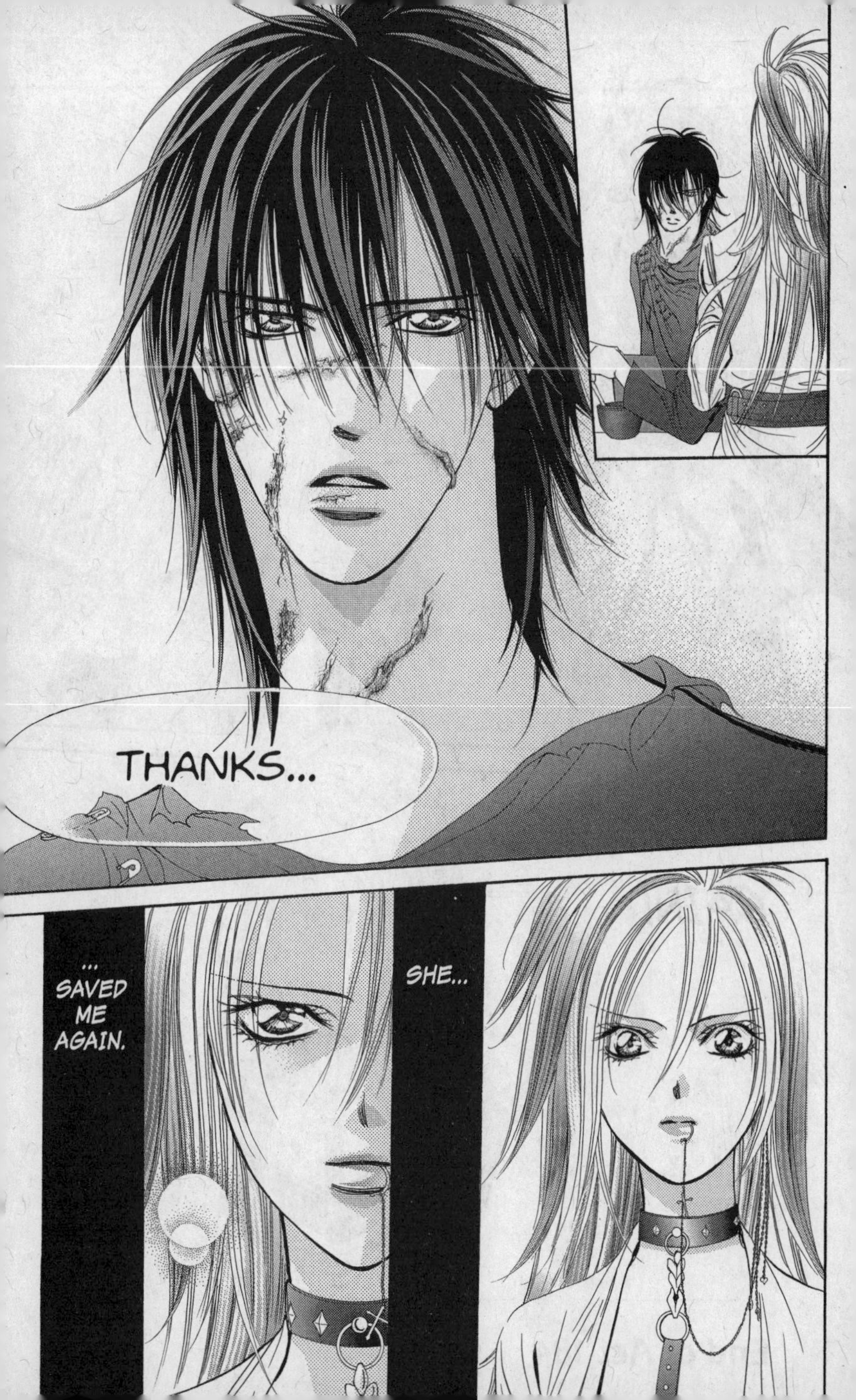
THANKS...
SHE...
... SAVED ME AGAIN.

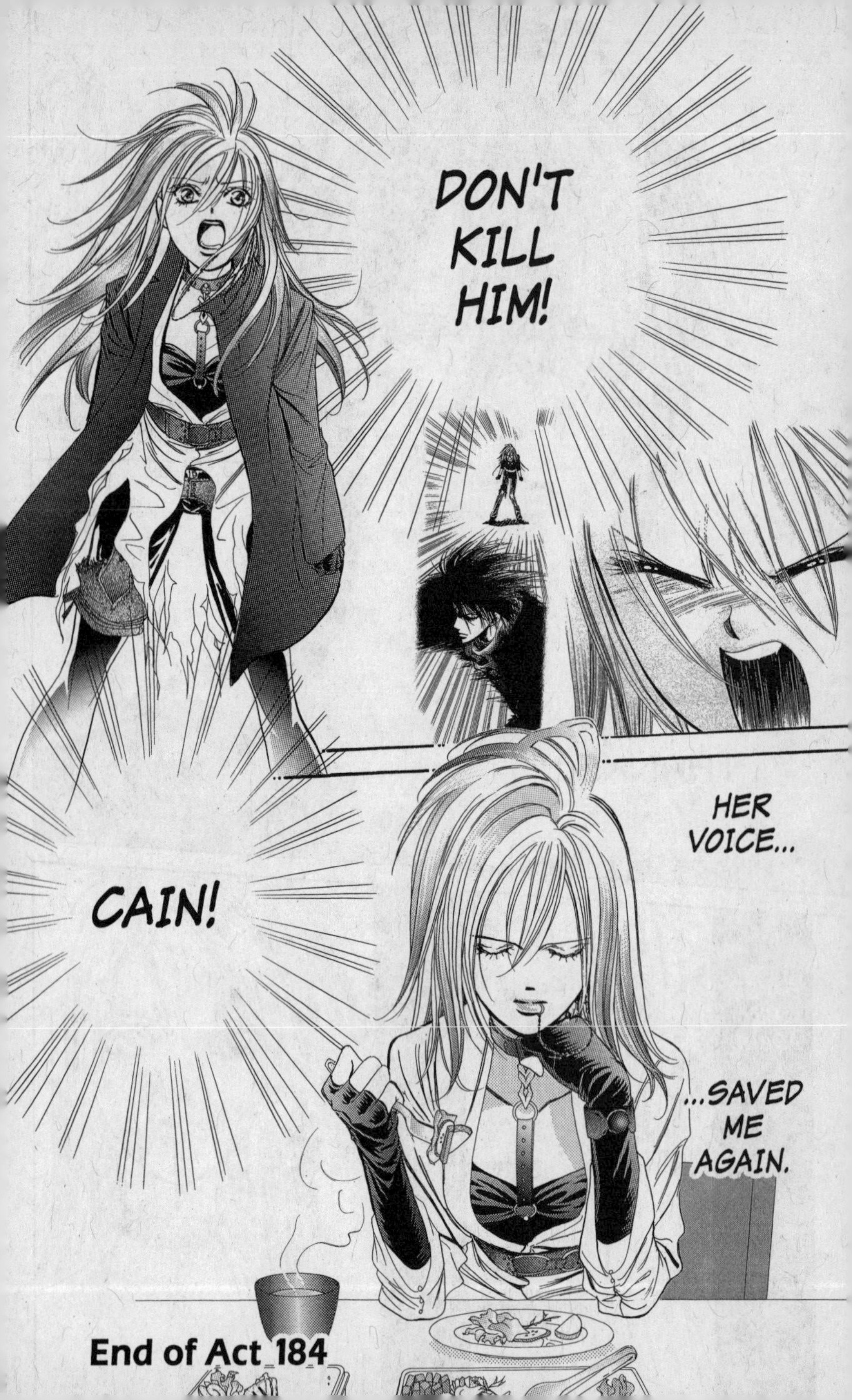
DON'T KILL HIM!
CAIN!
HER VOICE...
...SAVED ME AGAIN.
End of Act 184

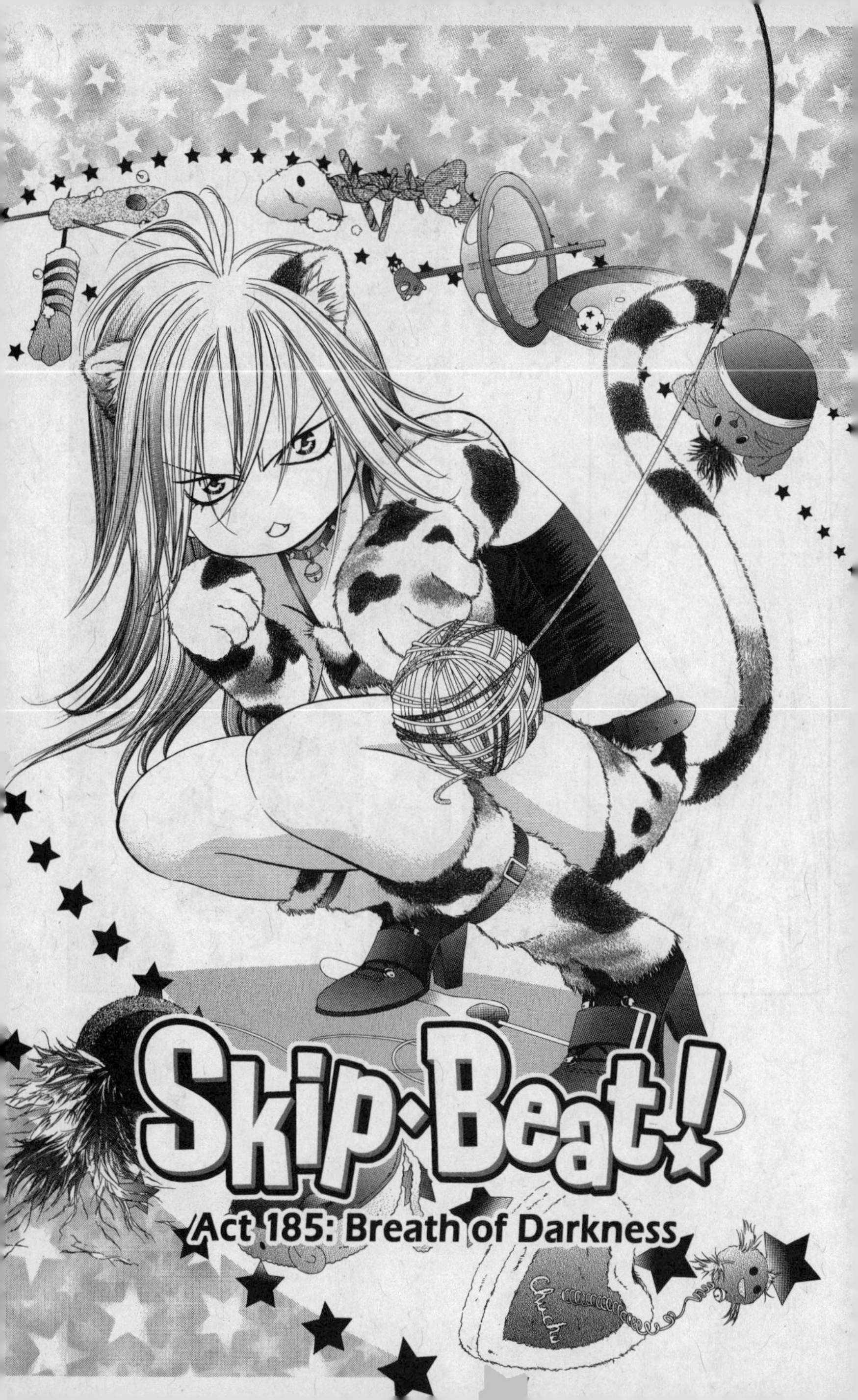
Skip·Beat!
Act 185: Breath of Darkness
Chuchu

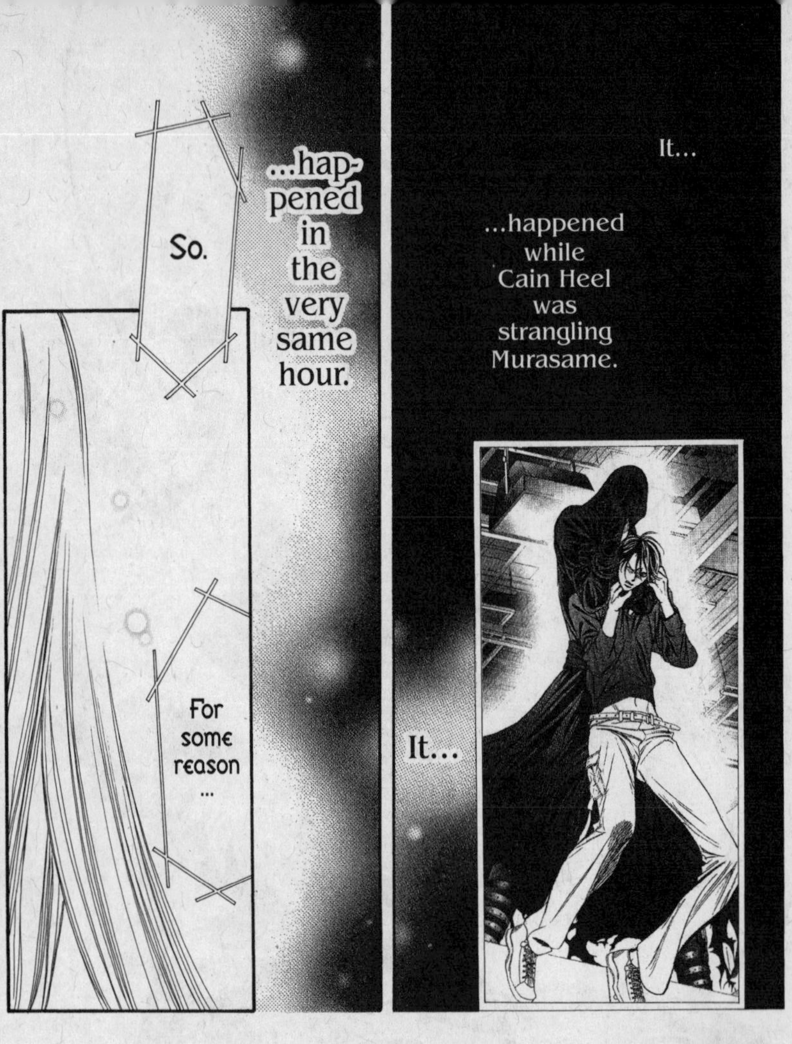
It...
...happened while Cain Heel was strangling Murasame.
It...
...hap-pened in the very same hour.
So.
For some reason ...

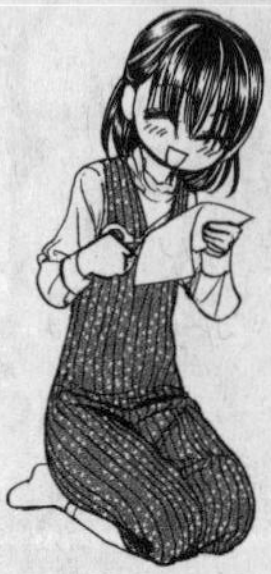

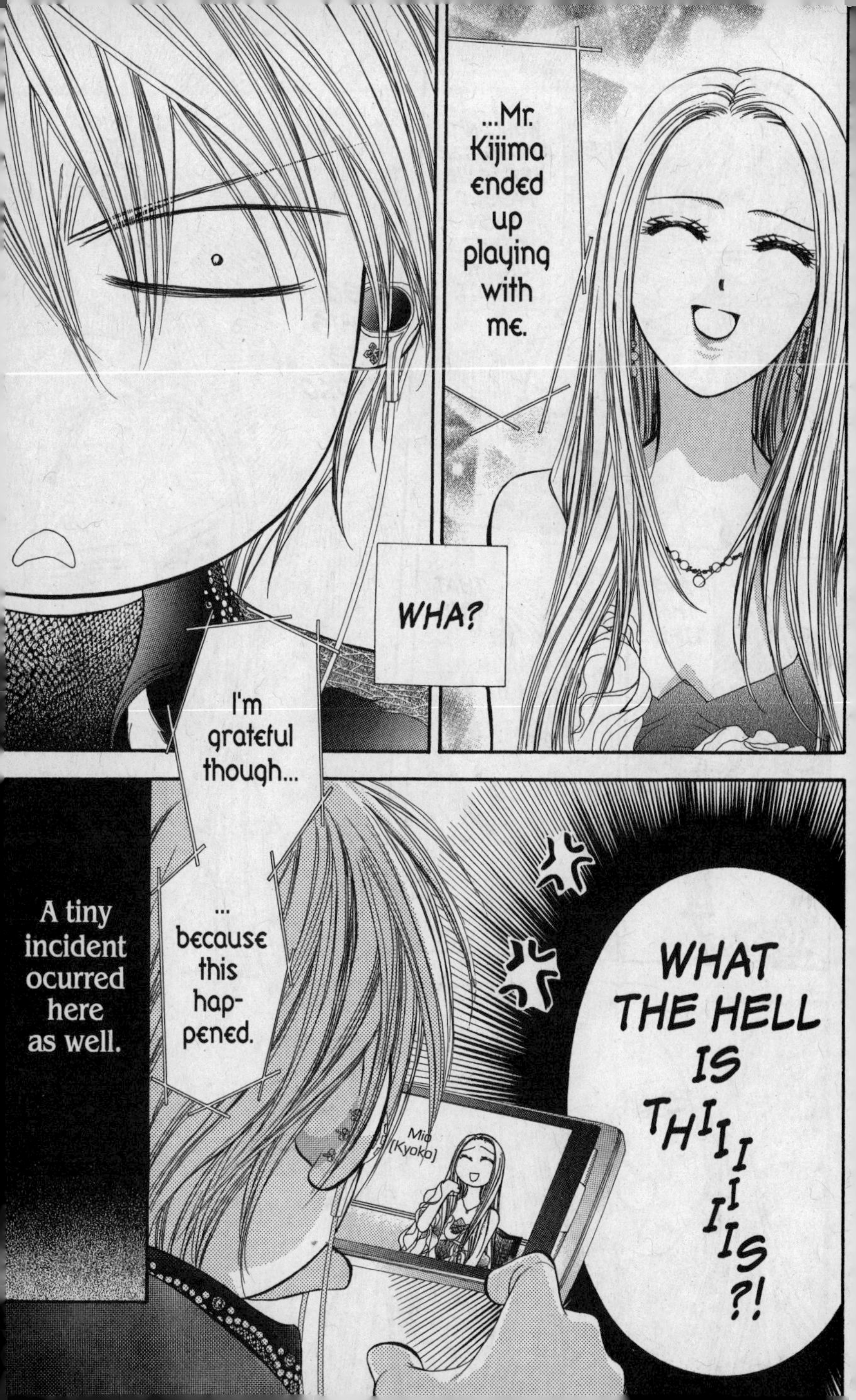
...Mr. Kijima ended up playing with me.
WHA?
I'm grateful though...
... because this hap-pened.
WHAT THE HELL IS THIIIIIIS?!
Mio [Kyoko]
A tiny incident ocurred here as well.

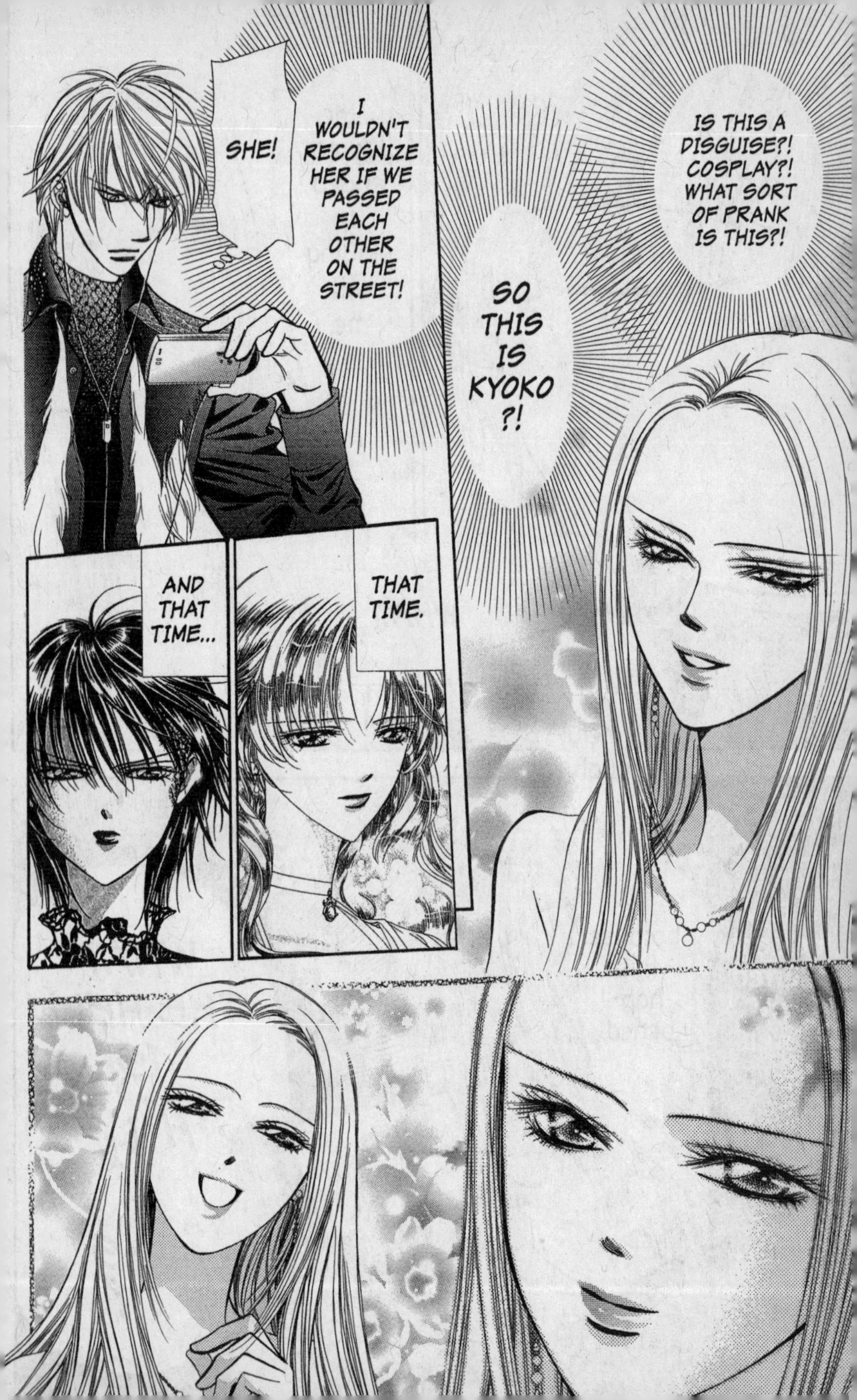
IS THIS A DISGUISE?! COSPLAY?! WHAT SORT OF PRANK IS THIS?!
SO THIS IS KYOKO ?!
I WOULDN'T RECOGNIZE HER IF WE PASSED EACH OTHER ON THE STREET!
SHE!
THAT TIME.
AND THAT TIME...

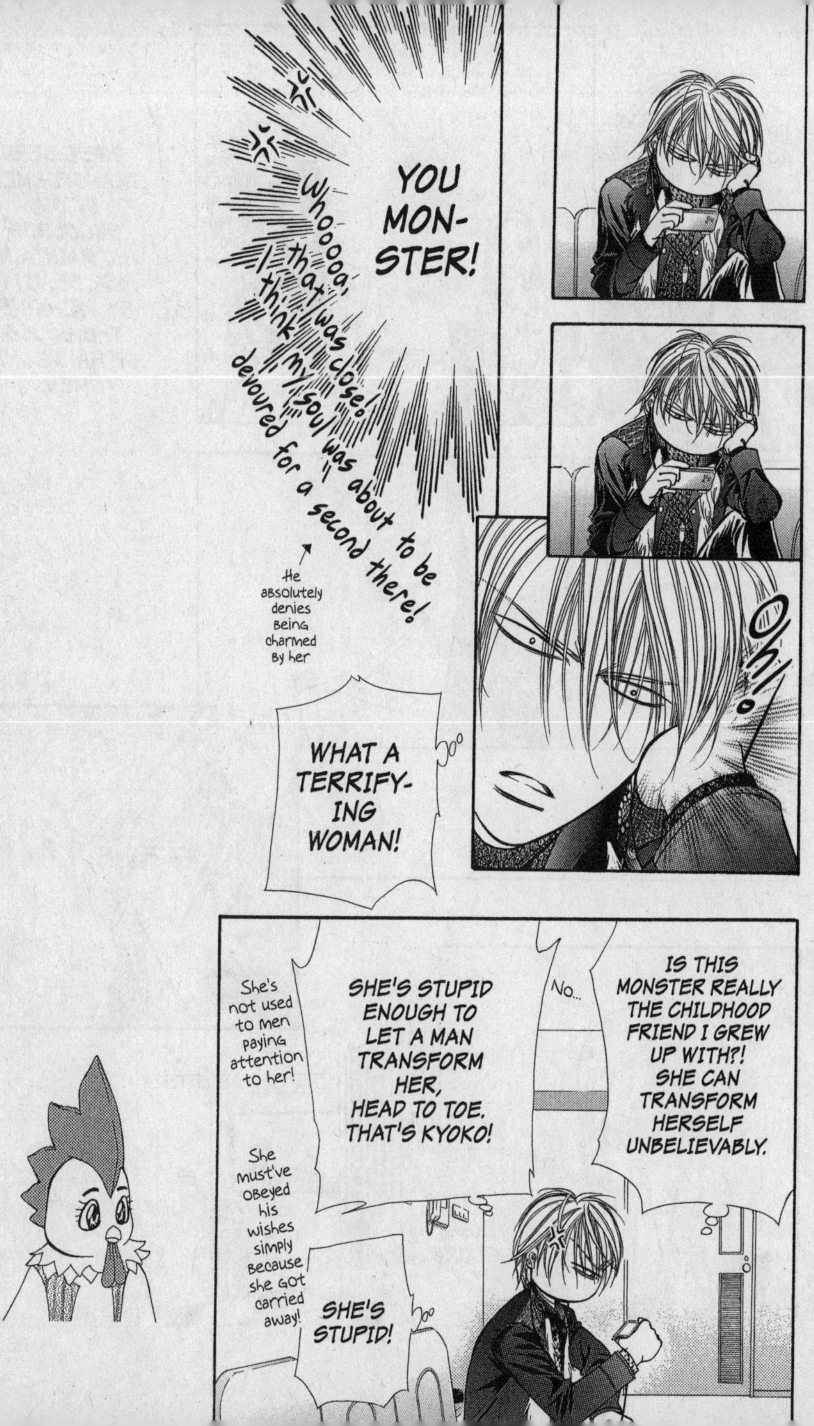
Oh!
YOU MONSTER!
Whoooa, that was close! I think my soul was about to be devoured for a second there!
He absolutely denies being charmed by her
WHAT A TERRIFYING WOMAN!
IS THIS MONSTER REALLY THE CHILDHOOD FRIEND I GREW UP WITH?! SHE CAN TRANSFORM HERSELF UNBELIEVABLY.
No...
SHE'S STUPID ENOUGH TO LET A MAN TRANSFORM HER, HEAD TO TOE. THAT'S KYOKO!
She's not used to men paying attention to her!
She must've obeyed his wishes simply because she got carried away!
SHE'S STUPID!

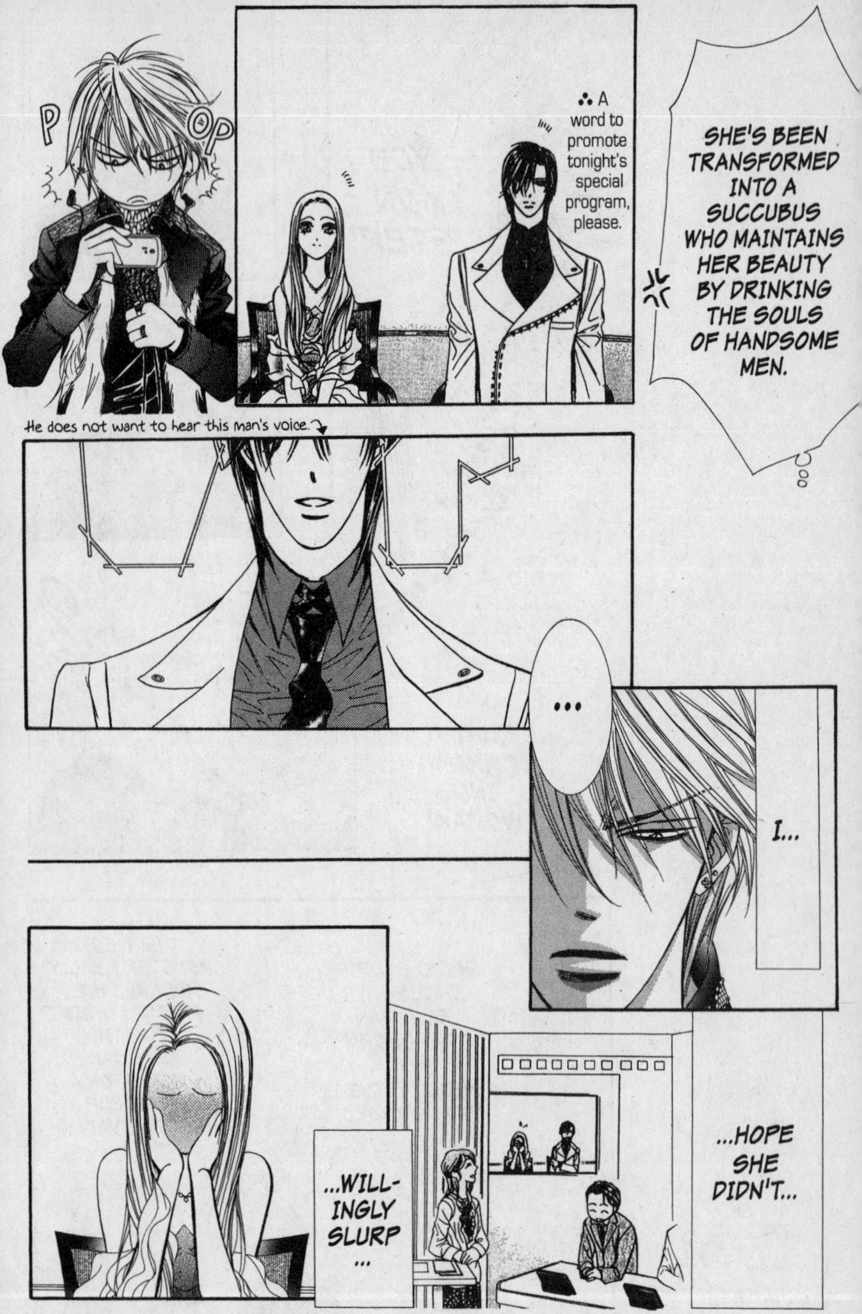
SHE'S BEEN TRANSFORMED INTO A SUCCUBUS WHO MAINTAINS HER BEAUTY BY DRINKING THE SOULS OF HANDSOME MEN.
A word to promote tonight's special program, please.
P OP
He does not want to hear this man's voice.
...
I...
...HOPE SHE DIDN'T...
...WILL-INGLY SLURP ...

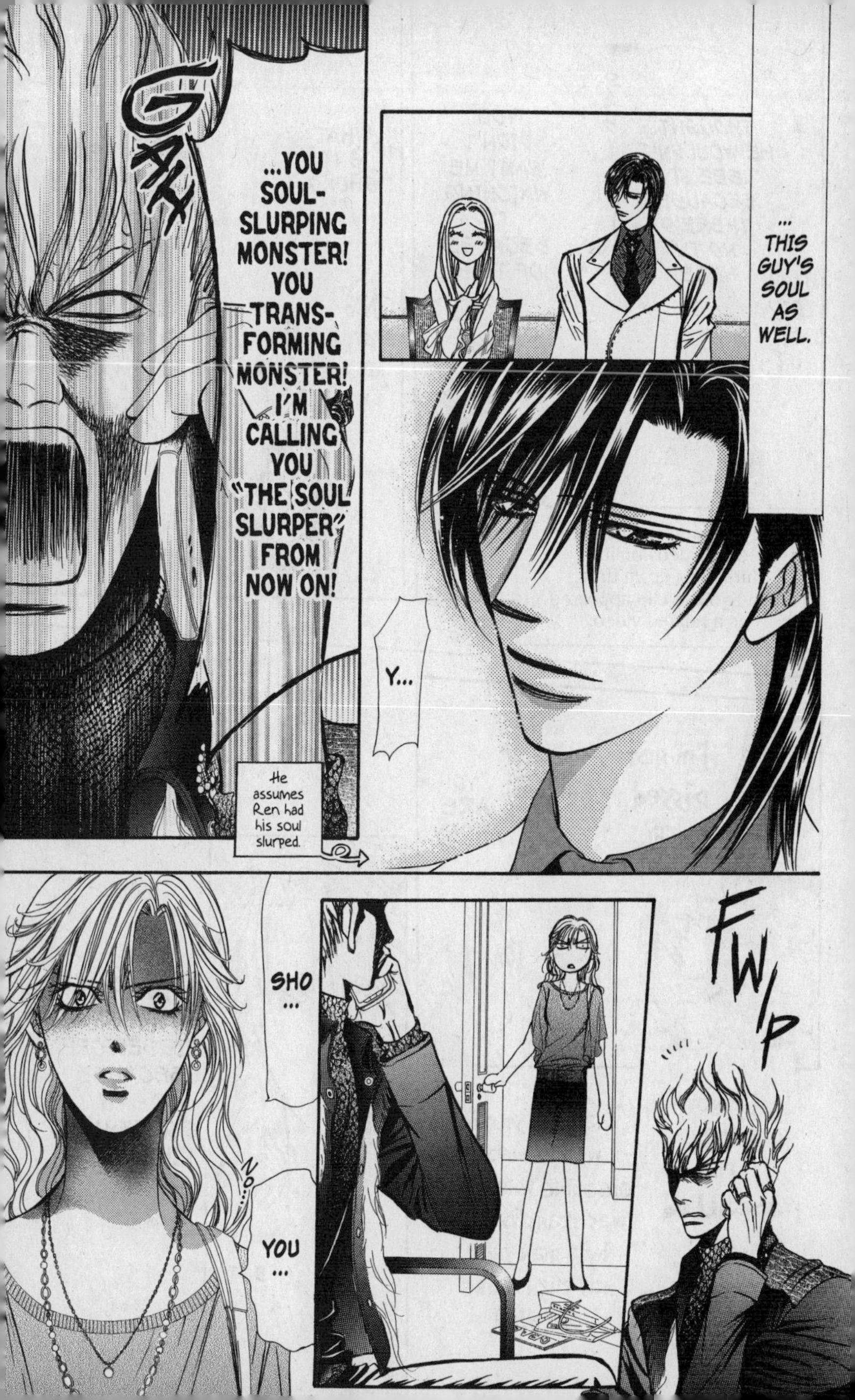
... THIS GUY'S SOUL AS WELL.
Y...
GAH
...YOU SOUL-SLURPING MONSTER! YOU TRANS-FORMING MONSTER! I'M CALLING YOU "THE SOUL SLURPER" FROM NOW ON!
He assumes Ren had his soul slurped.
FWIP
SHO ...
NO...
YOU ...

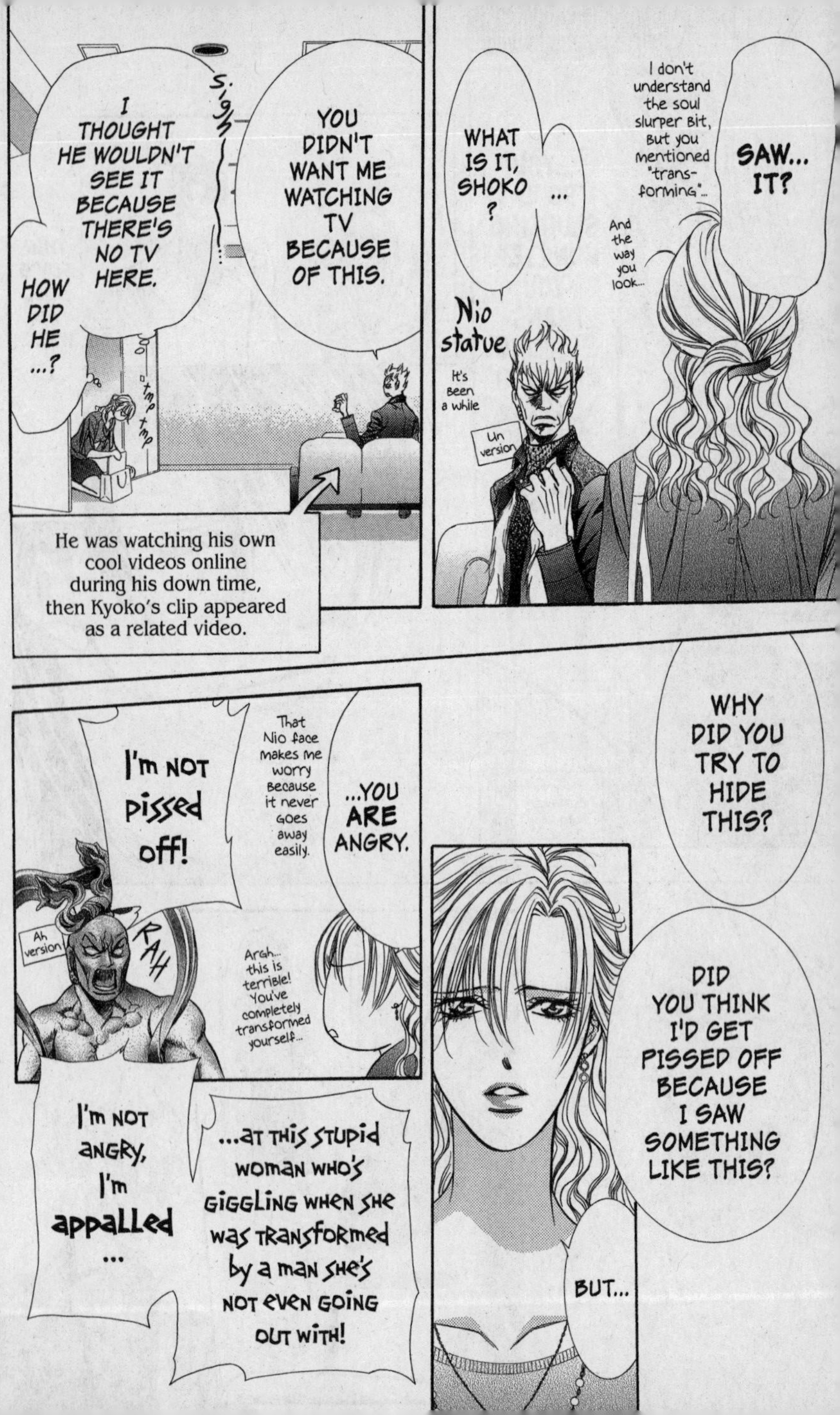
SAW... IT?
I don't understand the soul slurper bit, but you mentioned "transforming"...
And the way you look...
WHAT IS IT, SHOKO?
...
Nio statue
It's been a while
Un version
YOU DIDN'T WANT ME WATCHING TV BECAUSE OF THIS.
Sigh
I THOUGHT HE WOULDN'T SEE IT BECAUSE THERE'S NO TV HERE.
HOW DID HE ...?
tmp tmp
He was watching his own cool videos online during his down time, then Kyoko's clip appeared as a related video.
WHY DID YOU TRY TO HIDE THIS?
DID YOU THINK I'D GET PISSED OFF BECAUSE I SAW SOMETHING LIKE THIS?
BUT...
...YOU ARE ANGRY.
That Nio face makes me worry because it never goes away easily.
I'm NOT pissed off!
RAH
Ah version
Argh... this is terrible! You've completely transformed yourself...
I'm NOT angry, I'm appalled...
...at this stupid woman who's giggling when she was transformed by a man she's not even going out with!

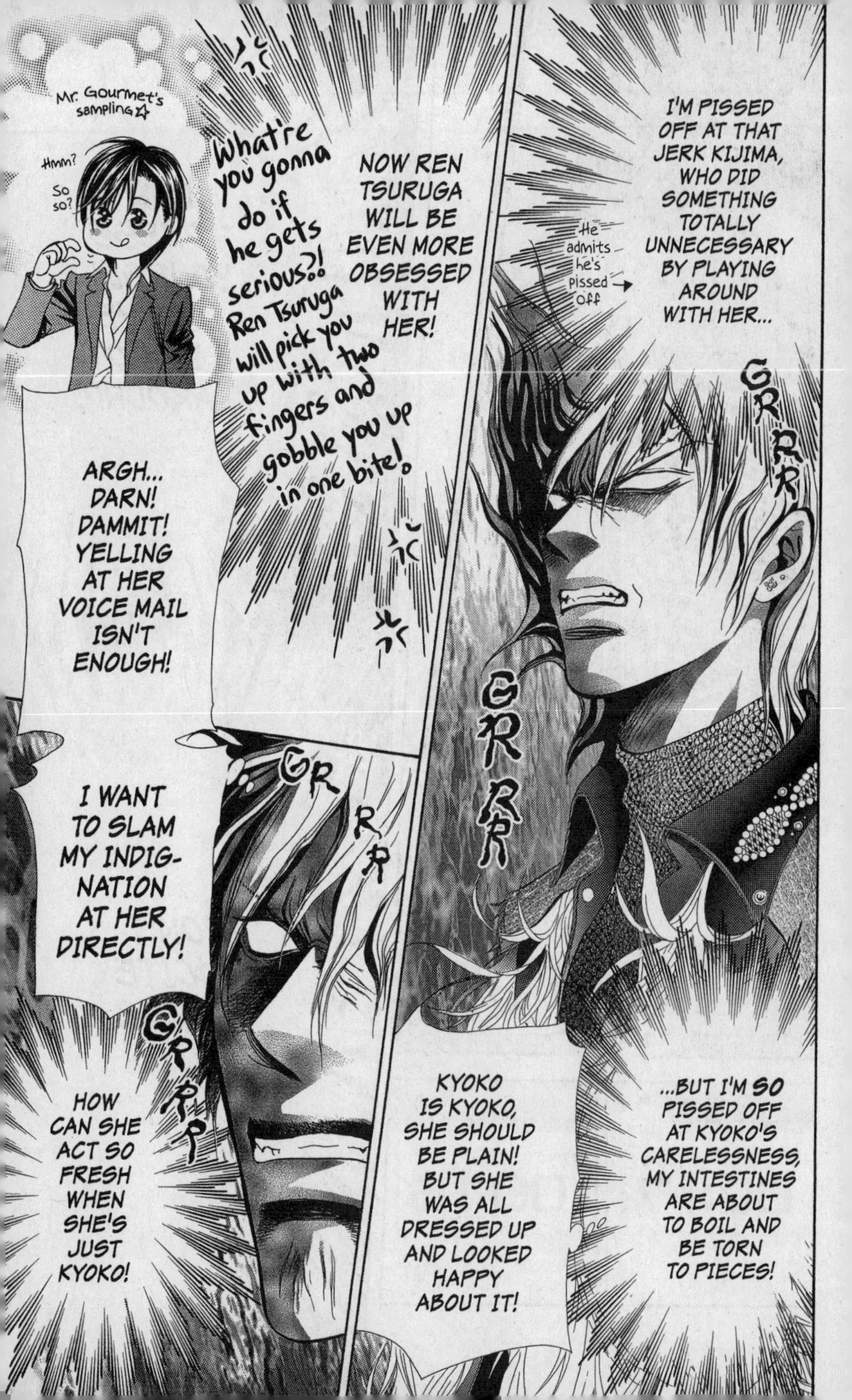
I'M PISSED OFF AT THAT JERK KIJIMA, WHO DID SOMETHING TOTALLY UNNECESSARY BY PLAYING AROUND WITH HER...
He admits he's pissed off
GRRR
NOW REN TSURUGA WILL BE EVEN MORE OBSESSED WITH HER!
What're you gonna do if he gets serious?! Ren Tsuruga will pick you up with two fingers and gobble you up in one bite!
Mr. Gourmet's sampling☆
Hmm?
So so?
ARGH... DARN! DAMMIT! YELLING AT HER VOICE MAIL ISN'T ENOUGH!
GRRR
...BUT I'M SO PISSED OFF AT KYOKO'S CARELESSNESS, MY INTESTINES ARE ABOUT TO BOIL AND BE TORN TO PIECES!
KYOKO IS KYOKO, SHE SHOULD BE PLAIN! BUT SHE WAS ALL DRESSED UP AND LOOKED HAPPY ABOUT IT!
GRRR
I WANT TO SLAM MY INDIG-NATION AT HER DIRECTLY!
GRRR
HOW CAN SHE ACT SO FRESH WHEN SHE'S JUST KYOKO!

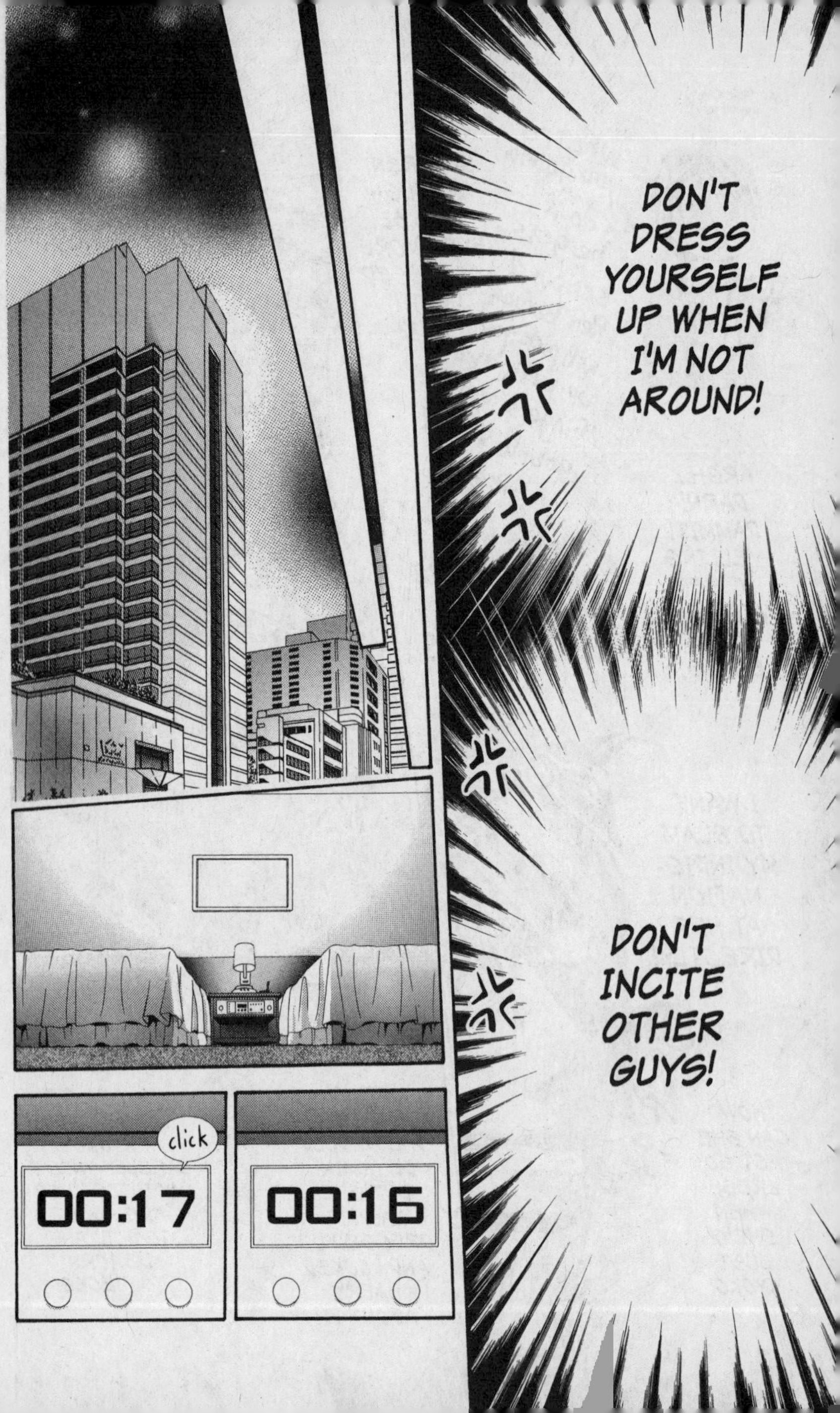
DON'T DRESS YOURSELF UP WHEN I'M NOT AROUND!
DON'T INCITE OTHER GUYS!
00:16
click
00:17

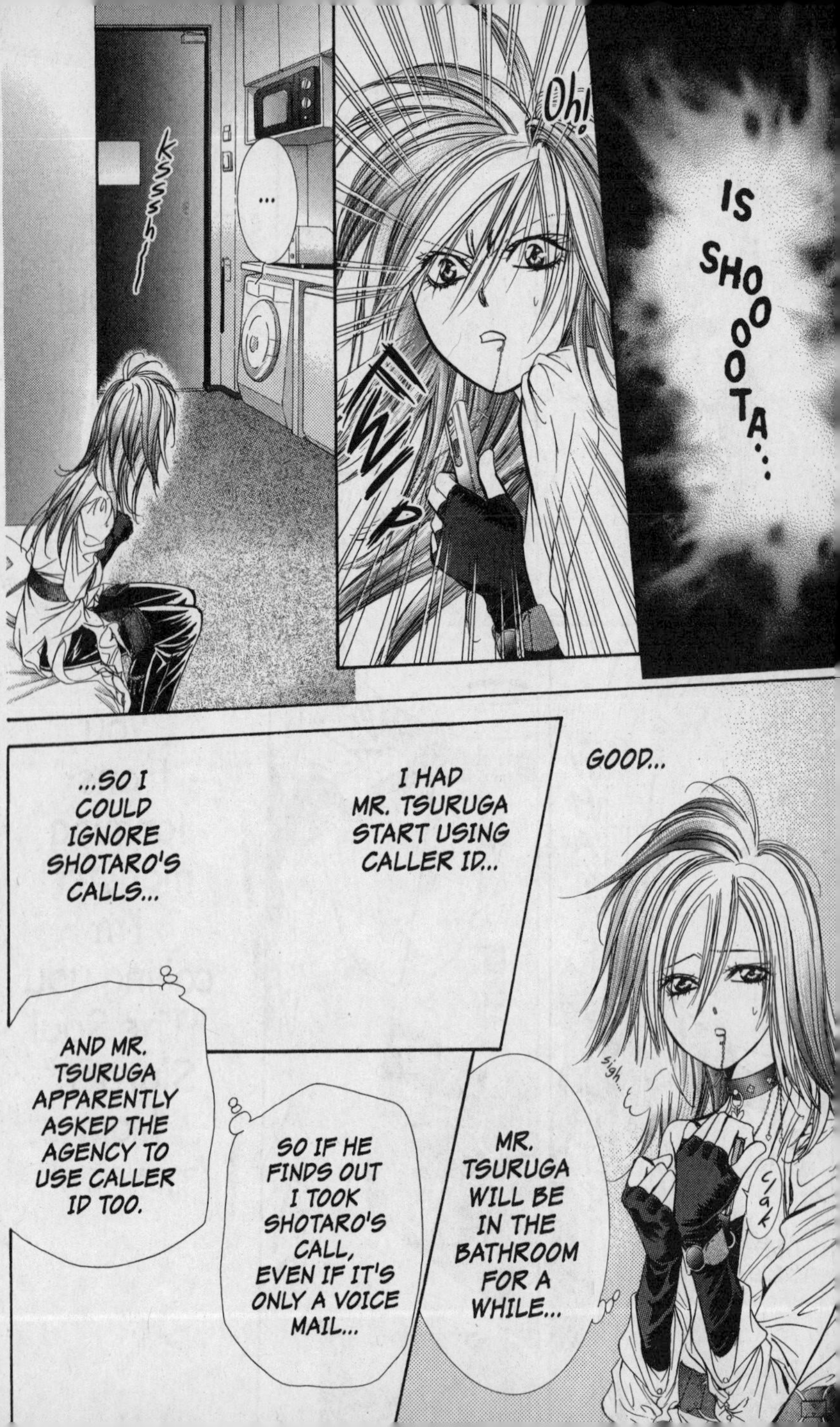
IS SHOOOOTA...
Oh!
FWIP
KSSSHH
...
GOOD...
I HAD MR. TSURUGA START USING CALLER ID...
...SO I COULD IGNORE SHOTARO'S CALLS...
AND MR. TSURUGA APPARENTLY ASKED THE AGENCY TO USE CALLER ID TOO.
SO IF HE FINDS OUT I TOOK SHOTARO'S CALL, EVEN IF IT'S ONLY A VOICE MAIL...
sigh...
MR. TSURUGA WILL BE IN THE BATHROOM FOR A WHILE...
clak

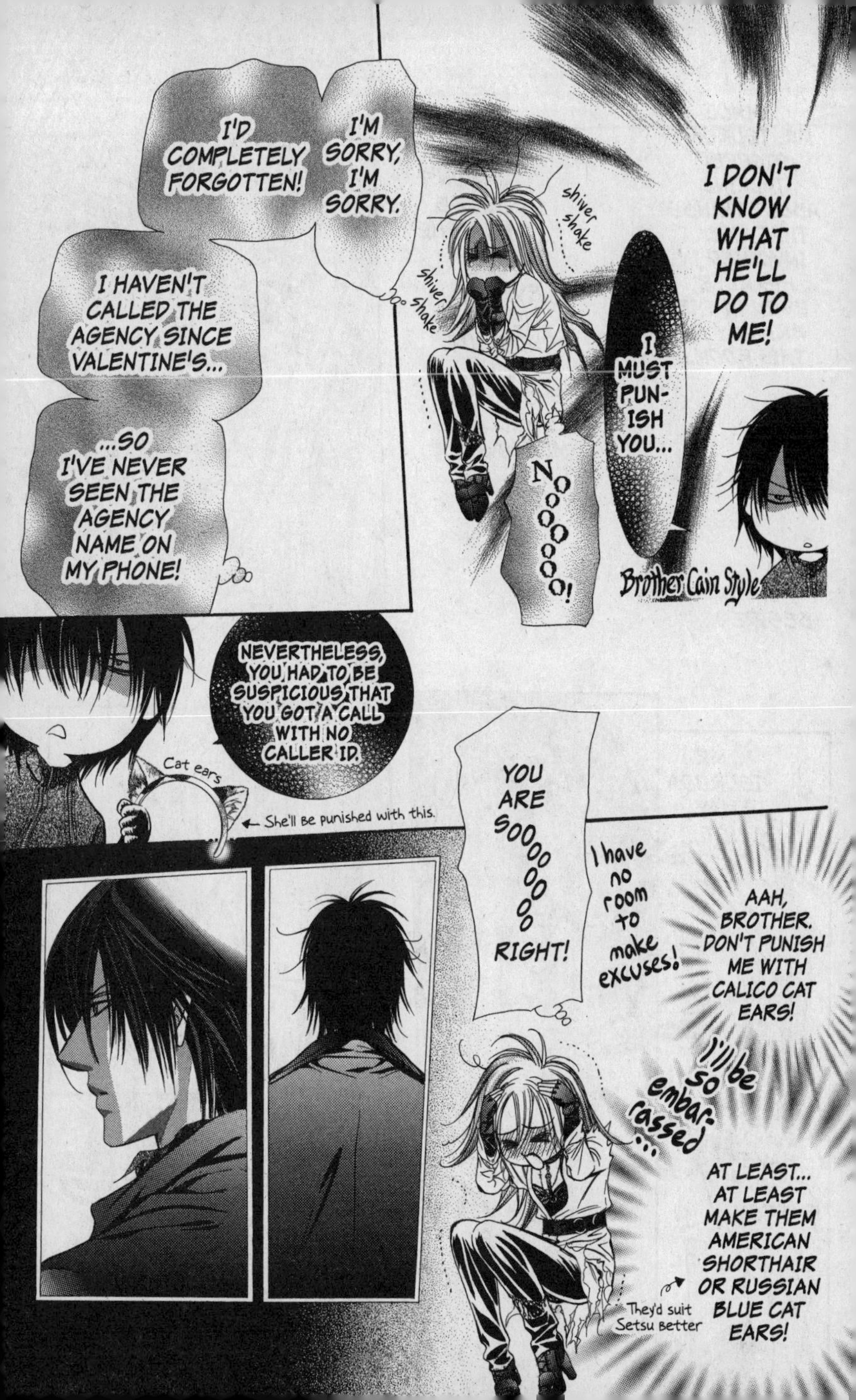
I DON'T KNOW WHAT HE'LL DO TO ME!
I MUST PUN-ISH YOU...
Brother Cain Style
shiver shake
shiver shake
NOOOOOOOO!
I'M SORRY, I'M SORRY.
I'D COMPLETELY FORGOTTEN!
I HAVEN'T CALLED THE AGENCY SINCE VALENTINE'S...
...SO I'VE NEVER SEEN THE AGENCY NAME ON MY PHONE!
AAH, BROTHER. DON'T PUNISH ME WITH CALICO CAT EARS!
I'll be so embar-rassed...
AT LEAST... AT LEAST MAKE THEM AMERICAN SHORTHAIR OR RUSSIAN BLUE CAT EARS!
They'd suit Setsu better
YOU ARE SOOOOOOOOOO RIGHT!
I have no room to make excuses!
NEVERTHELESS, YOU HAD TO BE SUSPICIOUS THAT YOU GOT A CALL WITH NO CALLER ID.
Cat ears
She'll be punished with this.

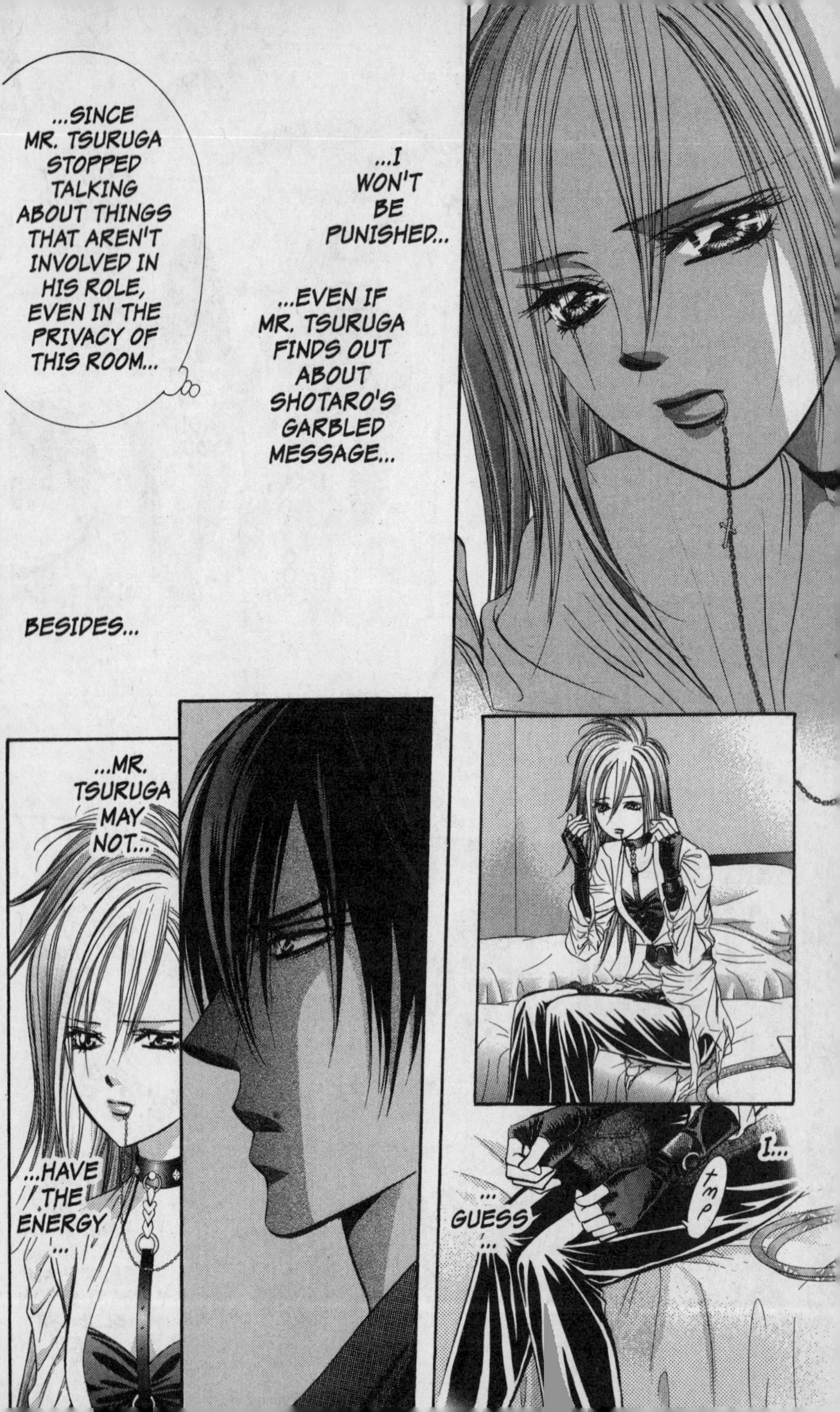
...I WON'T BE PUNISHED...
...EVEN IF MR. TSURUGA FINDS OUT ABOUT SHOTARO'S GARBLED MESSAGE...
...SINCE MR. TSURUGA STOPPED TALKING ABOUT THINGS THAT AREN'T INVOLVED IN HIS ROLE, EVEN IN THE PRIVACY OF THIS ROOM...
BESIDES...
I...
TMP
...GUESS...
...MR. TSURUGA MAY NOT...
...HAVE THE ENERGY...

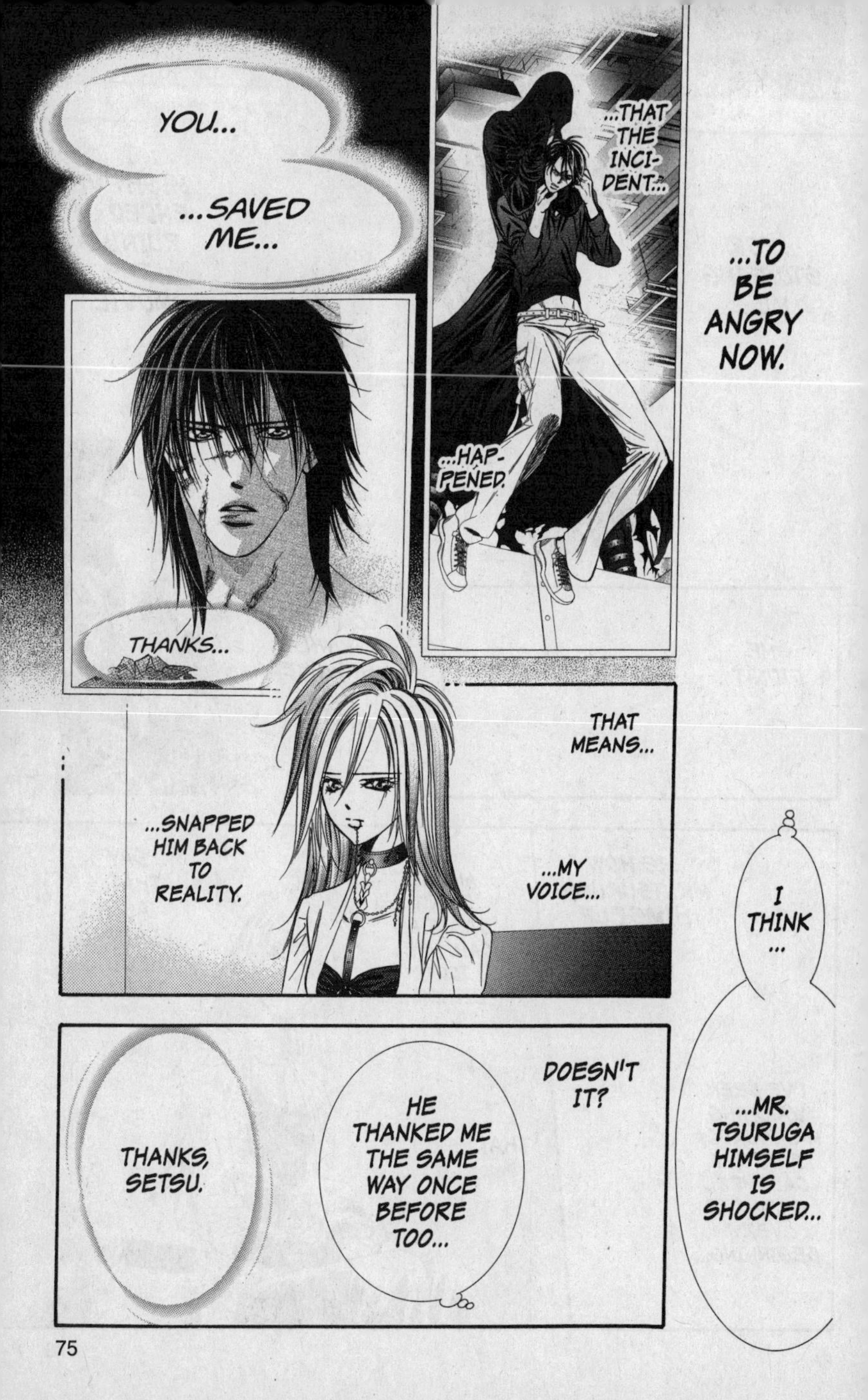
...TO BE ANGRY NOW.
...THAT THE INCIDENT...
...HAPPENED.
YOU...
...SAVED ME...
THANKS...
I THINK...
...MR. TSURUGA HIMSELF IS SHOCKED...
THAT MEANS...
...MY VOICE...
...SNAPPED HIM BACK TO REALITY.
DOESN'T IT?
HE THANKED ME THE SAME WAY ONCE BEFORE TOO...
THANKS, SETSU.

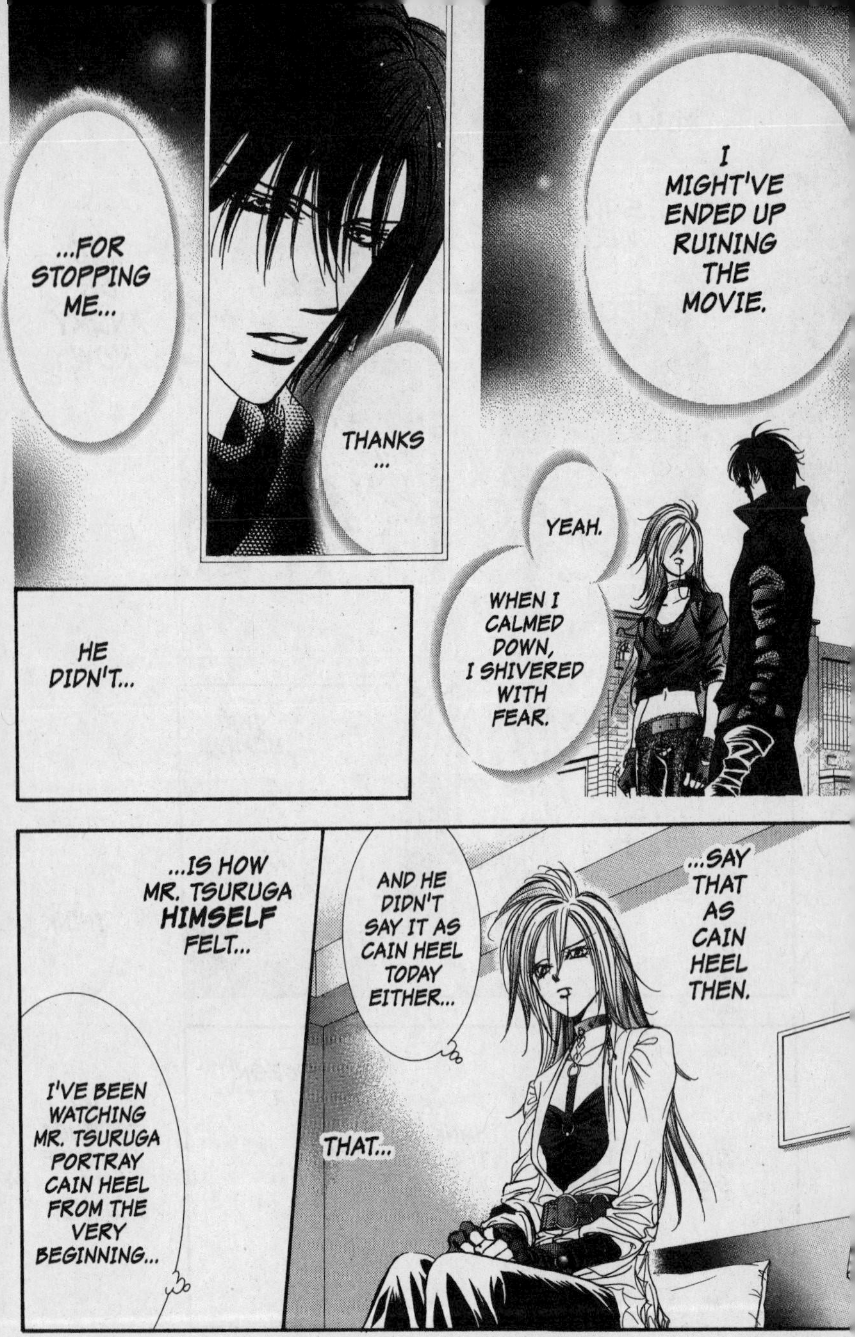
I MIGHT'VE ENDED UP RUINING THE MOVIE.
THANKS ...
...FOR STOPPING ME...
YEAH.
WHEN I CALMED DOWN, I SHIVERED WITH FEAR.
HE DIDN'T...
...SAY THAT AS CAIN HEEL THEN.
AND HE DIDN'T SAY IT AS CAIN HEEL TODAY EITHER...
THAT...
...IS HOW MR. TSURUGA **HIMSELF** FELT...
I'VE BEEN WATCHING MR. TSURUGA PORTRAY CAIN HEEL FROM THE VERY BEGINNING...

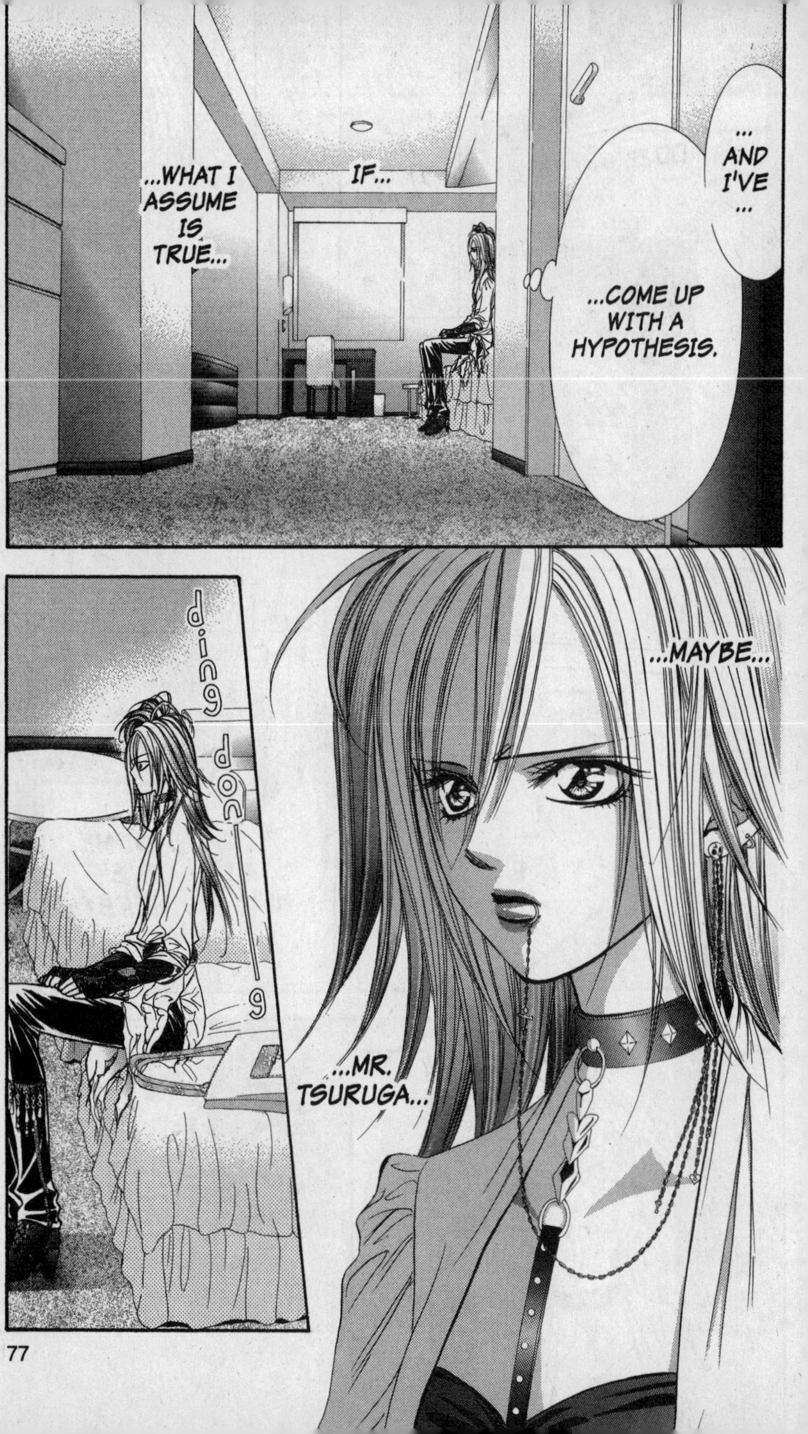
...AND I'VE...
...COME UP WITH A HYPOTHESIS.
IF...
...WHAT I ASSUME IS TRUE...
...MAYBE...
...MR. TSURUGA...
ding dong

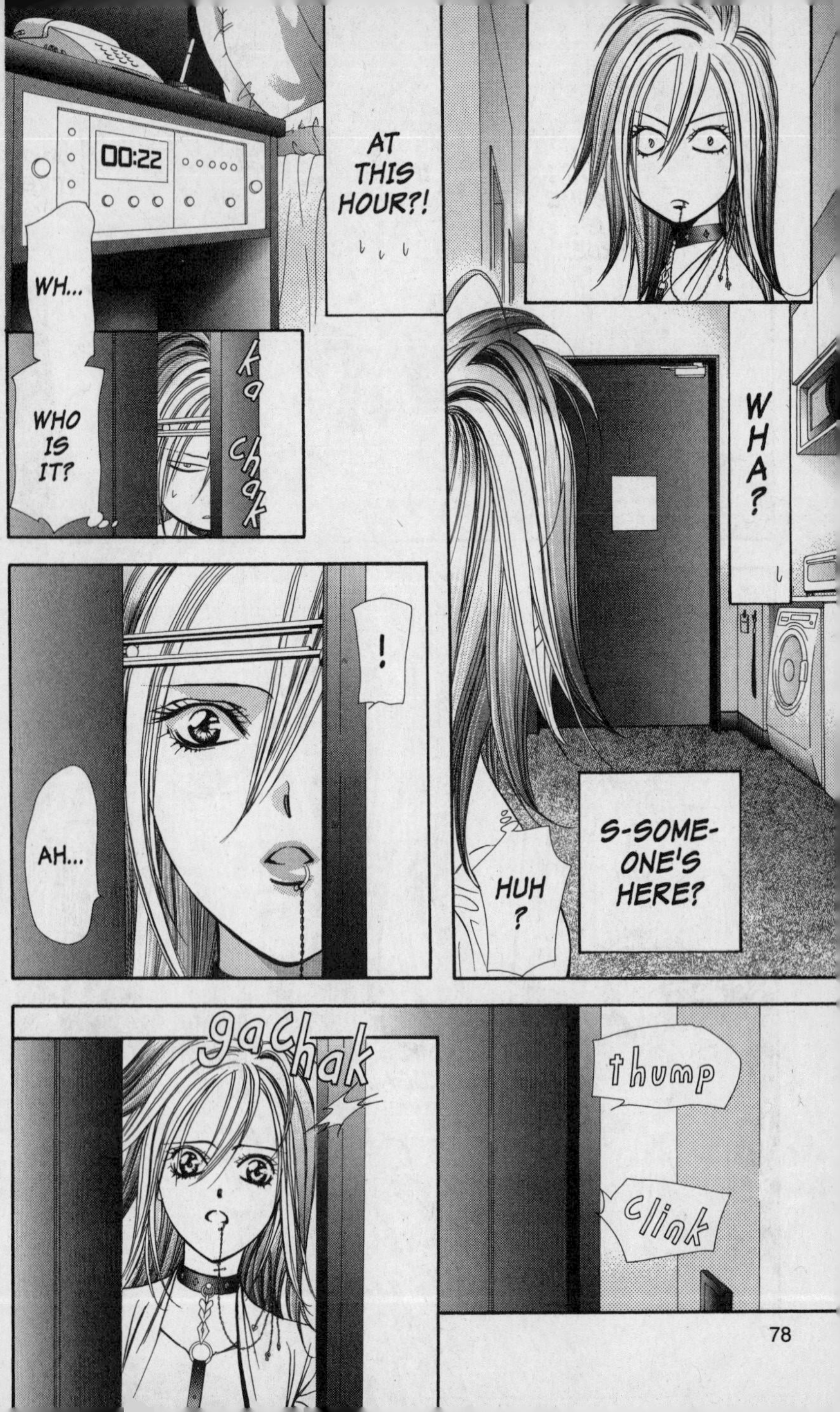

AT THIS HOUR?!
00:22
WH... WHO IS IT?
ka chak
WHA?
S-SOME-ONE'S HERE?
HUH?
!
AH...
thump
clink
gachak

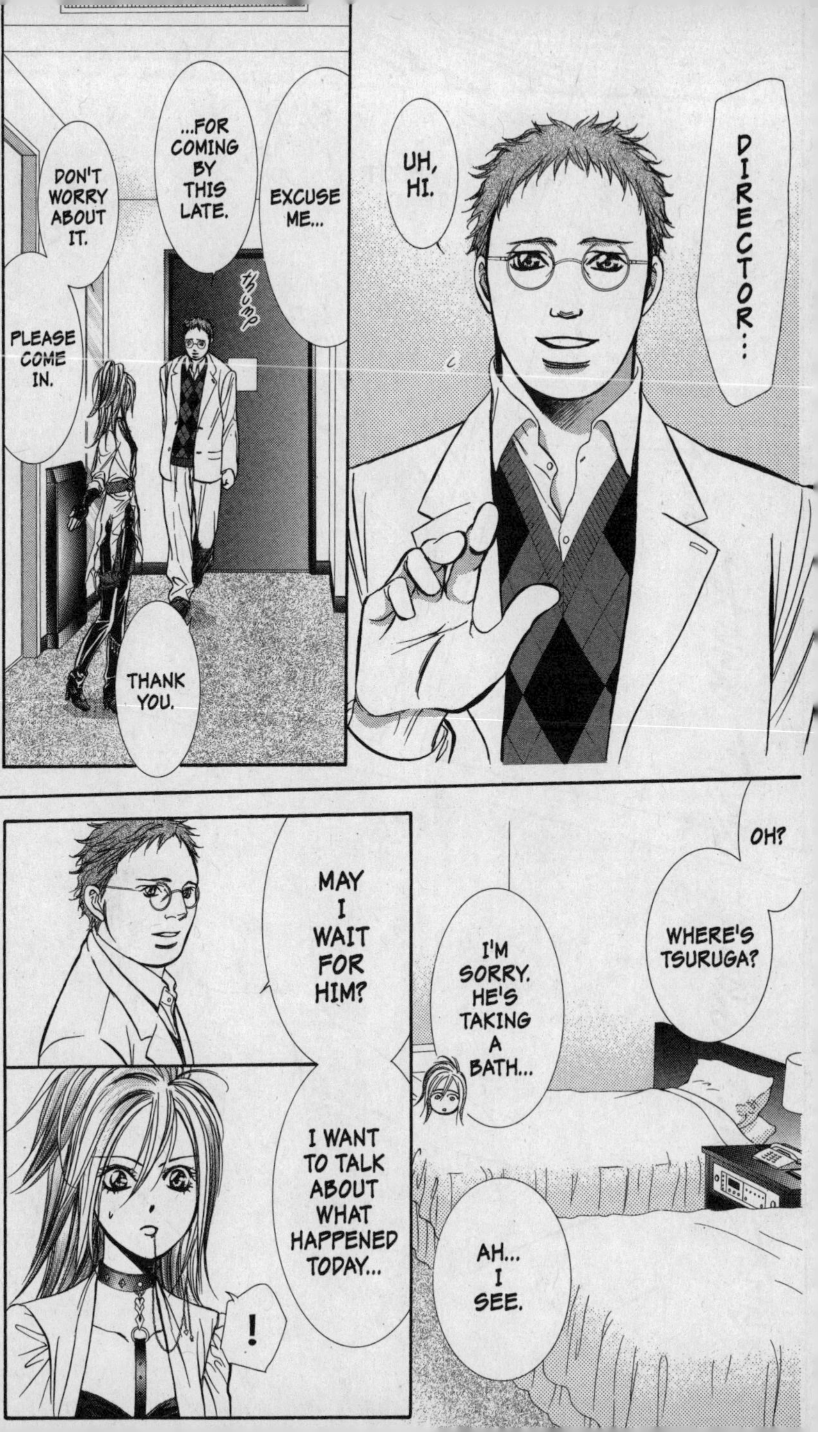
DIRECTOR...
UH, HI.
EXCUSE ME...
...FOR COMING BY THIS LATE.
DON'T WORRY ABOUT IT.
PLEASE COME IN.
THUMP
THANK YOU.
OH?
WHERE'S TSURUGA?
I'M SORRY. HE'S TAKING A BATH...
AH... I SEE.
MAY I WAIT FOR HIM?
I WANT TO TALK ABOUT WHAT HAPPENED TODAY...
!

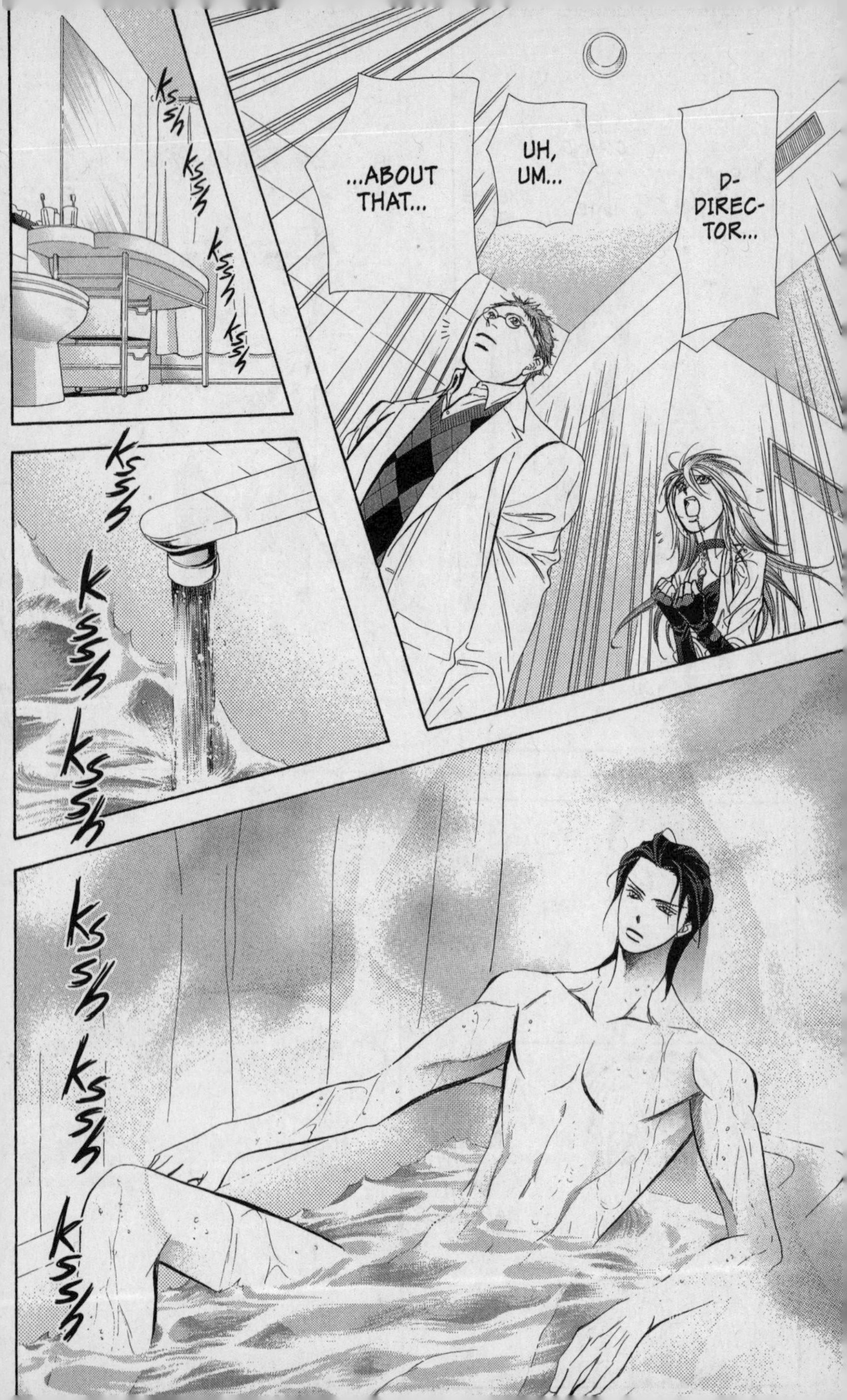
D-DIRECTOR...
UH, UM...
...ABOUT THAT...
KSSH
KSSH
KSSH
KSSH
KSSH
KSSH
KSSH
KSSH
KSSH
KSSH

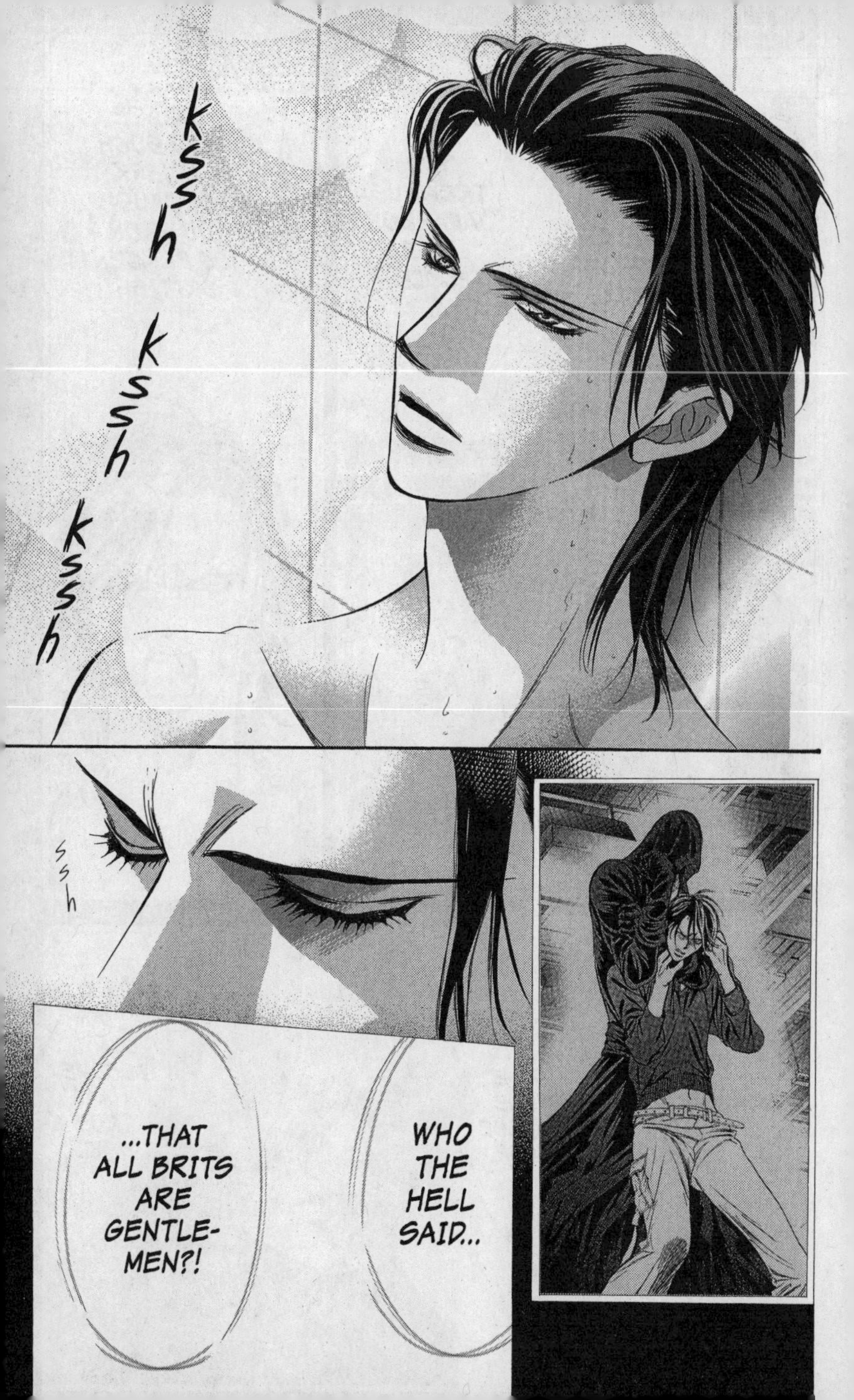
kssh
kssh
kssh
ssh
WHO THE HELL SAID...
...THAT ALL BRITS ARE GENTLE-MEN?!

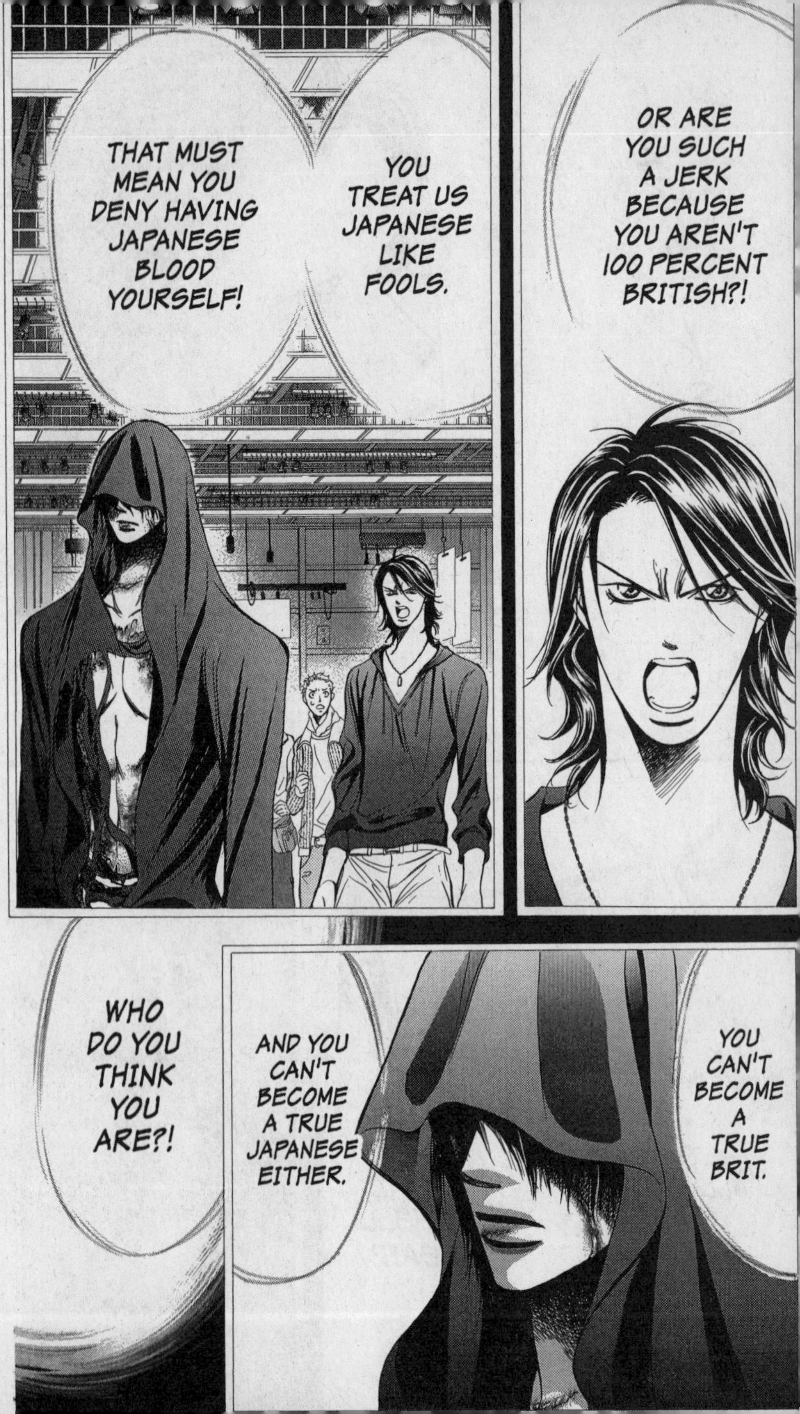
OR ARE YOU SUCH A JERK BECAUSE YOU AREN'T 100 PERCENT BRITISH?!
YOU TREAT US JAPANESE LIKE FOOLS.
THAT MUST MEAN YOU DENY HAVING JAPANESE BLOOD YOURSELF!
YOU CAN'T BECOME A TRUE BRIT.
AND YOU CAN'T BECOME A TRUE JAPANESE EITHER.
WHO DO YOU THINK YOU ARE?!

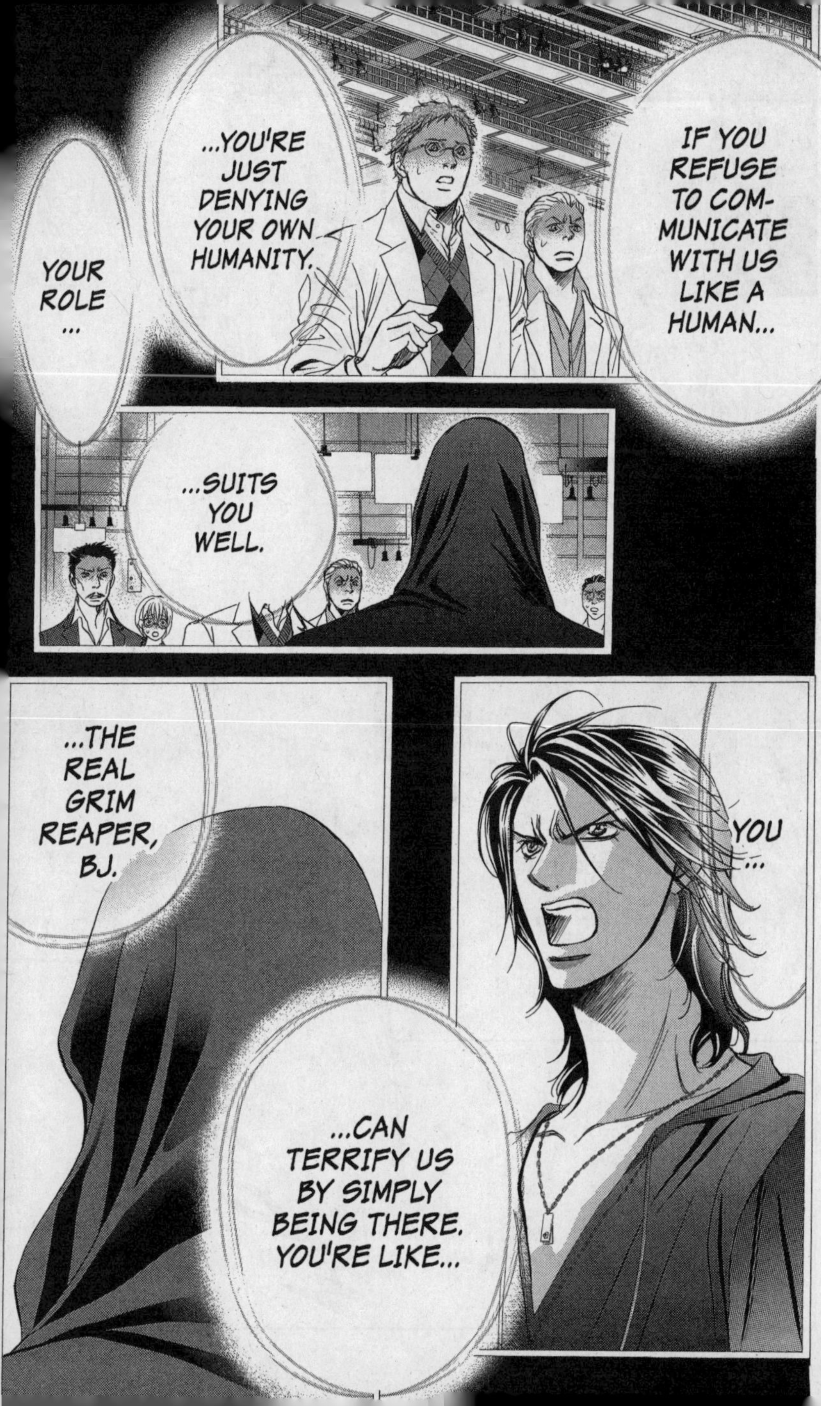
IF YOU REFUSE TO COMMUNICATE WITH US LIKE A HUMAN...
...YOU'RE JUST DENYING YOUR OWN HUMANITY.
YOUR ROLE ...
...SUITS YOU WELL.
YOU ...
...CAN TERRIFY US BY SIMPLY BEING THERE. YOU'RE LIKE...
...THE REAL GRIM REAPER, BJ.

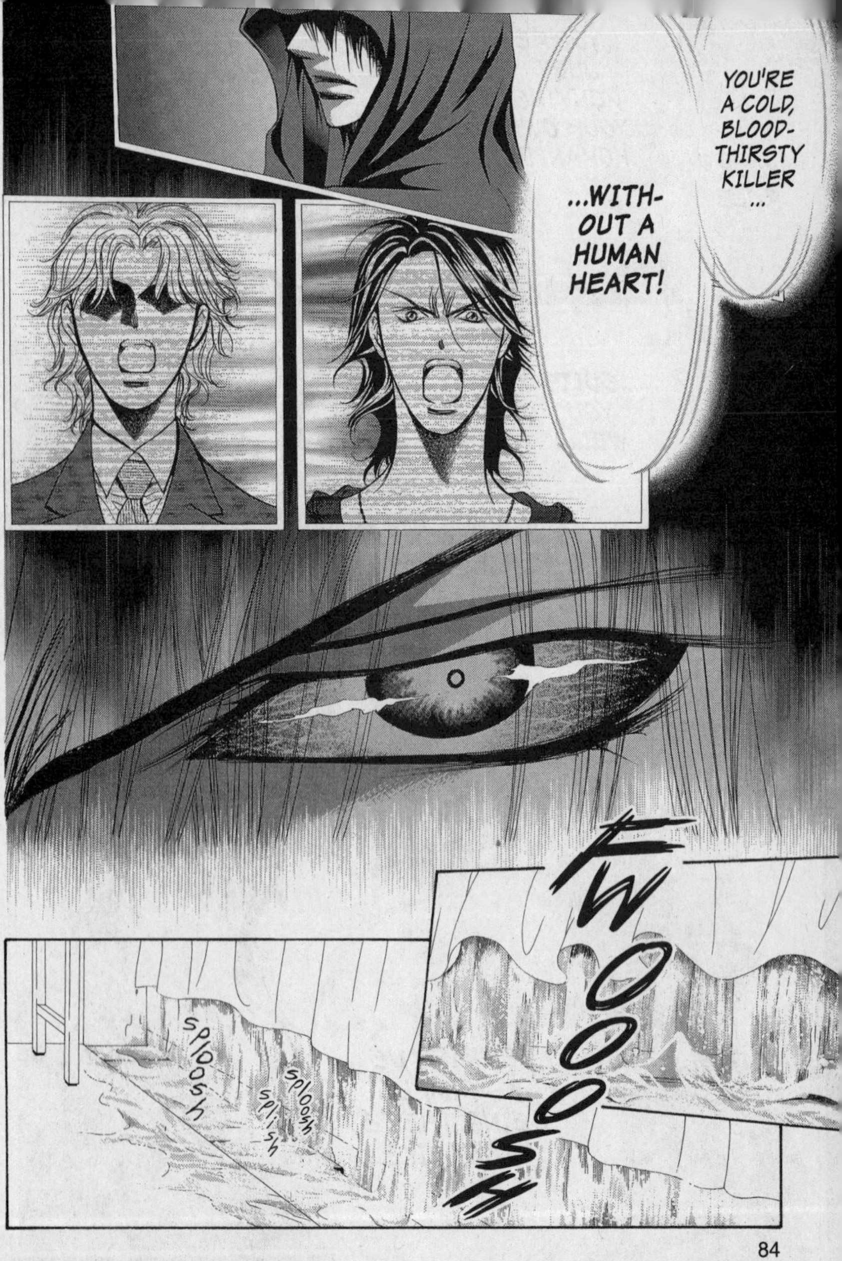
YOU'RE A COLD, BLOOD-THIRSTY KILLER ...
...WITH-OUT A HUMAN HEART!
FWOOOOSH
sploosh
splish
sploosh

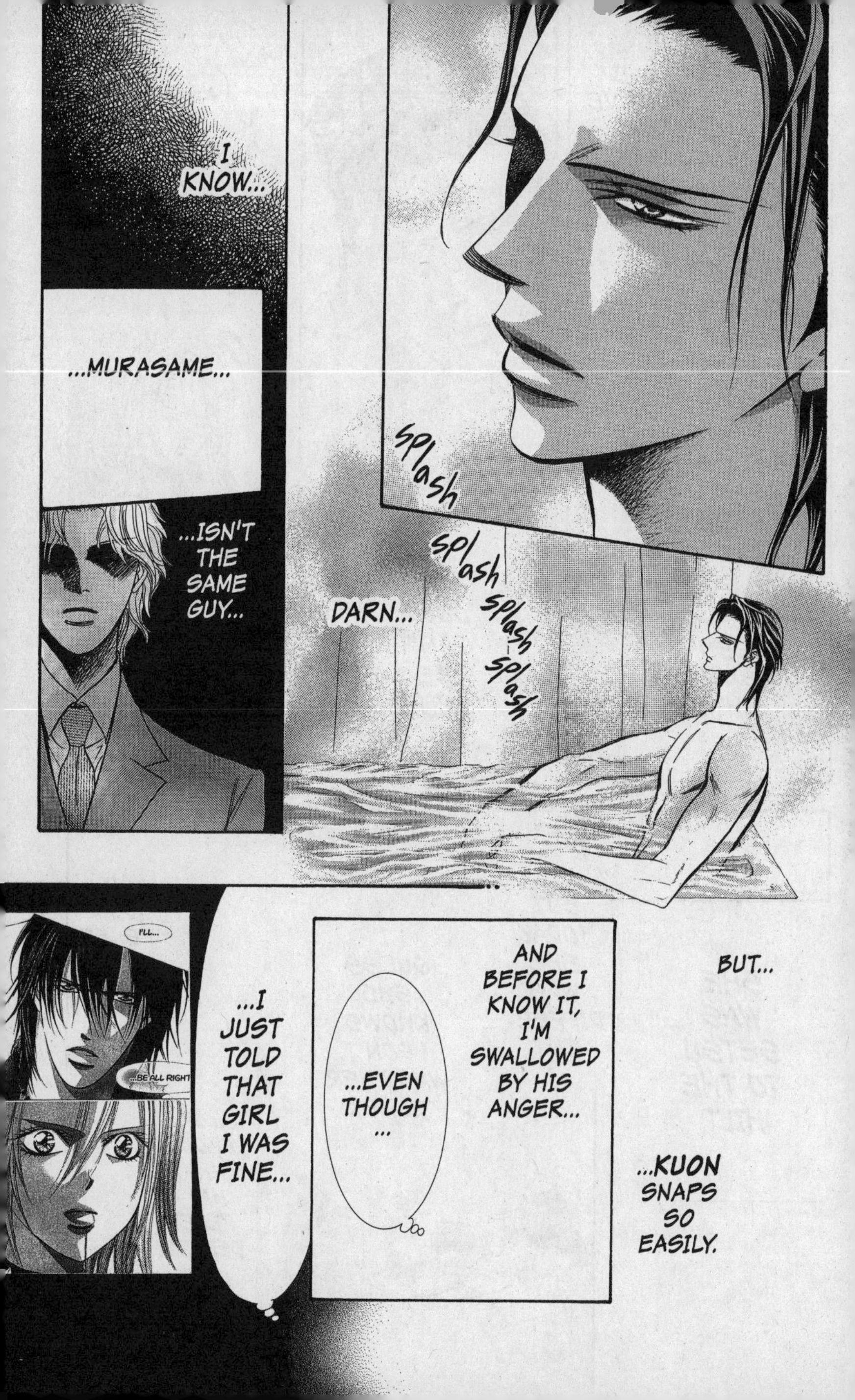
SPLASH
SPLASH
SPLASH
SPLASH
DARN...
I KNOW...
...MURASAME...
...ISN'T THE SAME GUY...
BUT...
...KUON SNAPS SO EASILY.
AND BEFORE I KNOW IT, I'M SWALLOWED BY HIS ANGER...
...EVEN THOUGH...
...I JUST TOLD THAT GIRL I WAS FINE...
I'LL...
...BE ALL RIGHT

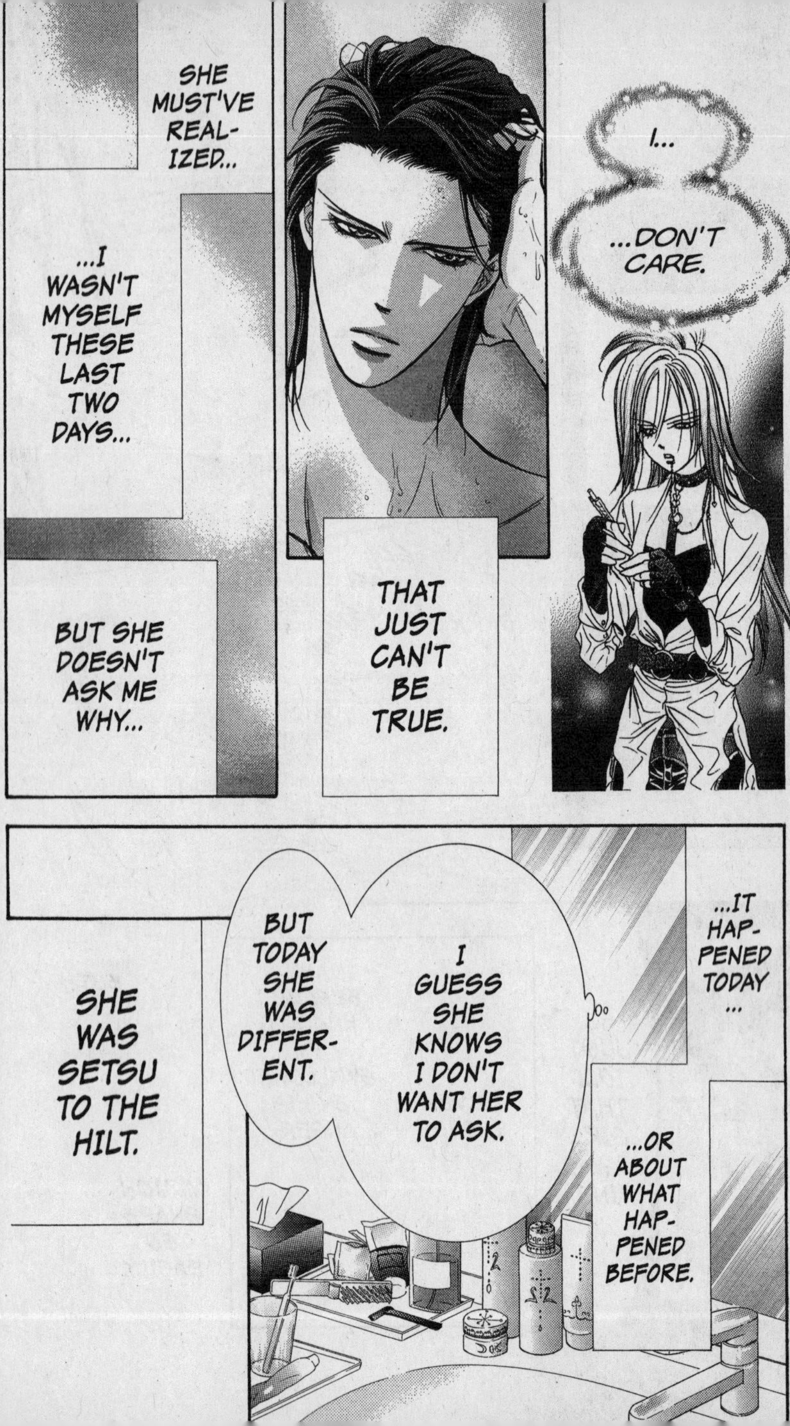
I...
...DON'T CARE.
THAT JUST CAN'T BE TRUE.
SHE MUST'VE REAL-IZED...
...I WASN'T MYSELF THESE LAST TWO DAYS...
BUT SHE DOESN'T ASK ME WHY...
...IT HAP-PENED TODAY...
...OR ABOUT WHAT HAP-PENED BEFORE.
I GUESS SHE KNOWS I DON'T WANT HER TO ASK.
BUT TODAY SHE WAS DIFFER-ENT.
SHE WAS SETSU TO THE HILT.

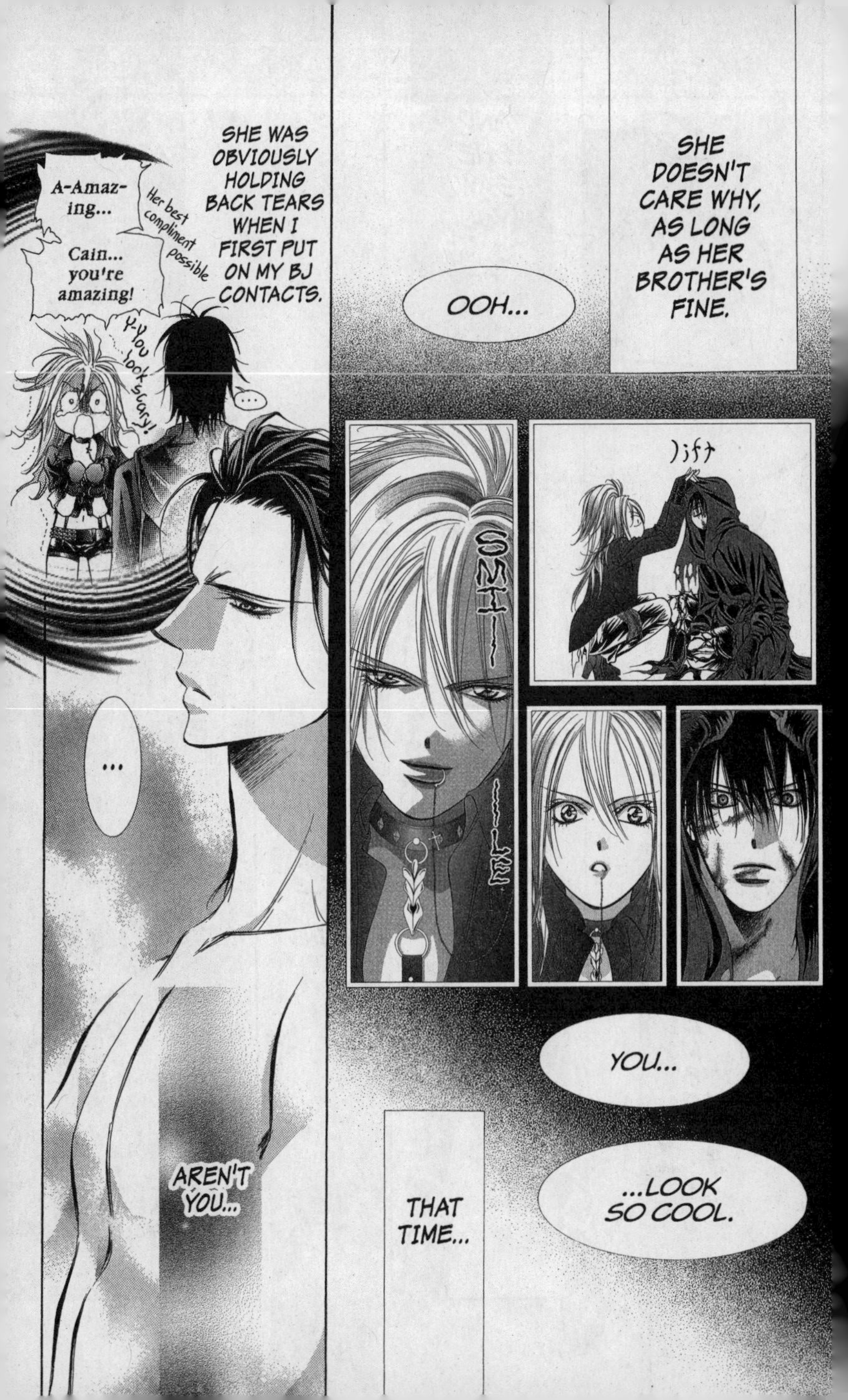
SHE DOESN'T CARE WHY, AS LONG AS HER BROTHER'S FINE.
OOH...
lift
SMILE
YOU...
...LOOK SO COOL.
THAT TIME...
SHE WAS OBVIOUSLY HOLDING BACK TEARS WHEN I FIRST PUT ON MY BJ CONTACTS.
A-Amazing...
Her best compliment possible
Cain... you're amazing!
Y-You look scary!
...
...
AREN'T YOU...

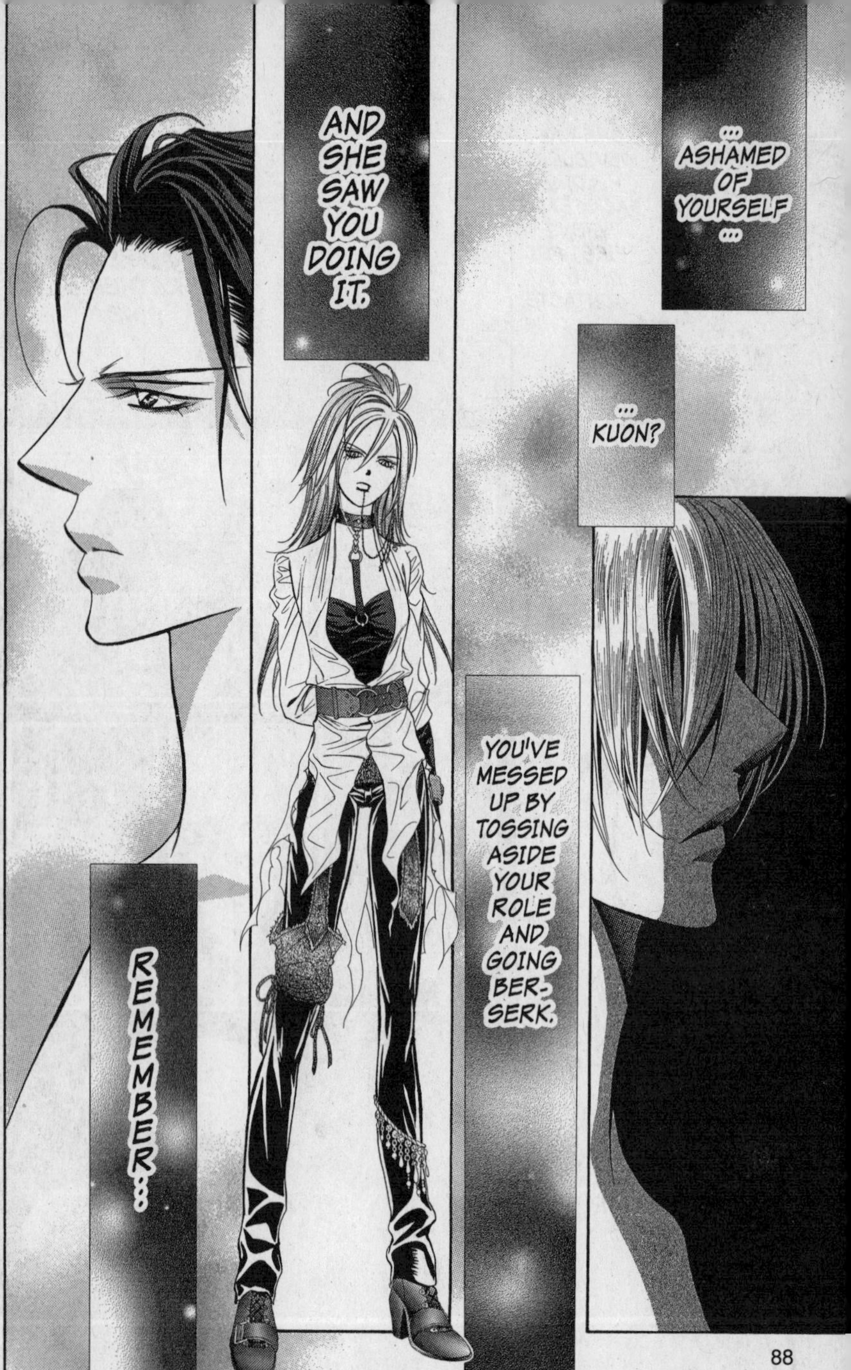
...ASHAMED OF YOURSELF...
...KUON?
YOU'VE MESSED UP BY TOSSING ASIDE YOUR ROLE AND GOING BER-SERK.
AND SHE SAW YOU DOING IT.
REMEMBER...

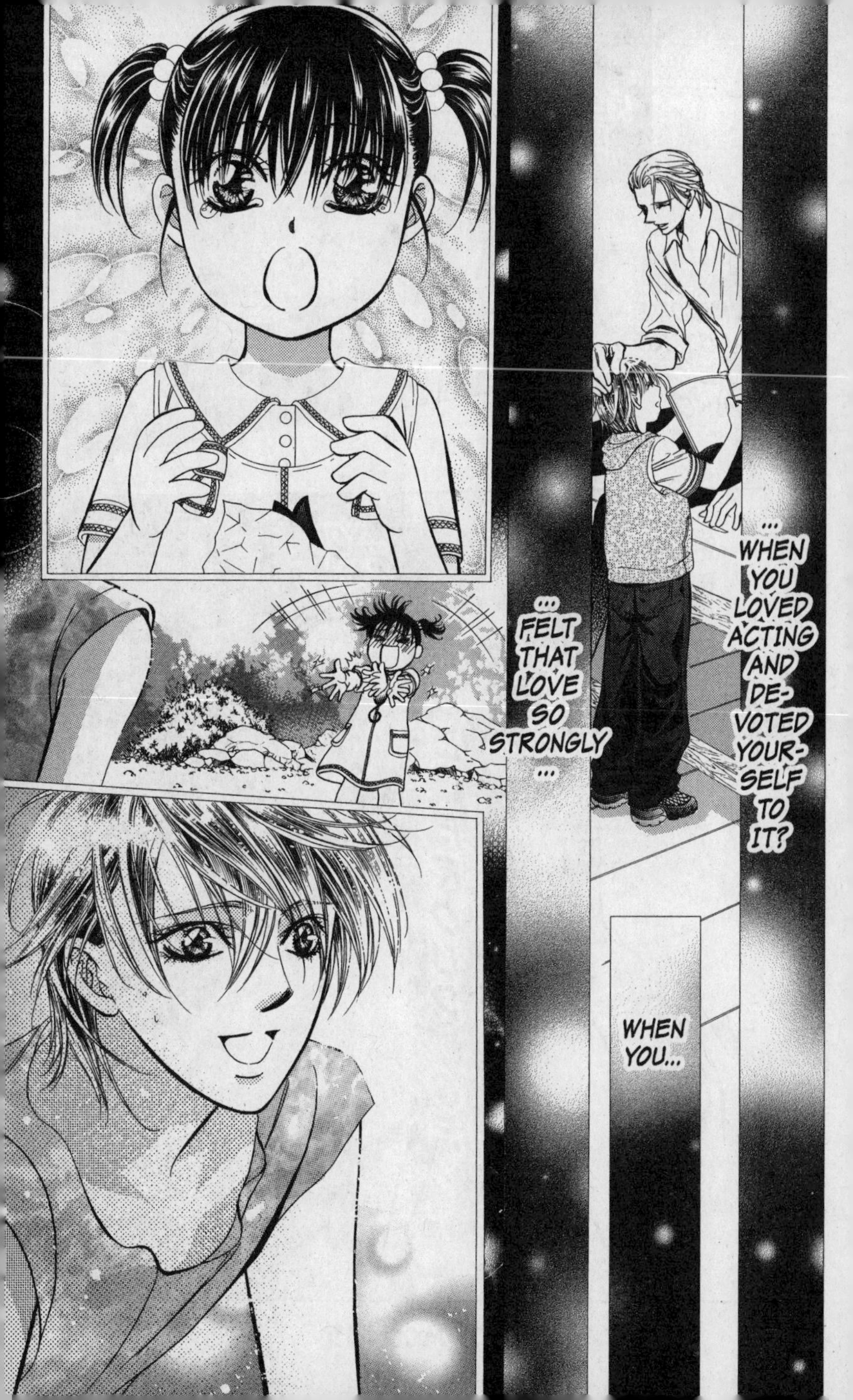

...WHEN YOU LOVED ACTING AND DE-VOTED YOUR-SELF TO IT?
WHEN YOU...
...FELT THAT LOVE SO STRONGLY...

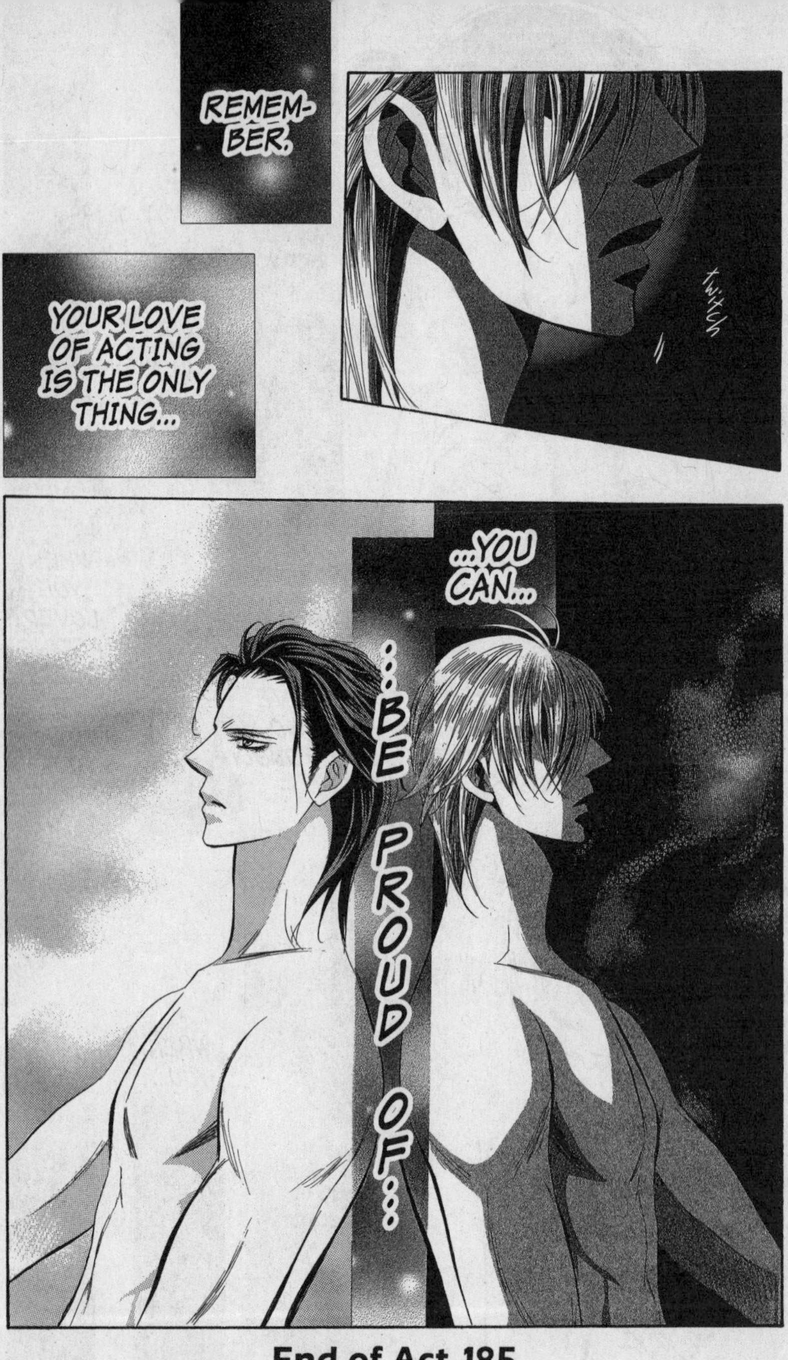
twitch
REMEM-BER.
YOUR LOVE OF ACTING IS THE ONLY THING...
...YOU CAN...
...BE PROUD OF...

End of Act 185

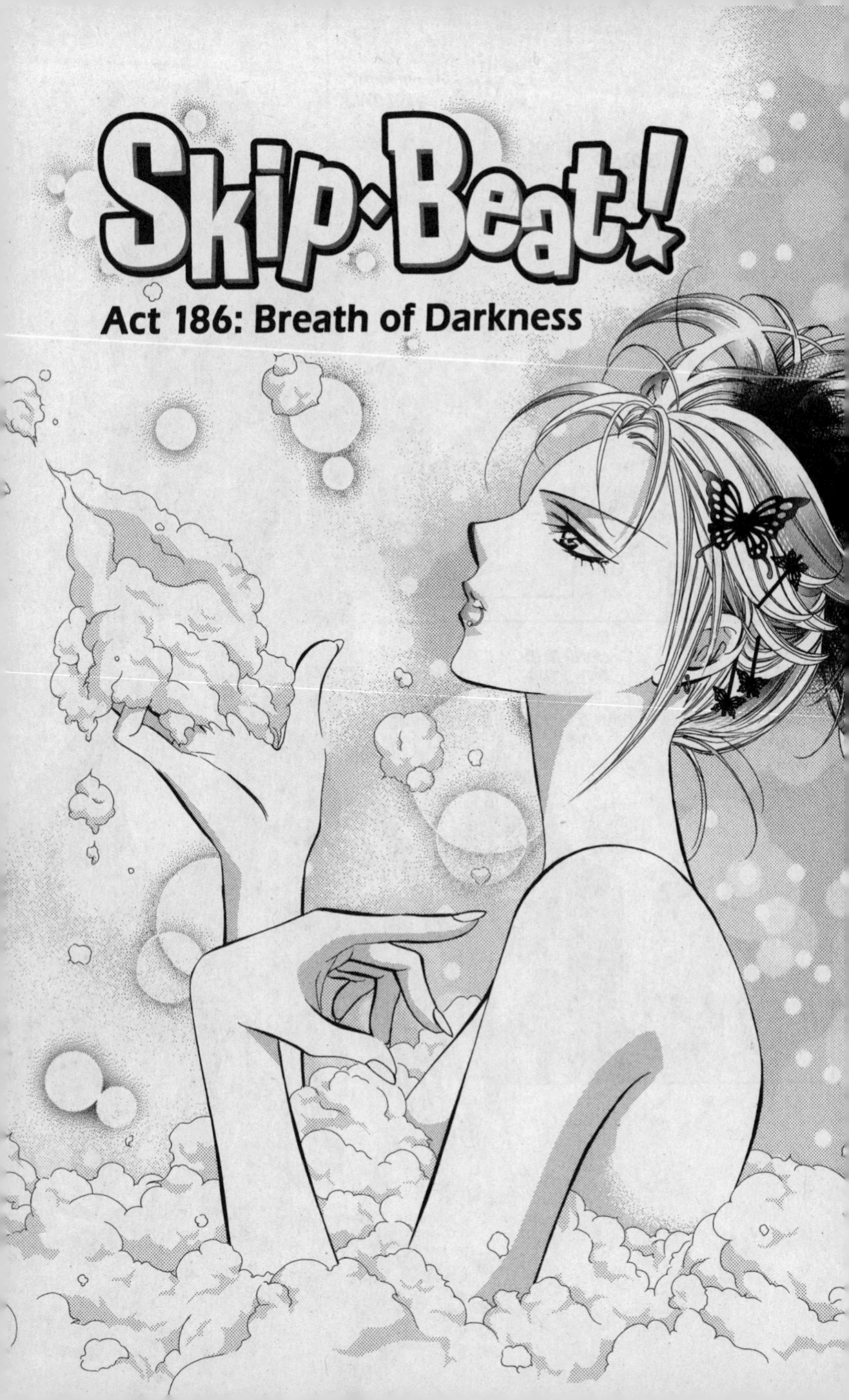
Skip·Beat!
Act 186: Breath of Darkness

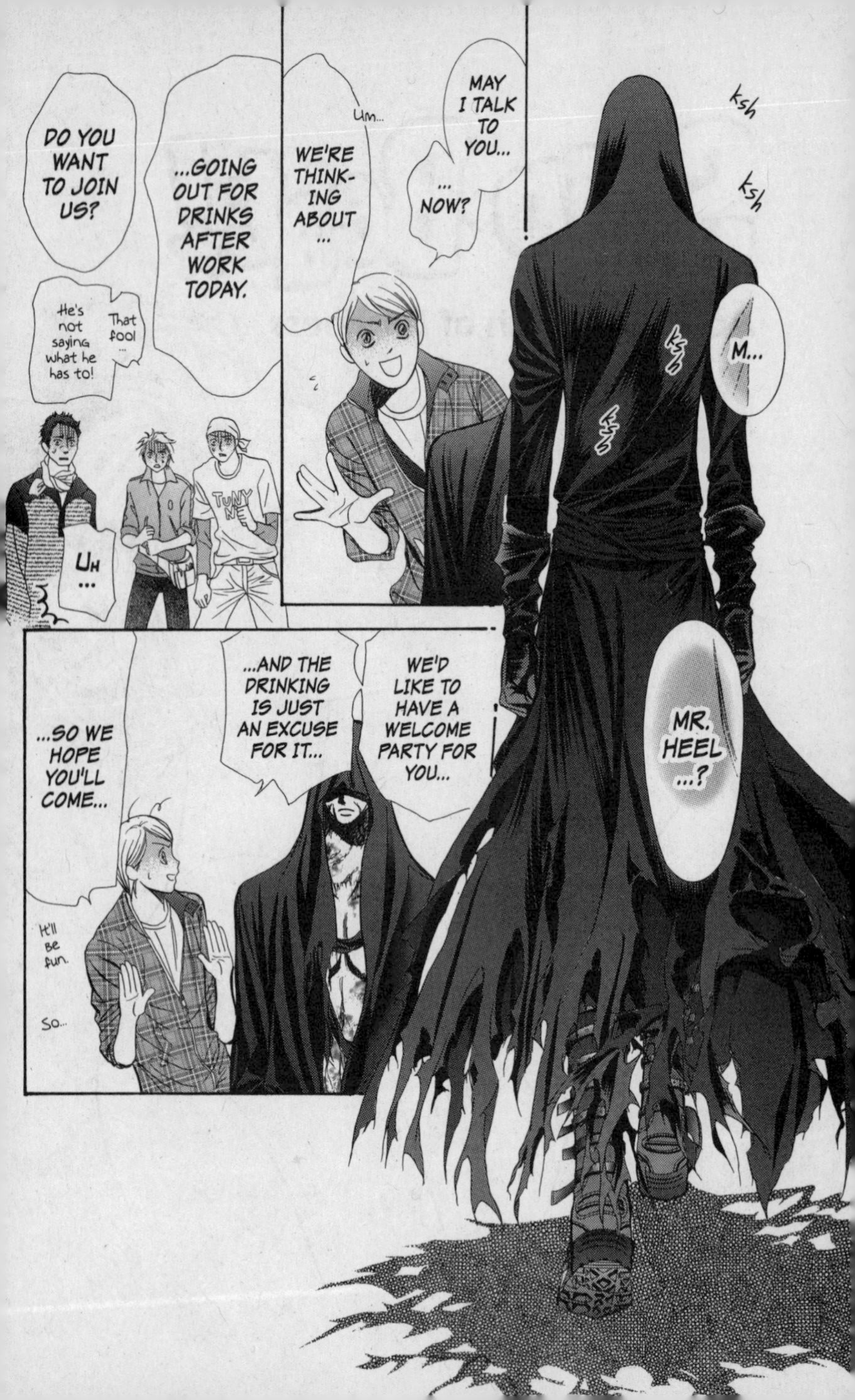
ksh
ksh
M...
ksh
ksh
MR. HEEL ...?
MAY I TALK TO YOU...
... NOW?
Um...
WE'RE THINK-ING ABOUT ...
...GOING OUT FOR DRINKS AFTER WORK TODAY.
DO YOU WANT TO JOIN US?
That fool ...
He's not saying what he has to!
UH ...
WE'D LIKE TO HAVE A WELCOME PARTY FOR YOU...
...AND THE DRINKING IS JUST AN EXCUSE FOR IT...
...SO WE HOPE YOU'LL COME...
It'll be fun.
So...

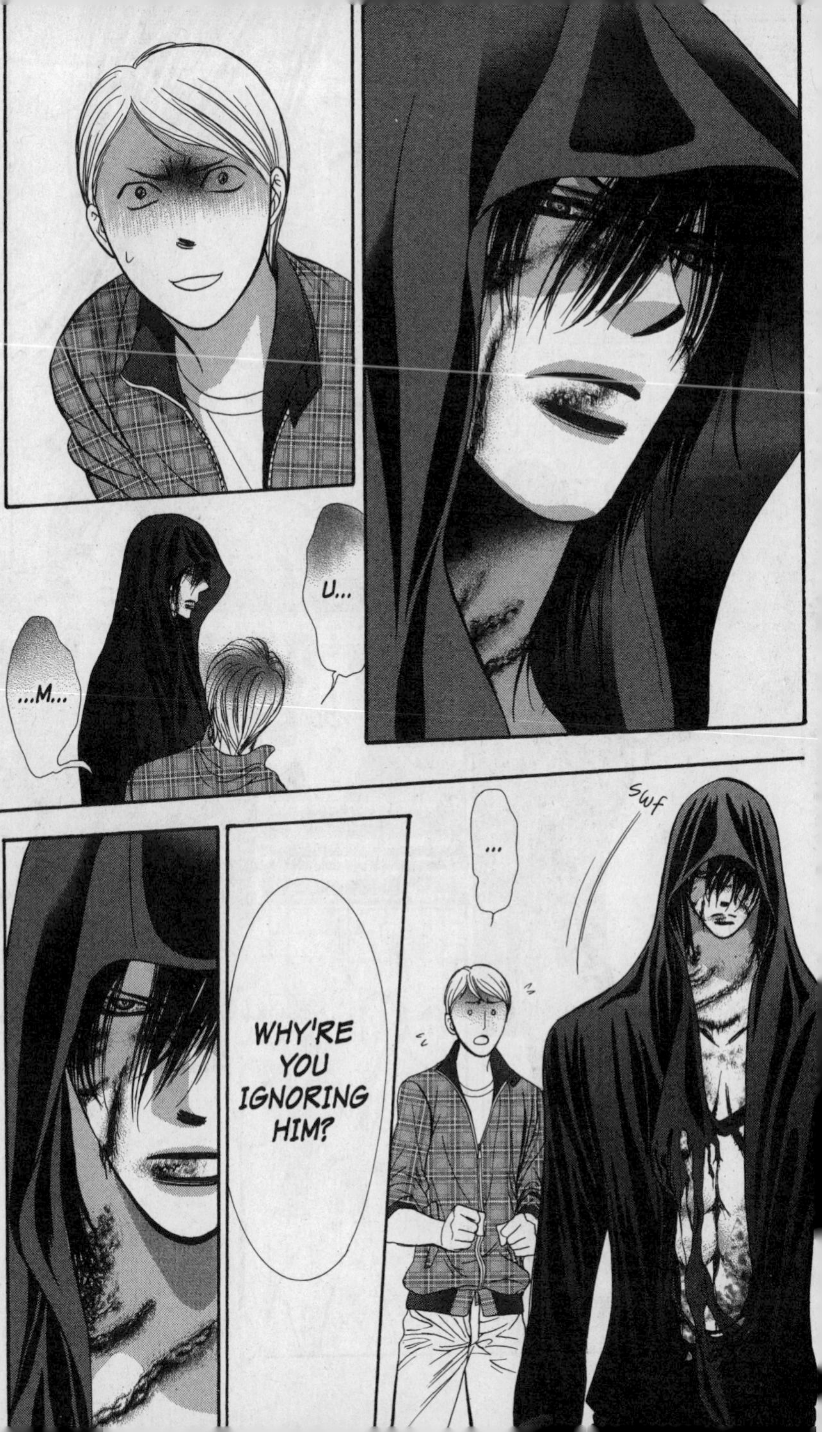
U...
...M...
SWf
...
WHY'RE YOU IGNORING HIM?

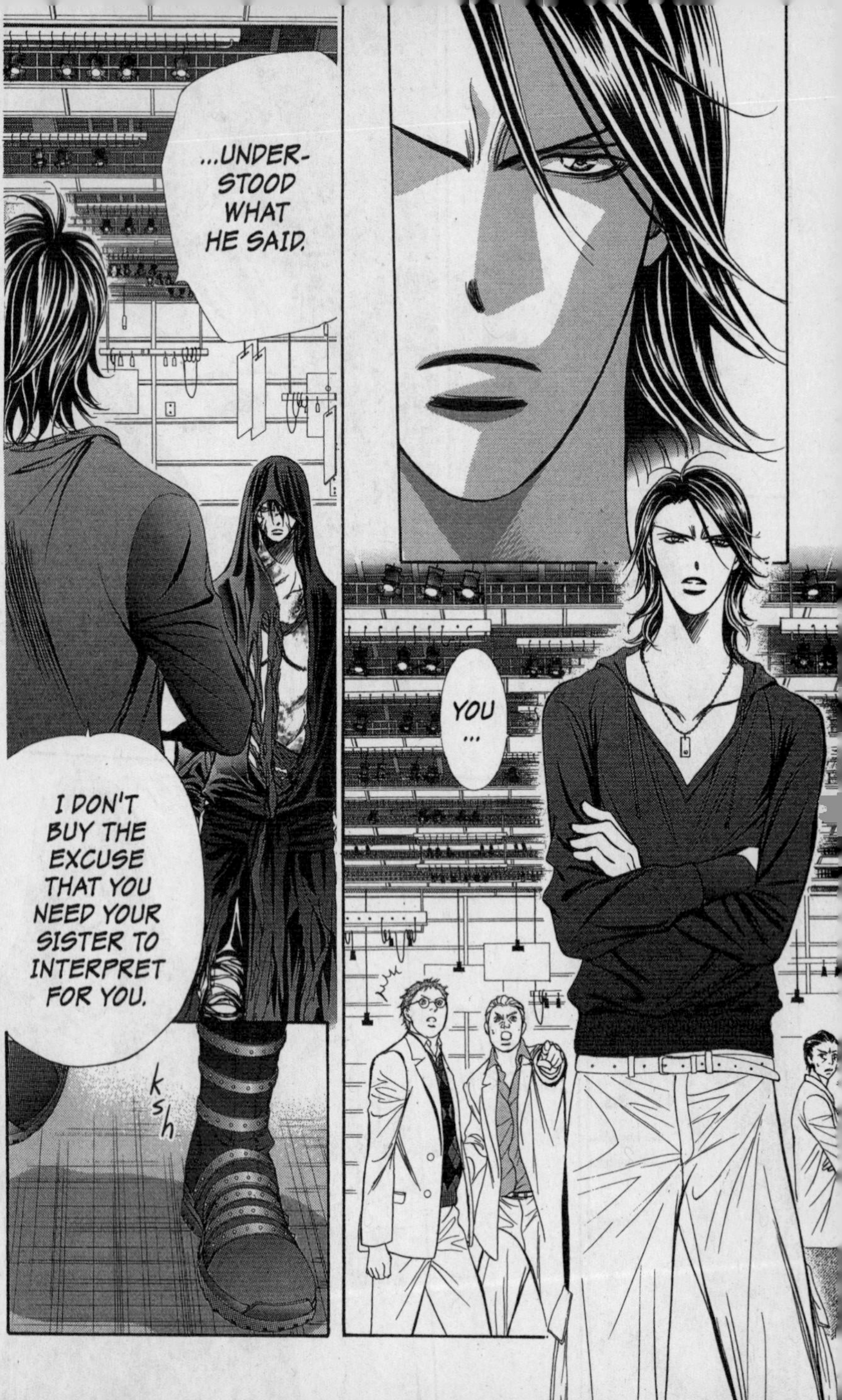
YOU ...
...UNDER-STOOD WHAT HE SAID.
I DON'T BUY THE EXCUSE THAT YOU NEED YOUR SISTER TO INTERPRET FOR YOU.
ksh

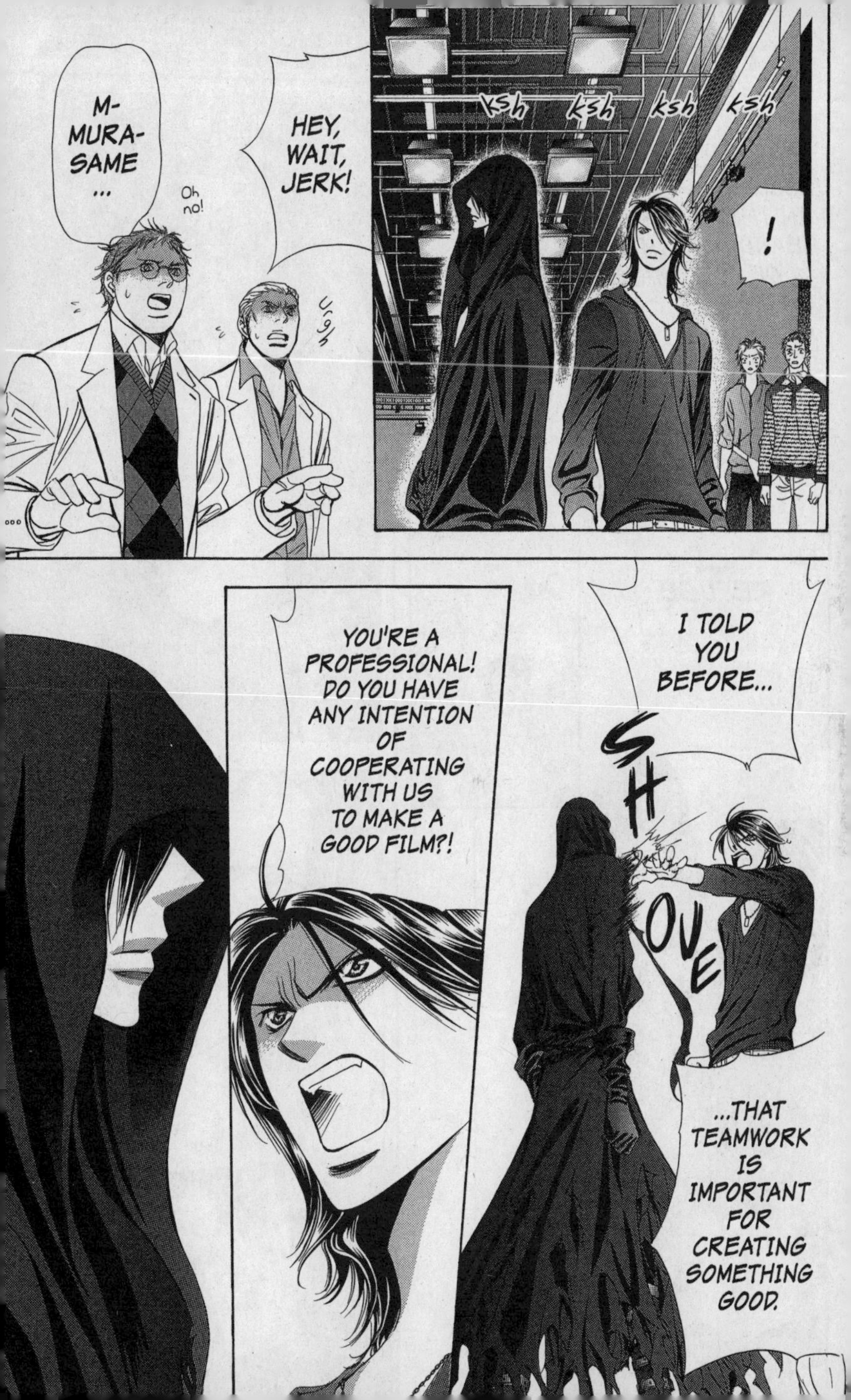
ksh ksh ksh ksh
!
HEY, WAIT, JERK!
M-MURASAME...
Oh no!
Urgh
I TOLD YOU BEFORE...
SHOVE
...THAT TEAMWORK IS IMPORTANT FOR CREATING SOMETHING GOOD.
YOU'RE A PROFESSIONAL! DO YOU HAVE ANY INTENTION OF COOPERATING WITH US TO MAKE A GOOD FILM?!

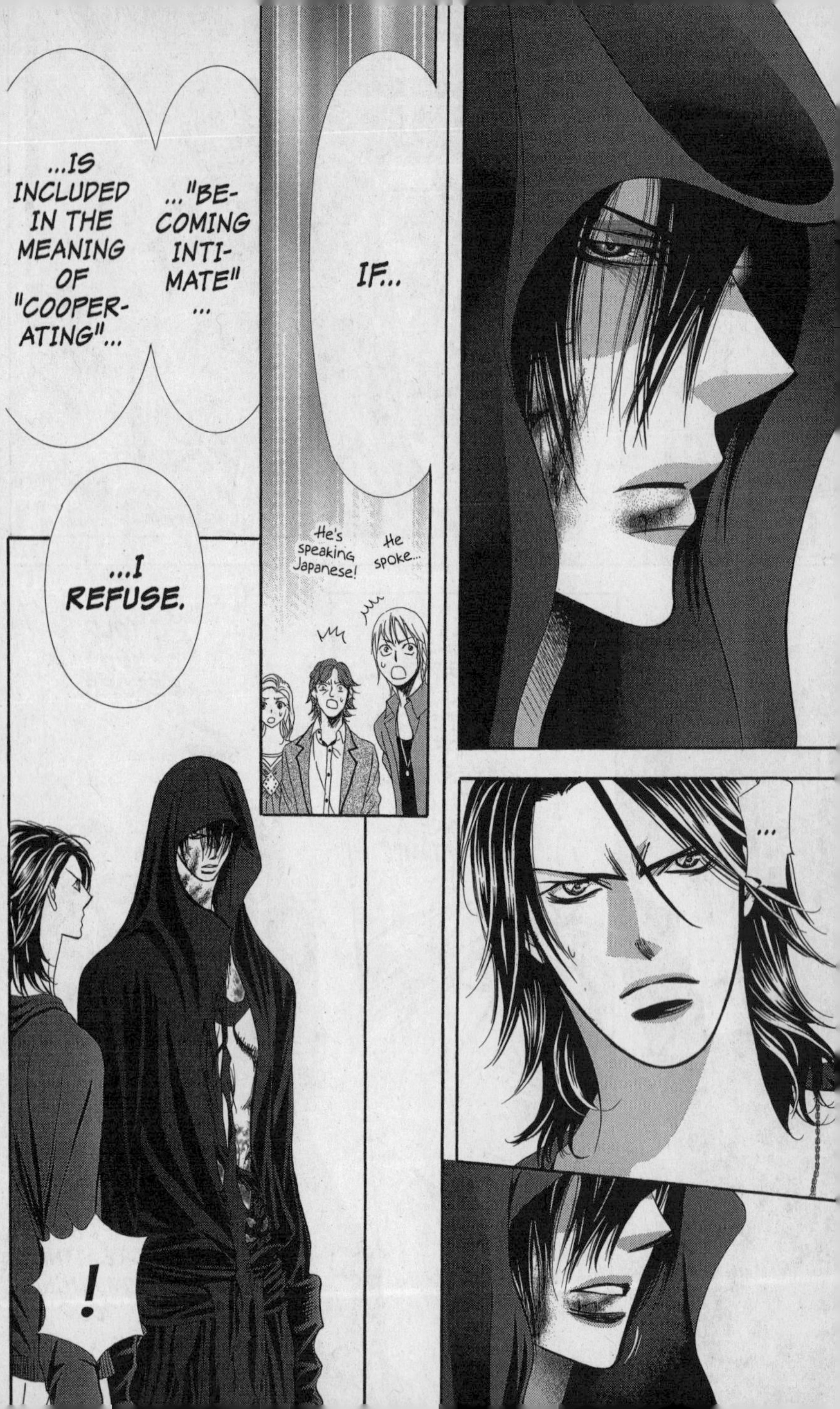
IF...
He spoke...
He's speaking Japanese!
..."BECOMING INTIMATE"...
...IS INCLUDED IN THE MEANING OF "COOPERATING"...
...I REFUSE.
!
...

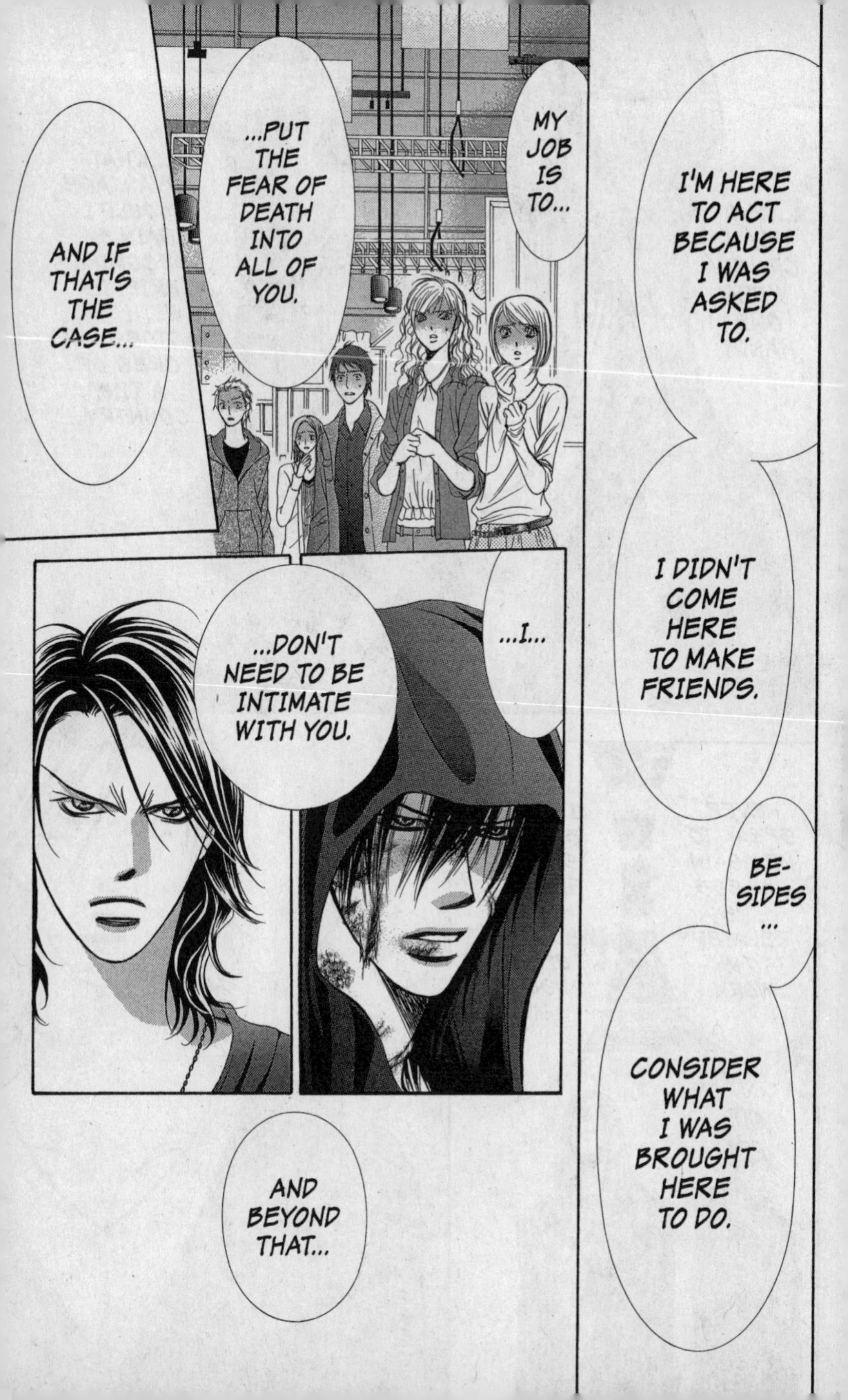
I'M HERE TO ACT BECAUSE I WAS ASKED TO.
I DIDN'T COME HERE TO MAKE FRIENDS.
BE-SIDES...
CONSIDER WHAT I WAS BROUGHT HERE TO DO.
MY JOB IS TO...
...PUT THE FEAR OF DEATH INTO ALL OF YOU.
AND IF THAT'S THE CASE...
...I...
...DON'T NEED TO BE INTIMATE WITH YOU.
AND BEYOND THAT...

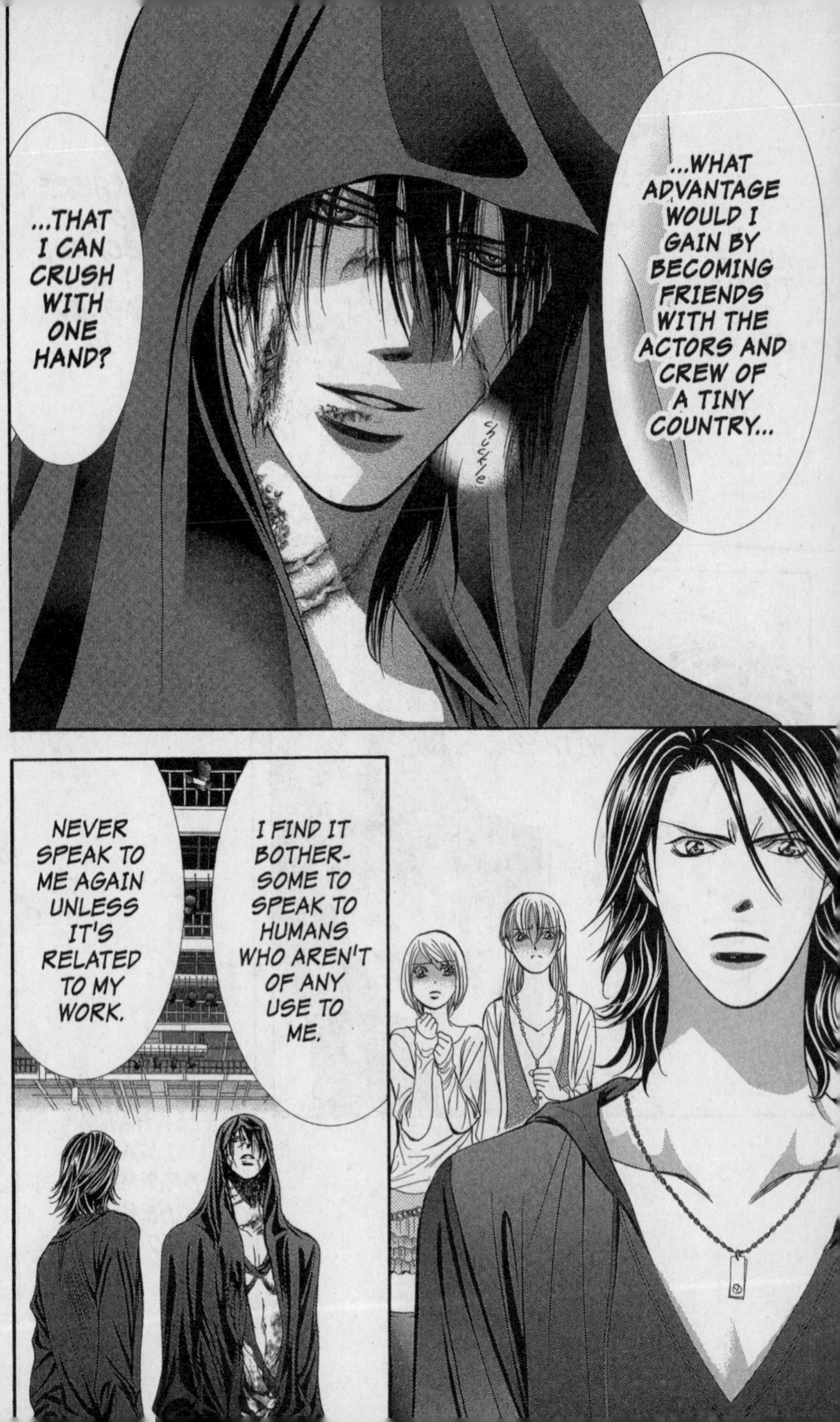
...WHAT ADVANTAGE WOULD I GAIN BY BECOMING FRIENDS WITH THE ACTORS AND CREW OF A TINY COUNTRY...
chuckle
...THAT I CAN CRUSH WITH ONE HAND?
I FIND IT BOTHER-SOME TO SPEAK TO HUMANS WHO AREN'T OF ANY USE TO ME.
NEVER SPEAK TO ME AGAIN UNLESS IT'S RELATED TO MY WORK.

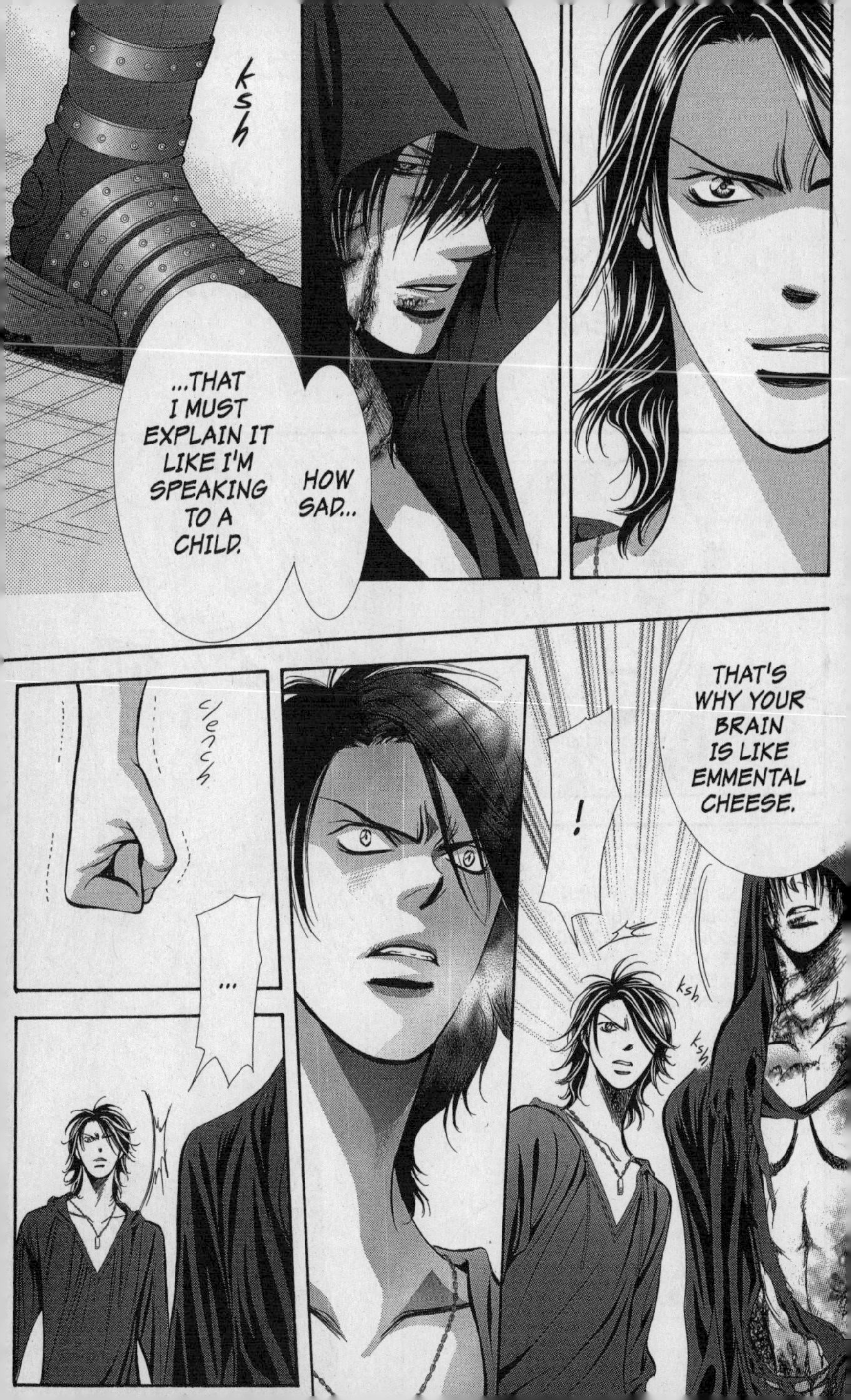
HOW SAD...
...THAT I MUST EXPLAIN IT LIKE I'M SPEAKING TO A CHILD.
ksh
THAT'S WHY YOUR BRAIN IS LIKE EMMENTAL CHEESE.
!
ksh
ksh
clench
...

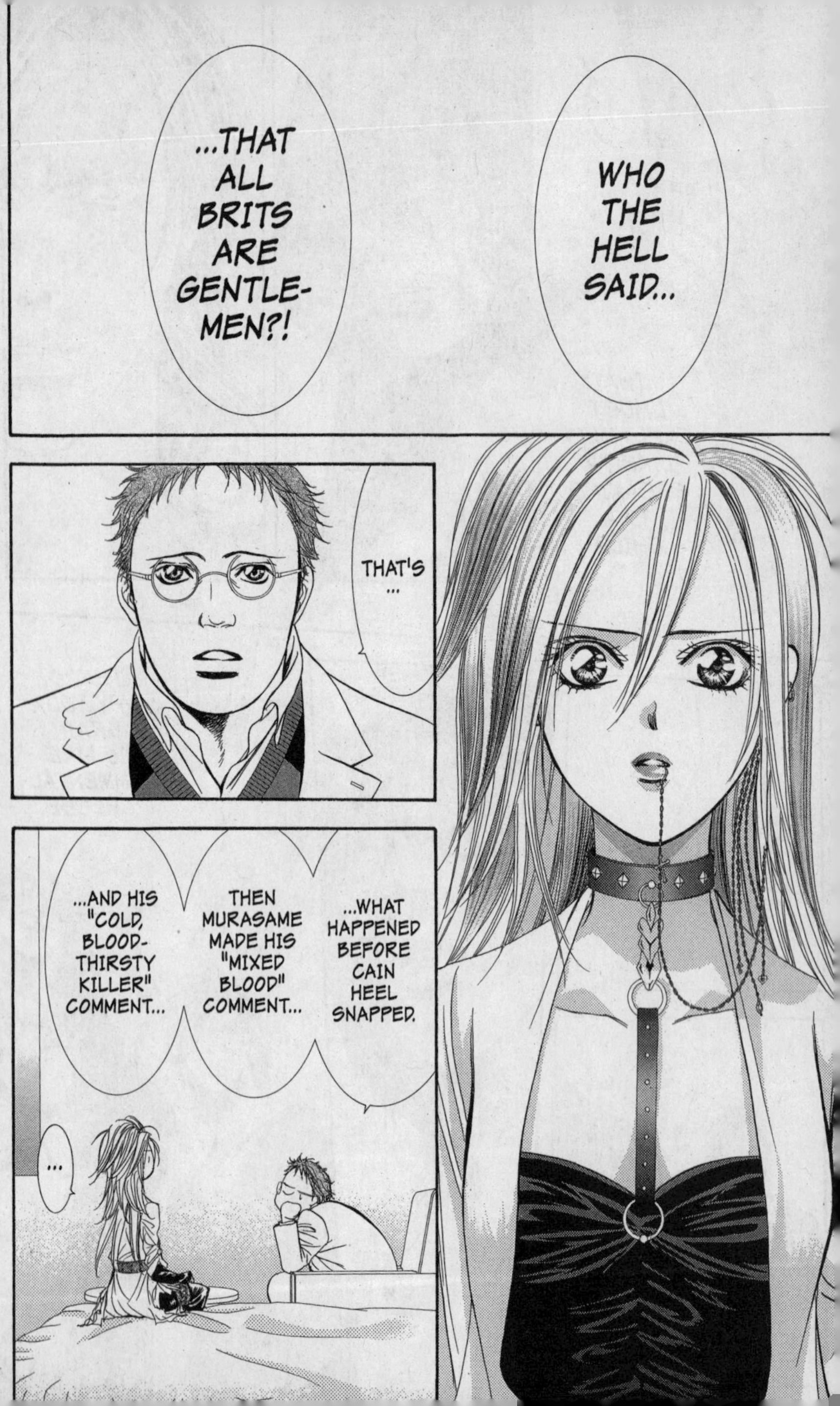
WHO THE HELL SAID...
...THAT ALL BRITS ARE GENTLEMEN?!
THAT'S ...
...WHAT HAPPENED BEFORE CAIN HEEL SNAPPED.
THEN MURASAME MADE HIS "MIXED BLOOD" COMMENT...
...AND HIS "COLD, BLOOD-THIRSTY KILLER" COMMENT...
...

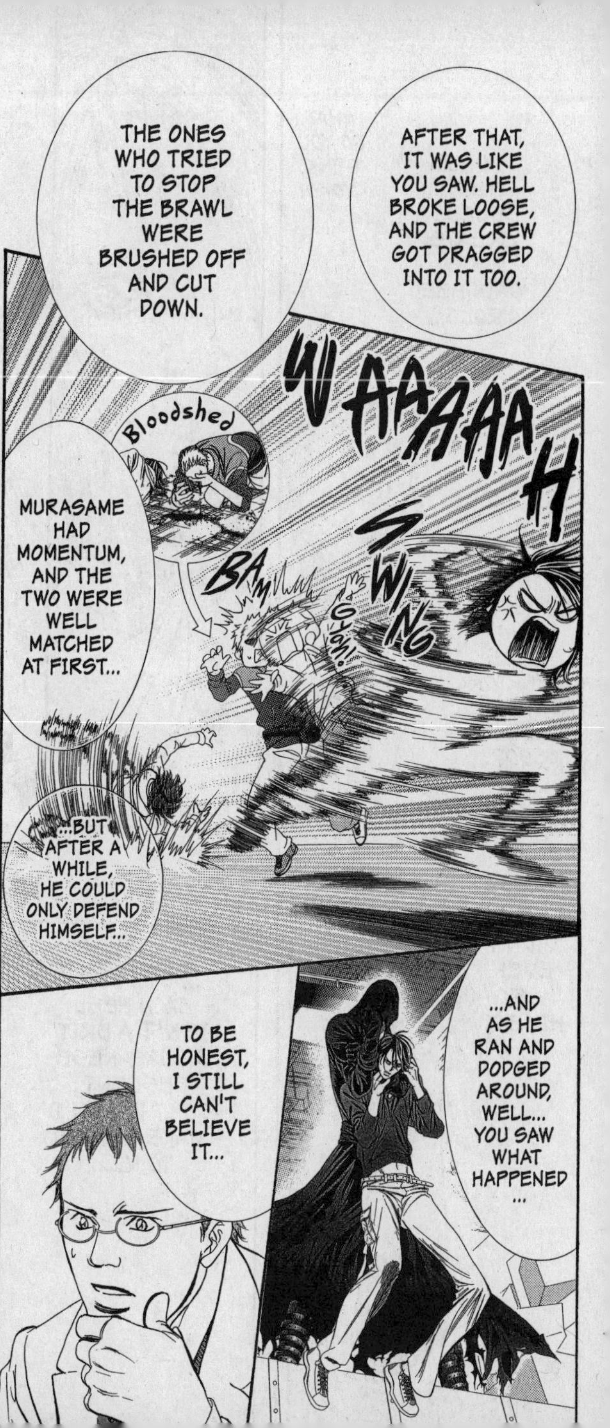
AFTER THAT, IT WAS LIKE YOU SAW. HELL BROKE LOOSE, AND THE CREW GOT DRAGGED INTO IT TOO.
THE ONES WHO TRIED TO STOP THE BRAWL WERE BRUSHED OFF AND CUT DOWN.
WAAAAAH
Bloodshed
MURASAME HAD MOMENTUM, AND THE TWO WERE WELL MATCHED AT FIRST...
SWING
BAM
...BUT AFTER A WHILE, HE COULD ONLY DEFEND HIMSELF...
...AND AS HE RAN AND DODGED AROUND, WELL... YOU SAW WHAT HAPPENED...
TO BE HONEST, I STILL CAN'T BELIEVE IT...

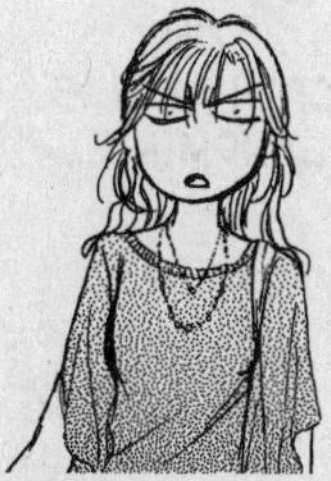

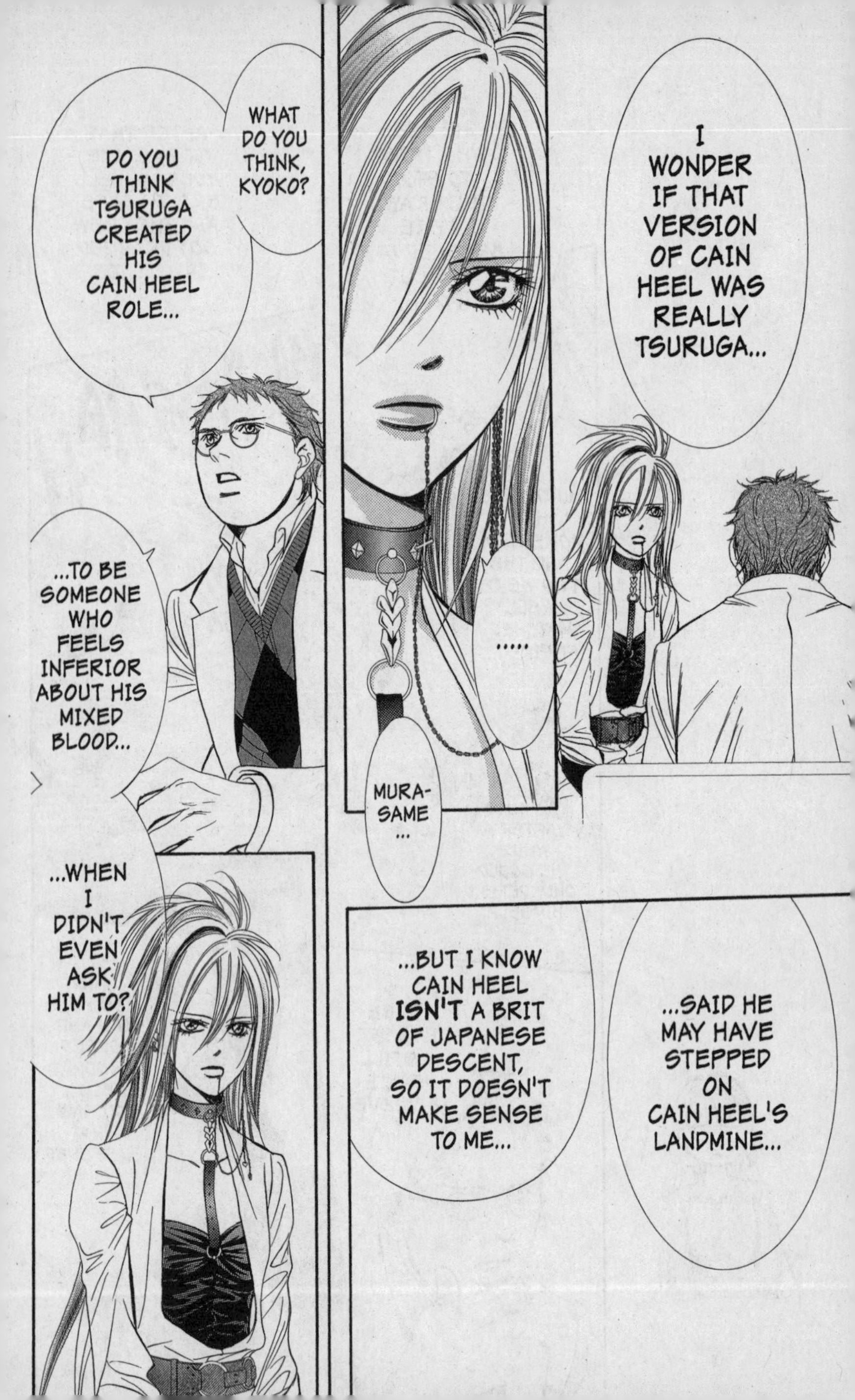
I WONDER IF THAT VERSION OF CAIN HEEL WAS REALLY TSURUGA...
.....
MURA-SAME...
WHAT DO YOU THINK, KYOKO?
DO YOU THINK TSURUGA CREATED HIS CAIN HEEL ROLE...
...TO BE SOMEONE WHO FEELS INFERIOR ABOUT HIS MIXED BLOOD...
...SAID HE MAY HAVE STEPPED ON CAIN HEEL'S LANDMINE...
...BUT I KNOW CAIN HEEL **ISN'T** A BRIT OF JAPANESE DESCENT, SO IT DOESN'T MAKE SENSE TO ME...
...WHEN I DIDN'T EVEN ASK HIM TO?

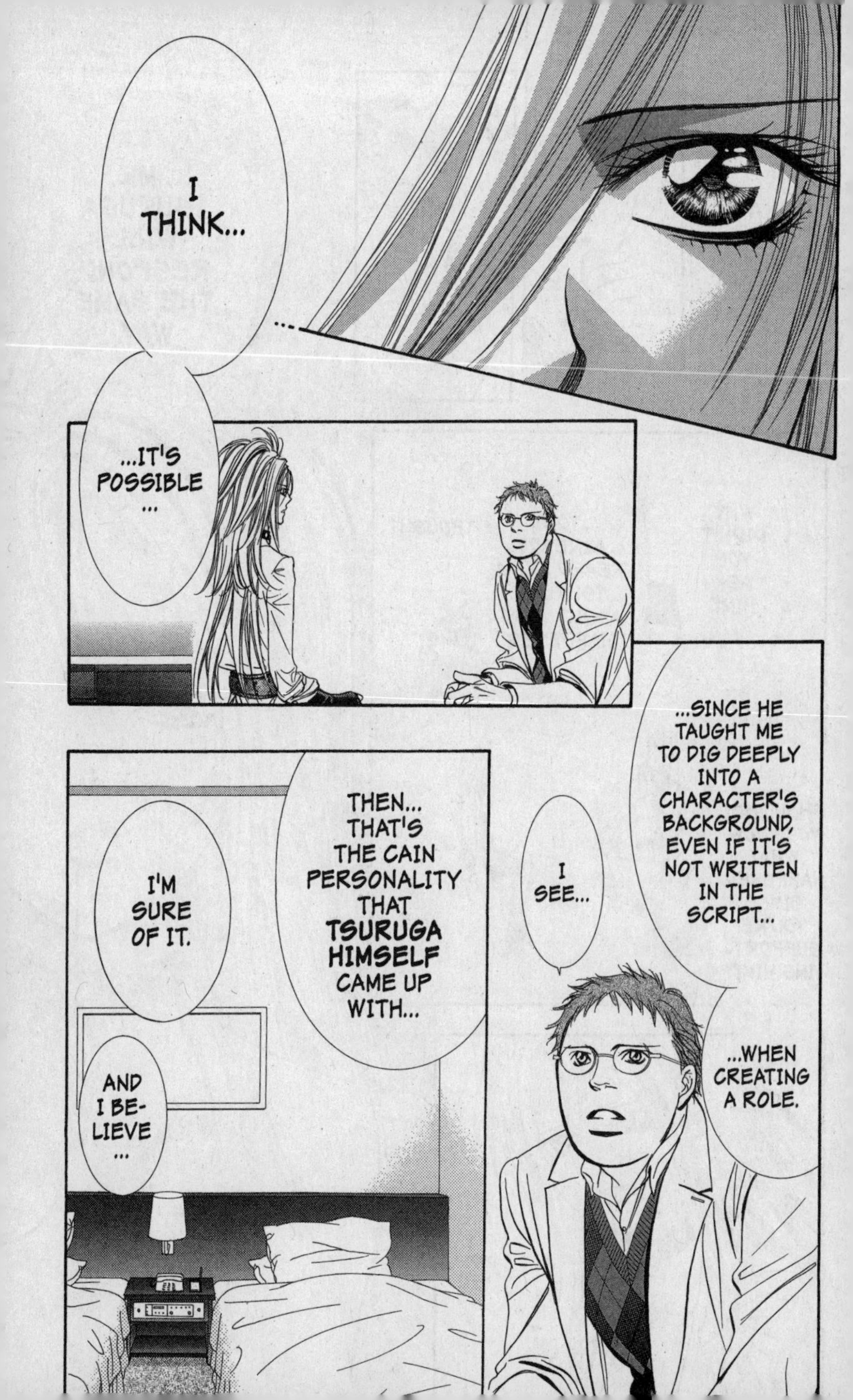
I THINK...
...IT'S POSSIBLE ...
...SINCE HE TAUGHT ME TO DIG DEEPLY INTO A CHARACTER'S BACKGROUND, EVEN IF IT'S NOT WRITTEN IN THE SCRIPT...
I SEE...
...WHEN CREATING A ROLE.
THEN... THAT'S THE CAIN PERSONALITY THAT **TSURUGA HIMSELF** CAME UP WITH...
I'M SURE OF IT.
AND I BE-LIEVE ...

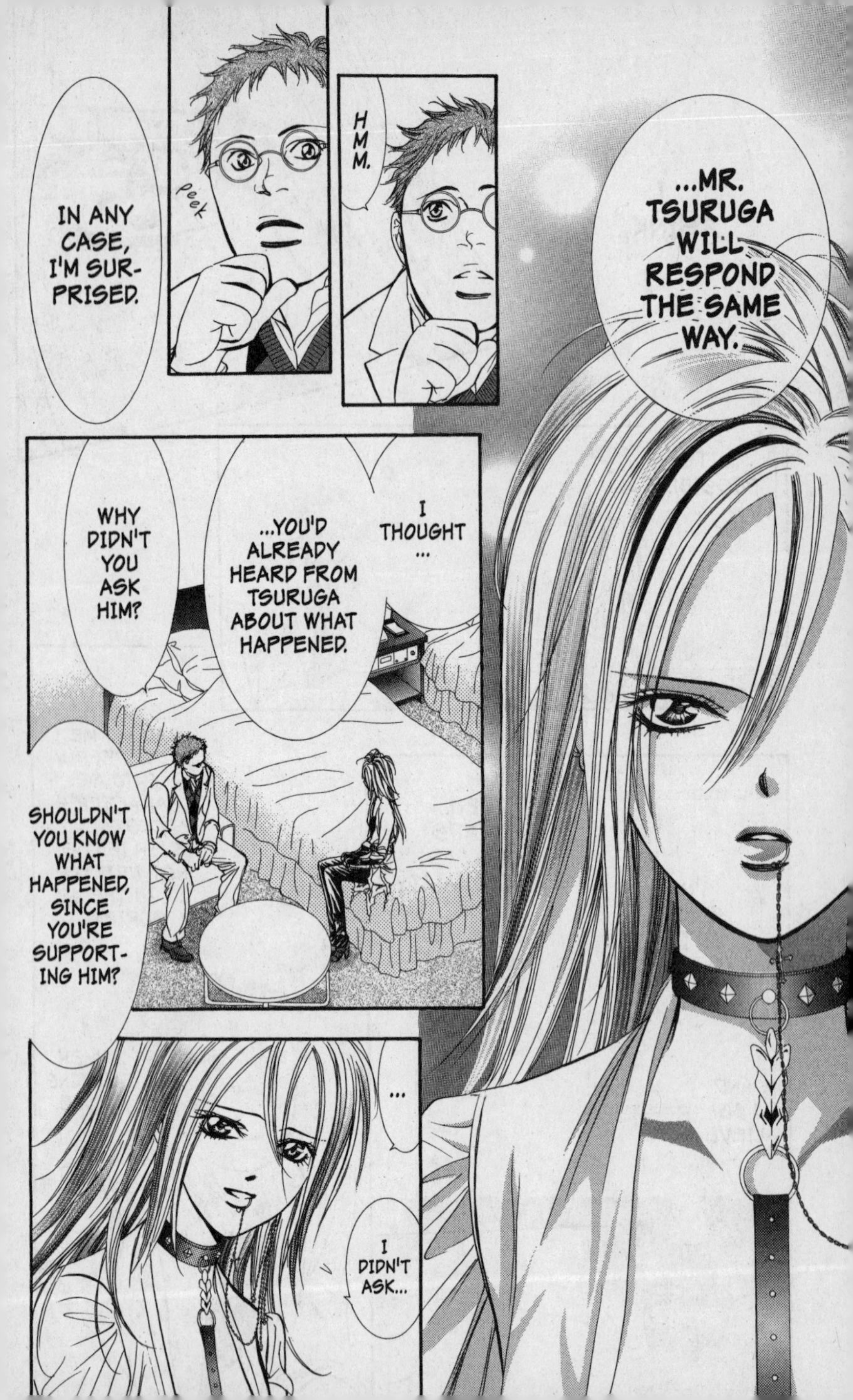
...MR. TSURUGA WILL RESPOND THE SAME WAY.
HMM.
peek
IN ANY CASE, I'M SURPRISED.
I THOUGHT...
...YOU'D ALREADY HEARD FROM TSURUGA ABOUT WHAT HAPPENED.
WHY DIDN'T YOU ASK HIM?
SHOULDN'T YOU KNOW WHAT HAPPENED, SINCE YOU'RE SUPPORTING HIM?
...
I DIDN'T ASK...

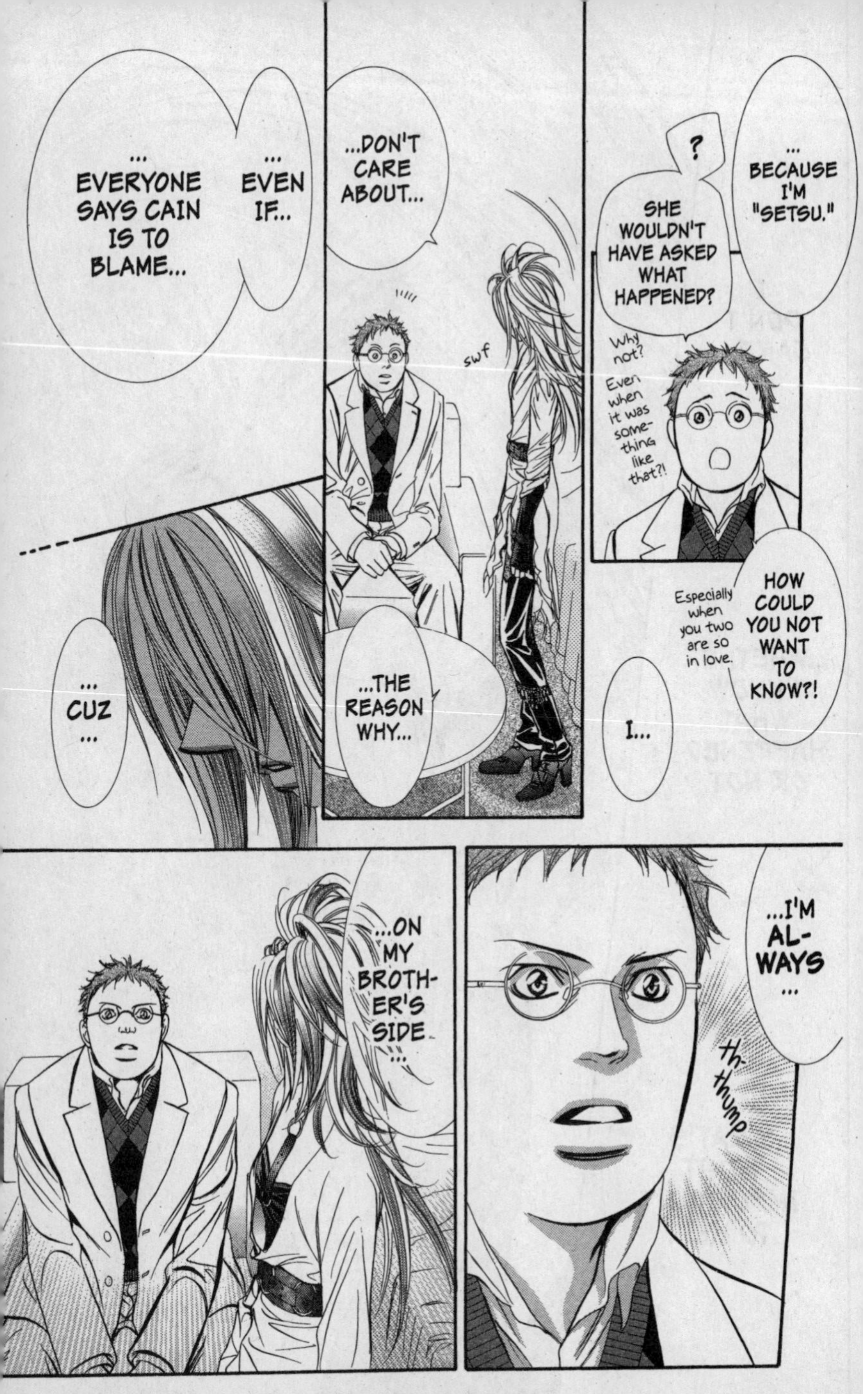
... BECAUSE I'M "SETSU."
?
SHE WOULDN'T HAVE ASKED WHAT HAPPENED?
Why not? Even when it was something like that?!
HOW COULD YOU NOT WANT TO KNOW?!
Especially when you two are so in love.
I...
...DON'T CARE ABOUT...
swf
...THE REASON WHY...
... EVEN IF...
... EVERYONE SAYS CAIN IS TO BLAME...
... CUZ ...
...I'M AL-WAYS ...
th-thump
...ON MY BROTH-ER'S SIDE ...

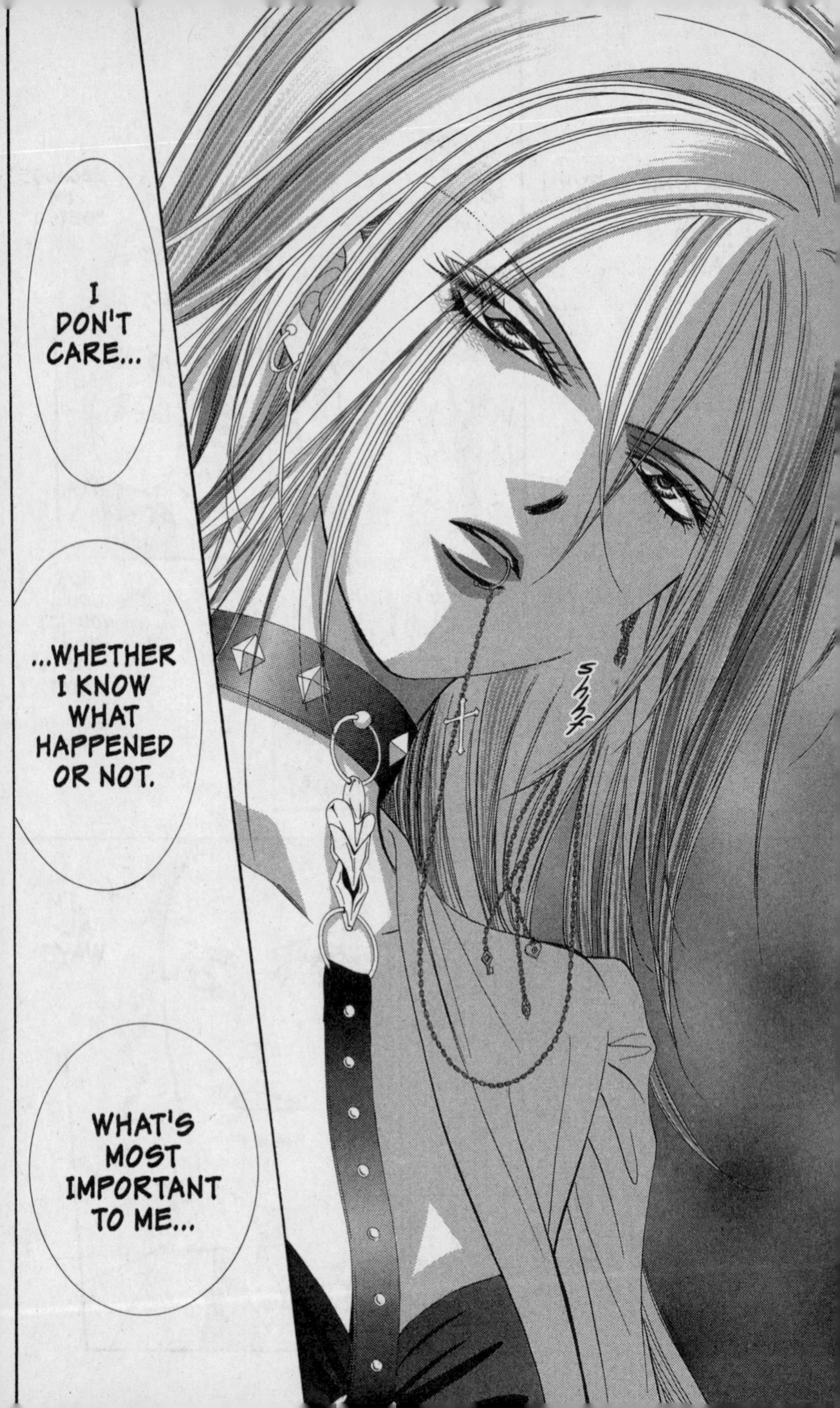
I DON'T CARE...
...WHETHER I KNOW WHAT HAPPENED OR NOT.
WHAT'S MOST IMPORTANT TO ME...

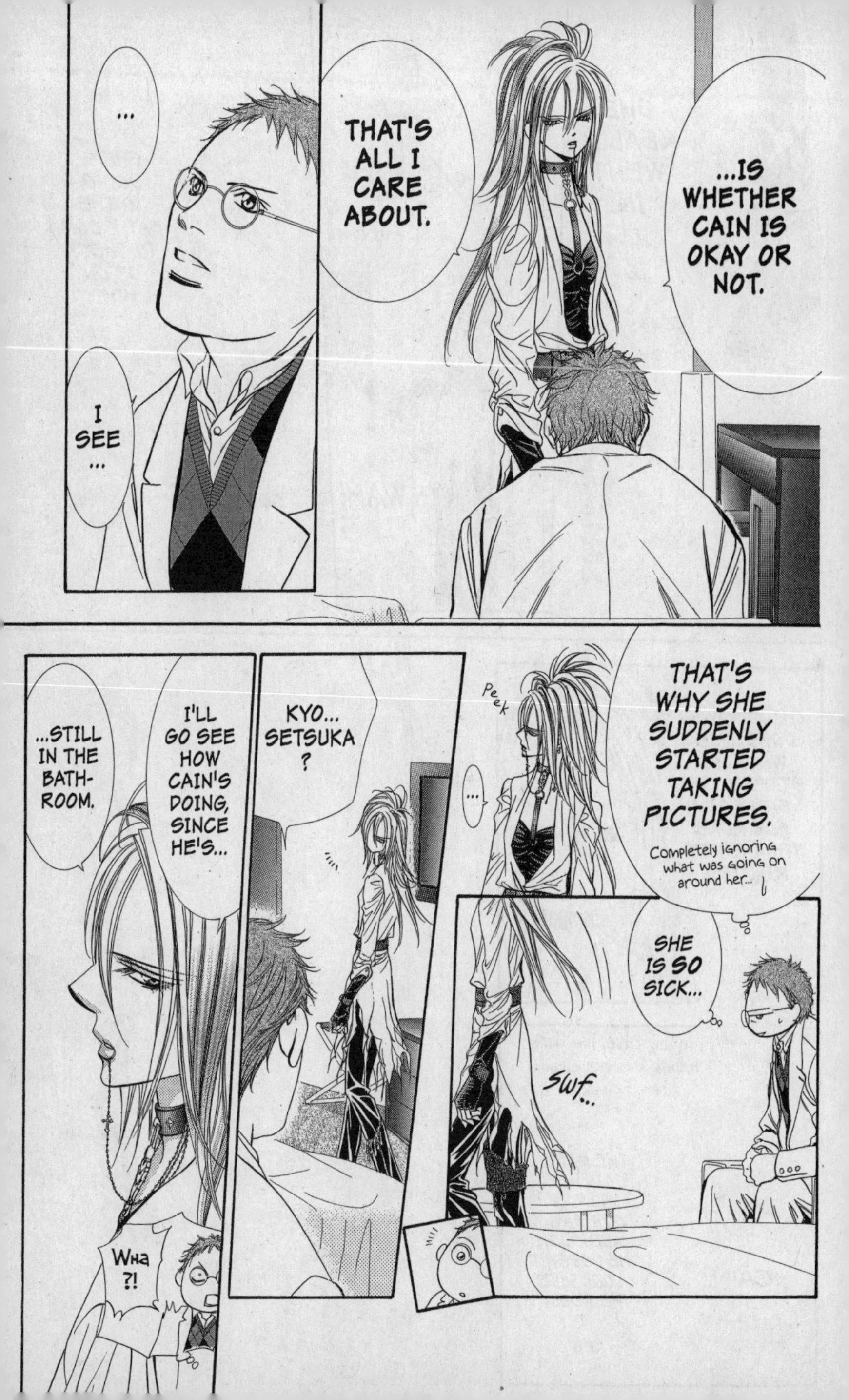
...IS WHETHER CAIN IS OKAY OR NOT.
THAT'S ALL I CARE ABOUT.
...
I SEE...
THAT'S WHY SHE SUDDENLY STARTED TAKING PICTURES.
Completely ignoring what was going on around her...
Peek
...
SHE IS SO SICK...
SWF...
KYO... SETSUKA?
I'LL GO SEE HOW CAIN'S DOING, SINCE HE'S...
...STILL IN THE BATH-ROOM.
Wha?!

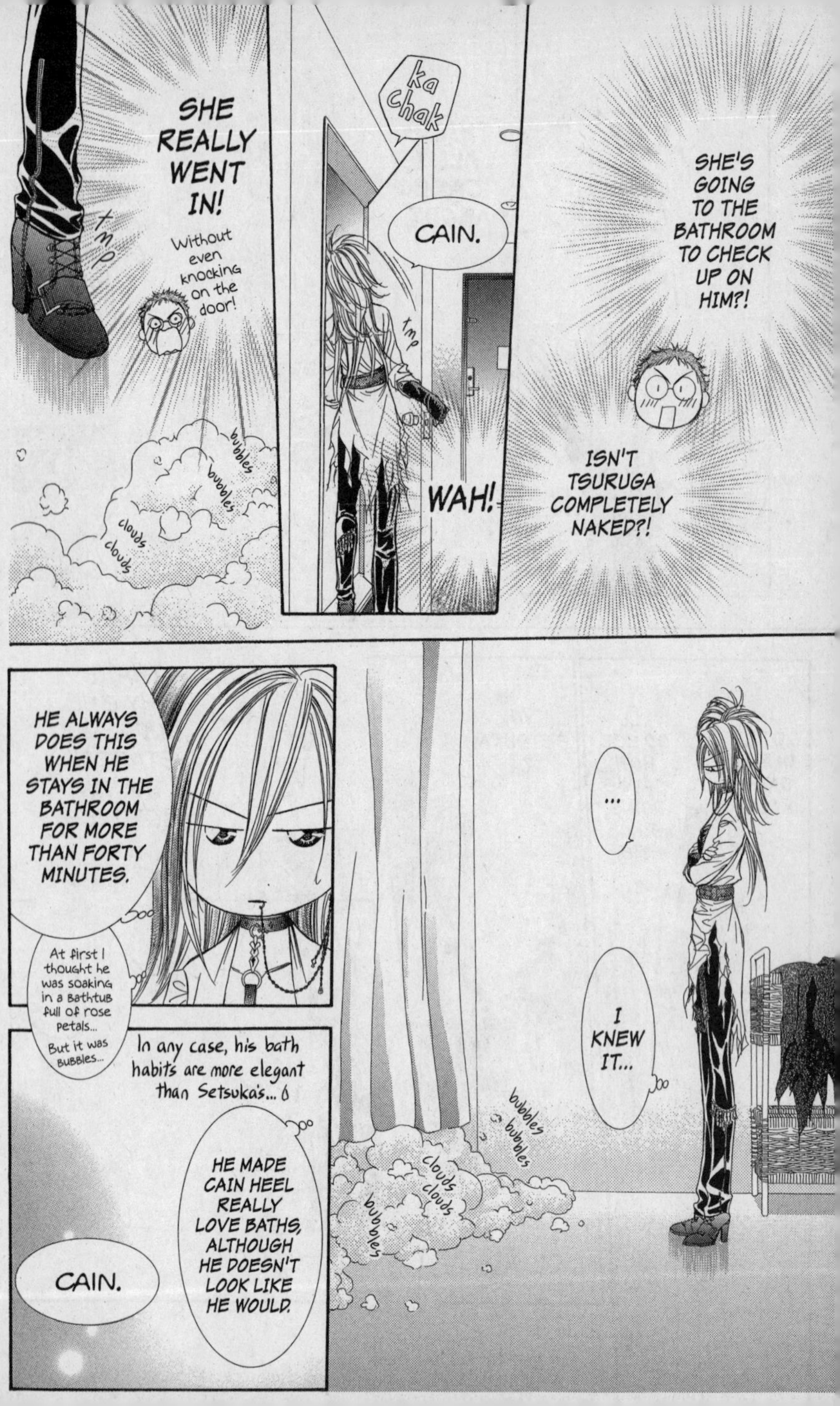
SHE'S GOING TO THE BATHROOM TO CHECK UP ON HIM?!
ISN'T TSURUGA COMPLETELY NAKED?!
ka chak
CAIN.
tmp
WAH!
SHE REALLY WENT IN!
Without even knocking on the door!
tmp
bubbles
bubbles
clouds
clouds
...
I KNEW IT...
bubbles
bubbles
clouds
clouds
bubbles
HE ALWAYS DOES THIS WHEN HE STAYS IN THE BATHROOM FOR MORE THAN FORTY MINUTES.
At first I thought he was soaking in a bathtub full of rose petals...
But it was bubbles...
In any case, his bath habits are more elegant than Setsuka's...
HE MADE CAIN HEEL REALLY LOVE BATHS, ALTHOUGH HE DOESN'T LOOK LIKE HE WOULD.
CAIN.

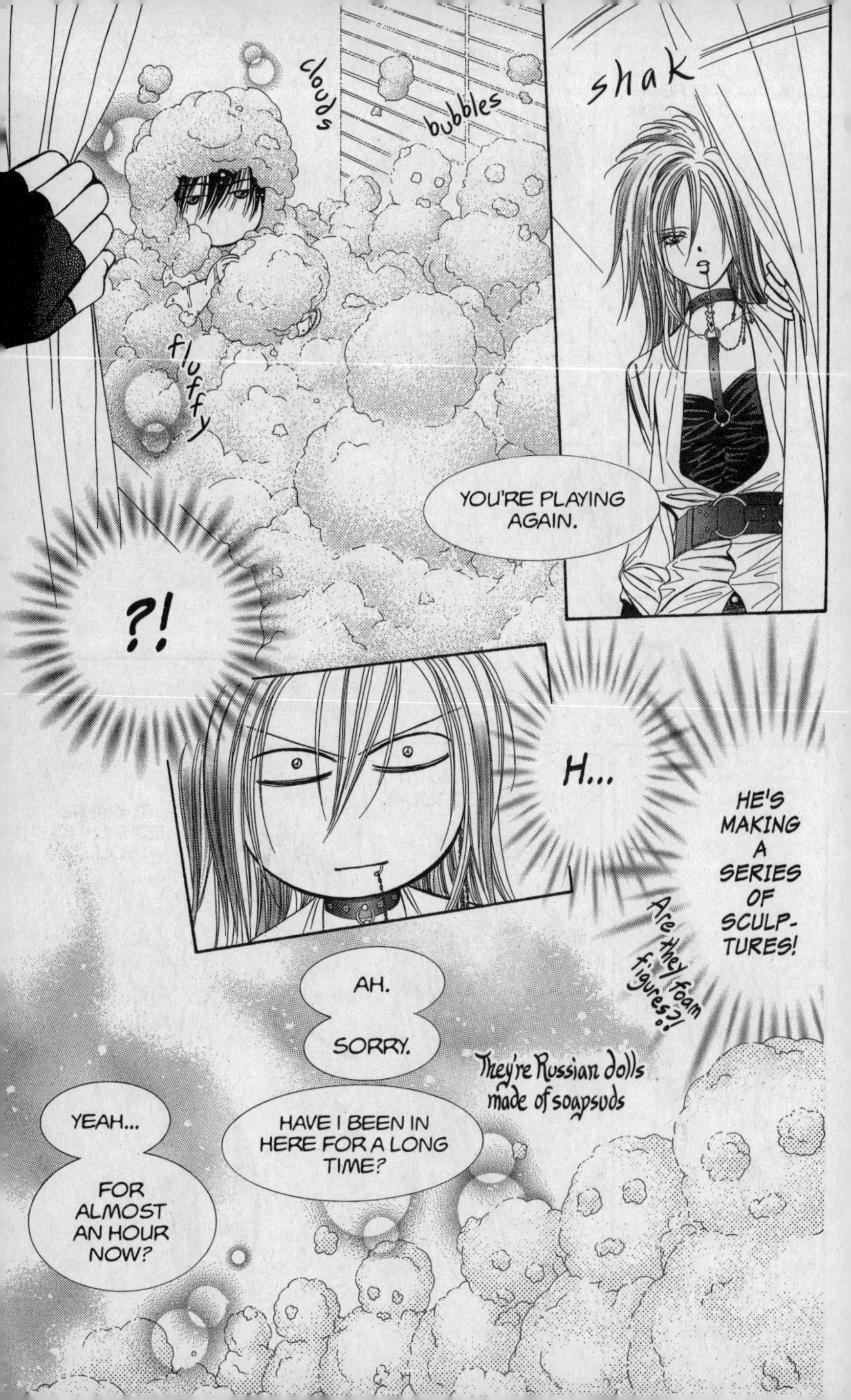
shak
YOU'RE PLAYING AGAIN.
bubbles
clouds
fluffy
?!
H...
HE'S MAKING A SERIES OF SCULPTURES!
Are they foam figures?!
AH.
SORRY.
They're Russian dolls made of soapsuds
HAVE I BEEN IN HERE FOR A LONG TIME?
YEAH...
FOR ALMOST AN HOUR NOW?

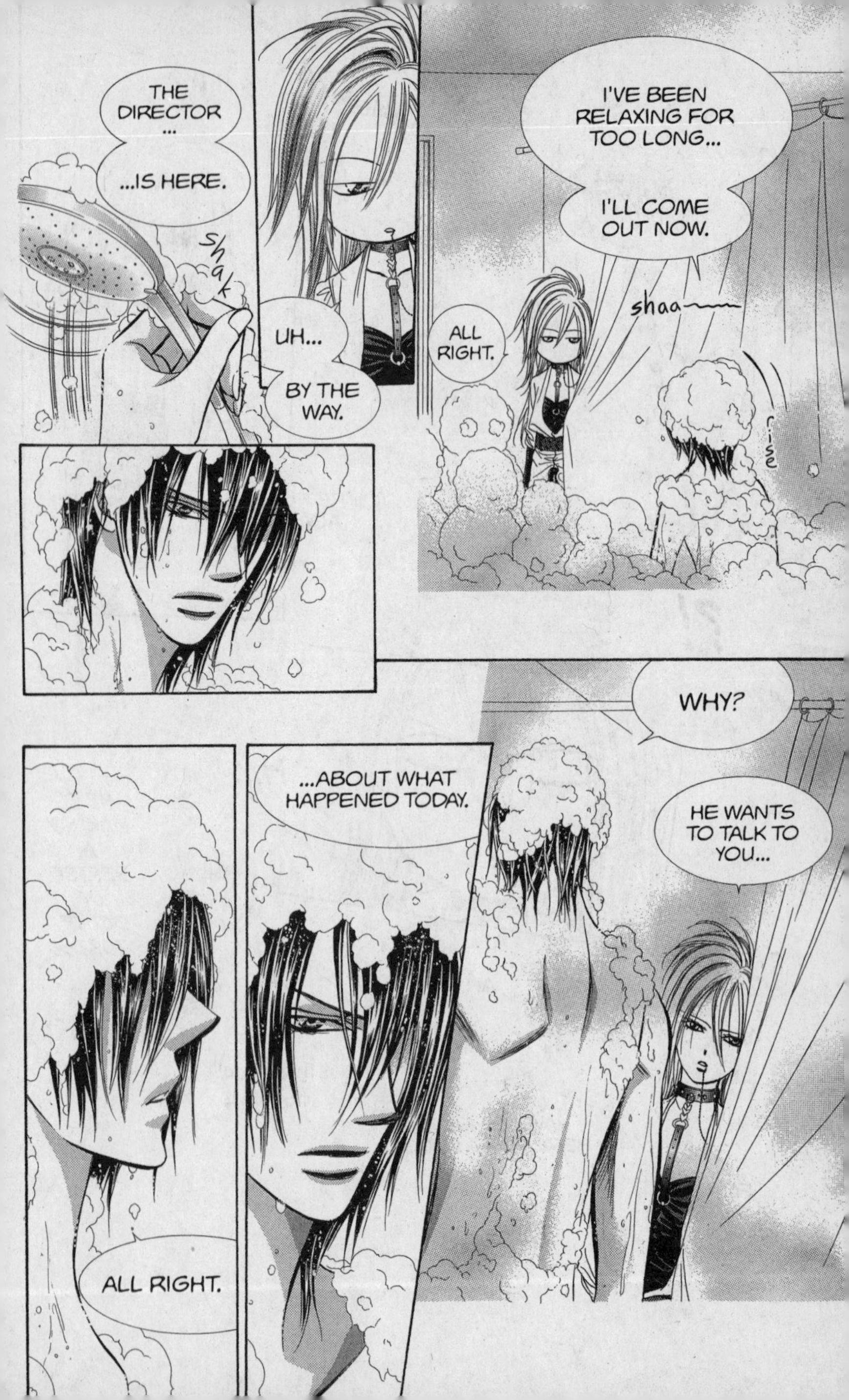
I'VE BEEN RELAXING FOR TOO LONG...
I'LL COME OUT NOW.
shaa
ALL RIGHT.
rise
UH... BY THE WAY.
THE DIRECTOR...
...IS HERE.
shak
WHY?
HE WANTS TO TALK TO YOU...
...ABOUT WHAT HAPPENED TODAY.
ALL RIGHT.

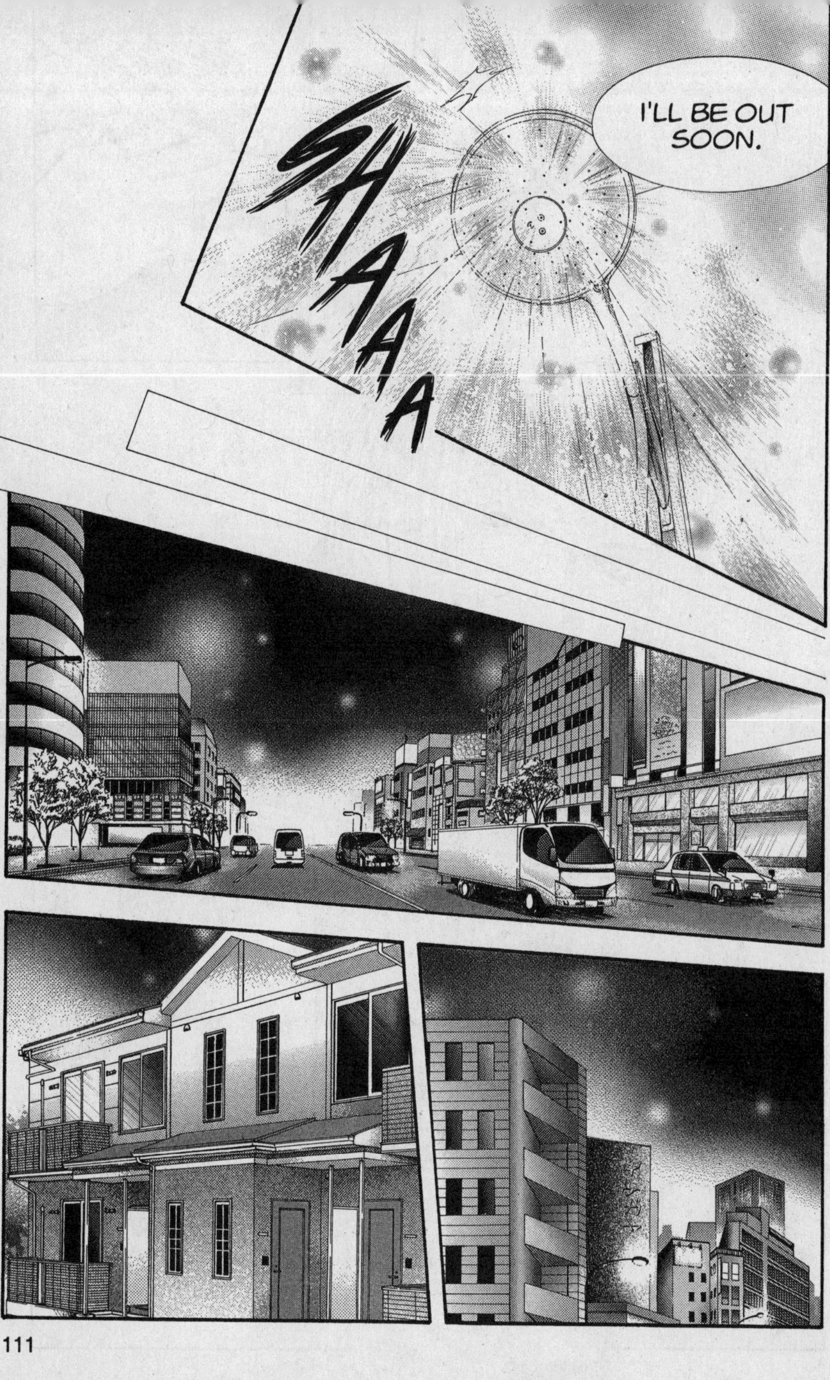
I'LL BE OUT SOON.
SHAAAA

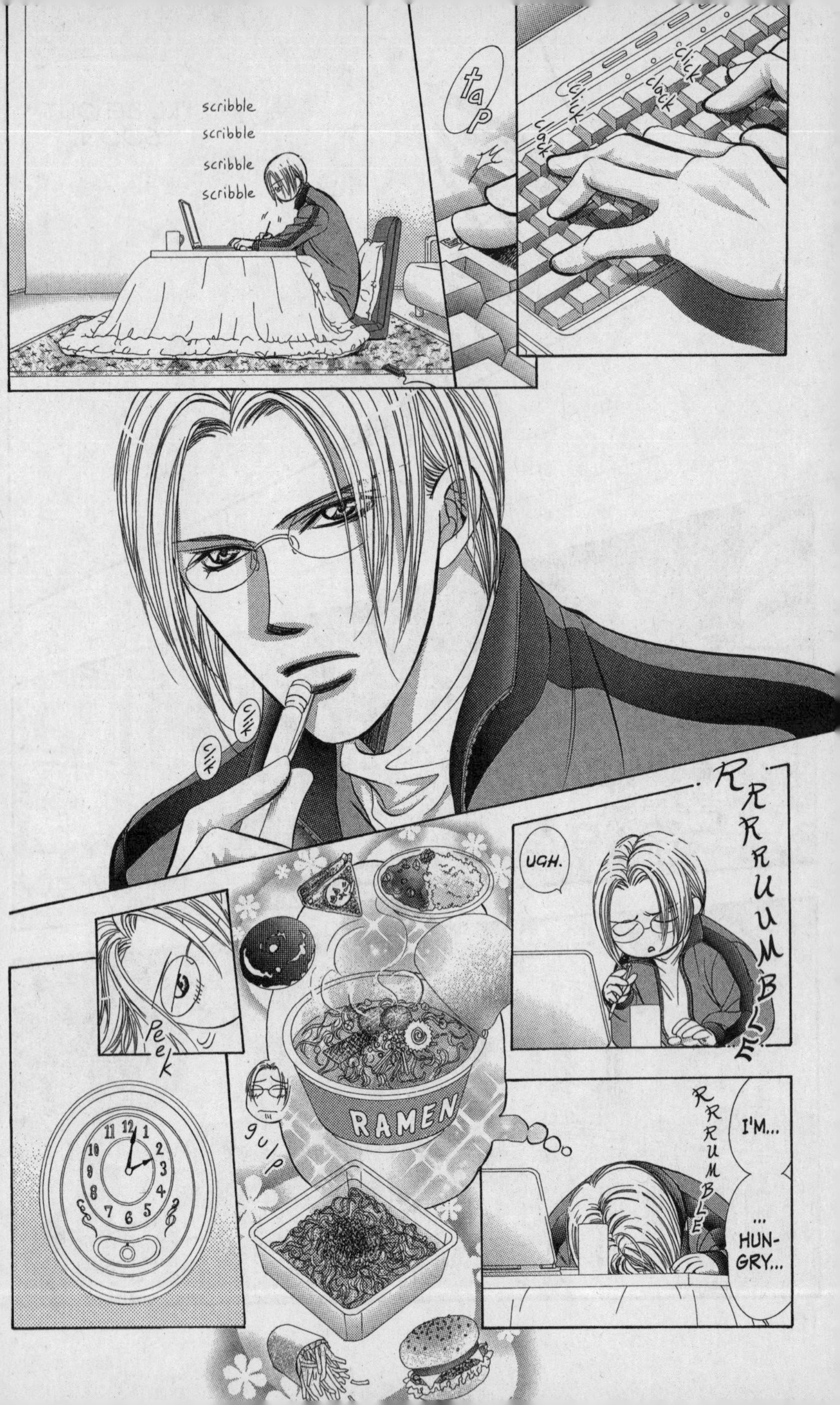
click
clack
click
clack
tap
scribble
scribble
scribble
scribble
click
click
RRRRUMBLE
UGH.
Peek
RAMEN
gulp
RRRUMBLE
I'M...
...HUNGRY...

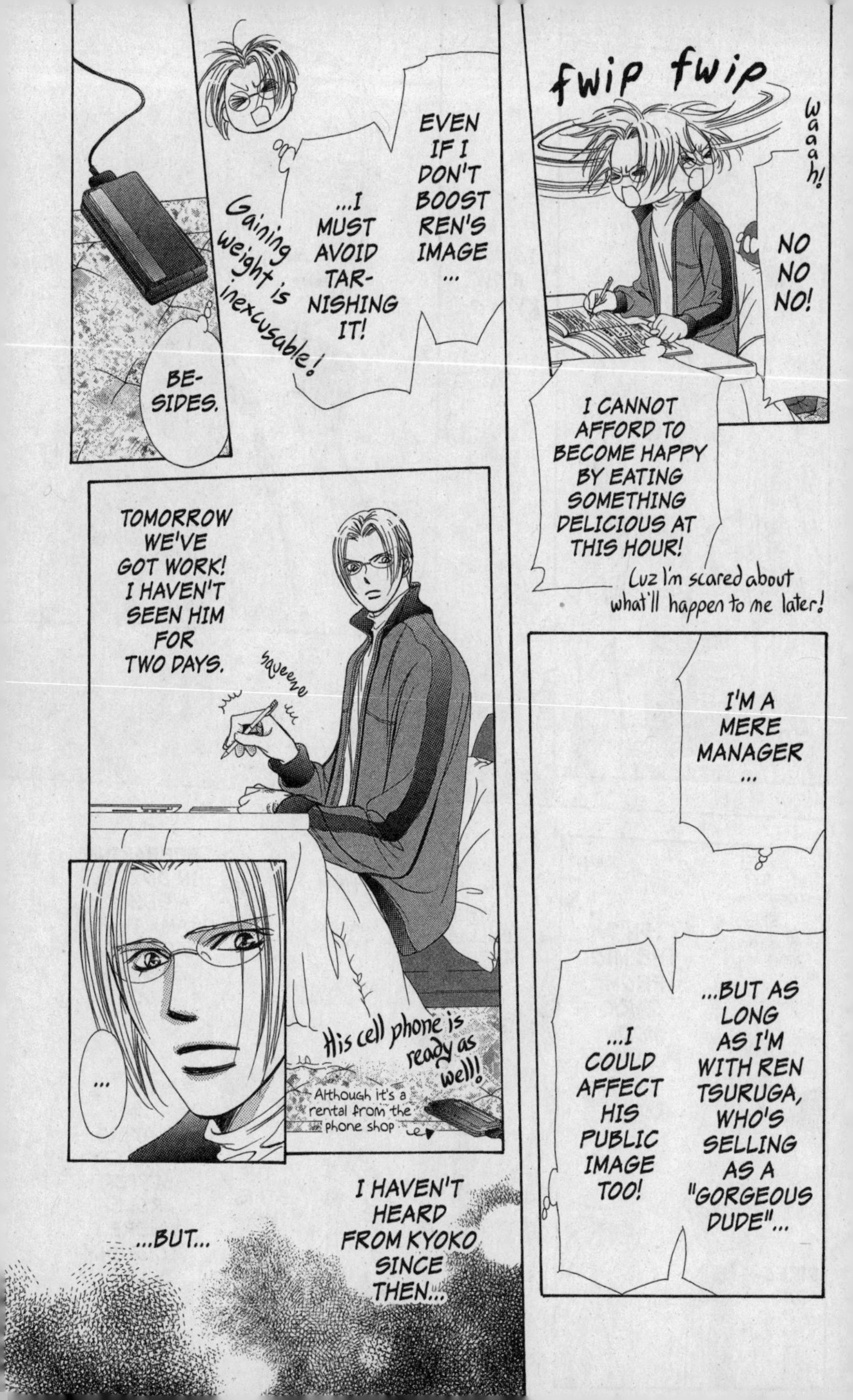
fwip fwip
Waaah!
NO NO NO!
I CANNOT AFFORD TO BECOME HAPPY BY EATING SOMETHING DELICIOUS AT THIS HOUR!
Cuz I'm scared about what'll happen to me later!
I'M A MERE MANAGER...
...BUT AS LONG AS I'M WITH REN TSURUGA, WHO'S SELLING AS A "GORGEOUS DUDE"...
...I COULD AFFECT HIS PUBLIC IMAGE TOO!
EVEN IF I DON'T BOOST REN'S IMAGE...
...I MUST AVOID TAR-NISHING IT!
Gaining weight is inexcusable!
BE-SIDES.
TOMORROW WE'VE GOT WORK! I HAVEN'T SEEN HIM FOR TWO DAYS.
squeeze
His cell phone is ready as well!
Although it's a rental from the phone shop
...
I HAVEN'T HEARD FROM KYOKO SINCE THEN...
...BUT...

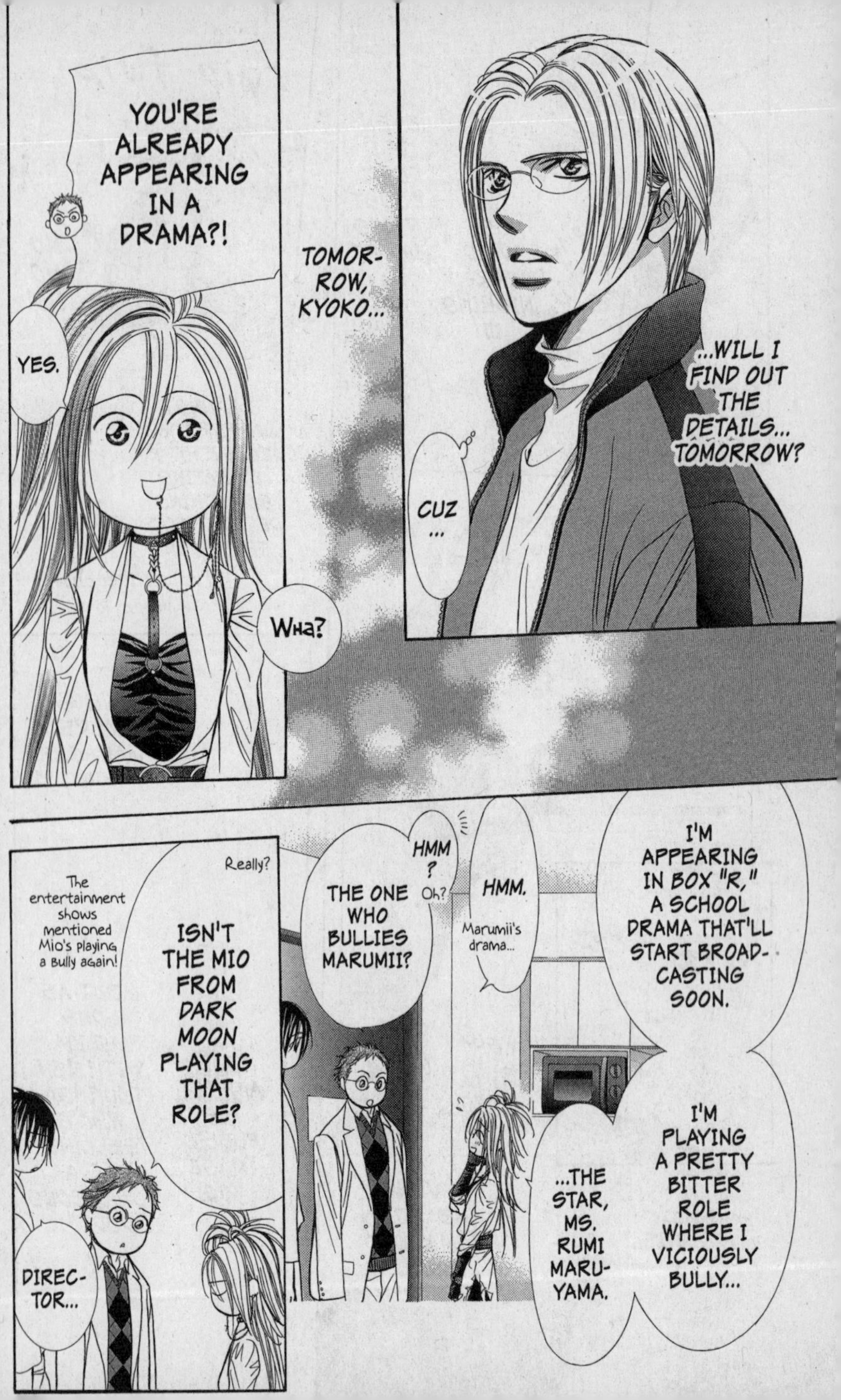
TOMOR-ROW, KYOKO...
...WILL I FIND OUT THE DETAILS... TOMORROW?
CUZ...
YOU'RE ALREADY APPEARING IN A DRAMA?!
YES.
Wha?
I'M APPEARING IN BOX "R," A SCHOOL DRAMA THAT'LL START BROAD-CASTING SOON.
I'M PLAYING A PRETTY BITTER ROLE WHERE I VICIOUSLY BULLY...
...THE STAR, MS. RUMI MARU-YAMA.
HMM.
Marumii's drama...
HMM?
Oh?
THE ONE WHO BULLIES MARUMII?
Really?
ISN'T THE MIO FROM DARK MOON PLAYING THAT ROLE?
The entertainment shows mentioned Mio's playing a bully again!
DIREC-TOR...

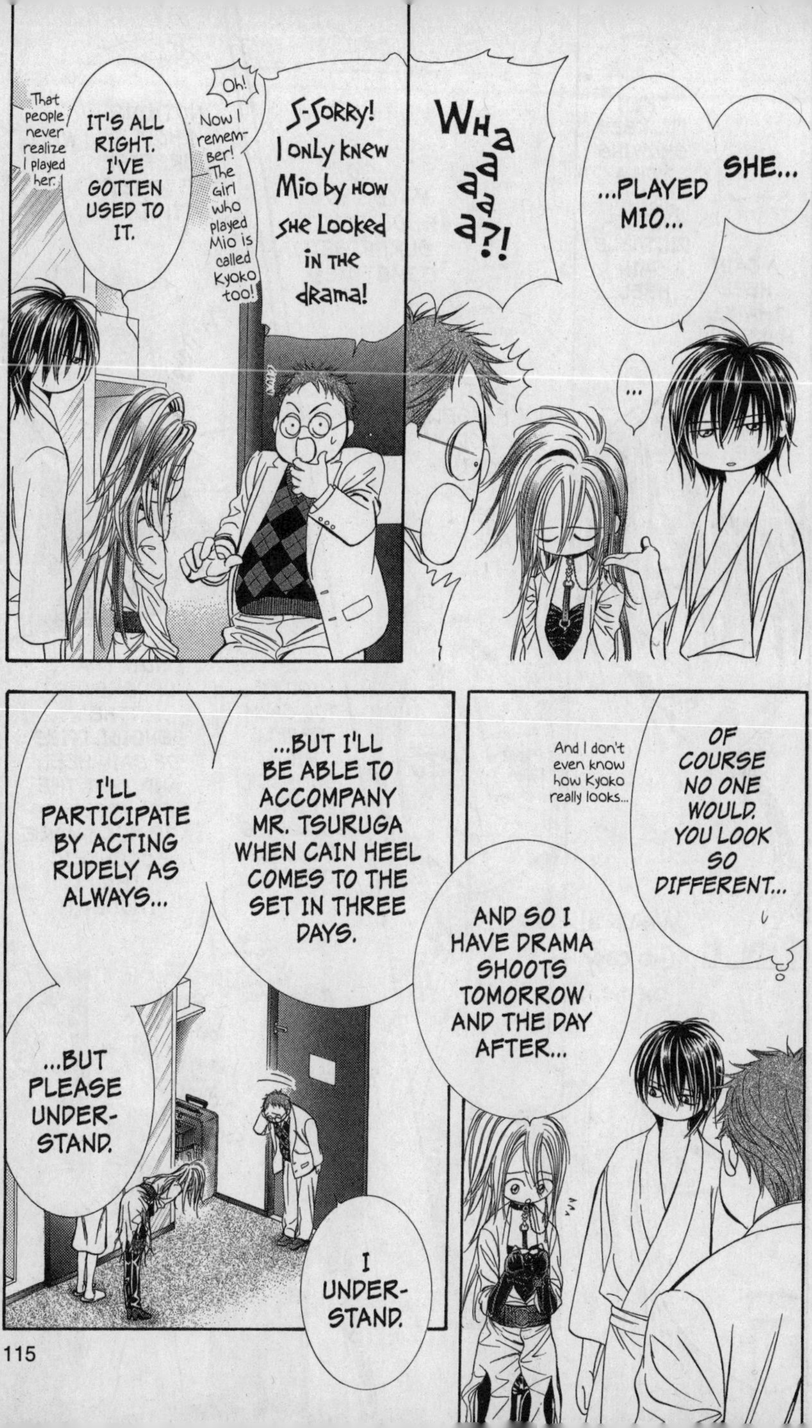
SHE...
...PLAYED MIO...
...
WHaaaaa?!
S-SORRY! I ONLY KNEW MIO BY HOW SHE LOOKED IN THE DRAMA!
Oh!
Now I remember! The girl who played Mio is called Kyoko too!
IT'S ALL RIGHT. I'VE GOTTEN USED TO IT.
That people never realize I played her.
OF COURSE NO ONE WOULD. YOU LOOK SO DIFFERENT...
And I don't even know how Kyoko really looks...
AND SO I HAVE DRAMA SHOOTS TOMORROW AND THE DAY AFTER...
...BUT I'LL BE ABLE TO ACCOMPANY MR. TSURUGA WHEN CAIN HEEL COMES TO THE SET IN THREE DAYS.
I'LL PARTICIPATE BY ACTING RUDELY AS ALWAYS...
...BUT PLEASE UNDER-STAND.
I UNDER-STAND.

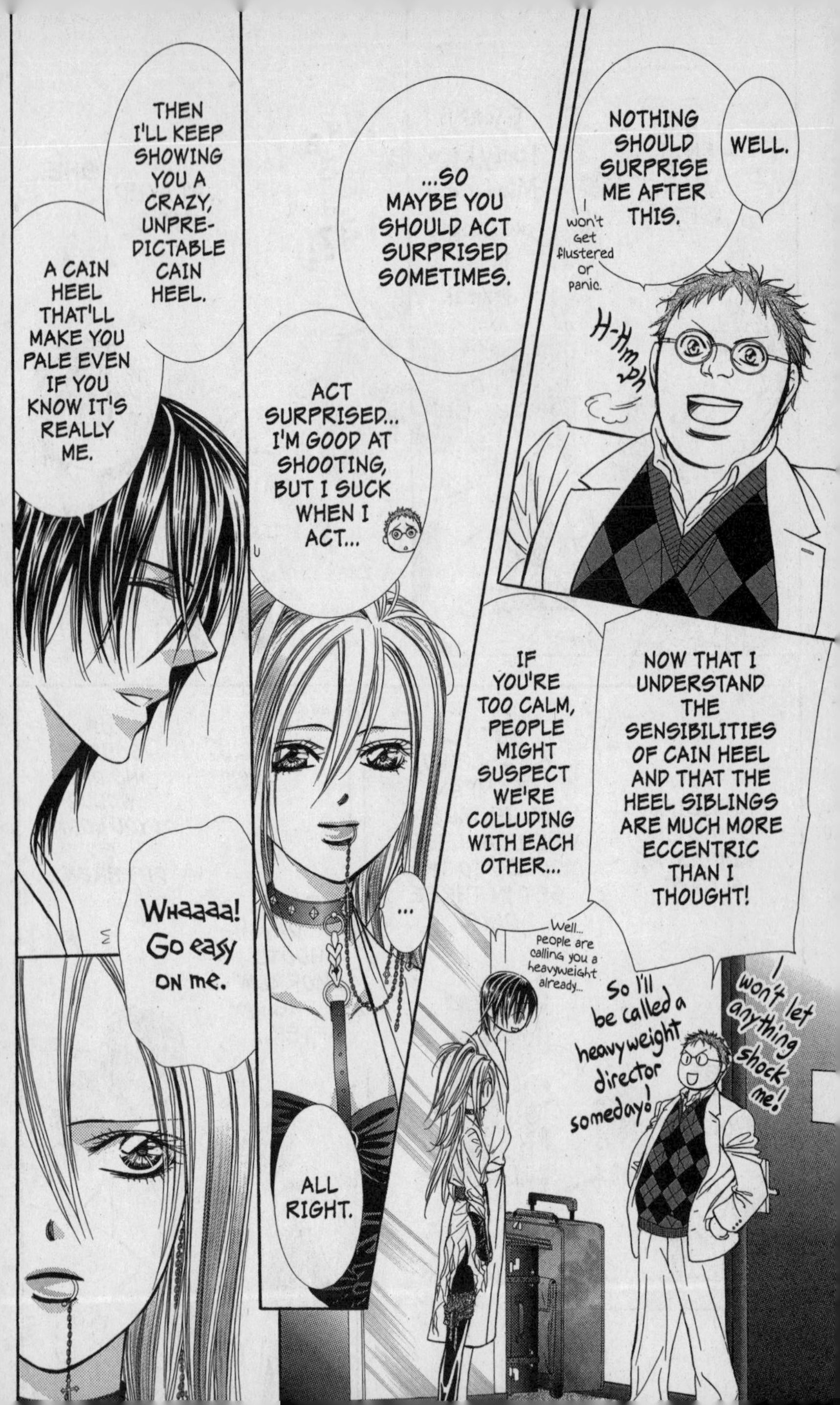
WELL.
NOTHING SHOULD SURPRISE ME AFTER THIS.
I won't get flustered or panic.
H-Hmph
...SO MAYBE YOU SHOULD ACT SURPRISED SOMETIMES.
ACT SURPRISED... I'M GOOD AT SHOOTING, BUT I SUCK WHEN I ACT...
THEN I'LL KEEP SHOWING YOU A CRAZY, UNPRE-DICTABLE CAIN HEEL.
A CAIN HEEL THAT'LL MAKE YOU PALE EVEN IF YOU KNOW IT'S REALLY ME.
NOW THAT I UNDERSTAND THE SENSIBILITIES OF CAIN HEEL AND THAT THE HEEL SIBLINGS ARE MUCH MORE ECCENTRIC THAN I THOUGHT!
IF YOU'RE TOO CALM, PEOPLE MIGHT SUSPECT WE'RE COLLUDING WITH EACH OTHER...
I won't let anything shock me!
So I'll be called a heavyweight director someday!
Well... People are calling you a heavyweight already...
...
ALL RIGHT.
Whaaaa! Go easy on me.

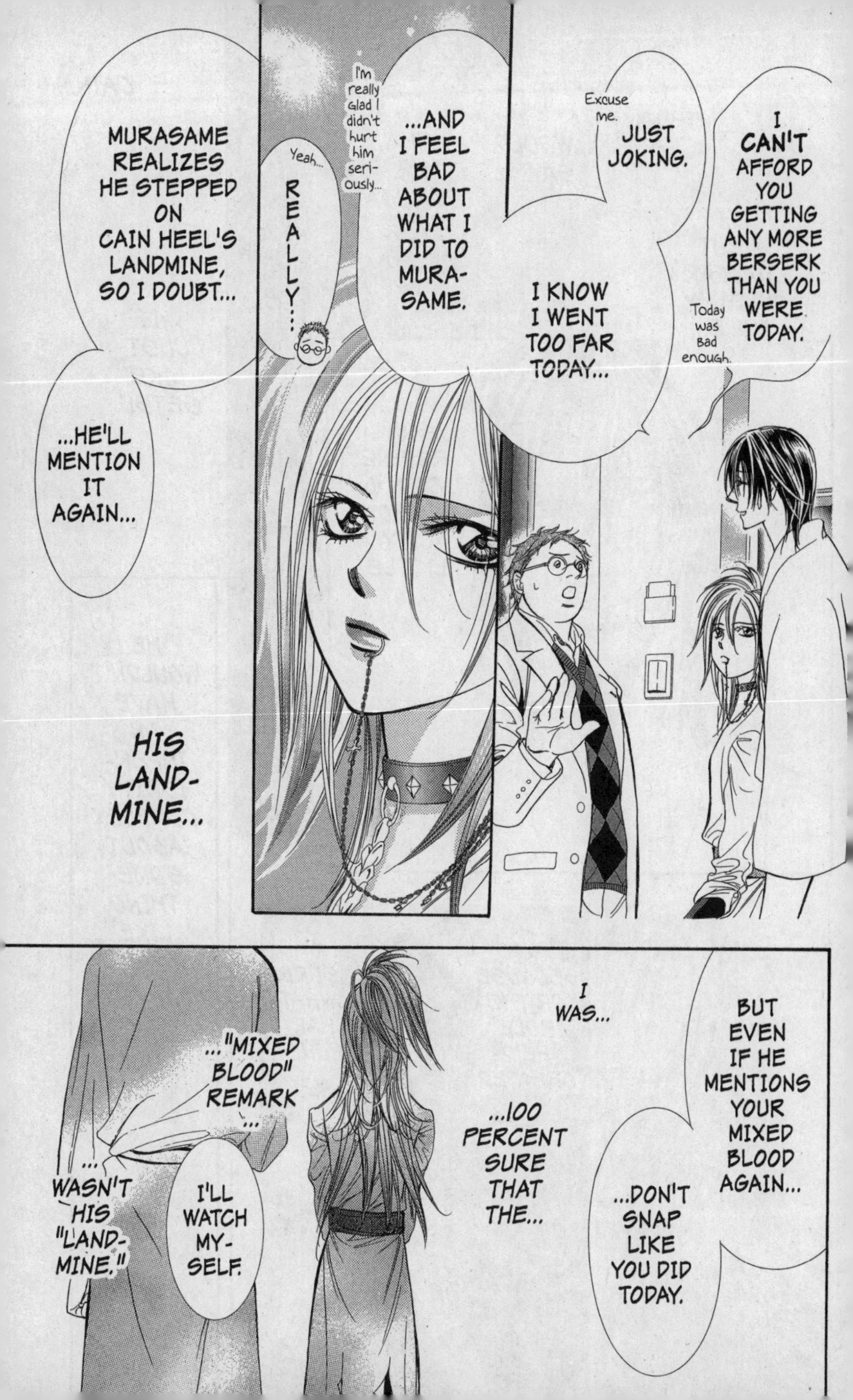

I CAN'T AFFORD YOU GETTING ANY MORE BERSERK THAN YOU WERE TODAY.
Today was bad enough.
JUST JOKING.
Excuse me.
I KNOW I WENT TOO FAR TODAY...
...AND I FEEL BAD ABOUT WHAT I DID TO MURASAME.
I'm really glad I didn't hurt him seriously...
Yeah...
REALLY...
MURASAME REALIZES HE STEPPED ON CAIN HEEL'S LANDMINE, SO I DOUBT...
...HE'LL MENTION IT AGAIN...
HIS LANDMINE...
BUT EVEN IF HE MENTIONS YOUR MIXED BLOOD AGAIN...
...DON'T SNAP LIKE YOU DID TODAY.
I'LL WATCH MYSELF.
I WAS...
...100 PERCENT SURE THAT THE...
..."MIXED BLOOD" REMARK...
...WASN'T HIS "LANDMINE."

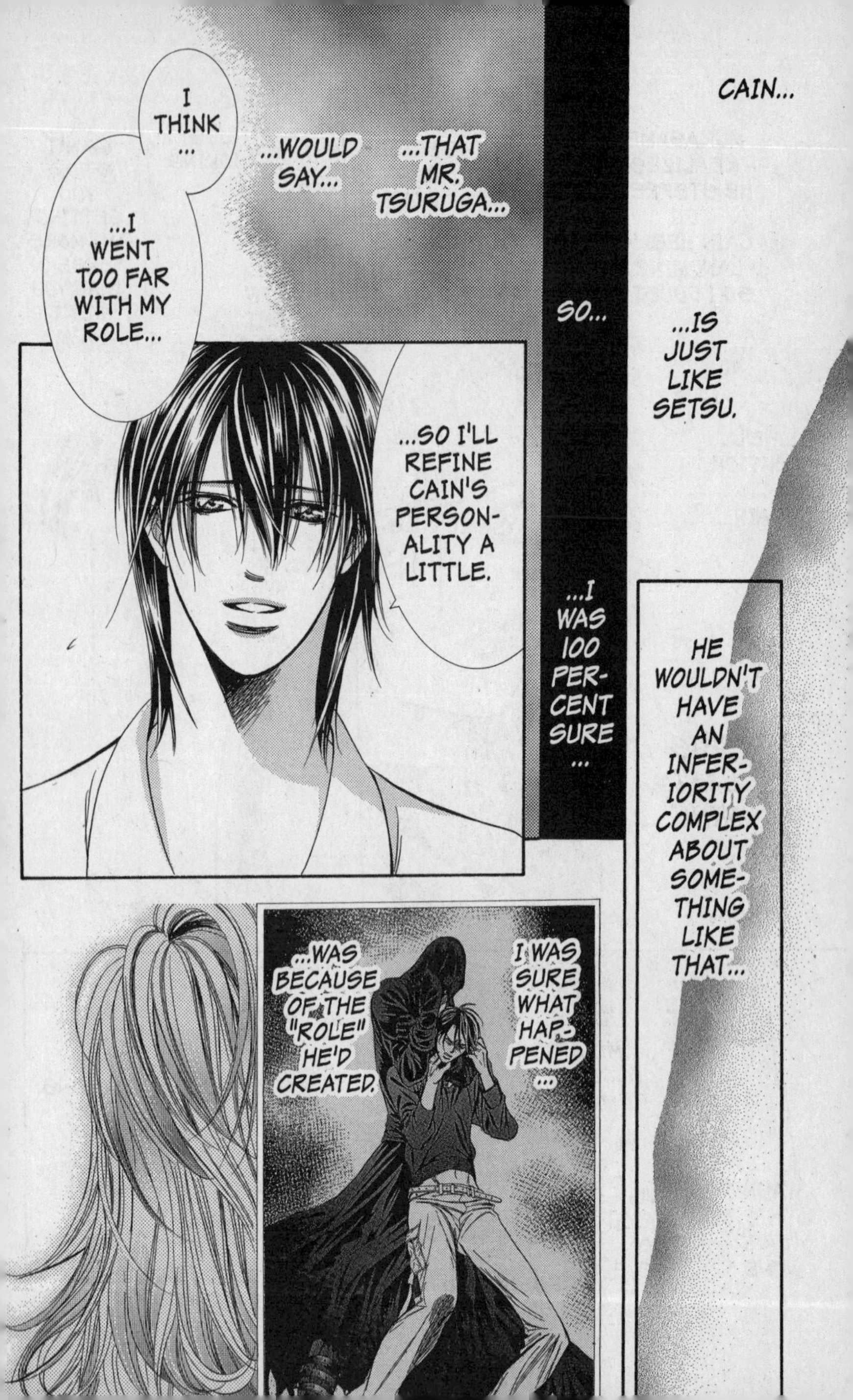

CAIN...
...IS JUST LIKE SETSU.
HE WOULDN'T HAVE AN INFERIORITY COMPLEX ABOUT SOMETHING LIKE THAT...
SO...
...I WAS 100 PERCENT SURE...
...THAT MR. TSURUGA...
...WOULD SAY...
I THINK...
...I WENT TOO FAR WITH MY ROLE...
...SO I'LL REFINE CAIN'S PERSONALITY A LITTLE.
I WAS SURE WHAT HAPPENED...
...WAS BECAUSE OF THE "ROLE" HE'D CREATED.

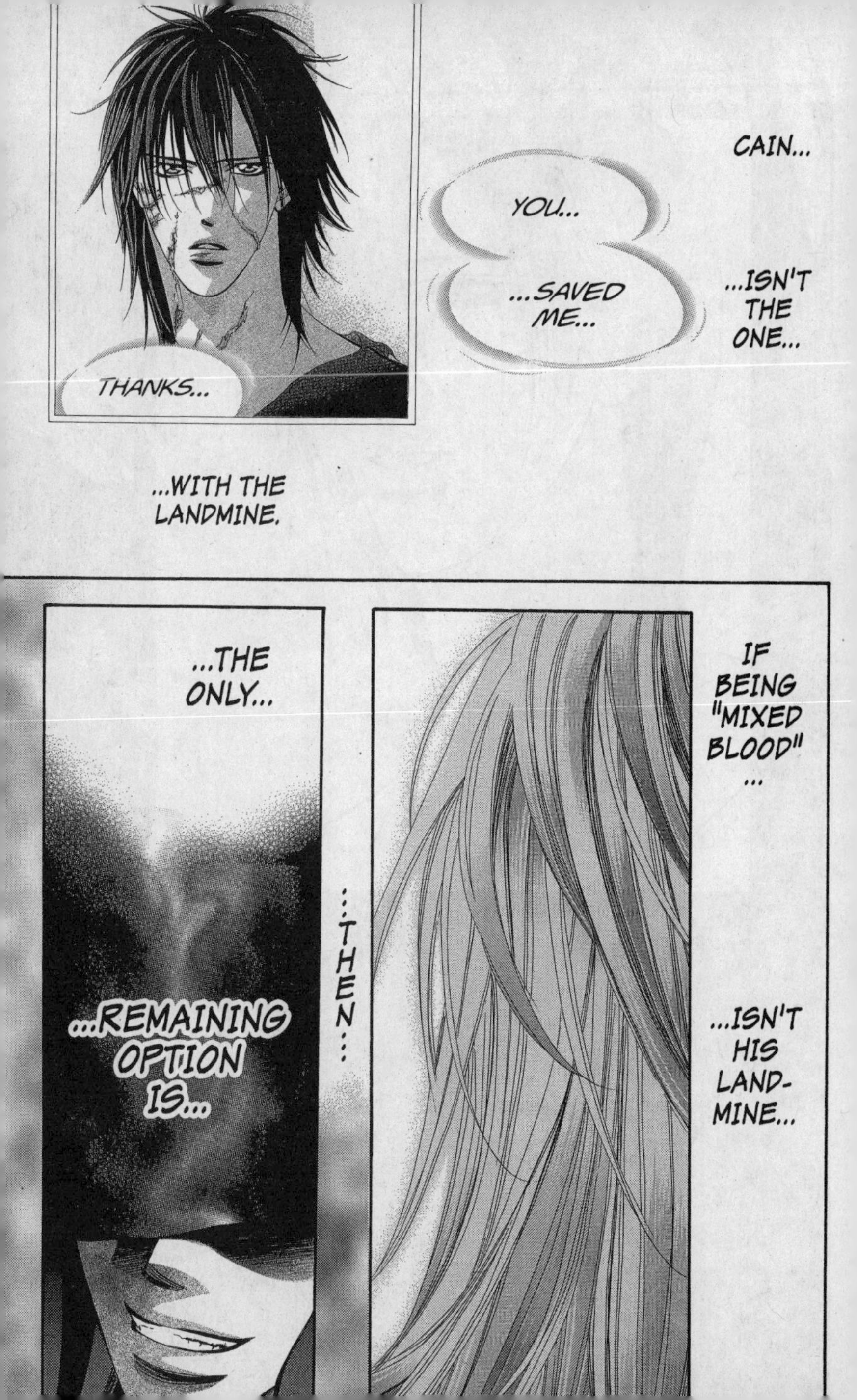
CAIN...
...ISN'T THE ONE...
YOU...
...SAVED ME...
THANKS...
...WITH THE LANDMINE.
IF BEING "MIXED BLOOD"...
...ISN'T HIS LAND-MINE...
...THEN...
...THE ONLY...
...REMAINING OPTION IS...

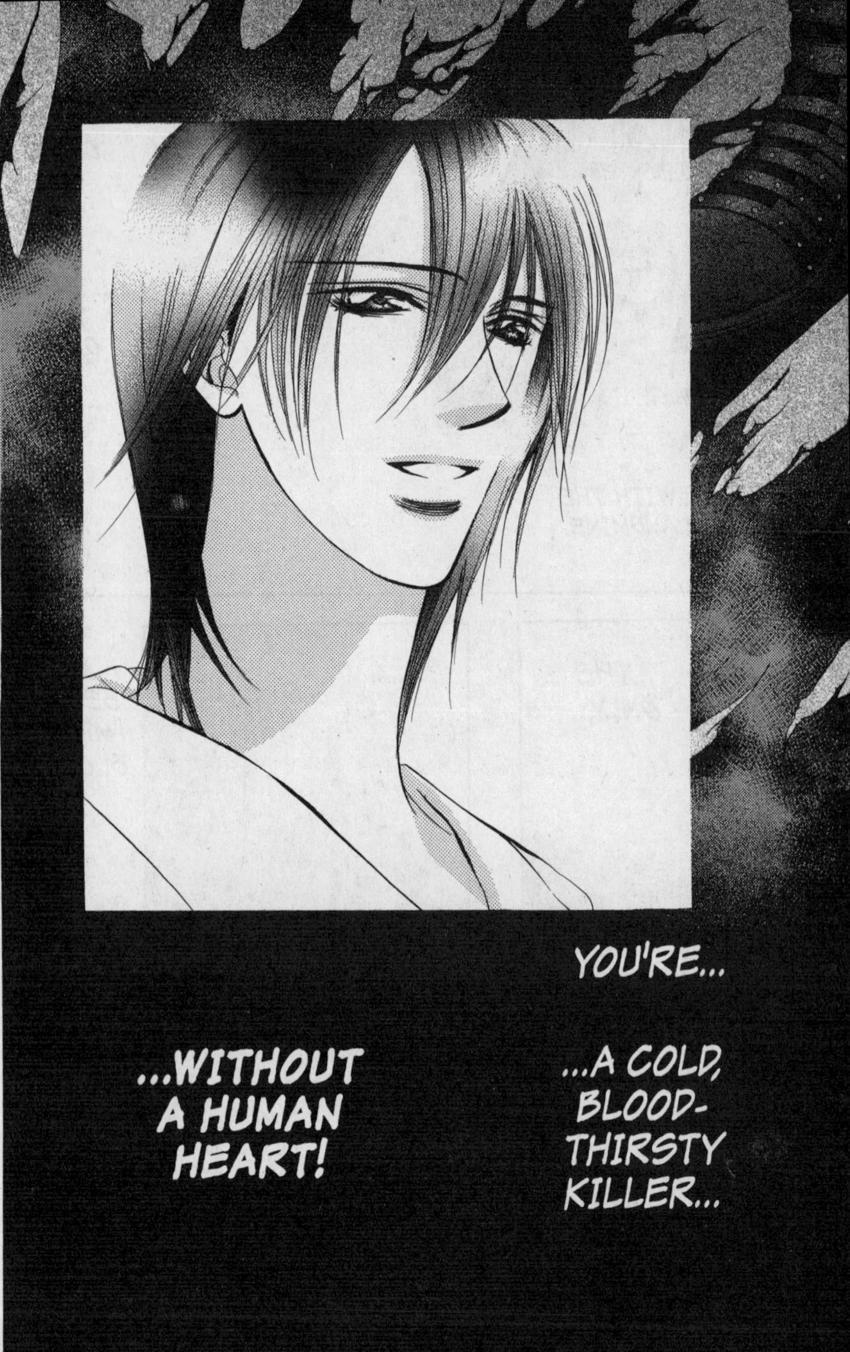
YOU'RE...
...A COLD, BLOOD-THIRSTY KILLER...
...WITHOUT A HUMAN HEART!

End of Act 186

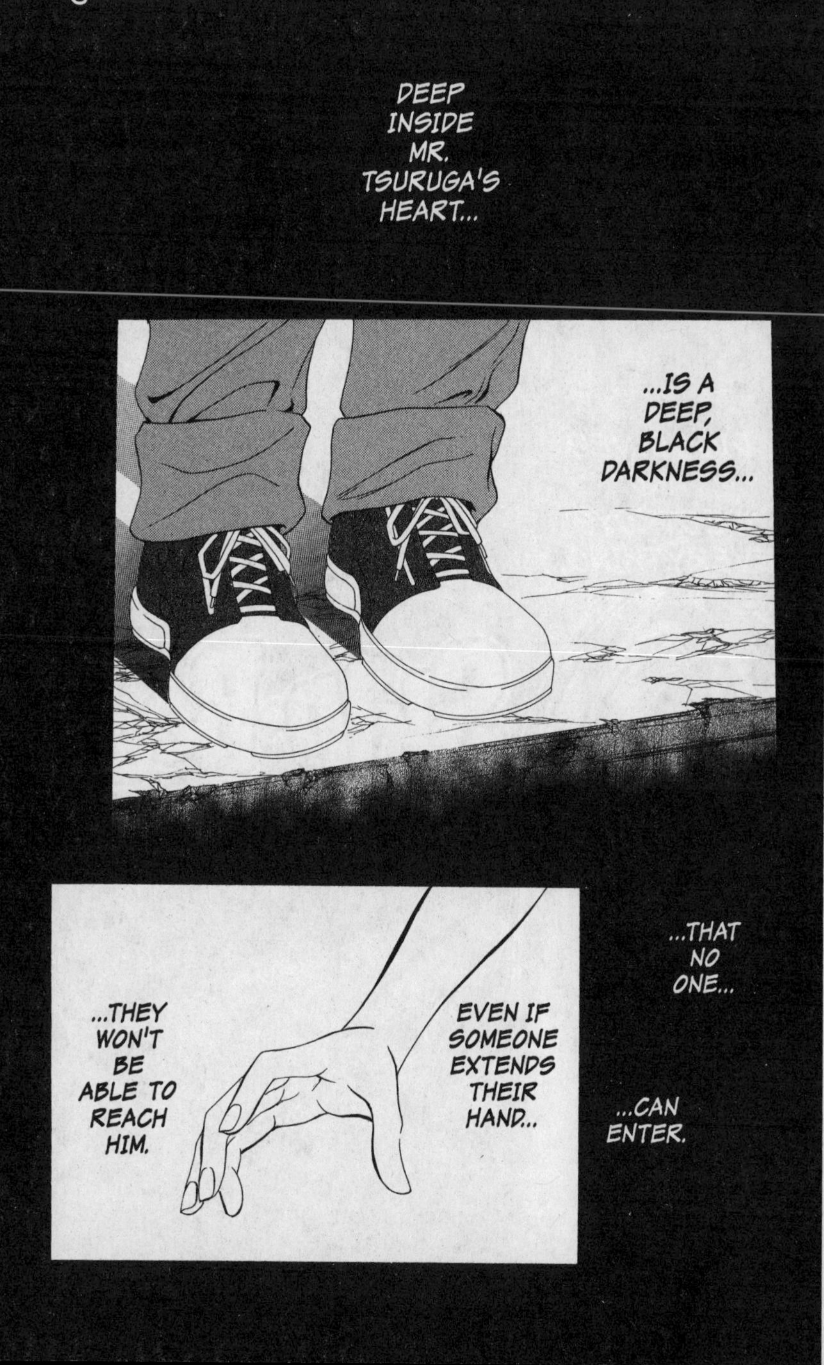
DEEP INSIDE MR. TSURUGA'S HEART...
...IS A DEEP, BLACK DARKNESS...
...THAT NO ONE...
...CAN ENTER.
EVEN IF SOMEONE EXTENDS THEIR HAND...
...THEY WON'T BE ABLE TO REACH HIM.

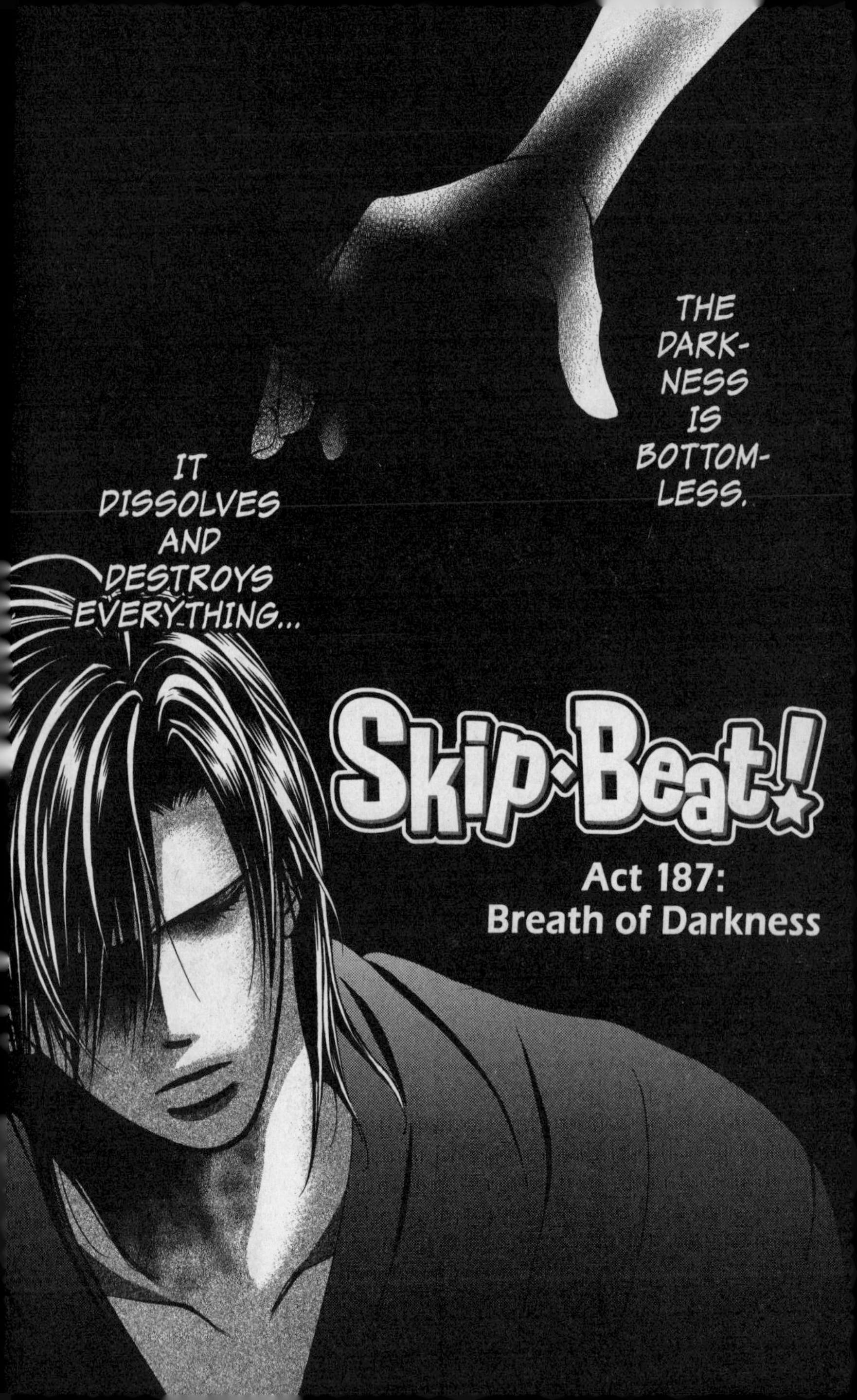
THE DARKNESS IS BOTTOMLESS.
IT DISSOLVES AND DESTROYS EVERYTHING...
Skip·Beat!
Act 187: Breath of Darkness

Morn-
ing...

...Kyo—

ka
chak

AH.

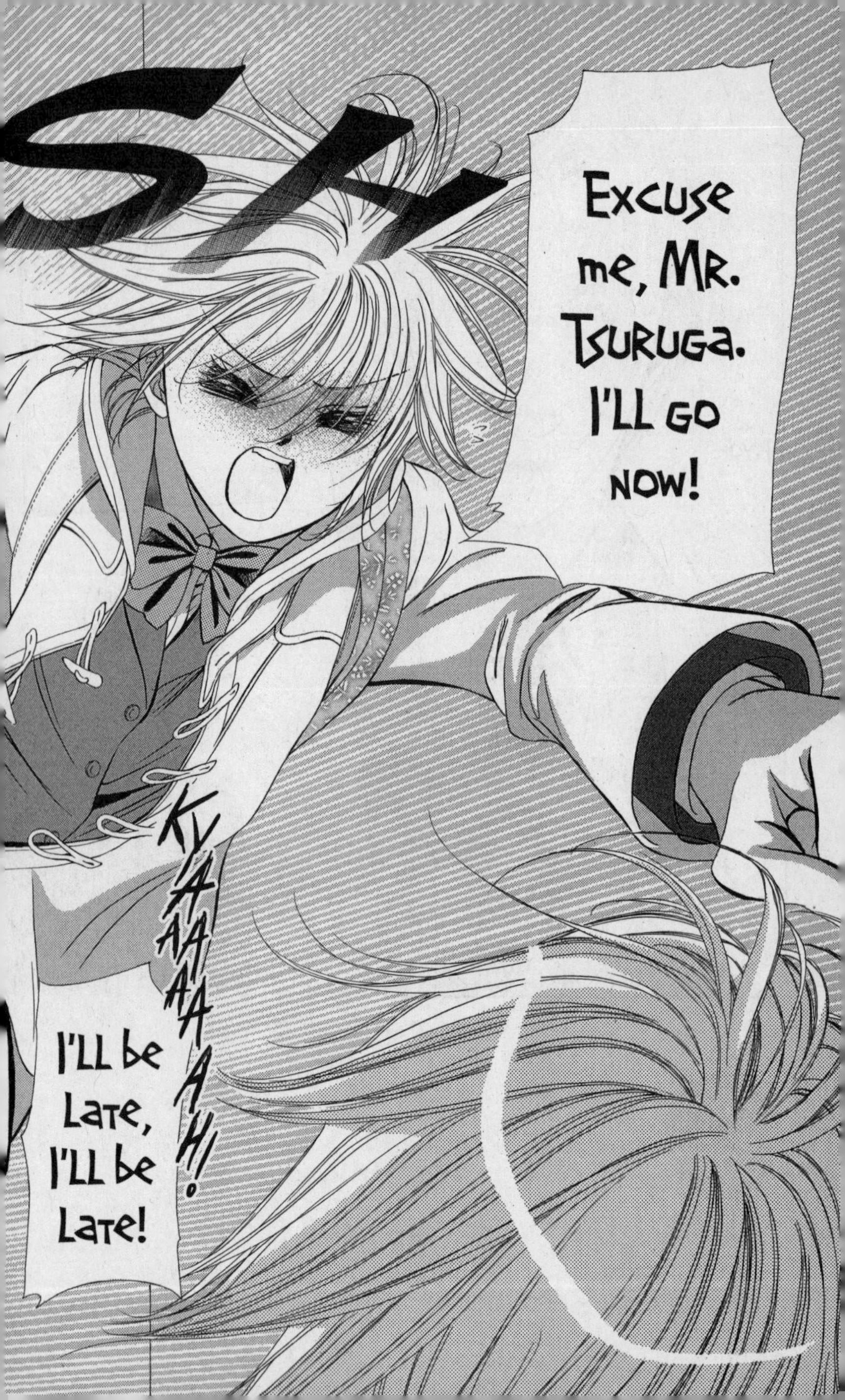
SHA
Excuse me, Mr. Tsuruga. I'll go now!
KYAAAAAAAH!
I'll be late, I'll be late!

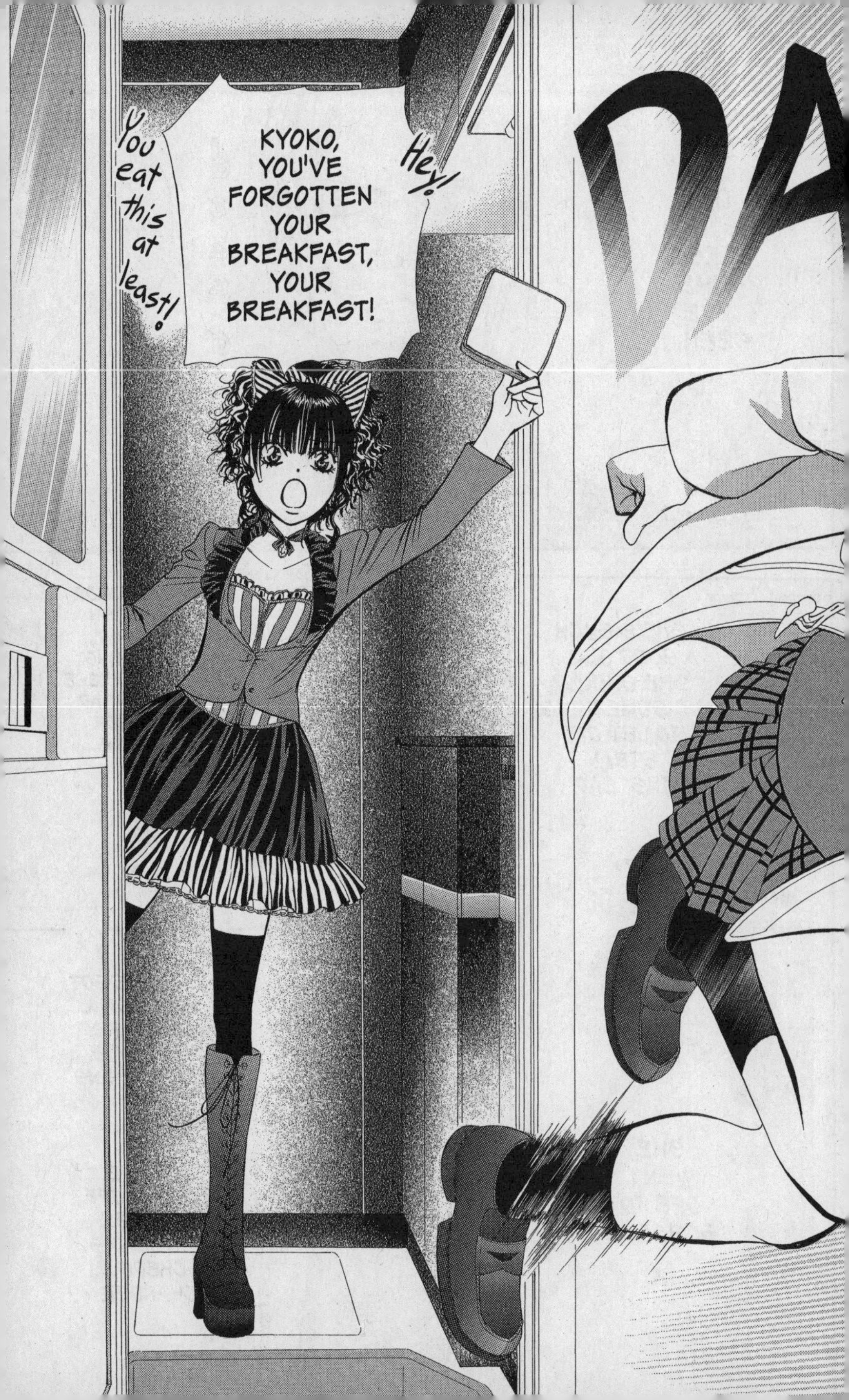
DA
Hey!
KYOKO, YOU'VE FORGOTTEN YOUR BREAKFAST, YOUR BREAKFAST!
You eat this at least!

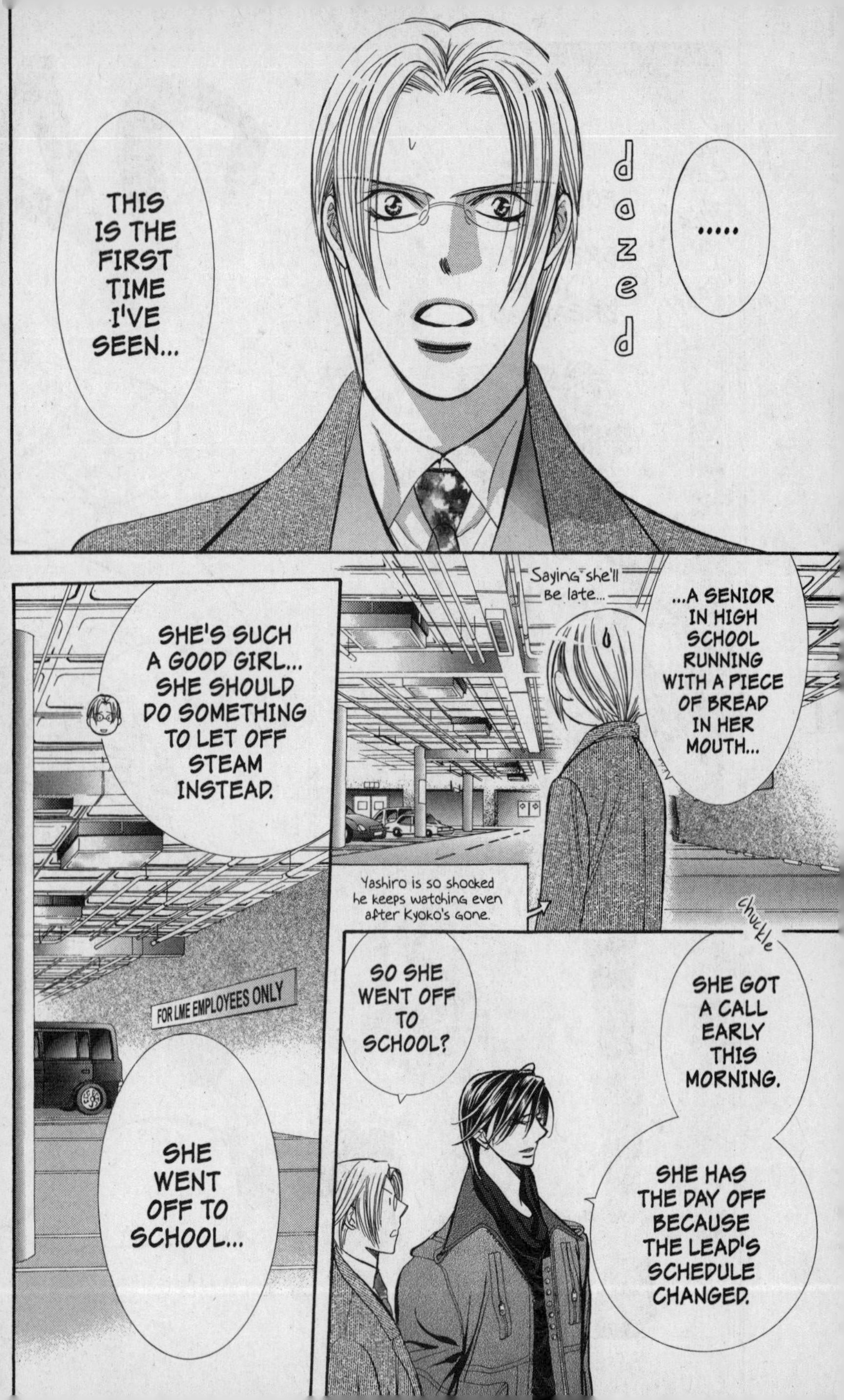
.....
dazed
THIS IS THE FIRST TIME I'VE SEEN...
Saying she'll be late...
...A SENIOR IN HIGH SCHOOL RUNNING WITH A PIECE OF BREAD IN HER MOUTH...
Yashiro is so shocked he keeps watching even after Kyoko's gone.
SO SHE WENT OFF TO SCHOOL?
chuckle
SHE GOT A CALL EARLY THIS MORNING.
SHE HAS THE DAY OFF BECAUSE THE LEAD'S SCHEDULE CHANGED.
SHE'S SUCH A GOOD GIRL... SHE SHOULD DO SOMETHING TO LET OFF STEAM INSTEAD.
FOR LME EMPLOYEES ONLY
SHE WENT OFF TO SCHOOL...

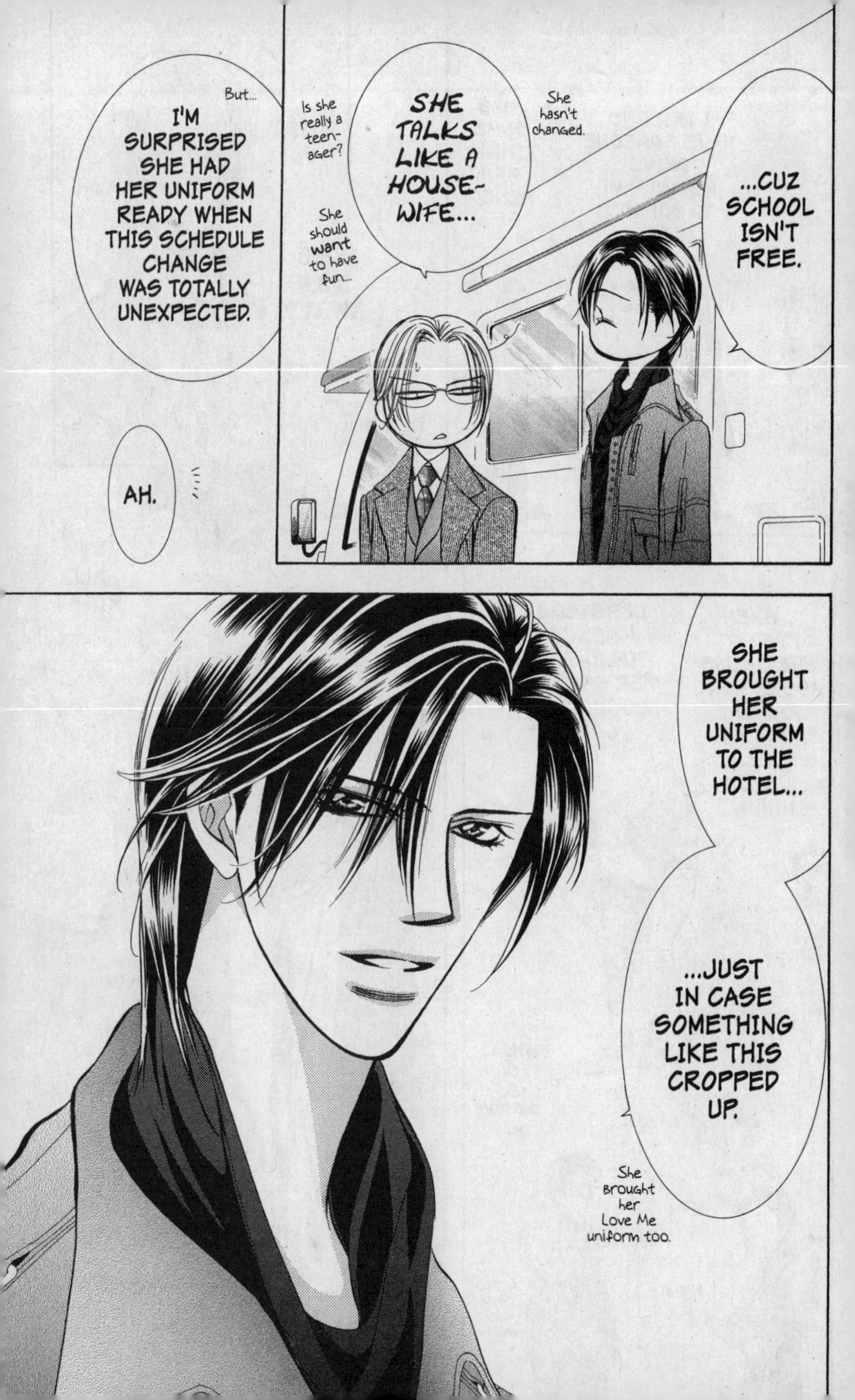
...CUZ SCHOOL ISN'T FREE.
She hasn't changed.
SHE TALKS LIKE A HOUSE-WIFE...
Is she really a teen-ager?
She should want to have fun...
But...
I'M SURPRISED SHE HAD HER UNIFORM READY WHEN THIS SCHEDULE CHANGE WAS TOTALLY UNEXPECTED.
AH.
SHE BROUGHT HER UNIFORM TO THE HOTEL...
...JUST IN CASE SOMETHING LIKE THIS CROPPED UP.
She brought her Love Me uniform too.

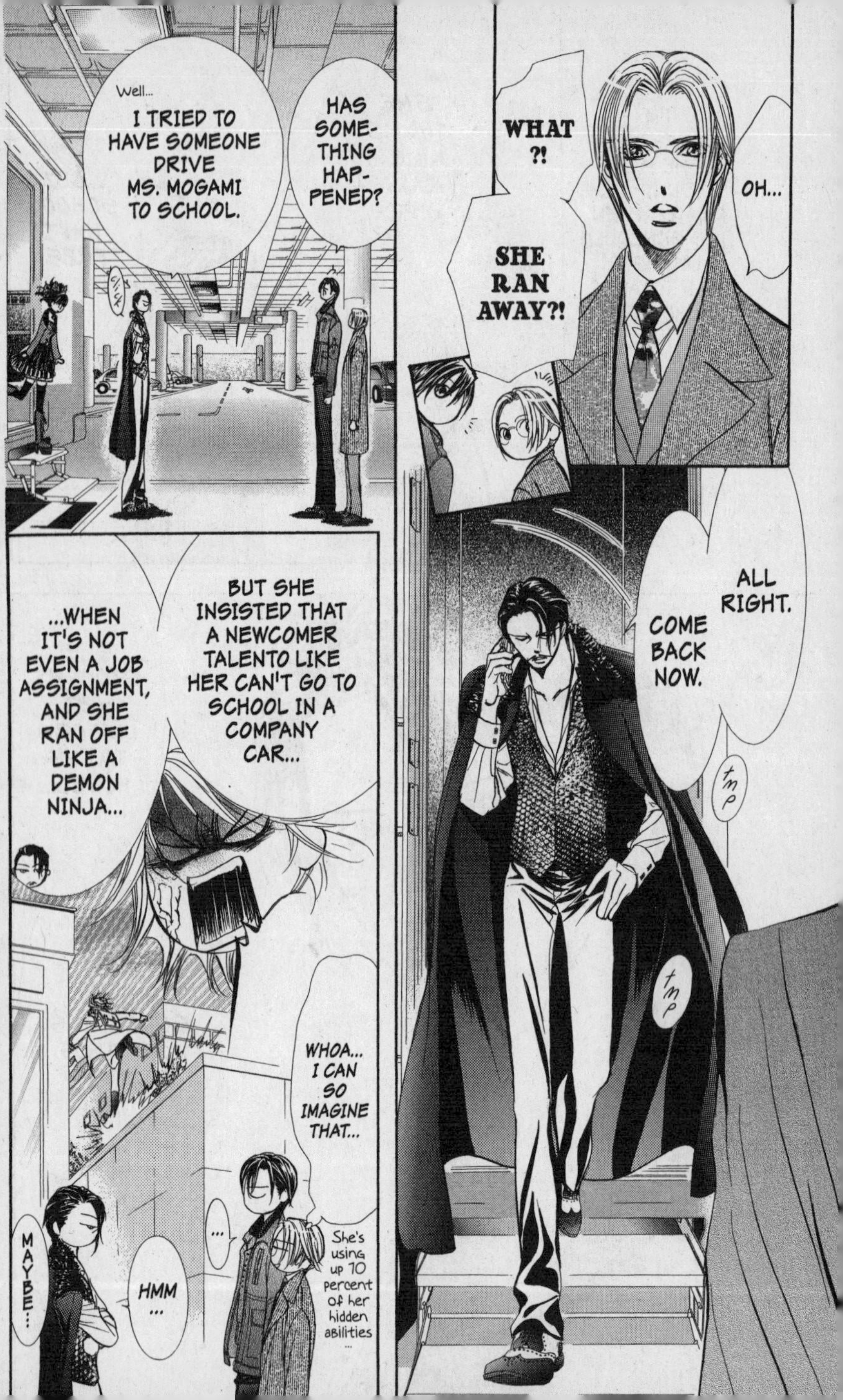
OH...
WHAT ?!
SHE RAN AWAY?!
ALL RIGHT. COME BACK NOW.
tmp
tmp
HAS SOMETHING HAPPENED?
Well... I TRIED TO HAVE SOMEONE DRIVE MS. MOGAMI TO SCHOOL.
click
BUT SHE INSISTED THAT A NEWCOMER TALENTO LIKE HER CAN'T GO TO SCHOOL IN A COMPANY CAR...
...WHEN IT'S NOT EVEN A JOB ASSIGNMENT, AND SHE RAN OFF LIKE A DEMON NINJA...
WHOA... I CAN SO IMAGINE THAT...
She's using up 10 percent of her hidden abilities...
...
HMM...
MAYBE...

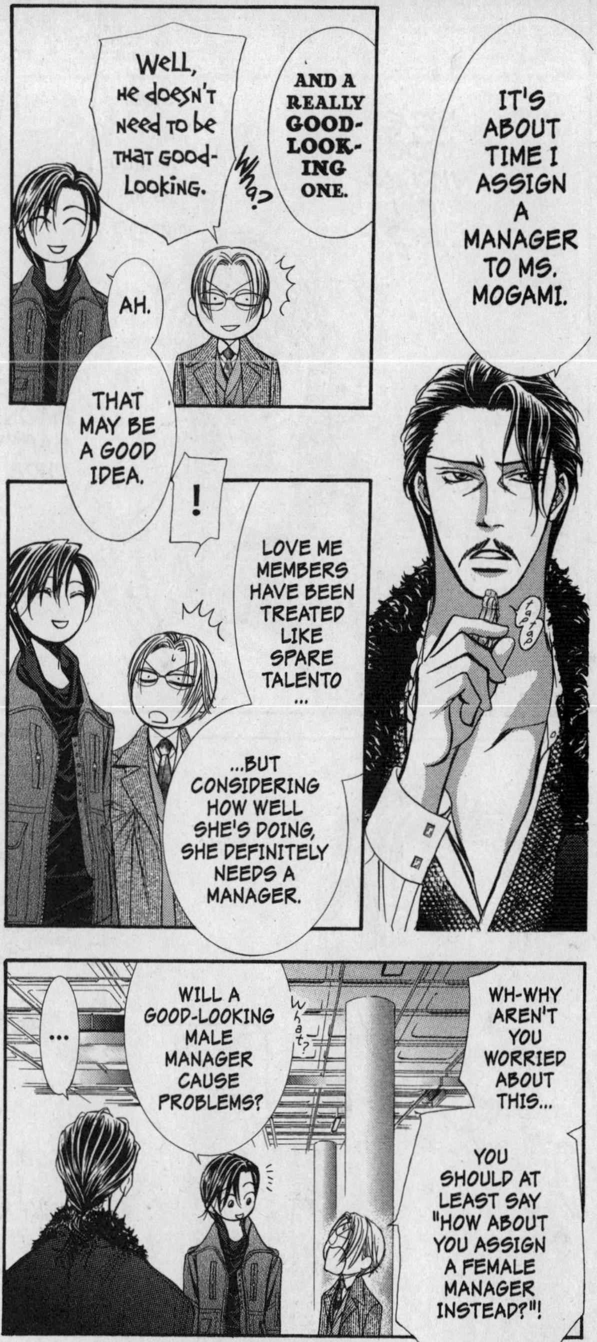
IT'S ABOUT TIME I ASSIGN A MANAGER TO MS. MOGAMI.
tap tap
AND A REALLY GOOD-LOOKING ONE.
Wha?
Well, he doesn't need to be that good-looking.
AH.
THAT MAY BE A GOOD IDEA.
!
LOVE ME MEMBERS HAVE BEEN TREATED LIKE SPARE TALENTO...
...BUT CONSIDERING HOW WELL SHE'S DOING, SHE DEFINITELY NEEDS A MANAGER.
WH-WHY AREN'T YOU WORRIED ABOUT THIS...
YOU SHOULD AT LEAST SAY "HOW ABOUT YOU ASSIGN A FEMALE MANAGER INSTEAD?"!
What?
WILL A GOOD-LOOKING MALE MANAGER CAUSE PROBLEMS?
...
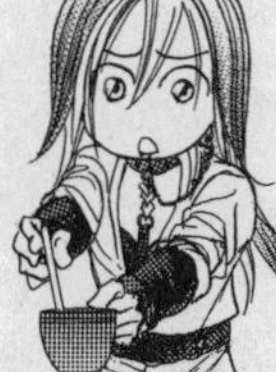

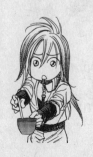

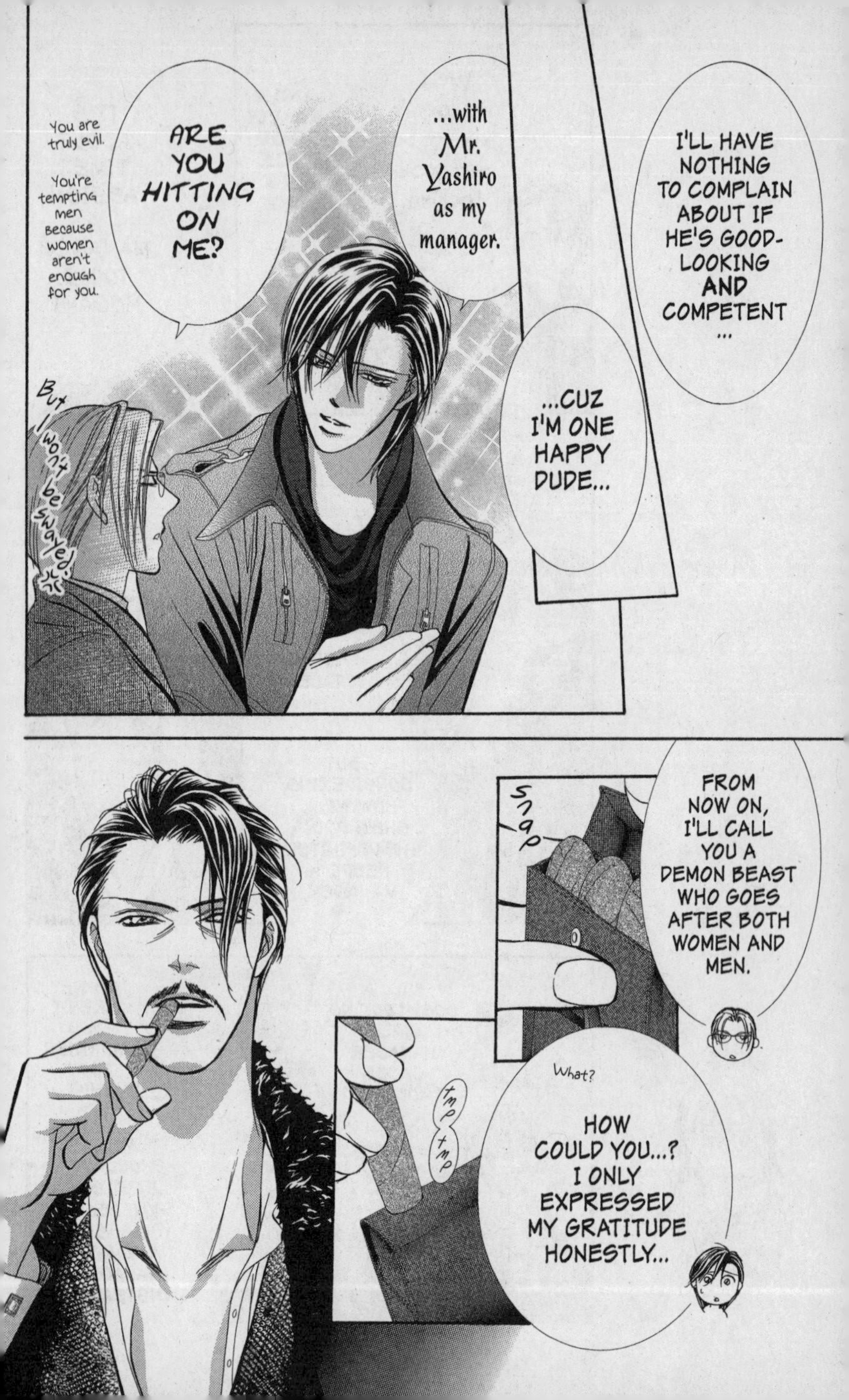

I'LL HAVE NOTHING TO COMPLAIN ABOUT IF HE'S GOOD-LOOKING AND COMPETENT...
...CUZ I'M ONE HAPPY DUDE...
...with Mr. Yashiro as my manager.
ARE YOU HITTING ON ME?
You are truly evil.
You're tempting men because women aren't enough for you.
But I won't be swayed.
snap
FROM NOW ON, I'LL CALL YOU A DEMON BEAST WHO GOES AFTER BOTH WOMEN AND MEN.
What?
HOW COULD YOU...? I ONLY EXPRESSED MY GRATITUDE HONESTLY...
tmp tmp

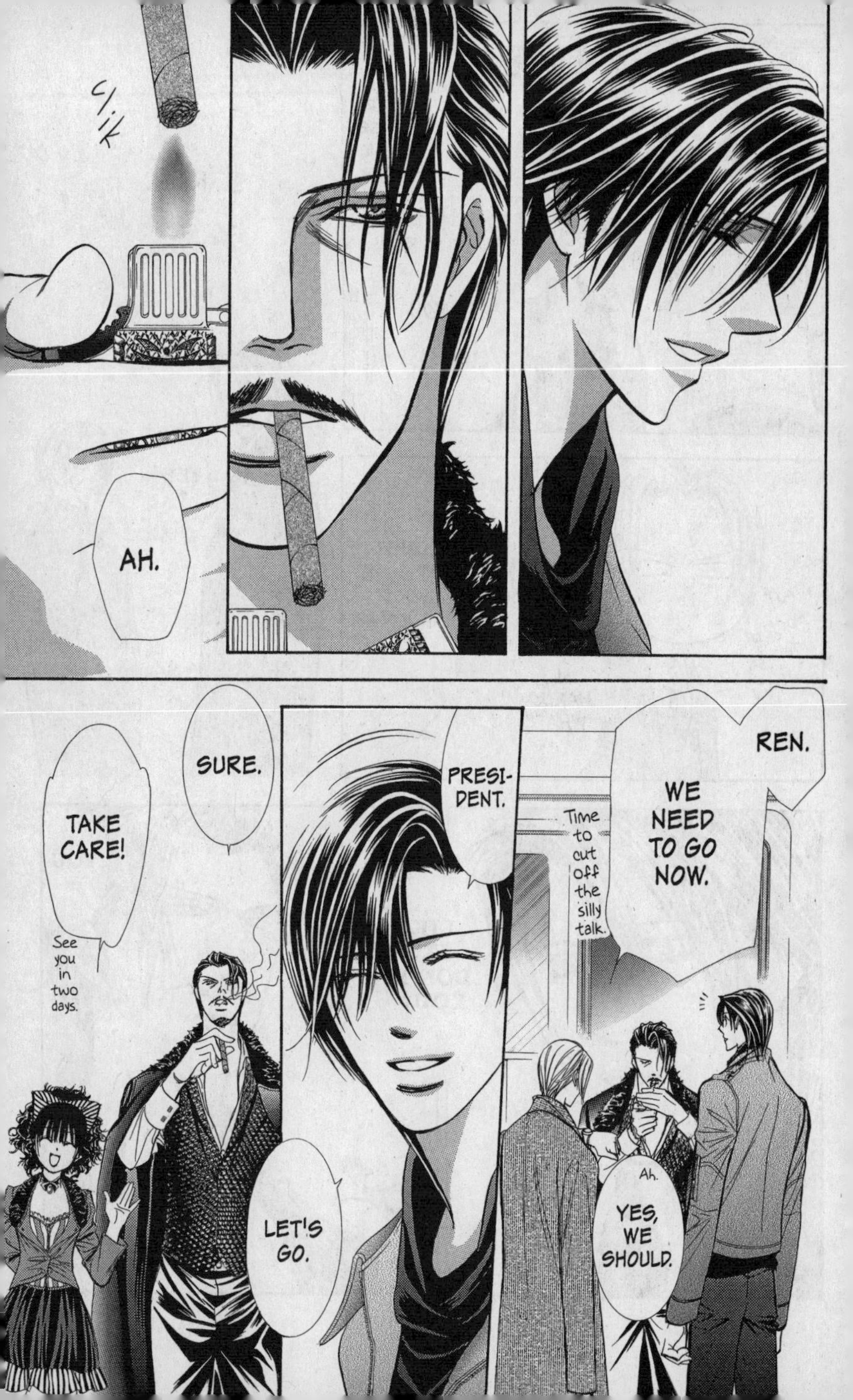
clik
AH.
REN.
WE NEED TO GO NOW.
Time to cut off the silly talk.
Ah.
YES, WE SHOULD.
PRESI-DENT.
LET'S GO.
SURE.
TAKE CARE!
See you in two days.

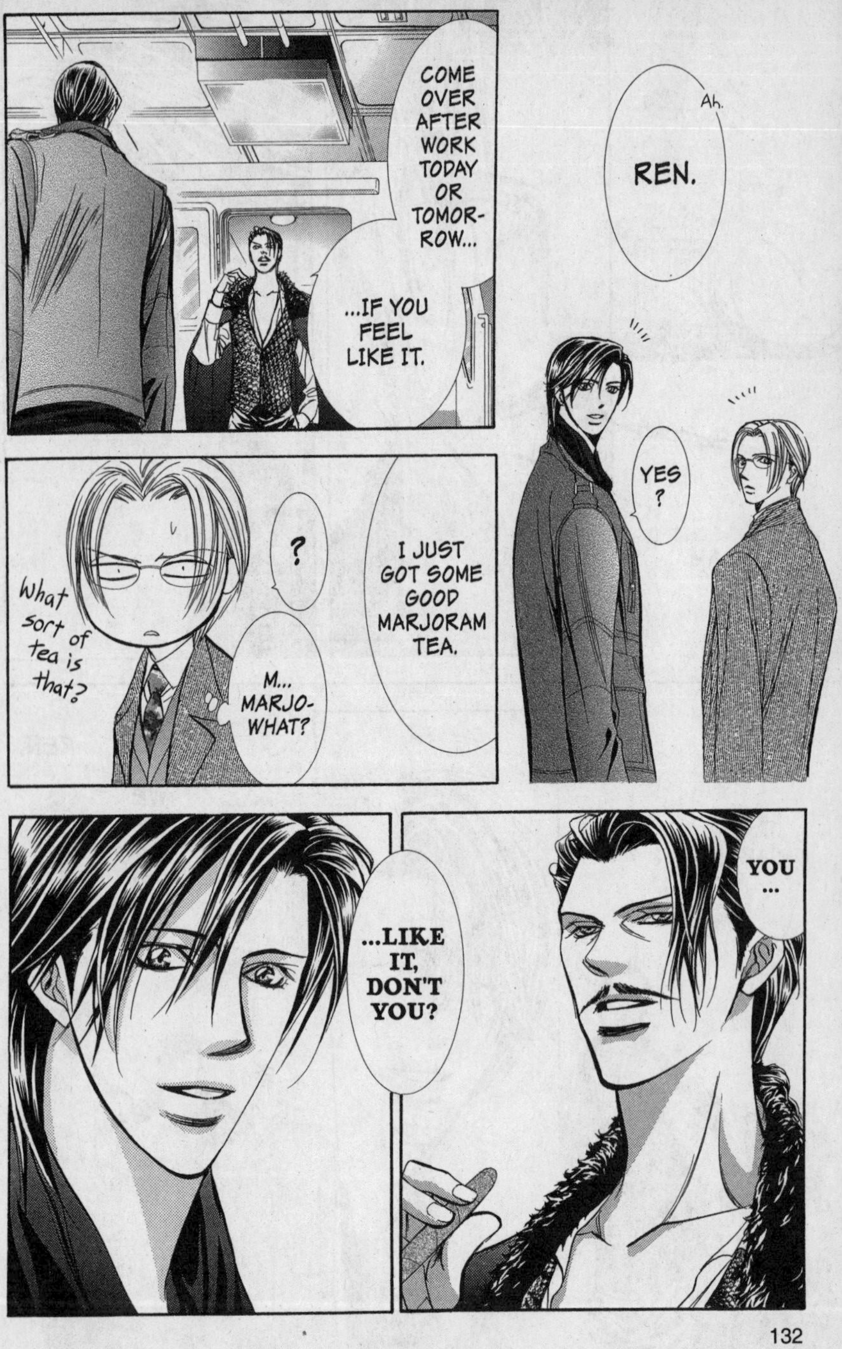
Ah.
REN.
YES?
COME OVER AFTER WORK TODAY OR TOMORROW...
...IF YOU FEEL LIKE IT.
I JUST GOT SOME GOOD MARJORAM TEA.
?
M... MARJO-WHAT?
What sort of tea is that?
YOU...
...LIKE IT, DON'T YOU?

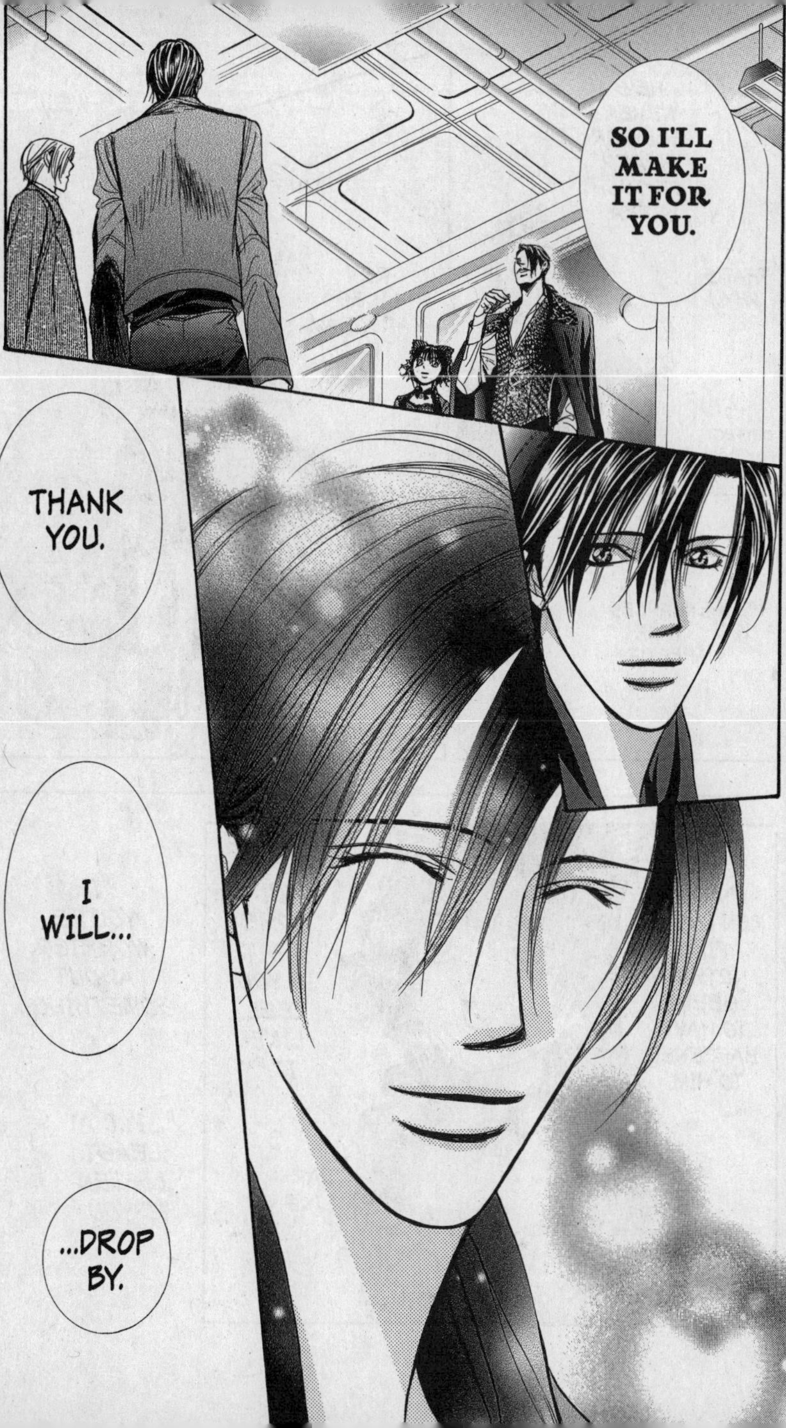
SO I'LL MAKE IT FOR YOU.
THANK YOU.
I WILL...
...DROP BY.

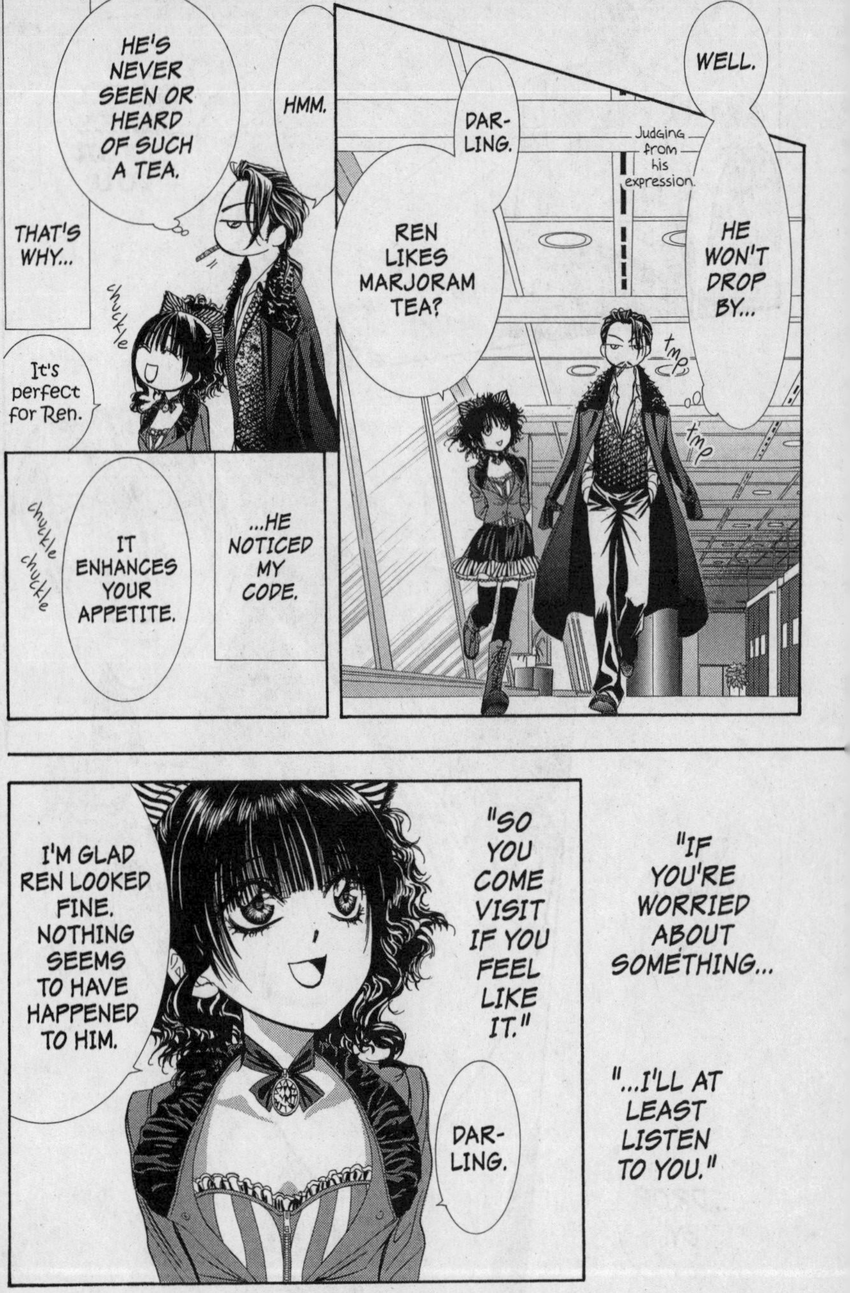
WELL.
Judging from his expression.
HE WON'T DROP BY...
tmp
tmp
DARLING.
REN LIKES MARJORAM TEA?
HMM.
HE'S NEVER SEEN OR HEARD OF SUCH A TEA.
THAT'S WHY...
chuckle
It's perfect for Ren.
...HE NOTICED MY CODE.
IT ENHANCES YOUR APPETITE.
chuckle chuckle
"IF YOU'RE WORRIED ABOUT SOMETHING...
"...I'LL AT LEAST LISTEN TO YOU."
"SO YOU COME VISIT IF YOU FEEL LIKE IT."
DARLING.
I'M GLAD REN LOOKED FINE. NOTHING SEEMS TO HAVE HAPPENED TO HIM.

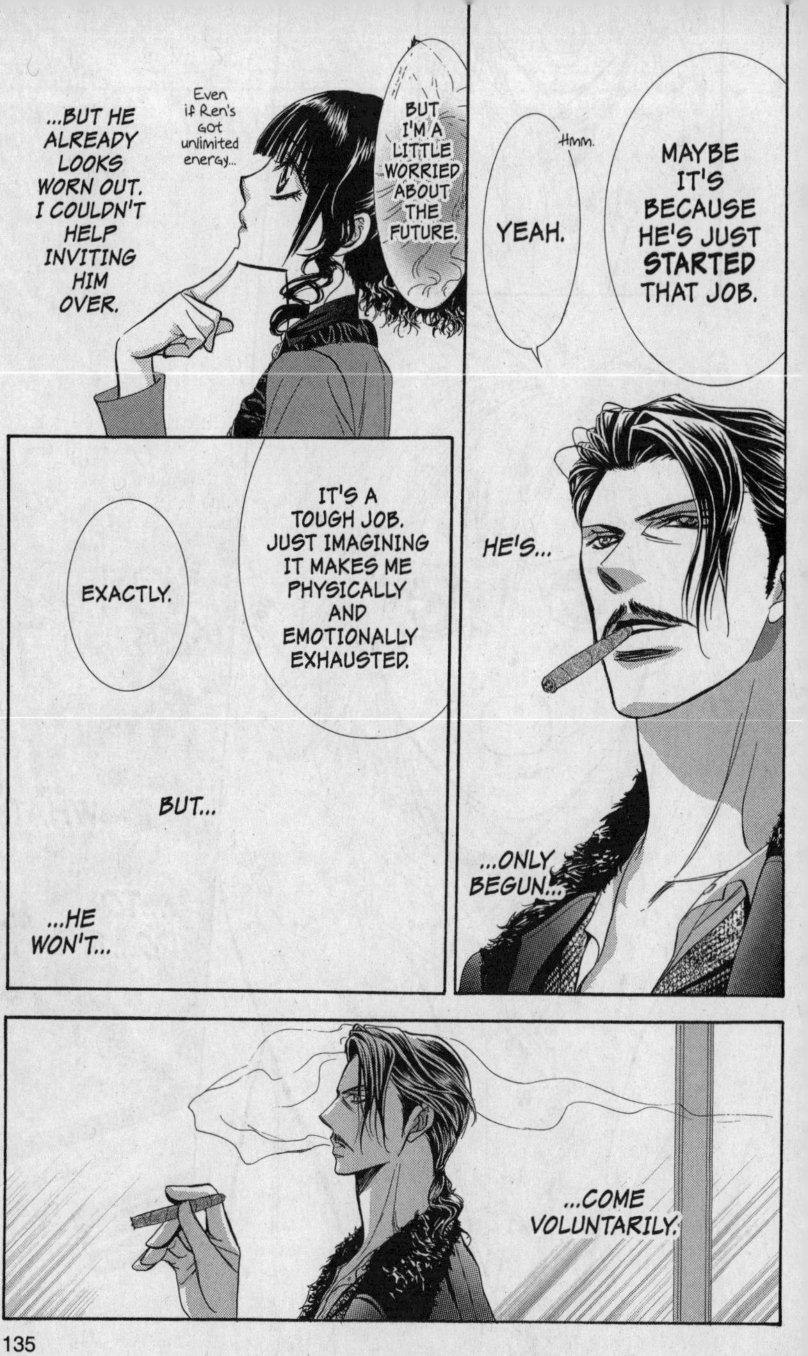
MAYBE IT'S BECAUSE HE'S JUST STARTED THAT JOB.
Hmm.
YEAH.
BUT I'M A LITTLE WORRIED ABOUT THE FUTURE.
Even if Ren's got unlimited energy...
...BUT HE ALREADY LOOKS WORN OUT. I COULDN'T HELP INVITING HIM OVER.
HE'S...
...ONLY BEGUN...
IT'S A TOUGH JOB. JUST IMAGINING IT MAKES ME PHYSICALLY AND EMOTIONALLY EXHAUSTED.
EXACTLY.
BUT...
...HE WON'T...
...COME VOLUNTARILY.

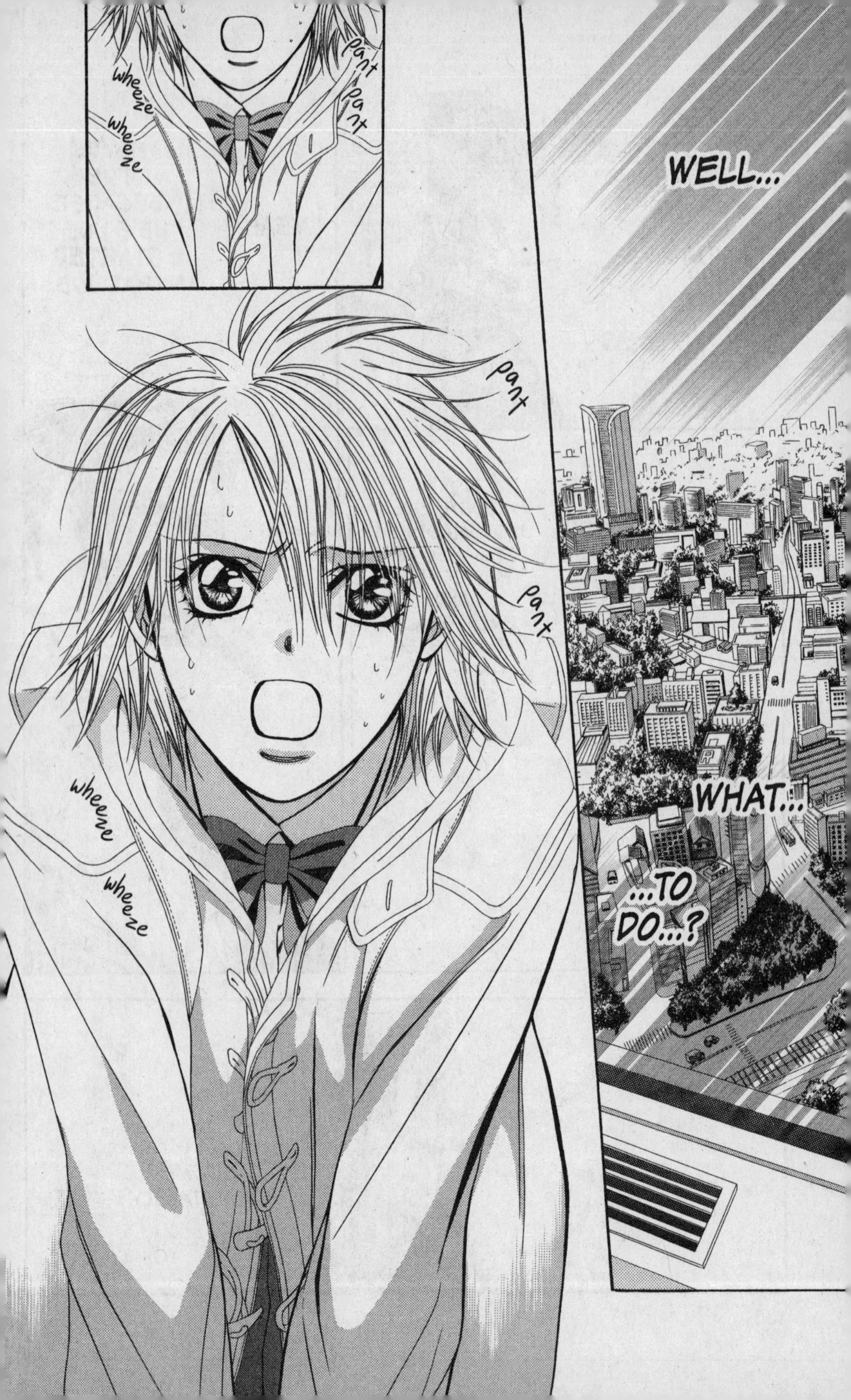
WELL...
WHAT...
...TO DO...?
pant pant
wheeze wheeze
pant pant
wheeze wheeze

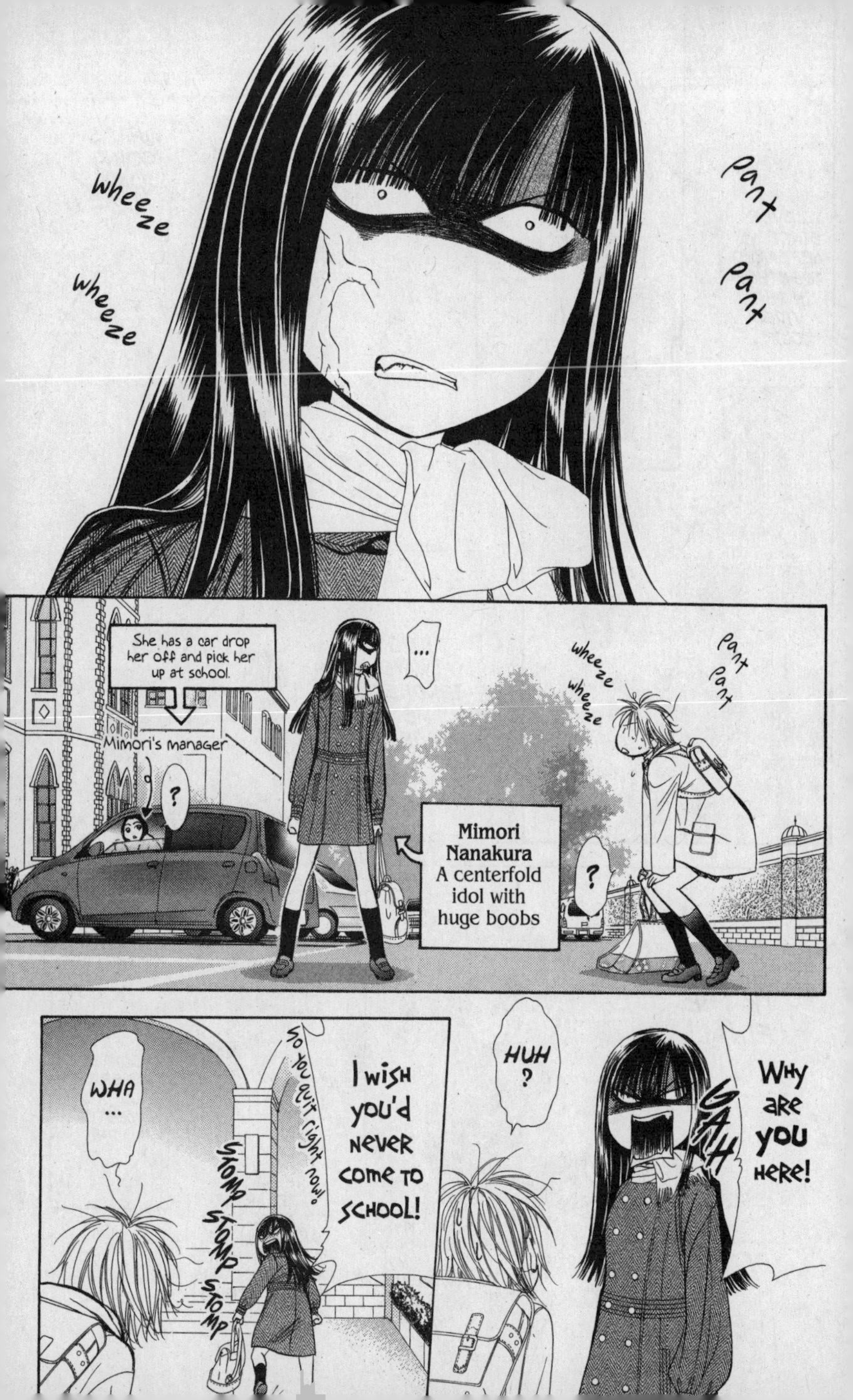
pant pant
wheeze wheeze
pant pant
wheeze wheeze
?
Mimori Nanakura A centerfold idol with huge boobs
...
She has a car drop her off and pick her up at school.
Mimori's manager
?
Why are you here!
GAH
HUH?
I wish you'd never come to school!
So you quit right now!
STOMP STOMP STOMP STOMP
WHA...

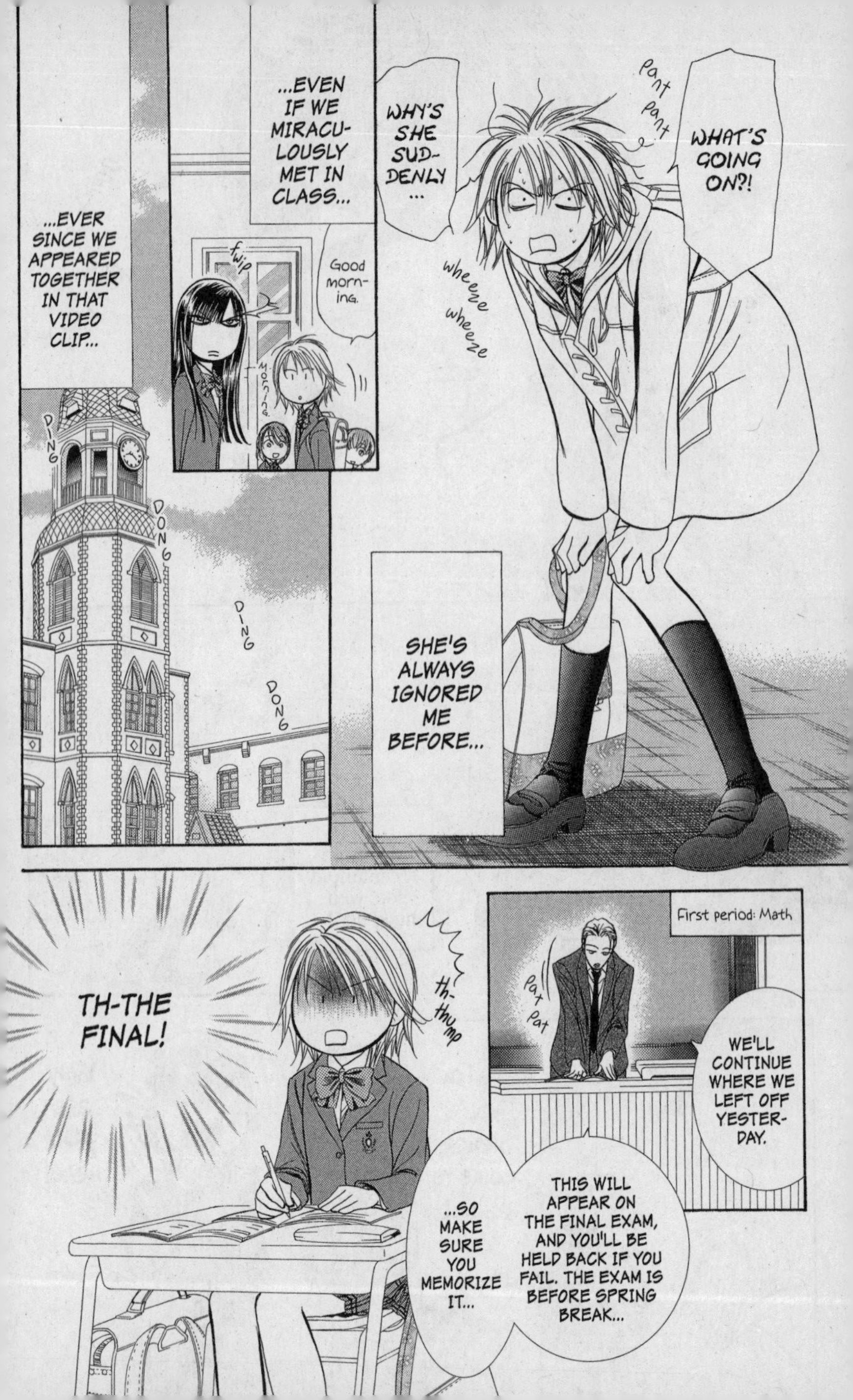
WHAT'S GOING ON?!
Pant pant
WHY'S SHE SUDDENLY...
wheeze wheeze
SHE'S ALWAYS IGNORED ME BEFORE...
...EVEN IF WE MIRACULOUSLY MET IN CLASS...
Good morning.
fwip
Morning.
...EVER SINCE WE APPEARED TOGETHER IN THAT VIDEO CLIP...
DING DONG DING DONG
First period: Math
Pat pat
WE'LL CONTINUE WHERE WE LEFT OFF YESTERDAY.
THIS WILL APPEAR ON THE FINAL EXAM, AND YOU'LL BE HELD BACK IF YOU FAIL. THE EXAM IS BEFORE SPRING BREAK...
...SO MAKE SURE YOU MEMORIZE IT...
th-thump
TH-THE FINAL!

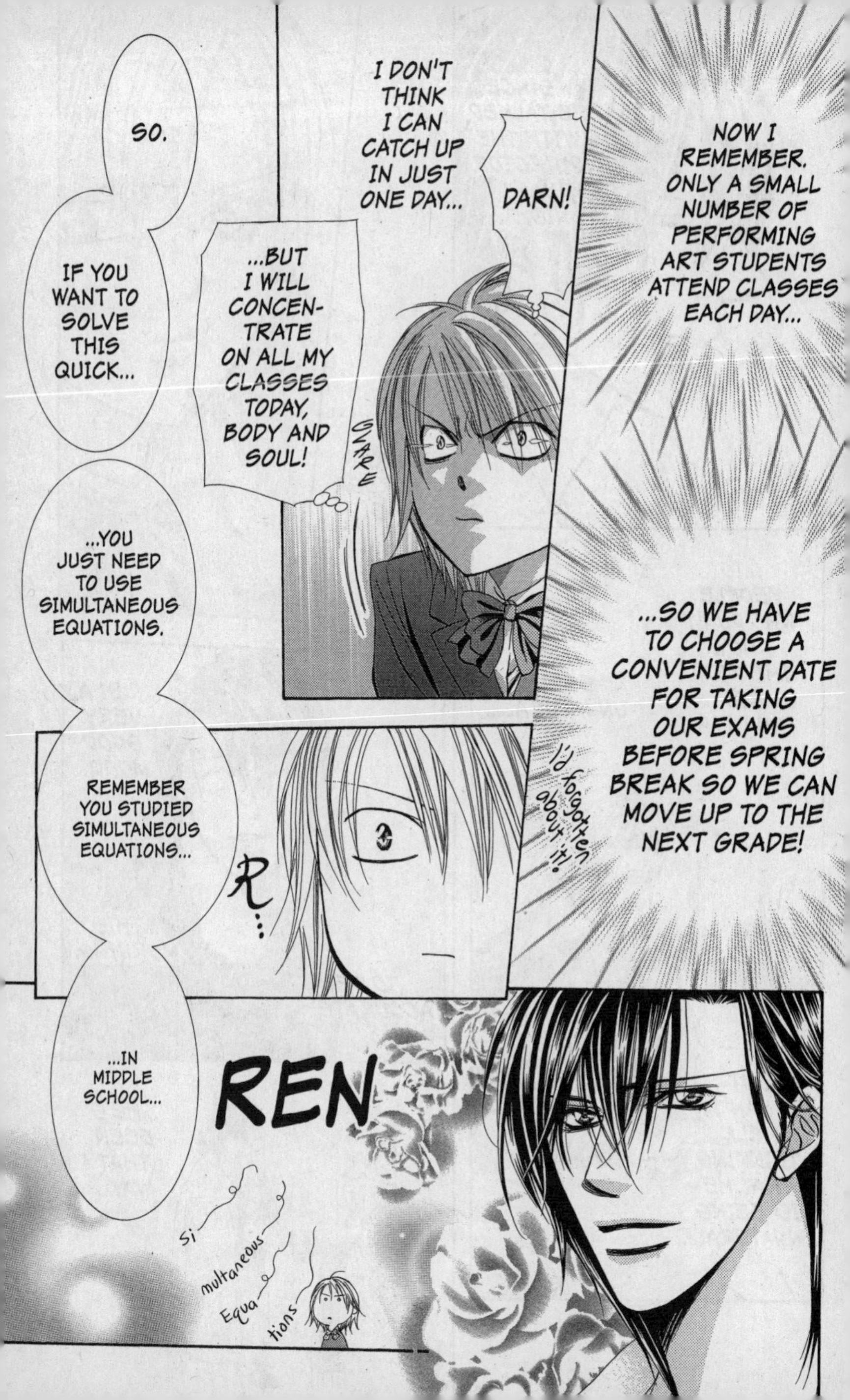
NOW I REMEMBER. ONLY A SMALL NUMBER OF PERFORMING ART STUDENTS ATTEND CLASSES EACH DAY...
...SO WE HAVE TO CHOOSE A CONVENIENT DATE FOR TAKING OUR EXAMS BEFORE SPRING BREAK SO WE CAN MOVE UP TO THE NEXT GRADE!
I DON'T THINK I CAN CATCH UP IN JUST ONE DAY...
DARN!
...BUT I WILL CONCENTRATE ON ALL MY CLASSES TODAY, BODY AND SOUL!
GLARE
I'd forgotten about it!!
R...
SO.
IF YOU WANT TO SOLVE THIS QUICK...
...YOU JUST NEED TO USE SIMULTANEOUS EQUATIONS.
REMEMBER YOU STUDIED SIMULTANEOUS EQUATIONS...
...IN MIDDLE SCHOOL...
REN
Si multaneous Equa tions

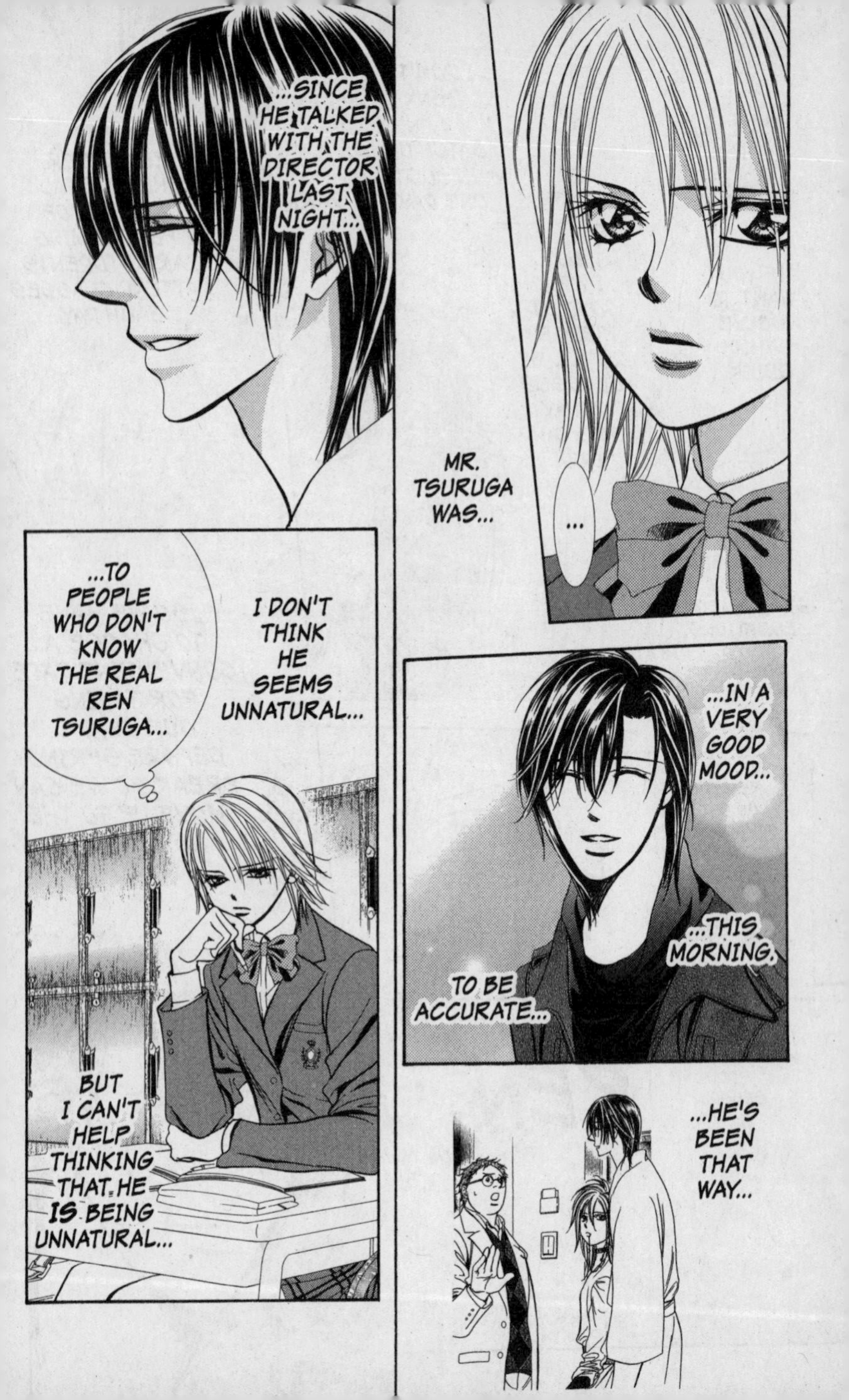
...
MR. TSURUGA WAS...
...IN A VERY GOOD MOOD...
...THIS MORNING.
TO BE ACCURATE...
...HE'S BEEN THAT WAY...
...SINCE HE TALKED WITH THE DIRECTOR LAST NIGHT...
I DON'T THINK HE SEEMS UNNATURAL...
...TO PEOPLE WHO DON'T KNOW THE REAL REN TSURUGA...
BUT I CAN'T HELP THINKING THAT HE **IS** BEING UNNATURAL...

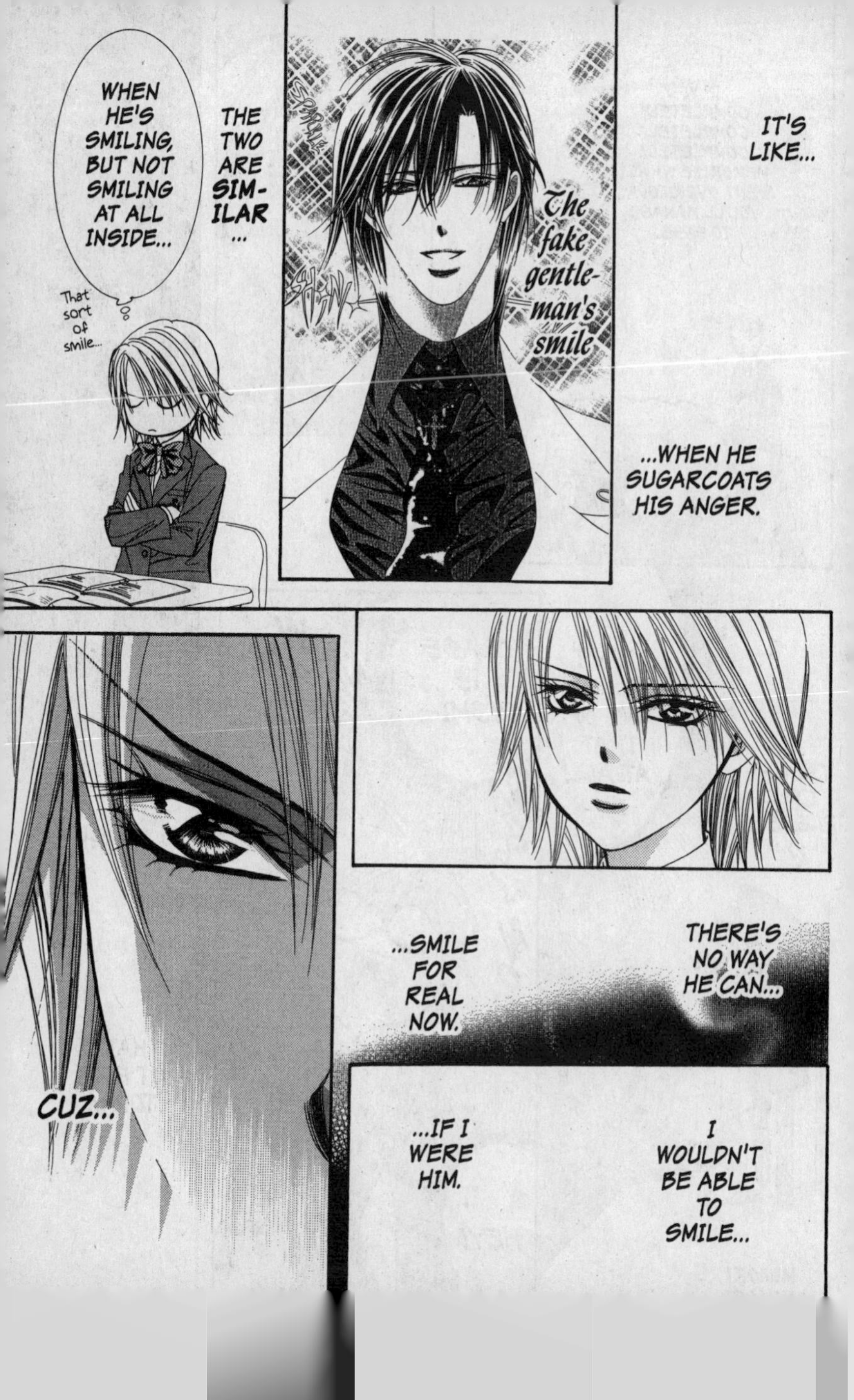

IT'S LIKE...
SPARKLE
SHINE
The fake gentleman's smile
...WHEN HE SUGARCOATS HIS ANGER.
THE TWO ARE SIMILAR...
WHEN HE'S SMILING, BUT NOT SMILING AT ALL INSIDE...
That sort of smile...
THERE'S NO WAY HE CAN...
...SMILE FOR REAL NOW.
I WOULDN'T BE ABLE TO SMILE...
...IF I WERE HIM.
CUZ...

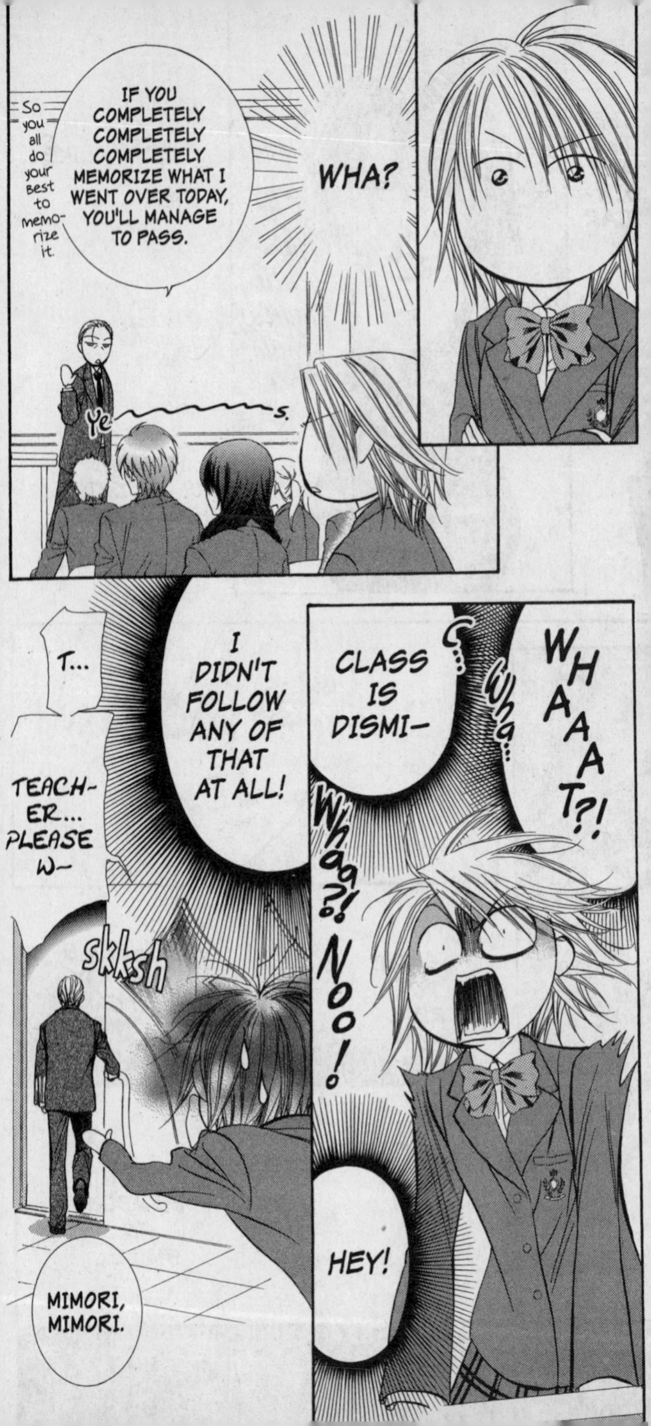
WHA?
IF YOU COMPLETELY COMPLETELY COMPLETELY MEMORIZE WHAT I WENT OVER TODAY, YOU'LL MANAGE TO PASS.
So you all do your Best to memorize it.
Ye~~~s.
CLASS IS DISMI-
WHAAAT?!
Wha...
Whaa?! Nooo!
HEY!
I DIDN'T FOLLOW ANY OF THAT AT ALL!
T...
TEACHER... PLEASE W-
skksh
MIMORI, MIMORI.

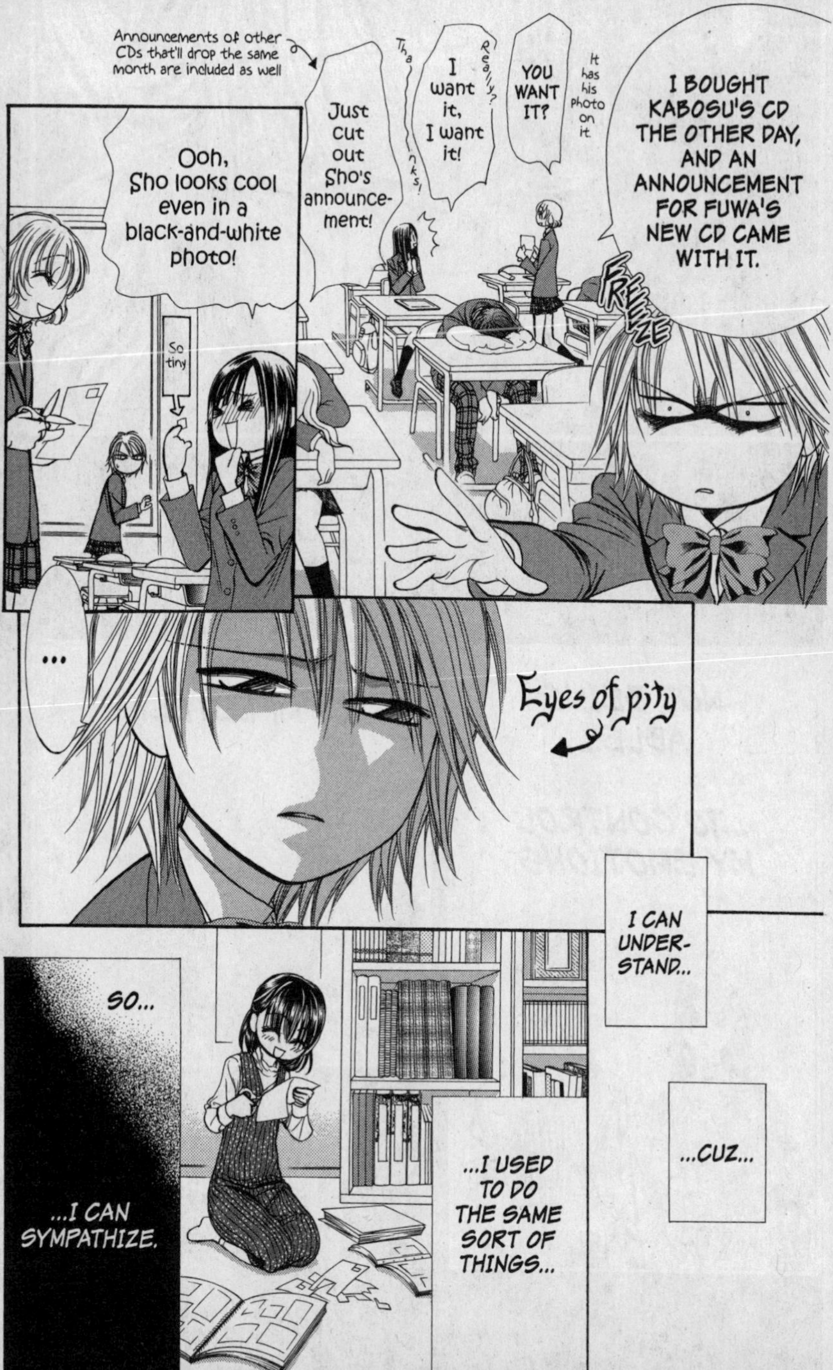
I BOUGHT KABOSU'S CD THE OTHER DAY, AND AN ANNOUNCEMENT FOR FUWA'S NEW CD CAME WITH IT.
It has his photo on it.
YOU WANT IT?
Really?
I want it, I want it!
Thanks!
Just cut out Sho's announcement!
Announcements of other CDs that'll drop the same month are included as well
FREEZE
Ooh, Sho looks cool even in a black-and-white photo!
So tiny
...
Eyes of pity
I CAN UNDER-STAND...
...CUZ...
...I USED TO DO THE SAME SORT OF THINGS...
SO...
...I CAN SYMPATHIZE.

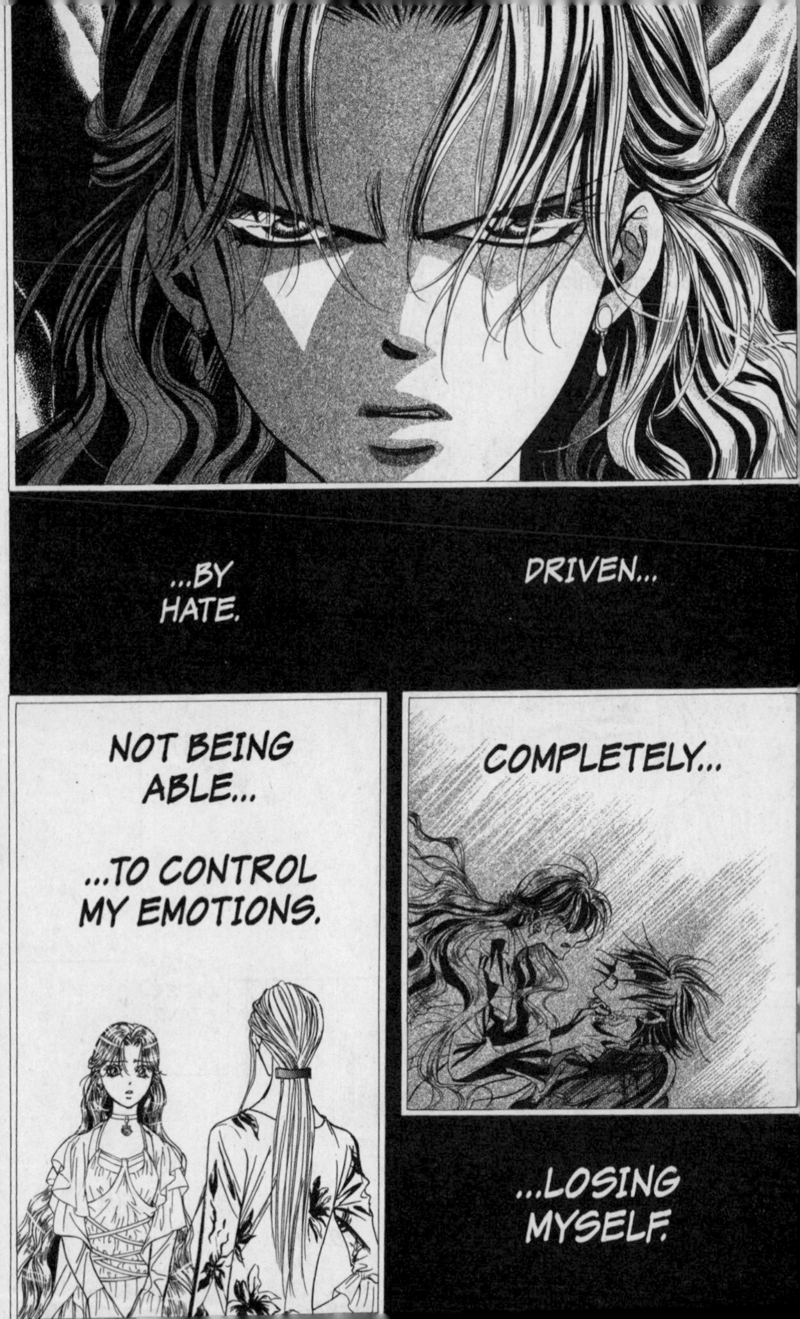
DRIVEN...
...BY HATE.
COMPLETELY...
...LOSING MYSELF.
NOT BEING ABLE...
...TO CONTROL MY EMOTIONS.

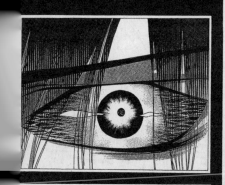

CRUSHED...

I...

...WAS SMILING?

...BY FEELINGS OF DESPAIR...

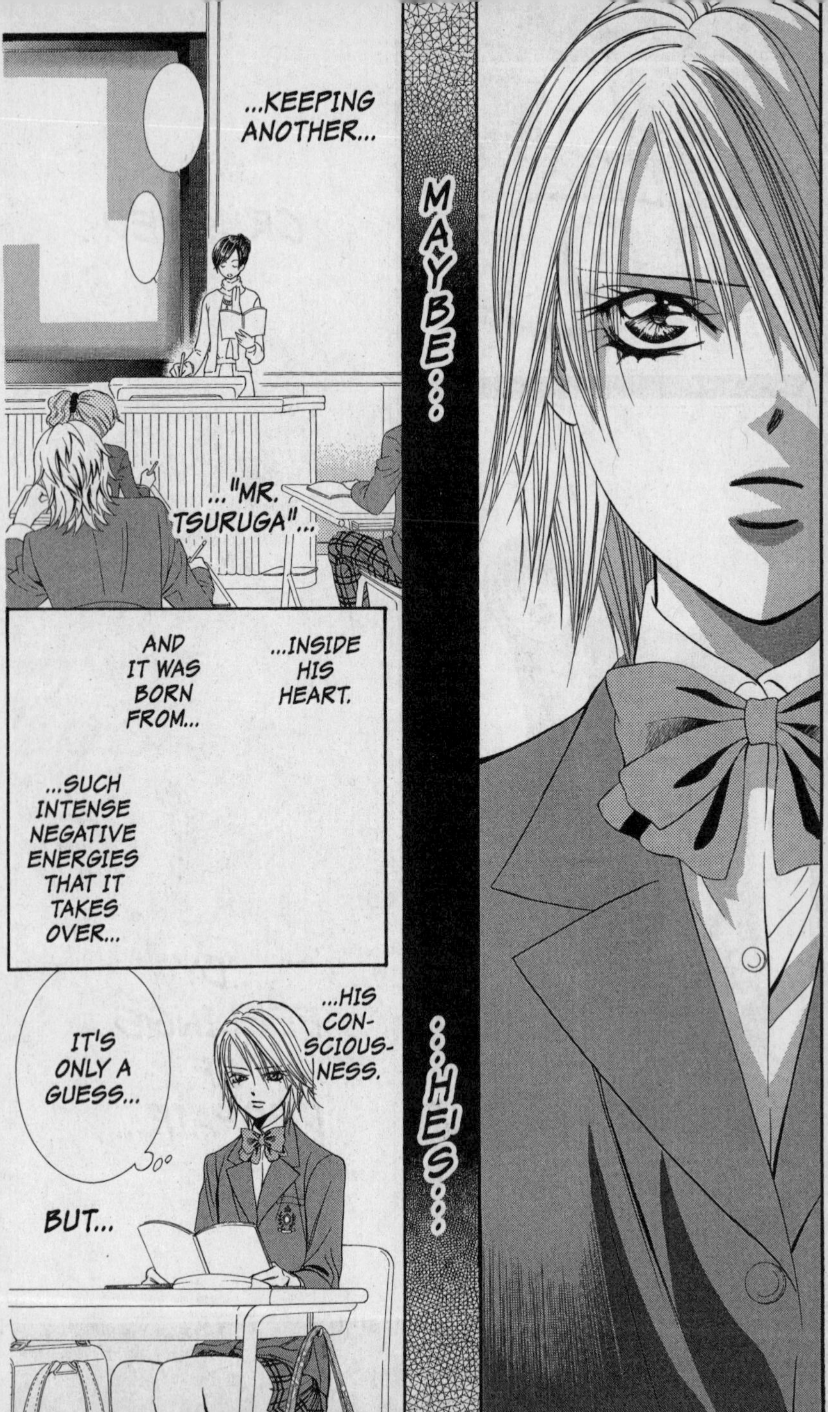

MAYBE...
...HE'S...
...KEEPING ANOTHER...
..."MR. TSURUGA"...
...INSIDE HIS HEART.
AND IT WAS BORN FROM...
...SUCH INTENSE NEGATIVE ENERGIES THAT IT TAKES OVER...
...HIS CON-SCIOUS-NESS.
IT'S SUCH ONLY A GUESS...
BUT...

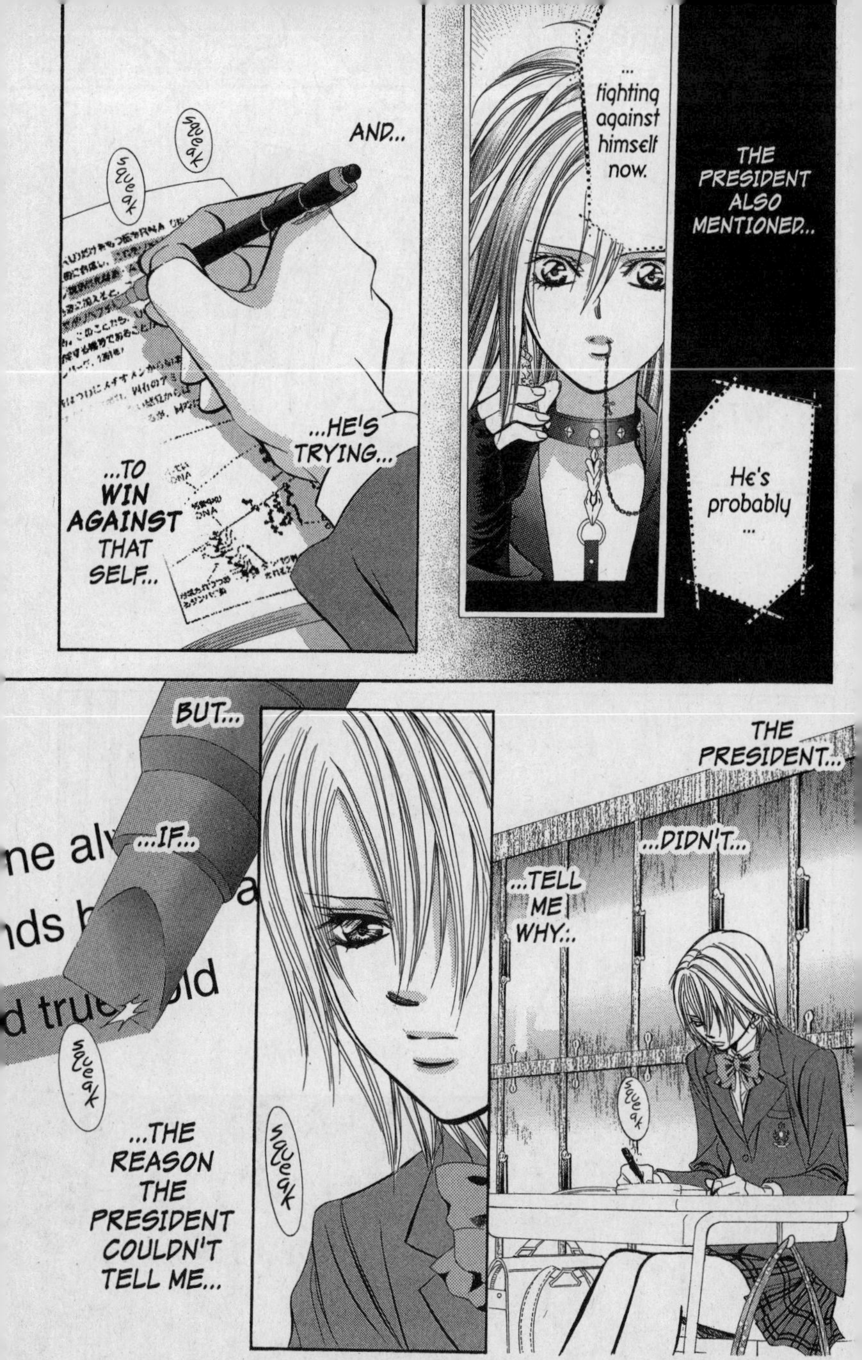
THE PRESIDENT ALSO MENTIONED...
He's probably...
...fighting against himself now.
AND...
squeak
squeak
...HE'S TRYING...
...TO WIN AGAINST THAT SELF...
THE PRESIDENT...
...DIDN'T...
...TELL ME WHY...
squeak
squeak
BUT...
...IF...
squeak
...THE REASON THE PRESIDENT COULDN'T TELL ME...

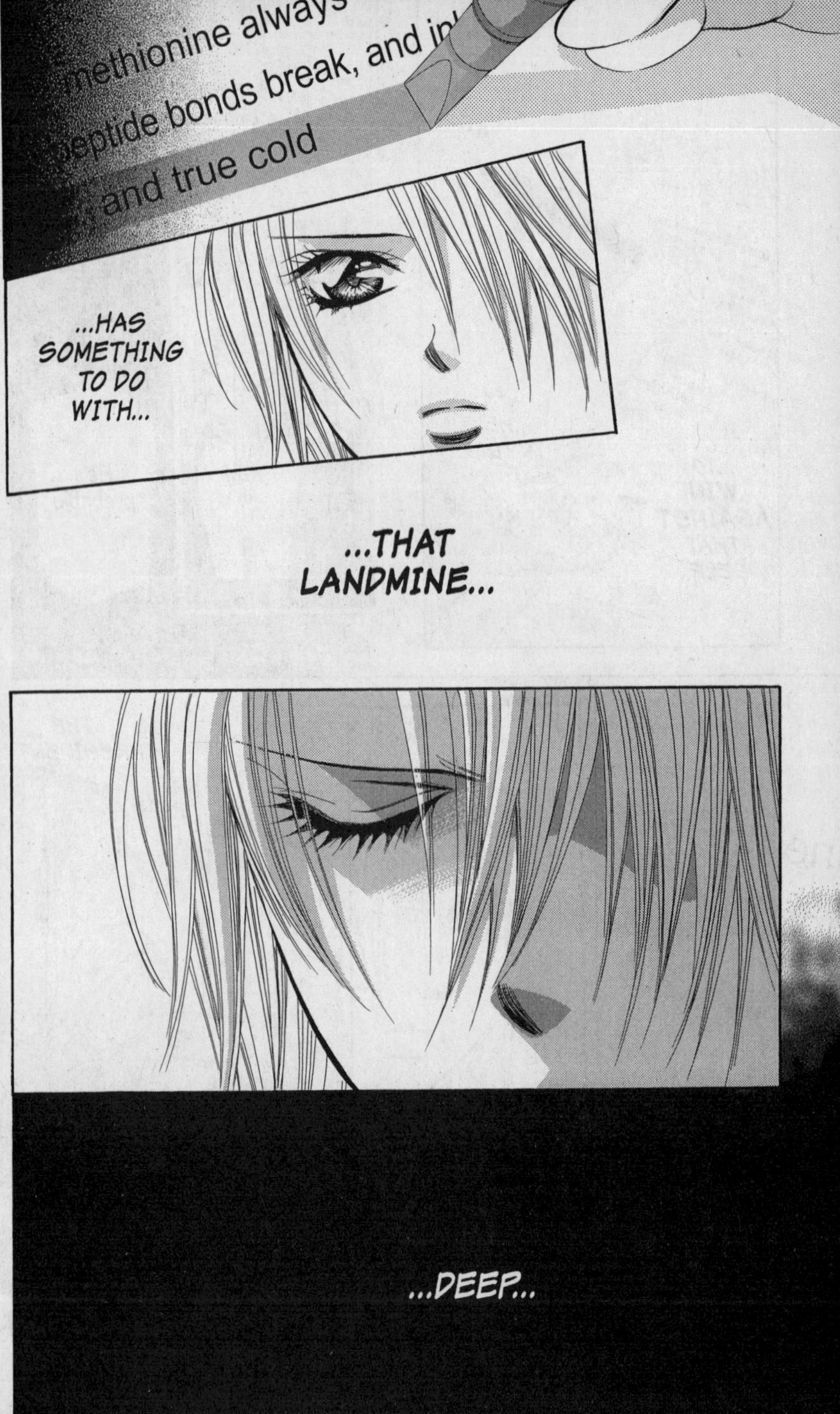
methionine always
peptide bonds break, and in
and true cold
...HAS SOMETHING TO DO WITH...
...THAT LANDMINE...
...DEEP...

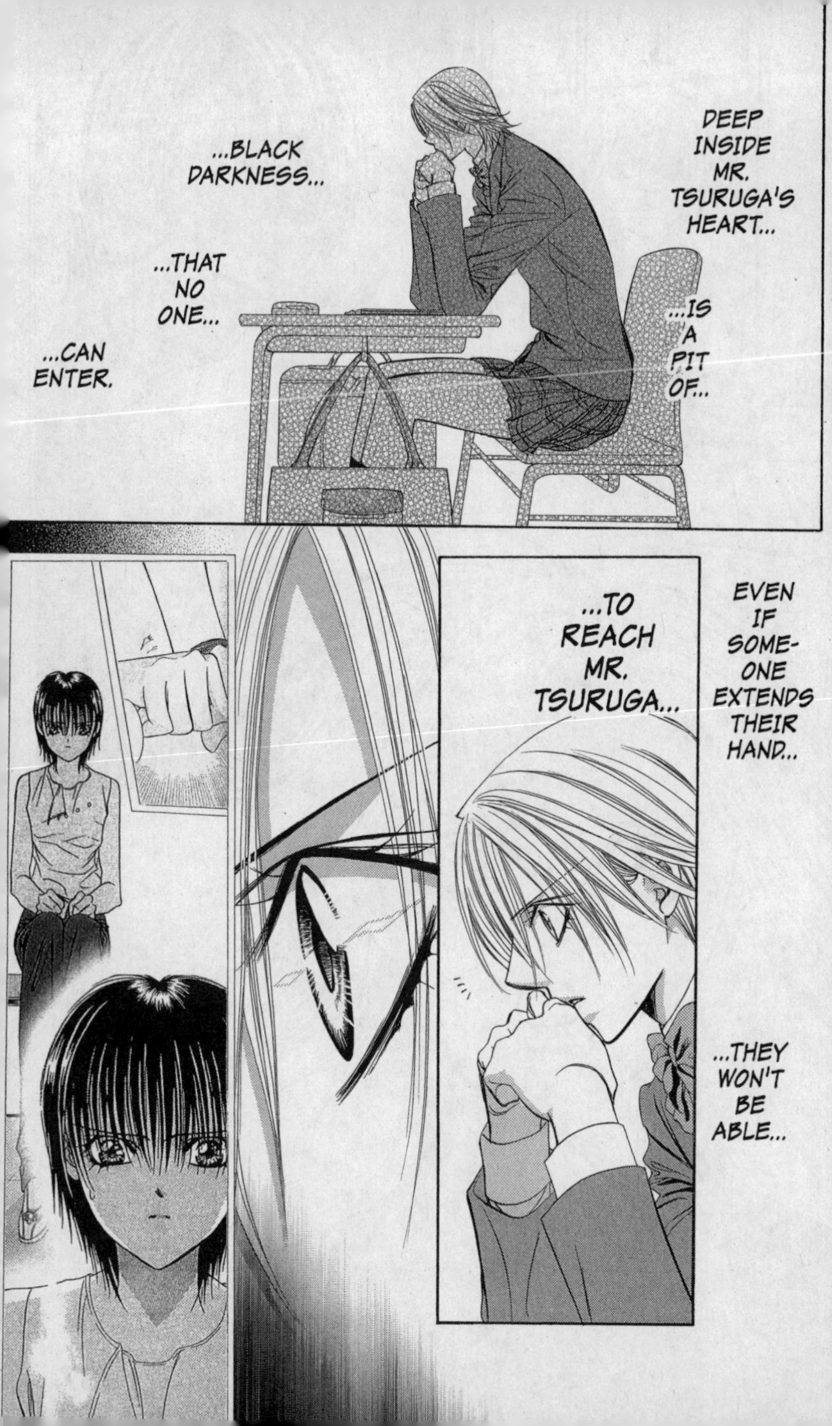
DEEP INSIDE MR. TSURUGA'S HEART...
...IS A PIT OF...
...BLACK DARKNESS...
...THAT NO ONE...
...CAN ENTER.
EVEN IF SOME-ONE EXTENDS THEIR HAND...
...TO REACH MR. TSURUGA...
...THEY WON'T BE ABLE...

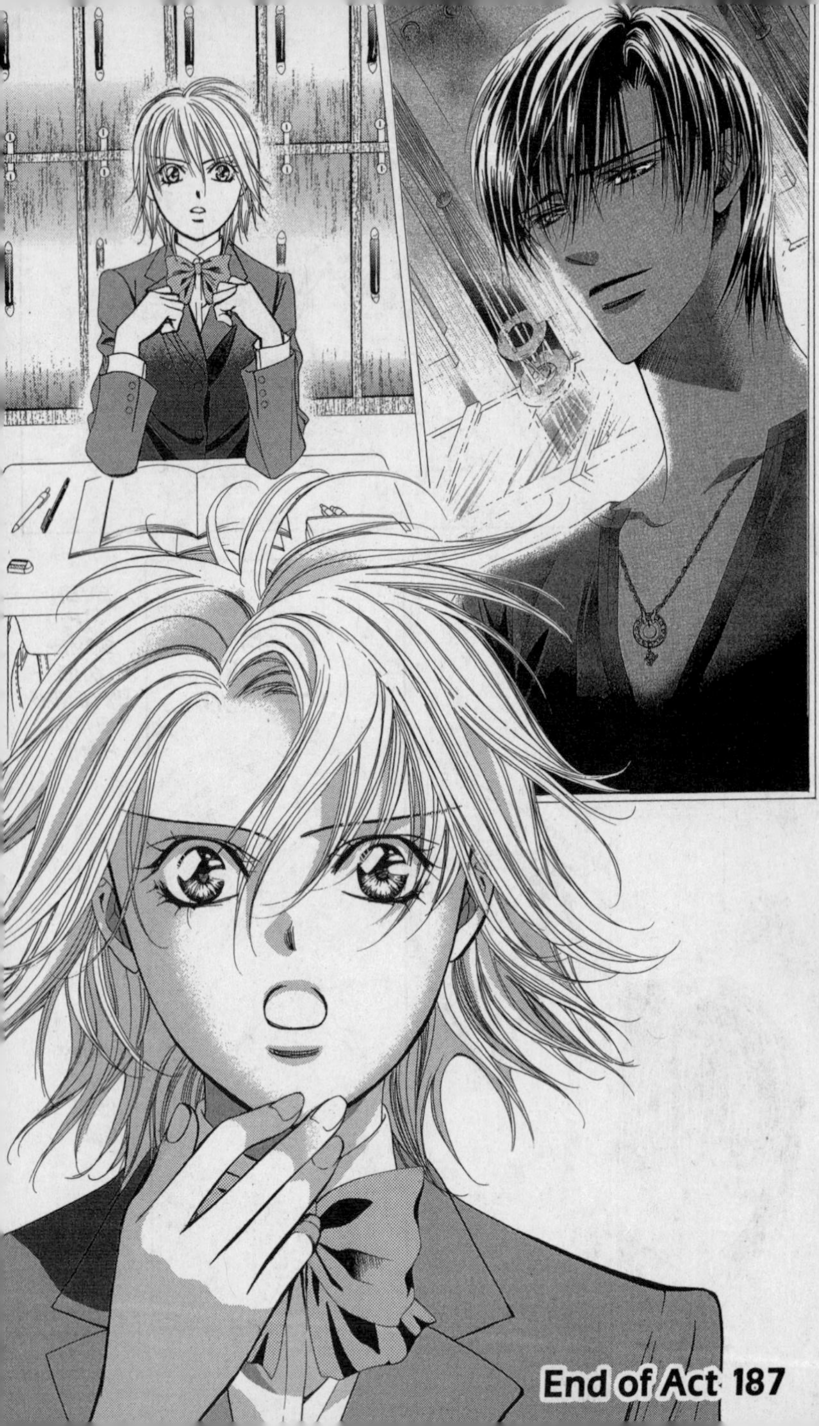
End of Act 187

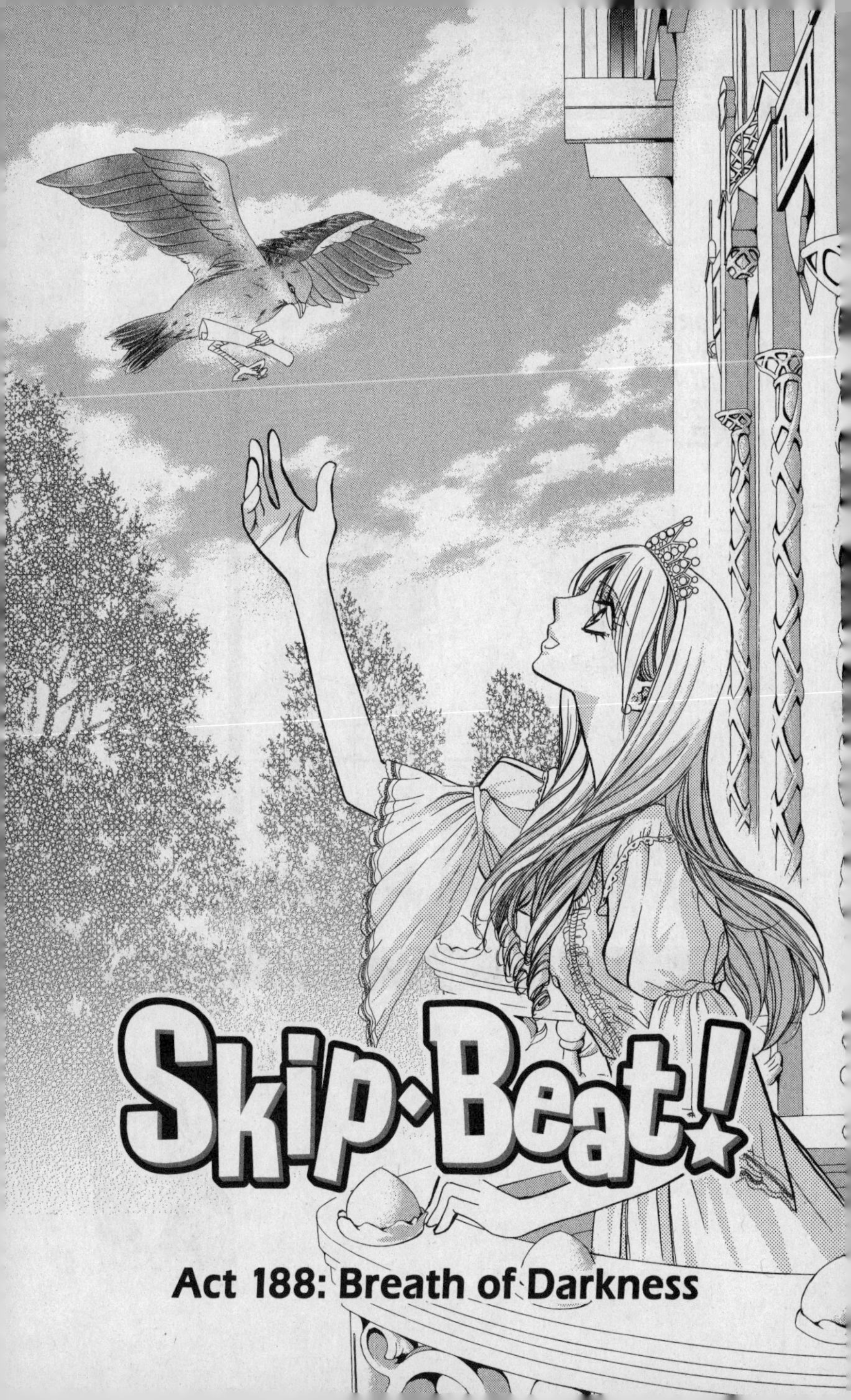
Skip·Beat!

Act 188: Breath of Darkness

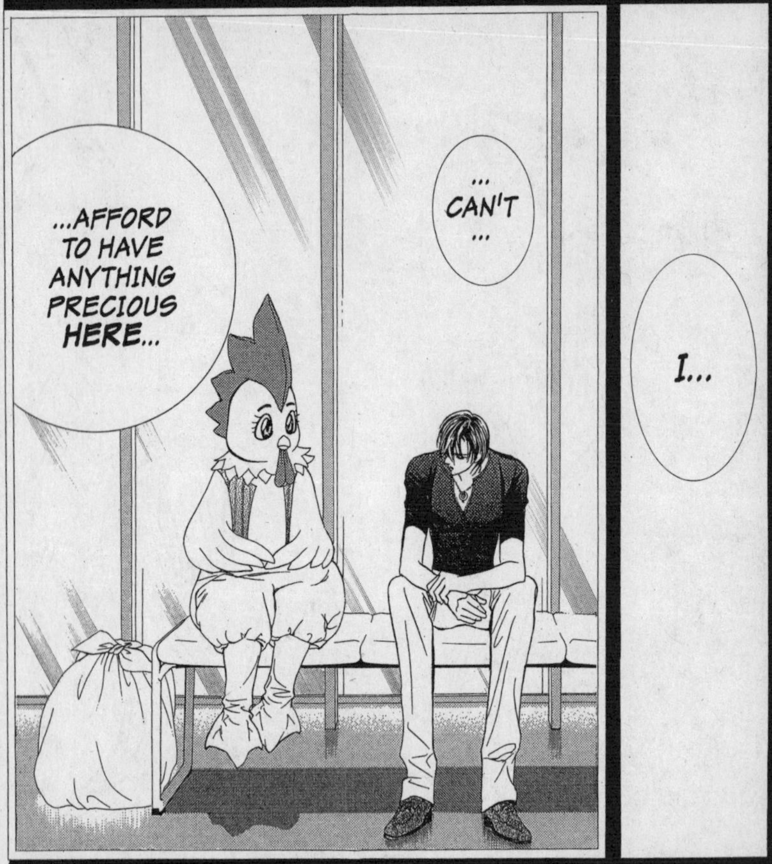
I...
...CAN'T...
...AFFORD TO HAVE ANYTHING PRECIOUS HERE...

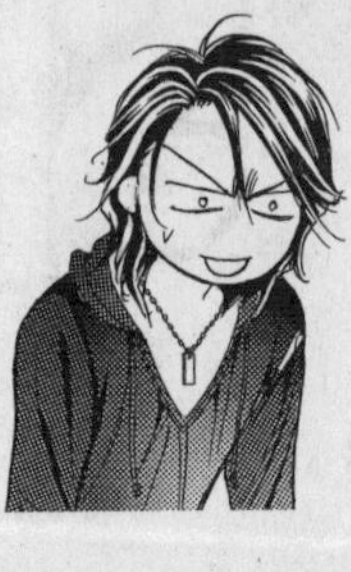

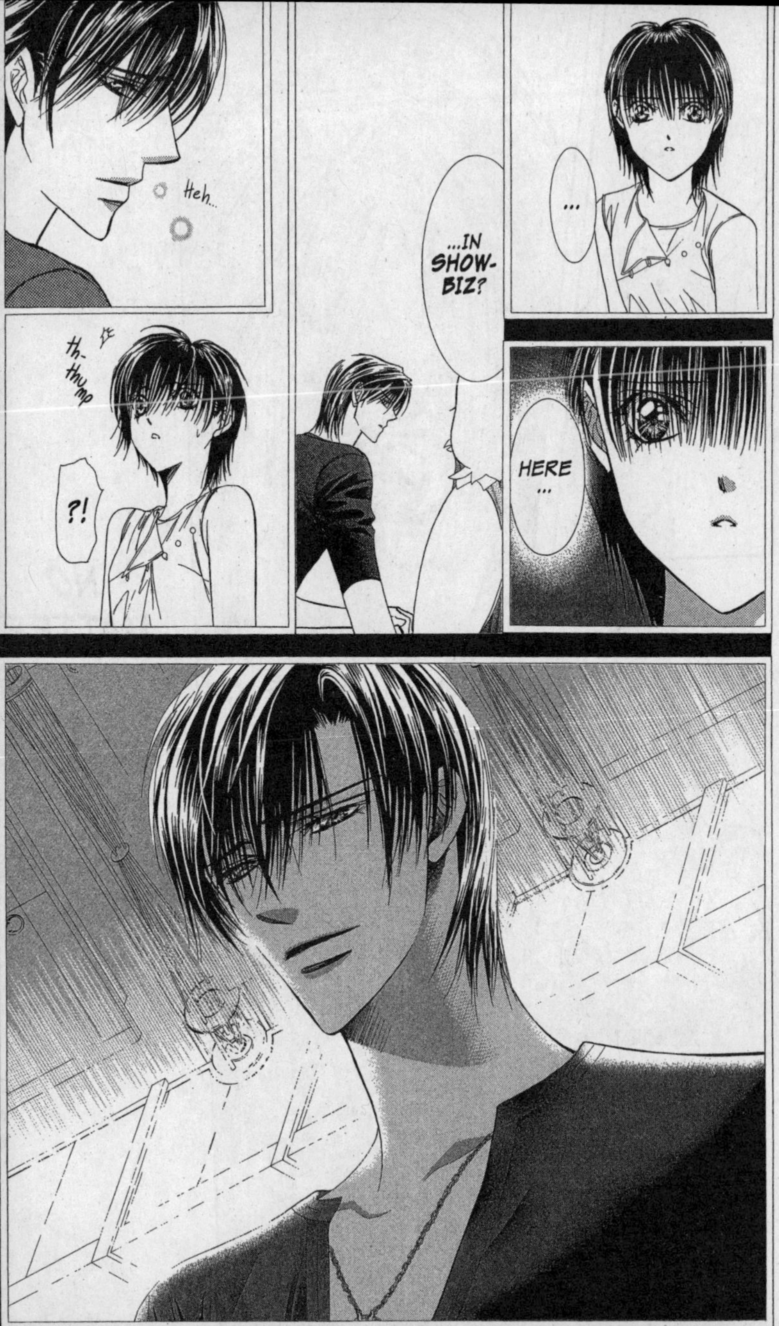
...
HERE ...
...IN SHOW-BIZ?
Heh...
Th-thump
?!

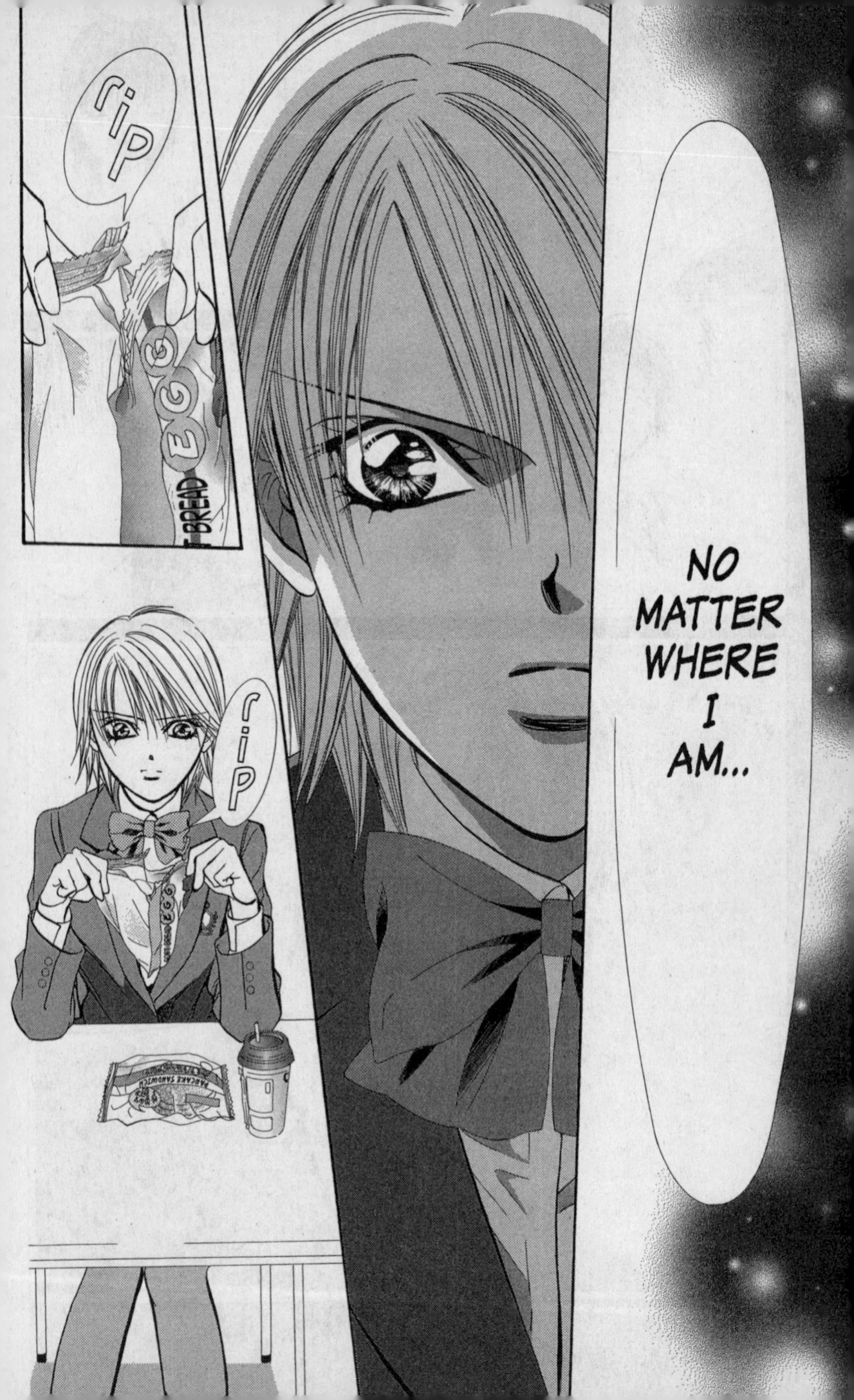
NO MATTER WHERE I AM...
rip
EGG
BREAD
rip

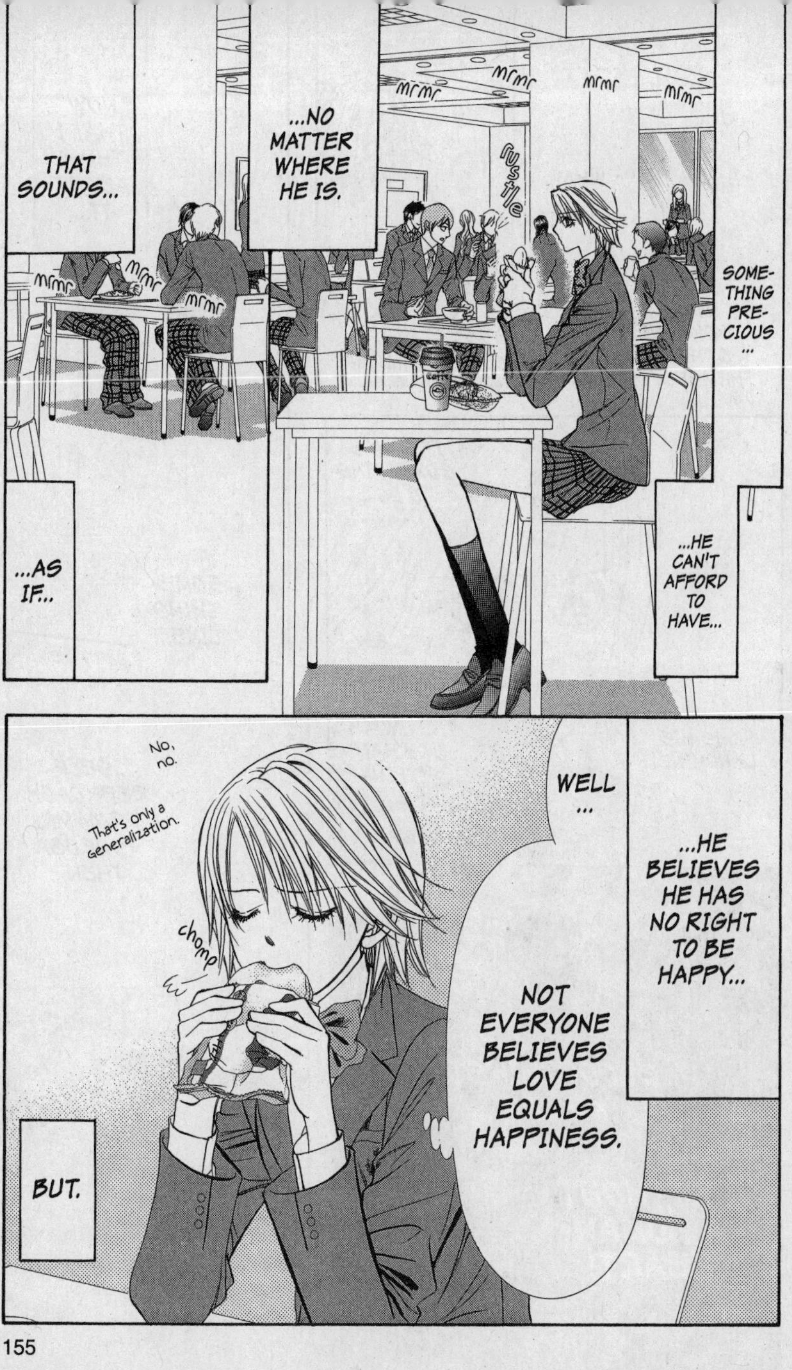
SOME-THING PRE-CIOUS...
...HE CAN'T AFFORD TO HAVE...
mrmr
mrmr
mrmr
rustle
...NO MATTER WHERE HE IS.
mrmr
THAT SOUNDS...
mrmr
mrmr
mrmr
...AS IF...
...HE BELIEVES HE HAS NO RIGHT TO BE HAPPY...
WELL...
NOT EVERYONE BELIEVES LOVE EQUALS HAPPINESS.
No, no.
That's only a generalization.
chomp
BUT.

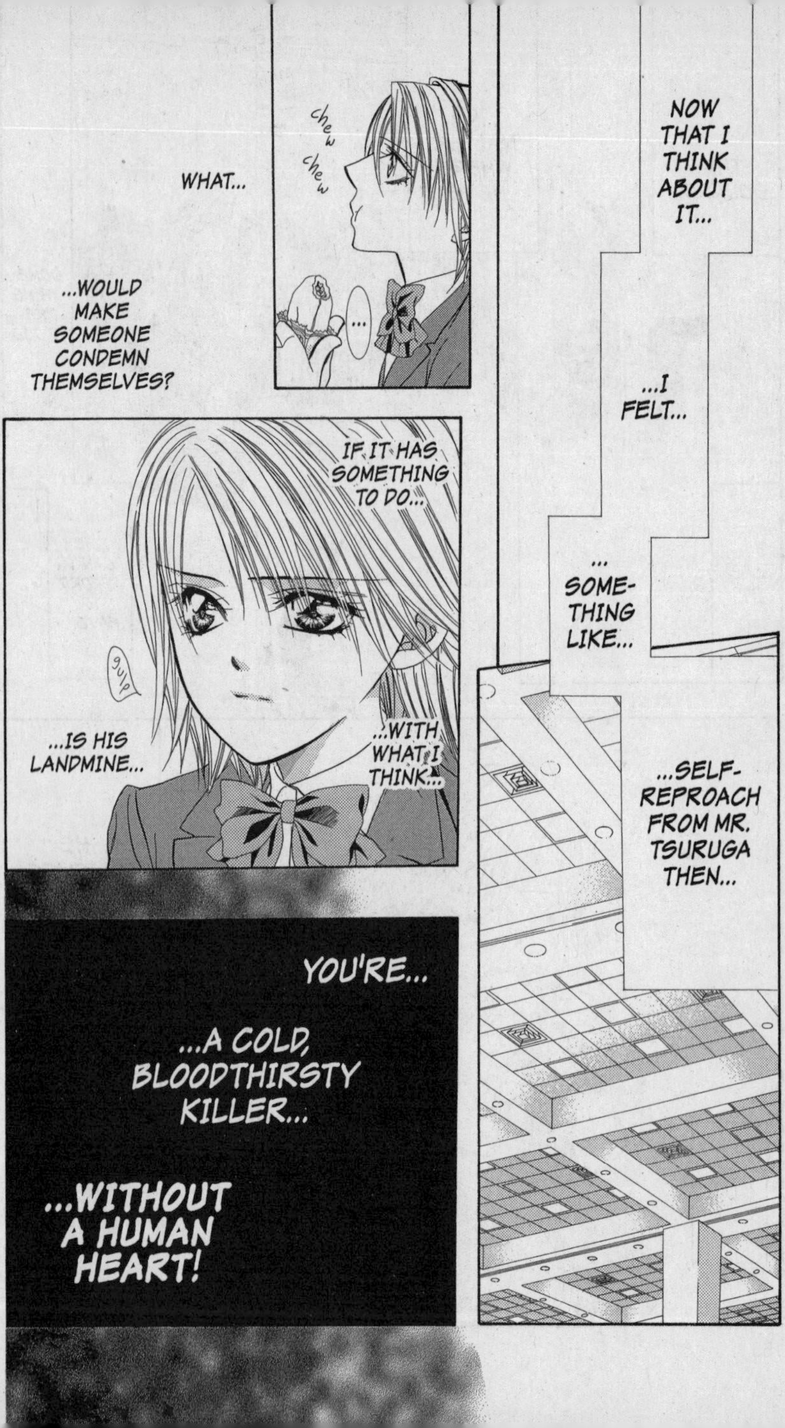
NOW THAT I THINK ABOUT IT...
...I FELT...
...SOMETHING LIKE...
...SELF-REPROACH FROM MR. TSURUGA THEN...
chew chew
WHAT...
...
...WOULD MAKE SOMEONE CONDEMN THEMSELVES?
IF IT HAS SOMETHING TO DO...
...WITH WHAT I THINK...
gulp
...IS HIS LANDMINE...
YOU'RE...
...A COLD, BLOODTHIRSTY KILLER...
...WITHOUT A HUMAN HEART!

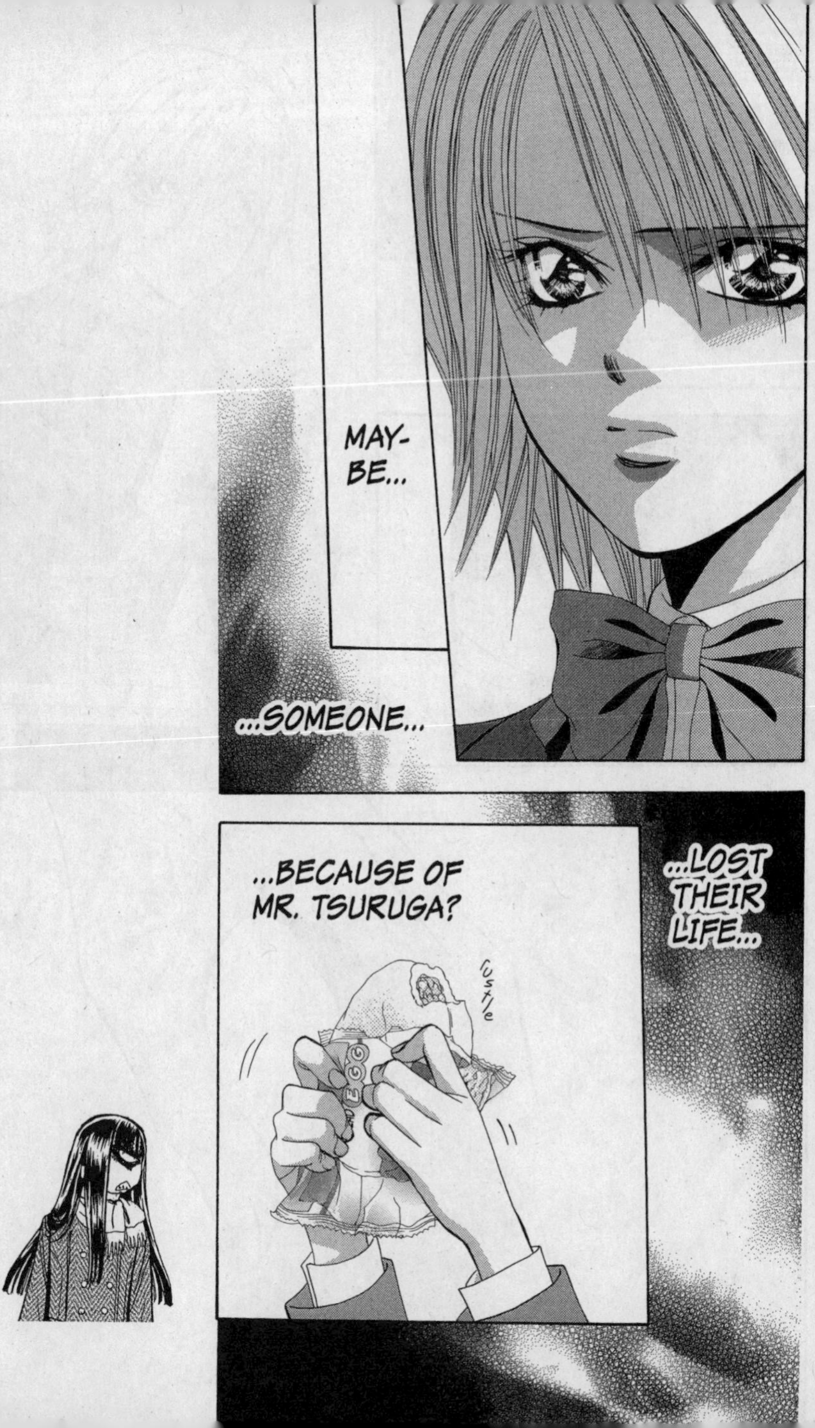
MAY-BE...
...SOMEONE...
...LOST THEIR LIFE...
...BECAUSE OF MR. TSURUGA?
rustle
EGG

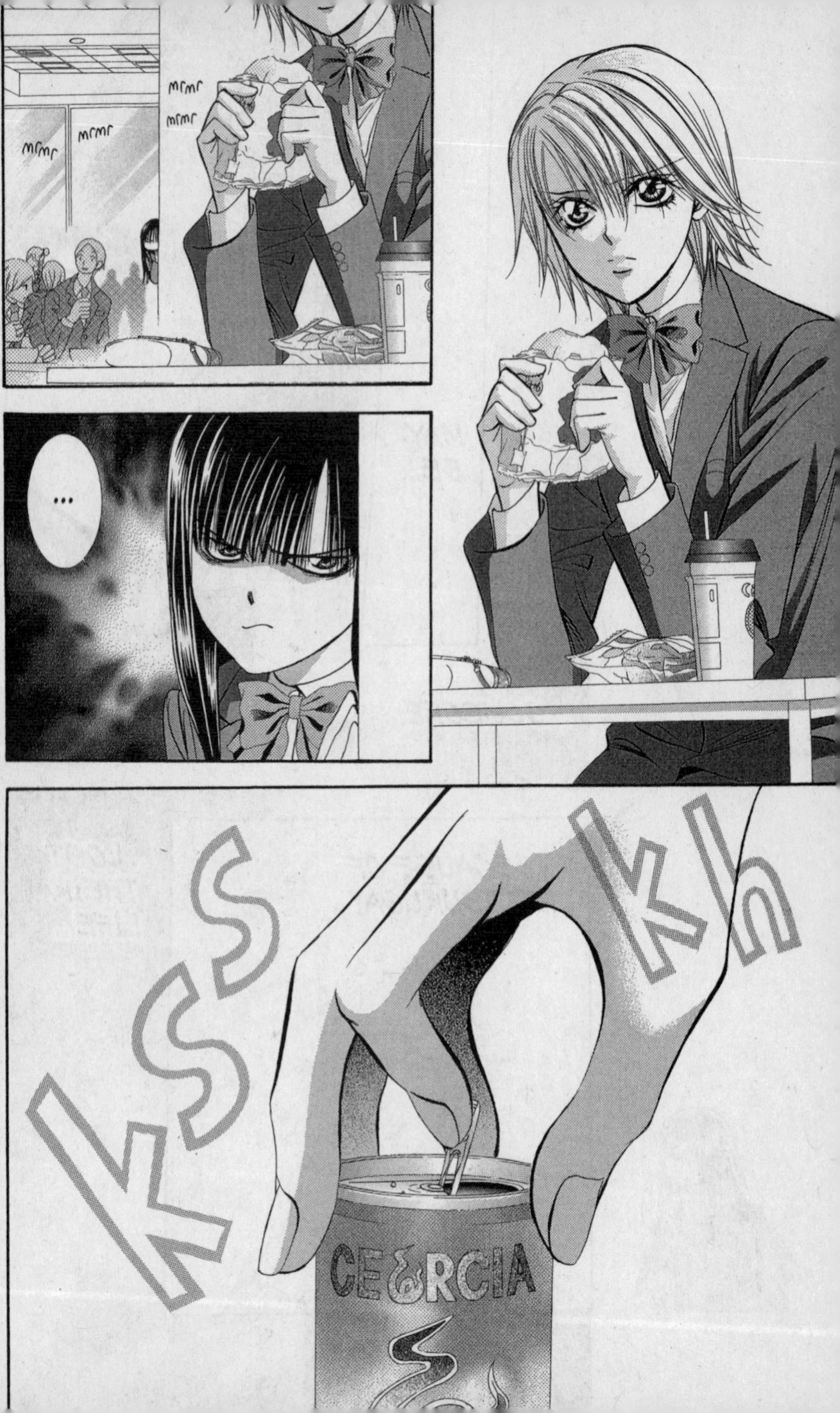
mrmr
mrmr
mrmr
mrmr
...
KSSKH

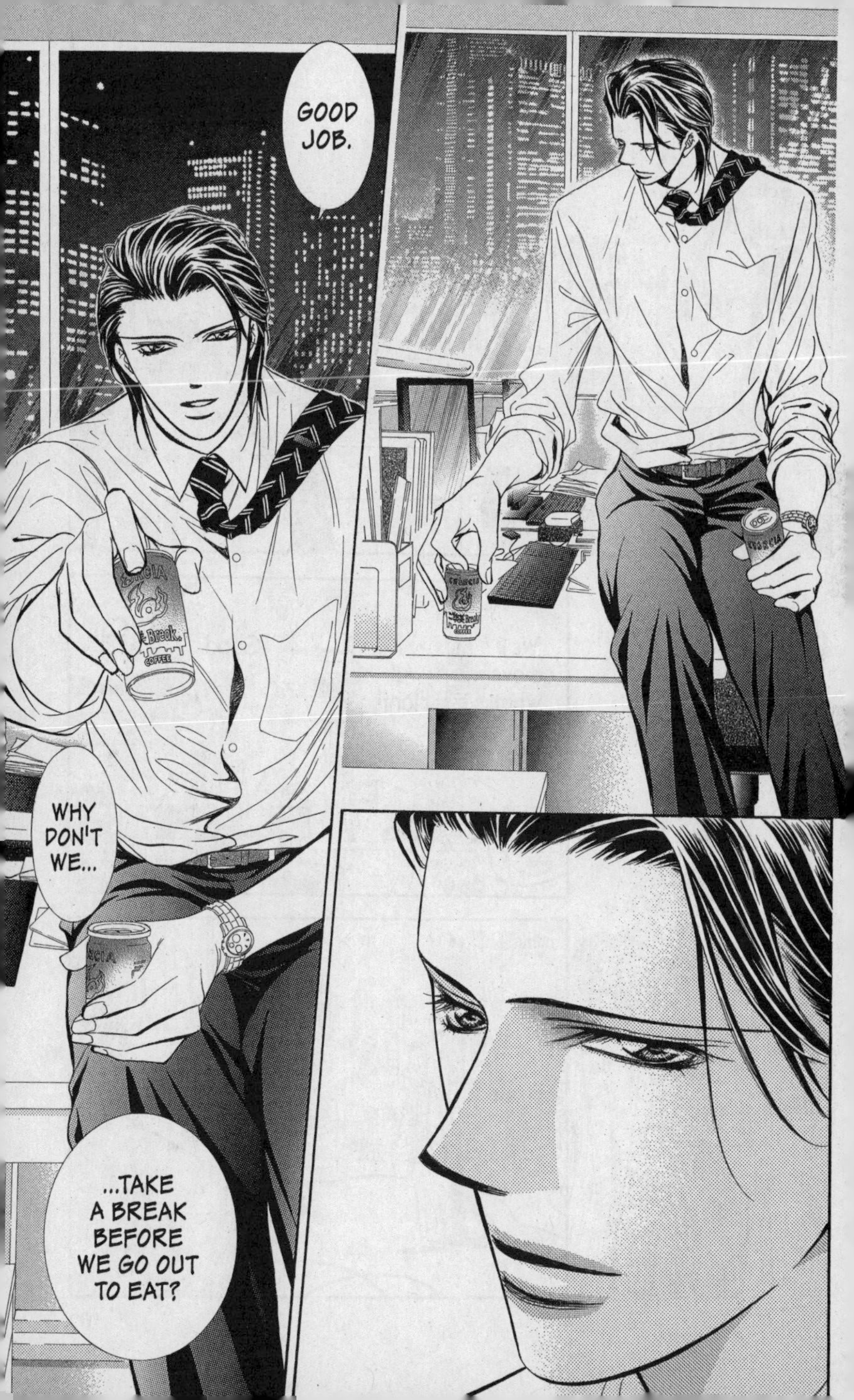
GOOD JOB.
WHY DON'T WE...
...TAKE A BREAK BEFORE WE GO OUT TO EAT?

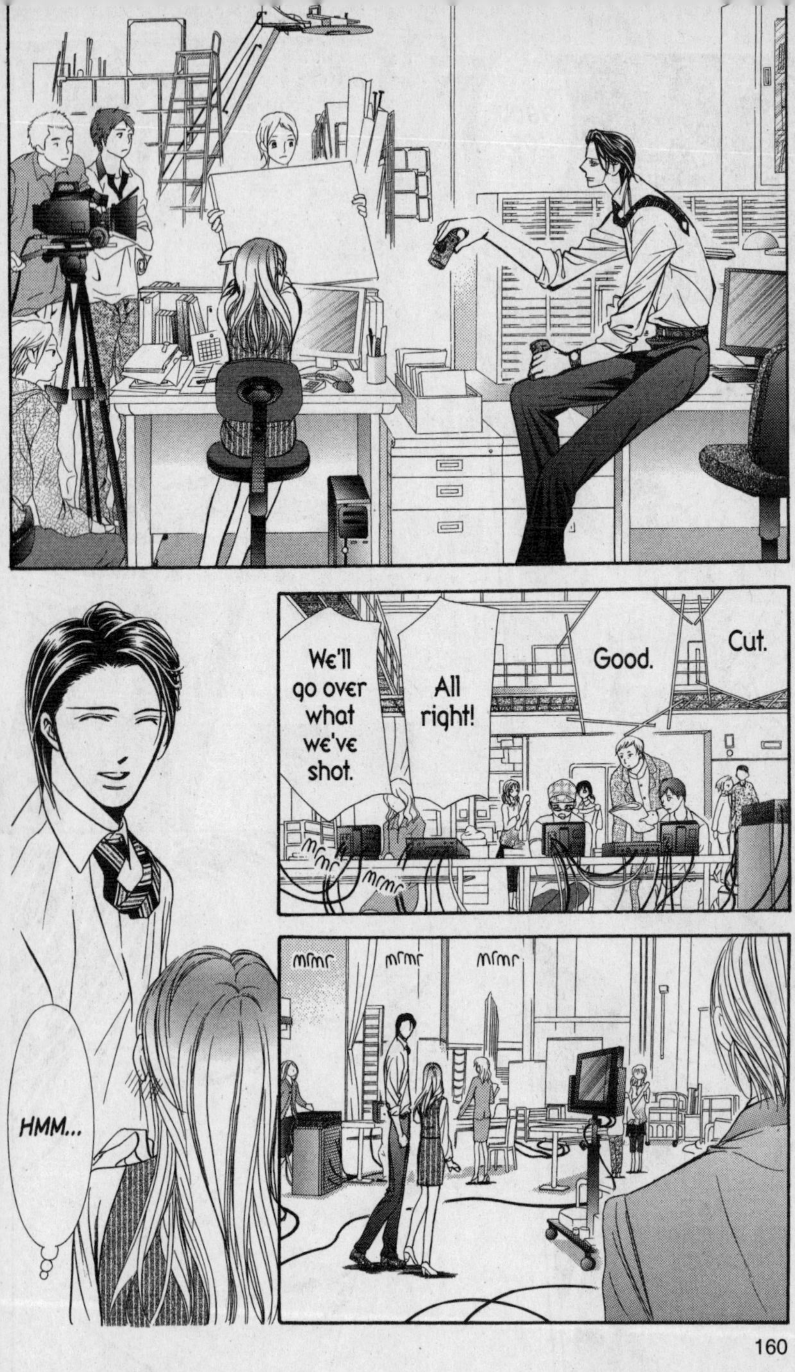
Cut.
Good.
All right!
We'll go over what we've shot.
mrmr
mrmr
mrmr
mrmr
mrmr
HMM...

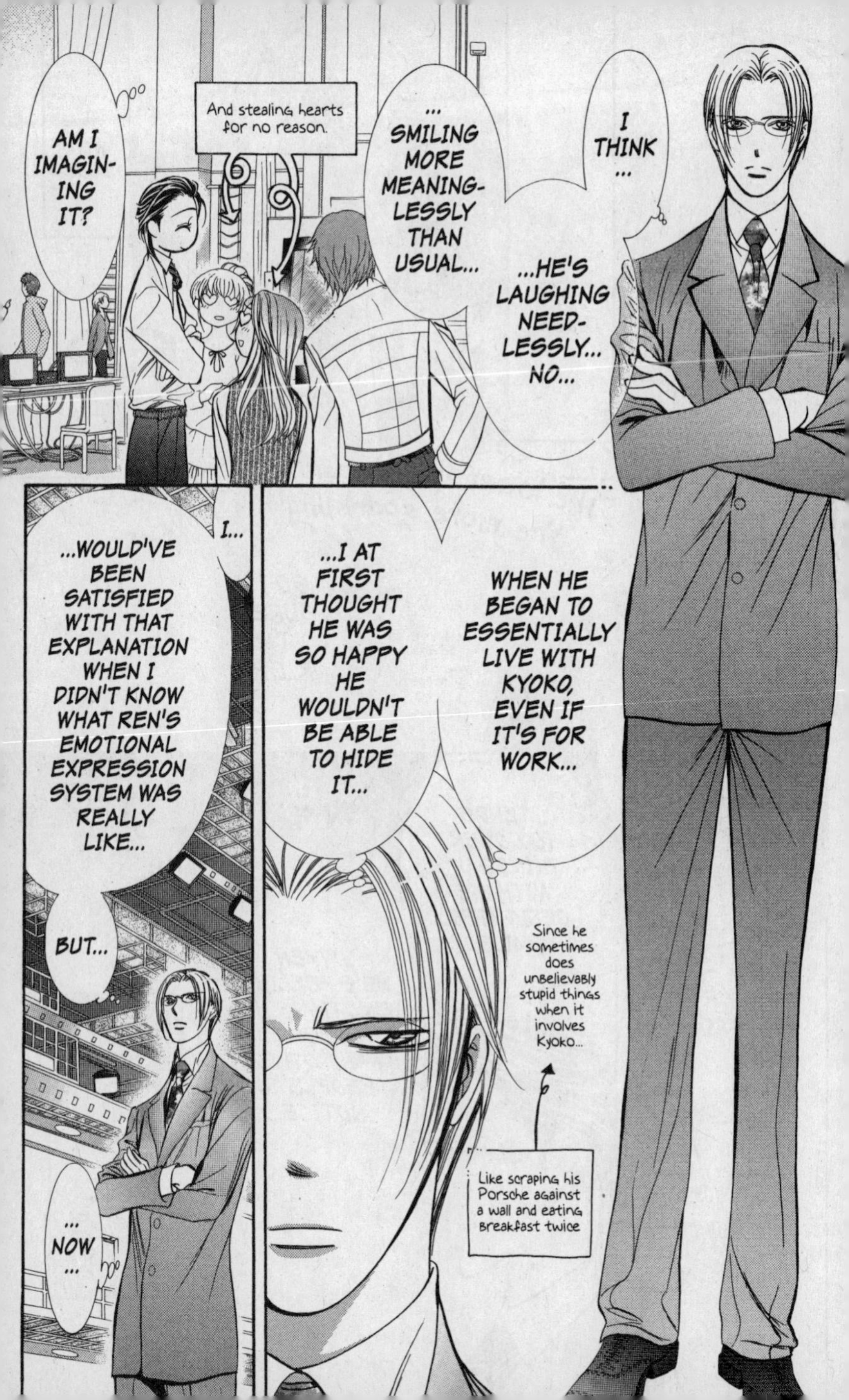
I THINK...
...HE'S LAUGHING NEEDLESSLY... NO...
...SMILING MORE MEANINGLESSLY THAN USUAL...
And stealing hearts for no reason.
AM I IMAGINING IT?
WHEN HE BEGAN TO ESSENTIALLY LIVE WITH KYOKO, EVEN IF IT'S FOR WORK...
...I AT FIRST THOUGHT HE WAS SO HAPPY HE WOULDN'T BE ABLE TO HIDE IT...
Since he sometimes does unbelievably stupid things when it involves Kyoko...
Like scraping his Porsche against a wall and eating breakfast twice
I...
...WOULD'VE BEEN SATISFIED WITH THAT EXPLANATION WHEN I DIDN'T KNOW WHAT REN'S EMOTIONAL EXPRESSION SYSTEM WAS REALLY LIKE...
BUT...
...NOW...

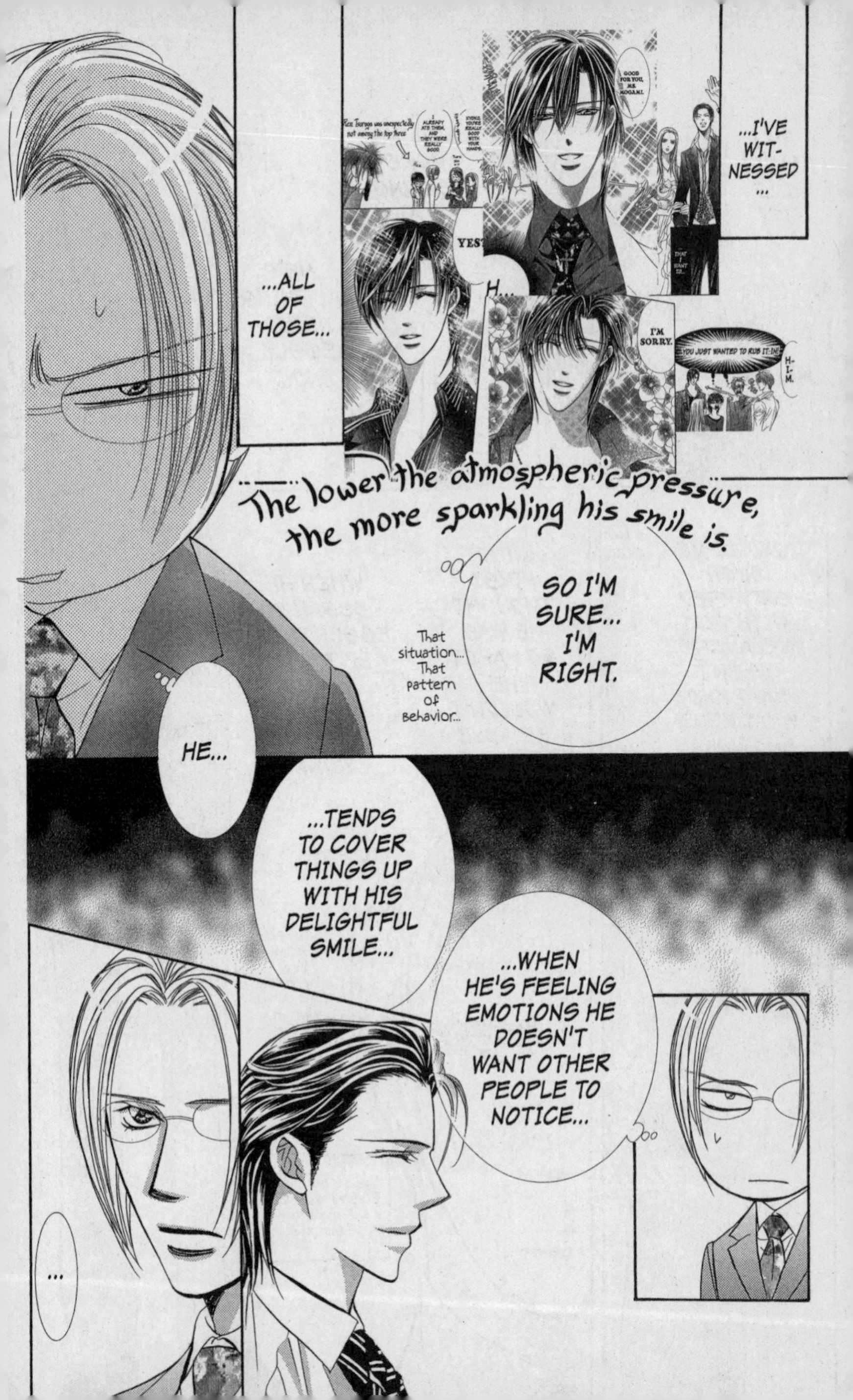
...I'VE WITNESSED...
GOOD FOR YOU, MS. MOGAMI.
YES!
H...
I'M SORRY.
YOU JUST WANTED TO RUB IT IN!
H-I-M.
...ALL OF THOSE...
...The lower the atmospheric pressure, the more sparkling his smile is.
SO I'M SURE... I'M RIGHT.
That situation... That pattern of behavior...
HE...
...TENDS TO COVER THINGS UP WITH HIS DELIGHTFUL SMILE...
...WHEN HE'S FEELING EMOTIONS HE DOESN'T WANT OTHER PEOPLE TO NOTICE...
...

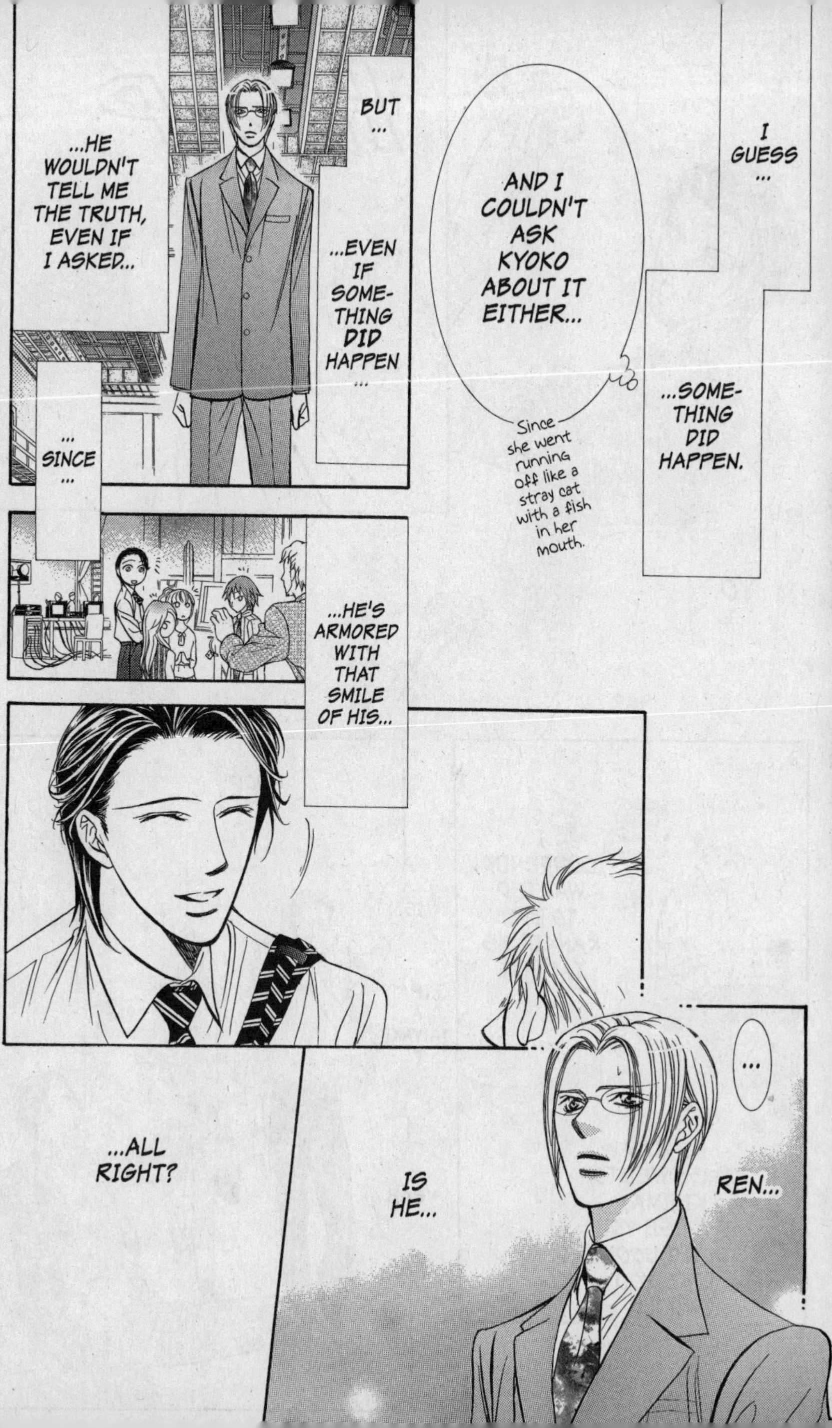
I GUESS...
...SOMETHING DID HAPPEN.
AND I COULDN'T ASK KYOKO ABOUT IT EITHER...
Since she went running off like a stray cat with a fish in her mouth.
BUT...
...EVEN IF SOMETHING DID HAPPEN...
...HE WOULDN'T TELL ME THE TRUTH, EVEN IF I ASKED...
...SINCE...
...HE'S ARMORED WITH THAT SMILE OF HIS...
...
REN...
IS HE...
...ALL RIGHT?

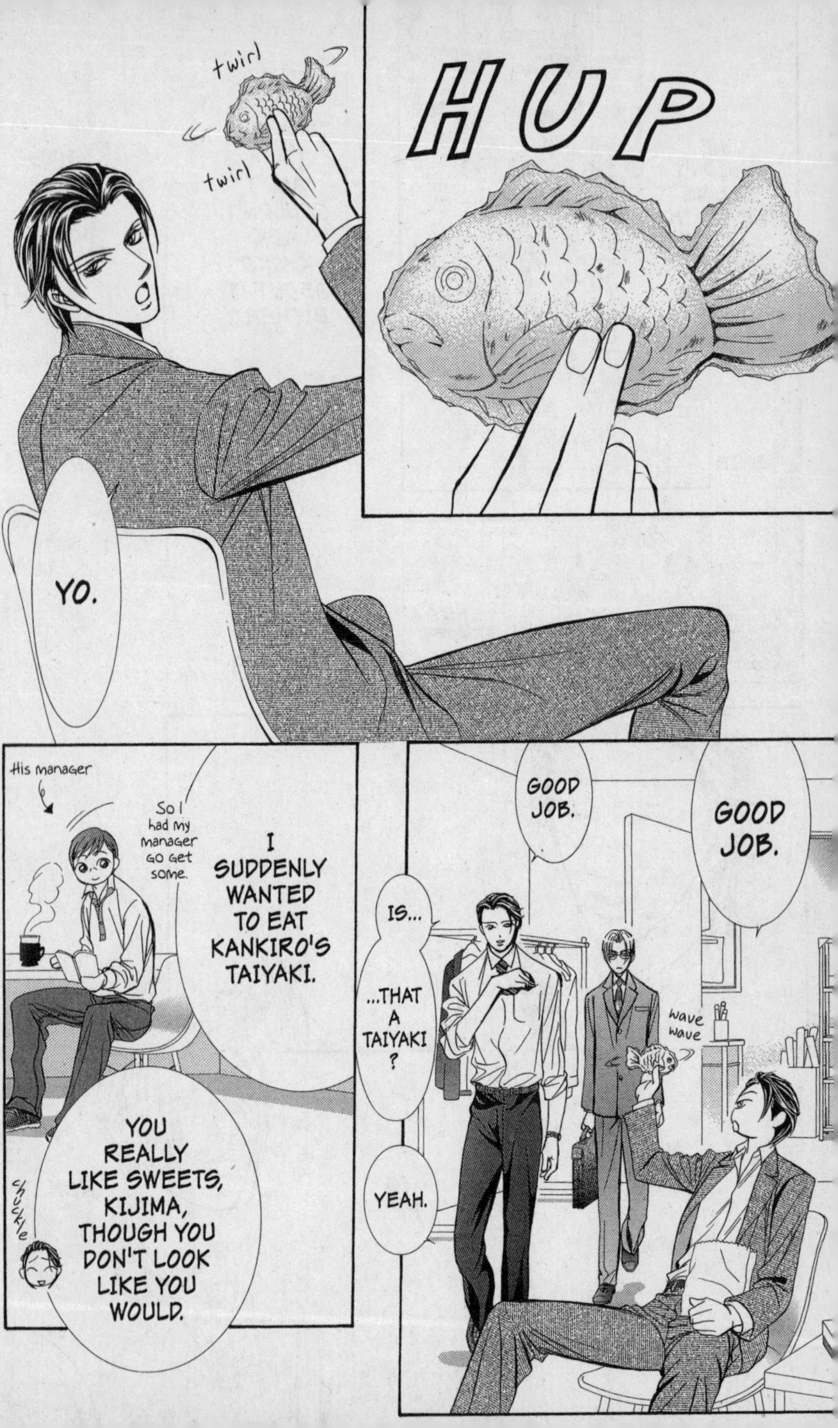
HUP
twirl
twirl
YO.
GOOD JOB.
GOOD JOB.
IS...
...THAT A TAIYAKI?
wave wave
YEAH.
I SUDDENLY WANTED TO EAT KANKIRO'S TAIYAKI.
So I had my manager go get some.
His manager
YOU REALLY LIKE SWEETS, KIJIMA, THOUGH YOU DON'T LOOK LIKE YOU WOULD.
chuckle

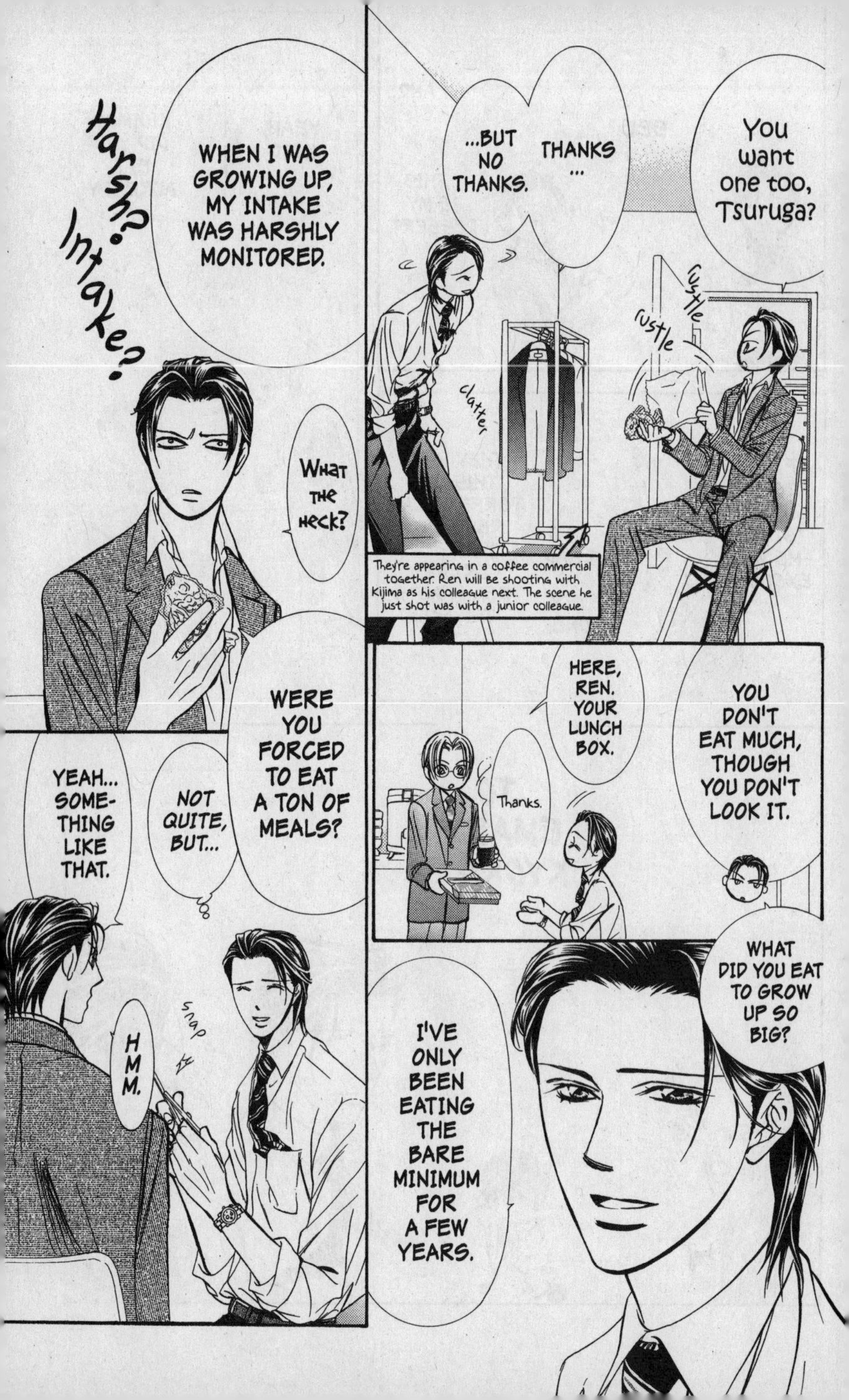

You want one too, Tsuruga?
THANKS ...
...BUT NO THANKS.
rustle
rustle
clatter
They're appearing in a coffee commercial together. Ren will be shooting with Kijima as his colleague next. The scene he just shot was with a junior colleague.
YOU DON'T EAT MUCH, THOUGH YOU DON'T LOOK IT.
HERE, REN. YOUR LUNCH BOX.
Thanks.
WHAT DID YOU EAT TO GROW UP SO BIG?
I'VE ONLY BEEN EATING THE BARE MINIMUM FOR A FEW YEARS.
WHEN I WAS GROWING UP, MY INTAKE WAS HARSHLY MONITORED.
Harsh? Intake?
What the heck?
WERE YOU FORCED TO EAT A TON OF MEALS?
NOT QUITE, BUT...
YEAH... SOMETHING LIKE THAT.
HMM.
snap

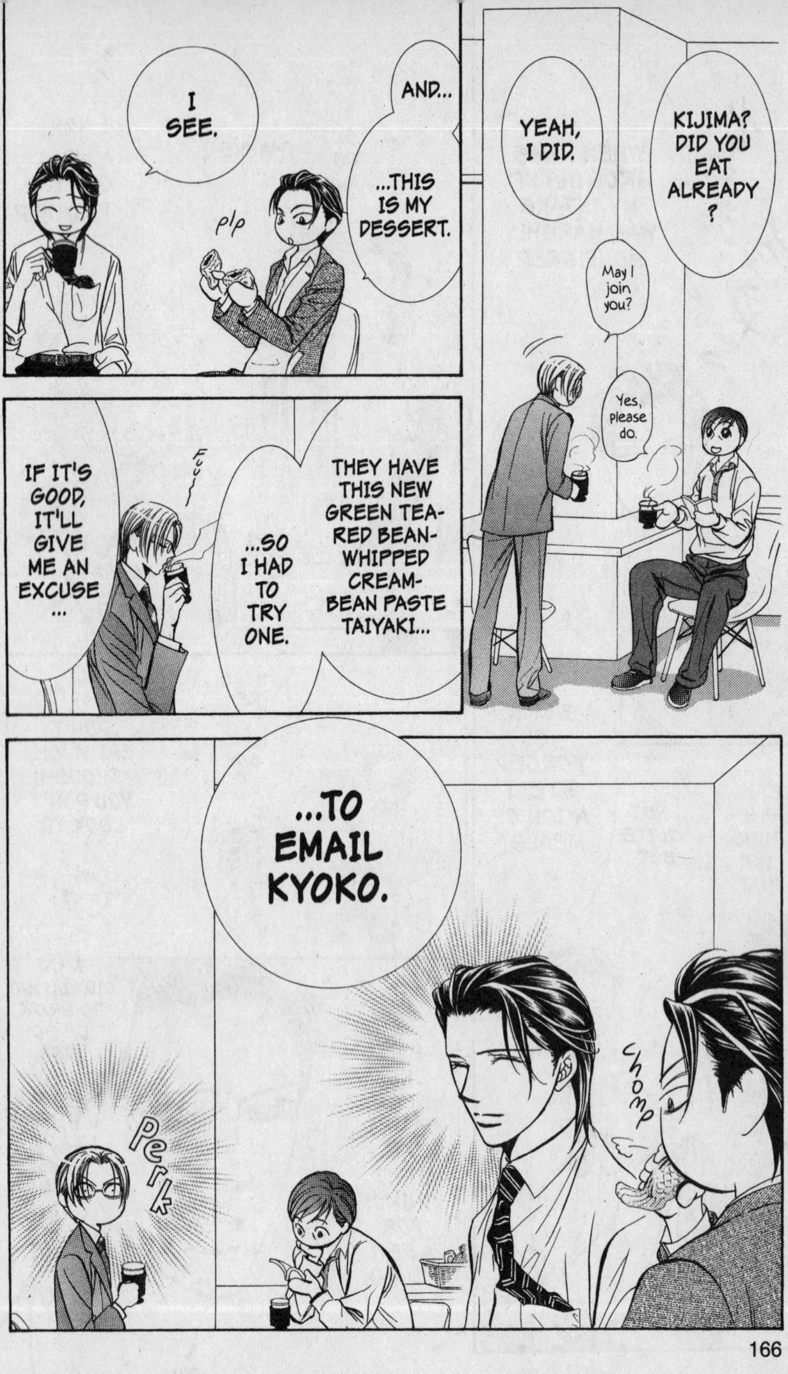
KIJIMA? DID YOU EAT ALREADY?
YEAH, I DID.
May I join you?
Yes, please do.
AND...
...THIS IS MY DESSERT.
I SEE.
THEY HAVE THIS NEW GREEN TEA-RED BEAN-WHIPPED CREAM-BEAN PASTE TAIYAKI...
...SO I HAD TO TRY ONE.
IF IT'S GOOD, IT'LL GIVE ME AN EXCUSE...
...TO EMAIL KYOKO.
chomp
Perk

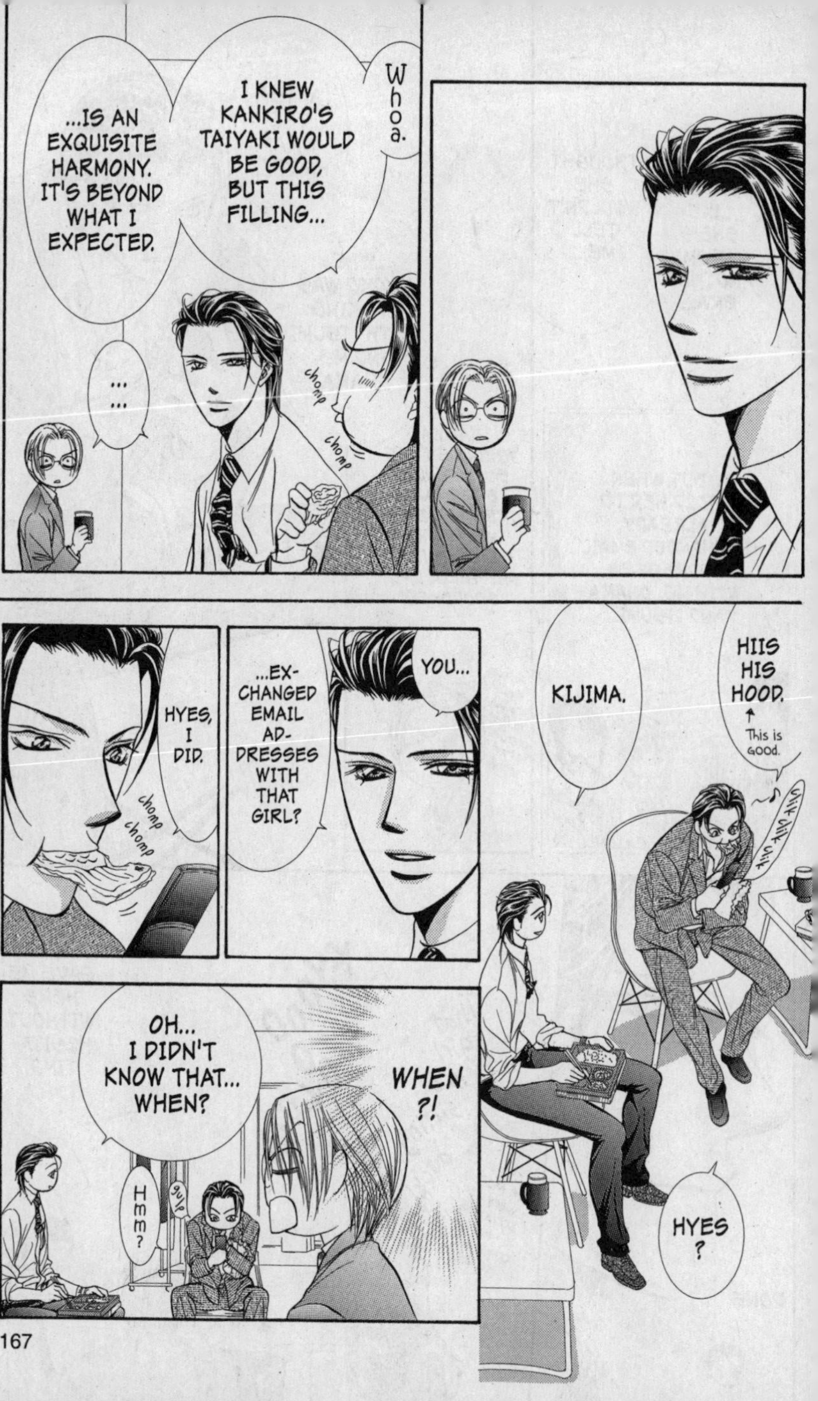
Whoa.
I KNEW KANKIRO'S TAIYAKI WOULD BE GOOD, BUT THIS FILLING...
...IS AN EXQUISITE HARMONY. IT'S BEYOND WHAT I EXPECTED.
chomp
chomp
......
HIIS HIS HOOD.
This is GOOD.
click click click
KIJIMA.
HYES?
YOU...
...EX-CHANGED EMAIL AD-DRESSES WITH THAT GIRL?
HYES, I DID.
chomp chomp
WHEN?!
OH... I DIDN'T KNOW THAT... WHEN?
gulp
Hmm?

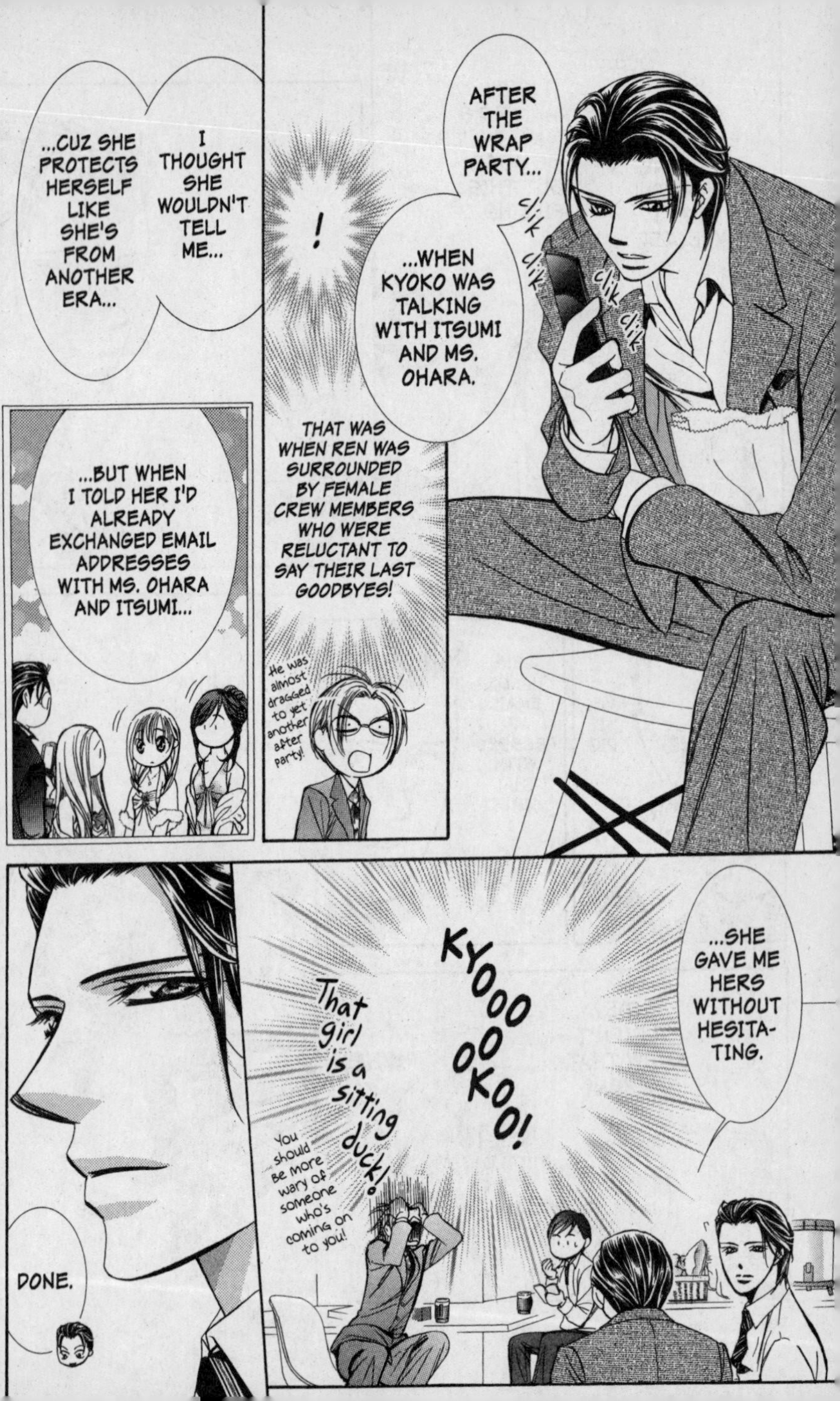

AFTER THE WRAP PARTY...
clik clik clik clik
...WHEN KYOKO WAS TALKING WITH ITSUMI AND MS. OHARA.
!
THAT WAS WHEN REN WAS SURROUNDED BY FEMALE CREW MEMBERS WHO WERE RELUCTANT TO SAY THEIR LAST GOODBYES!
He was almost dragged to yet another after party!
I THOUGHT SHE WOULDN'T TELL ME...
...CUZ SHE PROTECTS HERSELF LIKE SHE'S FROM ANOTHER ERA...
...BUT WHEN I TOLD HER I'D ALREADY EXCHANGED EMAIL ADDRESSES WITH MS. OHARA AND ITSUMI...
...SHE GAVE ME HERS WITHOUT HESITA-TING.
KYOOOOOOKOO!
That girl is a sitting duck!
You should be more wary of someone who's coming on to you!
DONE.

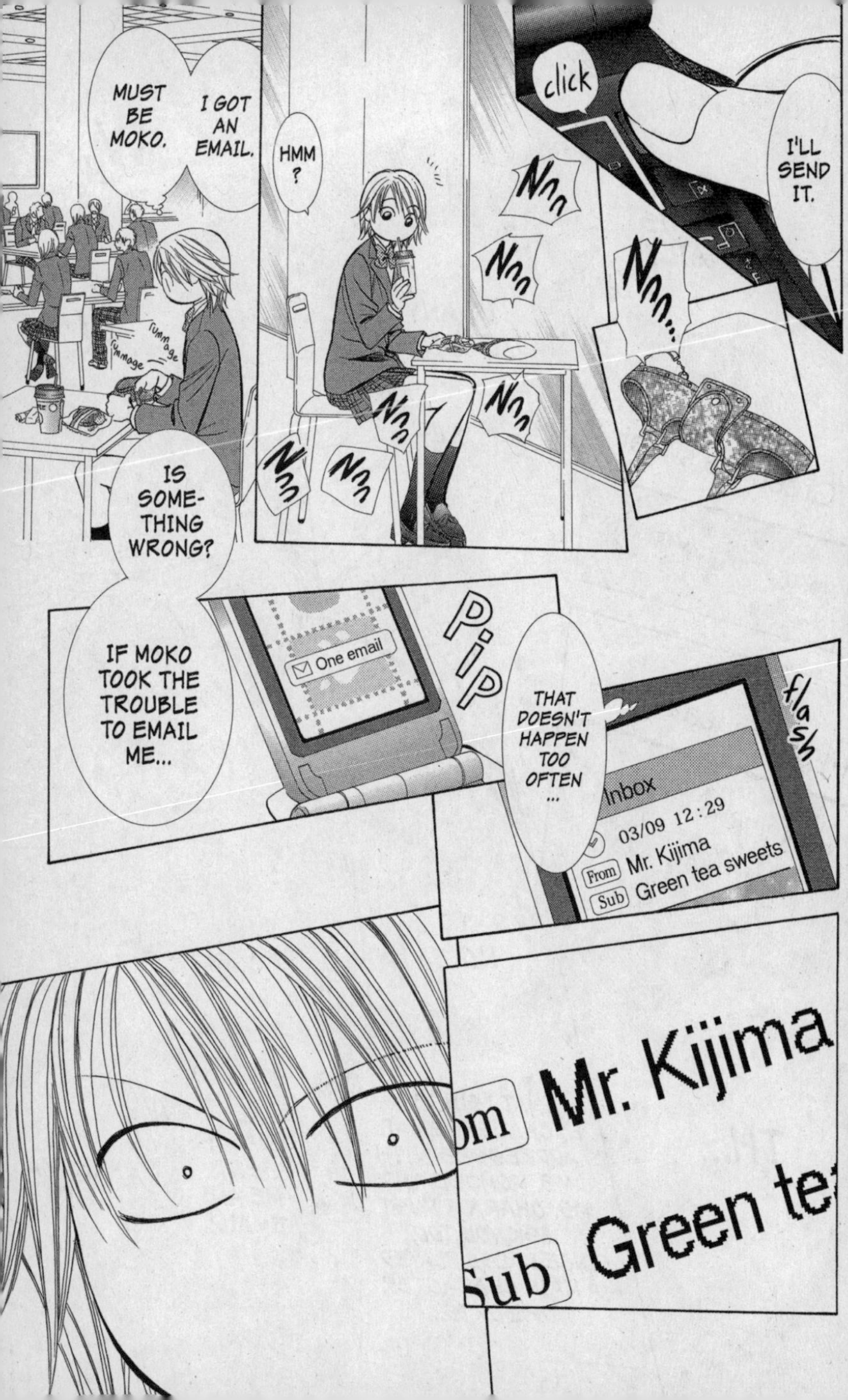
I'LL SEND IT.
click
Nnn...
Nnn
Nnn
HMM?
Nnn
Nnn
Nnn
I GOT AN EMAIL.
MUST BE MOKO.
rummage
rummage
IS SOMETHING WRONG?
IF MOKO TOOK THE TROUBLE TO EMAIL ME...
THAT DOESN'T HAPPEN TOO OFTEN...
flash
Inbox
03/09 12:29
From Mr. Kijima
Sub Green tea sweets
Pip
One email
om Mr. Kijima
Sub Green te

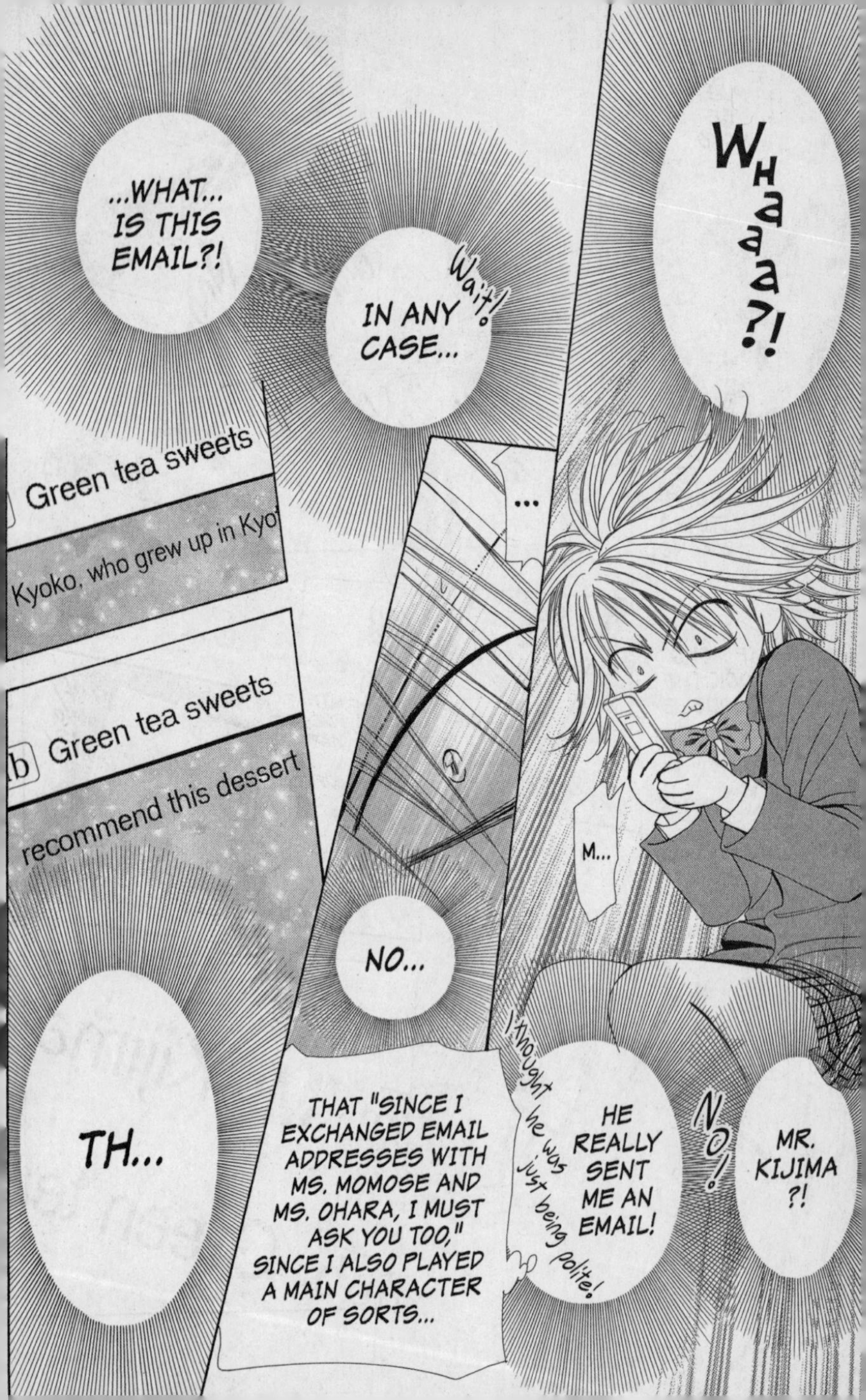
Whaaa?!
M...
MR. KIJIMA?!
NO!
HE REALLY SENT ME AN EMAIL!
I thought he was just being polite!
IN ANY CASE...
Wait!
...
NO...
THAT "SINCE I EXCHANGED EMAIL ADDRESSES WITH MS. MOMOSE AND MS. OHARA, I MUST ASK YOU TOO," SINCE I ALSO PLAYED A MAIN CHARACTER OF SORTS...
...WHAT... IS THIS EMAIL?!
Green tea sweets
Kyoko, who grew up in Kyo
Green tea sweets
recommend this dessert
TH...

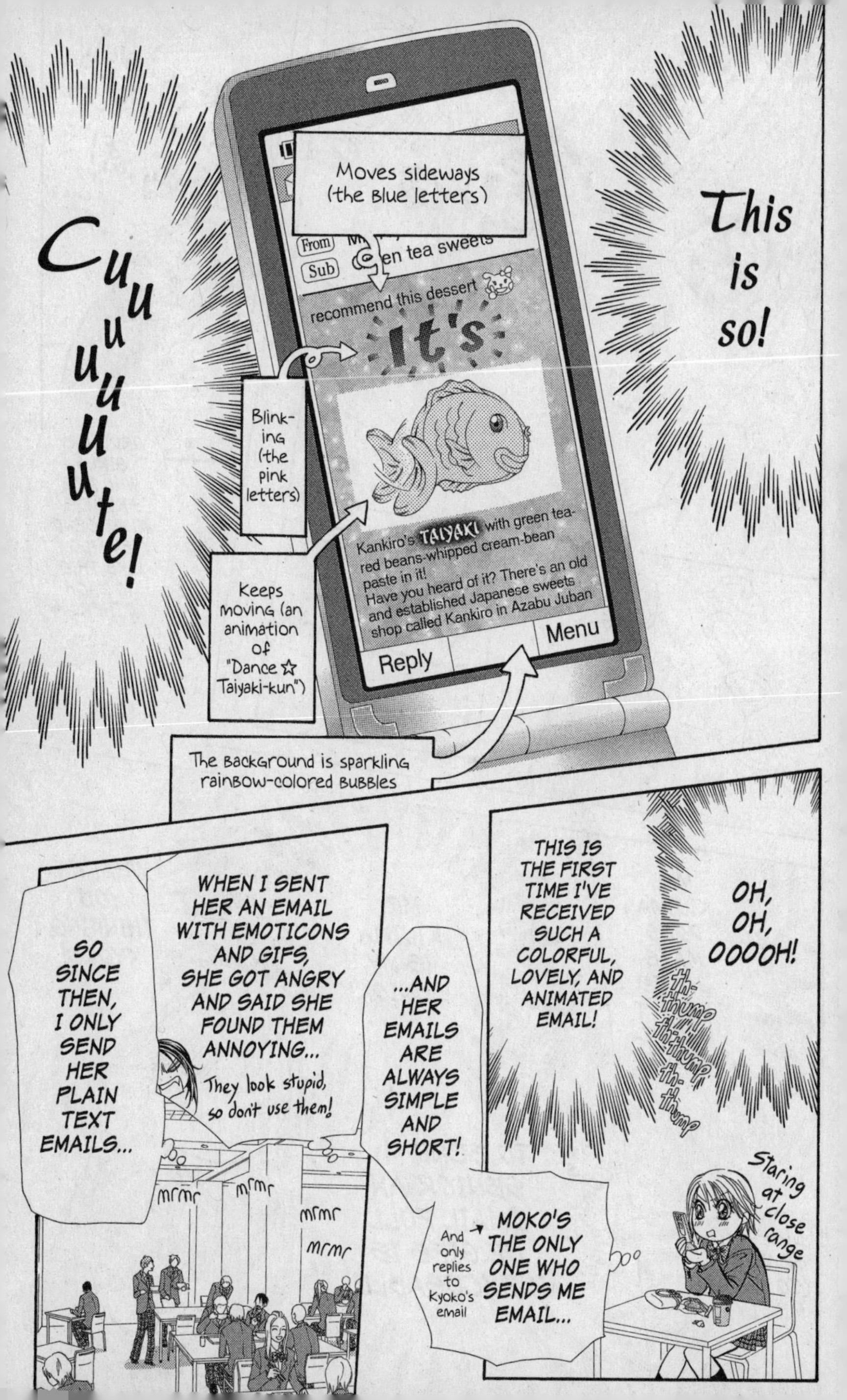
This is so!
Moves sideways (the Blue letters)
From
Sub
recommend this dessert
It's
Kankiro's TAIYAKI with green tea-red beans-whipped cream-bean paste in it!
Have you heard of it? There's an old and established Japanese sweets shop called Kankiro in Azabu Juban
Reply
Menu
Blinking (the pink letters)
Keeps moving (an animation of "Dance ☆ Taiyaki-kun")
The Background is sparkling rainbow-colored Bubbles
Cuuuuuuute!
OH, OH, OOOOH!
THIS IS THE FIRST TIME I'VE RECEIVED SUCH A COLORFUL, LOVELY, AND ANIMATED EMAIL!
th-thump th-thump th-thump
Staring at close range
MOKO'S THE ONLY ONE WHO SENDS ME EMAIL...
And only replies to Kyoko's email
...AND HER EMAILS ARE ALWAYS SIMPLE AND SHORT!
WHEN I SENT HER AN EMAIL WITH EMOTICONS AND GIFS, SHE GOT ANGRY AND SAID SHE FOUND THEM ANNOYING...
They look stupid, so don't use them!
SO SINCE THEN, I ONLY SEND HER PLAIN TEXT EMAILS...
mrmr
mrmr
mrmr
mrmr

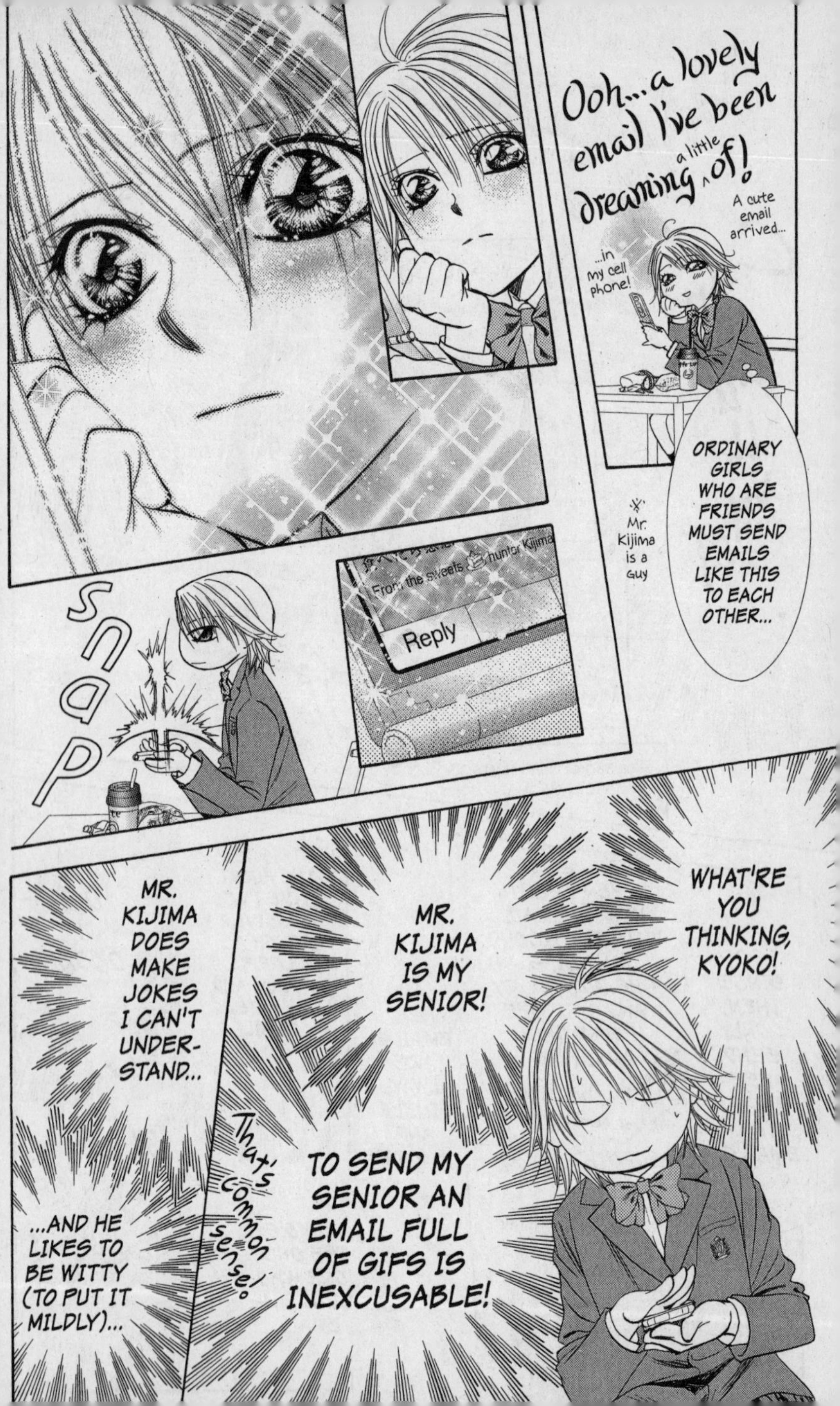

Ooh... a lovely email I've been dreaming a little of!
A cute email arrived...
...in my cell phone!
ORDINARY GIRLS WHO ARE FRIENDS MUST SEND EMAILS LIKE THIS TO EACH OTHER...
※ Mr. Kijima is a Guy
From the sweets hunter Kijima
Reply
snap
WHAT'RE YOU THINKING, KYOKO!
MR. KIJIMA IS MY SENIOR!
TO SEND MY SENIOR AN EMAIL FULL OF GIFS IS INEXCUSABLE!
That's common sense!
MR. KIJIMA DOES MAKE JOKES I CAN'T UNDER-STAND...
...AND HE LIKES TO BE WITTY (TO PUT IT MILDLY)...

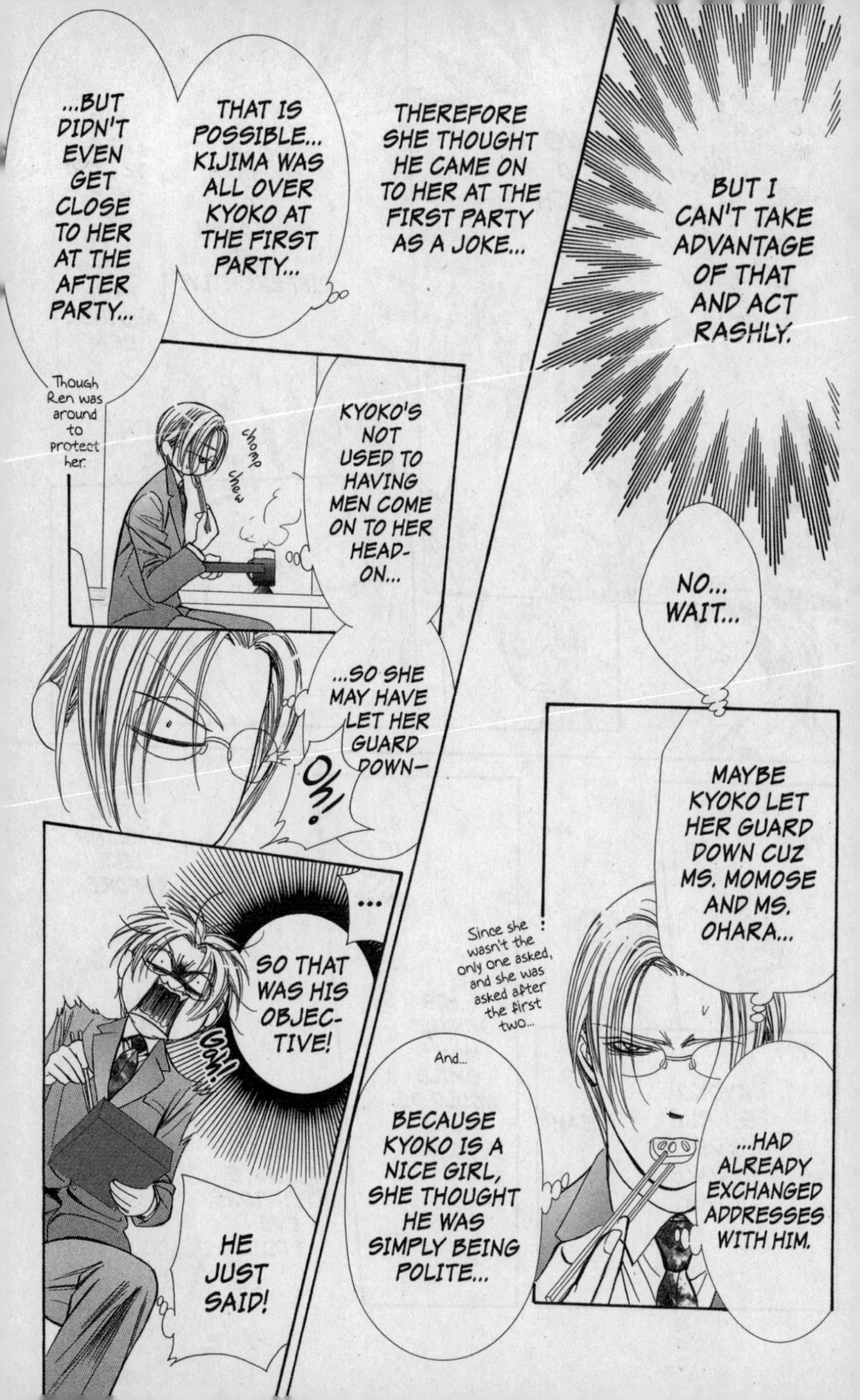
BUT I CAN'T TAKE ADVANTAGE OF THAT AND ACT RASHLY.
NO... WAIT...
MAYBE KYOKO LET HER GUARD DOWN CUZ MS. MOMOSE AND MS. OHARA...
...HAD ALREADY EXCHANGED ADDRESSES WITH HIM.
Since she wasn't the only one asked, and she was asked after the first two...
And...
BECAUSE KYOKO IS A NICE GIRL, SHE THOUGHT HE WAS SIMPLY BEING POLITE...
THEREFORE SHE THOUGHT HE CAME ON TO HER AT THE FIRST PARTY AS A JOKE...
THAT IS POSSIBLE... KIJIMA WAS ALL OVER KYOKO AT THE FIRST PARTY...
...BUT DIDN'T EVEN GET CLOSE TO HER AT THE AFTER PARTY...
Though Ren was around to protect her.
chomp
chew
KYOKO'S NOT USED TO HAVING MEN COME ON TO HER HEAD-ON...
...SO SHE MAY HAVE LET HER GUARD DOWN—
Oh!?
...
SO THAT WAS HIS OBJECTIVE!
Gah!
HE JUST SAID!

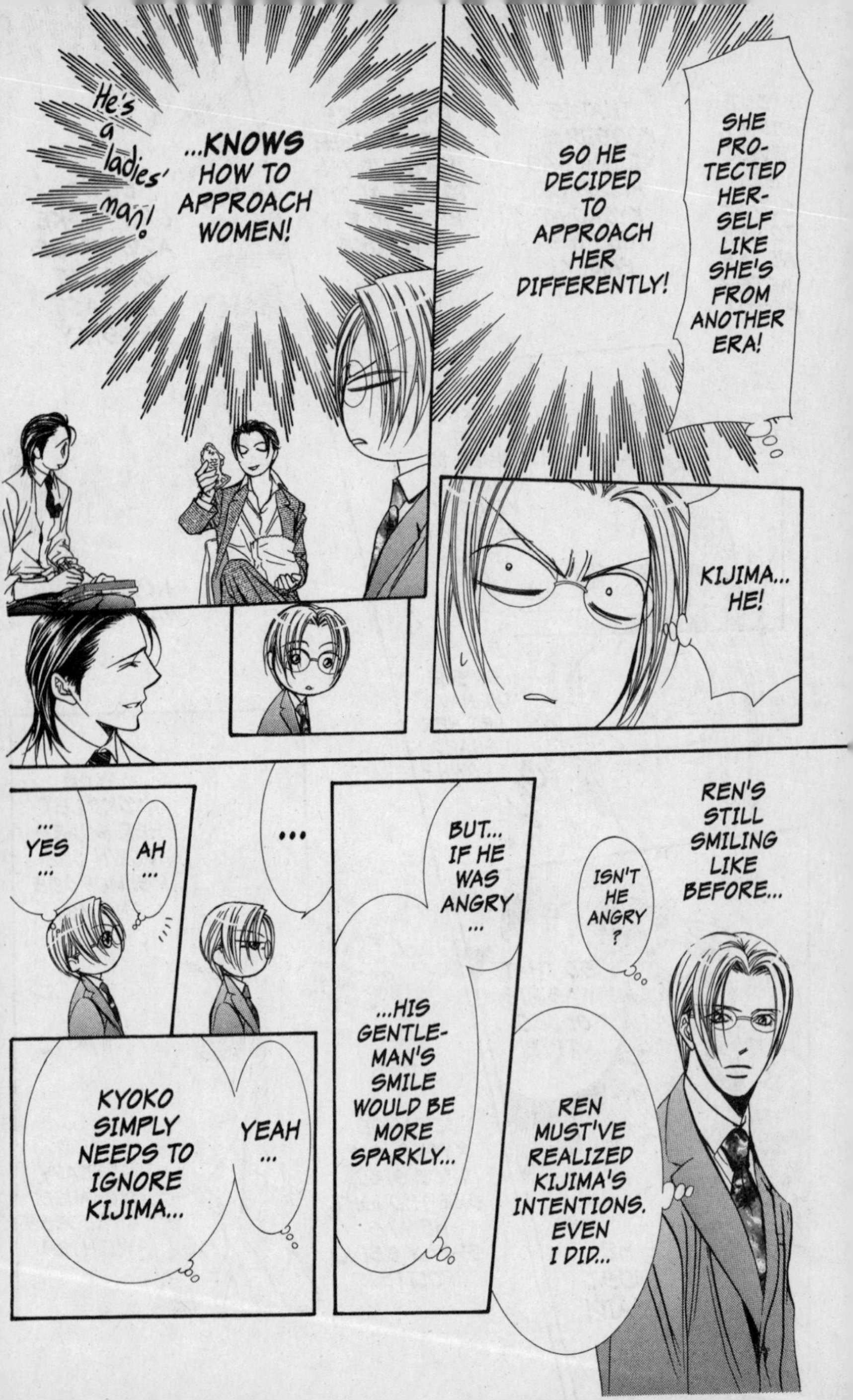
SHE PROTECTED HERSELF LIKE SHE'S FROM ANOTHER ERA!
SO HE DECIDED TO APPROACH HER DIFFERENTLY!
...KNOWS HOW TO APPROACH WOMEN!
He's a ladies' man!
KIJIMA... HE!
REN'S STILL SMILING LIKE BEFORE...
ISN'T HE ANGRY?
REN MUST'VE REALIZED KIJIMA'S INTENTIONS. EVEN I DID...
BUT... IF HE WAS ANGRY...
...HIS GENTLEMAN'S SMILE WOULD BE MORE SPARKLY...
...
AH...
...YES...
YEAH...
KYOKO SIMPLY NEEDS TO IGNORE KIJIMA...

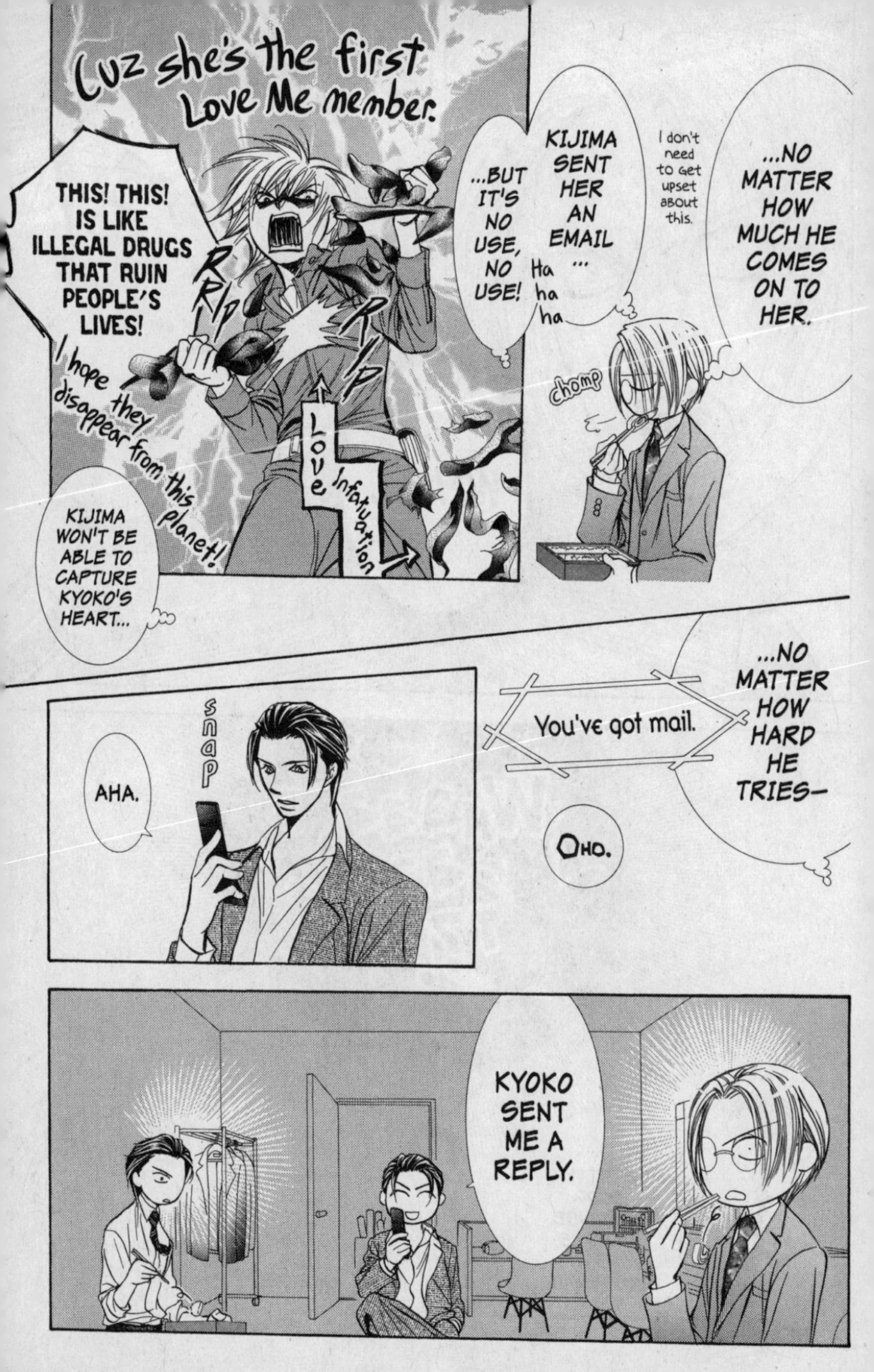
...NO MATTER HOW MUCH HE COMES ON TO HER.
I don't need to get upset about this.
KIJIMA SENT HER AN EMAIL...
...BUT IT'S NO USE, NO USE!
Ha ha ha
chomp
Cuz she's the first Love Me member.
THIS! THIS! IS LIKE ILLEGAL DRUGS THAT RUIN PEOPLE'S LIVES!
RIP
RIP
Love
Infatuation
I hope they disappear from this planet!
KIJIMA WON'T BE ABLE TO CAPTURE KYOKO'S HEART...
...NO MATTER HOW HARD HE TRIES—
You've got mail.
OHO.
snap
AHA.
KYOKO SENT ME A REPLY.

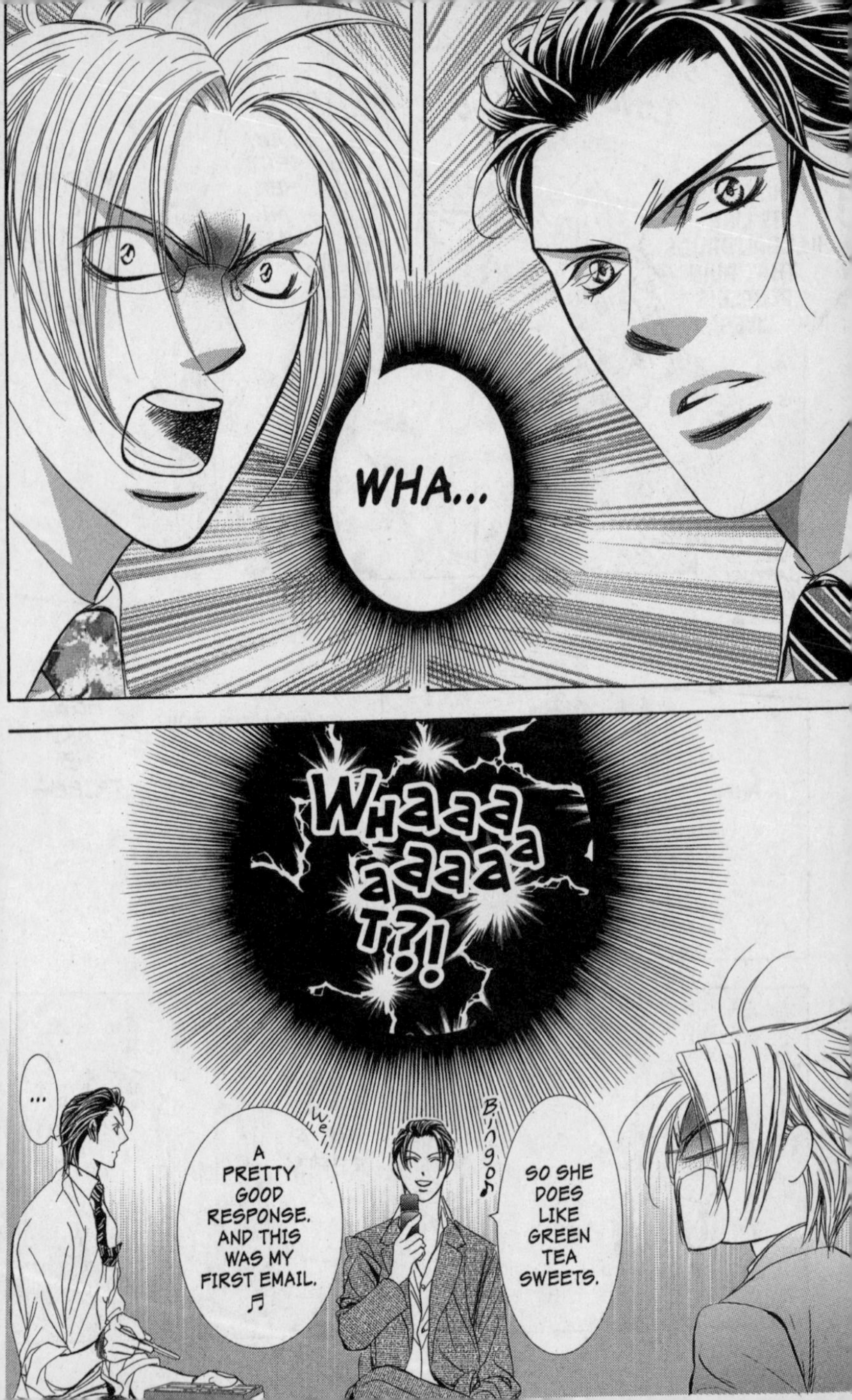
WHA...
WHAAAAAAAAAT?!
SO SHE DOES LIKE GREEN TEA SWEETS.
Bingo♪
A PRETTY GOOD RESPONSE. AND THIS WAS MY FIRST EMAIL. ♬
Well...
...

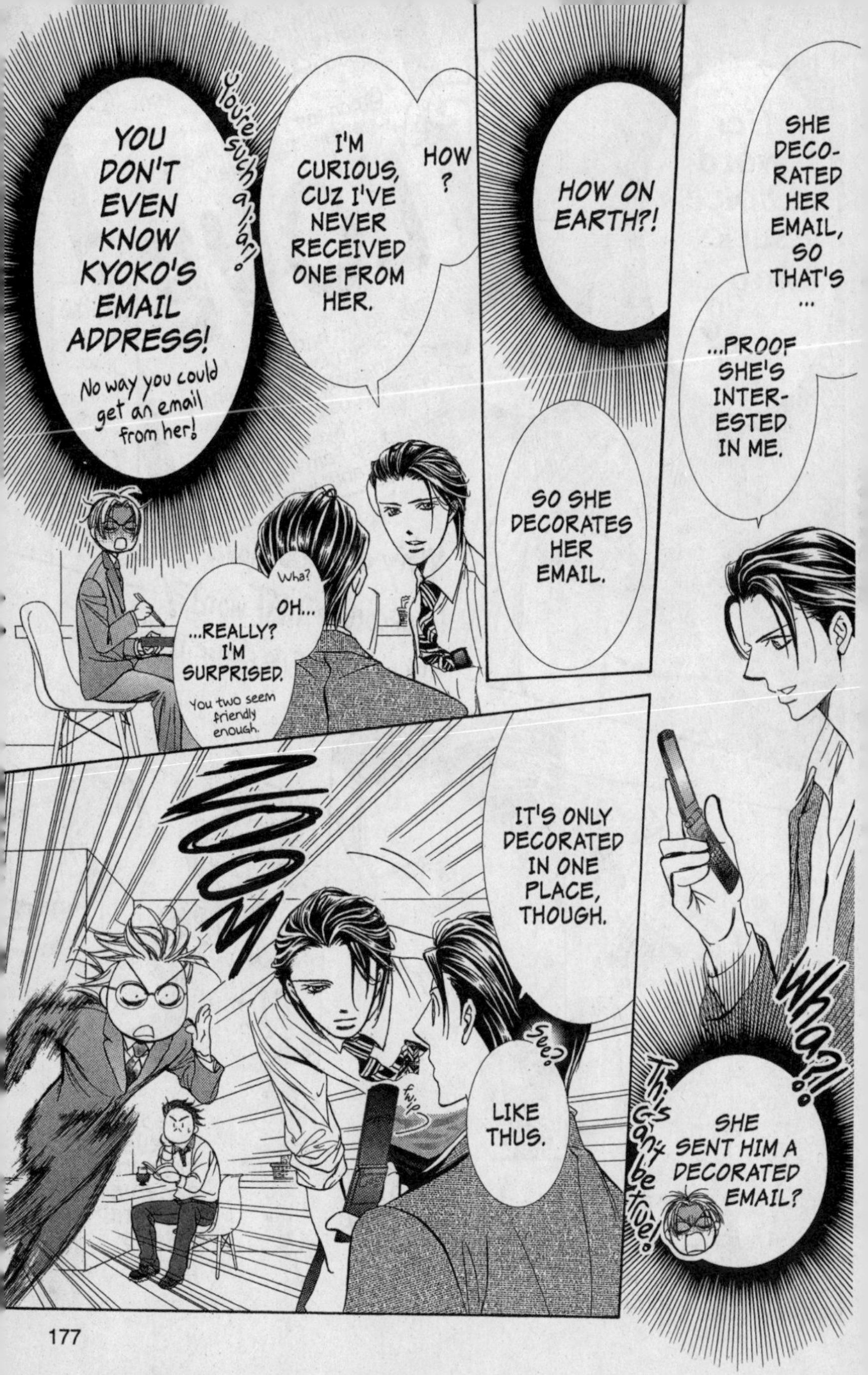
SHE DECORATED HER EMAIL, SO THAT'S ...
...PROOF SHE'S INTERESTED IN ME.
WHA?!!
SHE SENT HIM A DECORATED EMAIL?
This can't be true!
HOW ON EARTH?!
SO SHE DECORATES HER EMAIL.
You're such a liar!
YOU DON'T EVEN KNOW KYOKO'S EMAIL ADDRESS!
No way you could get an email from her!
HOW?
I'M CURIOUS, CUZ I'VE NEVER RECEIVED ONE FROM HER.
Wha?
OH...
...REALLY? I'M SURPRISED.
You two seem friendly enough.
IT'S ONLY DECORATED IN ONE PLACE, THOUGH.
See?
LIKE THUS.
fwip
ZOOM

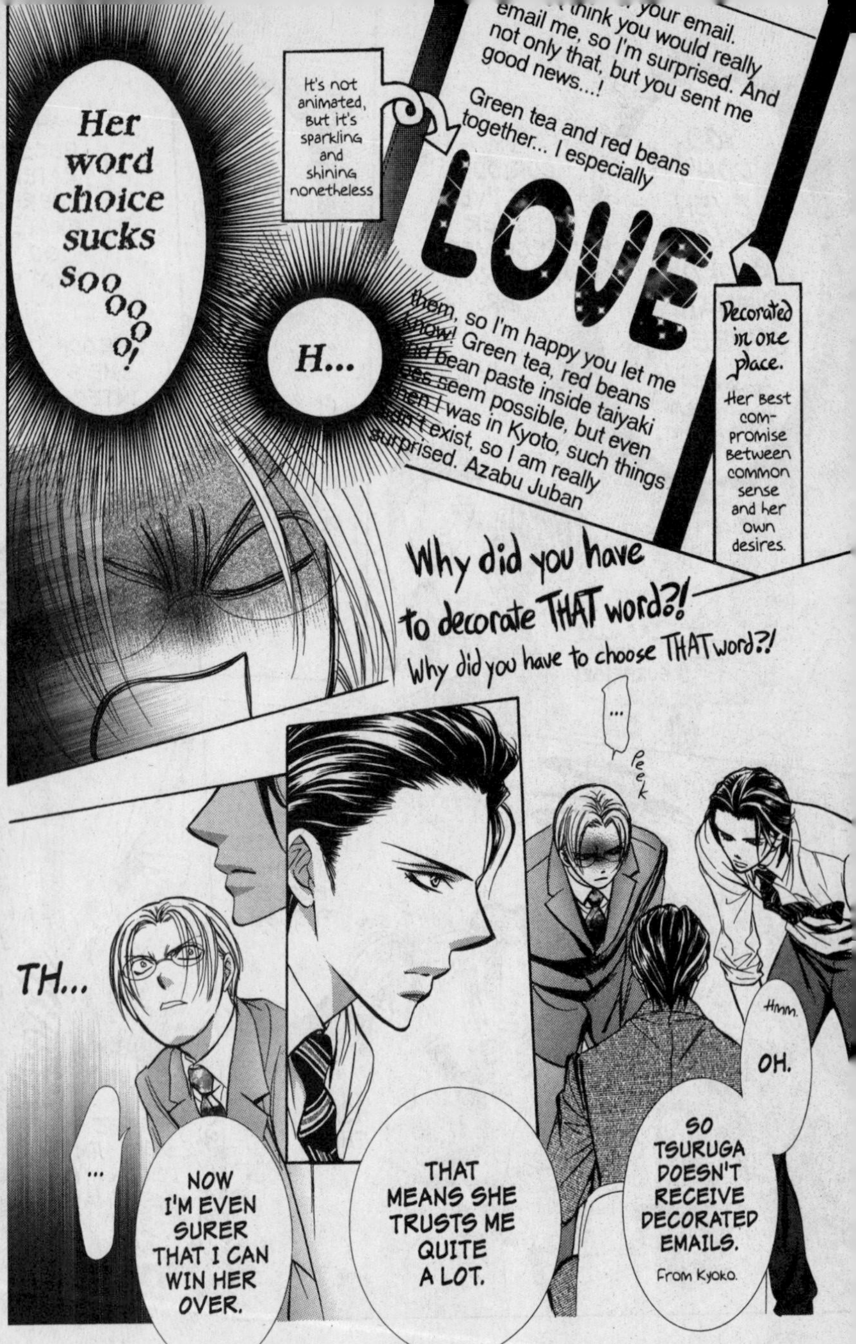

your email.
think you would really email me, so I'm surprised. And not only that, but you sent me good news...!
Green tea and red beans together... I especially
LOVE
them, so I'm happy you let me know! Green tea, red beans and bean paste inside taiyaki seem possible, but even when I was in Kyoto, such things t exist, so I am really surprised. Azabu Juban
Decorated in one place.
Her best compromise between common sense and her own desires.
It's not animated, but it's sparkling and shining nonetheless
H...
Her word choice sucks sooooo!
Why did you have to decorate THAT word?!
Why did you have to choose THAT word?!
...
Peek
Hmm.
OH.
SO TSURUGA DOESN'T RECEIVE DECORATED EMAILS.
From Kyoko.
THAT MEANS SHE TRUSTS ME QUITE A LOT.
TH...
...
NOW I'M EVEN SURER THAT I CAN WIN HER OVER.

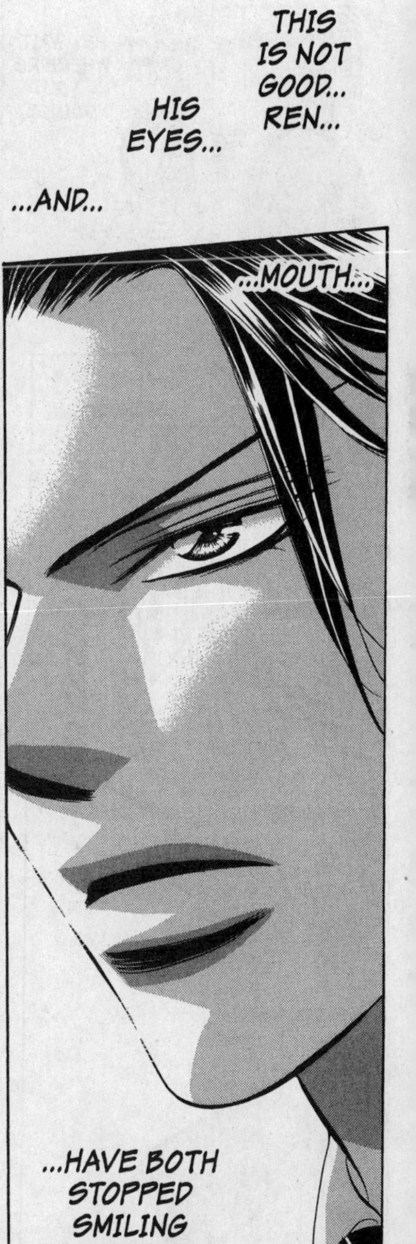
THIS IS NOT GOOD... REN...
HIS EYES...
...AND...
...MOUTH...
...HAVE BOTH STOPPED SMILING COMPLETELY...

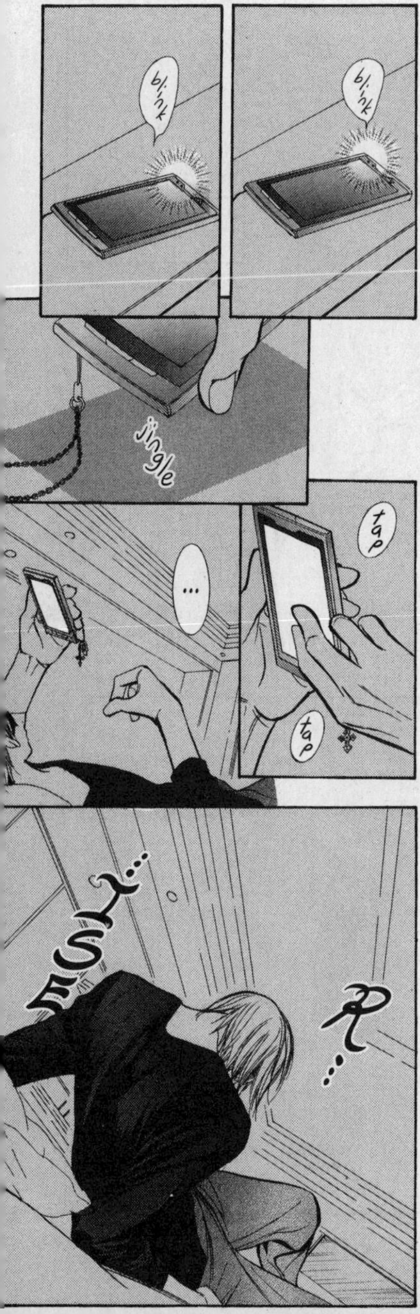
blink
blink
jingle
tap
tap
...
R...

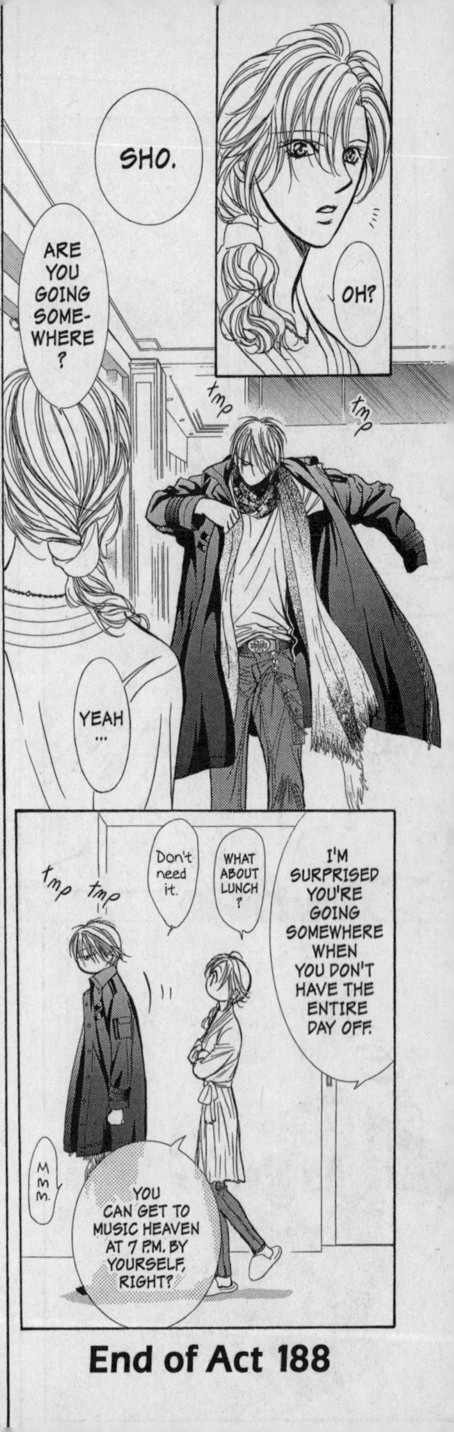
OH?
SHO.
ARE YOU GOING SOME-WHERE?
xmp
xmp
YEAH...
I'M SURPRISED YOU'RE GOING SOMEWHERE WHEN YOU DON'T HAVE THE ENTIRE DAY OFF.
WHAT ABOUT LUNCH?
Don't need it.
xmp tmp
YOU CAN GET TO MUSIC HEAVEN AT 7 P.M. BY YOURSELF, RIGHT?
Mmm.

End of Act 188

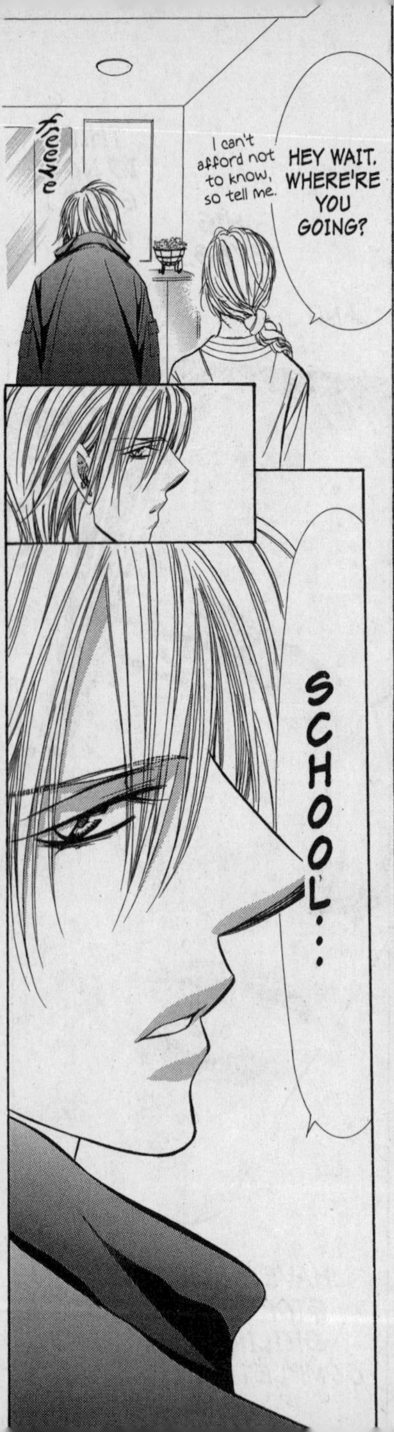
HEY WAIT. WHERE'RE YOU GOING?
I can't afford not to know, so tell me.
freeze
SCHOOL...

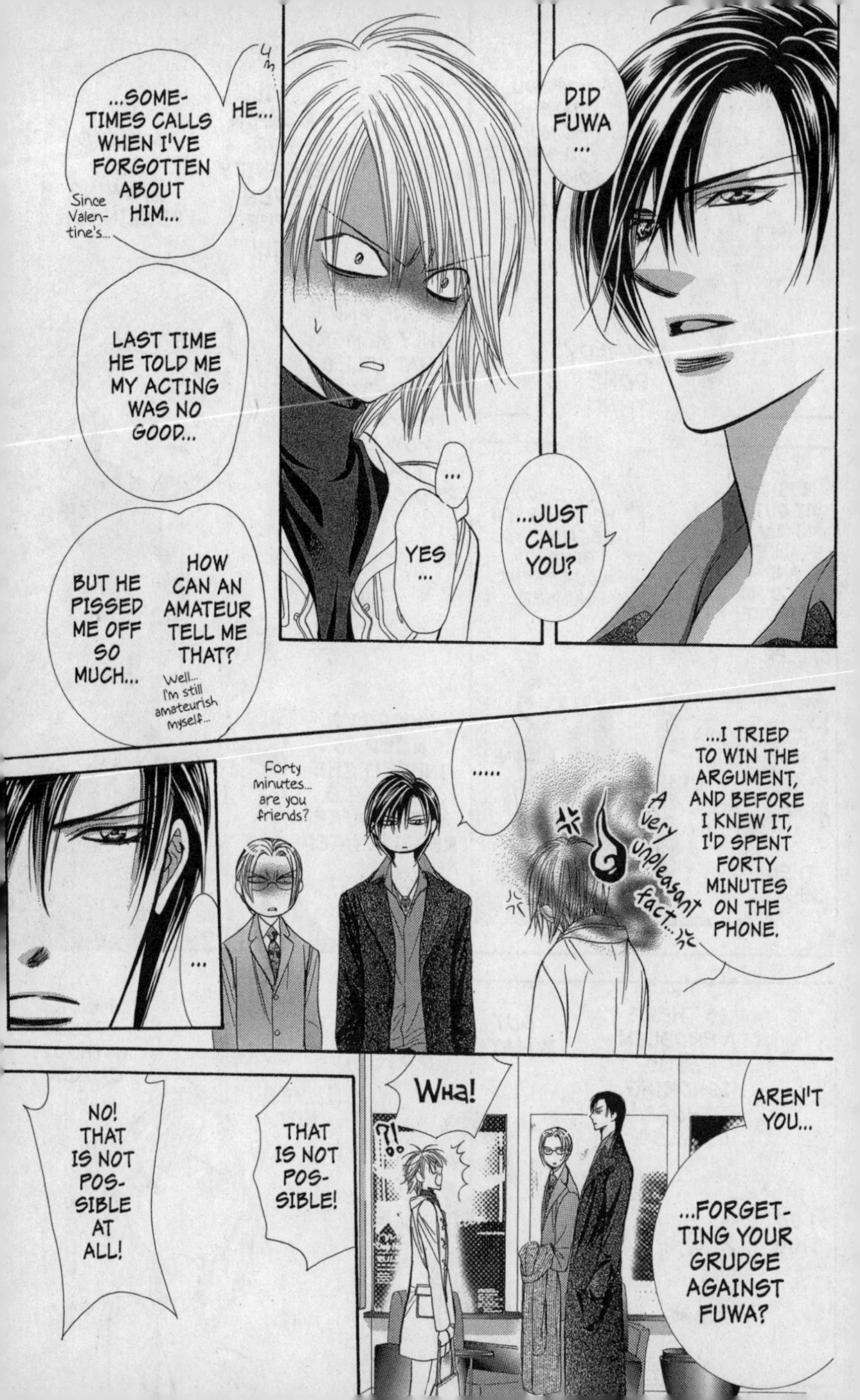
DID FUWA...
...JUST CALL YOU?
...
YES...
Um...
HE...
...SOMETIMES CALLS WHEN I'VE FORGOTTEN ABOUT HIM...
Since Valentine's...
LAST TIME HE TOLD ME MY ACTING WAS NO GOOD...
HOW CAN AN AMATEUR TELL ME THAT?
BUT HE PISSED ME OFF SO MUCH...
Well... I'm still amateurish myself...
...I TRIED TO WIN THE ARGUMENT, AND BEFORE I KNEW IT, I'D SPENT FORTY MINUTES ON THE PHONE.
A very unpleasant fact...
.....
Forty minutes... are you friends?
...
AREN'T YOU...
...FORGETTING YOUR GRUDGE AGAINST FUWA?
WHA!
?!
THAT IS NOT POSSIBLE!
NO! THAT IS NOT POSSIBLE AT ALL!

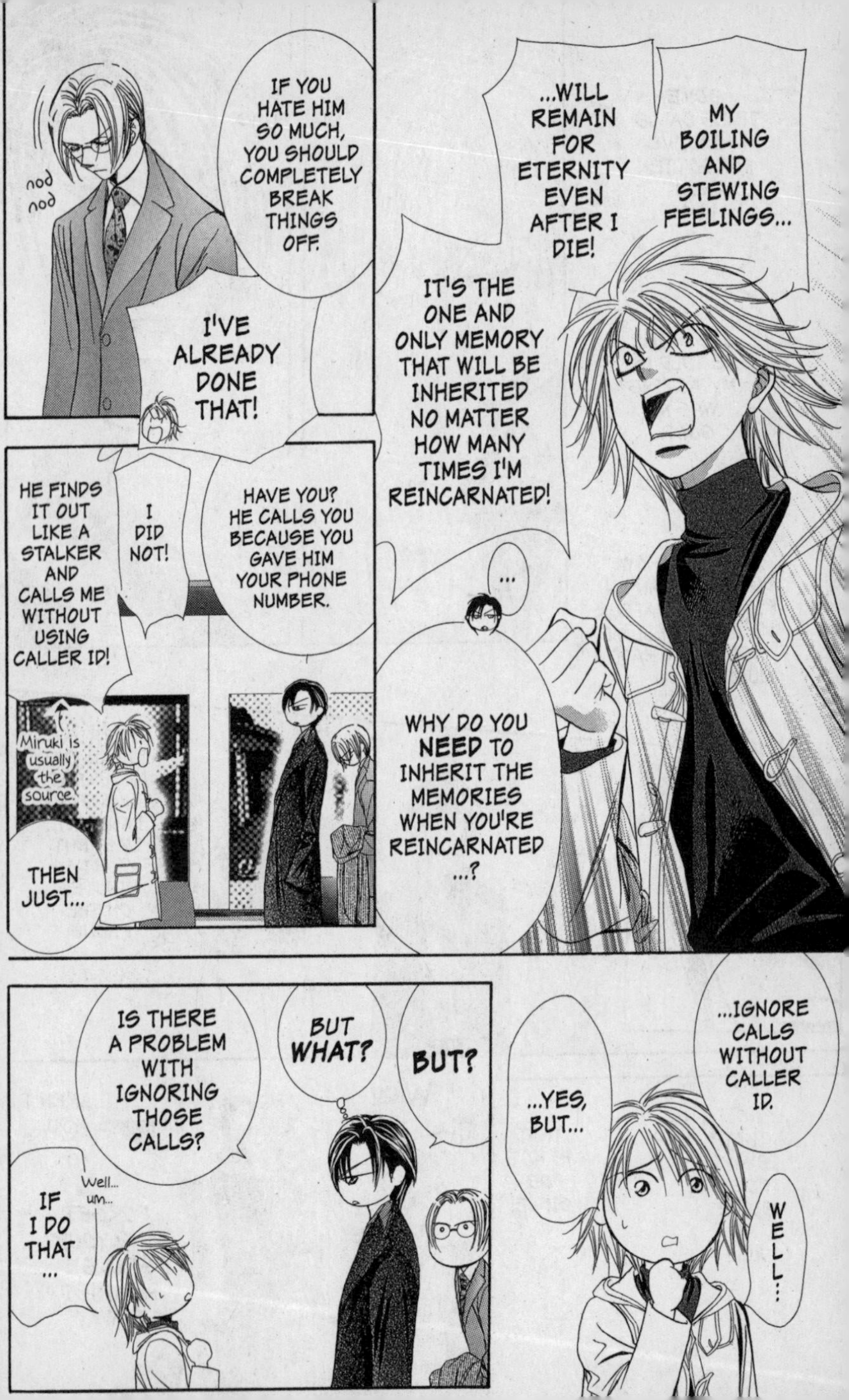
MY BOILING AND STEWING FEELINGS...
...WILL REMAIN FOR ETERNITY EVEN AFTER I DIE!
IT'S THE ONE AND ONLY MEMORY THAT WILL BE INHERITED NO MATTER HOW MANY TIMES I'M REINCARNATED!
...
WHY DO YOU NEED TO INHERIT THE MEMORIES WHEN YOU'RE REINCARNATED ...?
IF YOU HATE HIM SO MUCH, YOU SHOULD COMPLETELY BREAK THINGS OFF.
nod nod
I'VE ALREADY DONE THAT!
HAVE YOU? HE CALLS YOU BECAUSE YOU GAVE HIM YOUR PHONE NUMBER.
I DID NOT!
HE FINDS IT OUT LIKE A STALKER AND CALLS ME WITHOUT USING CALLER ID!
Miruki is usually the source.
THEN JUST...
...IGNORE CALLS WITHOUT CALLER ID.
...YES, BUT...
WELL...
BUT?
BUT WHAT?
IS THERE A PROBLEM WITH IGNORING THOSE CALLS?
Well... um...
IF I DO THAT ...

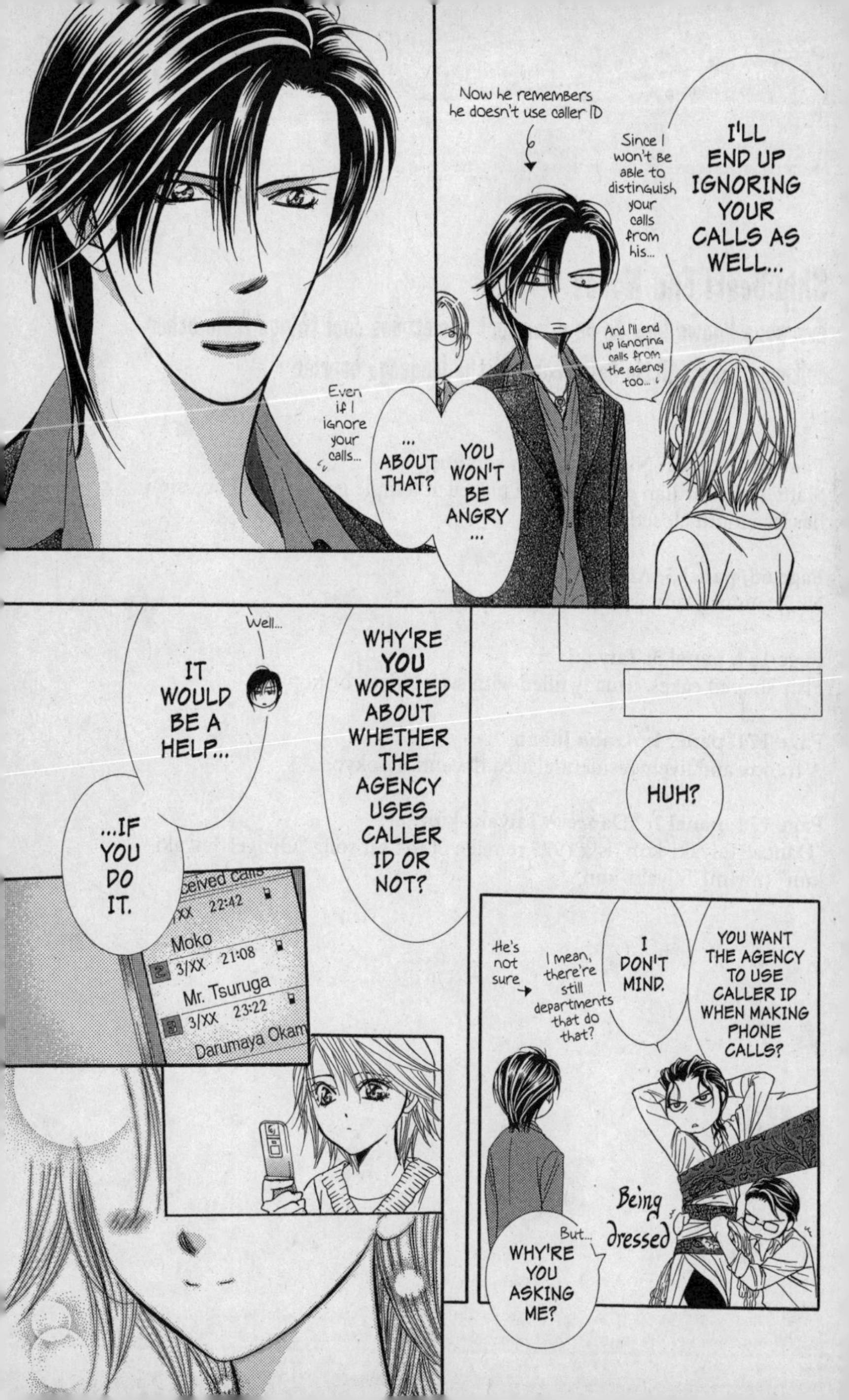
I'LL END UP IGNORING YOUR CALLS AS WELL...
Since I won't be able to distinguish your calls from his...
And I'll end up ignoring calls from the agency too...
Now he remembers he doesn't use caller ID
YOU WON'T BE ANGRY...
...ABOUT THAT?
Even if I ignore your calls...
HUH?
YOU WANT THE AGENCY TO USE CALLER ID WHEN MAKING PHONE CALLS?
I DON'T MIND.
I mean, there're still departments that do that?
He's not sure
Being dressed
But...
WHY'RE YOU ASKING ME?
WHY'RE YOU WORRIED ABOUT WHETHER THE AGENCY USES CALLER ID OR NOT?
Well...
IT WOULD BE A HELP...
...IF YOU DO IT.
Moko 3/XX 21:08
Mr. Tsuruga 3/XX 23:22
Darumaya Okam

Skip·Beat! End Notes
Everyone knows how to be a fan, but sometimes cool things from other cultures need a little help crossing the language barrier.

Page 68, panel 1: Nio statue, Un version
Statues of guardian gods that are placed at temple gates. The Un version has its mouth closed.

Page 68, panel 5: Ah version
Nio statue version with its mouth open.

Page 164, panel 3: Taiyaki
Fish-shaped cakes, usually filled with sweet black bean paste.

Page 171, panel 1: Azabu Juban
A trendy and lively residential area in central Tokyo.

Page 171, panel 1: "Dance ★ Taiyaki-kun"
"Dance! Taiyaki-kun" is a 1975 remake of the hit song "Oyoge! Taiyaki-kun" (Swim! Taiyaki-kun).

Shojo Beat

Skip·Beat!

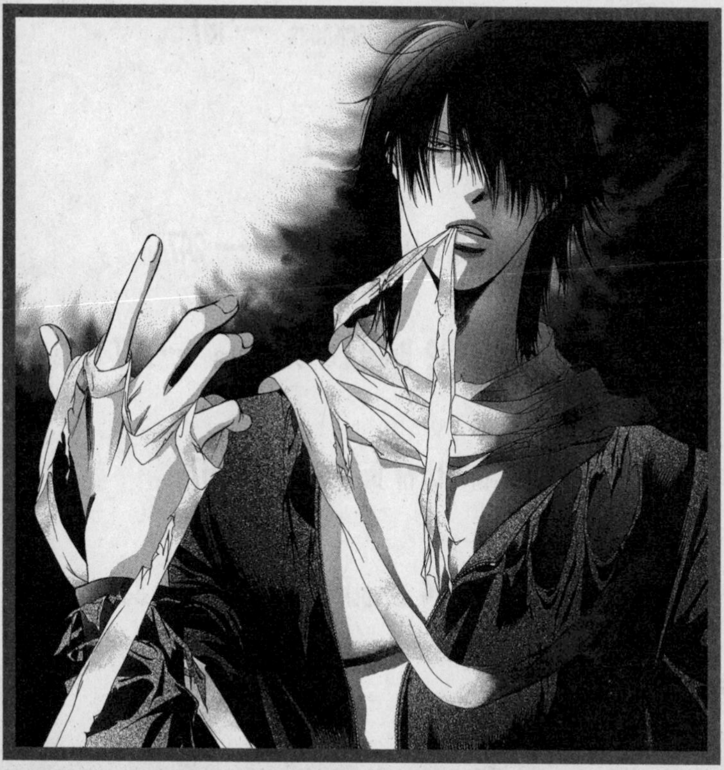

Skip·Beat!

Volume 32

CONTENTS

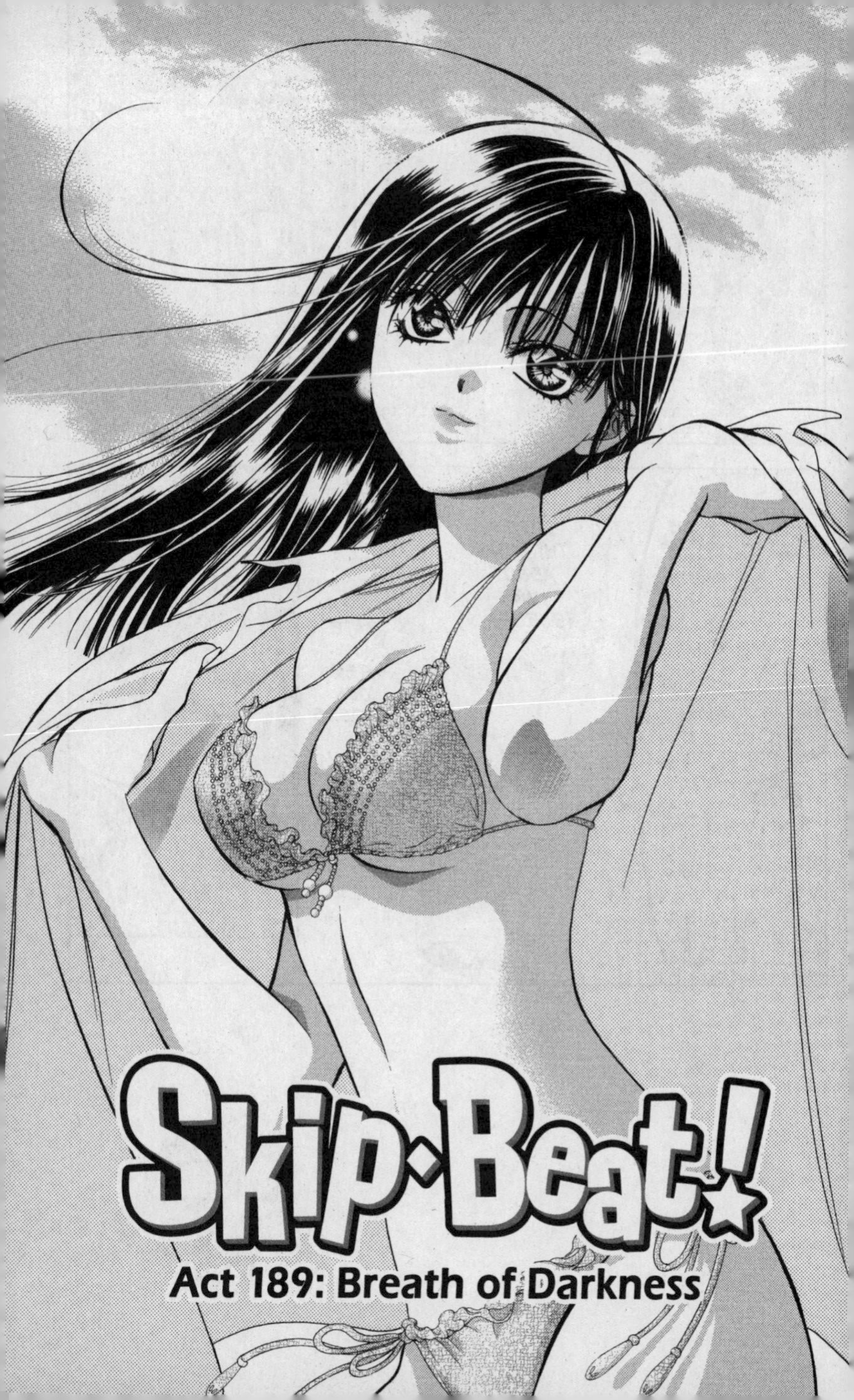
Skip·Beat!
Act 189: Breath of Darkness

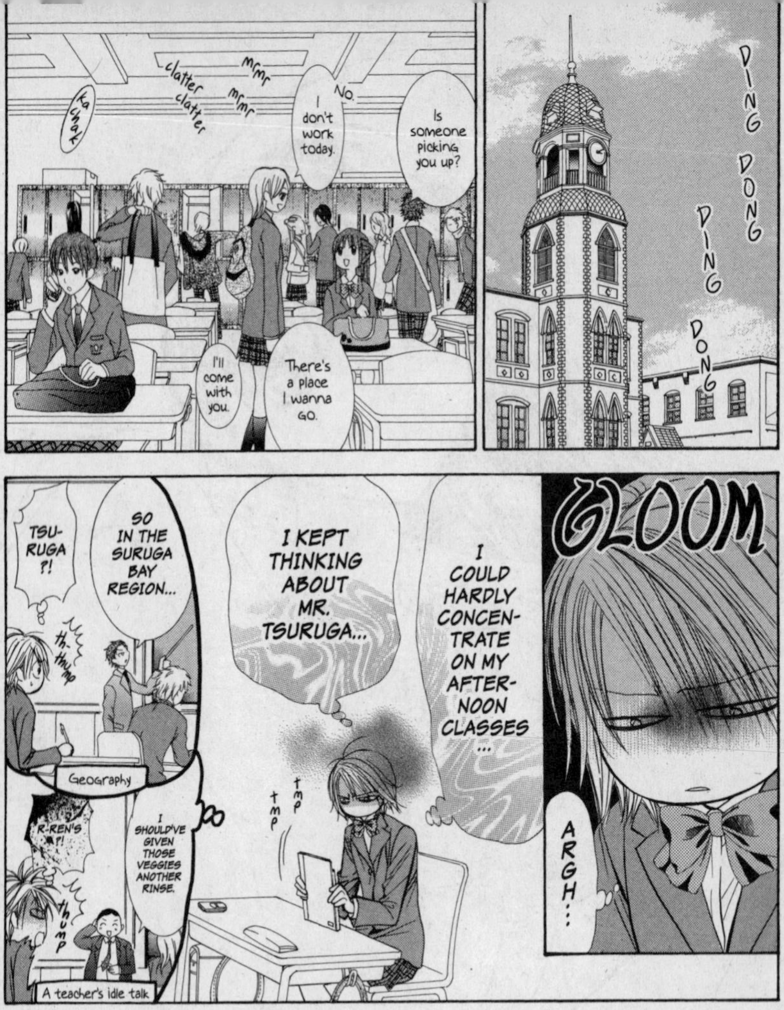
DING DONG
DING DONG
Is someone picking you up?
No.
I don't work today.
mrmr
mrmr
clatter clatter
ka chak
There's a place I wanna GO.
I'll come with you.
GLOOM
ARGH...
I COULD HARDLY CONCENTRATE ON MY AFTERNOON CLASSES...
I KEPT THINKING ABOUT MR. TSURUGA...
tmp
tmp
SO IN THE SURUGA BAY REGION...
TSURUGA?!
th-thump
Geography
I SHOULD'VE GIVEN THOSE VEGGIES ANOTHER RINSE.
R-REN'S?!
thump
A teacher's idle talk

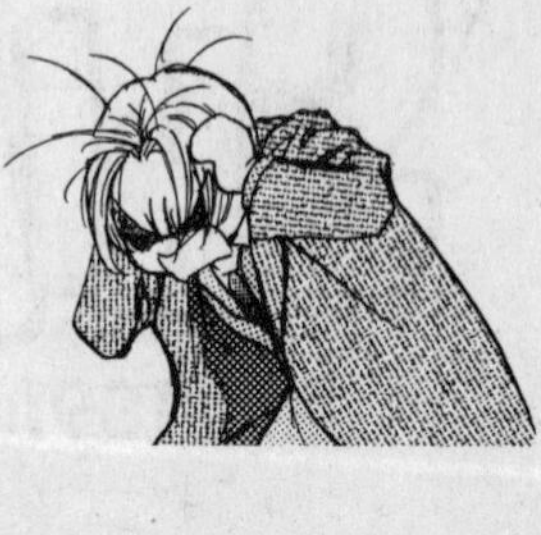

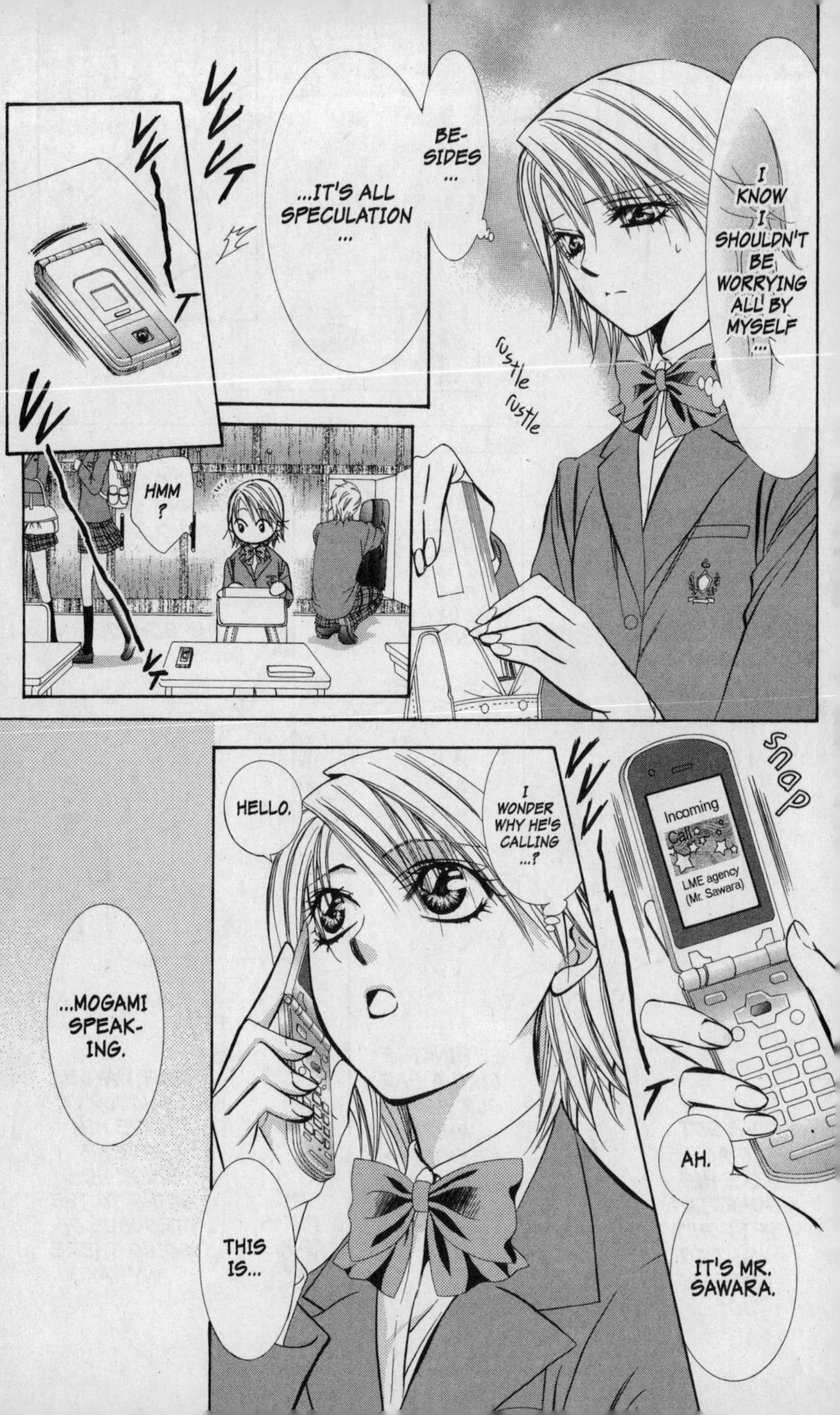
I KNOW I SHOULDN'T BE WORRYING ALL BY MYSELF...
BE-SIDES...
...IT'S ALL SPECULATION...
rustle rustle
VVVT
VVVT
HMM?
VVT
snap
Incoming Call
LME agency (Mr. Sawara)
VVVT
AH.
IT'S MR. SAWARA.
I WONDER WHY HE'S CALLING...?
HELLO.
THIS IS...
...MOGAMI SPEAK-ING.

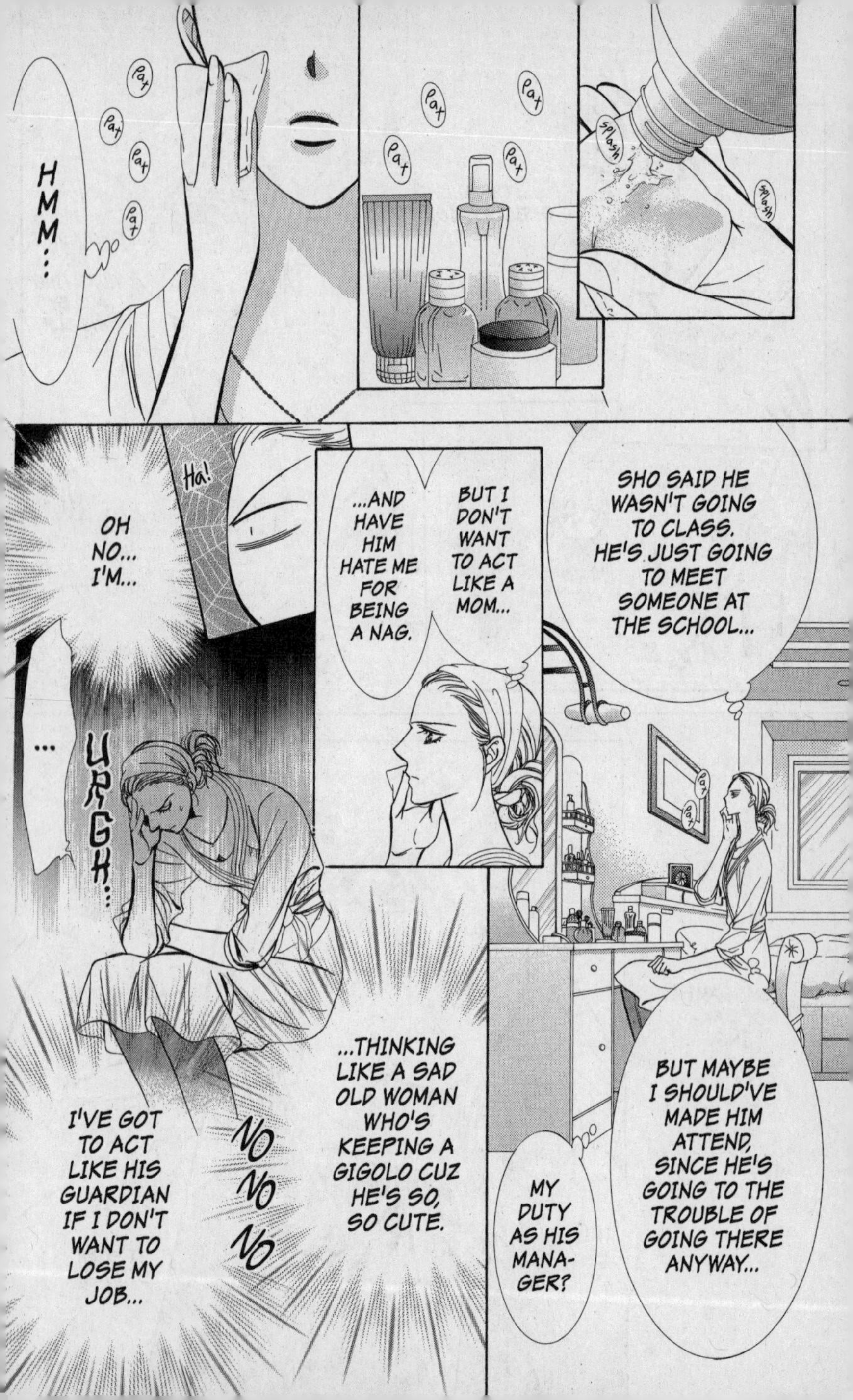
splash
splash
Pat
Pat
Pat
Pat
Pat
Pat
Pat
HMM...
SHO SAID HE WASN'T GOING TO CLASS. HE'S JUST GOING TO MEET SOMEONE AT THE SCHOOL...
Pat
Pat
BUT MAYBE I SHOULD'VE MADE HIM ATTEND, SINCE HE'S GOING TO THE TROUBLE OF GOING THERE ANYWAY...
MY DUTY AS HIS MANAGER?
BUT I DON'T WANT TO ACT LIKE A MOM...
...AND HAVE HIM HATE ME FOR BEING A NAG.
Ha!
OH NO... I'M...
...THINKING LIKE A SAD OLD WOMAN WHO'S KEEPING A GIGOLO CUZ HE'S SO, SO CUTE.
NO NO NO
I'VE GOT TO ACT LIKE HIS GUARDIAN IF I DON'T WANT TO LOSE MY JOB...
...
URGH...

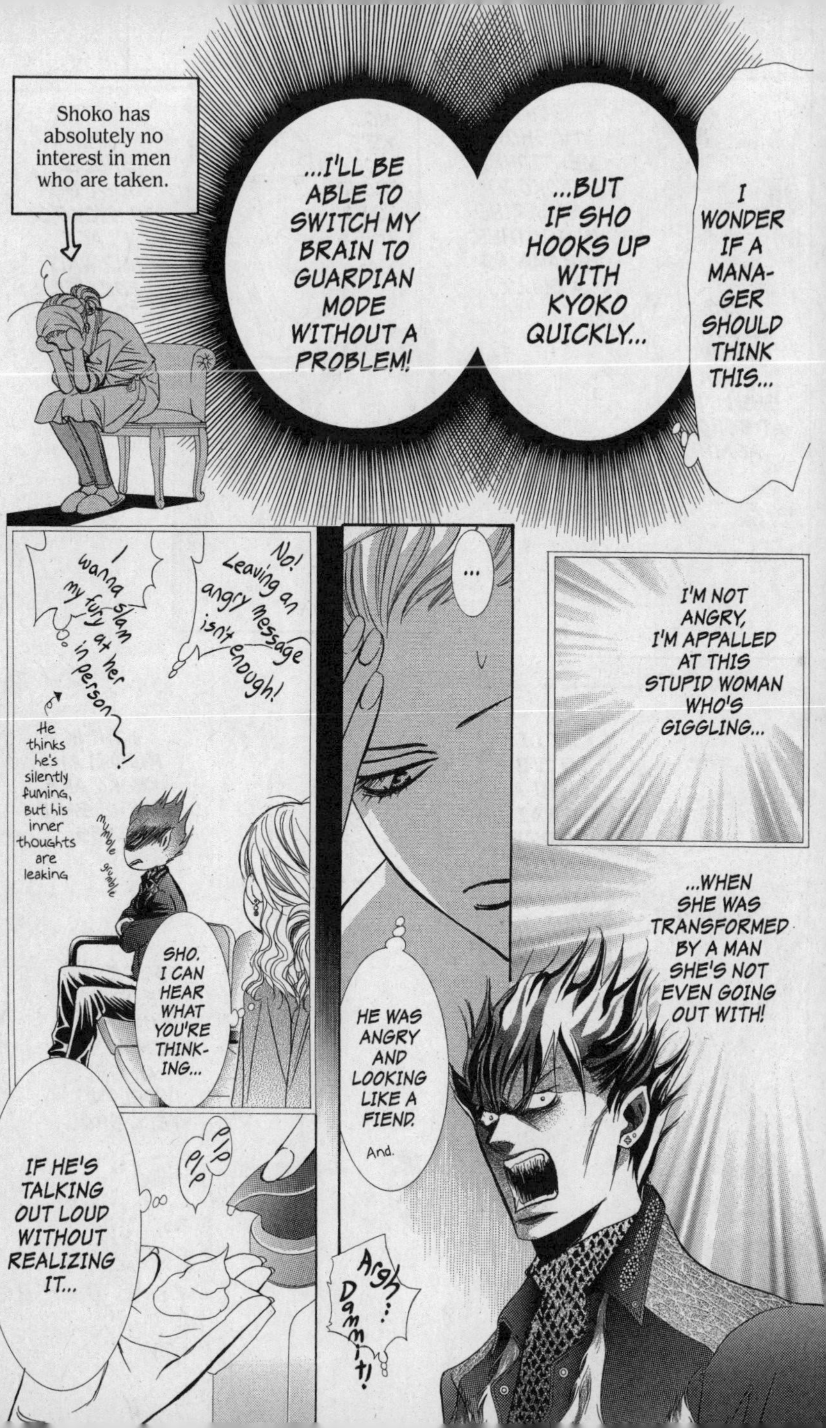
I WONDER IF A MANA-GER SHOULD THINK THIS...
...BUT IF SHO HOOKS UP WITH KYOKO QUICKLY...
...I'LL BE ABLE TO SWITCH MY BRAIN TO GUARDIAN MODE WITHOUT A PROBLEM!
Shoko has absolutely no interest in men who are taken.
...
I'M NOT ANGRY, I'M APPALLED AT THIS STUPID WOMAN WHO'S GIGGLING...
...WHEN SHE WAS TRANSFORMED BY A MAN SHE'S NOT EVEN GOING OUT WITH!
HE WAS ANGRY AND LOOKING LIKE A FIEND.
And.
Argh... Dammit!
No! Leaving an angry message isn't enough!
I wanna slam my fury at her in person~!
He thinks he's silently fuming, but his inner thoughts are leaking
mumble grumble
SHO. I CAN HEAR WHAT YOU'RE THINK-ING...
Pip pip
IF HE'S TALKING OUT LOUD WITHOUT REALIZING IT...

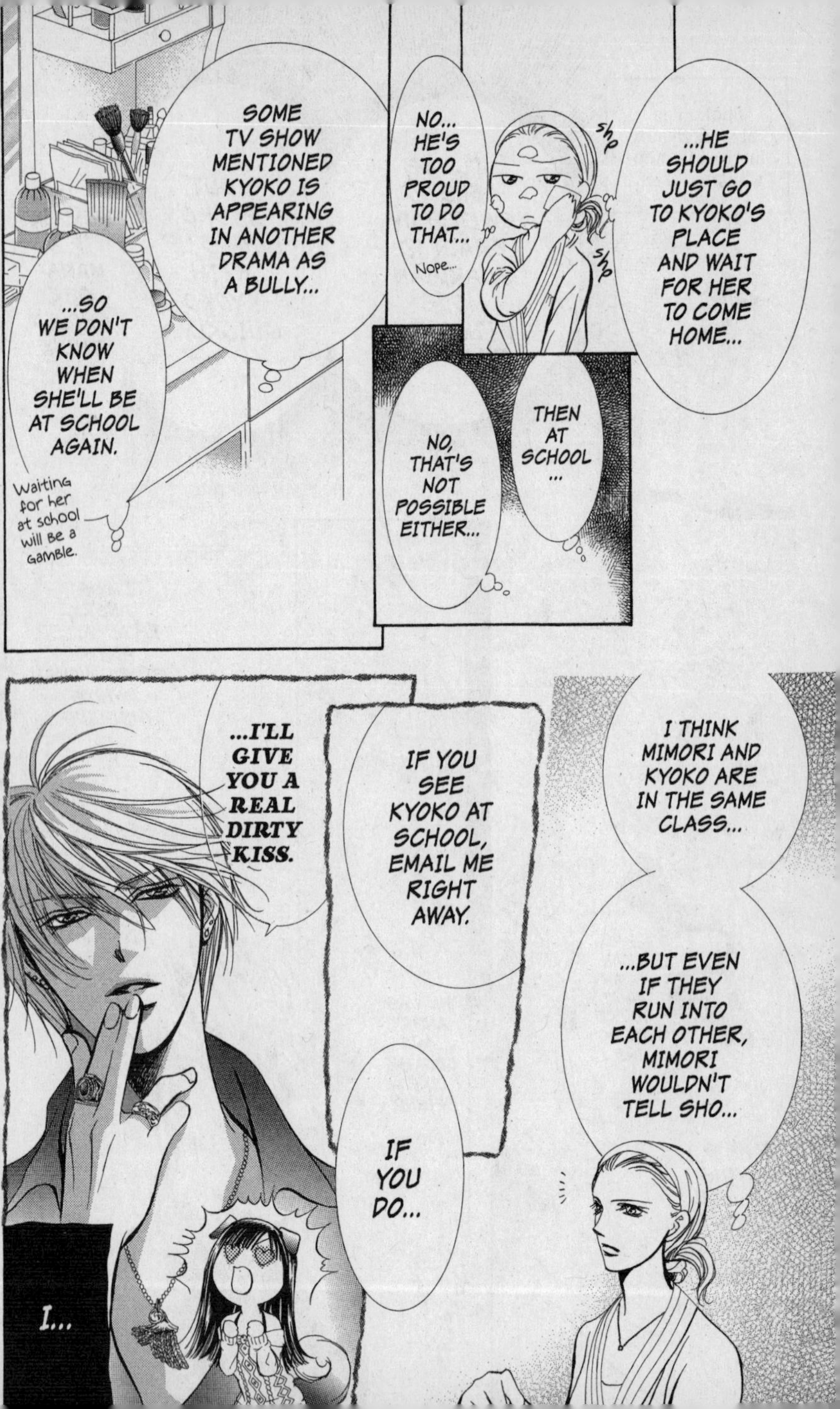
...HE SHOULD JUST GO TO KYOKO'S PLACE AND WAIT FOR HER TO COME HOME...
shp
shp
NO... HE'S TOO PROUD TO DO THAT...
Nope...
THEN AT SCHOOL...
NO, THAT'S NOT POSSIBLE EITHER...
SOME TV SHOW MENTIONED KYOKO IS APPEARING IN ANOTHER DRAMA AS A BULLY...
...SO WE DON'T KNOW WHEN SHE'LL BE AT SCHOOL AGAIN.
Waiting for her at school will be a gamble.
I THINK MIMORI AND KYOKO ARE IN THE SAME CLASS...
...BUT EVEN IF THEY RUN INTO EACH OTHER, MIMORI WOULDN'T TELL SHO...
IF YOU SEE KYOKO AT SCHOOL, EMAIL ME RIGHT AWAY.
IF YOU DO...
...I'LL GIVE YOU A REAL DIRTY KISS.
I...

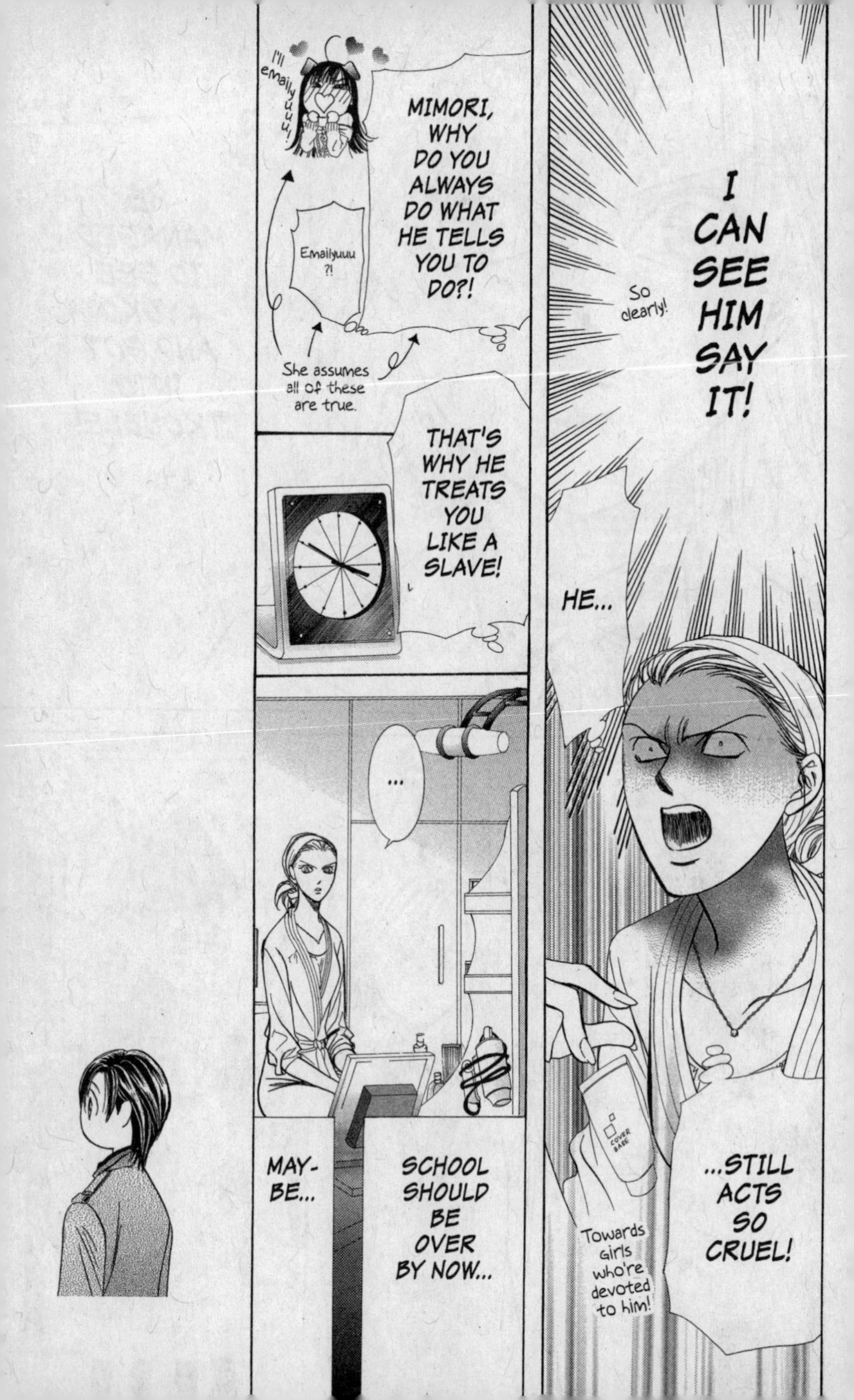

I CAN SEE HIM SAY IT!
So clearly!
HE...
...STILL ACTS SO CRUEL!
Towards Girls who're devoted to him!
COVER BASE
MIMORI, WHY DO YOU ALWAYS DO WHAT HE TELLS YOU TO DO?!
I'll emailyuuu!
Emailyuuu ?!
She assumes all of these are true.
THAT'S WHY HE TREATS YOU LIKE A SLAVE!
...
SCHOOL SHOULD BE OVER BY NOW...
MAY-BE...

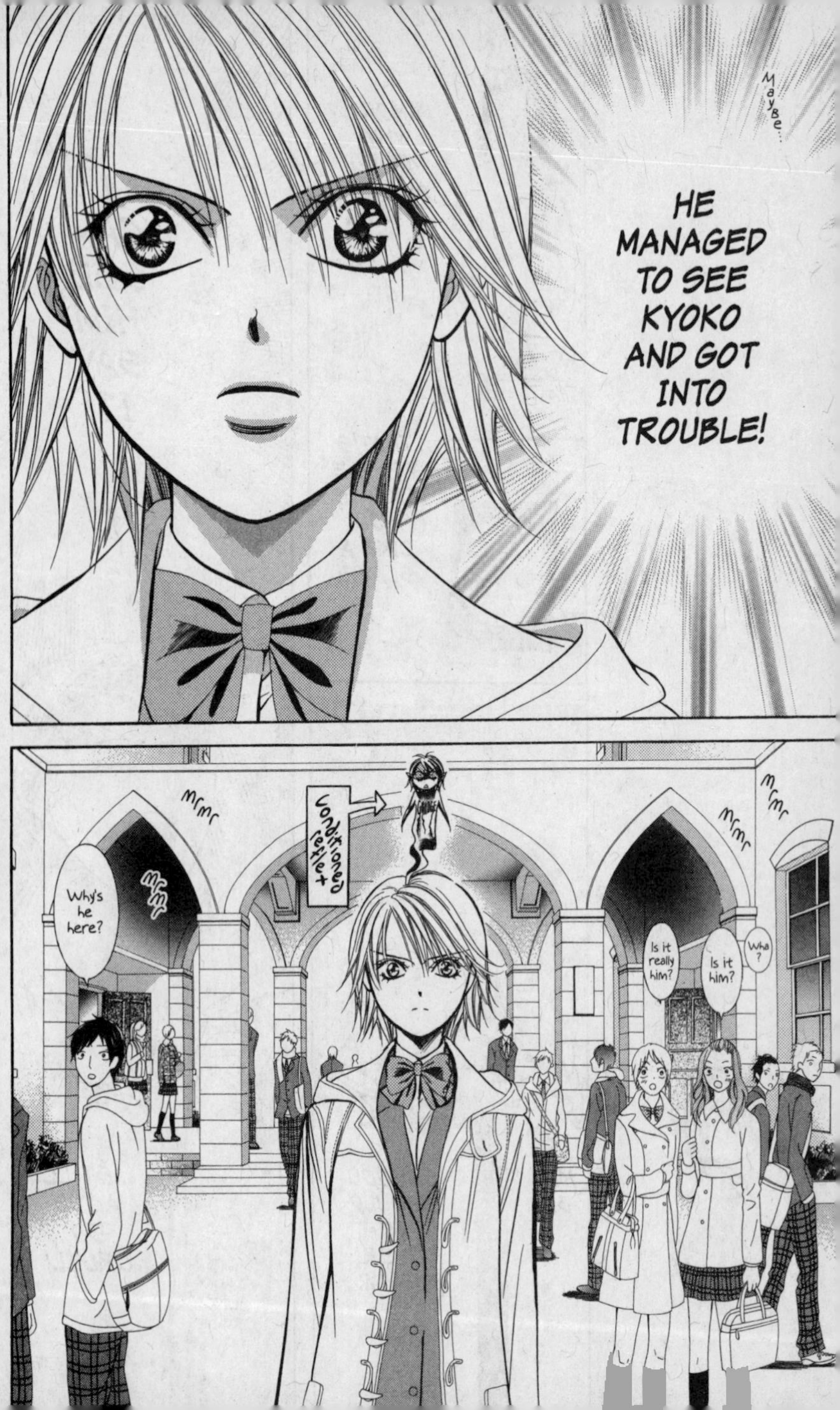
Maybe...
HE MANAGED TO SEE KYOKO AND GOT INTO TROUBLE!
mrmr
Wha?
Is it him?
Is it really him?
mrmr
Conditioned reflex
mrmr
mrmr
Why's he here?

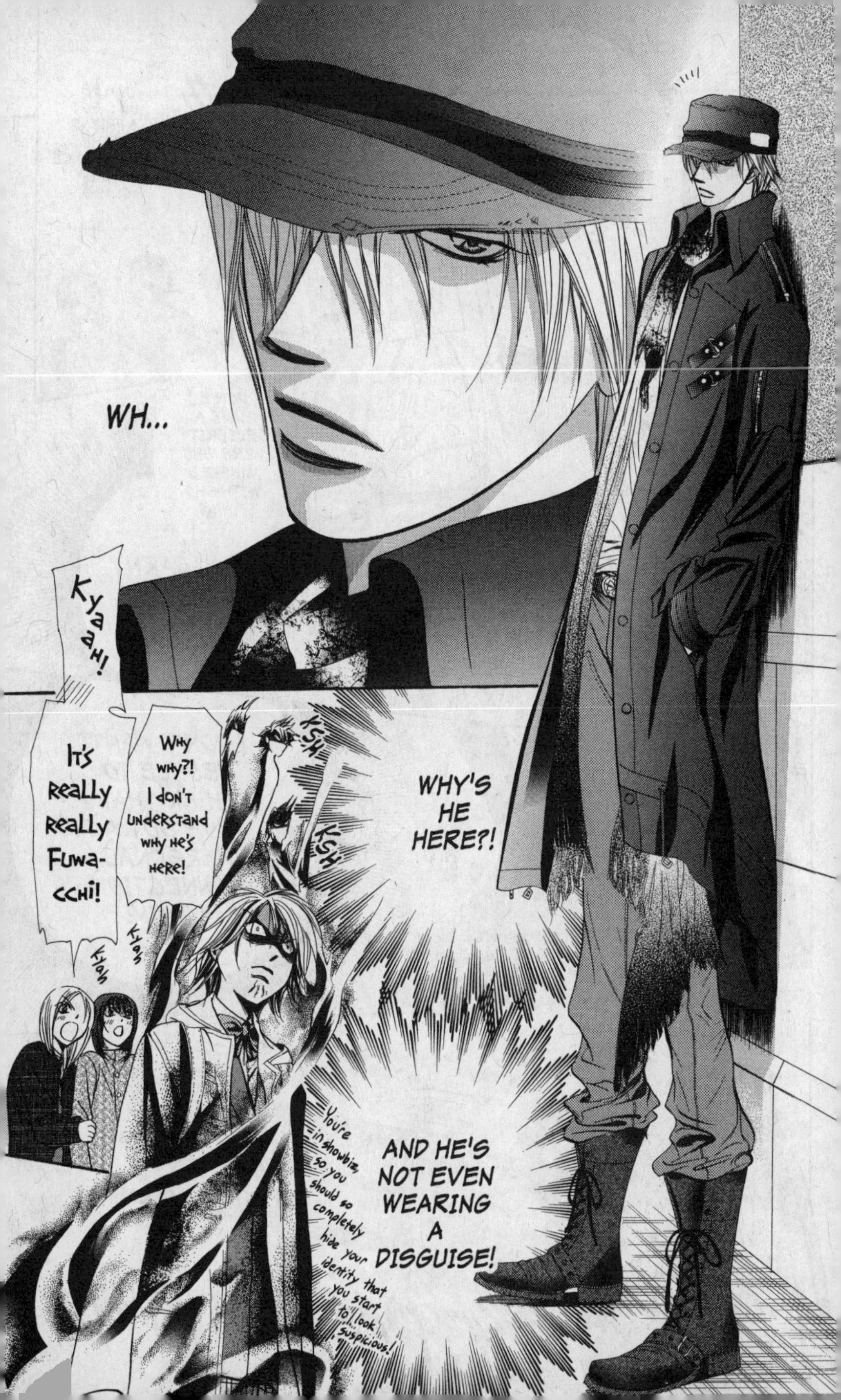
WH...
WHY'S HE HERE?!
Kyaah!
It's really really Fuwa-cchi!
Why why?! I don't understand why he's here!
KSH
KSH
Kyah kyah
AND HE'S NOT EVEN WEARING A DISGUISE!
You're in showbiz, so you should so completely hide your identity that you start to look suspicious!

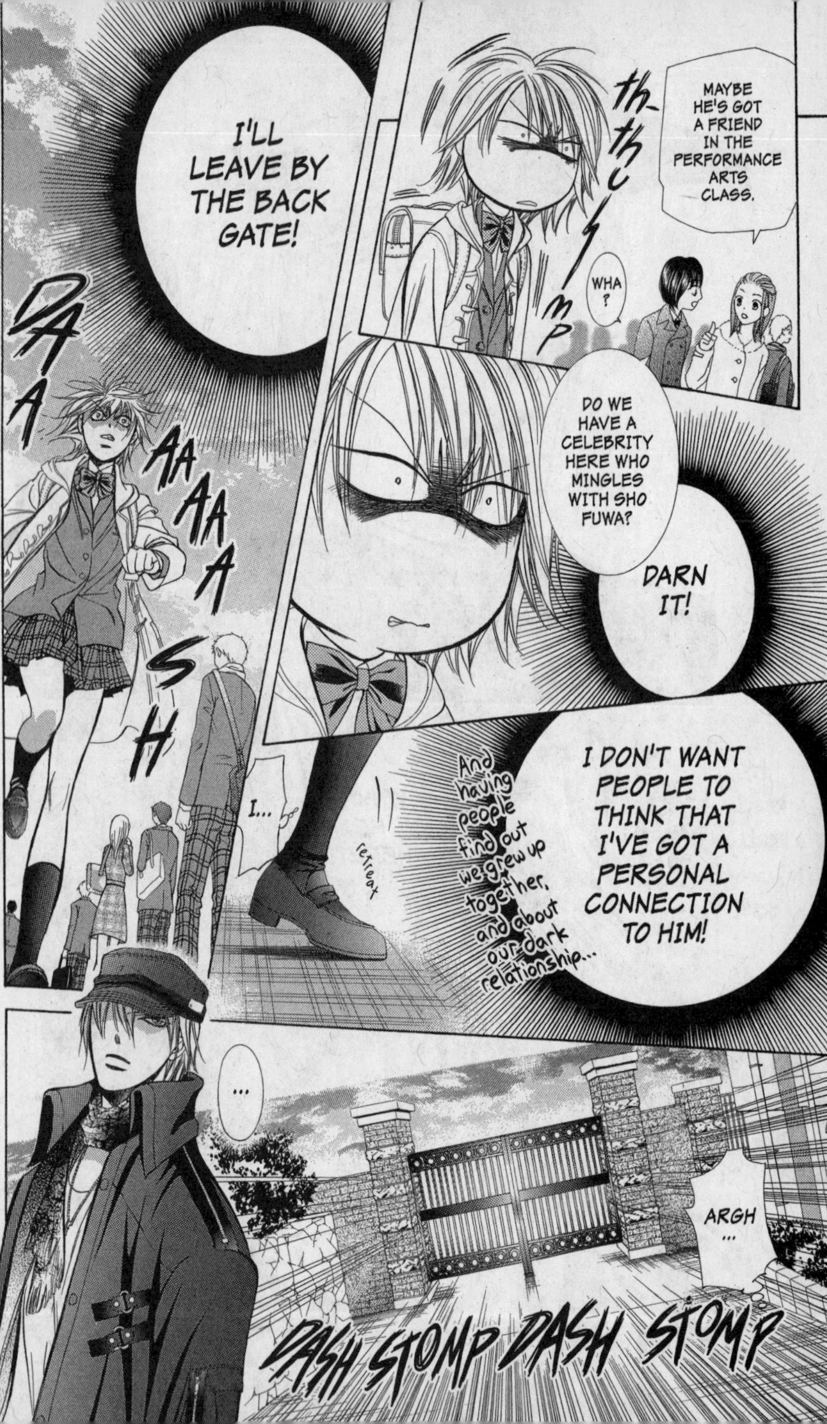
MAYBE HE'S GOT A FRIEND IN THE PERFORMANCE ARTS CLASS.
WHA?
th-thump
DO WE HAVE A CELEBRITY HERE WHO MINGLES WITH SHO FUWA?
DARN IT!
I DON'T WANT PEOPLE TO THINK THAT I'VE GOT A PERSONAL CONNECTION TO HIM!
And having people find out we grew up together, and about our dark relationship...
retreat
I...
I'LL LEAVE BY THE BACK GATE!
DAAAAAAAASH
ARGH...
...
DASH STOMP DASH STOMP

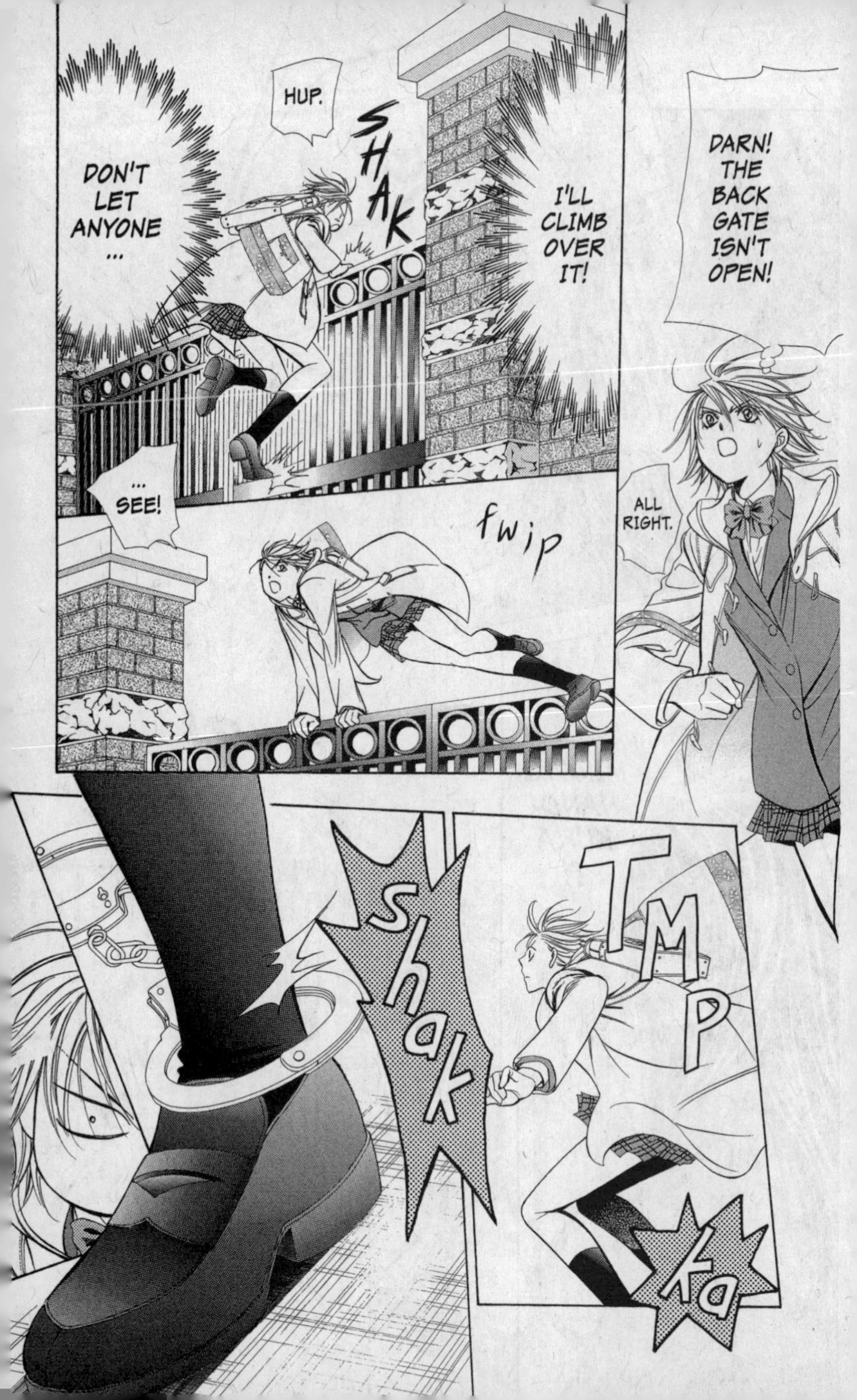
DARN! THE BACK GATE ISN'T OPEN!
ALL RIGHT.
I'LL CLIMB OVER IT!
HUP.
SHAK
DON'T LET ANYONE ...
... SEE!
fwip
TMP
ka
shak

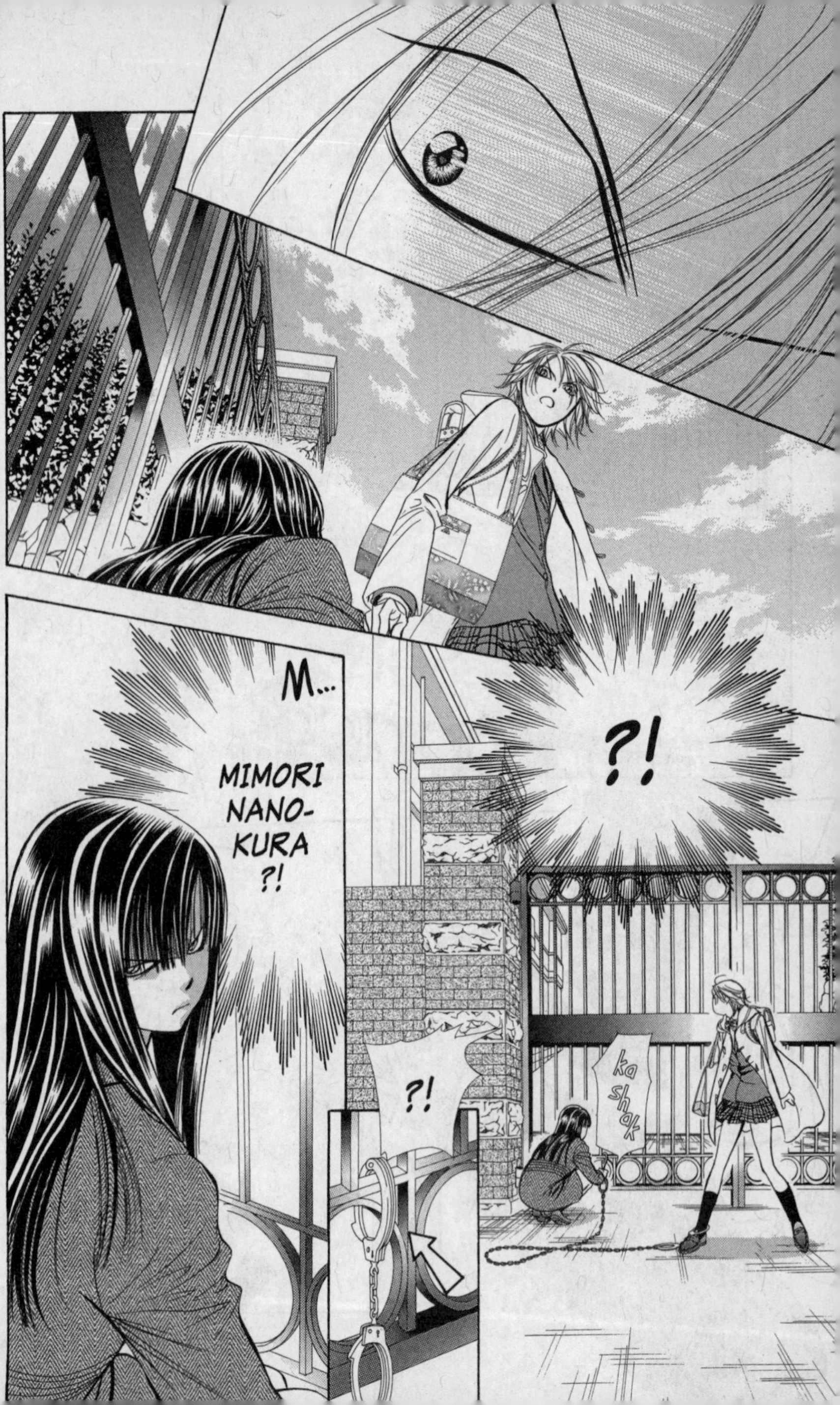
?!
ka shak
?!
M...
MIMORI NANO-KURA ?!

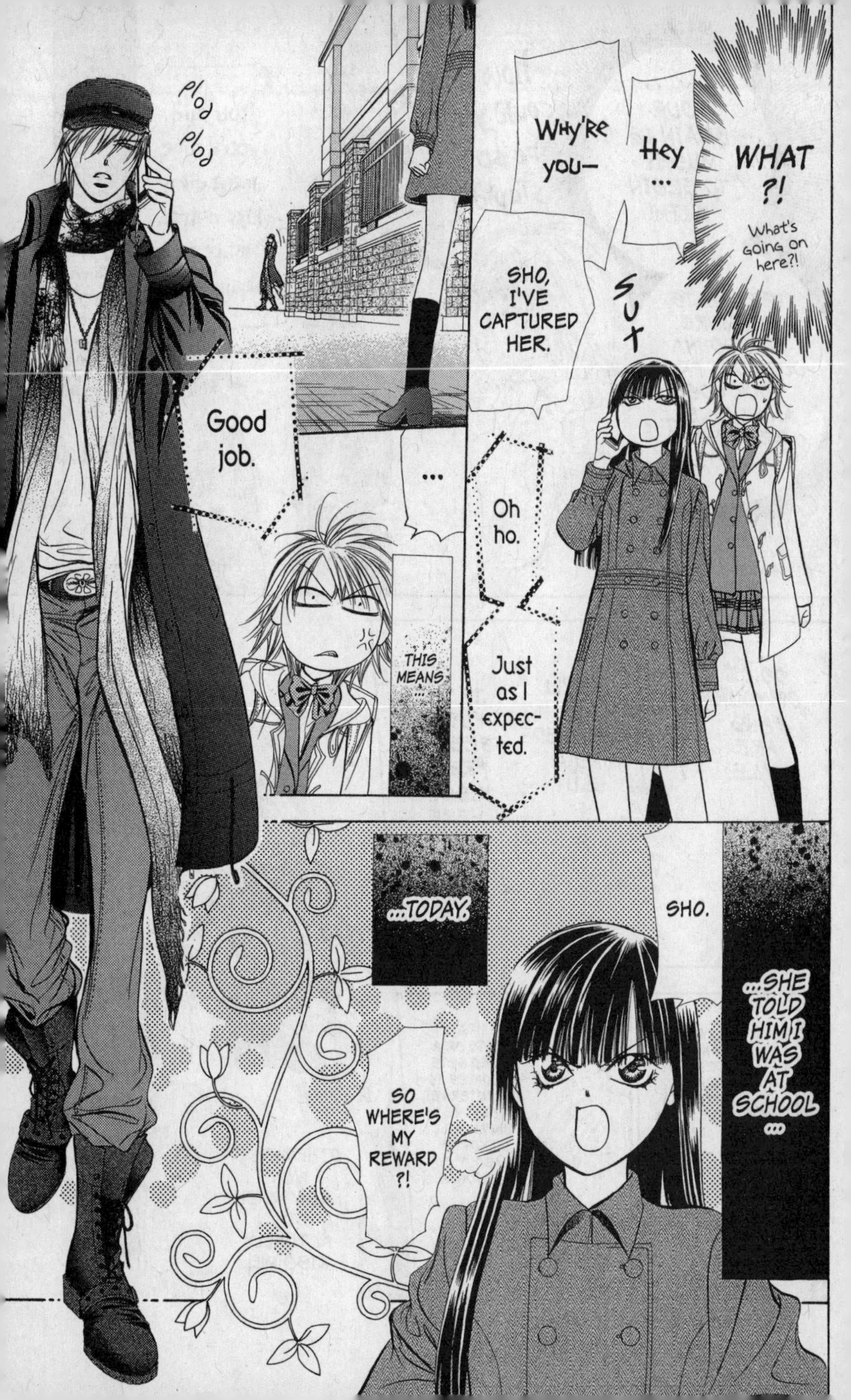
WHAT?!
What's going on here?!
Hey...
Why're you—
SUT
SHO, I'VE CAPTURED HER.
plod plod
Good job.
...
Oh ho.
Just as I expected.
THIS MEANS...
SHO.
...SHE TOLD HIM I WAS AT SCHOOL...
...TODAY.
SO WHERE'S MY REWARD?!

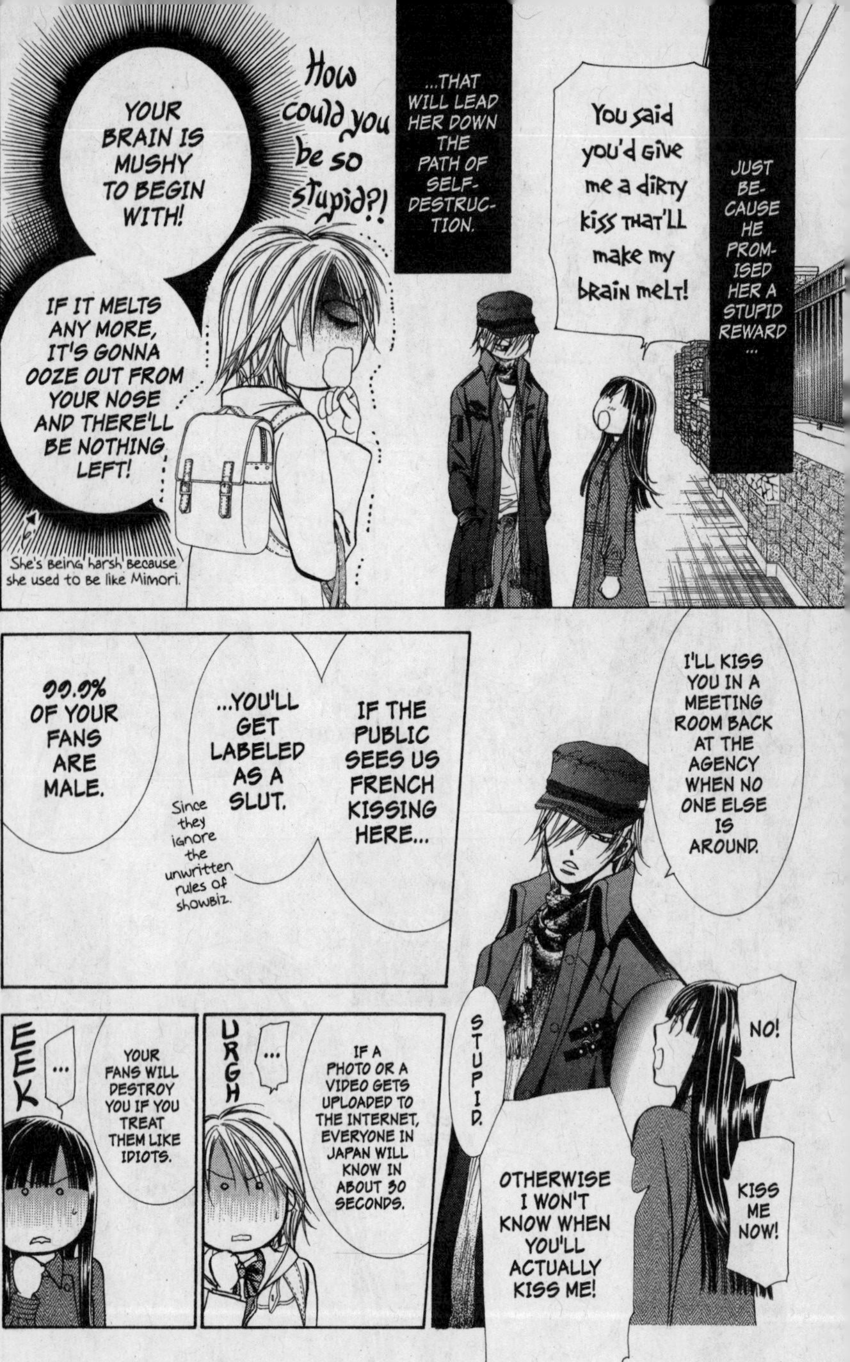
JUST BE-CAUSE HE PROM-ISED HER A STUPID REWARD...
You said you'd give me a dirty kiss that'll make my brain melt!
...THAT WILL LEAD HER DOWN THE PATH OF SELF-DESTRUC-TION.
How could you be so stupid?!
YOUR BRAIN IS MUSHY TO BEGIN WITH!
IF IT MELTS ANY MORE, IT'S GONNA OOZE OUT FROM YOUR NOSE AND THERE'LL BE NOTHING LEFT!
She's being harsh because she used to be like Mimori.
I'LL KISS YOU IN A MEETING ROOM BACK AT THE AGENCY WHEN NO ONE ELSE IS AROUND.
NO!
KISS ME NOW!
STUPID.
OTHERWISE I WON'T KNOW WHEN YOU'LL ACTUALLY KISS ME!
IF THE PUBLIC SEES US FRENCH KISSING HERE...
...YOU'LL GET LABELED AS A SLUT.
Since they ignore the unwritten rules of showbiz.
99.9% OF YOUR FANS ARE MALE.
IF A PHOTO OR A VIDEO GETS UPLOADED TO THE INTERNET, EVERYONE IN JAPAN WILL KNOW IN ABOUT 30 SECONDS.
...
URGH
YOUR FANS WILL DESTROY YOU IF YOU TREAT THEM LIKE IDIOTS.
...
EEK

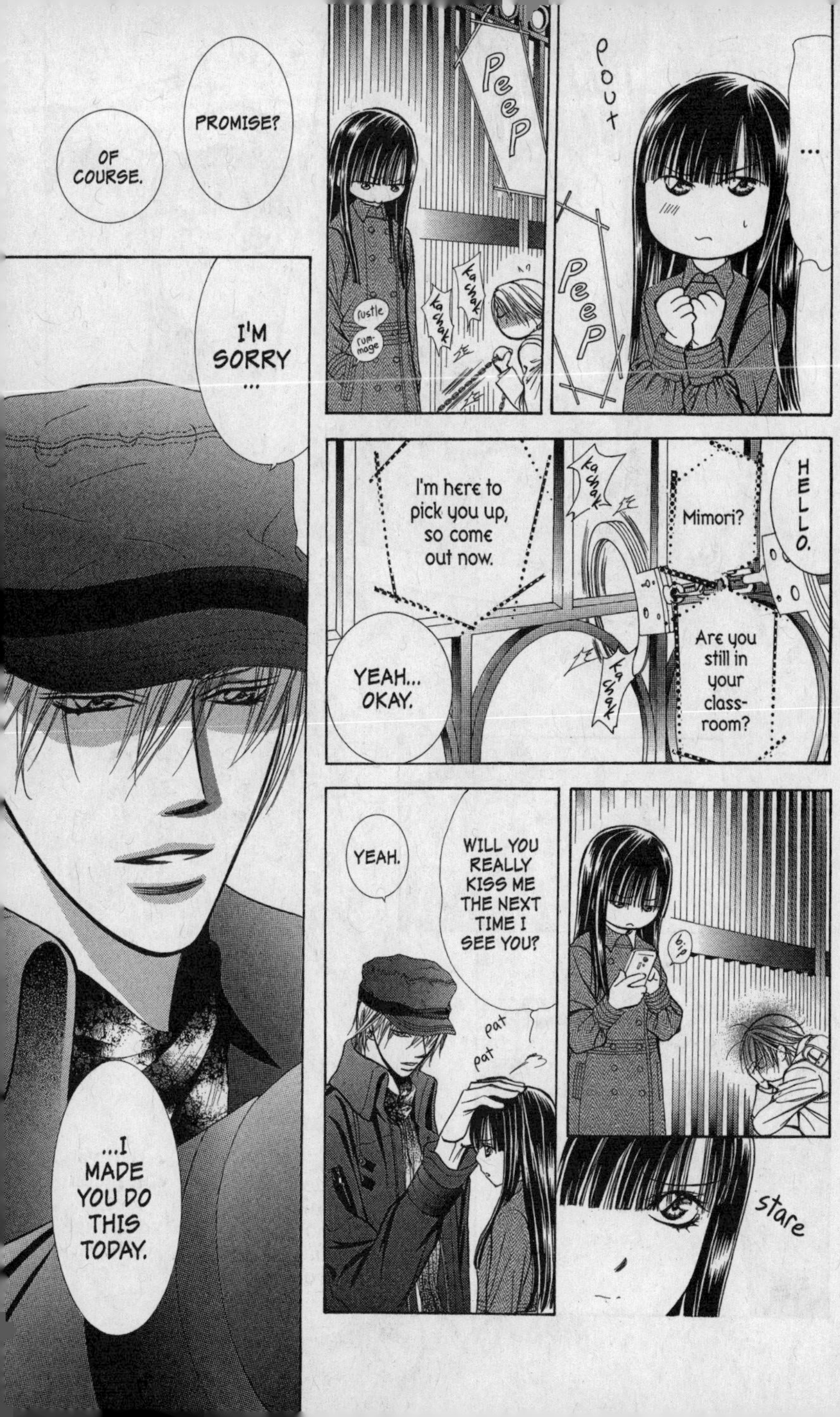
...
pout
Peep
Peep
Peep
ka chak
ka chak
rustle
rum-mage
HELLO.
Mimori?
Are you still in your class-room?
ka chak
ka chak
I'm here to pick you up, so come out now.
YEAH... OKAY.
bip
stare
WILL YOU REALLY KISS ME THE NEXT TIME I SEE YOU?
YEAH.
pat
pat
PROMISE?
OF COURSE.
I'M SORRY...
...I MADE YOU DO THIS TODAY.

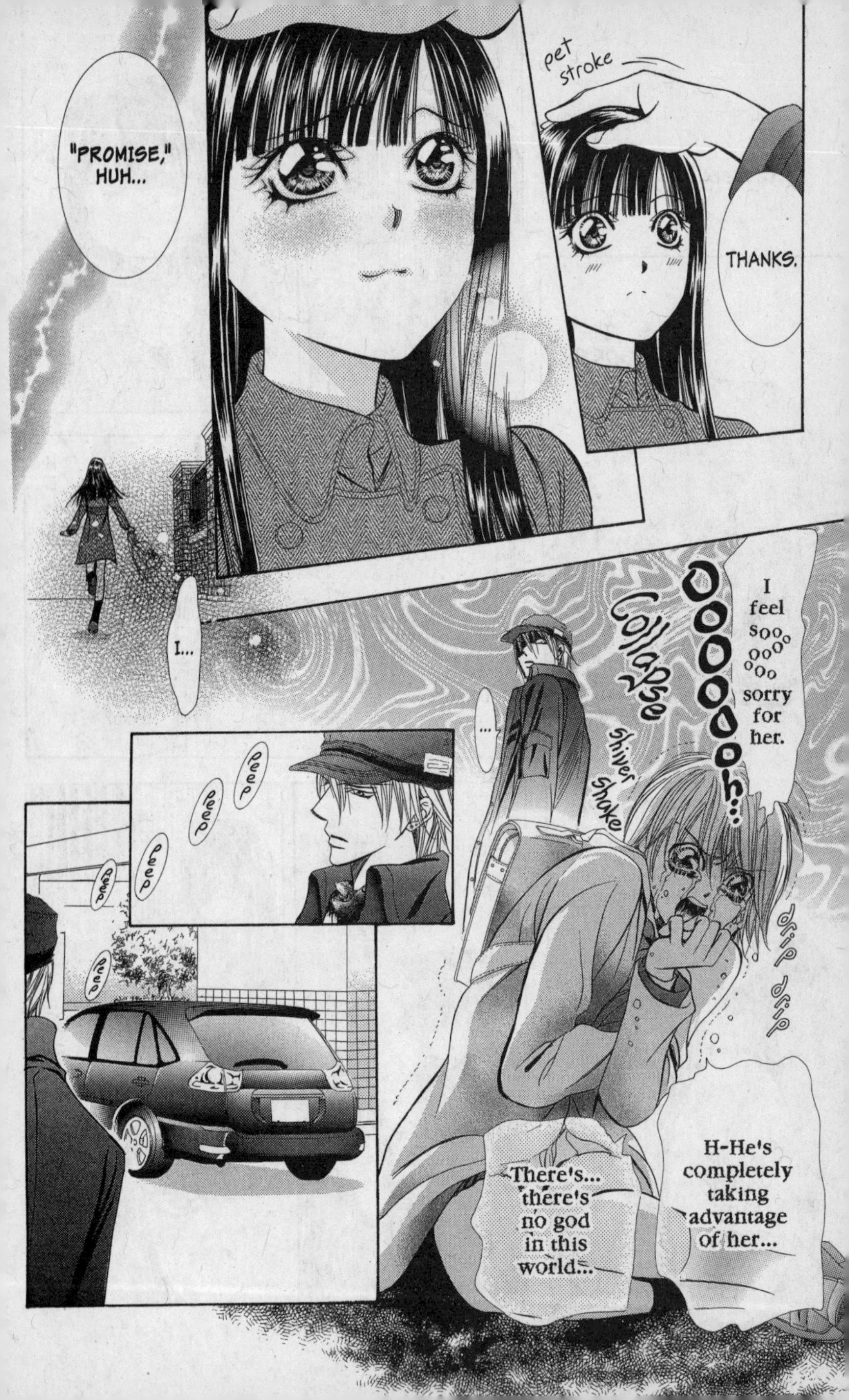
pet stroke
THANKS.
"PROMISE," HUH...
I...
I feel sooooooooo sorry for her.
OOOOOOh...
Collapse
shiver shake
...
peep peep peep peep peep
H-He's completely taking advantage of her...
There's... there's no god in this world...
drip drip

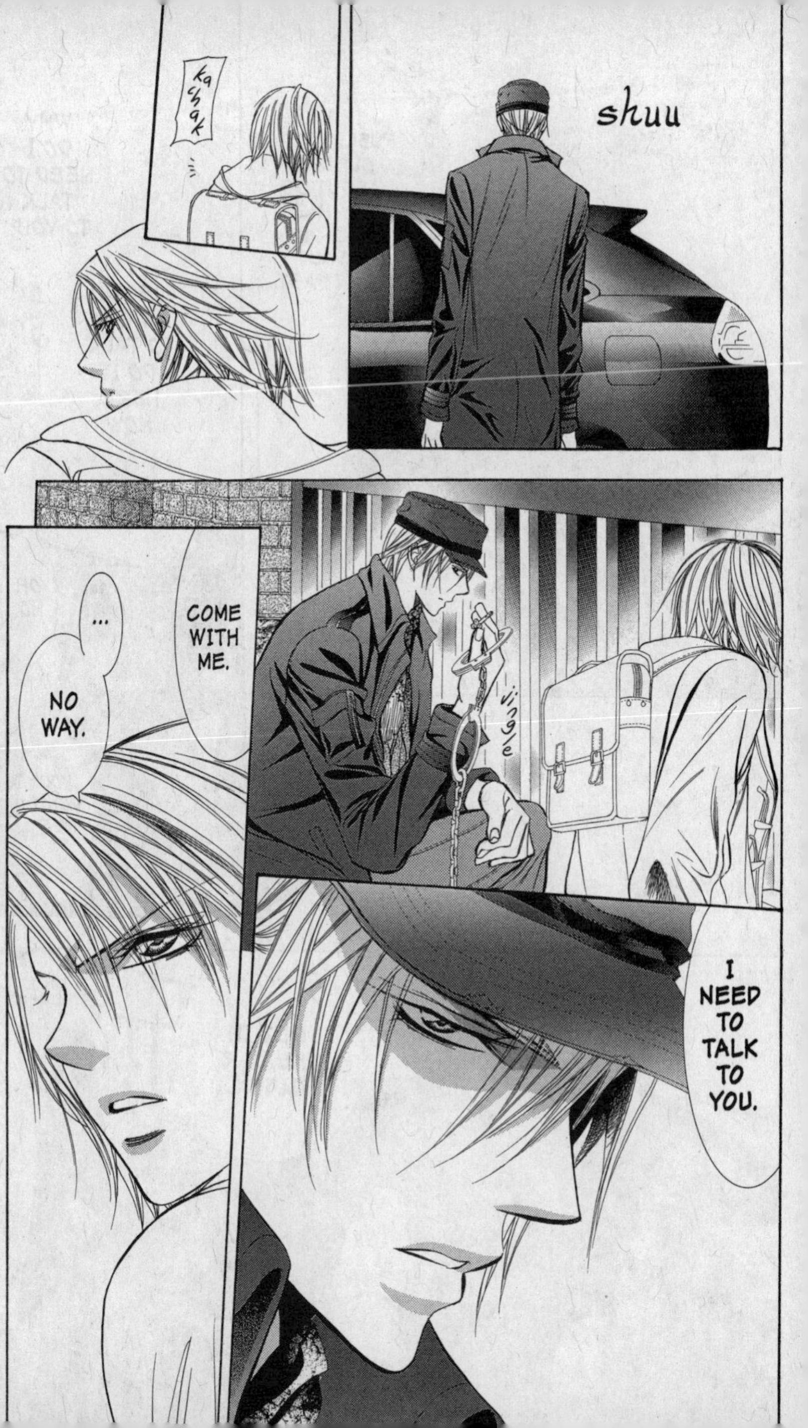
shuu
ka chak
jingle
COME WITH ME.
...
NO WAY.
I NEED TO TALK TO YOU.

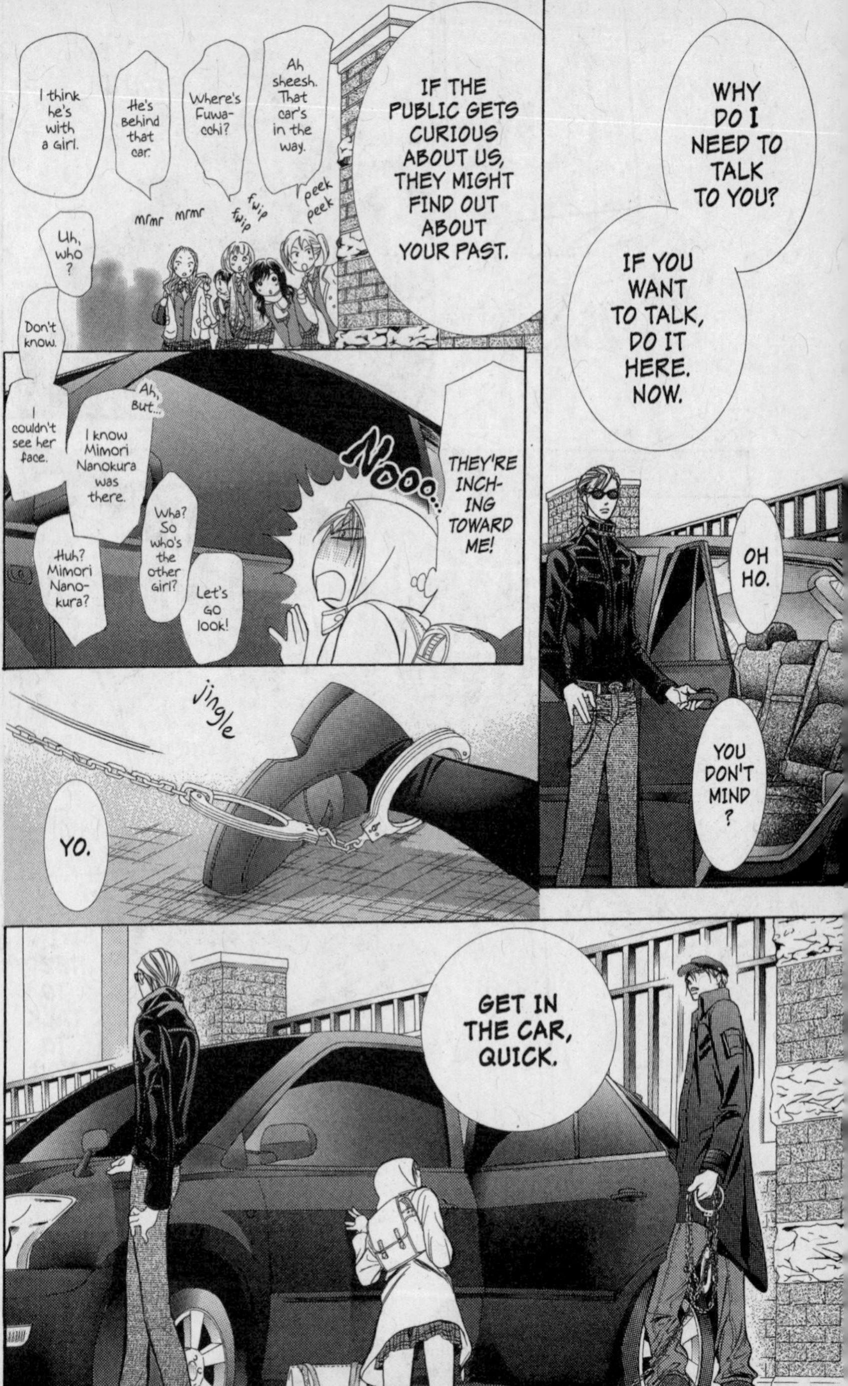
WHY DO I NEED TO TALK TO YOU?
IF YOU WANT TO TALK, DO IT HERE. NOW.
OH HO.
YOU DON'T MIND?
IF THE PUBLIC GETS CURIOUS ABOUT US, THEY MIGHT FIND OUT ABOUT YOUR PAST.
Ah sheesh. That car's in the way.
Where's Fuwa-cchi?
He's behind that car.
I think he's with a girl.
peek peek
fwip fwip
mrmr mrmr
Uh, who?
Don't know.
THEY'RE INCHING TOWARD ME!
Nooo...
Ah, But...
I couldn't see her face.
I know Mimori Nanokura was there.
Wha? So who's the other girl?
Huh? Mimori Nanokura?
Let's go look!
jingle
YO.
GET IN THE CAR, QUICK.

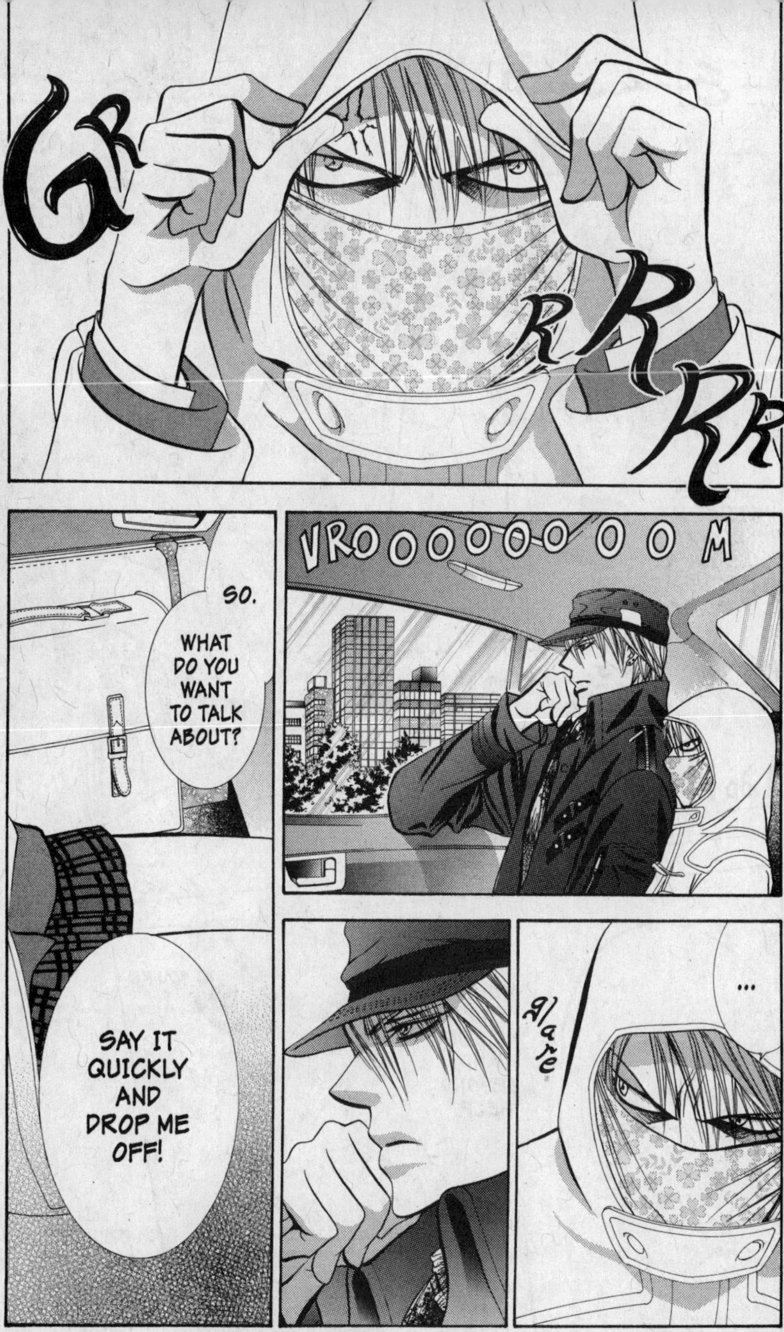
GRRRRRR
VROOOOOOOOOM
glare
...
SO.
WHAT DO YOU WANT TO TALK ABOUT?
SAY IT QUICKLY AND DROP ME OFF!

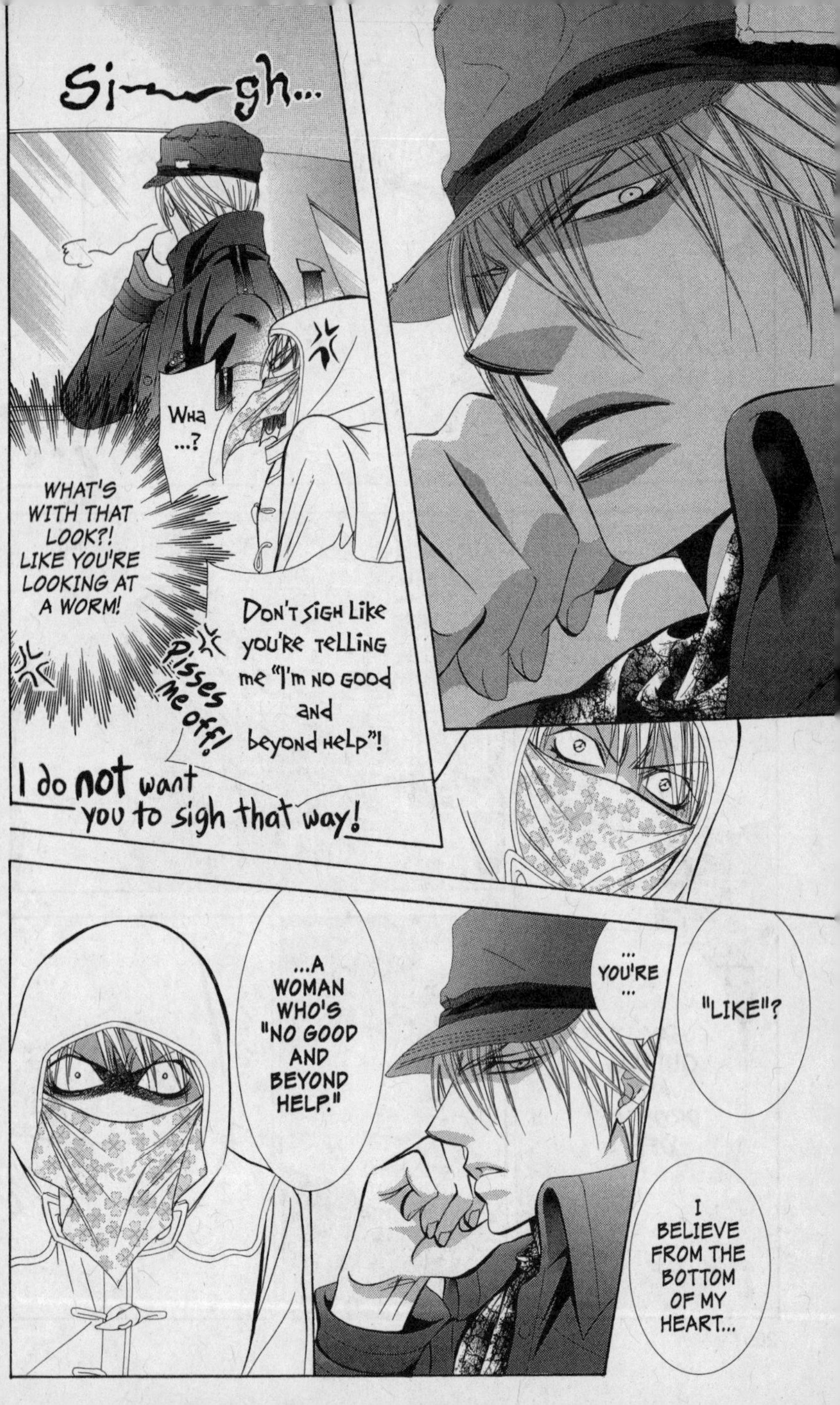
Si~~gh...
Wha ...?
WHAT'S WITH THAT LOOK?! LIKE YOU'RE LOOKING AT A WORM!
Don't sigh like you're telling me "I'm no good and beyond help"!
Pisses me off!
I do **not** want you to sigh that way!
"LIKE"?
I BELIEVE FROM THE BOTTOM OF MY HEART...
... YOU'RE ...
...A WOMAN WHO'S "NO GOOD AND BEYOND HELP."

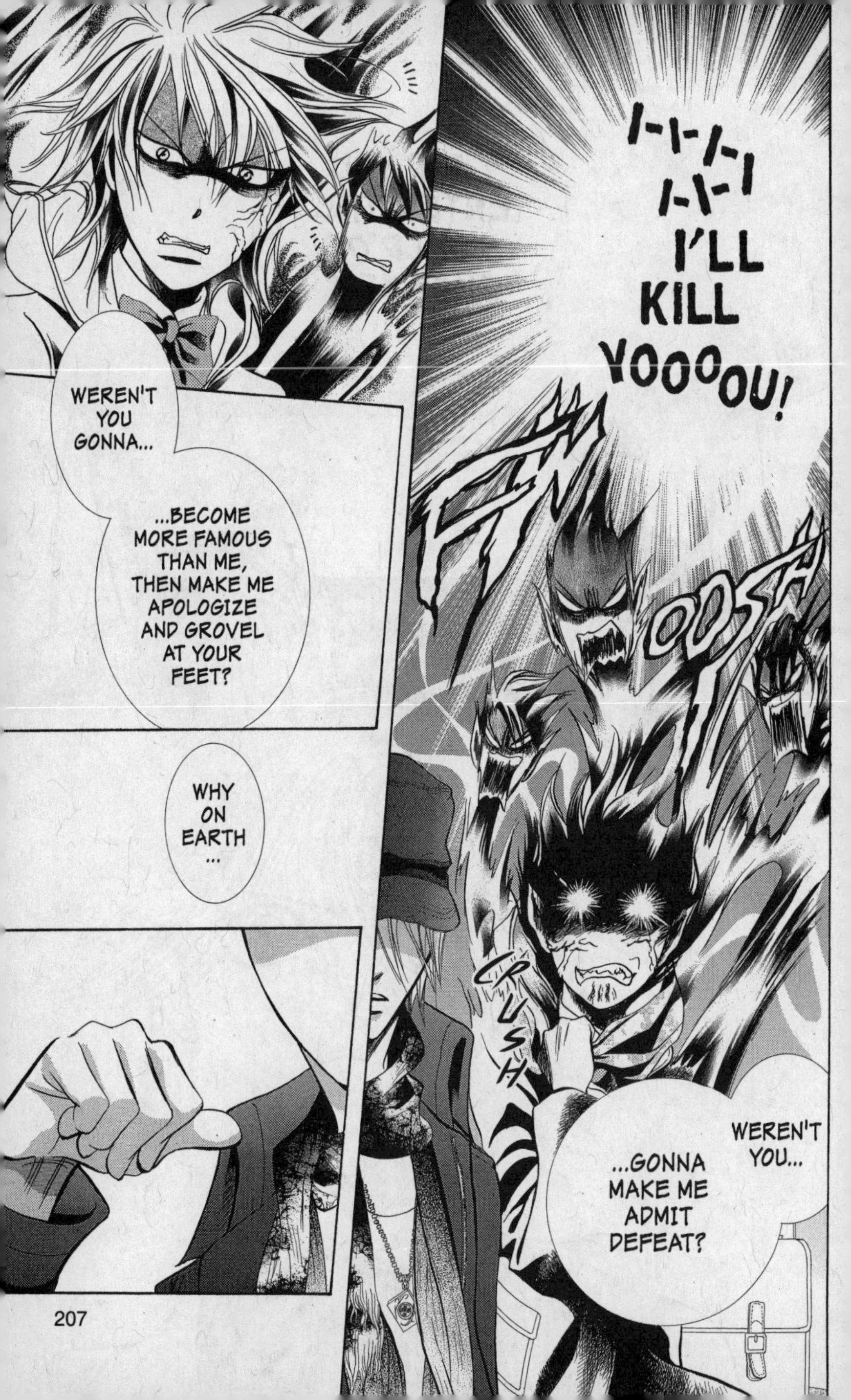
I-I-I-I I-I-I I'LL KILL YOOOOU!
CRUSH
WEREN'T YOU...
...GONNA MAKE ME ADMIT DEFEAT?
WEREN'T YOU GONNA...
...BECOME MORE FAMOUS THAN ME, THEN MAKE ME APOLOGIZE AND GROVEL AT YOUR FEET?
WHY ON EARTH ...

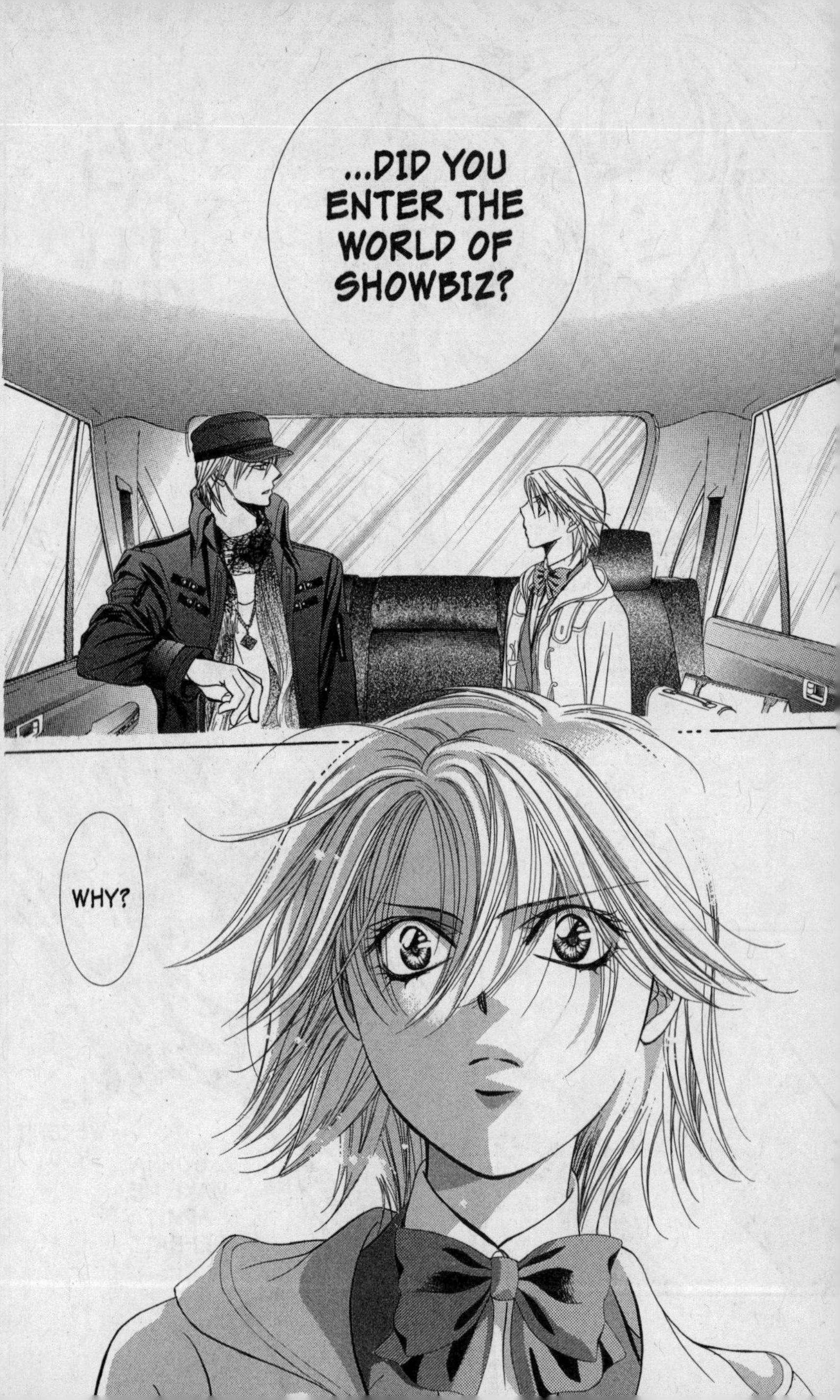
...DID YOU ENTER THE WORLD OF SHOWBIZ?
WHY?

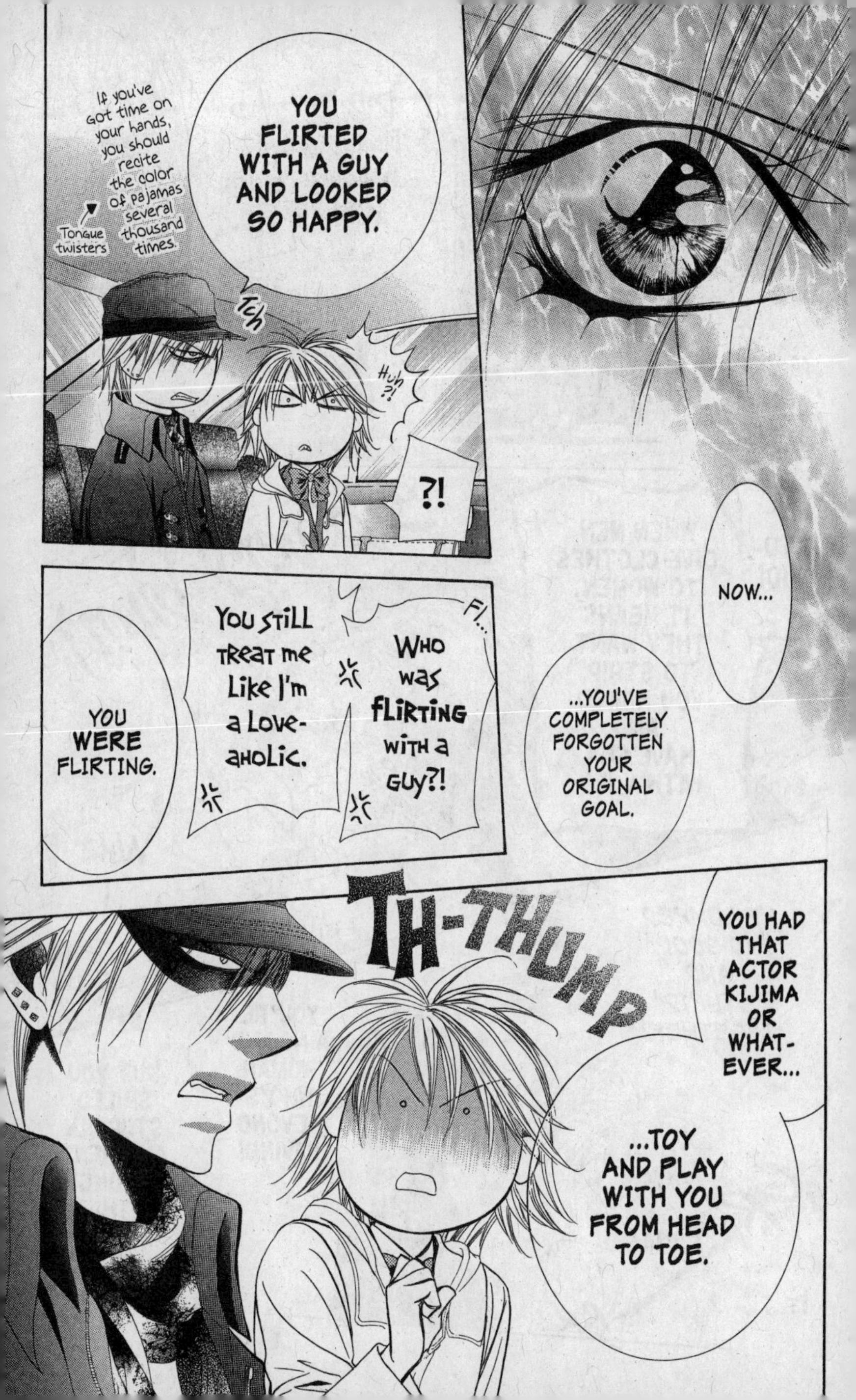

NOW...
...YOU'VE COMPLETELY FORGOTTEN YOUR ORIGINAL GOAL.
YOU FLIRTED WITH A GUY AND LOOKED SO HAPPY.
If you've got time on your hands, you should recite the color of pajamas several thousand times.
Tongue twisters
Tch
Huh?!
?!
Fl...
Who was flirting with a guy?!
You still treat me like I'm a love-aholic.
YOU WERE FLIRTING.
YOU HAD THAT ACTOR KIJIMA OR WHATEVER...
TH-THUMP
...TOY AND PLAY WITH YOU FROM HEAD TO TOE.

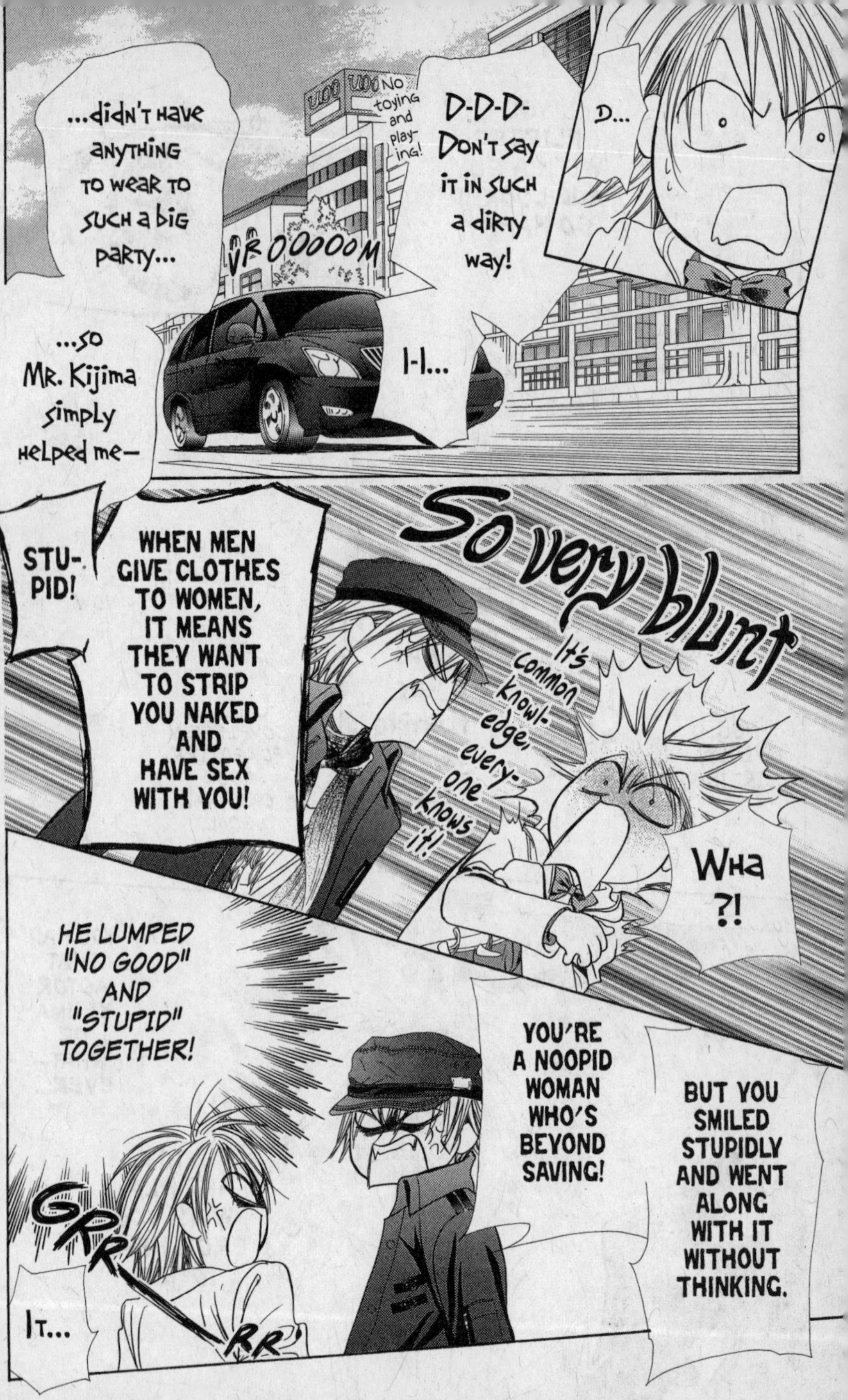
D...
D-D-D- Don't say it in such a dirty way!
No toying and playing!
I-I...
...didn't have anything to wear to such a big party...
VROOOOOM
...so Mr. Kijima simply helped me—
STUPID!
WHEN MEN GIVE CLOTHES TO WOMEN, IT MEANS THEY WANT TO STRIP YOU NAKED AND HAVE SEX WITH YOU!
WHA?!
It's common knowledge, everyone knows it!
So very blunt
BUT YOU SMILED STUPIDLY AND WENT ALONG WITH IT WITHOUT THINKING.
YOU'RE A NOOPID WOMAN WHO'S BEYOND SAVING!
HE LUMPED "NO GOOD" AND "STUPID" TOGETHER!
GRRRR
It...

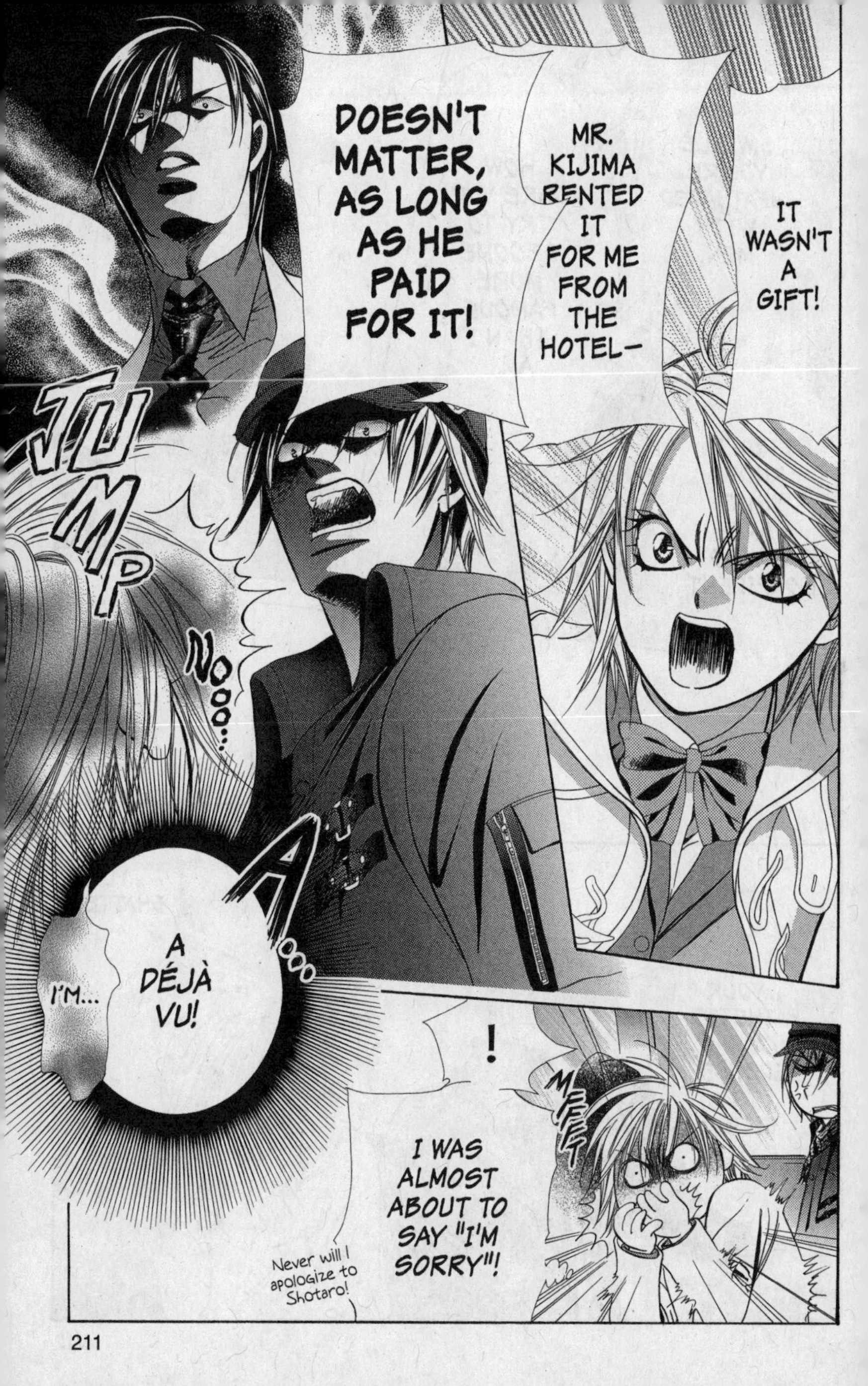
IT WASN'T A GIFT!
MR. KIJIMA RENTED IT FOR ME FROM THE HOTEL—
DOESN'T MATTER, AS LONG AS HE PAID FOR IT!
JUMP
NOOO...
A
AOOO
A DÉJÀ VU!
I'M...
!
MFF
I WAS ALMOST ABOUT TO SAY "I'M SORRY"!
Never will I apologize to Shotaro!

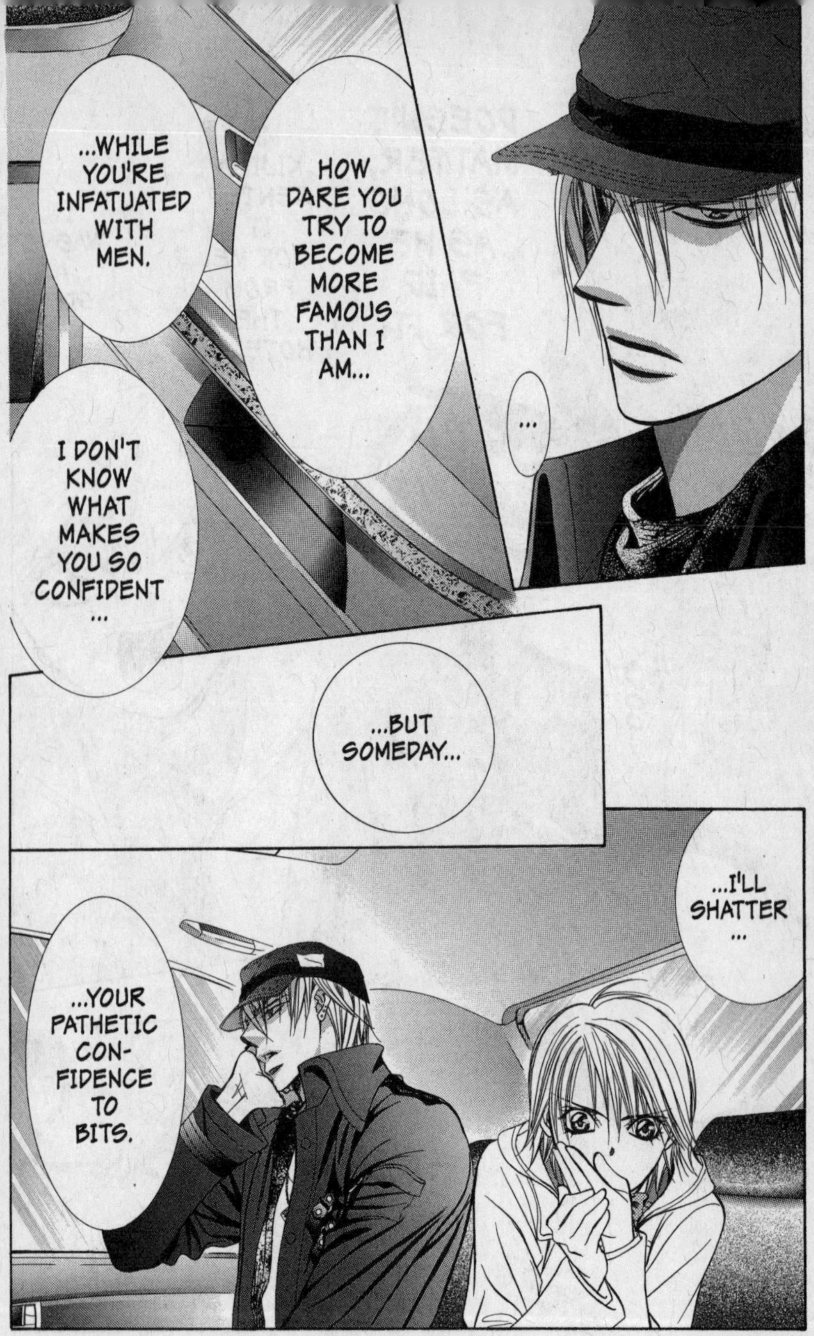
...
HOW DARE YOU TRY TO BECOME MORE FAMOUS THAN I AM...
...WHILE YOU'RE INFATUATED WITH MEN.
I DON'T KNOW WHAT MAKES YOU SO CONFIDENT...
...BUT SOMEDAY...
...I'LL SHATTER...
...YOUR PATHETIC CON-FIDENCE TO BITS.

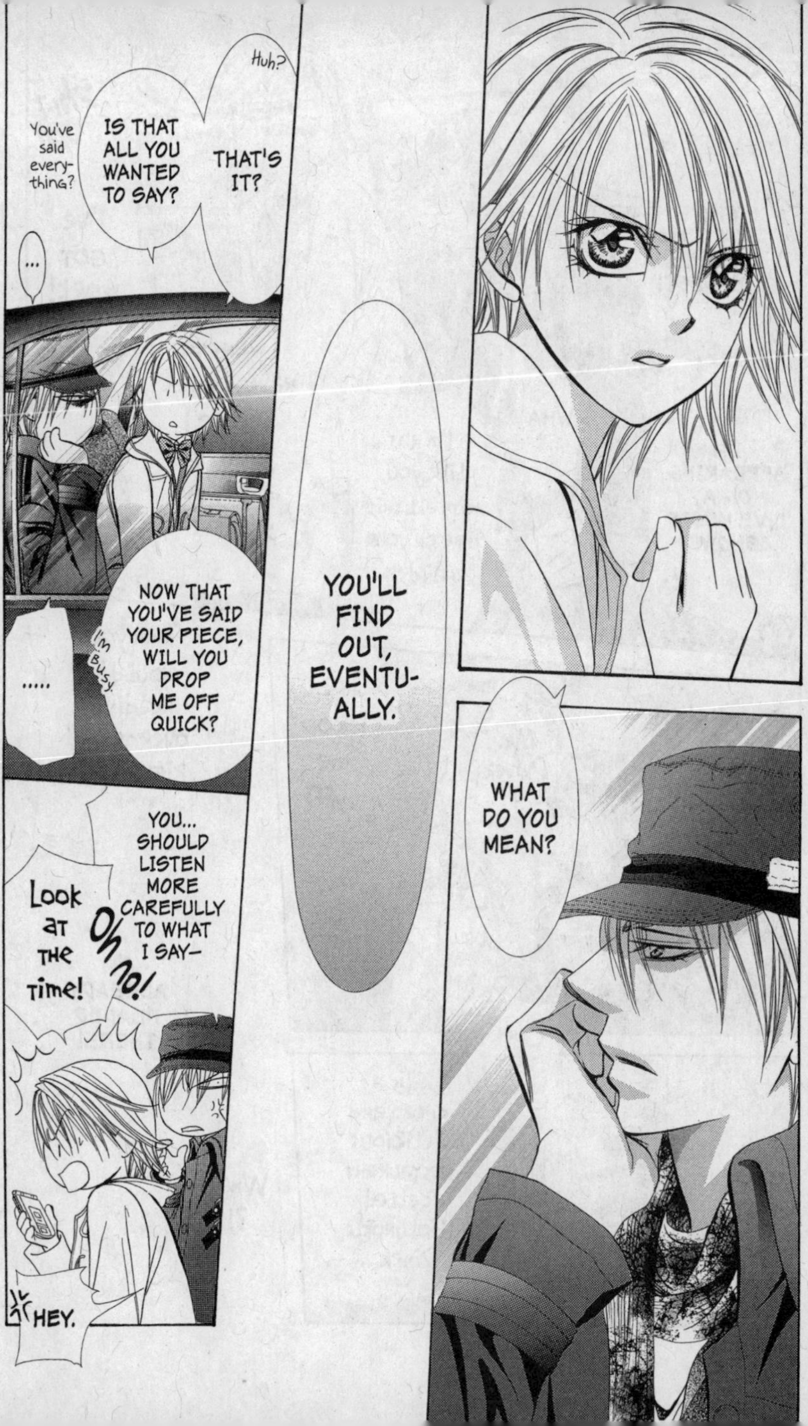

WHAT DO YOU MEAN?
YOU'LL FIND OUT, EVENTUALLY.
Huh?
THAT'S IT?
IS THAT ALL YOU WANTED TO SAY?
You've said every-thing?
...
NOW THAT YOU'VE SAID YOUR PIECE, WILL YOU DROP ME OFF QUICK?
I'm Busy.
.....
YOU... SHOULD LISTEN MORE CAREFULLY TO WHAT I SAY—
Oh no!
Look at the Time!
HEY.

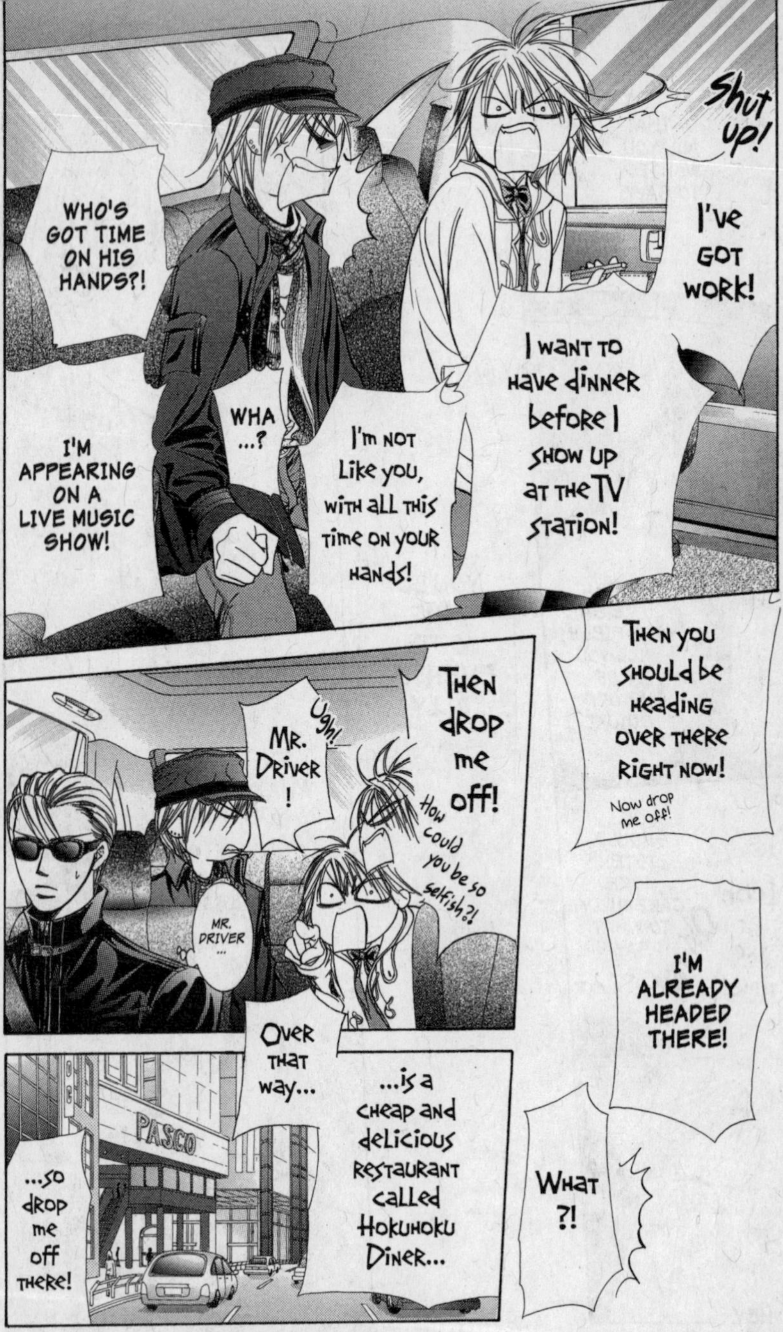
Shut up!
I've got work!
I want to have dinner before I show up at the TV station!
I'm not like you, with all this time on your hands!
Wha...?
Who's got time on his hands?!
I'm appearing on a live music show!
Then you should be heading over there right now!
Now drop me off!
Then drop me off!
Ugh!
Mr. Driver!
How could you be so selfish?!
Mr. Driver...
I'm already headed there!
What?!
Over that way...
...is a cheap and delicious restaurant called Hokuhoku Diner...
PASCO
...so drop me off there!

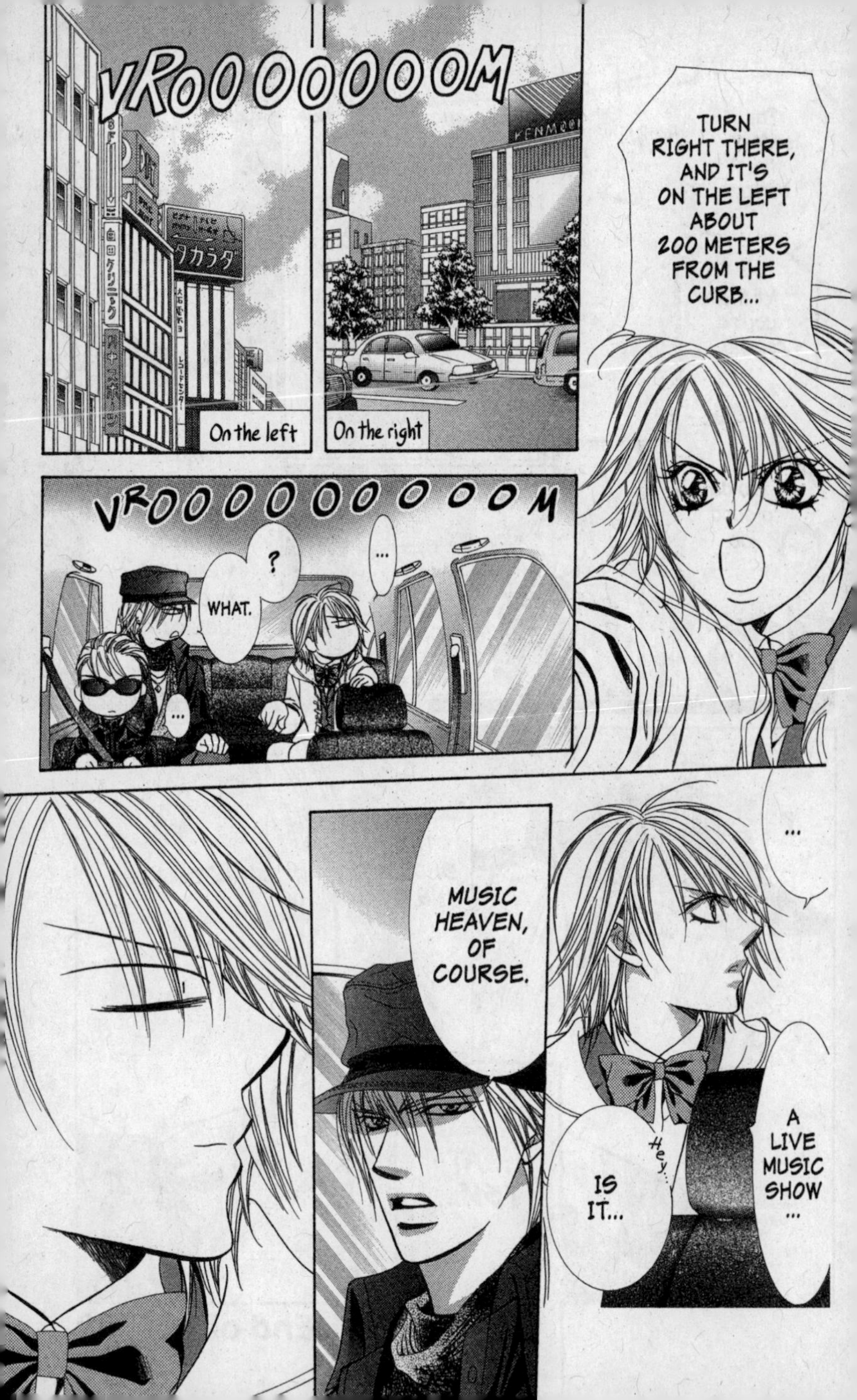
TURN RIGHT THERE, AND IT'S ON THE LEFT ABOUT 200 METERS FROM THE CURB...
VROOOOOOOM
On the right
On the left
VROOOOOOOOOOM
...
?
WHAT.
...
...
A LIVE MUSIC SHOW ...
Hey...
IS IT...
MUSIC HEAVEN, OF COURSE.

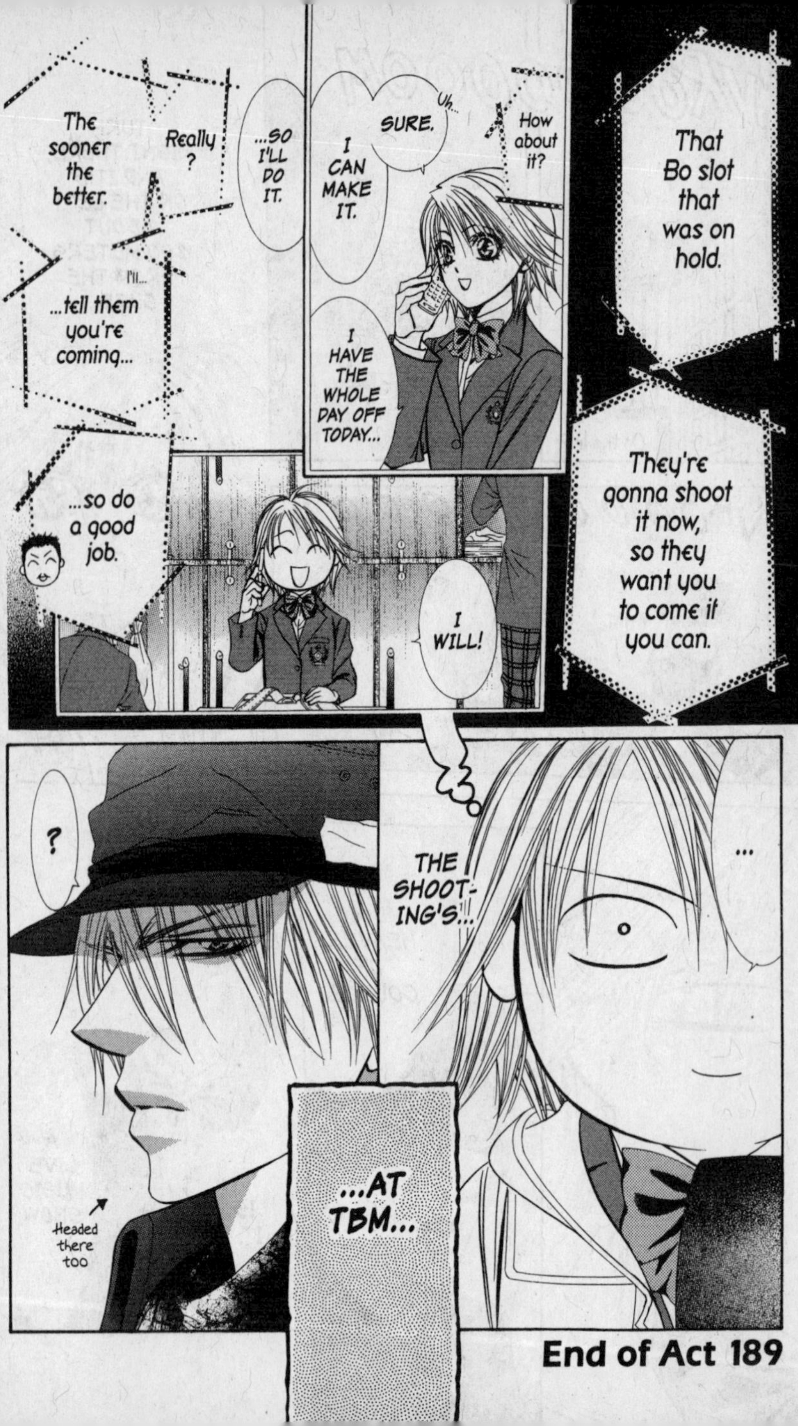
That Bo slot that was on hold.
They're gonna shoot it now, so they want you to come if you can.
How about it?
Uh...
SURE.
I CAN MAKE IT.
I HAVE THE WHOLE DAY OFF TODAY...
...SO I'LL DO IT.
Really?
The sooner the better.
I'll...
...tell them you're coming...
...so do a good job.
I WILL!
...
THE SHOOTING'S...
...AT TBM...
?
Headed there too

End of Act 189

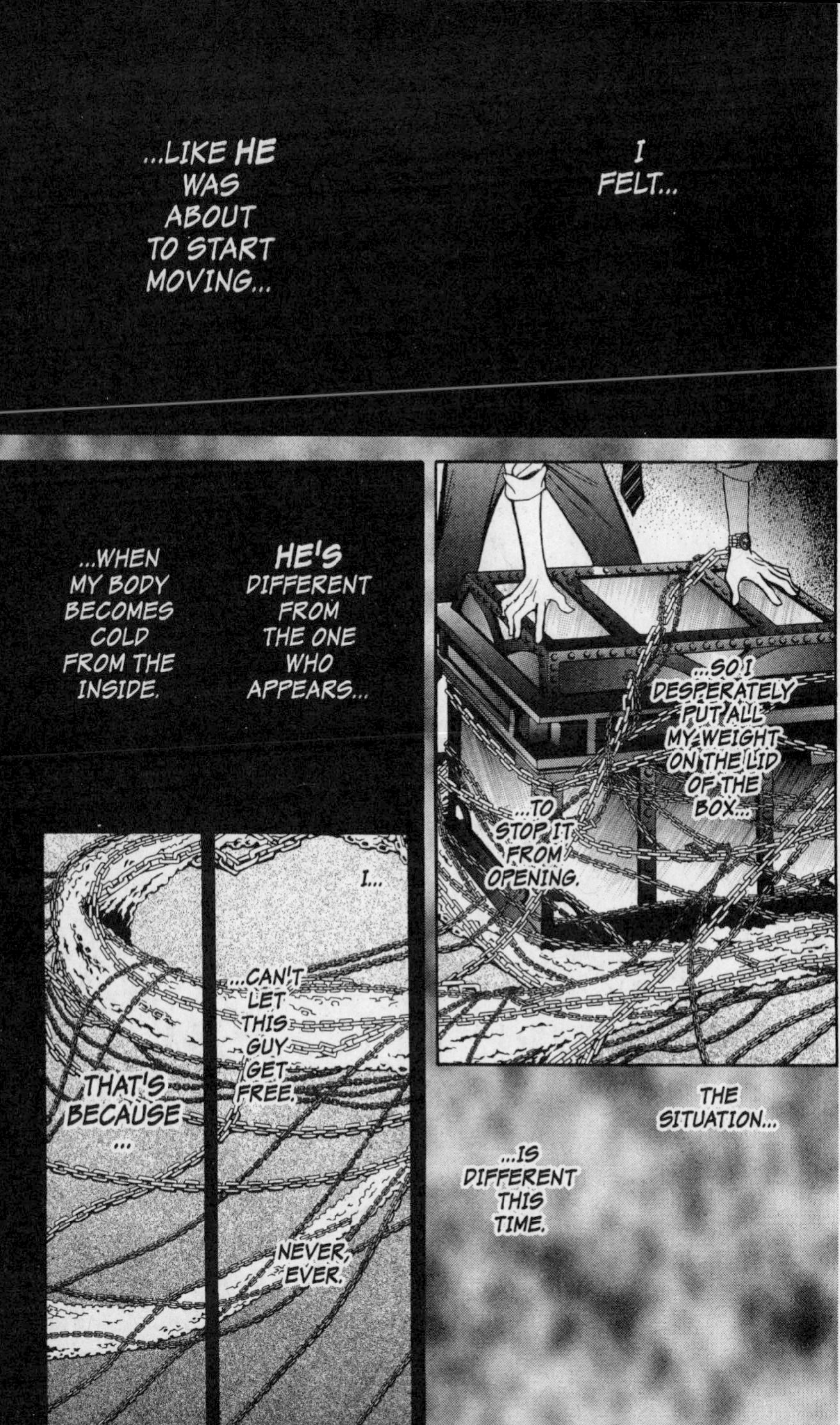
I FELT...
...LIKE HE WAS ABOUT TO START MOVING...
...SO I DESPERATELY PUT ALL MY WEIGHT ON THE LID OF THE BOX...
...TO STOP IT FROM OPENING.
HE'S DIFFERENT FROM THE ONE WHO APPEARS...
...WHEN MY BODY BECOMES COLD FROM THE INSIDE.
THE SITUATION...
...IS DIFFERENT THIS TIME.
I...
...CAN'T LET THIS GUY GET FREE.
NEVER, EVER.
THAT'S BECAUSE ...

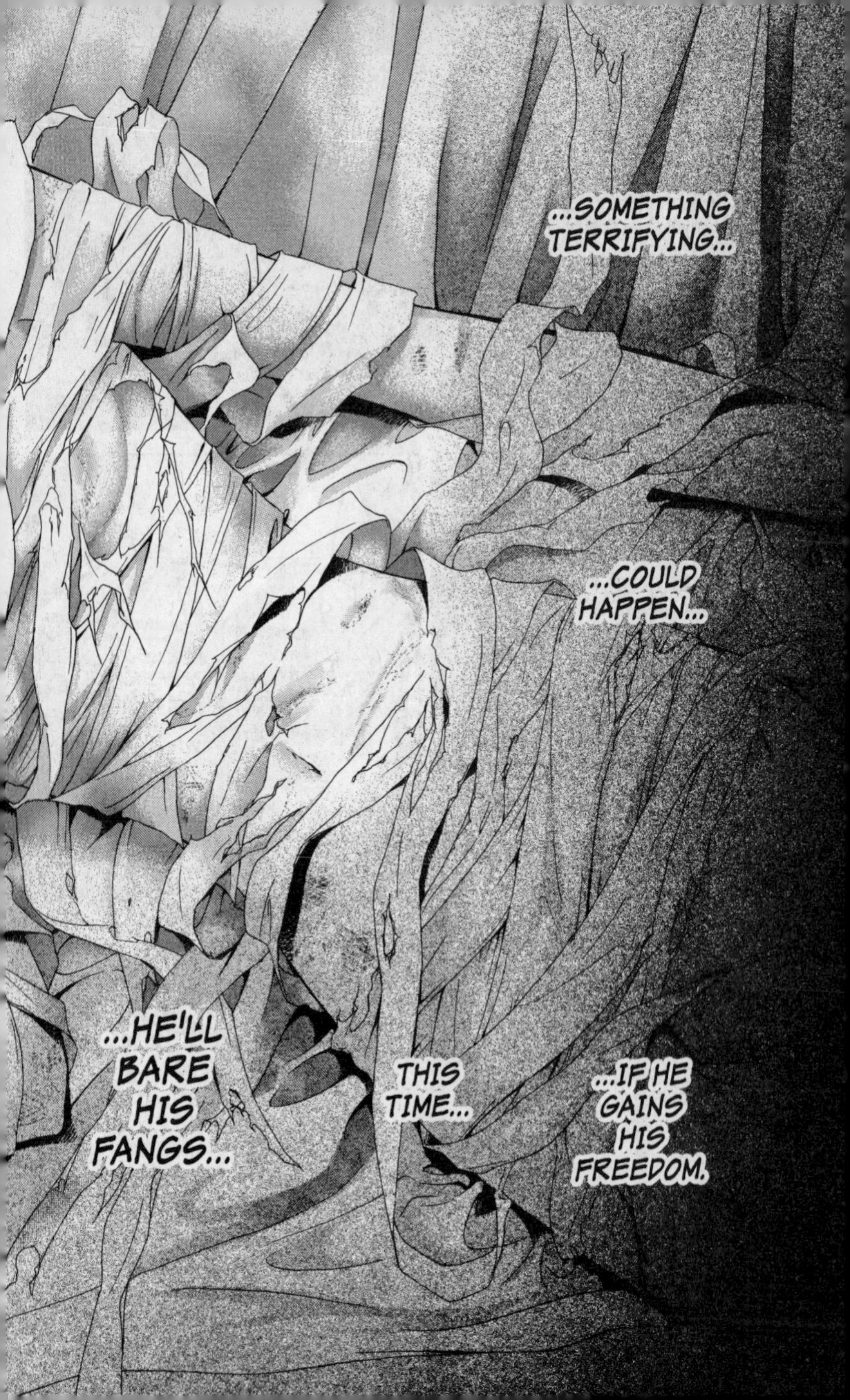
...SOMETHING TERRIFYING...
...COULD HAPPEN...
...IF HE GAINS HIS FREEDOM.
THIS TIME...
...HE'LL BARE HIS FANGS...

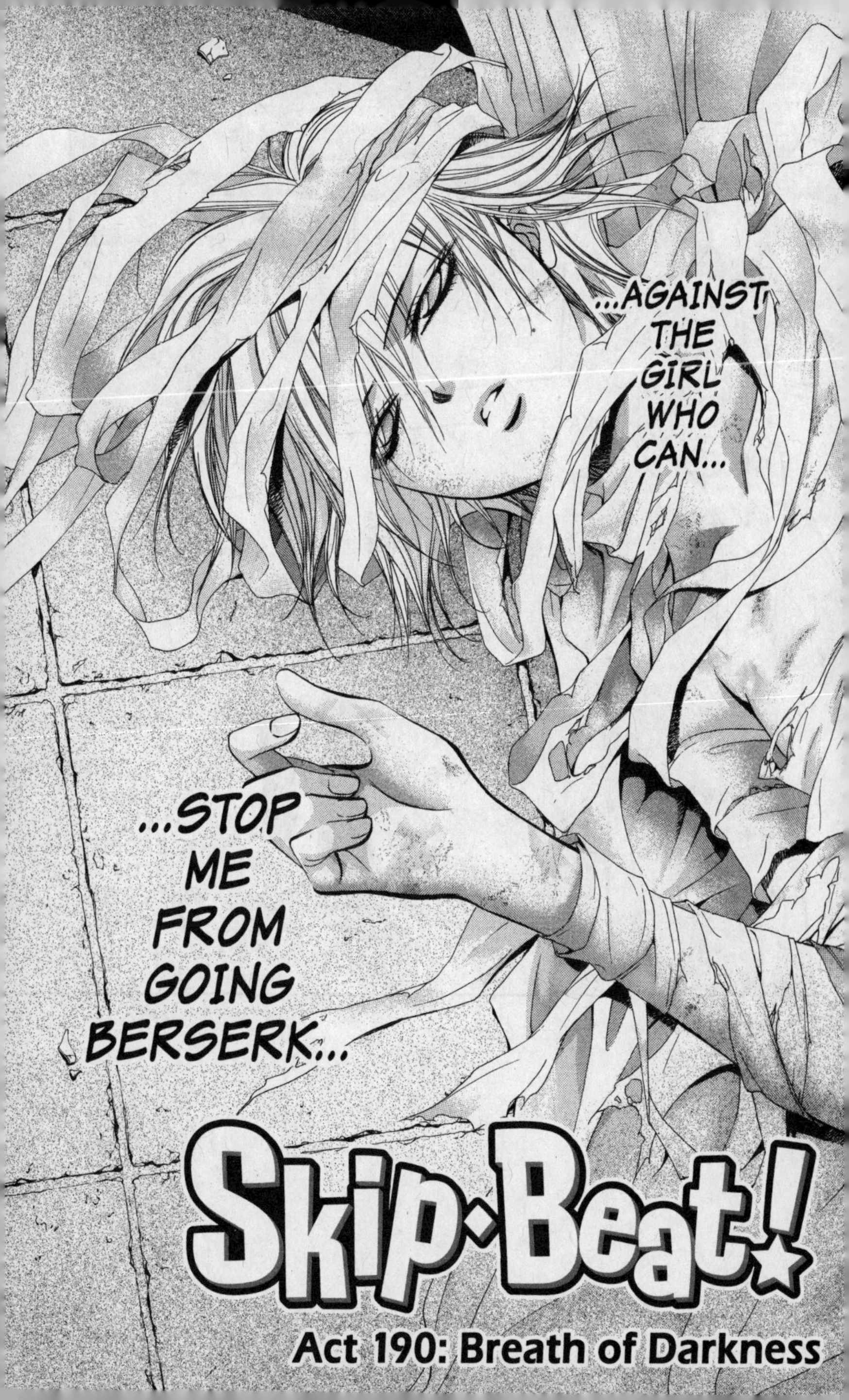
...AGAINST THE GIRL WHO CAN...
...STOP ME FROM GOING BERSERK...

Skip·Beat!

Act 190: Breath of Darkness

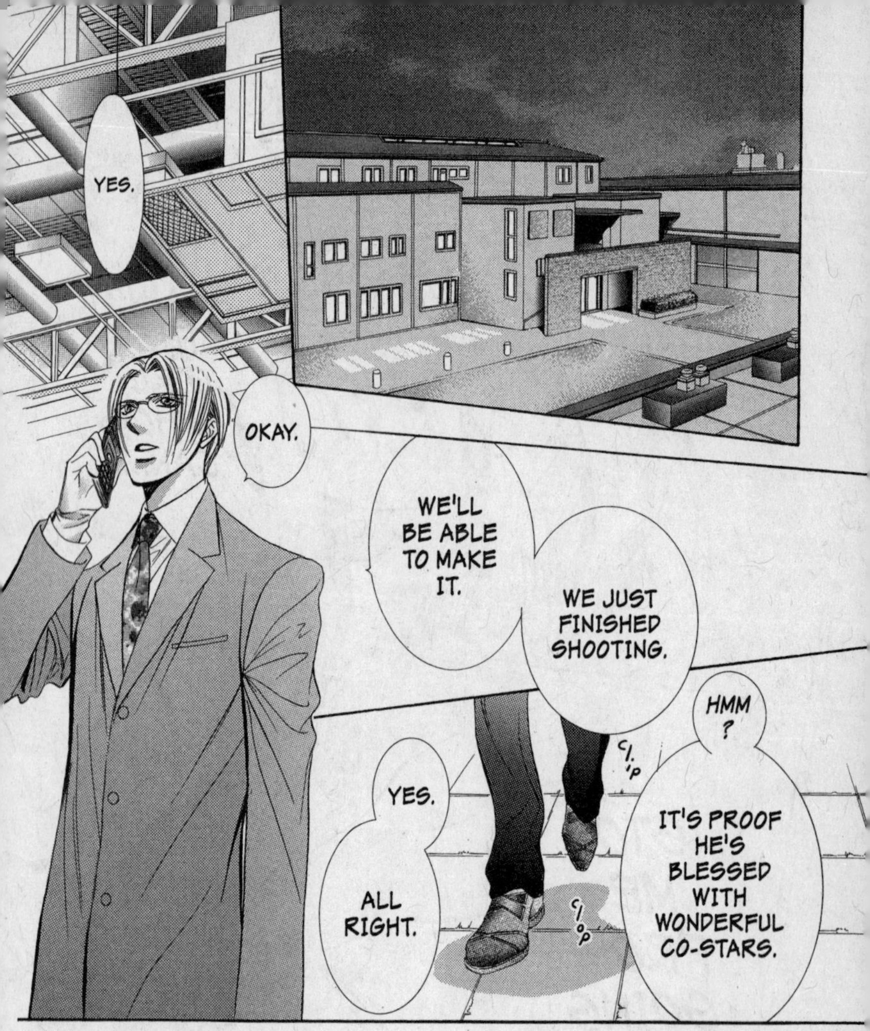
YES.
OKAY.
WE'LL BE ABLE TO MAKE IT.
WE JUST FINISHED SHOOTING.
HMM?
IT'S PROOF HE'S BLESSED WITH WONDERFUL CO-STARS.
CLIP
CLOP
YES.
ALL RIGHT.

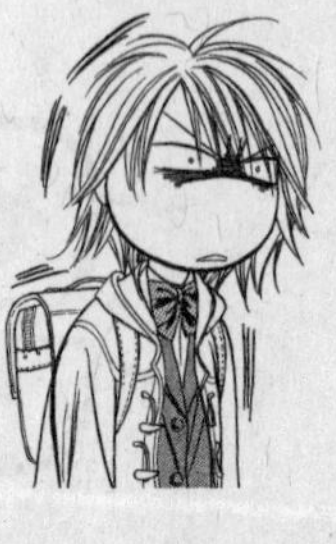

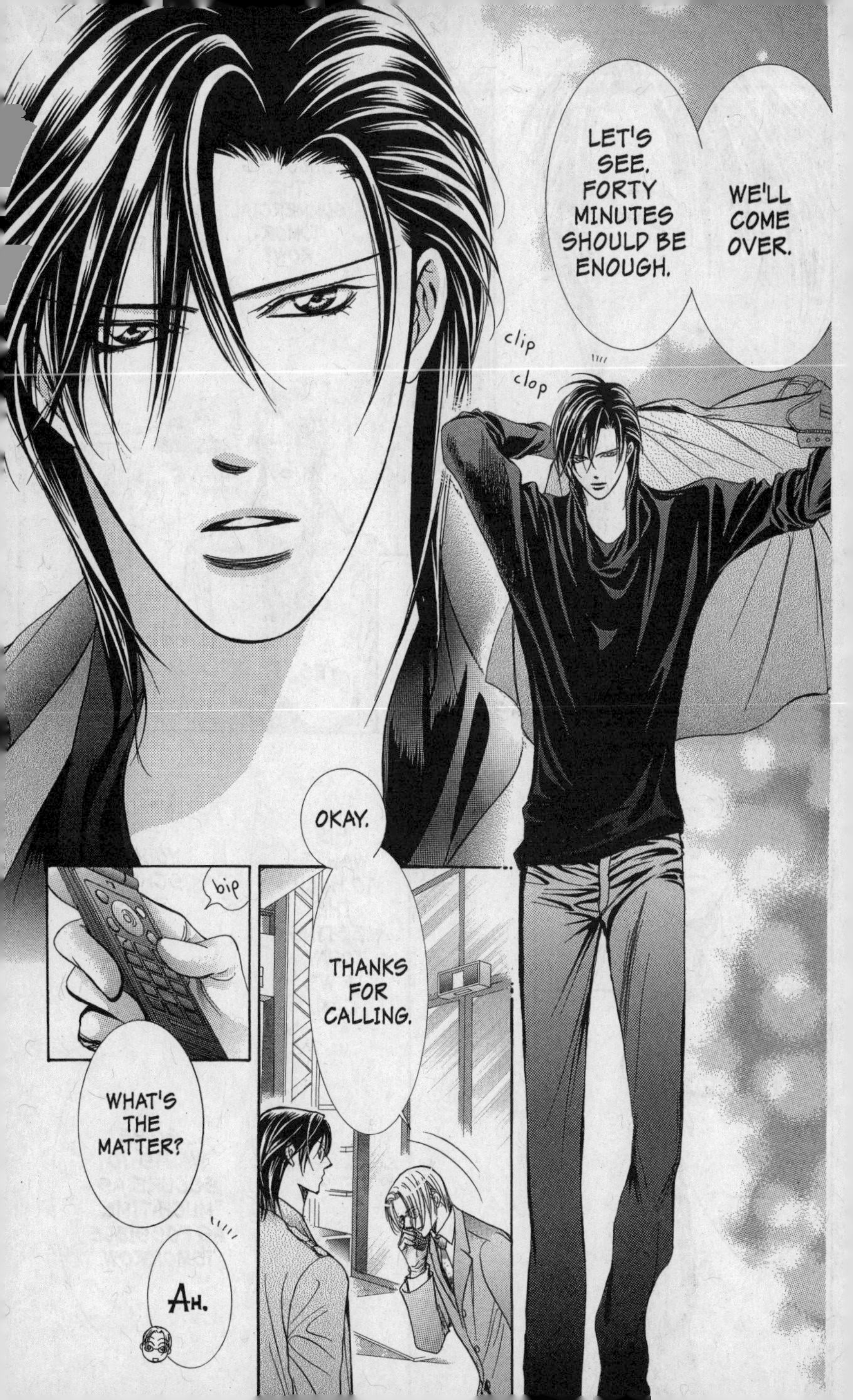
WE'LL COME OVER.
LET'S SEE. FORTY MINUTES SHOULD BE ENOUGH.
clip
clop
OKAY.
bip
THANKS FOR CALLING.
WHAT'S THE MATTER?
AH.

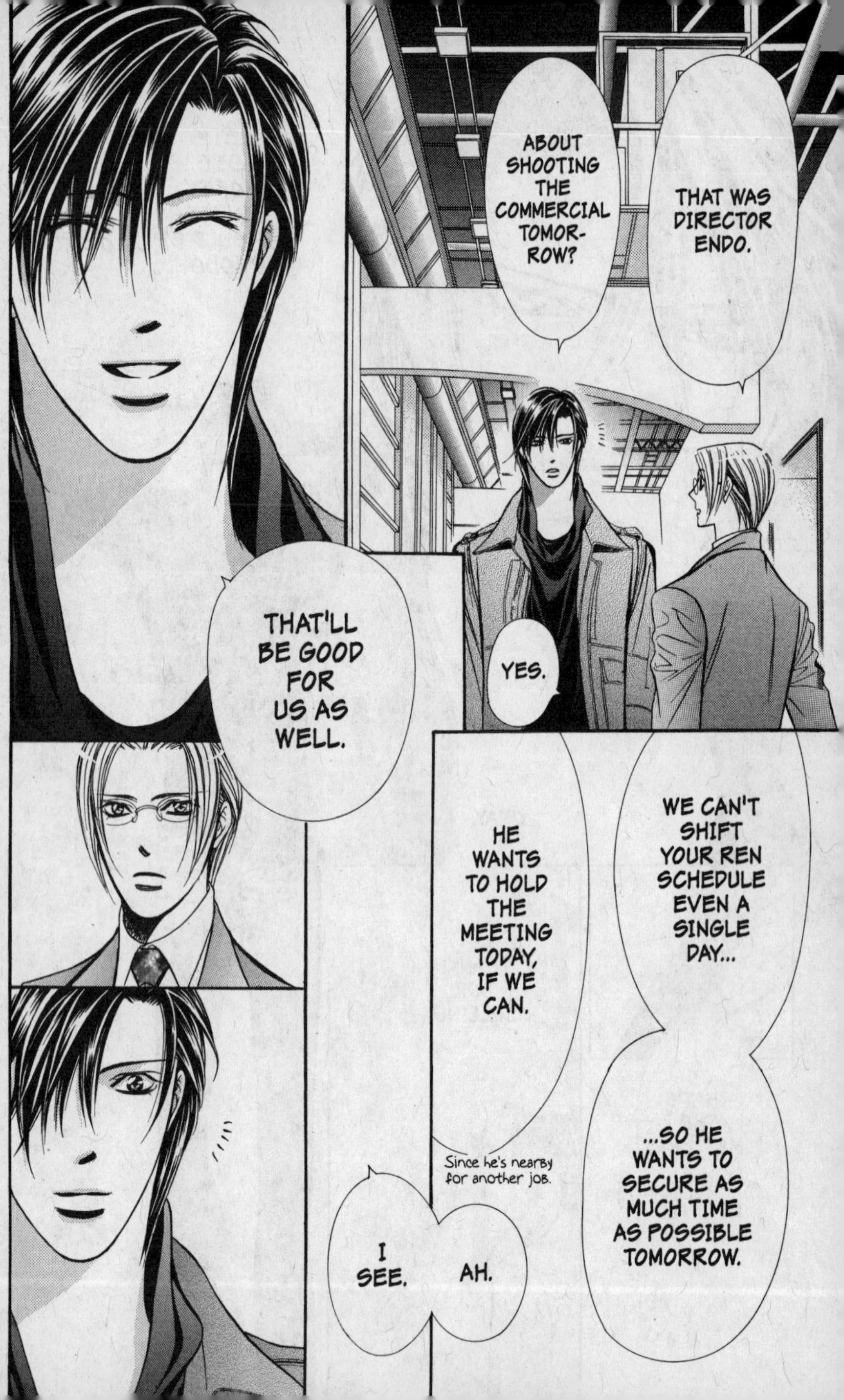
THAT WAS DIRECTOR ENDO.
ABOUT SHOOTING THE COMMERCIAL TOMOR-ROW?
YES.
WE CAN'T SHIFT YOUR REN SCHEDULE EVEN A SINGLE DAY...
...SO HE WANTS TO SECURE AS MUCH TIME AS POSSIBLE TOMORROW.
HE WANTS TO HOLD THE MEETING TODAY, IF WE CAN.
Since he's nearby for another job.
AH.
I SEE.
THAT'LL BE GOOD FOR US AS WELL.

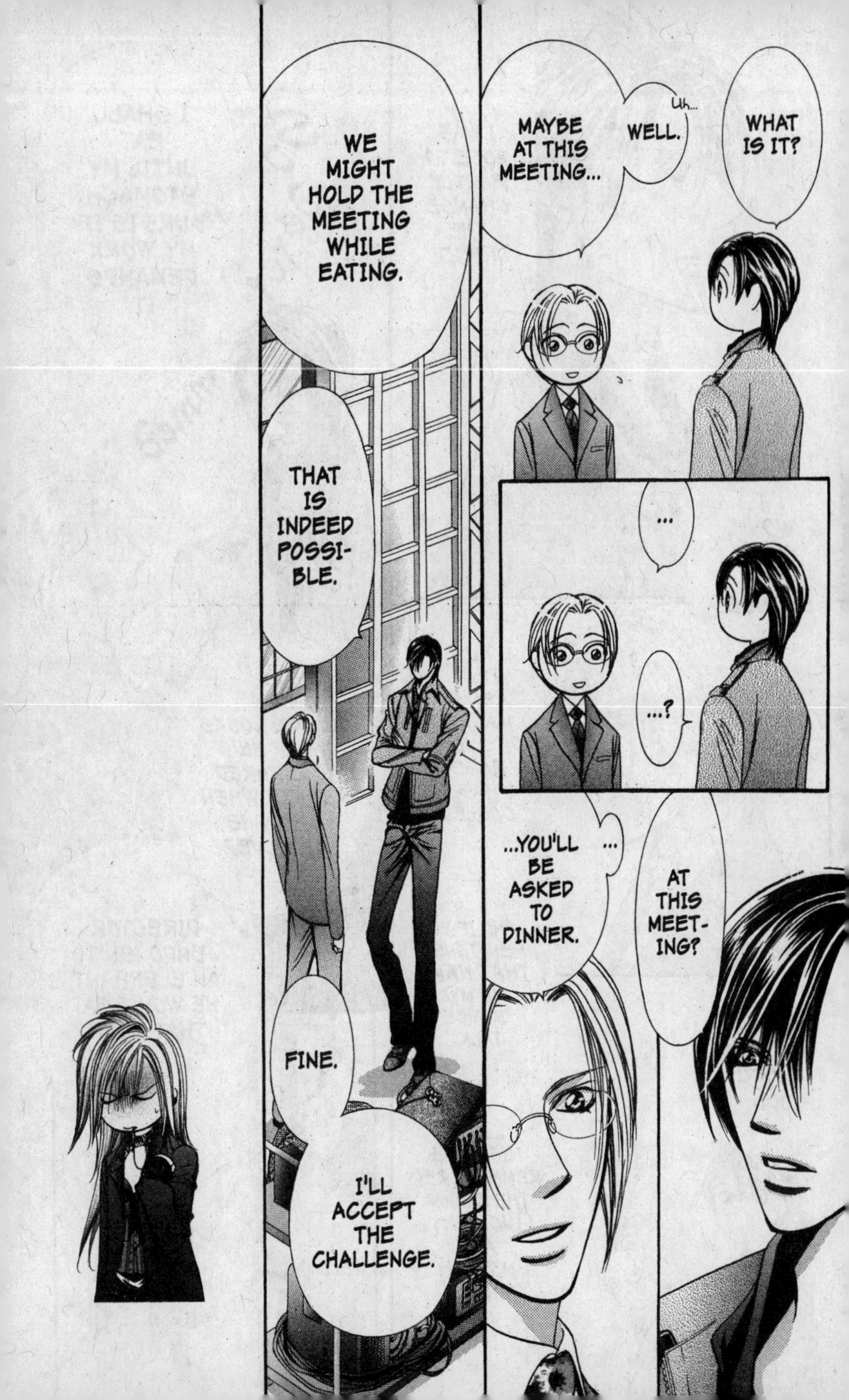
WHAT IS IT?
Uh...
WELL.
MAYBE AT THIS MEETING...
...
...?
AT THIS MEET-ING?
...
...YOU'LL BE ASKED TO DINNER.
WE MIGHT HOLD THE MEETING WHILE EATING.
THAT IS INDEED POSSIBLE.
FINE.
I'LL ACCEPT THE CHALLENGE.

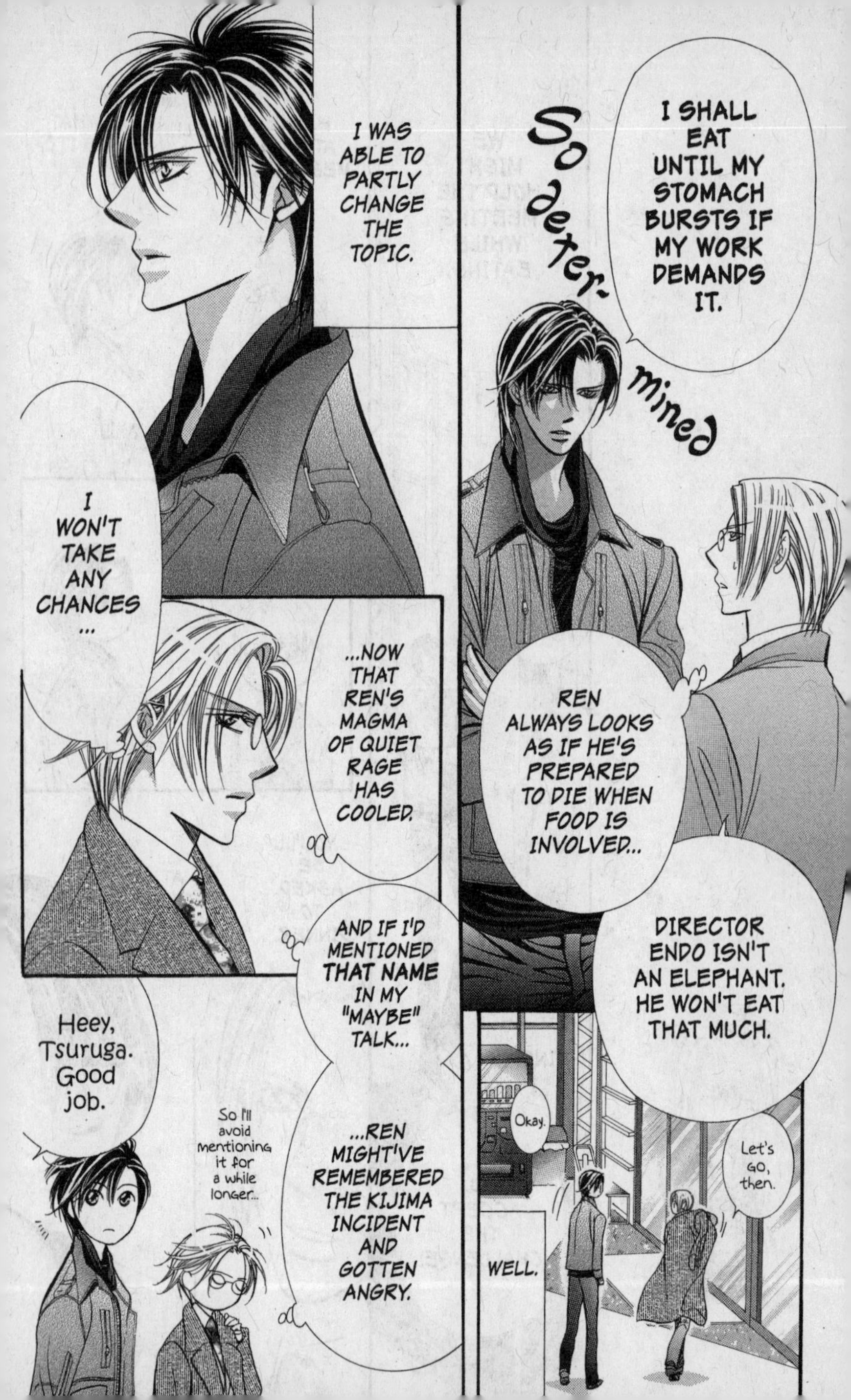
I SHALL EAT UNTIL MY STOMACH BURSTS IF MY WORK DEMANDS IT.
So deter-mined
REN ALWAYS LOOKS AS IF HE'S PREPARED TO DIE WHEN FOOD IS INVOLVED...
DIRECTOR ENDO ISN'T AN ELEPHANT. HE WON'T EAT THAT MUCH.
Let's GO, then.
Okay.
WELL.
I WAS ABLE TO PARTLY CHANGE THE TOPIC.
I WON'T TAKE ANY CHANCES ...
...NOW THAT REN'S MAGMA OF QUIET RAGE HAS COOLED.
AND IF I'D MENTIONED THAT NAME IN MY "MAYBE" TALK...
...REN MIGHT'VE REMEMBERED THE KIJIMA INCIDENT AND GOTTEN ANGRY.
So I'll avoid mentioning it for a while longer...
Heey, Tsuruga. Good job.

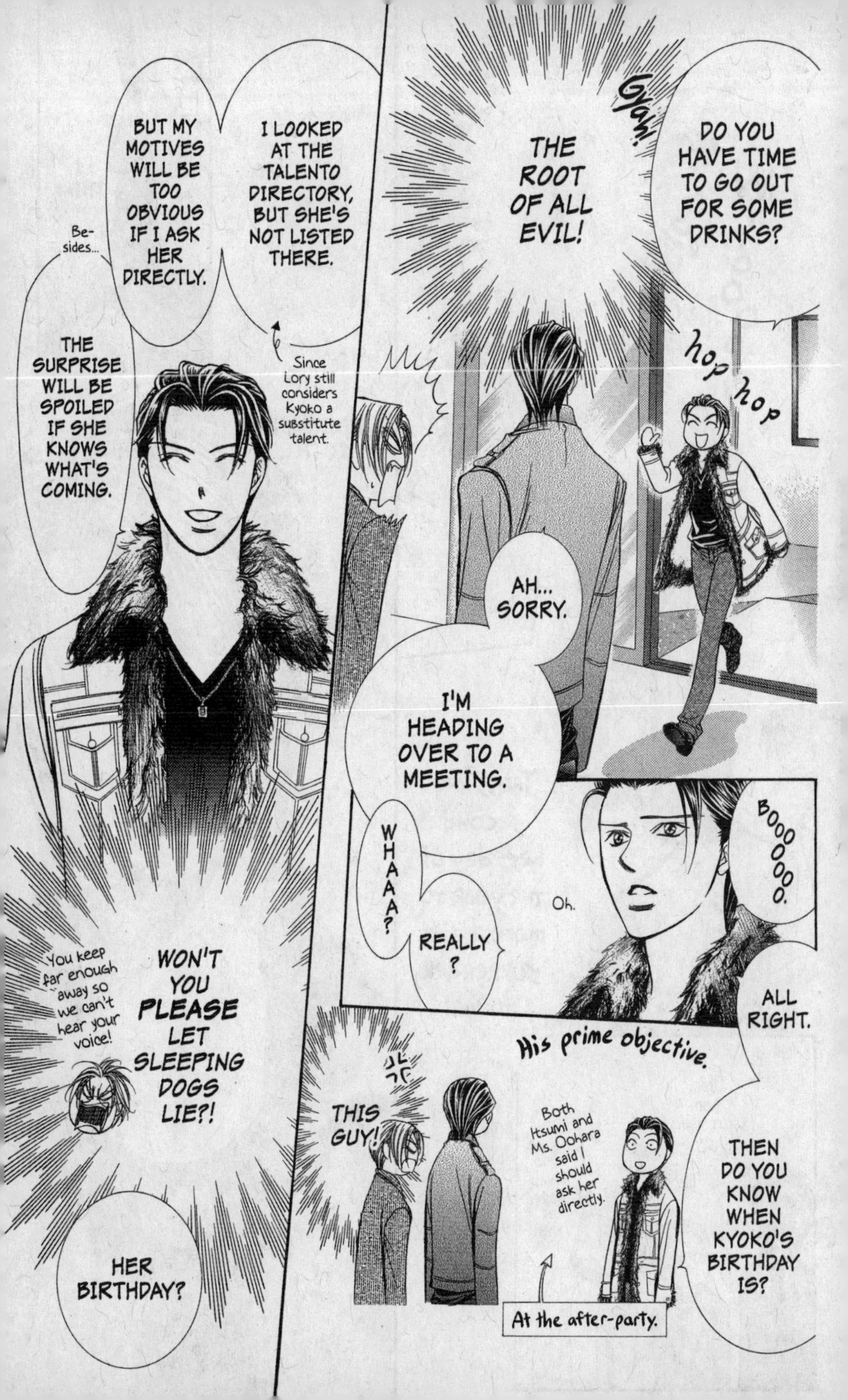
DO YOU HAVE TIME TO GO OUT FOR SOME DRINKS?
hop hop
Gyah!
THE ROOT OF ALL EVIL!
AH... SORRY.
I'M HEADING OVER TO A MEETING.
BOOOOOOO.
WHAAAA?
Oh.
REALLY?
ALL RIGHT.
His prime objective.
THEN DO YOU KNOW WHEN KYOKO'S BIRTHDAY IS?
Both Itsumi and Ms. Oohara said I should ask her directly.
At the after-party.
THIS GUY!
I LOOKED AT THE TALENTO DIRECTORY, BUT SHE'S NOT LISTED THERE.
Since Lory still considers Kyoko a substitute talent.
BUT MY MOTIVES WILL BE TOO OBVIOUS IF I ASK HER DIRECTLY.
Be-sides...
THE SURPRISE WILL BE SPOILED IF SHE KNOWS WHAT'S COMING.
WON'T YOU PLEASE LET SLEEPING DOGS LIE?!
You keep far enough away so we can't hear your voice!
HER BIRTHDAY?

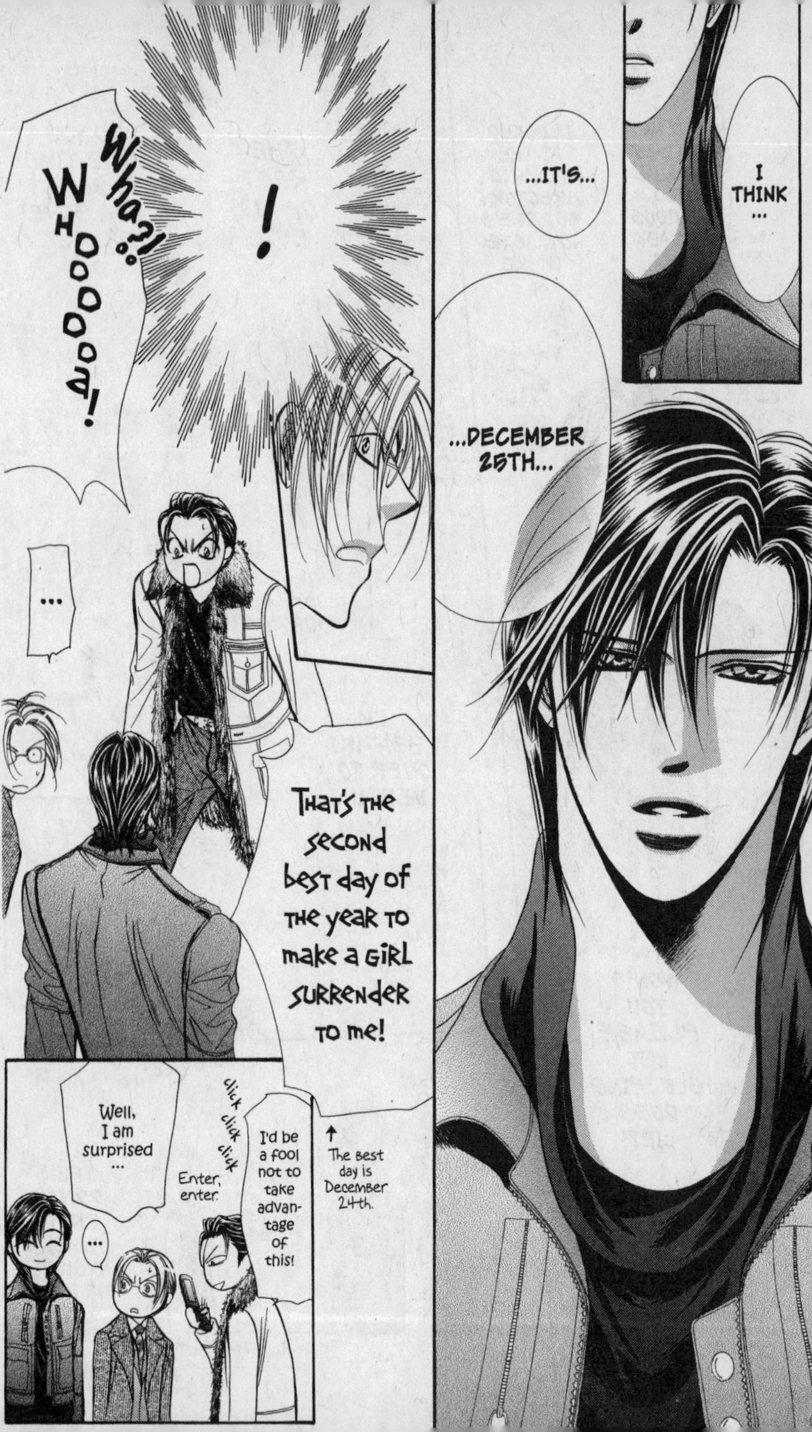
I THINK...
...IT'S...
...DECEMBER 25TH...
!
Wha?! WHOOOOOa!
...
That's the second best day of the year to make a girl surrender to me!
↑ The best day is December 24th.
I'd be a fool not to take advantage of this!
click click click
Enter, enter.
Well, I am surprised...
...

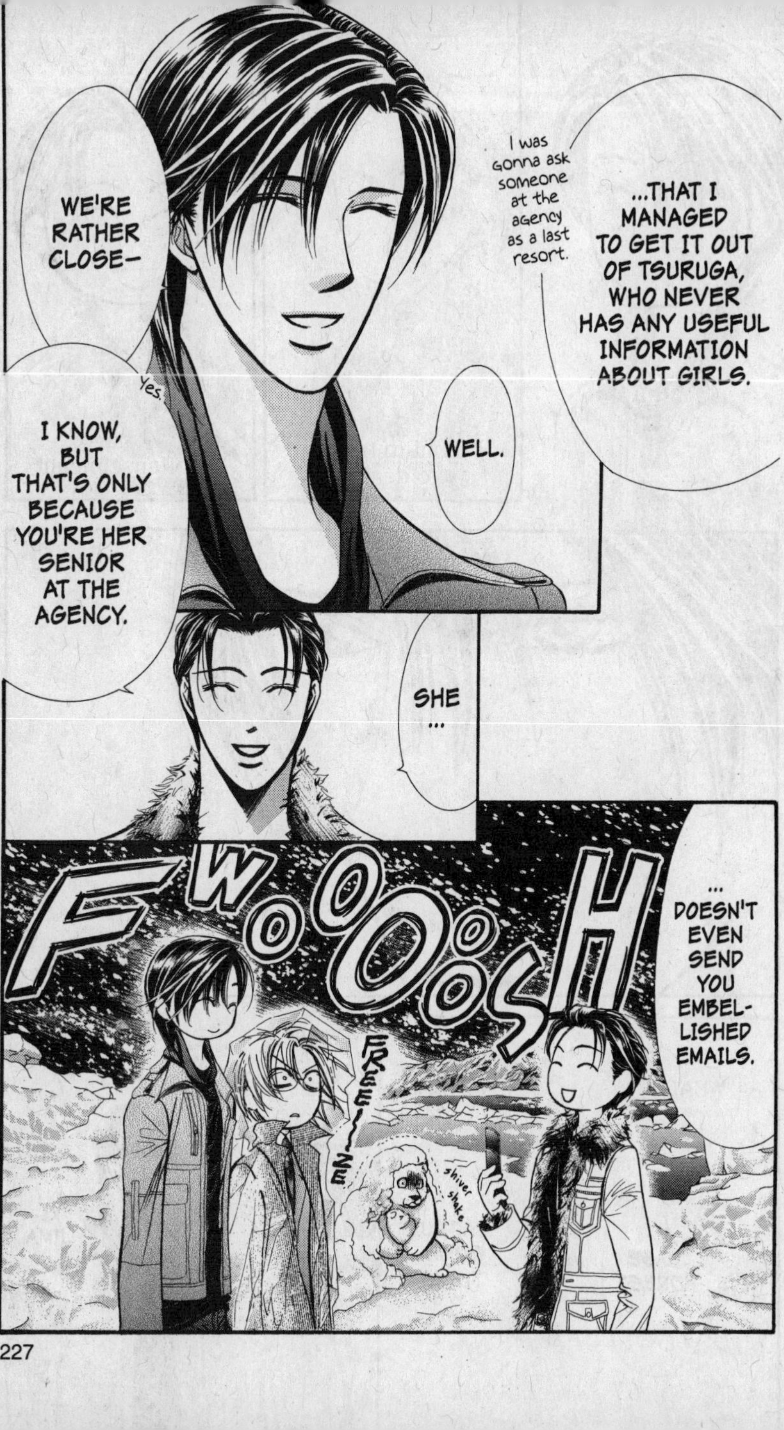

I was gonna ask someone at the agency as a last resort.
...THAT I MANAGED TO GET IT OUT OF TSURUGA, WHO NEVER HAS ANY USEFUL INFORMATION ABOUT GIRLS.
WE'RE RATHER CLOSE—
WELL.
Yes.
I KNOW, BUT THAT'S ONLY BECAUSE YOU'RE HER SENIOR AT THE AGENCY.
SHE ...
... DOESN'T EVEN SEND YOU EMBEL-LISHED EMAILS.
FWOOOOSH
FREE—NE
shiver shake

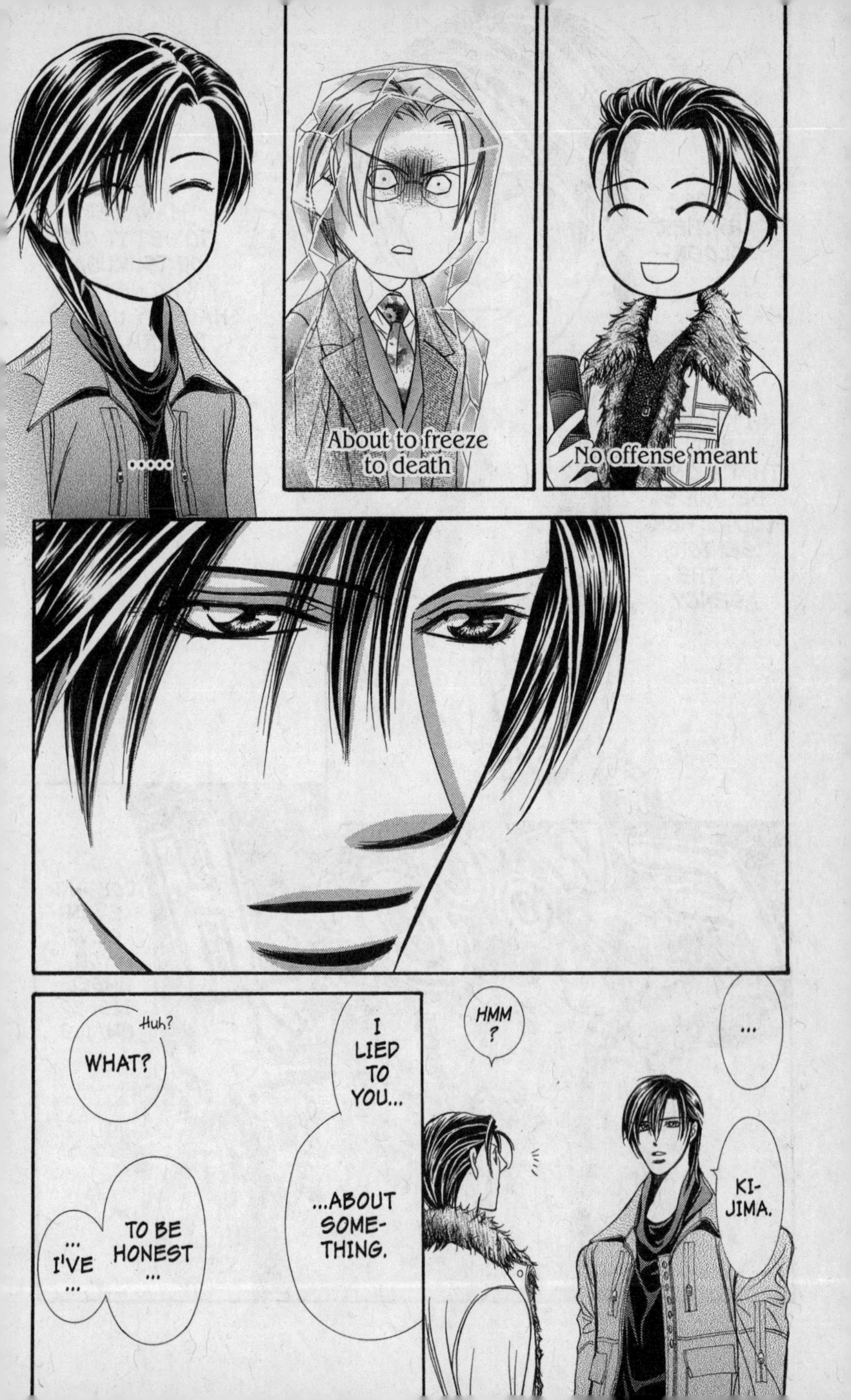

No offense meant
About to freeze to death
......
...
KI-JIMA.
HMM?
I LIED TO YOU...
...ABOUT SOMETHING.
Huh?
WHAT?
TO BE HONEST...
...I'VE...

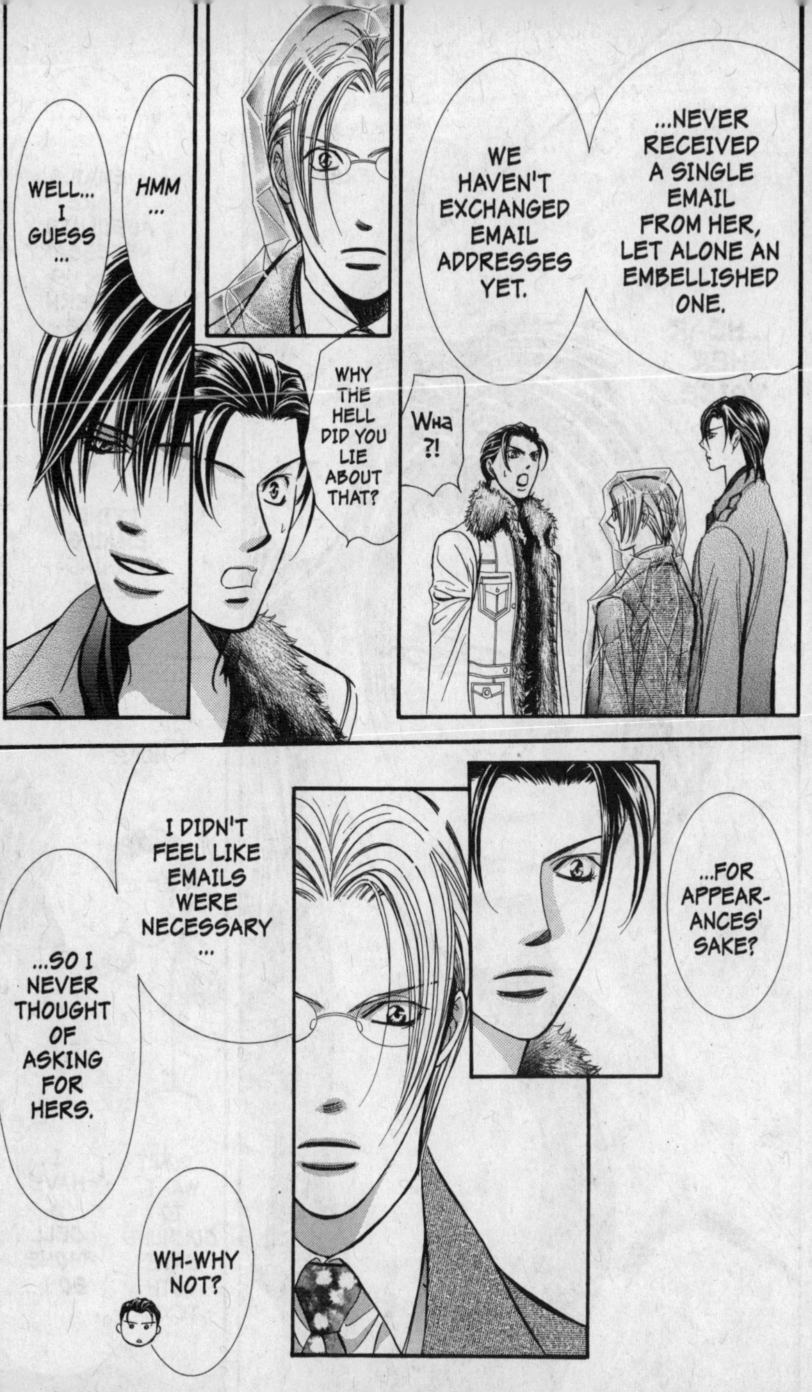
...NEVER RECEIVED A SINGLE EMAIL FROM HER, LET ALONE AN EMBELLISHED ONE.
WE HAVEN'T EXCHANGED EMAIL ADDRESSES YET.
WHA ?!
WHY THE HELL DID YOU LIE ABOUT THAT?
HMM ...
WELL... I GUESS ...
...FOR APPEARANCES' SAKE?
I DIDN'T FEEL LIKE EMAILS WERE NECESSARY ...
...SO I NEVER THOUGHT OF ASKING FOR HERS.
WH-WHY NOT?

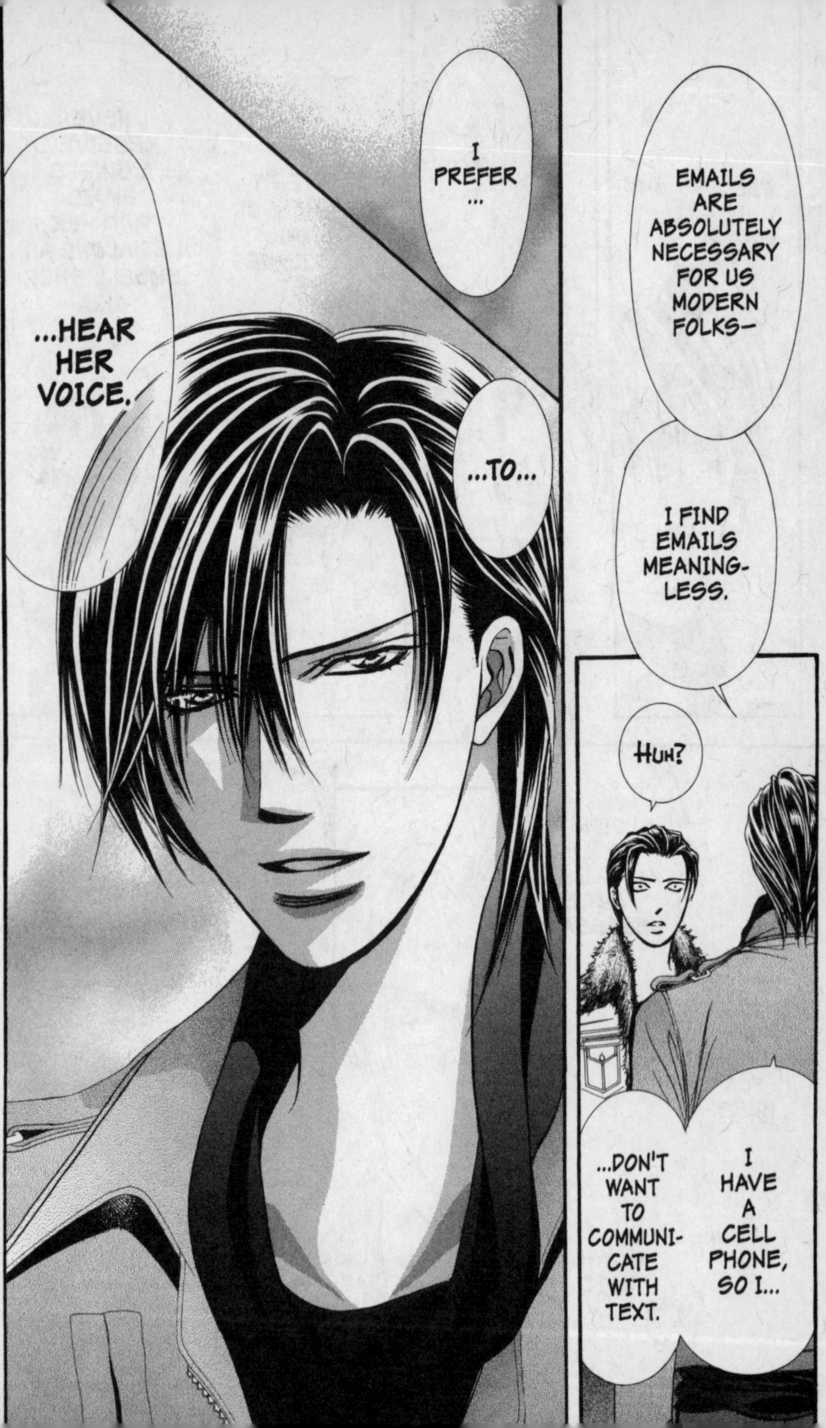
EMAILS ARE ABSOLUTELY NECESSARY FOR US MODERN FOLKS—
I FIND EMAILS MEANING-LESS.
HUH?
I HAVE A CELL PHONE, SO I...
...DON'T WANT TO COMMUNI-CATE WITH TEXT.
I PREFER ...
...TO...
...HEAR HER VOICE.

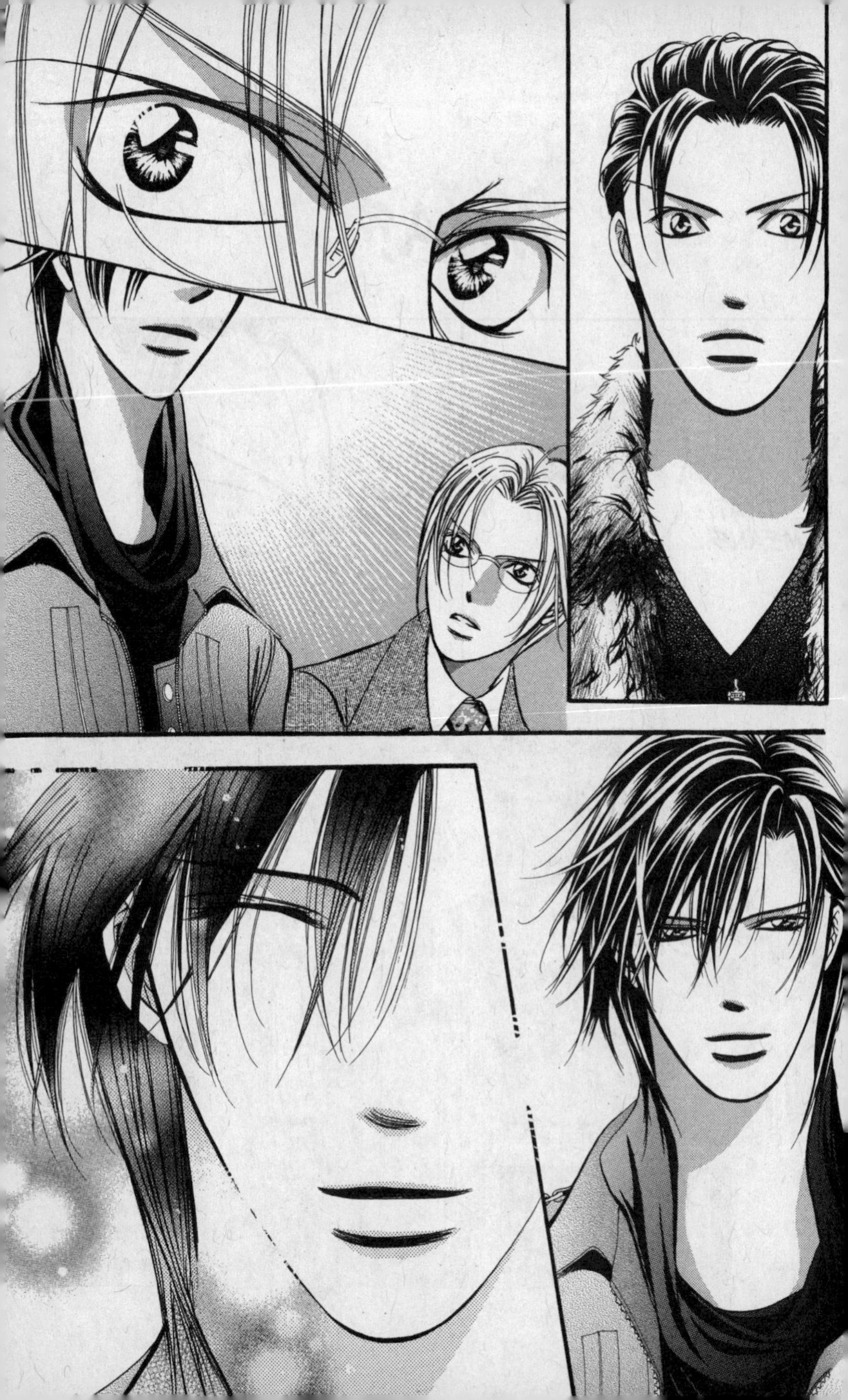

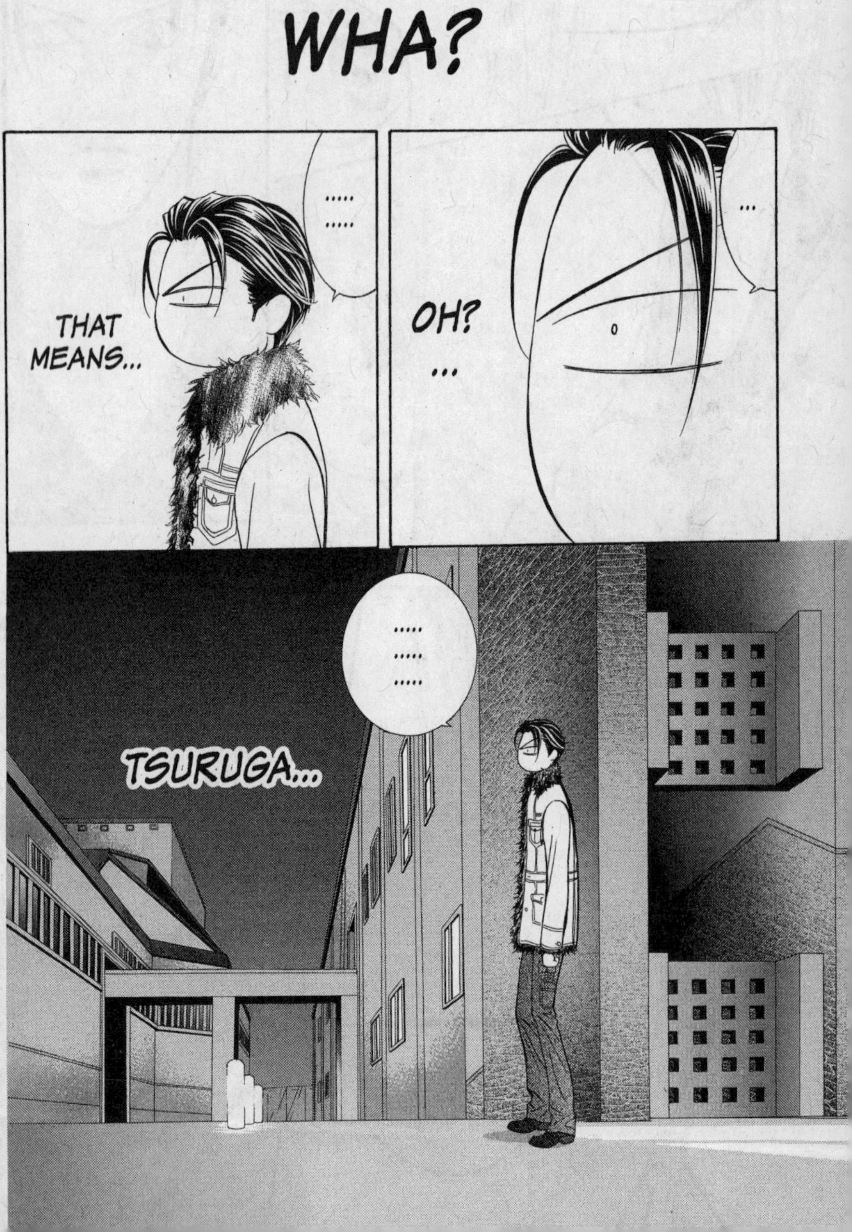
WHA?
...
OH? ...
....
THAT MEANS...
....
TSURUGA...

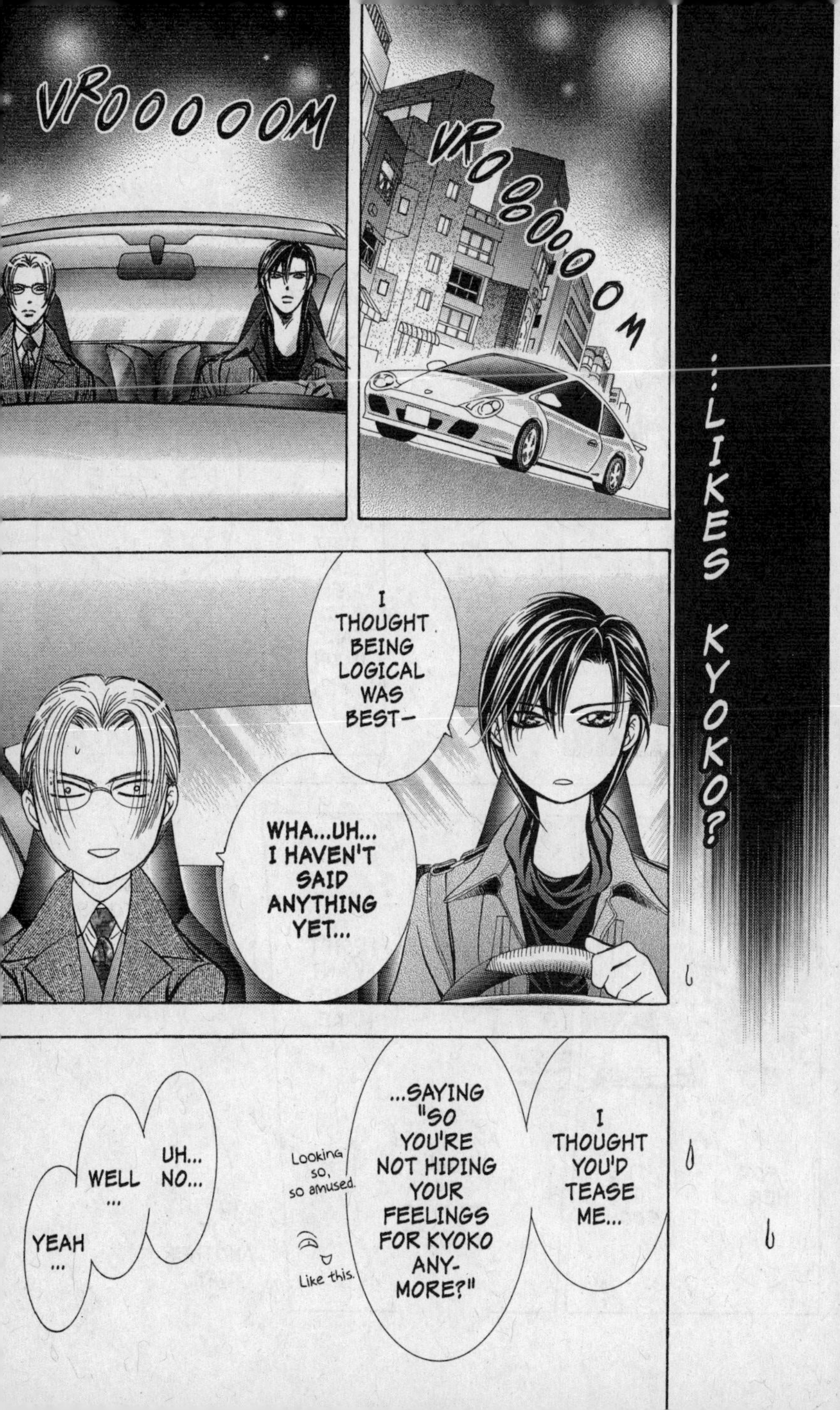
...LIKES KYOKO?
VROOOOOOOM
VROOOOOOM
I THOUGHT BEING LOGICAL WAS BEST—
WHA...UH... I HAVEN'T SAID ANYTHING YET...
I THOUGHT YOU'D TEASE ME...
...SAYING "SO YOU'RE NOT HIDING YOUR FEELINGS FOR KYOKO ANY-MORE?"
Looking so, so amused.
Like this.
UH... NO...
WELL...
YEAH...

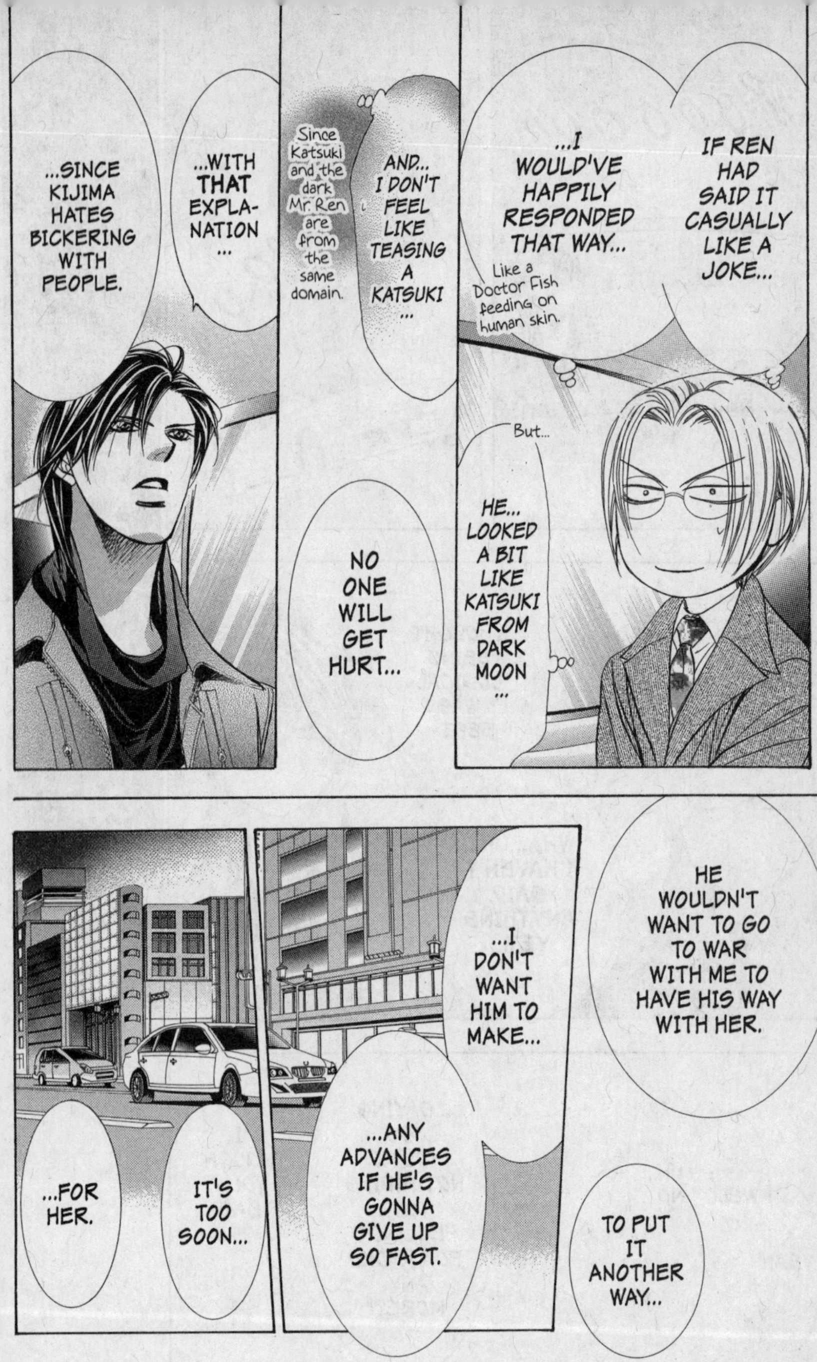
IF REN HAD SAID IT CASUALLY LIKE A JOKE...
...I WOULD'VE HAPPILY RESPONDED THAT WAY...
Like a Doctor Fish feeding on human skin.
But...
HE... LOOKED A BIT LIKE KATSUKI FROM DARK MOON...
AND... I DON'T FEEL LIKE TEASING A KATSUKI...
Since Katsuki and the dark Mr. Ren are from the same domain.
NO ONE WILL GET HURT...
...WITH THAT EXPLANATION...
...SINCE KIJIMA HATES BICKERING WITH PEOPLE.
HE WOULDN'T WANT TO GO TO WAR WITH ME TO HAVE HIS WAY WITH HER.
TO PUT IT ANOTHER WAY...
...I DON'T WANT HIM TO MAKE...
...ANY ADVANCES IF HE'S GONNA GIVE UP SO FAST.
IT'S TOO SOON...
...FOR HER.

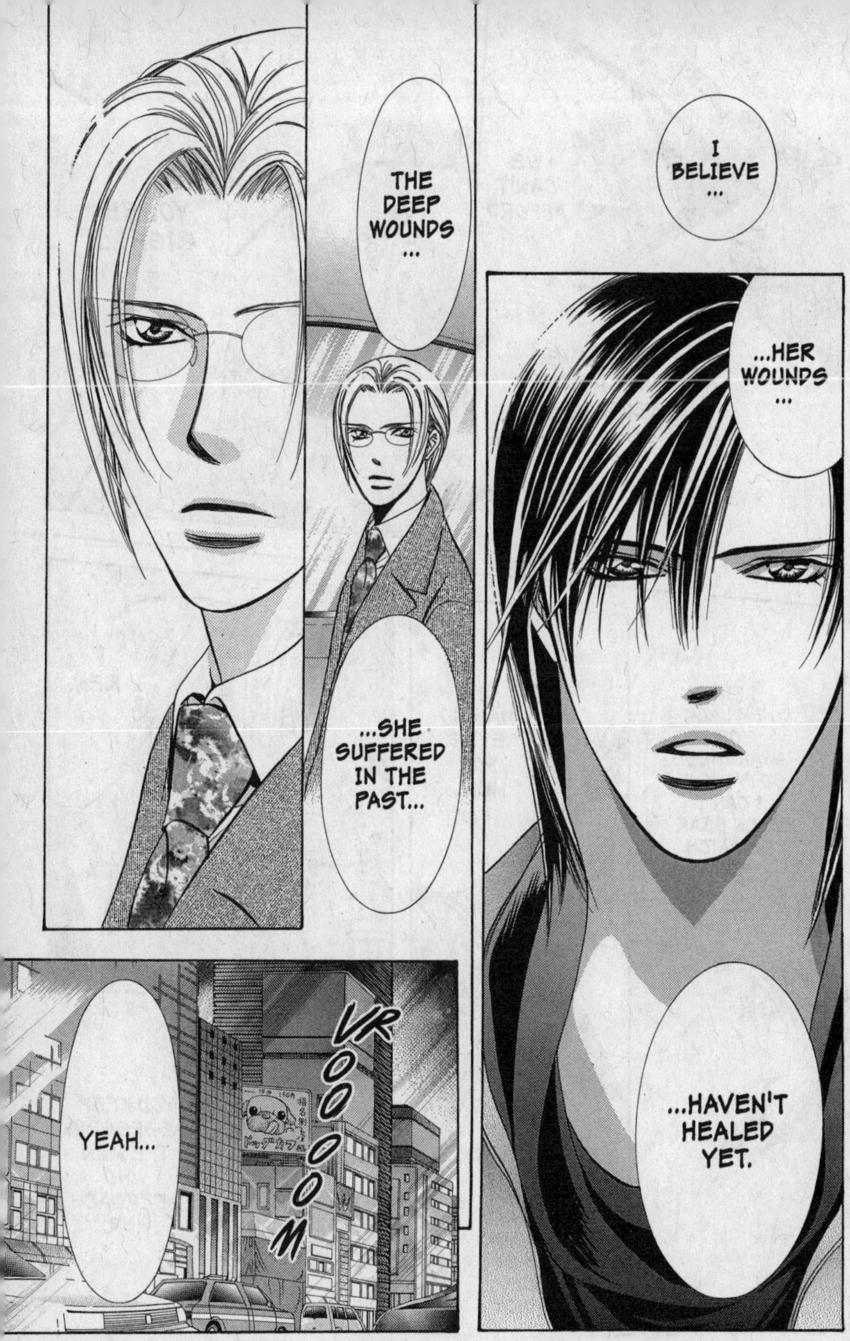
I BELIEVE...
...HER WOUNDS...
...HAVEN'T HEALED YET.
THE DEEP WOUNDS...
...SHE SUFFERED IN THE PAST...
VROOOOOOM
YEAH...

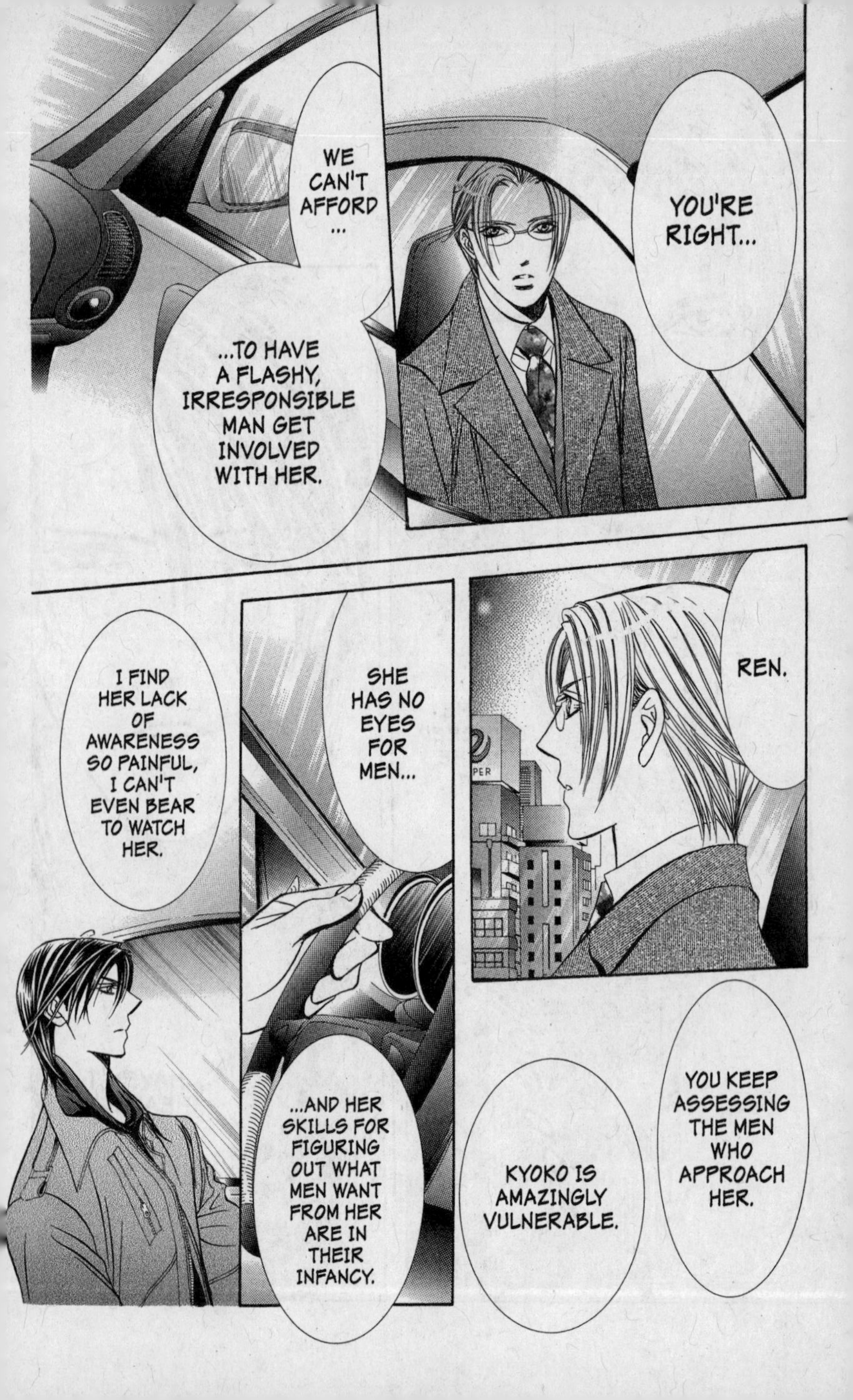
YOU'RE RIGHT...
WE CAN'T AFFORD ...
...TO HAVE A FLASHY, IRRESPONSIBLE MAN GET INVOLVED WITH HER.
REN.
YOU KEEP ASSESSING THE MEN WHO APPROACH HER.
KYOKO IS AMAZINGLY VULNERABLE.
SHE HAS NO EYES FOR MEN...
...AND HER SKILLS FOR FIGURING OUT WHAT MEN WANT FROM HER ARE IN THEIR INFANCY.
I FIND HER LACK OF AWARENESS SO PAINFUL, I CAN'T EVEN BEAR TO WATCH HER.

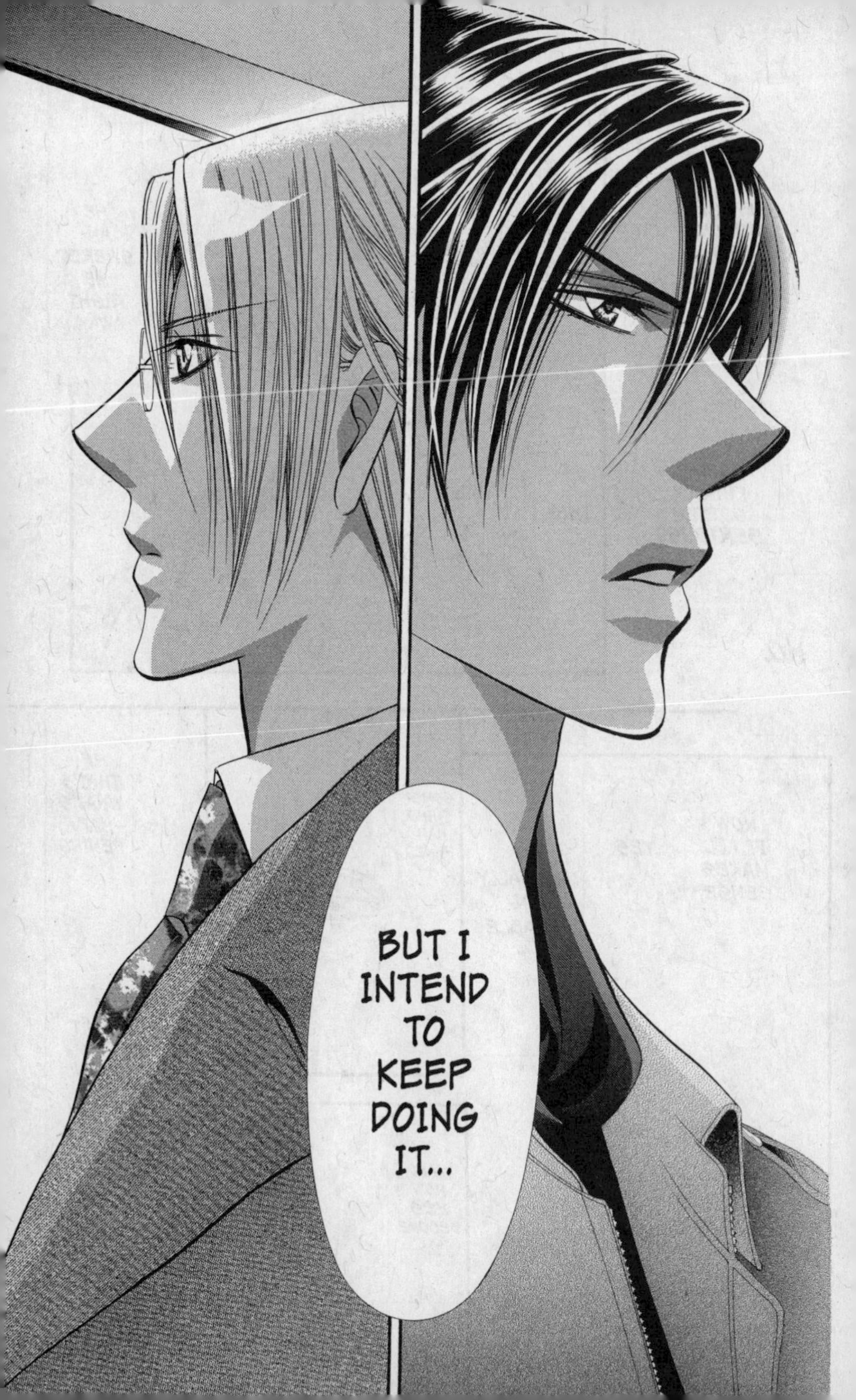
BUT I INTEND TO KEEP DOING IT...

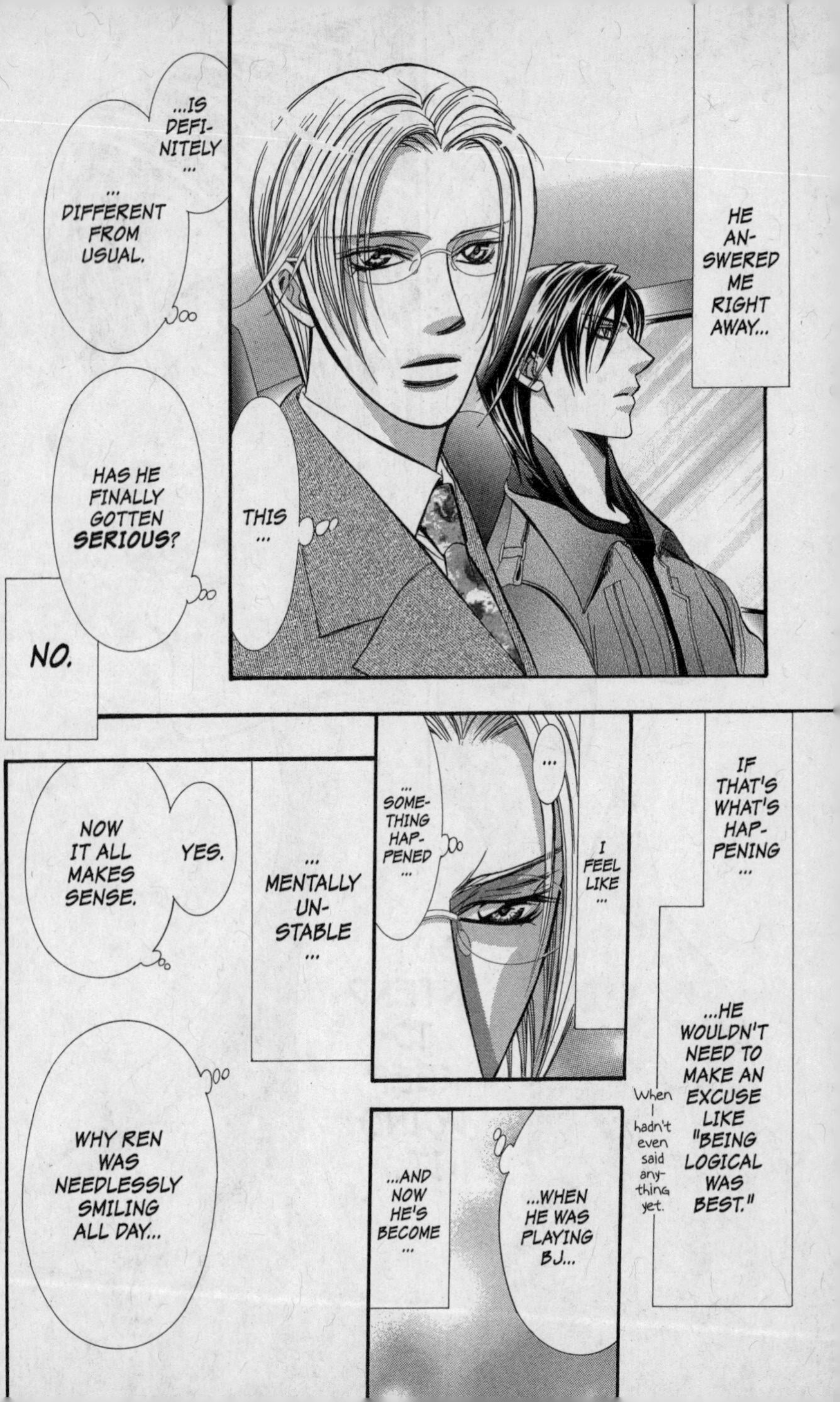

HE ANSWERED ME RIGHT AWAY...
THIS...
...IS DEFINITELY... ...DIFFERENT FROM USUAL.
HAS HE FINALLY GOTTEN SERIOUS?
NO.
IF THAT'S WHAT'S HAPPENING...
...HE WOULDN'T NEED TO MAKE AN EXCUSE LIKE "BEING LOGICAL WAS BEST."
When I hadn't even said anything yet.
I FEEL LIKE...
...
...SOMETHING HAPPENED...
...WHEN HE WAS PLAYING BJ...
...AND NOW HE'S BECOME...
...MENTALLY UNSTABLE...
YES.
NOW IT ALL MAKES SENSE.
WHY REN WAS NEEDLESSLY SMILING ALL DAY...

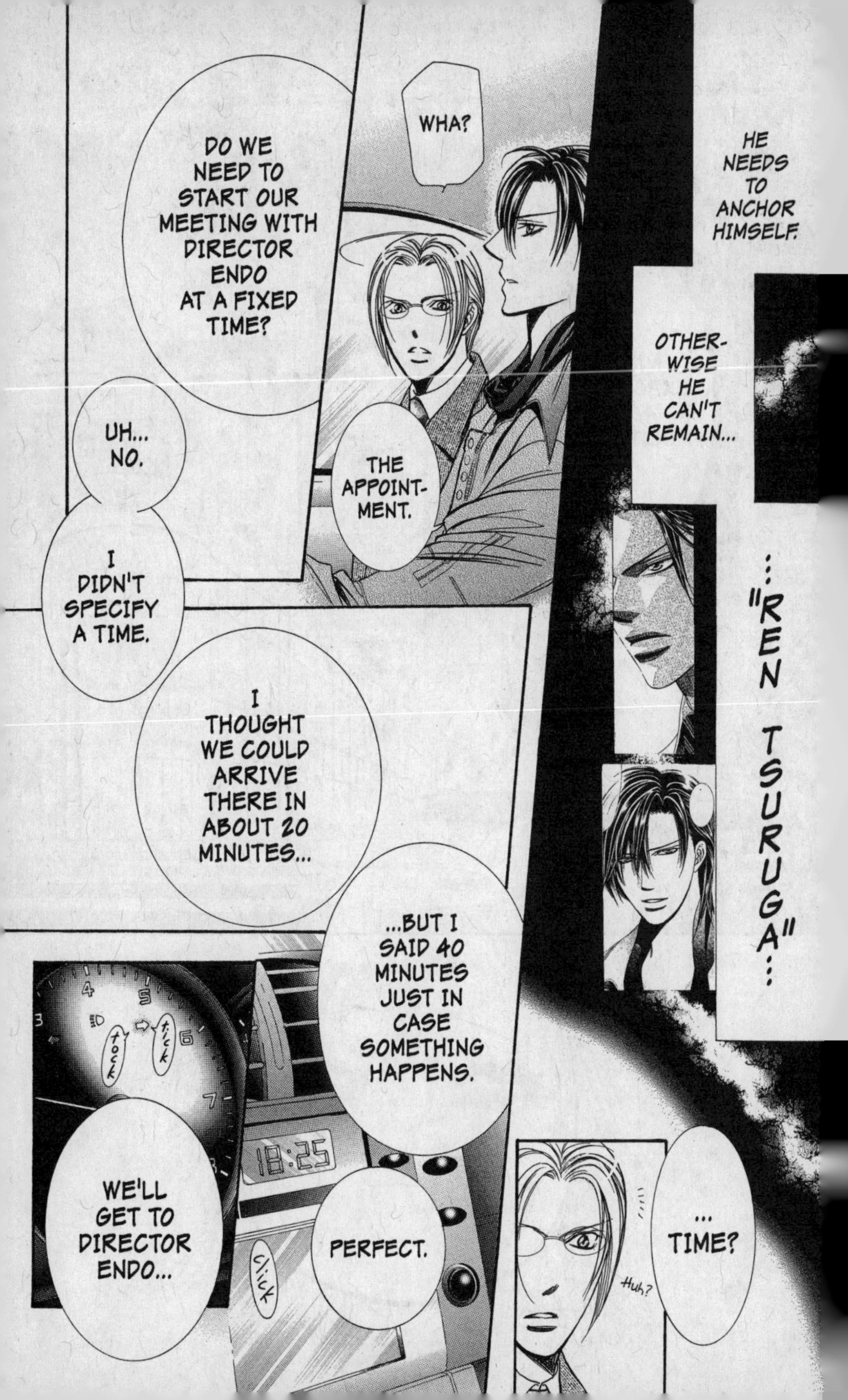
HE NEEDS TO ANCHOR HIMSELF.
OTHERWISE HE CAN'T REMAIN...
..."REN TSURUGA"...
WHA?
DO WE NEED TO START OUR MEETING WITH DIRECTOR ENDO AT A FIXED TIME?
THE APPOINTMENT.
UH... NO.
I DIDN'T SPECIFY A TIME.
I THOUGHT WE COULD ARRIVE THERE IN ABOUT 20 MINUTES...
...BUT I SAID 40 MINUTES JUST IN CASE SOMETHING HAPPENS.
... TIME?
Huh?
PERFECT.
click
WE'LL GET TO DIRECTOR ENDO...
tick
tock
18:25

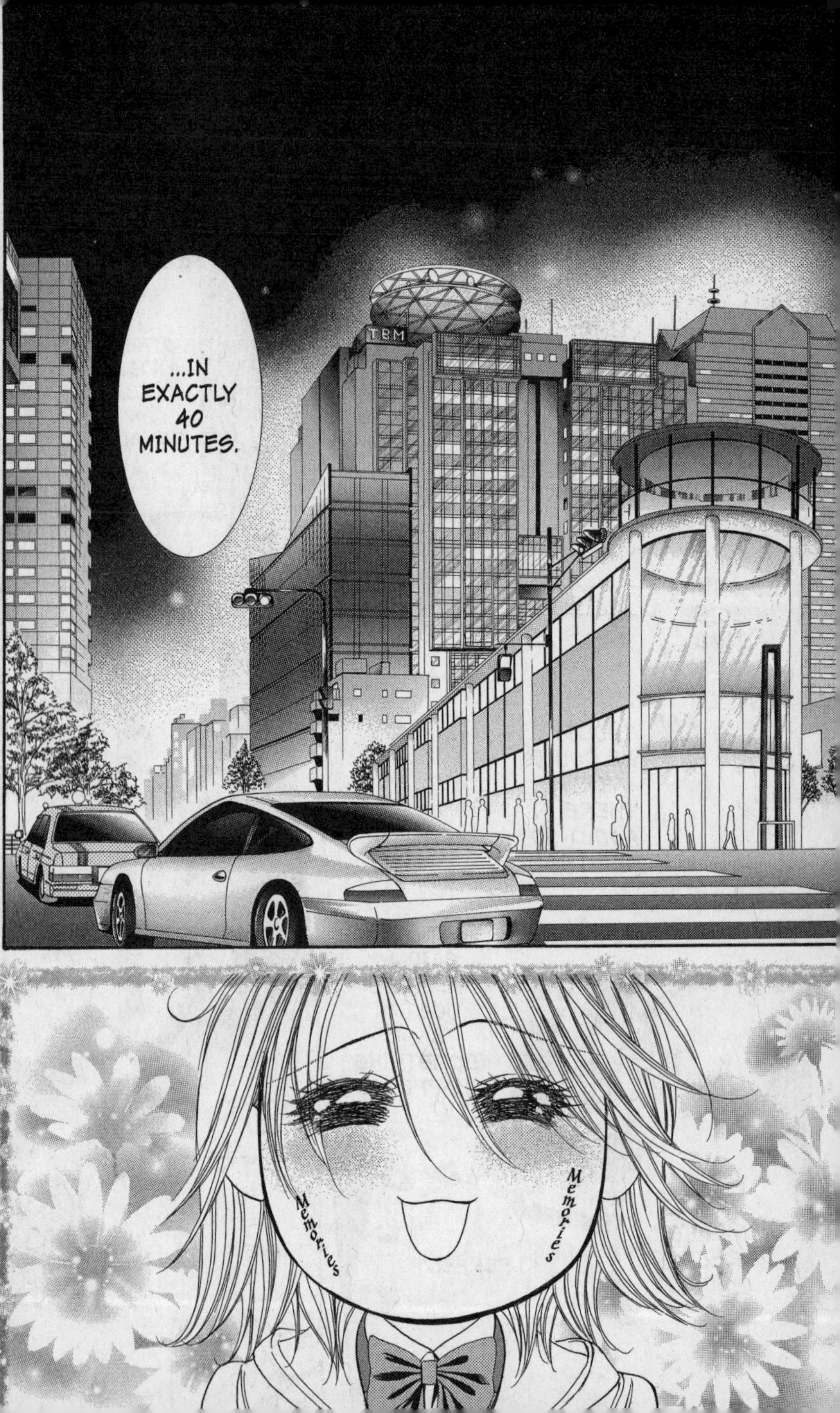
...IN EXACTLY 40 MINUTES.
TBM
Memories
Memories

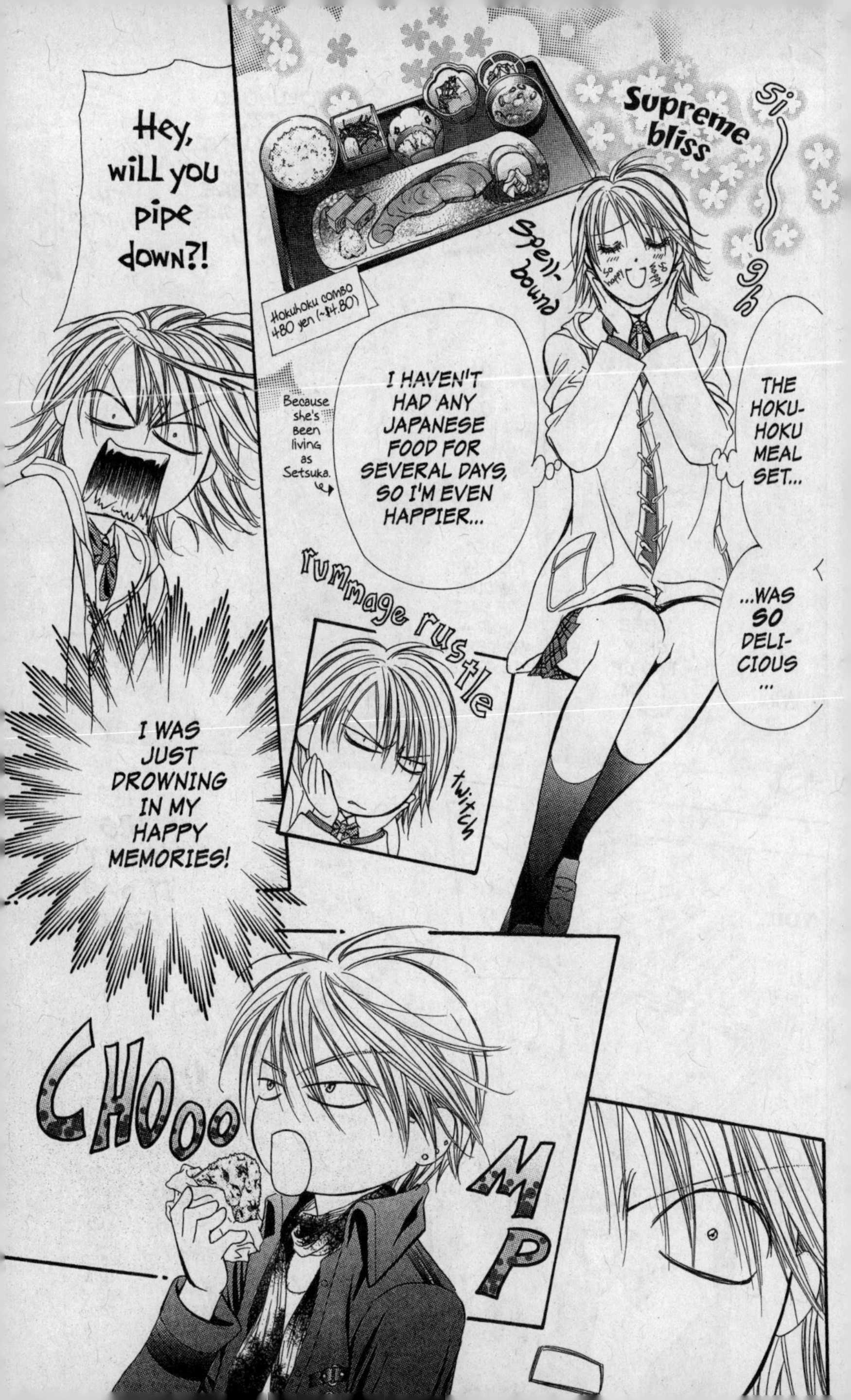
Supreme bliss
Si~gh
Spell-bound
So happy!
So happy
Hokuhoku combo 480 yen (~$4.80)
THE HOKU-HOKU MEAL SET...
...WAS SO DELICIOUS...
I HAVEN'T HAD ANY JAPANESE FOOD FOR SEVERAL DAYS, SO I'M EVEN HAPPIER...
Because she's been living as Setsuka.
rummage rustle
twitch
Hey, will you pipe down?!
I WAS JUST DROWNING IN MY HAPPY MEMORIES!
CHOOOMP

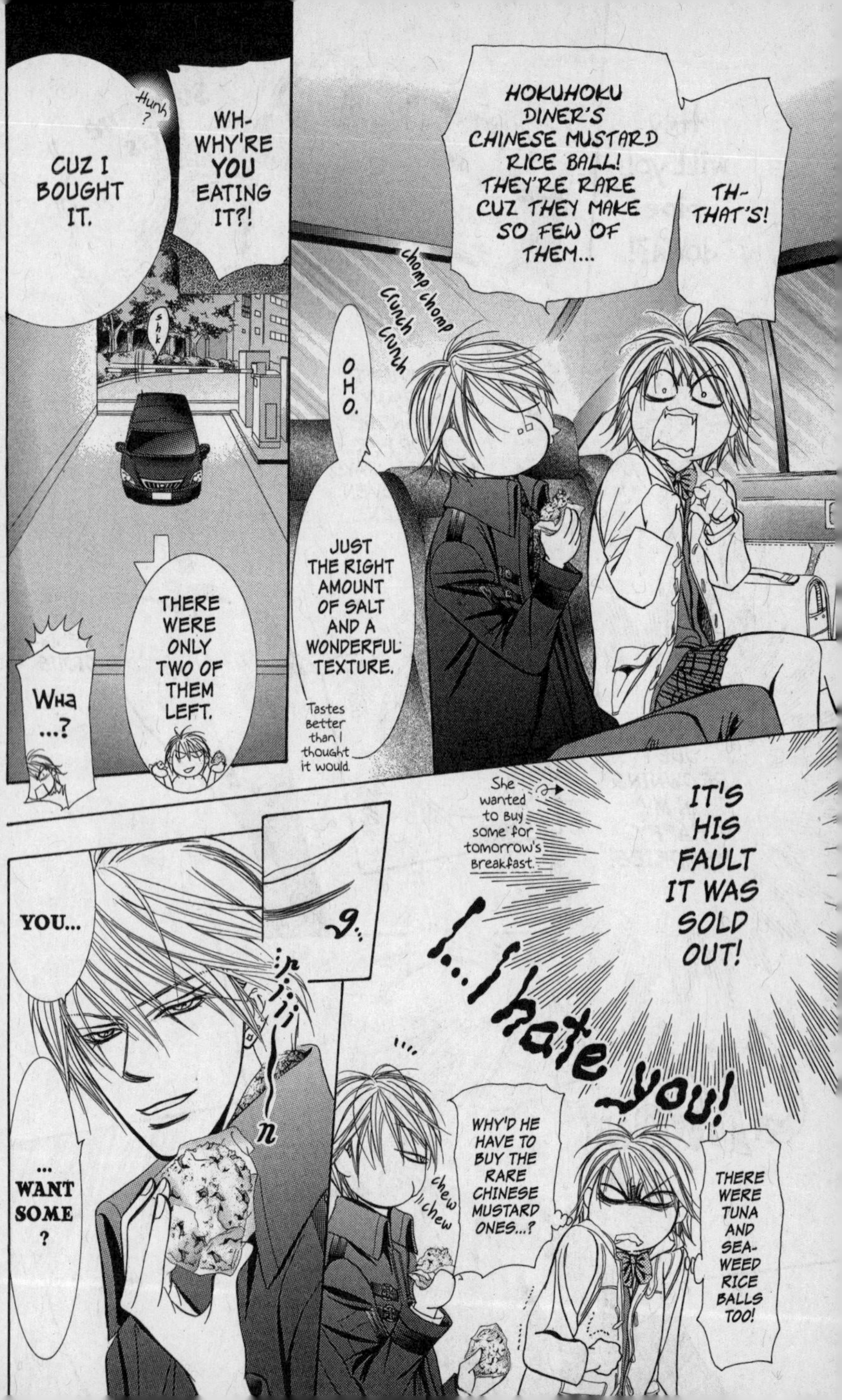
TH-THAT'S!
HOKUHOKU DINER'S CHINESE MUSTARD RICE BALL! THEY'RE RARE CUZ THEY MAKE SO FEW OF THEM...
chomp chomp
crunch crunch
OHO.
JUST THE RIGHT AMOUNT OF SALT AND A WONDERFUL TEXTURE.
Tastes better than I thought it would.
WH-WHY'RE YOU EATING IT?!
Hunh?
CUZ I BOUGHT IT.
shk
THERE WERE ONLY TWO OF THEM LEFT.
Wha...?
IT'S HIS FAULT IT WAS SOLD OUT!
She wanted to buy some for tomorrow's breakfast.
I... I hate you!
...
THERE WERE TUNA AND SEAWEED RICE BALLS TOO!
WHY'D HE HAVE TO BUY THE RARE CHINESE MUSTARD ONES...?
chew chew
YOU...
...WANT SOME?

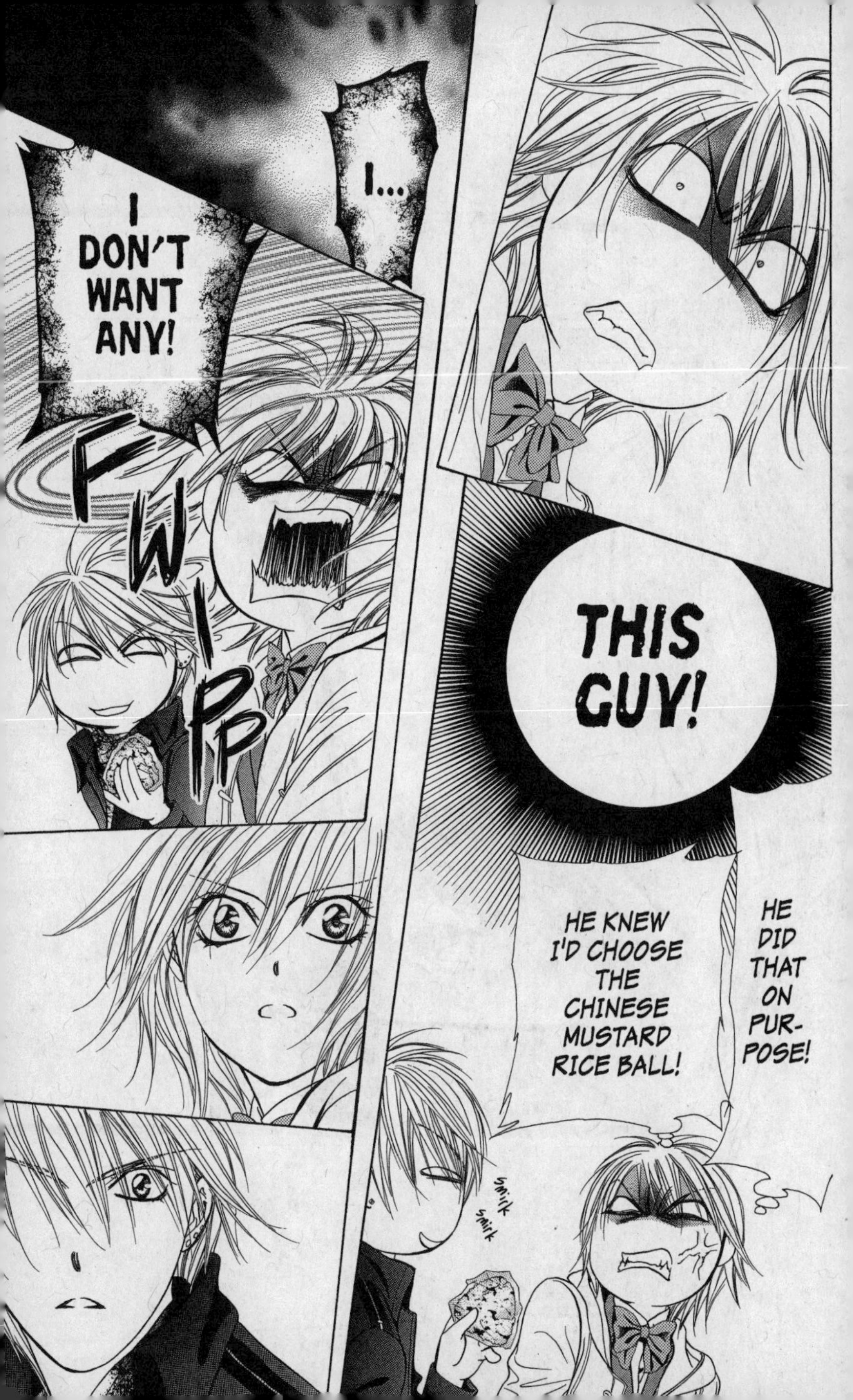
THIS GUY!
HE DID THAT ON PURPOSE!
HE KNEW I'D CHOOSE THE CHINESE MUSTARD RICE BALL!
smirk smirk
I...
I DON'T WANT ANY!
FWIPP

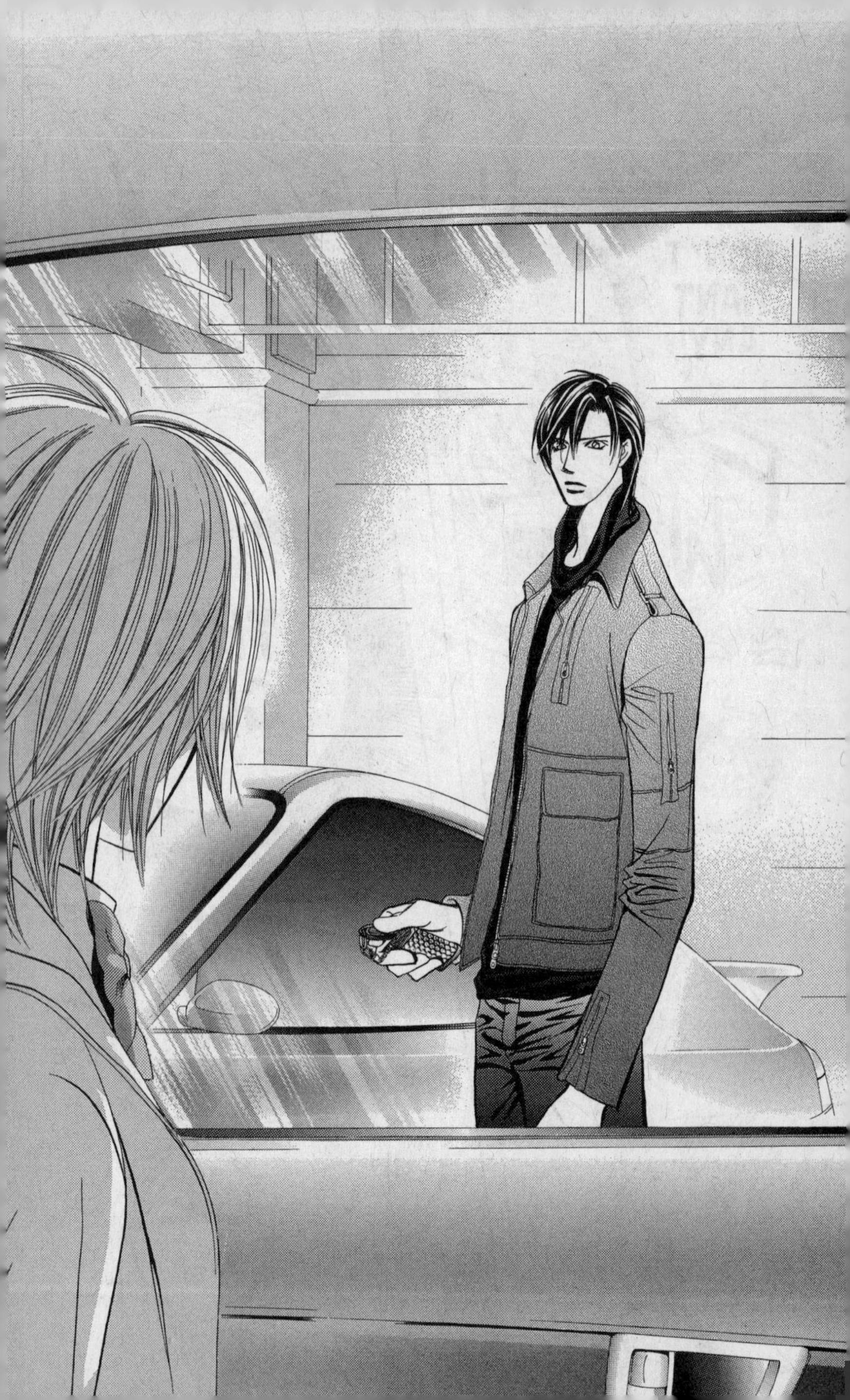

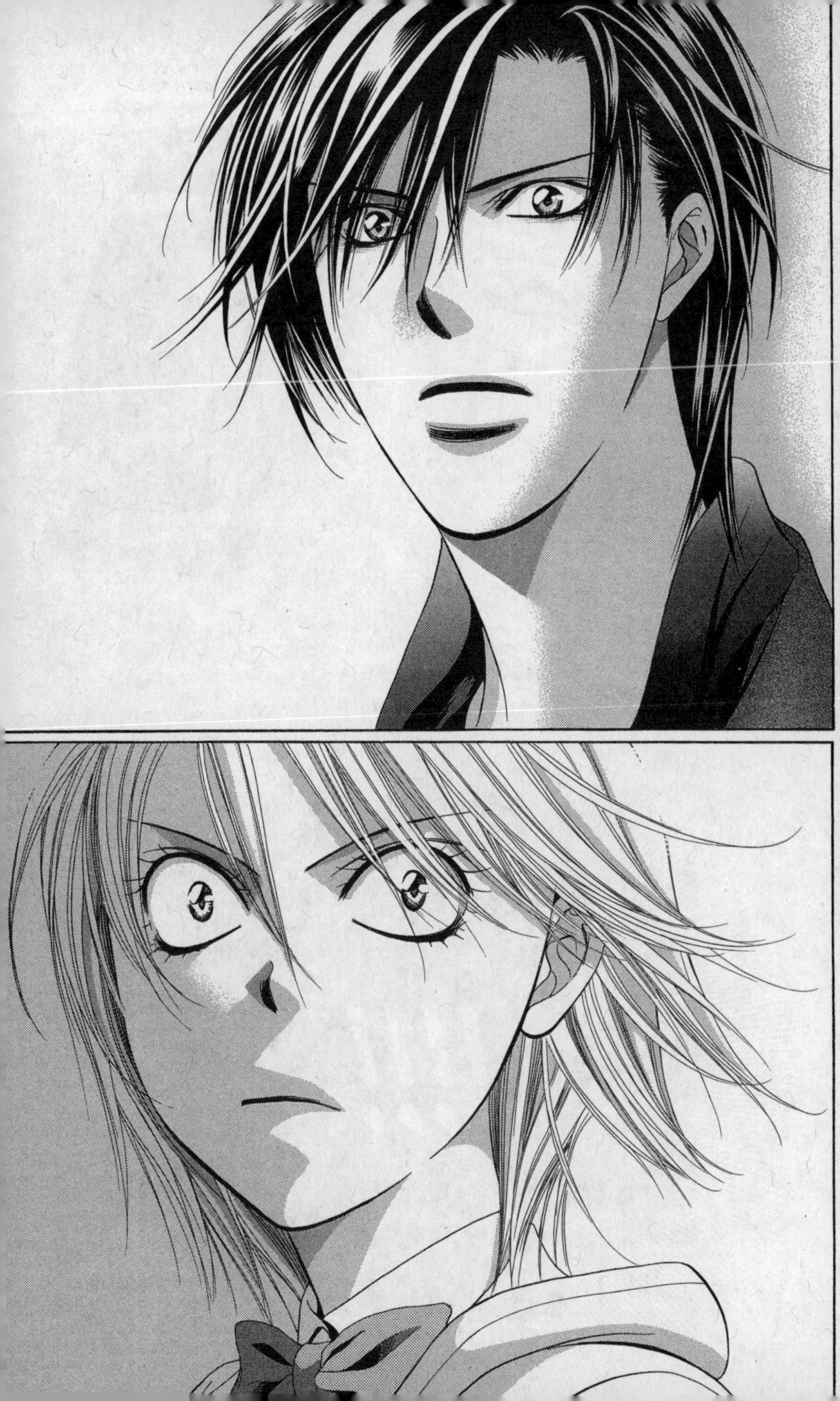

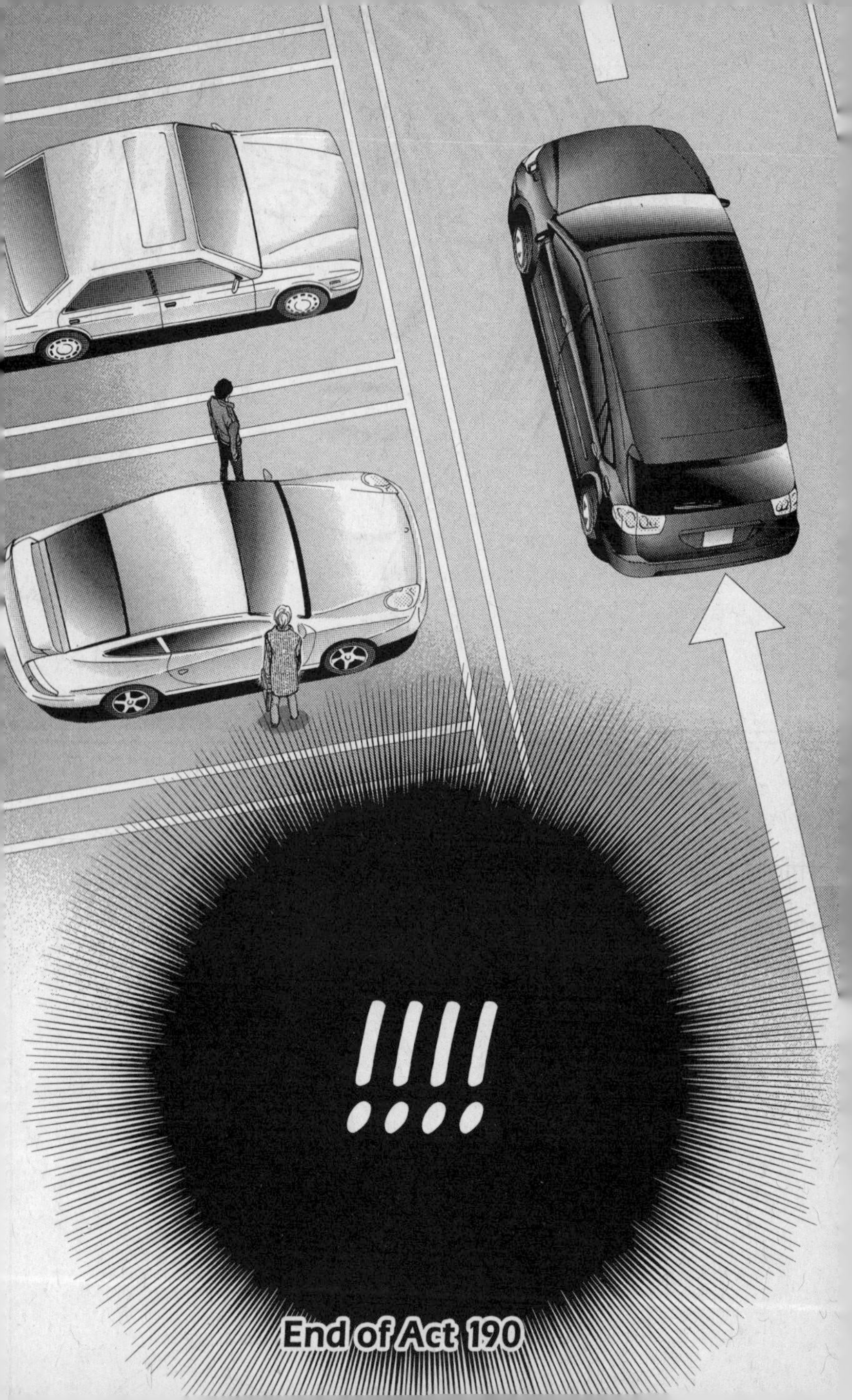
!!!!
End of Act 190

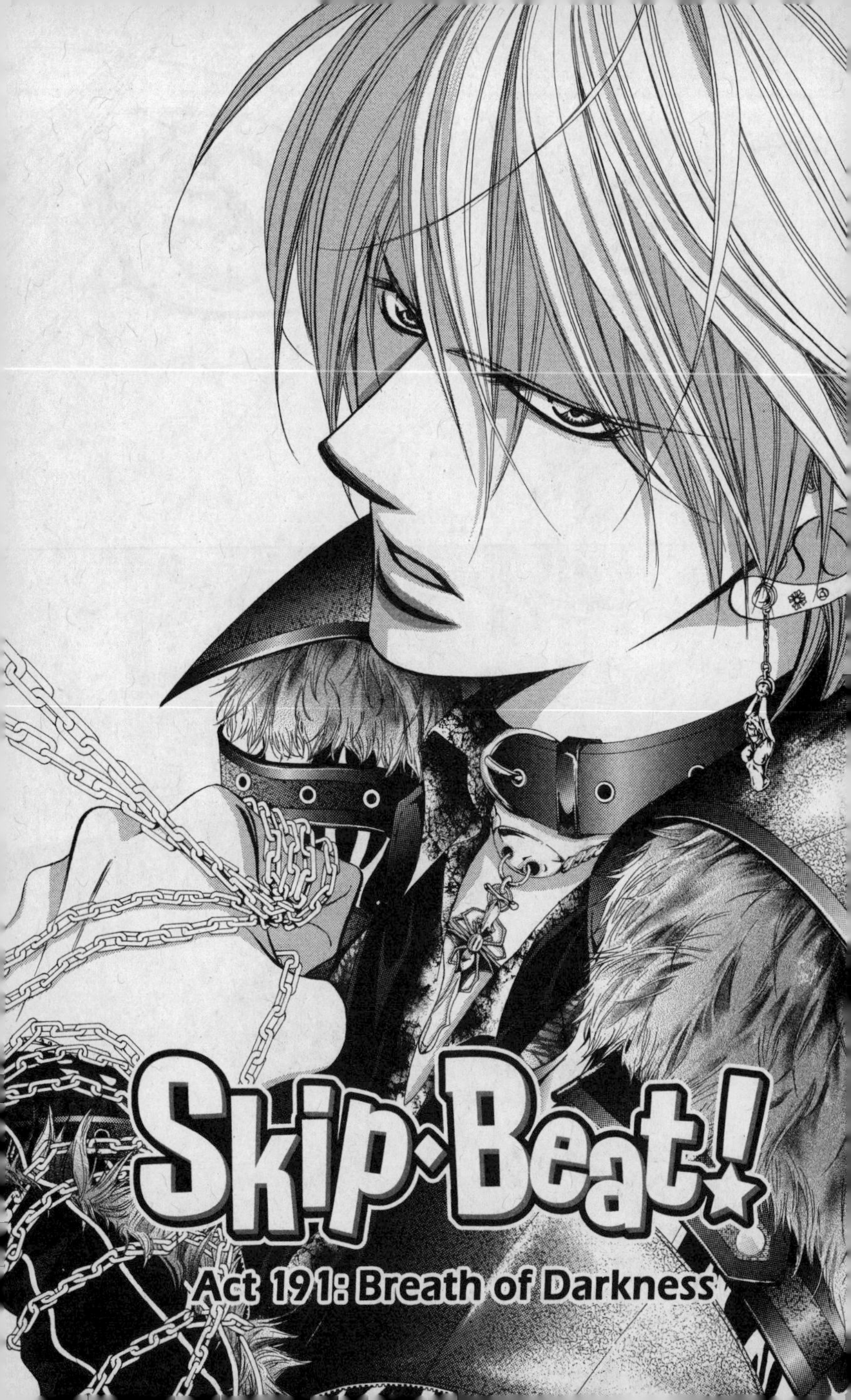

Skip·Beat!
Act 191: Breath of Darkness

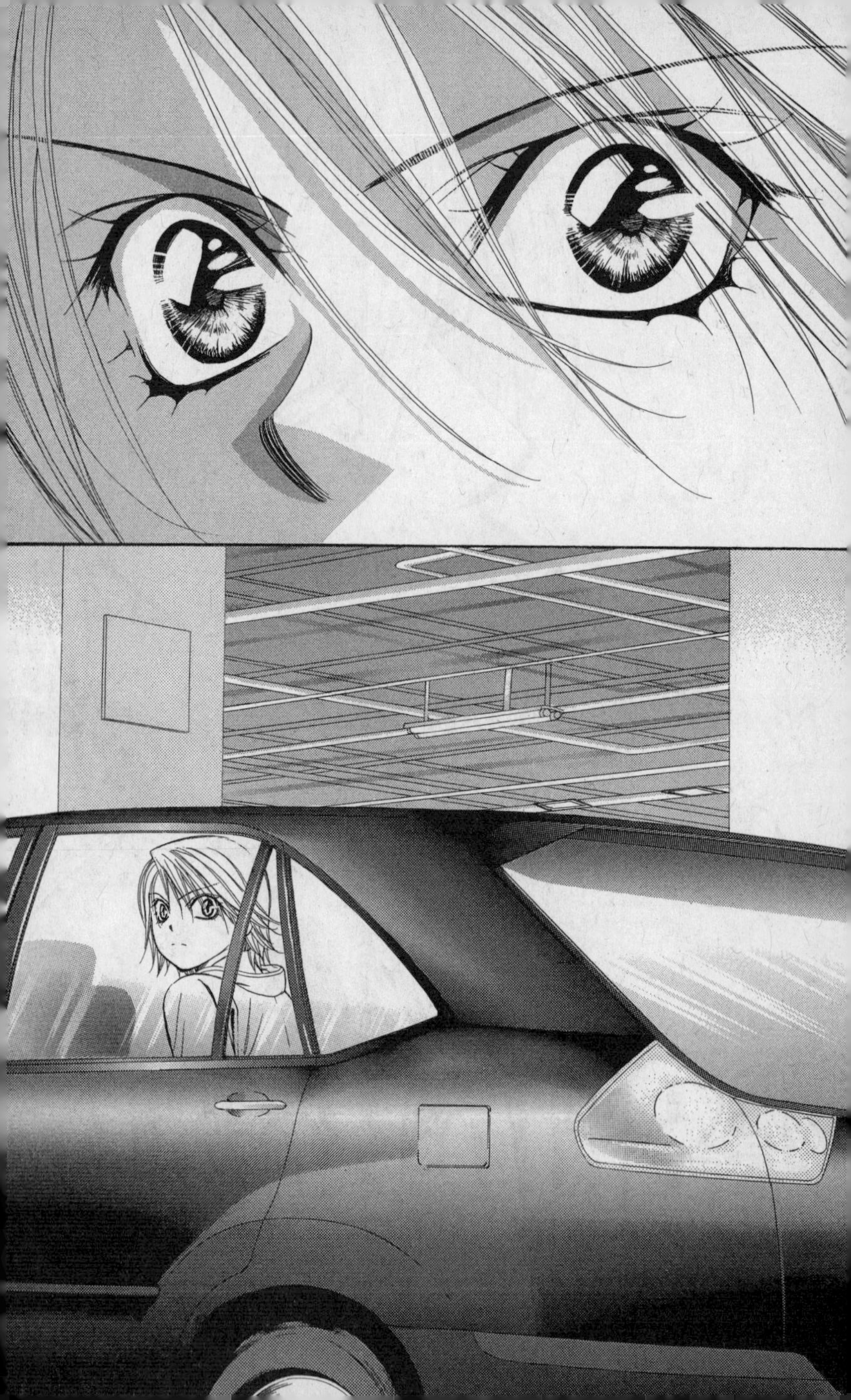

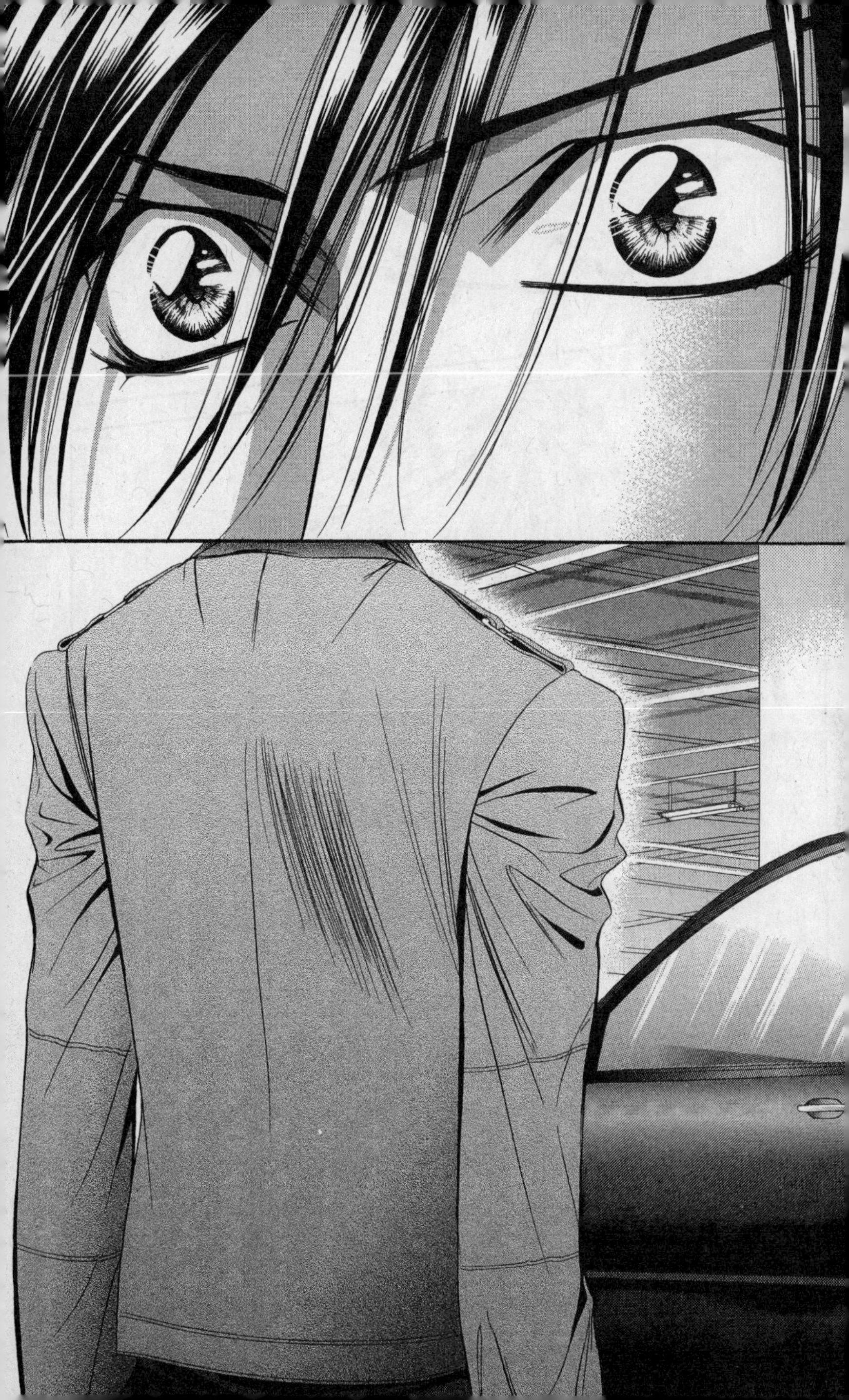

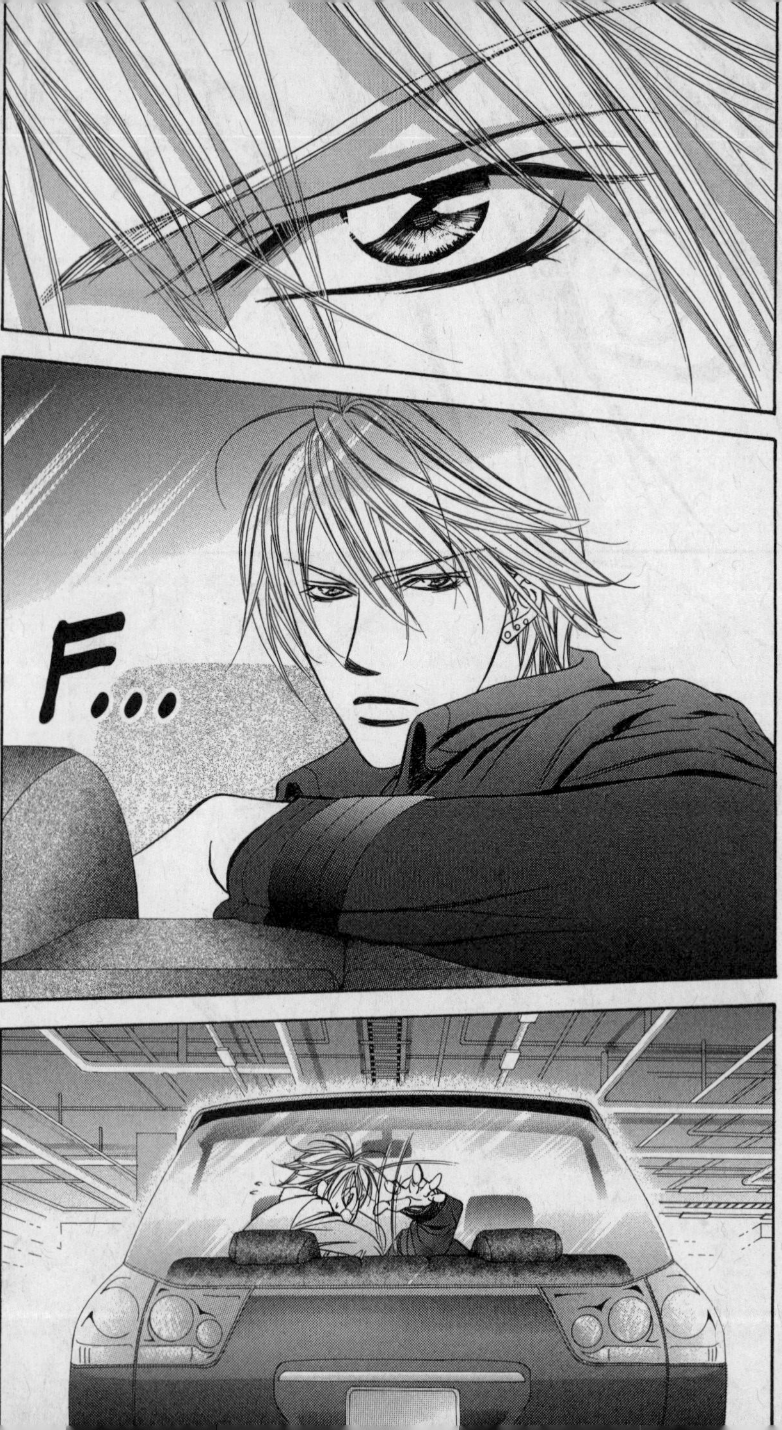
F...

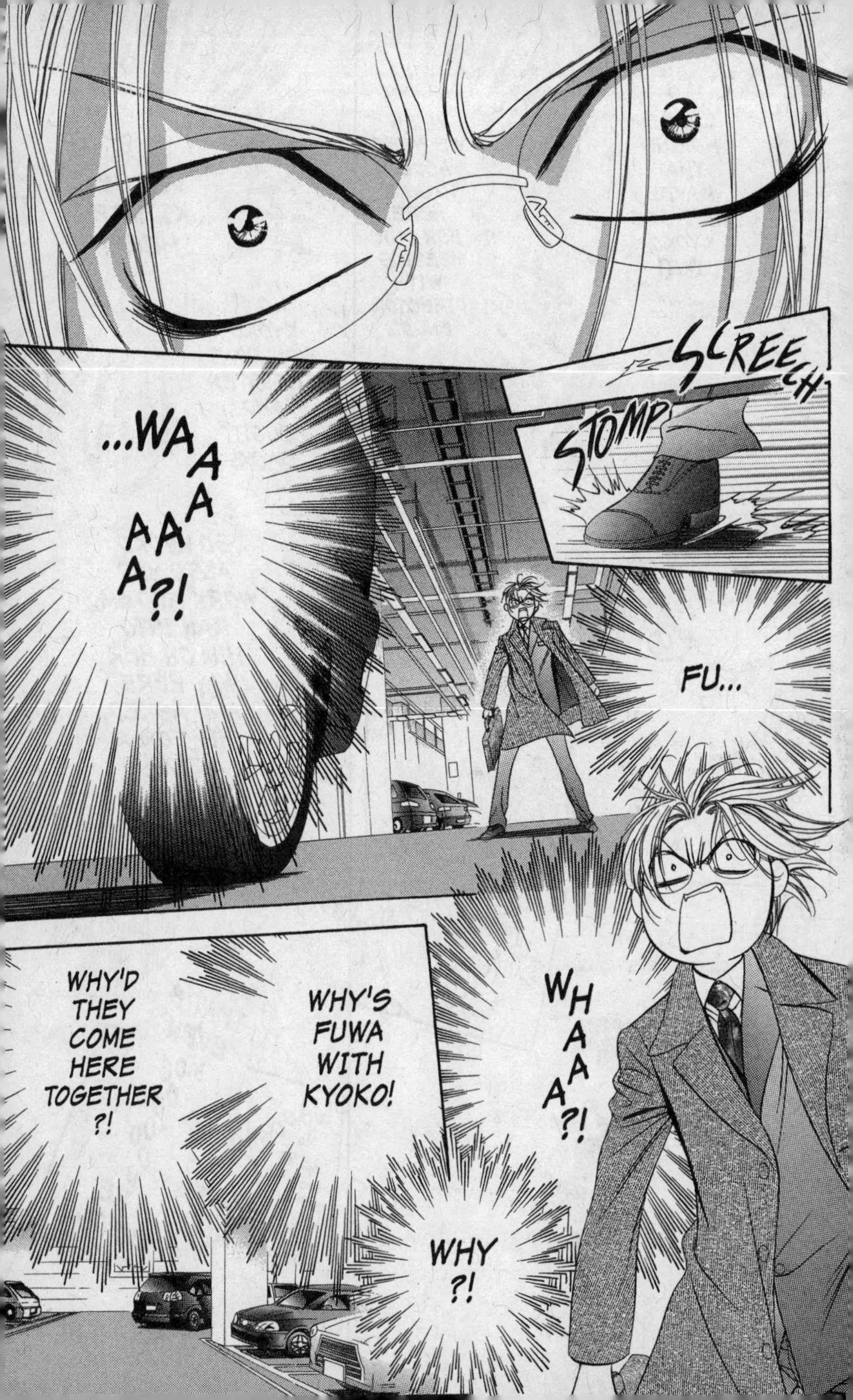
SCREECH
STOMP
FU...
...WAAAAAA?!
WHAAAA?!
WHY'S FUWA WITH KYOKO!
WHY'D THEY COME HERE TOGETHER?!
WHY?!

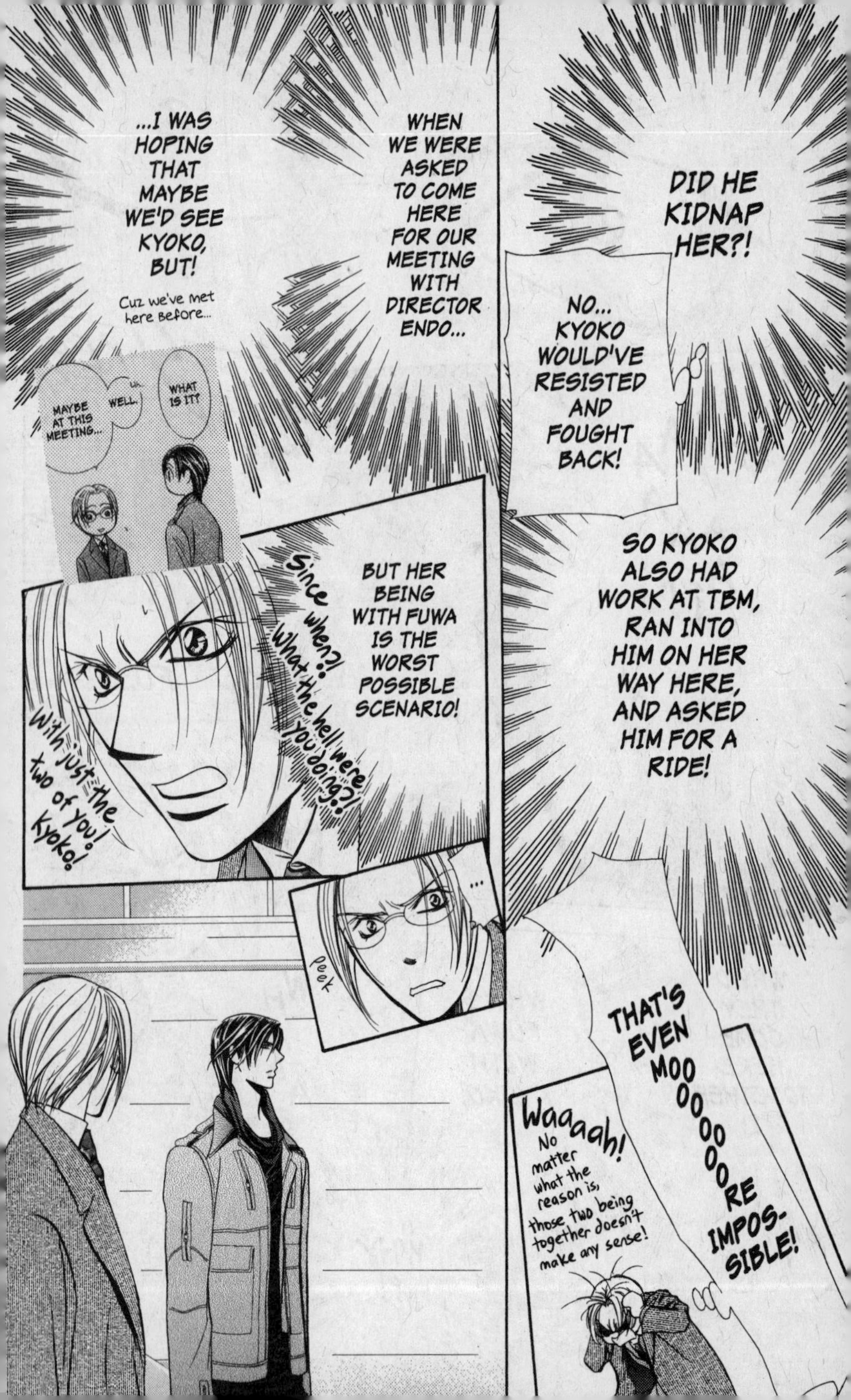
DID HE KIDNAP HER?!
NO... KYOKO WOULD'VE RESISTED AND FOUGHT BACK!
SO KYOKO ALSO HAD WORK AT TBM, RAN INTO HIM ON HER WAY HERE, AND ASKED HIM FOR A RIDE!
THAT'S EVEN MOOOOOOOORE IMPOS-SIBLE!
Waaaah!
No matter what the reason is, those two being together doesn't make any sense!
WHEN WE WERE ASKED TO COME HERE FOR OUR MEETING WITH DIRECTOR ENDO...
...I WAS HOPING THAT MAYBE WE'D SEE KYOKO, BUT!
Cuz we've met here before...
WHAT IS IT?
Uh... WELL.
MAYBE AT THIS MEETING...
BUT HER BEING WITH FUWA IS THE WORST POSSIBLE SCENARIO!
Since when?! What the hell were you doing?!
With just the two of you! Kyoko!
...
Peek

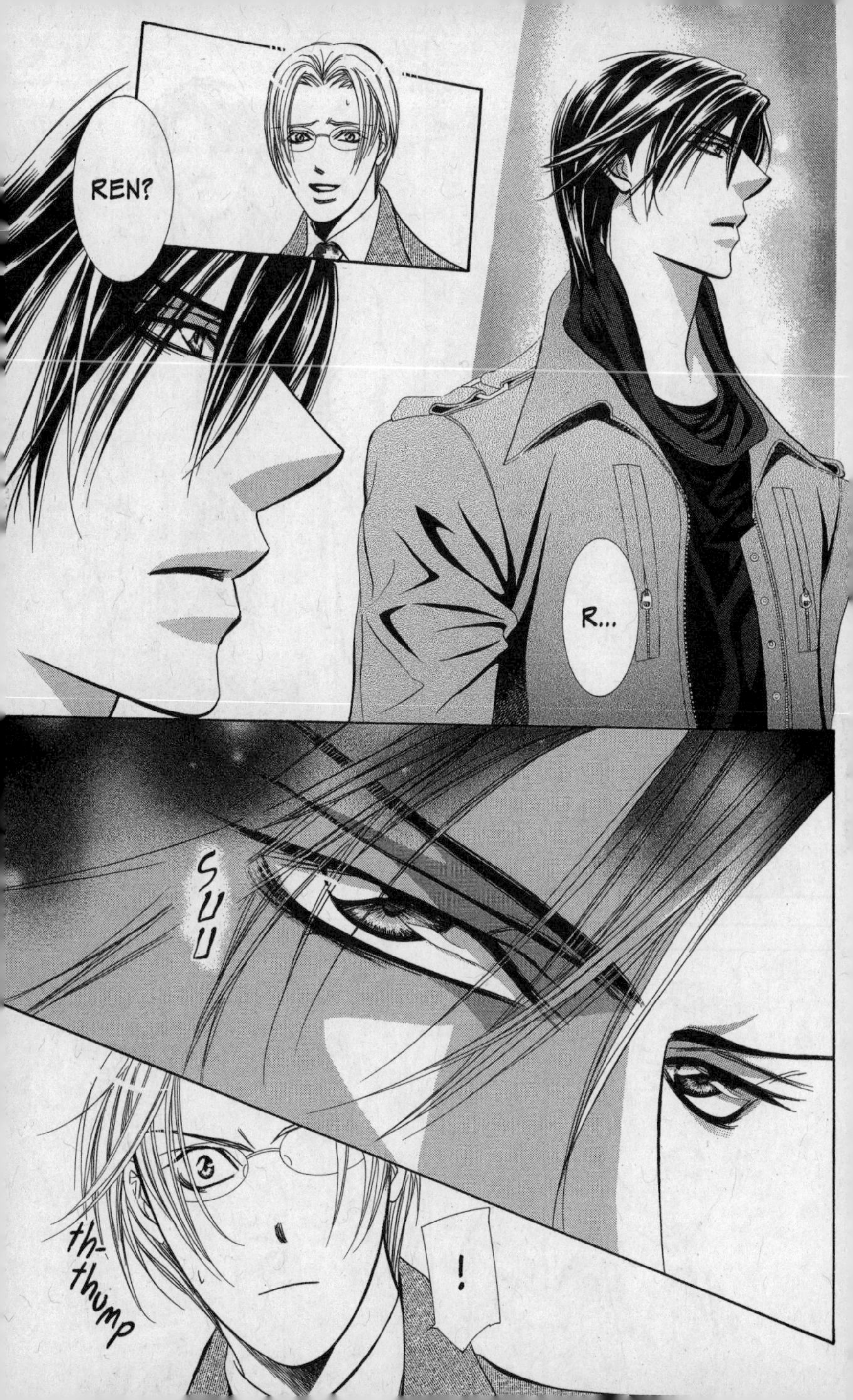
R...
REN?
SUU
!
th-thump

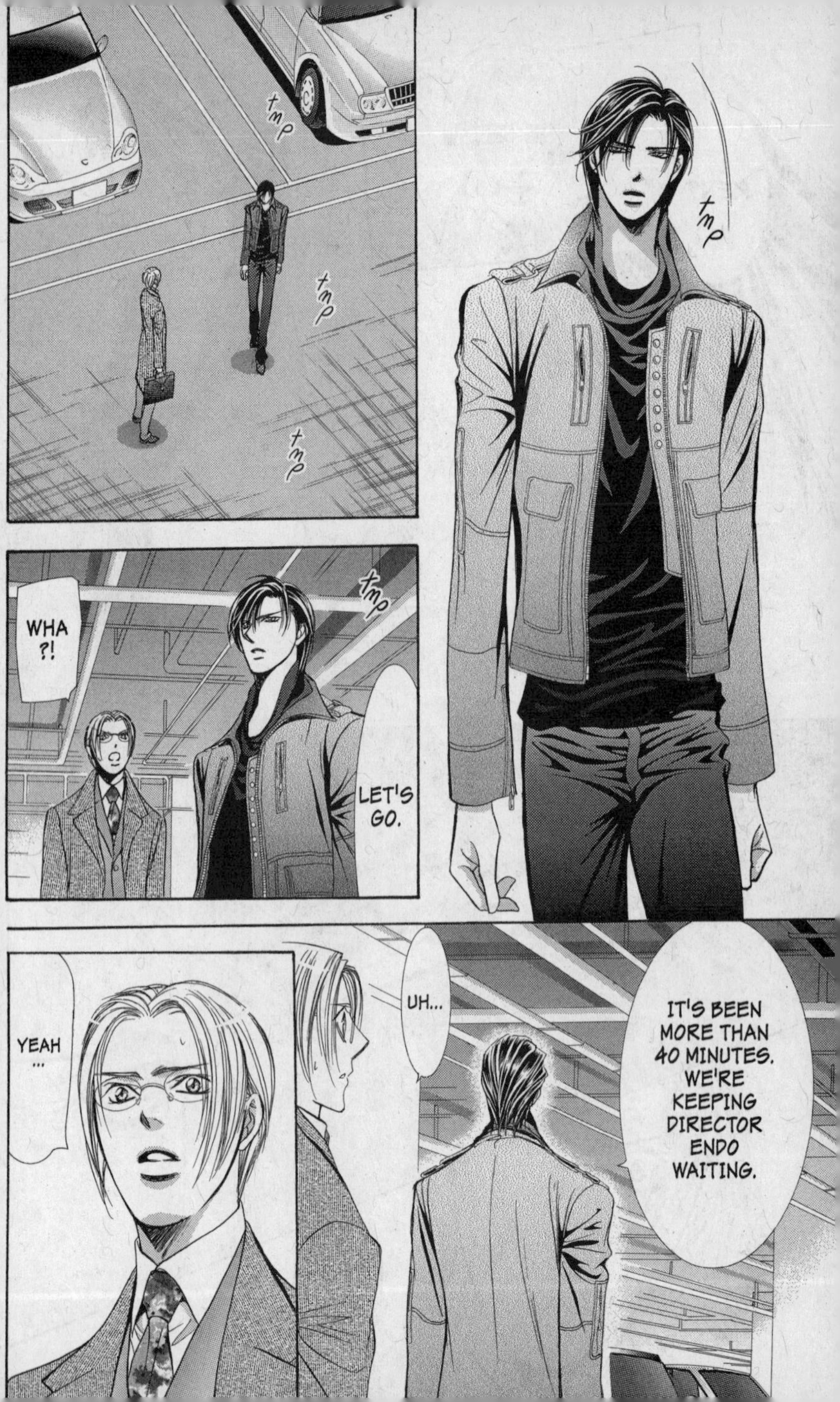
tmp
tmp
tmp
tmp
tmp
LET'S GO.
WHA ?!
IT'S BEEN MORE THAN 40 MINUTES. WE'RE KEEPING DIRECTOR ENDO WAITING.
UH...
YEAH ...

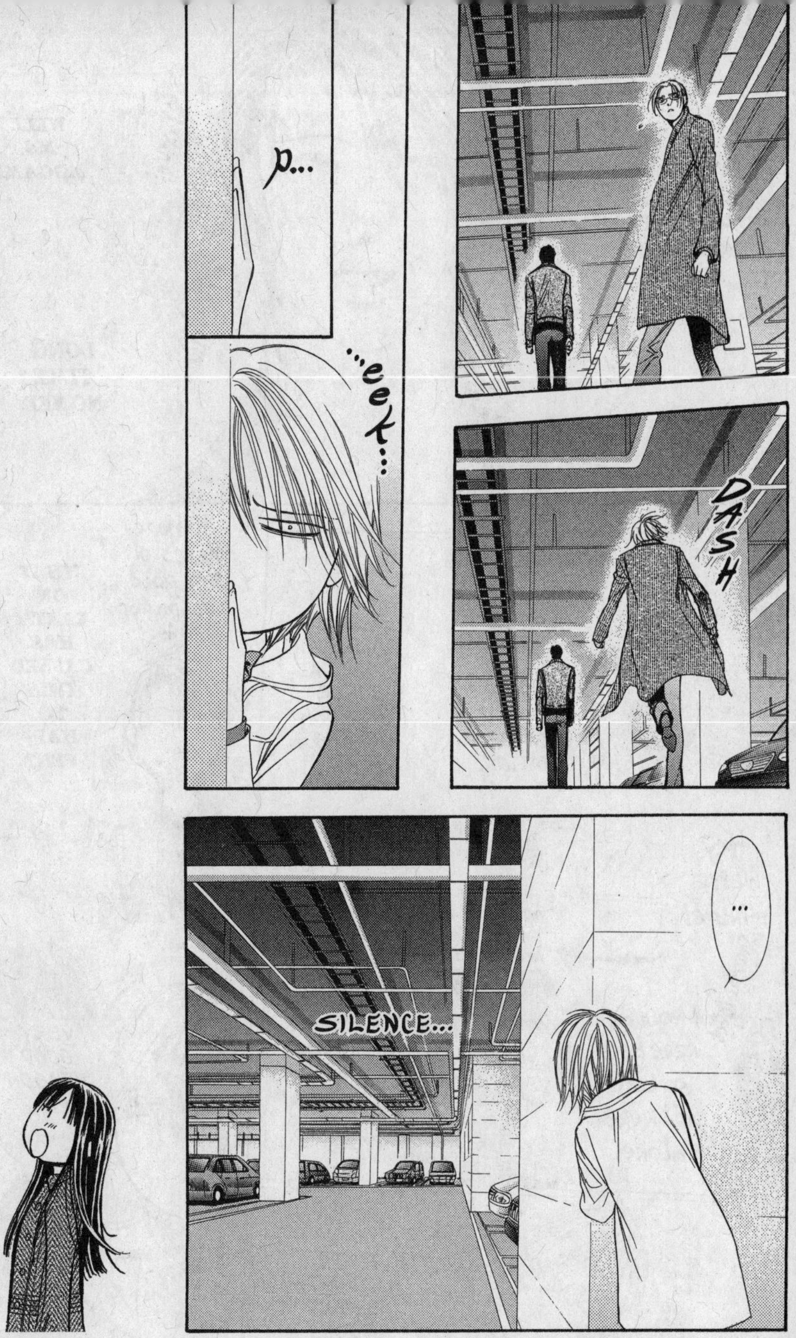
DASH
p...
...eek...
...
SILENCE...

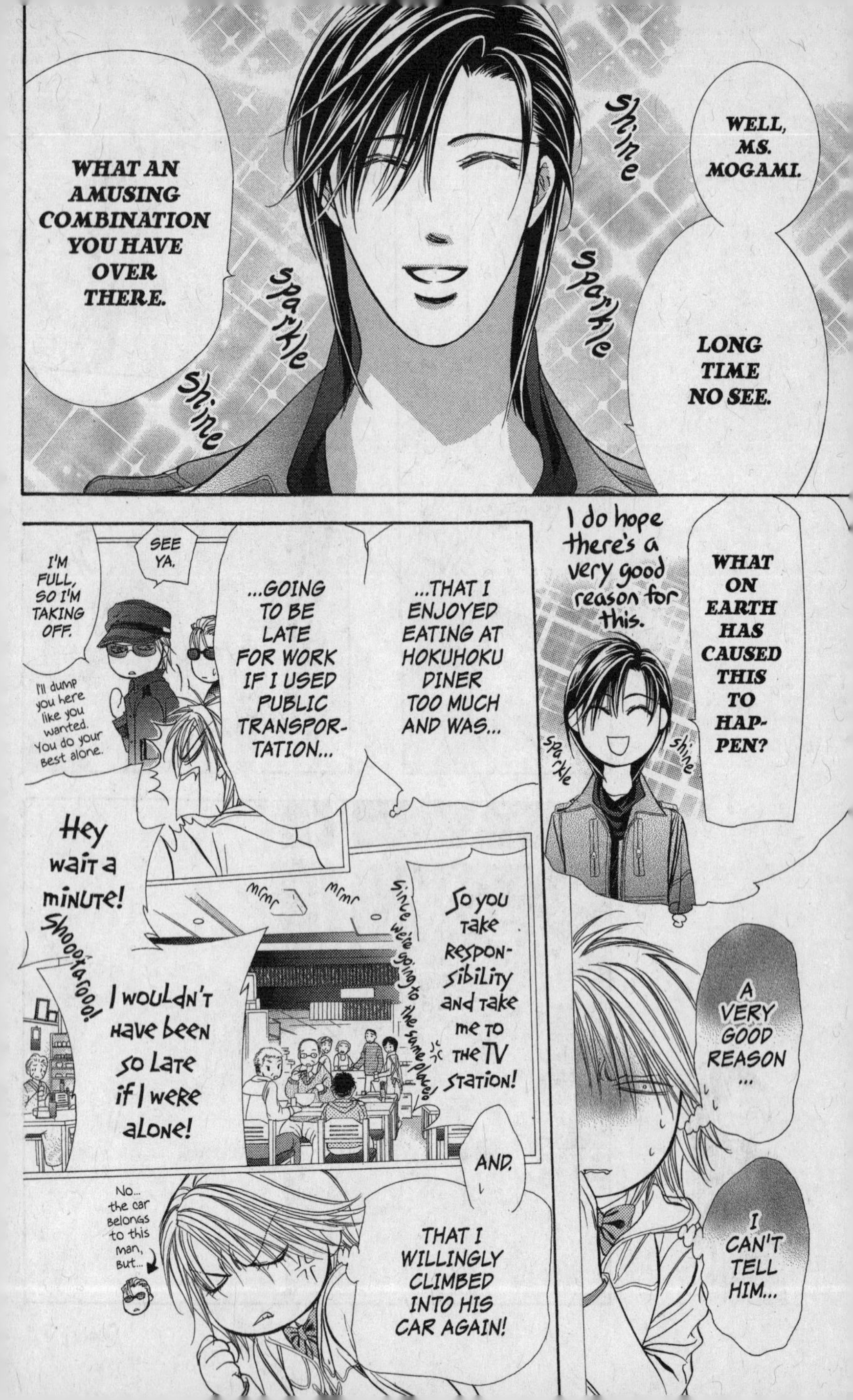
WELL, MS. MOGAMI.
LONG TIME NO SEE.
Shine
Sparkle
WHAT AN AMUSING COMBINATION YOU HAVE OVER THERE.
Sparkle
Shine
WHAT ON EARTH HAS CAUSED THIS TO HAP-PEN?
I do hope there's a very good reason for this.
Shine
Sparkle
A VERY GOOD REASON...
I CAN'T TELL HIM...
...THAT I ENJOYED EATING AT HOKUHOKU DINER TOO MUCH AND WAS...
...GOING TO BE LATE FOR WORK IF I USED PUBLIC TRANSPOR-TATION...
SEE YA.
I'M FULL, SO I'M TAKING OFF.
I'll dump you here like you wanted. You do your best alone.
Hey wait a minute!
Shoootarooo!
So you take respon-sibility and take me to the TV station!
Since we're going to the same place!
mrmr
mrmr
I wouldn't have been so late if I were alone!
AND.
THAT I WILLINGLY CLIMBED INTO HIS CAR AGAIN!
No... the car belongs to this man, but...

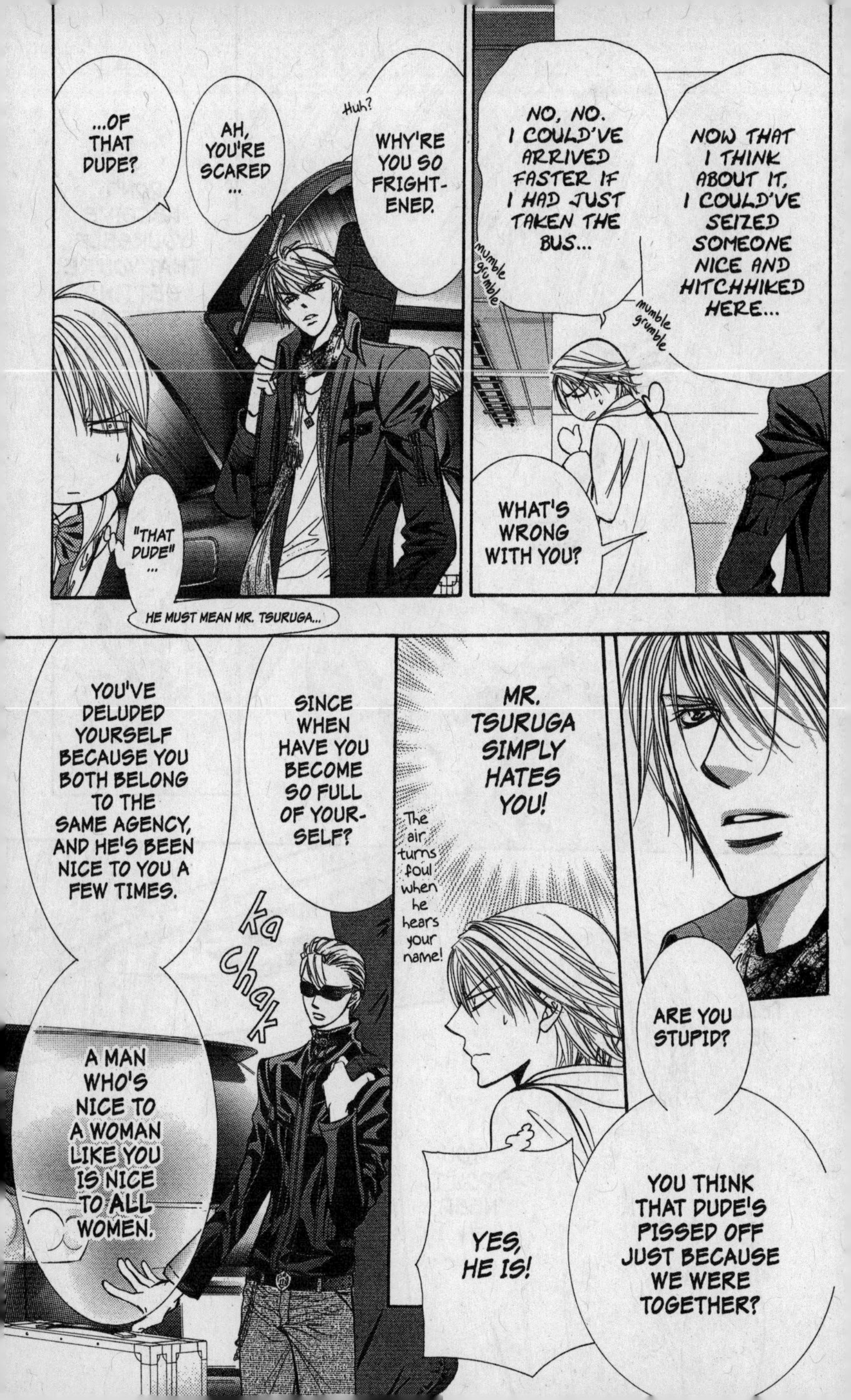
NOW THAT I THINK ABOUT IT, I COULD'VE SEIZED SOMEONE NICE AND HITCHHIKED HERE...
mumble grumble
NO, NO. I COULD'VE ARRIVED FASTER IF I HAD JUST TAKEN THE BUS...
mumble grumble
WHAT'S WRONG WITH YOU?
WHY'RE YOU SO FRIGHTENED.
Huh?
AH, YOU'RE SCARED...
...OF THAT DUDE?
"THAT DUDE"...
HE MUST MEAN MR. TSURUGA...
ARE YOU STUPID?
YOU THINK THAT DUDE'S PISSED OFF JUST BECAUSE WE WERE TOGETHER?
YES, HE IS!
MR. TSURUGA SIMPLY HATES YOU!
The air turns foul when he hears your name!
SINCE WHEN HAVE YOU BECOME SO FULL OF YOURSELF?
YOU'VE DELUDED YOURSELF BECAUSE YOU BOTH BELONG TO THE SAME AGENCY, AND HE'S BEEN NICE TO YOU A FEW TIMES.
ka chak
A MAN WHO'S NICE TO A WOMAN LIKE YOU IS NICE TO ALL WOMEN.

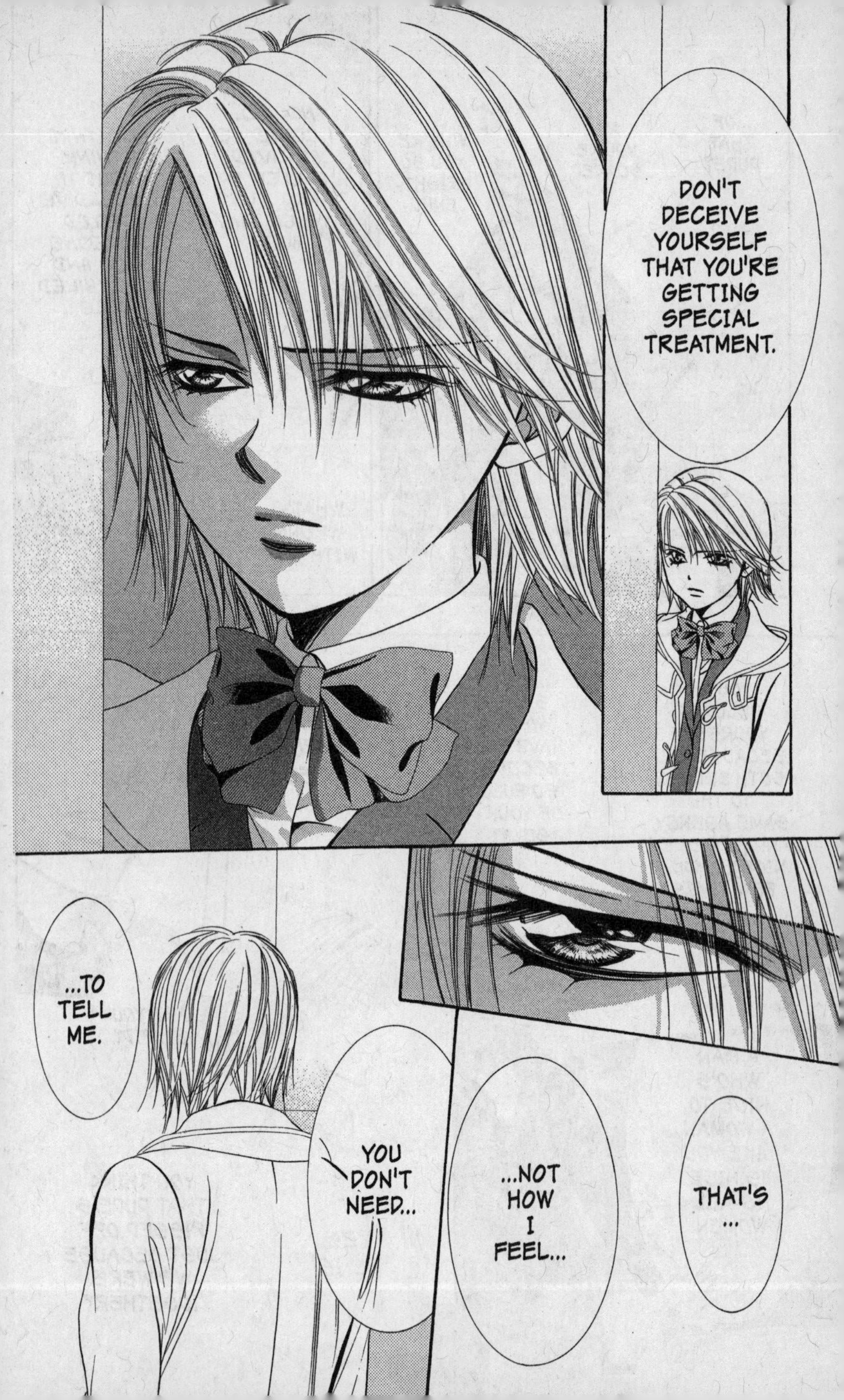
DON'T DECEIVE YOURSELF THAT YOU'RE GETTING SPECIAL TREATMENT.
THAT'S ...
...NOT HOW I FEEL...
YOU DON'T NEED...
...TO TELL ME.

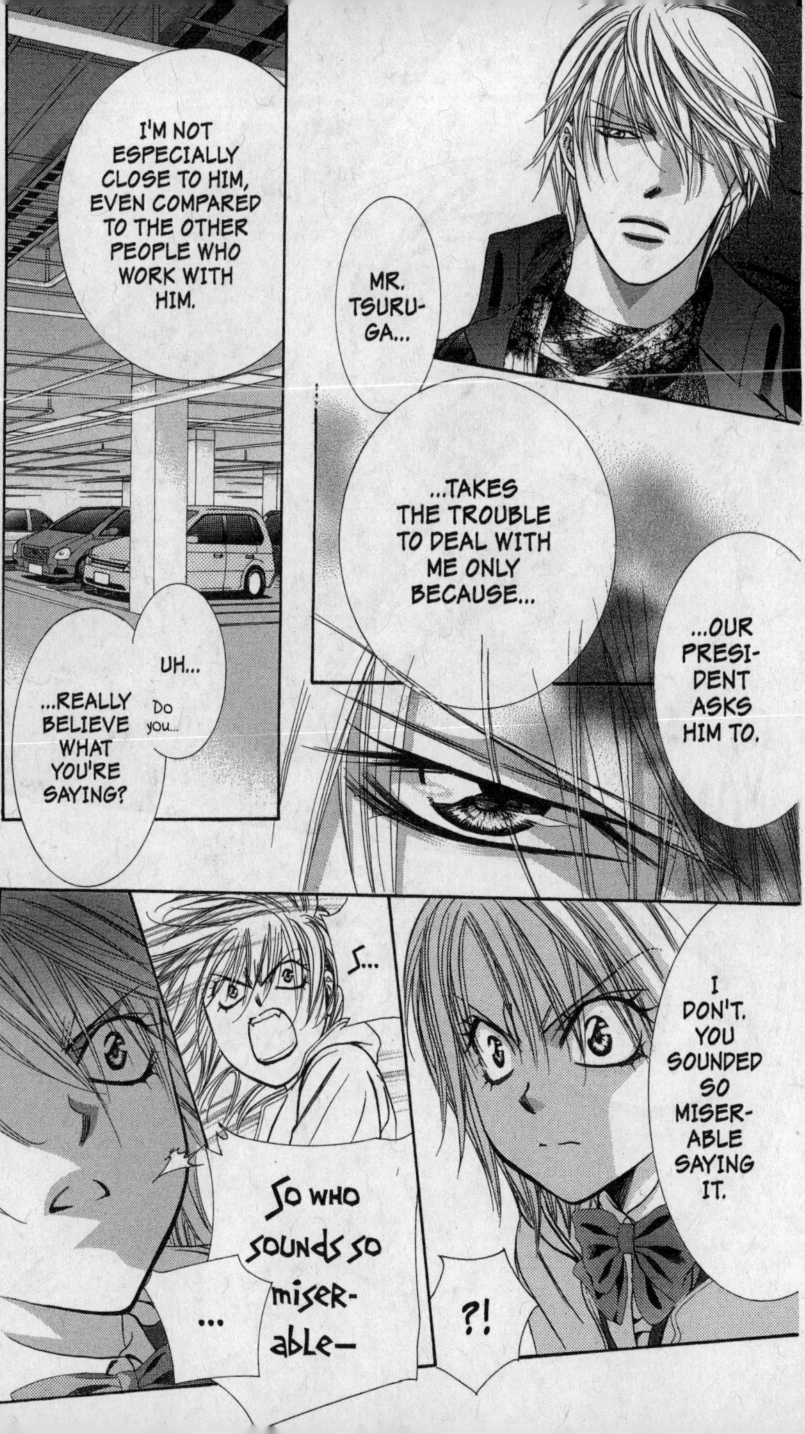
MR. TSURUGA...
...TAKES THE TROUBLE TO DEAL WITH ME ONLY BECAUSE...
...OUR PRESIDENT ASKS HIM TO.
I'M NOT ESPECIALLY CLOSE TO HIM, EVEN COMPARED TO THE OTHER PEOPLE WHO WORK WITH HIM.
UH...
Do you...
...REALLY BELIEVE WHAT YOU'RE SAYING?
I DON'T. YOU SOUNDED SO MISERABLE SAYING IT.
?!
S...
SO WHO SOUNDS SO MISERABLE—
...

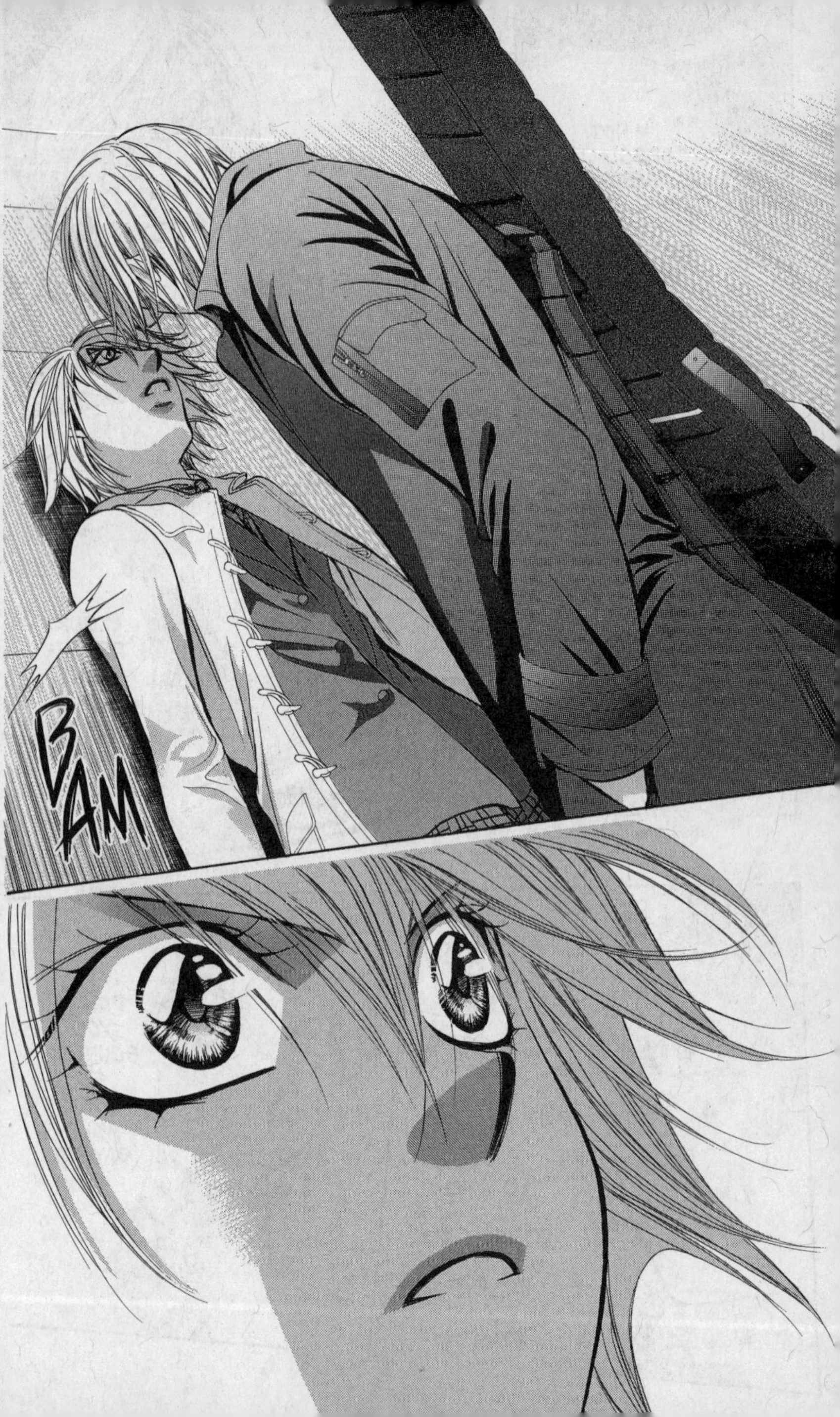
BAM

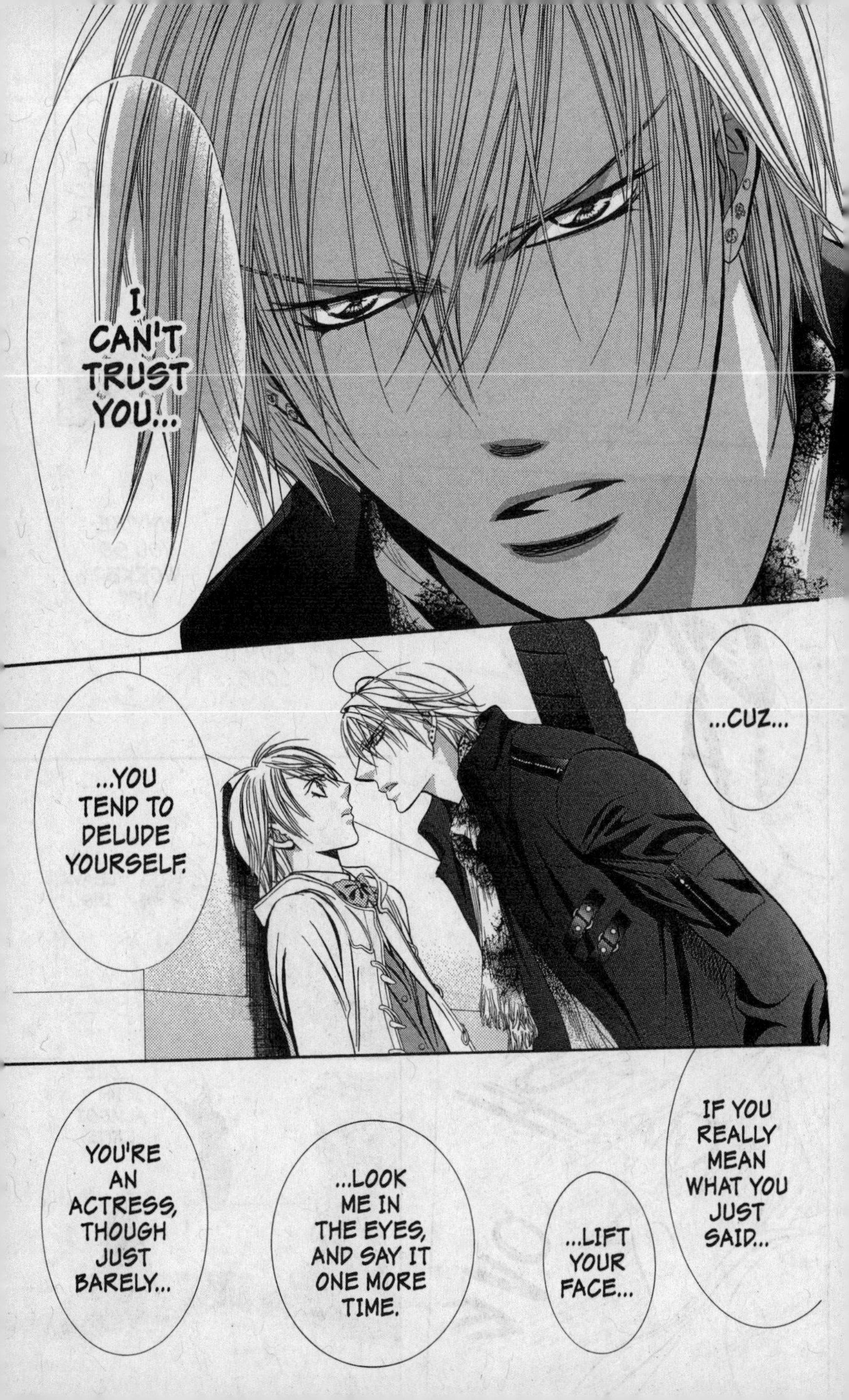
I CAN'T TRUST YOU...
...CUZ...
...YOU TEND TO DELUDE YOURSELF.
IF YOU REALLY MEAN WHAT YOU JUST SAID...
...LIFT YOUR FACE...
...LOOK ME IN THE EYES, AND SAY IT ONE MORE TIME.
YOU'RE AN ACTRESS, THOUGH JUST BARELY...

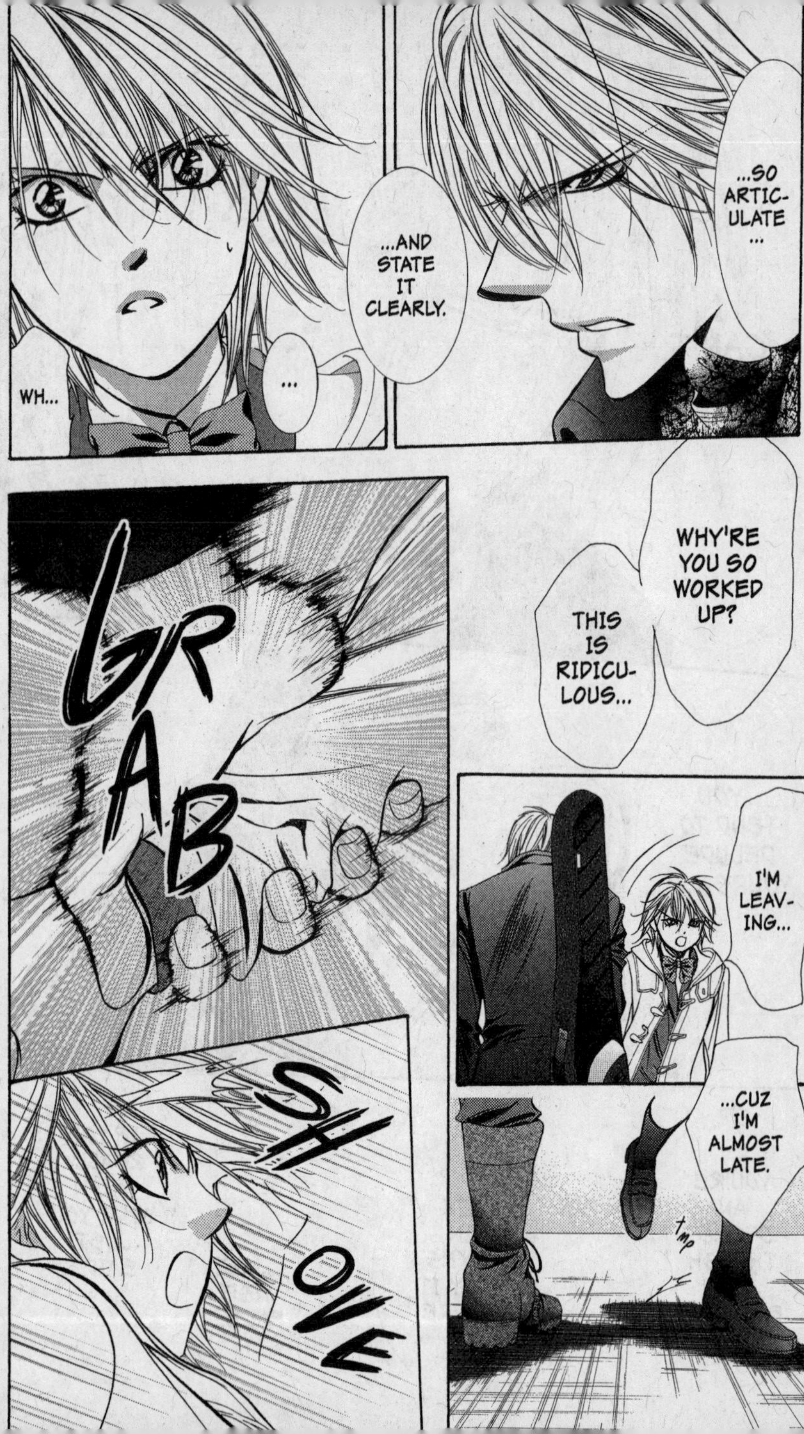
...SO ARTIC-ULATE...
...AND STATE IT CLEARLY.
...
WH...
WHY'RE YOU SO WORKED UP?
THIS IS RIDICU-LOUS...
I'M LEAV-ING...
...CUZ I'M ALMOST LATE.
TMP
GRAB
SHOVE

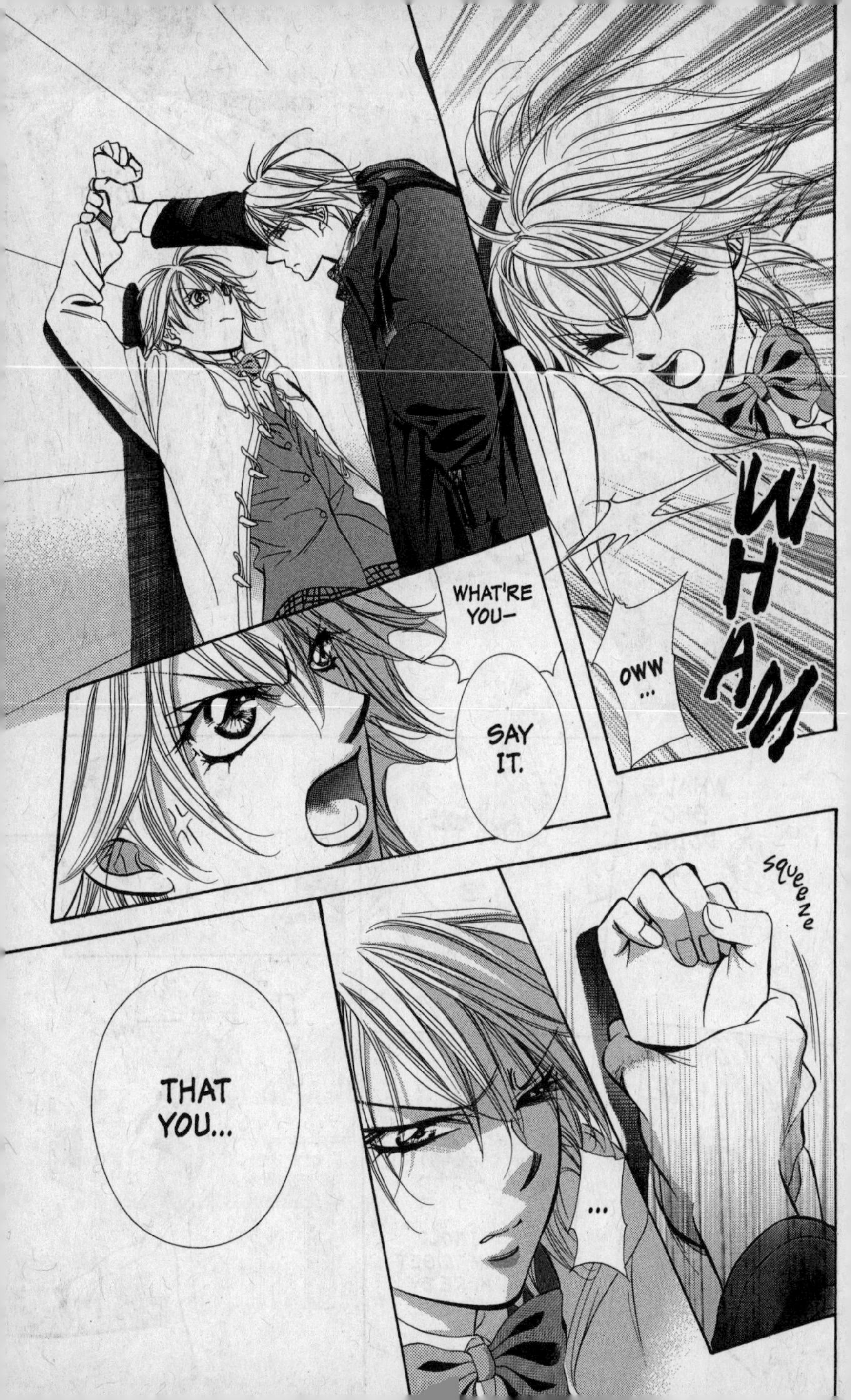
WHAM
OWW...
WHAT'RE YOU—
SAY IT.
squeeze
...
THAT YOU...

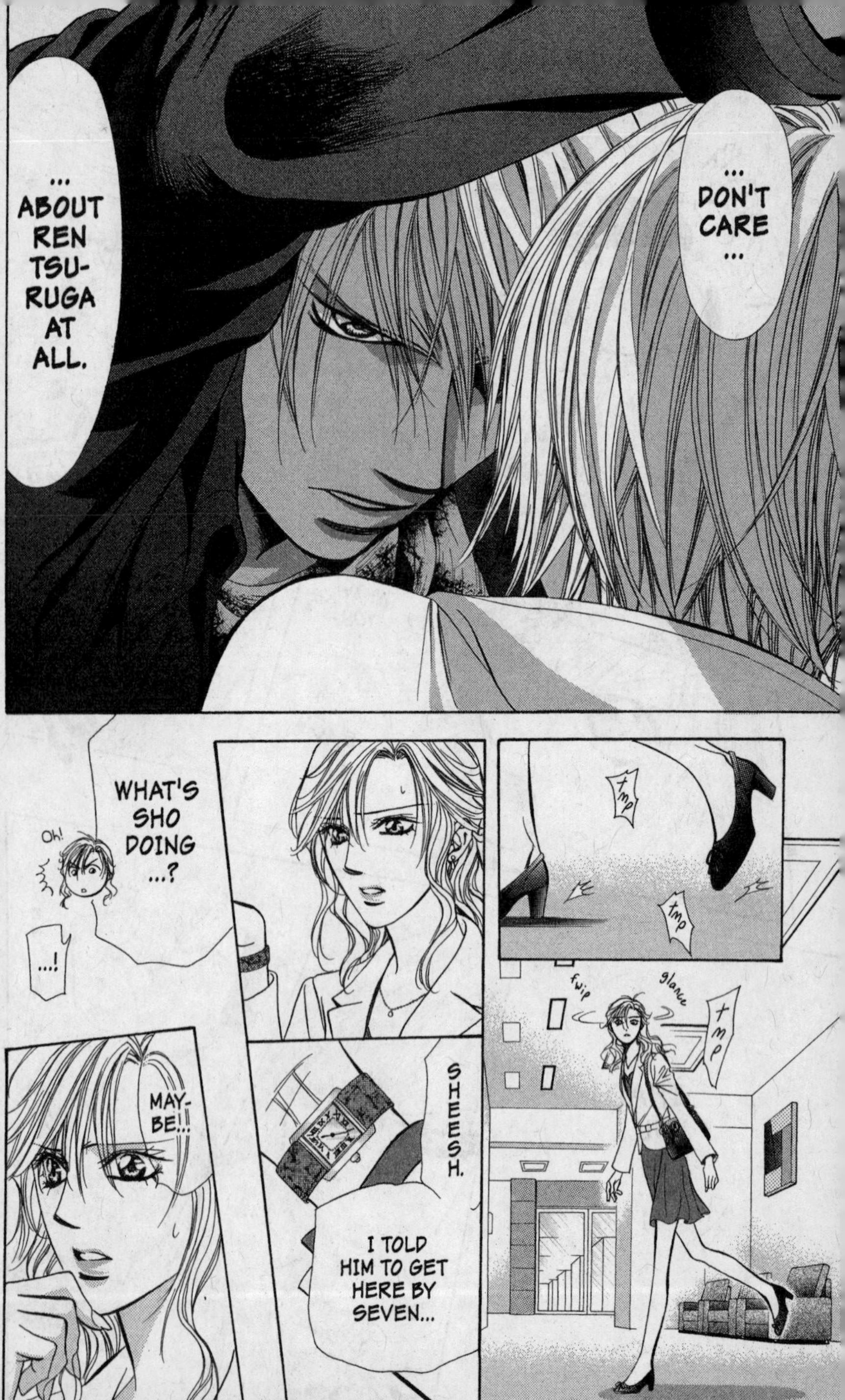
... DON'T CARE ...
... ABOUT REN TSURUGA AT ALL.
tmp
tmp
WHAT'S SHO DOING ...?
Oh!
...!
fwip
glance
tmp
SHEESH.
I TOLD HIM TO GET HERE BY SEVEN...
MAY-BE...!

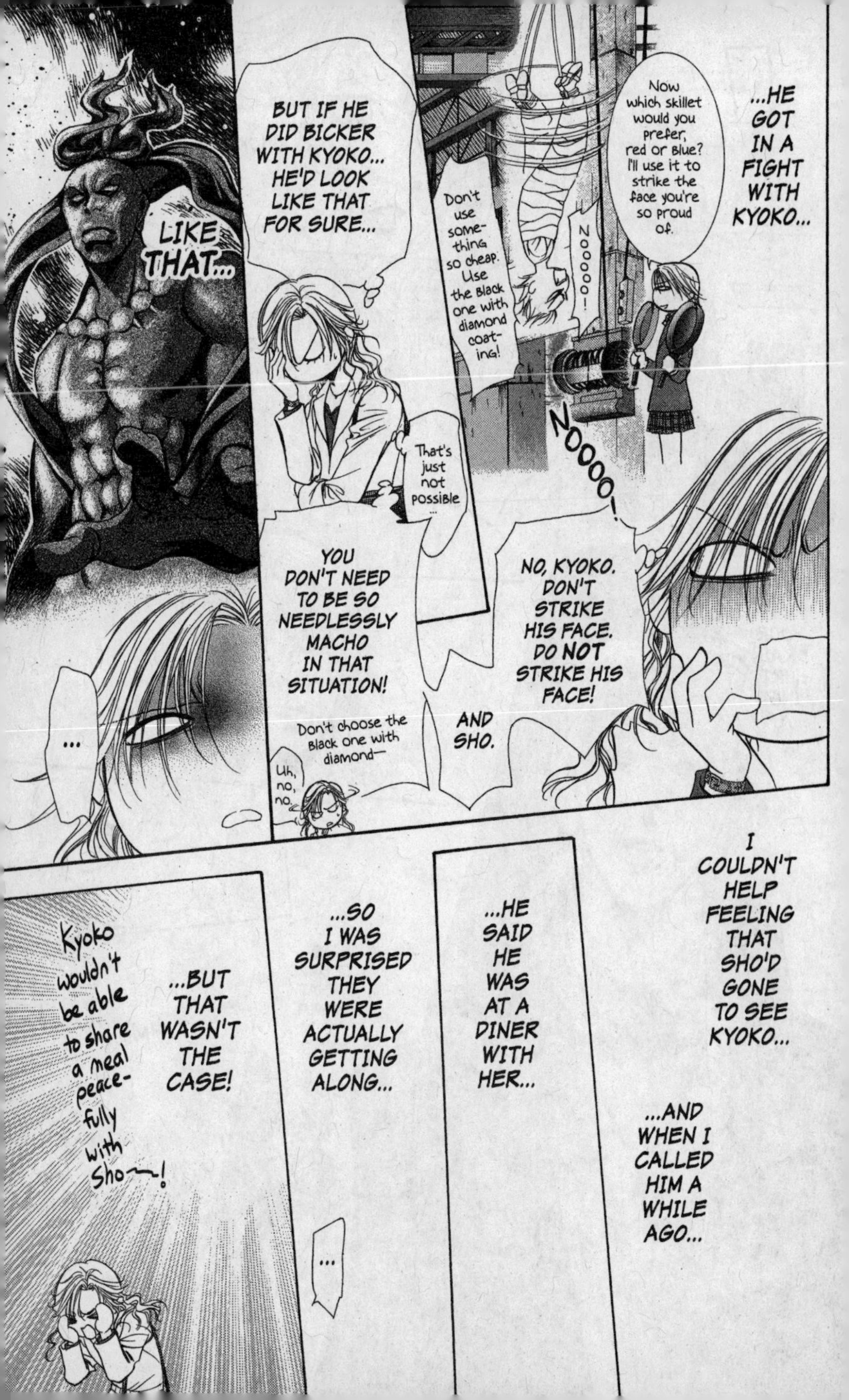

...HE GOT IN A FIGHT WITH KYOKO...
Now which skillet would you prefer, red or blue? I'll use it to strike the face you're so proud of.
Don't use something so cheap. Use the black one with diamond coating!
NOOOOO!
NOOOO!
BUT IF HE DID BICKER WITH KYOKO... HE'D LOOK LIKE THAT FOR SURE...
That's just not possible...
LIKE THAT...
NO, KYOKO. DON'T STRIKE HIS FACE. DO NOT STRIKE HIS FACE!
AND SHO.
YOU DON'T NEED TO BE SO NEEDLESSLY MACHO IN THAT SITUATION!
Don't choose the black one with diamond—
Uh, no, no.
...
I COULDN'T HELP FEELING THAT SHO'D GONE TO SEE KYOKO...
...AND WHEN I CALLED HIM A WHILE AGO...
...HE SAID HE WAS AT A DINER WITH HER...
...SO I WAS SURPRISED THEY WERE ACTUALLY GETTING ALONG...
...
...BUT THAT WASN'T THE CASE!
Kyoko wouldn't be able to share a meal peacefully with Sho—!

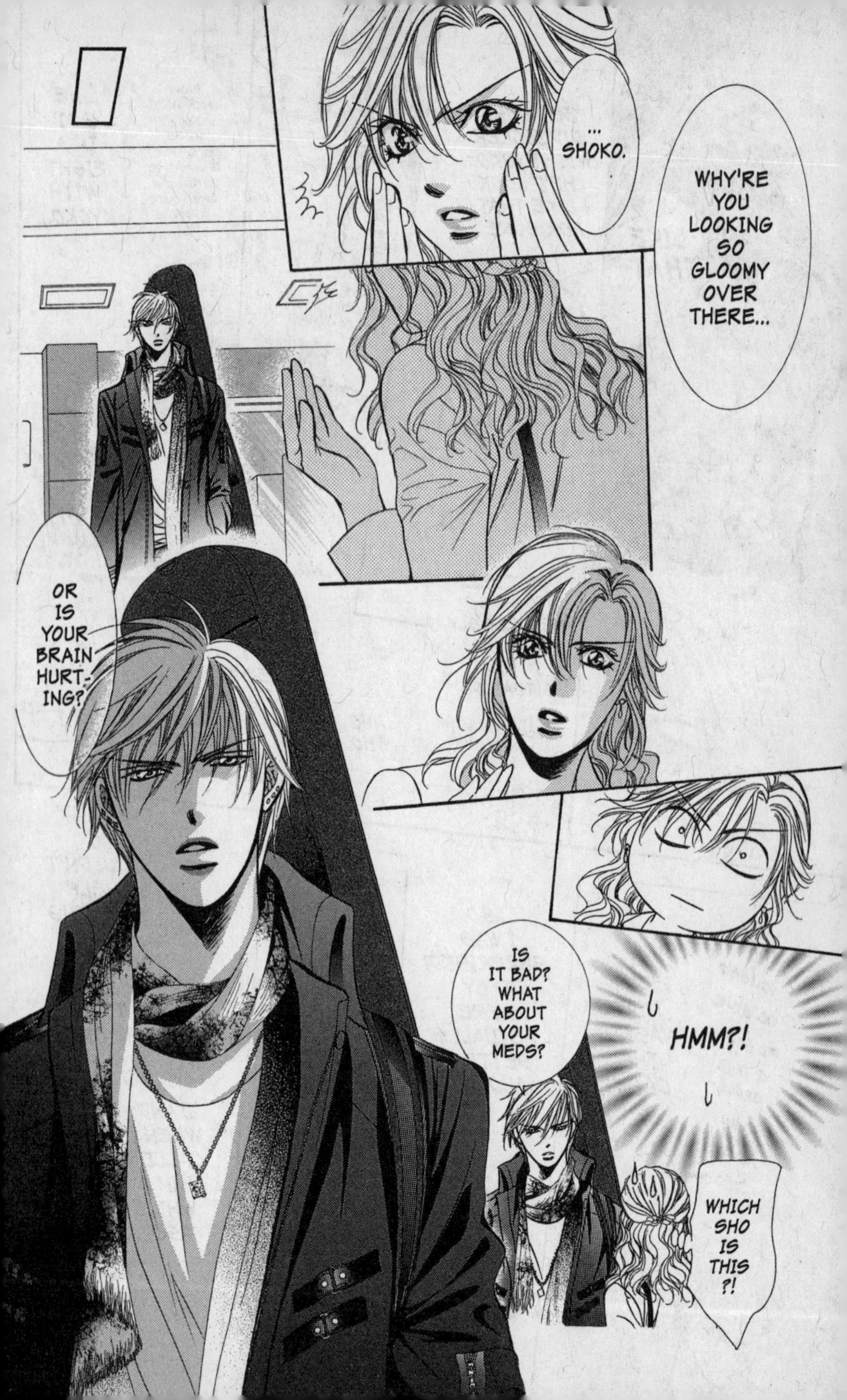

... SHOKO.
WHY'RE YOU LOOKING SO GLOOMY OVER THERE...
OR IS YOUR BRAIN HURTING?
IS IT BAD? WHAT ABOUT YOUR MEDS?
HMM?!
WHICH SHO IS THIS?!

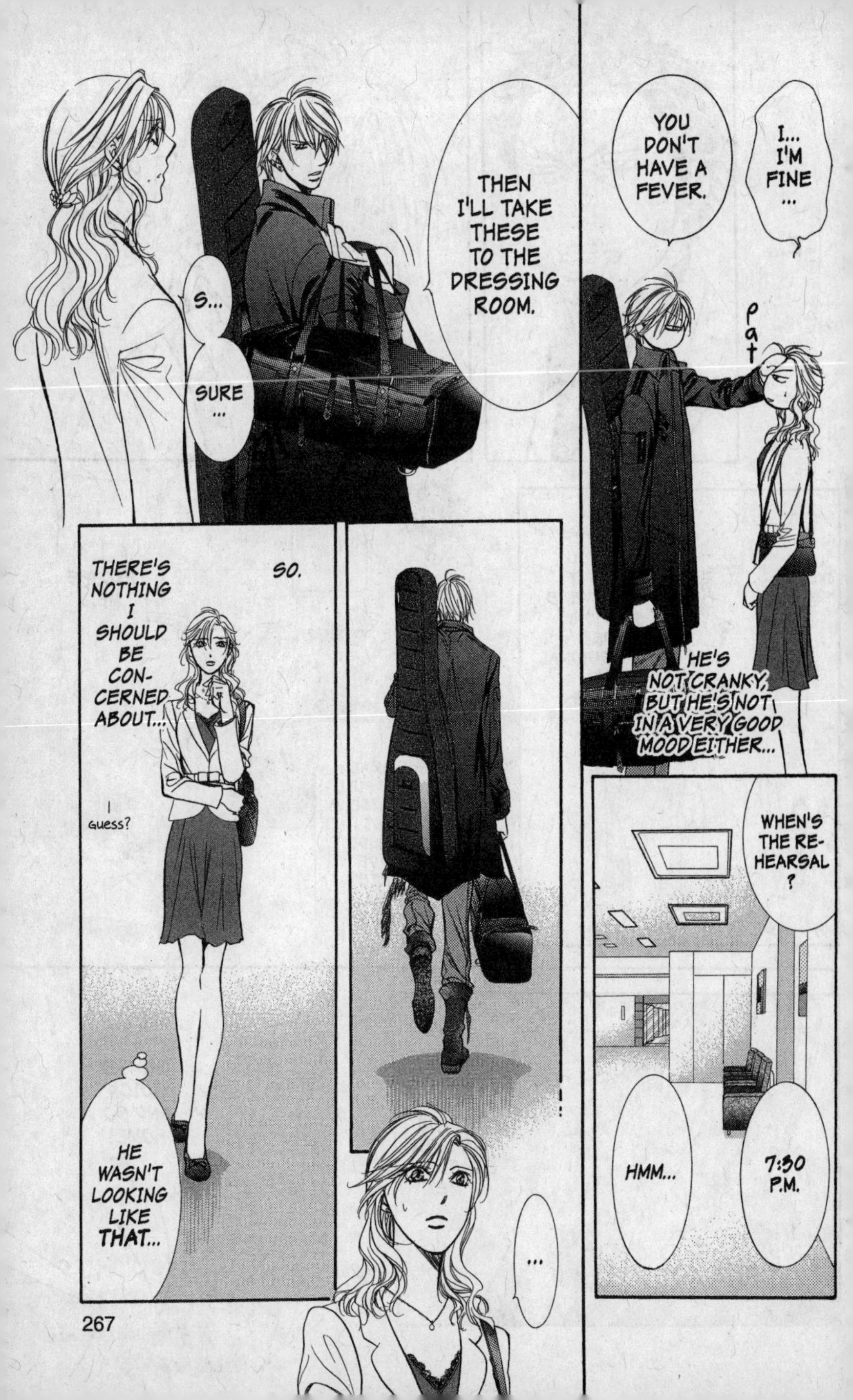
I... I'M FINE...
YOU DON'T HAVE A FEVER.
pat
HE'S NOT CRANKY, BUT HE'S NOT IN A VERY GOOD MOOD EITHER...
WHEN'S THE RE-HEARSAL?
7:30 P.M.
HMM...
THEN I'LL TAKE THESE TO THE DRESSING ROOM.
S...
SURE...
SO.
THERE'S NOTHING I SHOULD BE CON-CERNED ABOUT...
I guess?
HE WASN'T LOOKING LIKE THAT...
...

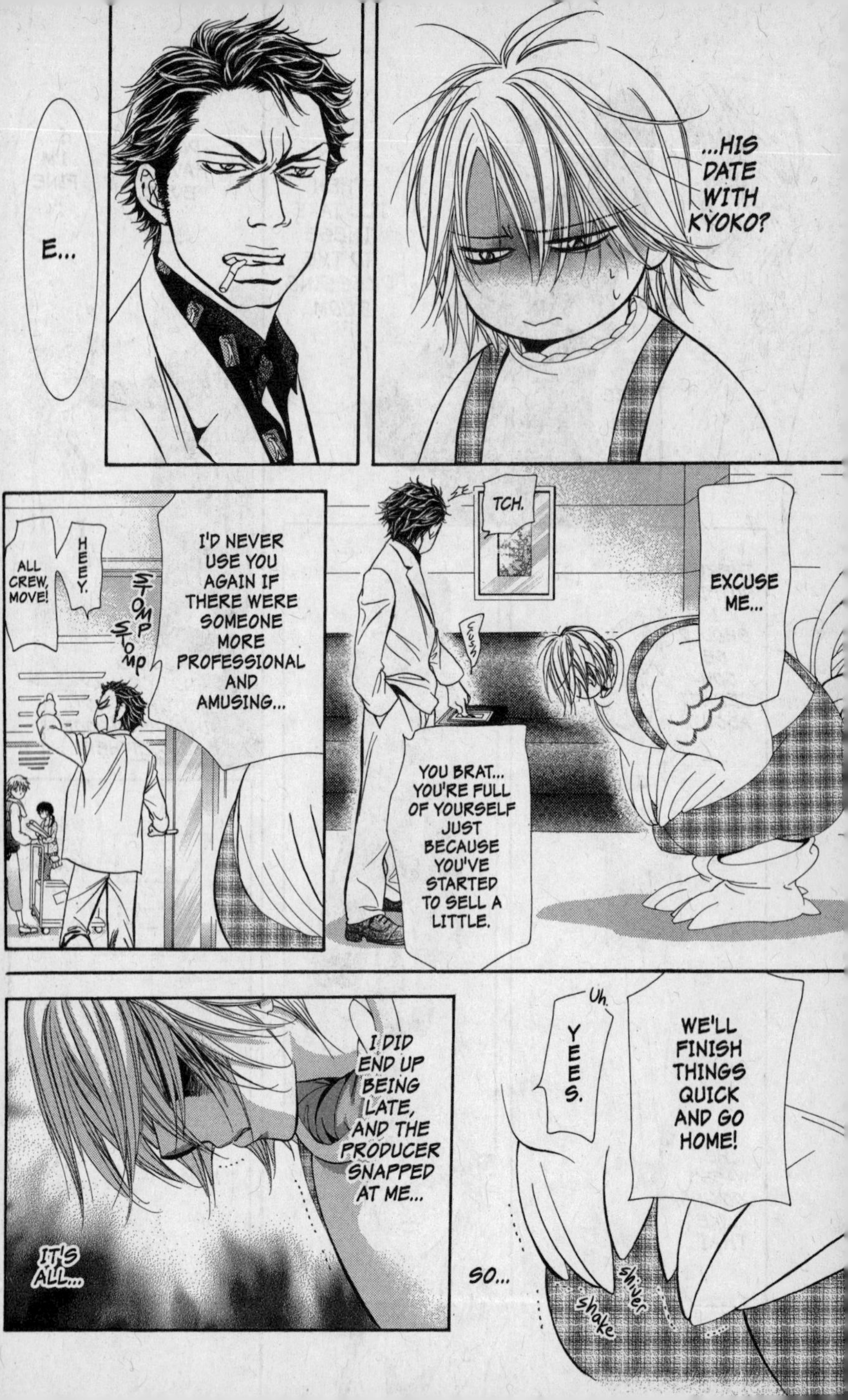
...HIS DATE WITH KYOKO?
E...
EXCUSE ME...
TCH.
YOU BRAT... YOU'RE FULL OF YOURSELF JUST BECAUSE YOU'VE STARTED TO SELL A LITTLE.
I'D NEVER USE YOU AGAIN IF THERE WERE SOMEONE MORE PROFESSIONAL AND AMUSING...
HEEY.
ALL CREW, MOVE!
STOMP STOMP
WE'LL FINISH THINGS QUICK AND GO HOME!
Uh.
YEES.
shiver
shake
SO...
I DID END UP BEING LATE, AND THE PRODUCER SNAPPED AT ME...
IT'S ALL...

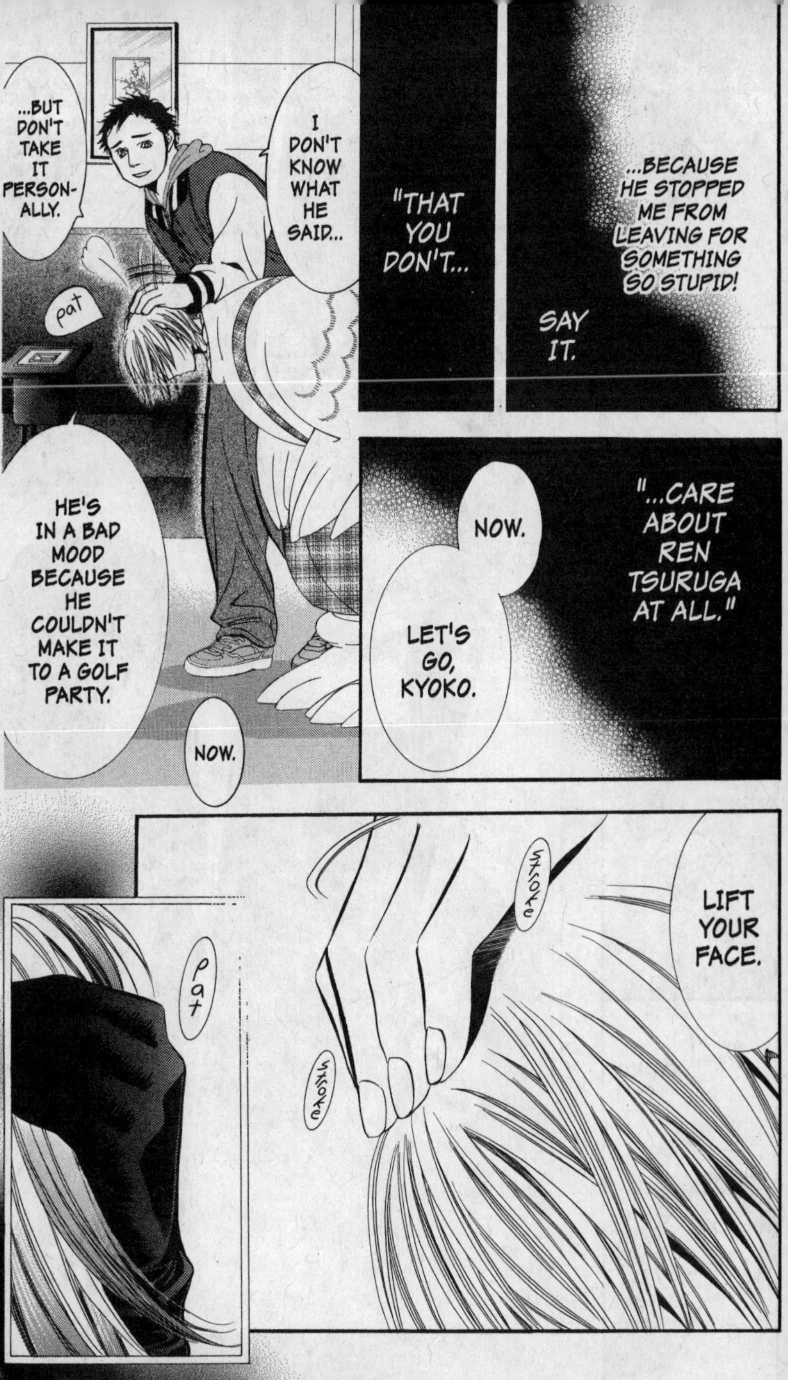
...BECAUSE HE STOPPED ME FROM LEAVING FOR SOMETHING SO STUPID!
SAY IT.
"THAT YOU DON'T...
"...CARE ABOUT REN TSURUGA AT ALL."
NOW.
LET'S GO, KYOKO.
I DON'T KNOW WHAT HE SAID...
...BUT DON'T TAKE IT PERSONALLY.
pat
HE'S IN A BAD MOOD BECAUSE HE COULDN'T MAKE IT TO A GOLF PARTY.
NOW.
LIFT YOUR FACE.
stroke
stroke
pat

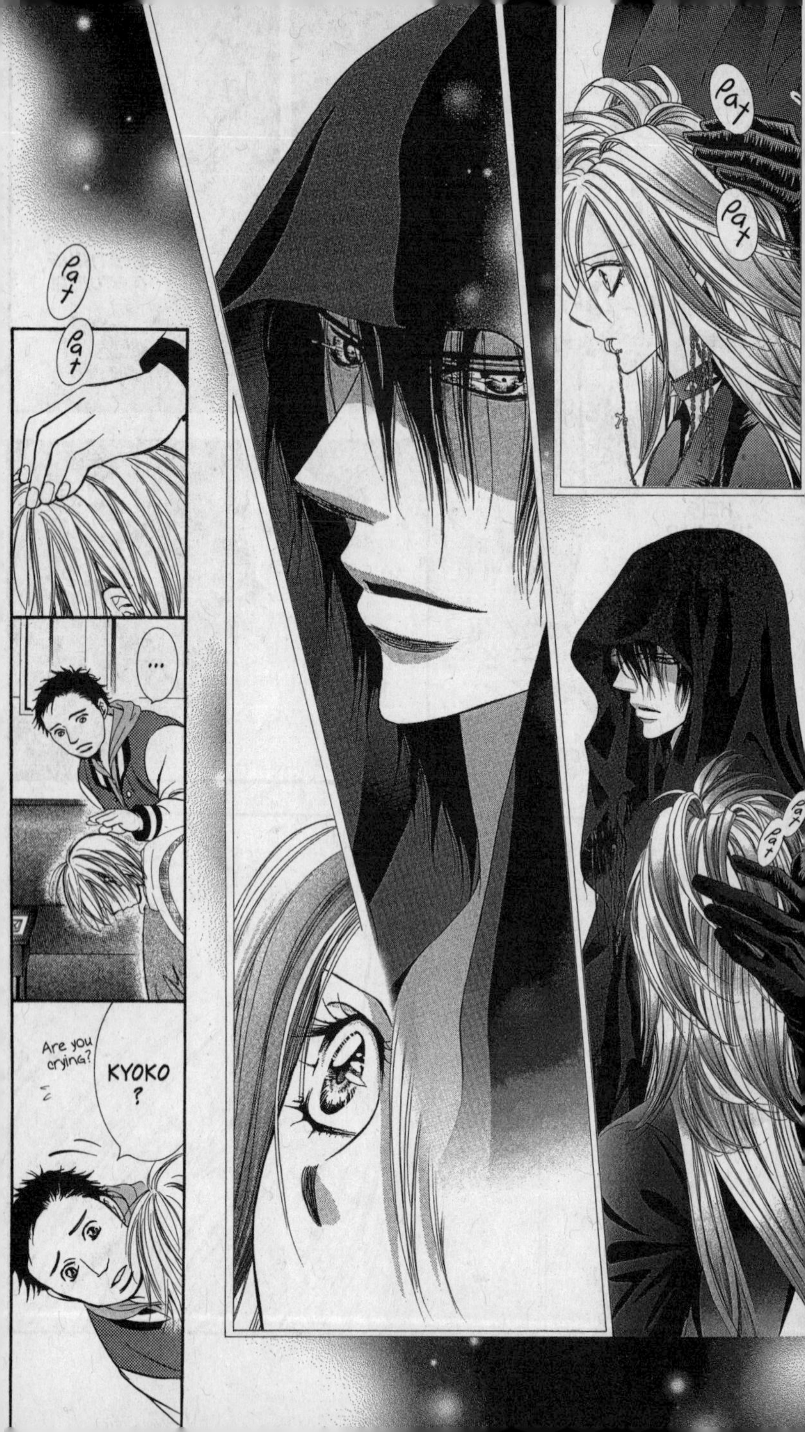
pat
pat
pat
pat
pat
pat
...
KYOKO ?
Are you crying?

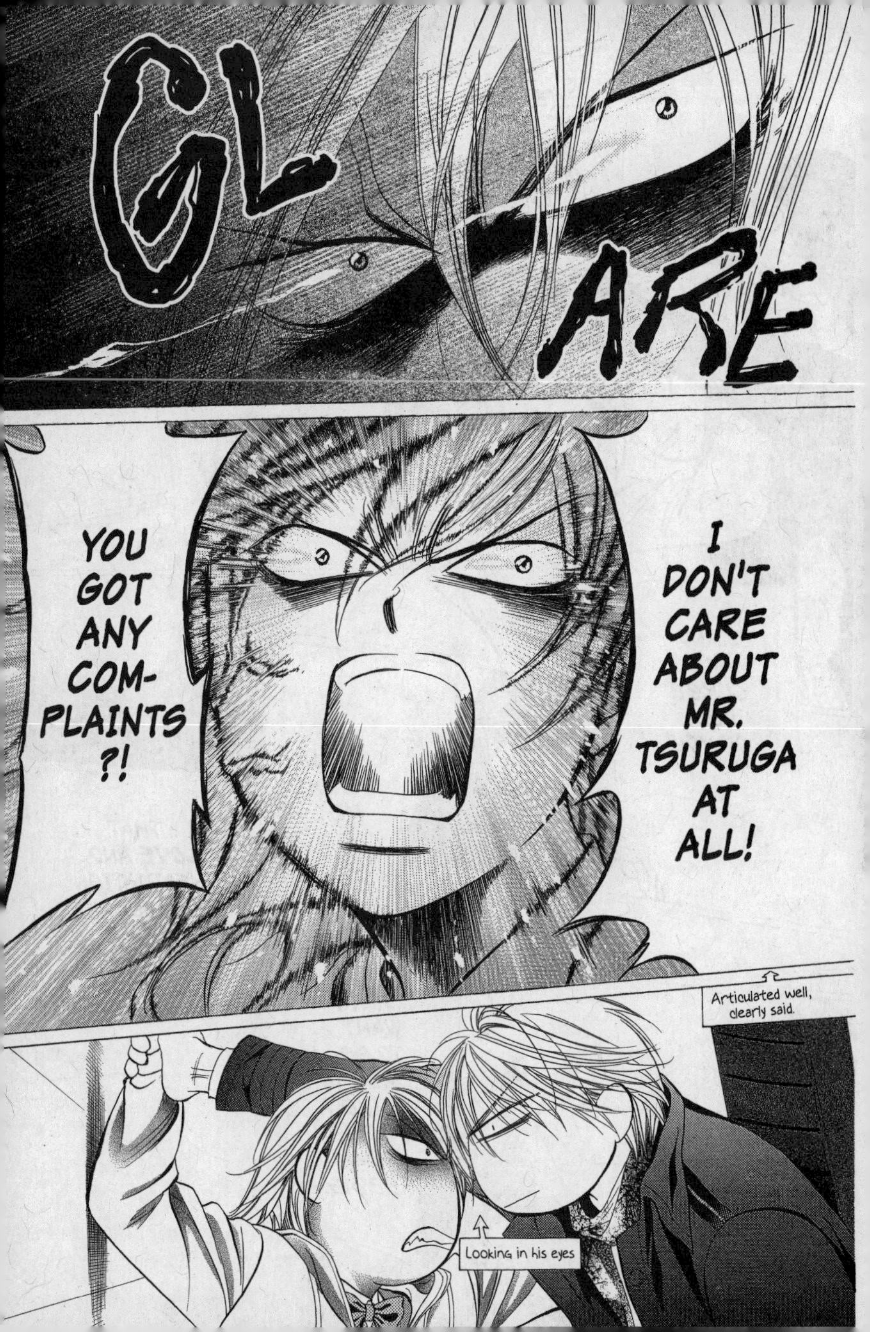
GLARE
I DON'T CARE ABOUT MR. TSURUGA AT ALL!
YOU GOT ANY COM-PLAINTS?!
Articulated well, clearly said.
Looking in his eyes

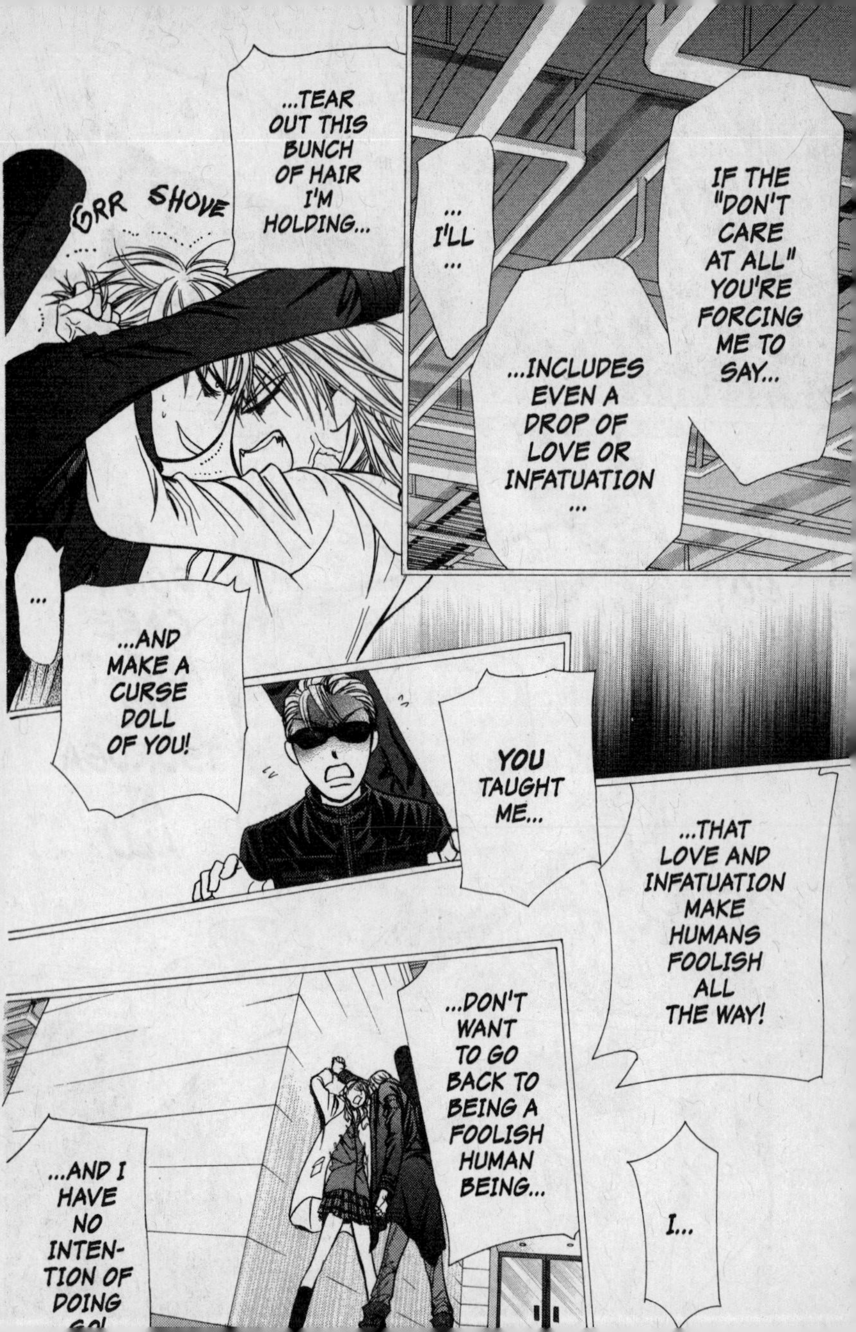
IF THE "DON'T CARE AT ALL" YOU'RE FORCING ME TO SAY...
...INCLUDES EVEN A DROP OF LOVE OR INFATUATION ...
... I'LL ...
...TEAR OUT THIS BUNCH OF HAIR I'M HOLDING...
GRR
SHOVE
...
...AND MAKE A CURSE DOLL OF YOU!
YOU TAUGHT ME...
...THAT LOVE AND INFATUATION MAKE HUMANS FOOLISH ALL THE WAY!
I...
...DON'T WANT TO GO BACK TO BEING A FOOLISH HUMAN BEING...
...AND I HAVE NO INTEN-TION OF DOING

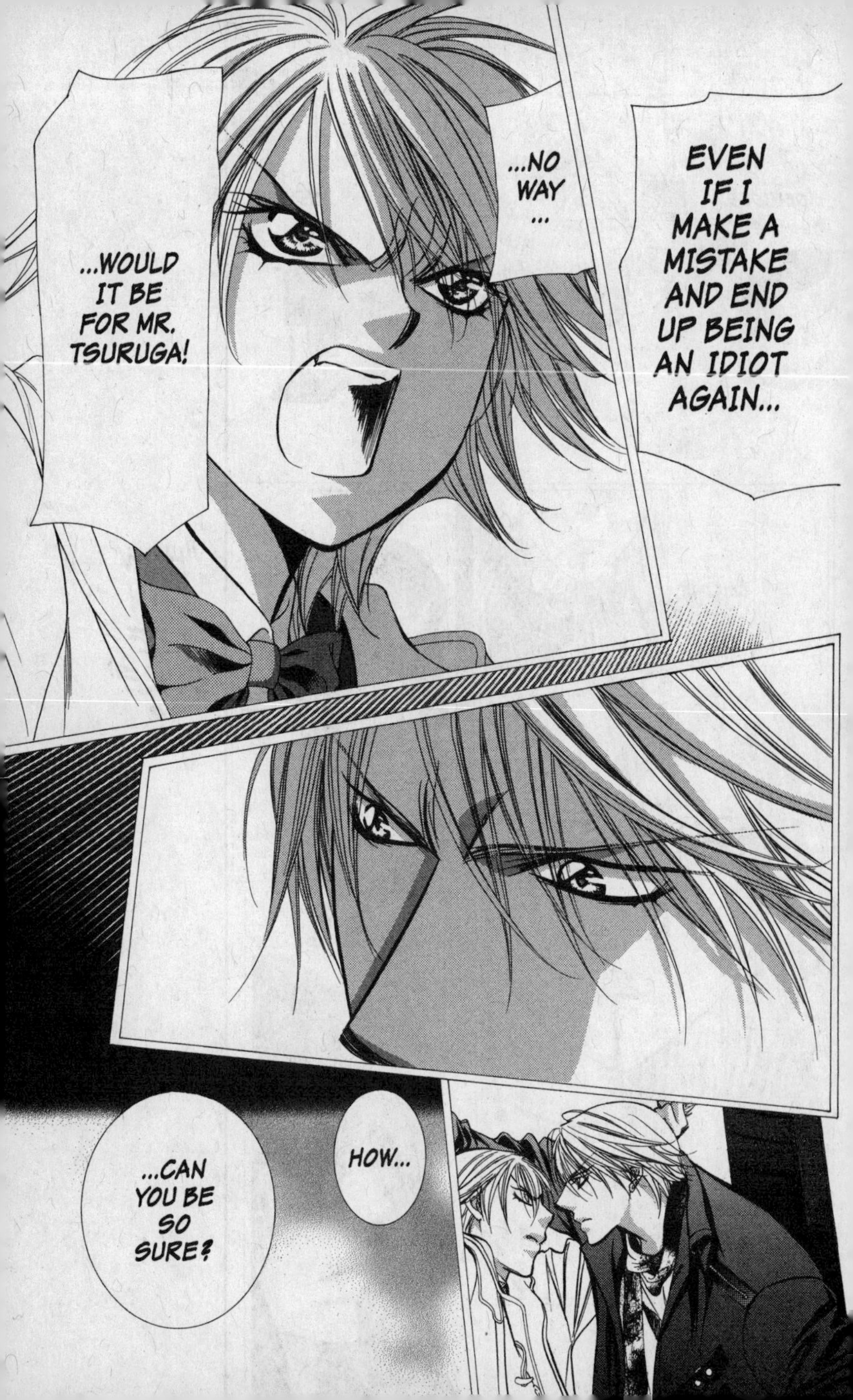
EVEN IF I MAKE A MISTAKE AND END UP BEING AN IDIOT AGAIN...
...NO WAY...
...WOULD IT BE FOR MR. TSURUGA!
HOW...
...CAN YOU BE SO SURE?

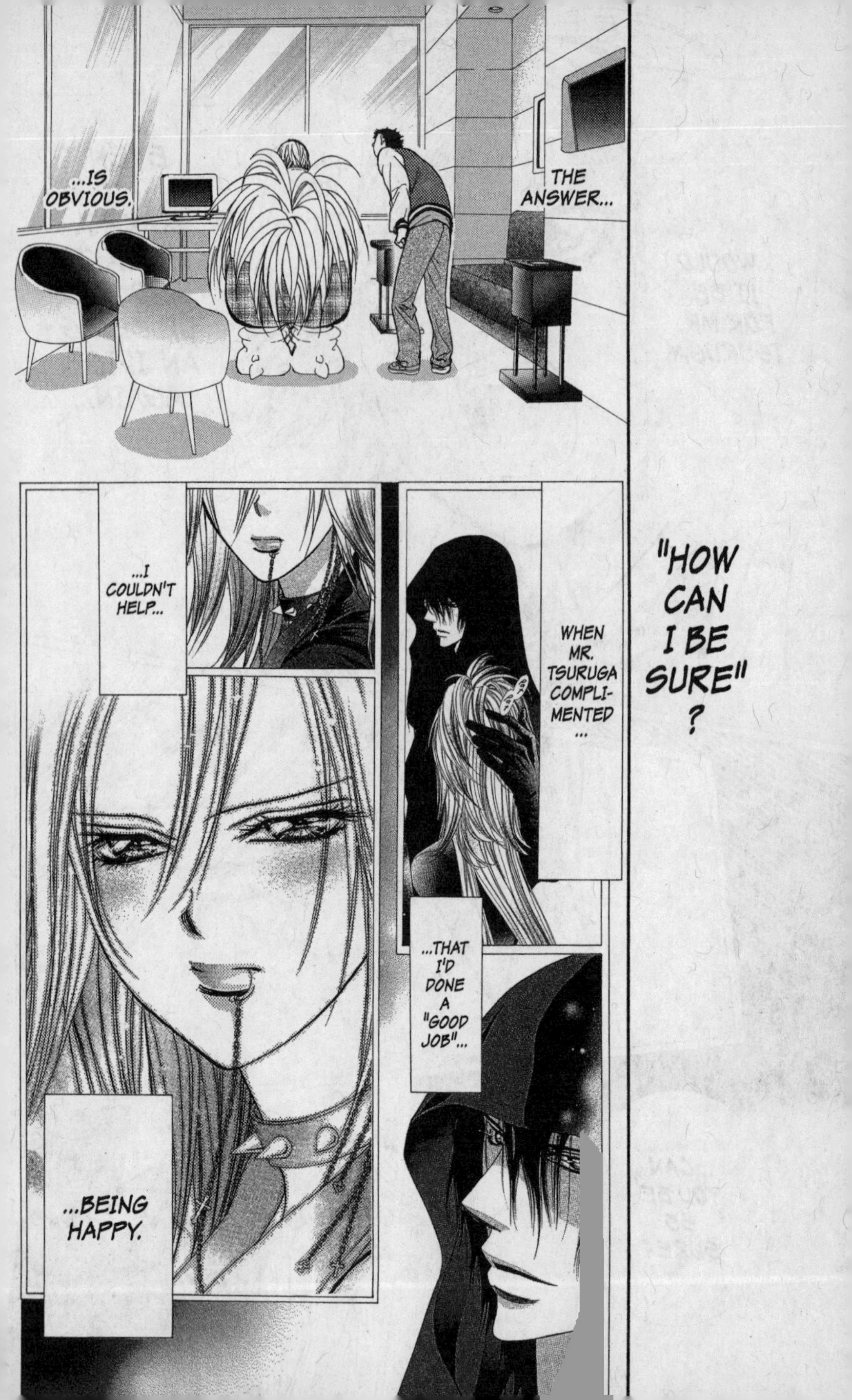
"HOW CAN I BE SURE"?
THE ANSWER...
...IS OBVIOUS.
WHEN MR. TSURUGA COMPLIMENTED...
...THAT I'D DONE A "GOOD JOB"...
...I COULDN'T HELP...
...BEING HAPPY.

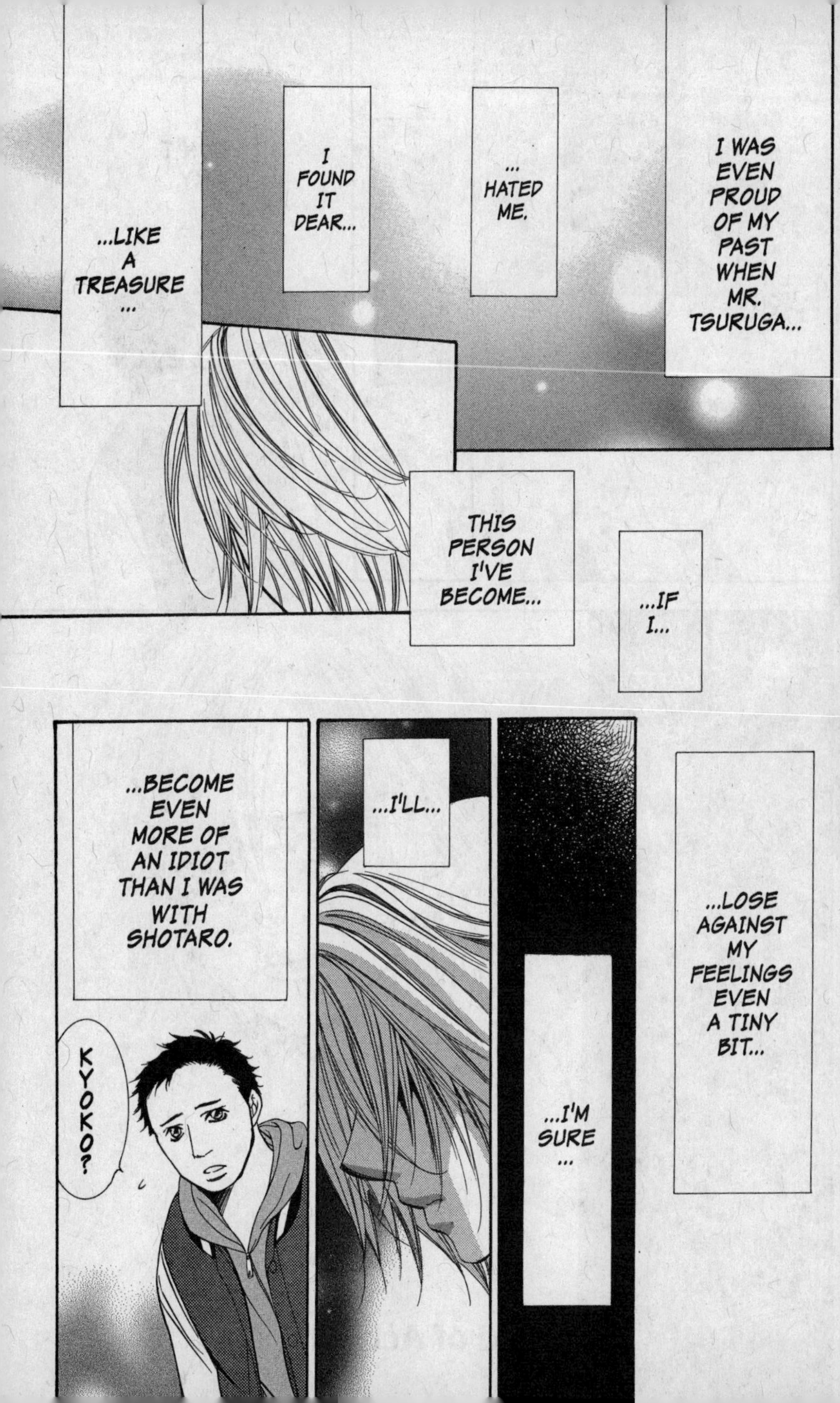

I WAS EVEN PROUD OF MY PAST WHEN MR. TSURUGA...
... HATED ME.
I FOUND IT DEAR...
...LIKE A TREASURE ...
THIS PERSON I'VE BECOME...
...IF I...
...LOSE AGAINST MY FEELINGS EVEN A TINY BIT...
...I'M SURE ...
...I'LL...
...BECOME EVEN MORE OF AN IDIOT THAN I WAS WITH SHOTARO.
KYOKO?

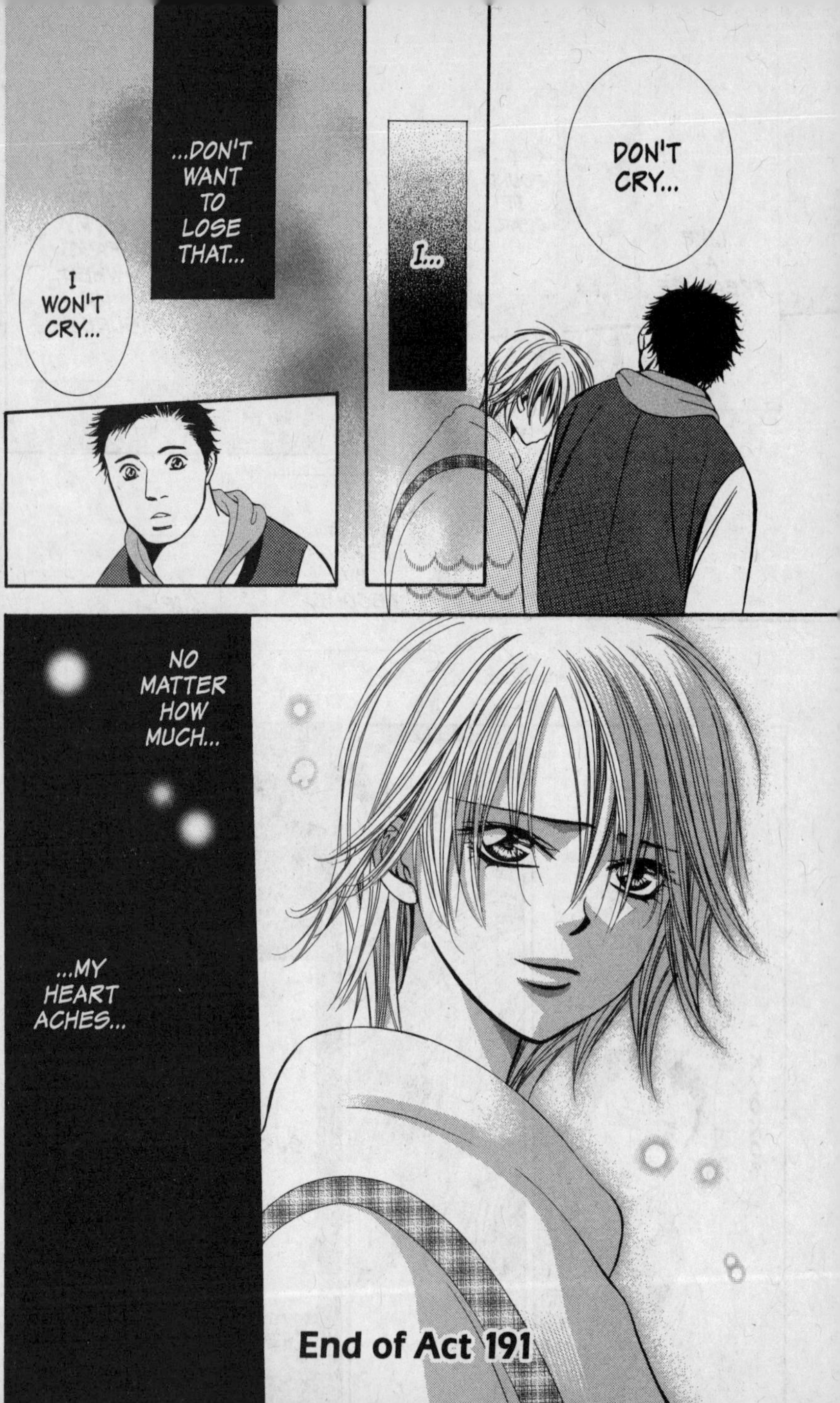
DON'T CRY...
I...
...DON'T WANT TO LOSE THAT...
I WON'T CRY...
NO MATTER HOW MUCH...
...MY HEART ACHES...
End of Act 191

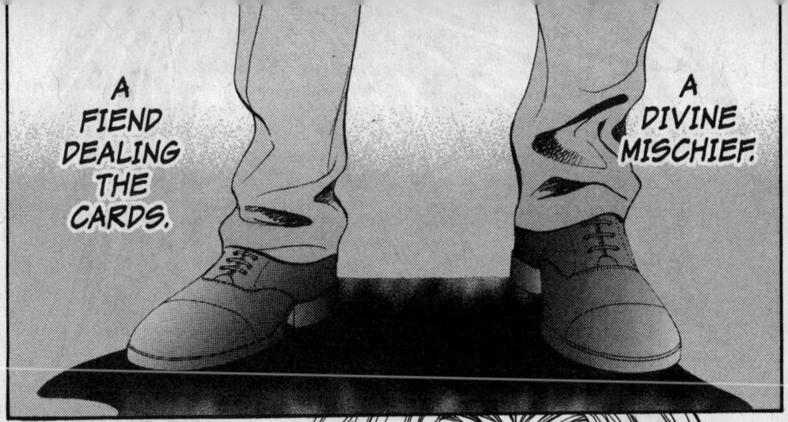
A DIVINE MISCHIEF.
A FIEND DEALING THE CARDS.

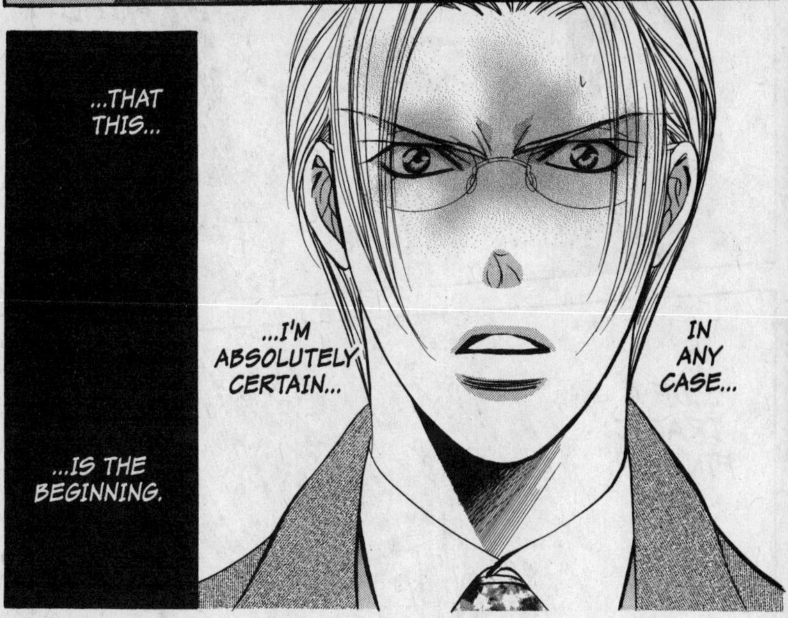
IN ANY CASE...
...I'M ABSOLUTELY CERTAIN...
...THAT THIS...
...IS THE BEGINNING.

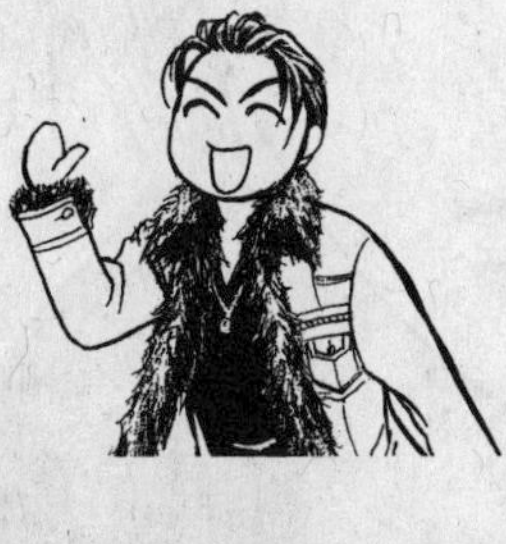

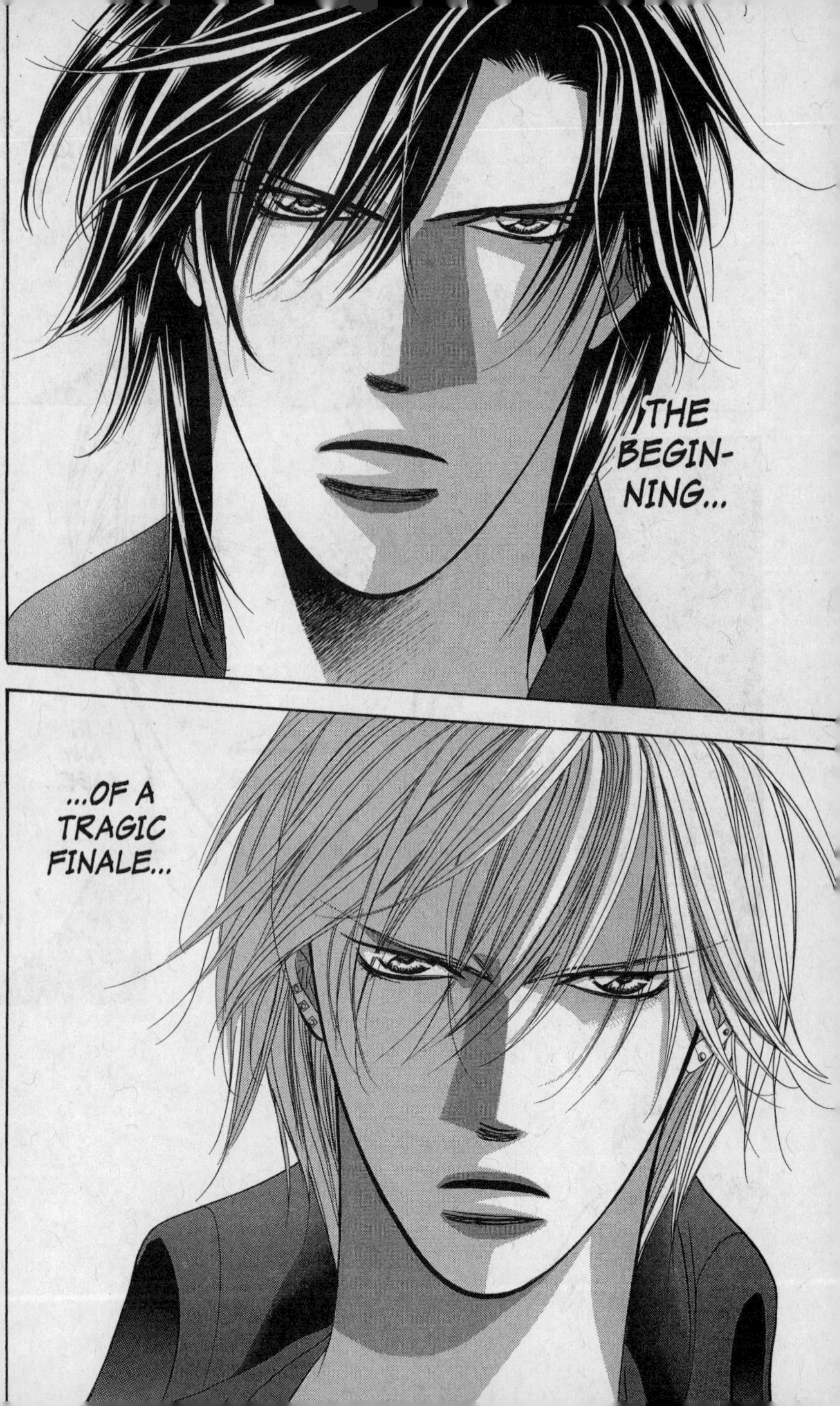
THE BEGINNING...
...OF A TRAGIC FINALE...

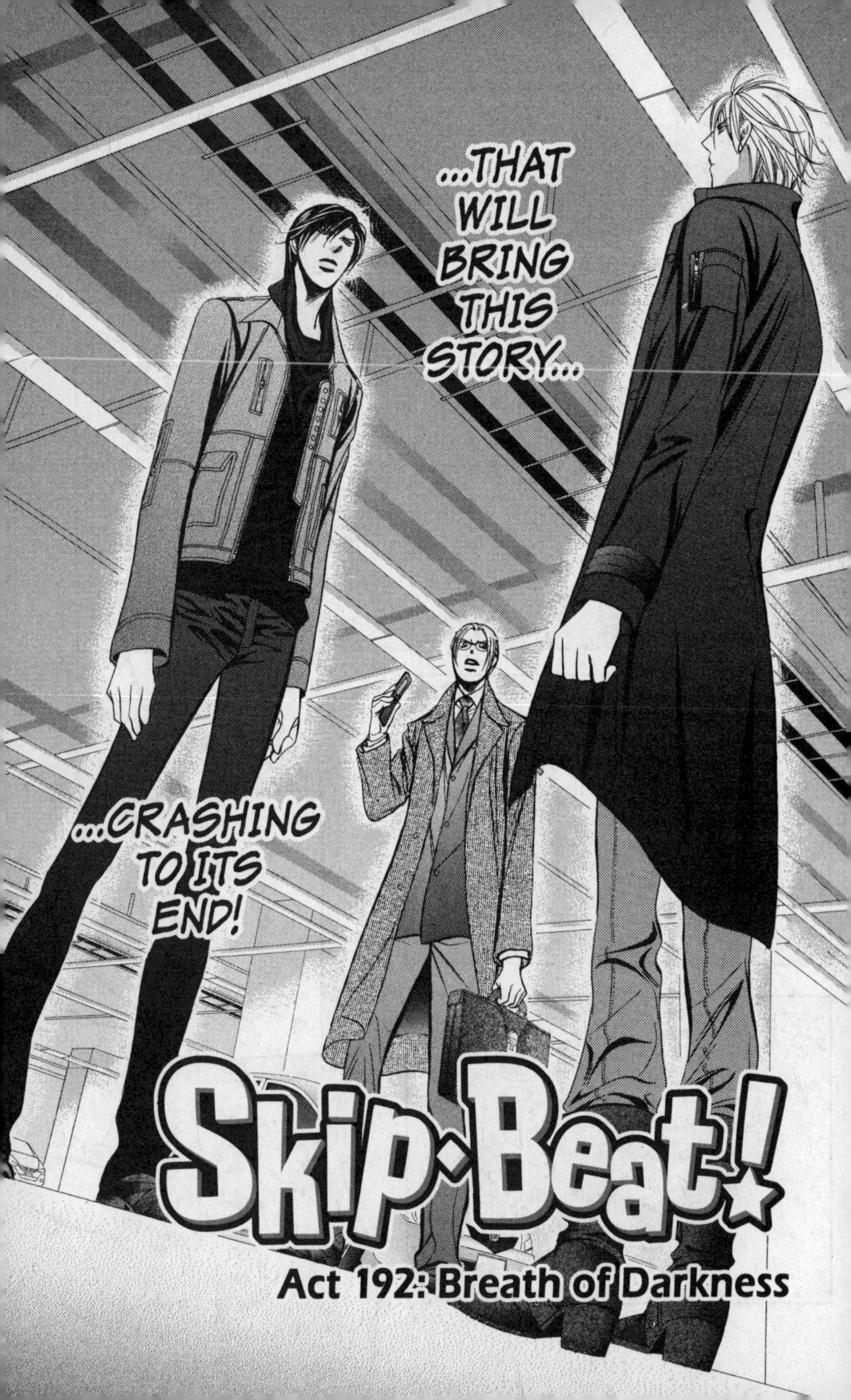
...THAT WILL BRING THIS STORY...
...CRASHING TO ITS END!
Skip·Beat!
Act 192: Breath of Darkness

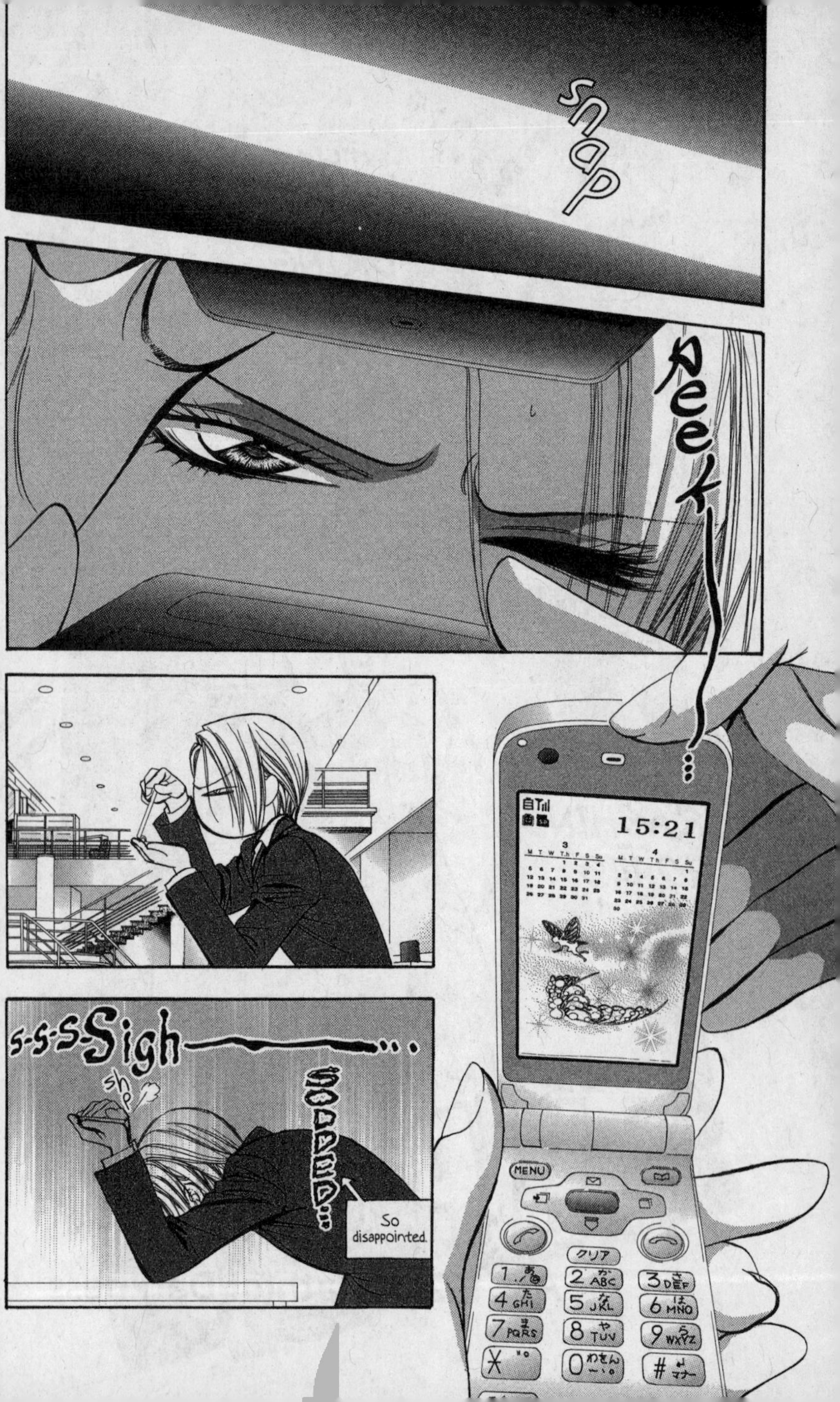
snap
peek...
15:21
MENU
クリア
s-s-s-Sigh...
shp
SOBBBED...
So disappointed.

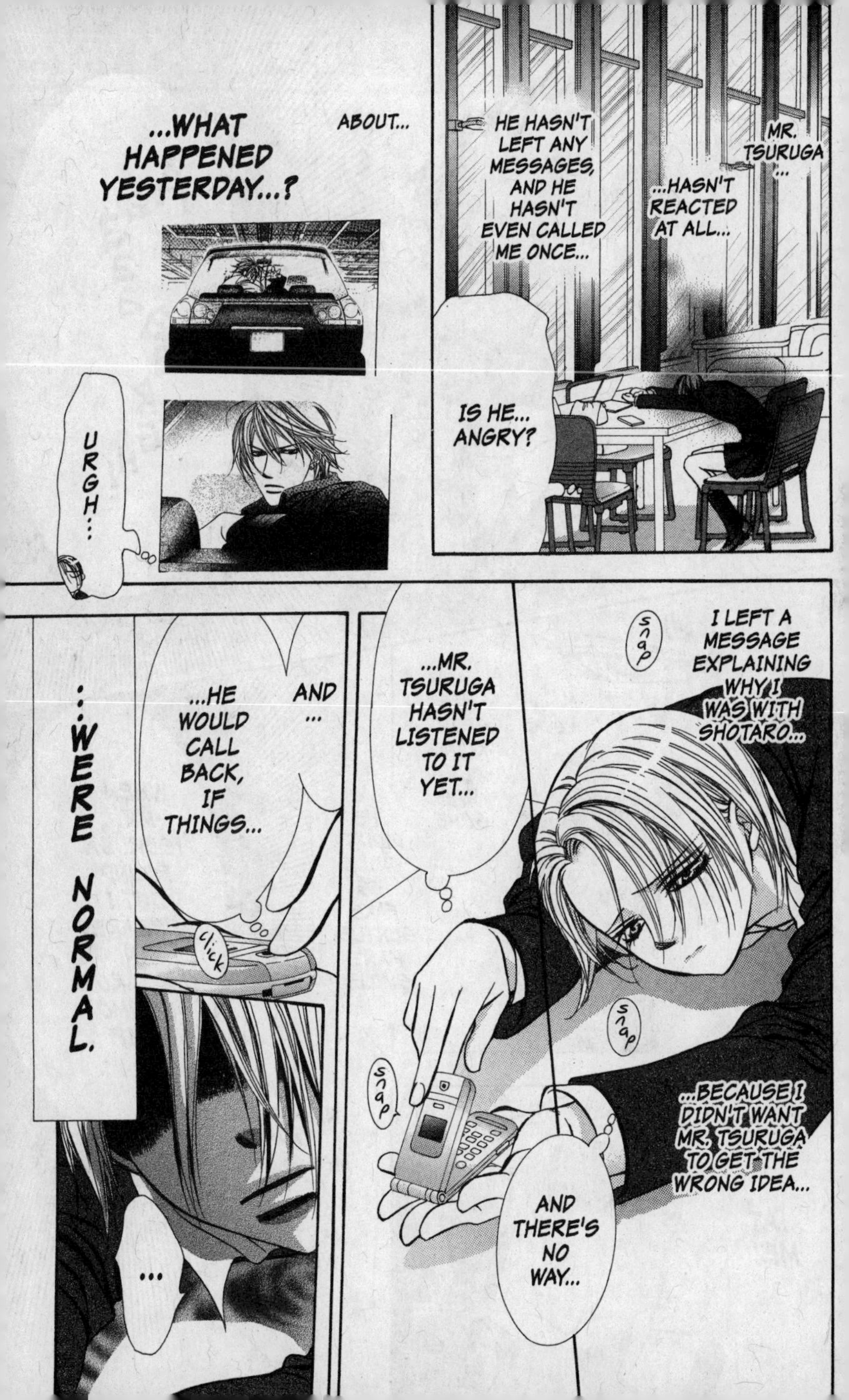
MR. TSURUGA...
...HASN'T REACTED AT ALL...
HE HASN'T LEFT ANY MESSAGES, AND HE HASN'T EVEN CALLED ME ONCE...
IS HE... ANGRY?
ABOUT...
...WHAT HAPPENED YESTERDAY...?
URGH...
snap
I LEFT A MESSAGE EXPLAINING WHY I WAS WITH SHOTARO...
snap
snap
...BECAUSE I DIDN'T WANT MR. TSURUGA TO GET THE WRONG IDEA...
AND THERE'S NO WAY...
...MR. TSURUGA HASN'T LISTENED TO IT YET...
AND...
...HE WOULD CALL BACK, IF THINGS...
click
...
...WERE NORMAL.

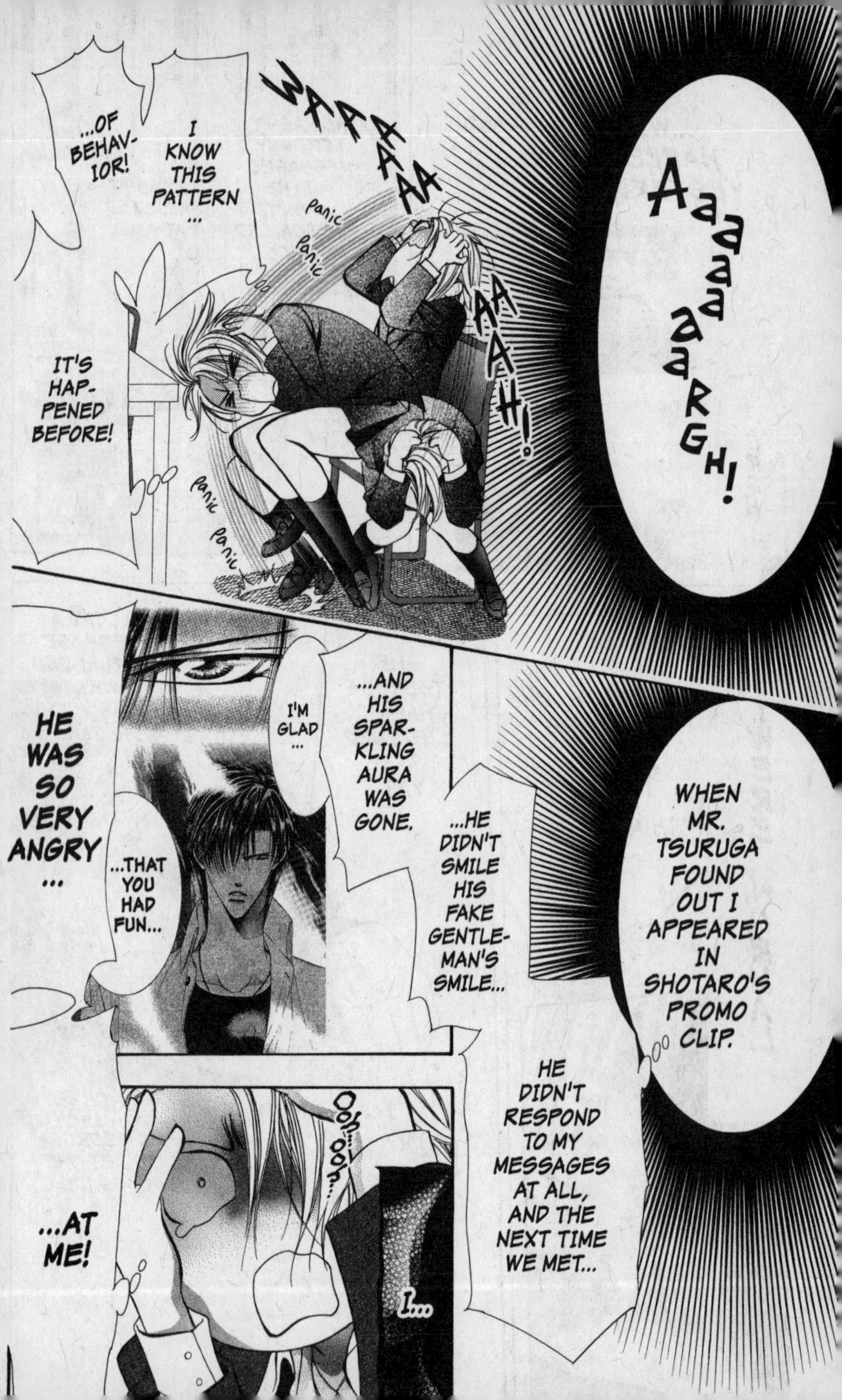
Aaaaaaargh!
WAAAAAAAAAH!
Panic Panic
I KNOW THIS PATTERN...
...OF BEHAVIOR!
IT'S HAPPENED BEFORE!
Panic Panic
WHEN MR. TSURUGA FOUND OUT I APPEARED IN SHOTARO'S PROMO CLIP.
HE DIDN'T RESPOND TO MY MESSAGES AT ALL, AND THE NEXT TIME WE MET...
...HE DIDN'T SMILE HIS FAKE GENTLEMAN'S SMILE...
...AND HIS SPARKLING AURA WAS GONE.
I'M GLAD...
...THAT YOU HAD FUN...
HE WAS SO VERY ANGRY...
Ooh... ooh... ooh...
I...
...AT ME!

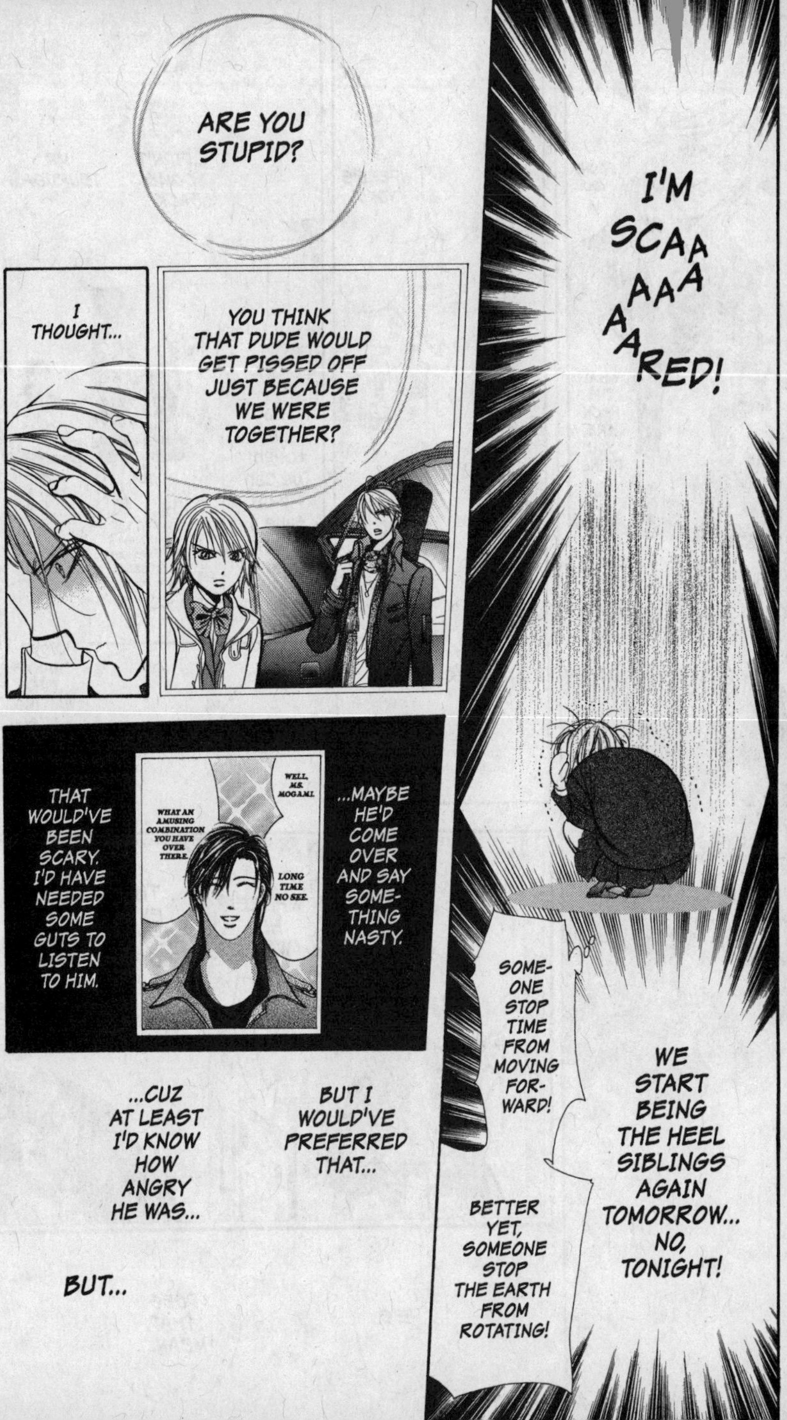
I'M SCAAAAAAARED!
WE START BEING THE HEEL SIBLINGS AGAIN TOMORROW... NO, TONIGHT!
SOME-ONE STOP TIME FROM MOVING FOR-WARD!
BETTER YET, SOMEONE STOP THE EARTH FROM ROTATING!
ARE YOU STUPID?
YOU THINK THAT DUDE WOULD GET PISSED OFF JUST BECAUSE WE WERE TOGETHER?
I THOUGHT...
...MAYBE HE'D COME OVER AND SAY SOME-THING NASTY.
WELL, MS. MOGAMI.
LONG TIME NO SEE.
WHAT AN AMUSING COMBINATION YOU HAVE OVER THERE.
THAT WOULD'VE BEEN SCARY. I'D HAVE NEEDED SOME GUTS TO LISTEN TO HIM.
BUT I WOULD'VE PREFERRED THAT...
...CUZ AT LEAST I'D KNOW HOW ANGRY HE WAS...
BUT...

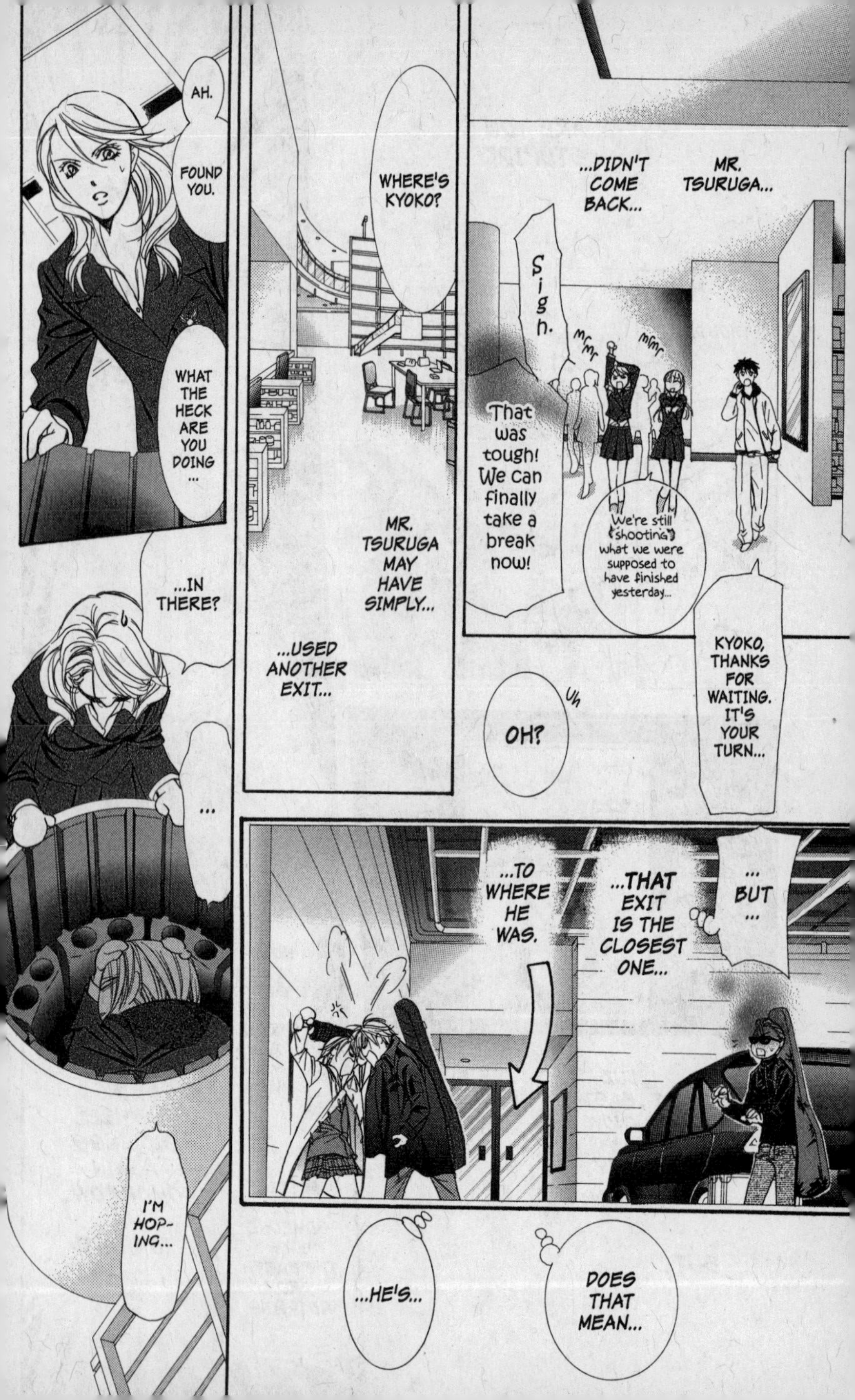
MR. TSURUGA...
...DIDN'T COME BACK...
Sigh.
mrmr
mrmr
That was tough! We can finally take a break now!
We're still "shooting" what we were supposed to have finished yesterday...
KYOKO, THANKS FOR WAITING. IT'S YOUR TURN...
Uh
OH?
WHERE'S KYOKO?
MR. TSURUGA MAY HAVE SIMPLY...
...USED ANOTHER EXIT...
...BUT...
...THAT EXIT IS THE CLOSEST ONE...
...TO WHERE HE WAS.
DOES THAT MEAN...
...HE'S...
AH.
FOUND YOU.
WHAT THE HECK ARE YOU DOING...
...IN THERE?
...
I'M HOPING...

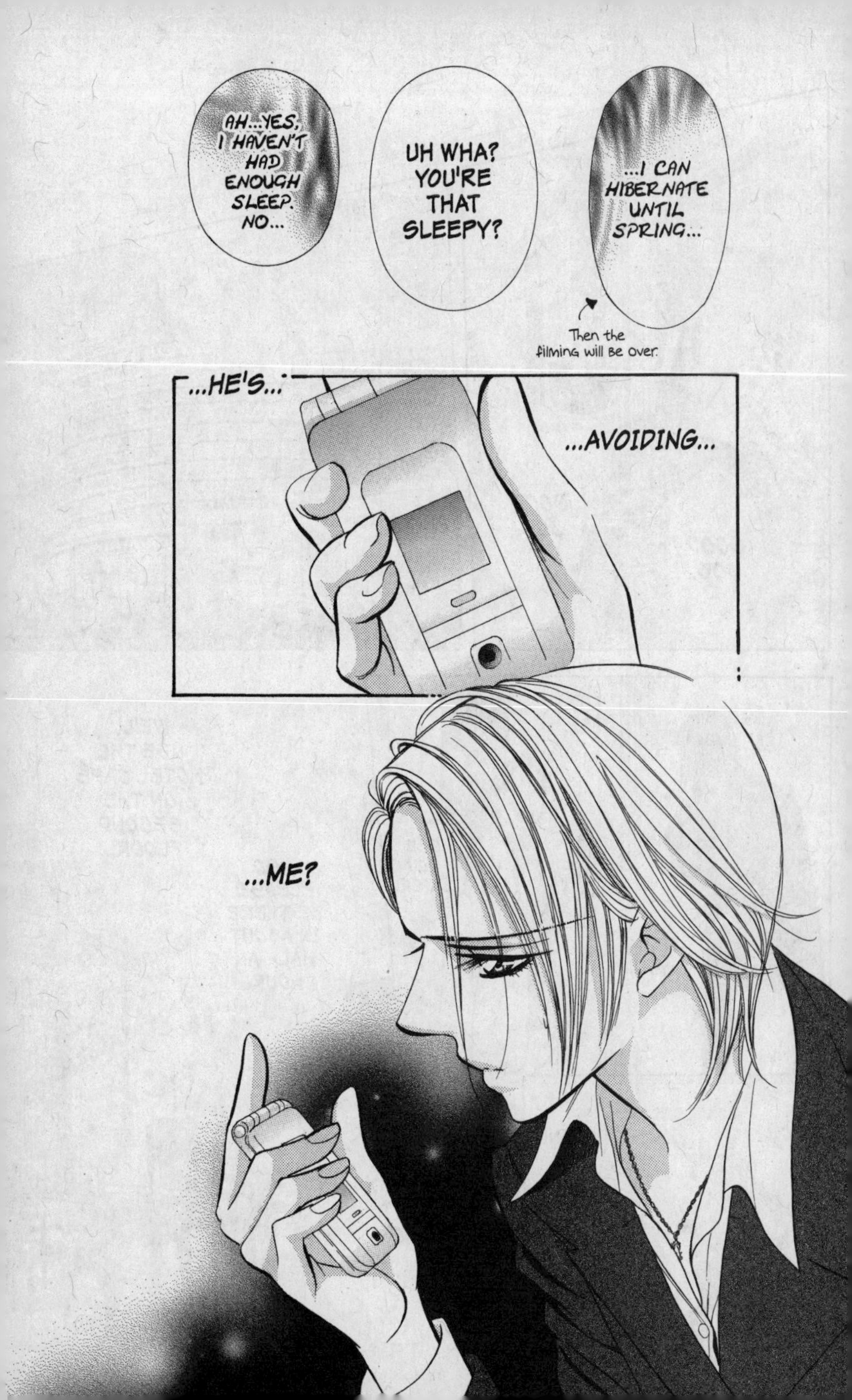
...I CAN HIBERNATE UNTIL SPRING...
Then the filming will be over.
UH WHA? YOU'RE THAT SLEEPY?
AH...YES, I HAVEN'T HAD ENOUGH SLEEP. NO...
...HE'S...
...AVOIDING...
...ME?

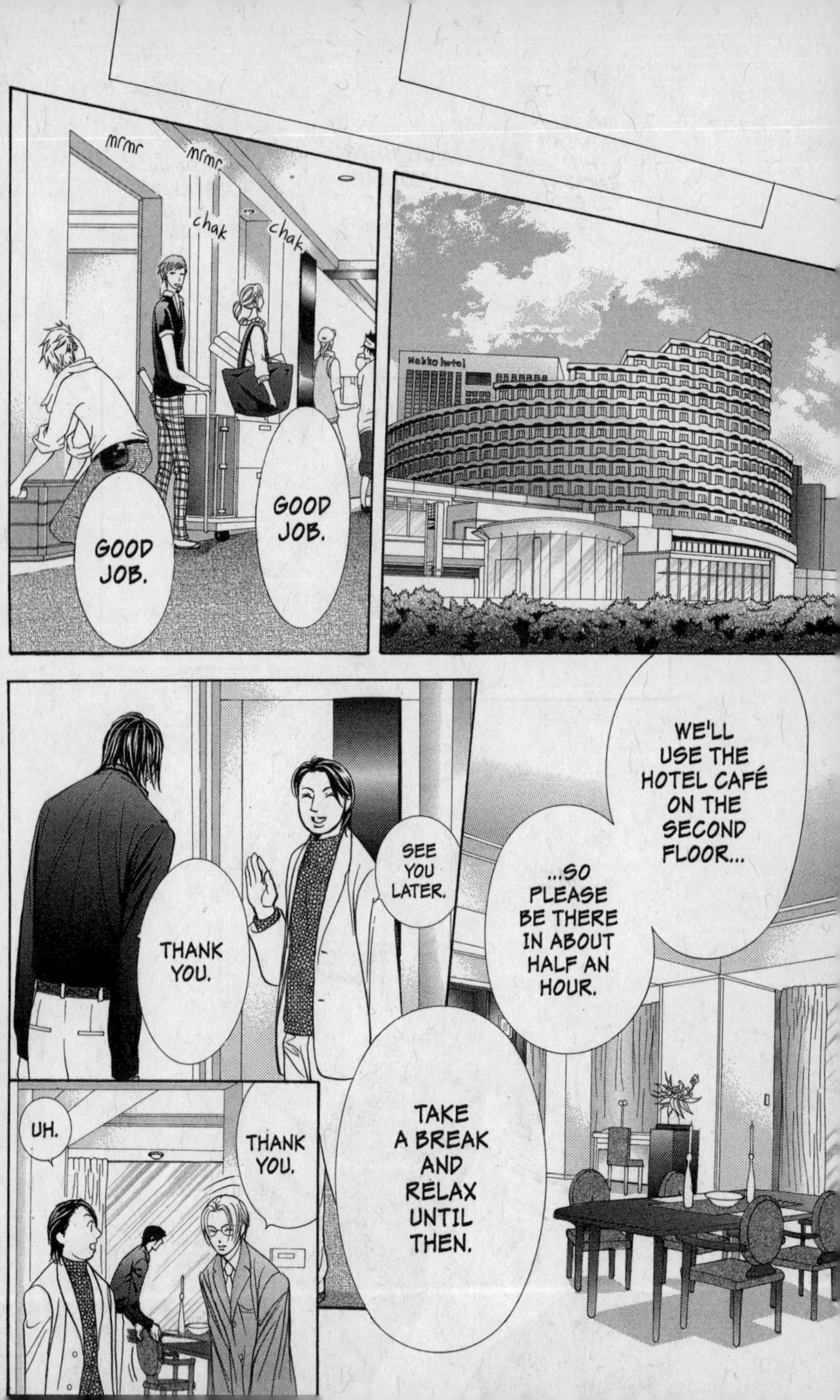
mrmr
mrmr
chak
chak
GOOD JOB.
GOOD JOB.
WE'LL USE THE HOTEL CAFÉ ON THE SECOND FLOOR...
...SO PLEASE BE THERE IN ABOUT HALF AN HOUR.
TAKE A BREAK AND RELAX UNTIL THEN.
SEE YOU LATER.
THANK YOU.
THANK YOU.
UH.

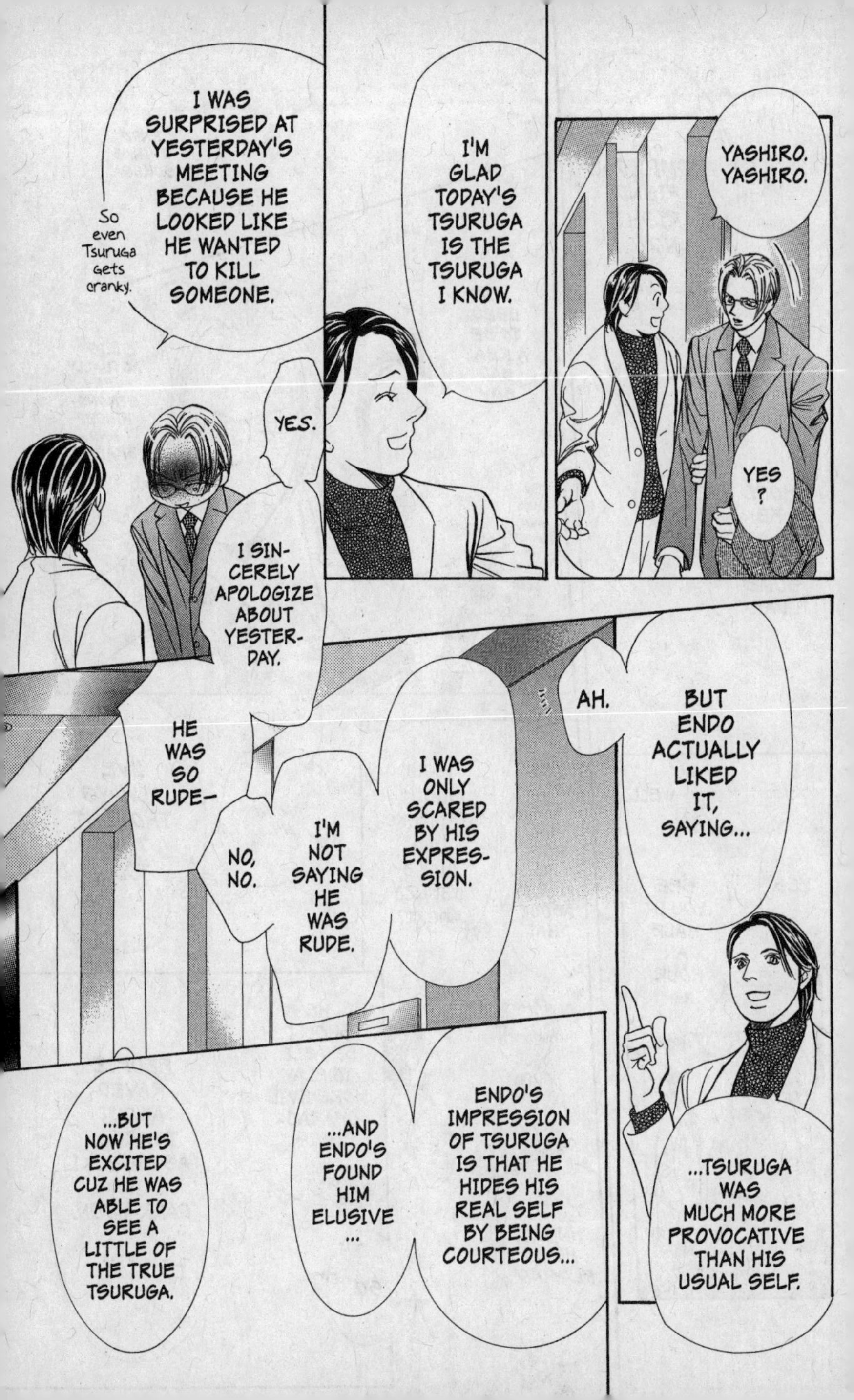
YASHIRO. YASHIRO.
YES?
I'M GLAD TODAY'S TSURUGA IS THE TSURUGA I KNOW.
I WAS SURPRISED AT YESTERDAY'S MEETING BECAUSE HE LOOKED LIKE HE WANTED TO KILL SOMEONE.
So even Tsuruga gets cranky.
YES.
I SINCERELY APOLOGIZE ABOUT YESTERDAY.
HE WAS SO RUDE–
NO, NO.
I'M NOT SAYING HE WAS RUDE.
I WAS ONLY SCARED BY HIS EXPRESSION.
AH.
BUT ENDO ACTUALLY LIKED IT, SAYING...
...TSURUGA WAS MUCH MORE PROVOCATIVE THAN HIS USUAL SELF.
ENDO'S IMPRESSION OF TSURUGA IS THAT HE HIDES HIS REAL SELF BY BEING COURTEOUS...
...AND ENDO'S FOUND HIM ELUSIVE...
...BUT NOW HE'S EXCITED CUZ HE WAS ABLE TO SEE A LITTLE OF THE TRUE TSURUGA.

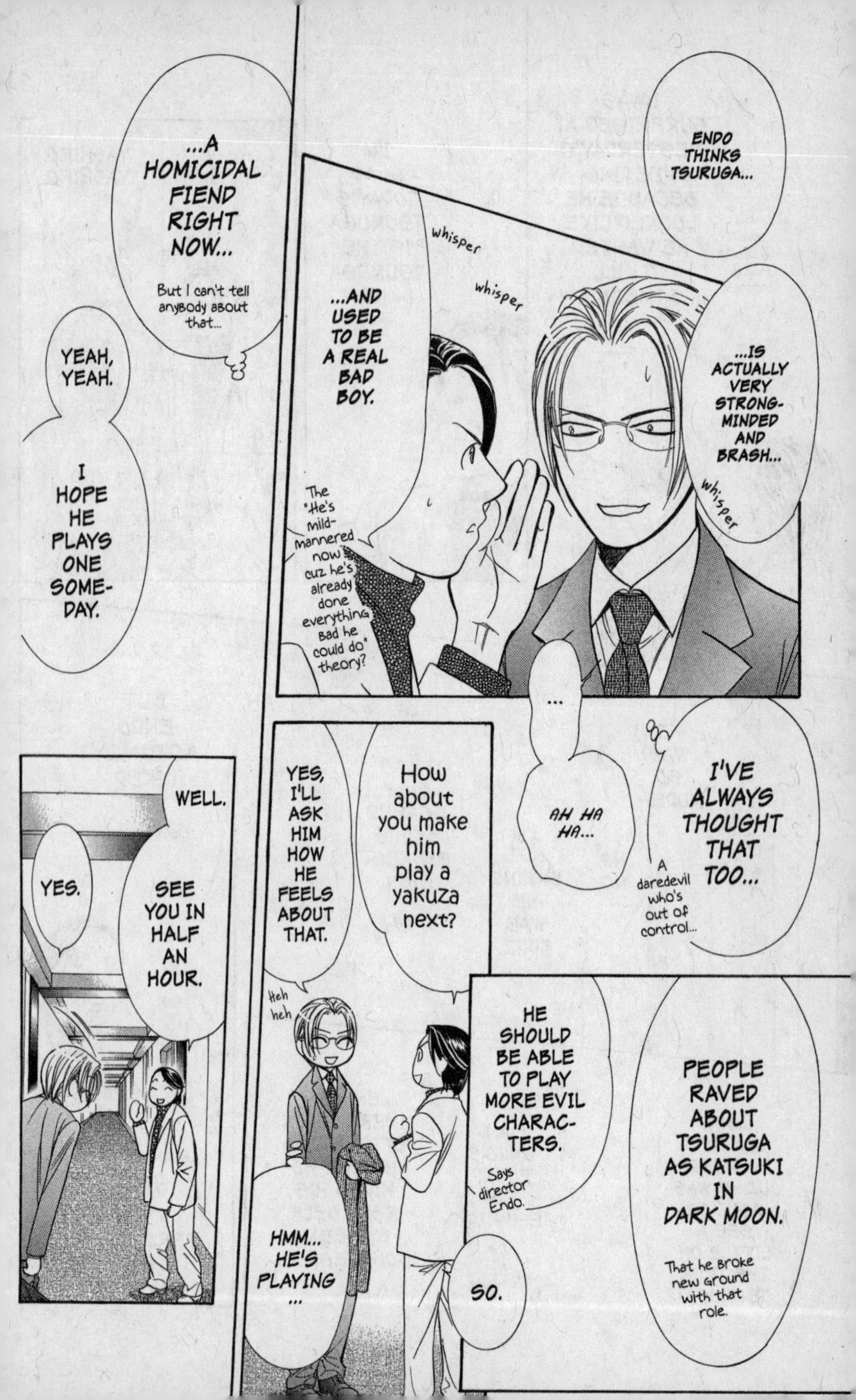
ENDO THINKS TSURUGA...
...IS ACTUALLY VERY STRONG-MINDED AND BRASH...
whisper
whisper
whisper
...AND USED TO BE A REAL BAD BOY.
The "He's mild-mannered now cuz he's already done everything bad he could do" theory?
...
I'VE ALWAYS THOUGHT THAT TOO...
A daredevil who's out of control...
AH HA HA...
PEOPLE RAVED ABOUT TSURUGA AS KATSUKI IN DARK MOON.
That he broke new ground with that role.
HE SHOULD BE ABLE TO PLAY MORE EVIL CHARACTERS.
Says director Endo.
SO.
How about you make him play a yakuza next?
YES, I'LL ASK HIM HOW HE FEELS ABOUT THAT.
Heh heh
HMM... HE'S PLAYING ...
...A HOMICIDAL FIEND RIGHT NOW...
But I can't tell anybody about that...
YEAH, YEAH.
I HOPE HE PLAYS ONE SOME-DAY.
WELL.
SEE YOU IN HALF AN HOUR.
YES.

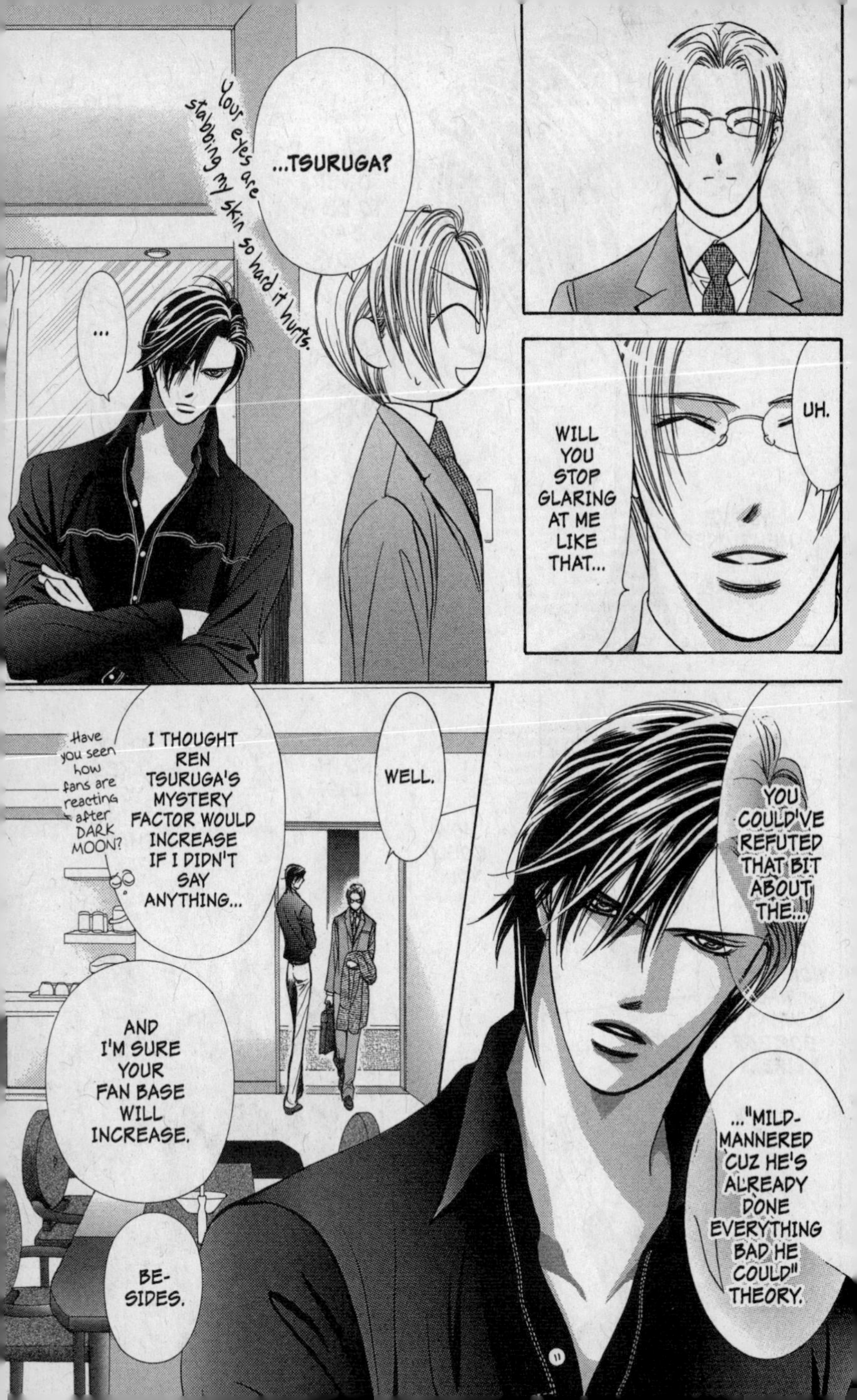
UH.
WILL YOU STOP GLARING AT ME LIKE THAT...
...TSURUGA?
Your eyes are stabbing my skin so hard it hurts.
...
YOU COULD'VE REFUTED THAT BIT ABOUT THE...
..."MILD-MANNERED CUZ HE'S ALREADY DONE EVERYTHING BAD HE COULD" THEORY.
WELL.
I THOUGHT REN TSURUGA'S MYSTERY FACTOR WOULD INCREASE IF I DIDN'T SAY ANYTHING...
Have you seen how fans are reacting after DARK MOON?
AND I'M SURE YOUR FAN BASE WILL INCREASE.
BE-SIDES.

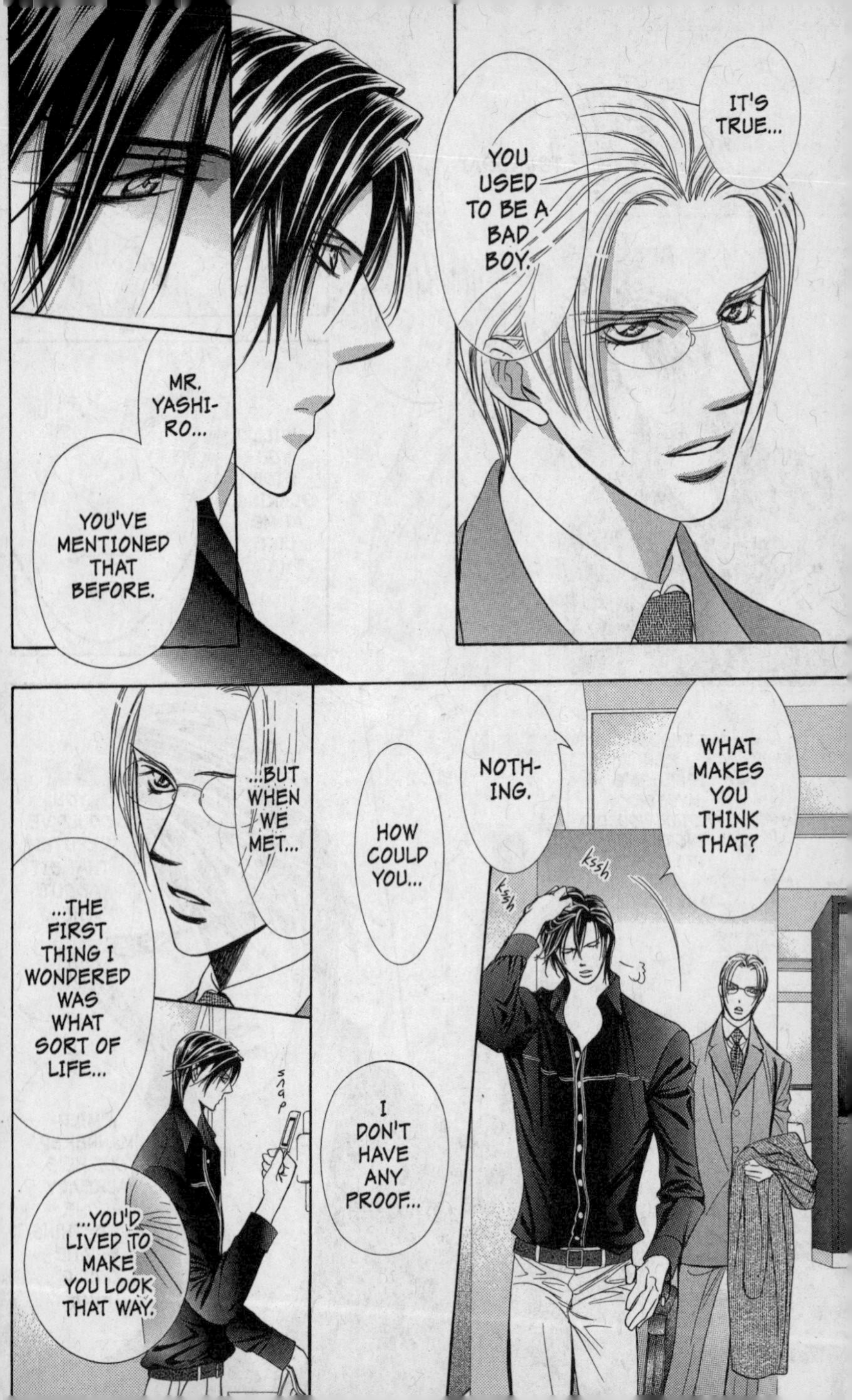
IT'S TRUE...
YOU USED TO BE A BAD BOY.
MR. YASHIRO...
YOU'VE MENTIONED THAT BEFORE.
WHAT MAKES YOU THINK THAT?
NOTHING.
kssh
kssh
HOW COULD YOU...
I DON'T HAVE ANY PROOF...
...BUT WHEN WE MET...
...THE FIRST THING I WONDERED WAS WHAT SORT OF LIFE...
snap
...YOU'D LIVED TO MAKE YOU LOOK THAT WAY.

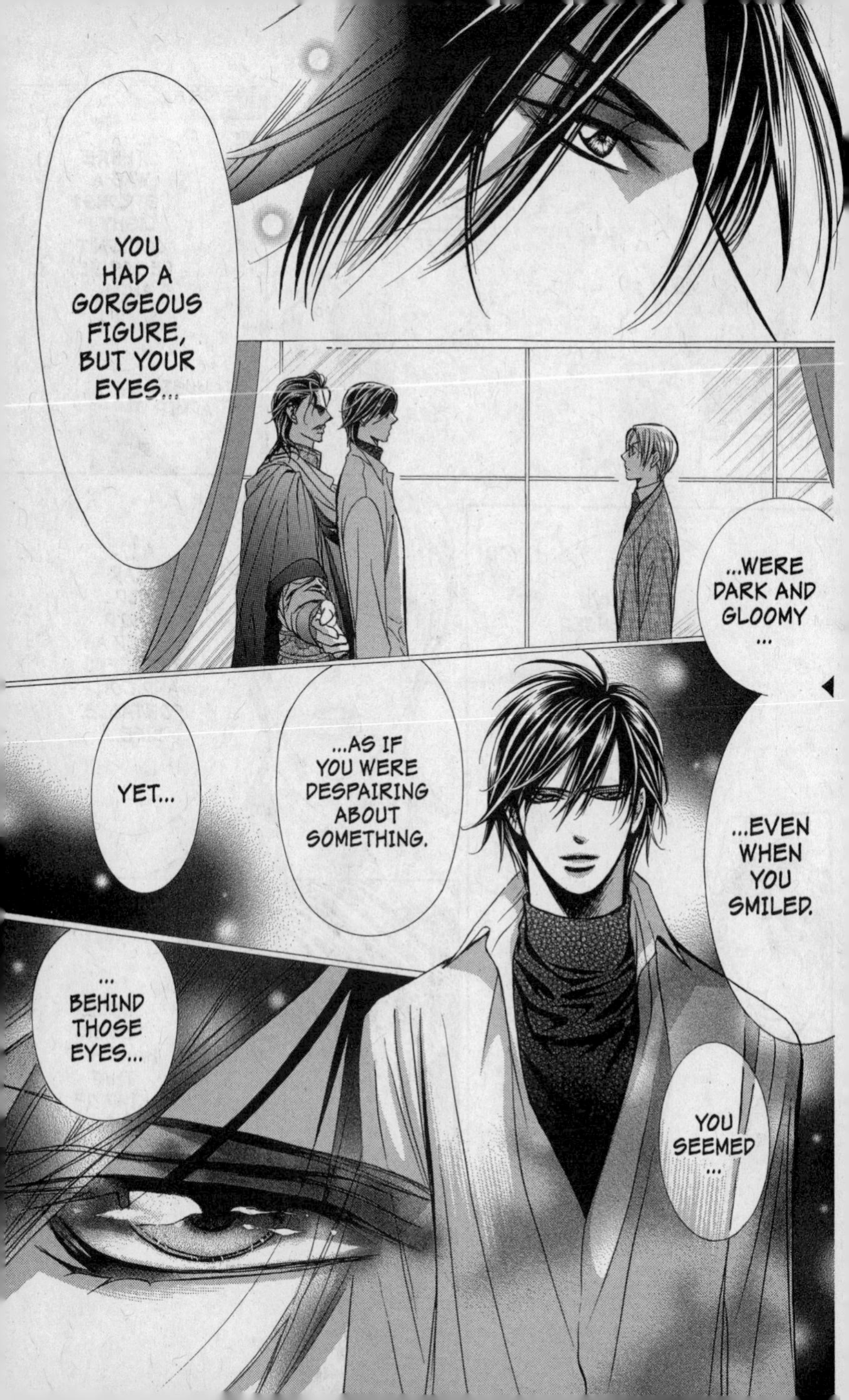
YOU HAD A GORGEOUS FIGURE, BUT YOUR EYES...
...WERE DARK AND GLOOMY ...
...EVEN WHEN YOU SMILED.
YET...
... BEHIND THOSE EYES...
YOU SEEMED ...
...AS IF YOU WERE DESPAIRING ABOUT SOMETHING.

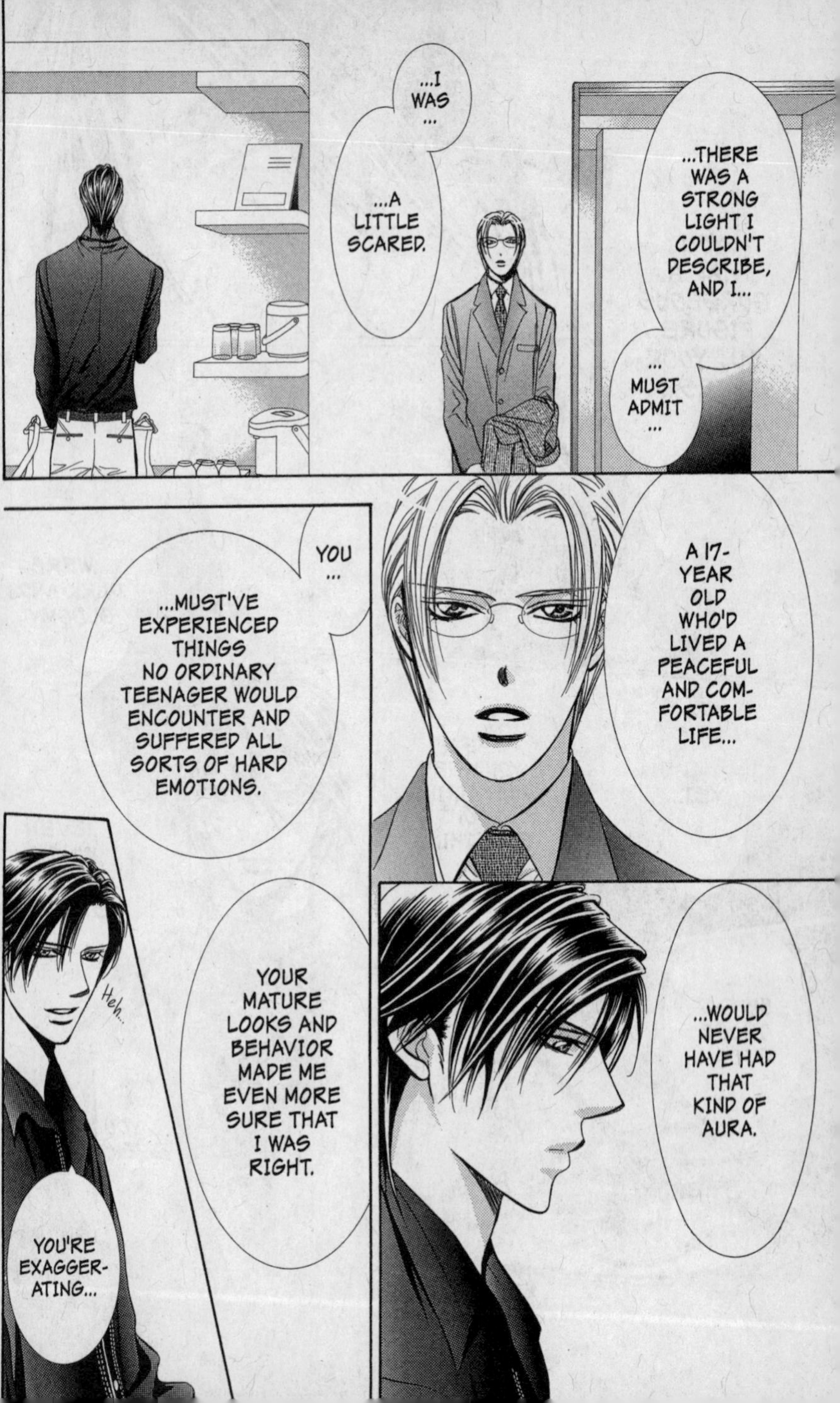
...THERE WAS A STRONG LIGHT I COULDN'T DESCRIBE, AND I...
...MUST ADMIT...
...I WAS...
...A LITTLE SCARED.
A 17-YEAR OLD WHO'D LIVED A PEACEFUL AND COMFORTABLE LIFE...
...WOULD NEVER HAVE HAD THAT KIND OF AURA.
YOU...
...MUST'VE EXPERIENCED THINGS NO ORDINARY TEENAGER WOULD ENCOUNTER AND SUFFERED ALL SORTS OF HARD EMOTIONS.
YOUR MATURE LOOKS AND BEHAVIOR MADE ME EVEN MORE SURE THAT I WAS RIGHT.
Heh...
YOU'RE EXAGGERATING...

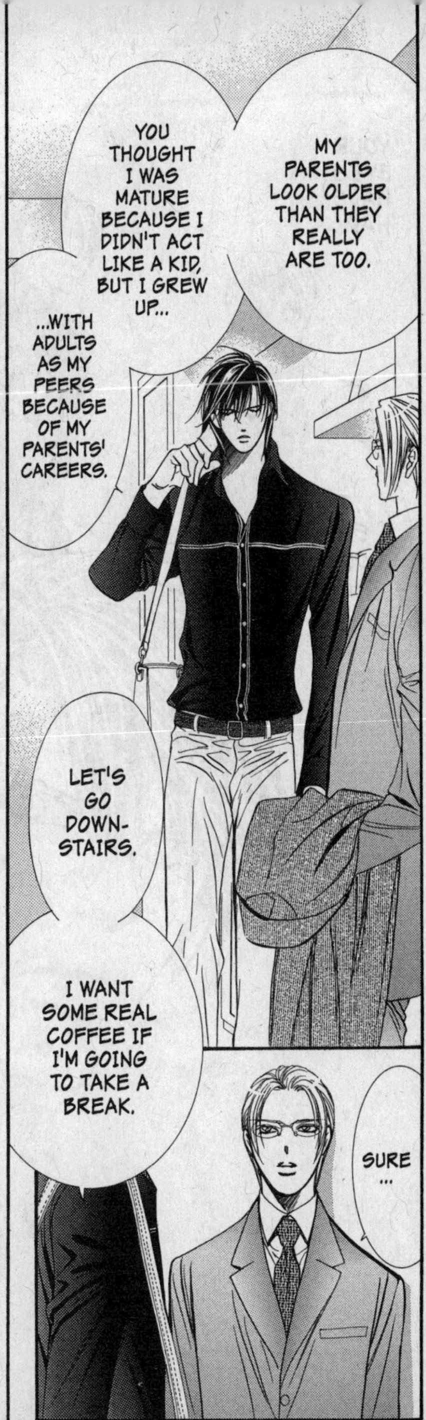
MY PARENTS LOOK OLDER THAN THEY REALLY ARE TOO.
YOU THOUGHT I WAS MATURE BECAUSE I DIDN'T ACT LIKE A KID, BUT I GREW UP...
...WITH ADULTS AS MY PEERS BECAUSE OF MY PARENTS' CAREERS.
LET'S GO DOWN-STAIRS.
...I WANT SOME REAL COFFEE IF I'M GOING TO TAKE A BREAK.
SURE...
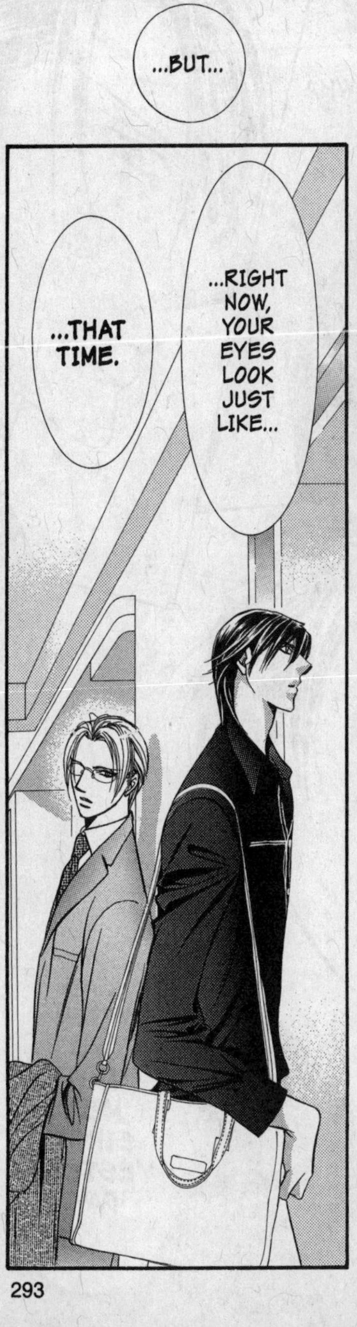
...BUT...
...RIGHT NOW, YOUR EYES LOOK JUST LIKE...
...THAT TIME.

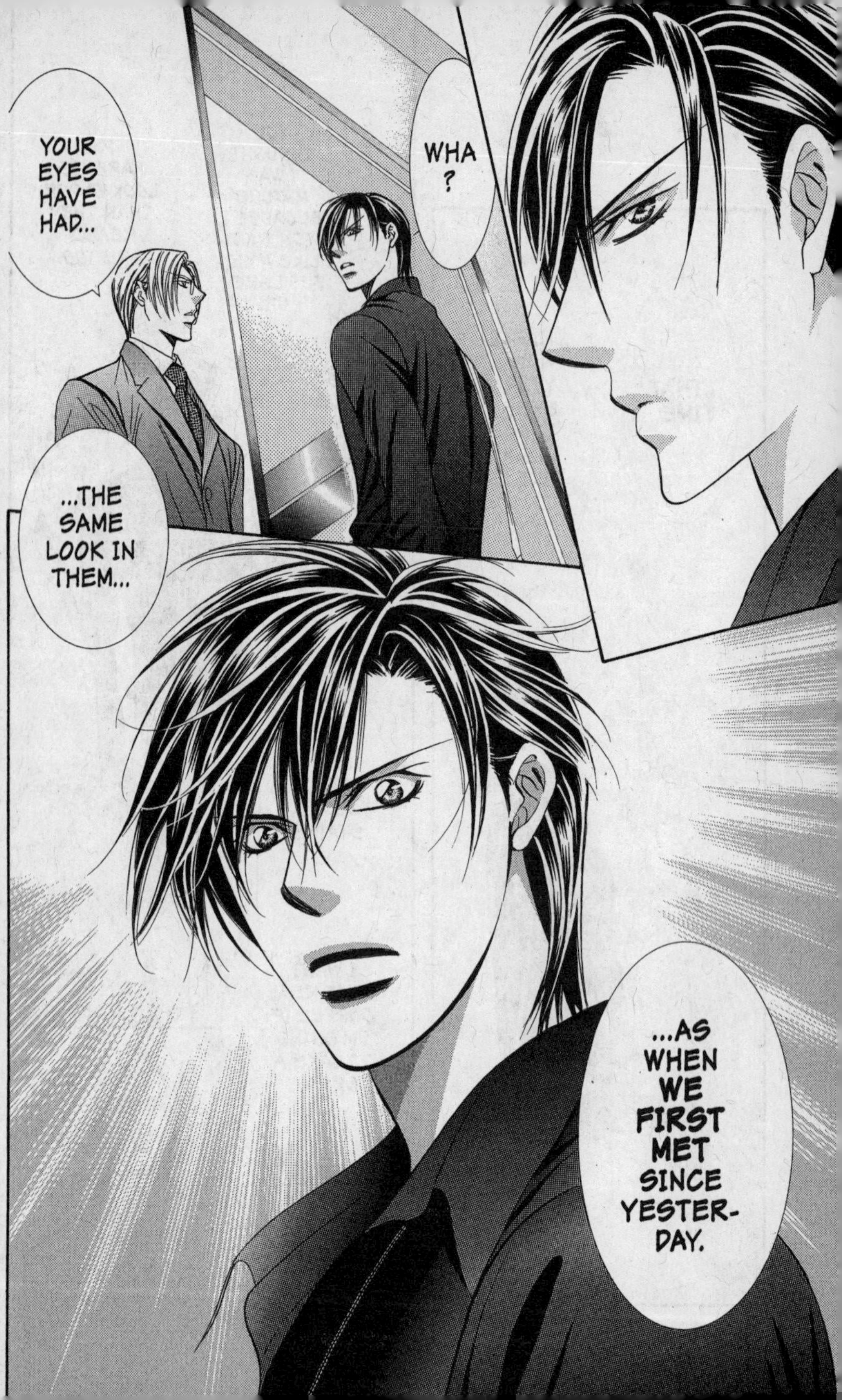
WHA ?
YOUR EYES HAVE HAD...
...THE SAME LOOK IN THEM...
...AS WHEN WE FIRST MET SINCE YESTER-DAY.

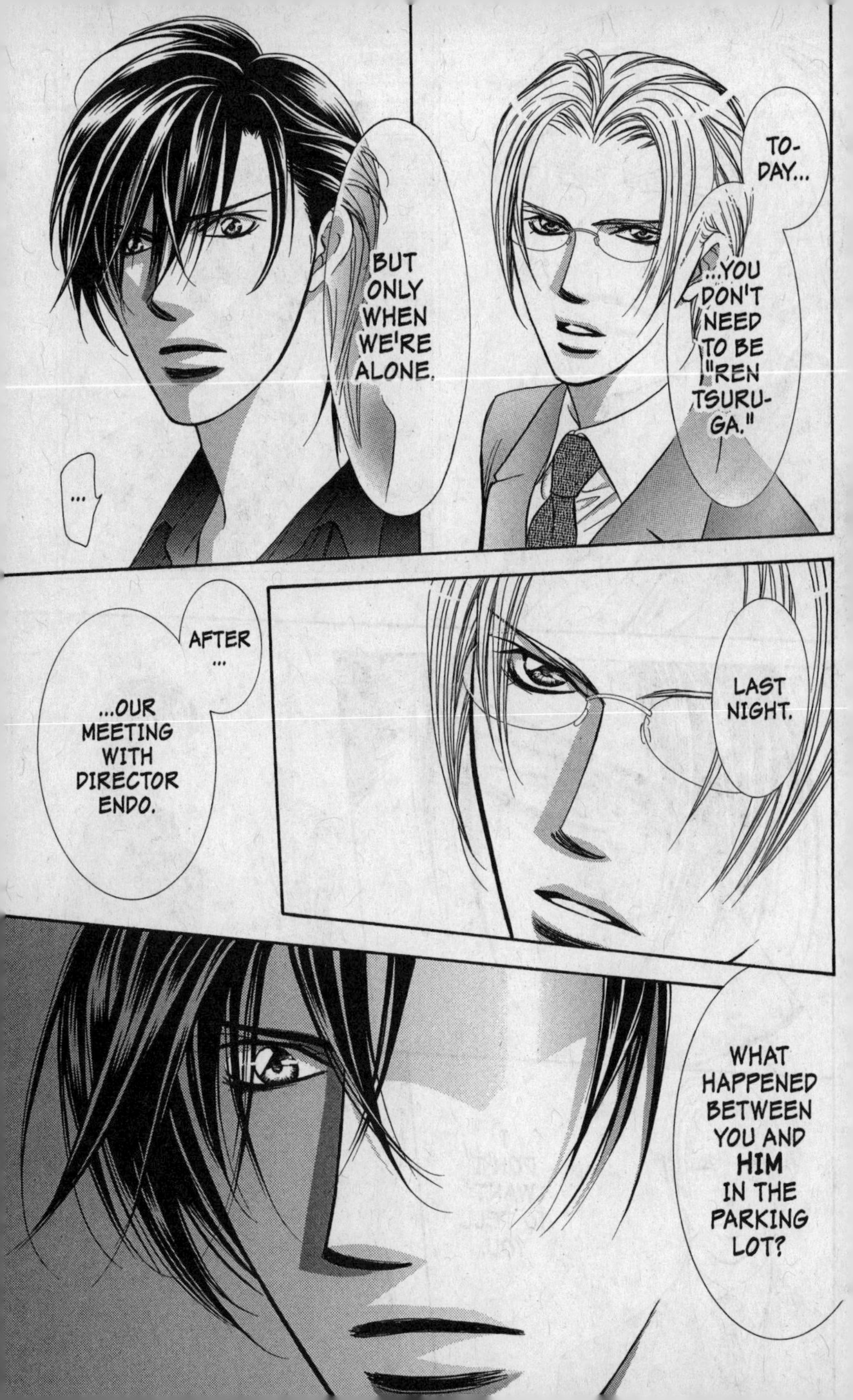
TO-DAY...
...YOU DON'T NEED TO BE "REN TSURU-GA."
BUT ONLY WHEN WE'RE ALONE.
...
LAST NIGHT.
AFTER...
...OUR MEETING WITH DIRECTOR ENDO.
WHAT HAPPENED BETWEEN YOU AND HIM IN THE PARKING LOT?

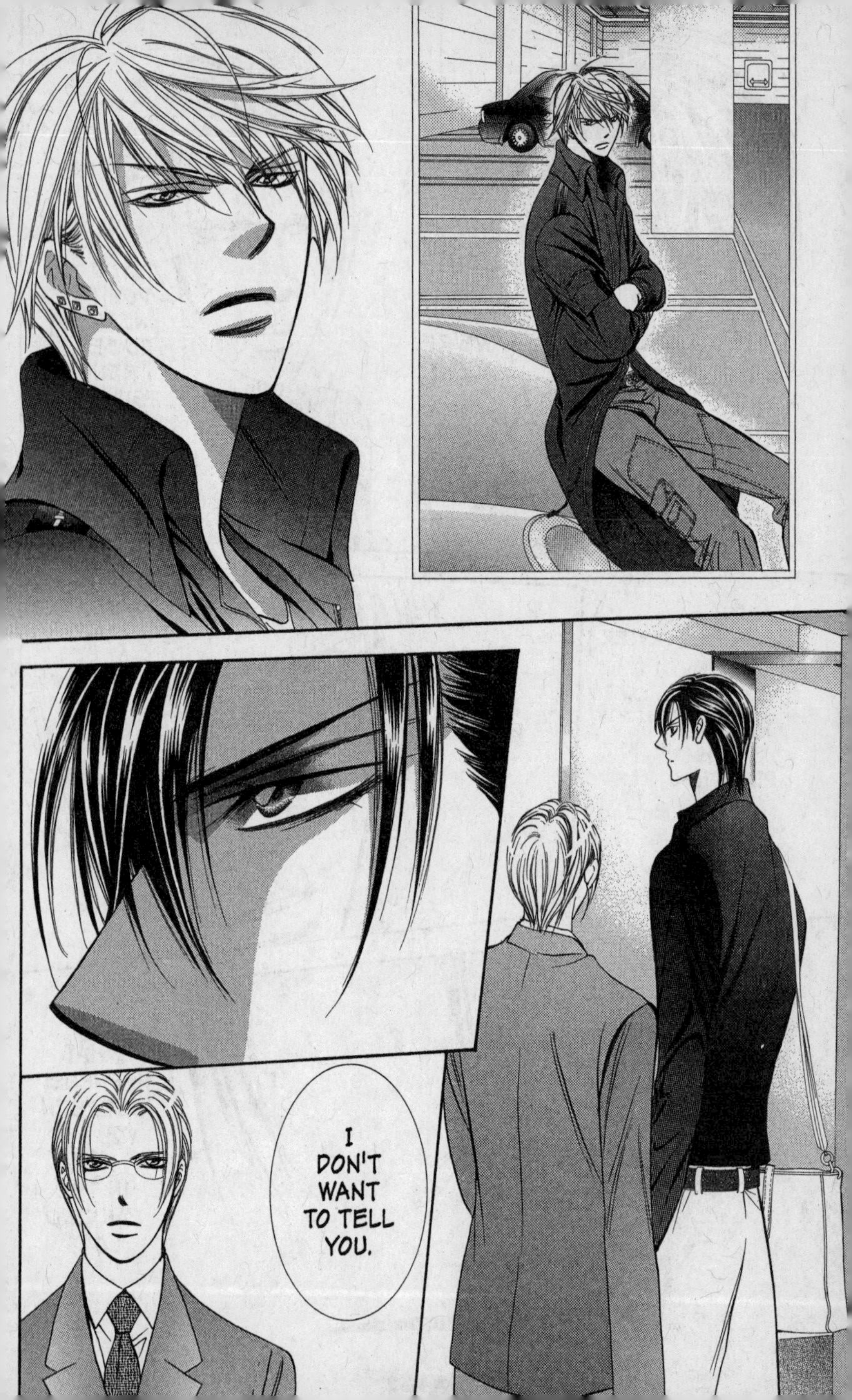
I DON'T WANT TO TELL YOU.

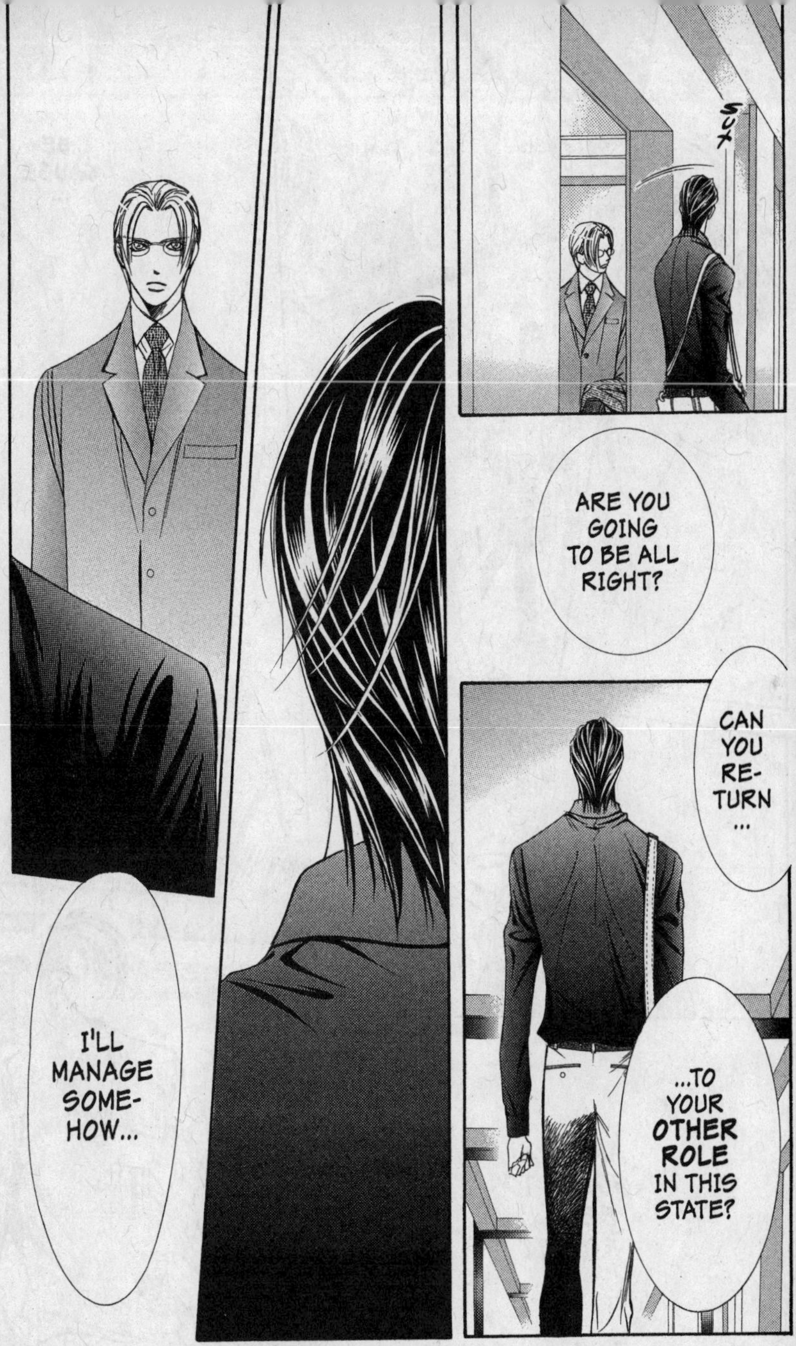
SUX
ARE YOU GOING TO BE ALL RIGHT?
CAN YOU RE-TURN...
...TO YOUR OTHER ROLE IN THIS STATE?
I'LL MANAGE SOME-HOW...

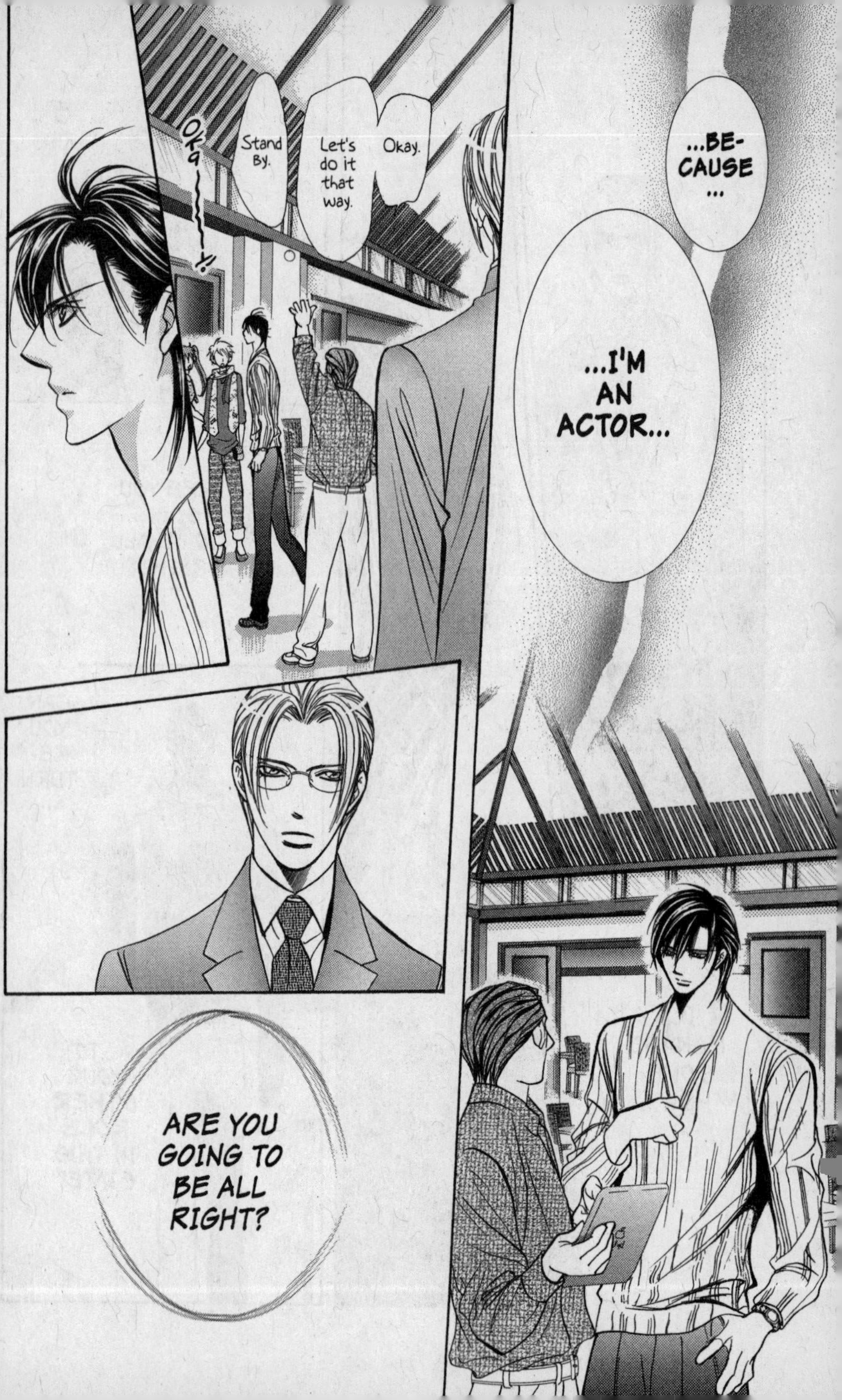
...BE-CAUSE...
...I'M AN ACTOR...
Okay.
Let's do it that way.
Stand by.
Okay---y!
ARE YOU GOING TO BE ALL RIGHT?

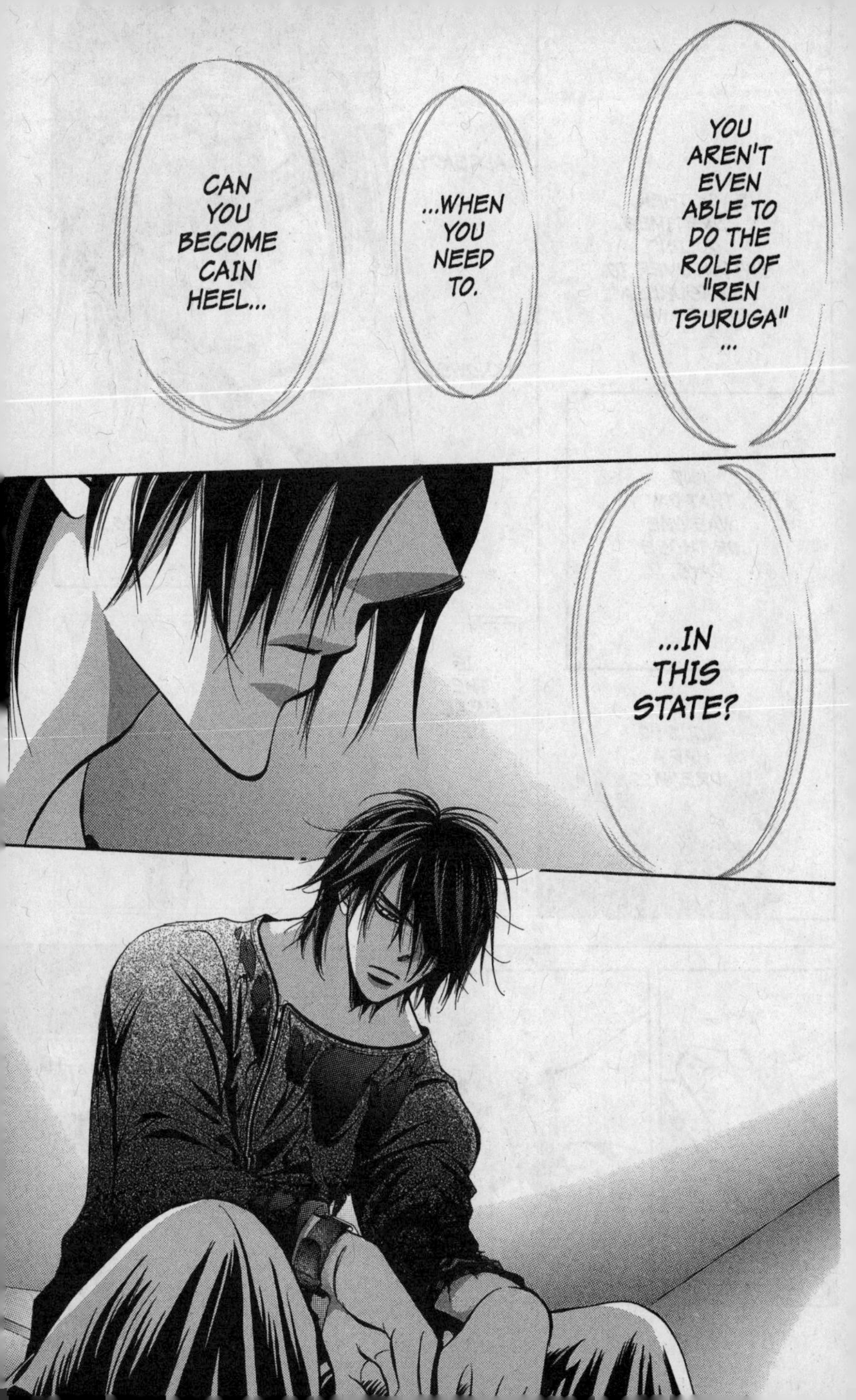
YOU AREN'T EVEN ABLE TO DO THE ROLE OF "REN TSURUGA" ...
...WHEN YOU NEED TO.
CAN YOU BECOME CAIN HEEL...
...IN THIS STATE?

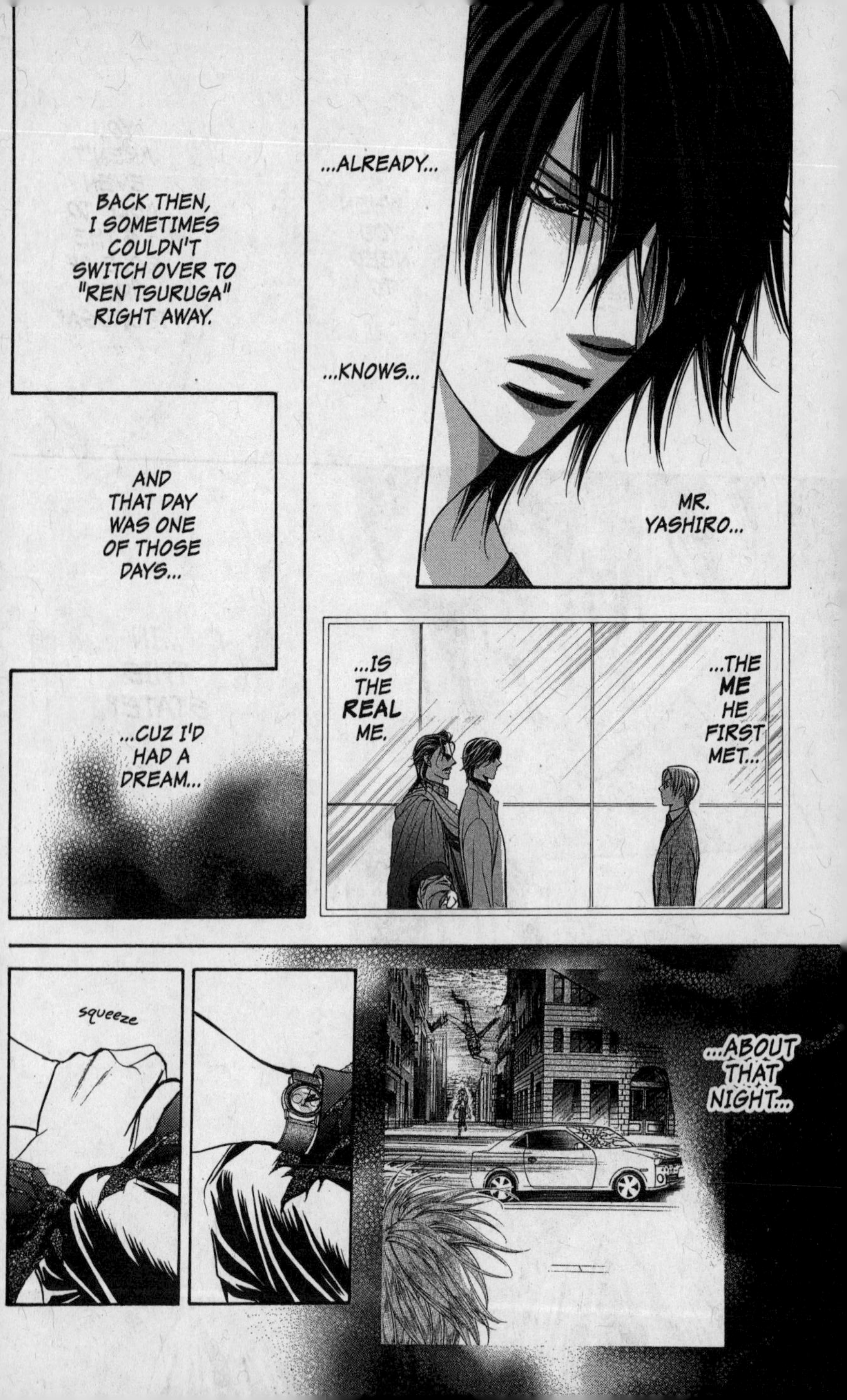
MR. YASHIRO...
...ALREADY...
...KNOWS...
...THE ME HE FIRST MET...
...IS THE REAL ME.
BACK THEN, I SOMETIMES COULDN'T SWITCH OVER TO "REN TSURUGA" RIGHT AWAY.
AND THAT DAY WAS ONE OF THOSE DAYS...
...CUZ I'D HAD A DREAM...
...ABOUT THAT NIGHT...
squeeze

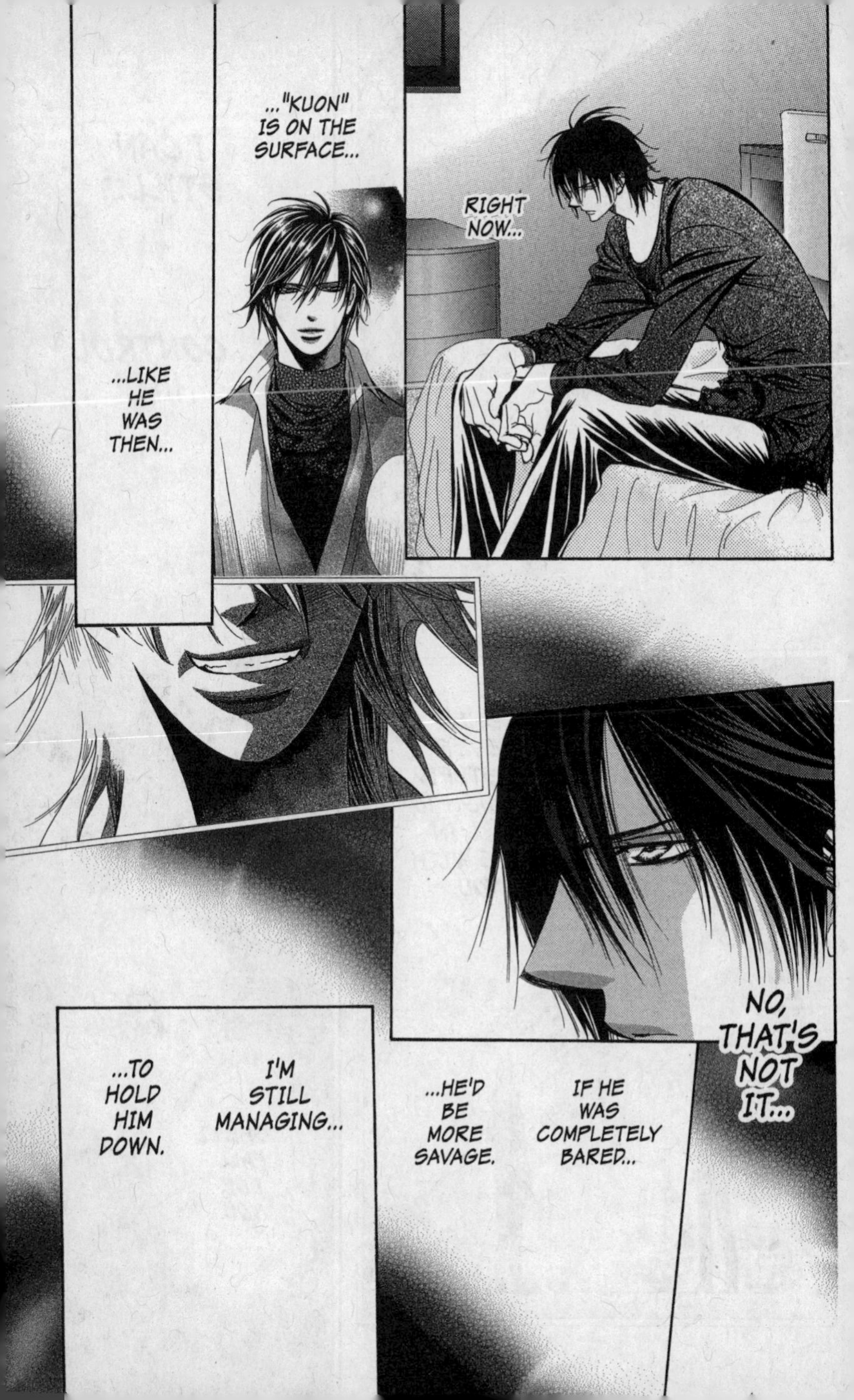
RIGHT NOW...
..."KUON" IS ON THE SURFACE...
...LIKE HE WAS THEN...
NO, THAT'S NOT IT...
IF HE WAS COMPLETELY BARED...
...HE'D BE MORE SAVAGE.
I'M STILL MANAGING...
...TO HOLD HIM DOWN.

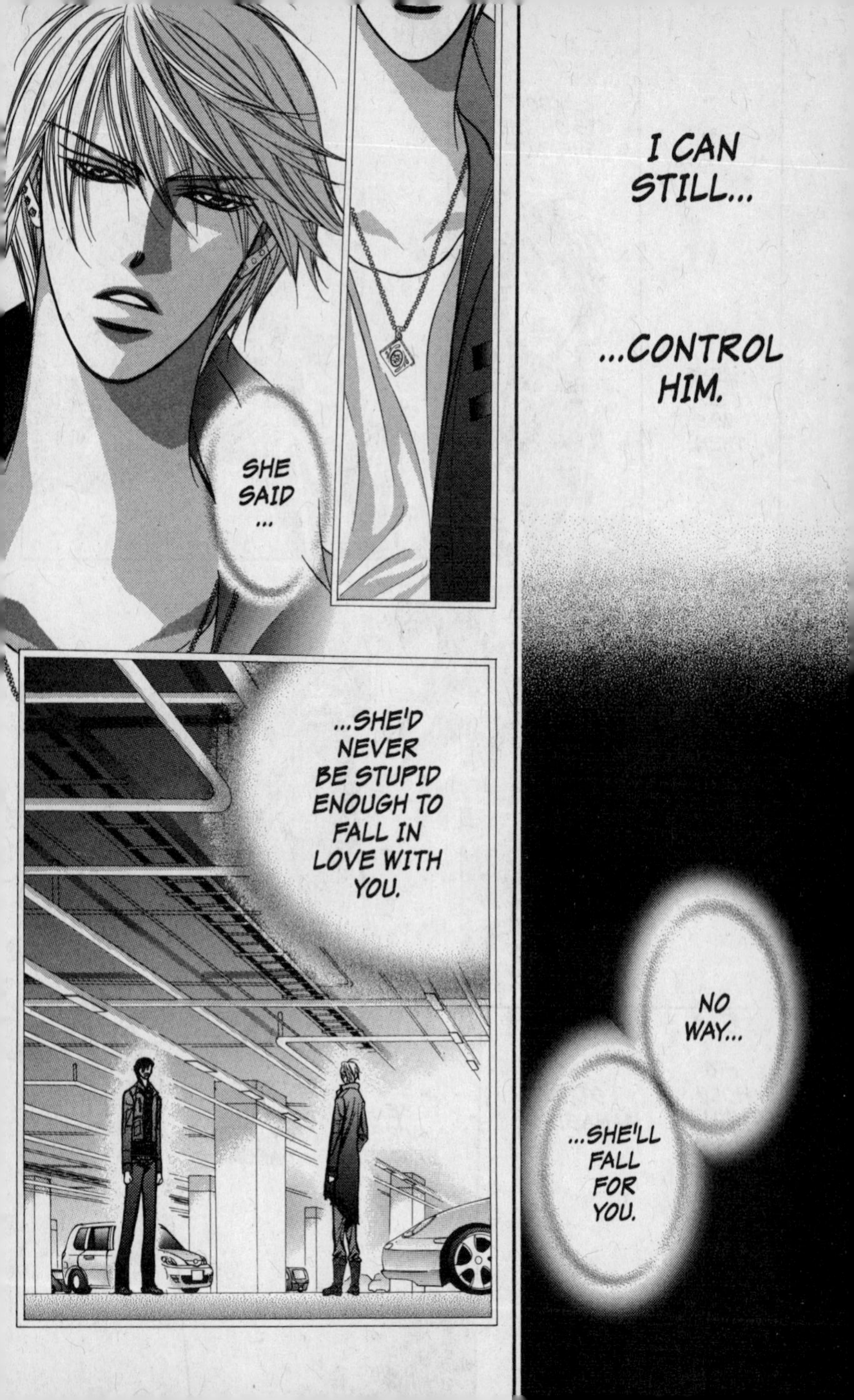
I CAN STILL...
...CONTROL HIM.
NO WAY...
...SHE'LL FALL FOR YOU.
SHE SAID ...
...SHE'D NEVER BE STUPID ENOUGH TO FALL IN LOVE WITH YOU.

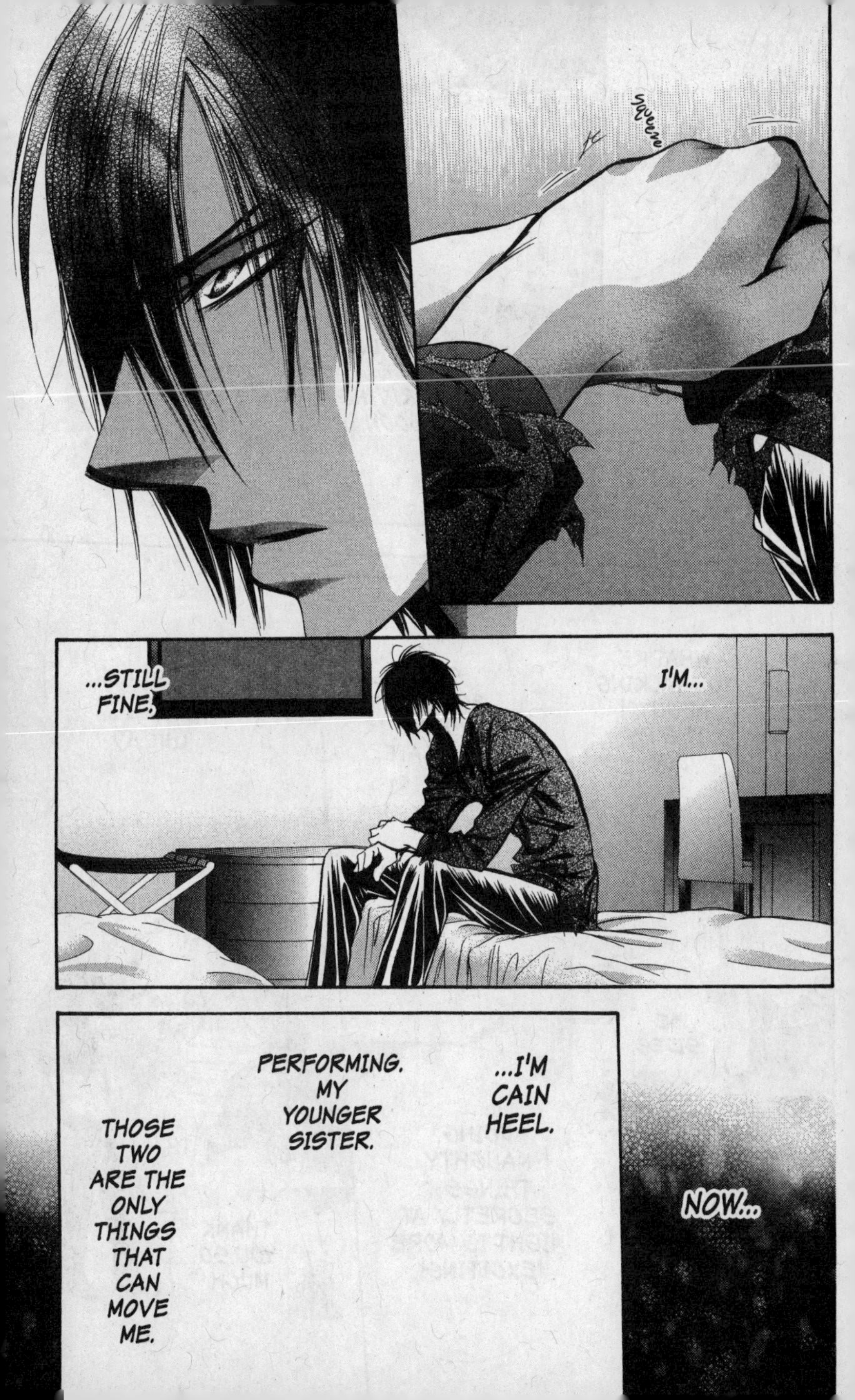
squeeze
I'M...
...STILL FINE.
NOW...
...I'M CAIN HEEL.
PERFORMING. MY YOUNGER SISTER.
THOSE TWO ARE THE ONLY THINGS THAT CAN MOVE ME.

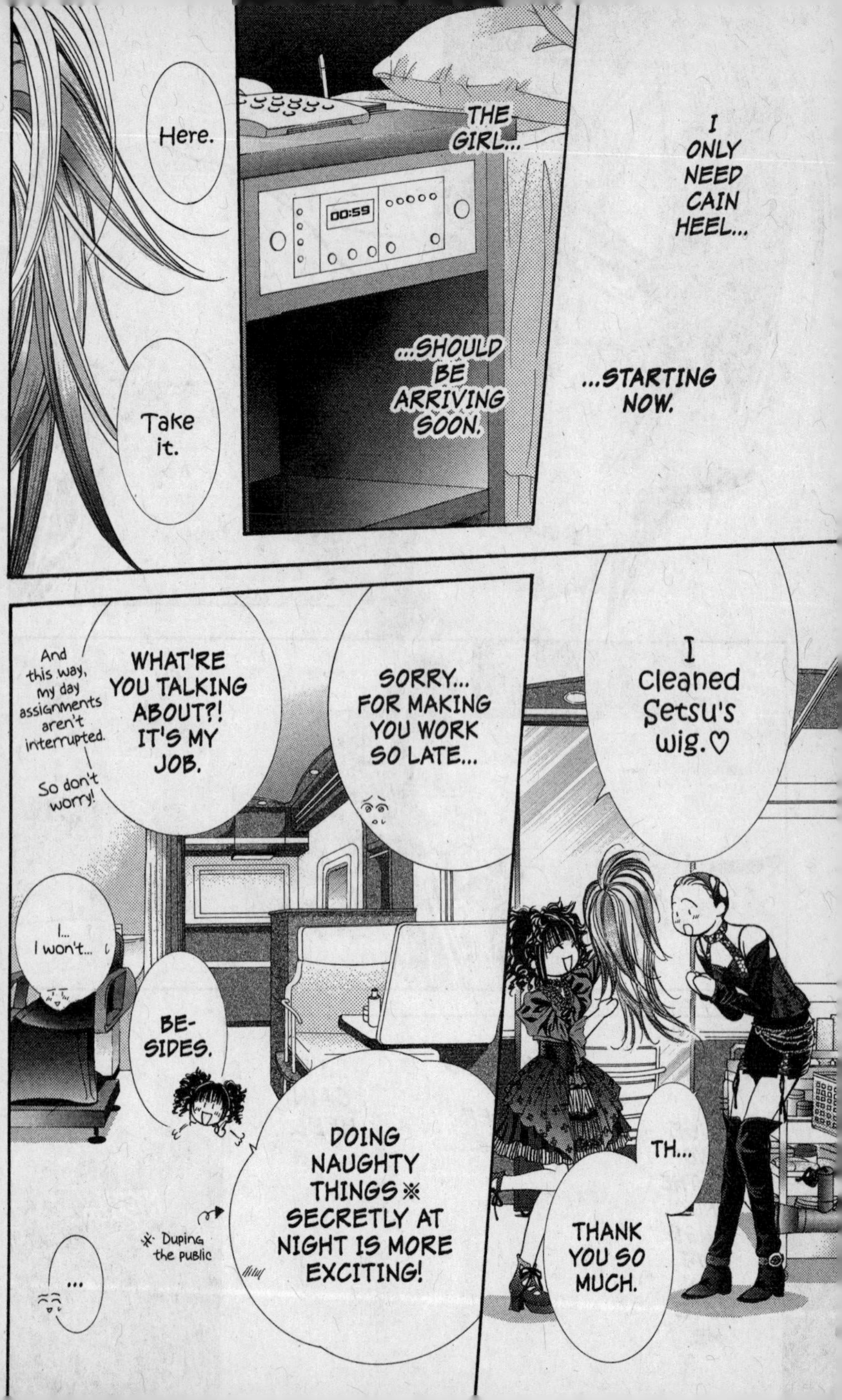
I ONLY NEED CAIN HEEL...
...STARTING NOW.
THE GIRL...
...SHOULD BE ARRIVING SOON.
Here.
Take it.
I cleaned Setsu's wig.♡
SORRY... FOR MAKING YOU WORK SO LATE...
WHAT'RE YOU TALKING ABOUT?! IT'S MY JOB.
And this way, my day assignments aren't interrupted.
So don't worry!
TH...
THANK YOU SO MUCH.
DOING NAUGHTY THINGS※ SECRETLY AT NIGHT IS MORE EXCITING!
※ Duping the public
BE-SIDES.
I... I won't...
...

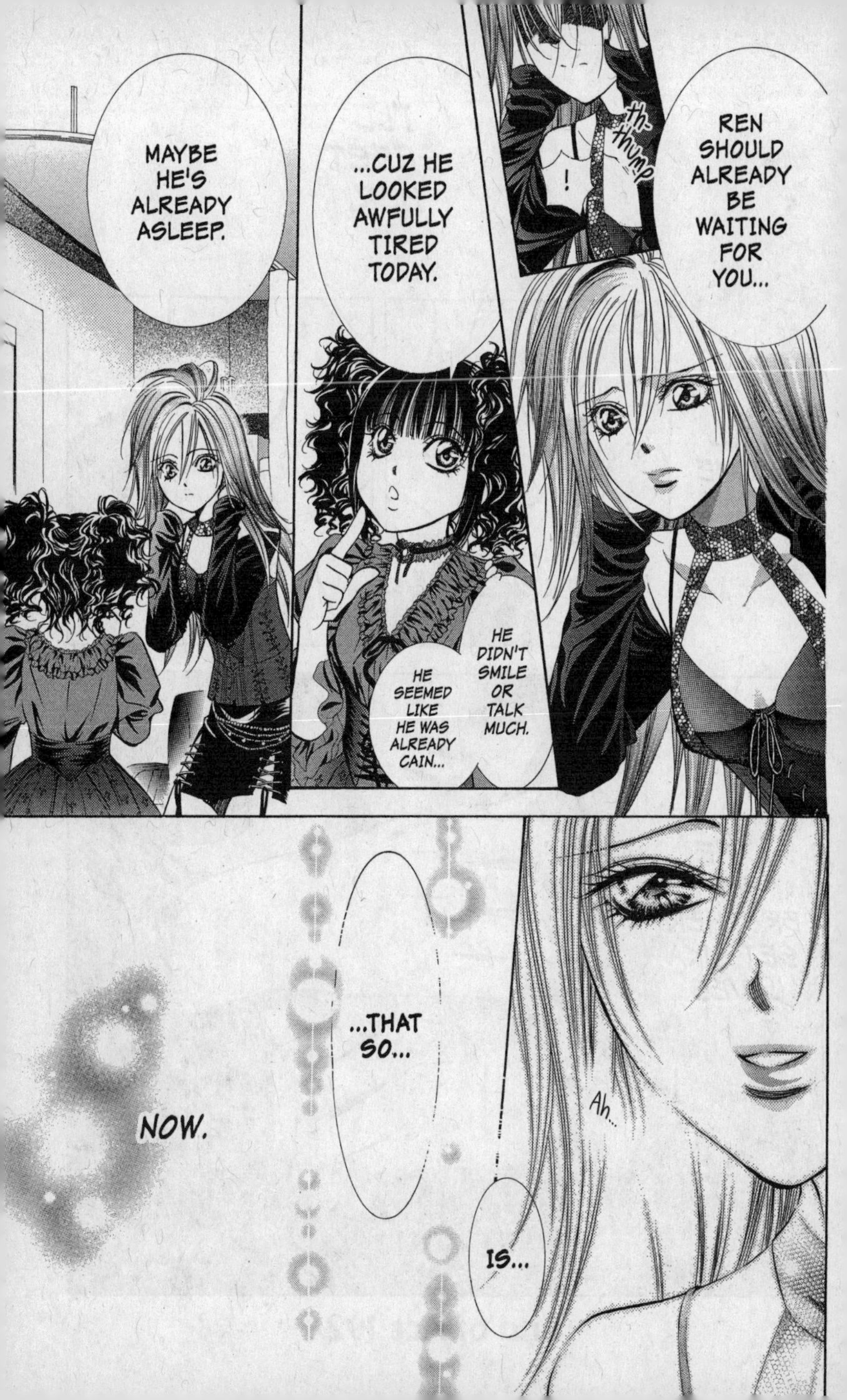
REN SHOULD ALREADY BE WAITING FOR YOU...
th-thump
!
...CUZ HE LOOKED AWFULLY TIRED TODAY.
HE DIDN'T SMILE OR TALK MUCH.
HE SEEMED LIKE HE WAS ALREADY CAIN...
MAYBE HE'S ALREADY ASLEEP.
Ah...
IS...
...THAT SO...
NOW.

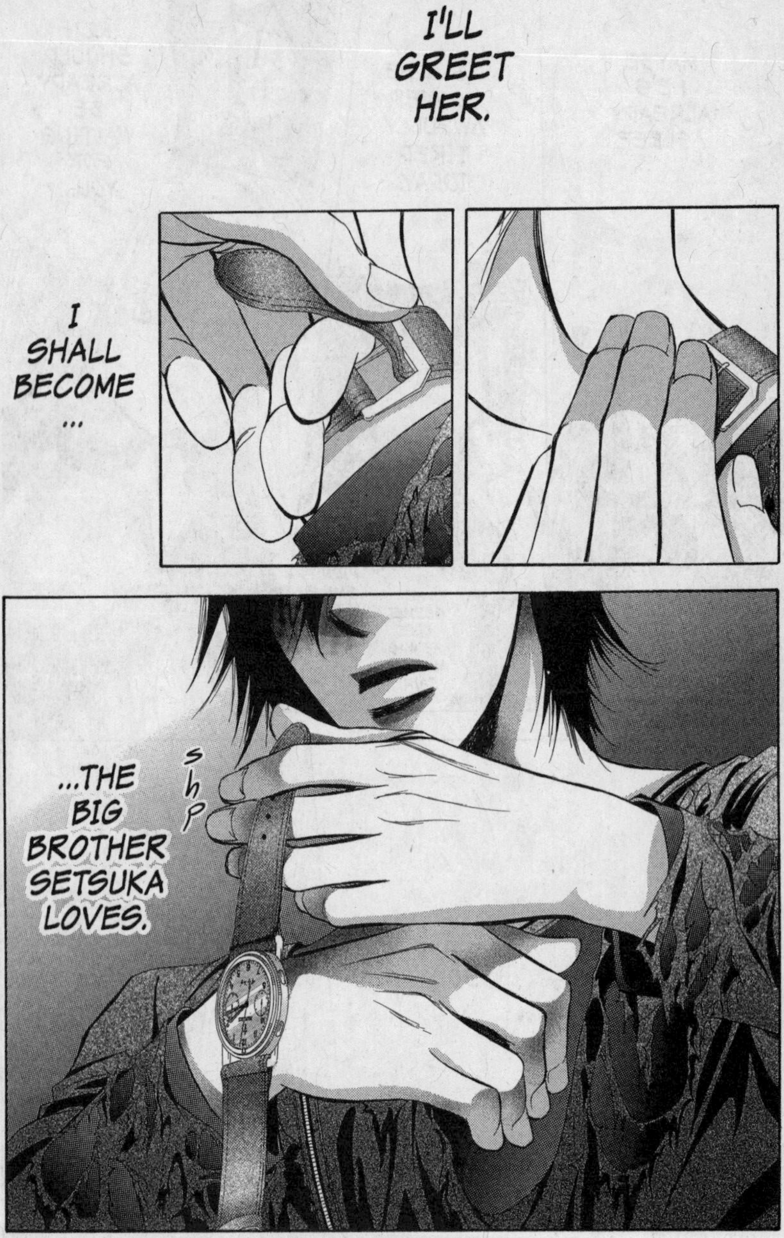
I'LL GREET HER.
I SHALL BECOME...
shp
...THE BIG BROTHER SETSUKA LOVES.

End of Act 192

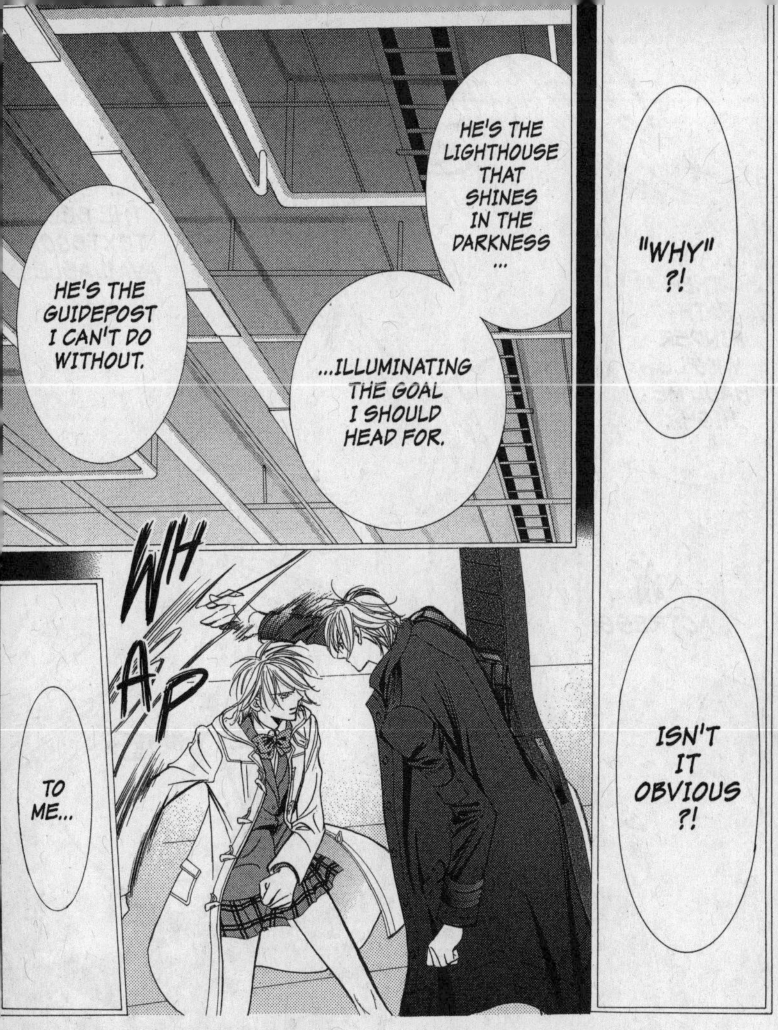
"WHY"?!
ISN'T IT OBVIOUS?!
HE'S THE LIGHTHOUSE THAT SHINES IN THE DARKNESS...
...ILLUMINATING THE GOAL I SHOULD HEAD FOR.
HE'S THE GUIDEPOST I CAN'T DO WITHOUT.
WHAP
TO ME...

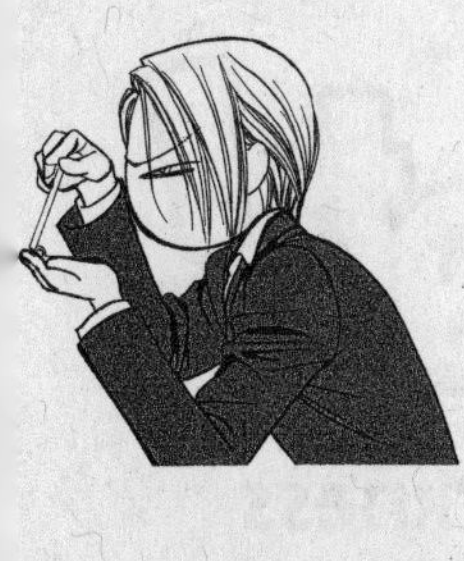

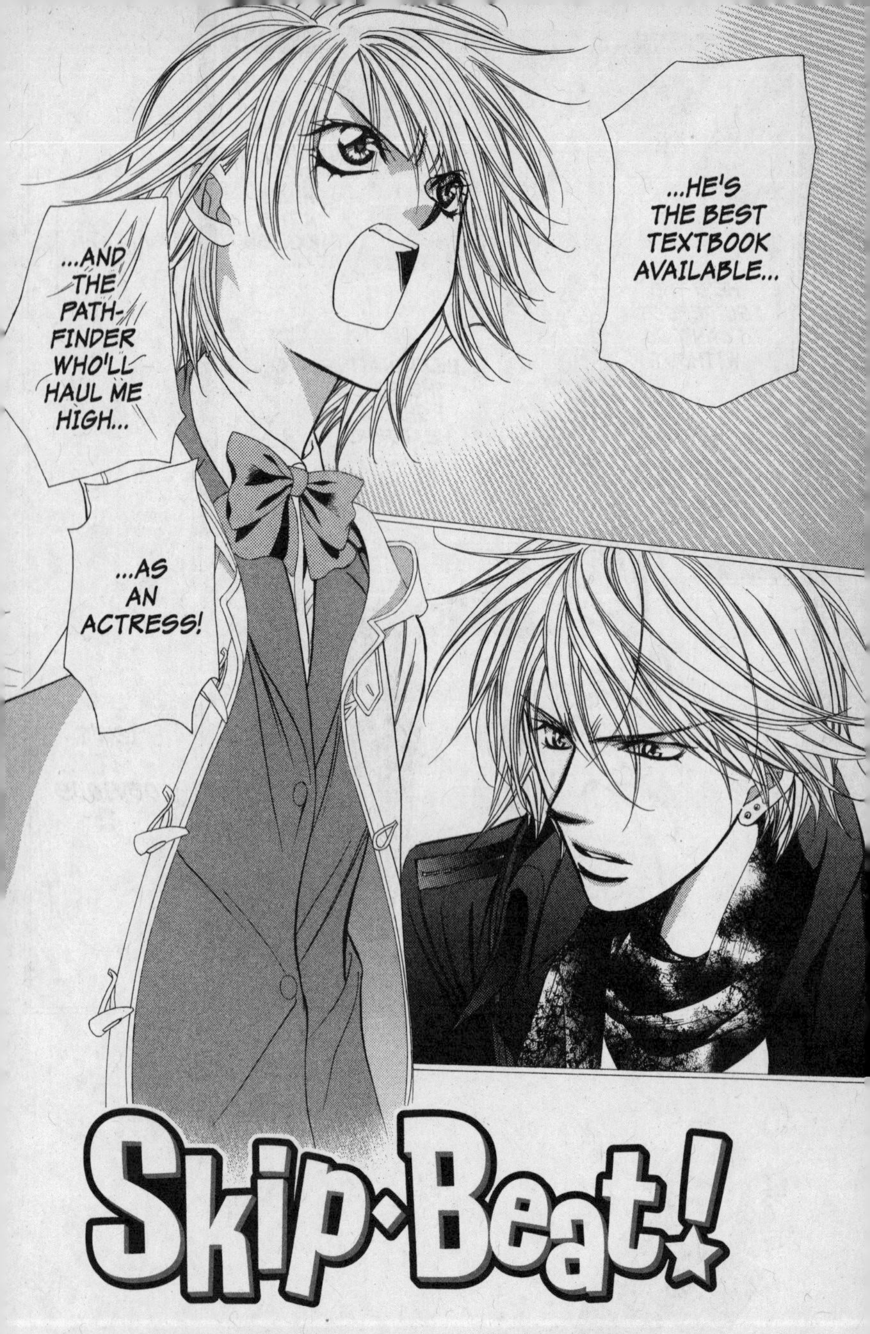
...HE'S THE BEST TEXTBOOK AVAILABLE...
...AND THE PATH-FINDER WHO'LL HAUL ME HIGH...
...AS AN ACTRESS!
Skip·Beat!

Act 193: Breath of Darkness

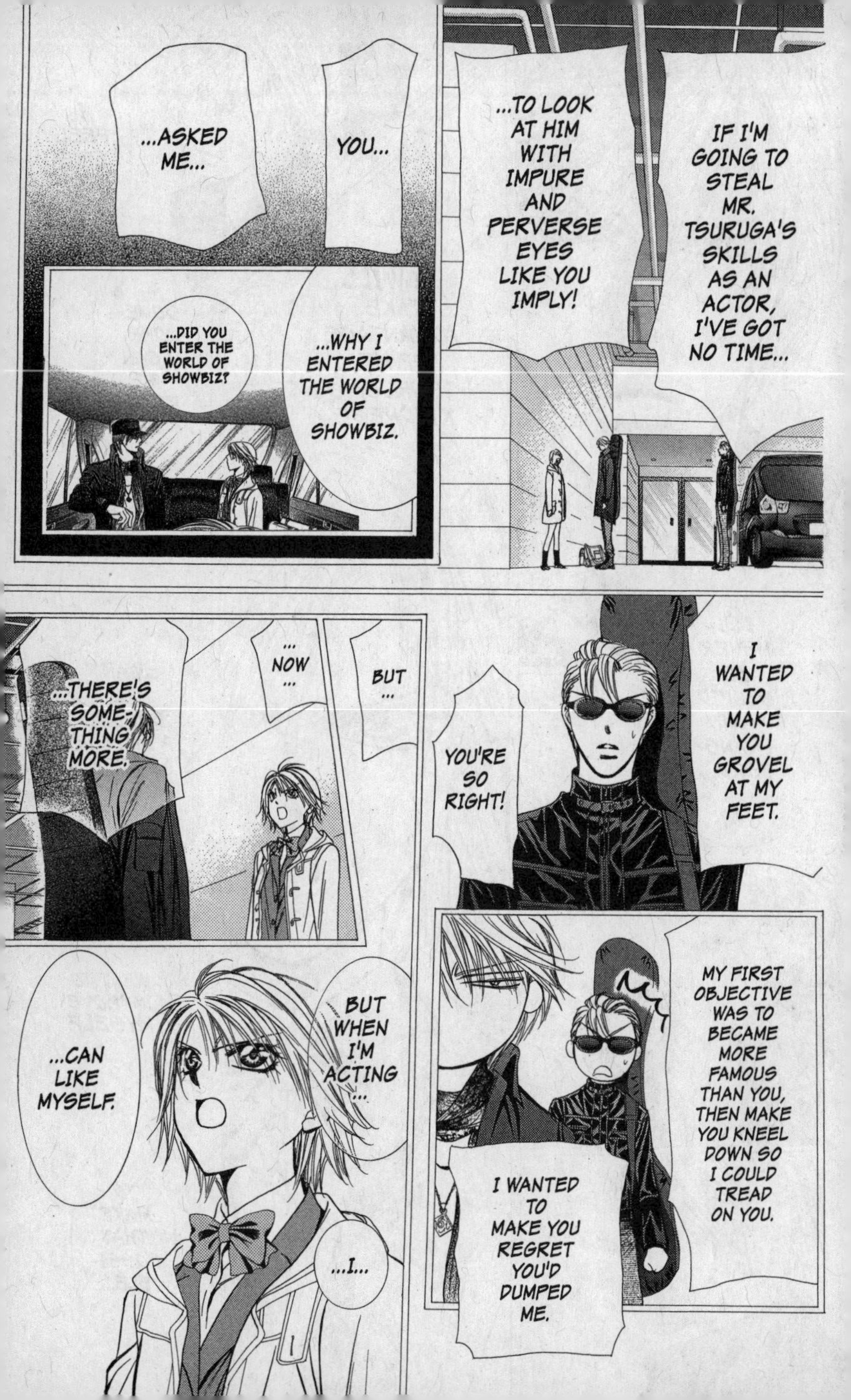
IF I'M GOING TO STEAL MR. TSURUGA'S SKILLS AS AN ACTOR, I'VE GOT NO TIME...
...TO LOOK AT HIM WITH IMPURE AND PERVERSE EYES LIKE YOU IMPLY!
YOU...
...ASKED ME...
...WHY I ENTERED THE WORLD OF SHOWBIZ.
...DID YOU ENTER THE WORLD OF SHOWBIZ?
I WANTED TO MAKE YOU GROVEL AT MY FEET.
YOU'RE SO RIGHT!
MY FIRST OBJECTIVE WAS TO BECAME MORE FAMOUS THAN YOU, THEN MAKE YOU KNEEL DOWN SO I COULD TREAD ON YOU.
I WANTED TO MAKE YOU REGRET YOU'D DUMPED ME.
BUT...
...NOW...
...THERE'S SOMETHING MORE.
BUT WHEN I'M ACTING...
...I...
...CAN LIKE MYSELF.

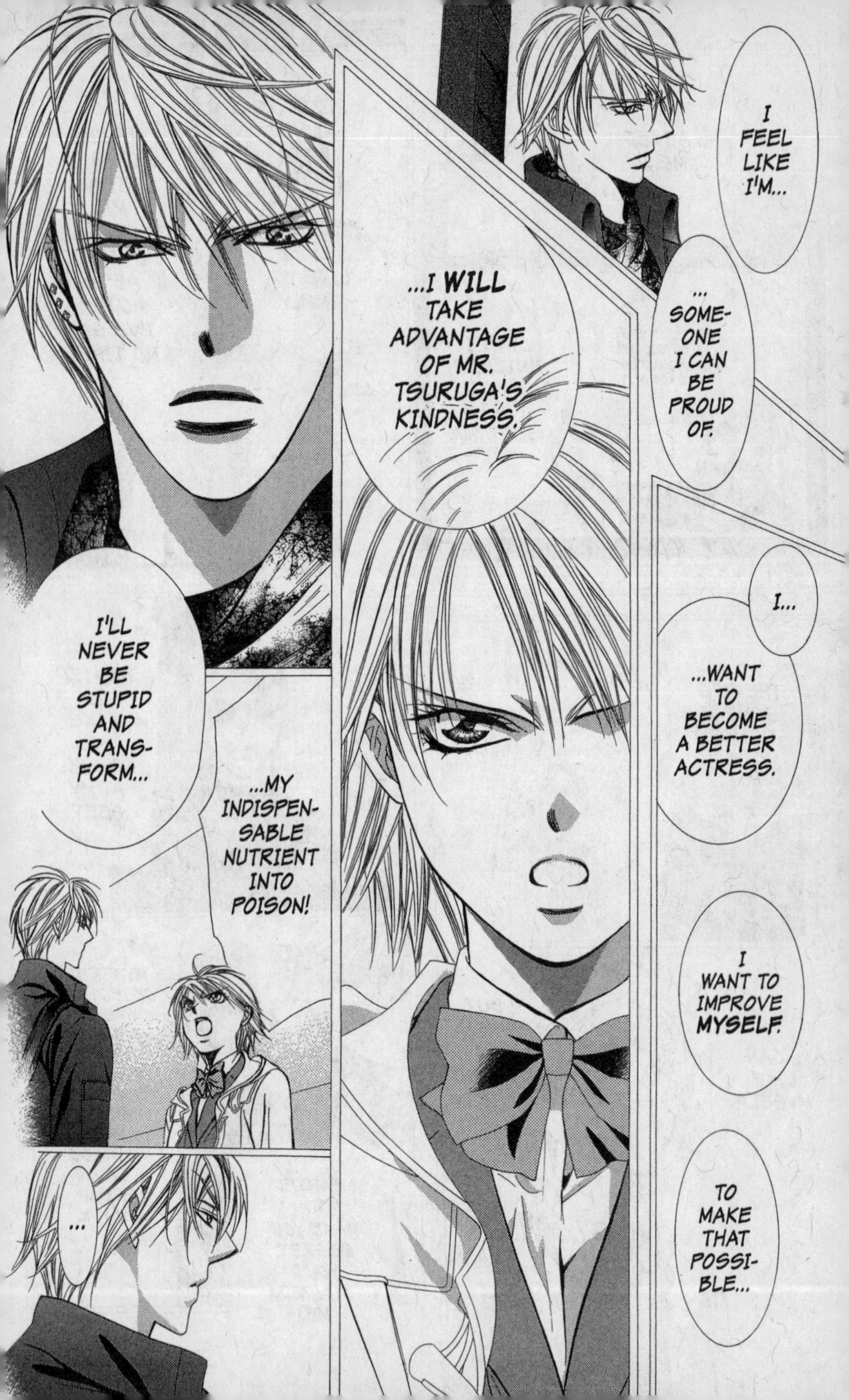
I FEEL LIKE I'M...
...SOMEONE I CAN BE PROUD OF.
I...
...WANT TO BECOME A BETTER ACTRESS.
I WANT TO IMPROVE MYSELF.
TO MAKE THAT POSSIBLE...
...I WILL TAKE ADVANTAGE OF MR. TSURUGA'S KINDNESS.
I'LL NEVER BE STUPID AND TRANSFORM...
...MY INDISPENSABLE NUTRIENT INTO POISON!
...

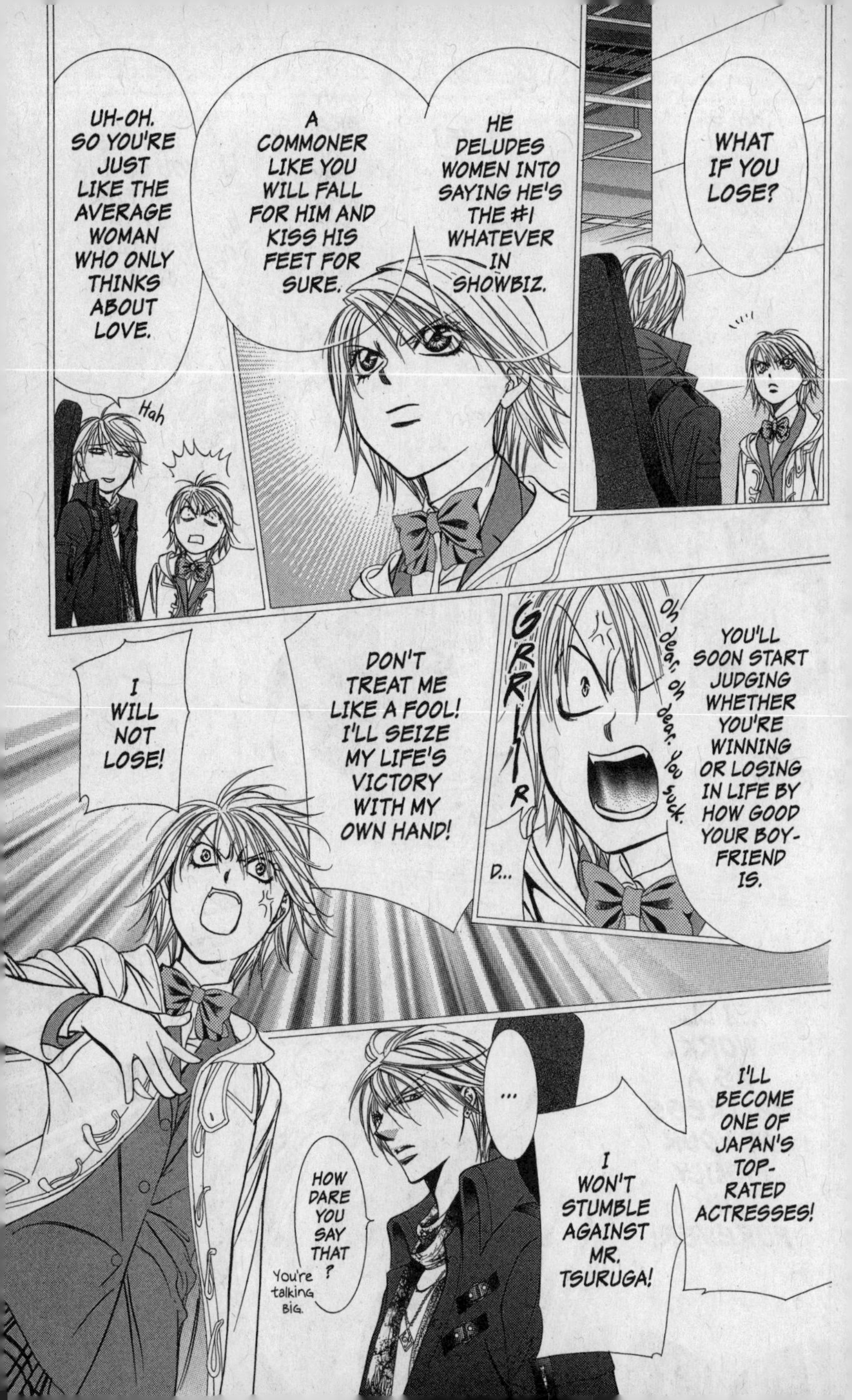
WHAT IF YOU LOSE?
HE DELUDES WOMEN INTO SAYING HE'S THE #1 WHATEVER IN SHOWBIZ.
A COMMONER LIKE YOU WILL FALL FOR HIM AND KISS HIS FEET FOR SURE.
UH-OH. SO YOU'RE JUST LIKE THE AVERAGE WOMAN WHO ONLY THINKS ABOUT LOVE.
Hah
YOU'LL SOON START JUDGING WHETHER YOU'RE WINNING OR LOSING IN LIFE BY HOW GOOD YOUR BOY-FRIEND IS.
Oh dear, oh dear. You suck.
GRRR
D...
DON'T TREAT ME LIKE A FOOL! I'LL SEIZE MY LIFE'S VICTORY WITH MY OWN HAND!
I WILL NOT LOSE!
I'LL BECOME ONE OF JAPAN'S TOP-RATED ACTRESSES!
I WON'T STUMBLE AGAINST MR. TSURUGA!
...
HOW DARE YOU SAY THAT?
You're talking BIG.

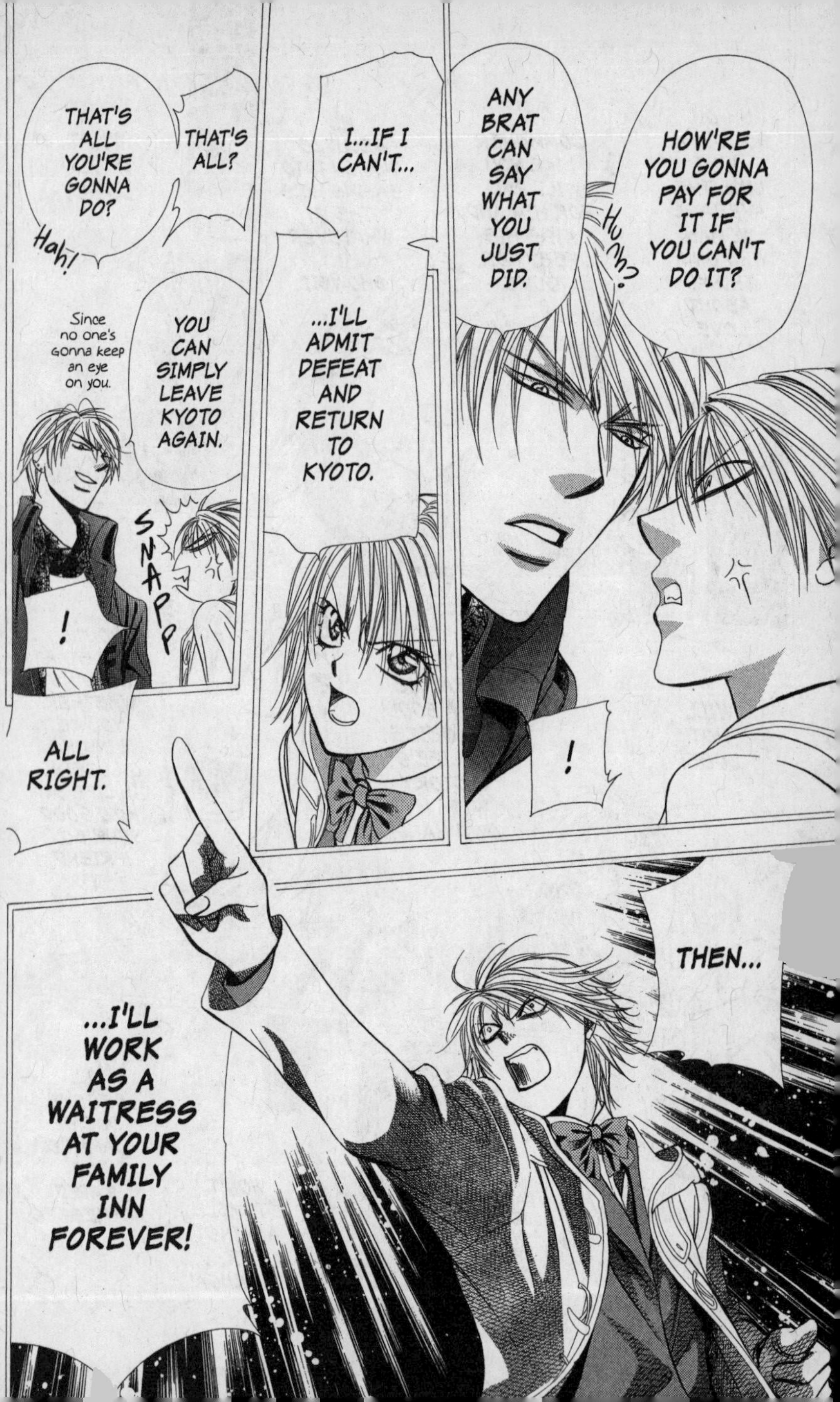
HOW'RE YOU GONNA PAY FOR IT IF YOU CAN'T DO IT?
Hunh?
ANY BRAT CAN SAY WHAT YOU JUST DID.
!
I...IF I CAN'T...
...I'LL ADMIT DEFEAT AND RETURN TO KYOTO.
THAT'S ALL?
THAT'S ALL YOU'RE GONNA DO?
Hah!
YOU CAN SIMPLY LEAVE KYOTO AGAIN.
Since no one's gonna keep an eye on you.
SNAPP
!
ALL RIGHT.
THEN...
...I'LL WORK AS A WAITRESS AT YOUR FAMILY INN FOREVER!

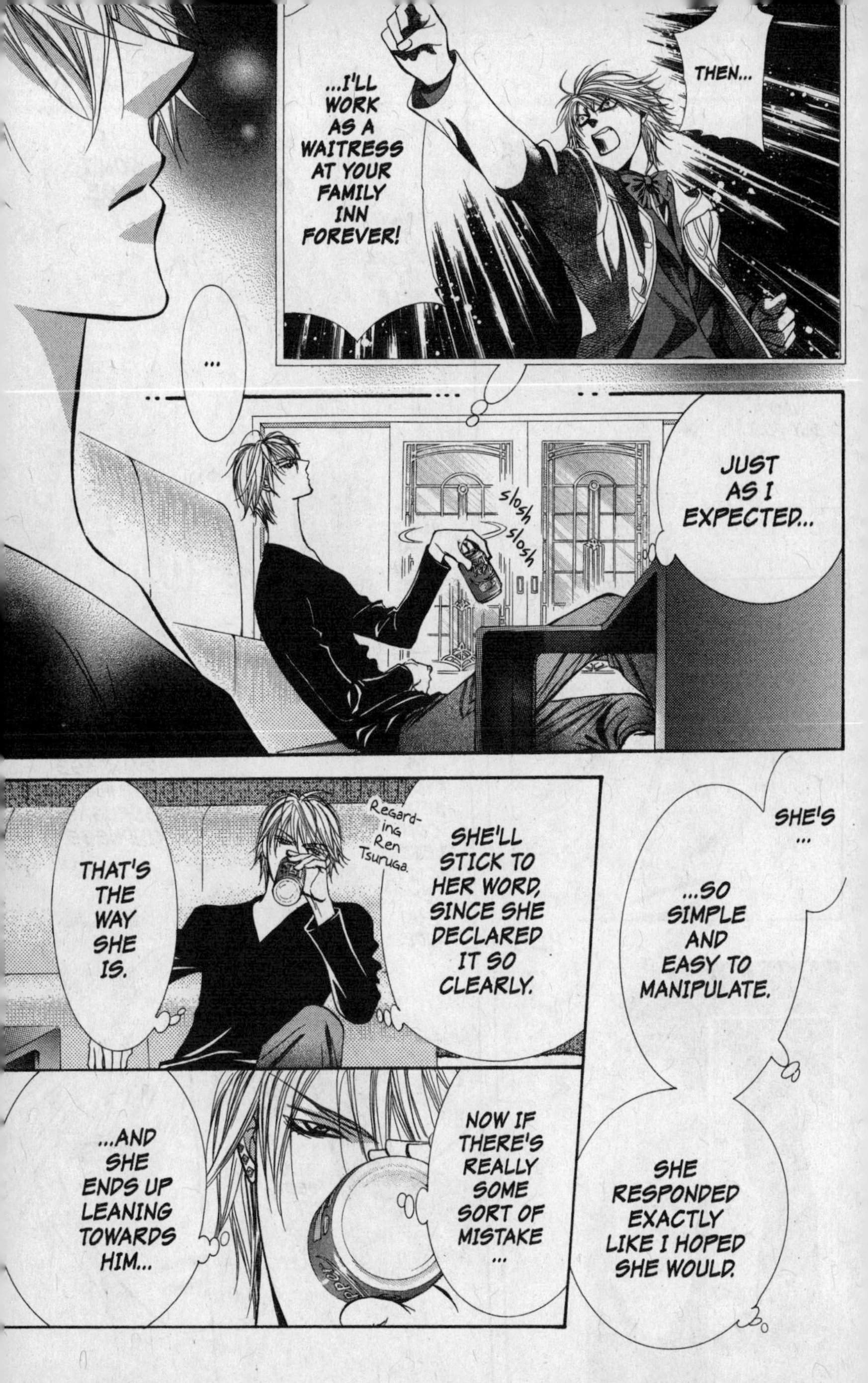

THEN...
...I'LL WORK AS A WAITRESS AT YOUR FAMILY INN FOREVER!
...
JUST AS I EXPECTED...
slosh slosh
SHE'S ...
...SO SIMPLE AND EASY TO MANIPULATE.
SHE'LL STICK TO HER WORD, SINCE SHE DECLARED IT SO CLEARLY.
Regarding Ren Tsuruga.
THAT'S THE WAY SHE IS.
SHE RESPONDED EXACTLY LIKE I HOPED SHE WOULD.
NOW IF THERE'S REALLY SOME SORT OF MISTAKE ...
...AND SHE ENDS UP LEANING TOWARDS HIM...

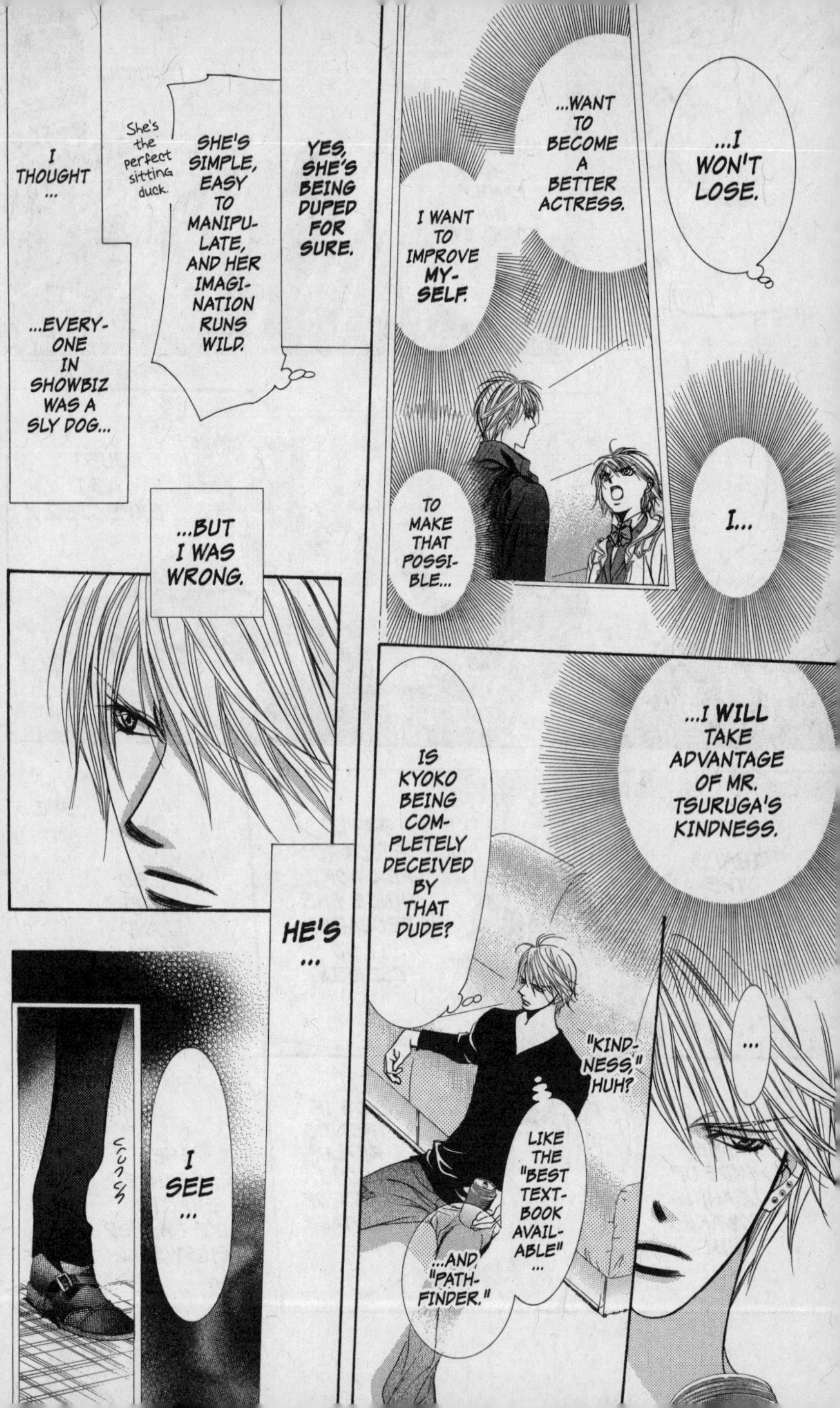

...I WON'T LOSE.
...WANT TO BECOME A BETTER ACTRESS.
I WANT TO IMPROVE MY-SELF.
I...
TO MAKE THAT POSSI-BLE...
...I WILL TAKE ADVANTAGE OF MR. TSURUGA'S KINDNESS.
IS KYOKO BEING COM-PLETELY DECEIVED BY THAT DUDE?
...
"KIND-NESS," HUH?
LIKE THE "BEST TEXT-BOOK AVAIL-ABLE" ...
...AND "PATH-FINDER."
YES, SHE'S BEING DUPED FOR SURE.
SHE'S SIMPLE, EASY TO MANIPU-LATE, AND HER IMAGI-NATION RUNS WILD.
She's the perfect sitting duck.
I THOUGHT ...
...EVERY-ONE IN SHOWBIZ WAS A SLY DOG...
...BUT I WAS WRONG.
HE'S ...
I SEE ...

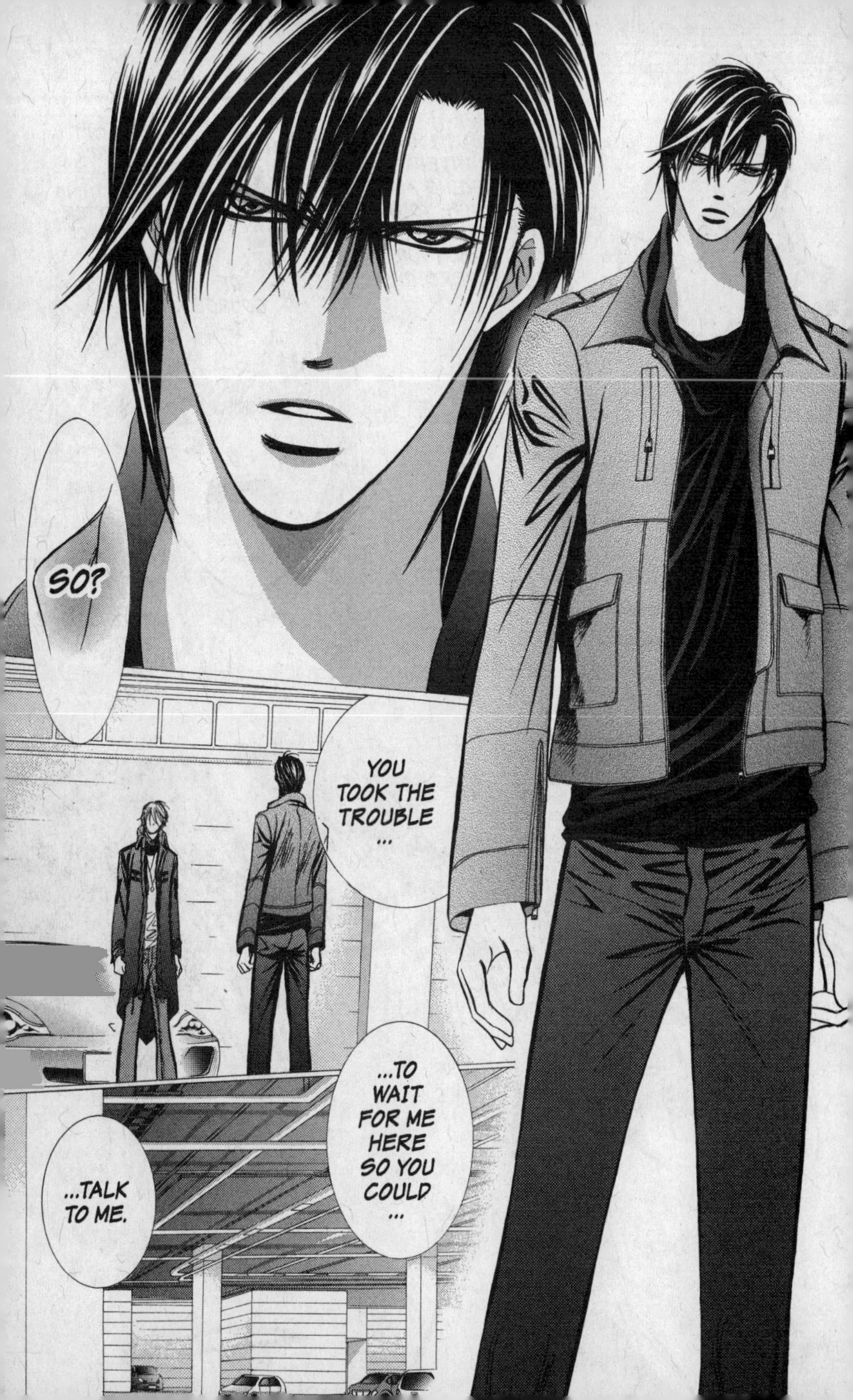
YOU TOOK THE TROUBLE ...
...TO WAIT FOR ME HERE SO YOU COULD ...
...TALK TO ME.
SO?

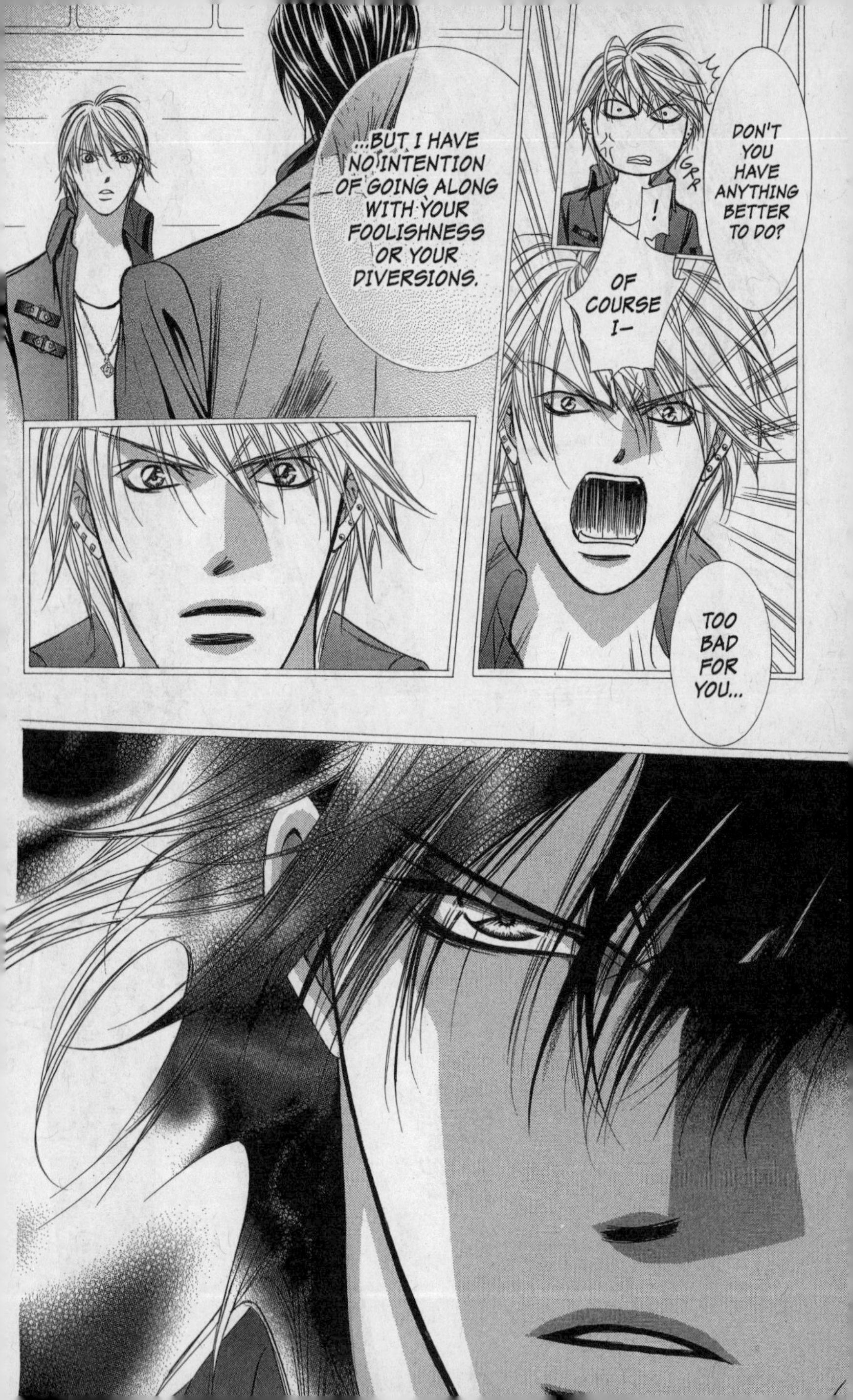
DON'T YOU HAVE ANYTHING BETTER TO DO?
GRR
!
...BUT I HAVE NO INTENTION OF GOING ALONG WITH YOUR FOOLISHNESS OR YOUR DIVERSIONS.
OF COURSE I—
TOO BAD FOR YOU...

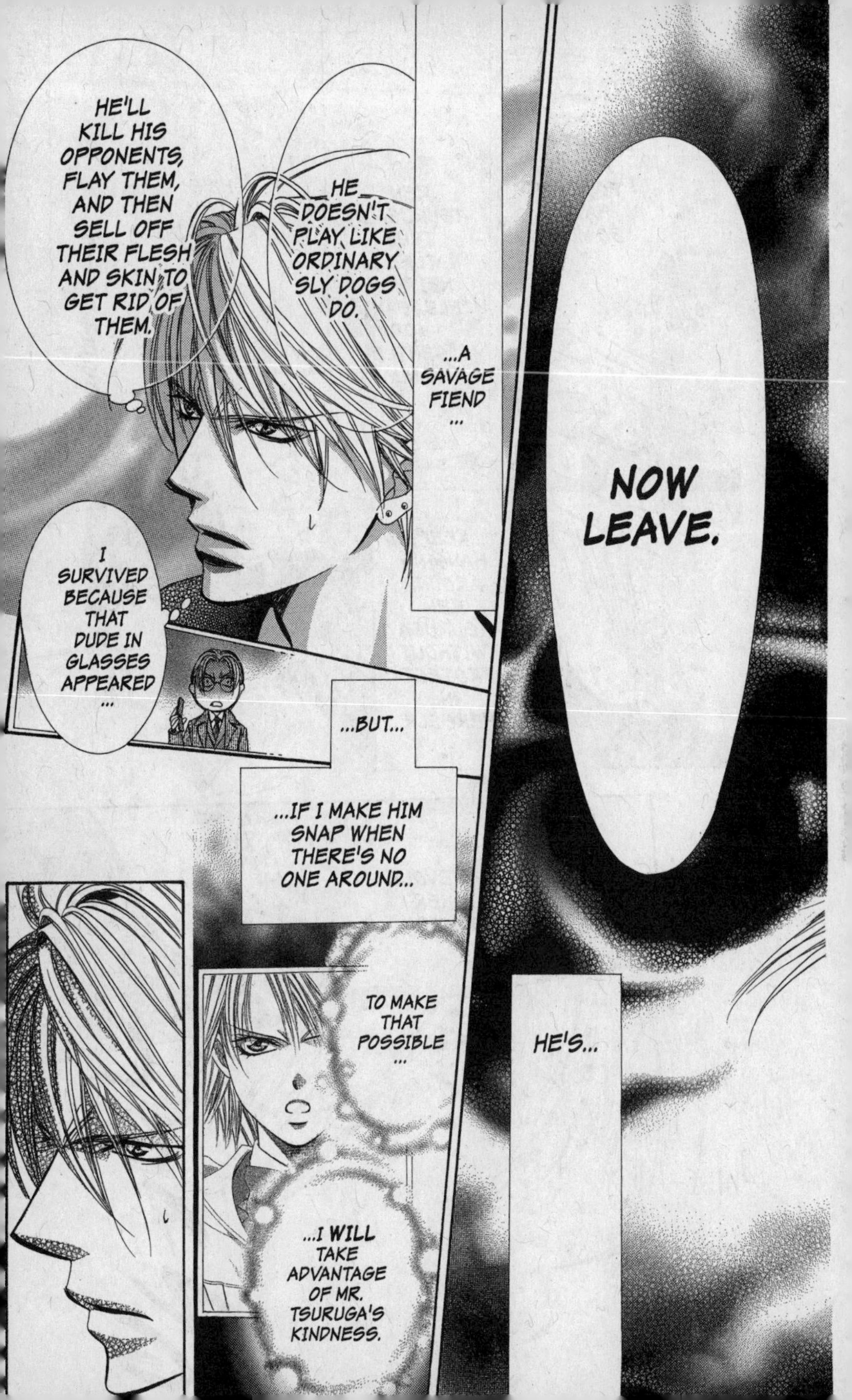
NOW LEAVE.
HE'S...
...A SAVAGE FIEND...
HE DOESN'T PLAY LIKE ORDINARY SLY DOGS DO.
HE'LL KILL HIS OPPONENTS, FLAY THEM, AND THEN SELL OFF THEIR FLESH AND SKIN TO GET RID OF THEM.
I SURVIVED BECAUSE THAT DUDE IN GLASSES APPEARED...
...BUT...
...IF I MAKE HIM SNAP WHEN THERE'S NO ONE AROUND...
TO MAKE THAT POSSIBLE...
...I WILL TAKE ADVANTAGE OF MR. TSURUGA'S KINDNESS.

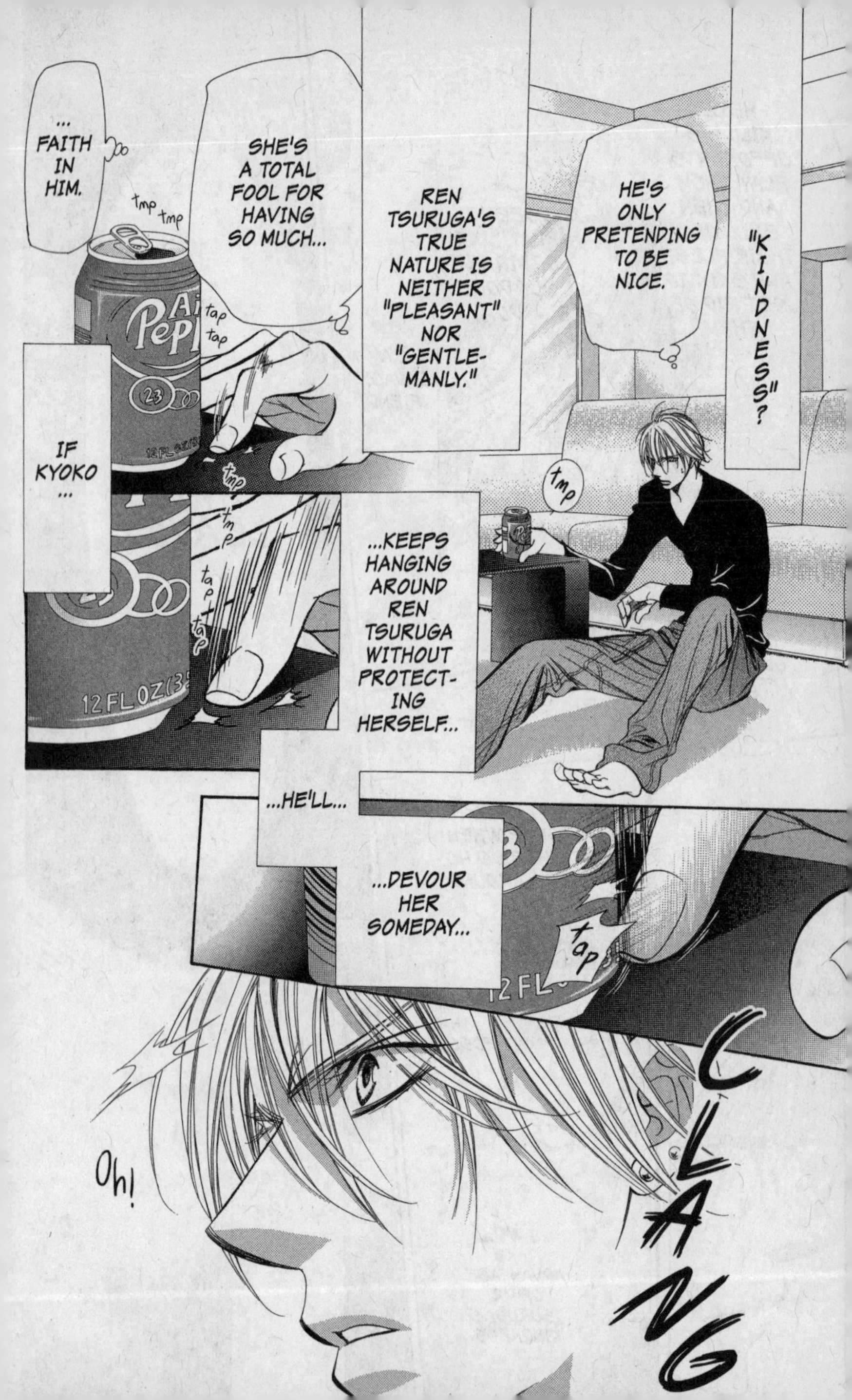
"KINDNESS"?
HE'S ONLY PRETENDING TO BE NICE.
REN TSURUGA'S TRUE NATURE IS NEITHER "PLEASANT" NOR "GENTLE-MANLY."
SHE'S A TOTAL FOOL FOR HAVING SO MUCH...
...FAITH IN HIM.
tmp tmp
tap tap
tmp
IF KYOKO...
...KEEPS HANGING AROUND REN TSURUGA WITHOUT PROTECT-ING HERSELF...
tmp tmp
tap tap
...HE'LL...
...DEVOUR HER SOMEDAY...
tap
CLANG
Oh!

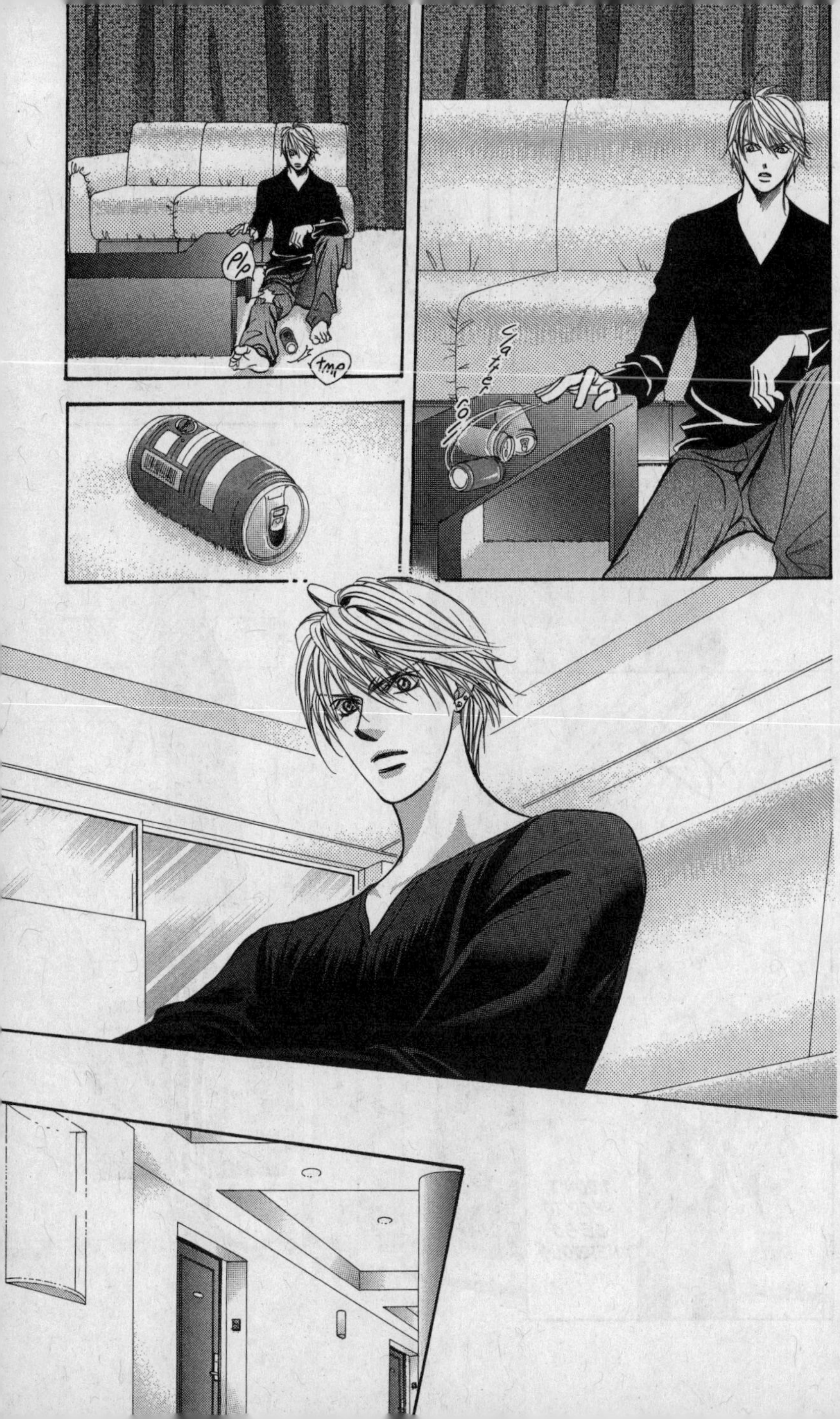
clatter roll
plp
tmp

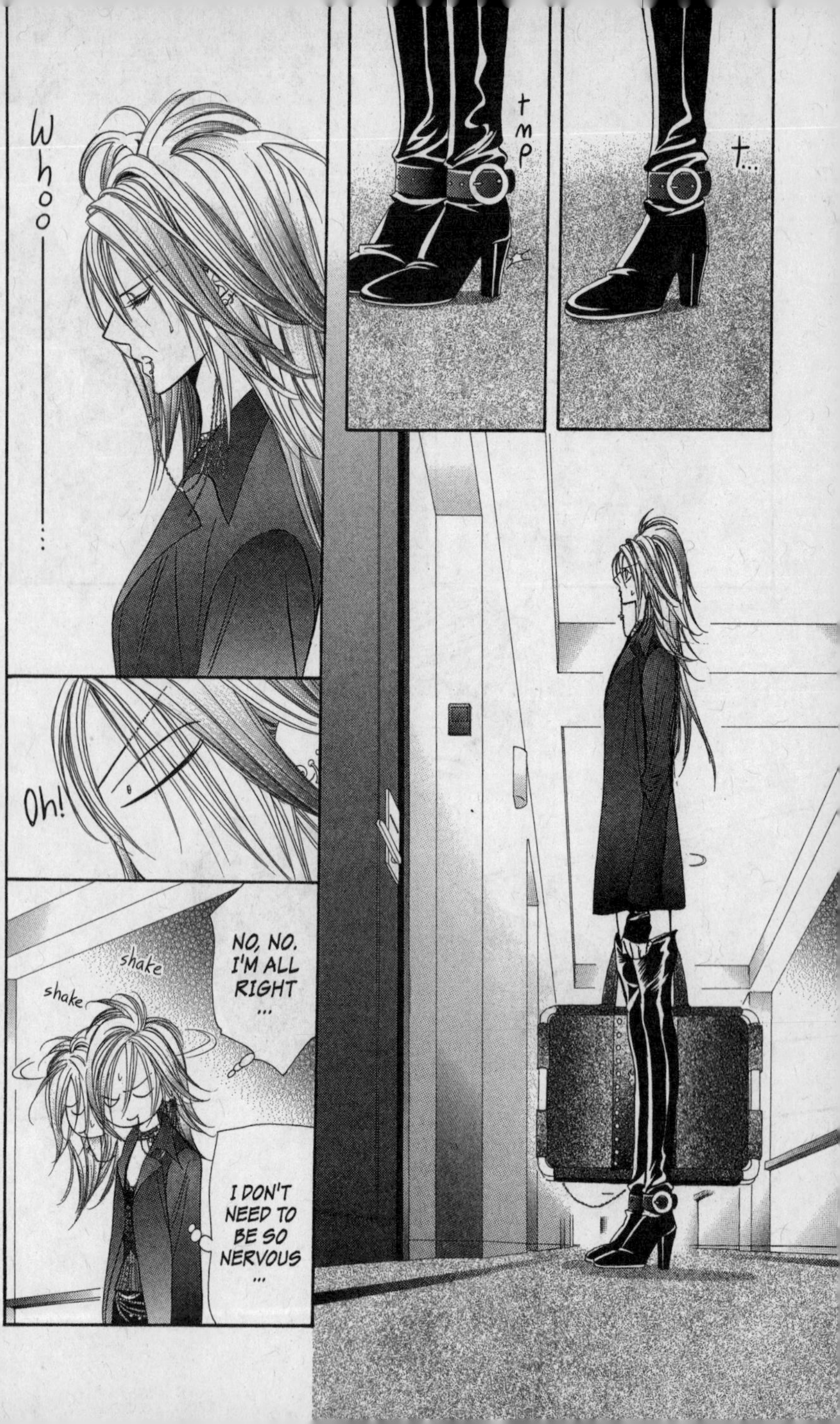
t...
tmp
Whoo—...
Oh!
shake
shake
NO, NO. I'M ALL RIGHT...
I DON'T NEED TO BE SO NERVOUS...

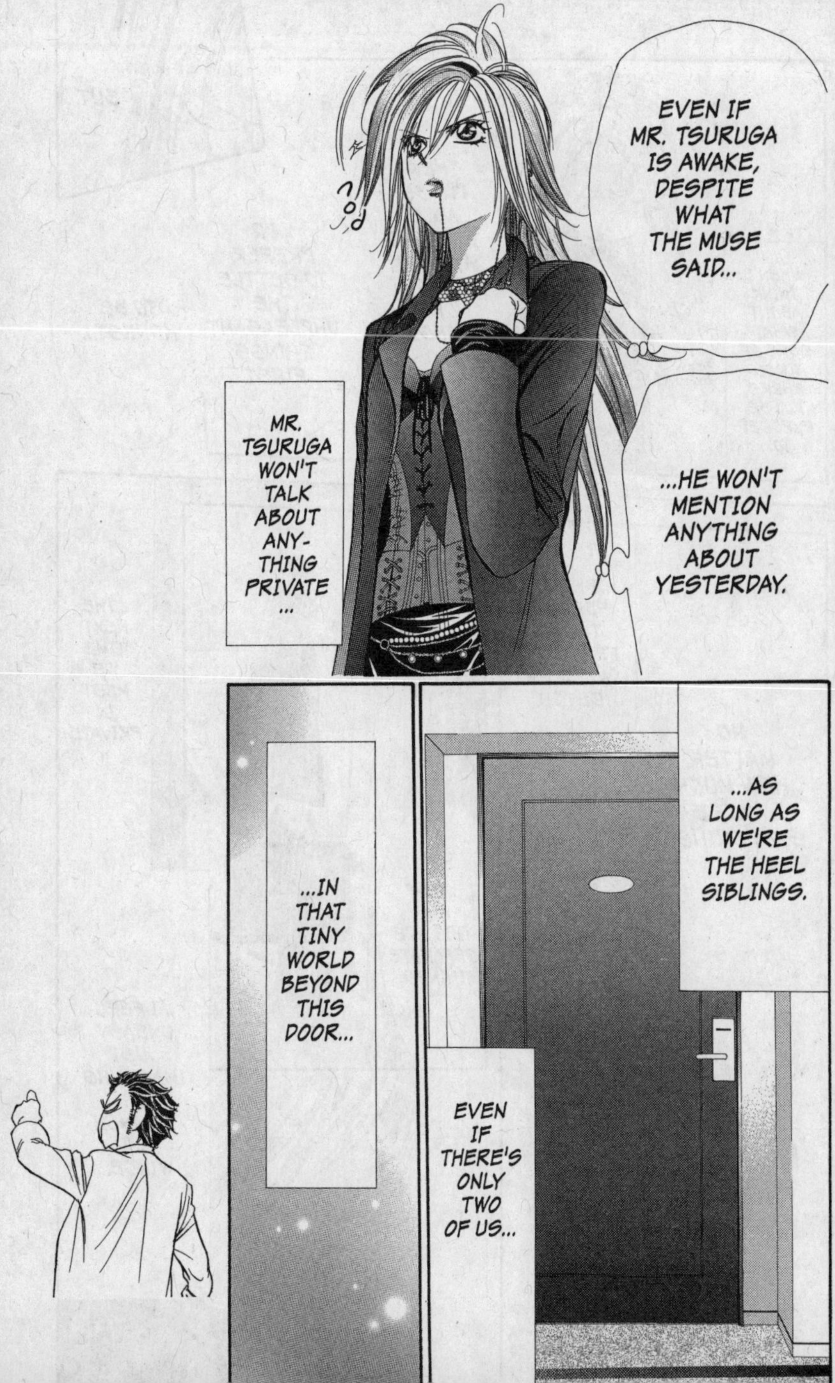
EVEN IF MR. TSURUGA IS AWAKE, DESPITE WHAT THE MUSE SAID...
...HE WON'T MENTION ANYTHING ABOUT YESTERDAY.
MR. TSURUGA WON'T TALK ABOUT ANY-THING PRIVATE...
...AS LONG AS WE'RE THE HEEL SIBLINGS.
EVEN IF THERE'S ONLY TWO OF US...
...IN THAT TINY WORLD BEYOND THIS DOOR...

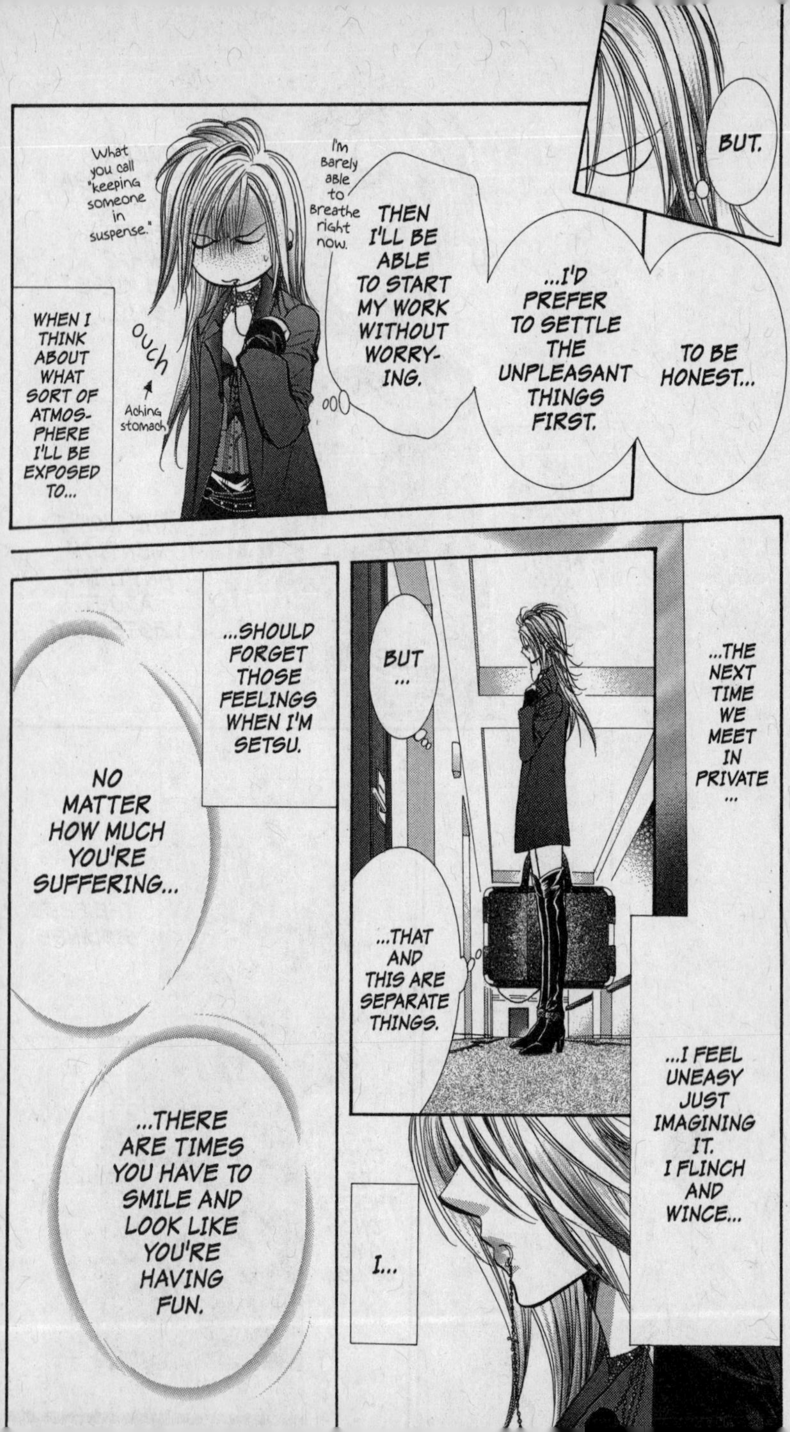
BUT.
TO BE HONEST...
...I'D PREFER TO SETTLE THE UNPLEASANT THINGS FIRST.
THEN I'LL BE ABLE TO START MY WORK WITHOUT WORRY-ING.
I'm barely able to breathe right now.
What you call "keeping someone in suspense."
ouch
Aching stomach
WHEN I THINK ABOUT WHAT SORT OF ATMOS-PHERE I'LL BE EXPOSED TO...
...THE NEXT TIME WE MEET IN PRIVATE...
BUT...
...THAT AND THIS ARE SEPARATE THINGS.
...I FEEL UNEASY JUST IMAGINING IT. I FLINCH AND WINCE...
I...
...SHOULD FORGET THOSE FEELINGS WHEN I'M SETSU.
NO MATTER HOW MUCH YOU'RE SUFFERING...
...THERE ARE TIMES YOU HAVE TO SMILE AND LOOK LIKE YOU'RE HAVING FUN.

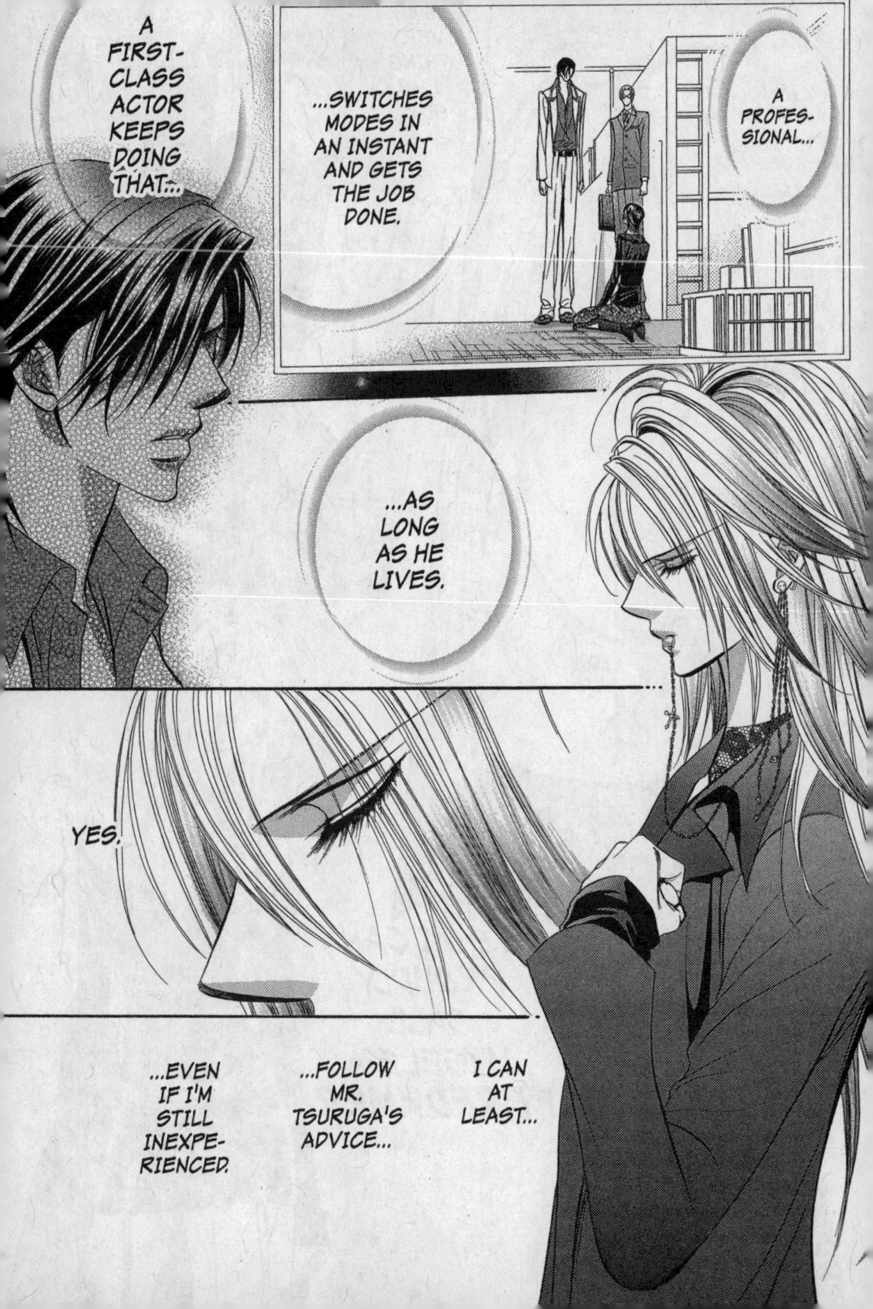
A PROFESSIONAL...
...SWITCHES MODES IN AN INSTANT AND GETS THE JOB DONE.
A FIRST-CLASS ACTOR KEEPS DOING THAT...
...AS LONG AS HE LIVES.
YES.
I CAN AT LEAST...
...FOLLOW MR. TSURUGA'S ADVICE...
...EVEN IF I'M STILL INEXPERIENCED.

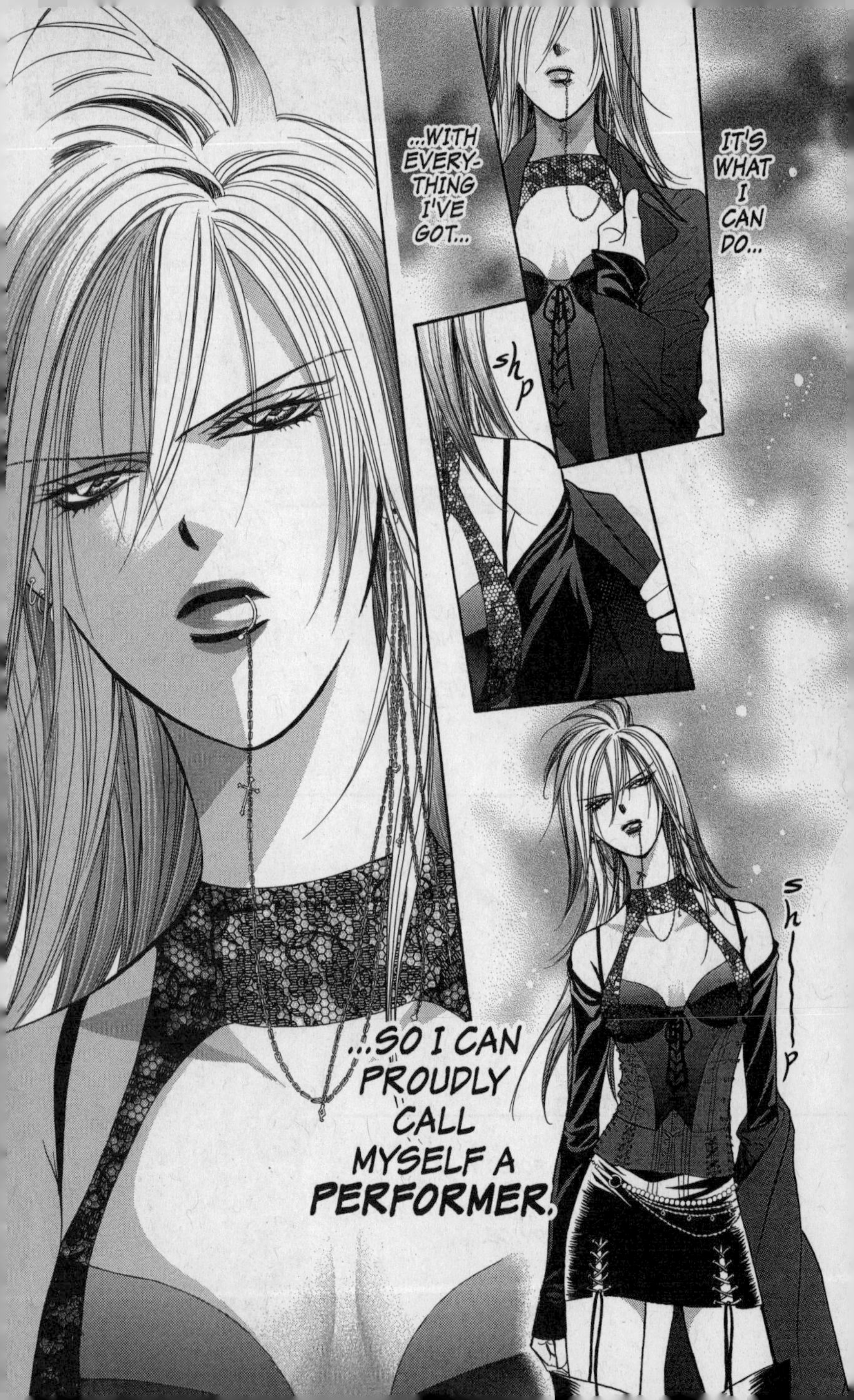
IT'S WHAT I CAN DO...
...WITH EVERYTHING I'VE GOT...
shp
shp
...SO I CAN PROUDLY CALL MYSELF A PERFORMER.

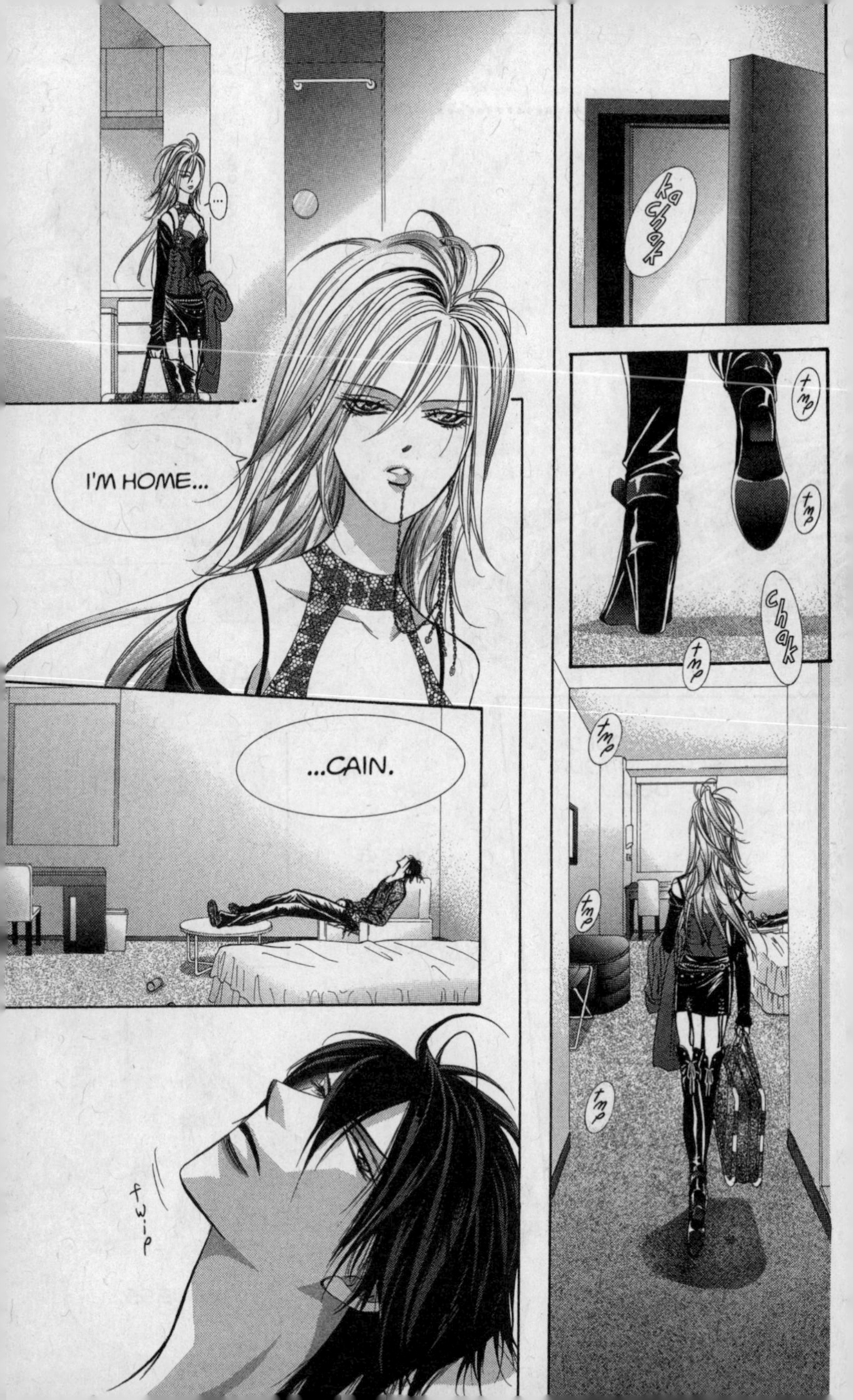
ka chak
tmp
tmp
chak
tmp
tmp
tmp
tmp
...
I'M HOME...
...CAIN.
fwip

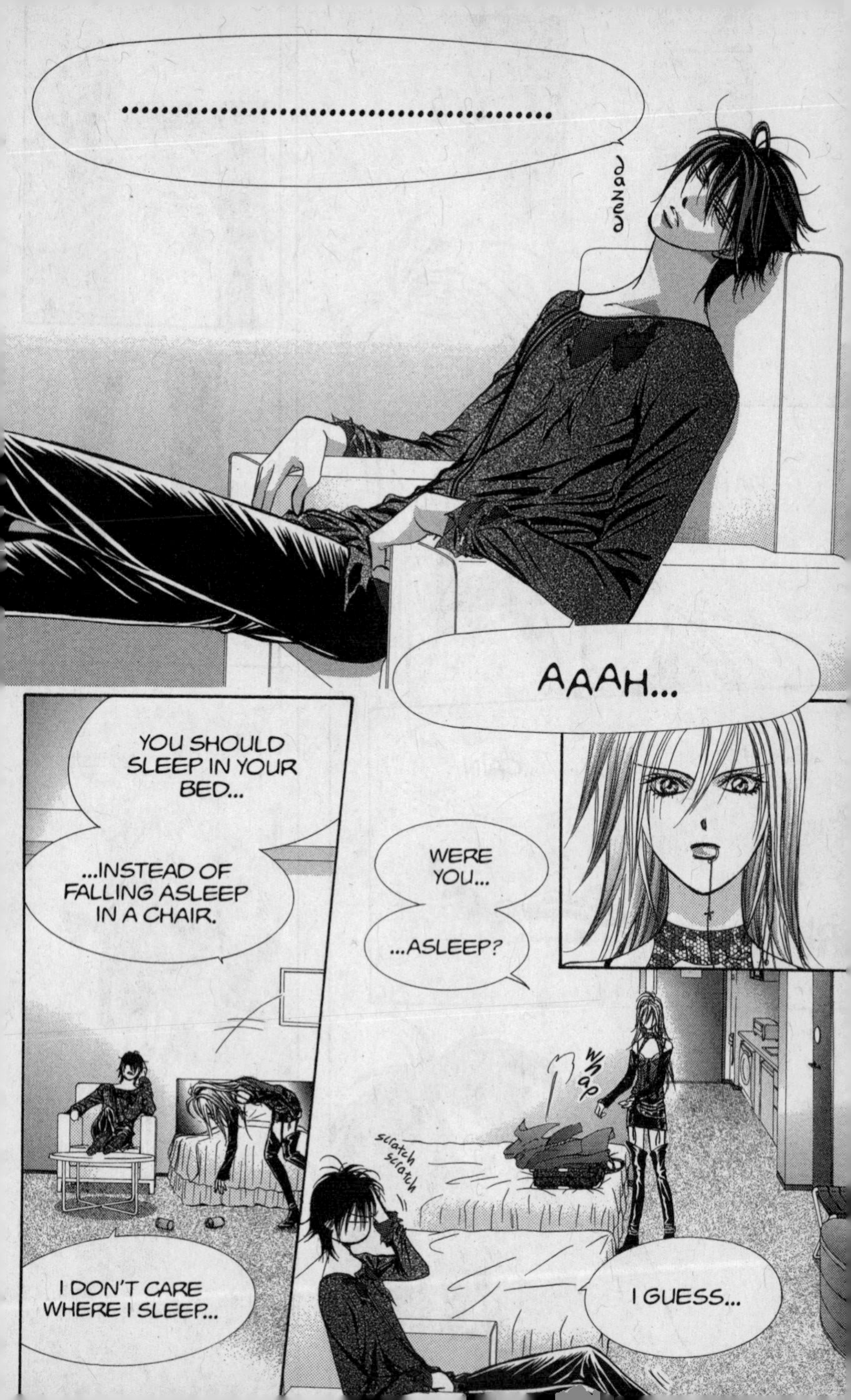
....
AAAH...
WERE YOU...
...ASLEEP?
WHAP
SCRATCH SCRATCH
I GUESS...
YOU SHOULD SLEEP IN YOUR BED...
...INSTEAD OF FALLING ASLEEP IN A CHAIR.
I DON'T CARE WHERE I SLEEP...

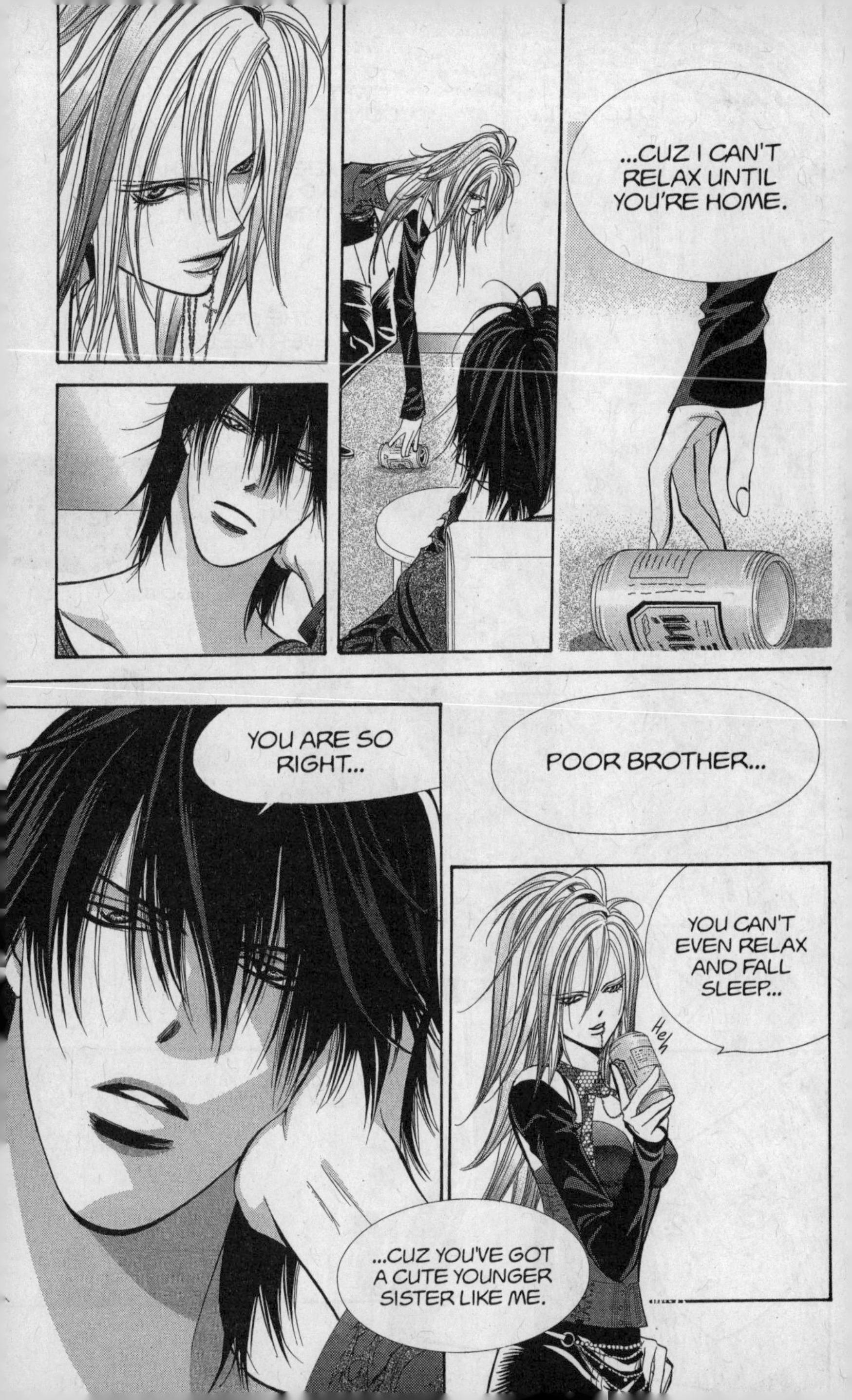
...CUZ I CAN'T RELAX UNTIL YOU'RE HOME.
POOR BROTHER...
YOU CAN'T EVEN RELAX AND FALL SLEEP...
Heh
...CUZ YOU'VE GOT A CUTE YOUNGER SISTER LIKE ME.
YOU ARE SO RIGHT...

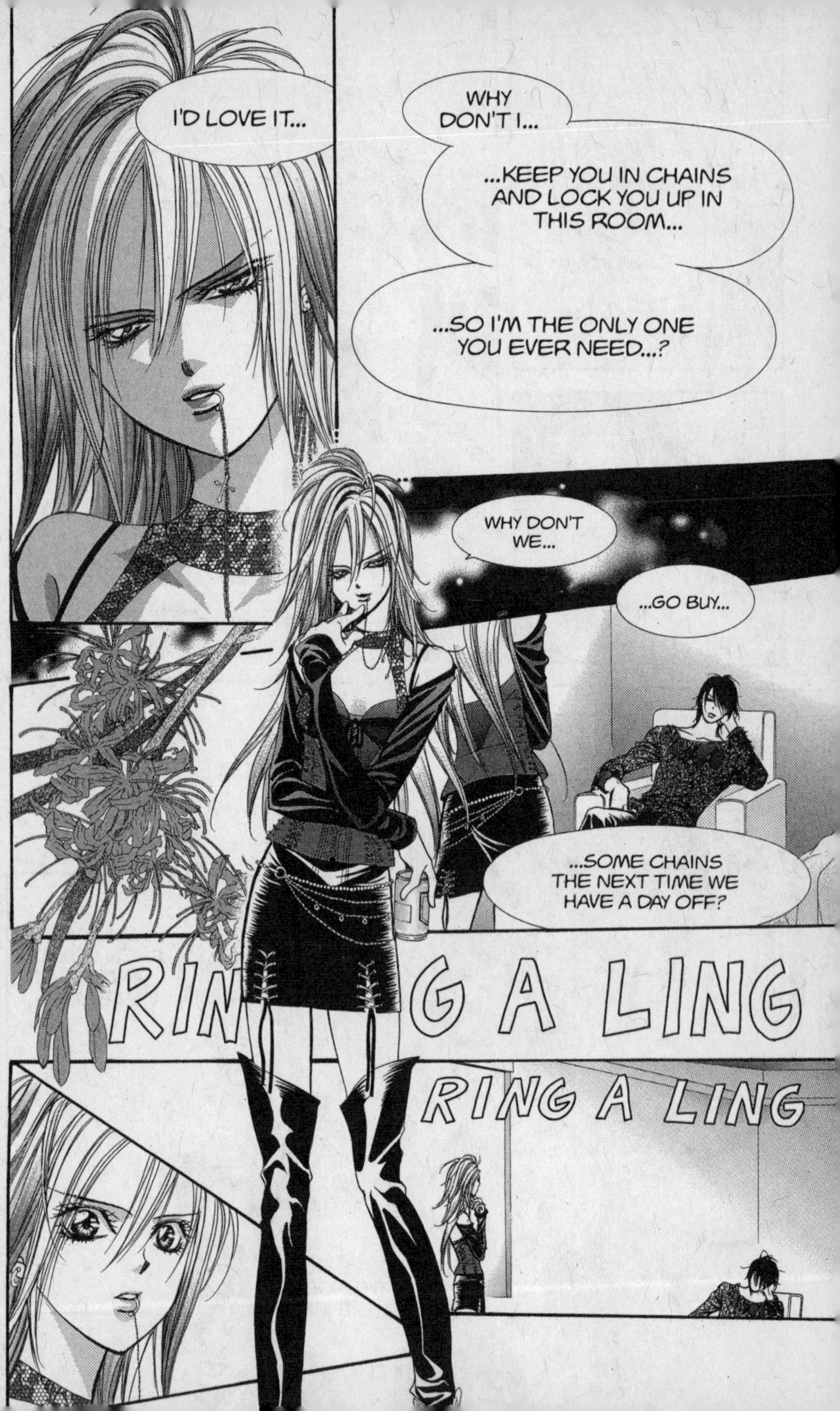
WHY DON'T I...
...KEEP YOU IN CHAINS AND LOCK YOU UP IN THIS ROOM...
...SO I'M THE ONLY ONE YOU EVER NEED...?
I'D LOVE IT...
WHY DON'T WE...
...GO BUY...
...SOME CHAINS THE NEXT TIME WE HAVE A DAY OFF?
RING A LING
RING A LING

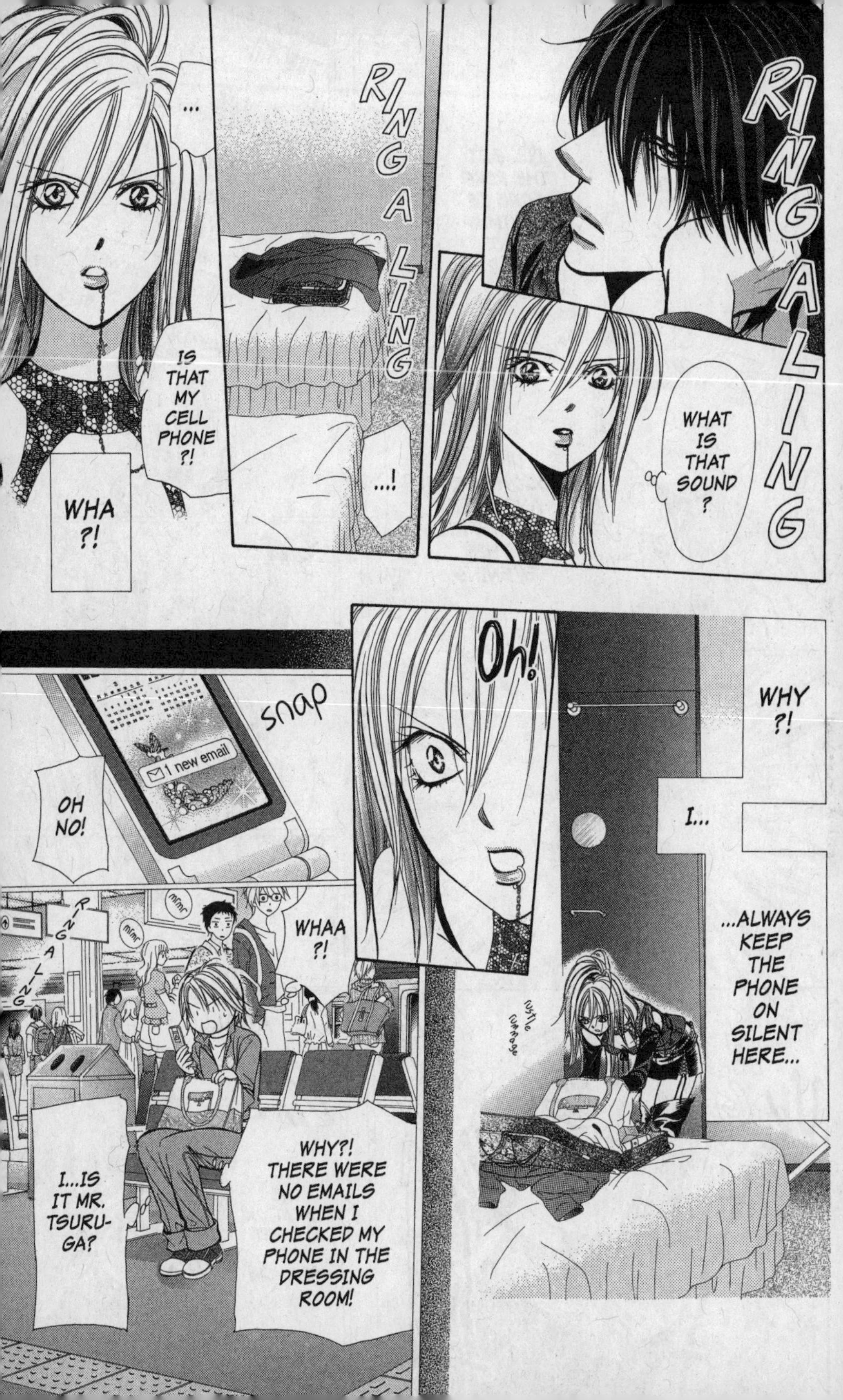
RINGALING
WHAT IS THAT SOUND?
RINGALING
...!
...
IS THAT MY CELL PHONE?!
WHA?!
Oh!
WHY?!
I...
...ALWAYS KEEP THE PHONE ON SILENT HERE...
rustle rummage
snap
1 new email
OH NO!
RING A LING
WHAA?!
WHY?! THERE WERE NO EMAILS WHEN I CHECKED MY PHONE IN THE DRESSING ROOM!
I...IS IT MR. TSURUGA?

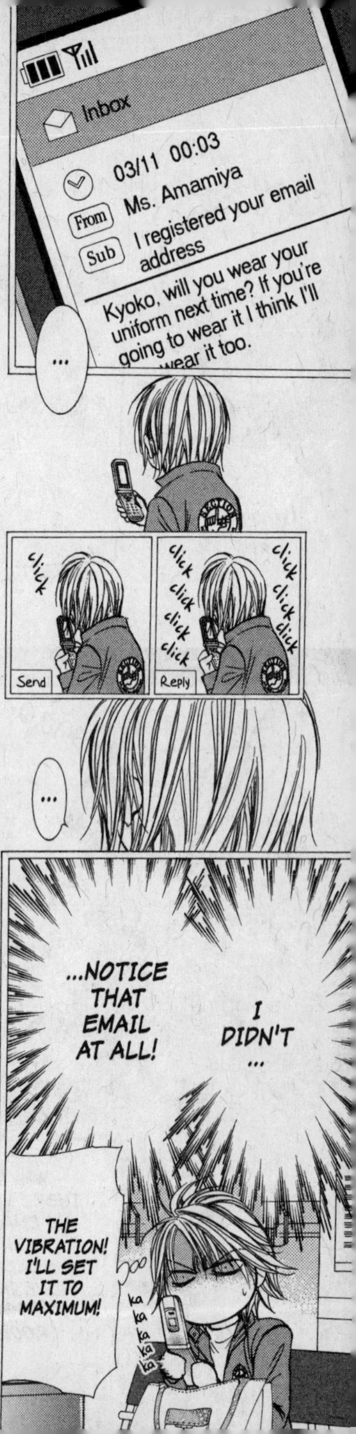
Inbox
03/11 00:03
From Ms. Amamiya
Sub I registered your email address
Kyoko, will you wear your uniform next time? If you're going to wear it I think I'll wear it too.
...
Reply
click click click click
click click click
Send
click
...
I DIDN'T ...
...NOTICE THAT EMAIL AT ALL!
THE VIBRATION! I'LL SET IT TO MAXIMUM!
ka ka ka ka ka
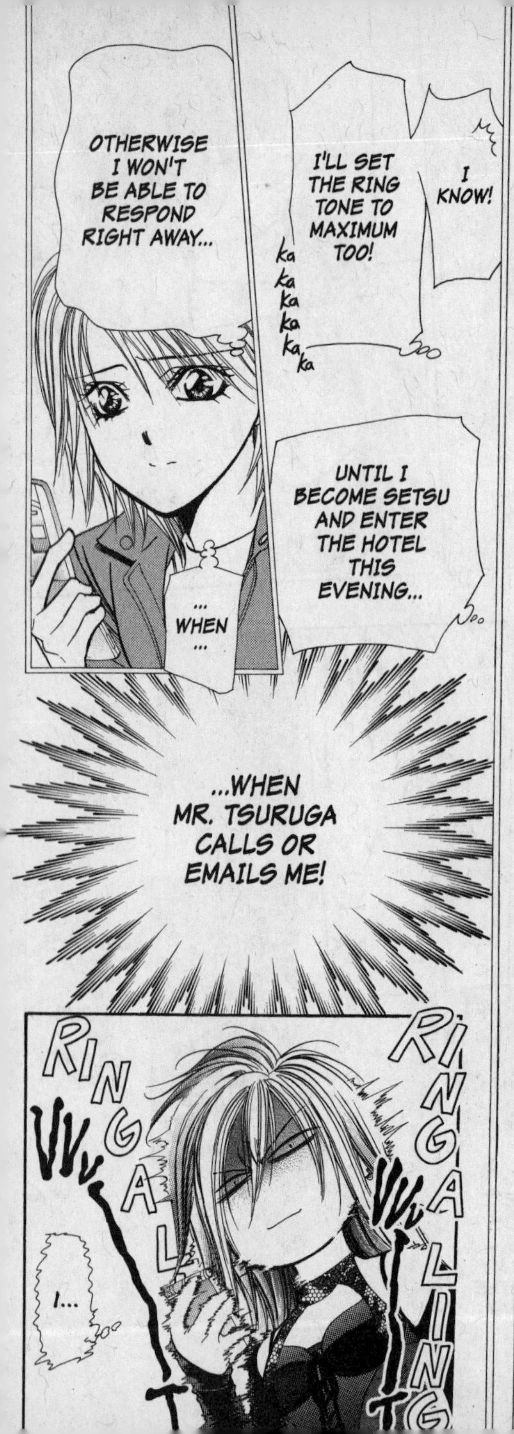
I KNOW!
I'LL SET THE RING TONE TO MAXIMUM TOO!
ka ka ka ka ka ka
UNTIL I BECOME SETSU AND ENTER THE HOTEL THIS EVENING...
OTHERWISE I WON'T BE ABLE TO RESPOND RIGHT AWAY...
... WHEN ...
...WHEN MR. TSURUGA CALLS OR EMAILS ME!
RINGALING
VVV
RINGALING
VVV
I...

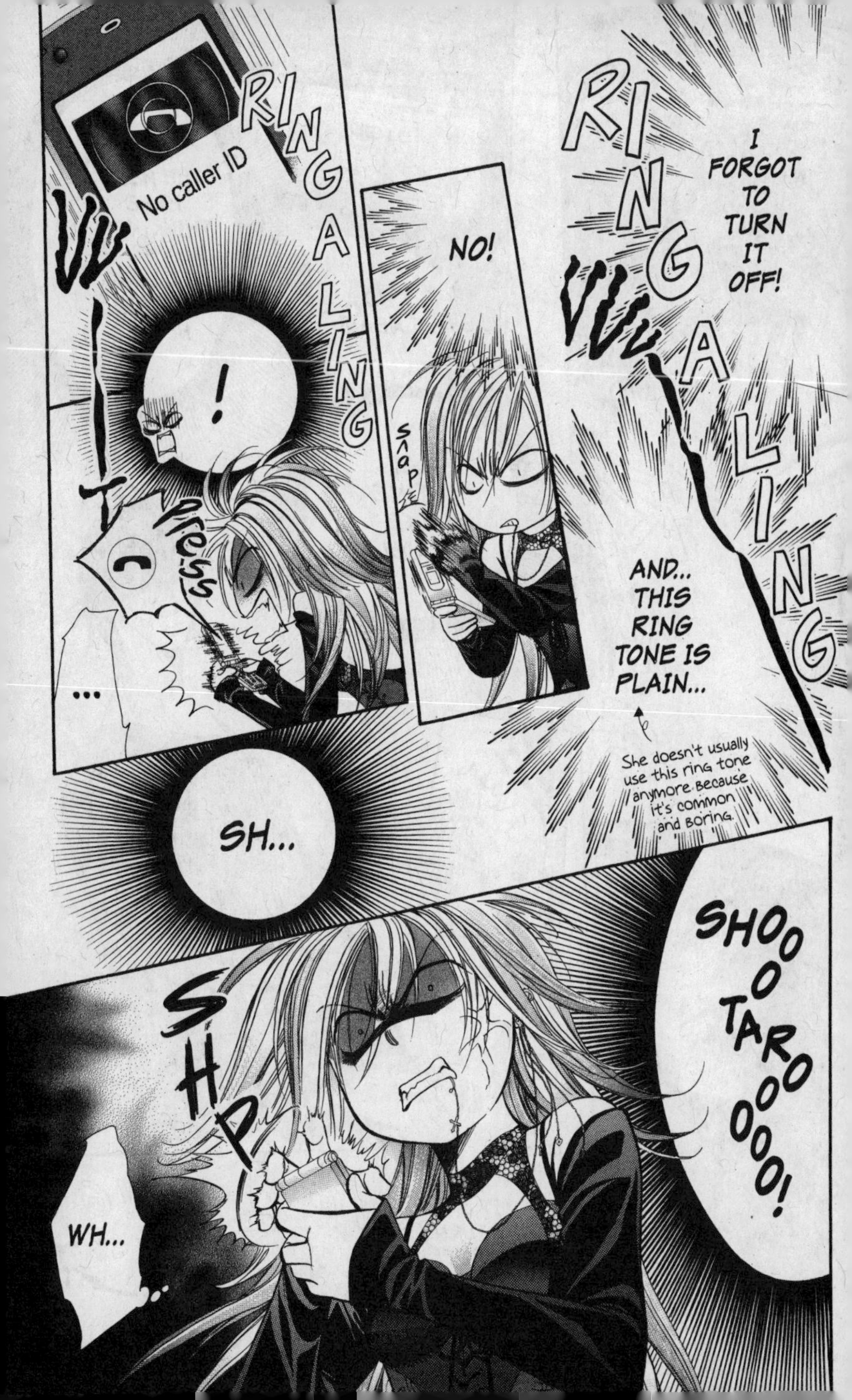
RING A LING
I FORGOT TO TURN IT OFF!
VVV
RING A LING
AND... THIS RING TONE IS PLAIN...
She doesn't usually use this ring tone anymore because it's common and boring.
NO!
snap
No caller ID
RING A LING
VV
!
Press
...
SH...
SHOOOTAROOOOOOO!
SHP
WH...

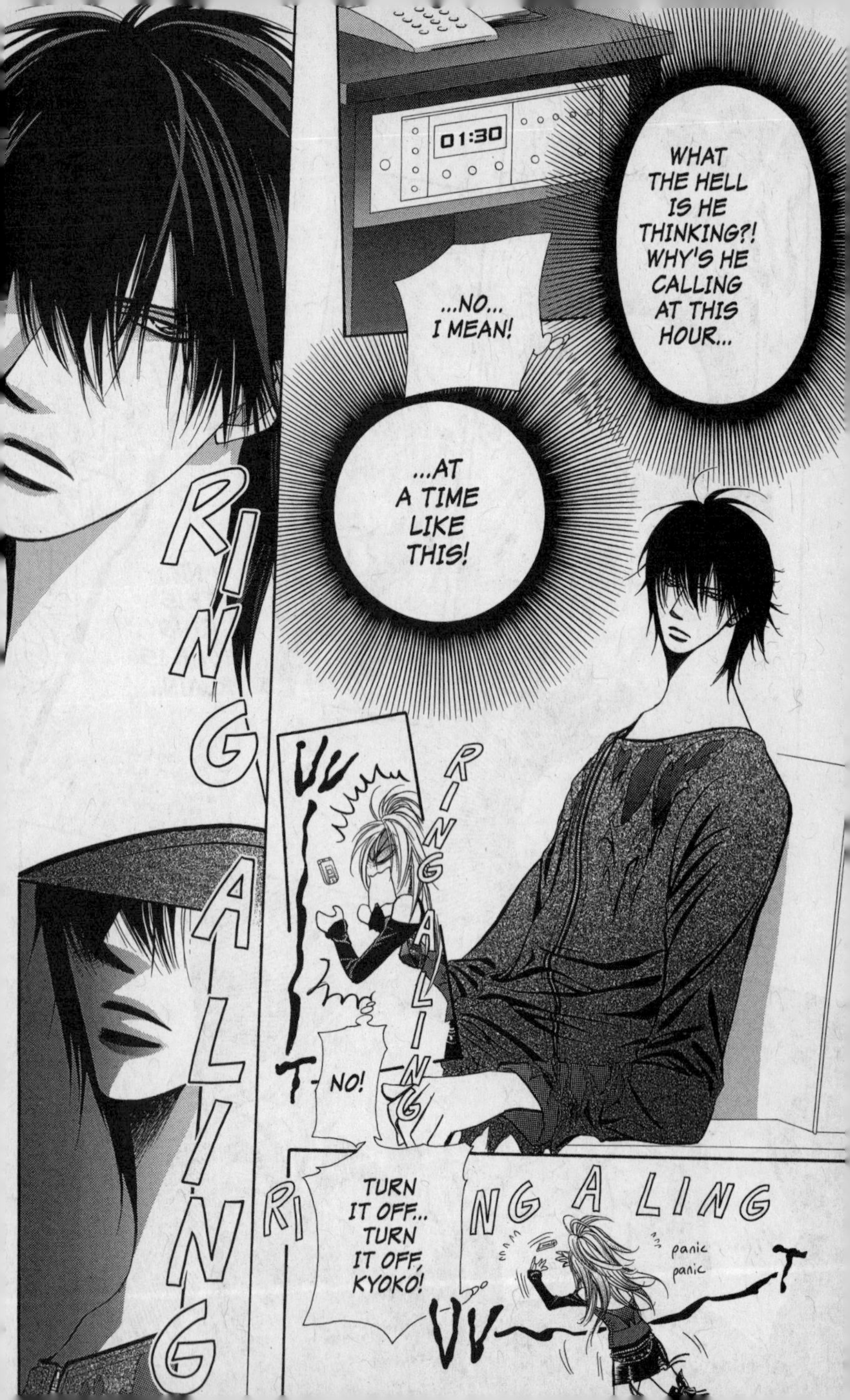
WHAT THE HELL IS HE THINKING?! WHY'S HE CALLING AT THIS HOUR...
...NO... I MEAN!
...AT A TIME LIKE THIS!
VV-T
RINGALING
NO!
TURN IT OFF... TURN IT OFF, KYOKO!
RI NG A LING
panic panic
VV-T
RINGALING

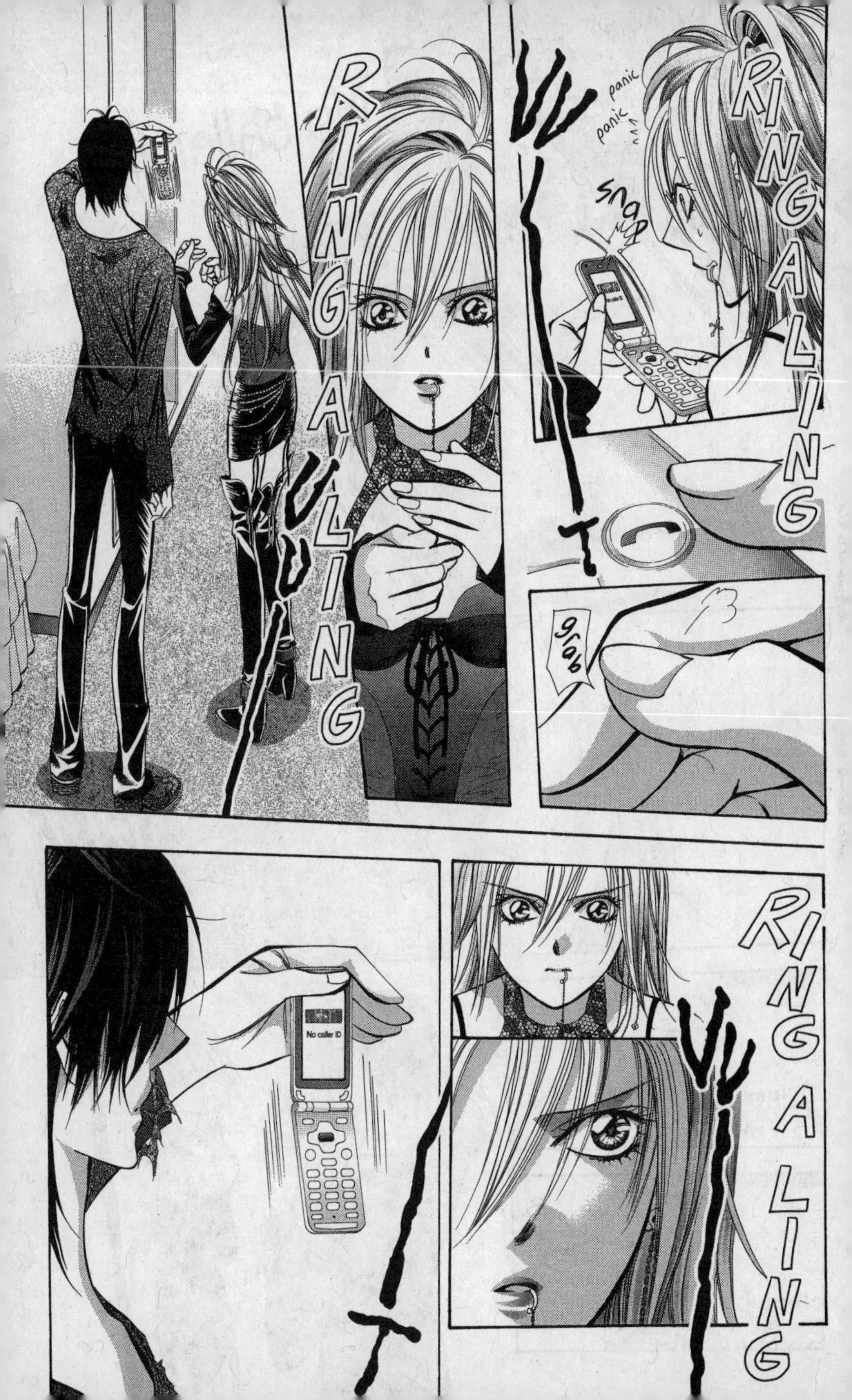
RINGALLING
panic
panic
snap
grab
RINGALLING
RINGALLING
No caller ID

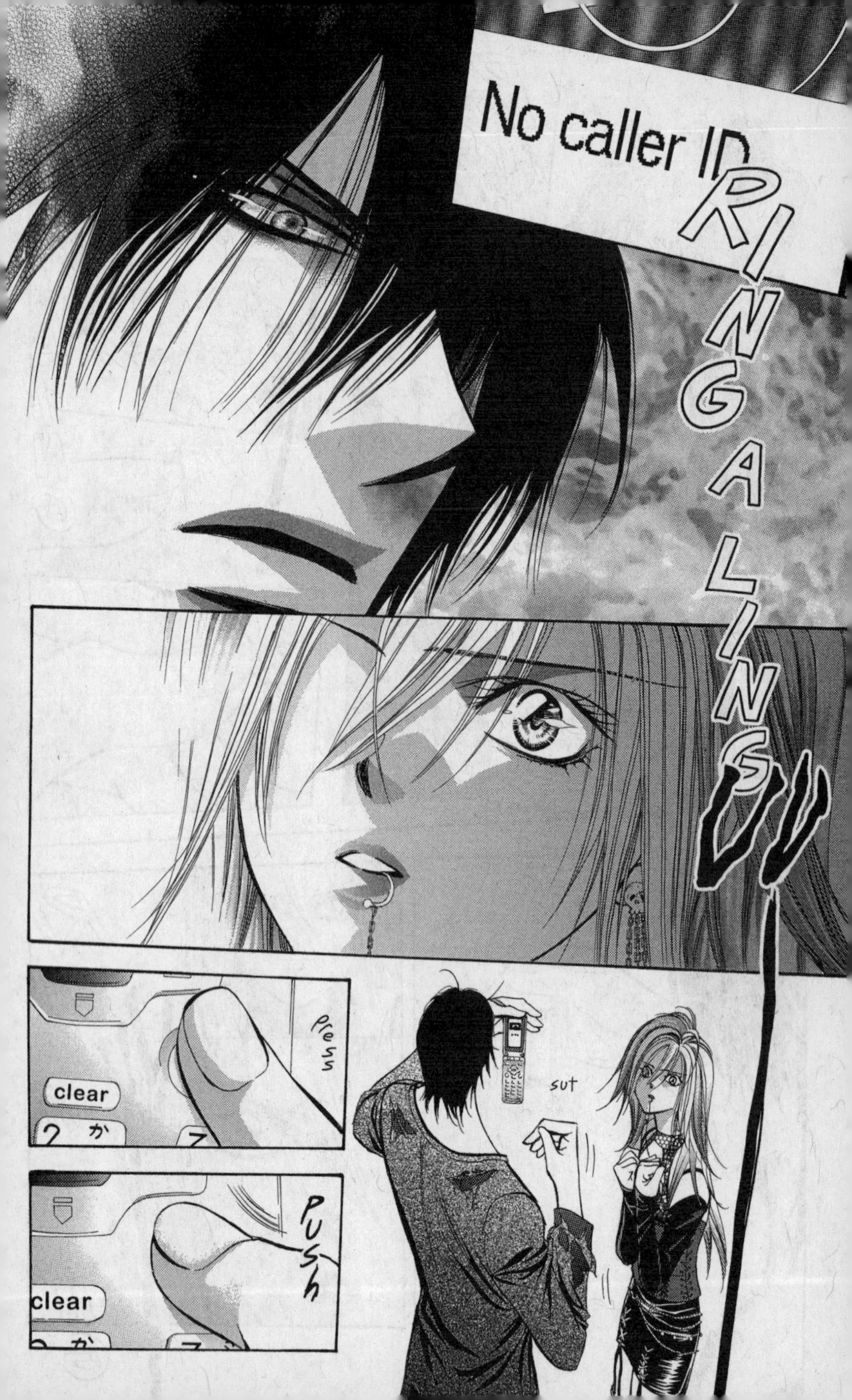
No caller ID
RINGALLING
sut
Press
clear
Push
clear

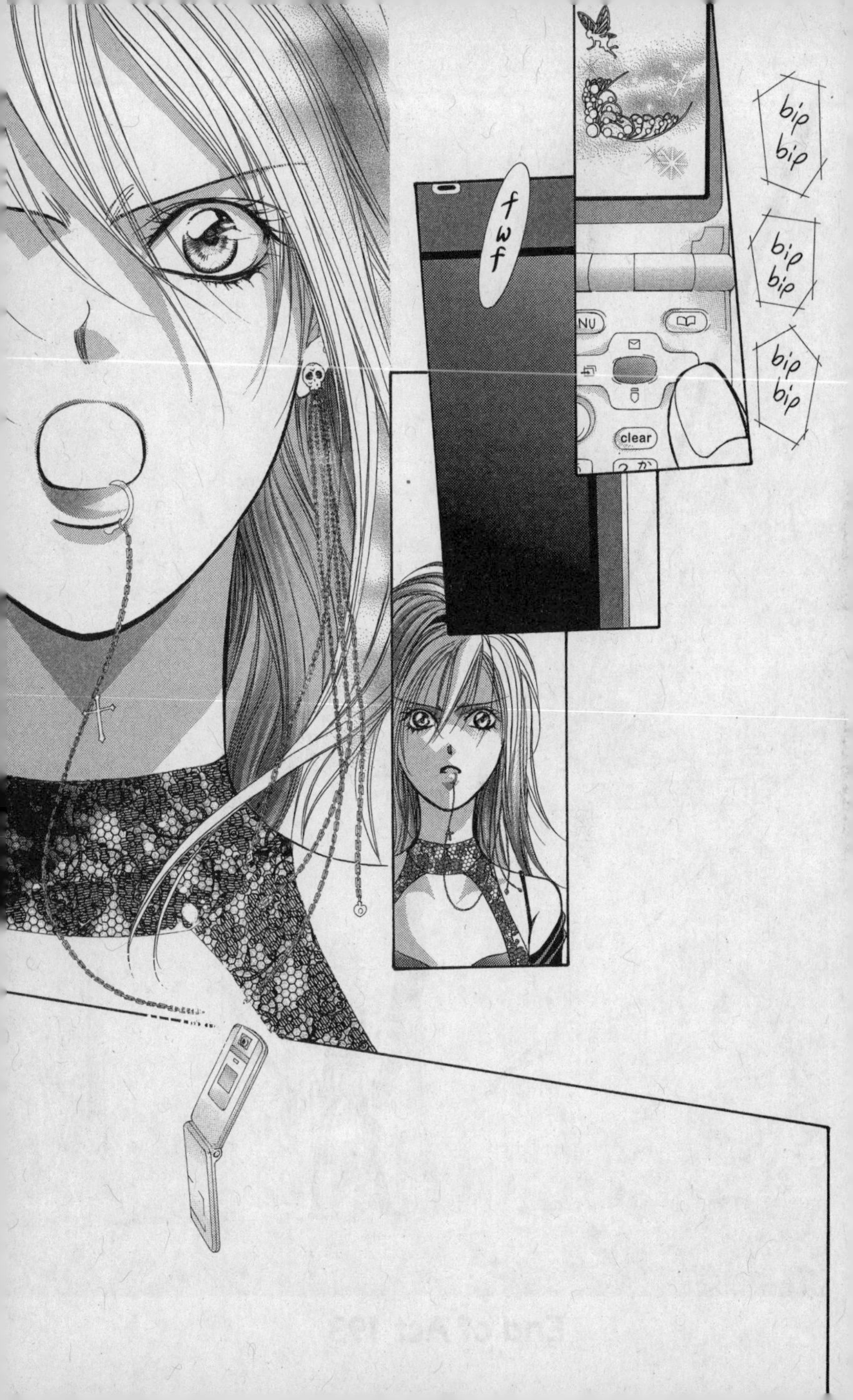
bip bip
bip bip
bip bip
fwf
clear

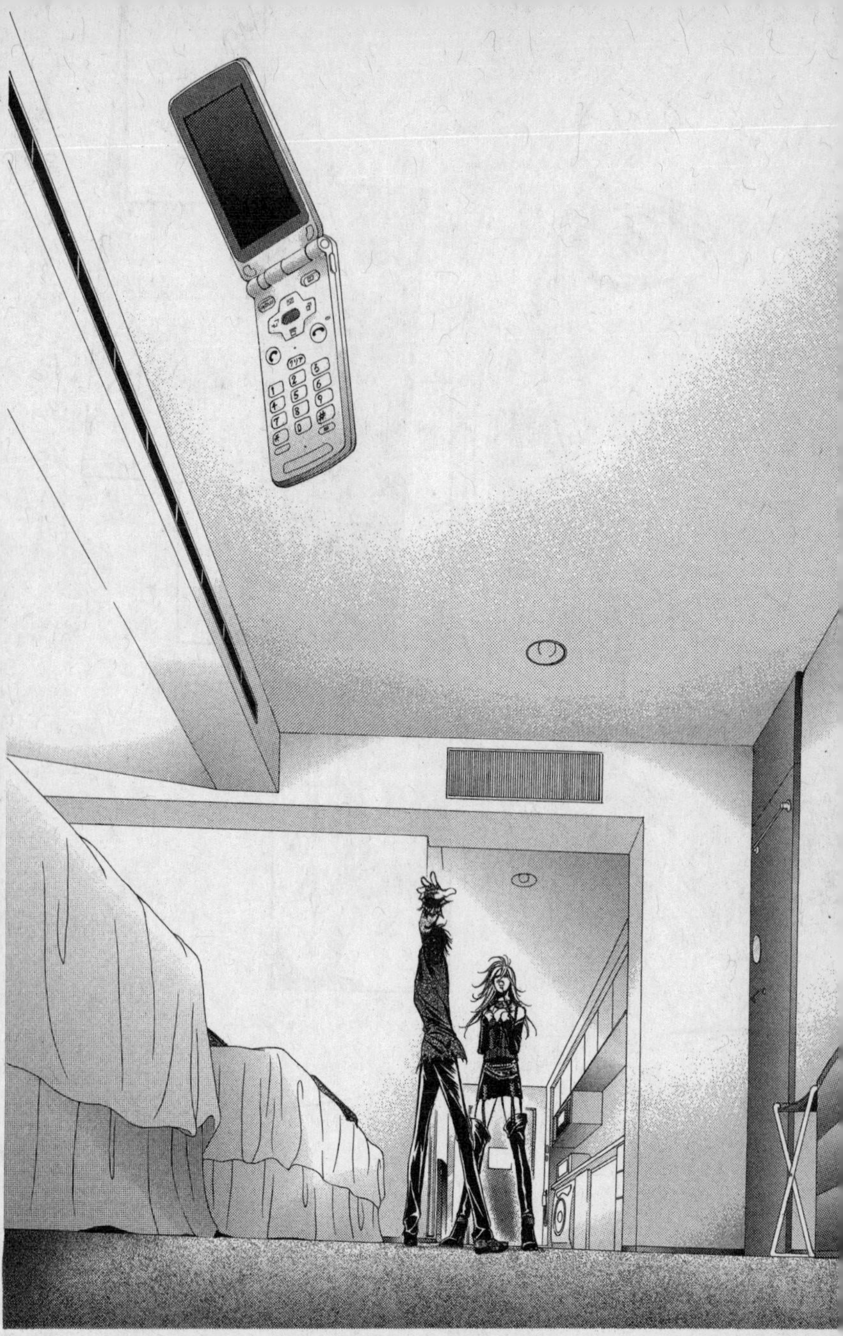

End of Act 193

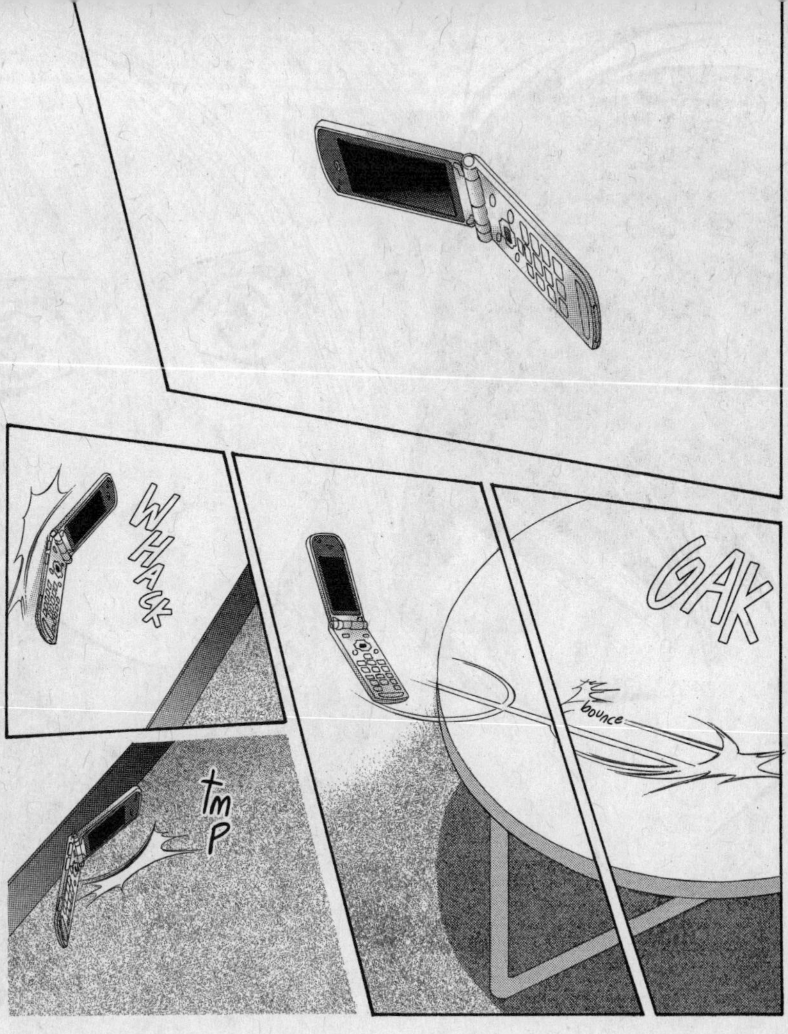
GAK
bounce
WHACK
tmp
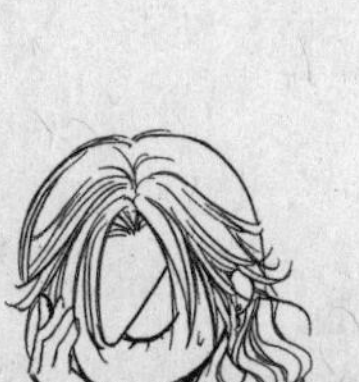

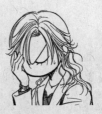

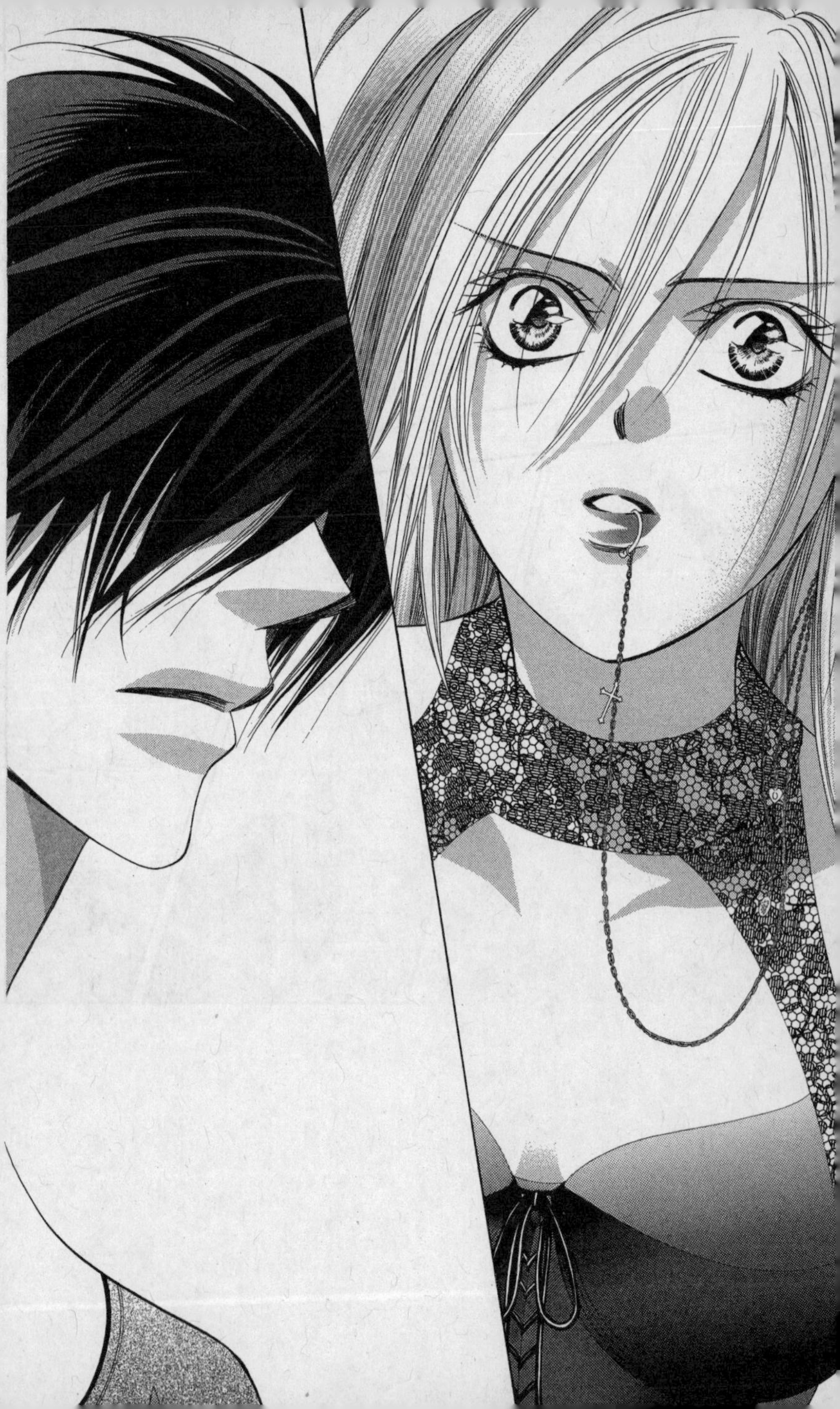

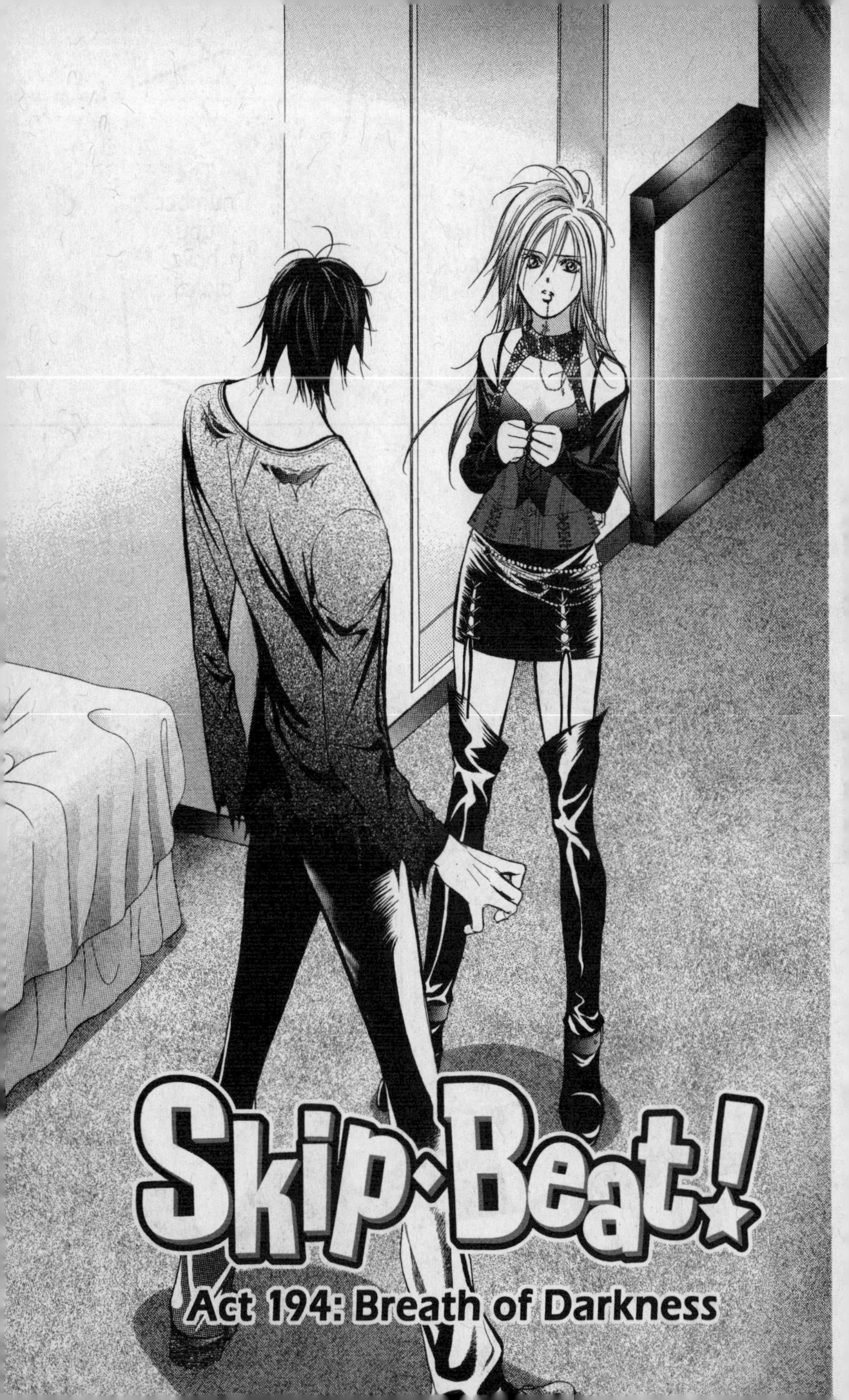
Skip·Beat!
Act 194: Breath of Darkness

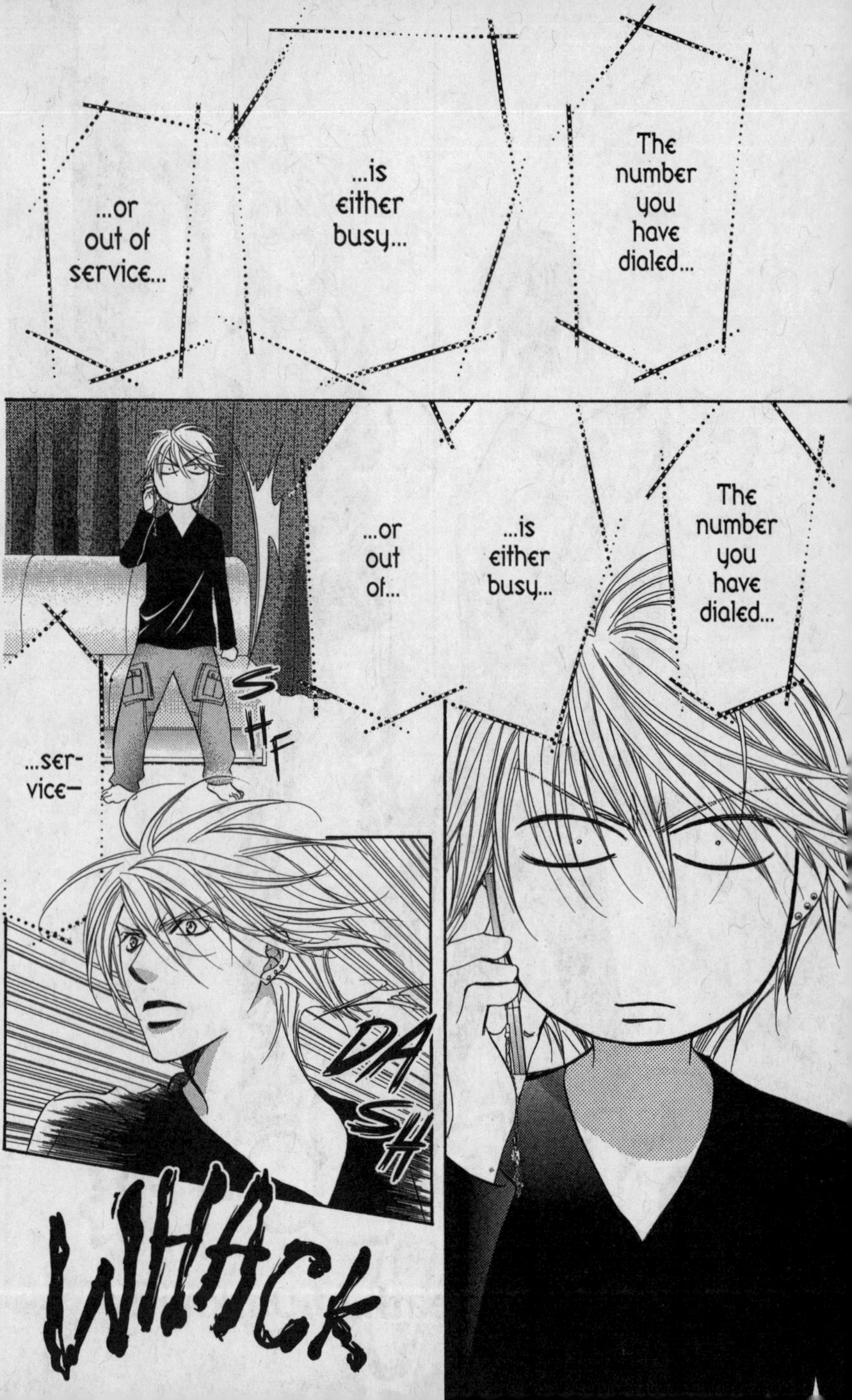
The number you have dialed...
...is either busy...
...or out of service...
The number you have dialed...
...is either busy...
...or out of...
SHF
...ser- vice—
DASH
WHACK

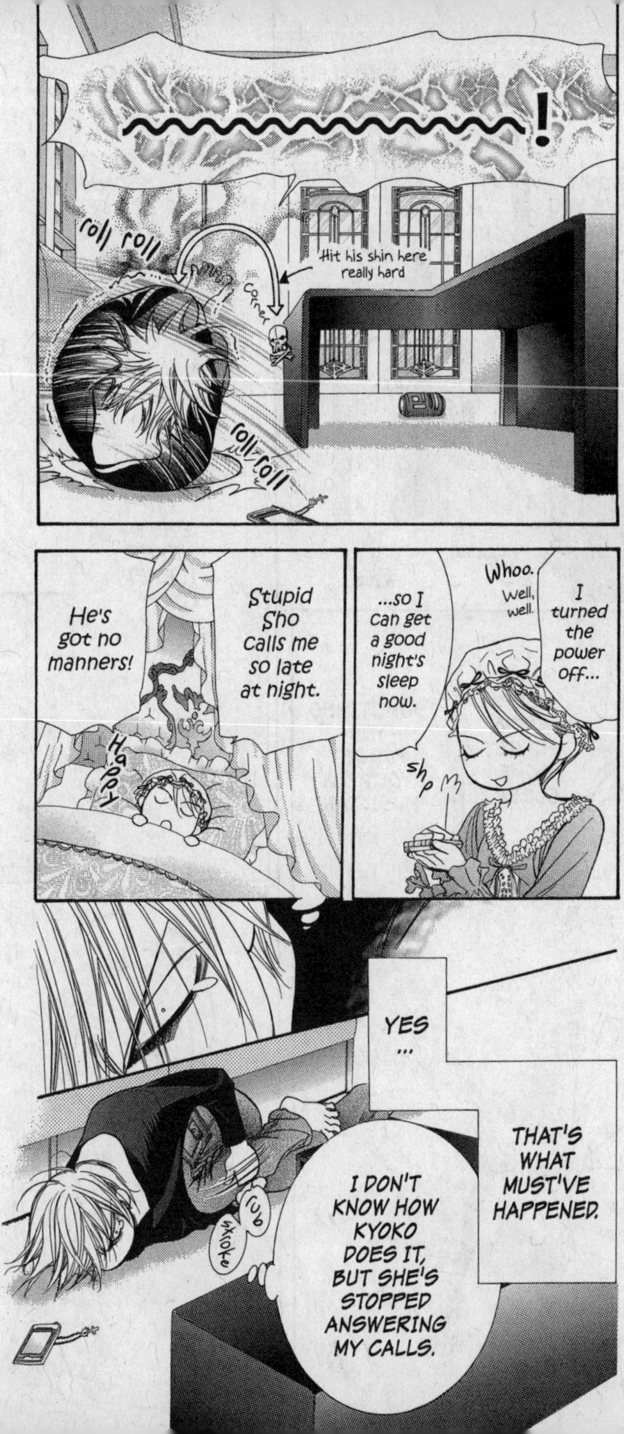

!
roll roll
Hit his shin here really hard
Corner
roll roll
Whoo.
Well, well.
I turned the power off...
...so I can get a good night's sleep now.
shp
Stupid Sho calls me so late at night.
He's got no manners!
Happy
YES...
THAT'S WHAT MUST'VE HAPPENED.
I DON'T KNOW HOW KYOKO DOES IT, BUT SHE'S STOPPED ANSWERING MY CALLS.
rub
stroke

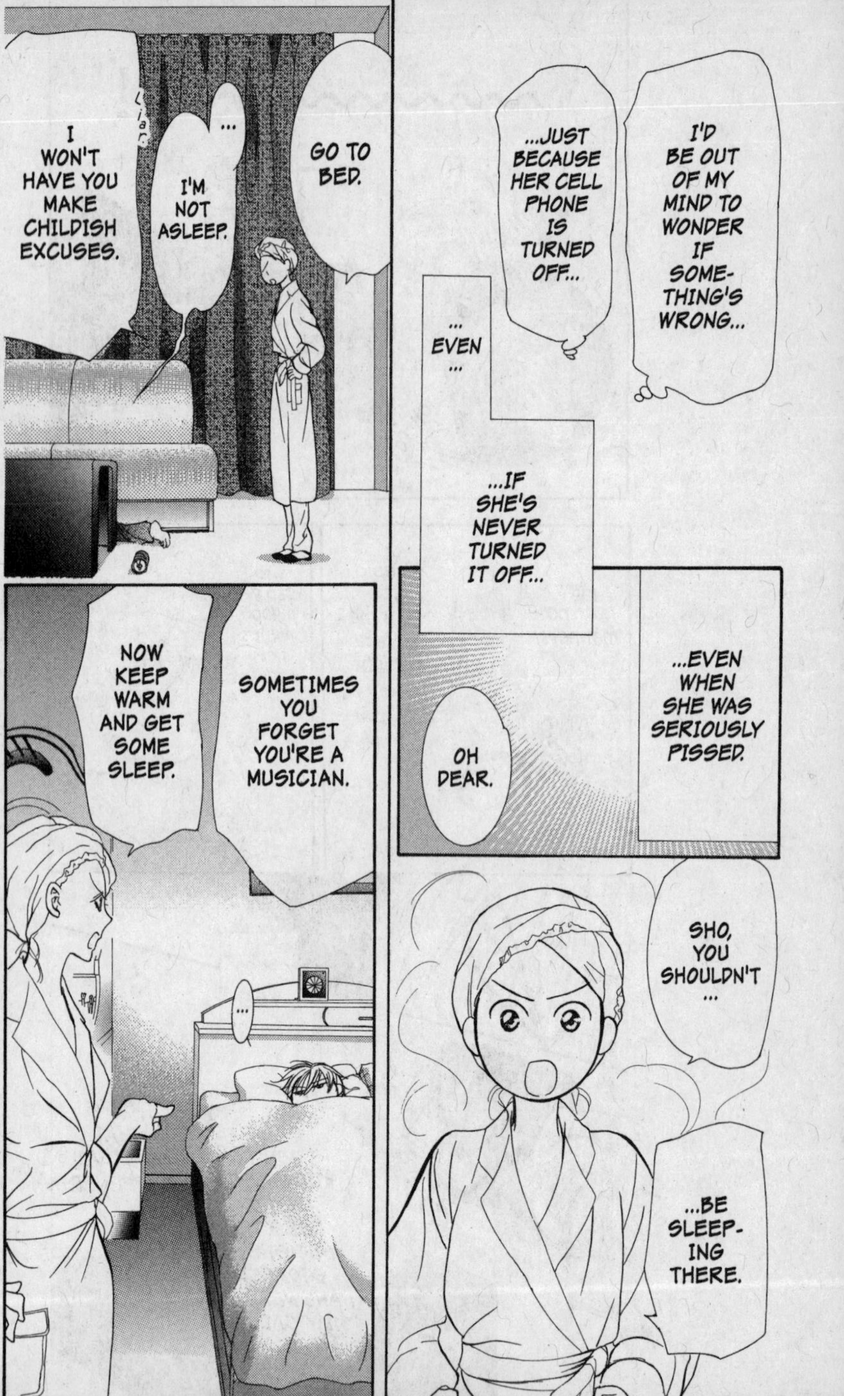
I'D BE OUT OF MY MIND TO WONDER IF SOME-THING'S WRONG...
...JUST BECAUSE HER CELL PHONE IS TURNED OFF...
...EVEN...
...IF SHE'S NEVER TURNED IT OFF...
...EVEN WHEN SHE WAS SERIOUSLY PISSED.
OH DEAR.
SHO, YOU SHOULDN'T...
...BE SLEEP-ING THERE.
GO TO BED.
...
I'M NOT ASLEEP.
Liar.
I WON'T HAVE YOU MAKE CHILDISH EXCUSES.
SOMETIMES YOU FORGET YOU'RE A MUSICIAN.
NOW KEEP WARM AND GET SOME SLEEP.
...

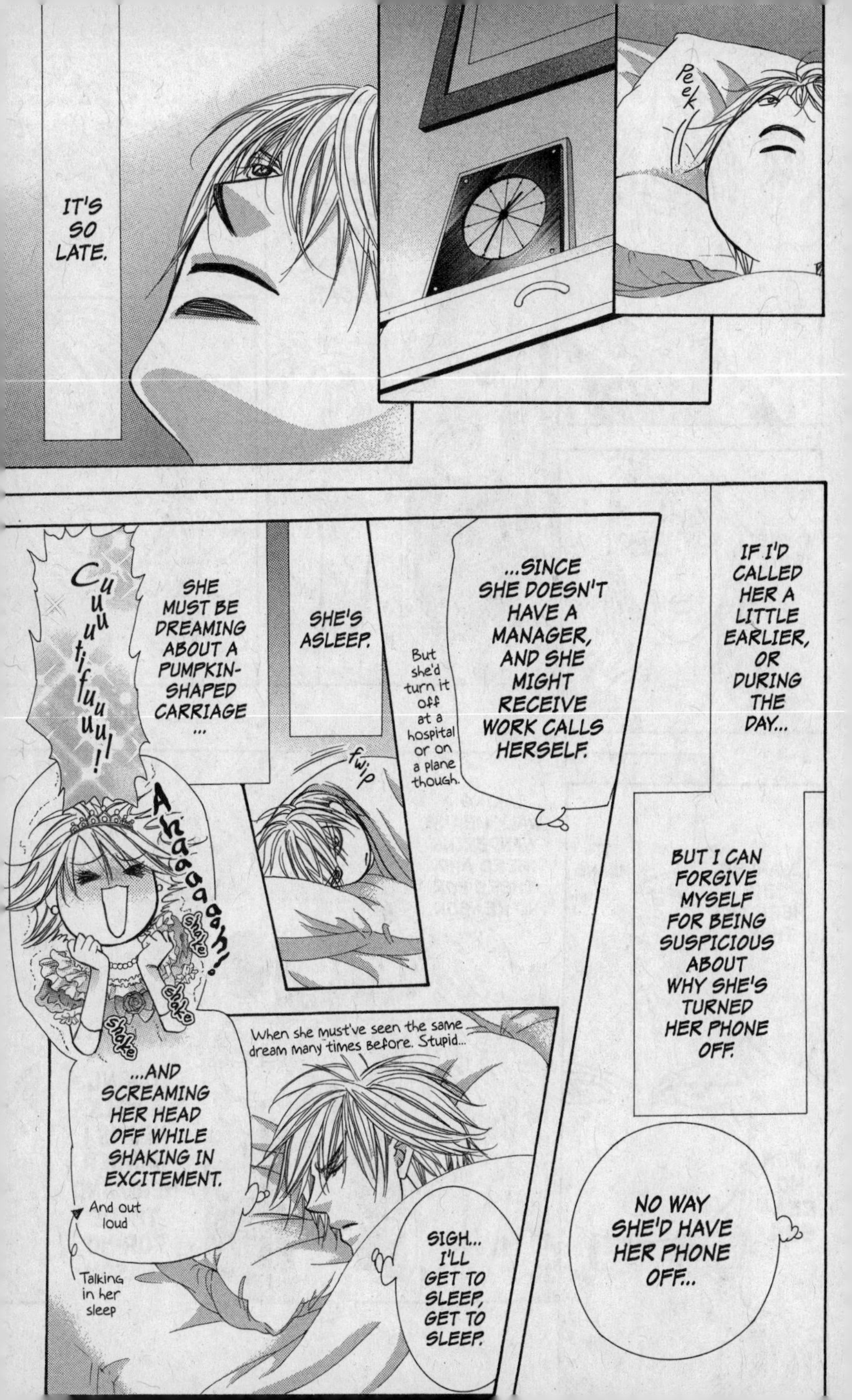
Peek
IT'S SO LATE.
IF I'D CALLED HER A LITTLE EARLIER, OR DURING THE DAY...
BUT I CAN FORGIVE MYSELF FOR BEING SUSPICIOUS ABOUT WHY SHE'S TURNED HER PHONE OFF.
NO WAY SHE'D HAVE HER PHONE OFF...
...SINCE SHE DOESN'T HAVE A MANAGER, AND SHE MIGHT RECEIVE WORK CALLS HERSELF.
But she'd turn it off at a hospital or on a plane though.
SHE'S ASLEEP.
fwip
SHE MUST BE DREAMING ABOUT A PUMPKIN-SHAPED CARRIAGE ...
Cuuuutifuuuul!
Ahaaaaah!
shake
shake
shake
...AND SCREAMING HER HEAD OFF WHILE SHAKING IN EXCITEMENT.
And out loud
Talking in her sleep
When she must've seen the same dream many times before. Stupid...
SIGH... I'LL GET TO SLEEP, GET TO SLEEP.

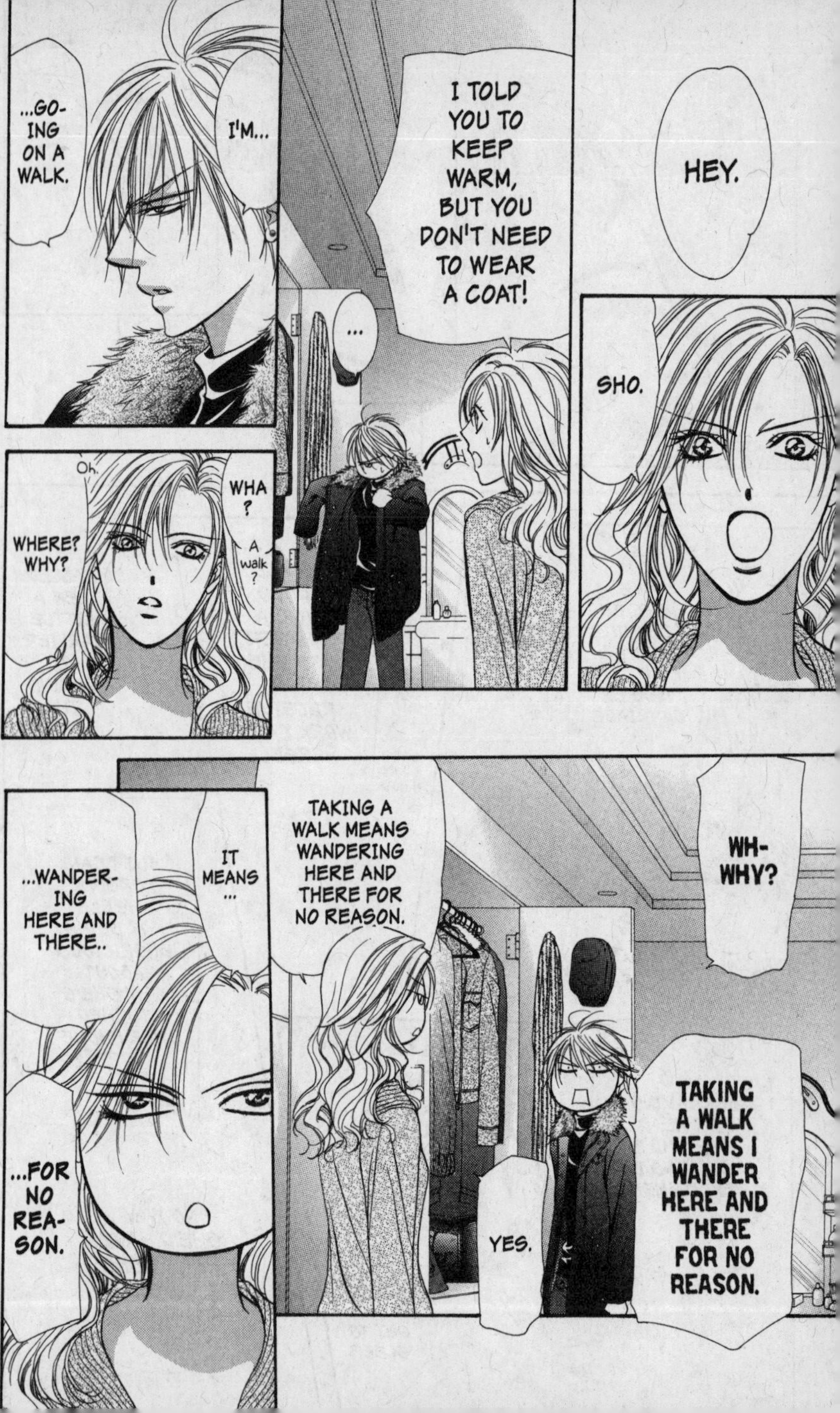
HEY.
SHO.
I TOLD YOU TO KEEP WARM, BUT YOU DON'T NEED TO WEAR A COAT!
...
I'M...
...GO-ING ON A WALK.
WHA?
A walk?
Oh.
WHERE? WHY?
WH-WHY?
TAKING A WALK MEANS I WANDER HERE AND THERE FOR NO REASON.
YES.
TAKING A WALK MEANS WANDERING HERE AND THERE FOR NO REASON.
IT MEANS...
...WANDER-ING HERE AND THERE..
...FOR NO REA-SON.

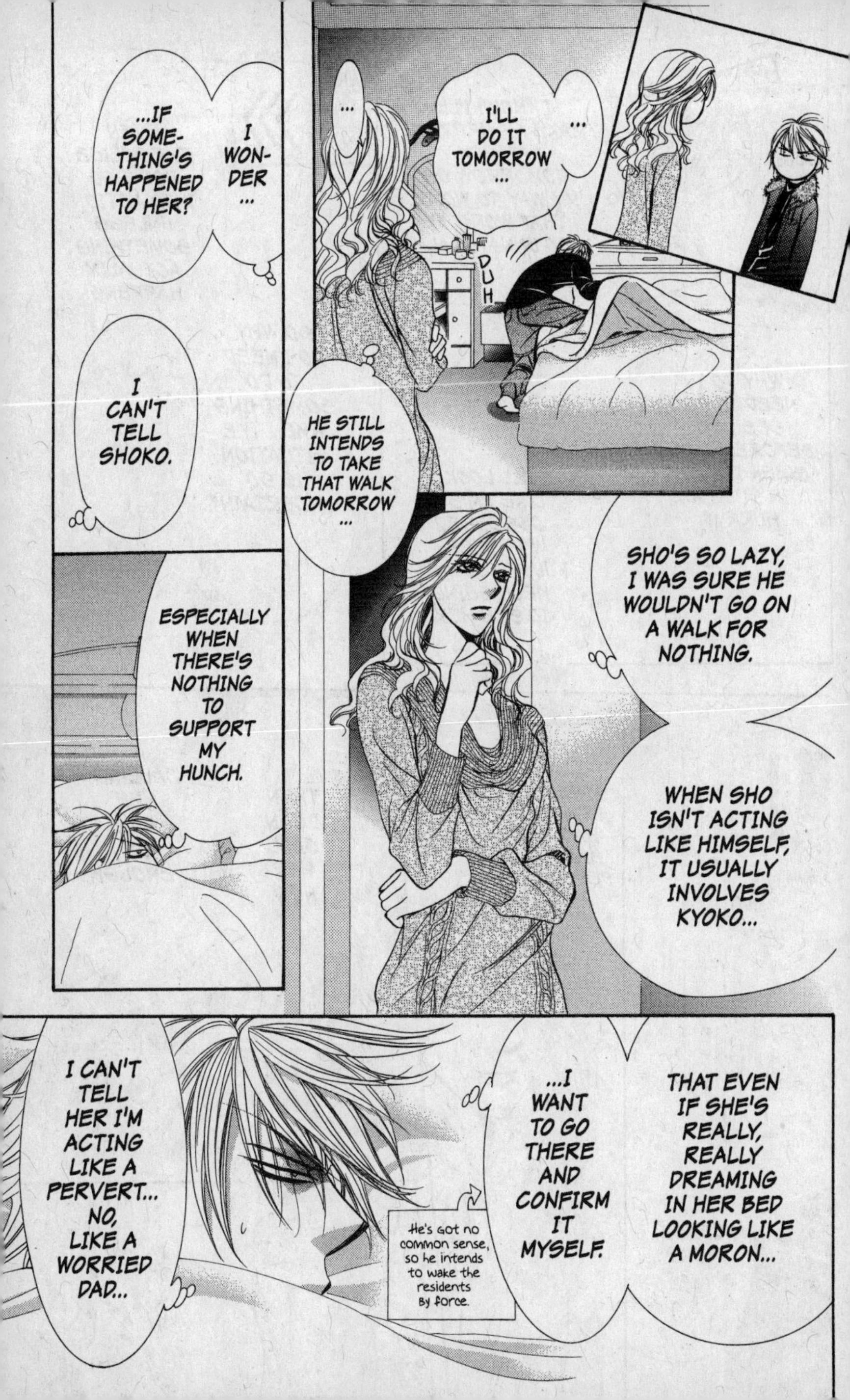
...
I'LL DO IT TOMORROW ...
...
DUH
HE STILL INTENDS TO TAKE THAT WALK TOMORROW ...
SHO'S SO LAZY, I WAS SURE HE WOULDN'T GO ON A WALK FOR NOTHING.
WHEN SHO ISN'T ACTING LIKE HIMSELF, IT USUALLY INVOLVES KYOKO...
I WONDER ...
...IF SOMETHING'S HAPPENED TO HER?
I CAN'T TELL SHOKO.
ESPECIALLY WHEN THERE'S NOTHING TO SUPPORT MY HUNCH.
THAT EVEN IF SHE'S REALLY, REALLY DREAMING IN HER BED LOOKING LIKE A MORON...
...I WANT TO GO THERE AND CONFIRM IT MYSELF.
He's got no common sense, so he intends to wake the residents by force.
I CAN'T TELL HER I'M ACTING LIKE A PERVERT... NO, LIKE A WORRIED DAD...

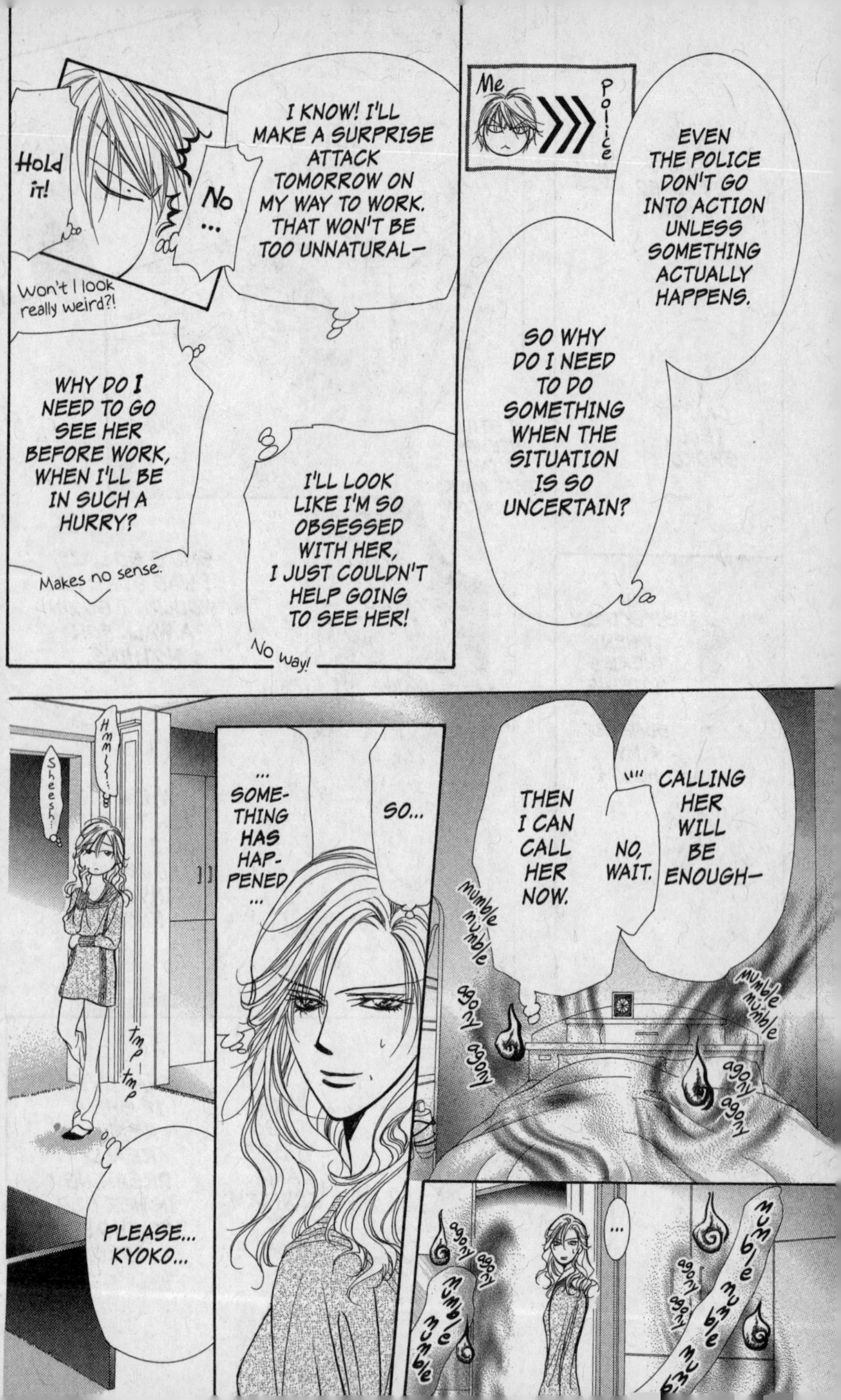
Me
Police
EVEN THE POLICE DON'T GO INTO ACTION UNLESS SOMETHING ACTUALLY HAPPENS.
SO WHY DO I NEED TO DO SOMETHING WHEN THE SITUATION IS SO UNCERTAIN?
I KNOW! I'LL MAKE A SURPRISE ATTACK TOMORROW ON MY WAY TO WORK. THAT WON'T BE TOO UNNATURAL—
No...
Hold it!
Won't I look really weird?!
WHY DO I NEED TO GO SEE HER BEFORE WORK, WHEN I'LL BE IN SUCH A HURRY?
Makes no sense.
I'LL LOOK LIKE I'M SO OBSESSED WITH HER, I JUST COULDN'T HELP GOING TO SEE HER!
No way!
CALLING HER WILL BE ENOUGH—
NO, WAIT.
THEN I CAN CALL HER NOW.
mumble mumble
agony agony
mumble mumble
agony agony
...
mumble mumble
agony agony
mumble mumble
agony agony
SO...
...SOMETHING HAS HAPPENED...
Hmm~~...
Sheesh...
tmp tmp
PLEASE... KYOKO...

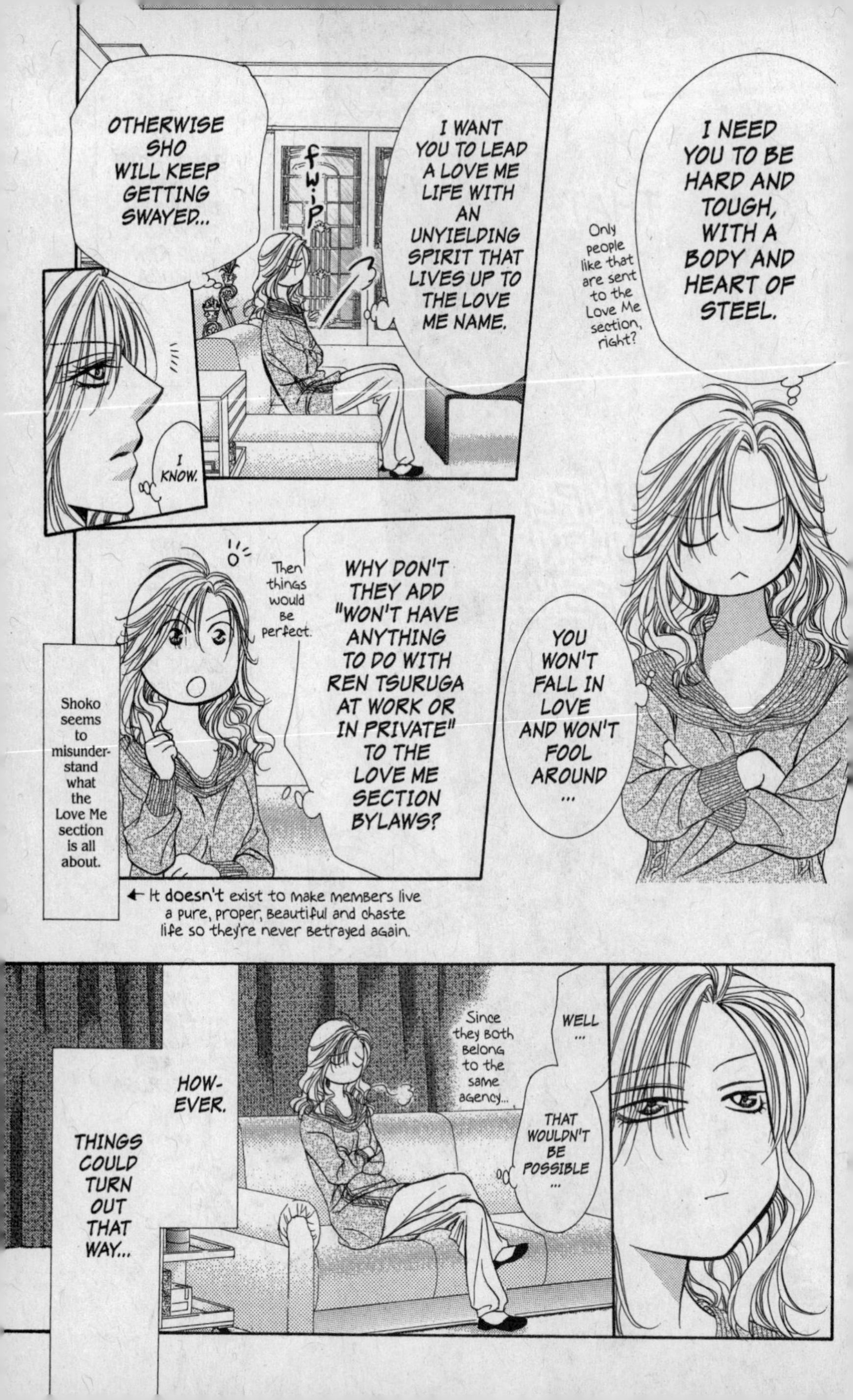
I NEED YOU TO BE HARD AND TOUGH, WITH A BODY AND HEART OF STEEL.
Only people like that are sent to the Love Me section, right?
I WANT YOU TO LEAD A LOVE ME LIFE WITH AN UNYIELDING SPIRIT THAT LIVES UP TO THE LOVE ME NAME.
fwip
OTHERWISE SHO WILL KEEP GETTING SWAYED...
I KNOW.
YOU WON'T FALL IN LOVE AND WON'T FOOL AROUND ...
WHY DON'T THEY ADD "WON'T HAVE ANYTHING TO DO WITH REN TSURUGA AT WORK OR IN PRIVATE" TO THE LOVE ME SECTION BYLAWS?
Then things would be perfect.
Shoko seems to misunderstand what the Love Me section is all about.
← It doesn't exist to make members live a pure, proper, beautiful and chaste life so they're never betrayed again.
WELL ...
THAT WOULDN'T BE POSSIBLE ...
Since they both belong to the same agency...
HOW-EVER.
THINGS COULD TURN OUT THAT WAY...

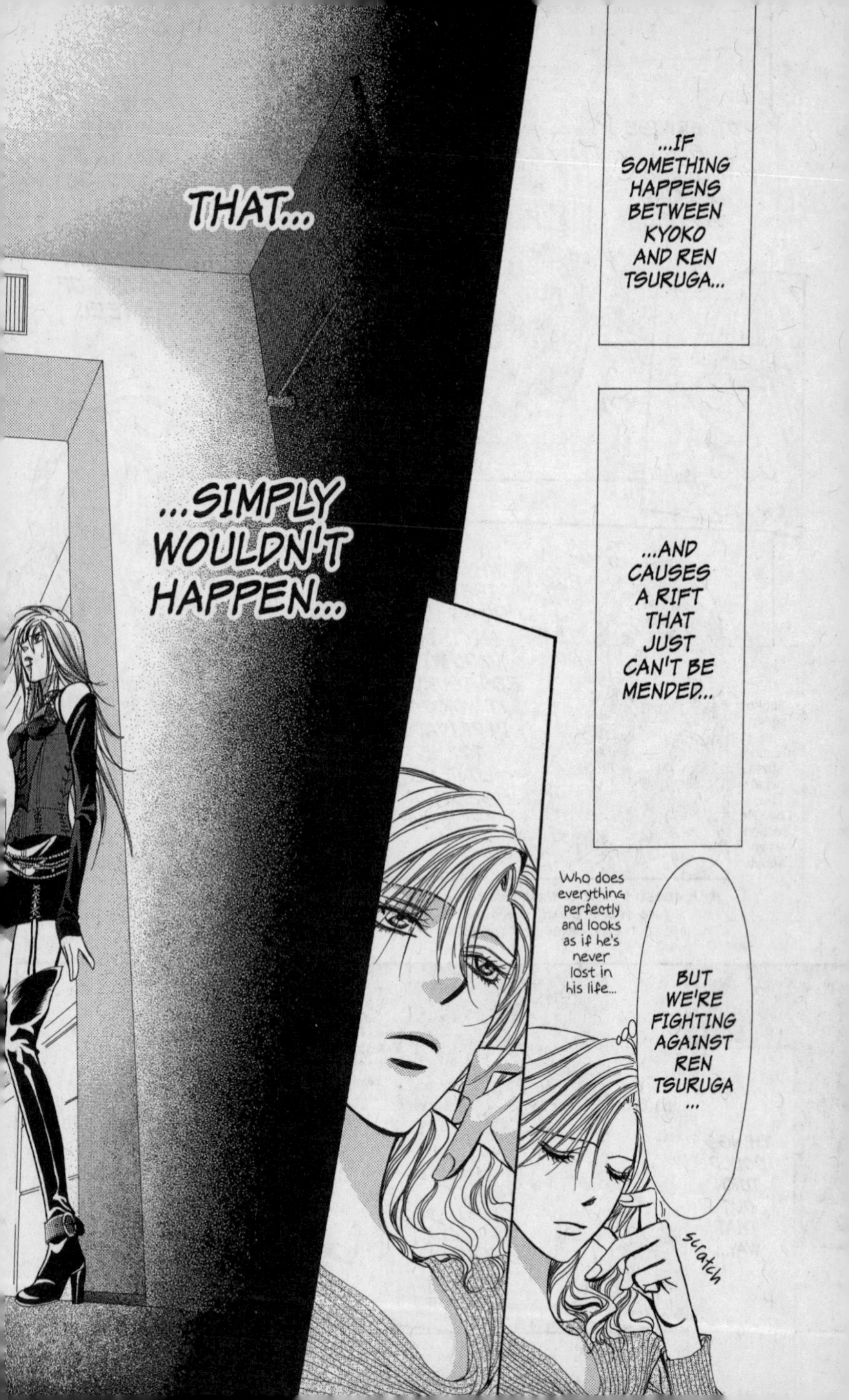
...IF SOMETHING HAPPENS BETWEEN KYOKO AND REN TSURUGA...
...AND CAUSES A RIFT THAT JUST CAN'T BE MENDED...
BUT WE'RE FIGHTING AGAINST REN TSURUGA ...
Who does everything perfectly and looks as if he's never lost in his life...
Scratch
THAT...
...SIMPLY WOULDN'T HAPPEN...

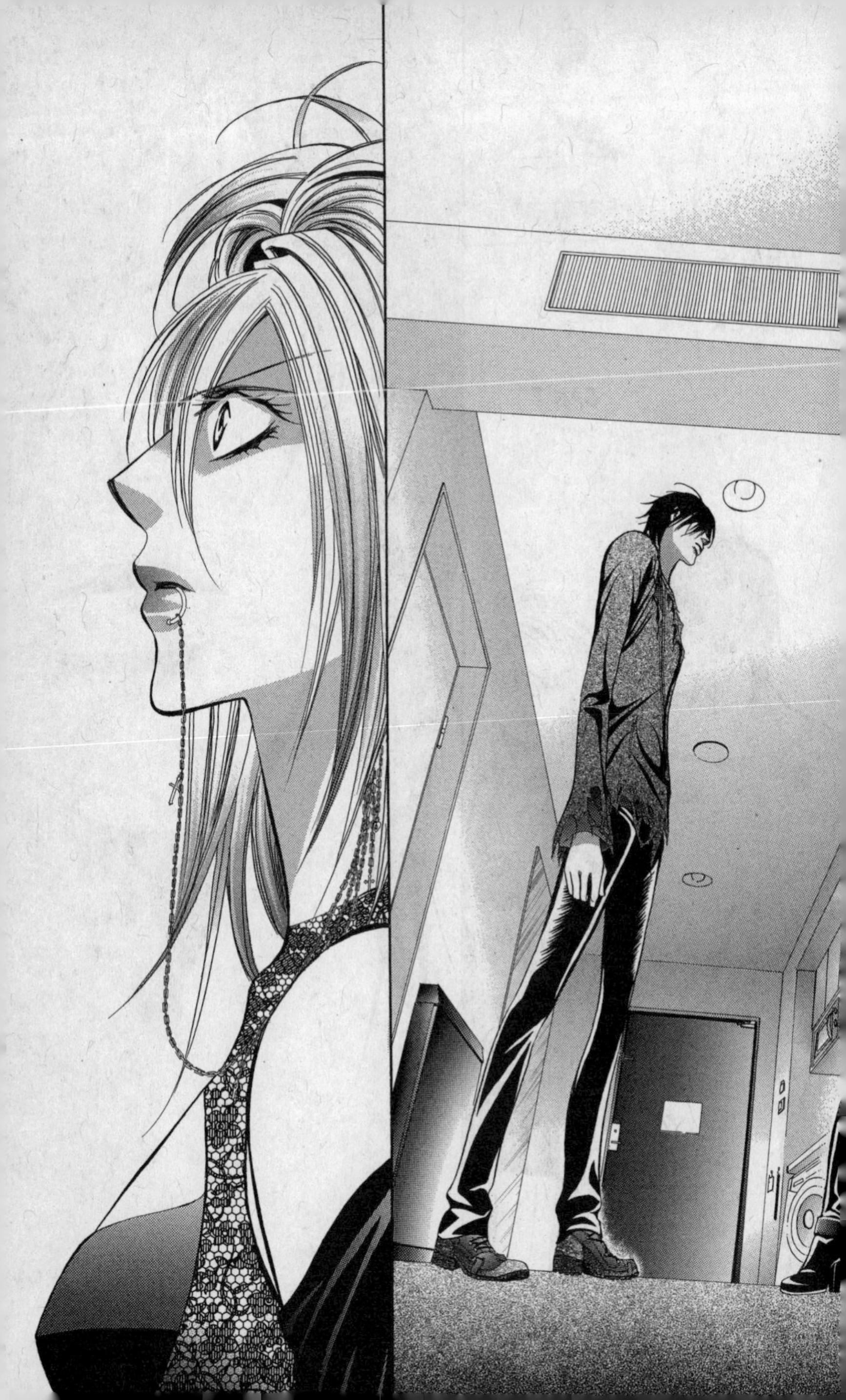

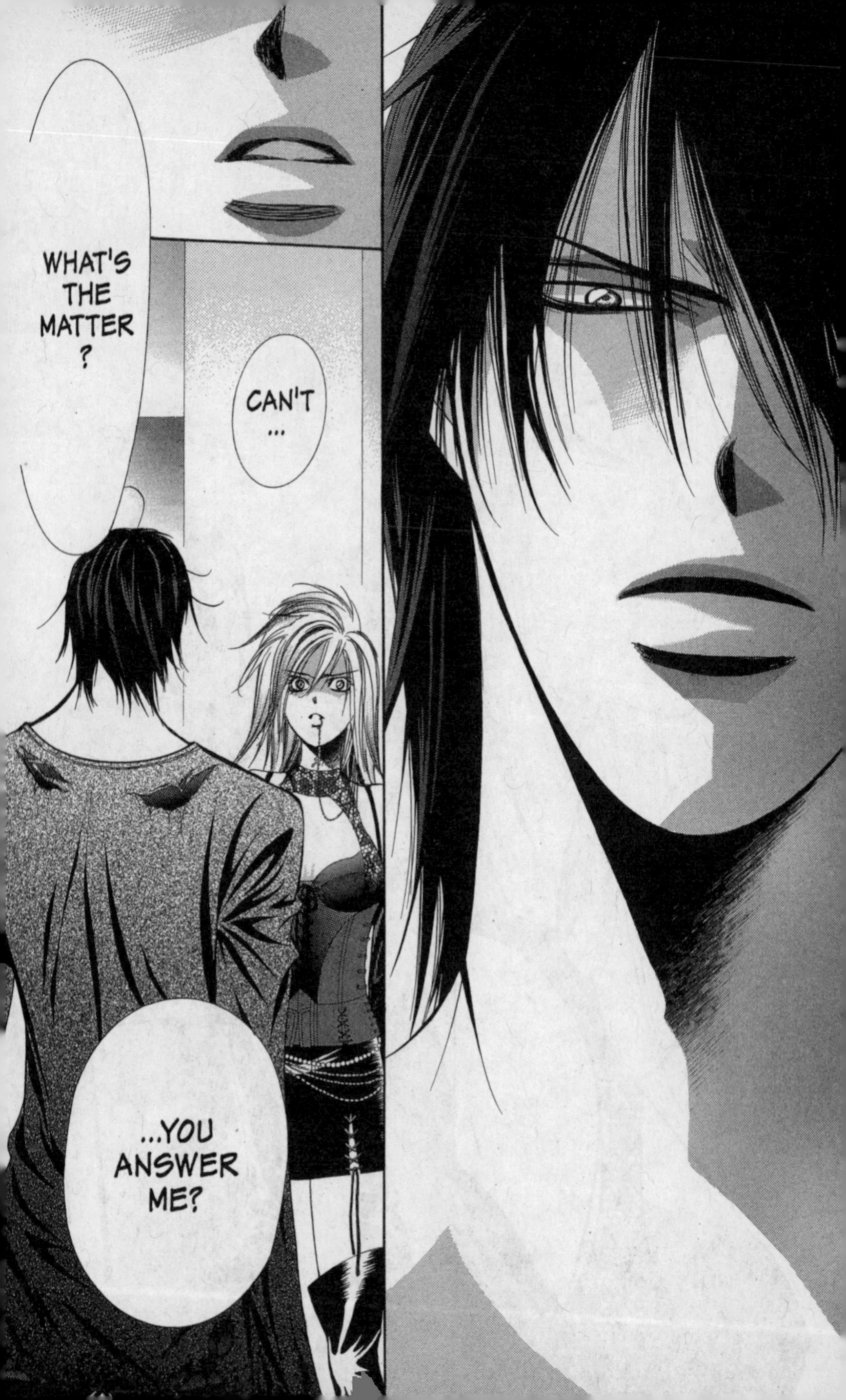
WHAT'S THE MATTER?
CAN'T ...
...YOU ANSWER ME?

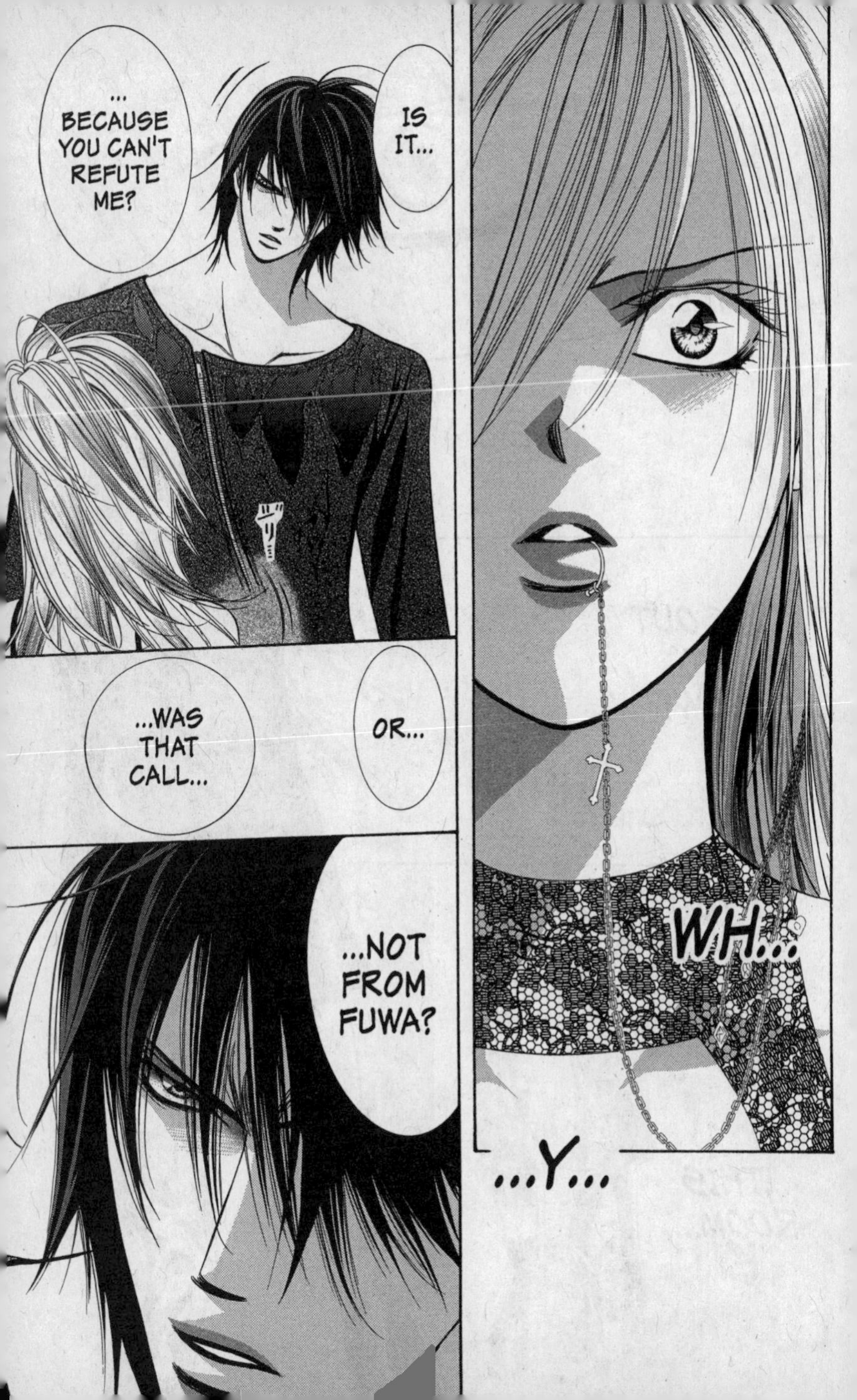
WH...
...Y...
IS IT...
... BECAUSE YOU CAN'T REFUTE ME?
OR...
...WAS THAT CALL...
...NOT FROM FUWA?

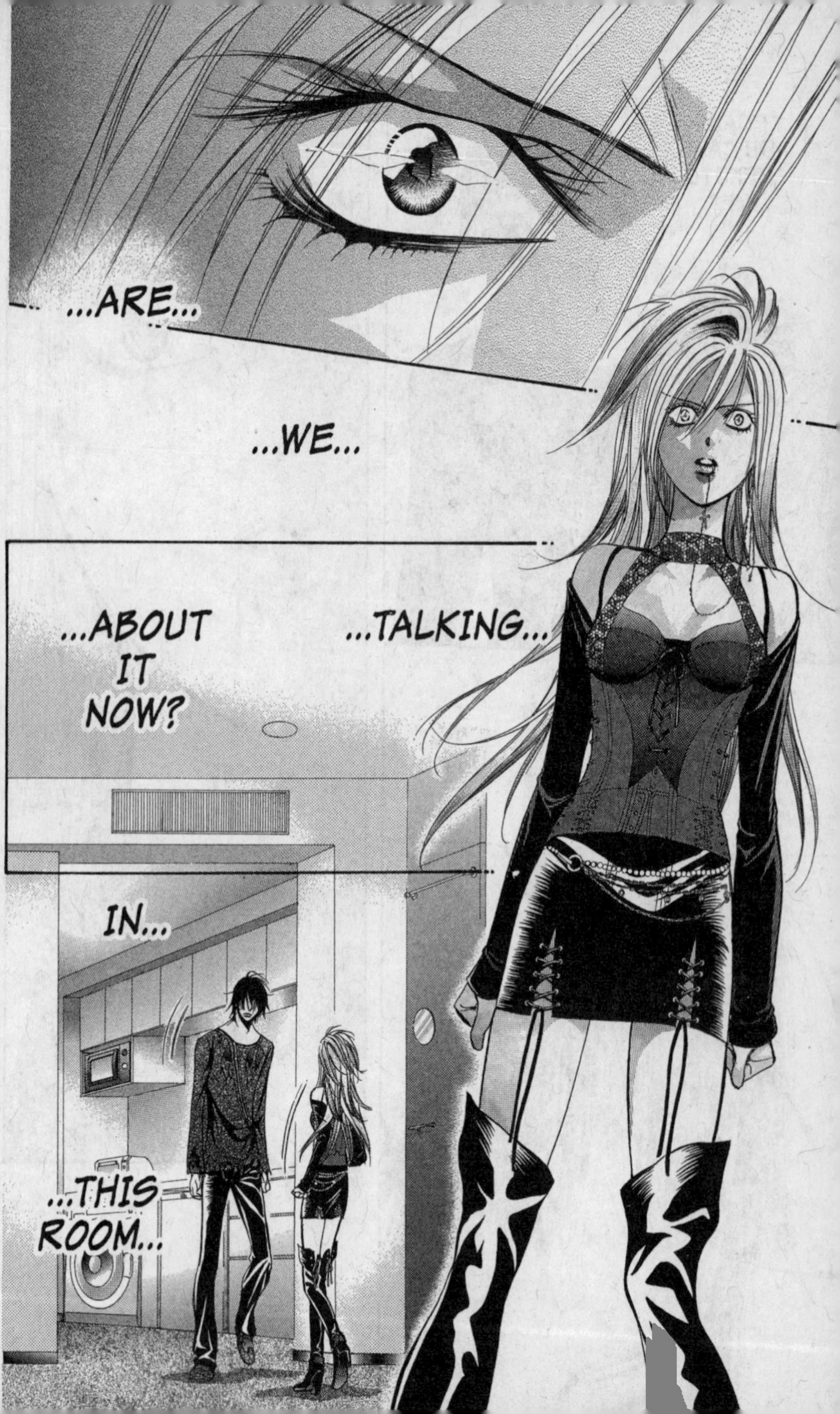
...ARE...
...WE...
...TALKING...
...ABOUT IT NOW?
IN...
...THIS ROOM...

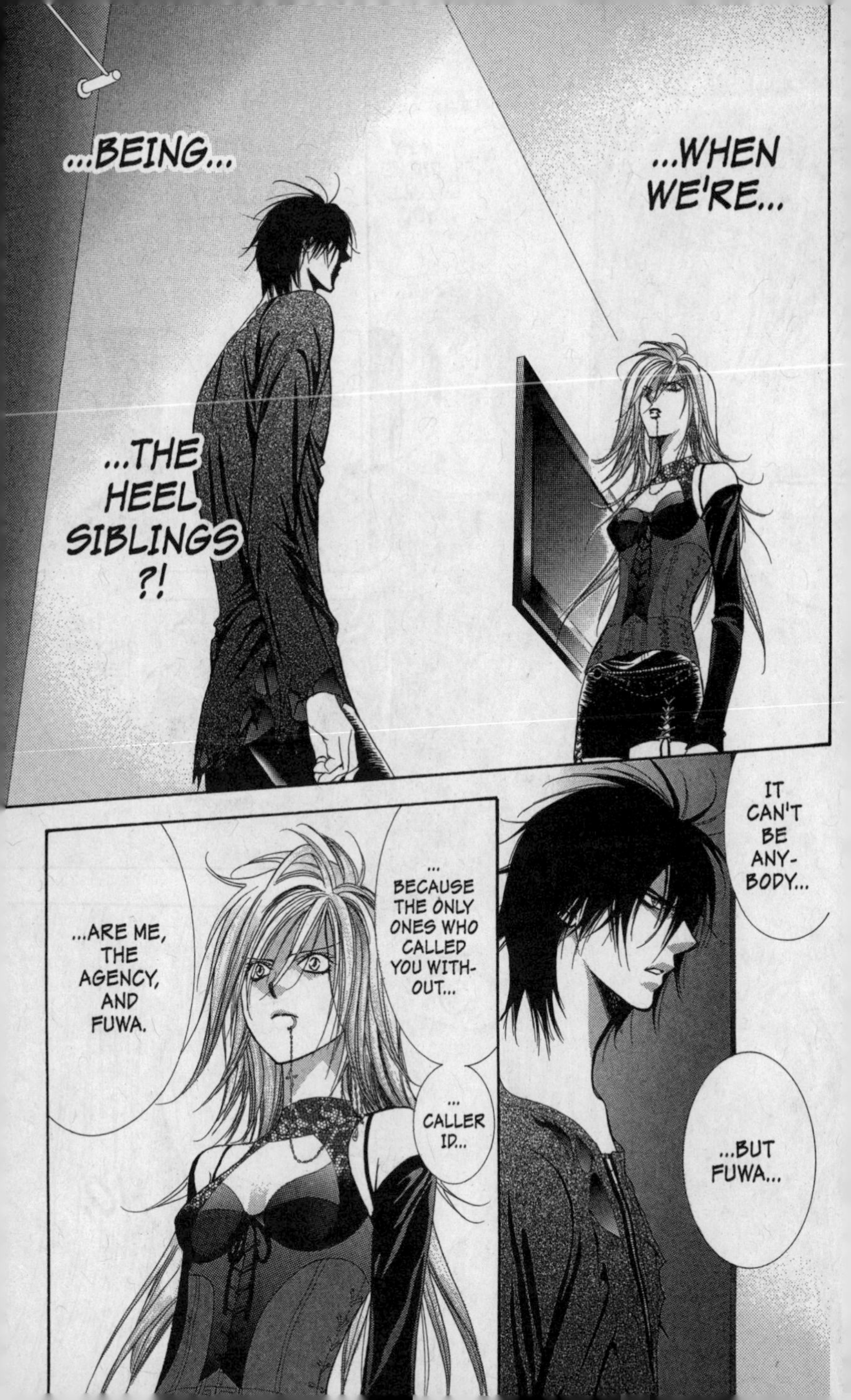
...WHEN WE'RE...
...BEING...
...THE HEEL SIBLINGS?!
IT CAN'T BE ANYBODY...
...BUT FUWA...
...BECAUSE THE ONLY ONES WHO CALLED YOU WITHOUT...
...CALLER ID...
...ARE ME, THE AGENCY, AND FUWA.

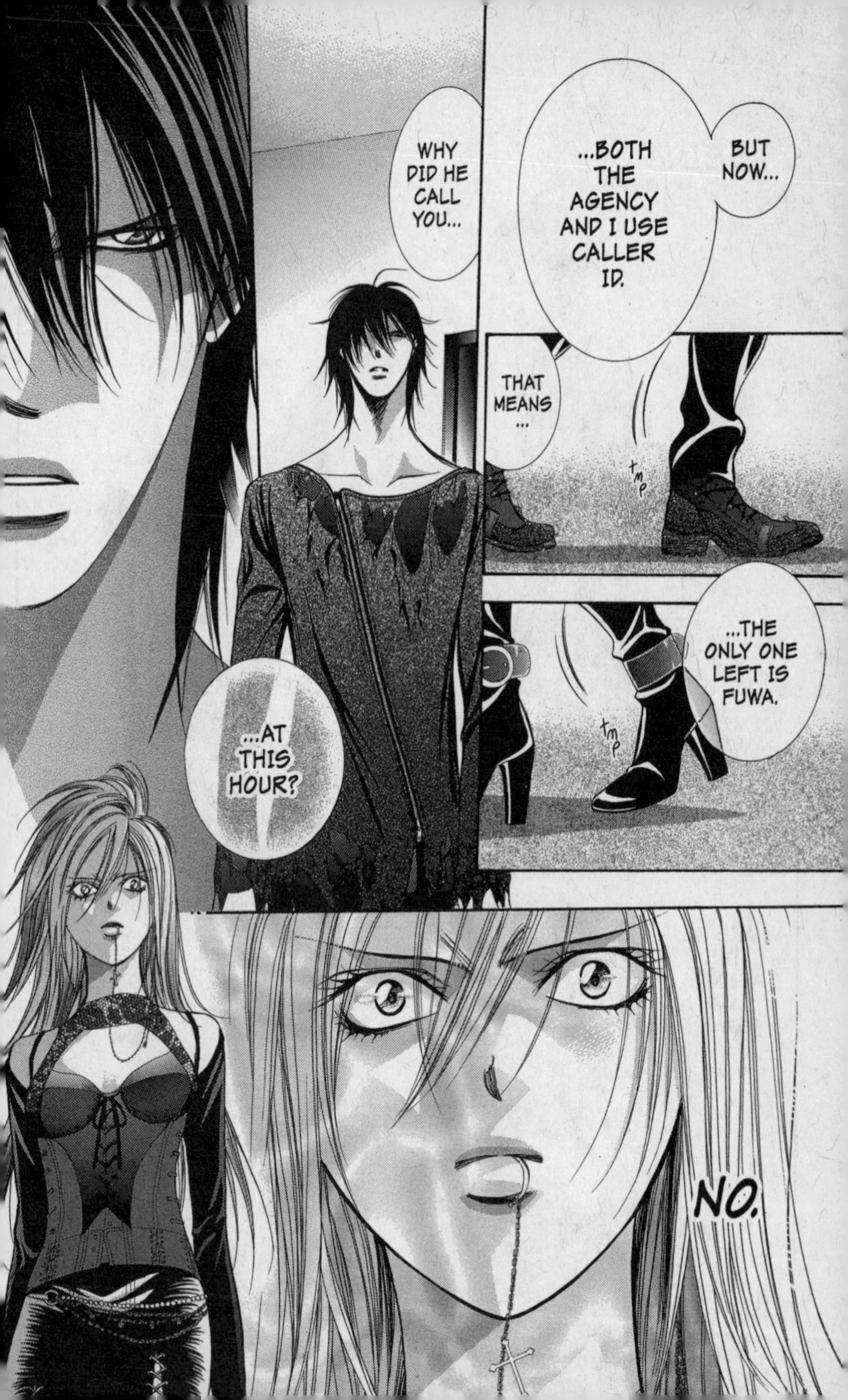
BUT NOW...
...BOTH THE AGENCY AND I USE CALLER ID.
THAT MEANS...
tmp
...THE ONLY ONE LEFT IS FUWA.
tmp
WHY DID HE CALL YOU...
...AT THIS HOUR?
NO.

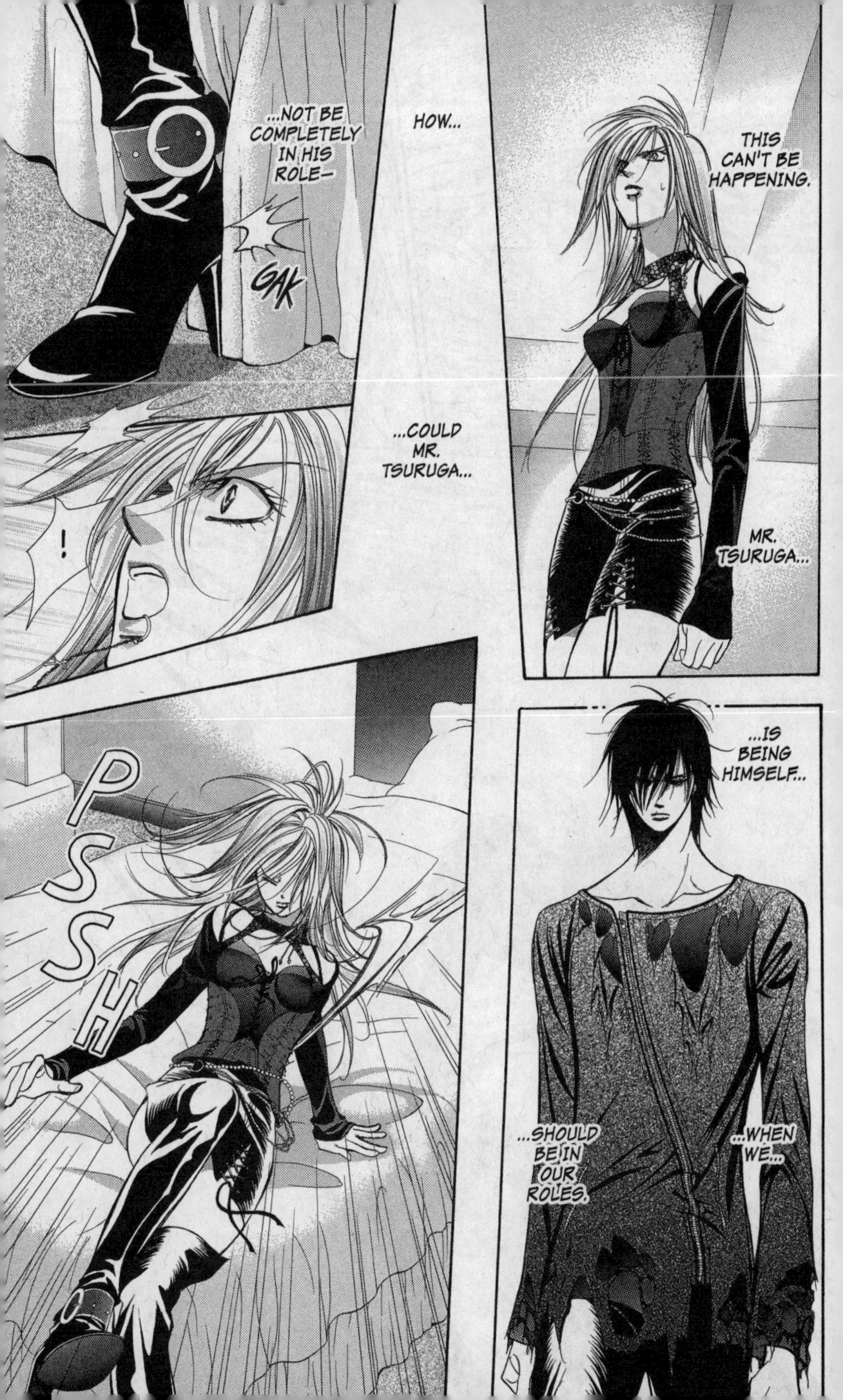
THIS CAN'T BE HAPPENING.
MR. TSURUGA...
HOW...
...COULD MR. TSURUGA...
...NOT BE COMPLETELY IN HIS ROLE—
GAK
!
...IS BEING HIMSELF...
...WHEN WE...
...SHOULD BE IN OUR ROLES.
PSSSH

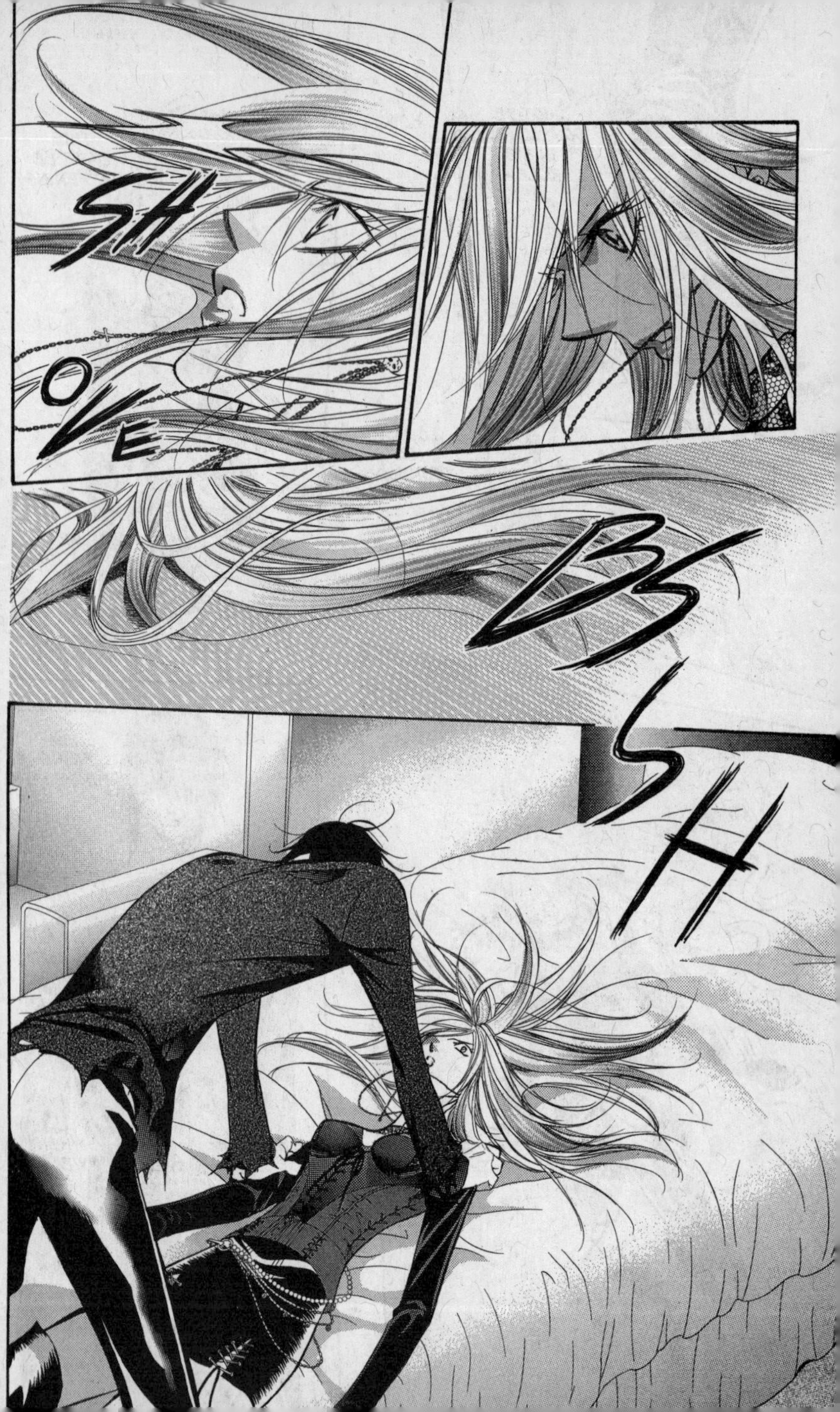
SHOVE
BSSH

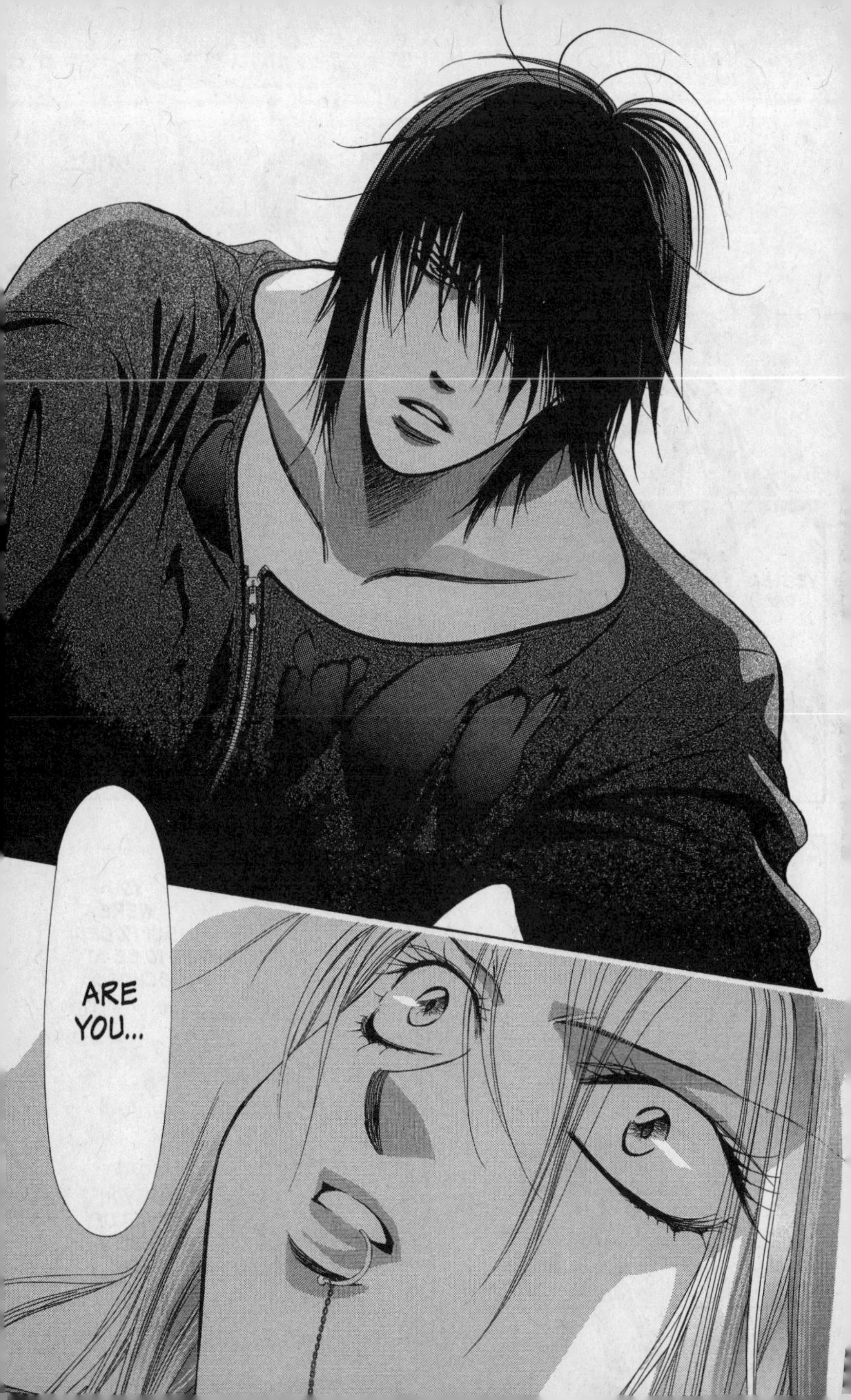
ARE YOU...

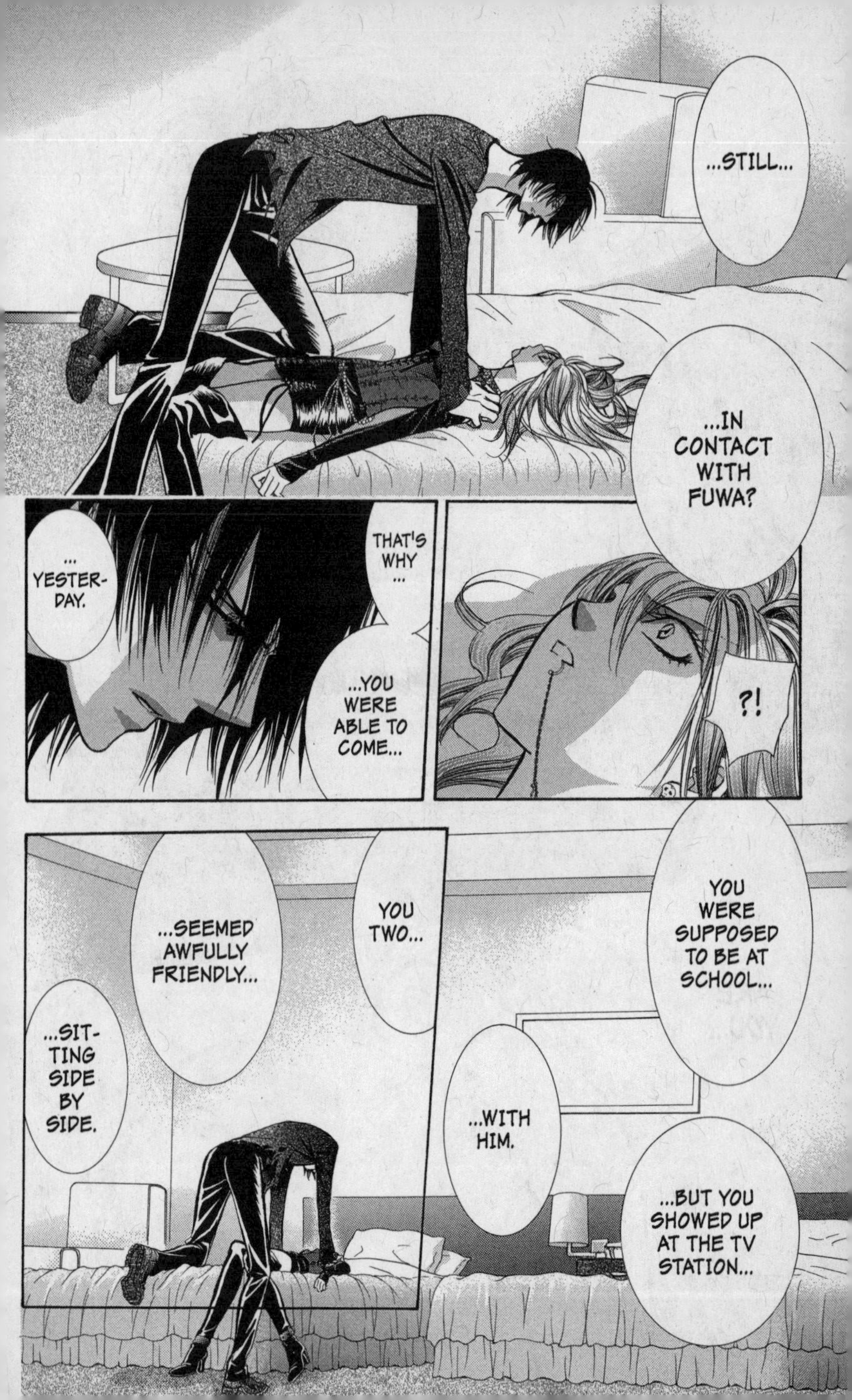
...STILL...
...IN CONTACT WITH FUWA?
?!
THAT'S WHY ...
... YESTER-DAY.
...YOU WERE ABLE TO COME...
YOU WERE SUPPOSED TO BE AT SCHOOL...
...BUT YOU SHOWED UP AT THE TV STATION...
...WITH HIM.
YOU TWO...
...SEEMED AWFULLY FRIENDLY...
...SIT-TING SIDE BY SIDE.

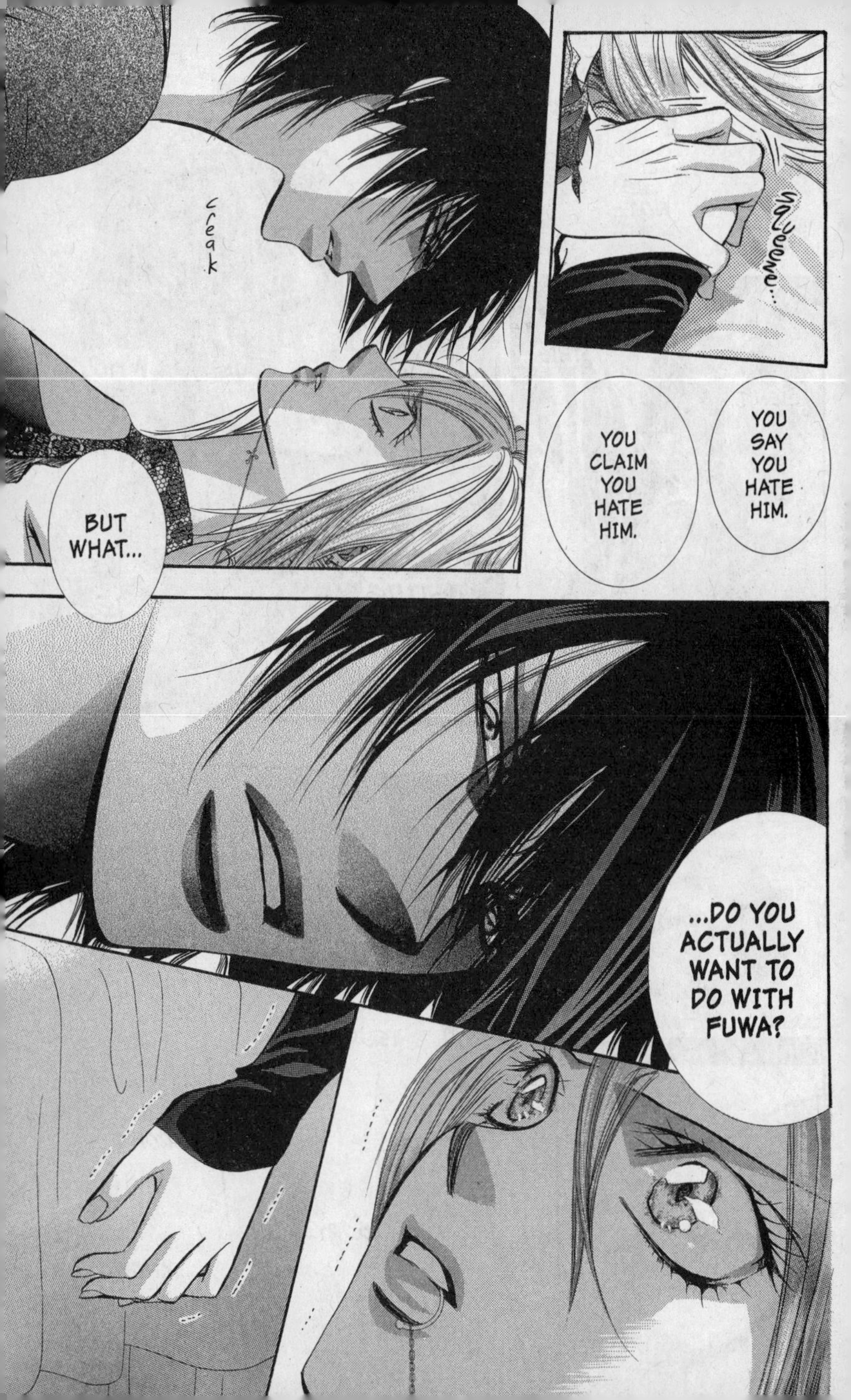
squeeze...
creak
YOU SAY YOU HATE HIM.
YOU CLAIM YOU HATE HIM.
BUT WHAT...
...DO YOU ACTUALLY WANT TO DO WITH FUWA?

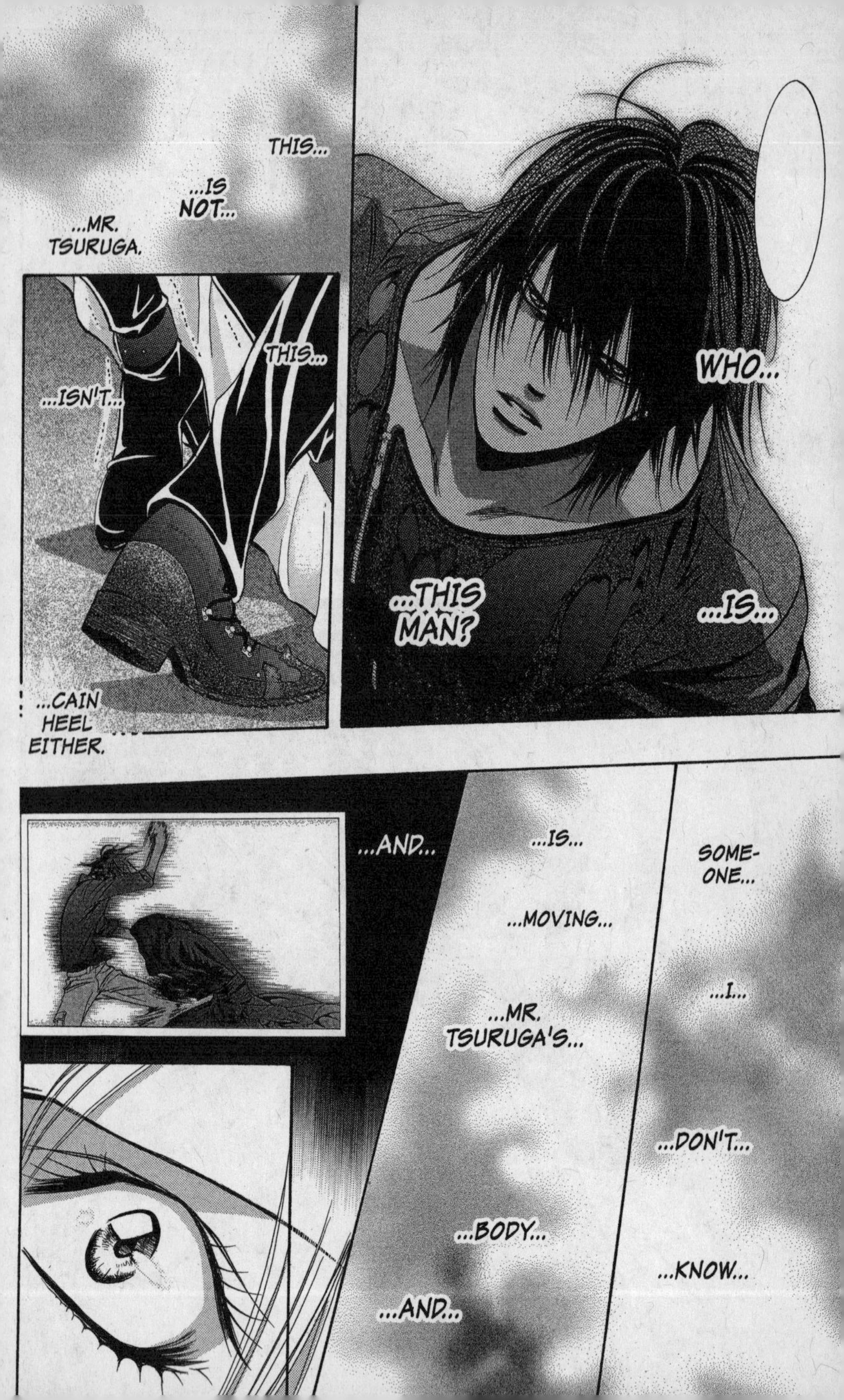
WHO...
...IS...
...THIS MAN?
THIS...
...IS NOT...
...MR. TSURUGA.
THIS...
...ISN'T...
...CAIN HEEL EITHER.
SOME-ONE...
...I...
...DON'T...
...KNOW...
...IS...
...MOVING...
...MR. TSURUGA'S...
...BODY...
...AND...
...AND...

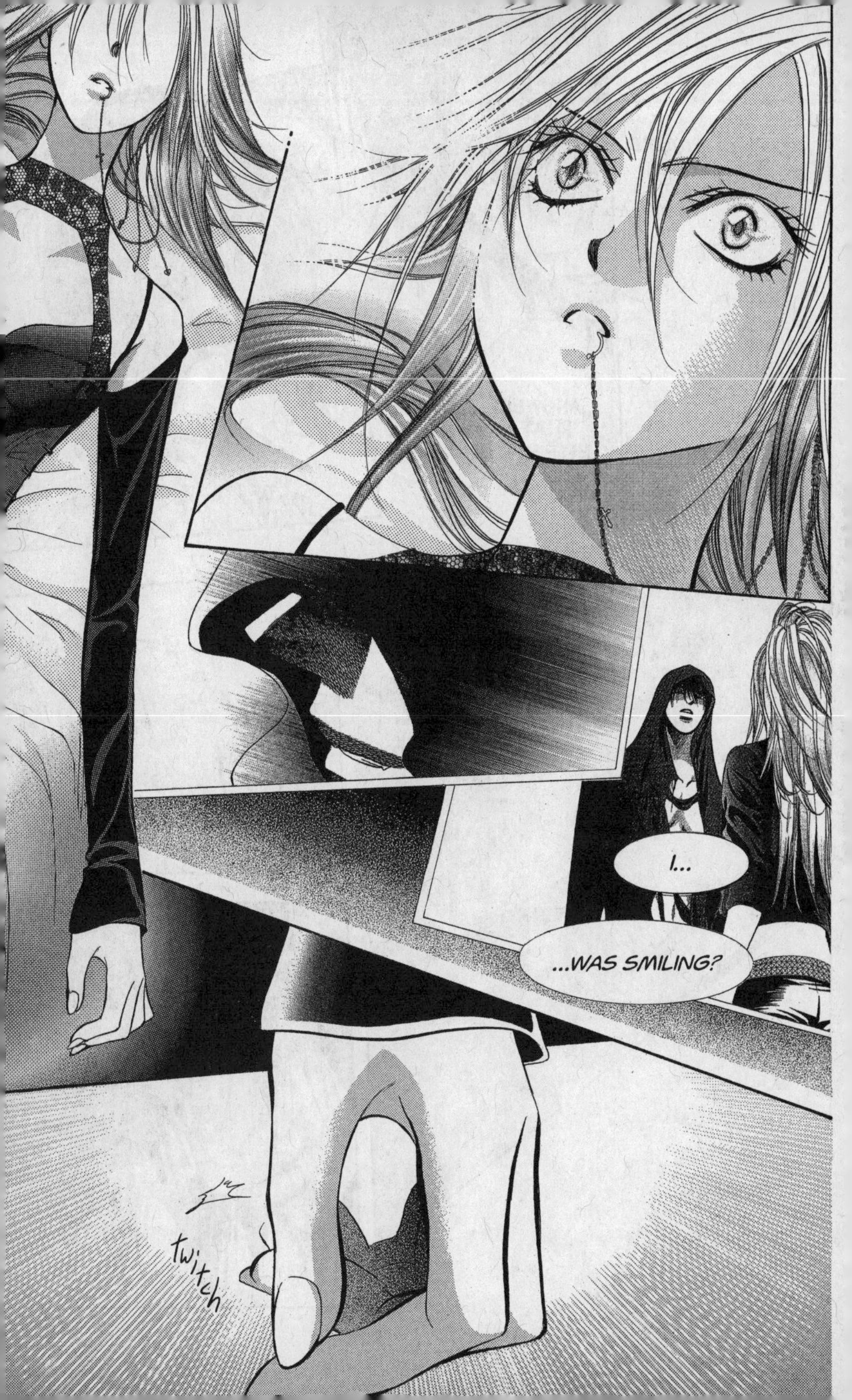
I...
...WAS SMILING?
twitch

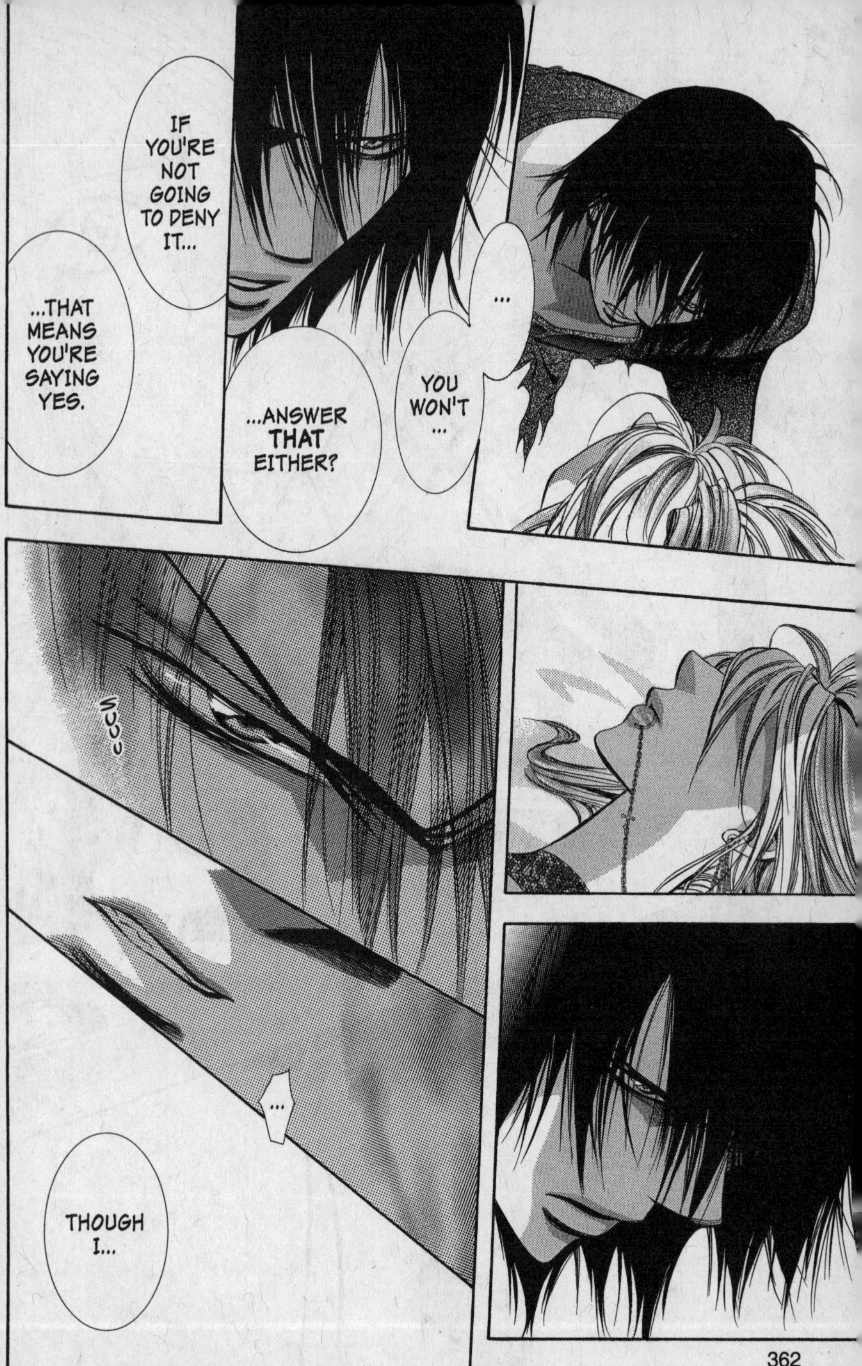
...
YOU WON'T ...
...ANSWER THAT EITHER?
IF YOU'RE NOT GOING TO DENY IT...
...THAT MEANS YOU'RE SAYING YES.
SUUU
...
THOUGH I...

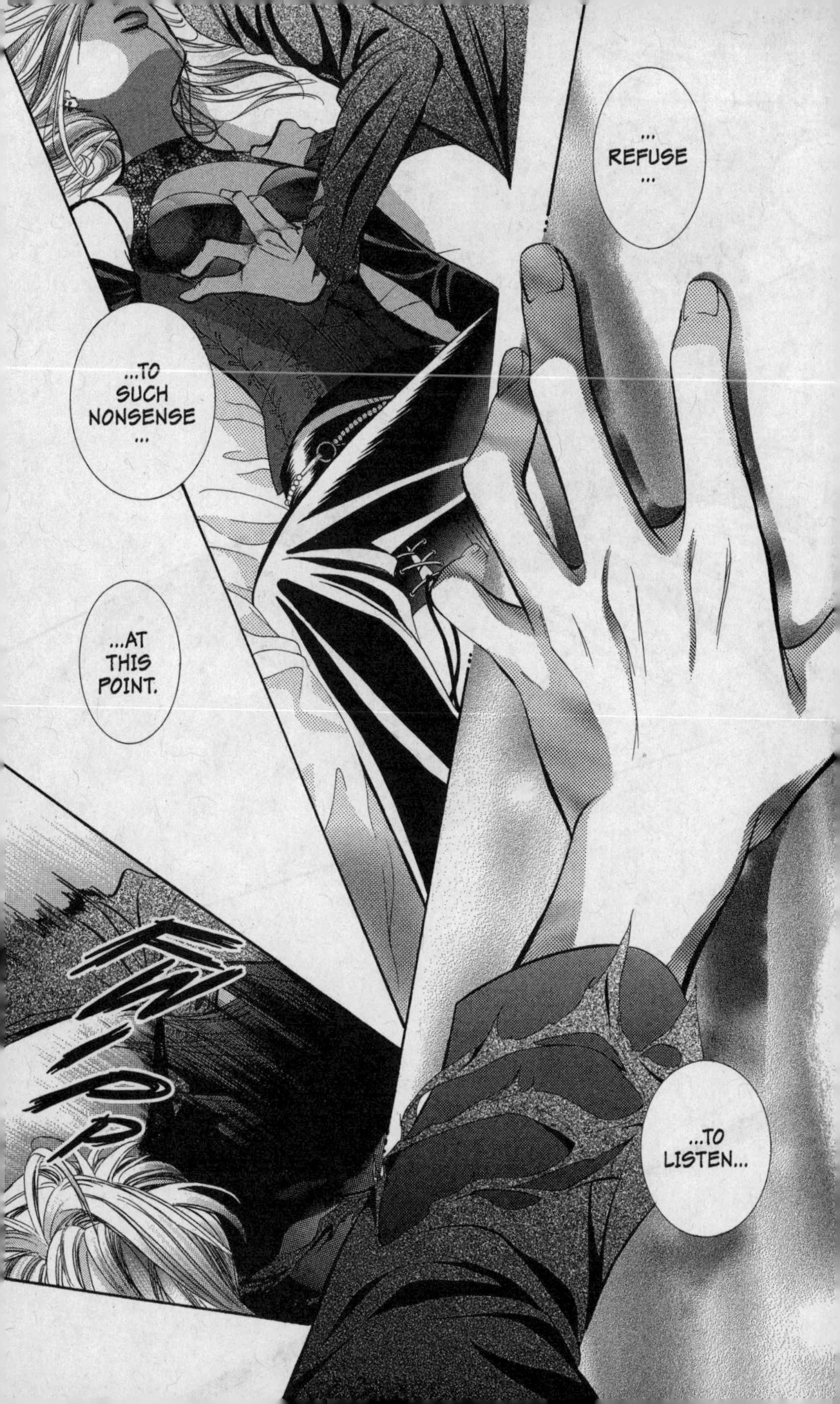
...REFUSE...
...TO LISTEN...
...TO SUCH NONSENSE...
...AT THIS POINT.
FWIPP

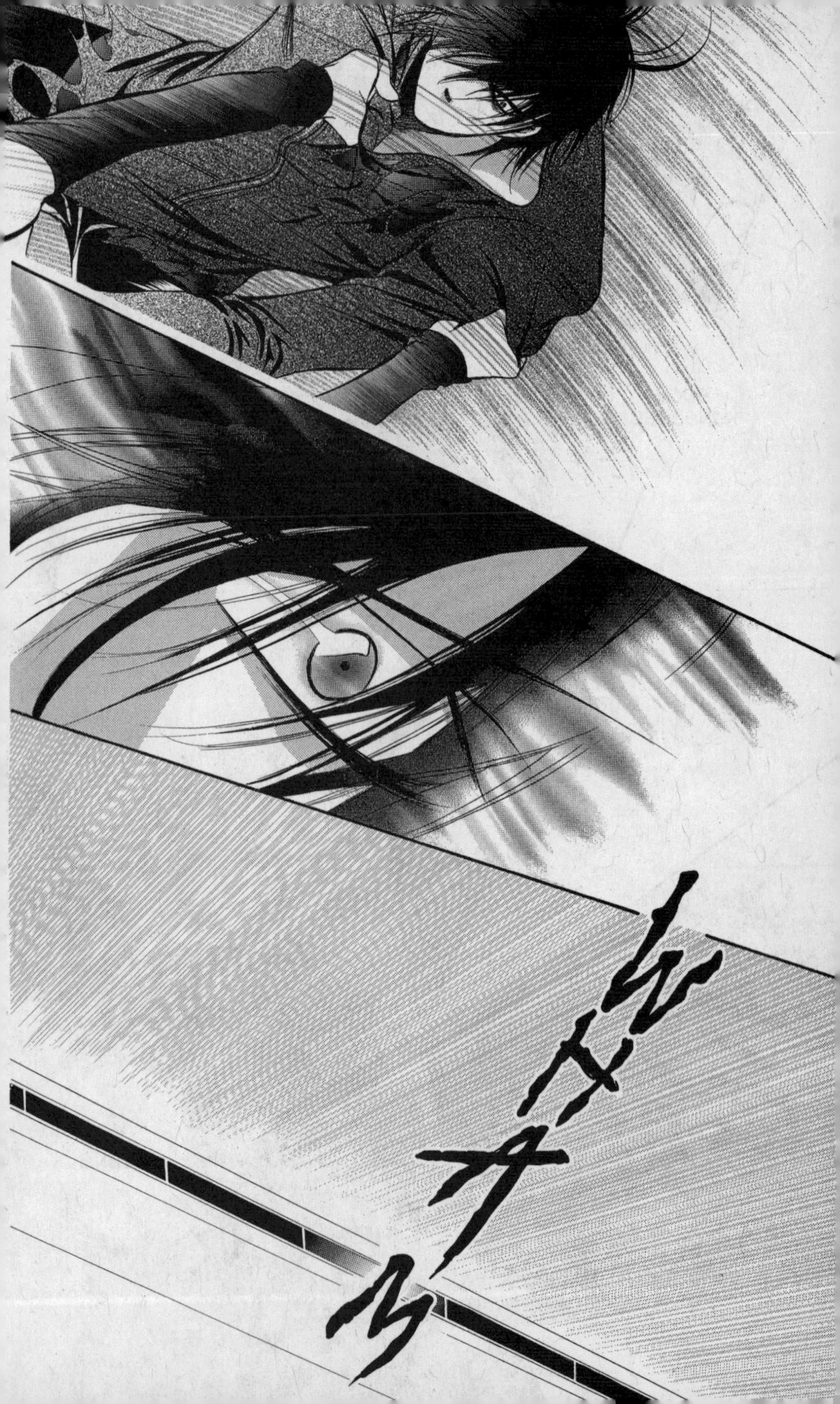
WHAM

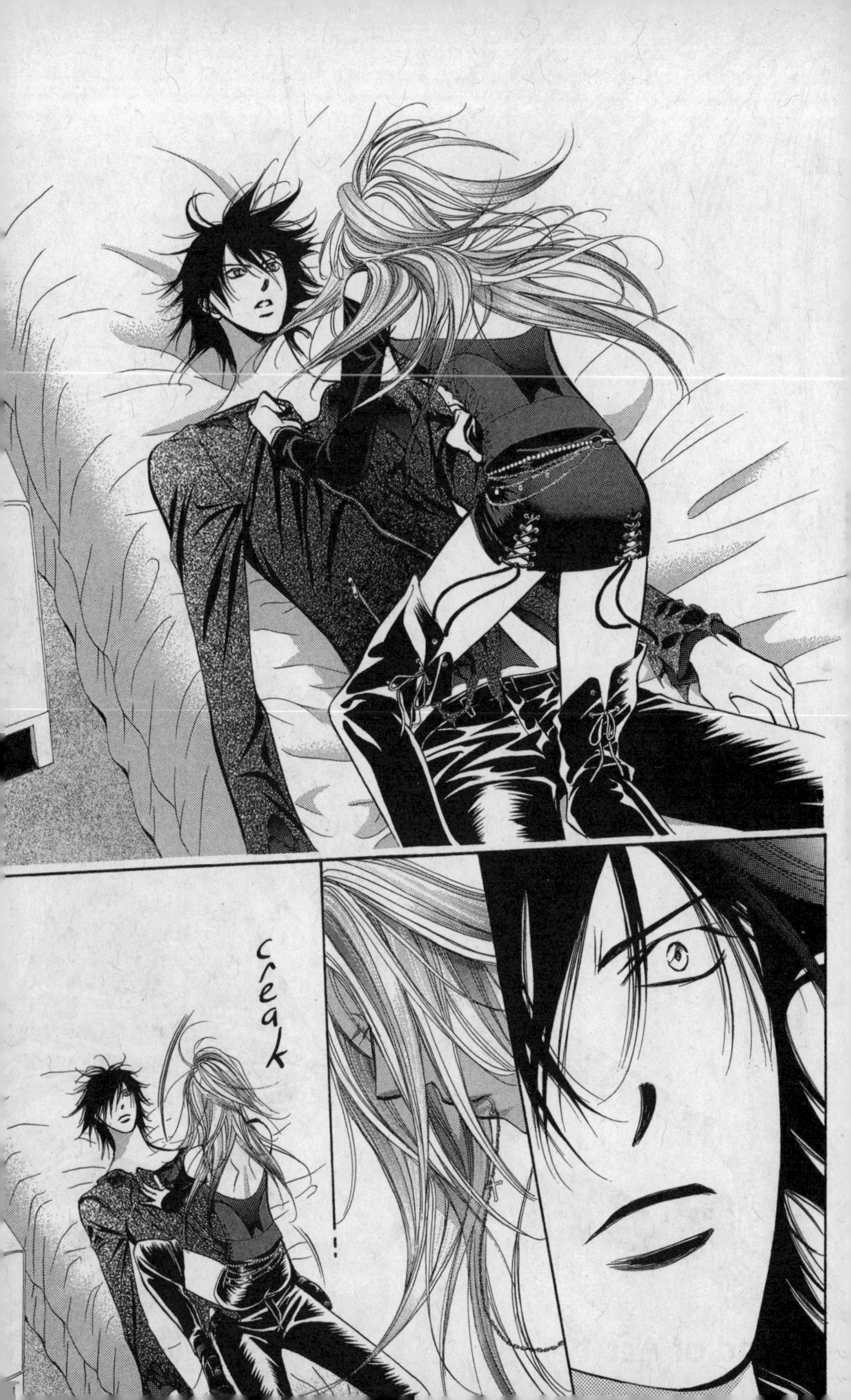

...!
creak

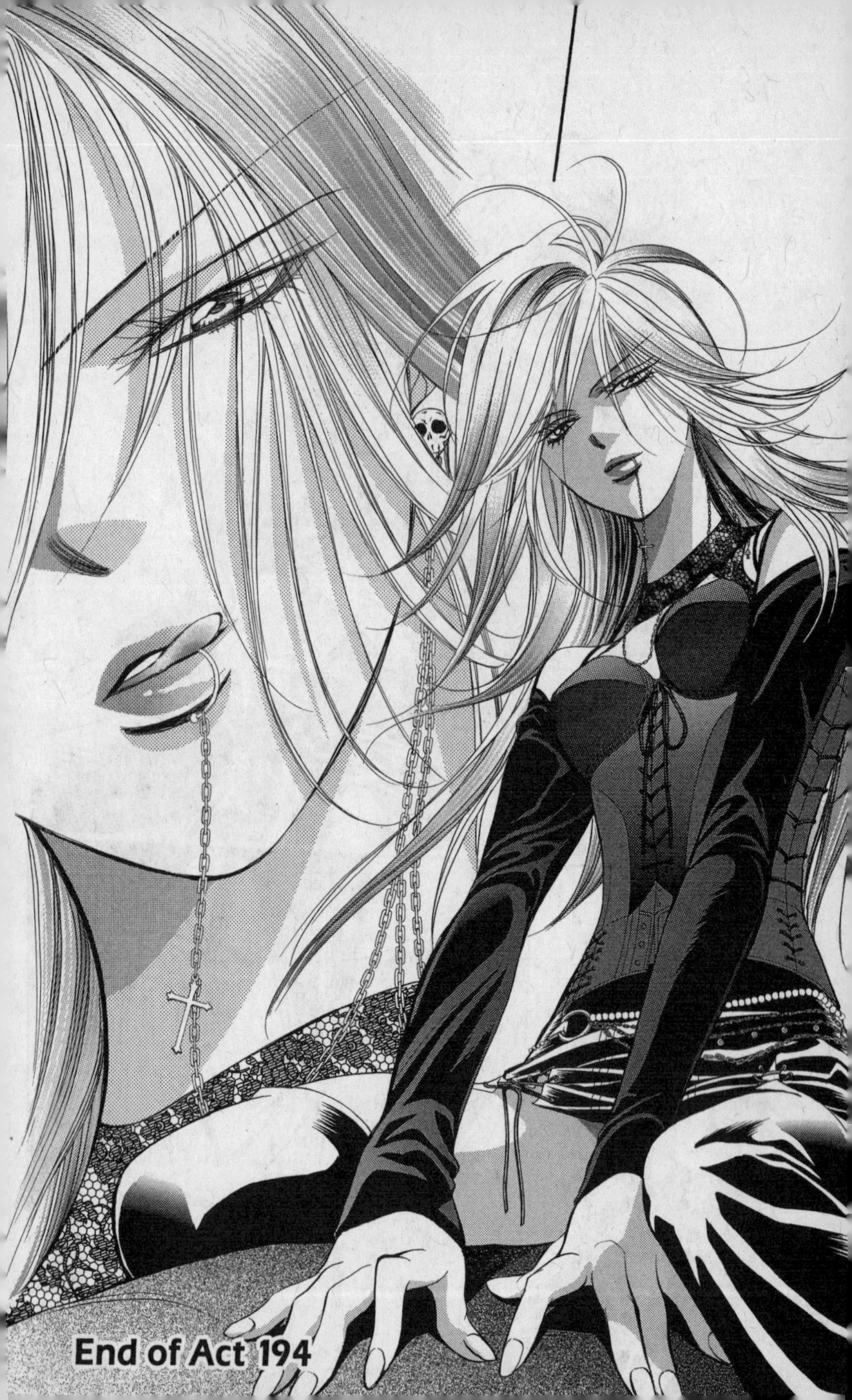
End of Act 194

Shojo Beat

Skip·Beat!

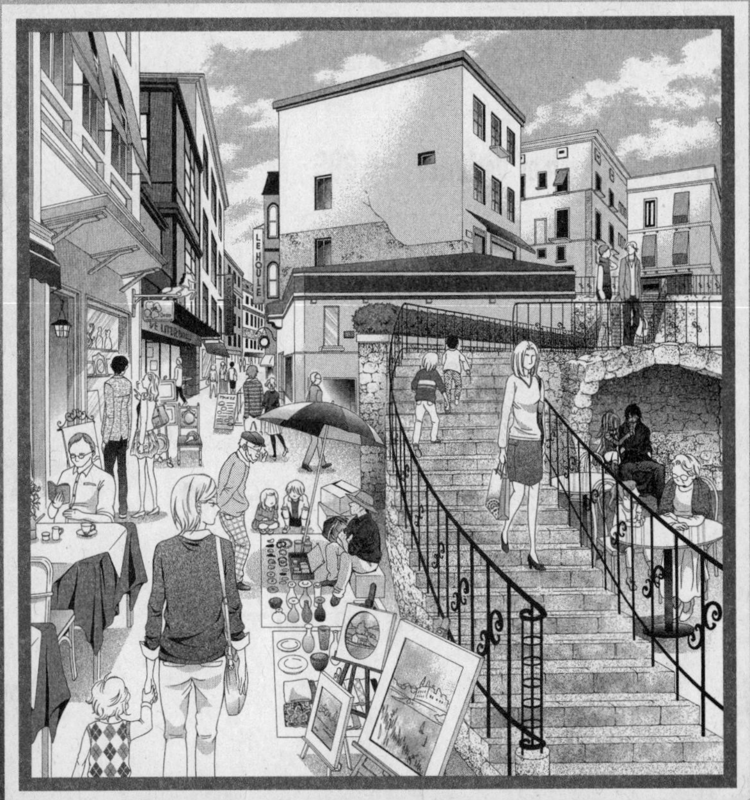

Skip·Beat!

Volume 33

CONTENTS

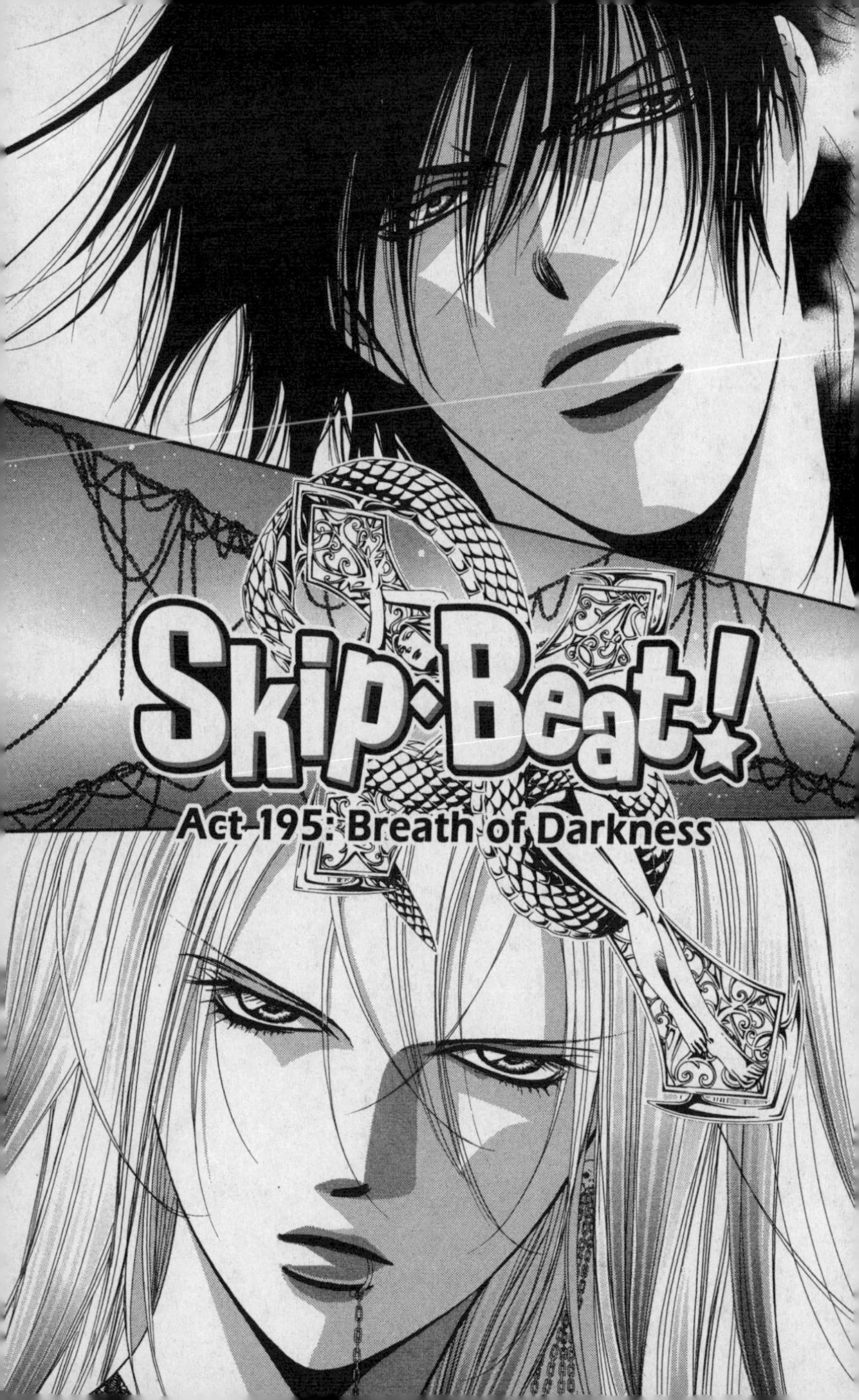
Skip·Beat!
Act 195: Breath of Darkness

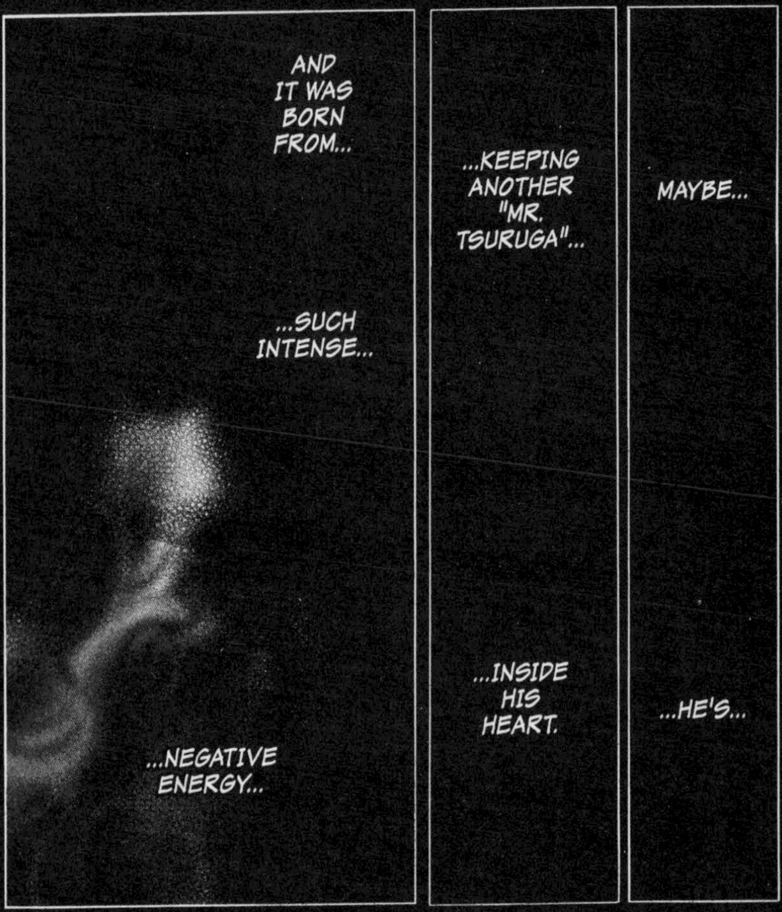
MAYBE...
...HE'S...
...KEEPING ANOTHER "MR. TSURUGA"...
...INSIDE HIS HEART.
AND IT WAS BORN FROM...
...SUCH INTENSE...
...NEGATIVE ENERGY...

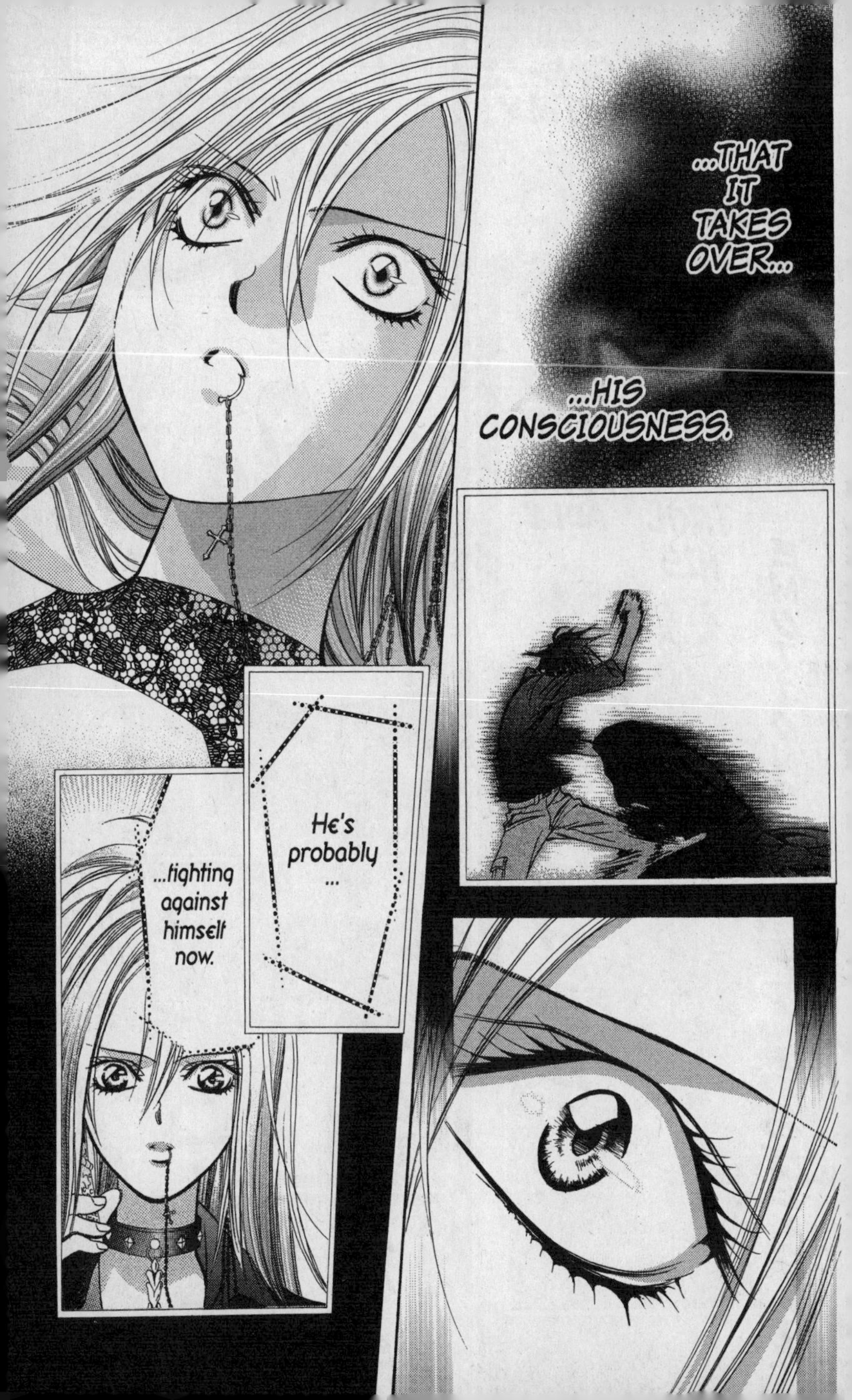
...THAT IT TAKES OVER...
...HIS CONSCIOUSNESS.
He's probably ...
...fighting against himself now.

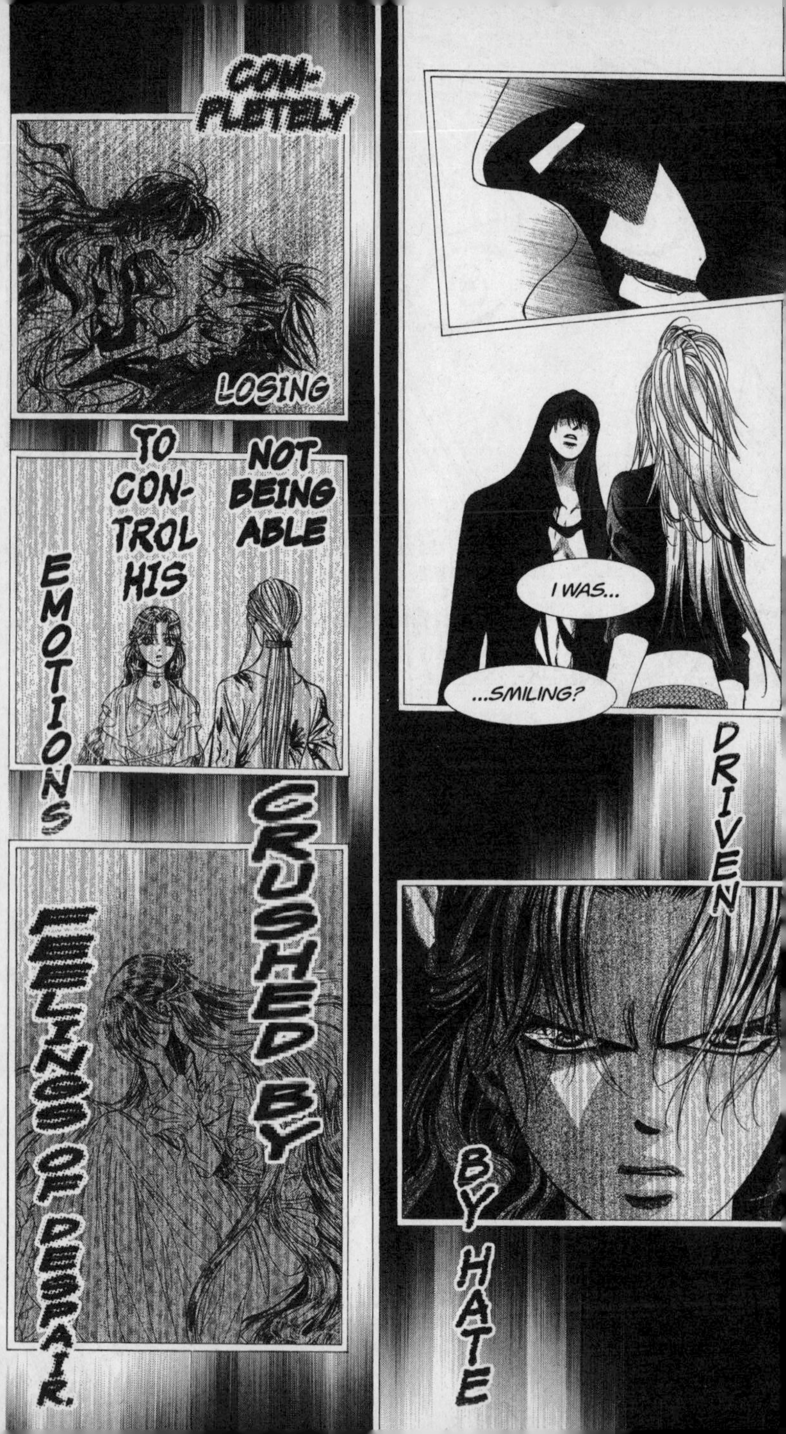
I WAS...
...SMILING?
DRIVEN BY HATE
COM-PLETELY LOSING
NOT BEING ABLE TO CON-TROL HIS EMOTIONS
CRUSHED BY FEELINGS OF DESPAIR.

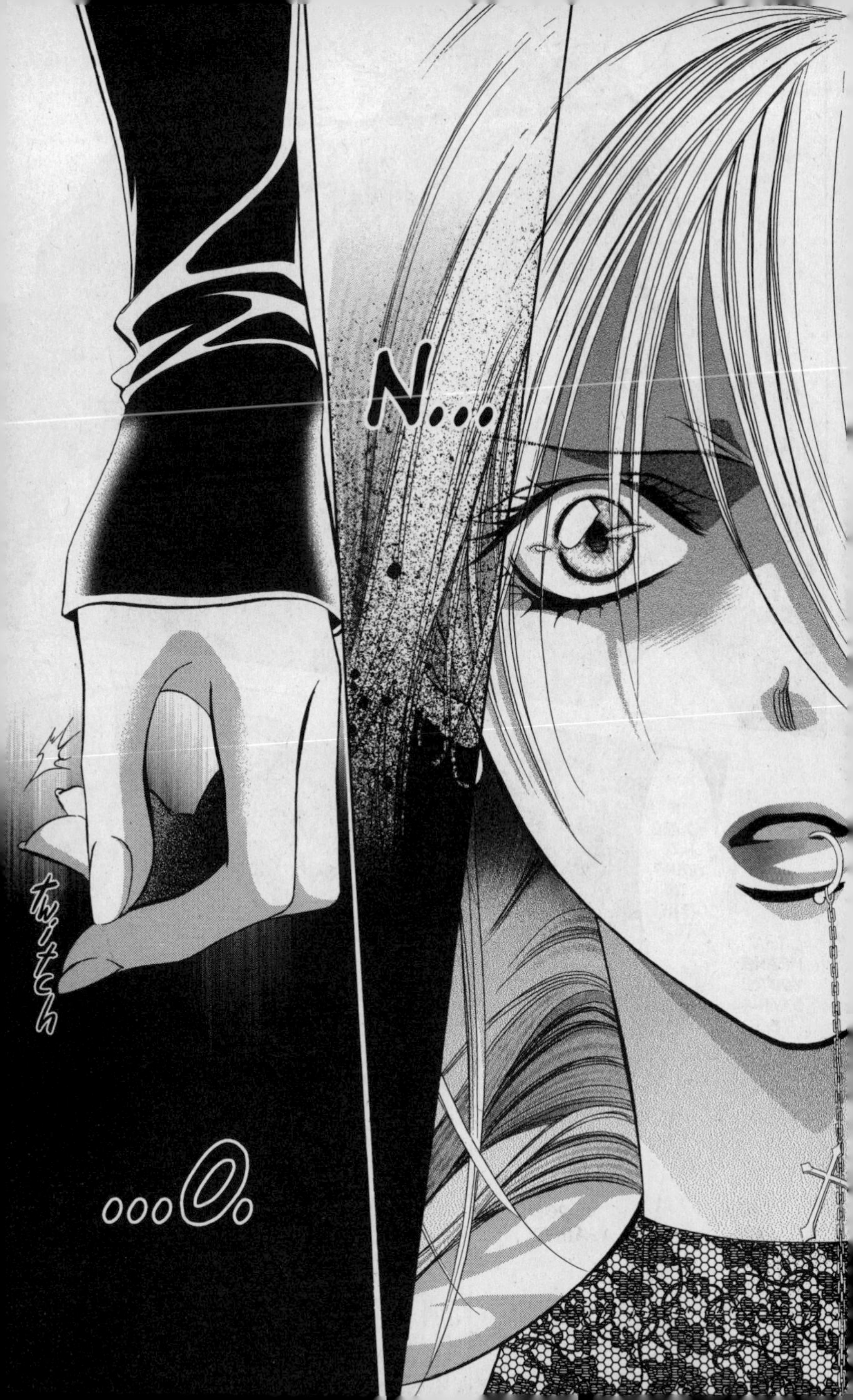
N...
twitch
oooO.

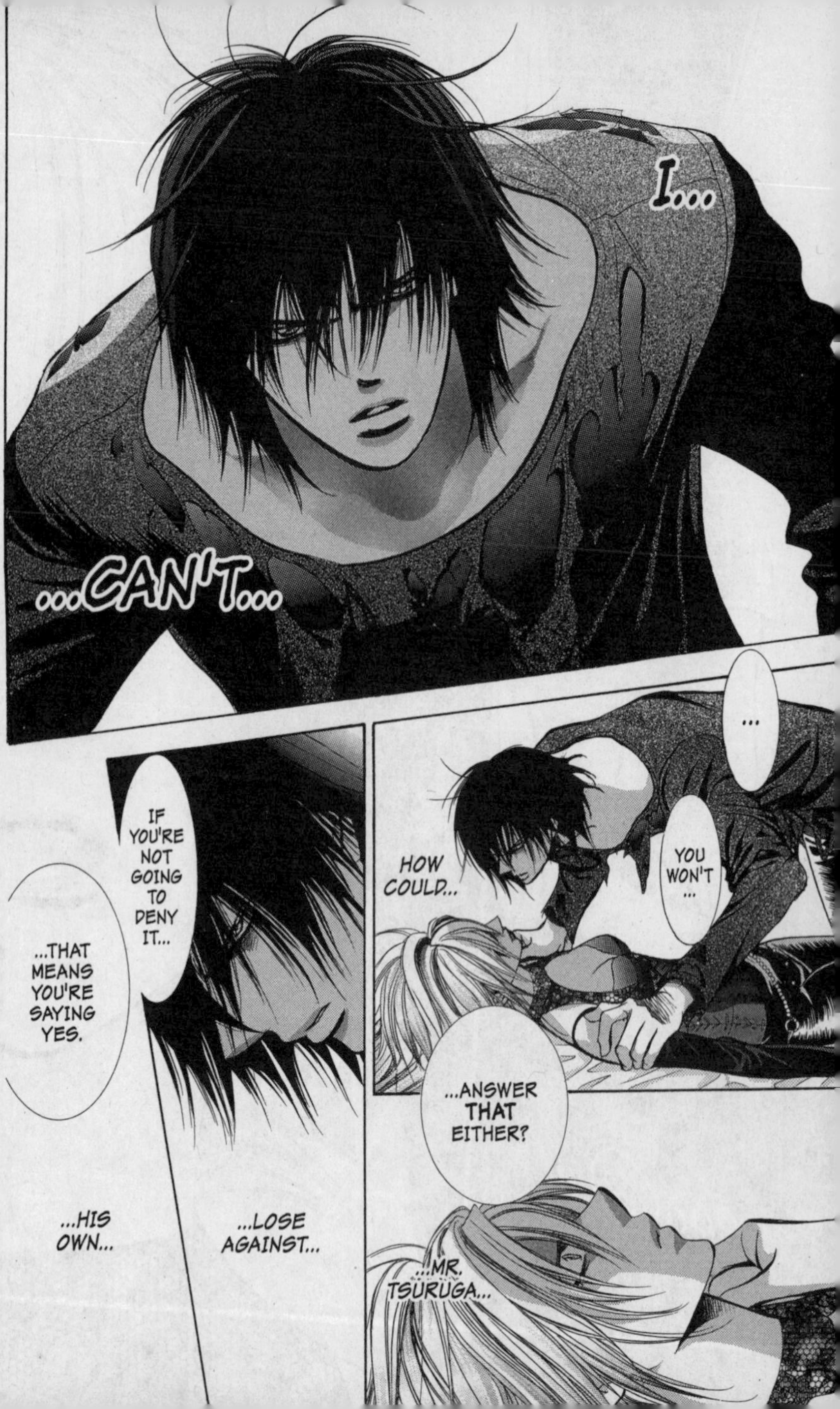
I...
...CAN'T...
...
YOU WON'T ...
HOW COULD...
...ANSWER THAT EITHER?
IF YOU'RE NOT GOING TO DENY IT...
...THAT MEANS YOU'RE SAYING YES.
...MR. TSURUGA...
...LOSE AGAINST...
...HIS OWN...

...
...DARK-
NESS?

THOUGH
...

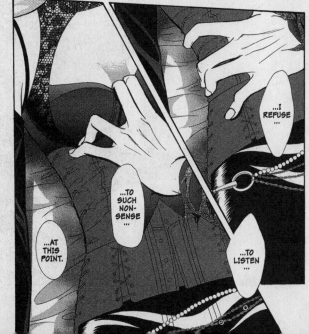

...I REFUSE
...

...TO
SUCH
NON-
SENSE
...

...AT
THIS
POINT.

...TO
LISTEN
...

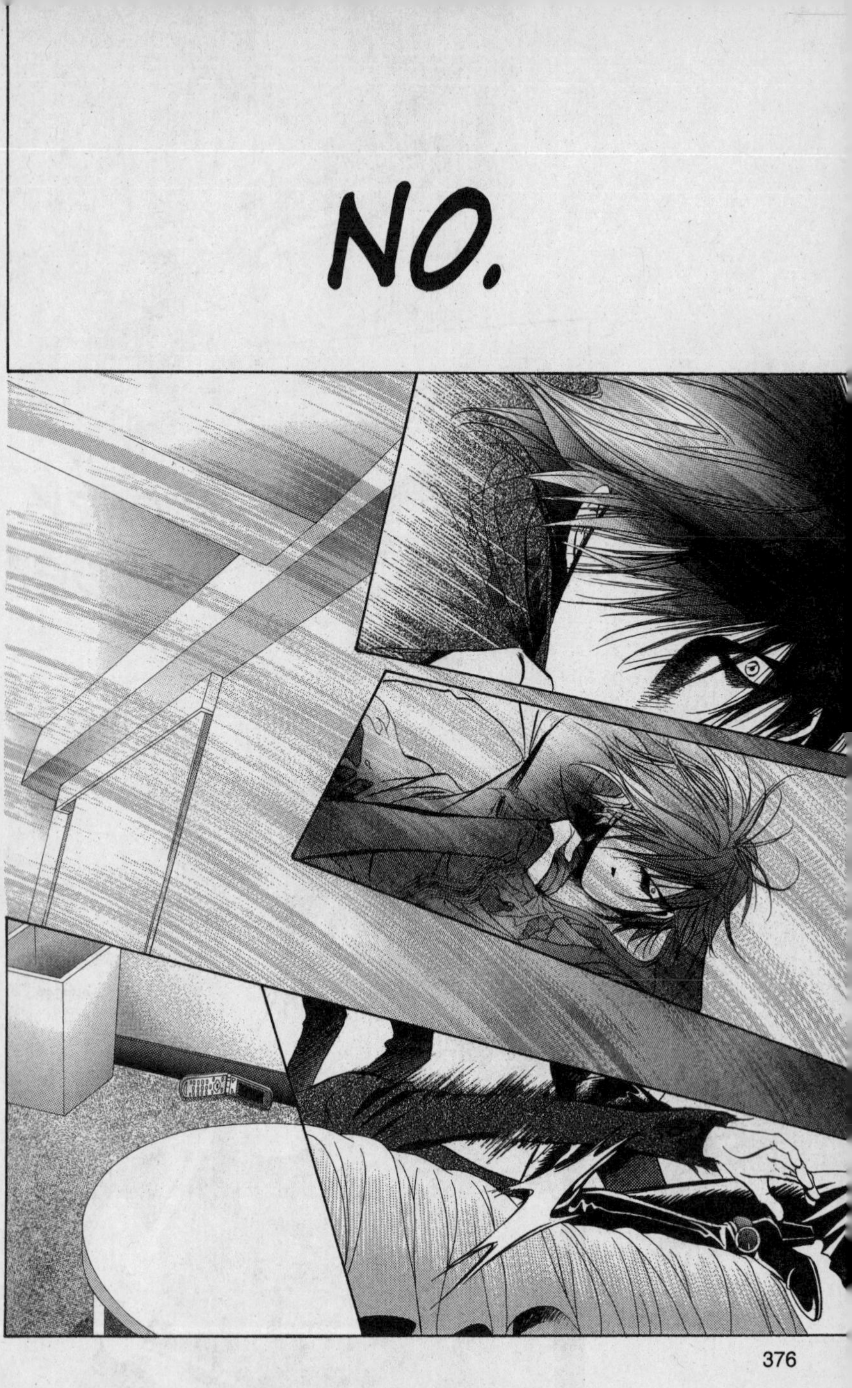
NO.

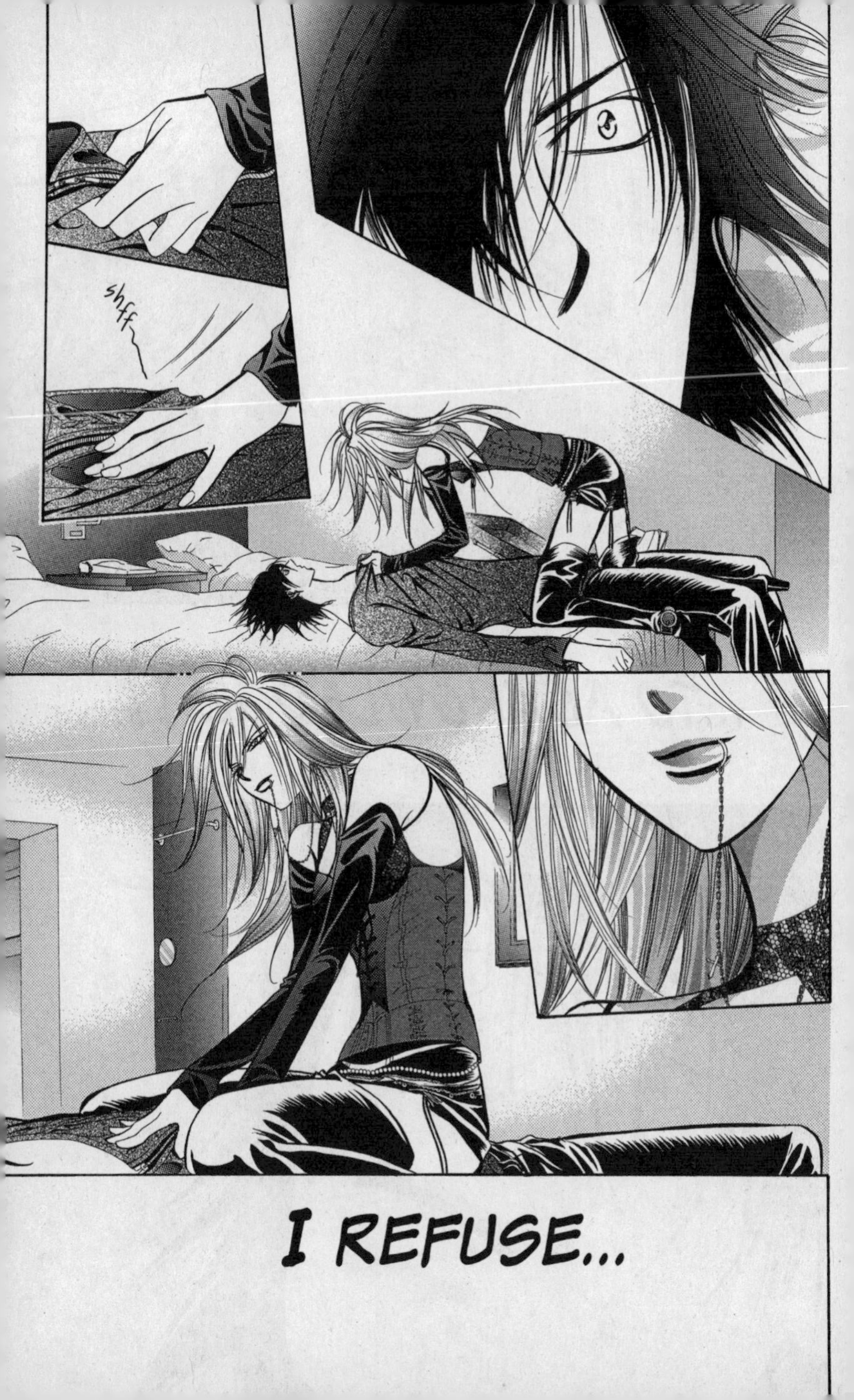
shff~
I REFUSE...

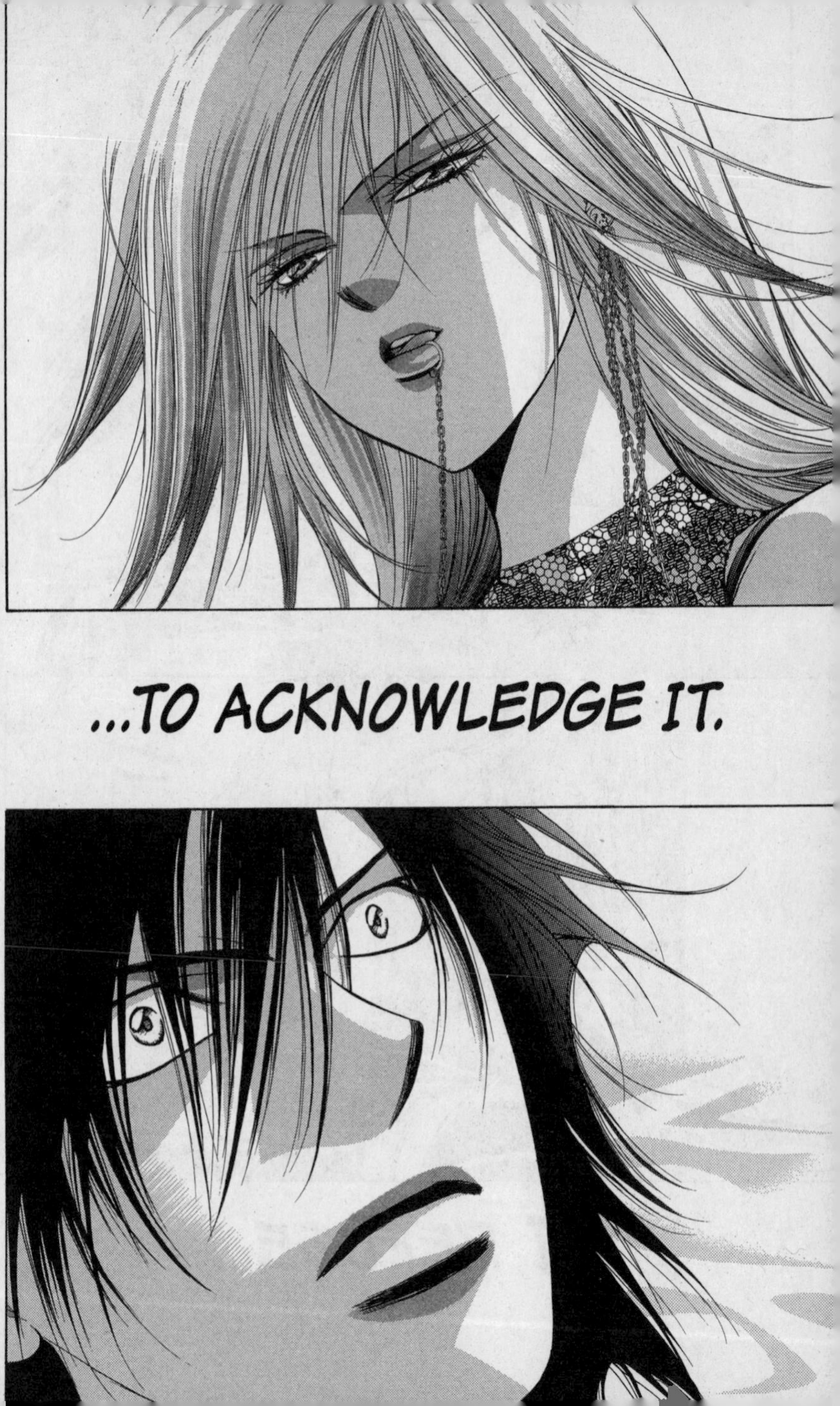
...TO ACKNOWLEDGE IT.

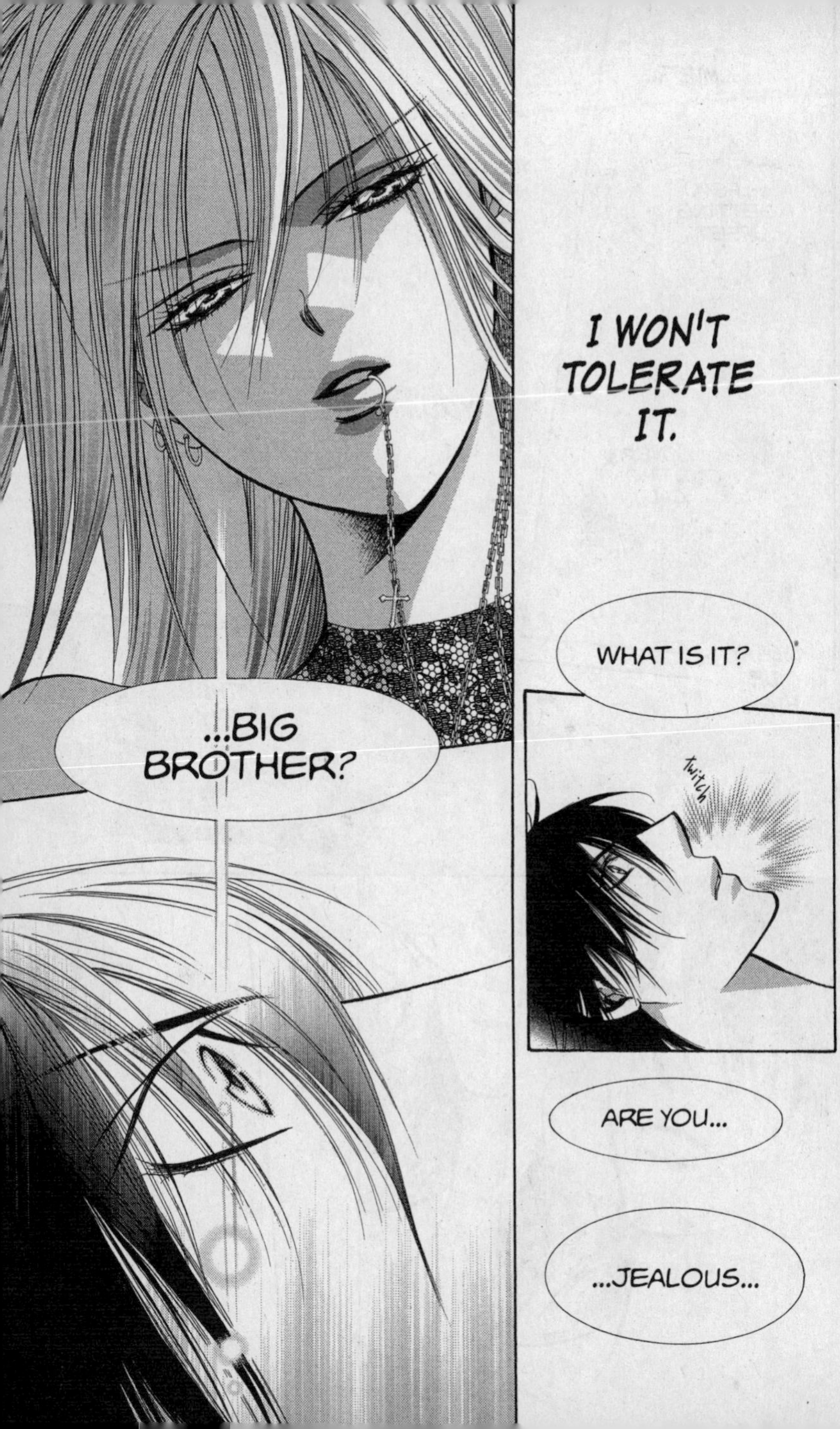
I WON'T TOLERATE IT.
WHAT IS IT?
twitch
ARE YOU...
...JEALOUS...
...BIG BROTHER?

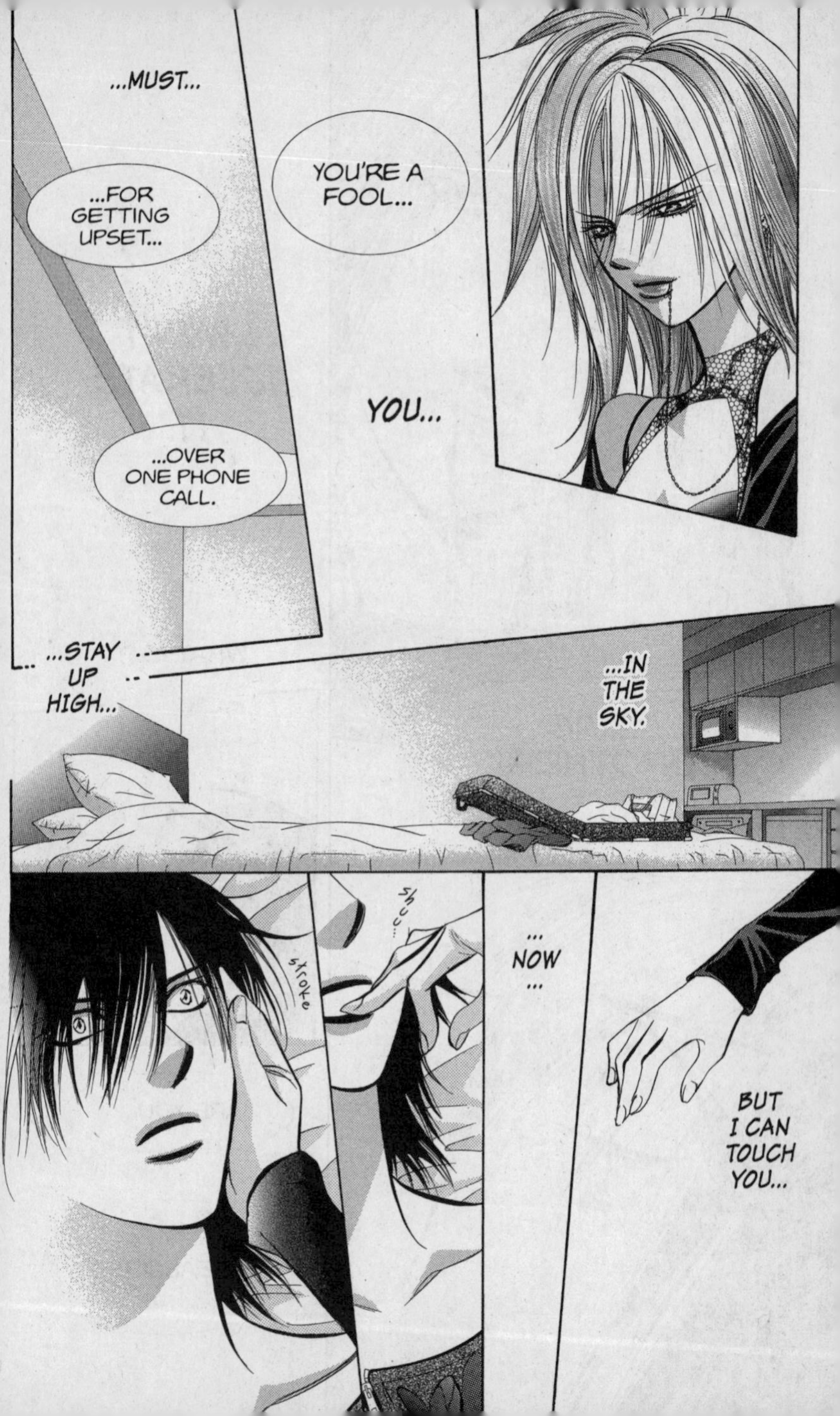
YOU'RE A FOOL...
...FOR GETTING UPSET...
...OVER ONE PHONE CALL.
YOU...
...MUST...
...STAY UP HIGH...
...IN THE SKY.
BUT I CAN TOUCH YOU...
...NOW...
shuu...
stroke

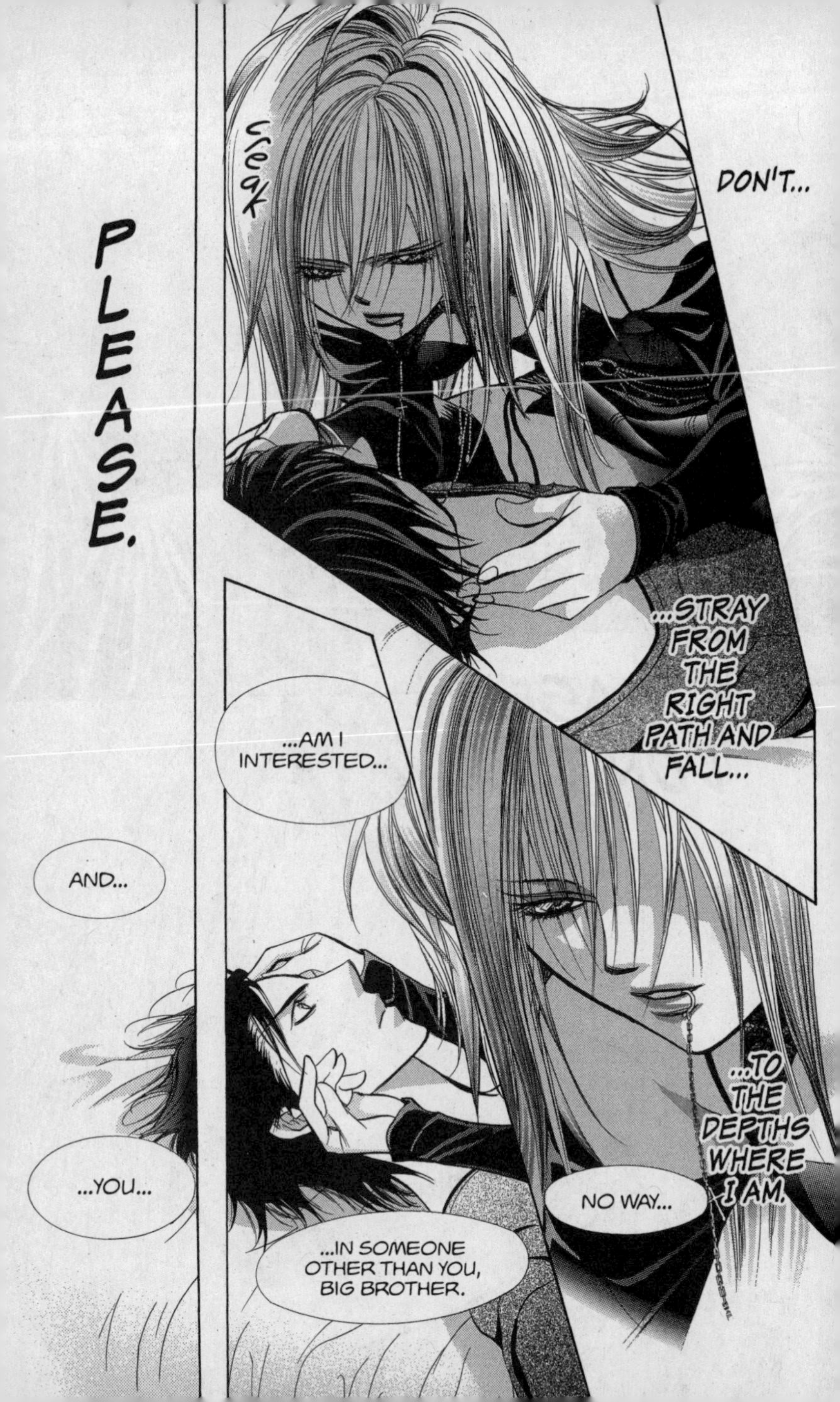
creak
DON'T...
...STRAY FROM THE RIGHT PATH AND FALL...
...AM I INTERESTED...
...TO THE DEPTHS WHERE I AM.
NO WAY...
...IN SOMEONE OTHER THAN YOU, BIG BROTHER.
PLEASE.
AND...
...YOU...

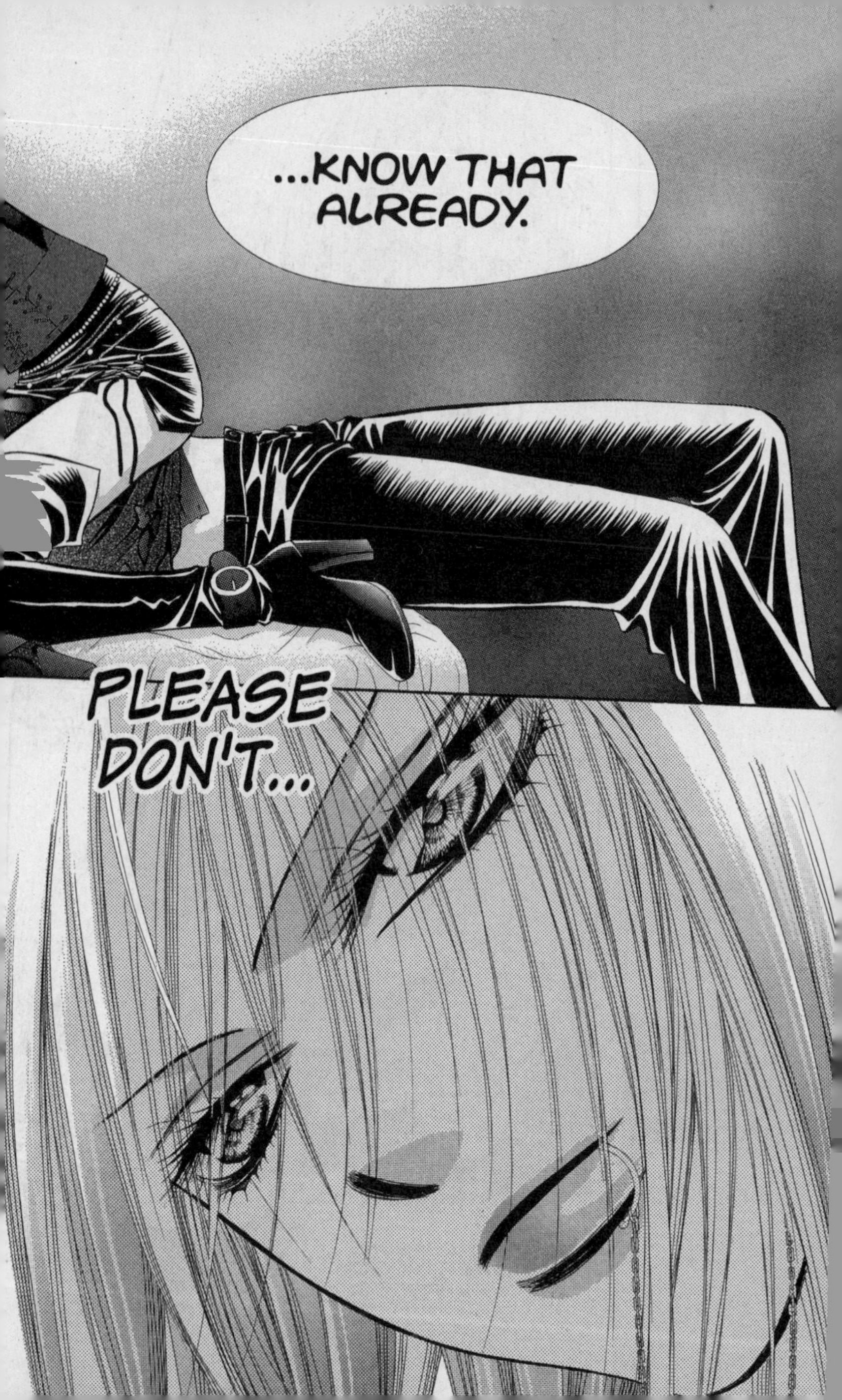
...KNOW THAT ALREADY.
PLEASE DON'T...

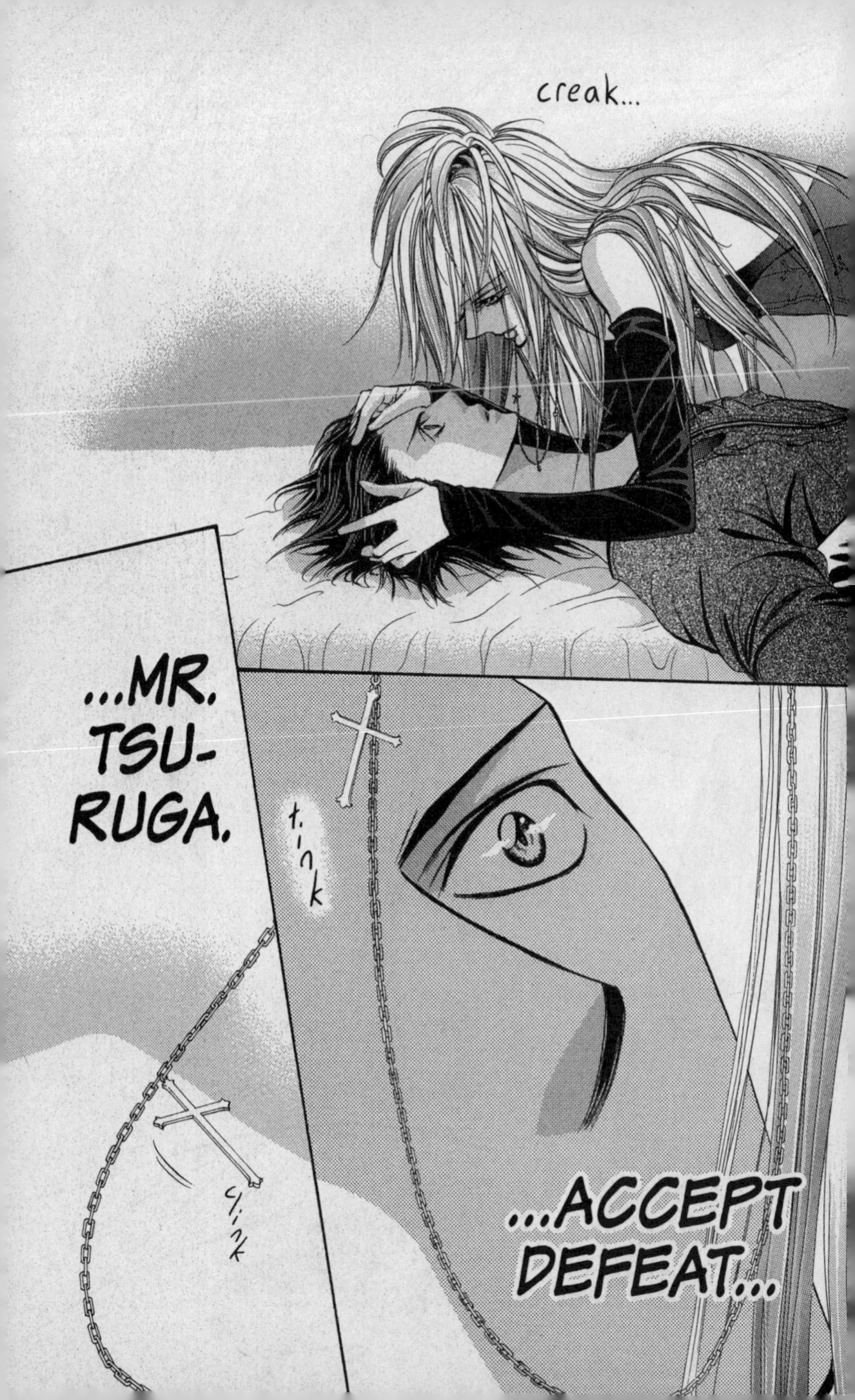
creak...
...MR. TSURUGA.
tink
...ACCEPT DEFEAT...
clink

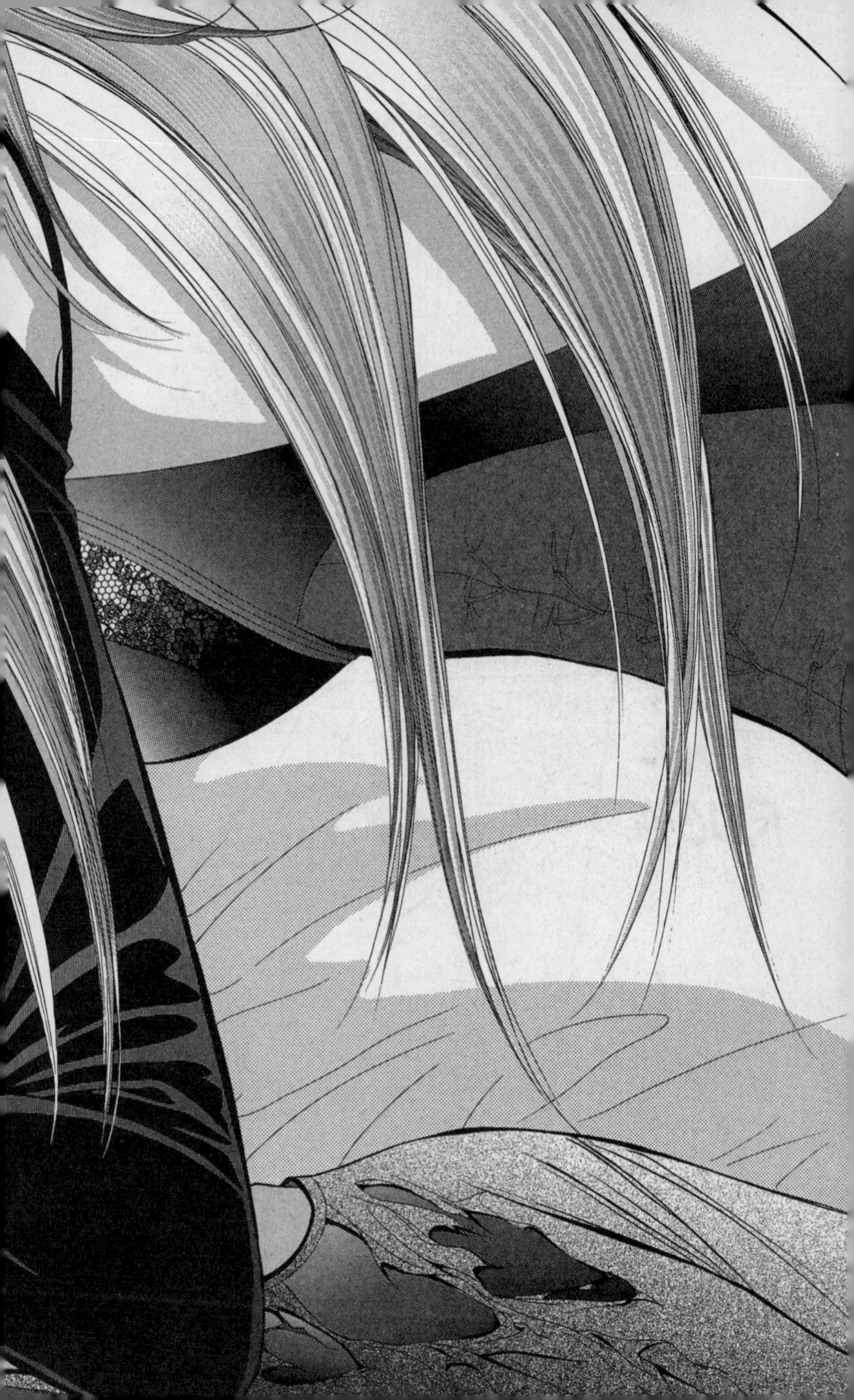

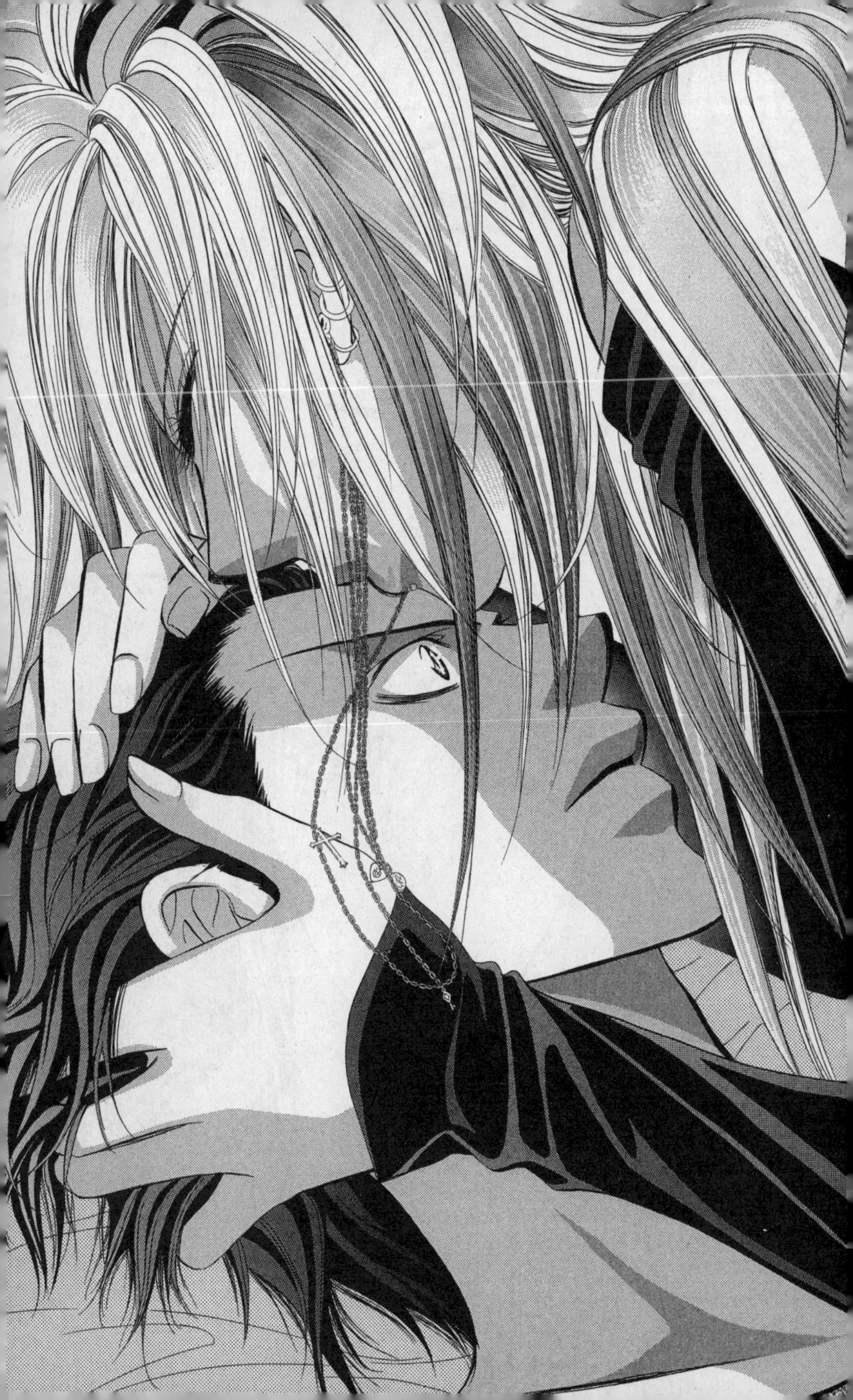

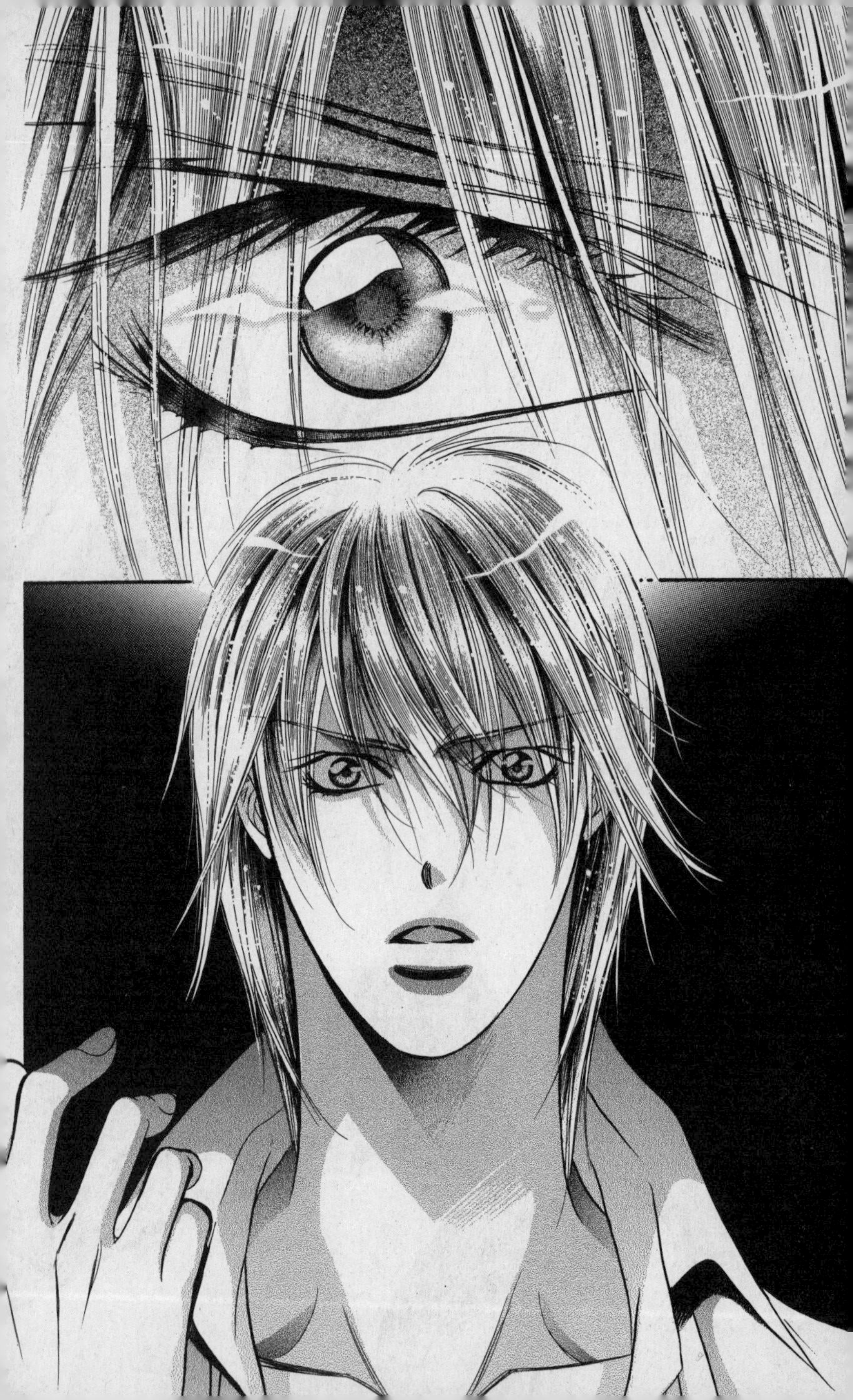

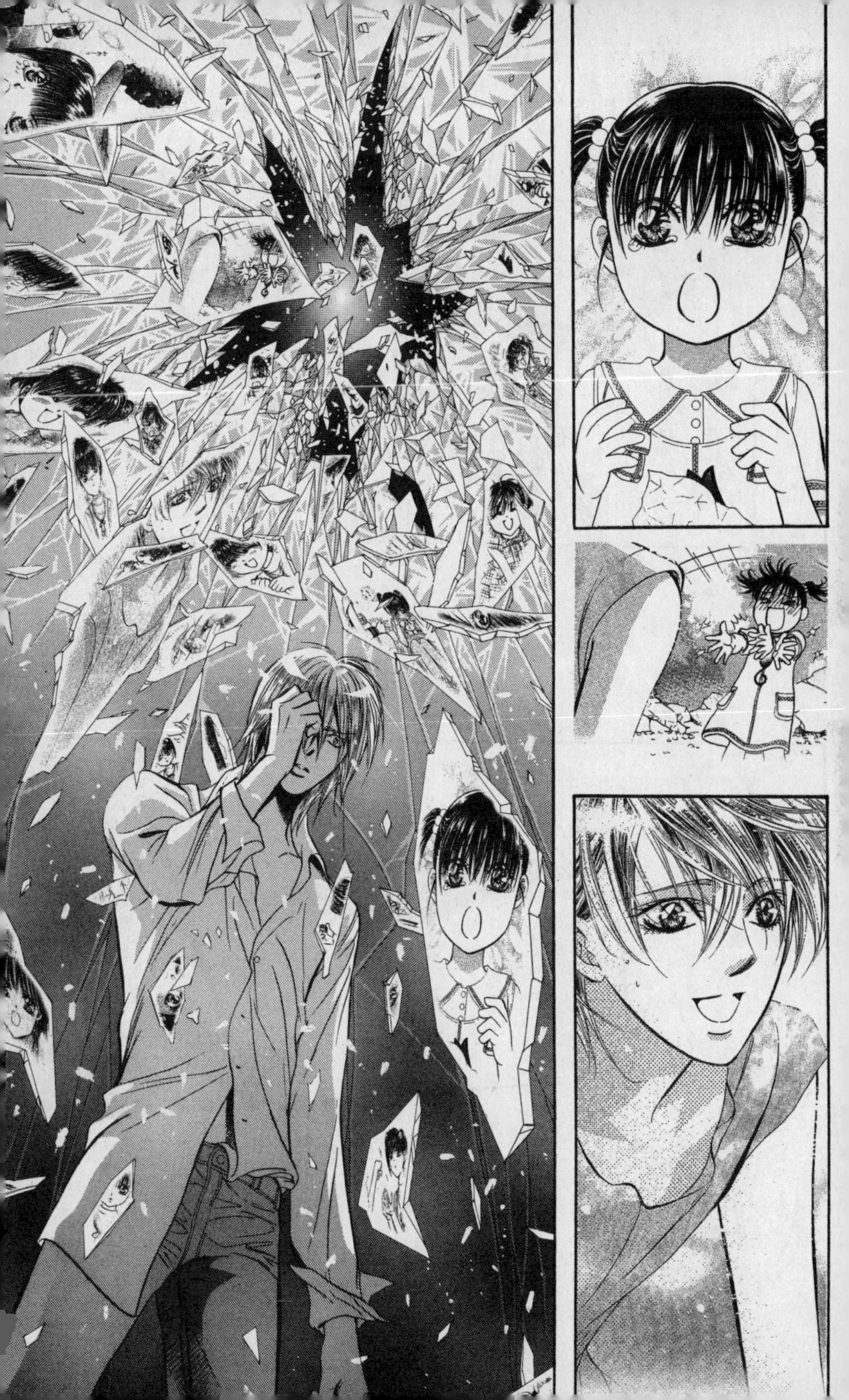

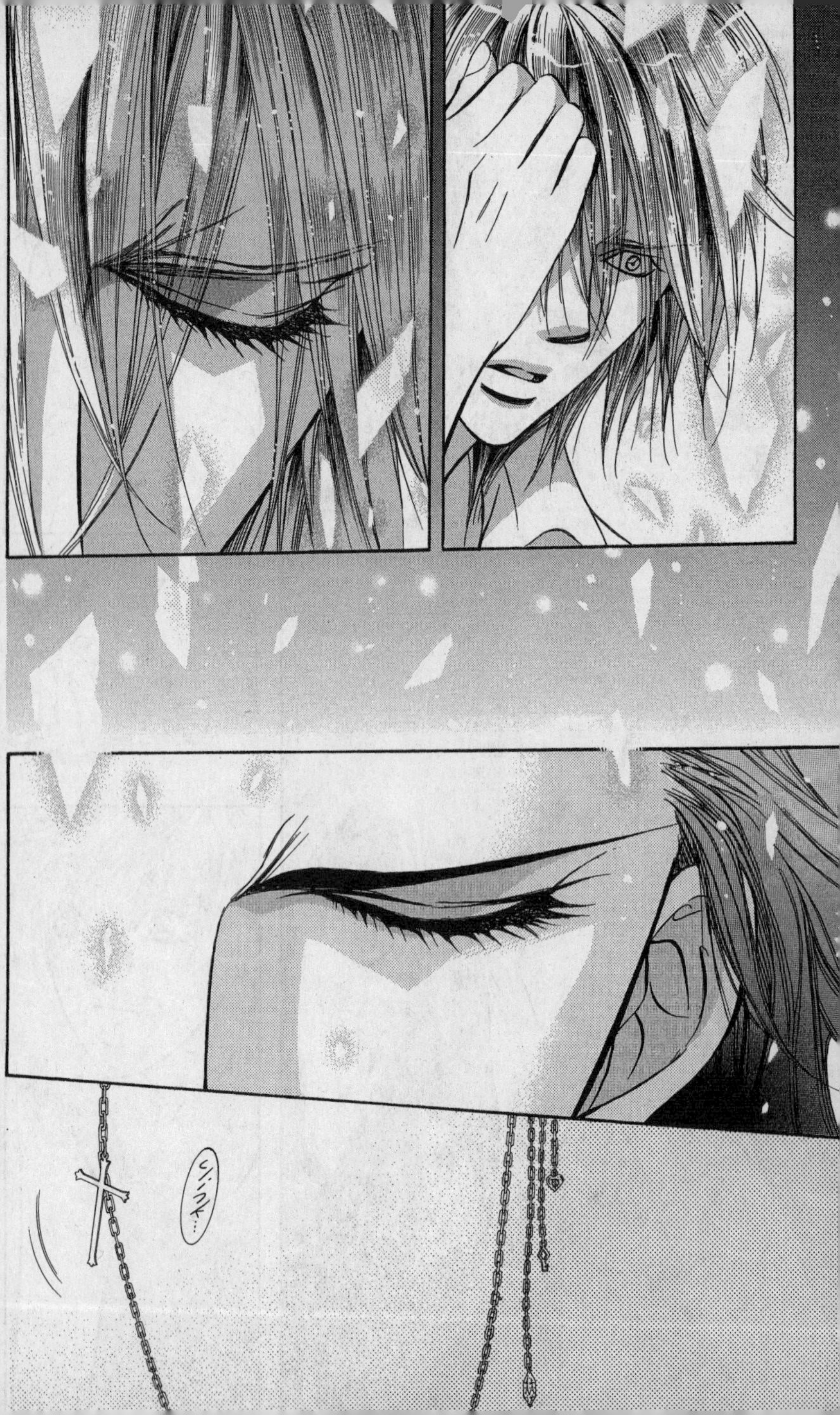
clink...

creak...

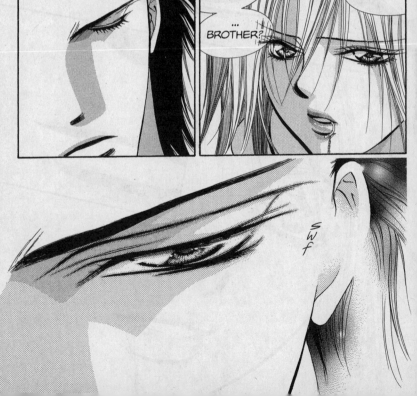

BIG...

...

...BROTHER?

swf

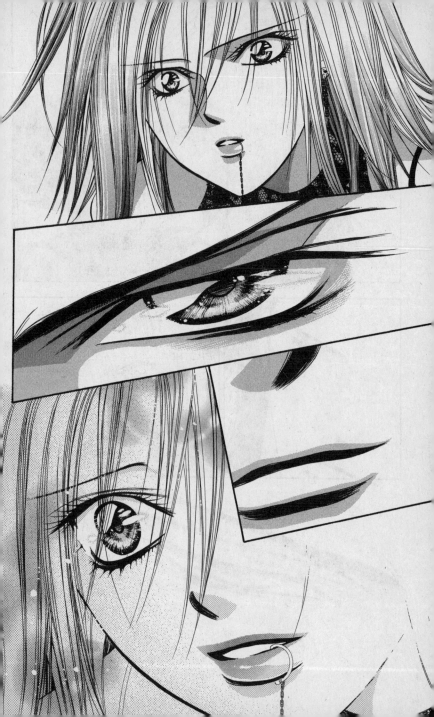

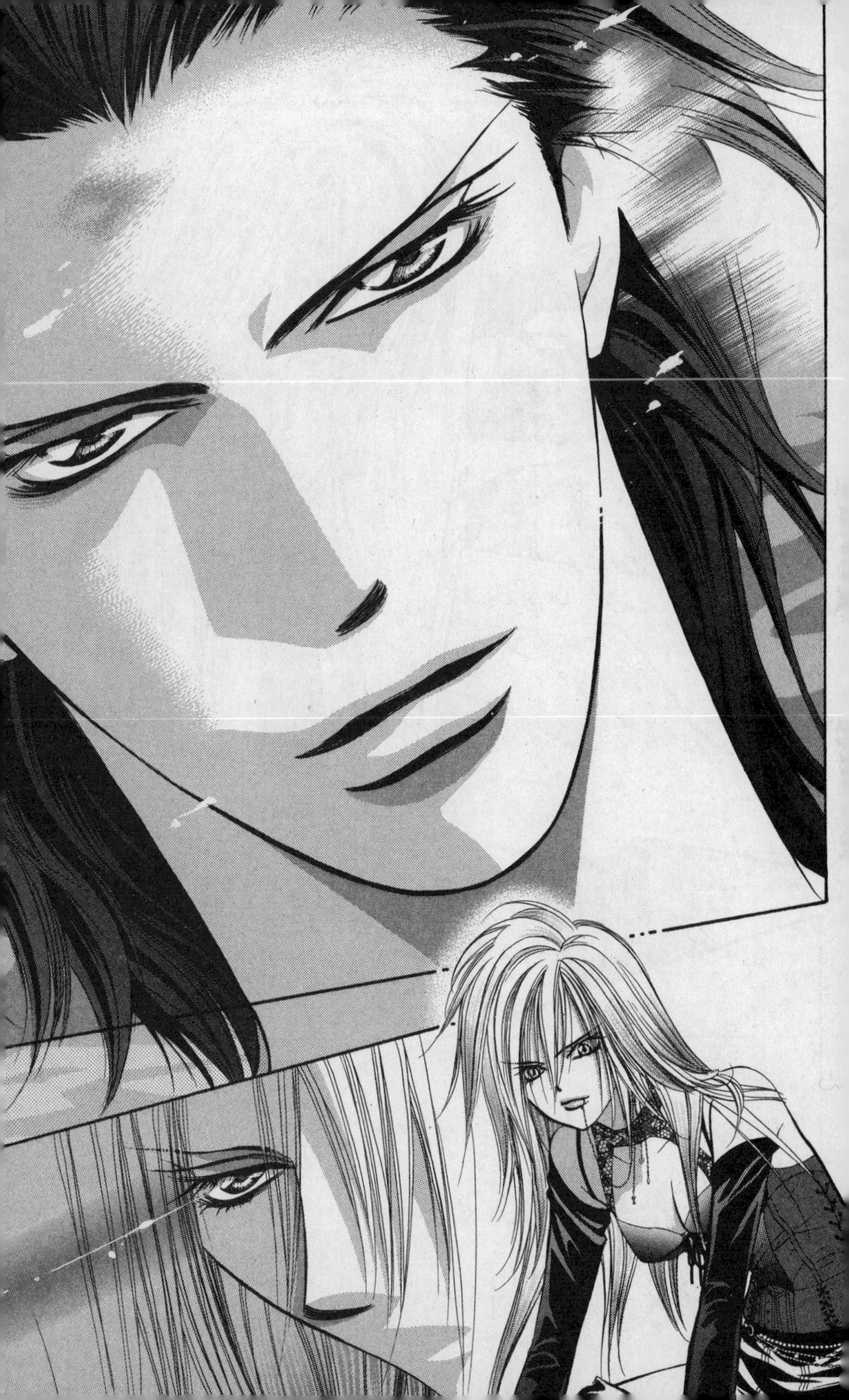

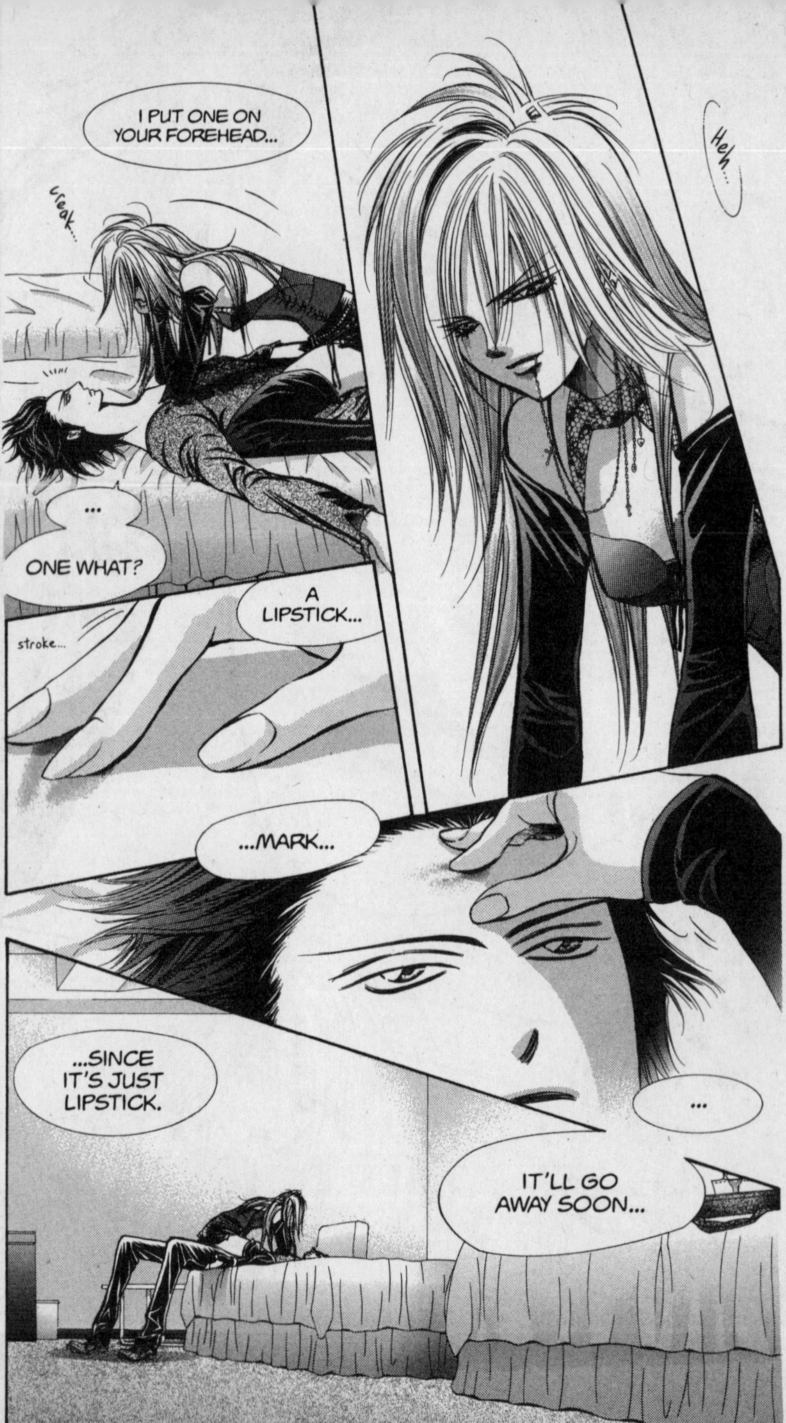
Heh...
I PUT ONE ON YOUR FOREHEAD...
creak...
...
ONE WHAT?
A LIPSTICK...
stroke...
...MARK...
...
IT'LL GO AWAY SOON...
...SINCE IT'S JUST LIPSTICK.

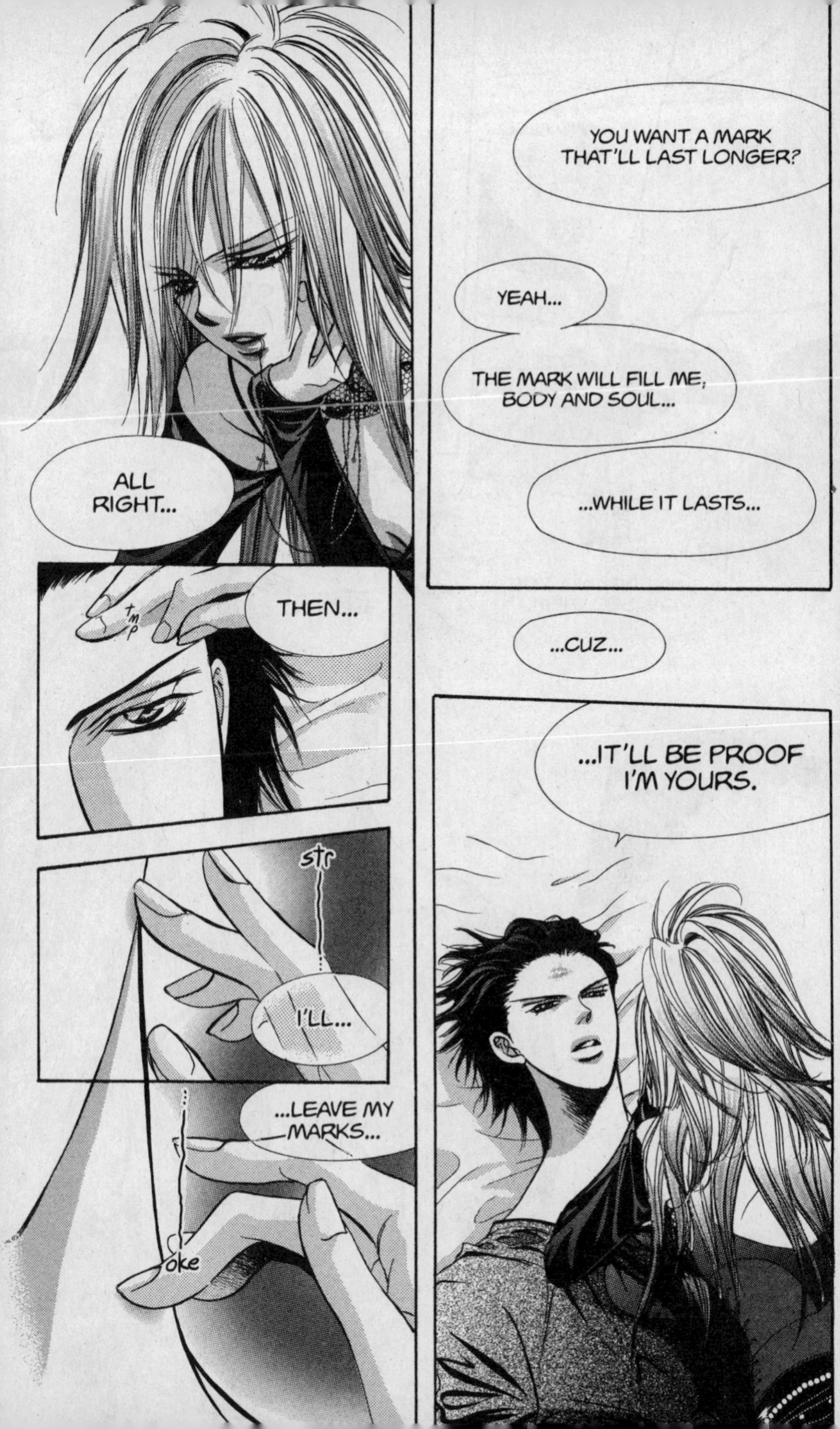
YOU WANT A MARK THAT'LL LAST LONGER?
YEAH...
THE MARK WILL FILL ME, BODY AND SOUL...
...WHILE IT LASTS...
...CUZ...
...IT'LL BE PROOF I'M YOURS.
ALL RIGHT...
THEN...
tmp
str
I'LL...
...LEAVE MY MARKS...
oke

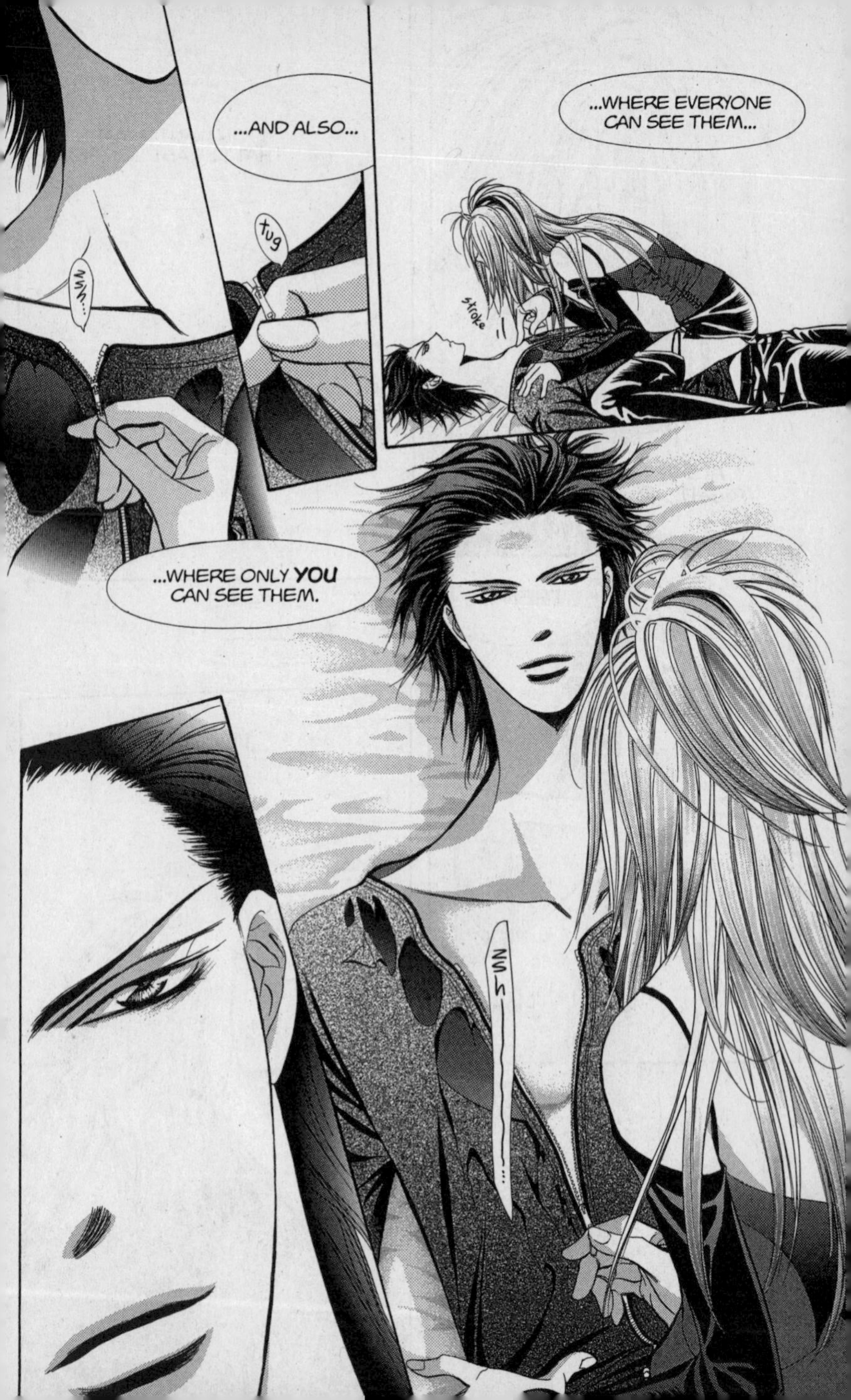
...WHERE EVERYONE CAN SEE THEM...
stroke
...AND ALSO...
tug
Nnn...
...WHERE ONLY **YOU** CAN SEE THEM.
Nnn—...

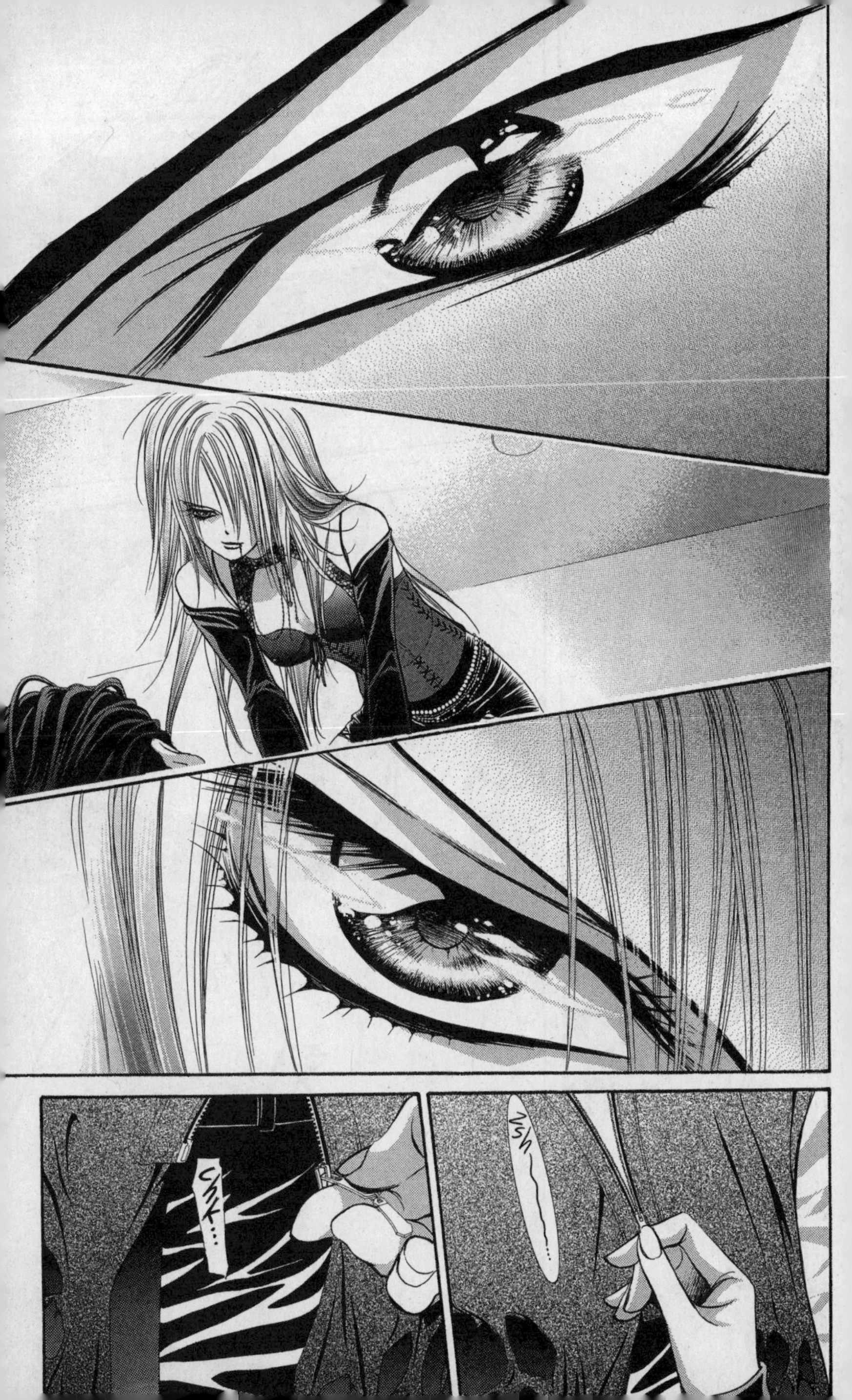
Zsh—...
Chik...

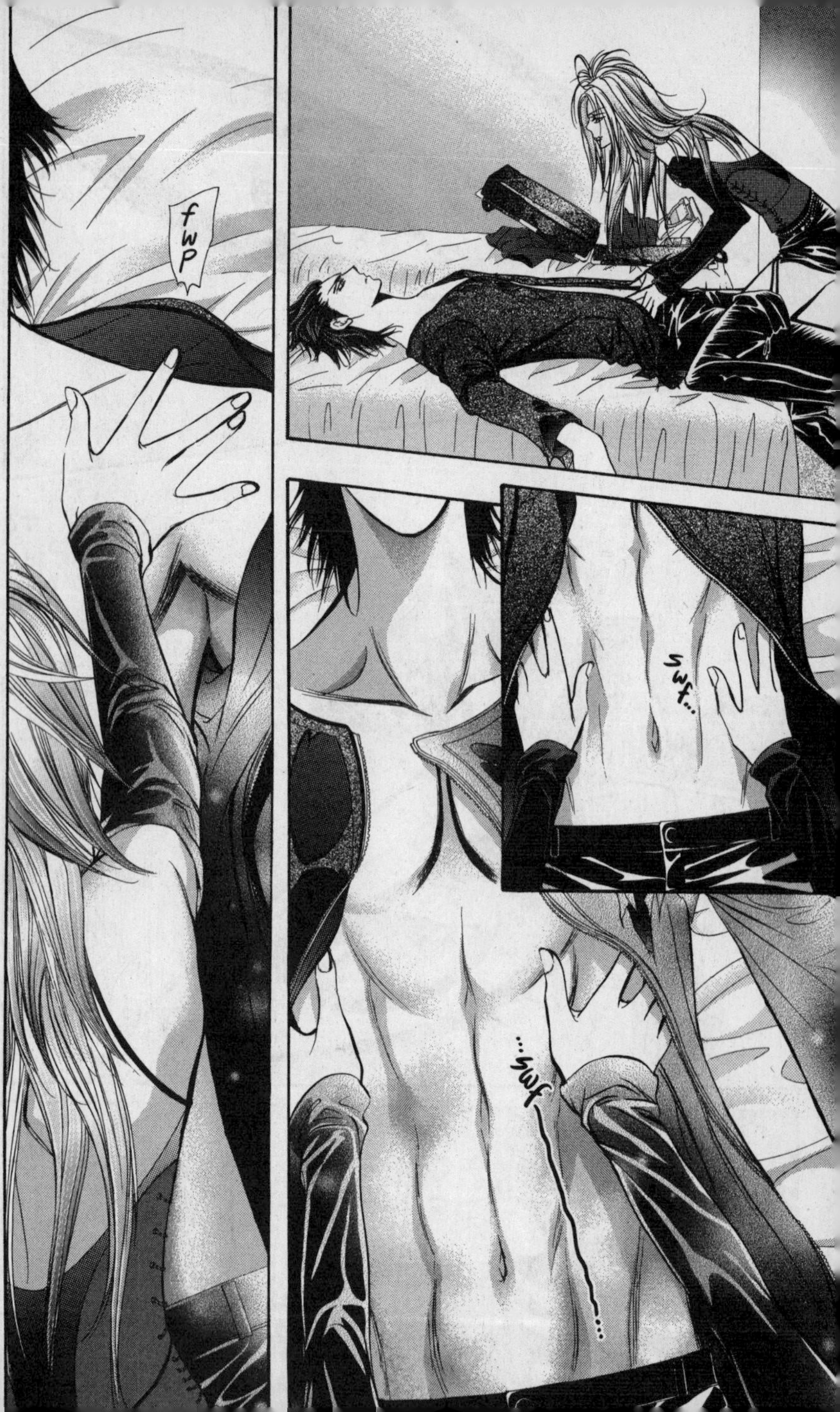
swf...
swf...
fwp

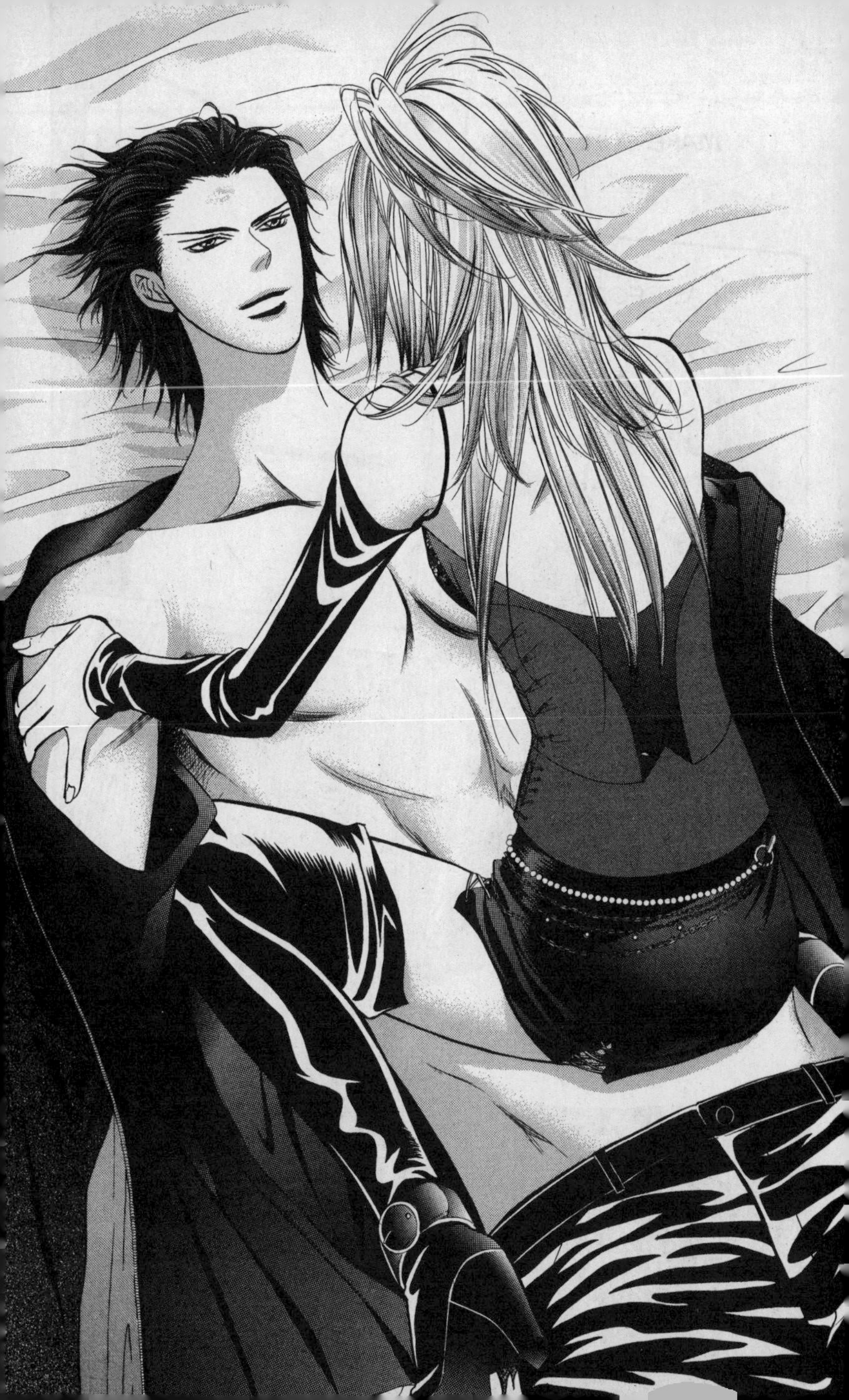

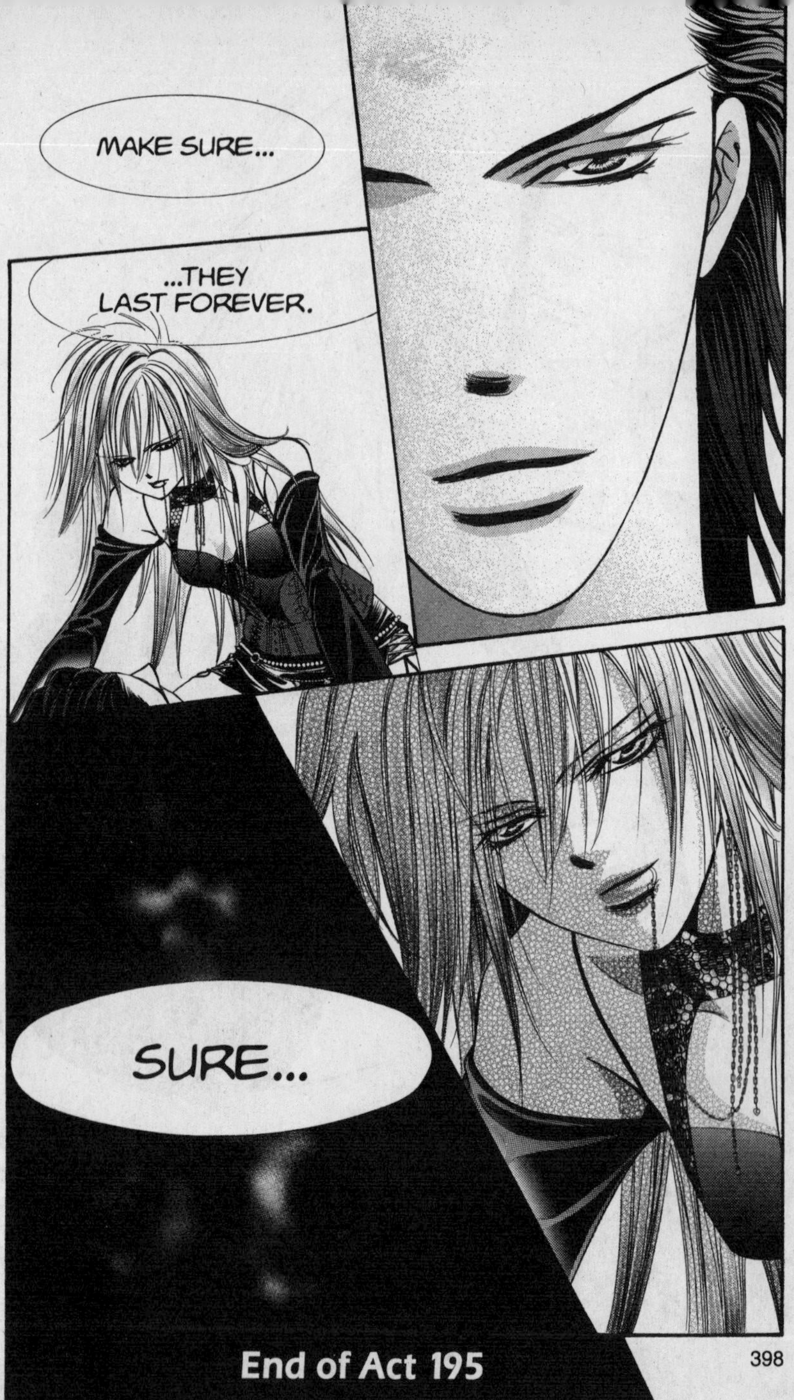
MAKE SURE...
...THEY LAST FOREVER.
SURE...
End of Act 195

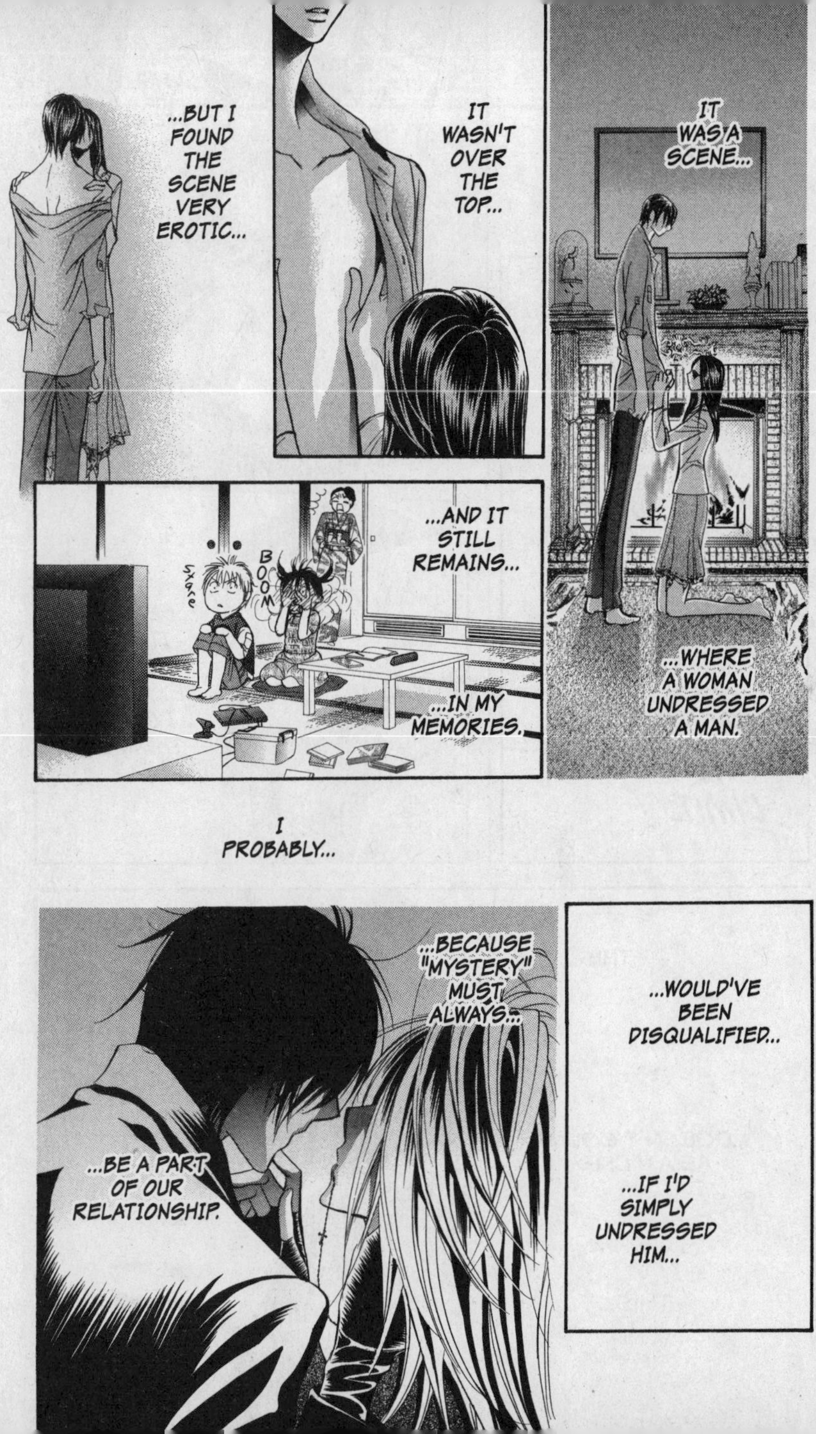
IT WAS A SCENE...
...WHERE A WOMAN UNDRESSED A MAN.
IT WASN'T OVER THE TOP...
...BUT I FOUND THE SCENE VERY EROTIC...
...AND IT STILL REMAINS...
BOOM
STARE
...IN MY MEMORIES.
I PROBABLY...
...WOULD'VE BEEN DISQUALIFIED...
...IF I'D SIMPLY UNDRESSED HIM...
...BECAUSE "MYSTERY" MUST ALWAYS...
...BE A PART OF OUR RELATIONSHIP.

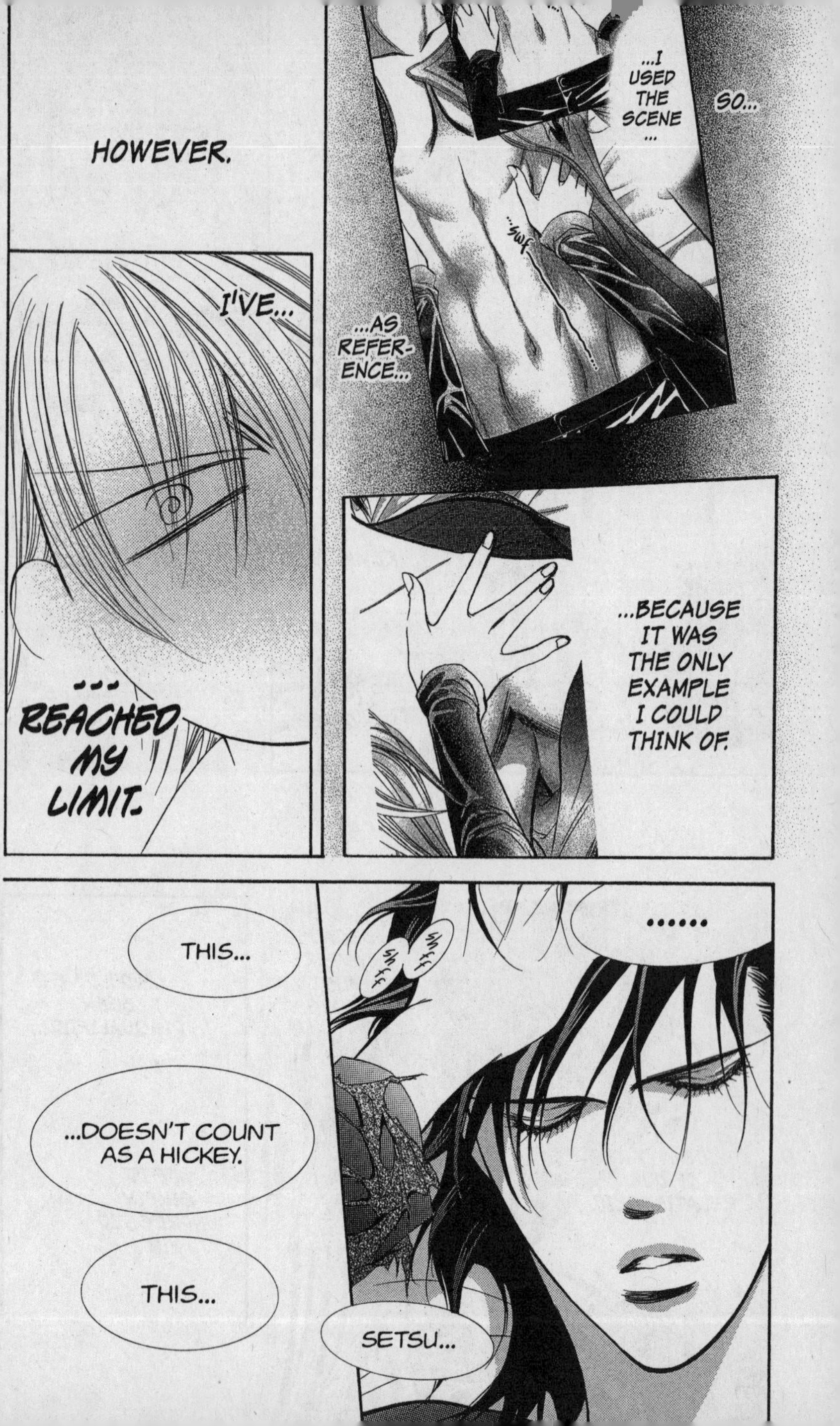
SO...
...I USED THE SCENE...
...swf
...AS REFERENCE...
HOWEVER.
...BECAUSE IT WAS THE ONLY EXAMPLE I COULD THINK OF.
I'VE...
...REACHED MY LIMIT.
......
swff swff
THIS...
...DOESN'T COUNT AS A HICKEY.
THIS...
SETSU...

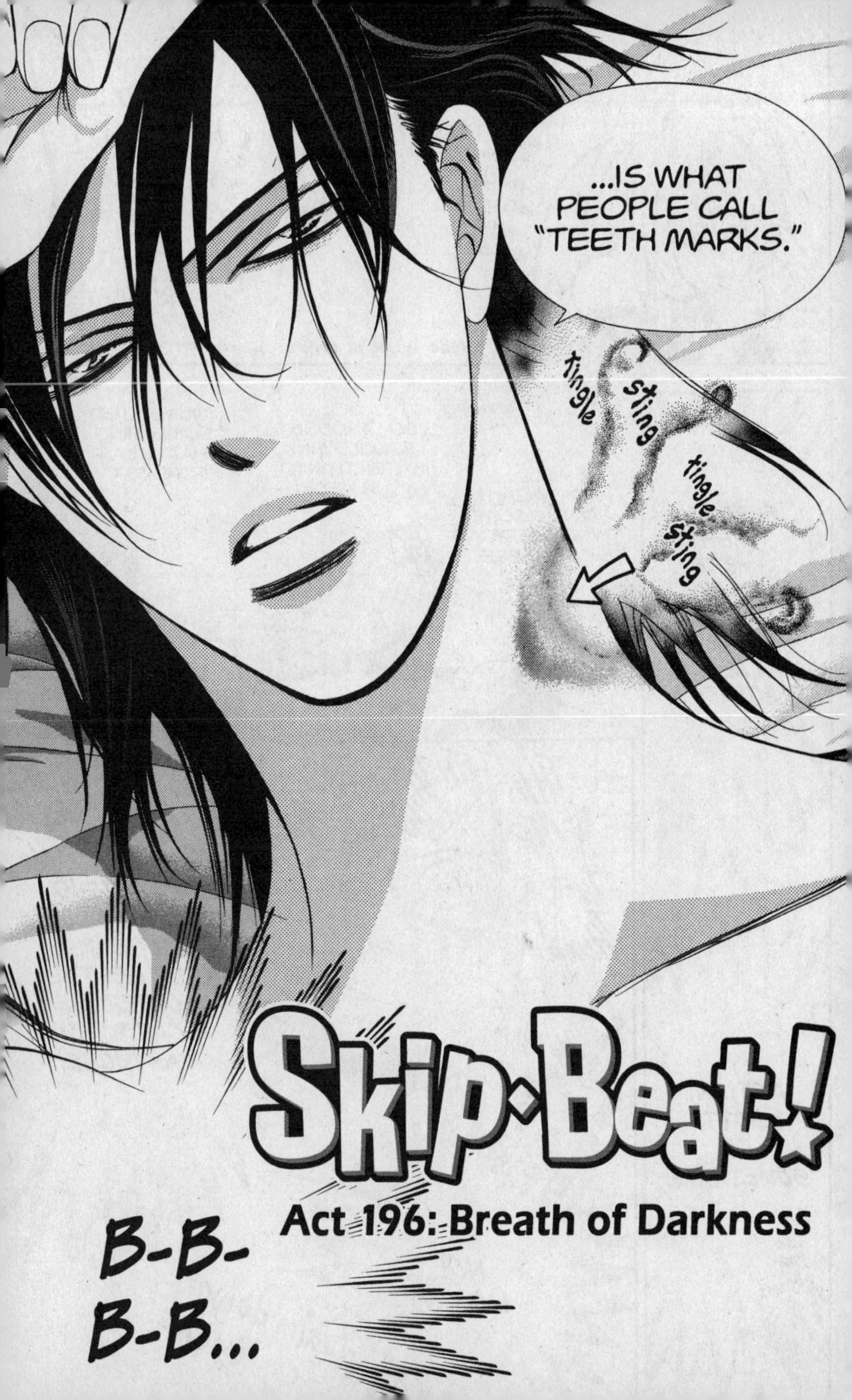
...IS WHAT PEOPLE CALL "TEETH MARKS."
tingle
sting
tingle
sting
Skip·Beat!
Act 196: Breath of Darkness
B-B-B-B...

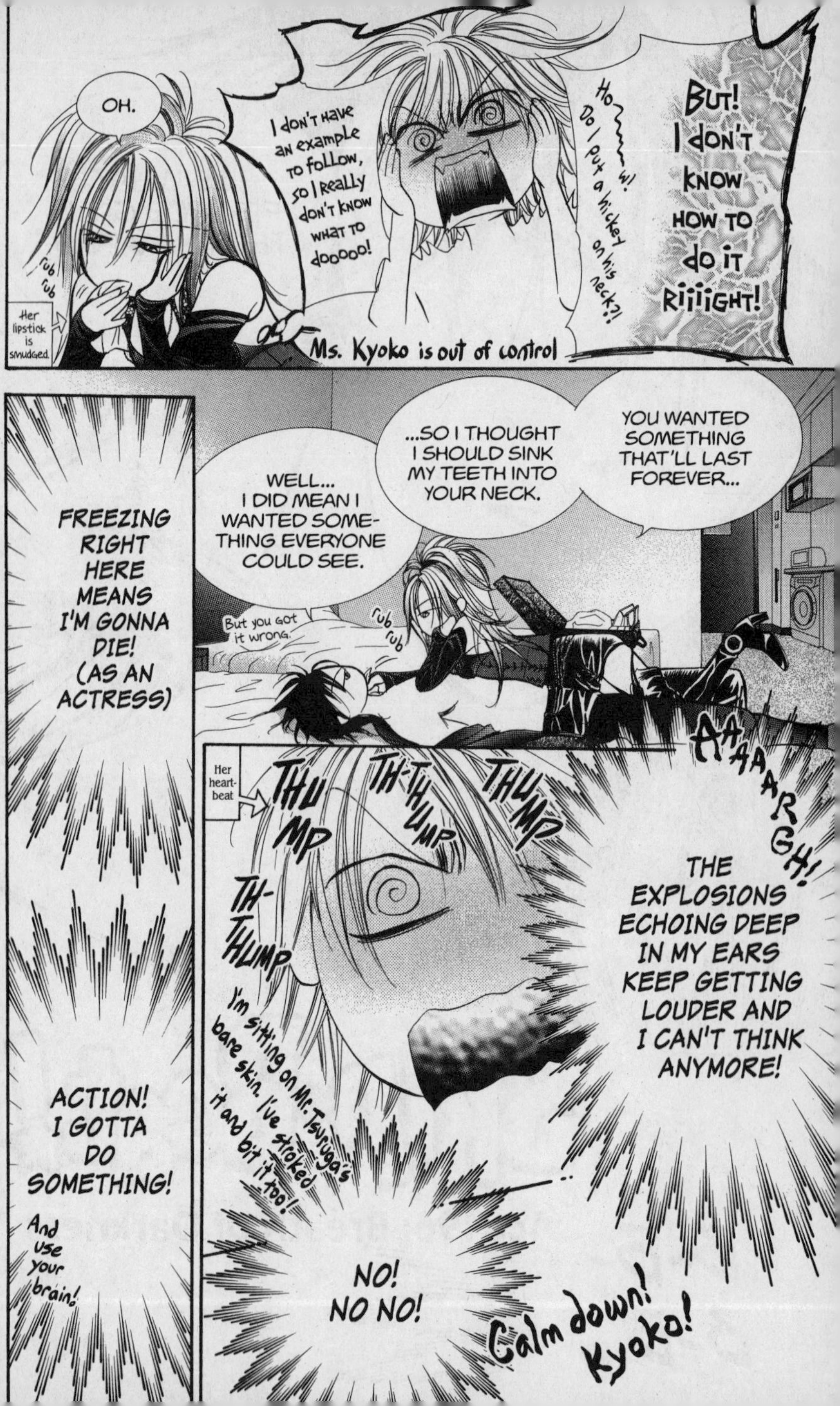
BUT! I DON'T KNOW HOW TO DO IT RIIIIGHT!
Ho~w! Do I put a hickey on his neck?!
I don't have an example to follow, so I really don't know what to doooooo!
Ms. Kyoko is out of control
OH.
rub rub
Her lipstick is smudged.
YOU WANTED SOMETHING THAT'LL LAST FOREVER...
...SO I THOUGHT I SHOULD SINK MY TEETH INTO YOUR NECK.
WELL... I DID MEAN I WANTED SOME-THING EVERYONE COULD SEE.
But you got it wrong.
rub rub
AAAARGH!
THUMP
TH-THUMP
THUMP
Her heartbeat
TH-THUMP
THE EXPLOSIONS ECHOING DEEP IN MY EARS KEEP GETTING LOUDER AND I CAN'T THINK ANYMORE!
I'm sitting on Mr. Tsuruga's bare skin. I've stroked it and bit it too!
NO! NO NO!
Calm down! Kyoko!
FREEZING RIGHT HERE MEANS I'M GONNA DIE! (AS AN ACTRESS)
ACTION! I GOTTA DO SOMETHING!
And use your brain!

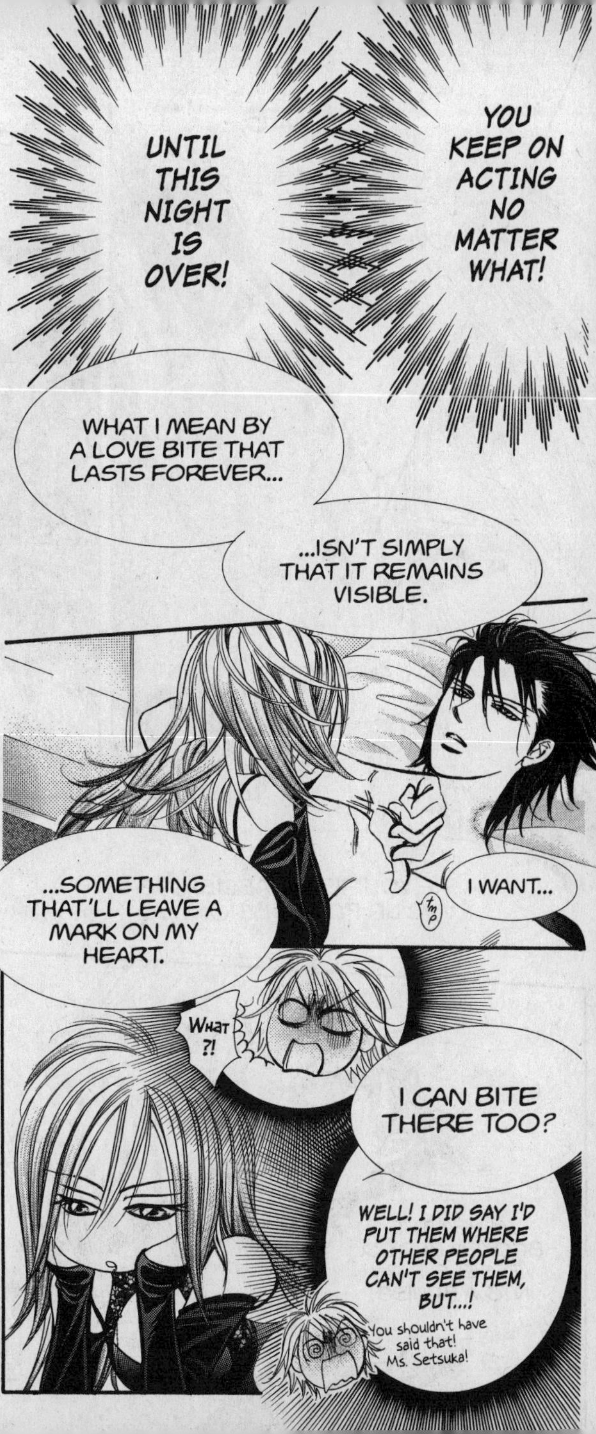
YOU KEEP ON ACTING NO MATTER WHAT!
UNTIL THIS NIGHT IS OVER!
WHAT I MEAN BY A LOVE BITE THAT LASTS FOREVER...
...ISN'T SIMPLY THAT IT REMAINS VISIBLE.
I WANT...
...SOMETHING THAT'LL LEAVE A MARK ON MY HEART.
WHAT ?!
I CAN BITE THERE TOO?
WELL! I DID SAY I'D PUT THEM WHERE OTHER PEOPLE CAN'T SEE THEM, BUT...!
You shouldn't have said that! Ms. Setsuka!

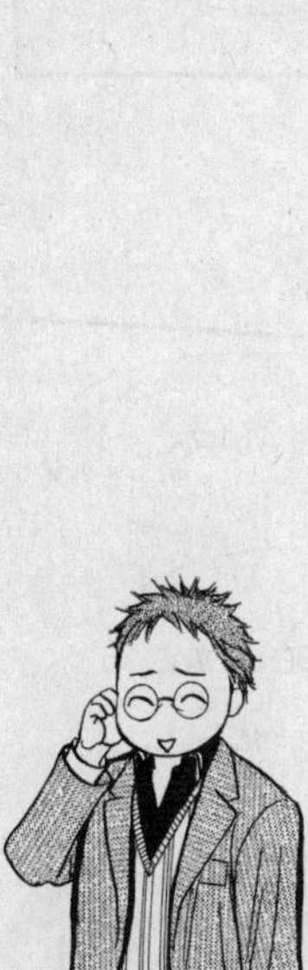

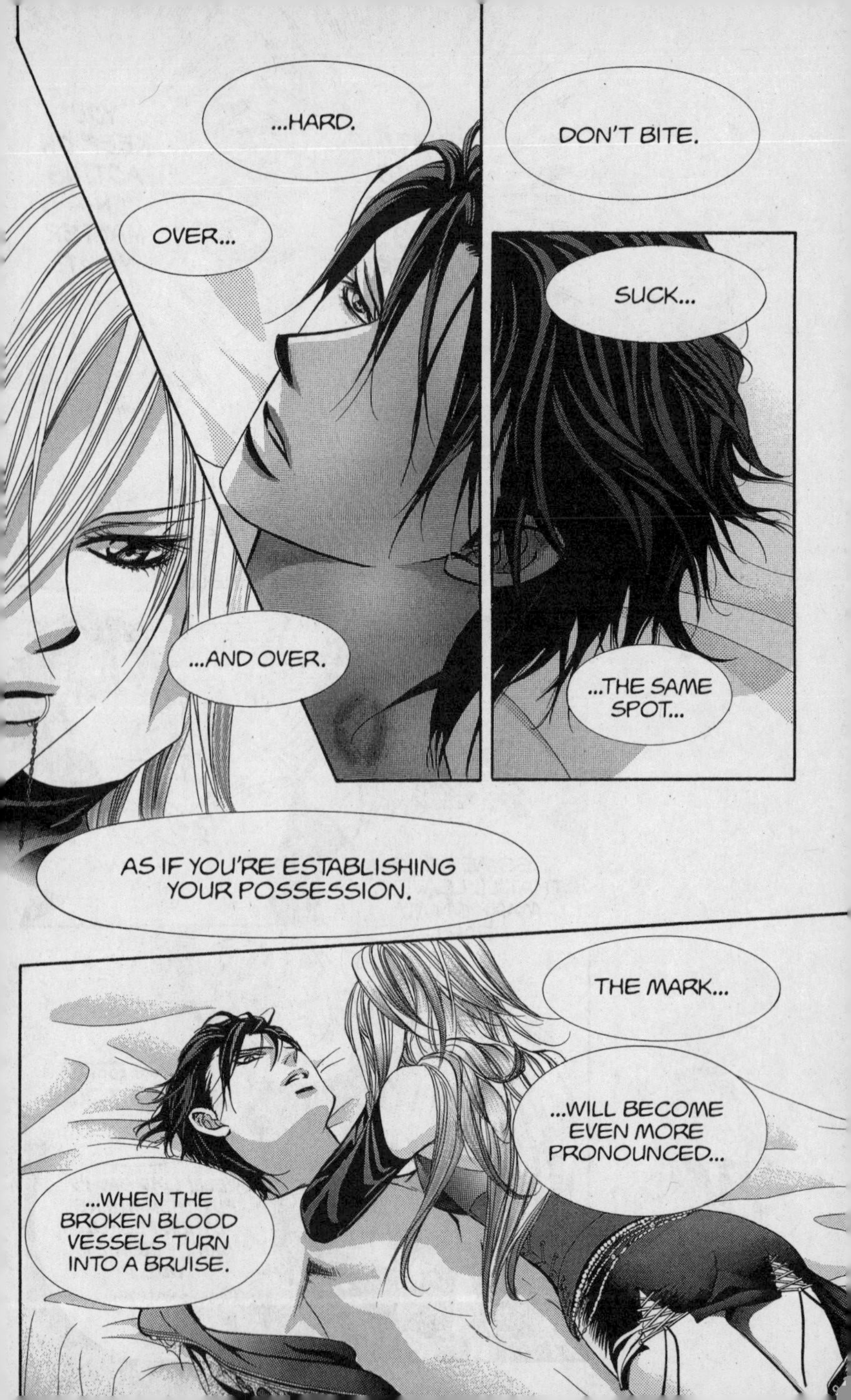
DON'T BITE.
SUCK...
...THE SAME SPOT...
...HARD.
OVER...
...AND OVER.
AS IF YOU'RE ESTABLISHING YOUR POSSESSION.
THE MARK...
...WILL BECOME EVEN MORE PRONOUNCED...
...WHEN THE BROKEN BLOOD VESSELS TURN INTO A BRUISE.

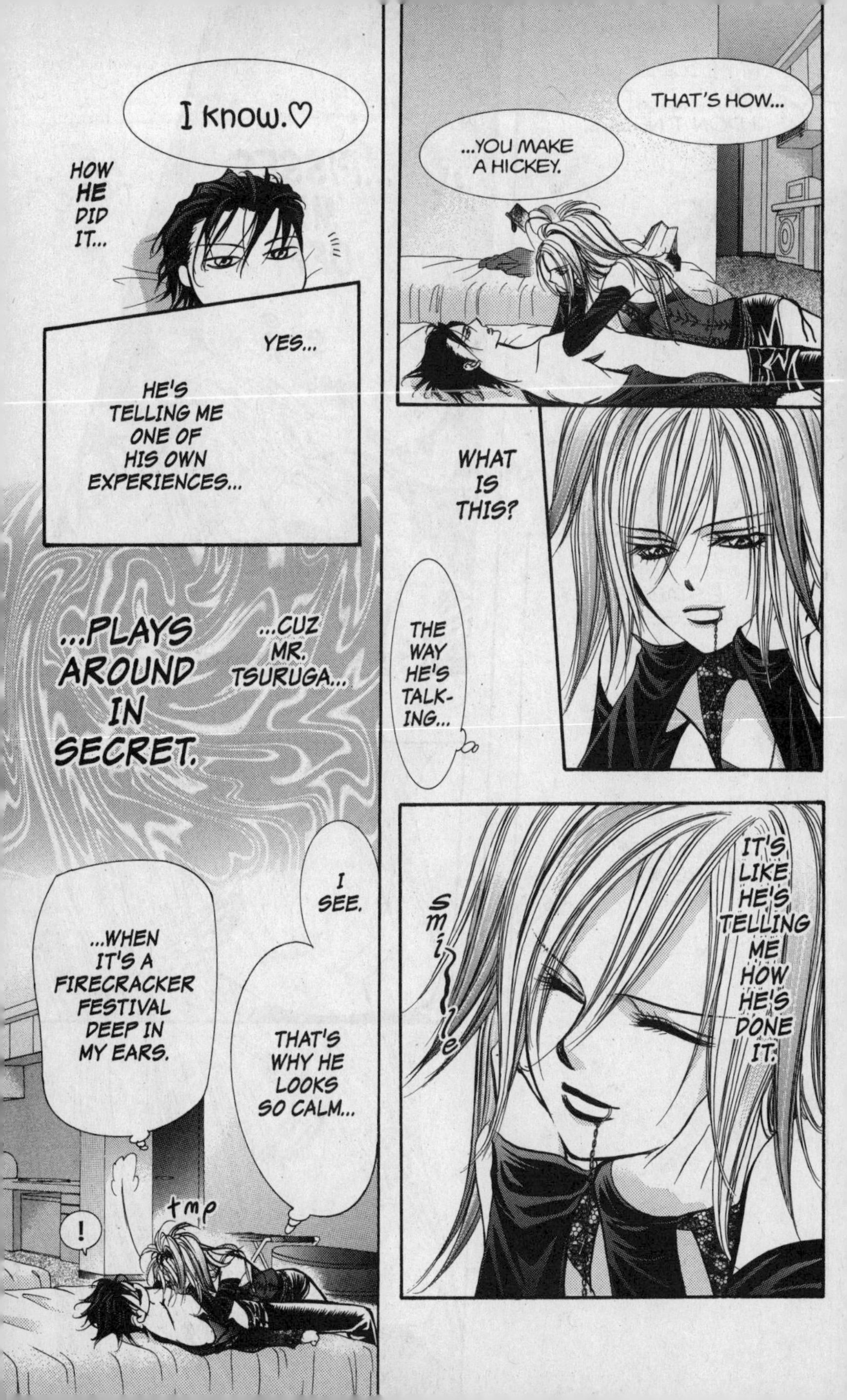
THAT'S HOW...
...YOU MAKE A HICKEY.
WHAT IS THIS?
THE WAY HE'S TALK-ING...
IT'S LIKE HE'S TELLING ME HOW HE'S DONE IT.
smi~le
I know.♡
HOW HE DID IT...
YES...
HE'S TELLING ME ONE OF HIS OWN EXPERIENCES...
...CUZ MR. TSURUGA...
...PLAYS AROUND IN SECRET.
I SEE.
THAT'S WHY HE LOOKS SO CALM...
...WHEN IT'S A FIRECRACKER FESTIVAL DEEP IN MY EARS.
tmp
!

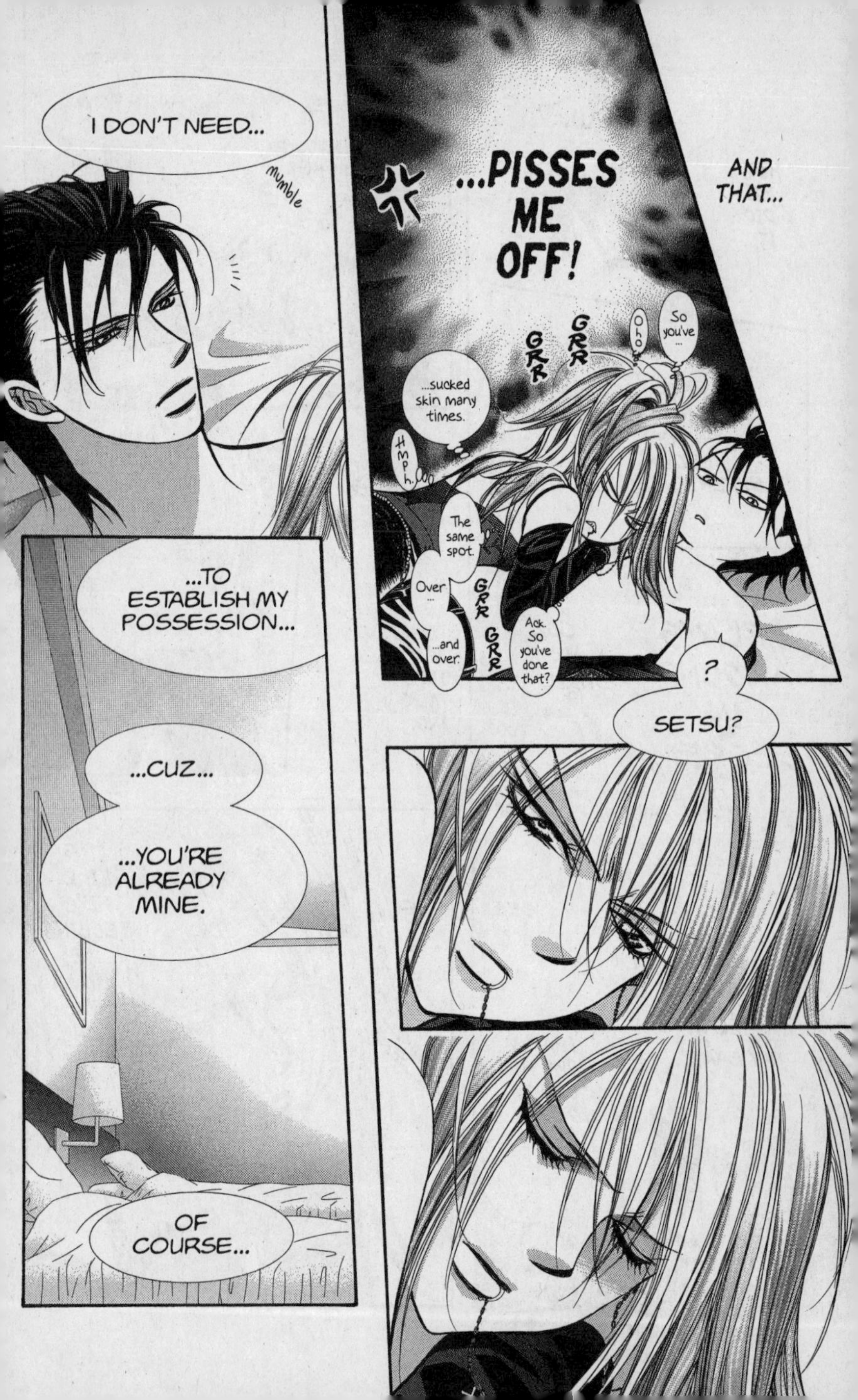
AND THAT...
...PISSES ME OFF!
GRR GRR
Oho
So you've ...
...sucked skin many times.
Hmph.
The same spot.
Over...
...and over.
GRR GRR
Ack. So you've done that?
?
SETSU?
I DON'T NEED...
mumble
...TO ESTABLISH MY POSSESSION...
...CUZ...
...YOU'RE ALREADY MINE.
OF COURSE...

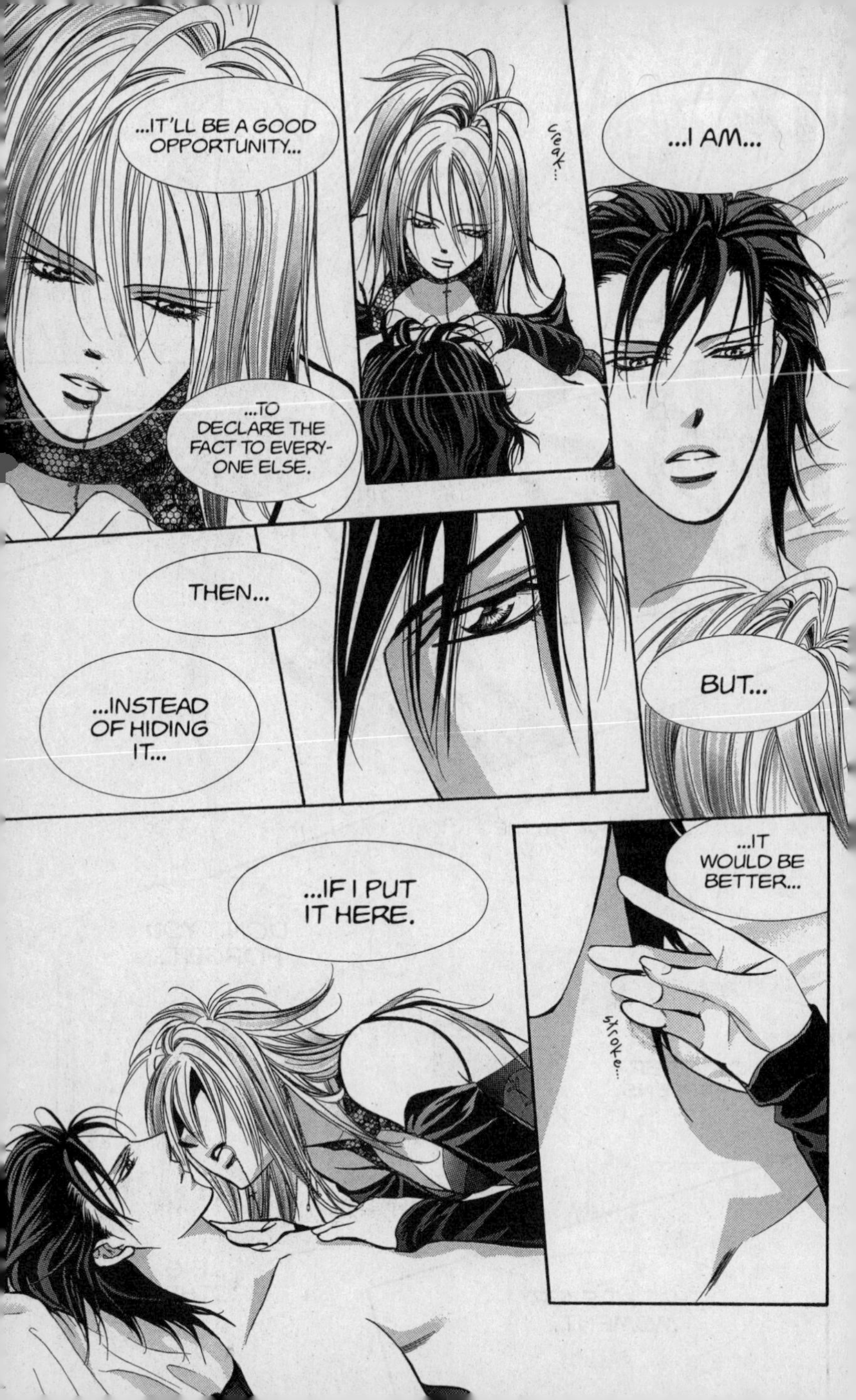
...I AM...
BUT...
creak...
...IT'LL BE A GOOD OPPORTUNITY...
...TO DECLARE THE FACT TO EVERY-ONE ELSE.
THEN...
...INSTEAD OF HIDING IT...
...IT WOULD BE BETTER...
stroke...
...IF I PUT IT HERE.

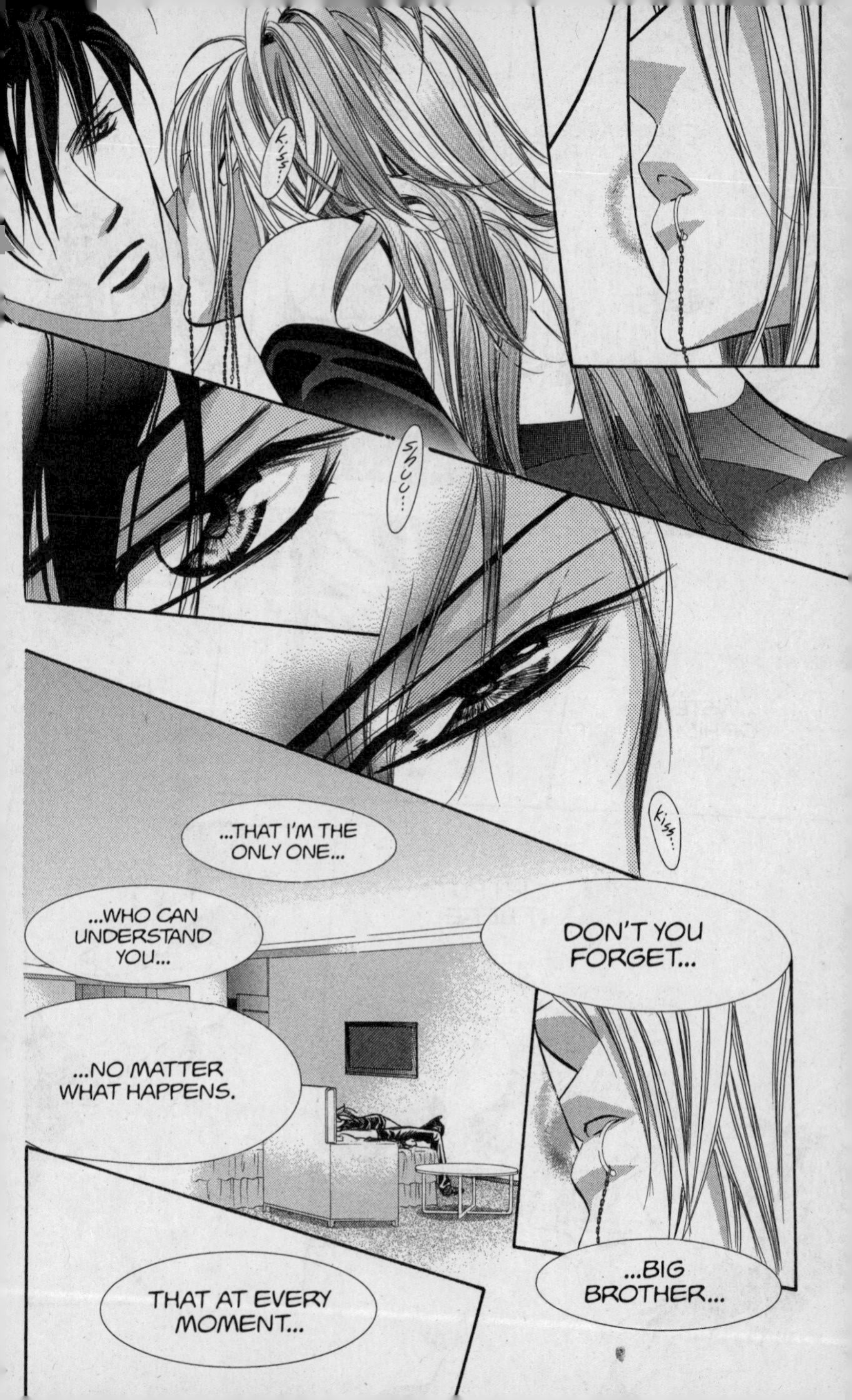
kiss...
shuu...
kiss...
DON'T YOU FORGET...
...THAT I'M THE ONLY ONE...
...WHO CAN UNDERSTAND YOU...
...NO MATTER WHAT HAPPENS.
...BIG BROTHER...
THAT AT EVERY MOMENT...

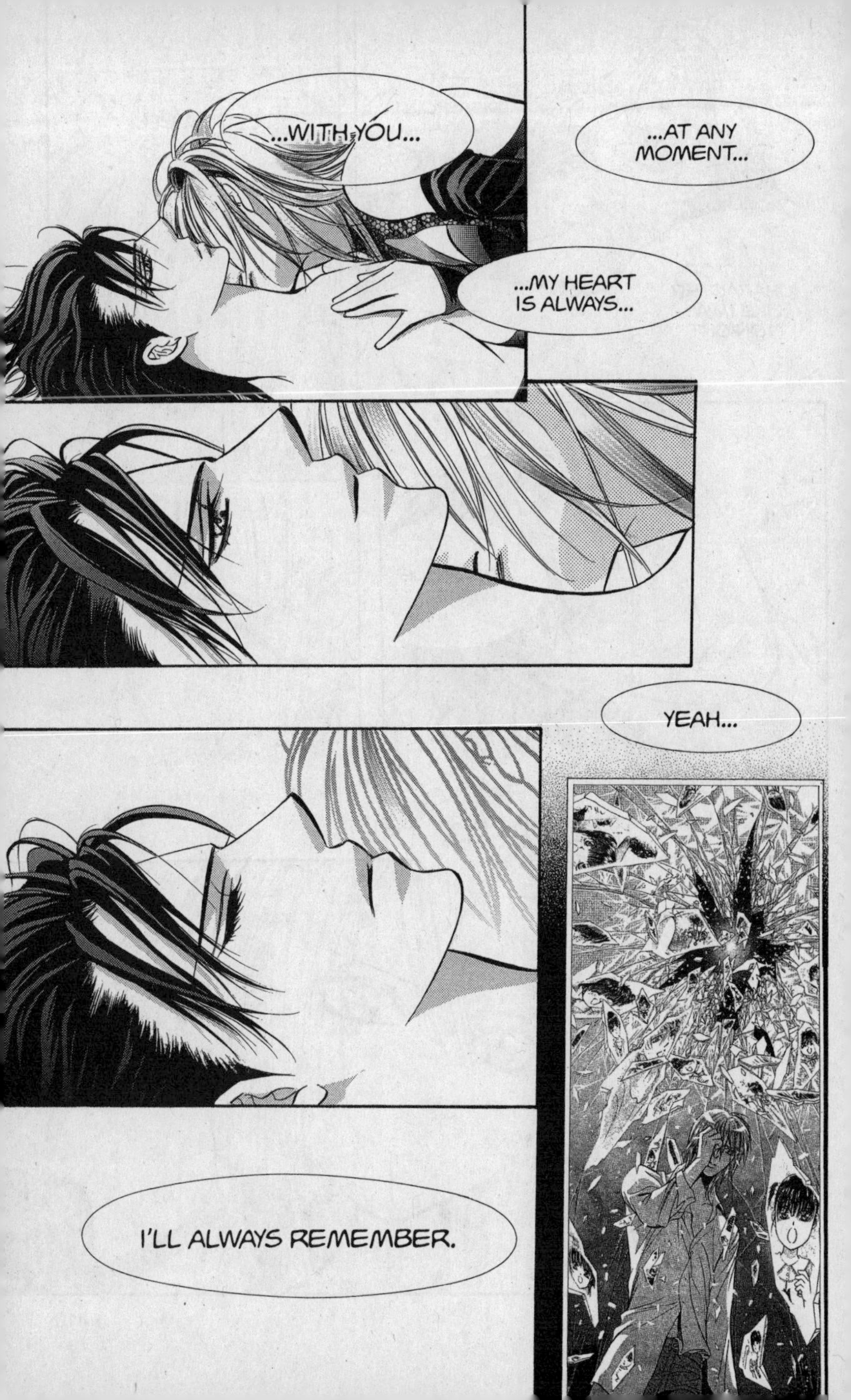
...AT ANY MOMENT...
...MY HEART IS ALWAYS...
...WITH YOU...
YEAH...
I'LL ALWAYS REMEMBER.

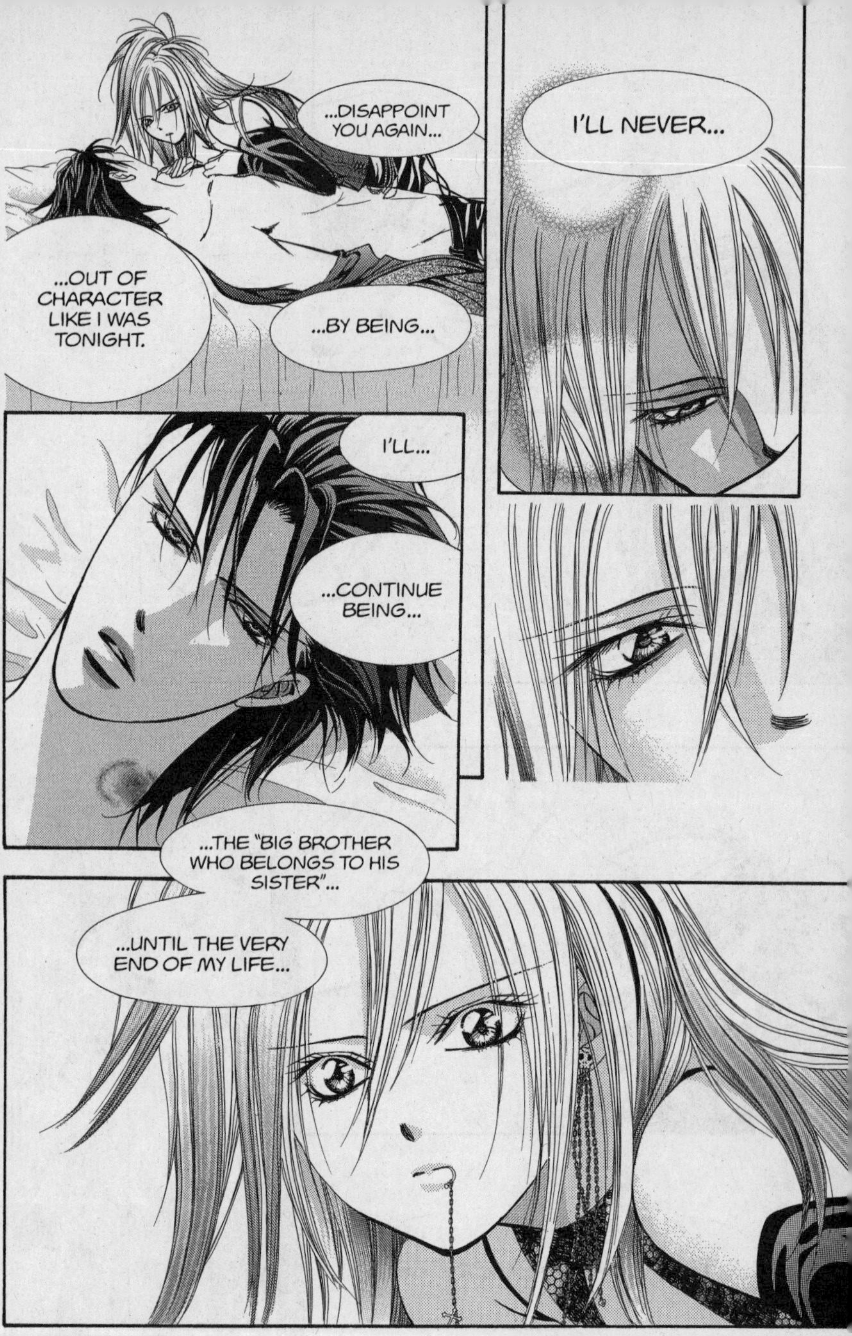
I'LL NEVER...
...DISAPPOINT YOU AGAIN...
...BY BEING...
...OUT OF CHARACTER LIKE I WAS TONIGHT.
I'LL...
...CONTINUE BEING...
...THE "BIG BROTHER WHO BELONGS TO HIS SISTER"...
...UNTIL THE VERY END OF MY LIFE...

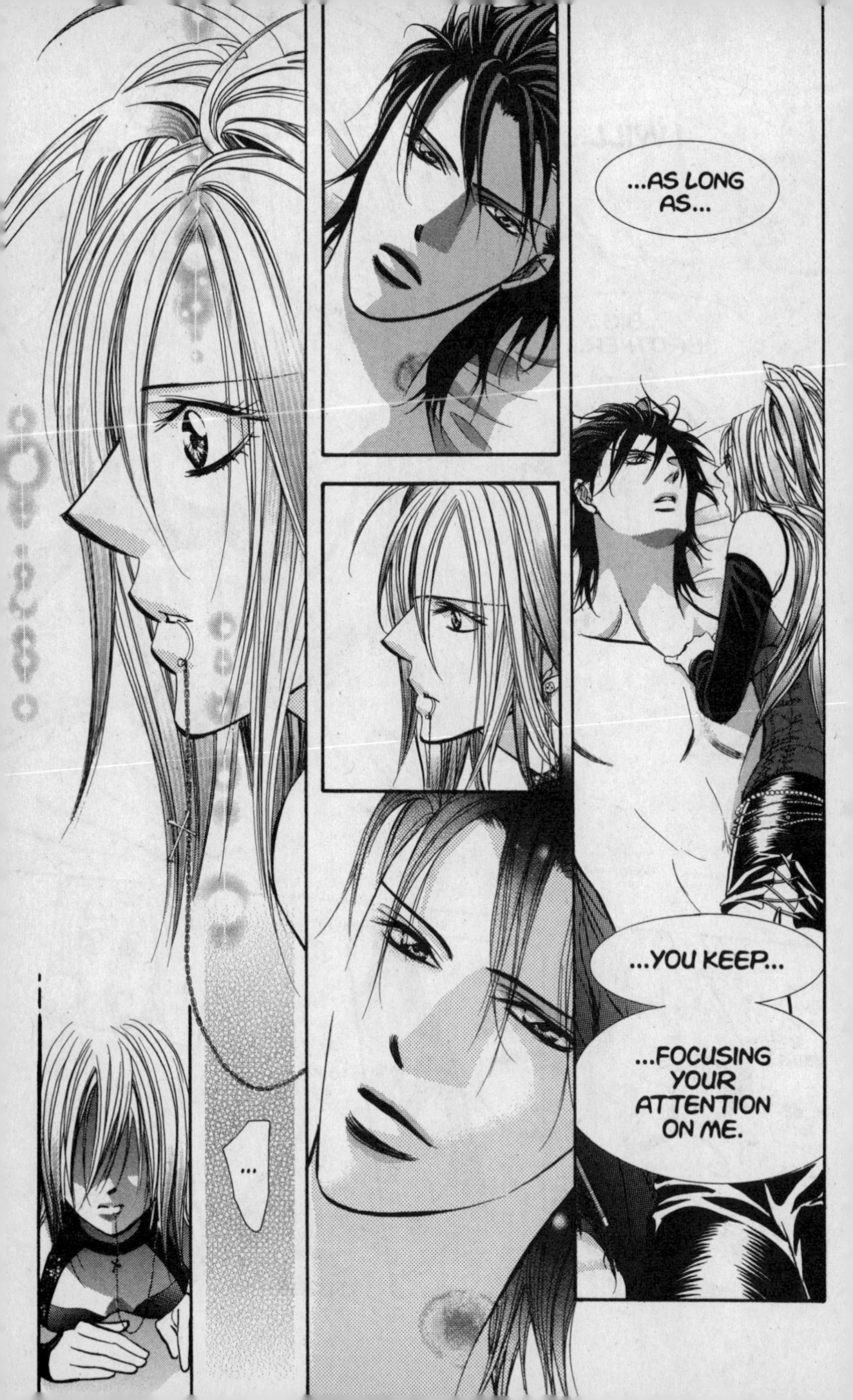
...AS LONG AS...
...YOU KEEP...
...FOCUSING YOUR ATTENTION ON ME.
...

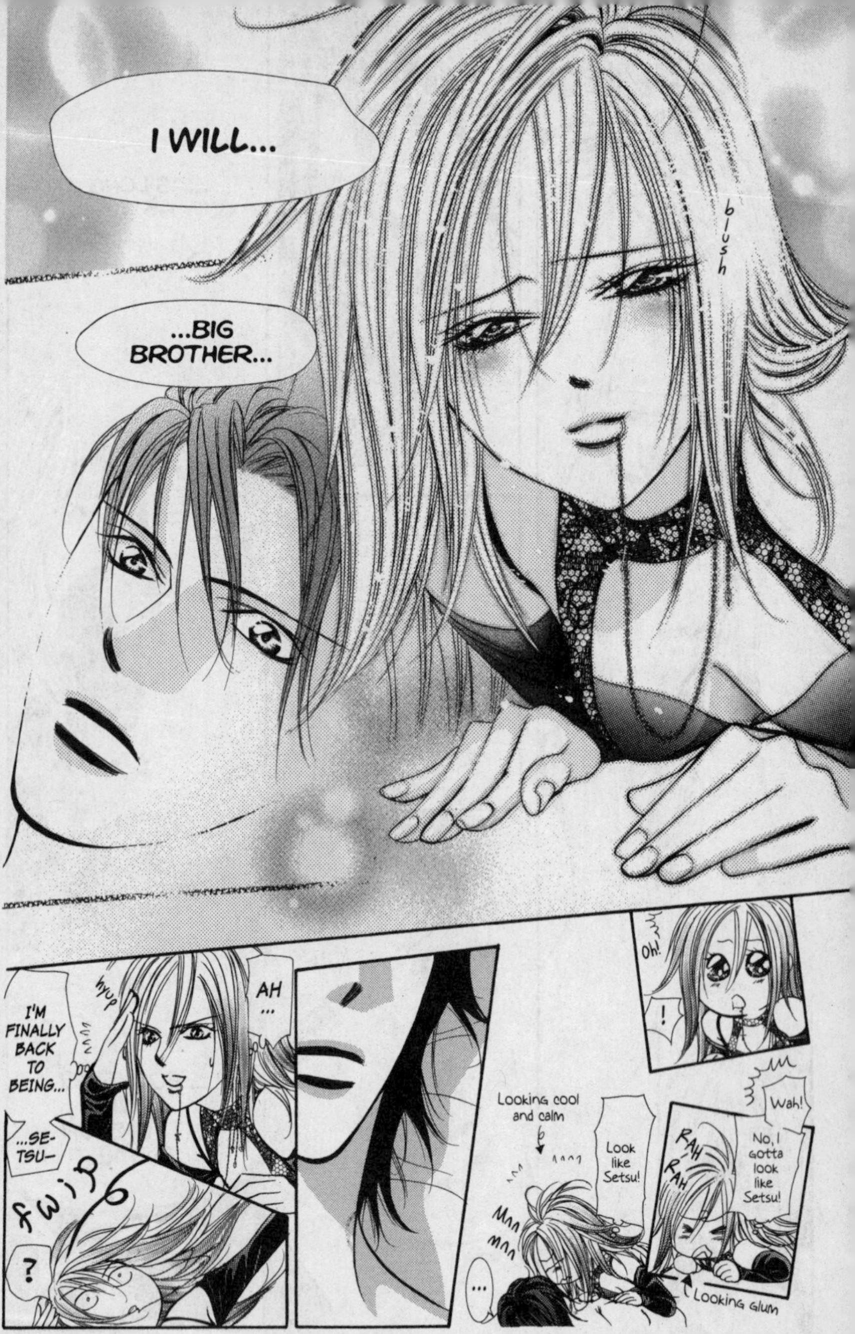
I WILL...
...BIG BROTHER...
blush
Oh!
!
Wah!
No, I gotta look like Setsu!
RAH RAH
Looking Glum
Look like Setsu!
Looking cool and calm
Mnn Mnn
...
AH...
hyup
I'M FINALLY BACK TO BEING...
...SE-TSU-
fwip
?

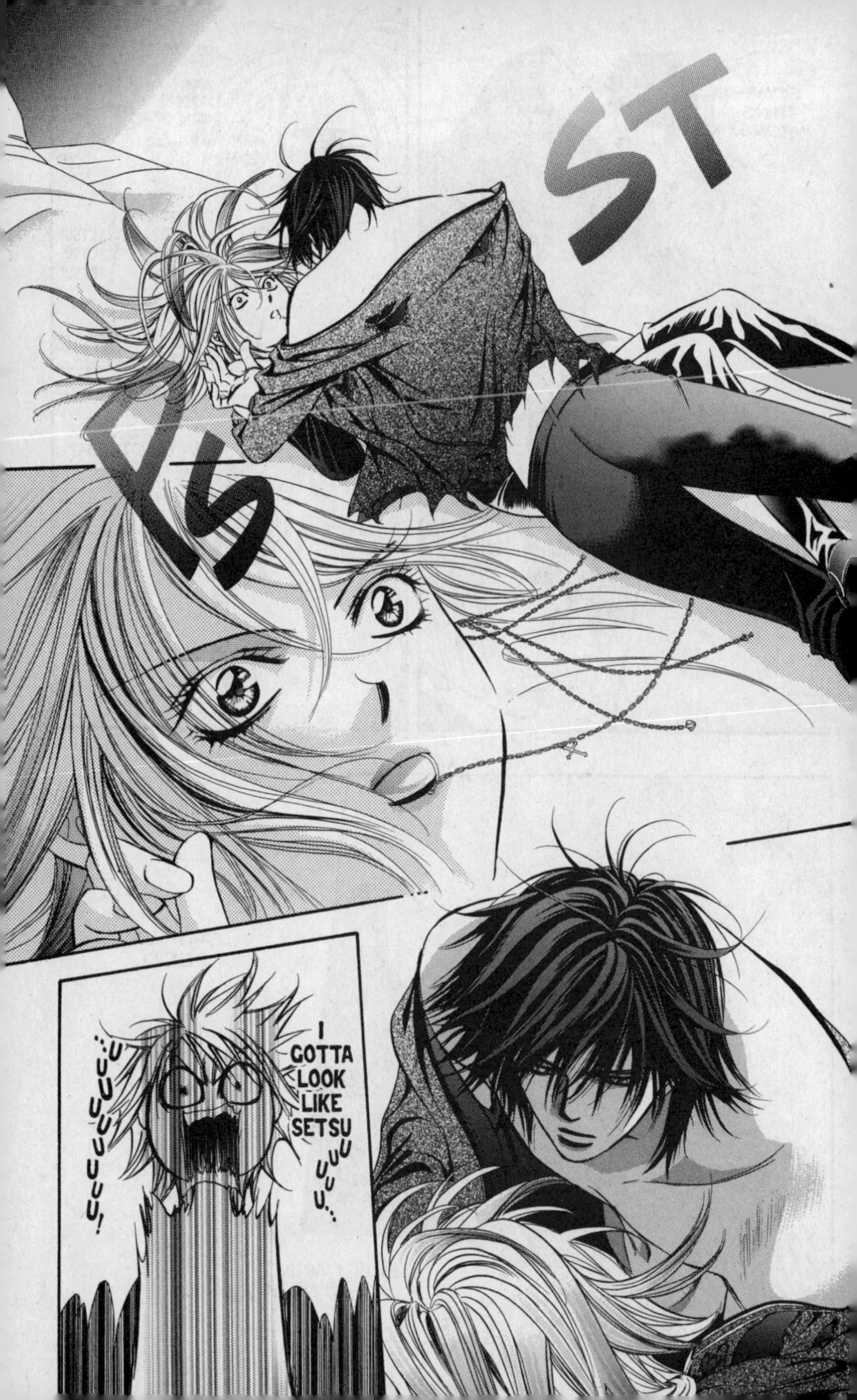
ST
I GOTTA LOOK LIKE SETSU
UUUUUU...
...UUUUUUUUUU!

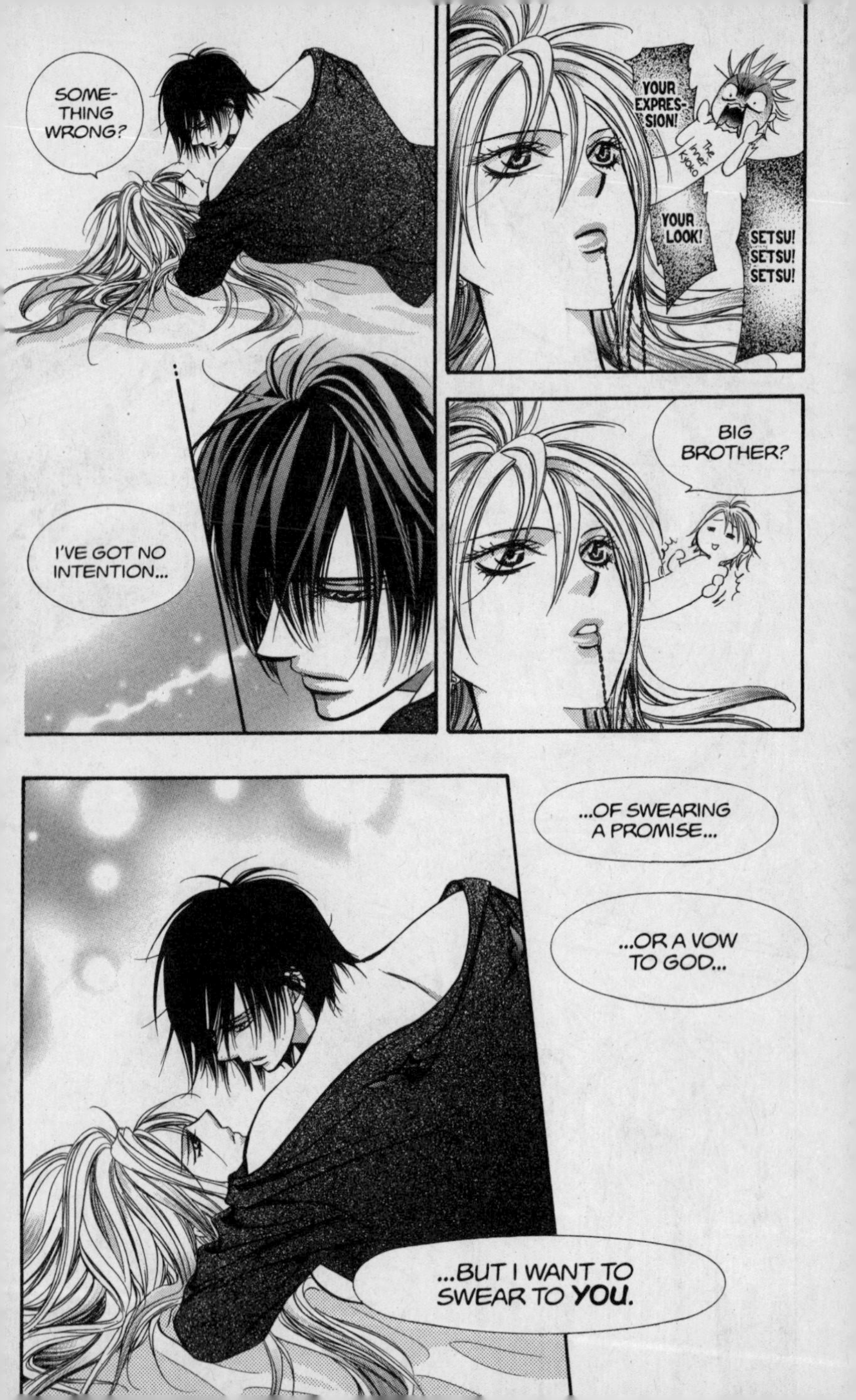
YOUR EXPRESSION!
The Inner Kyoko
YOUR LOOK!
SETSU! SETSU! SETSU!
SOME-THING WRONG?
BIG BROTHER?
I'VE GOT NO INTENTION...
...OF SWEARING A PROMISE...
...OR A VOW TO GOD...
...BUT I WANT TO SWEAR TO **YOU**.

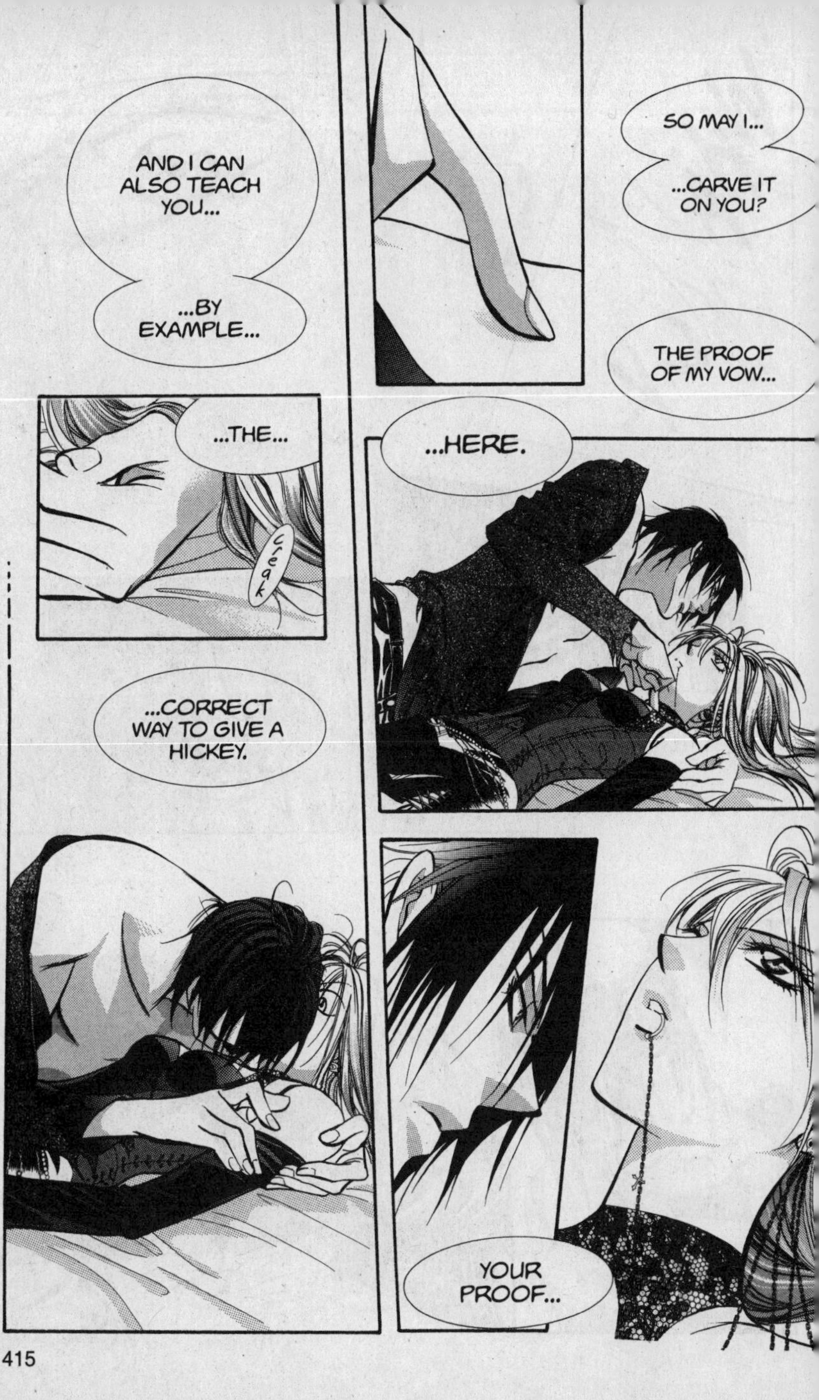
SO MAY I...
...CARVE IT ON YOU?
THE PROOF OF MY VOW...
...HERE.
YOUR PROOF...
AND I CAN ALSO TEACH YOU...
...BY EXAMPLE...
...THE...
Creak
...CORRECT WAY TO GIVE A HICKEY.

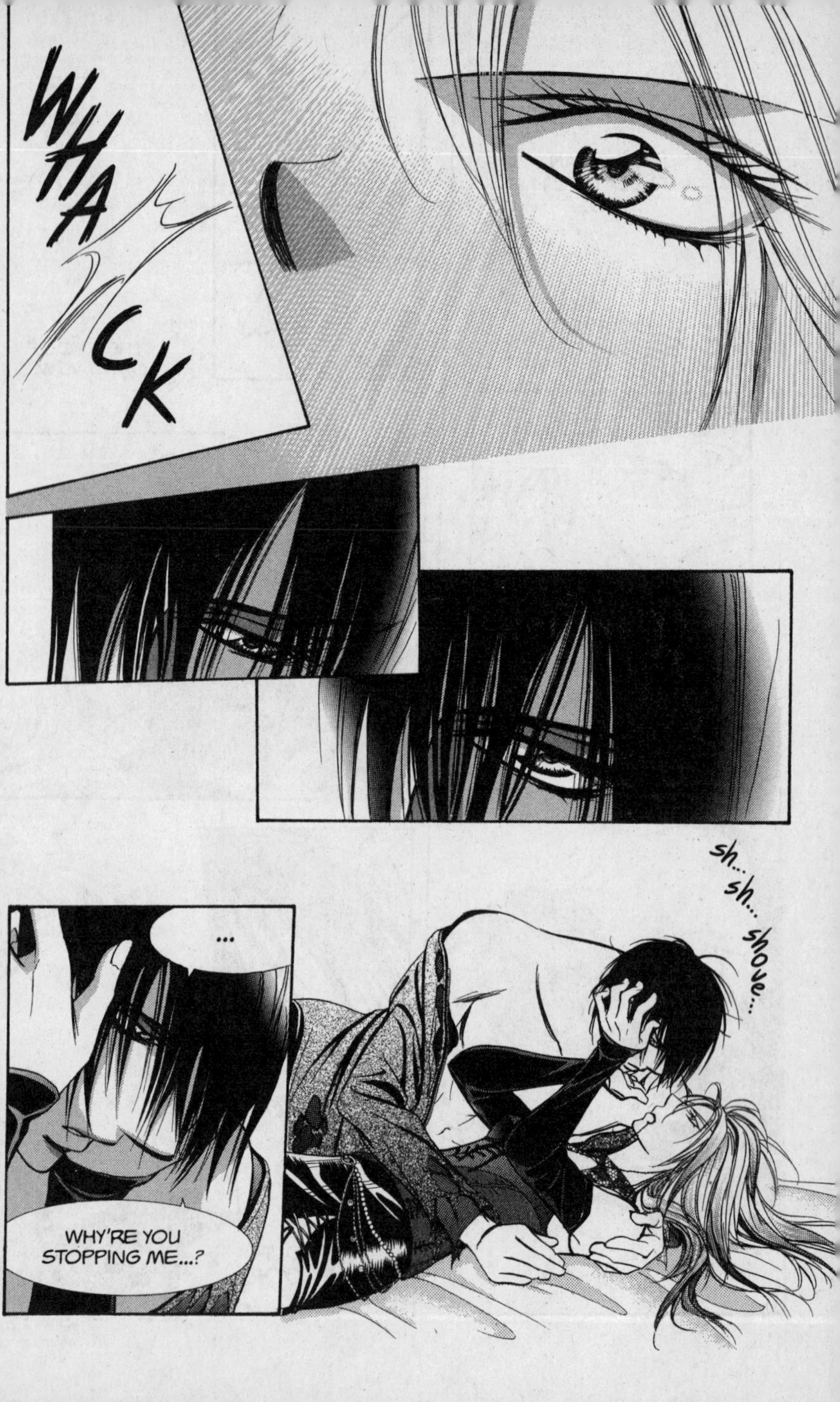
WHAMACK
sh... sh... shove...
...
WHY'RE YOU STOPPING ME...?

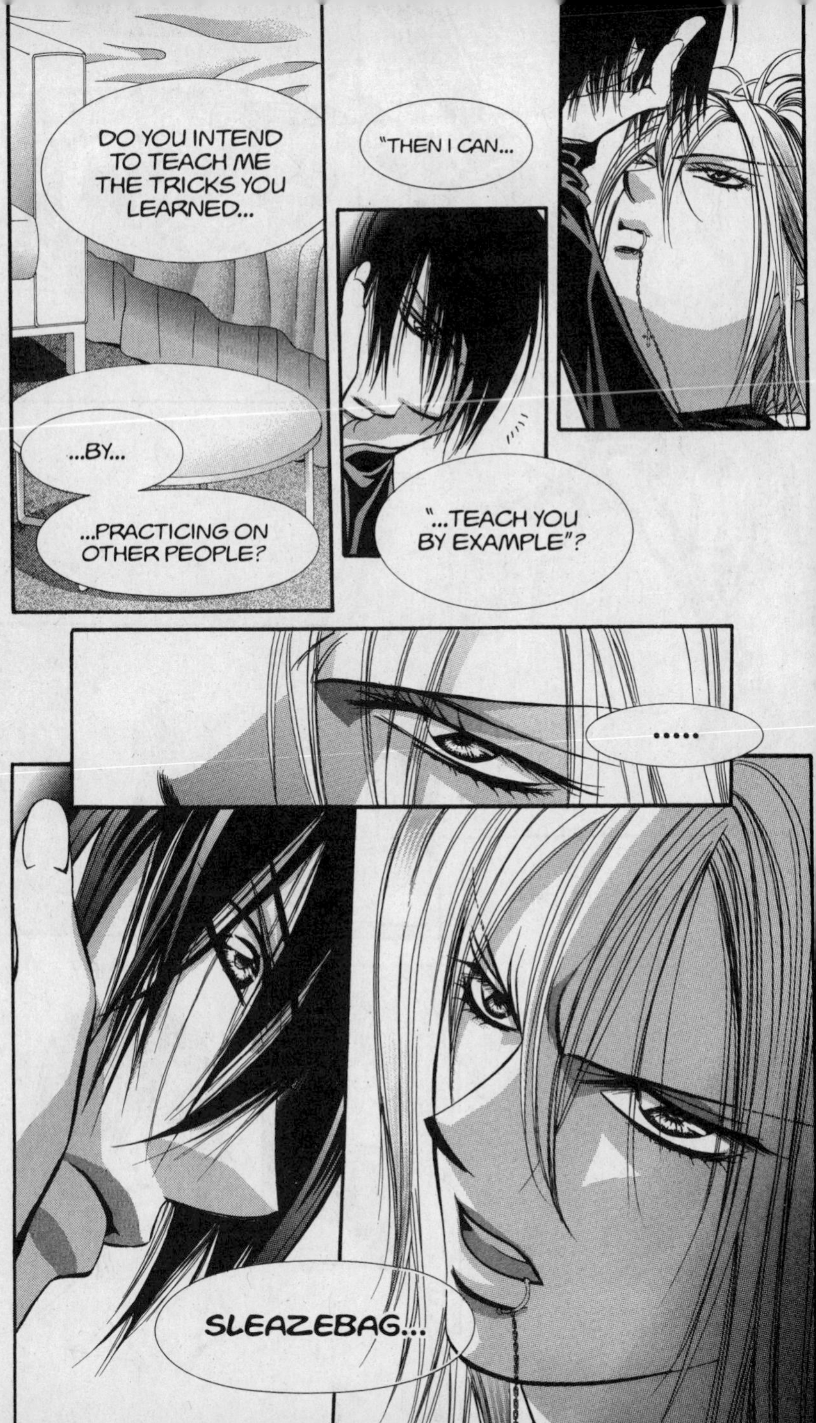
"THEN I CAN...
"...TEACH YOU BY EXAMPLE"?
DO YOU INTEND TO TEACH ME THE TRICKS YOU LEARNED...
...BY...
...PRACTICING ON OTHER PEOPLE?
.....
SLEAZEBAG...

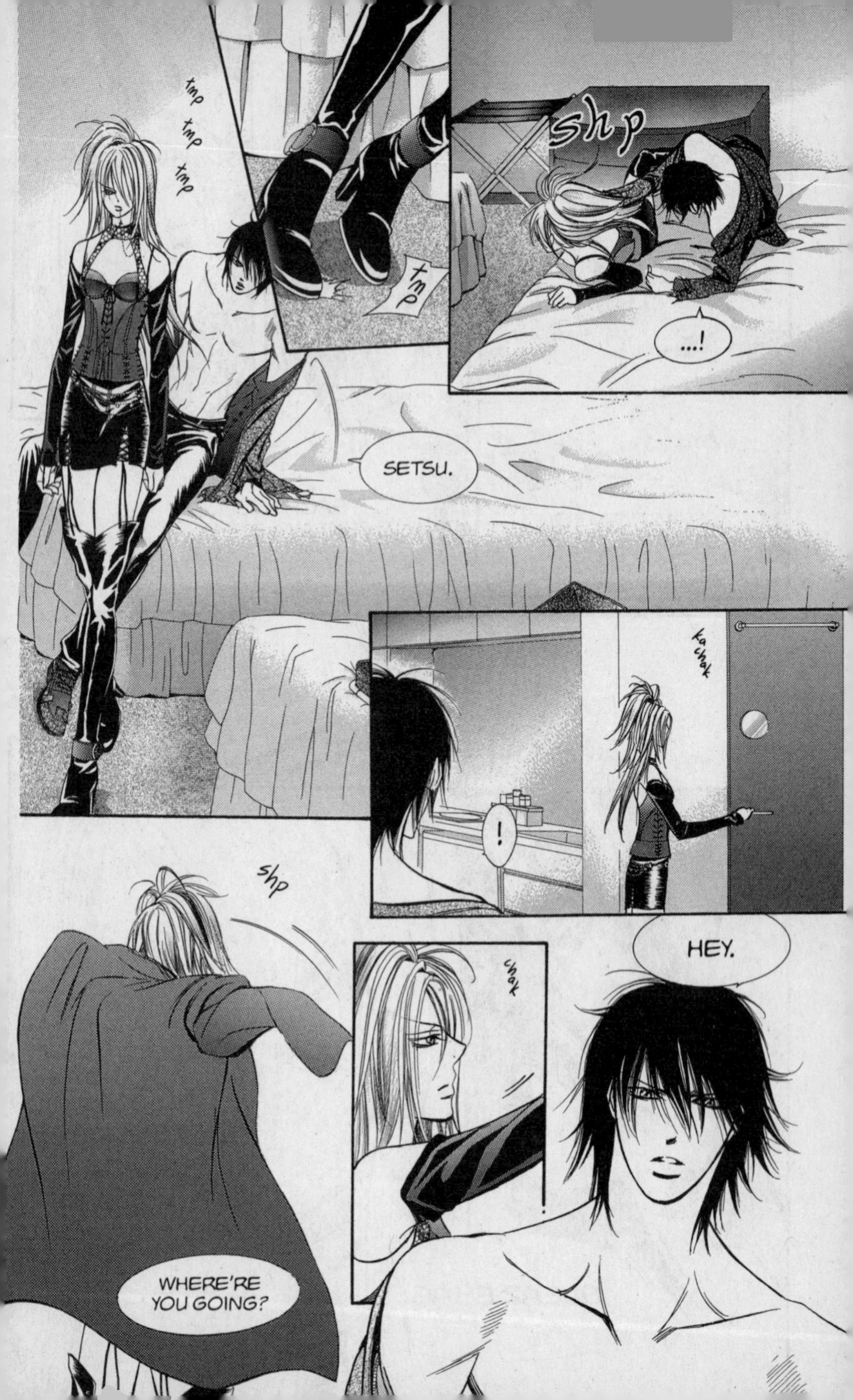
shp
...!
tmp
tmp tmp tmp
SETSU.
ka chak
!
HEY.
chak
shp
WHERE'RE YOU GOING?

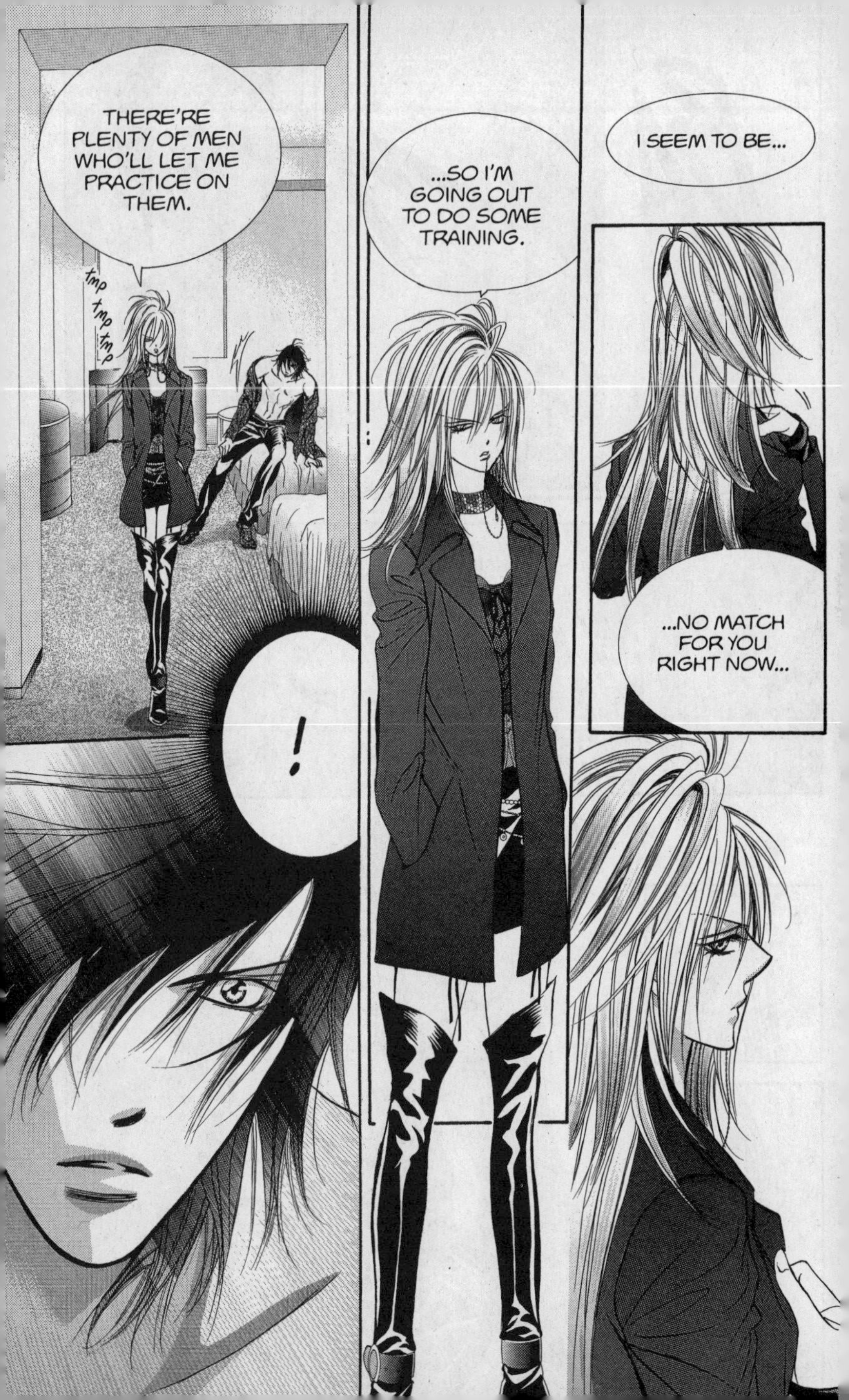
I SEEM TO BE...
...NO MATCH FOR YOU RIGHT NOW...
...SO I'M GOING OUT TO DO SOME TRAINING.
THERE'RE PLENTY OF MEN WHO'LL LET ME PRACTICE ON THEM.
tmp tmp tmp
!

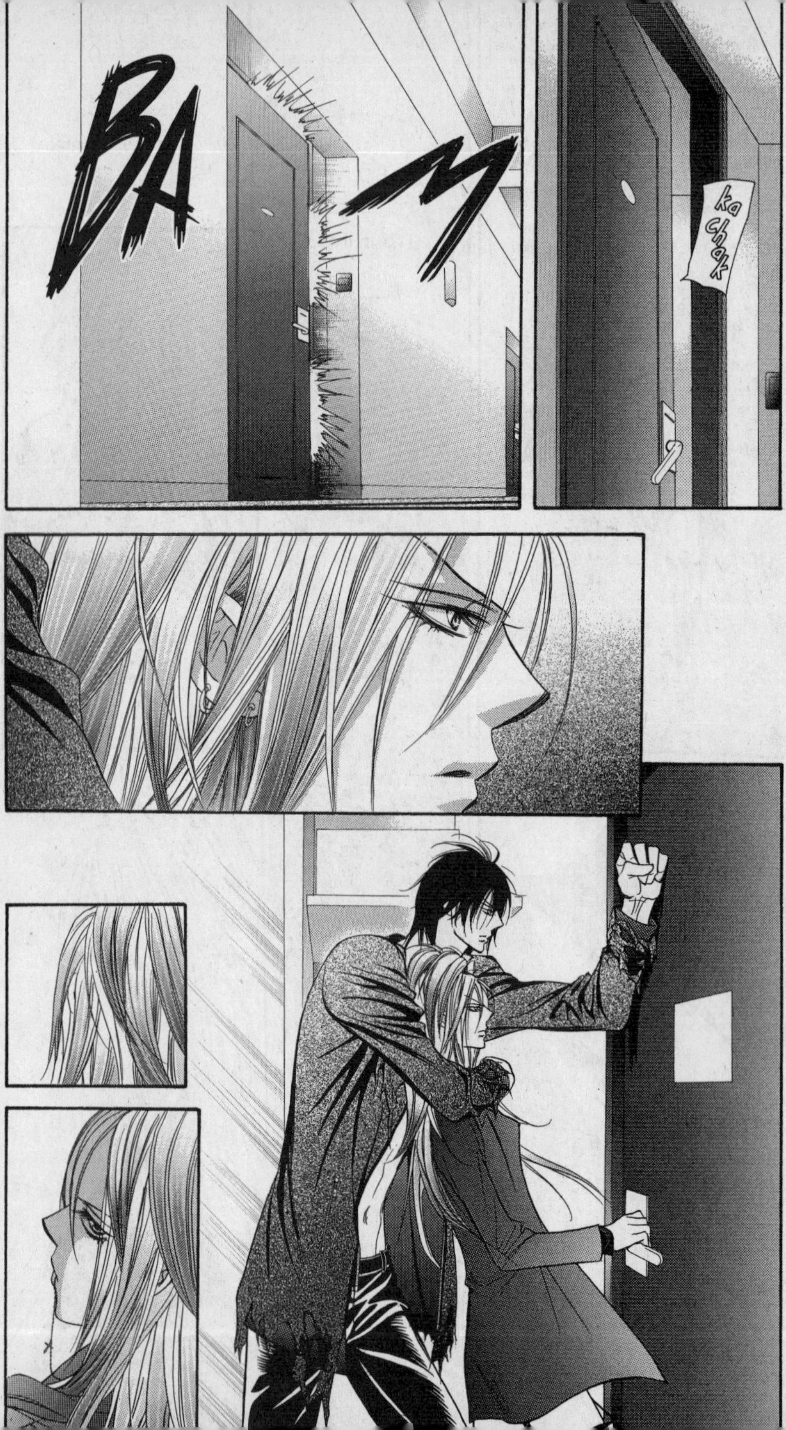
ka chak
BAM

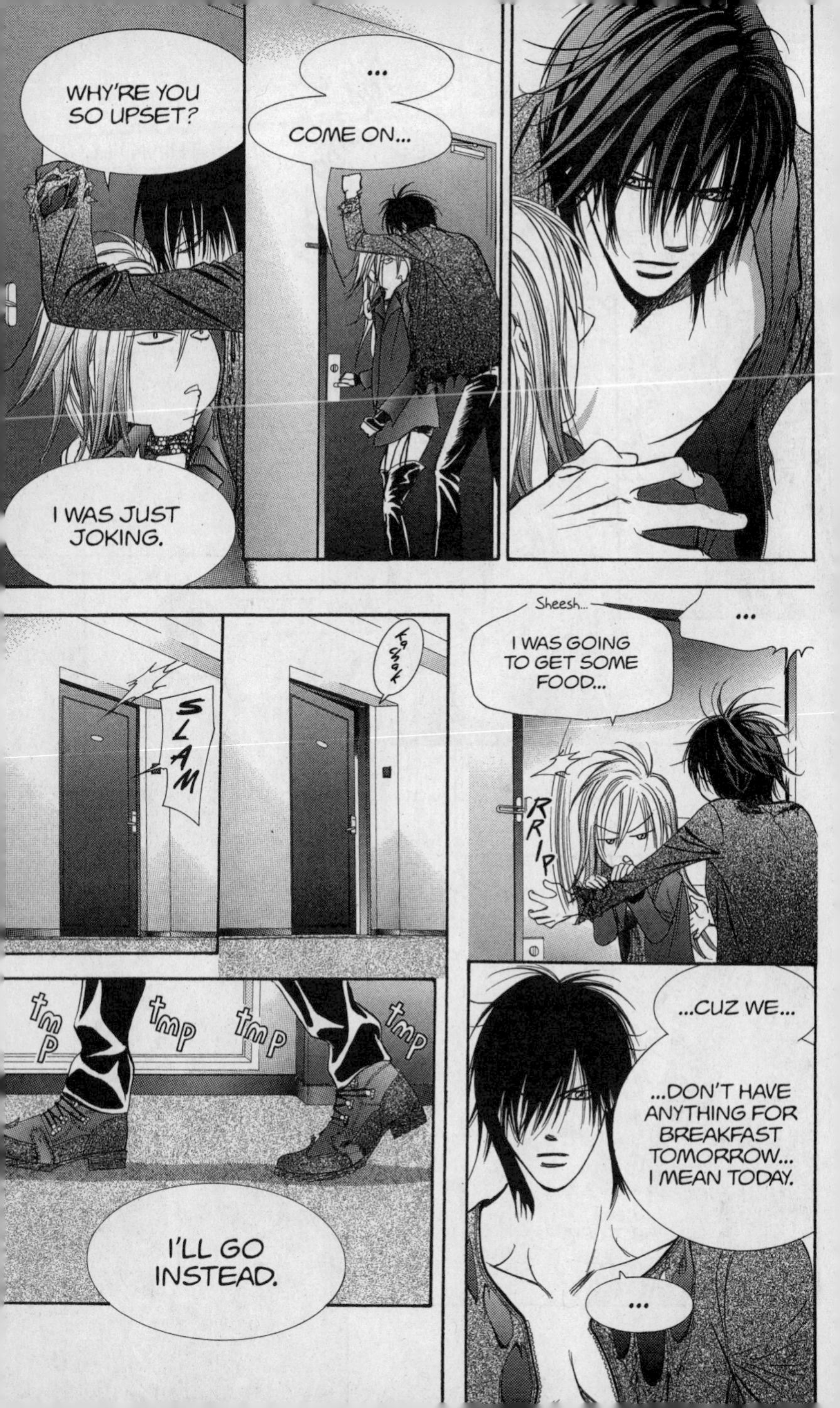
...
COME ON...
WHY'RE YOU SO UPSET?
I WAS JUST JOKING.
Sheesh...
I WAS GOING TO GET SOME FOOD...
...
RRIP
ka chak
SLAM
...CUZ WE...
...DON'T HAVE ANYTHING FOR BREAKFAST TOMORROW... I MEAN TODAY.
...
tmp
tmp
tmp
tmp
I'LL GO INSTEAD.

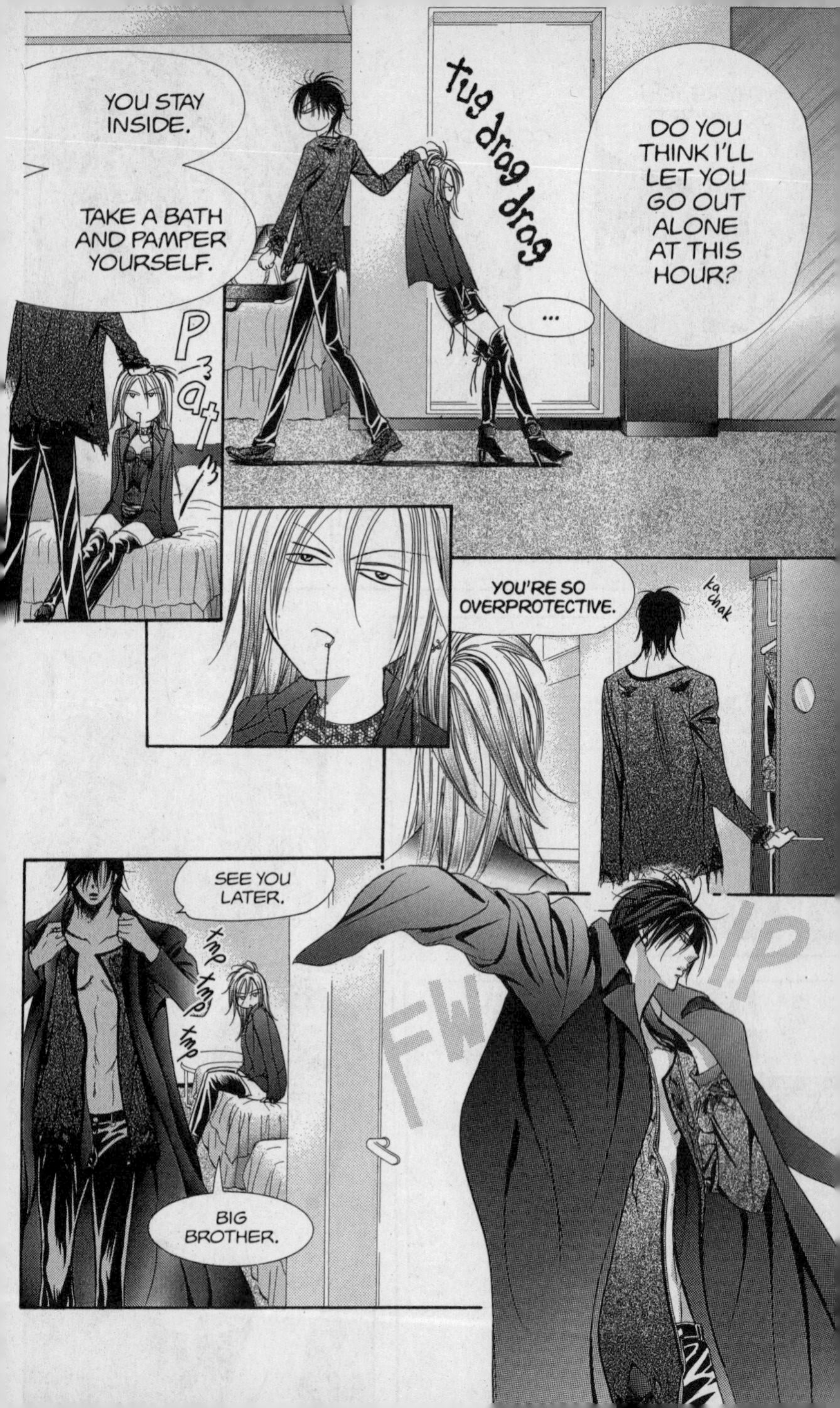

DO YOU THINK I'LL LET YOU GO OUT ALONE AT THIS HOUR?
tug drag drag
...
YOU STAY INSIDE.
TAKE A BATH AND PAMPER YOURSELF.
Pat
YOU'RE SO OVERPROTECTIVE.
ka chak
FWIP
SEE YOU LATER.
tmp tmp tmp
BIG BROTHER.

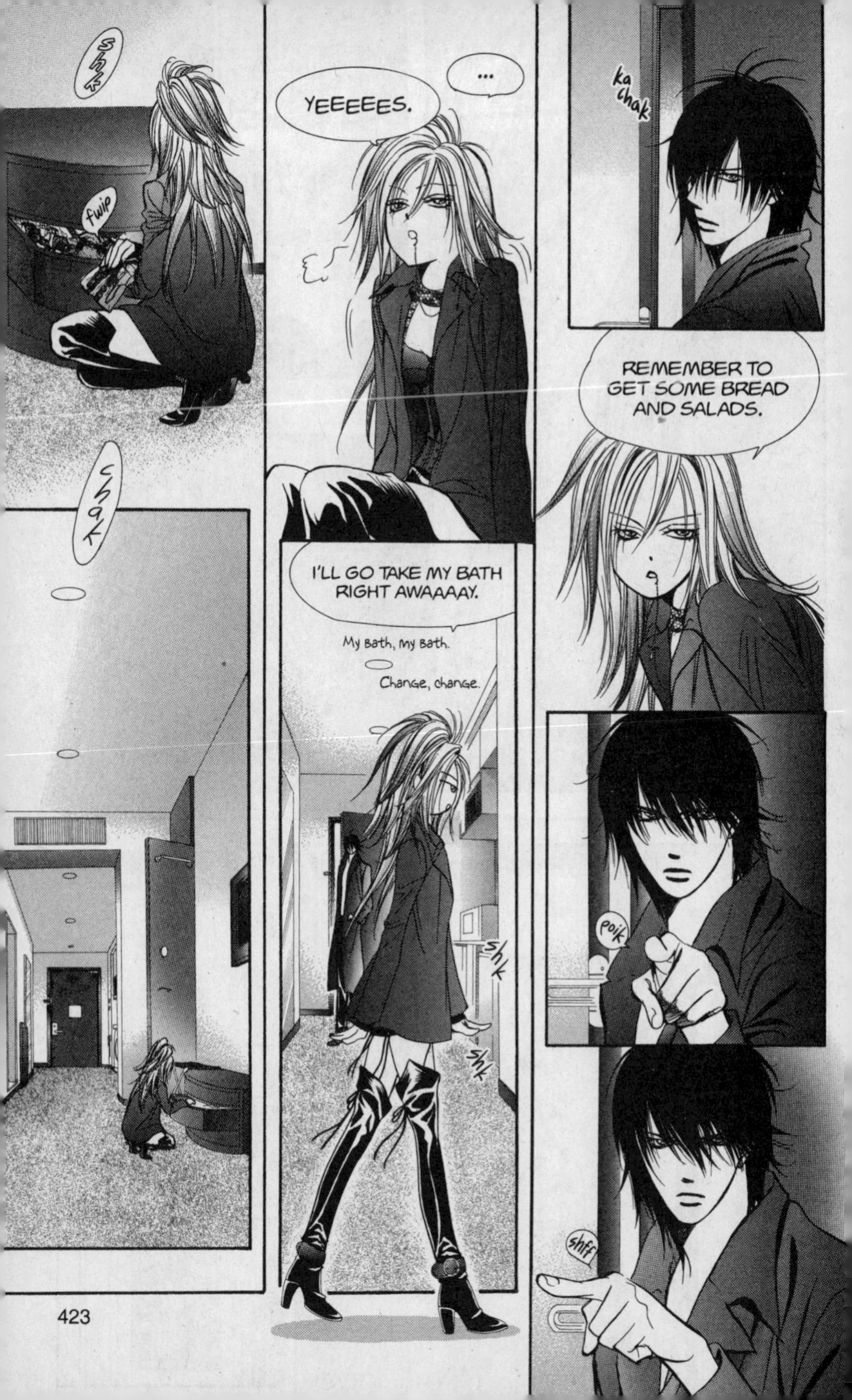
ka chak
REMEMBER TO GET SOME BREAD AND SALADS.
poik
shff
...
YEEEEEES.
I'LL GO TAKE MY BATH RIGHT AWAAAAY.
My Bath, my Bath.
Change, change.
shk
shk
shk
fwip
chak

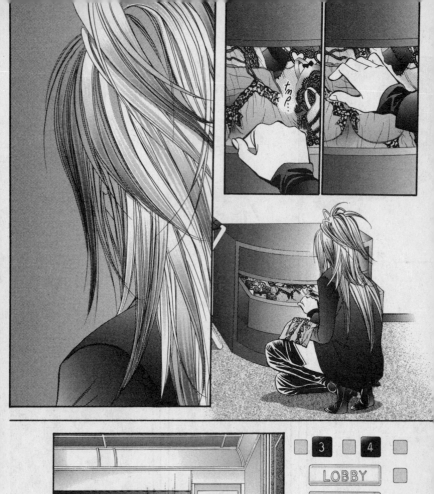

tmp...

COME
ON.

.....

3 4

LOBBY

B1

fsh

8

fsh

10

fsh

9

vree

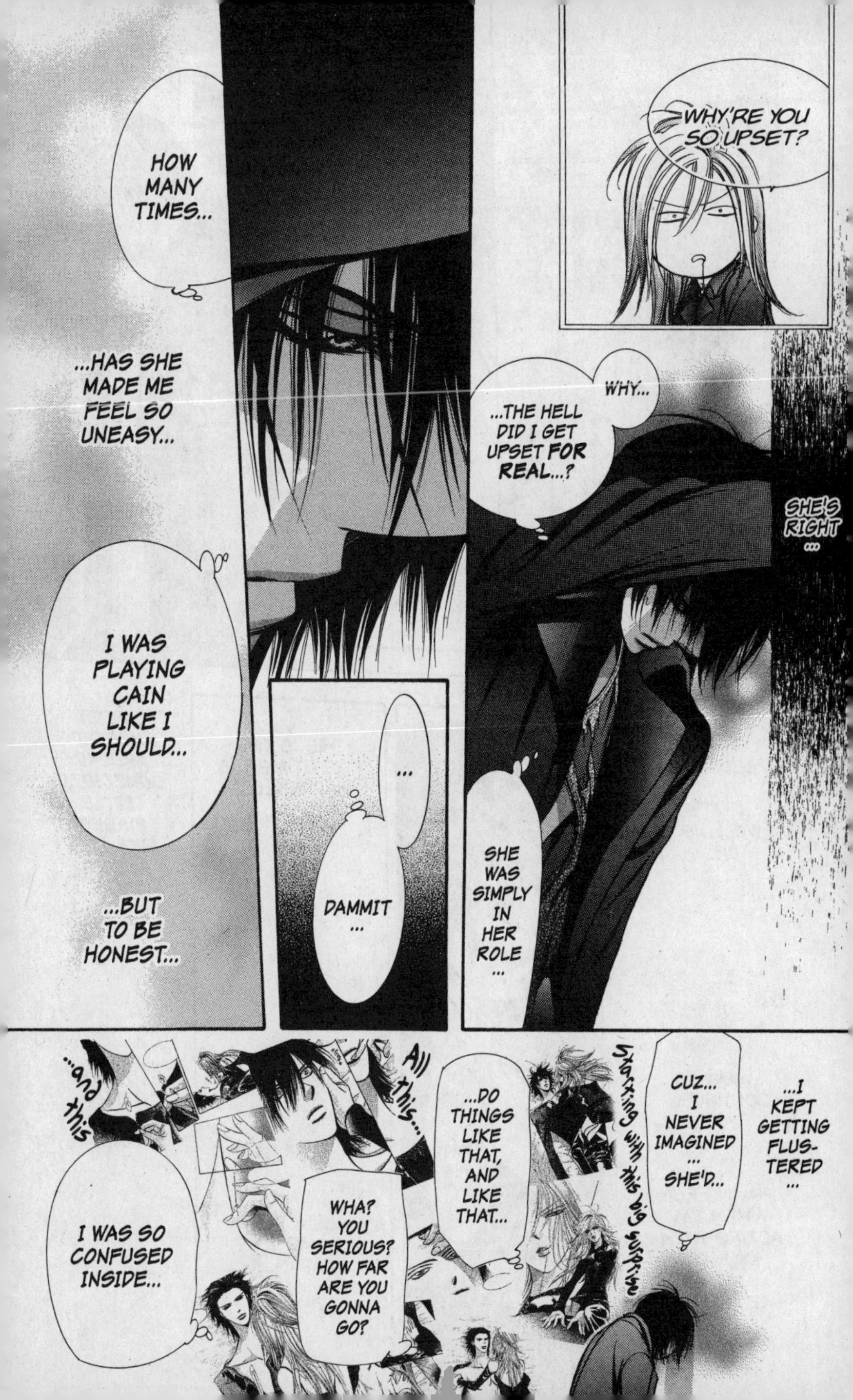
WHY'RE YOU SO UPSET?
SHE'S RIGHT...
WHY...
...THE HELL DID I GET UPSET FOR REAL...?
SHE WAS SIMPLY IN HER ROLE...
HOW MANY TIMES...
...HAS SHE MADE ME FEEL SO UNEASY...
...
DAMMIT...
I WAS PLAYING CAIN LIKE I SHOULD...
...BUT TO BE HONEST...
...I KEPT GETTING FLUSTERED...
CUZ... I NEVER IMAGINED... SHE'D...
Starting with this big surprise
...DO THINGS LIKE THAT, AND LIKE THAT...
All this...
WHA? YOU SERIOUS? HOW FAR ARE YOU GONNA GO?
...and this
I WAS SO CONFUSED INSIDE...

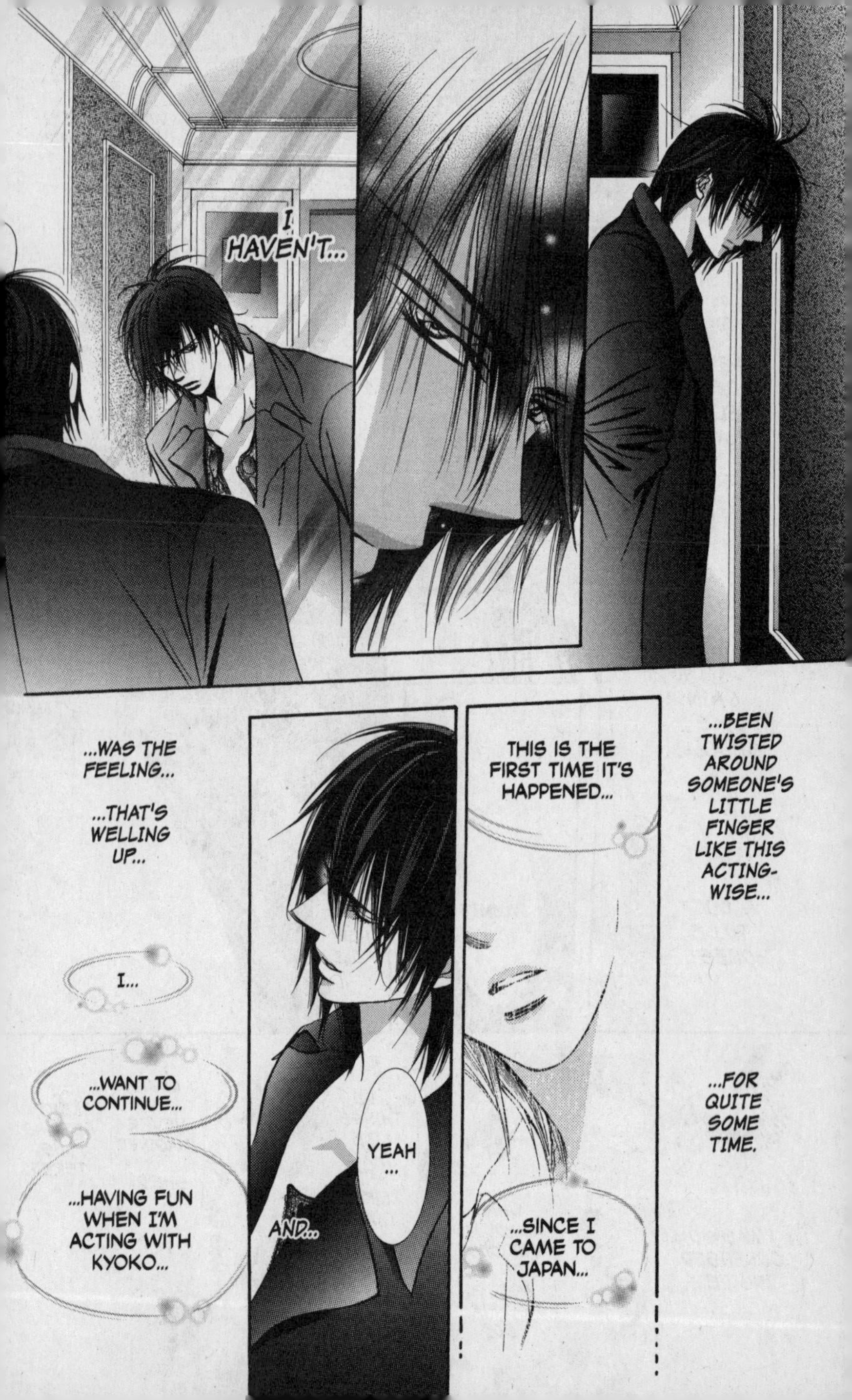
I HAVEN'T...
...BEEN TWISTED AROUND SOMEONE'S LITTLE FINGER LIKE THIS ACTING-WISE...
...FOR QUITE SOME TIME.
THIS IS THE FIRST TIME IT'S HAPPENED...
...SINCE I CAME TO JAPAN...
YEAH...
AND...
I...
...WANT TO CONTINUE...
...HAVING FUN WHEN I'M ACTING WITH KYOKO...
...WAS THE FEELING...
...THAT'S WELLING UP...

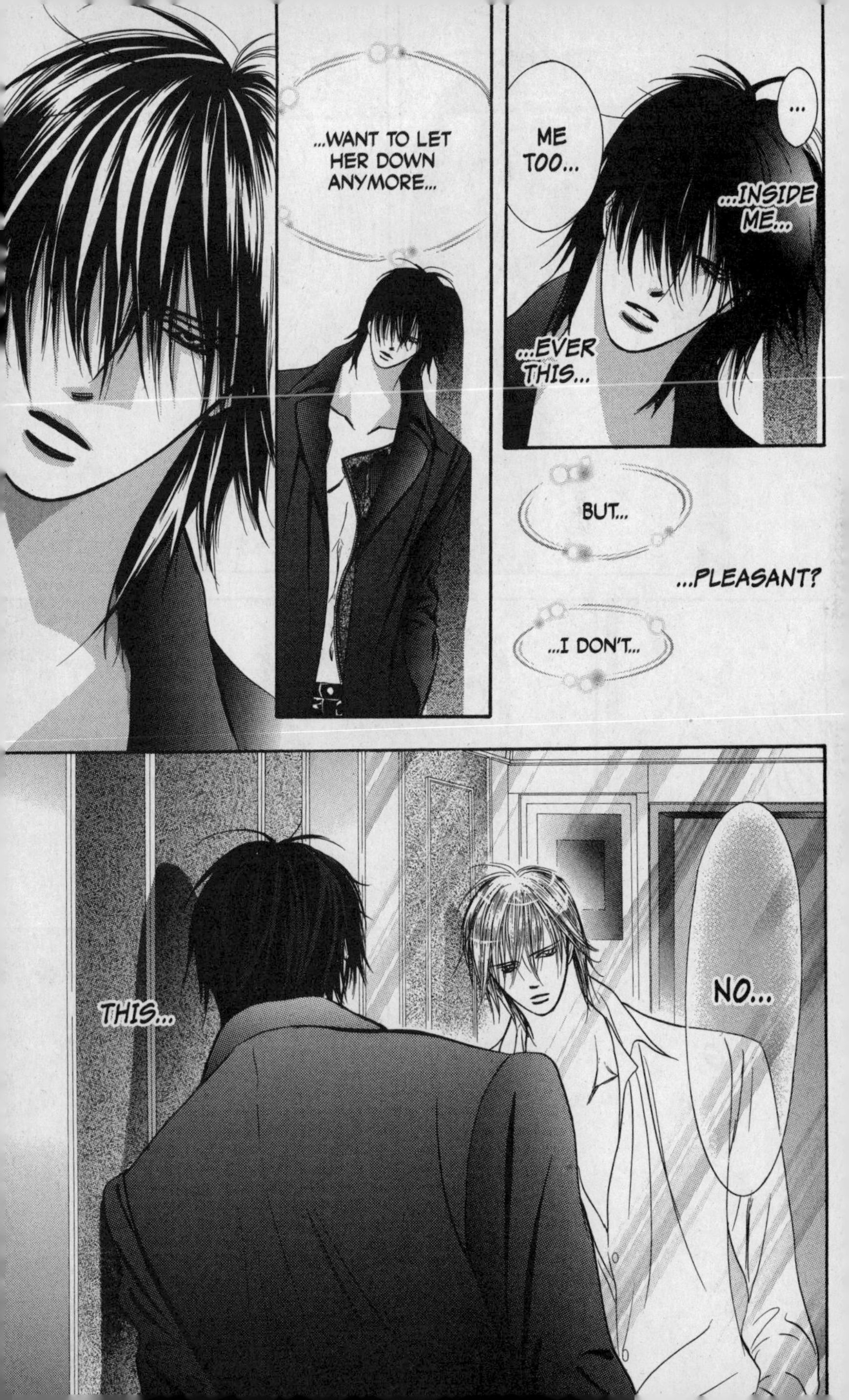
...
...INSIDE ME...
ME TOO...
...EVER THIS...
BUT...
...PLEASANT?
...I DON'T...
...WANT TO LET HER DOWN ANYMORE...
NO...
THIS...

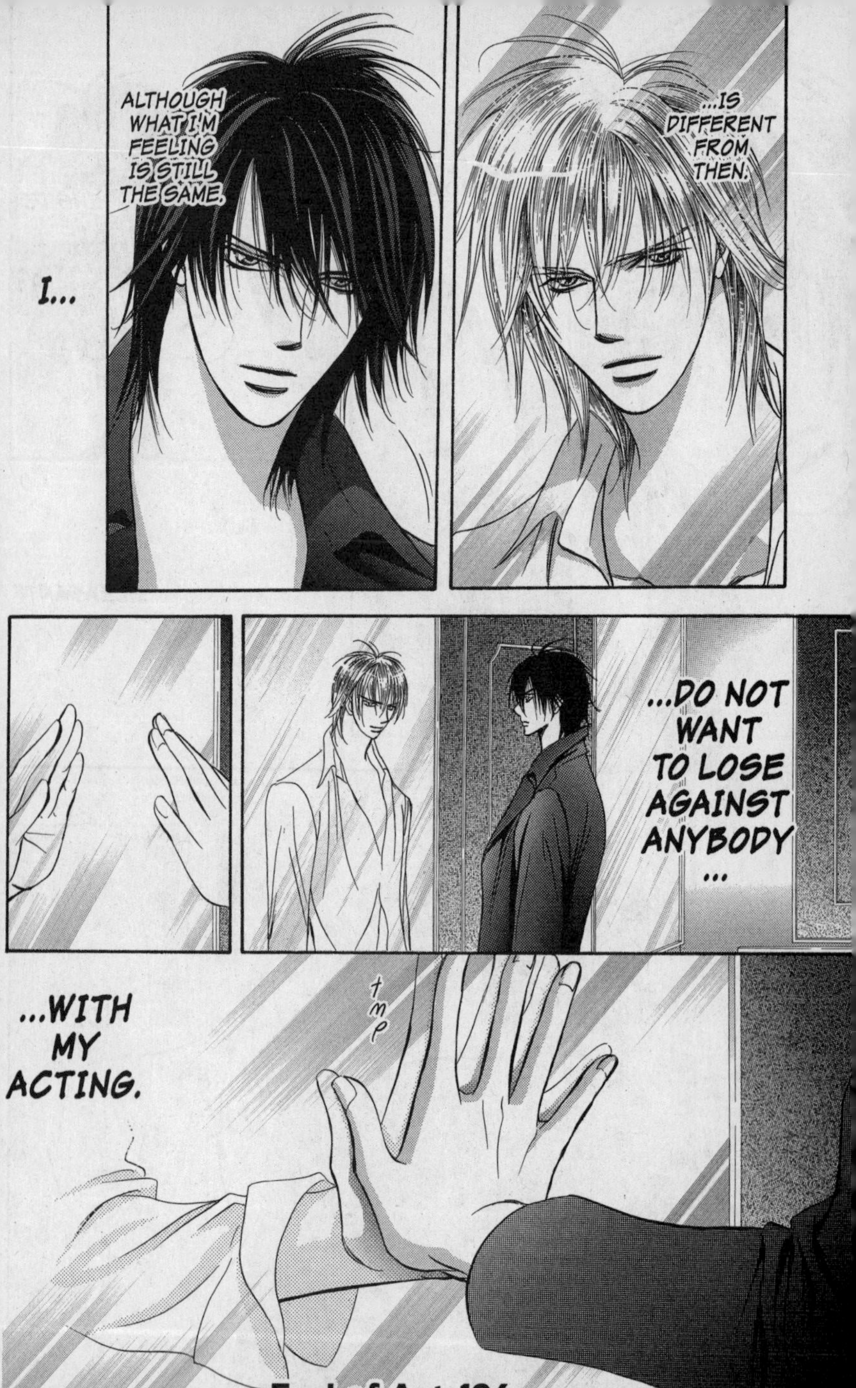
...IS DIFFERENT FROM THEN.
ALTHOUGH WHAT I'M FEELING IS STILL THE SAME.
I...
...DO NOT WANT TO LOSE AGAINST ANYBODY ...
tmp
...WITH MY ACTING.

End of Act 196

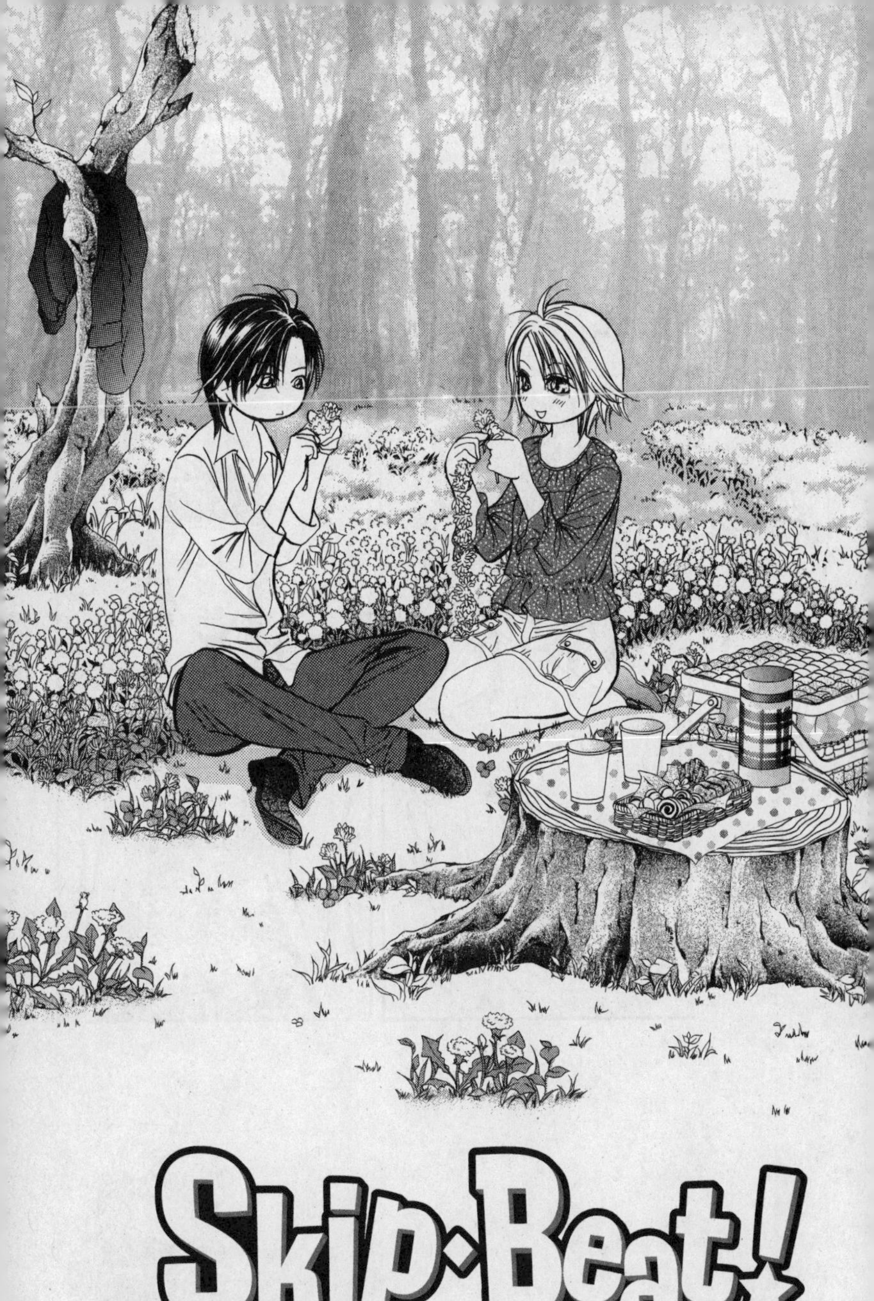

Skip·Beat!

Act 197: Turning Point

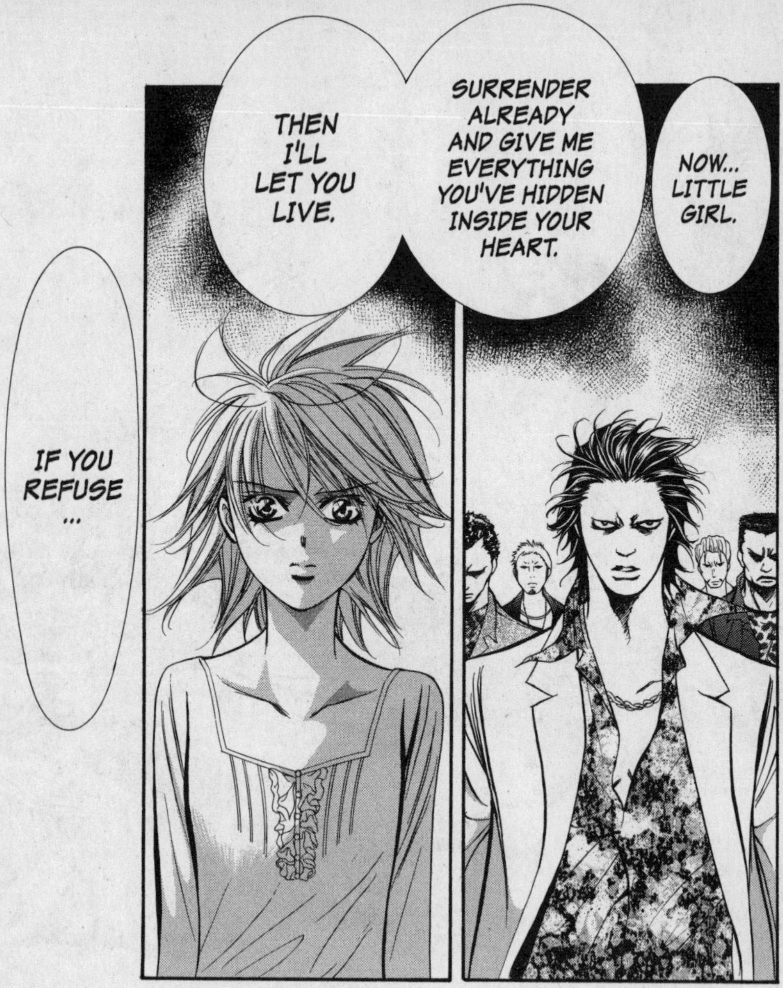
NOW... LITTLE GIRL.
SURRENDER ALREADY AND GIVE ME EVERYTHING YOU'VE HIDDEN INSIDE YOUR HEART.
THEN I'LL LET YOU LIVE.
IF YOU REFUSE ...

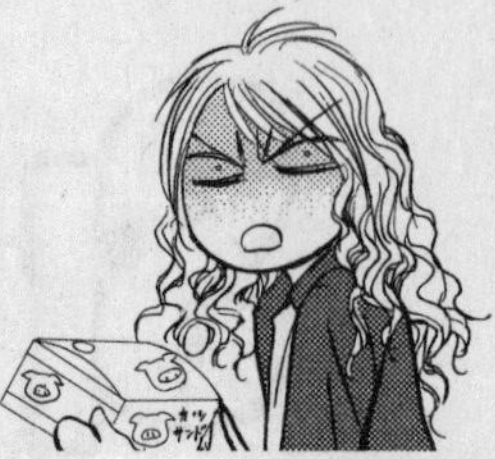

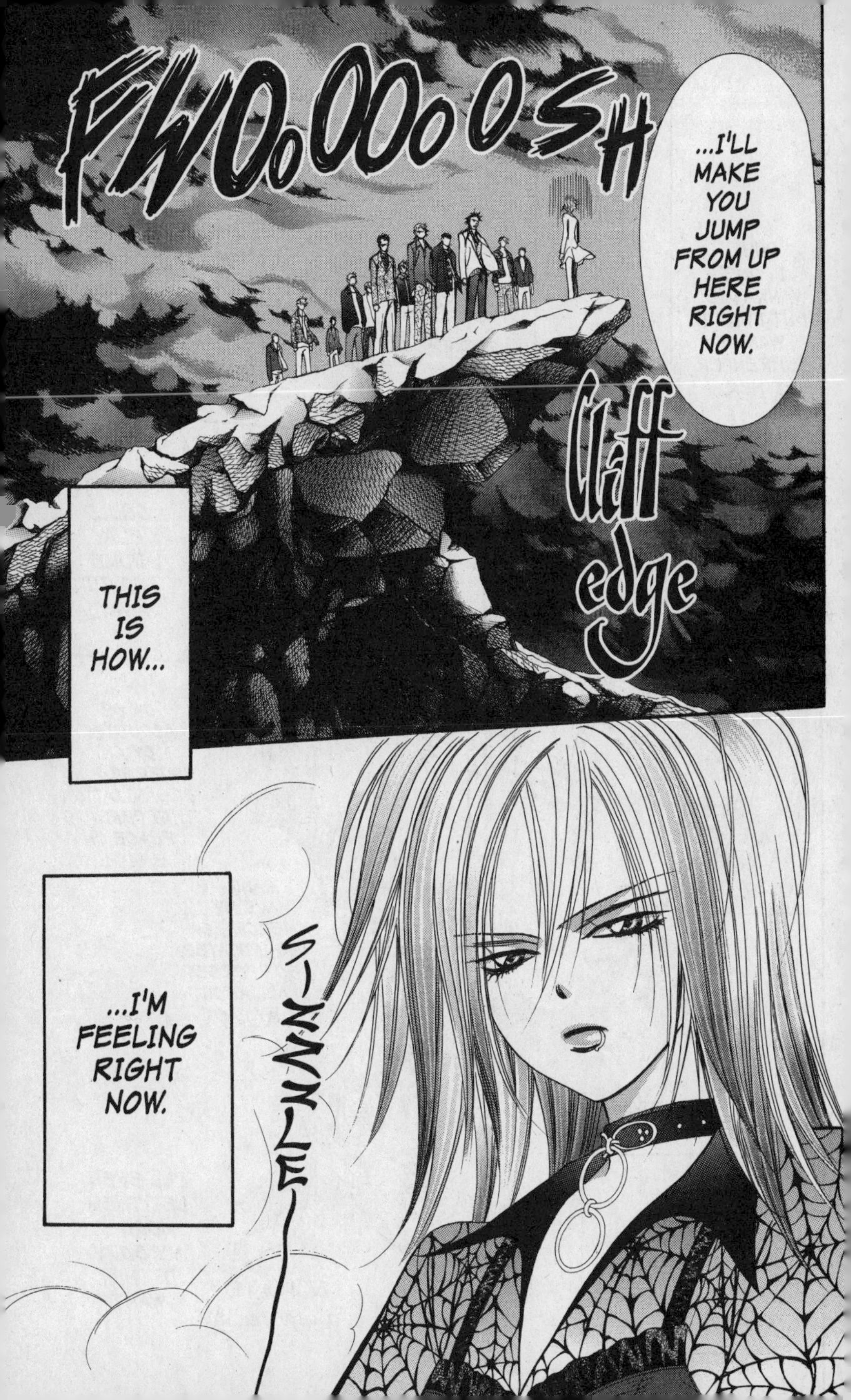
...I'LL MAKE YOU JUMP FROM UP HERE RIGHT NOW.
FWOoOOoOSH
Cliff edge
THIS IS HOW...
S-I-ZZZLE
...I'M FEELING RIGHT NOW.

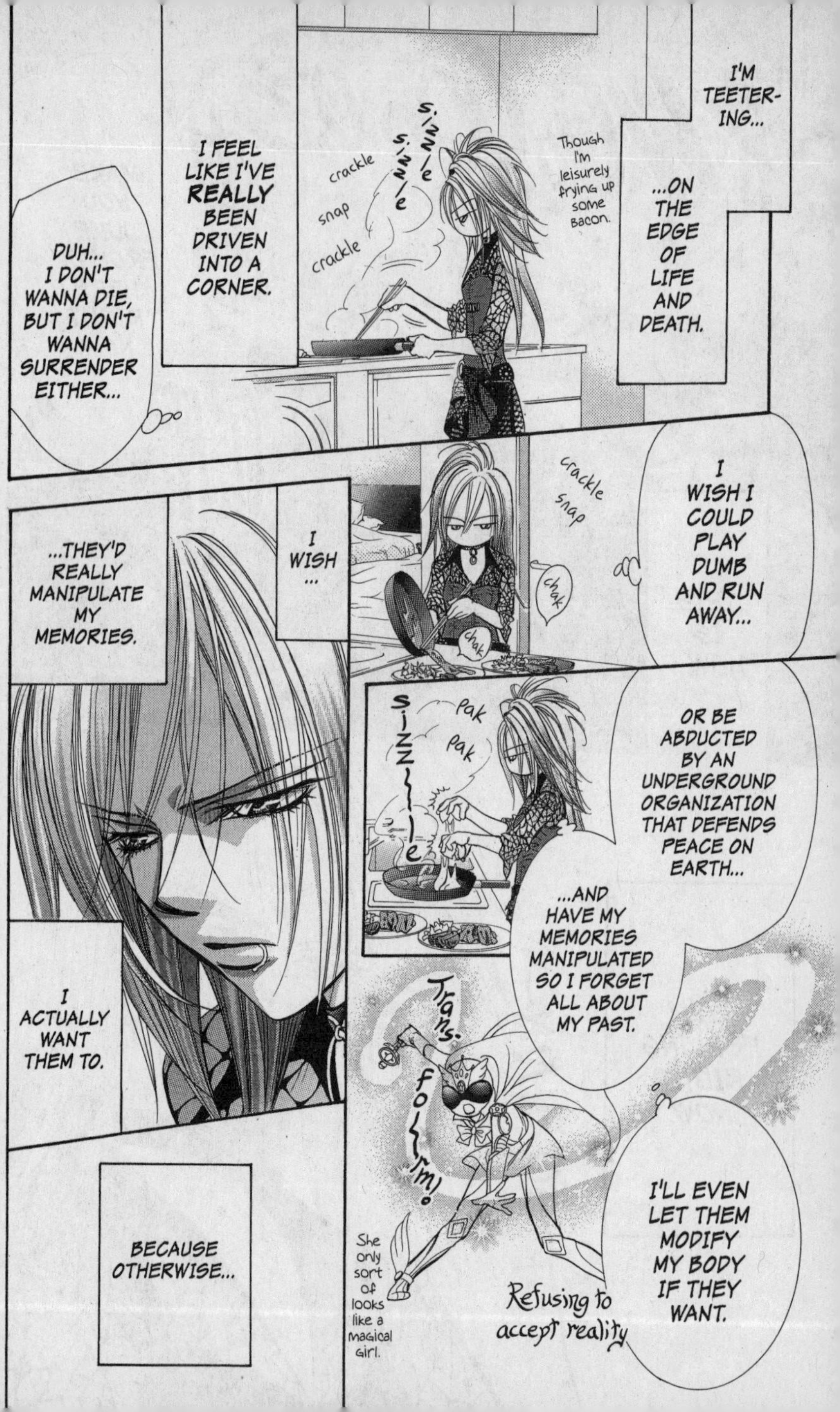

I'M TEETERING-ING...
...ON THE EDGE OF LIFE AND DEATH.
Though I'm leisurely frying up some bacon.
sizzle
sizzle
crackle
snap
crackle
I FEEL LIKE I'VE REALLY BEEN DRIVEN INTO A CORNER.
DUH... I DON'T WANNA DIE, BUT I DON'T WANNA SURRENDER EITHER...
I WISH I COULD PLAY DUMB AND RUN AWAY...
crackle
snap
chak
chak
OR BE ABDUCTED BY AN UNDERGROUND ORGANIZATION THAT DEFENDS PEACE ON EARTH...
sizz~~le
pak
pak
...AND HAVE MY MEMORIES MANIPULATED SO I FORGET ALL ABOUT MY PAST.
I'LL EVEN LET THEM MODIFY MY BODY IF THEY WANT.
Trans-fo~~rm!
She only sort of looks like a magical girl.
Refusing to accept reality
I WISH...
...THEY'D REALLY MANIPULATE MY MEMORIES.
I ACTUALLY WANT THEM TO.
BECAUSE OTHERWISE...

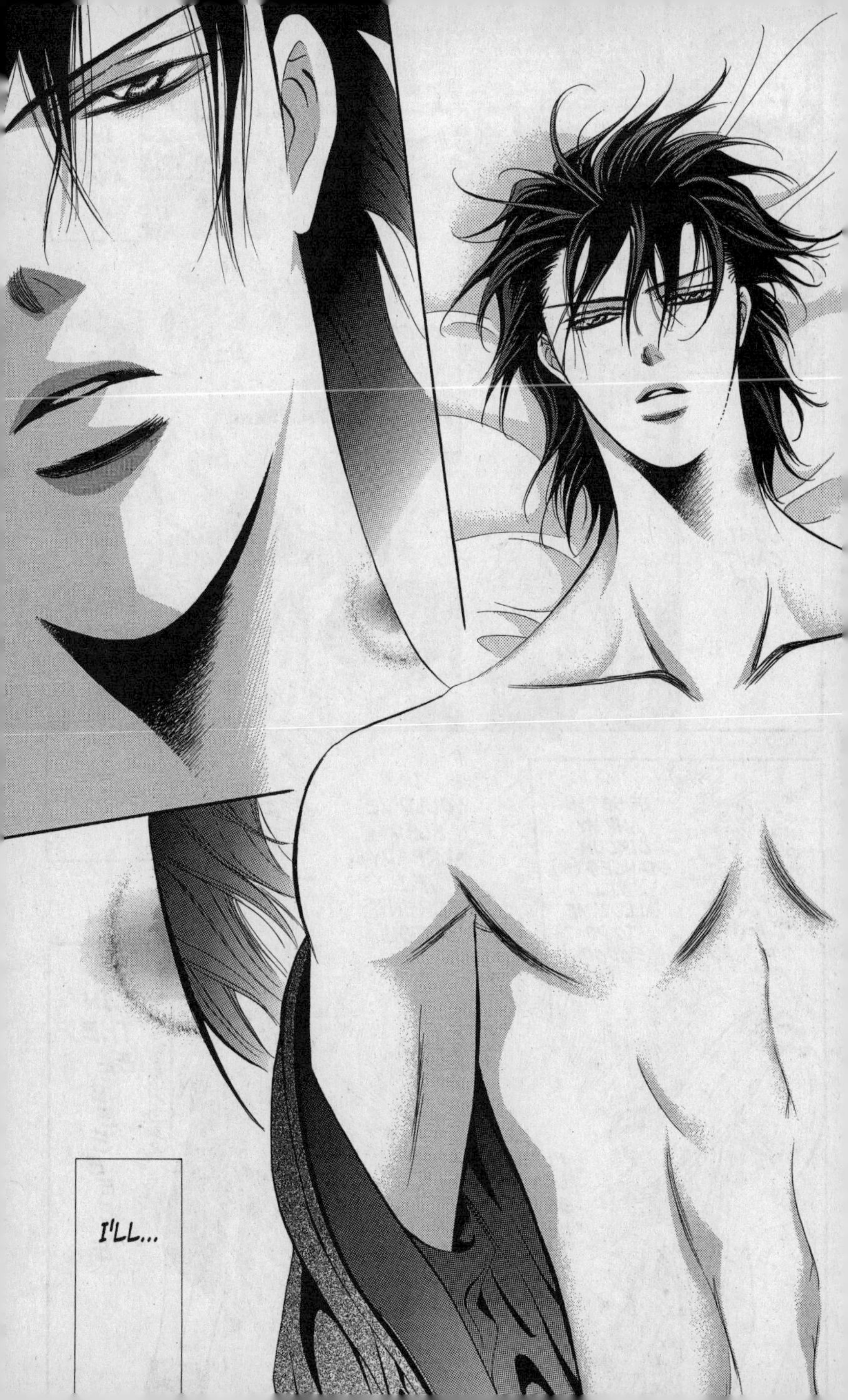
I'LL...

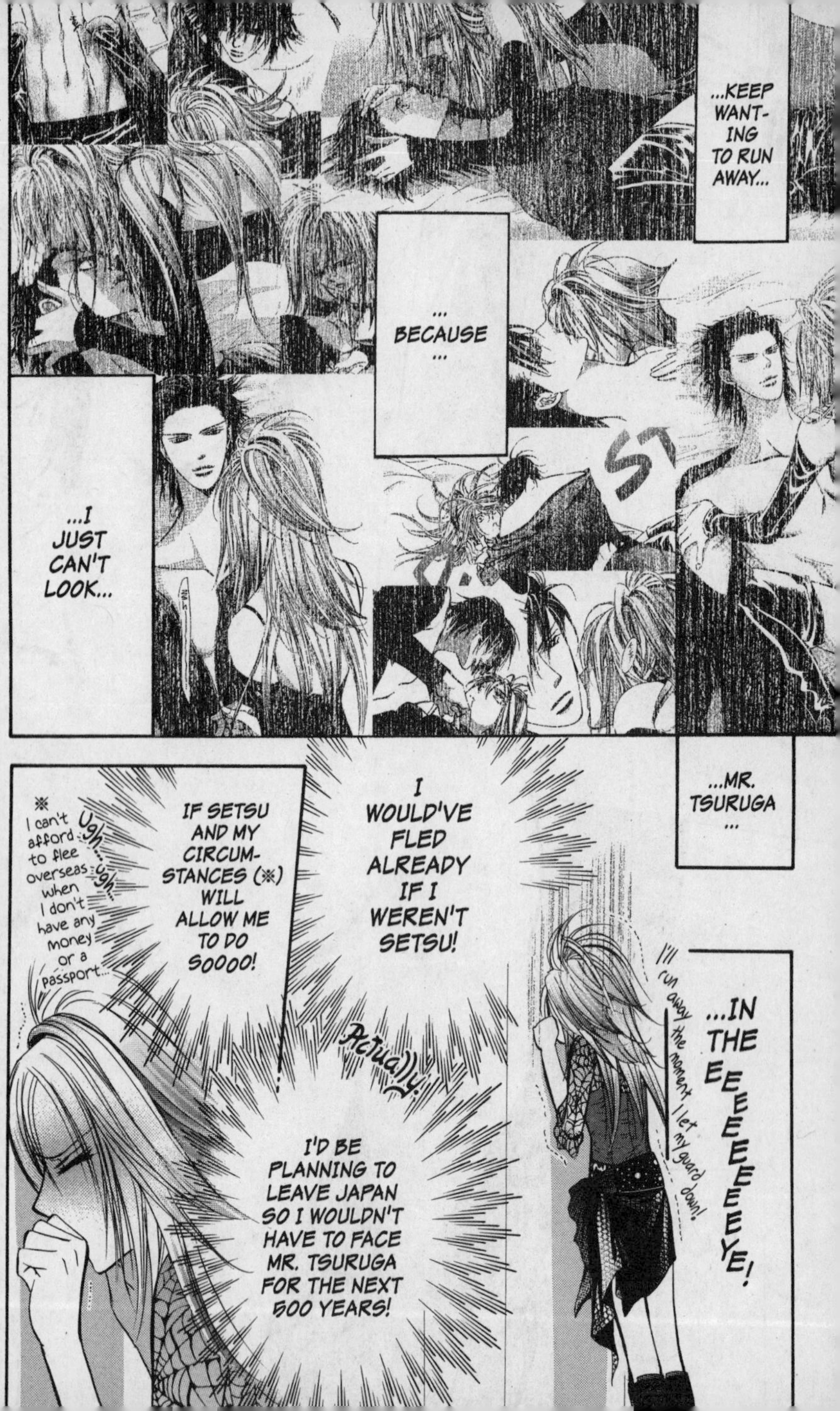
...KEEP WANTING TO RUN AWAY...
...BECAUSE...
...I JUST CAN'T LOOK...
...MR. TSURUGA...
...IN THE EEEEEEEEYE!
I'll run away the moment I let my guard down!
I WOULD'VE FLED ALREADY IF I WEREN'T SETSU!
IF SETSU AND MY CIRCUMSTANCES (※) WILL ALLOW ME TO DO SOOOO!
Ugh... ugh...
※ I can't afford to flee overseas when I don't have any money or a passport...
Actually,
I'D BE PLANNING TO LEAVE JAPAN SO I WOULDN'T HAVE TO FACE MR. TSURUGA FOR THE NEXT 500 YEARS!

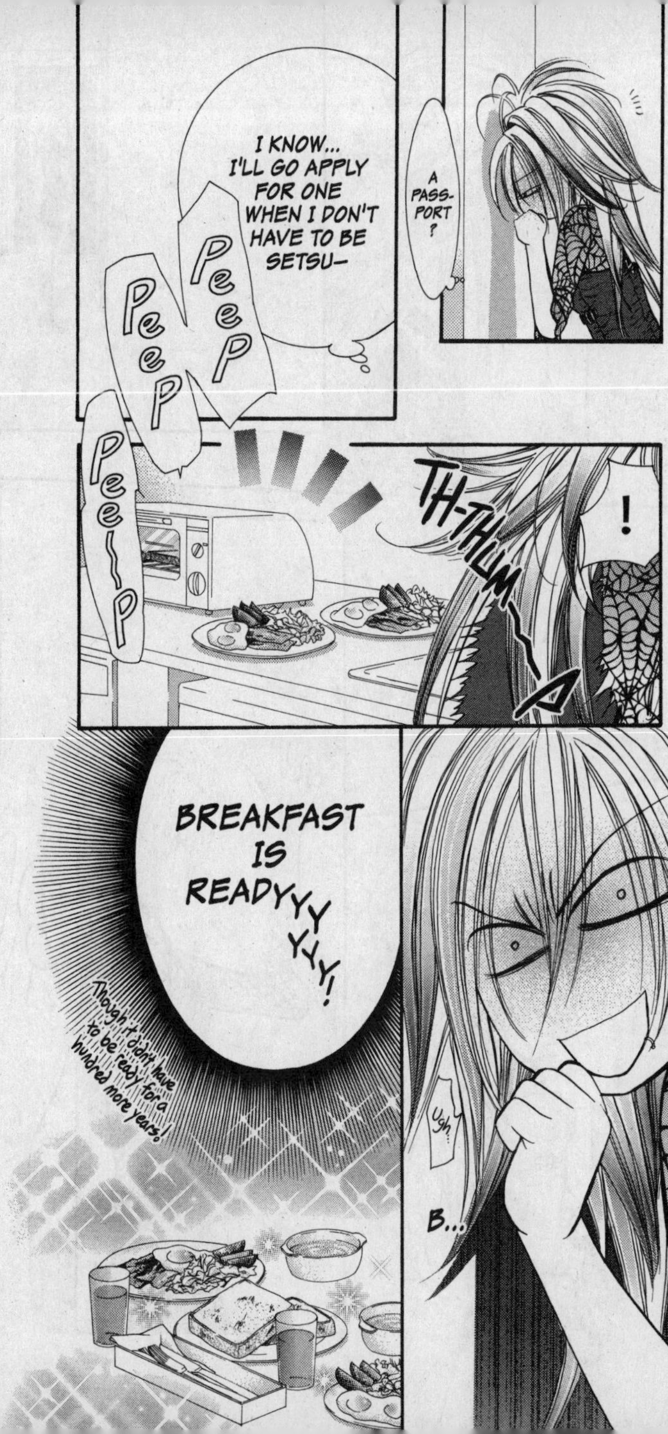
A PASSPORT?
I KNOW... I'LL GO APPLY FOR ONE WHEN I DON'T HAVE TO BE SETSU—
Peep
Peep
Pee~p
TH-THUM~A
!
Ugh...
B...
BREAKFAST IS READYYYYYY!
Though it didn't have to be ready for a hundred more years!

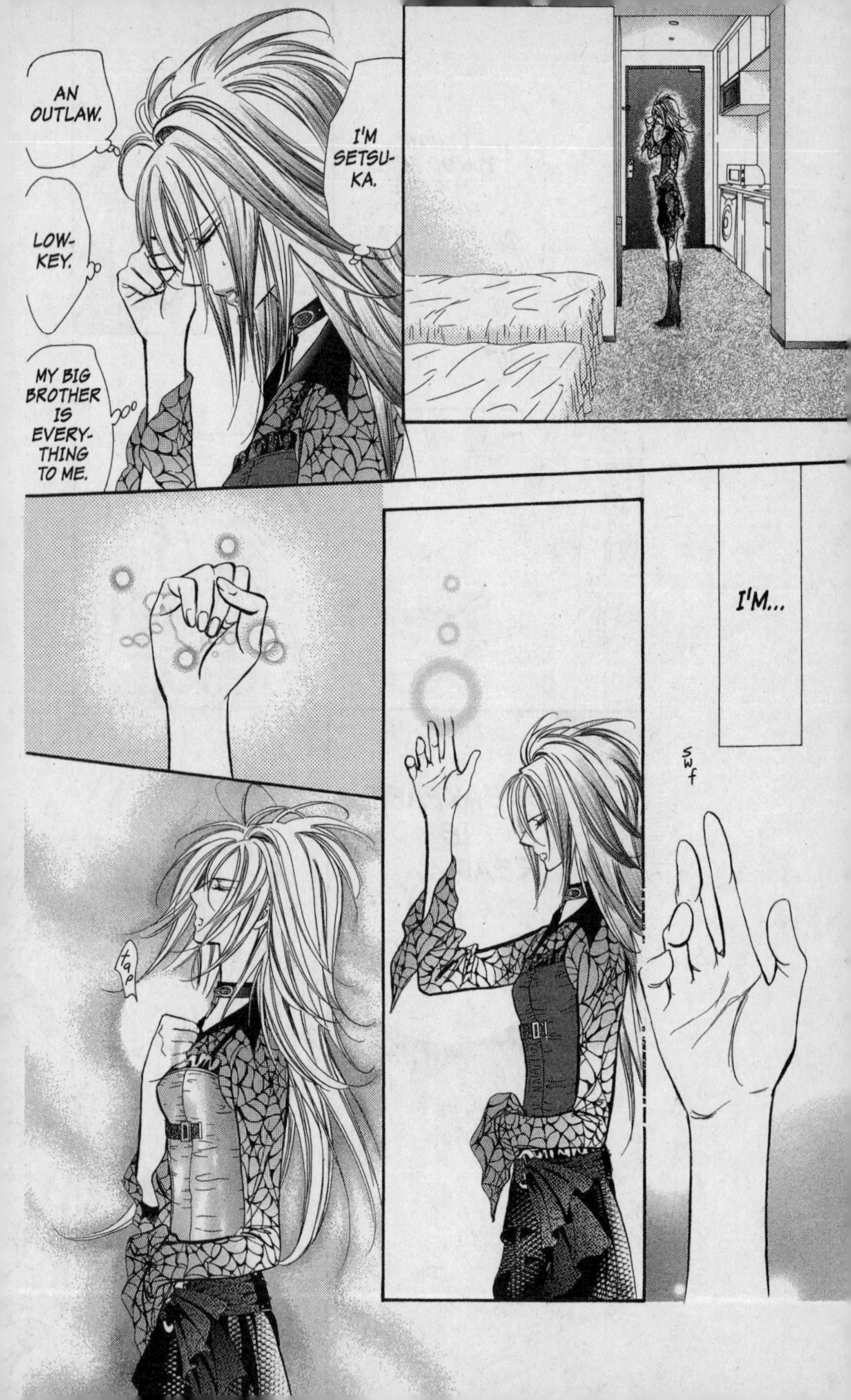
I'M SETSUKA.
AN OUTLAW.
LOW-KEY.
MY BIG BROTHER IS EVERYTHING TO ME.
I'M...
SWF
TAP

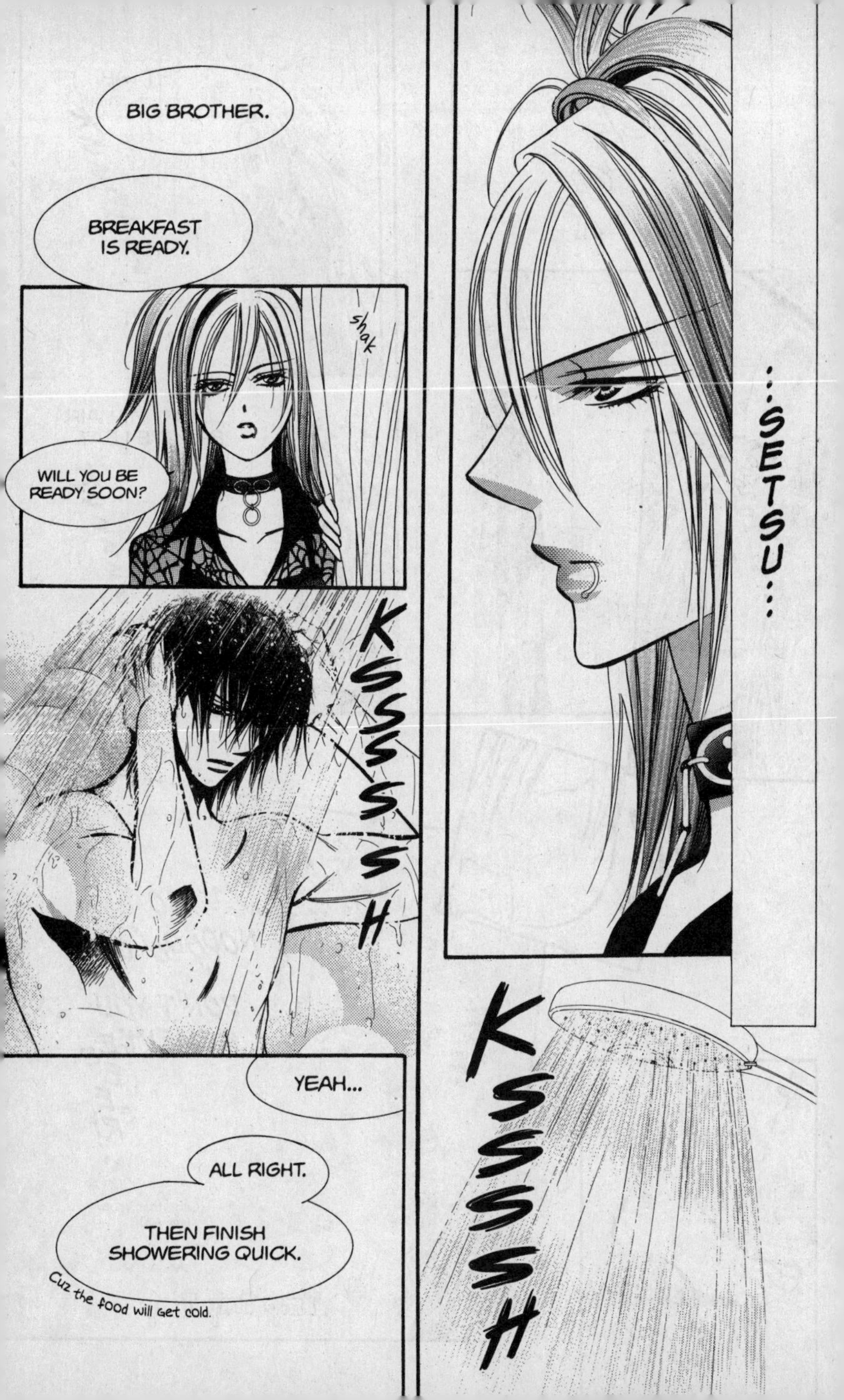
...SETSU...
KSSSSSH
BIG BROTHER.
BREAKFAST IS READY.
shak
WILL YOU BE READY SOON?
KSSSSSH
YEAH...
ALL RIGHT.
THEN FINISH SHOWERING QUICK.
Cuz the food will get cold.

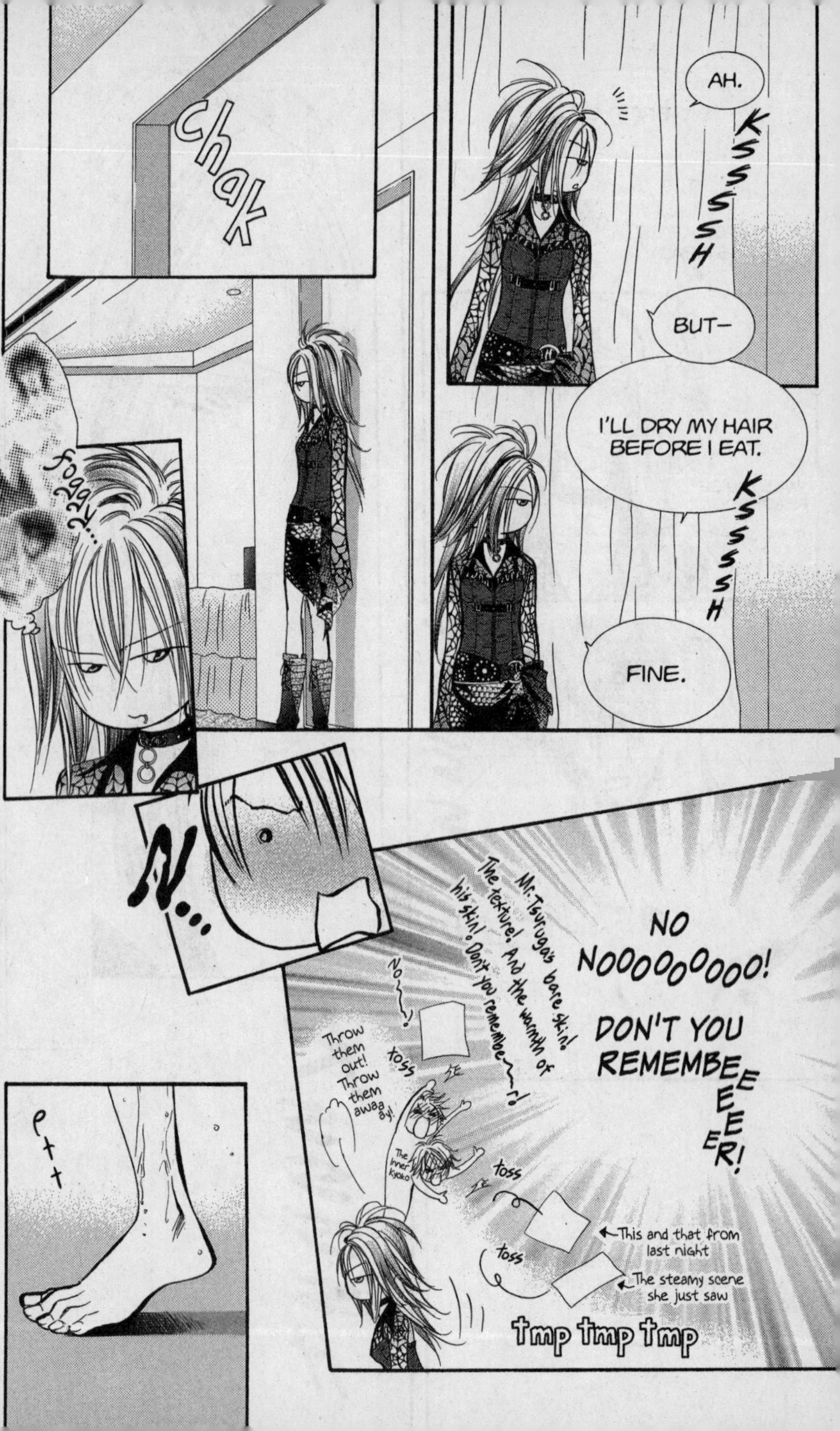
AH.
KSSSSH
BUT—
chak
I'LL DRY MY HAIR BEFORE I EAT.
KSSSSSH
FINE.
foggy...
N...
NO NOOOOOOOOO!
DON'T YOU REMEMBEEEEER!
Mr. Tsuruga's bare skin! The texture! And the warmth of his skin! Don't you remembe~r!
No~!
Throw them out! Throw them awaaay!
toss
The Inner Kyoko
toss
toss
This and that from last night
The steamy scene she just saw
tmp tmp tmp
ptt

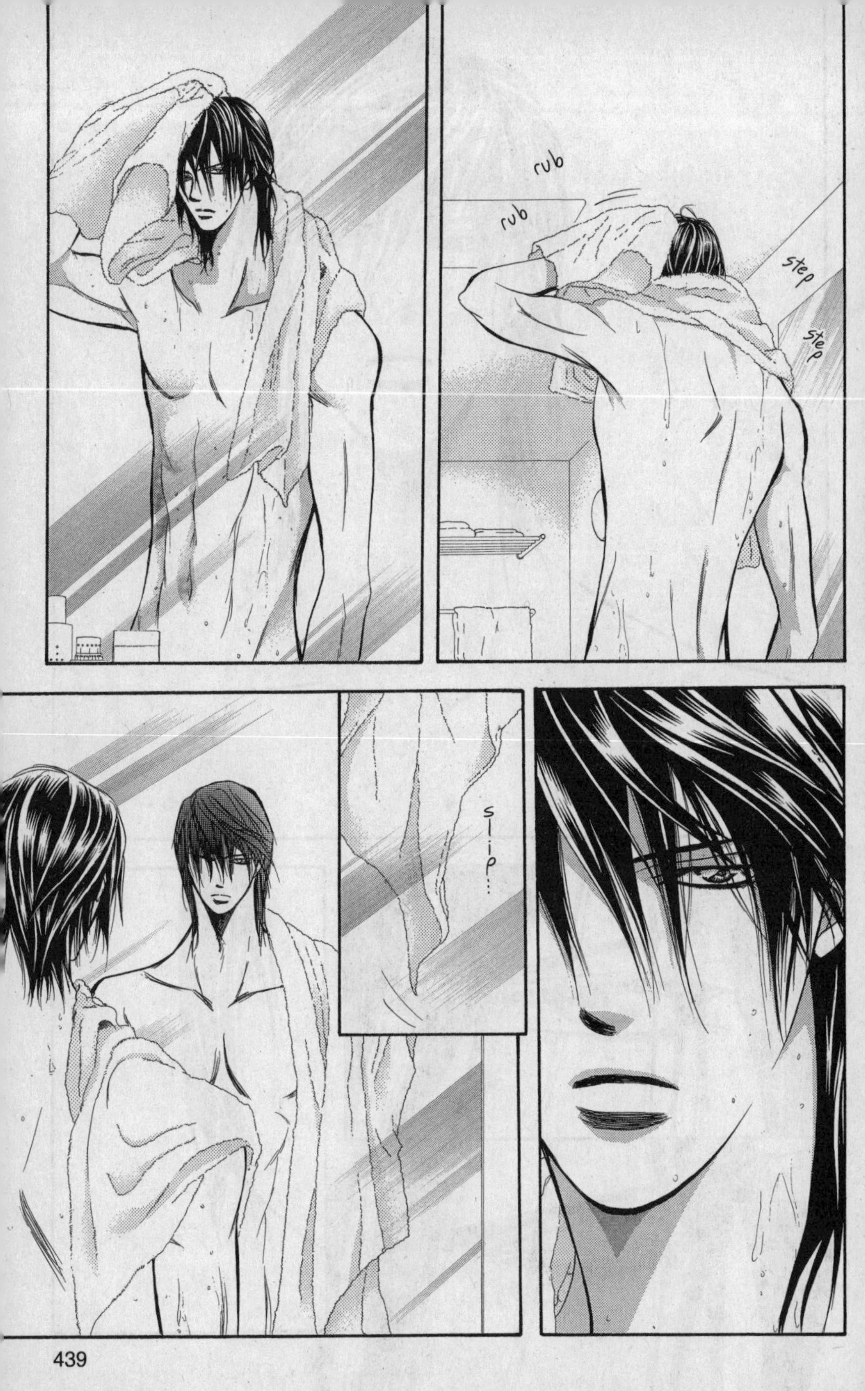
rub
rub
step
step
slip...

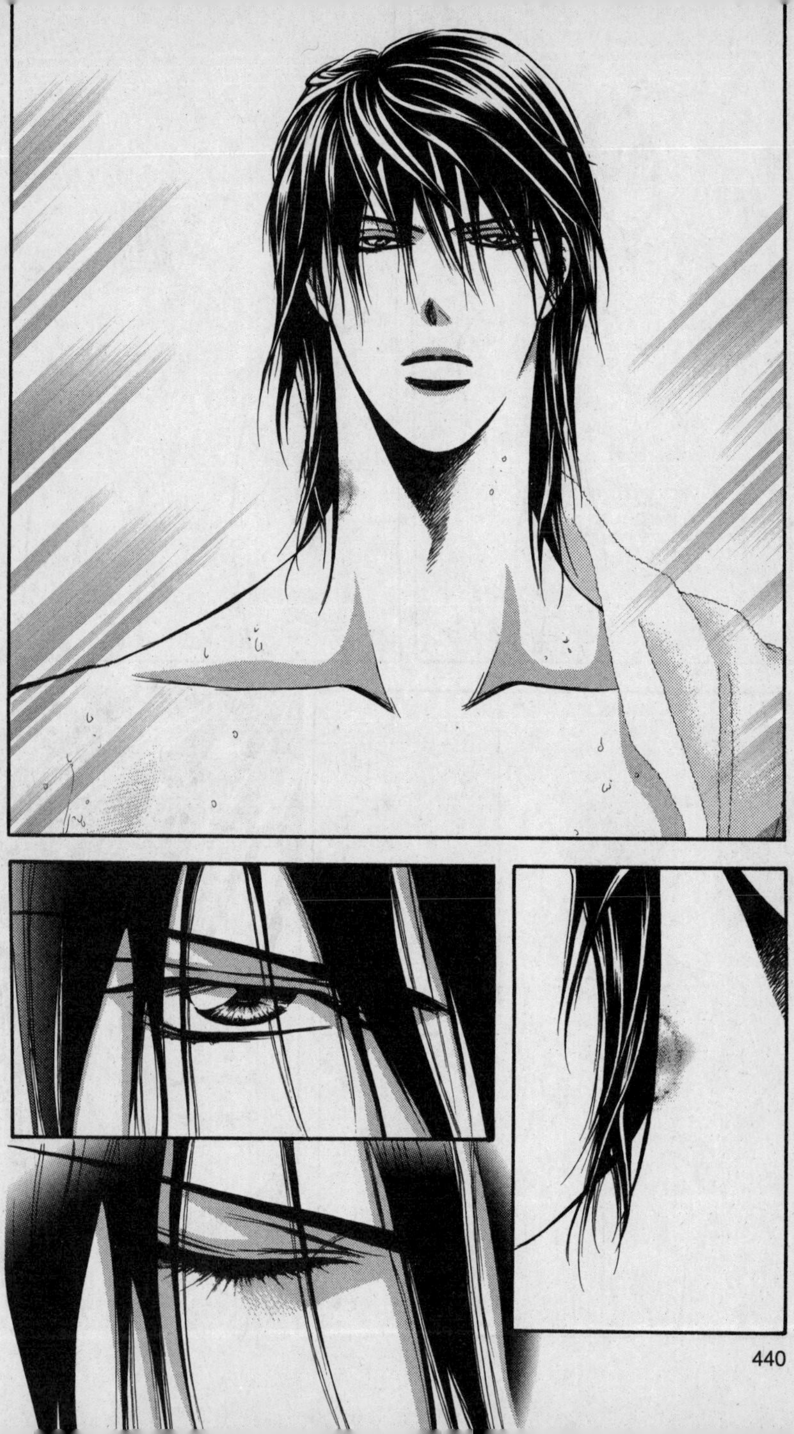

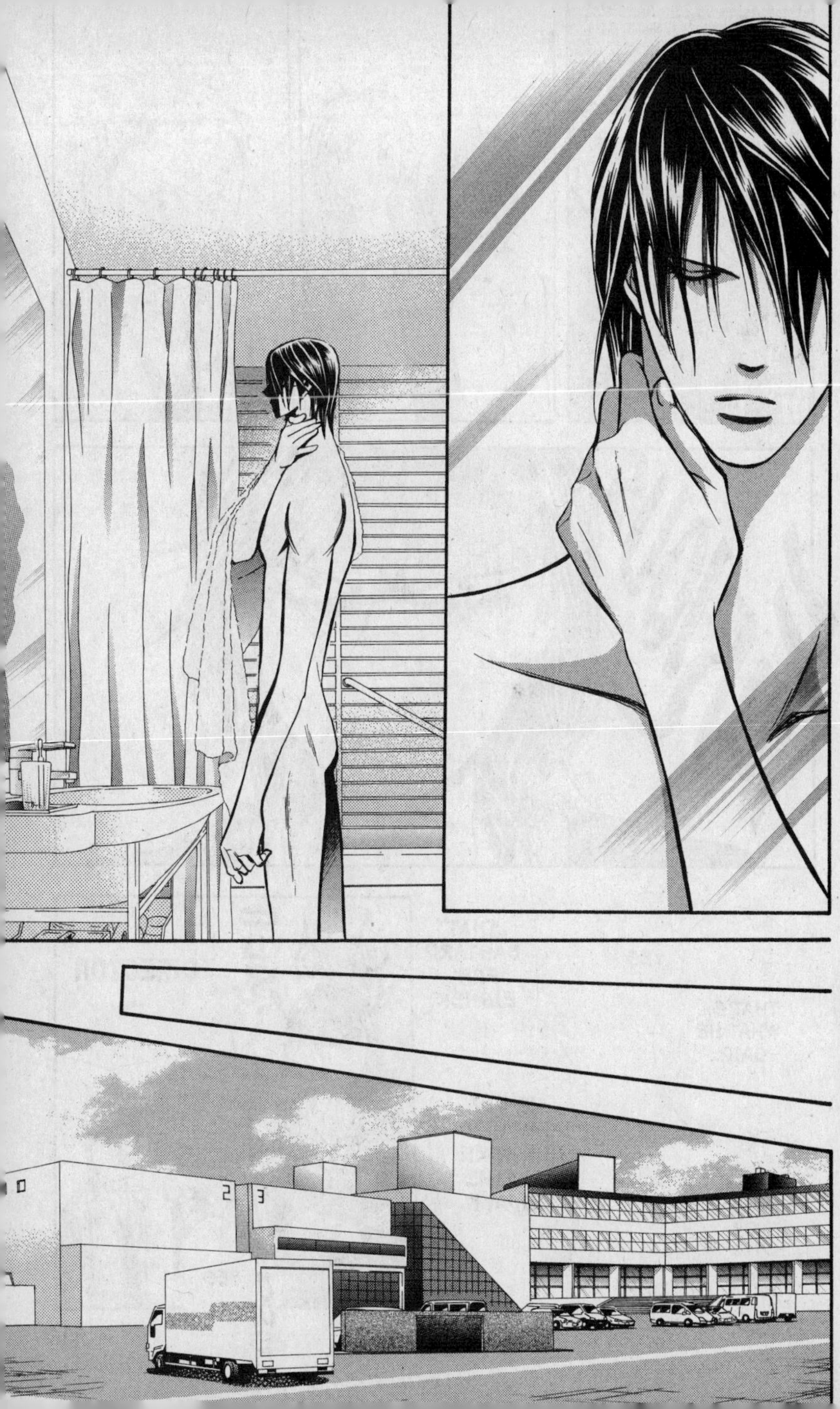

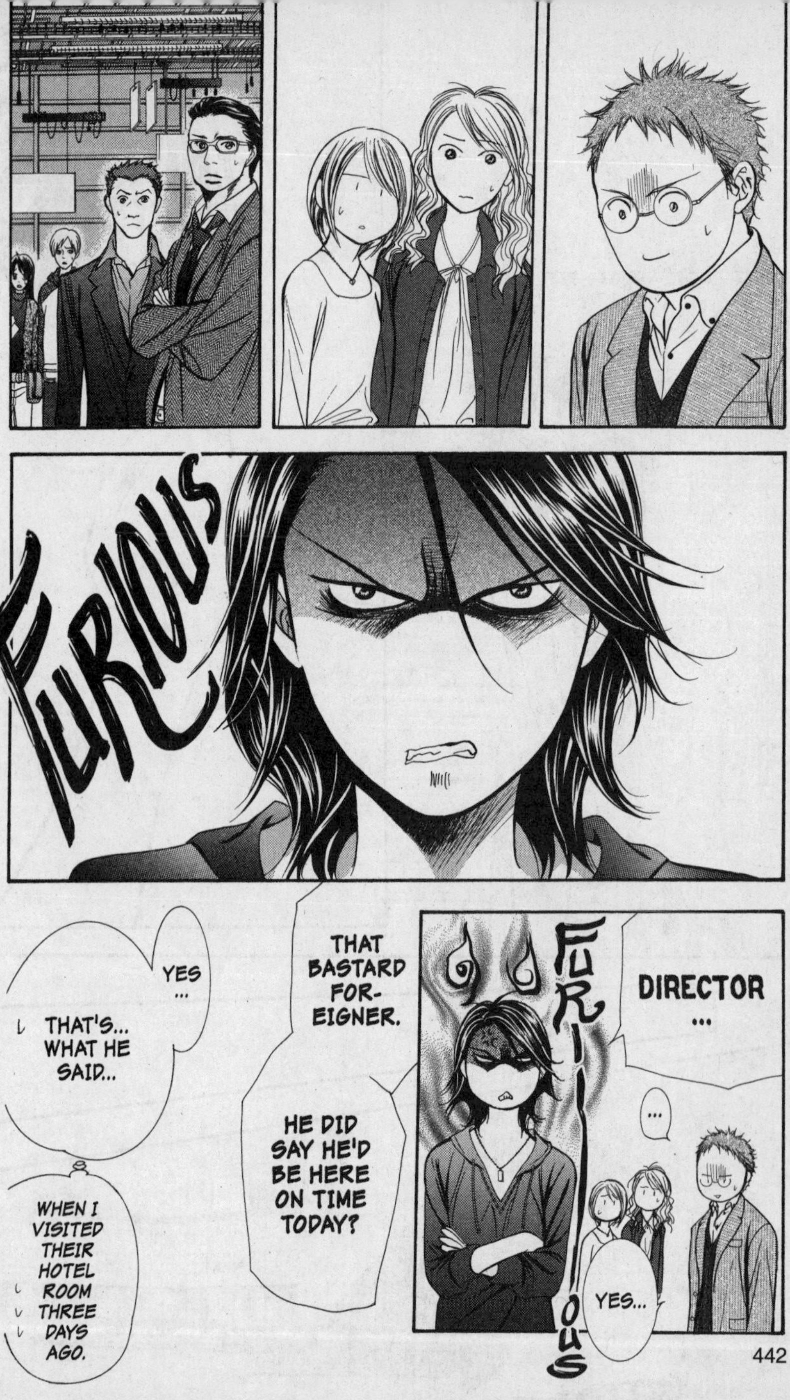
FURIOUS
DIRECTOR ...
...
FURI-I-I-OUS
YES...
THAT BASTARD FOR-EIGNER.
HE DID SAY HE'D BE HERE ON TIME TODAY?
YES ... THAT'S... WHAT HE SAID...
WHEN I VISITED THEIR HOTEL ROOM THREE DAYS AGO.

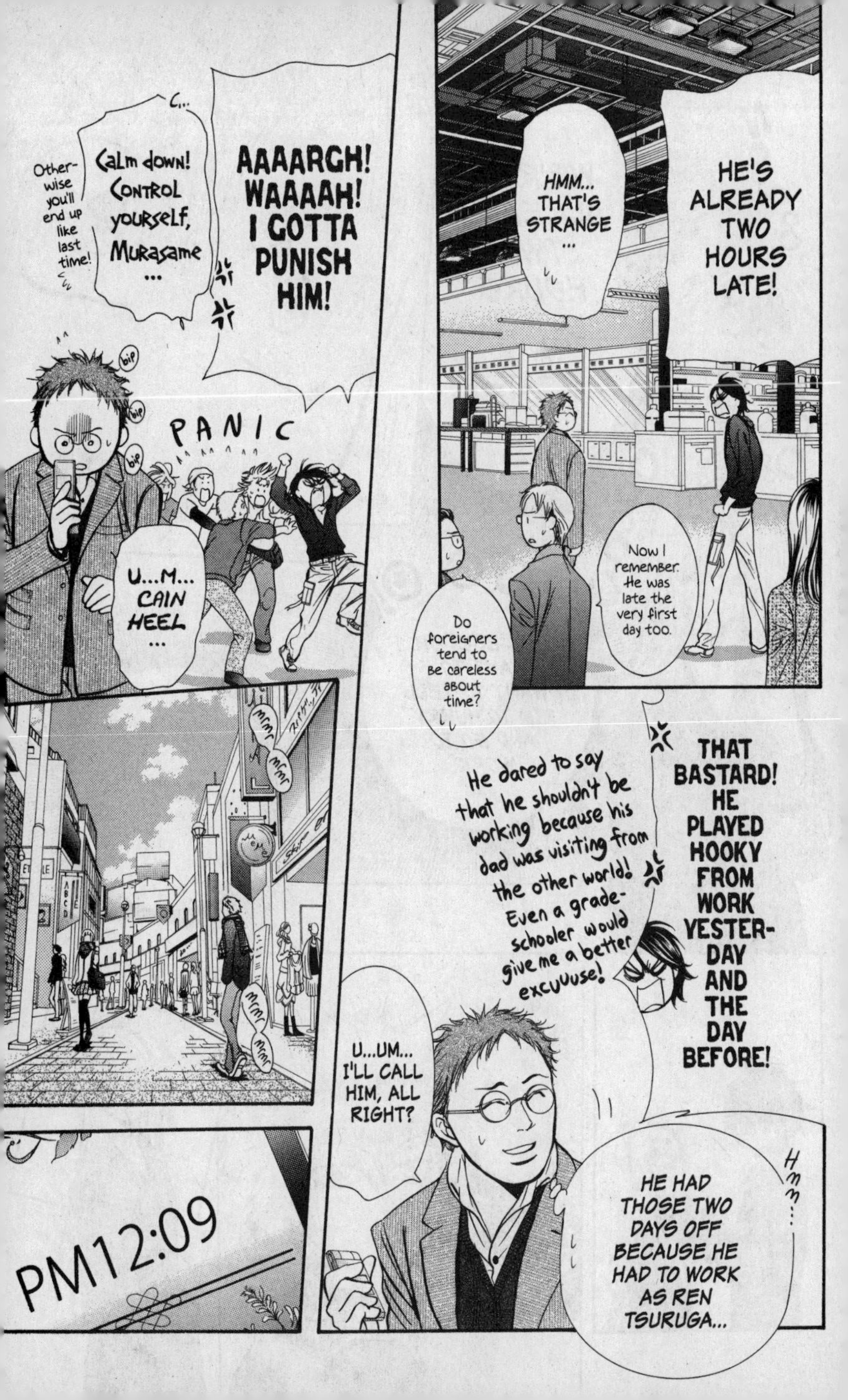
HE'S ALREADY TWO HOURS LATE!
HMM... THAT'S STRANGE ...
Now I remember. He was late the very first day too.
Do foreigners tend to be careless about time?
AAAARGH! WAAAAH! I GOTTA PUNISH HIM!
C...
Calm down! Control yourself, Murasame ...
Other-wise you'll end up like last time!
PANIC
bip
bip
bip
U...M... CAIN HEEL ...
THAT BASTARD! HE PLAYED HOOKY FROM WORK YESTER-DAY AND THE DAY BEFORE!
He dared to say that he shouldn't be working because his dad was visiting from the other world! Even a grade-schooler would give me a better excuuuse!
U...UM... I'LL CALL HIM, ALL RIGHT?
Hmm...
HE HAD THOSE TWO DAYS OFF BECAUSE HE HAD TO WORK AS REN TSURUGA...
mrmr
mrmr
mrmr
mrmr
PM12:09

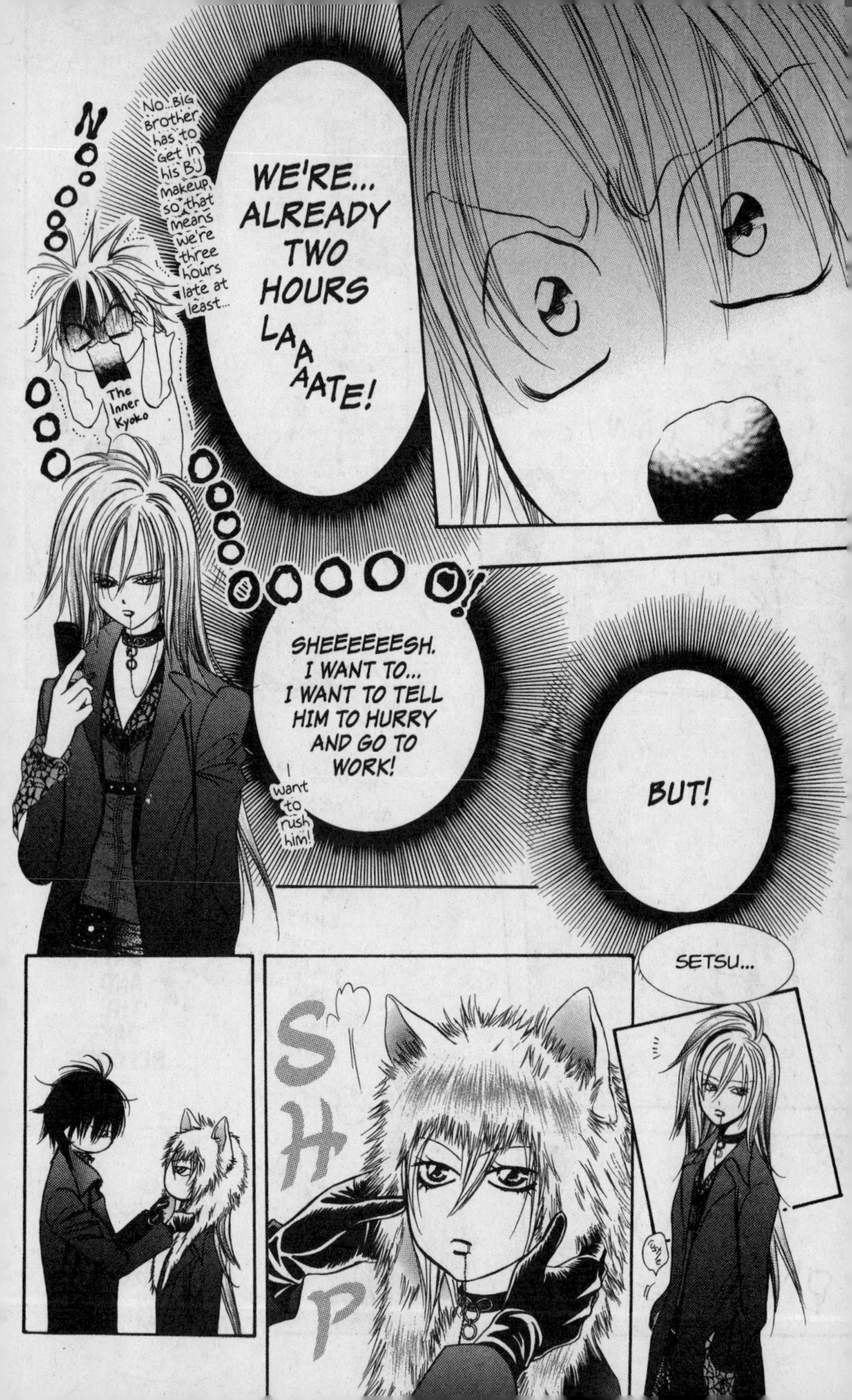
WE'RE... ALREADY TWO HOURS LAAAATE!
No...BIG Brother has to get in his BJ makeup, so that means we're three hours late at least...
The Inner Kyoko
NOOOOOOOOOOOOOOOOOO!
BUT!
SHEEEEEESH. I WANT TO... I WANT TO TELL HIM TO HURRY AND GO TO WORK!
I want to rush him!
SETSU...
rustle
SHP

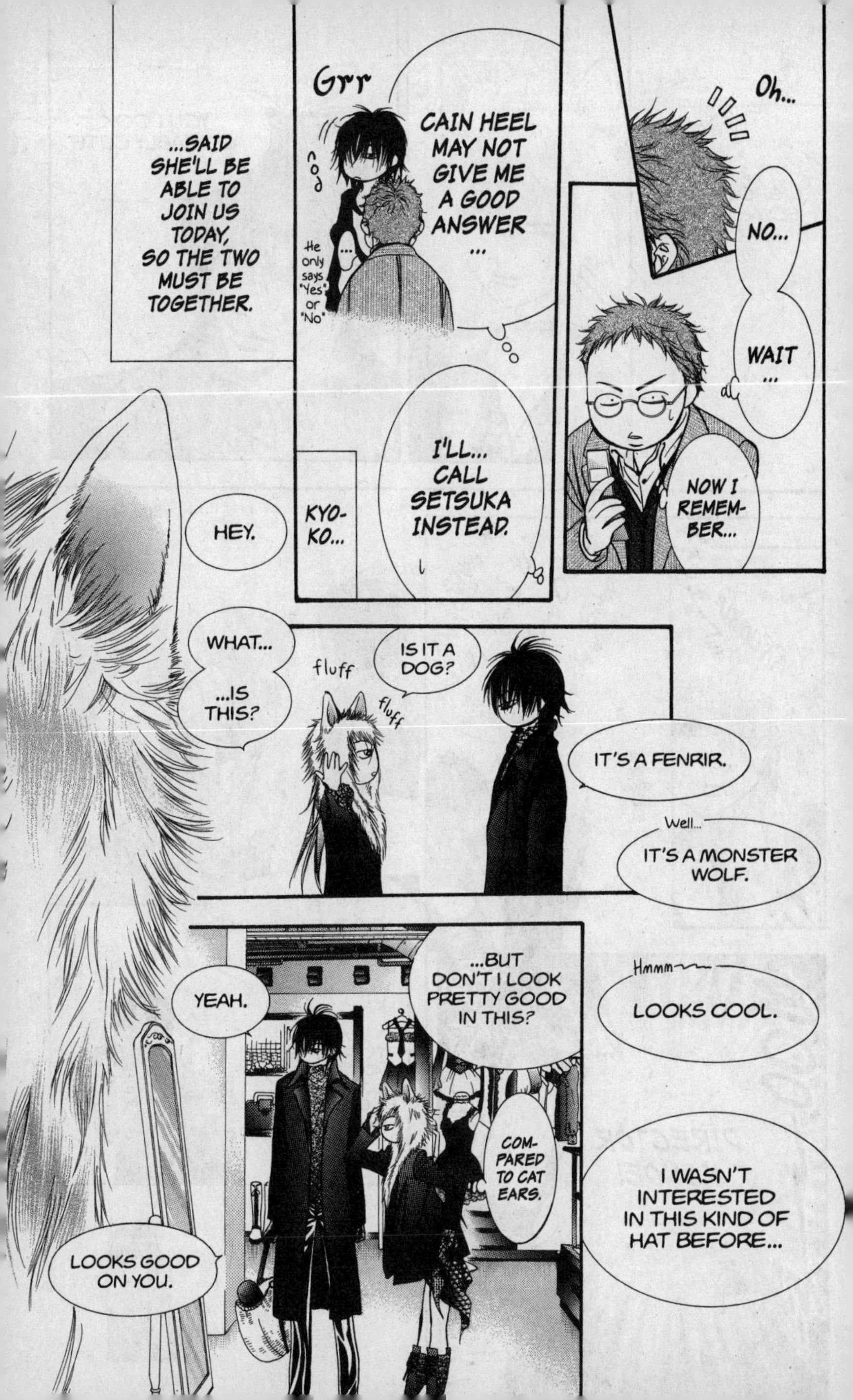
Oh...
NO...
WAIT...
NOW I REMEMBER...
Grr
CAIN HEEL MAY NOT GIVE ME A GOOD ANSWER...
He only says "Yes" or "No"
...
I'LL... CALL SETSUKA INSTEAD.
KYO-KO...
...SAID SHE'LL BE ABLE TO JOIN US TODAY, SO THE TWO MUST BE TOGETHER.
HEY.
WHAT... ...IS THIS?
fluff fluff
IS IT A DOG?
IT'S A FENRIR.
Well...
IT'S A MONSTER WOLF.
I WASN'T INTERESTED IN THIS KIND OF HAT BEFORE...
Hmmm
LOOKS COOL.
COMPARED TO CAT EARS.
...BUT DON'T I LOOK PRETTY GOOD IN THIS?
YEAH.
LOOKS GOOD ON YOU.

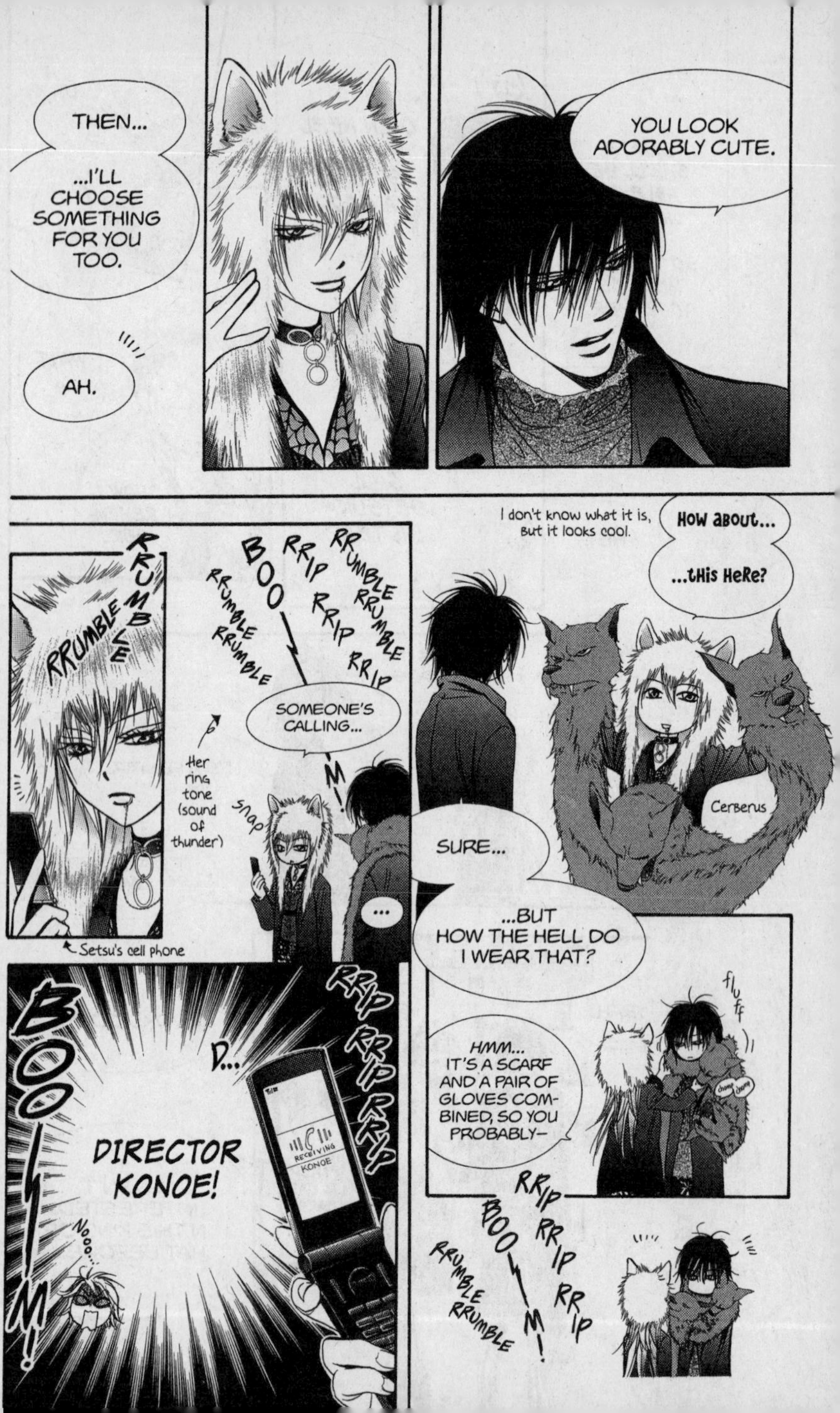

YOU LOOK ADORABLY CUTE.
THEN...
...I'LL CHOOSE SOMETHING FOR YOU TOO.
AH.
I don't know what it is, but it looks cool.
HOW ABOUT...
...THIS HERE?
Cerberus
SURE...
...BUT HOW THE HELL DO I WEAR THAT?
fluff
HMM... IT'S A SCARF AND A PAIR OF GLOVES COMBINED, SO YOU PROBABLY—
chomp chomp
RRIP RRIP RRIP RRIP
BOOM!
RRUMBLE RRUMBLE
RRUMBLE RRUMBLE
BOOM!
RRIP RRIP RRIP
RRUMBLE RRUMBLE RRUMBLE RRUMBLE
SOMEONE'S CALLING...
Her ring tone (sound of thunder)
snap
...
RRUMBLE RRUMBLE
Setsu's cell phone
RRIP RRIP RRIP RRIP
D...
RECEIVING KONOE
DIRECTOR KONOE!
BOOM!
Nooo...

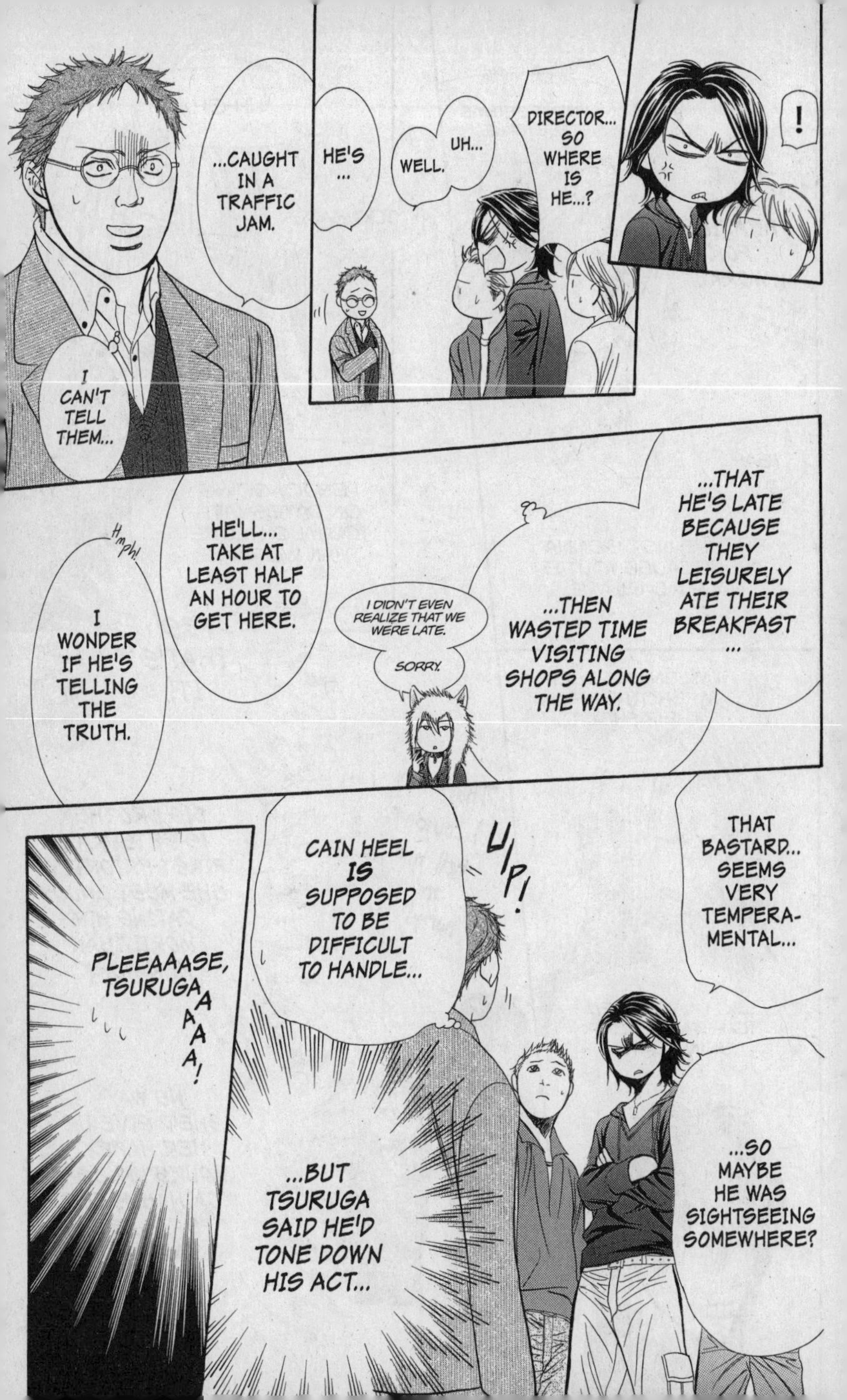
!
DIRECTOR... SO WHERE IS HE...?
UH... WELL.
HE'S ...
...CAUGHT IN A TRAFFIC JAM.
I CAN'T TELL THEM...
...THAT HE'S LATE BECAUSE THEY LEISURELY ATE THEIR BREAKFAST ...
...THEN WASTED TIME VISITING SHOPS ALONG THE WAY.
I DIDN'T EVEN REALIZE THAT WE WERE LATE.
SORRY.
HE'LL... TAKE AT LEAST HALF AN HOUR TO GET HERE.
Hmph!
I WONDER IF HE'S TELLING THE TRUTH.
THAT BASTARD... SEEMS VERY TEMPERA-MENTAL...
...SO MAYBE HE WAS SIGHTSEEING SOMEWHERE?
CAIN HEEL IS SUPPOSED TO BE DIFFICULT TO HANDLE...
...BUT TSURUGA SAID HE'D TONE DOWN HIS ACT...
PLEEAAASE, TSURUGAAAAA!

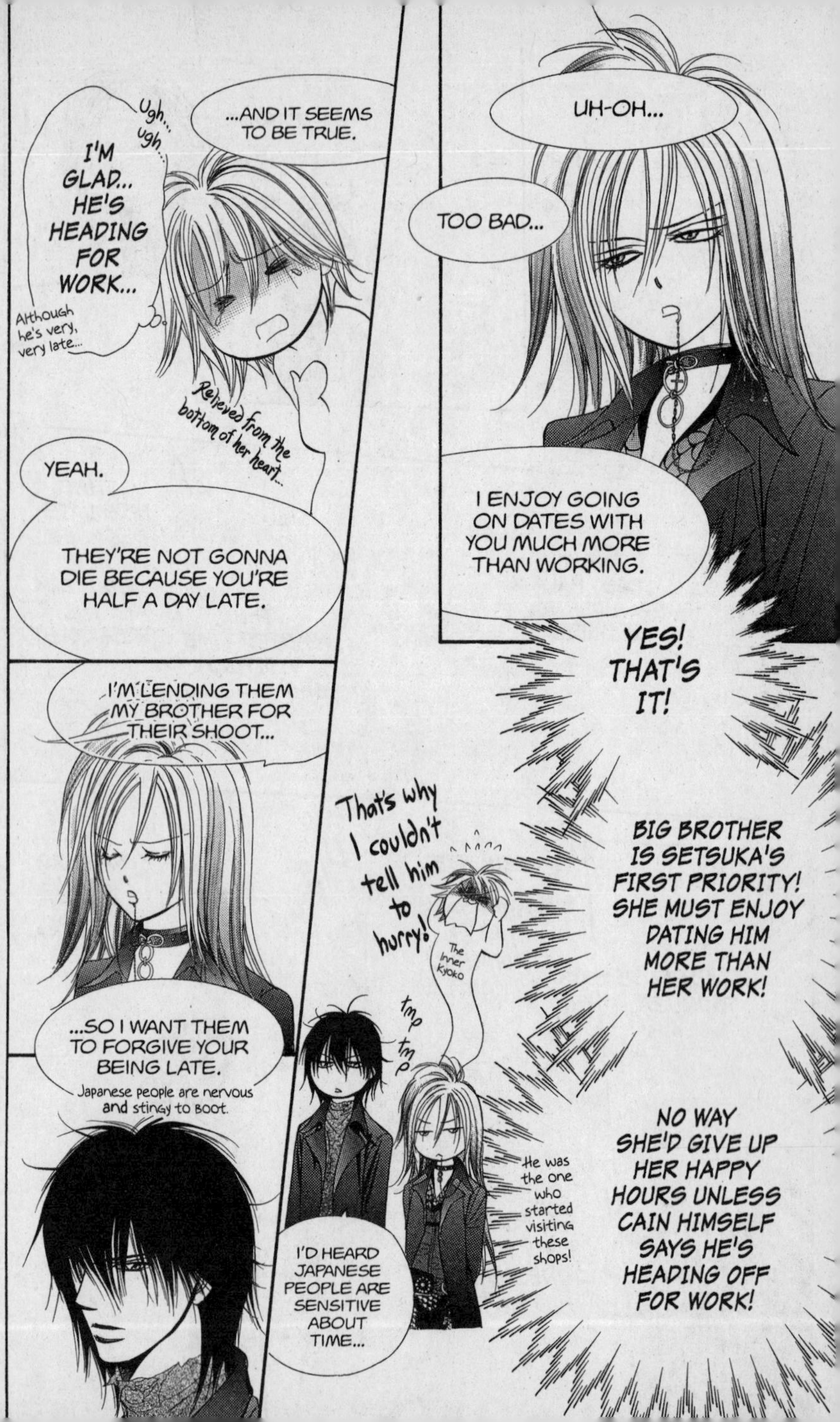
UH-OH...
TOO BAD...
I ENJOY GOING ON DATES WITH YOU MUCH MORE THAN WORKING.
...AND IT SEEMS TO BE TRUE.
Ugh... ugh...
I'M GLAD... HE'S HEADING FOR WORK...
Although he's very, very late...
Relieved from the bottom of her heart...
YEAH.
THEY'RE NOT GONNA DIE BECAUSE YOU'RE HALF A DAY LATE.
YES! THAT'S IT!
BIG BROTHER IS SETSUKA'S FIRST PRIORITY! SHE MUST ENJOY DATING HIM MORE THAN HER WORK!
NO WAY SHE'D GIVE UP HER HAPPY HOURS UNLESS CAIN HIMSELF SAYS HE'S HEADING OFF FOR WORK!
That's why I couldn't tell him to hurry!
The Inner Kyoko
tmp tmp
He was the one who started visiting these shops!
I'D HEARD JAPANESE PEOPLE ARE SENSITIVE ABOUT TIME...
I'M LENDING THEM MY BROTHER FOR THEIR SHOOT...
...SO I WANT THEM TO FORGIVE YOUR BEING LATE.
Japanese people are nervous and stingy to boot.

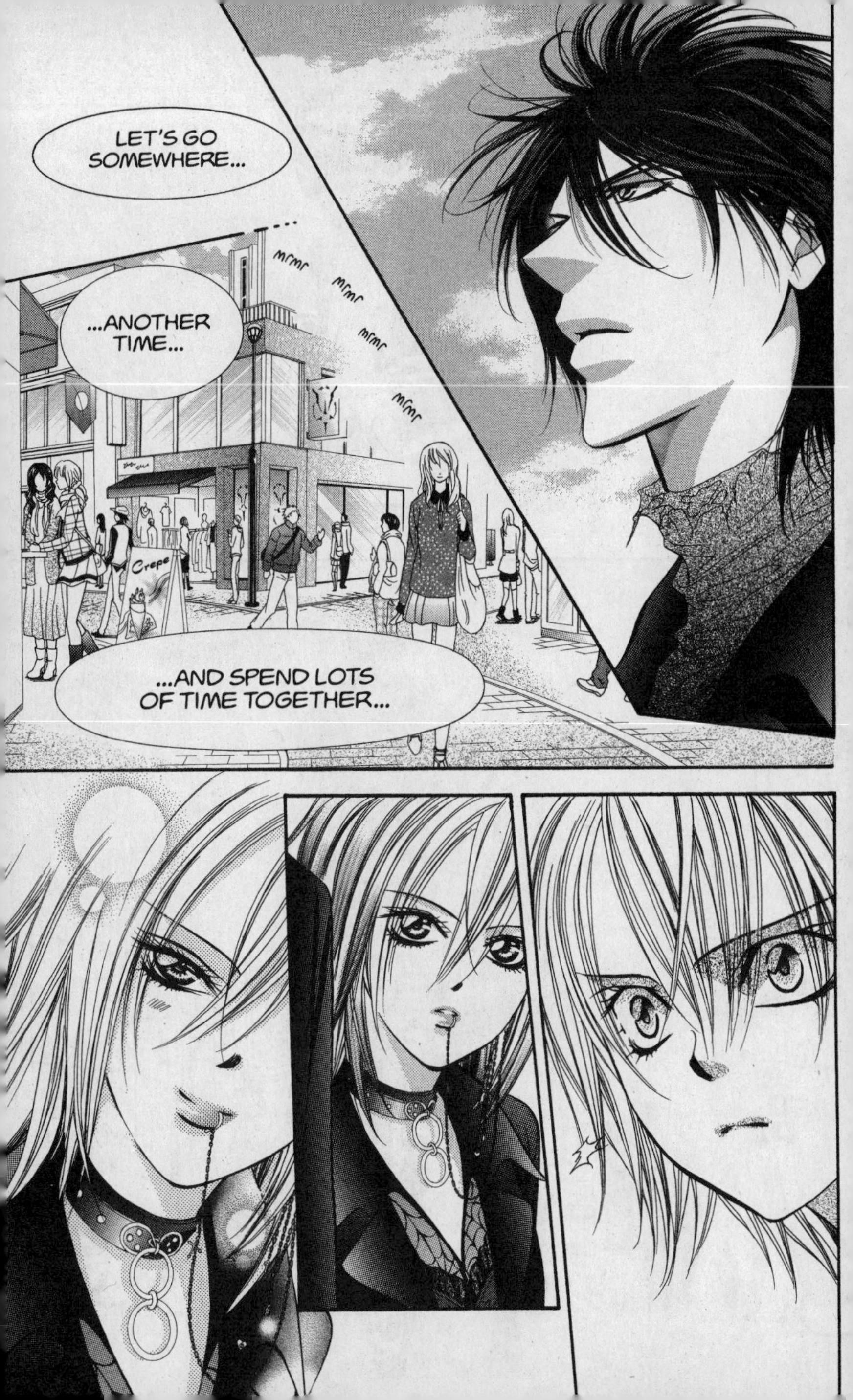
LET'S GO SOMEWHERE...
...ANOTHER TIME...
mrmr
mrmr
mrmr
mrmr
...AND SPEND LOTS OF TIME TOGETHER...

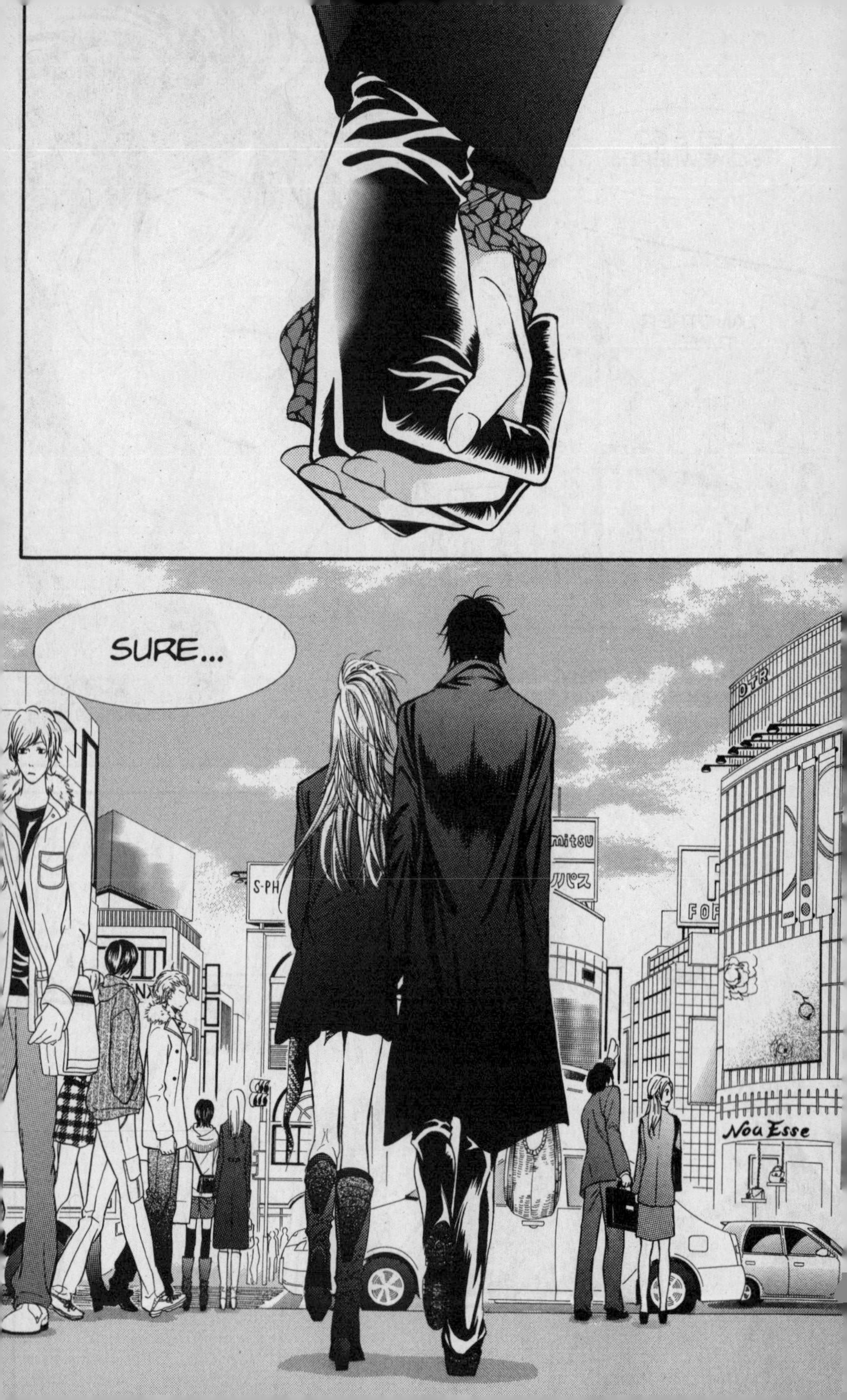
SURE...
OTR
mitsu
S-PH
FOF
Noa Esse

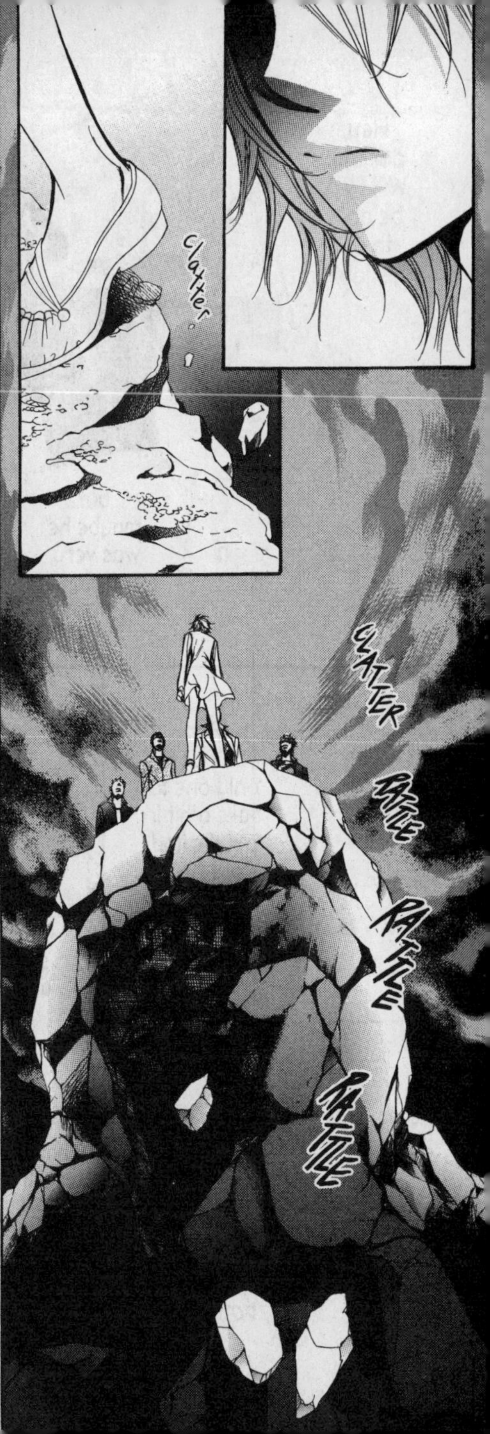
Clatter.
CLATTER
RATTLE
RATTLE
RATTLE
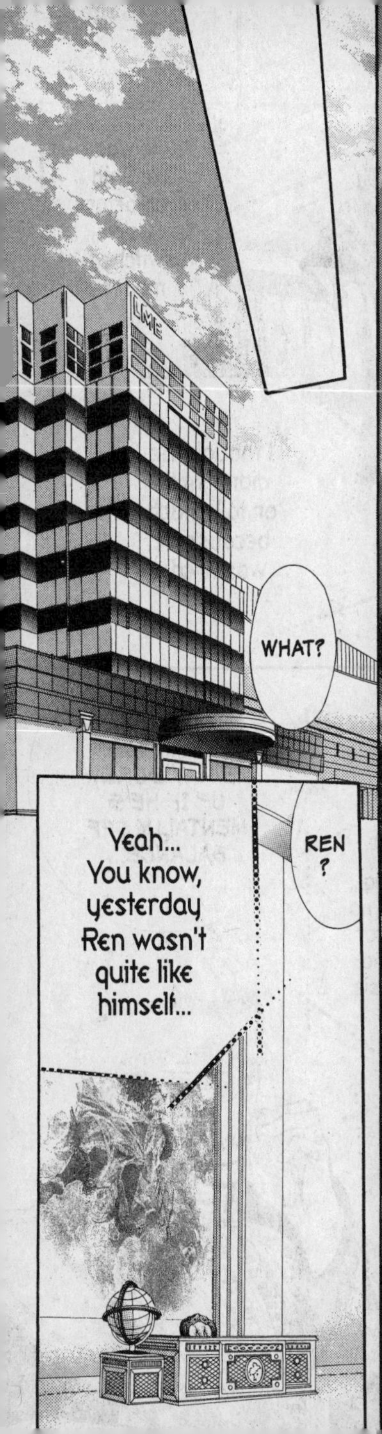
WHAT?
REN ?
Yeah... You know, yesterday Ren wasn't quite like himself...

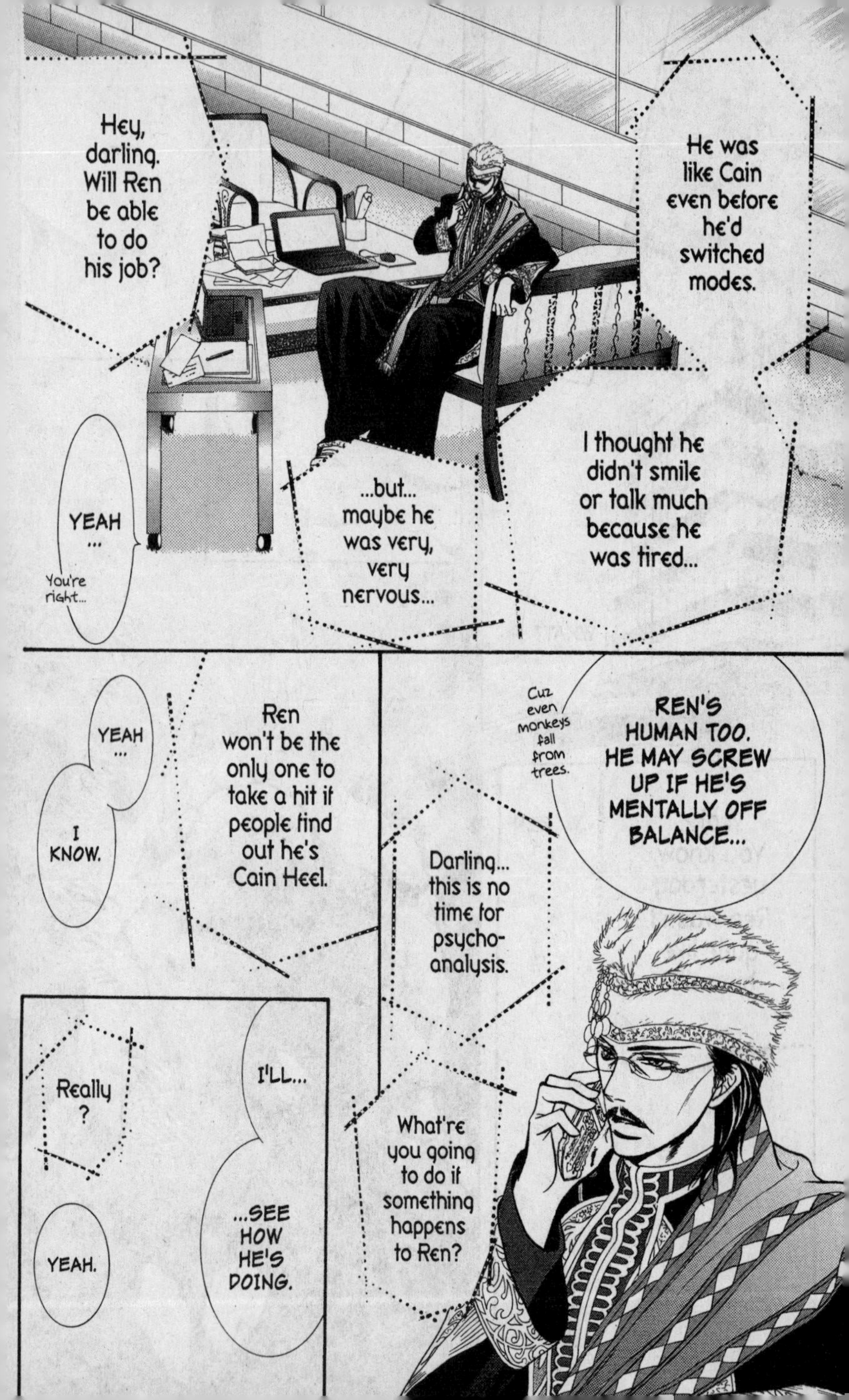
He was like Cain even before he'd switched modes.
I thought he didn't smile or talk much because he was tired...
...but... maybe he was very, very nervous...
Hey, darling. Will Ren be able to do his job?
YEAH...
You're right...
REN'S HUMAN TOO. HE MAY SCREW UP IF HE'S MENTALLY OFF BALANCE...
Cuz even monkeys fall from trees.
Darling... this is no time for psycho-analysis.
What're you going to do if something happens to Ren?
Ren won't be the only one to take a hit if people find out he's Cain Heel.
YEAH...
I KNOW.
I'LL...
...SEE HOW HE'S DOING.
Really?
YEAH.

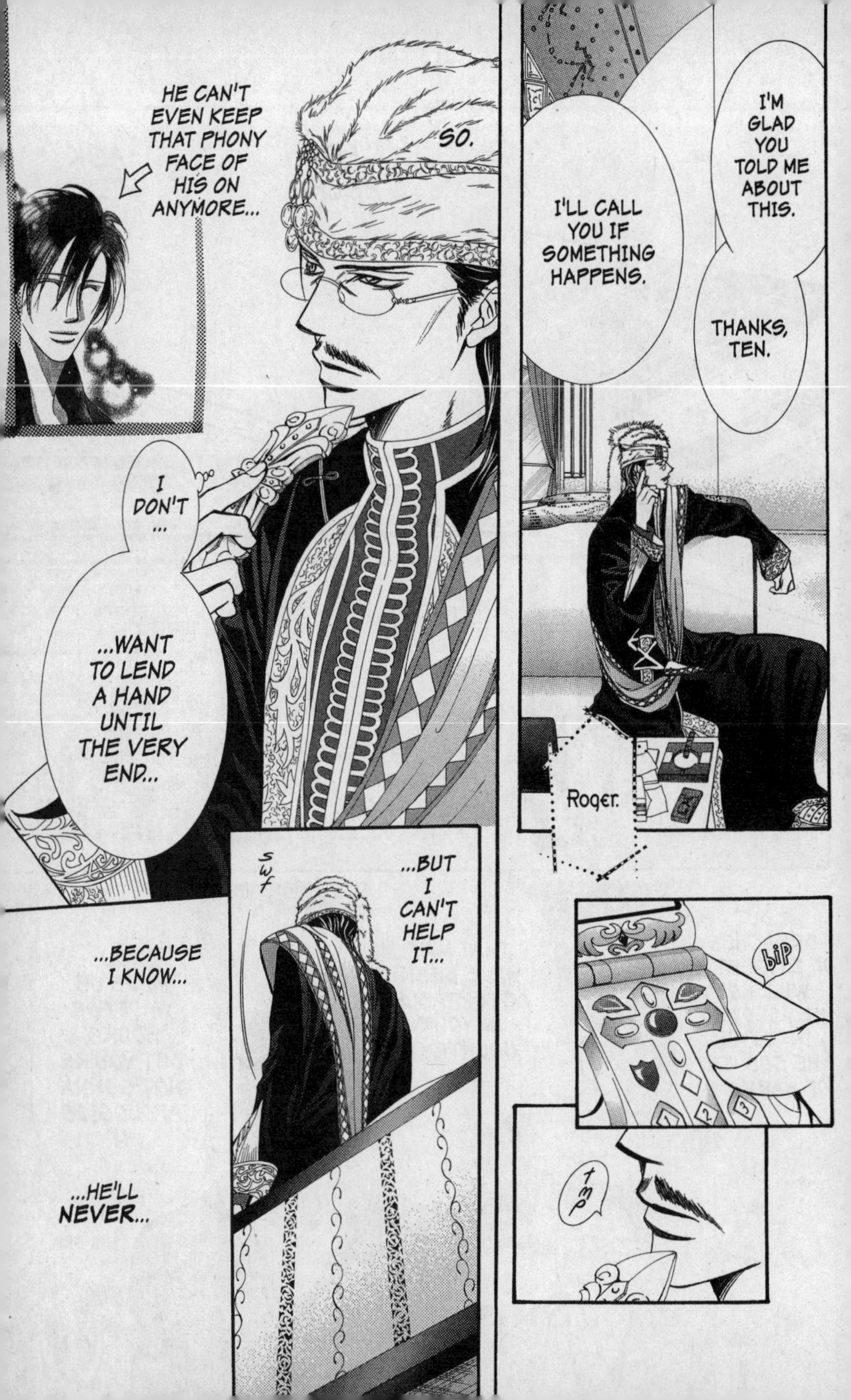

I'M GLAD YOU TOLD ME ABOUT THIS.
THANKS, TEN.
I'LL CALL YOU IF SOMETHING HAPPENS.
Roger.
SO.
HE CAN'T EVEN KEEP THAT PHONY FACE OF HIS ON ANYMORE...
I DON'T ...
...WANT TO LEND A HAND UNTIL THE VERY END...
biP
tmp
swf
...BUT I CAN'T HELP IT...
...BECAUSE I KNOW...
...HE'LL NEVER...

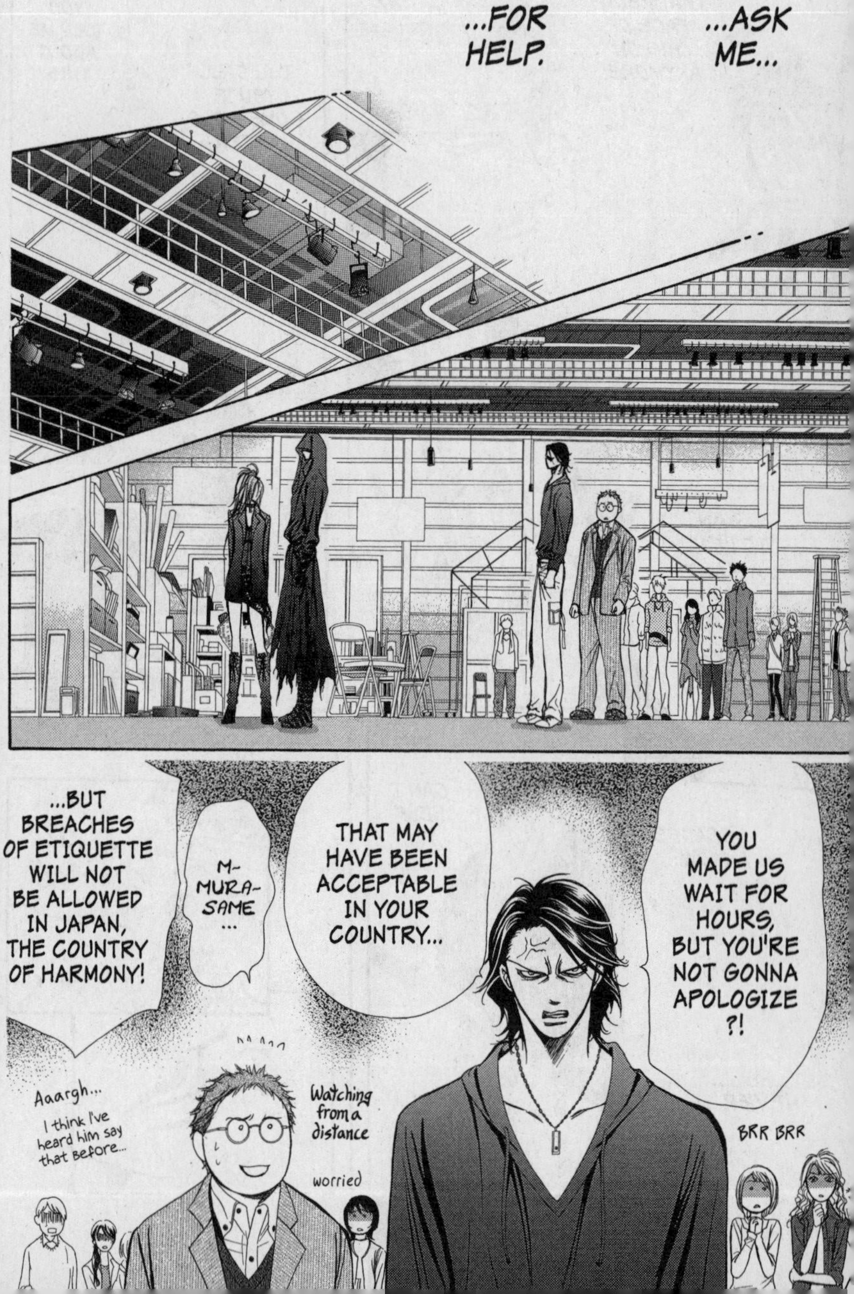
...ASK ME...
...FOR HELP.
YOU MADE US WAIT FOR HOURS, BUT YOU'RE NOT GONNA APOLOGIZE ?!
THAT MAY HAVE BEEN ACCEPTABLE IN YOUR COUNTRY...
M-MURASAME...
...BUT BREACHES OF ETIQUETTE WILL NOT BE ALLOWED IN JAPAN, THE COUNTRY OF HARMONY!
BRR BRR
Watching from a distance
worried
Aaargh...
I think I've heard him say that before...

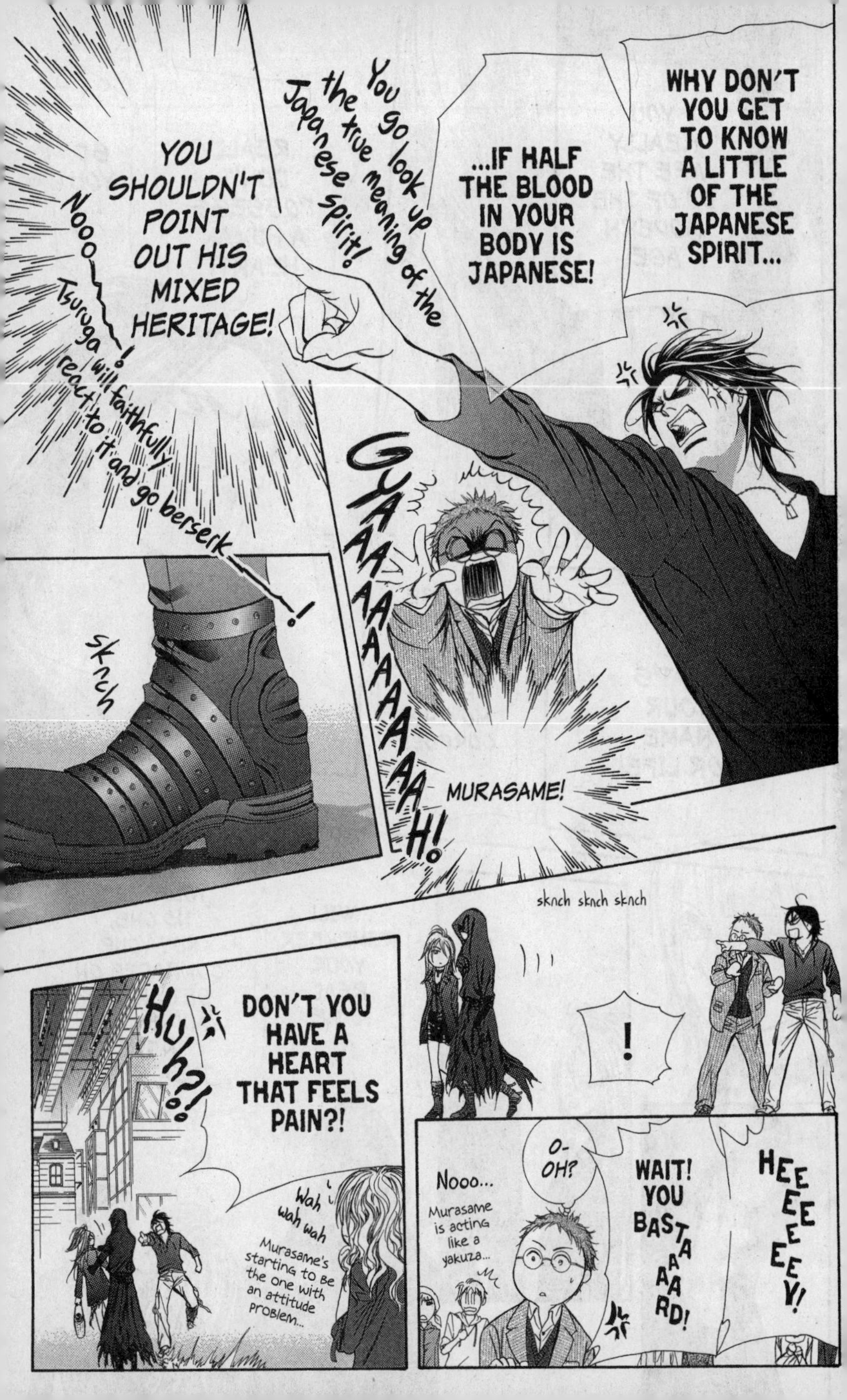
WHY DON'T YOU GET TO KNOW A LITTLE OF THE JAPANESE SPIRIT...
...IF HALF THE BLOOD IN YOUR BODY IS JAPANESE!
You go look up the true meaning of the Japanese spirit!
YOU SHOULDN'T POINT OUT HIS MIXED HERITAGE!
Nooo—! Tsuruga will faithfully react to it and go berserk—!
GYAAAAAAAAAAAAAH!
MURASAME!
sknch
sknch sknch sknch
!
HEEEEEEY!
WAIT! YOU BASTAAAARD!
O-OH?
Nooo...
Murasame is acting like a yakuza...
DON'T YOU HAVE A HEART THAT FEELS PAIN?!
Huh?!
Wah wah wah
Murasame's starting to be the one with an attitude problem...

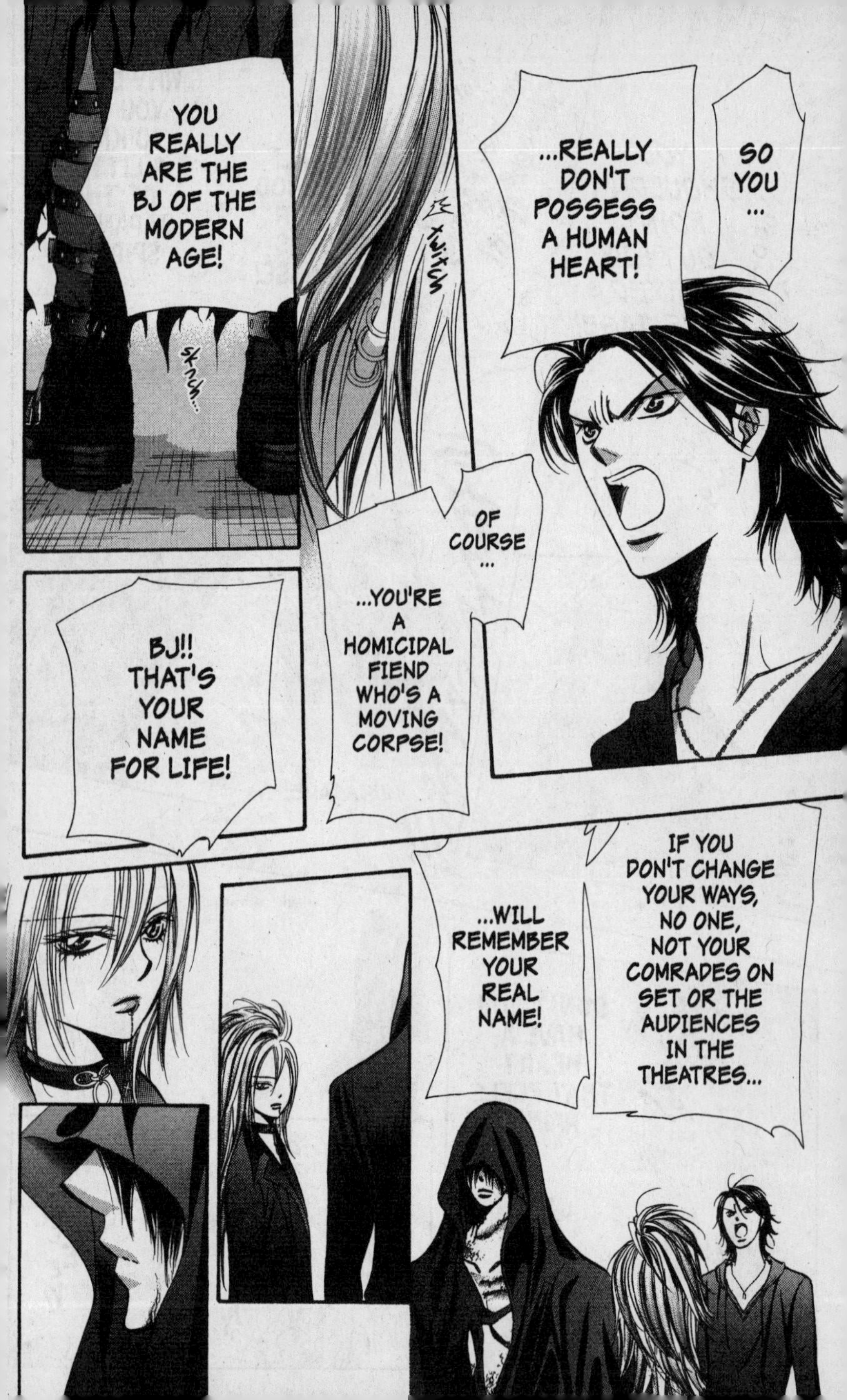
SO YOU ...
...REALLY DON'T POSSESS A HUMAN HEART!
OF COURSE ...
...YOU'RE A HOMICIDAL FIEND WHO'S A MOVING CORPSE!
twitch
YOU REALLY ARE THE BJ OF THE MODERN AGE!
skritch...
BJ!! THAT'S YOUR NAME FOR LIFE!
IF YOU DON'T CHANGE YOUR WAYS, NO ONE, NOT YOUR COMRADES ON SET OR THE AUDIENCES IN THE THEATRES...
...WILL REMEMBER YOUR REAL NAME!

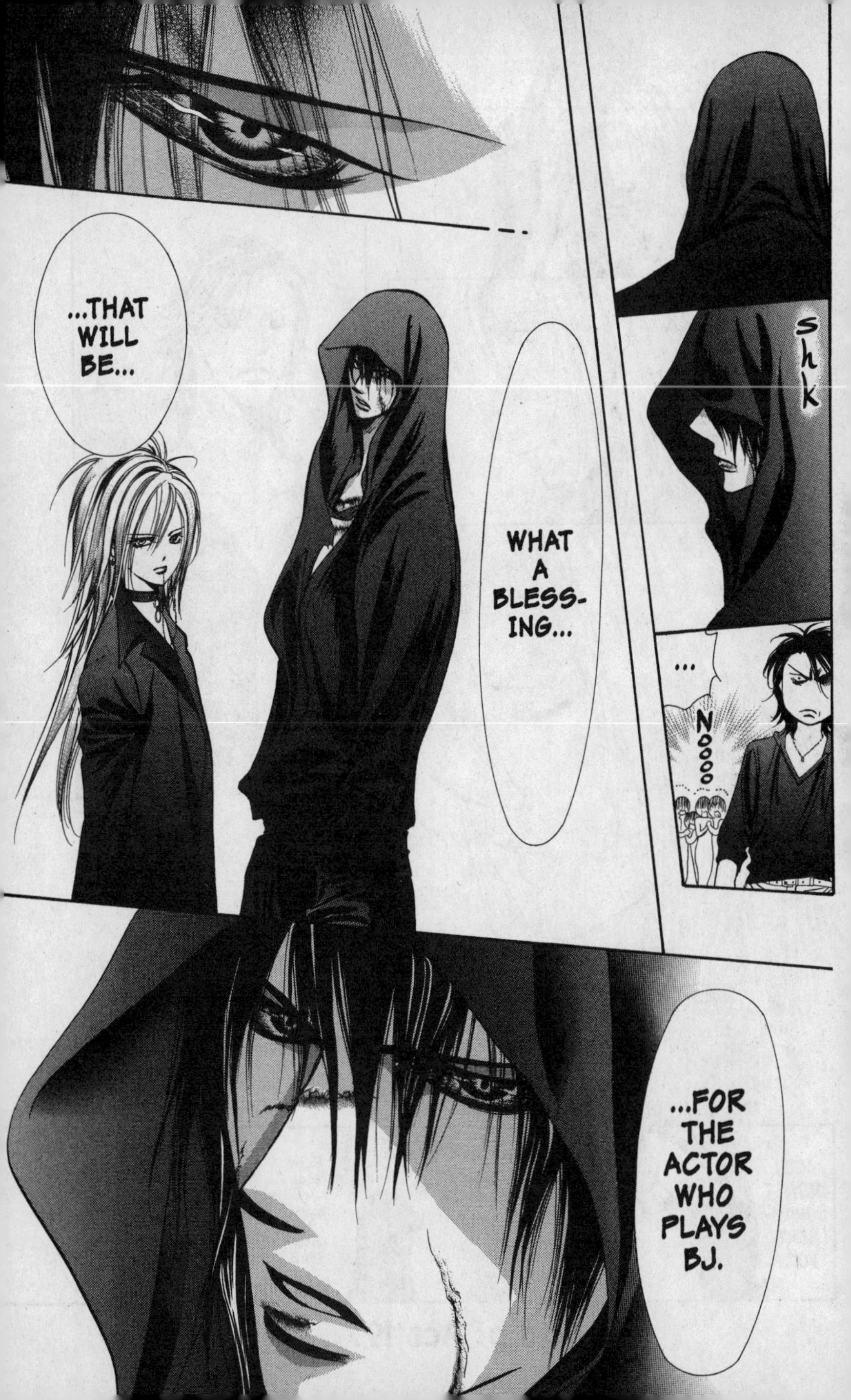
SHK
...
NOOOO
WHAT A BLESS-ING...
...THAT WILL BE...
...FOR THE ACTOR WHO PLAYS BJ.

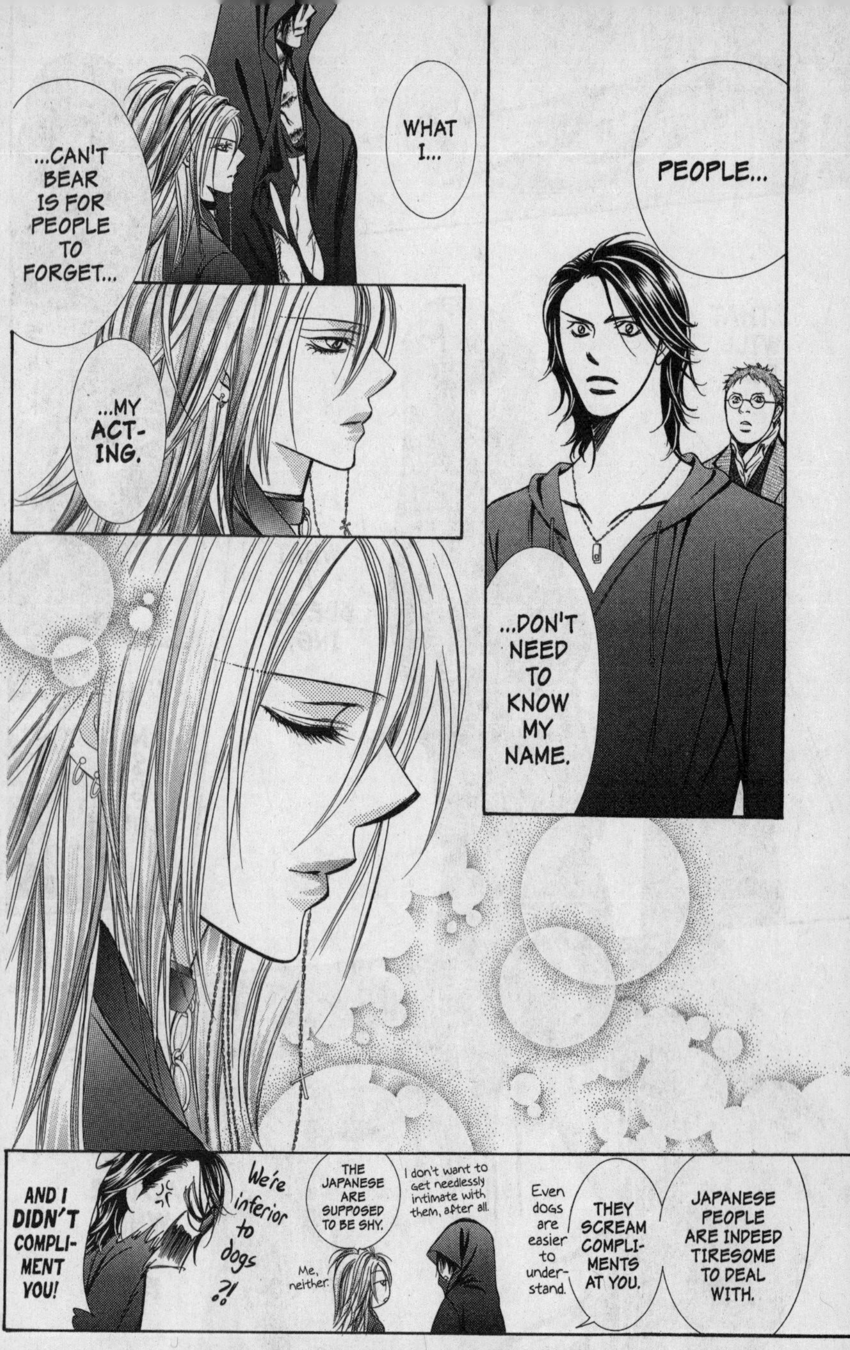
PEOPLE...
...DON'T NEED TO KNOW MY NAME.
WHAT I...
...CAN'T BEAR IS FOR PEOPLE TO FORGET...
...MY ACTING.
JAPANESE PEOPLE ARE INDEED TIRESOME TO DEAL WITH.
THEY SCREAM COMPLIMENTS AT YOU.
Even dogs are easier to understand.
I don't want to get needlessly intimate with them, after all.
THE JAPANESE ARE SUPPOSED TO BE SHY.
Me, neither.
We're inferior to dogs?!
AND I DIDN'T COMPLIMENT YOU!

End of Act 197

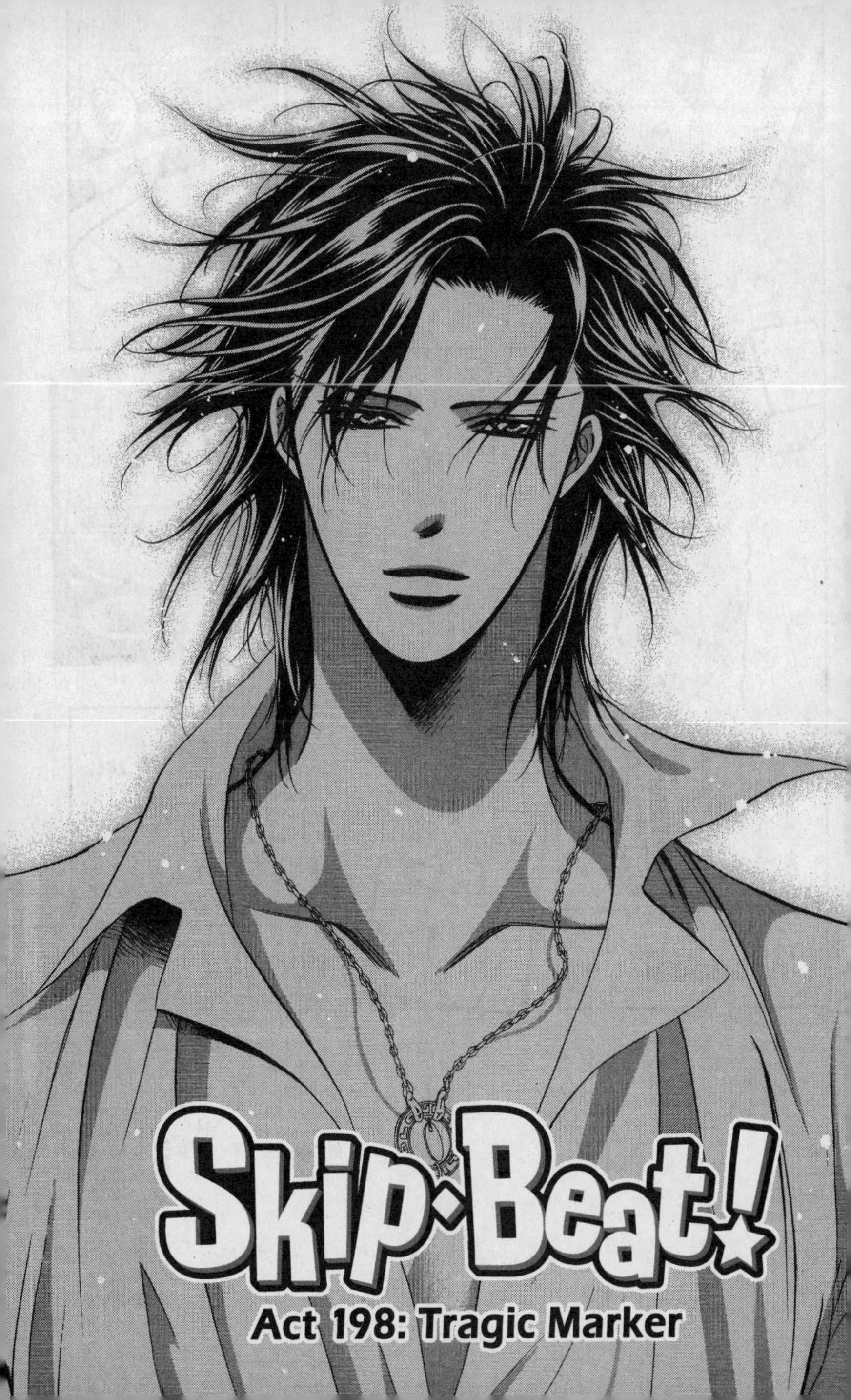
Skip·Beat!
Act 198: Tragic Marker

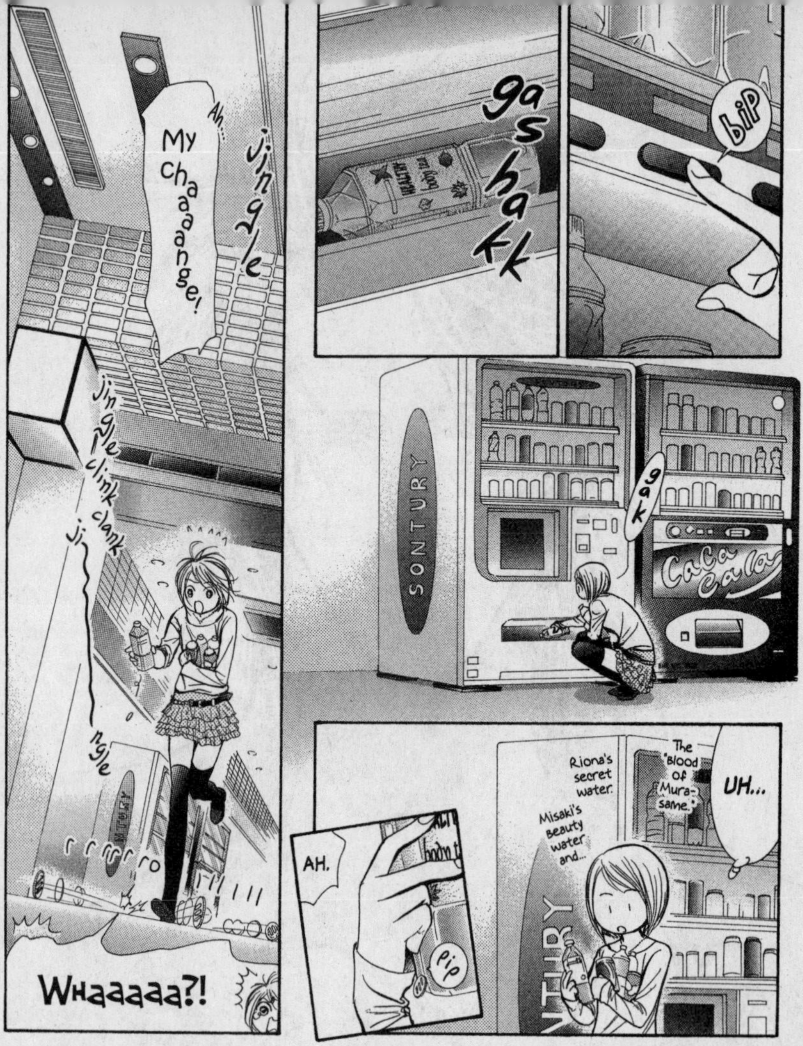
bip
gashakk
HEALTHY body tea
gak
SONTURY
Caca cola
UH...
The "Blood of Murasame."
Riona's secret water.
Misaki's Beauty water and...
pip
AH.
jingle
Ah... My chaaaaange!
jingle clink clank
ji
ngle
rrrrrro
Whaaaaa?!

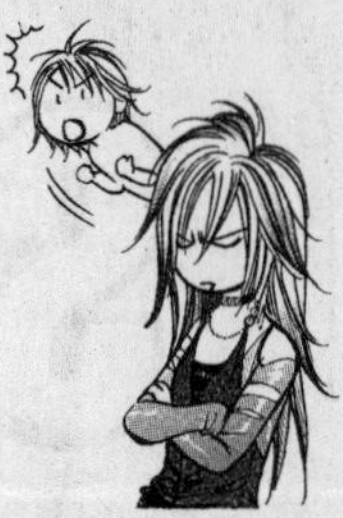

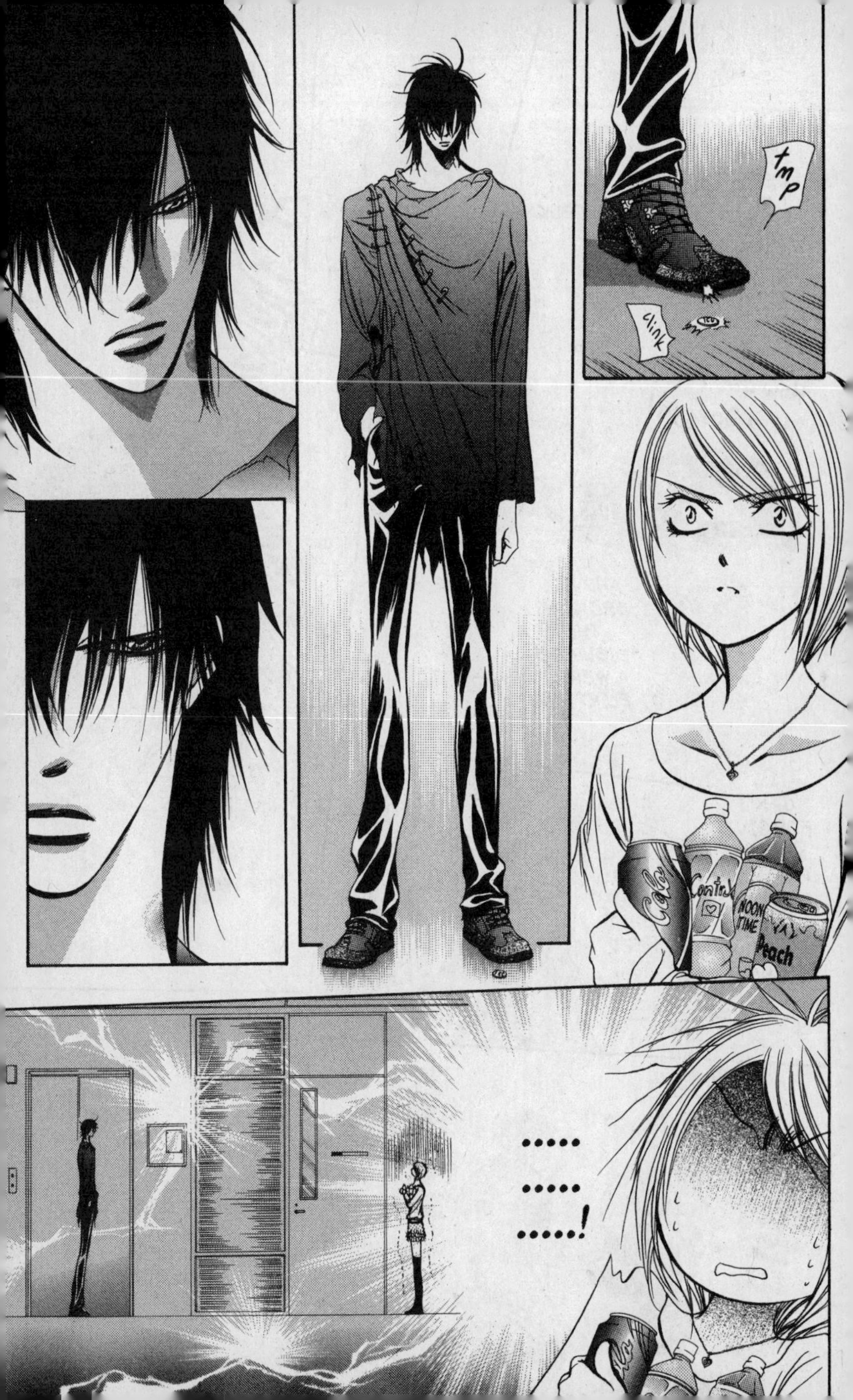
tmp
clink
NOON TIME
Peach
.....
.....
.....!

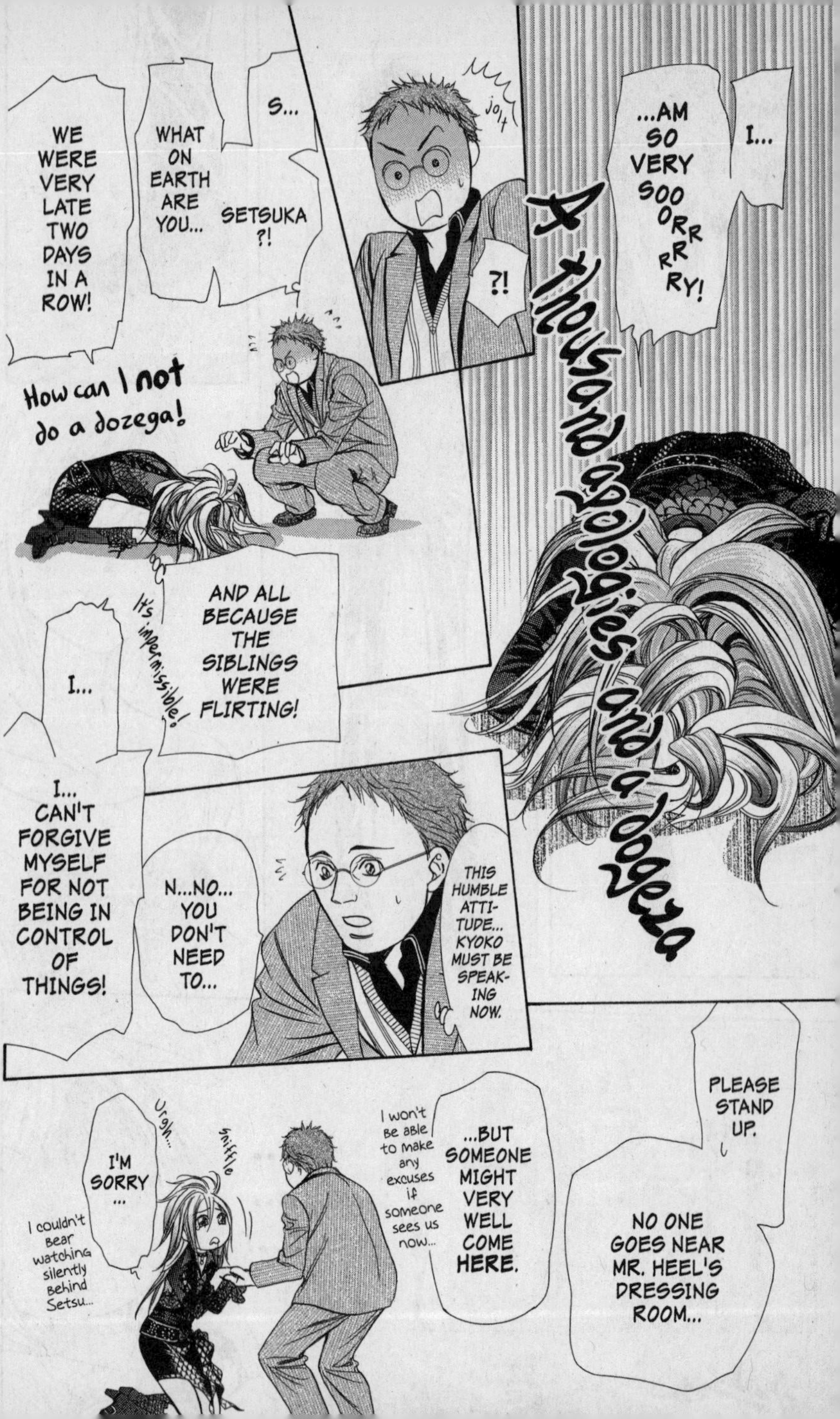
I...
...AM SO VERY SOOORRRRRRY!
A thousand apologies and a dogeza
jolt
?!
S...
SETSUKA ?!
WHAT ON EARTH ARE YOU...
WE WERE VERY LATE TWO DAYS IN A ROW!
How can I not do a dozega!
AND ALL BECAUSE THE SIBLINGS WERE FLIRTING!
It's impermissible!
I...
THIS HUMBLE ATTI-TUDE... KYOKO MUST BE SPEAK-ING NOW.
N...NO... YOU DON'T NEED TO...
I... CAN'T FORGIVE MYSELF FOR NOT BEING IN CONTROL OF THINGS!
PLEASE STAND UP.
NO ONE GOES NEAR MR. HEEL'S DRESSING ROOM...
...BUT SOMEONE MIGHT VERY WELL COME HERE.
I won't be able to make any excuses if someone sees us now...
sniffle
Urgh...
I'M SORRY ...
I couldn't bear watching silently behind Setsu...

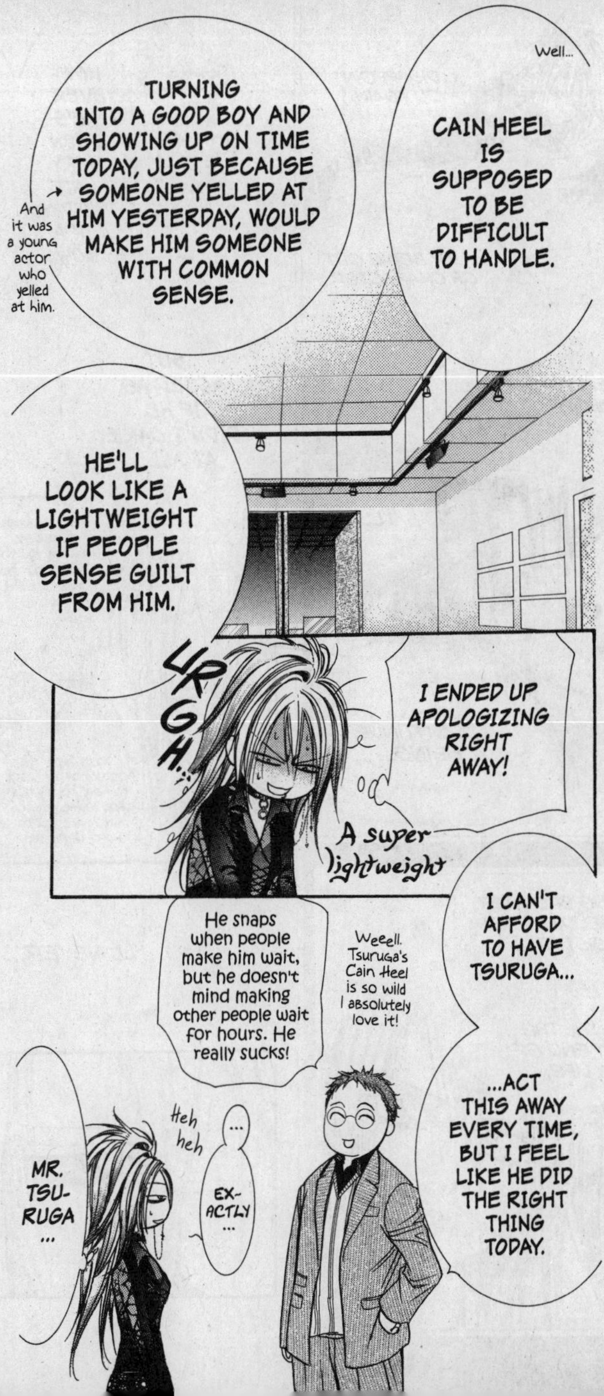
Well...
CAIN HEEL IS SUPPOSED TO BE DIFFICULT TO HANDLE.
TURNING INTO A GOOD BOY AND SHOWING UP ON TIME TODAY, JUST BECAUSE SOMEONE YELLED AT HIM YESTERDAY, WOULD MAKE HIM SOMEONE WITH COMMON SENSE.
And it was a young actor who yelled at him.
HE'LL LOOK LIKE A LIGHTWEIGHT IF PEOPLE SENSE GUILT FROM HIM.
I ENDED UP APOLOGIZING RIGHT AWAY!
URGH...
A super lightweight
I CAN'T AFFORD TO HAVE TSURUGA...
Weeell. Tsuruga's Cain Heel is so wild I absolutely love it!
He snaps when people make him wait, but he doesn't mind making other people wait for hours. He really sucks!
...ACT THIS AWAY EVERY TIME, BUT I FEEL LIKE HE DID THE RIGHT THING TODAY.
...
Heh heh
EX-ACTLY...
MR. TSU-RUGA...

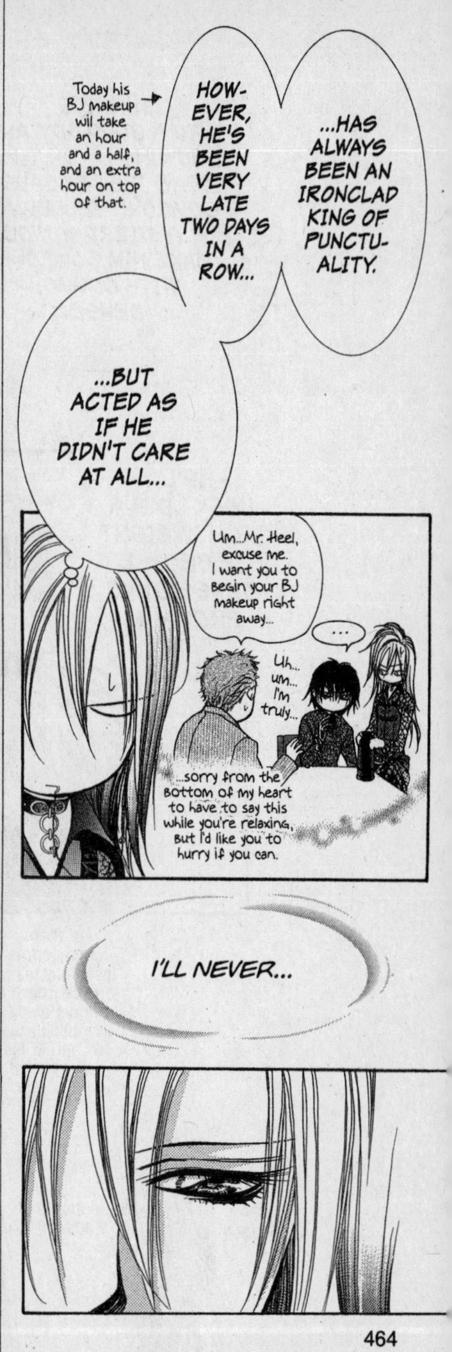
...HAS ALWAYS BEEN AN IRONCLAD KING OF PUNCTUALITY.
HOW-EVER, HE'S BEEN VERY LATE TWO DAYS IN A ROW...
Today his BJ makeup wil take an hour and a half, and an extra hour on top of that.
...BUT ACTED AS IF HE DIDN'T CARE AT ALL...
Um...Mr. Heel, excuse me. I want you to begin your BJ makeup right away...
...
Uh... um... I'm truly...
...sorry from the bottom of my heart to have to say this while you're relaxing, but I'd like you to hurry if you can.
I'LL NEVER...

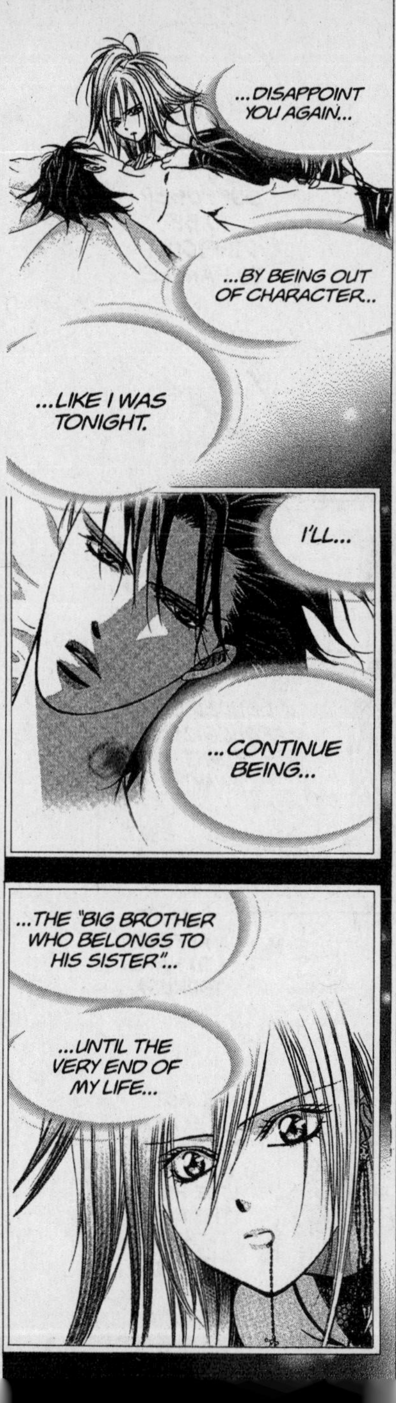
...DISAPPOINT YOU AGAIN...
...BY BEING OUT OF CHARACTER...
...LIKE I WAS TONIGHT.
I'LL...
...CONTINUE BEING...
...THE "BIG BROTHER WHO BELONGS TO HIS SISTER"...
...UNTIL THE VERY END OF MY LIFE...

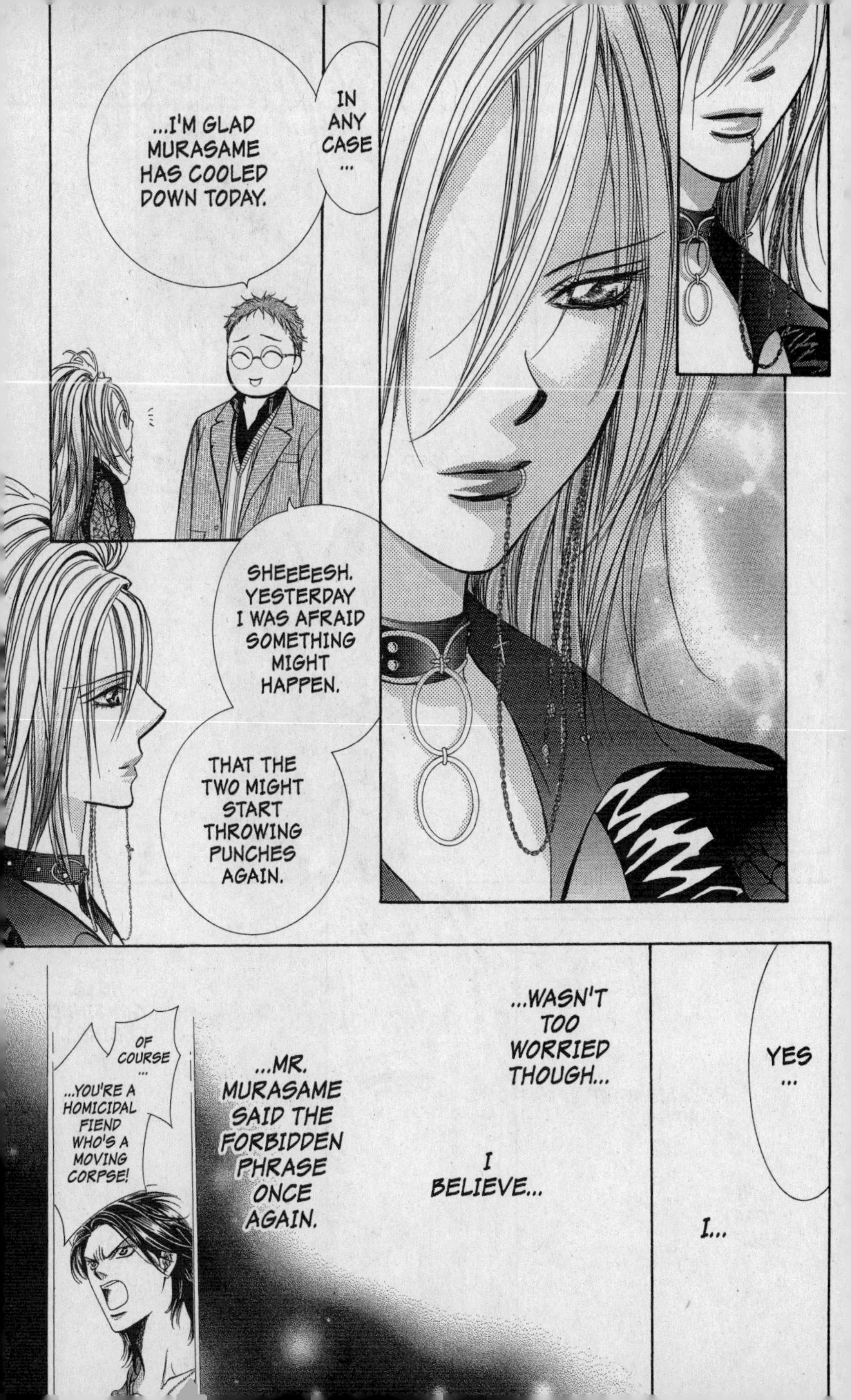
IN ANY CASE ...
...I'M GLAD MURASAME HAS COOLED DOWN TODAY.
SHEEEESH. YESTERDAY I WAS AFRAID SOMETHING MIGHT HAPPEN.
THAT THE TWO MIGHT START THROWING PUNCHES AGAIN.
YES ...
I...
...WASN'T TOO WORRIED THOUGH...
I BELIEVE...
...MR. MURASAME SAID THE FORBIDDEN PHRASE ONCE AGAIN.
OF COURSE ...
...YOU'RE A HOMICIDAL FIEND WHO'S A MOVING CORPSE!

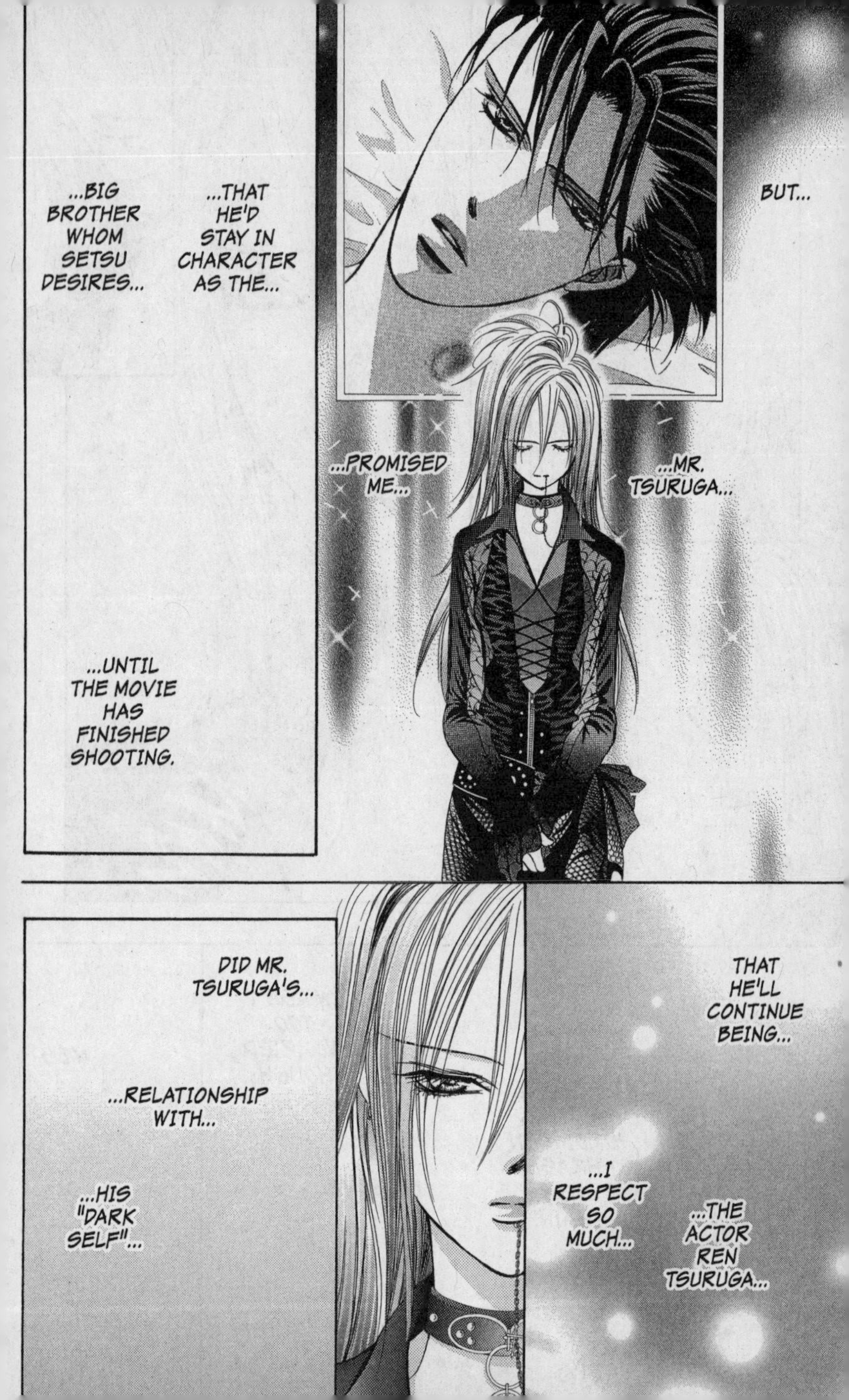
BUT...
...MR. TSURUGA...
...PROMISED ME...
...THAT HE'D STAY IN CHARACTER AS THE...
...BIG BROTHER WHOM SETSU DESIRES...
...UNTIL THE MOVIE HAS FINISHED SHOOTING.
THAT HE'LL CONTINUE BEING...
...THE ACTOR REN TSURUGA...
...I RESPECT SO MUCH...
DID MR. TSURUGA'S...
...RELATIONSHIP WITH...
...HIS "DARK SELF"...

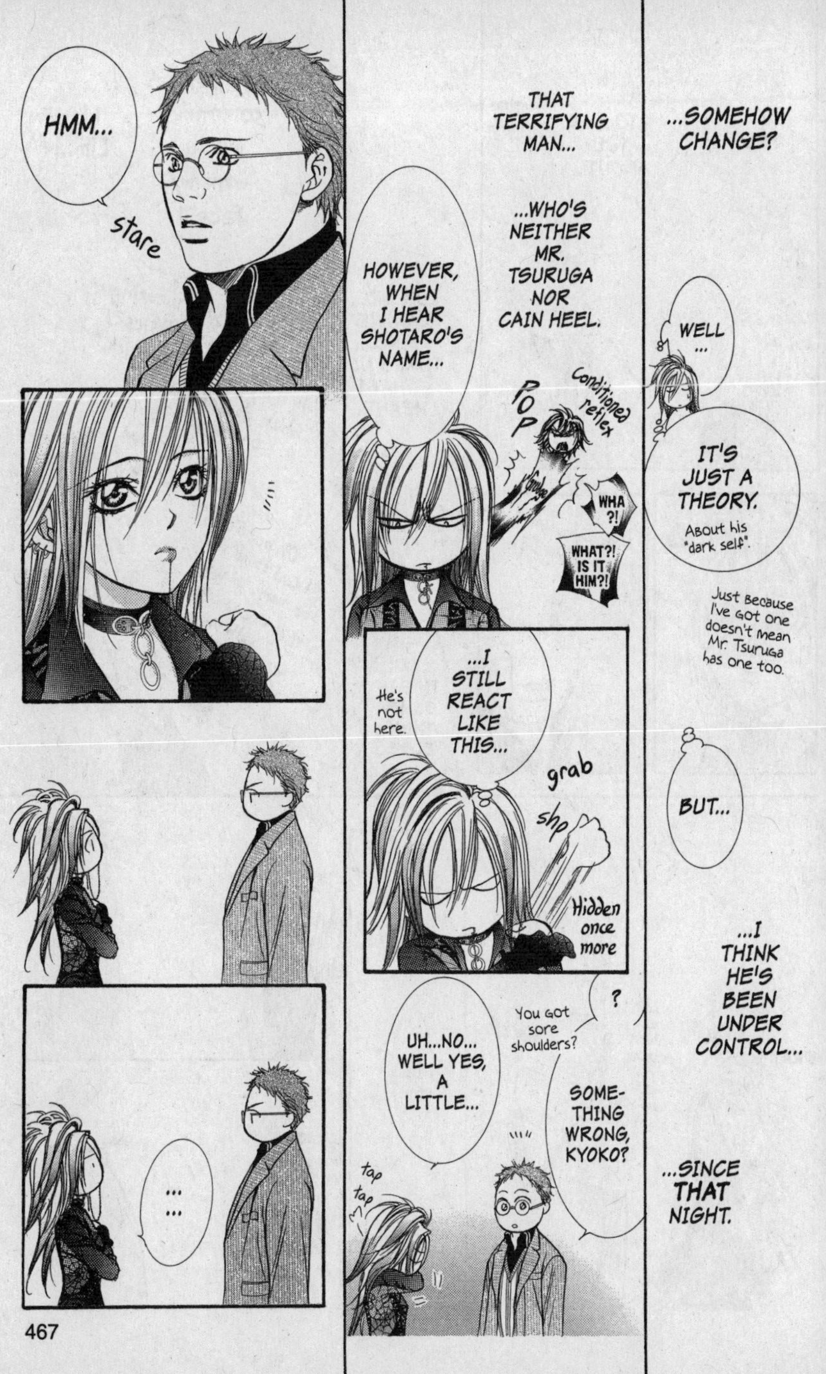
...SOMEHOW CHANGE?
WELL...
IT'S JUST A THEORY.
About his "dark self".
Just because I've got one doesn't mean Mr. Tsuruga has one too.
BUT...
...I THINK HE'S BEEN UNDER CONTROL...
...SINCE THAT NIGHT.
THAT TERRIFYING MAN...
...WHO'S NEITHER MR. TSURUGA NOR CAIN HEEL.
HOWEVER, WHEN I HEAR SHOTARO'S NAME...
POP
Conditioned reflex
WHA?!
WHAT?! IS IT HIM?!
...I STILL REACT LIKE THIS...
He's not here.
grab
shp
Hidden once more
?
SOME-THING WRONG, KYOKO?
You got sore shoulders?
UH...NO... WELL YES, A LITTLE...
tap
tap
HMM...
stare
......

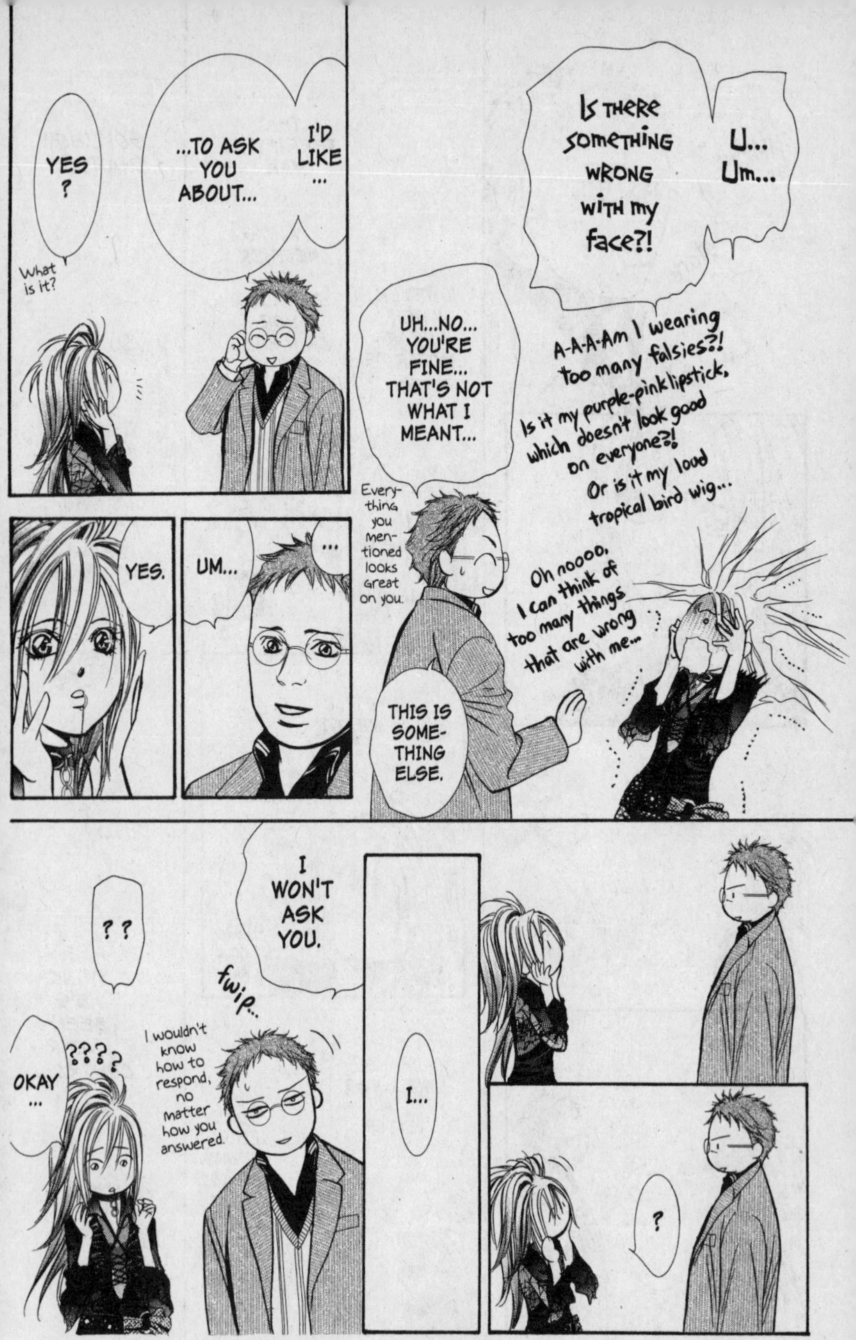

U... Um...
Is there something wrong with my face?!
A-A-A-Am I wearing too many falsies?! Is it my purple-pink lipstick, which doesn't look good on everyone?! Or is it my loud tropical bird wig...
UH...NO... YOU'RE FINE... THAT'S NOT WHAT I MEANT...
Everything you mentioned looks great on you.
Oh noooo, I can think of too many things that are wrong with me...
THIS IS SOMETHING ELSE.
I'D LIKE...
...TO ASK YOU ABOUT...
YES?
What is it?
...
UM...
YES.
?
I...
I WON'T ASK YOU.
? ?
fwip..
I wouldn't know how to respond, no matter how you answered.
OKAY...
???

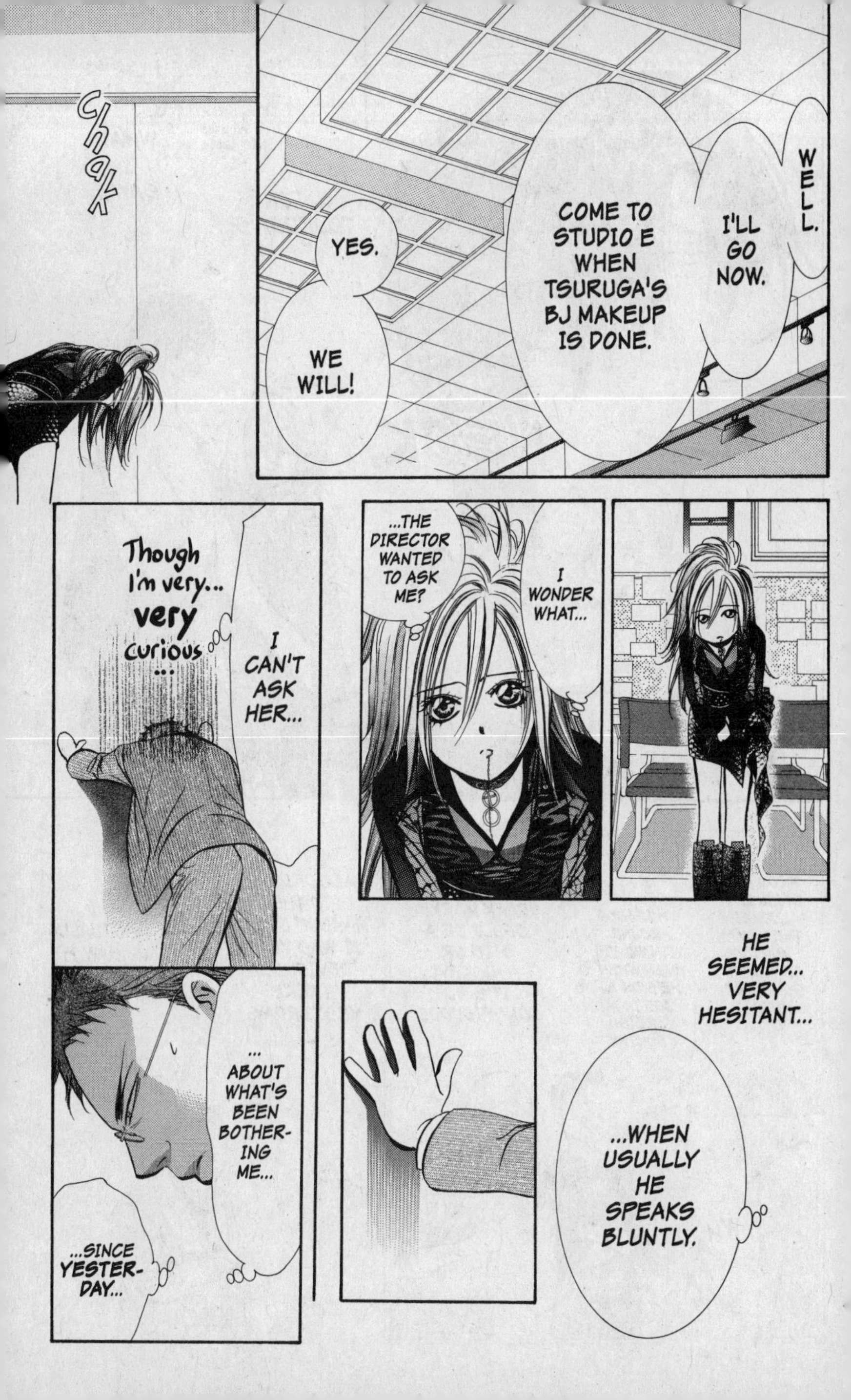
WELL.
I'LL GO NOW.
COME TO STUDIO E WHEN TSURUGA'S BJ MAKEUP IS DONE.
YES.
WE WILL!
Chak
I WONDER WHAT...
...THE DIRECTOR WANTED TO ASK ME?
I CAN'T ASK HER...
Though I'm very... very curious...
HE SEEMED... VERY HESITANT...
...WHEN USUALLY HE SPEAKS BLUNTLY.
...ABOUT WHAT'S BEEN BOTHER-ING ME...
...SINCE YESTER-DAY...

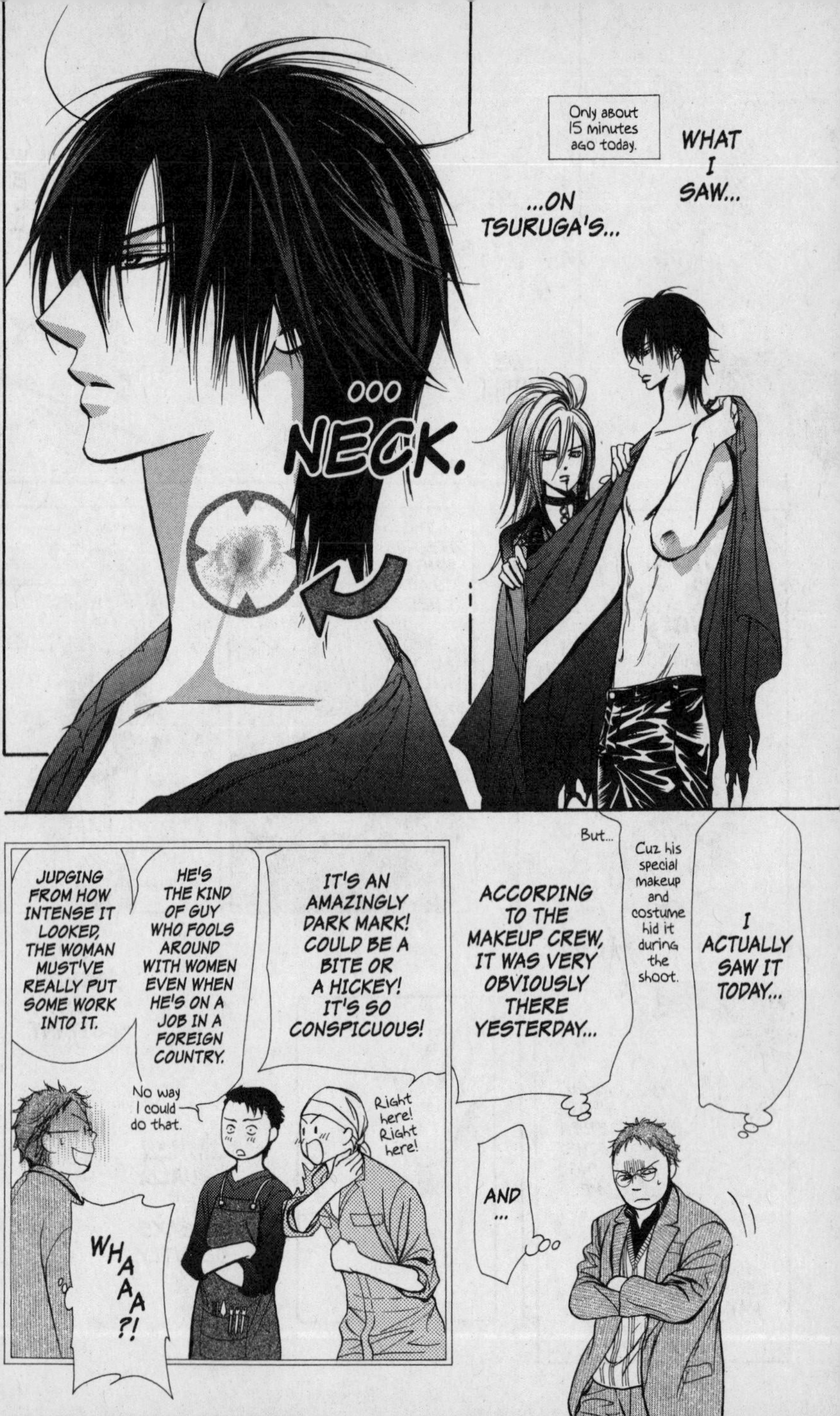
Only about 15 minutes ago today.
WHAT I SAW...
...ON TSURUGA'S...
ooo
NECK.
I ACTUALLY SAW IT TODAY...
Cuz his special makeup and costume hid it during the shoot.
But...
ACCORDING TO THE MAKEUP CREW, IT WAS VERY OBVIOUSLY THERE YESTERDAY...
AND ...
IT'S AN AMAZINGLY DARK MARK! COULD BE A BITE OR A HICKEY! IT'S SO CONSPICUOUS!
HE'S THE KIND OF GUY WHO FOOLS AROUND WITH WOMEN EVEN WHEN HE'S ON A JOB IN A FOREIGN COUNTRY.
JUDGING FROM HOW INTENSE IT LOOKED, THE WOMAN MUST'VE REALLY PUT SOME WORK INTO IT.
Right here! Right here!
No way I could do that.
WHAAAA?!

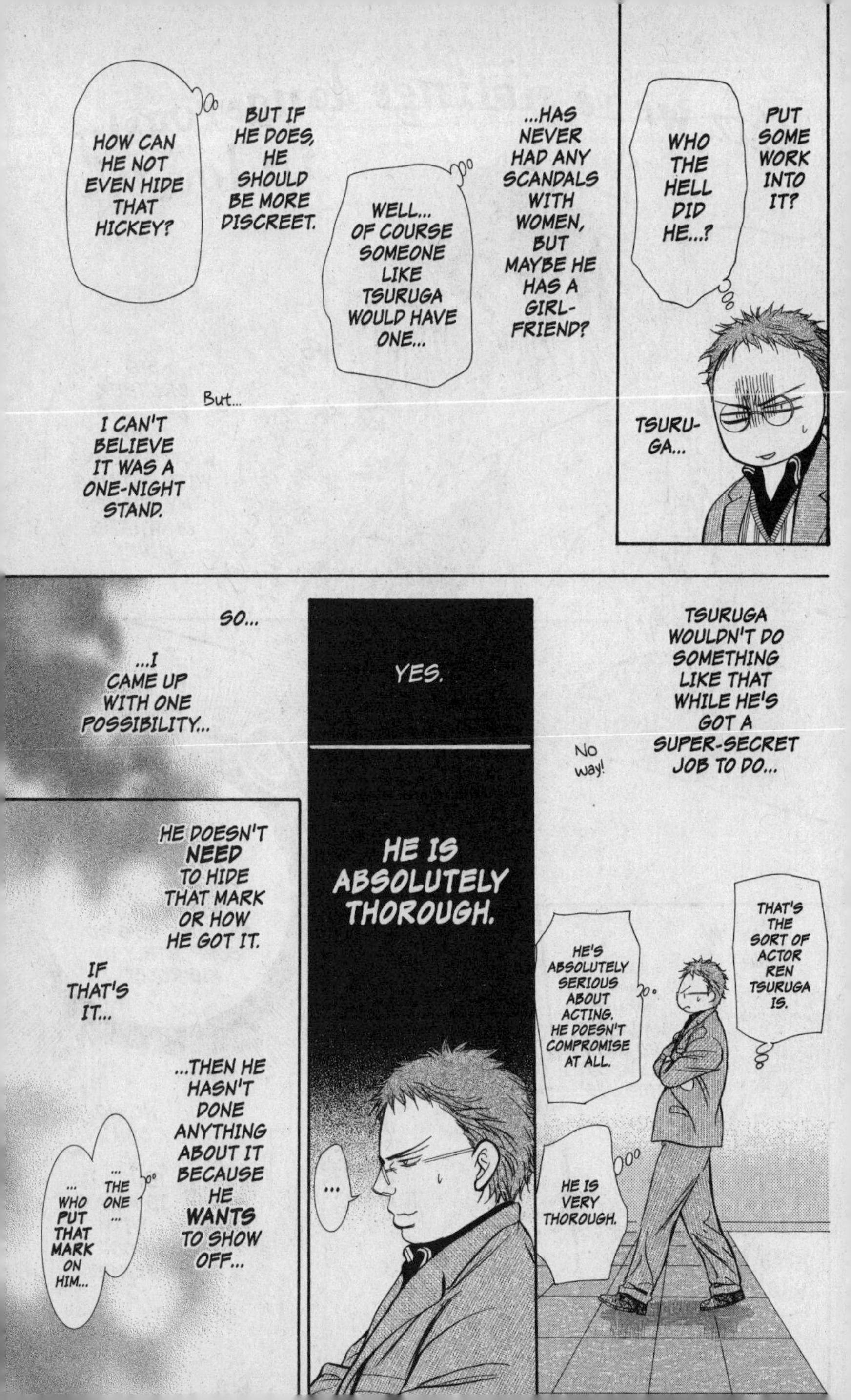
PUT SOME WORK INTO IT?
WHO THE HELL DID HE...?
TSURU-GA...
...HAS NEVER HAD ANY SCANDALS WITH WOMEN, BUT MAYBE HE HAS A GIRL-FRIEND?
WELL... OF COURSE SOMEONE LIKE TSURUGA WOULD HAVE ONE...
BUT IF HE DOES, HE SHOULD BE MORE DISCREET.
HOW CAN HE NOT EVEN HIDE THAT HICKEY?
But...
I CAN'T BELIEVE IT WAS A ONE-NIGHT STAND.
TSURUGA WOULDN'T DO SOMETHING LIKE THAT WHILE HE'S GOT A SUPER-SECRET JOB TO DO...
No way!
THAT'S THE SORT OF ACTOR REN TSURUGA IS.
HE'S ABSOLUTELY SERIOUS ABOUT ACTING. HE DOESN'T COMPROMISE AT ALL.
HE IS VERY THOROUGH.
YES.
HE IS ABSOLUTELY THOROUGH.
...
SO...
...I CAME UP WITH ONE POSSIBILITY...
HE DOESN'T NEED TO HIDE THAT MARK OR HOW HE GOT IT.
IF THAT'S IT...
...THEN HE HASN'T DONE ANYTHING ABOUT IT BECAUSE HE WANTS TO SHOW OFF...
...THE ONE...
...WHO PUT THAT MARK ON HIM...

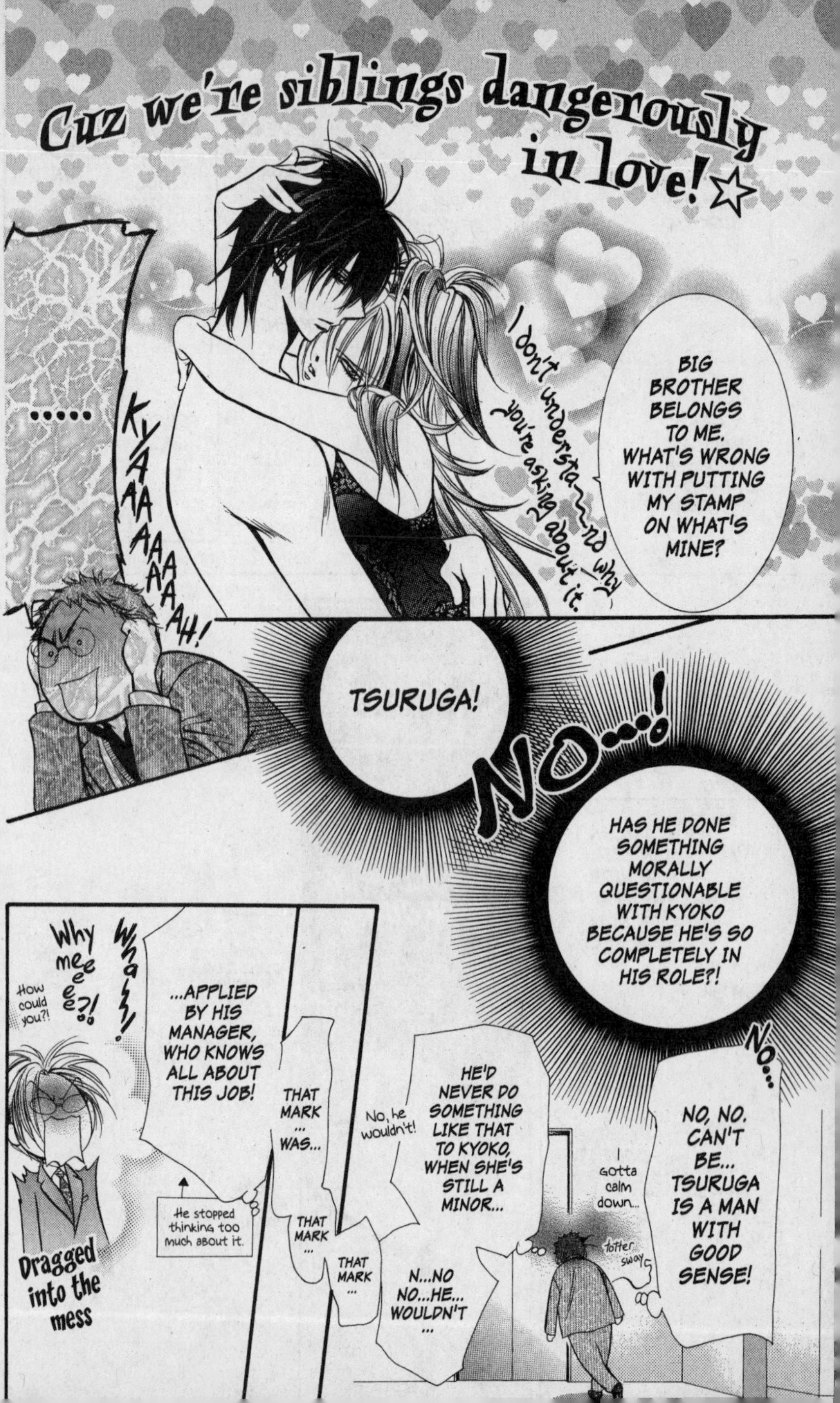
Cuz we're siblings dangerously in love!☆
BIG BROTHER BELONGS TO ME. WHAT'S WRONG WITH PUTTING MY STAMP ON WHAT'S MINE?
I don't understa~nd why you're asking about it.
KYAAAAAAAAAAAH!
.....
TSURUGA!
NO...!
HAS HE DONE SOMETHING MORALLY QUESTIONABLE WITH KYOKO BECAUSE HE'S SO COMPLETELY IN HIS ROLE?!
No...
NO, NO. CAN'T BE... TSURUGA IS A MAN WITH GOOD SENSE!
I gotta calm down...
totter sway
HE'D NEVER DO SOMETHING LIKE THAT TO KYOKO, WHEN SHE'S STILL A MINOR...
No, he wouldn't!
N...NO NO...HE... WOULDN'T ...
THAT MARK ... WAS...
THAT MARK ...
THAT MARK ...
...APPLIED BY HIS MANAGER, WHO KNOWS ALL ABOUT THIS JOB!
Whaa!
Why meeeee?!
How could you?!
He stopped thinking too much about it.
Dragged into the mess

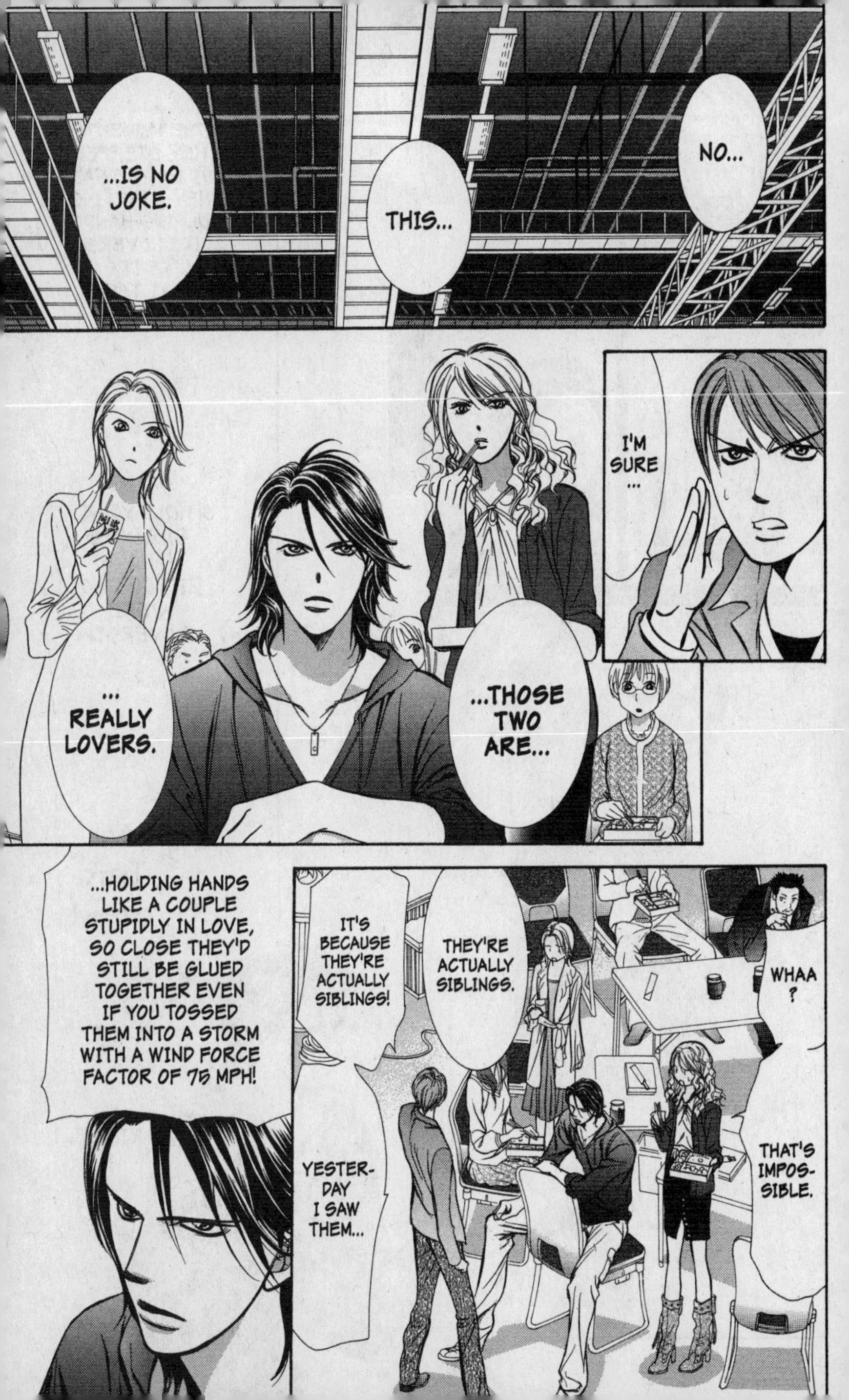
NO...
THIS...
...IS NO JOKE.
I'M SURE...
...THOSE TWO ARE...
...REALLY LOVERS.
WHAA?
THAT'S IMPOSSIBLE.
THEY'RE ACTUALLY SIBLINGS.
IT'S BECAUSE THEY'RE ACTUALLY SIBLINGS!
YESTERDAY I SAW THEM...
...HOLDING HANDS LIKE A COUPLE STUPIDLY IN LOVE, SO CLOSE THEY'D STILL BE GLUED TOGETHER EVEN IF YOU TOSSED THEM INTO A STORM WITH A WIND FORCE FACTOR OF 75 MPH!

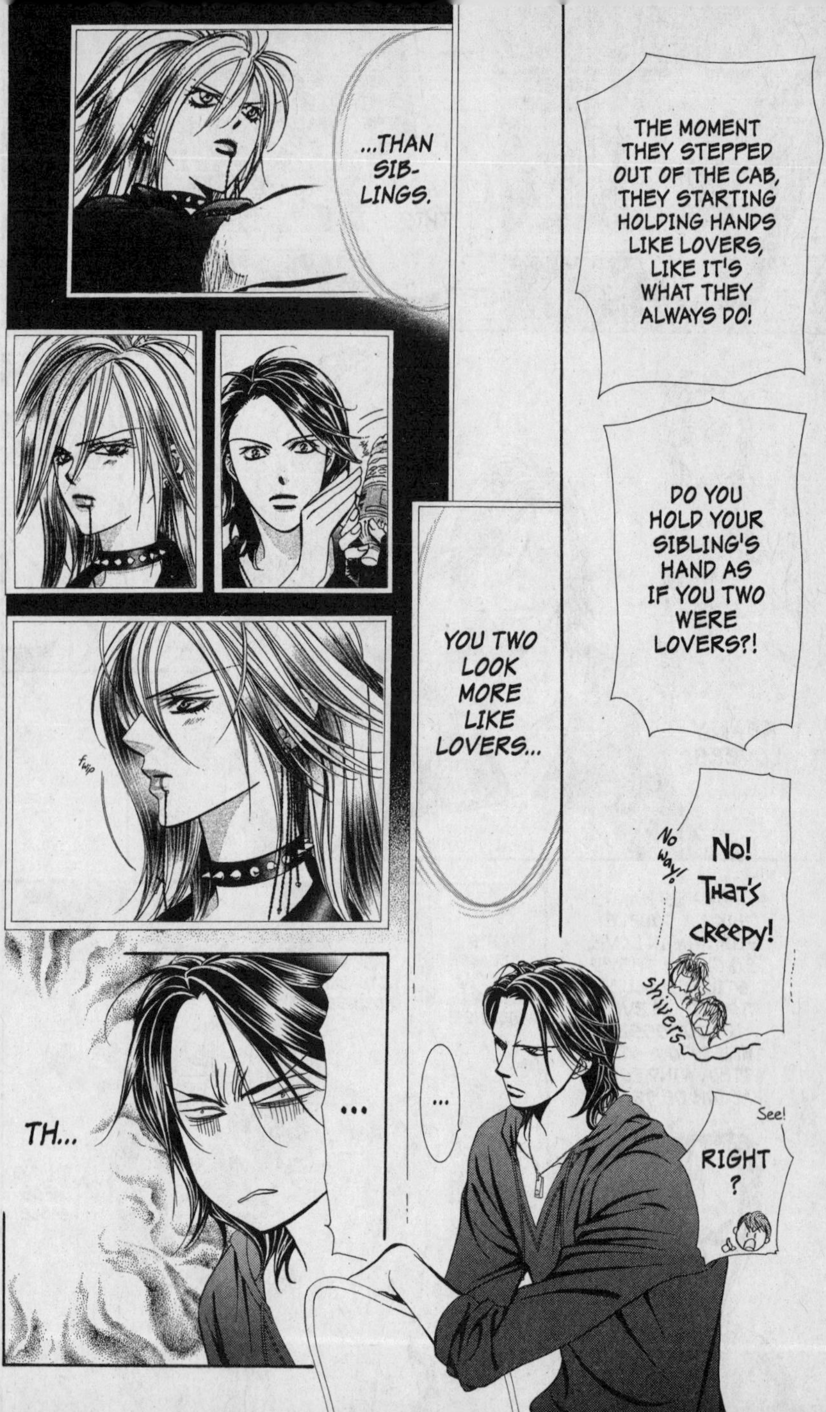
THE MOMENT THEY STEPPED OUT OF THE CAB, THEY STARTING HOLDING HANDS LIKE LOVERS, LIKE IT'S WHAT THEY ALWAYS DO!
...THAN SIB-LINGS.
DO YOU HOLD YOUR SIBLING'S HAND AS IF YOU TWO WERE LOVERS?!
YOU TWO LOOK MORE LIKE LOVERS...
fwip
No way!
No! That's creepy!
shivers
See!
RIGHT?
...
...
TH...

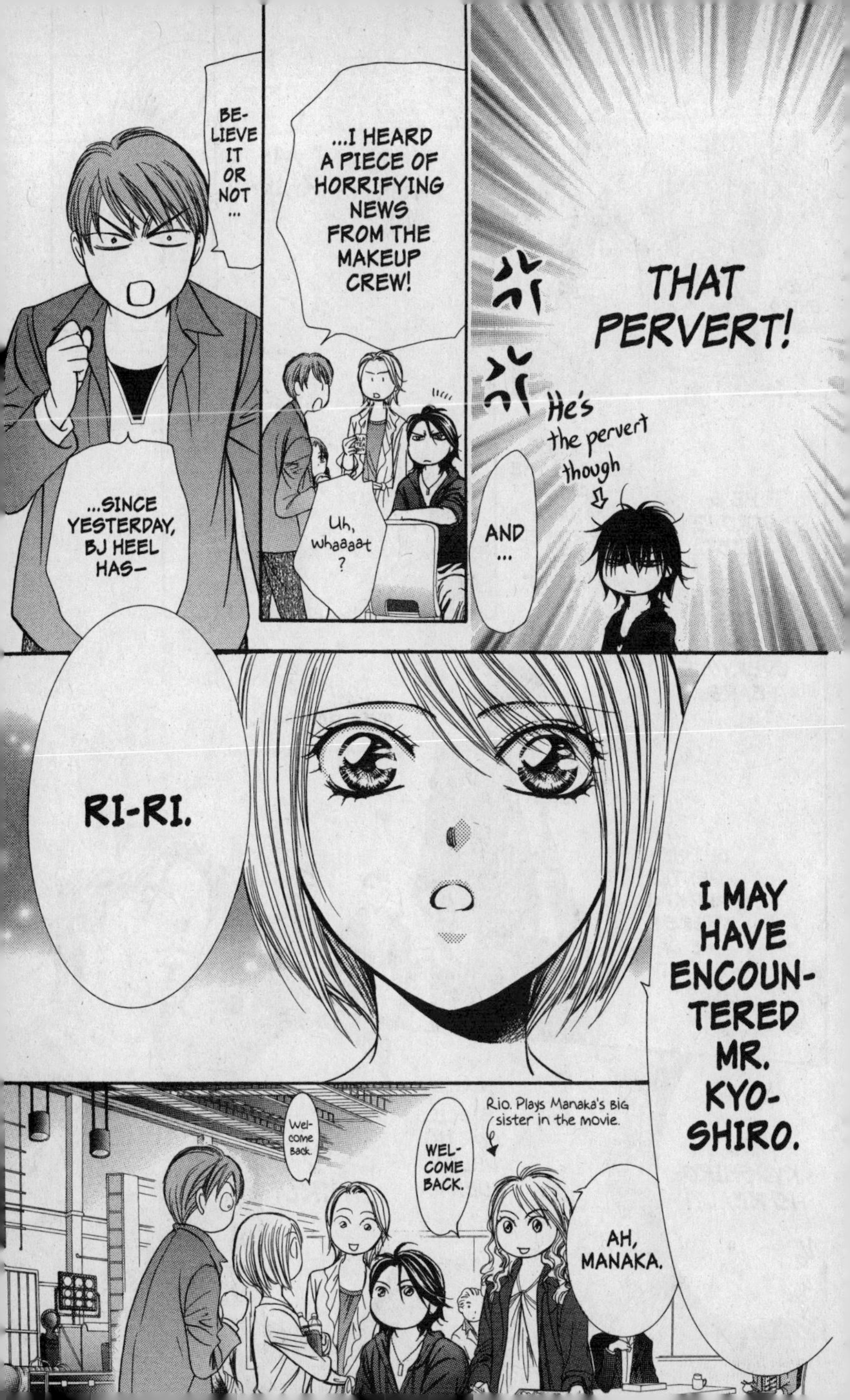
THAT PERVERT!
He's the pervert though
AND ...
...I HEARD A PIECE OF HORRIFYING NEWS FROM THE MAKEUP CREW!
Uh, whaaaat?
BE-LIEVE IT OR NOT ...
...SINCE YESTERDAY, BJ HEEL HAS—
I MAY HAVE ENCOUNTERED MR. KYO-SHIRO.
RI-RI.
AH, MANAKA.
Rio. Plays Manaka's big sister in the movie.
WEL-COME BACK.
Wel-come back.

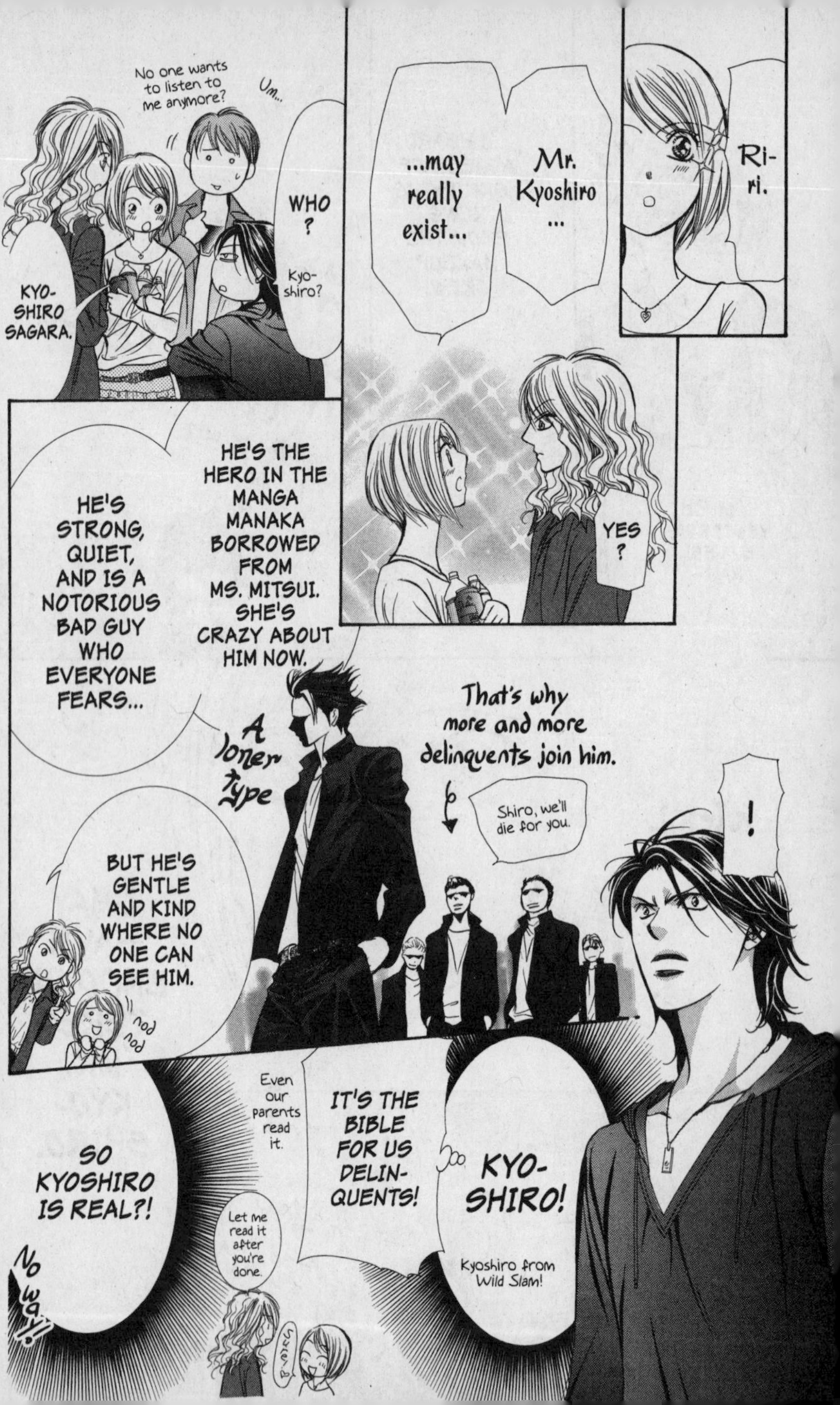
Ri-ri.
Mr. Kyoshiro ...
...may really exist...
YES?
Um...
No one wants to listen to me anymore?
WHO?
Kyo-shiro?
KYO-SHIRO SAGARA.
HE'S THE HERO IN THE MANGA MANAKA BORROWED FROM MS. MITSUI. SHE'S CRAZY ABOUT HIM NOW.
HE'S STRONG, QUIET, AND IS A NOTORIOUS BAD GUY WHO EVERYONE FEARS...
A loner type
That's why more and more delinquents join him.
Shiro, we'll die for you.
BUT HE'S GENTLE AND KIND WHERE NO ONE CAN SEE HIM.
nod nod
!
KYO-SHIRO!
Kyoshiro from Wild Slam!
IT'S THE BIBLE FOR US DELIN-QUENTS!
Even our parents read it.
SO KYOSHIRO IS REAL?!
Let me read it after you're done.
No way!!

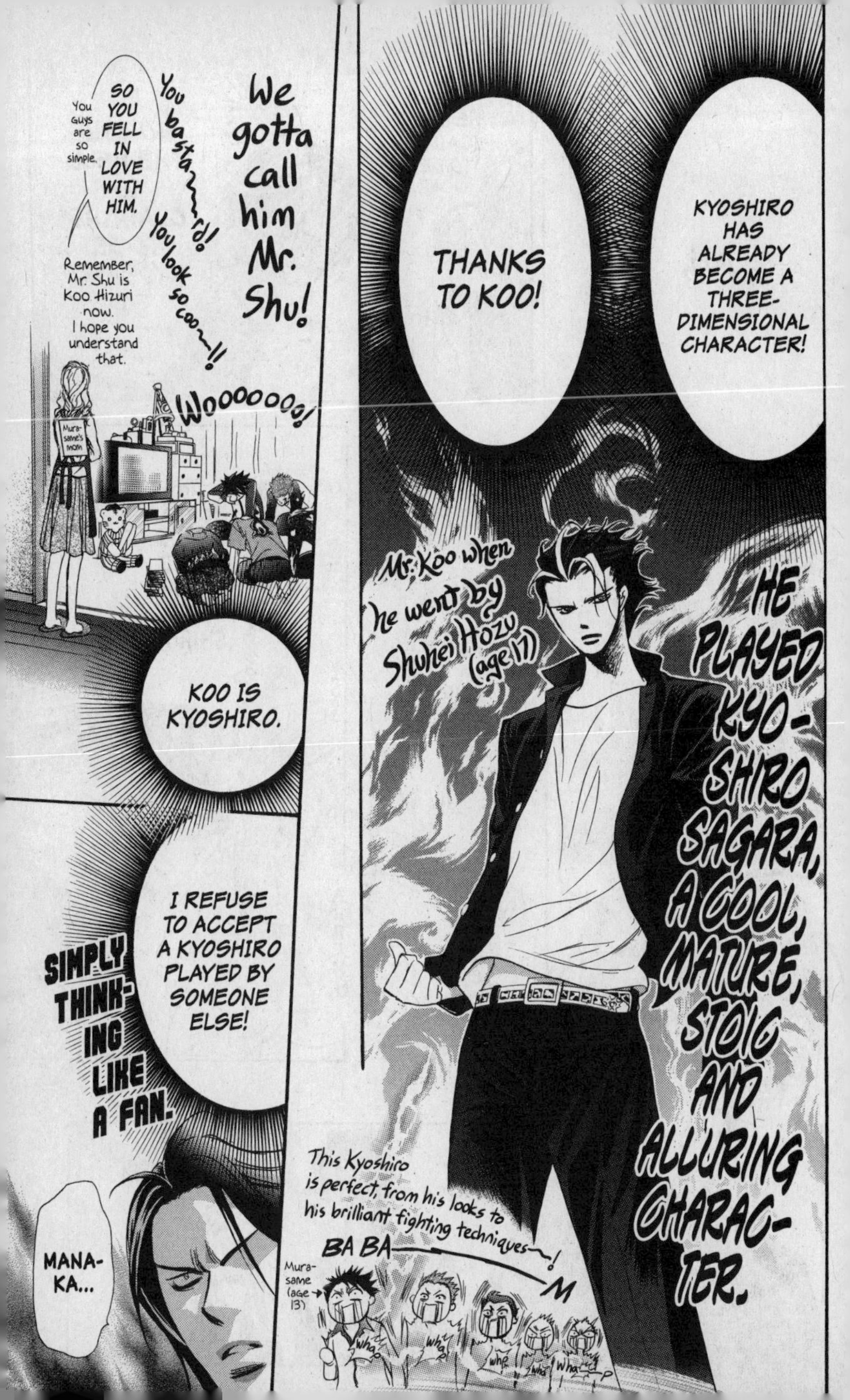
KYOSHIRO HAS ALREADY BECOME A THREE-DIMENSIONAL CHARACTER!
THANKS TO KOO!
HE PLAYED KYO-SHIRO SAGARA, A COOL, MATURE, STOIC AND ALLURING CHARAC-TER.
Mr. Koo when he went by Shuhei Hozu (age 17)
This Kyoshiro is perfect, from his looks to his brilliant fighting techniques~!
BA BA—M
Mura-same (age 13)
Wha
Wha
Wha
Wha
Wha
We gotta call him Mr. Shu!
You basta~~rd! You look so coo~~!!
SO YOU FELL IN LOVE WITH HIM.
You Guys are so simple.
Remember, Mr. Shu is Koo Hizuri now. I hope you understand that.
Mura-same's mom
Wooooooo!
KOO IS KYOSHIRO.
I REFUSE TO ACCEPT A KYOSHIRO PLAYED BY SOMEONE ELSE!
SIMPLY THINK-ING LIKE A FAN.
MANA-KA...

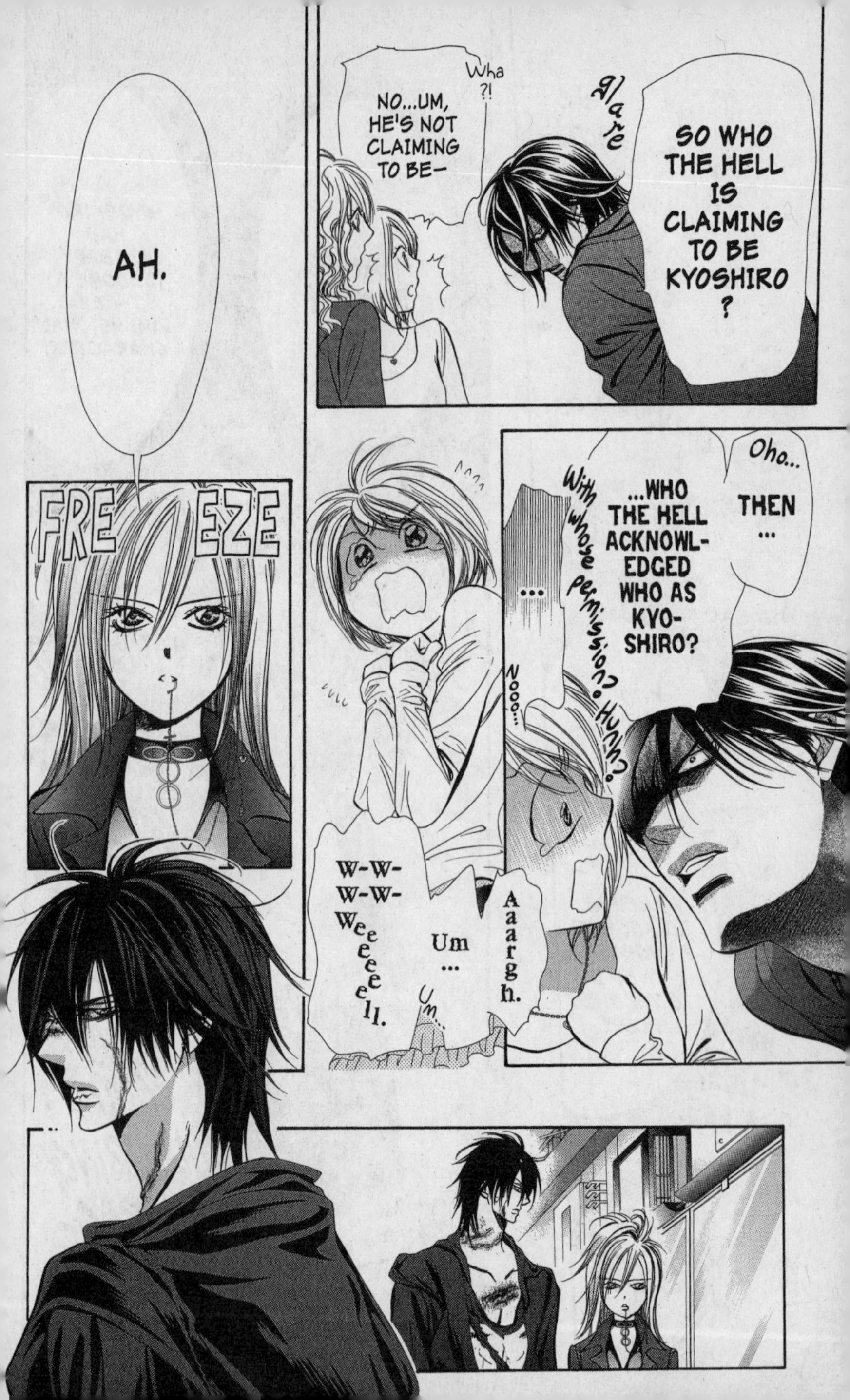
glare
SO WHO THE HELL IS CLAIMING TO BE KYOSHIRO?
Wha?!
NO...UM, HE'S NOT CLAIMING TO BE—
Oho...
THEN...
...WHO THE HELL ACKNOWLEDGED WHO AS KYOSHIRO?
With whose permission? Hunh?
...
Nooo...
W-W-W-W-Weeeeeell.
Um...
Um...
Aaargh.
AH.
FREEZE
...

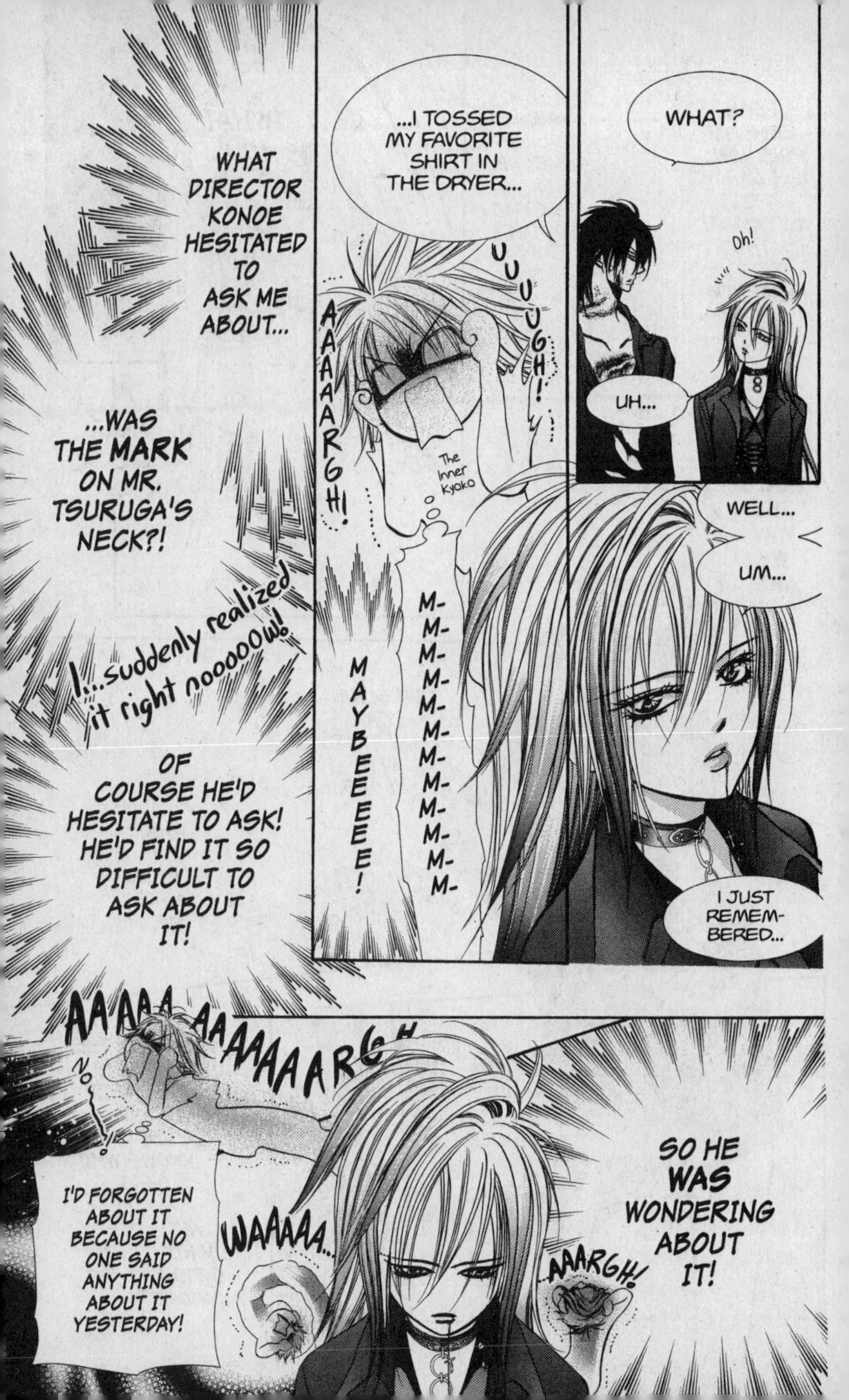
WHAT?
Oh!
UH...
WELL...
UM...
I JUST REMEMBERED...
...I TOSSED MY FAVORITE SHIRT IN THE DRYER...
UUUUGH!
AAAAAARGH!
The Inner Kyoko
M-MM-MMM-MMMM-MMMMM-MMMMMM-MMMMMMM-
MAYBEEEEE!
WHAT DIRECTOR KONOE HESITATED TO ASK ME ABOUT...
...WAS THE MARK ON MR. TSURUGA'S NECK?!
I...suddenly realized it right noooooow!
OF COURSE HE'D HESITATE TO ASK! HE'D FIND IT SO DIFFICULT TO ASK ABOUT IT!
SO HE WAS WONDERING ABOUT IT!
AAAARGH!
AAAAAAAAAARGH
NO--!!
WAAAAA...
I'D FORGOTTEN ABOUT IT BECAUSE NO ONE SAID ANYTHING ABOUT IT YESTERDAY!

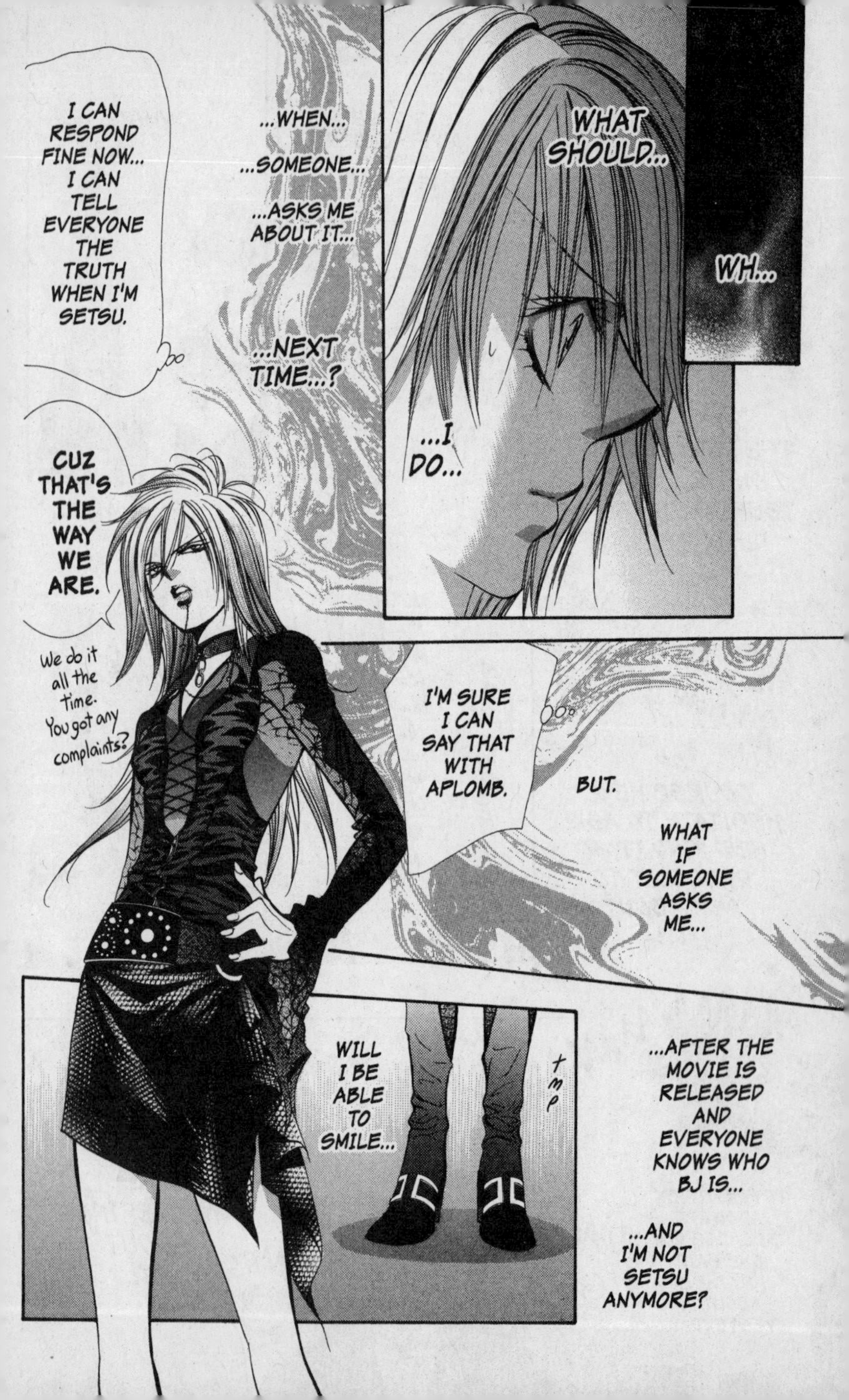
WH...
WHAT SHOULD...
...I DO...
...WHEN...
...SOMEONE...
...ASKS ME ABOUT IT...
...NEXT TIME...?
I CAN RESPOND FINE NOW... I CAN TELL EVERYONE THE TRUTH WHEN I'M SETSU.
CUZ THAT'S THE WAY WE ARE.
We do it all the time. You got any complaints?
I'M SURE I CAN SAY THAT WITH APLOMB.
BUT.
WHAT IF SOMEONE ASKS ME...
...AFTER THE MOVIE IS RELEASED AND EVERYONE KNOWS WHO BJ IS...
...AND I'M NOT SETSU ANYMORE?
tmp
WILL I BE ABLE TO SMILE...

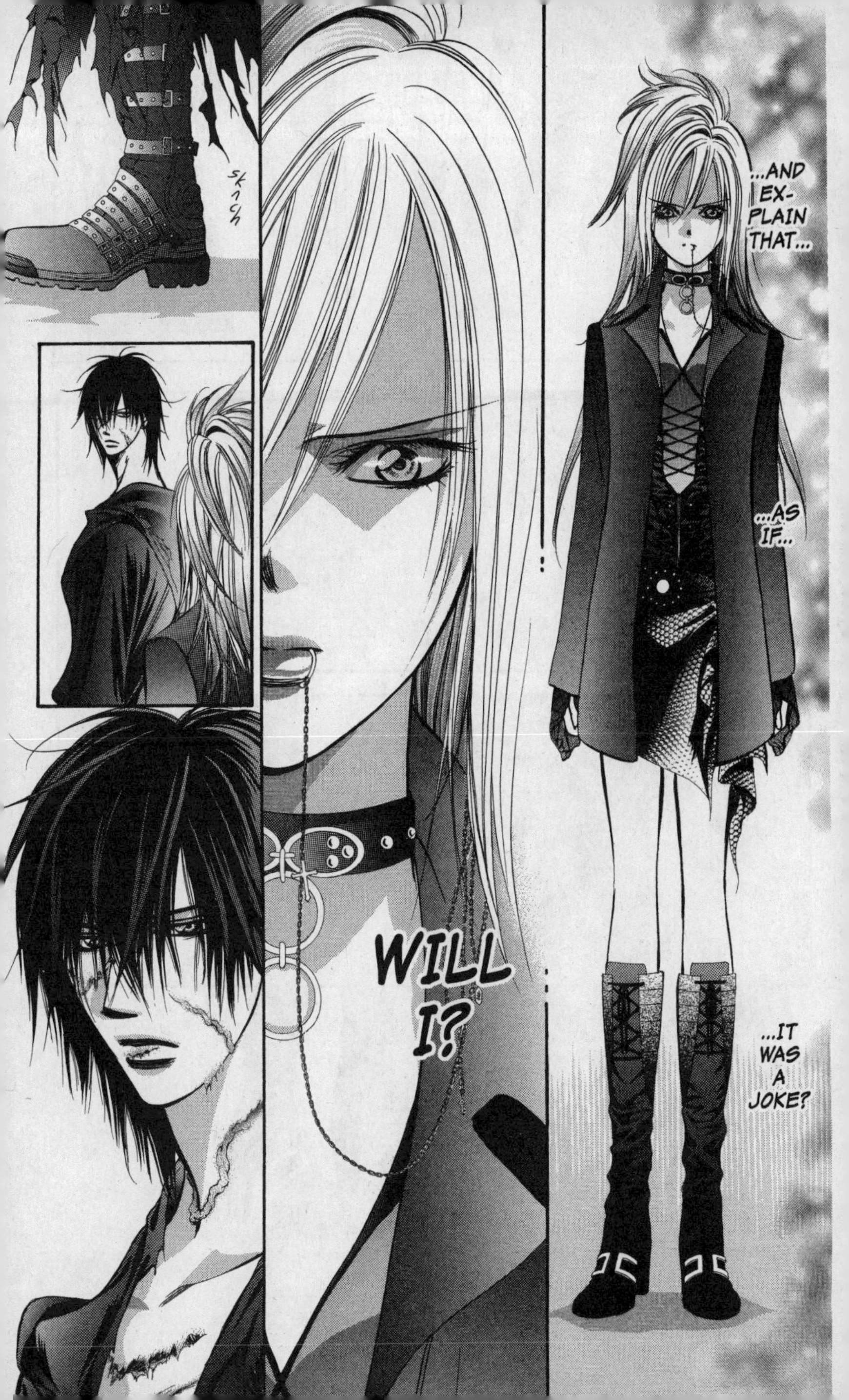
...AND EX-PLAIN THAT...
...AS IF...
...IT WAS A JOKE?
WILL I?
skrch

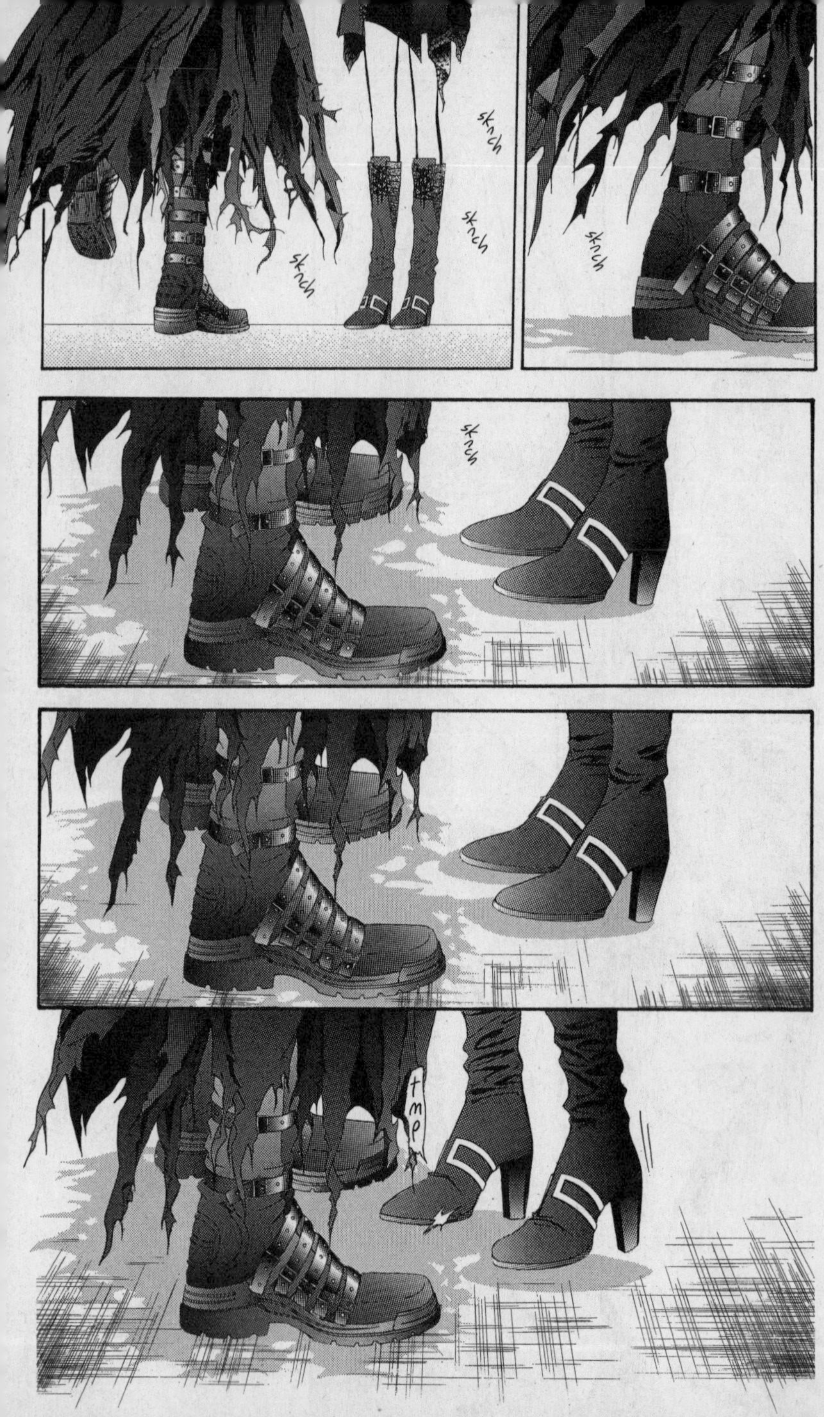
sknch
sknch
sknch
sknch
sknch
tmp

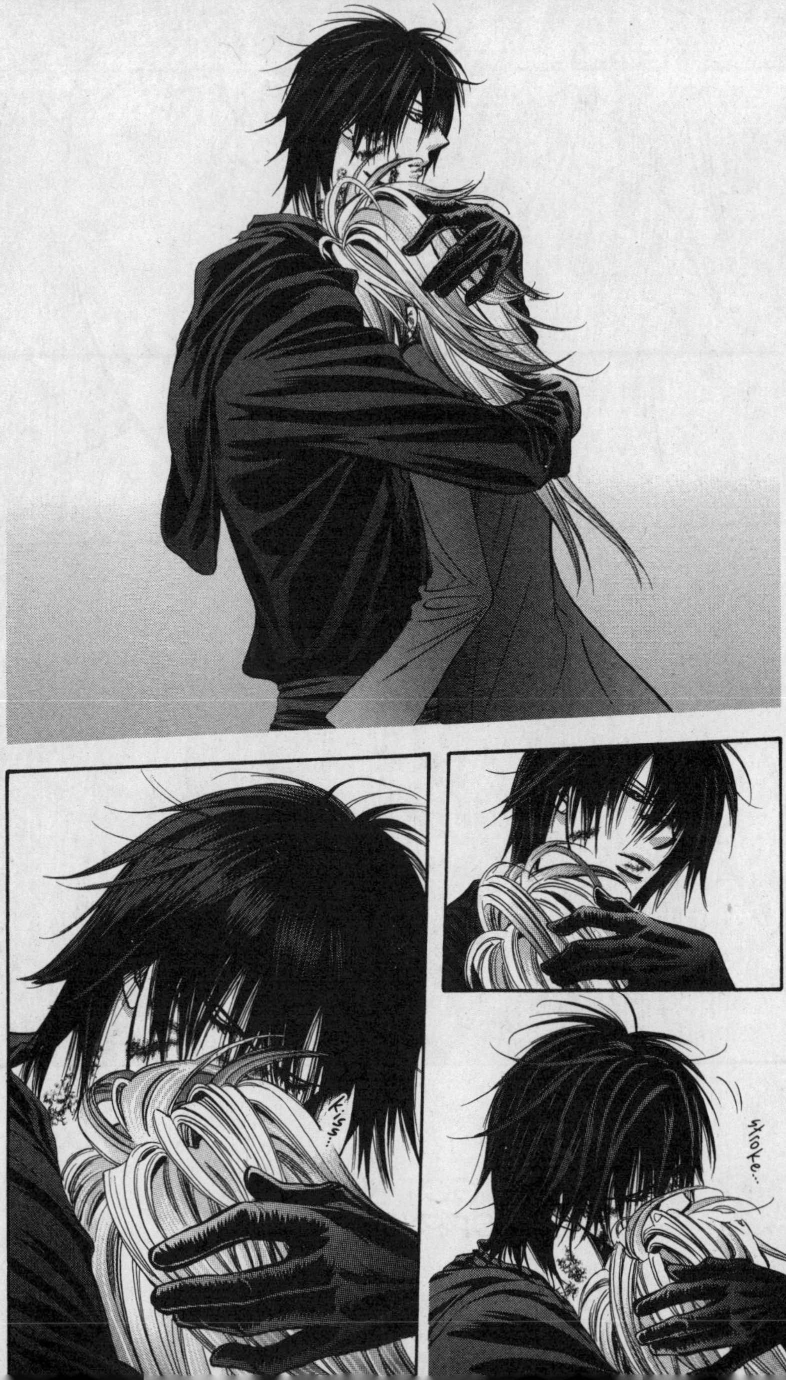
stroke...
kiss...

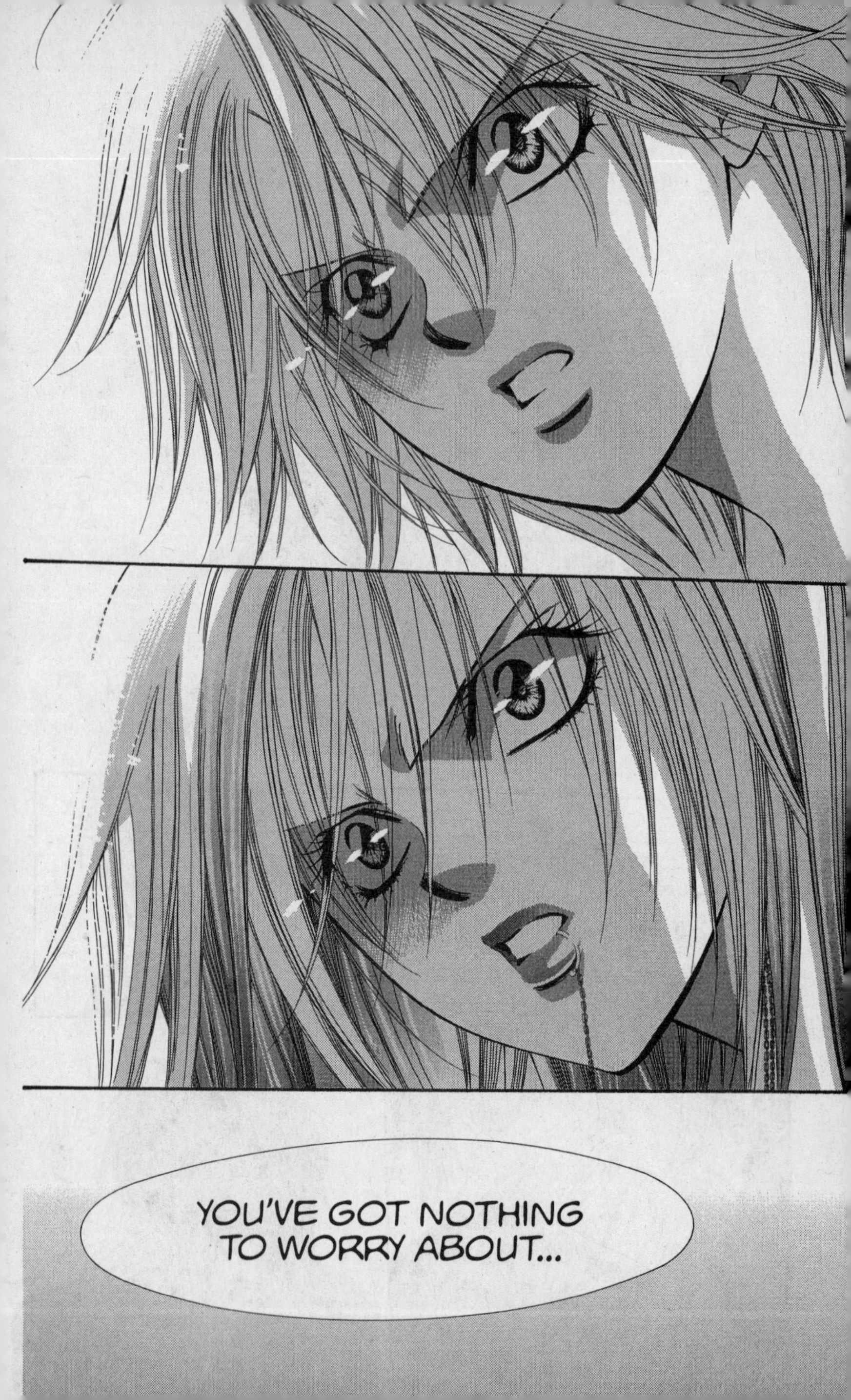
YOU'VE GOT NOTHING TO WORRY ABOUT...

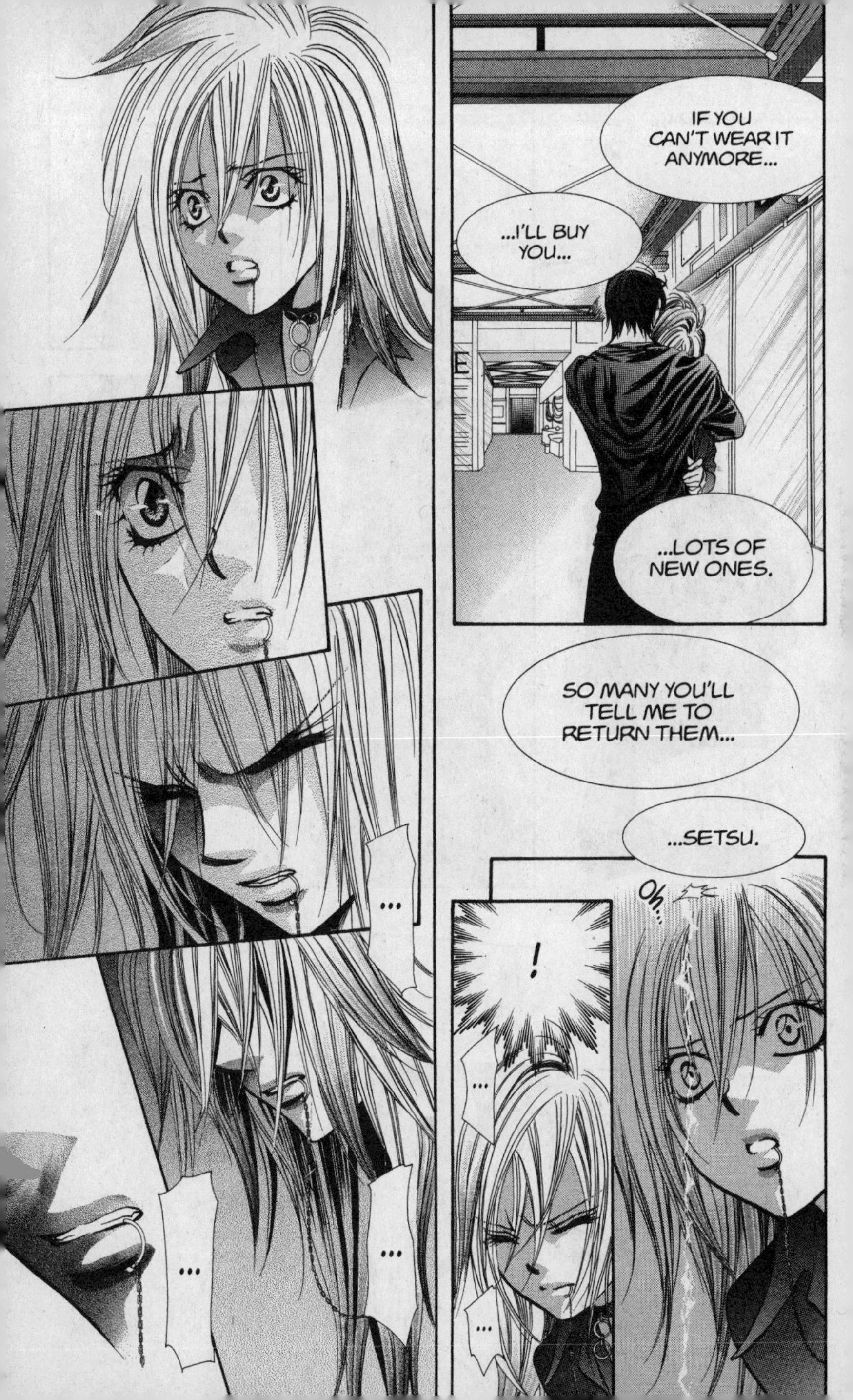
IF YOU CAN'T WEAR IT ANYMORE...
...I'LL BUY YOU...
...LOTS OF NEW ONES.
SO MANY YOU'LL TELL ME TO RETURN THEM...
...SETSU.
Oh...
!
...
...
...
...
...

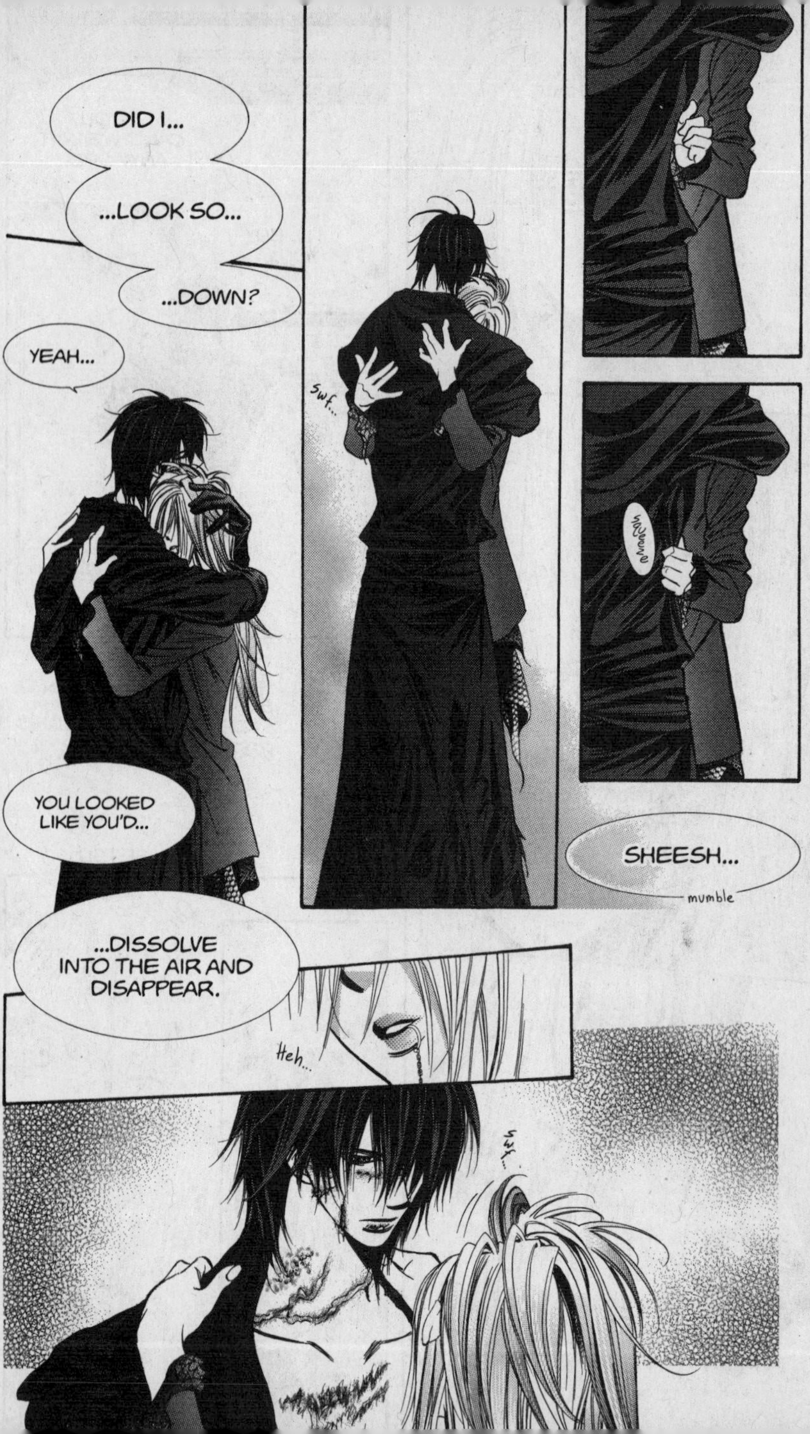
squeeze
SHEESH...
mumble
swf...
DID I...
...LOOK SO...
...DOWN?
YEAH...
YOU LOOKED LIKE YOU'D...
...DISSOLVE INTO THE AIR AND DISAPPEAR.
Heh...
swf...

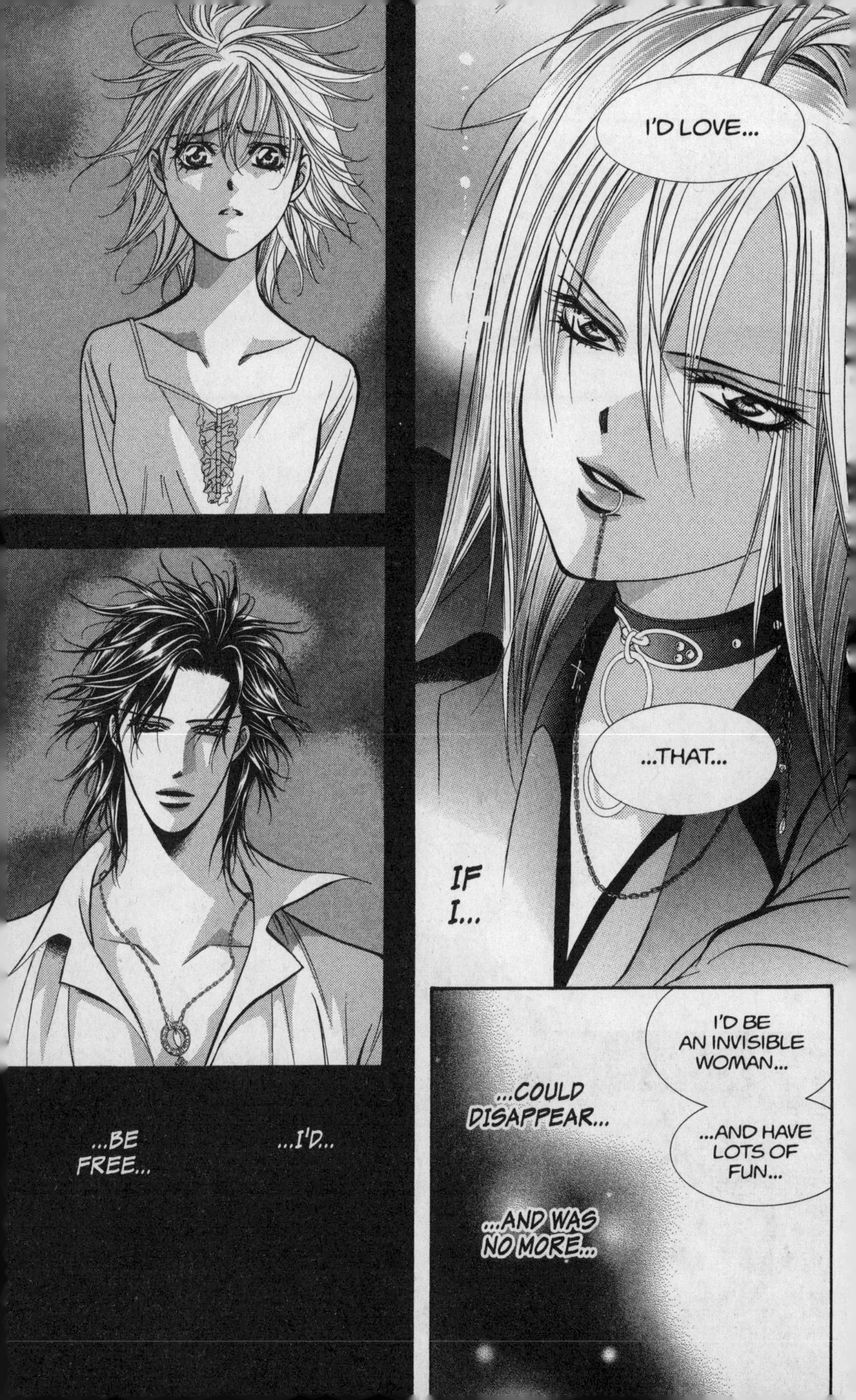
I'D LOVE...
...THAT...
IF I...
I'D BE AN INVISIBLE WOMAN...
...COULD DISAPPEAR...
...AND HAVE LOTS OF FUN...
...AND WAS NO MORE...
...I'D...
...BE FREE...

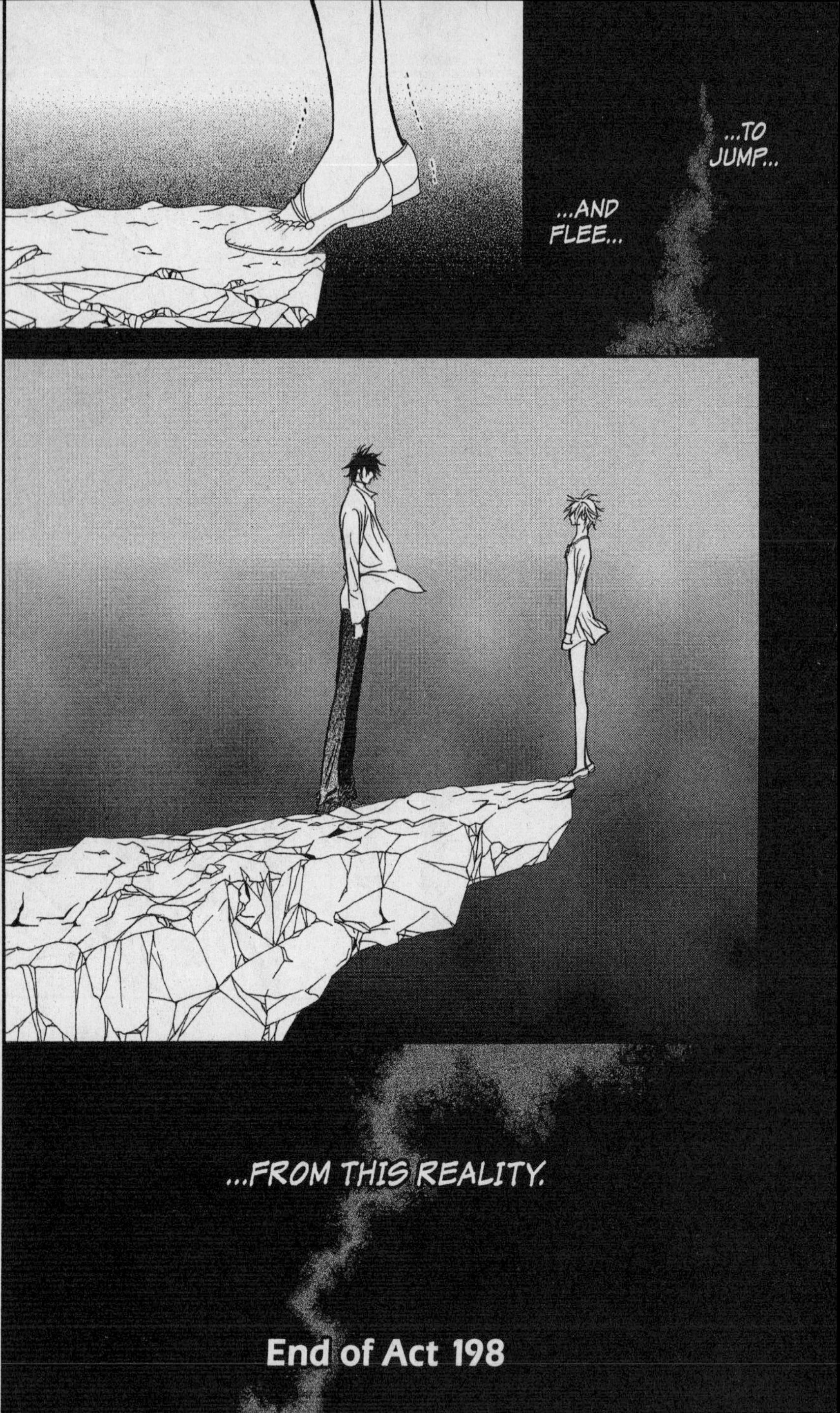
...TO JUMP...
...AND FLEE...
...FROM THIS REALITY.
End of Act 198

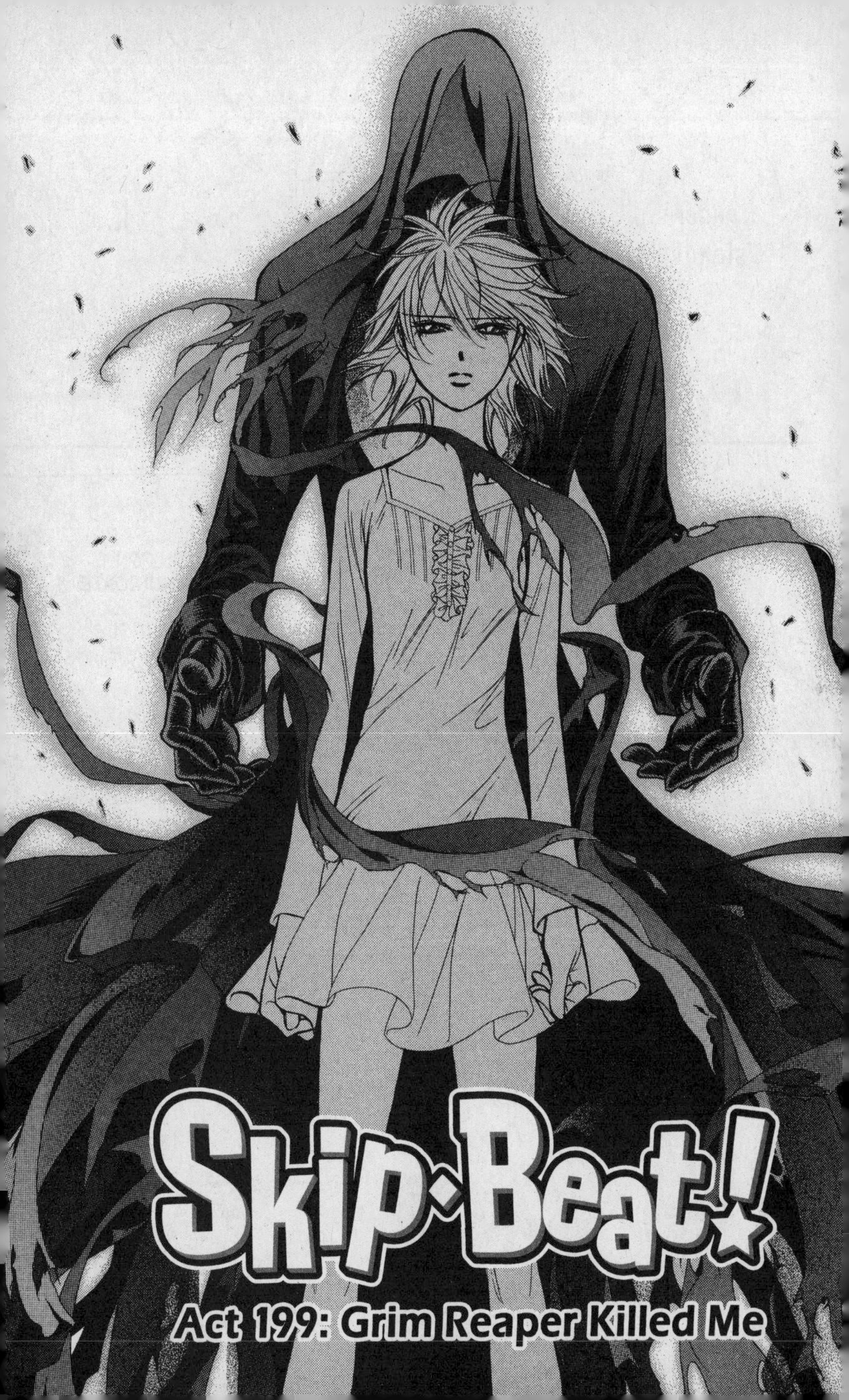
Skip·Beat!
Act 199: Grim Reaper Killed Me

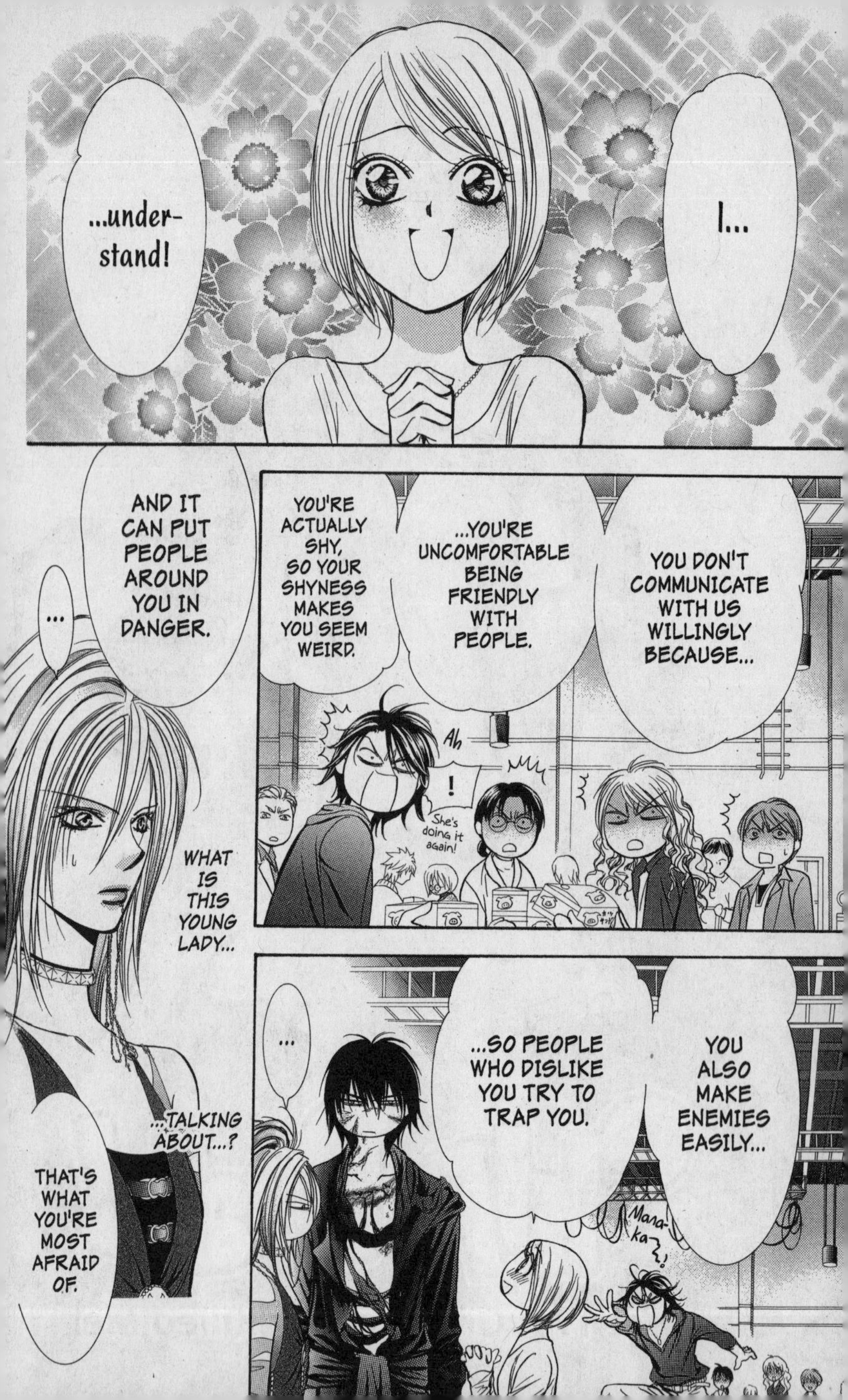
I...
...under-stand!
YOU DON'T COMMUNICATE WITH US WILLINGLY BECAUSE...
...YOU'RE UNCOMFORTABLE BEING FRIENDLY WITH PEOPLE.
YOU'RE ACTUALLY SHY, SO YOUR SHYNESS MAKES YOU SEEM WEIRD.
Ah
!
She's doing it again!
YOU ALSO MAKE ENEMIES EASILY...
...SO PEOPLE WHO DISLIKE YOU TRY TO TRAP YOU.
Mana-ka~!
...
AND IT CAN PUT PEOPLE AROUND YOU IN DANGER.
...
WHAT IS THIS YOUNG LADY...
...TALKING ABOUT...?
THAT'S WHAT YOU'RE MOST AFRAID OF.

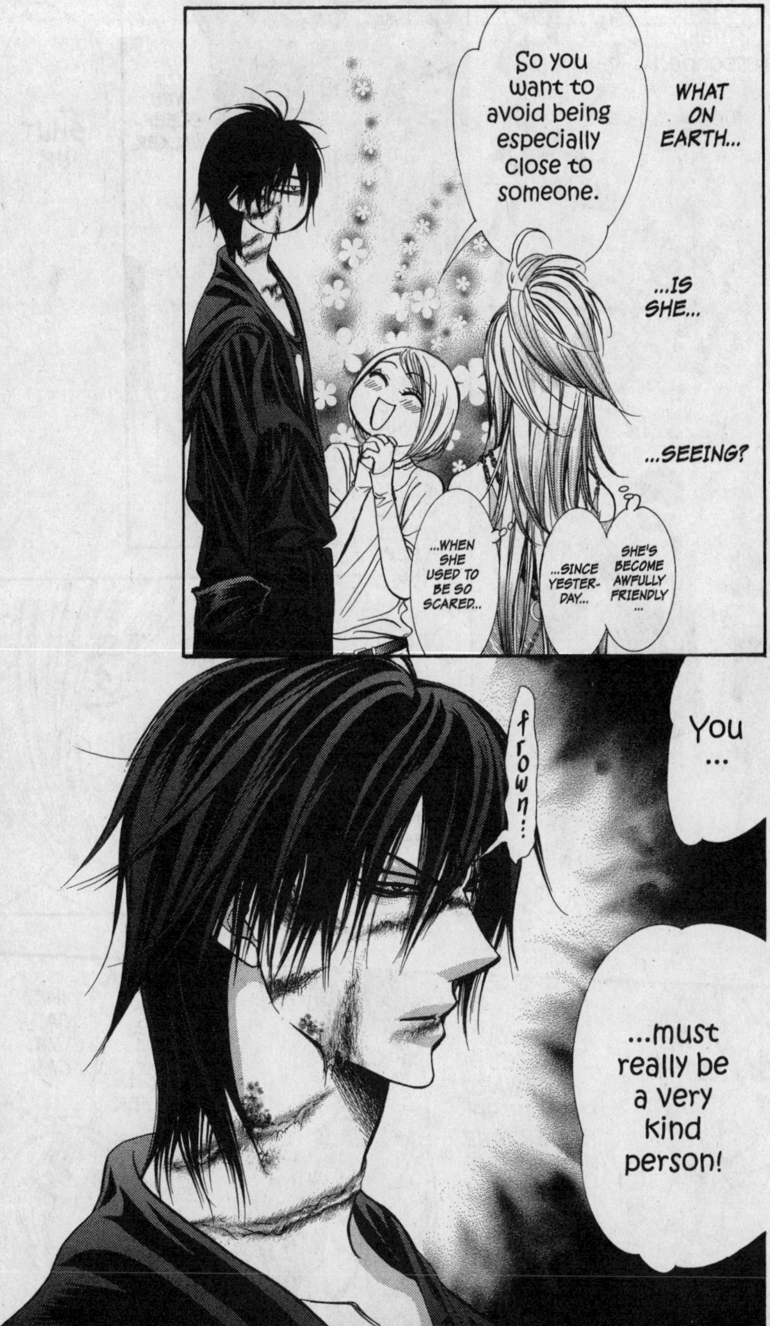
So you want to avoid being especially close to someone.
WHAT ON EARTH...
...IS SHE...
...SEEING?
SHE'S BECOME AWFULLY FRIENDLY ...
...SINCE YESTERDAY...
...WHEN SHE USED TO BE SO SCARED...
You ...
frown...
...must really be a very kind person!

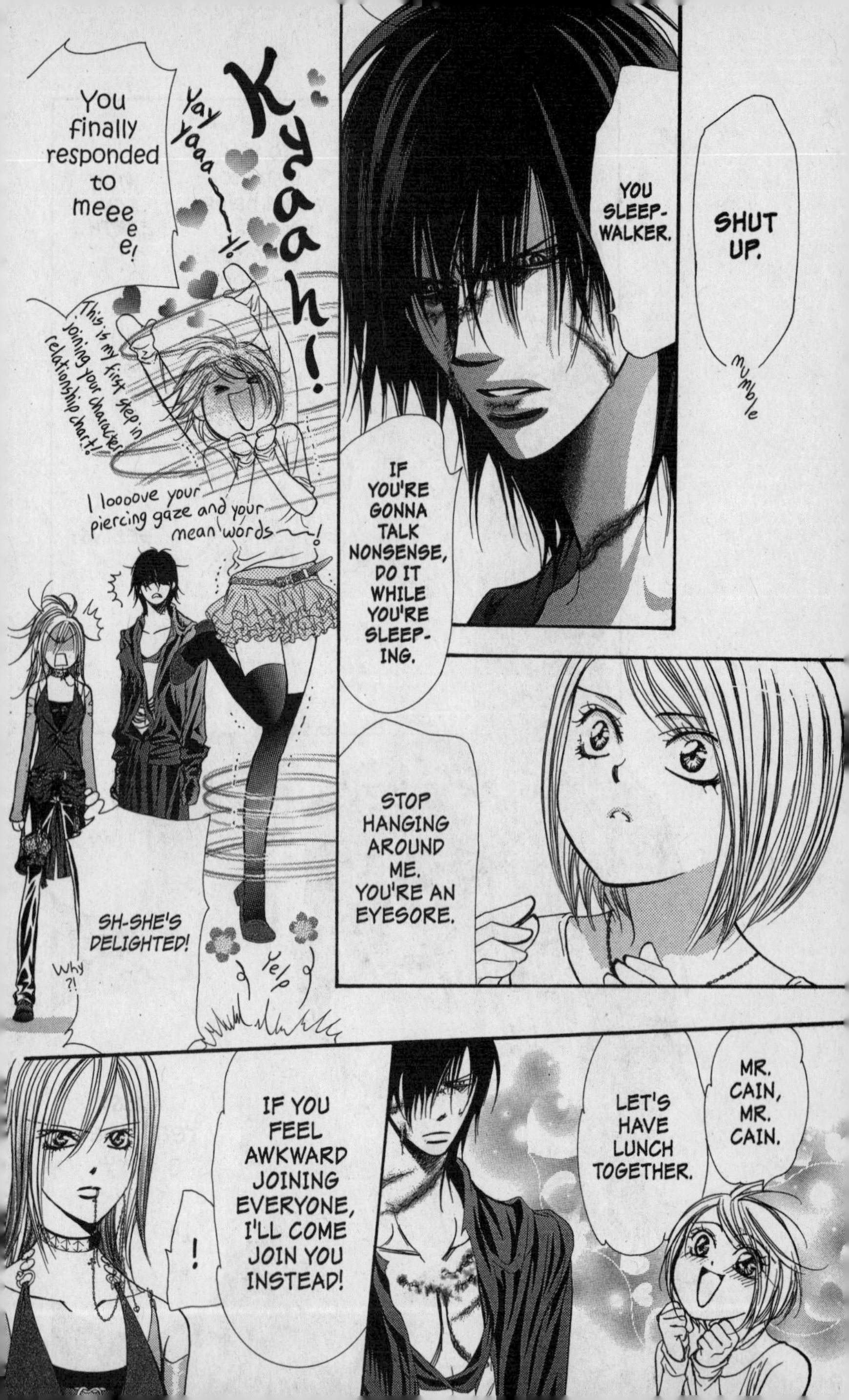
SHUT UP.
mumble
YOU SLEEP-WALKER.
IF YOU'RE GONNA TALK NONSENSE, DO IT WHILE YOU'RE SLEEPING.
STOP HANGING AROUND ME. YOU'RE AN EYESORE.
Kyaaah!
Yay yaaa~~y!
You finally responded to meeeee!
This is my first step in joining your character relationship chart!
I loooove your piercing gaze and your mean words~~!
SH-SHE'S DELIGHTED!
Why?!
Yelp
MR. CAIN, MR. CAIN.
LET'S HAVE LUNCH TOGETHER.
IF YOU FEEL AWKWARD JOINING EVERYONE, I'LL COME JOIN YOU INSTEAD!
!

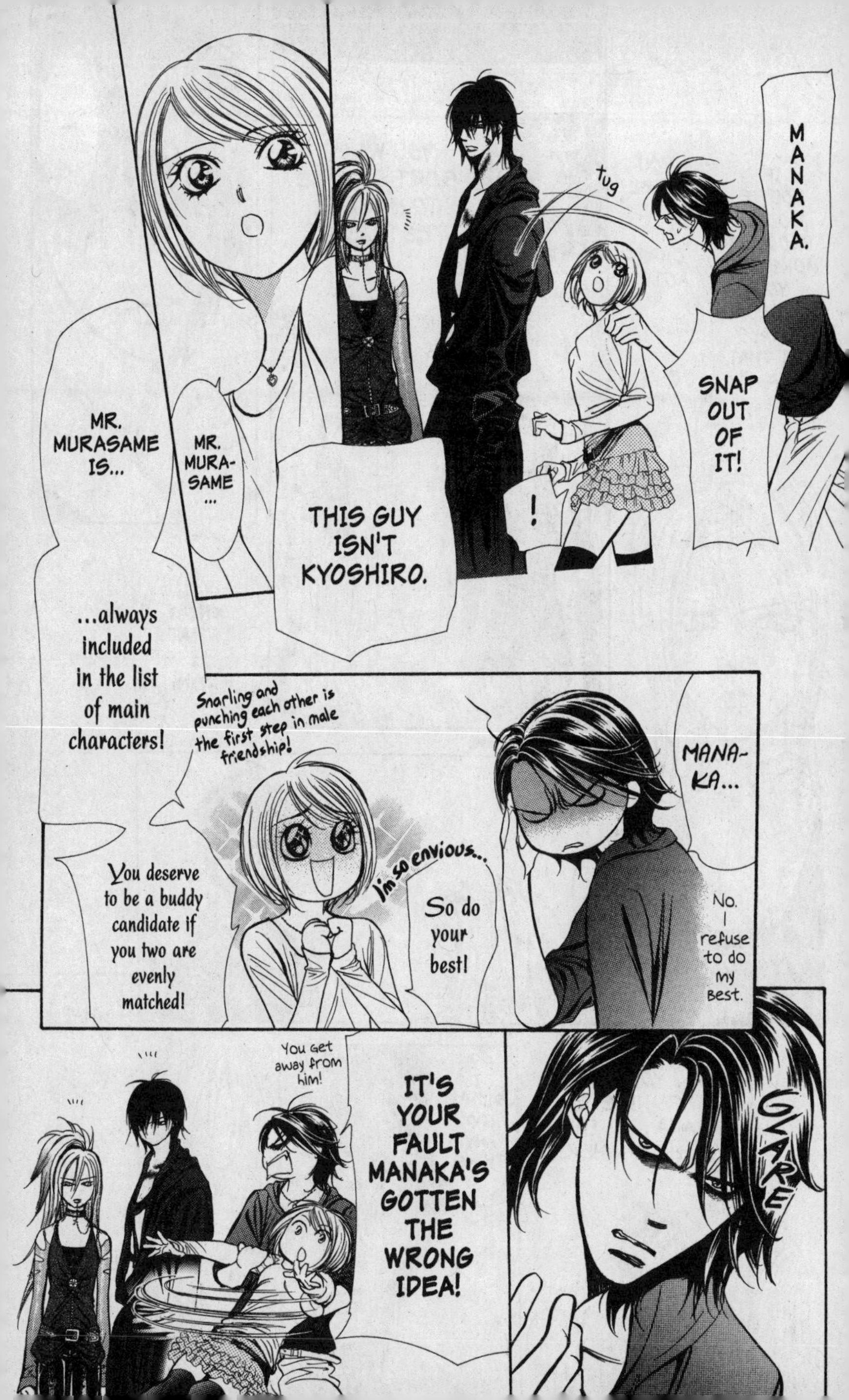
MANAKA.
tug
SNAP OUT OF IT!
!
THIS GUY ISN'T KYOSHIRO.
MR. MURA-SAME...
MR. MURASAME IS...
...always included in the list of main characters!
MANA-KA...
No. I refuse to do my Best.
Snarling and punching each other is the first step in male friendship!
I'm so envious...
So do your best!
You deserve to be a buddy candidate if you two are evenly matched!
GLARE
IT'S YOUR FAULT MANAKA'S GOTTEN THE WRONG IDEA!
You get away from him!

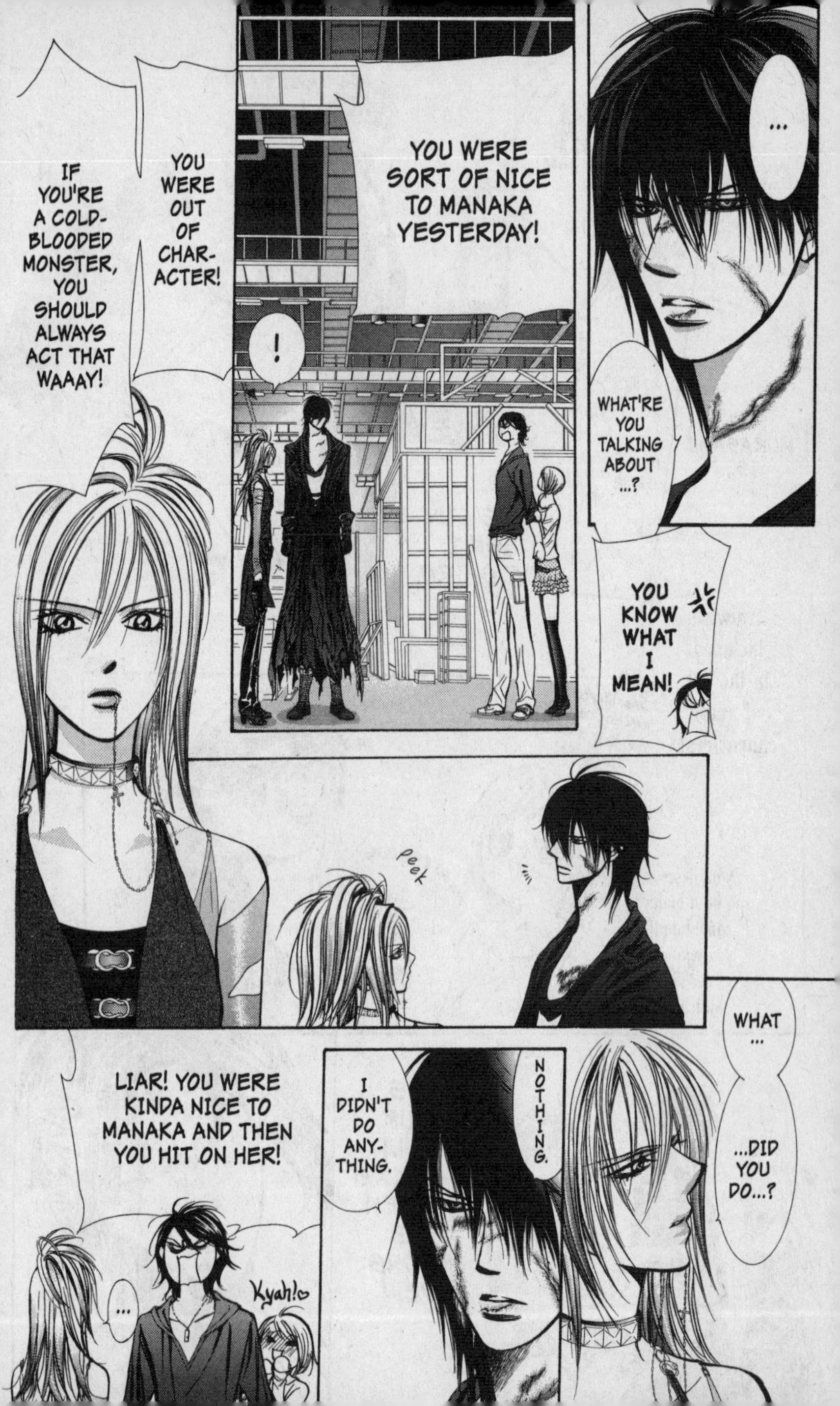
...
WHAT'RE YOU TALKING ABOUT ...?
YOU KNOW WHAT I MEAN!
YOU WERE SORT OF NICE TO MANAKA YESTERDAY!
!
YOU WERE OUT OF CHARACTER!
IF YOU'RE A COLD-BLOODED MONSTER, YOU SHOULD ALWAYS ACT THAT WAAAY!
Peek
WHAT ... ...DID YOU DO...?
NOTHING.
I DIDN'T DO ANYTHING.
LIAR! YOU WERE KINDA NICE TO MANAKA AND THEN YOU HIT ON HER!
...
Kyah!♡

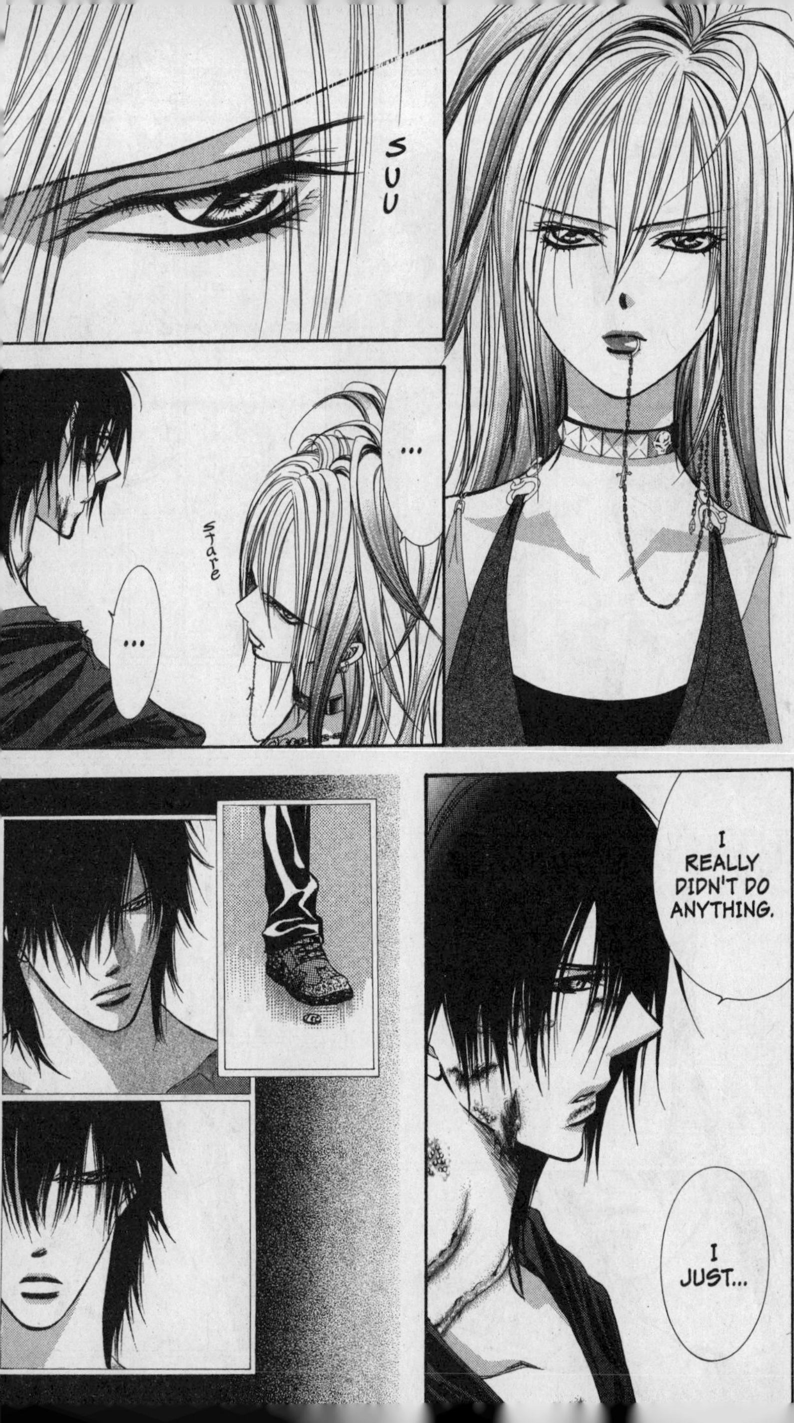
SUU
...
Stare
...
I REALLY DIDN'T DO ANYTHING.
I JUST...

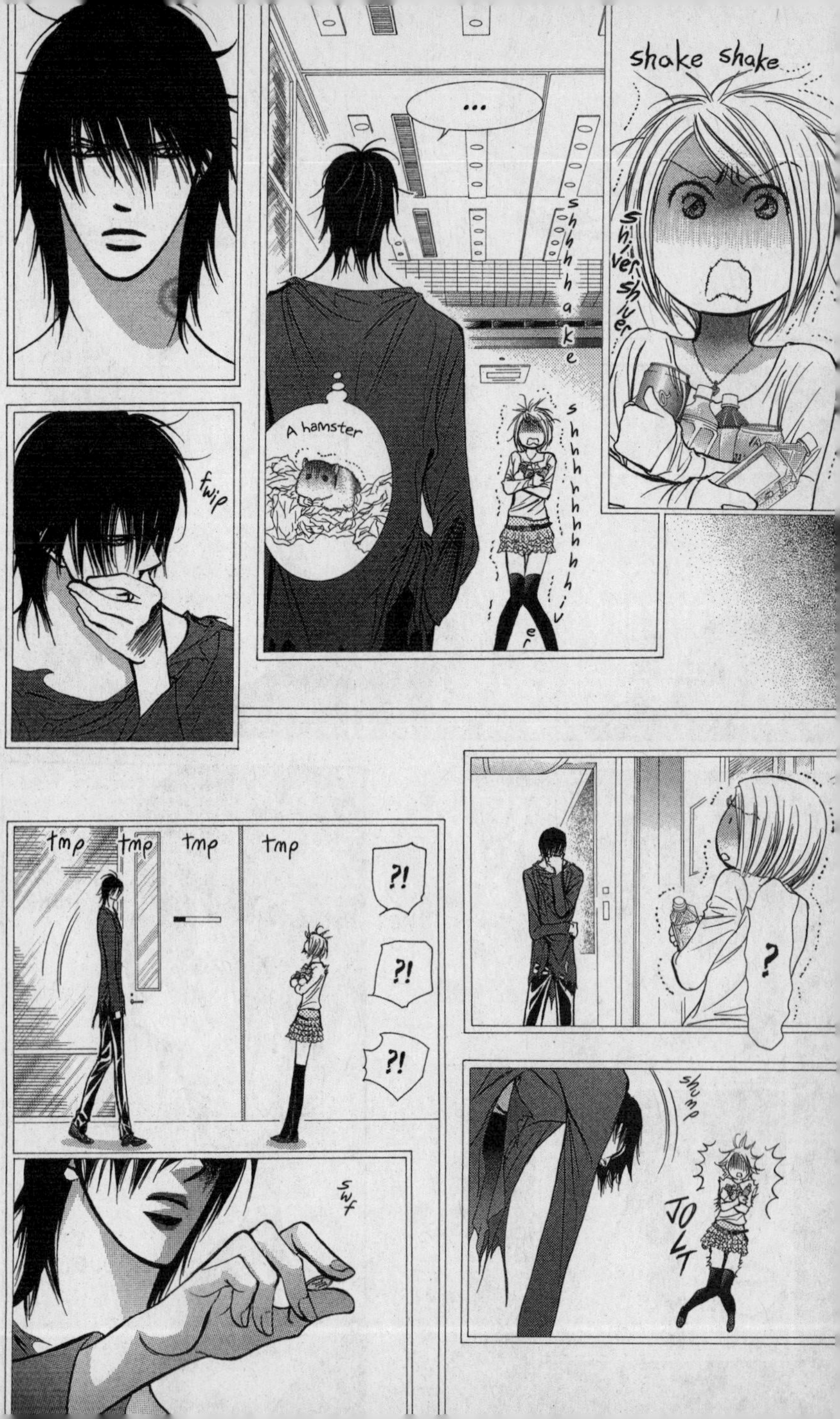
shake shake
shiver shiver
...
A hamster
shhhhake
shhhhhhhhhiver
fwip
?
shump
JOLT
tmp tmp tmp tmp
?!
?!
?!
swf

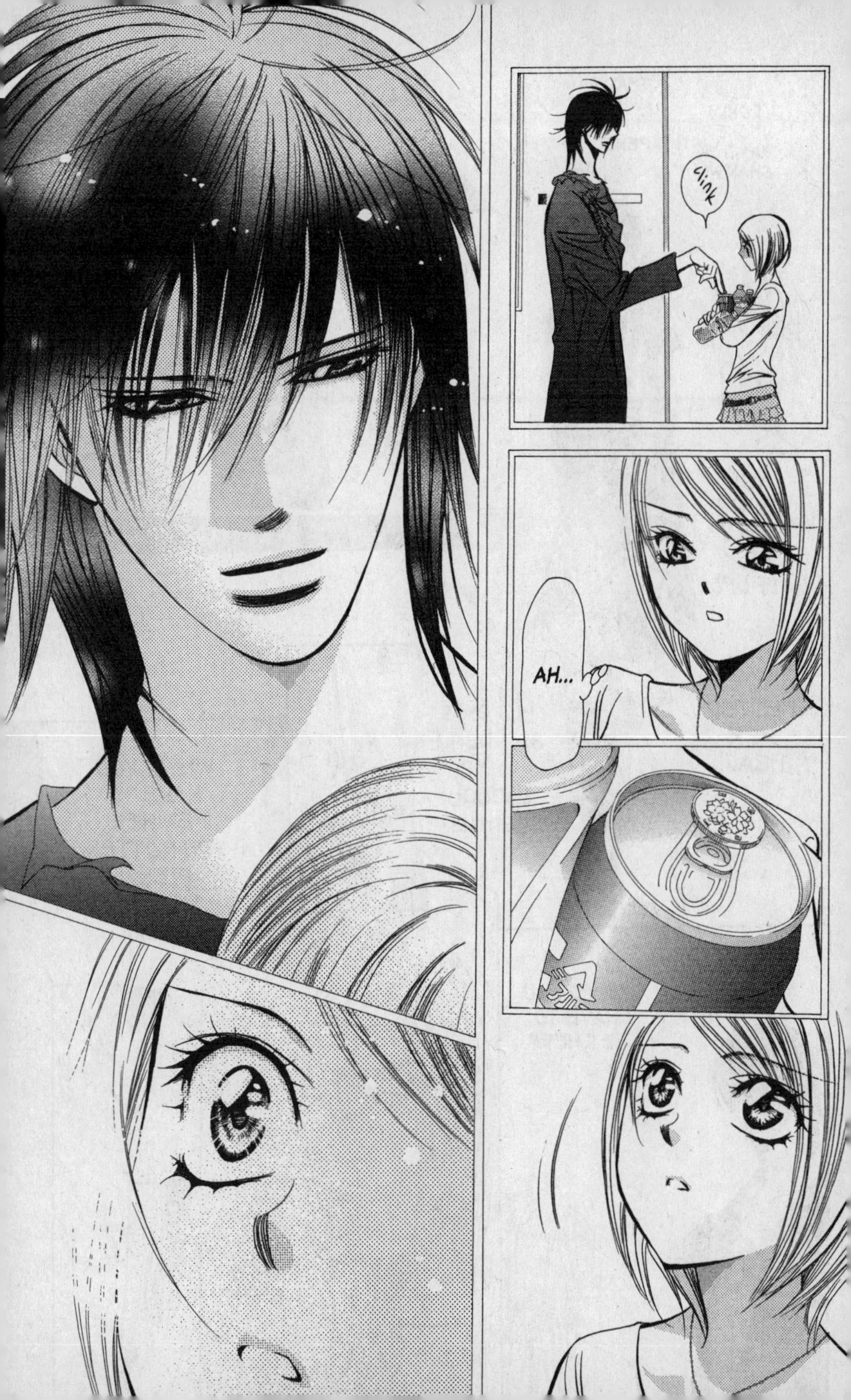
clink
AH...

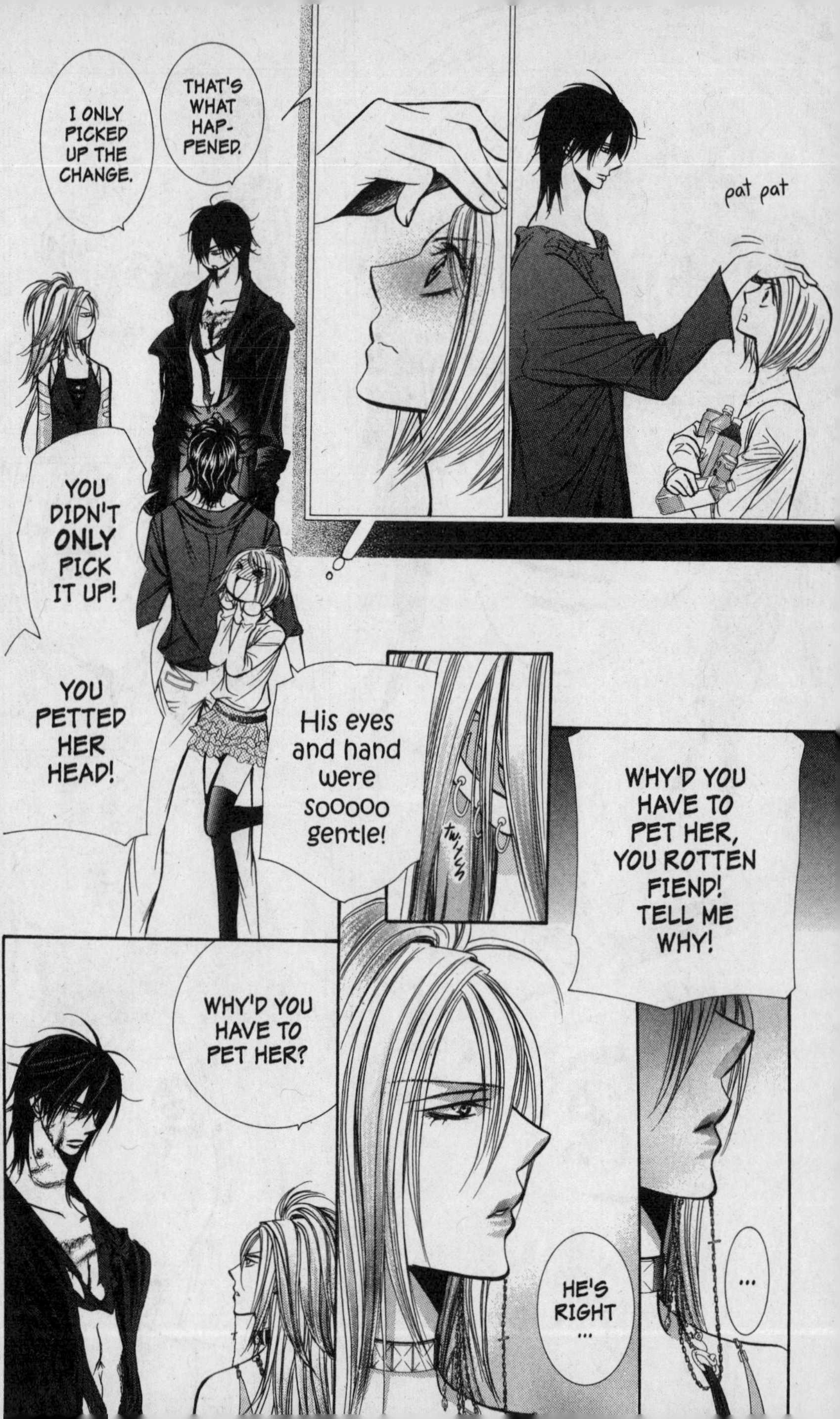
pat pat
THAT'S WHAT HAP-PENED.
I ONLY PICKED UP THE CHANGE.
YOU DIDN'T ONLY PICK IT UP!
YOU PETTED HER HEAD!
His eyes and hand were sooooo gentle!
TWITCH
WHY'D YOU HAVE TO PET HER, YOU ROTTEN FIEND! TELL ME WHY!
...
HE'S RIGHT ...
WHY'D YOU HAVE TO PET HER?

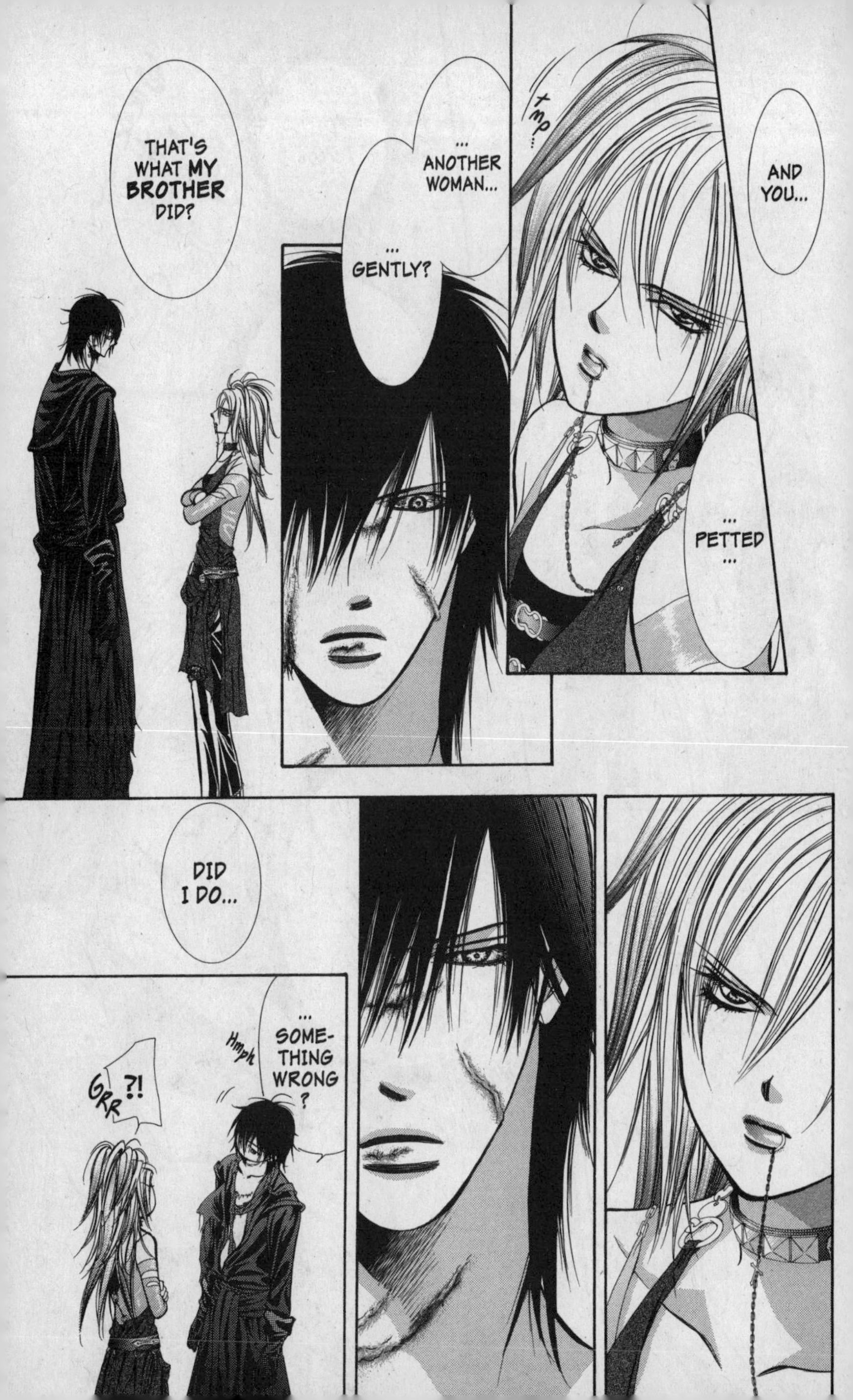
tmp...
AND YOU...
... PETTED ...
... ANOTHER WOMAN...
... GENTLY?
THAT'S WHAT MY BROTHER DID?
DID I DO...
... SOMETHING WRONG?
Hmph
?!
GRR

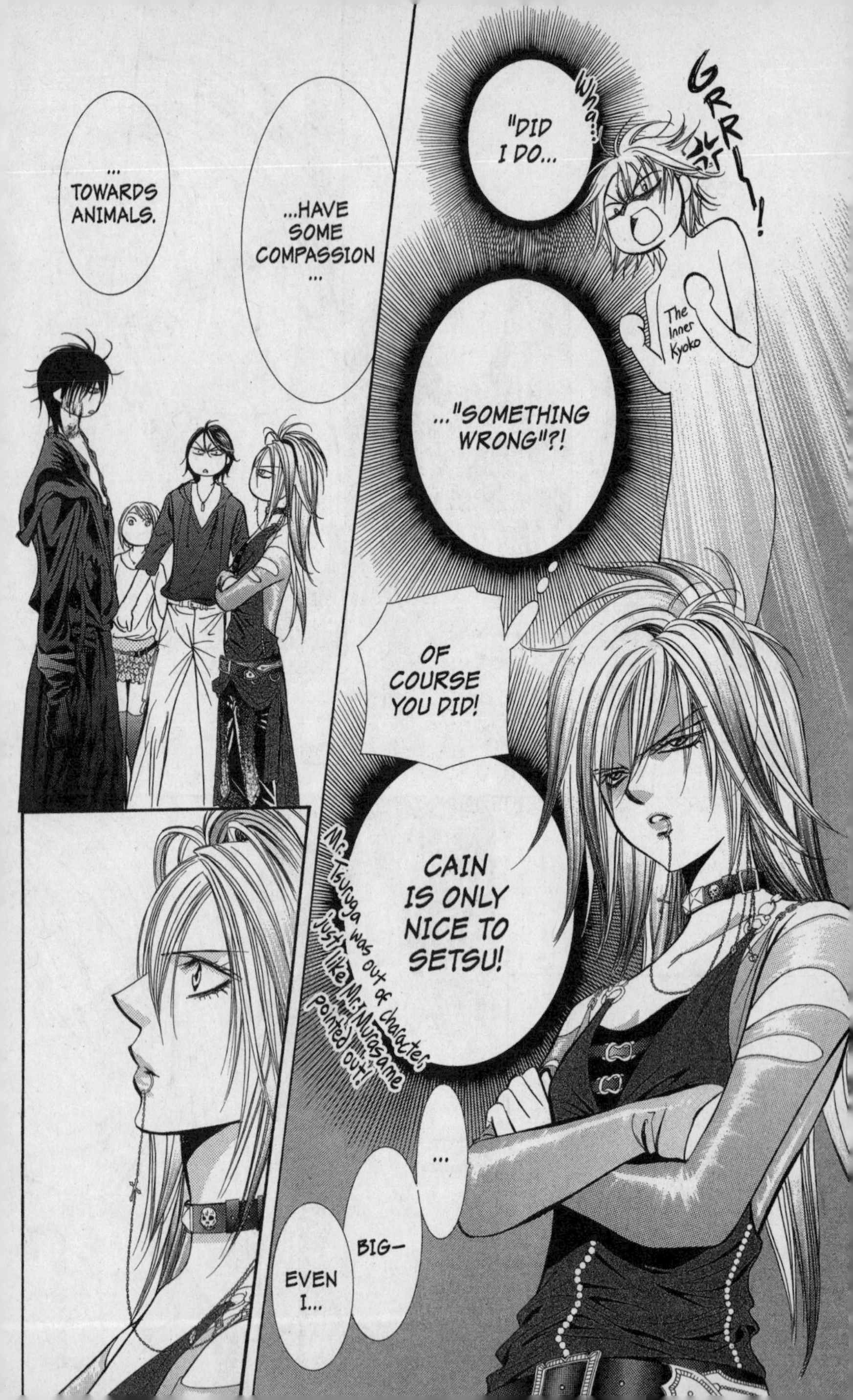
Wha...
"DID I DO...
GRRR!
The Inner Kyoko
..."SOMETHING WRONG"?!
OF COURSE YOU DID!
CAIN IS ONLY NICE TO SETSU!
Mr. Tsuruga was out of character, just like Mr. Murasame pointed out!
...
BIG—
EVEN I...
...HAVE SOME COMPASSION ...
... TOWARDS ANIMALS.

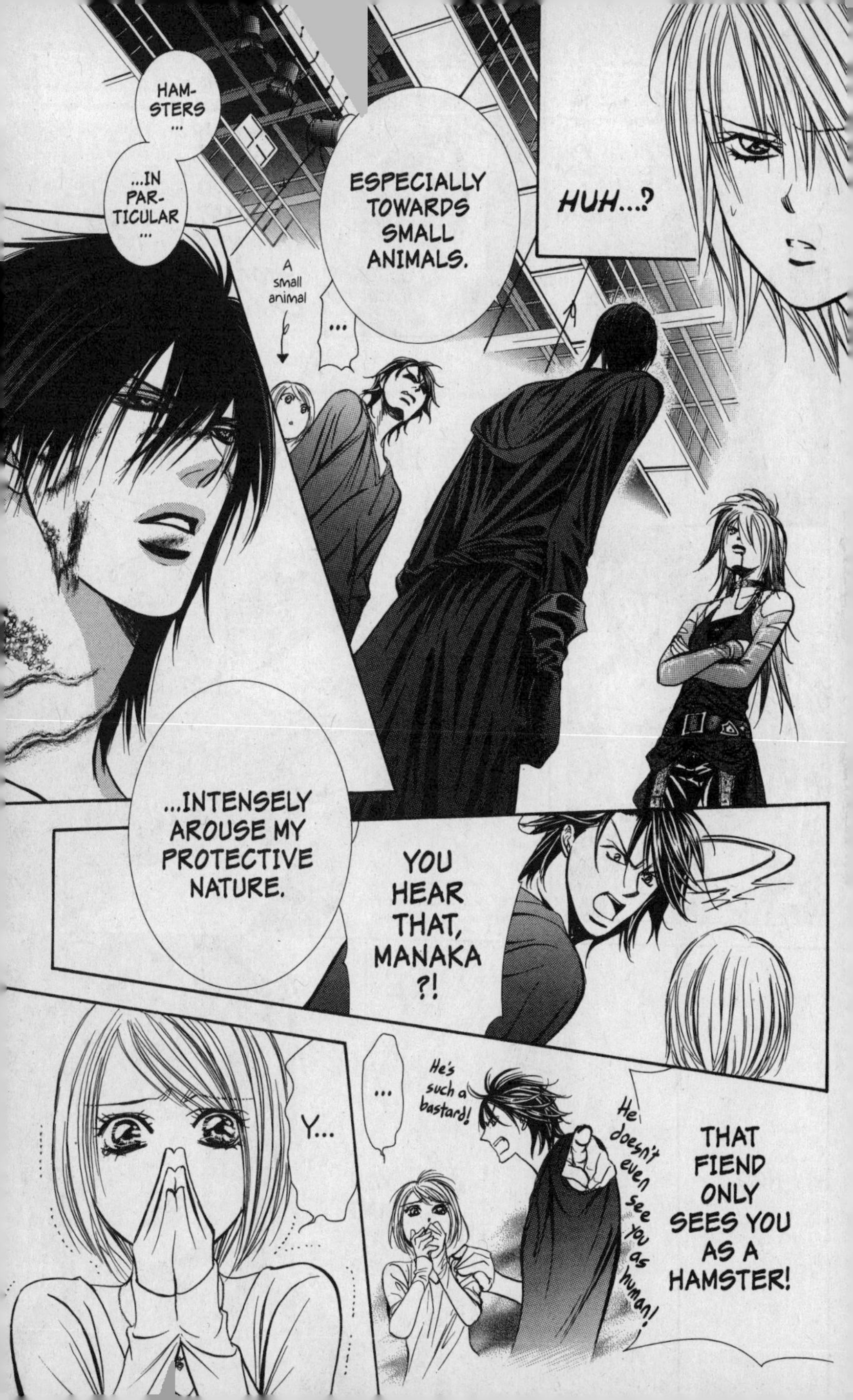
HUH...?
ESPECIALLY TOWARDS SMALL ANIMALS.
...
A small animal
HAM-STERS...
...IN PAR-TICULAR...
...INTENSELY AROUSE MY PROTECTIVE NATURE.
YOU HEAR THAT, MANAKA?!
THAT FIEND ONLY SEES YOU AS A HAMSTER!
He doesn't even see you as human!
He's such a bastard!
...
Y...

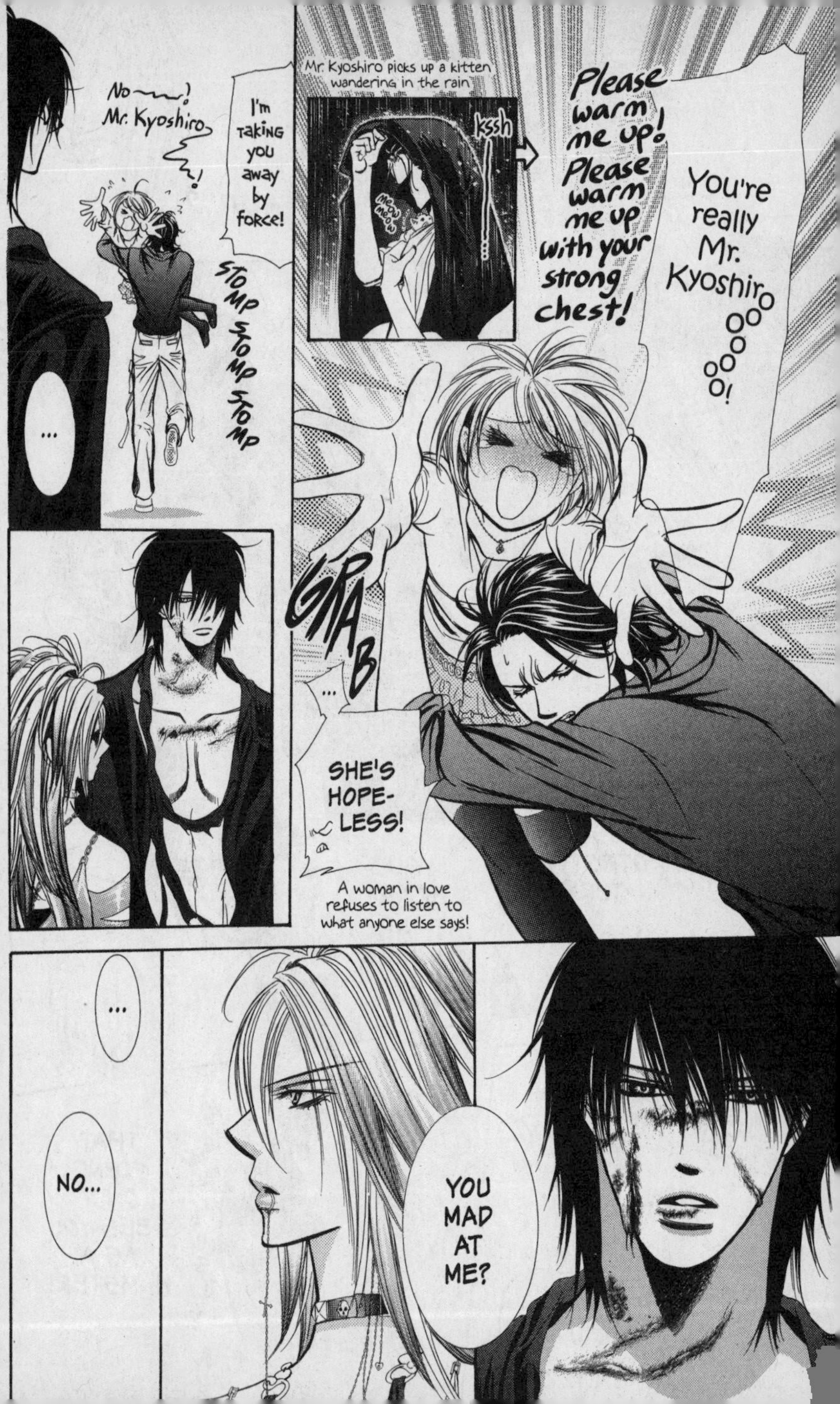
You're really Mr. Kyoshiroooooooo!
Please warm me up! Please warm me up with your strong chest!
Mr. Kyoshiro picks up a kitten wandering in the rain
kssh
Meow meow
GRAB
...
SHE'S HOPE-LESS!
A woman in love refuses to listen to what anyone else says!
I'm taking you away by force!
No~~! Mr. Kyoshiro~!
STOMP STOMP STOMP STOMP
...
YOU MAD AT ME?
...
NO...

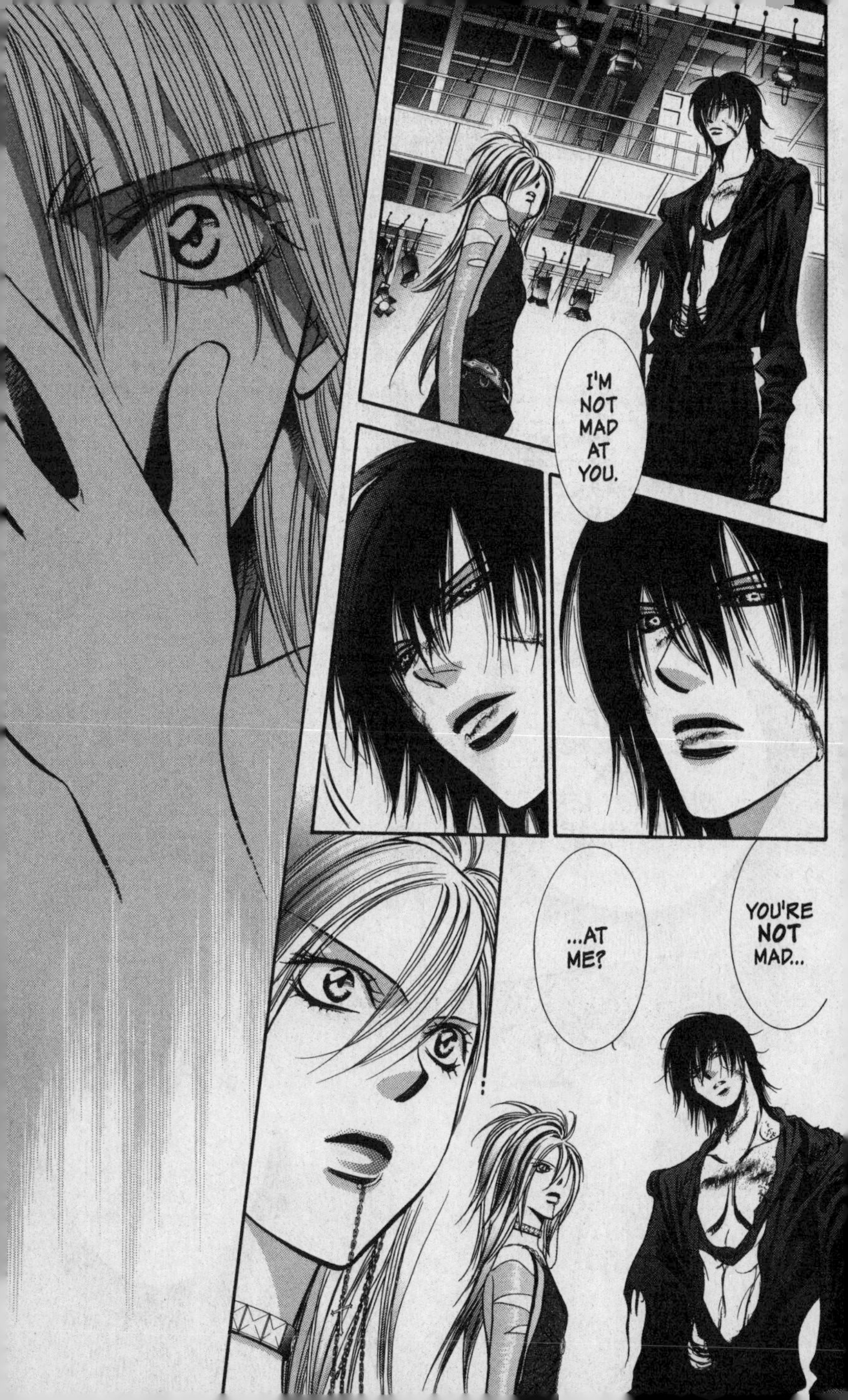
I'M NOT MAD AT YOU.
YOU'RE NOT MAD...
...AT ME?

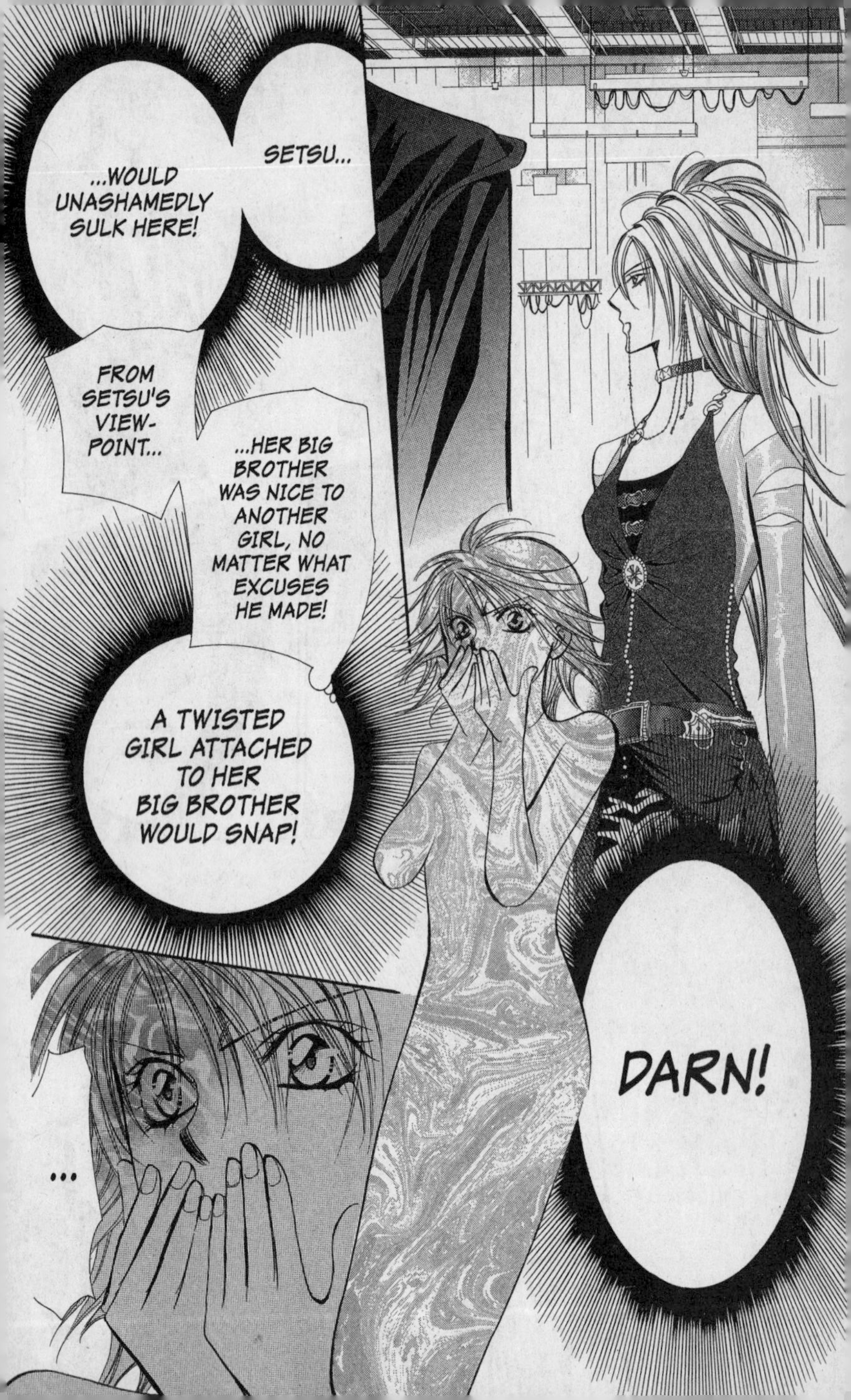
SETSU...
...WOULD UNASHAMEDLY SULK HERE!
FROM SETSU'S VIEW-POINT...
...HER BIG BROTHER WAS NICE TO ANOTHER GIRL, NO MATTER WHAT EXCUSES HE MADE!
A TWISTED GIRL ATTACHED TO HER BIG BROTHER WOULD SNAP!
DARN!
...

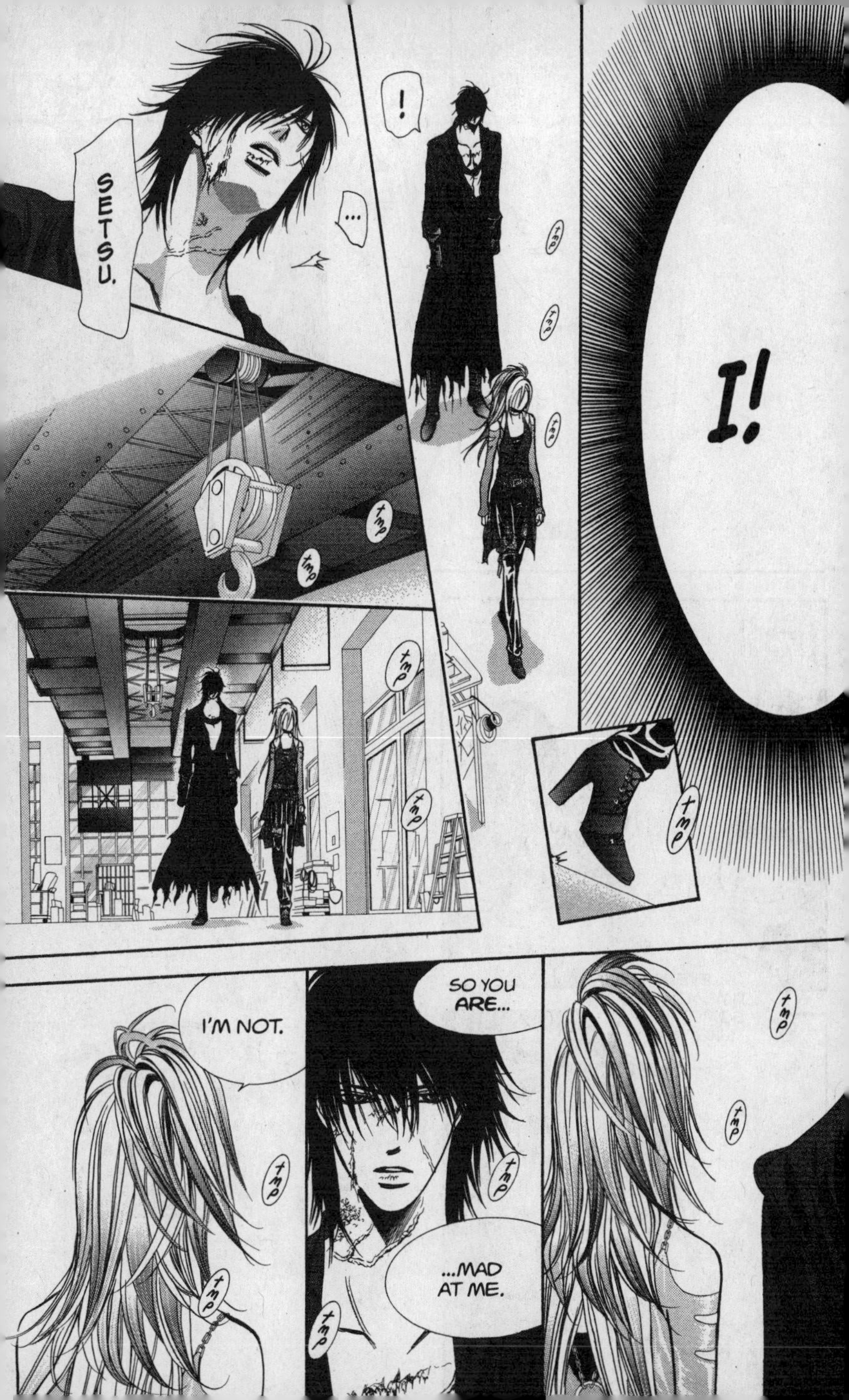

I!
tmp
!
tmp
tmp
tmp
SETSU.
...
tmp
tmp
tmp
tmp
tmp
tmp
SO YOU ARE...
tmp
...MAD AT ME.
tmp
I'M NOT.
tmp
tmp

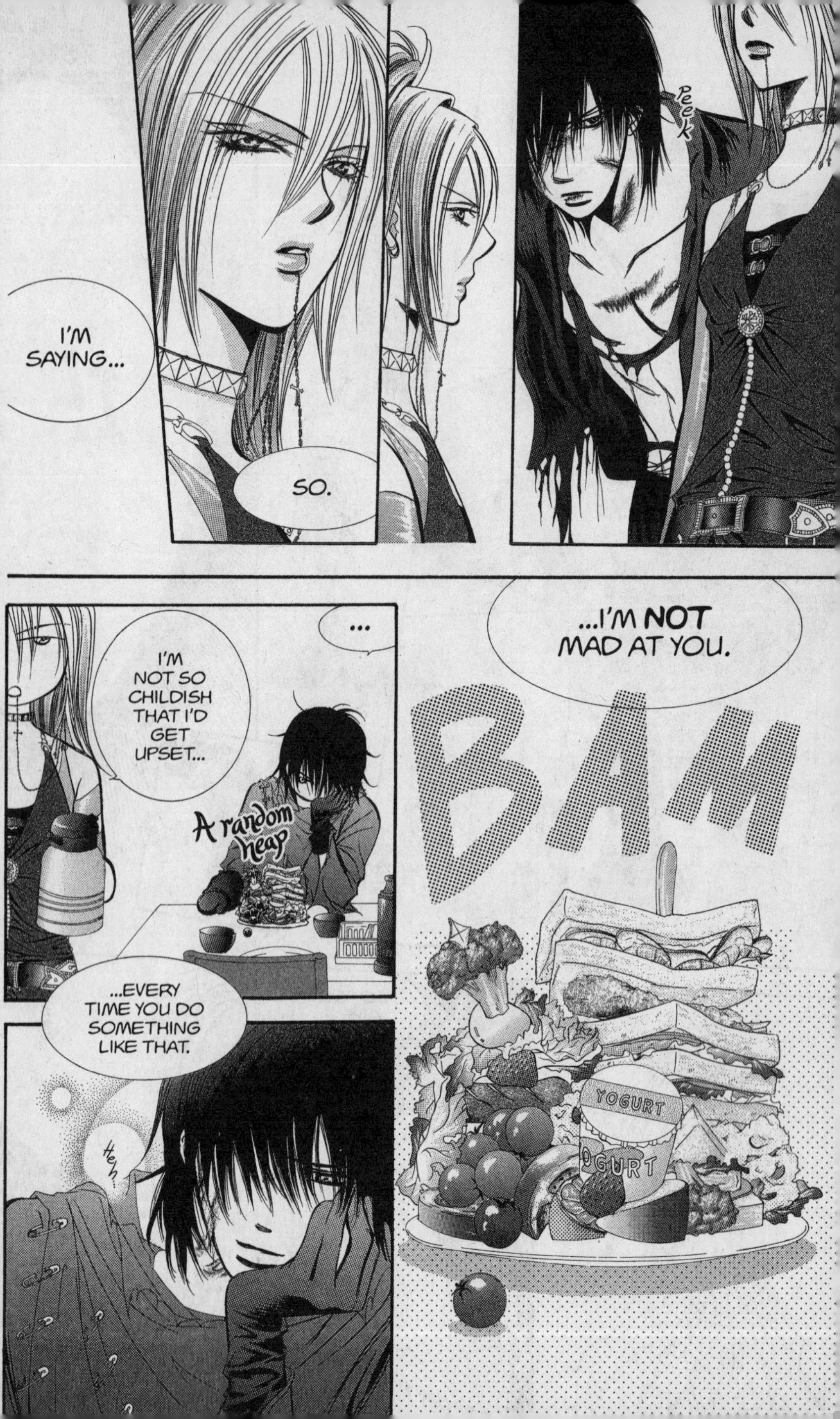

Peek
I'M SAYING...
SO.
...I'M NOT MAD AT YOU.
BAM
YOGURT
OGURT
...
I'M NOT SO CHILDISH THAT I'D GET UPSET...
A random heap
...EVERY TIME YOU DO SOMETHING LIKE THAT.
Heh.

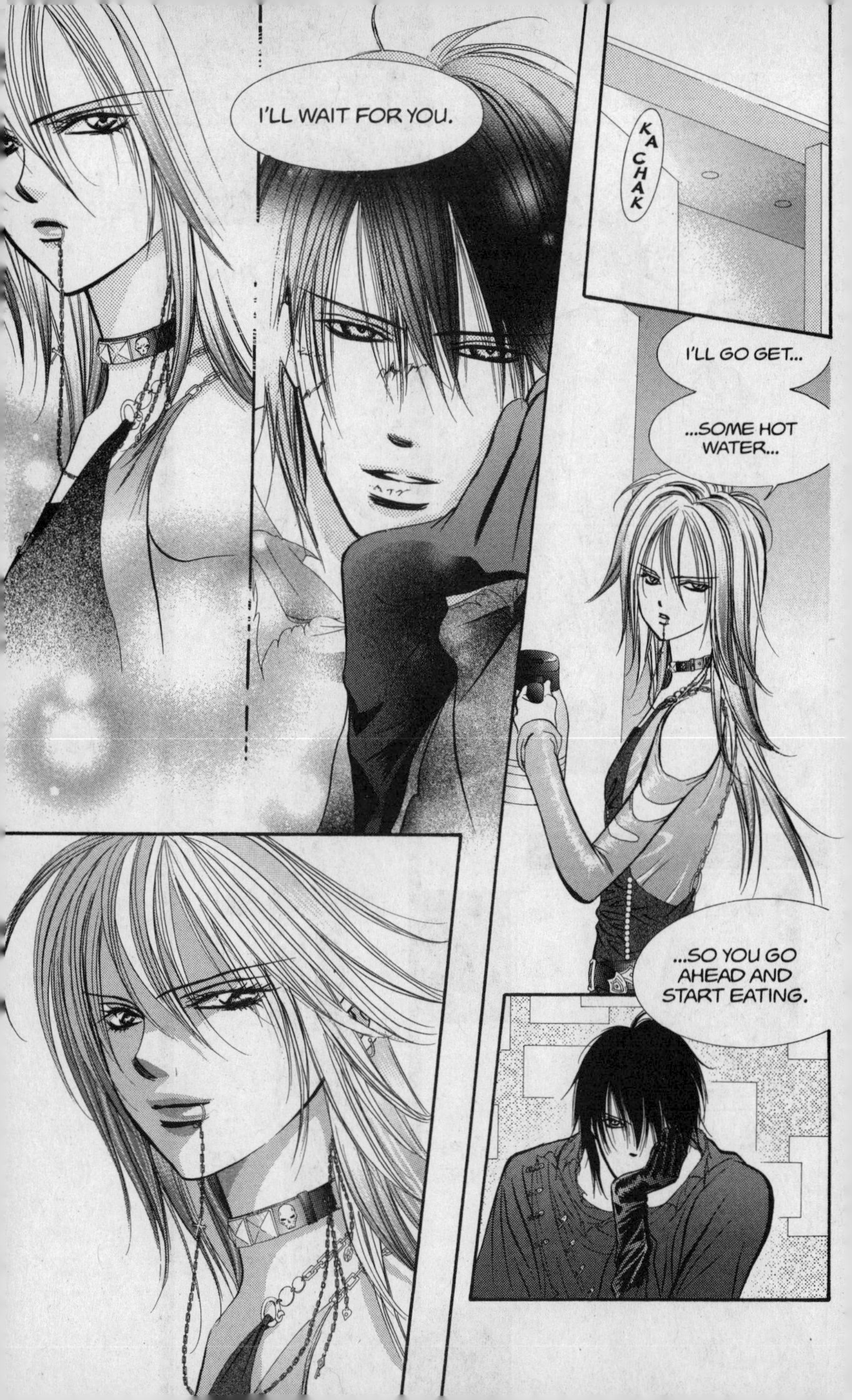
KA CHAK
I'LL GO GET...
...SOME HOT WATER...
...SO YOU GO AHEAD AND START EATING.
I'LL WAIT FOR YOU.

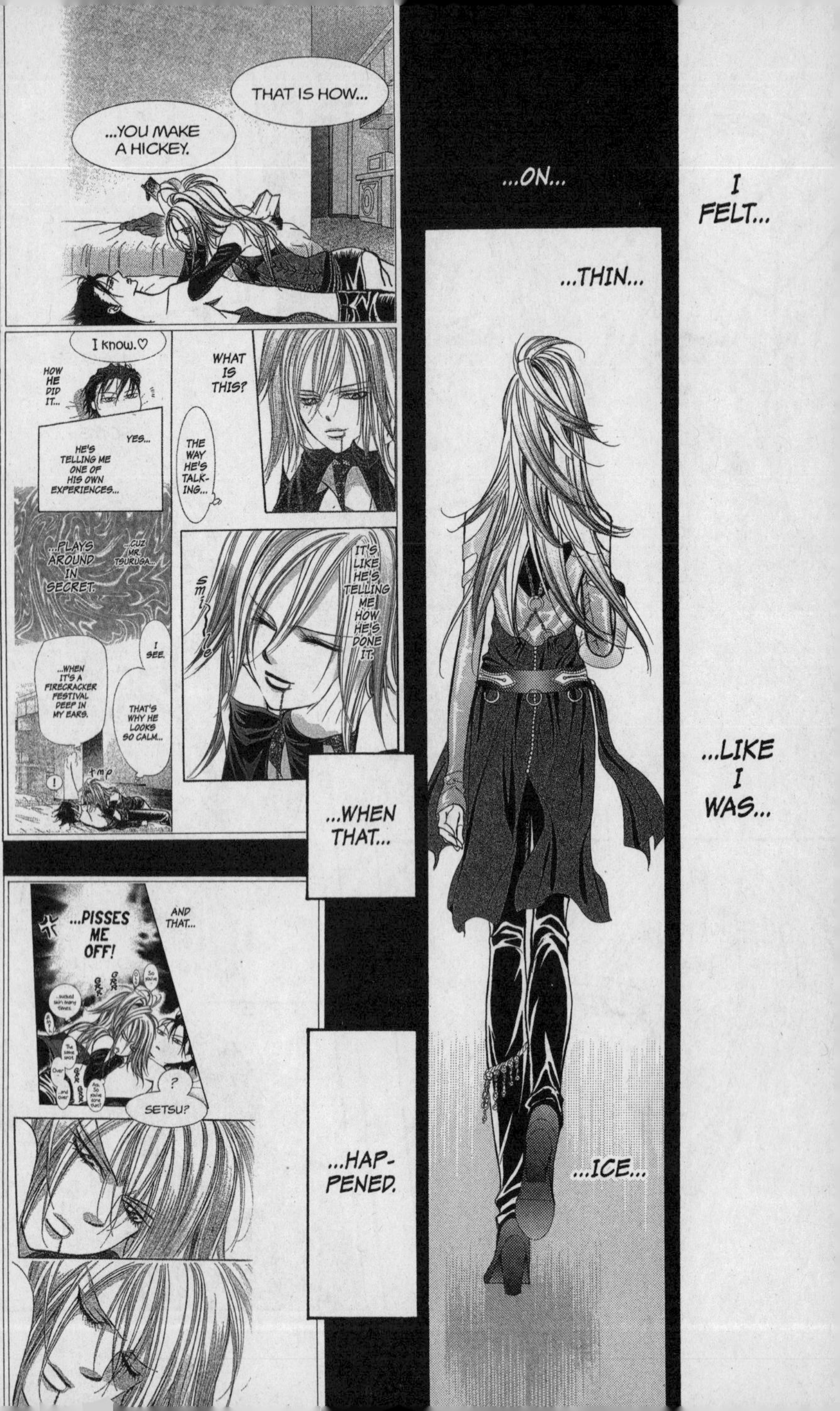
I FELT...
...LIKE I WAS...
...ON...
...THIN...
...ICE...
THAT IS HOW...
...YOU MAKE A HICKEY.
WHAT IS THIS?
THE WAY HE'S TALKING...
I know.♡
HOW HE DID IT...
YES...
HE'S TELLING ME ONE OF HIS OWN EXPERIENCES...
IT'S LIKE HE'S TELLING ME HOW HE'S DONE IT.
smile
...CUZ MR. TSURUGA...
...PLAYS AROUND IN SECRET.
I SEE.
THAT'S WHY HE LOOKS SO CALM...
...WHEN IT'S A FIRECRACKER FESTIVAL DEEP IN MY EARS.
!
tmp
...WHEN THAT...
...HAPPENED.
AND THAT...
...PISSES ME OFF!
?
SETSU?

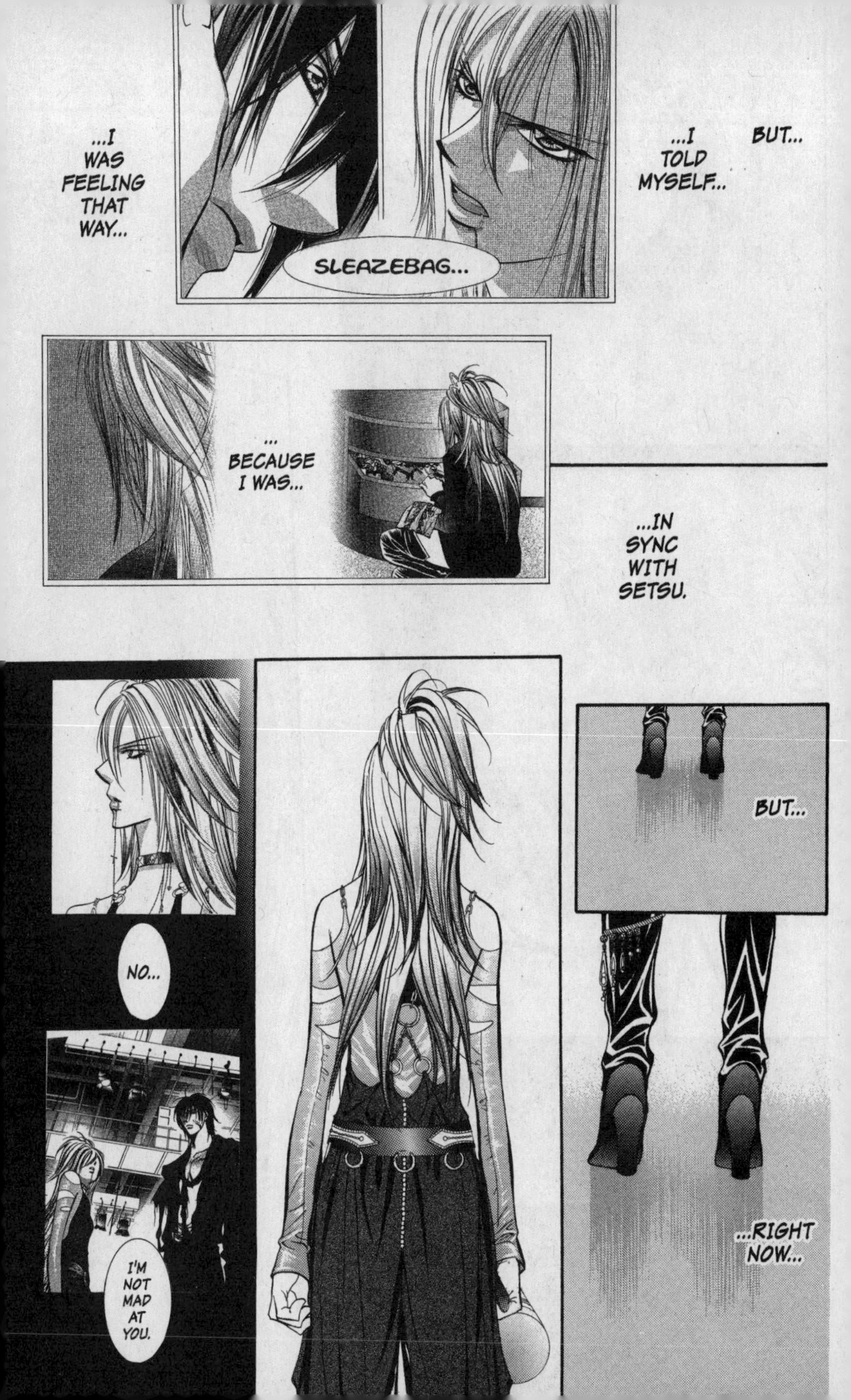
BUT...
...I TOLD MYSELF...
...I WAS FEELING THAT WAY...
SLEAZEBAG...
...BECAUSE I WAS...
...IN SYNC WITH SETSU.
BUT...
...RIGHT NOW...
NO...
I'M NOT MAD AT YOU.

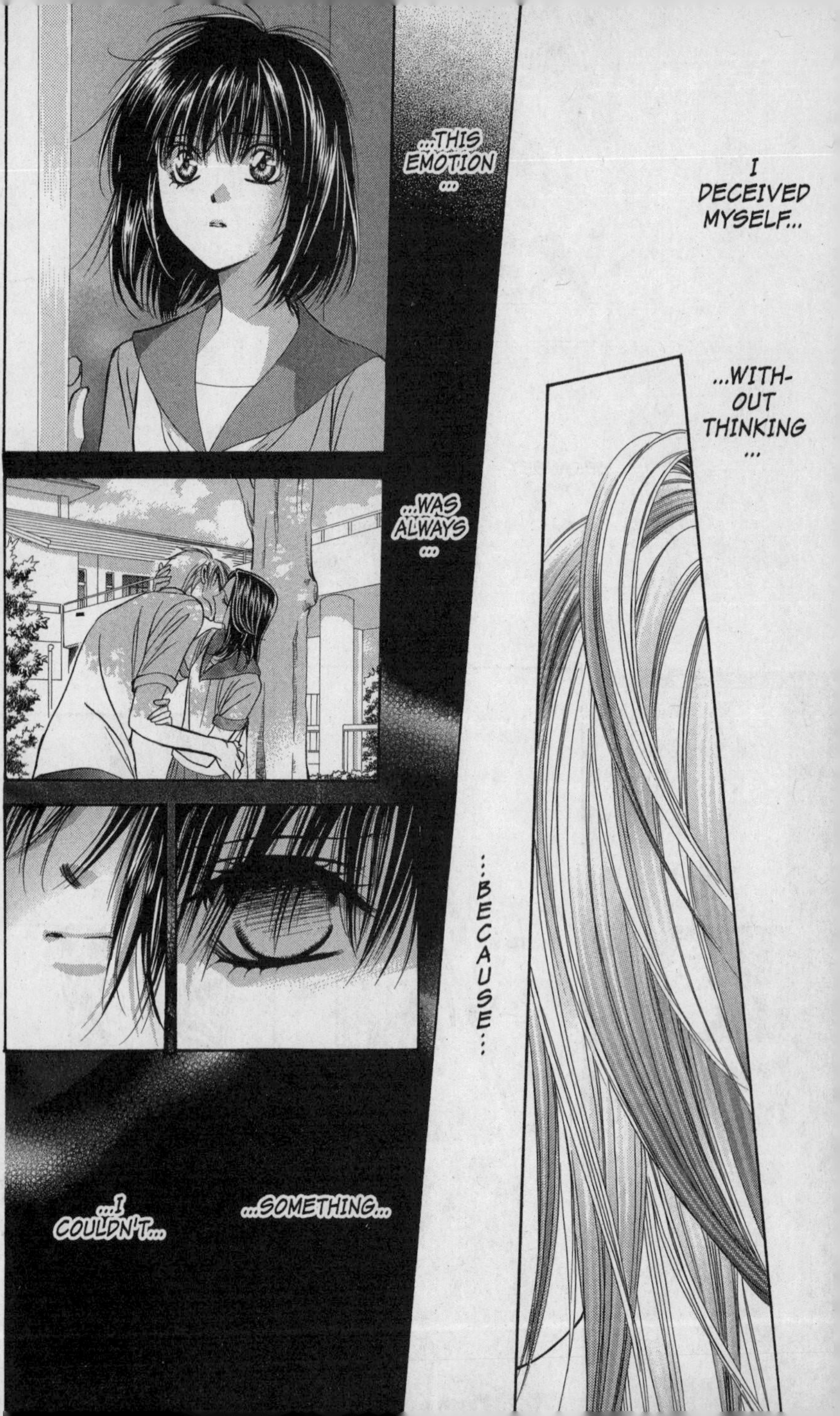
I DECEIVED MYSELF...
...WITH-OUT THINKING...
...BECAUSE...
...THIS EMOTION...
...WAS ALWAYS...
...SOMETHING...
...I COULDN'T...

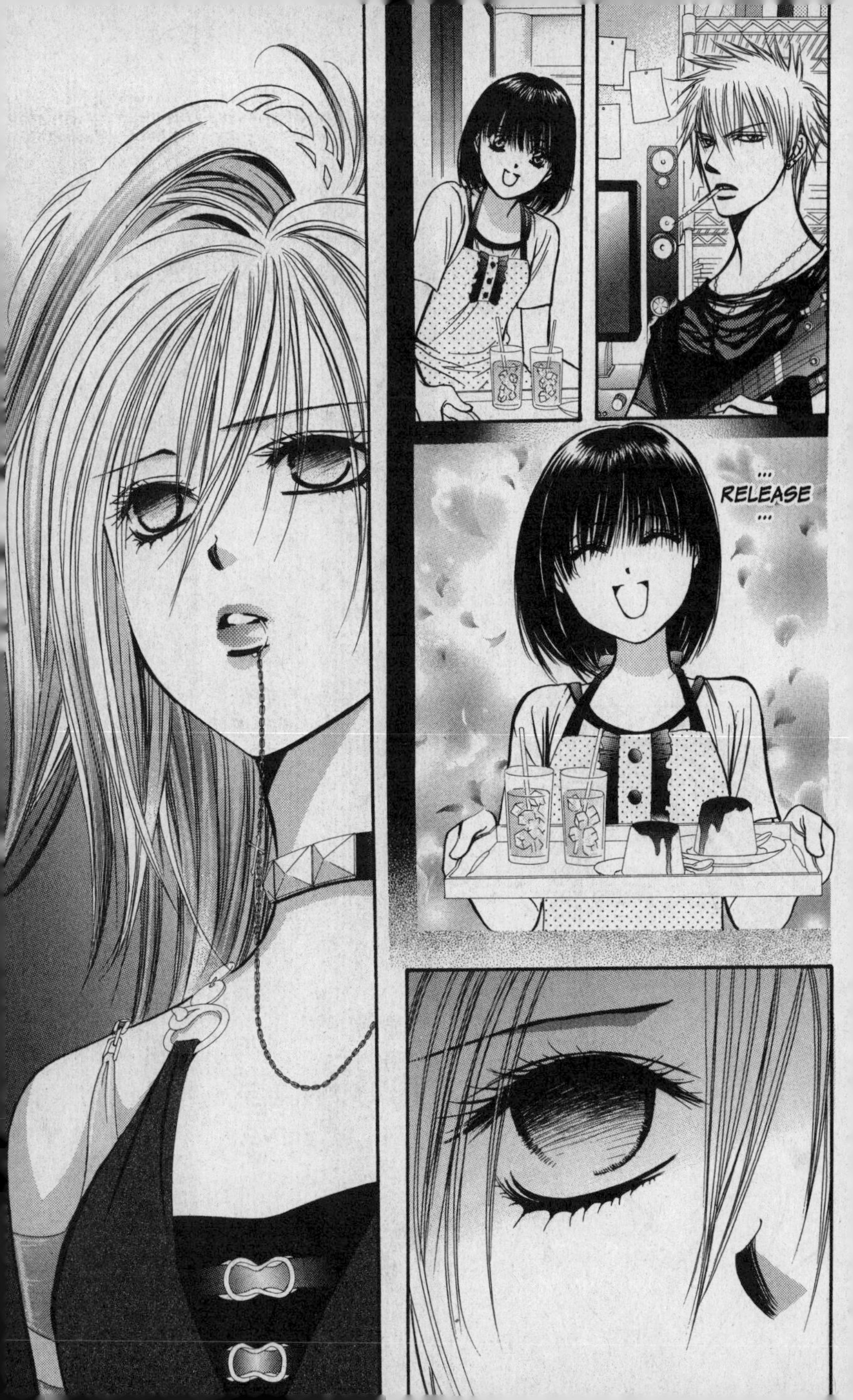
...RELEASE...

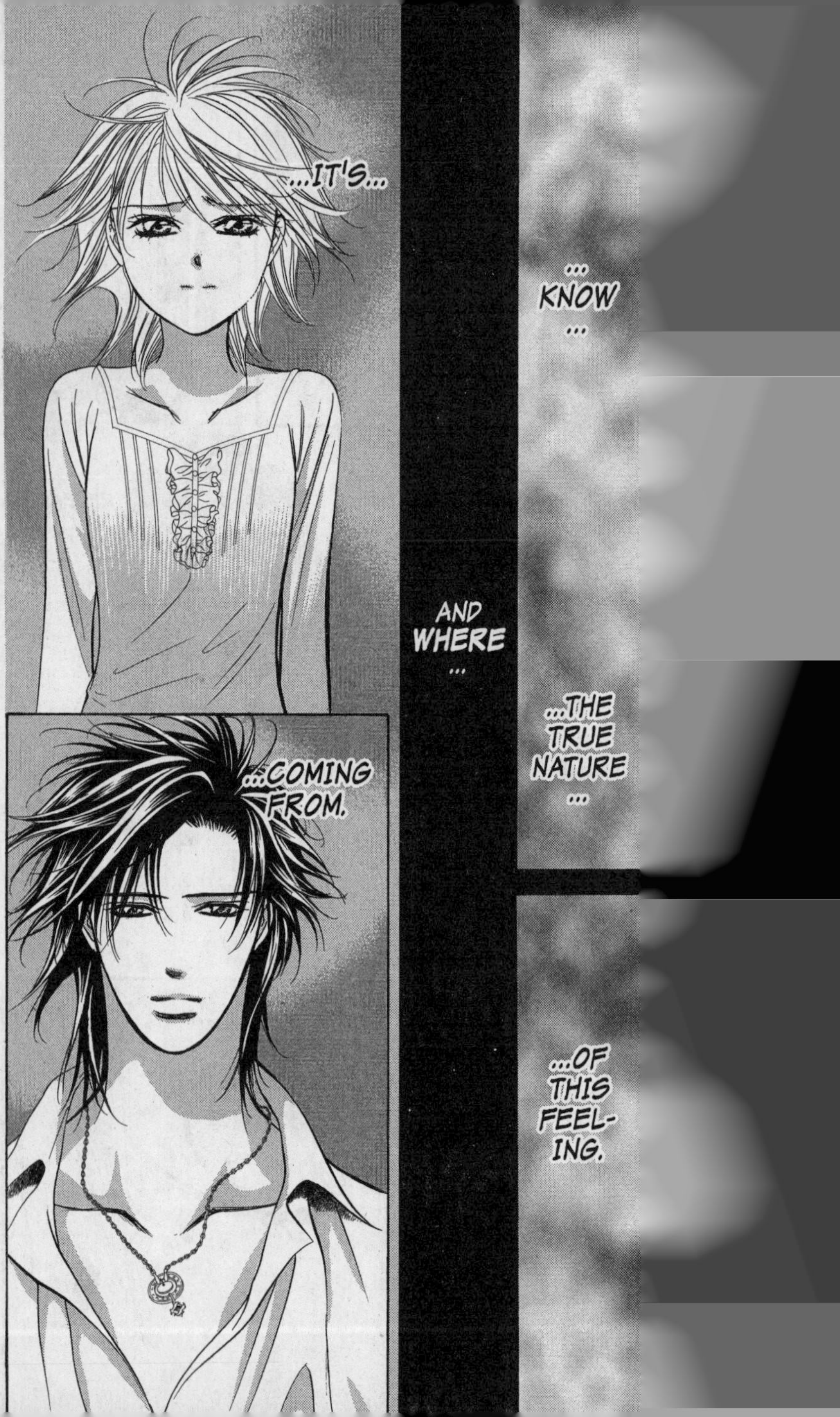

...KNOW...
...THE TRUE NATURE...
...OF THIS FEEL-ING.
AND WHERE...
...IT'S...
...COMING FROM.

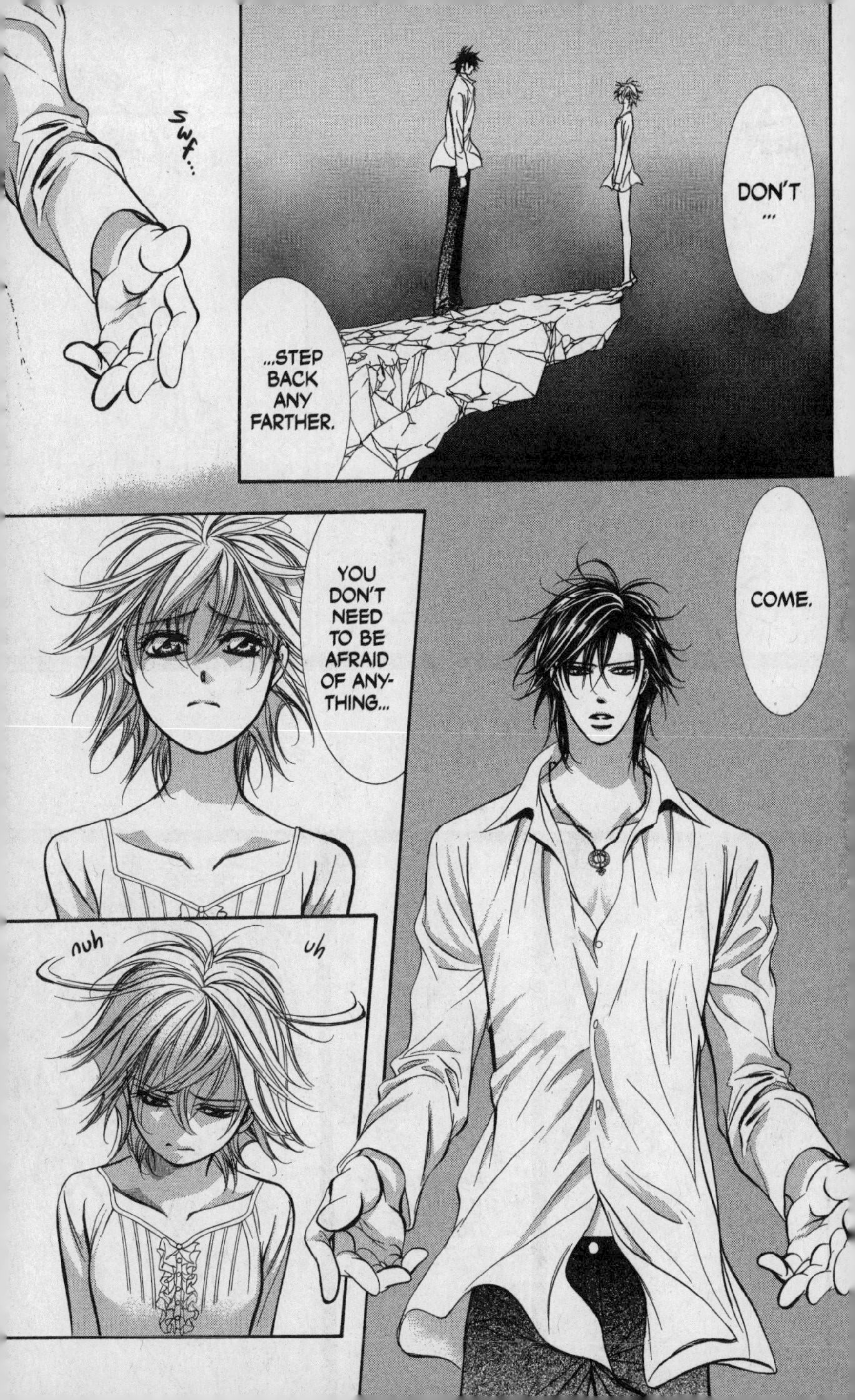
DON'T ...
...STEP BACK ANY FARTHER.
swf...
COME.
YOU DON'T NEED TO BE AFRAID OF ANY-THING...
uh
nuh

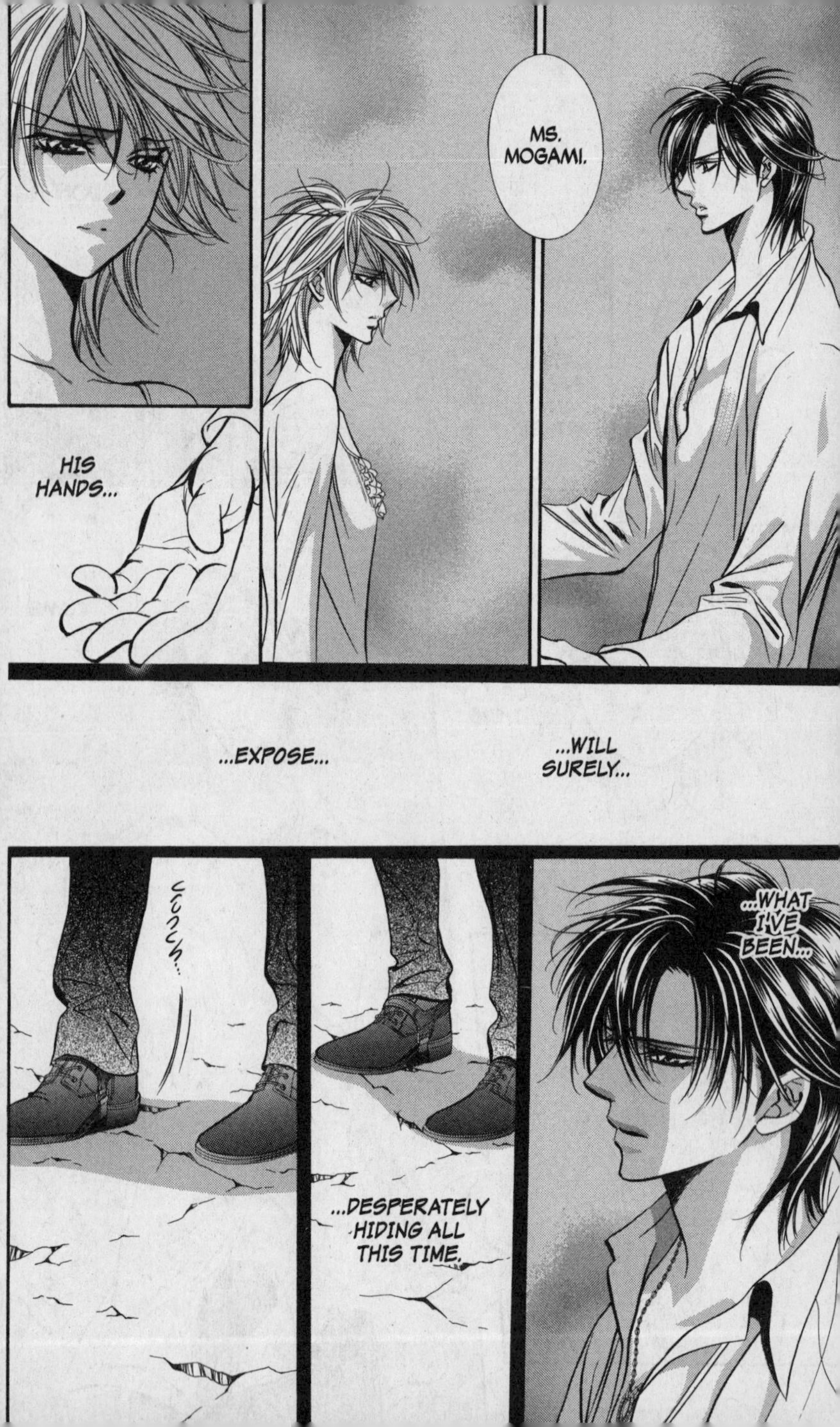
MS. MOGAMI.
HIS HANDS...
...WILL SURELY...
...EXPOSE...
...WHAT I'VE BEEN...
...DESPERATELY HIDING ALL THIS TIME.

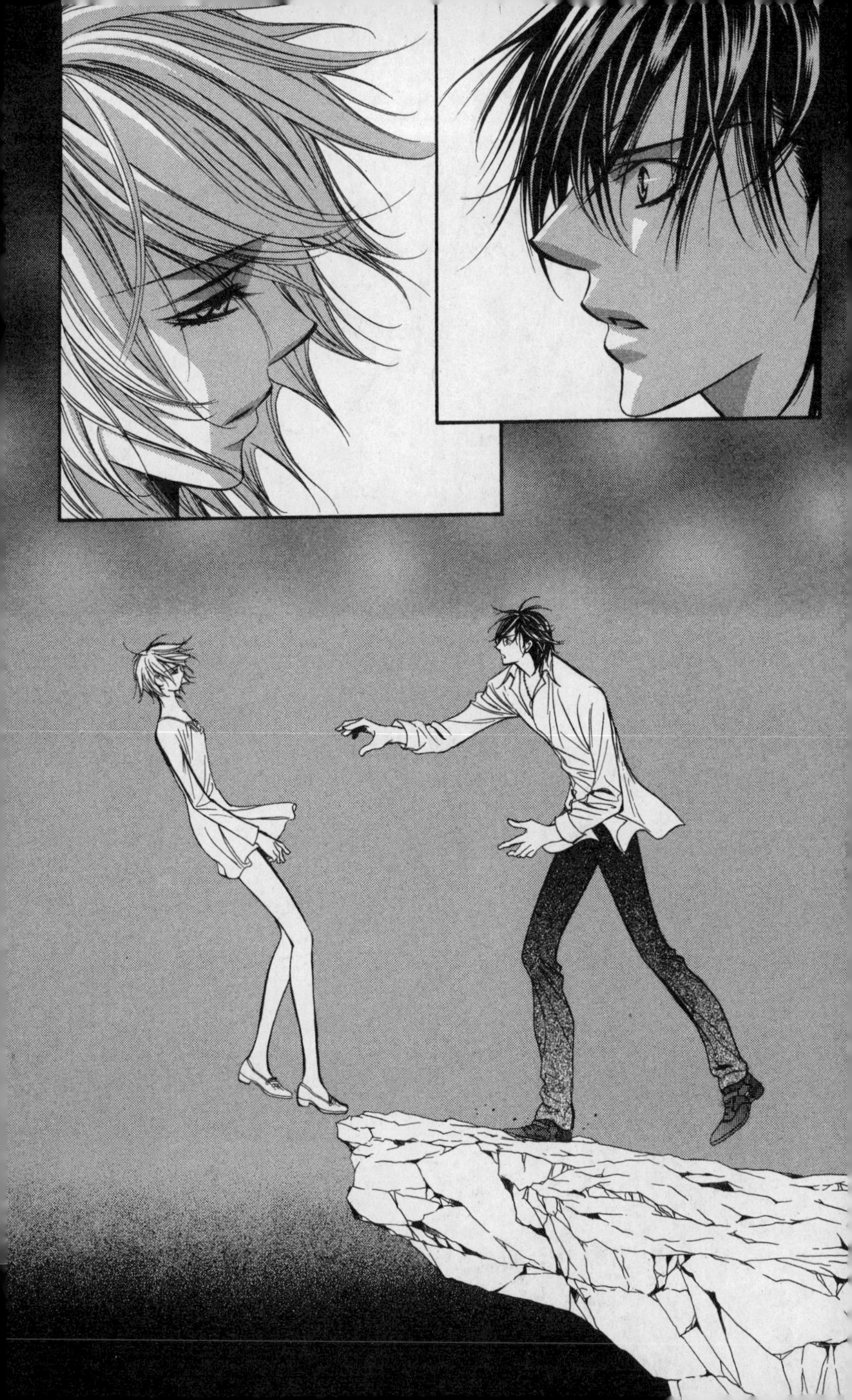

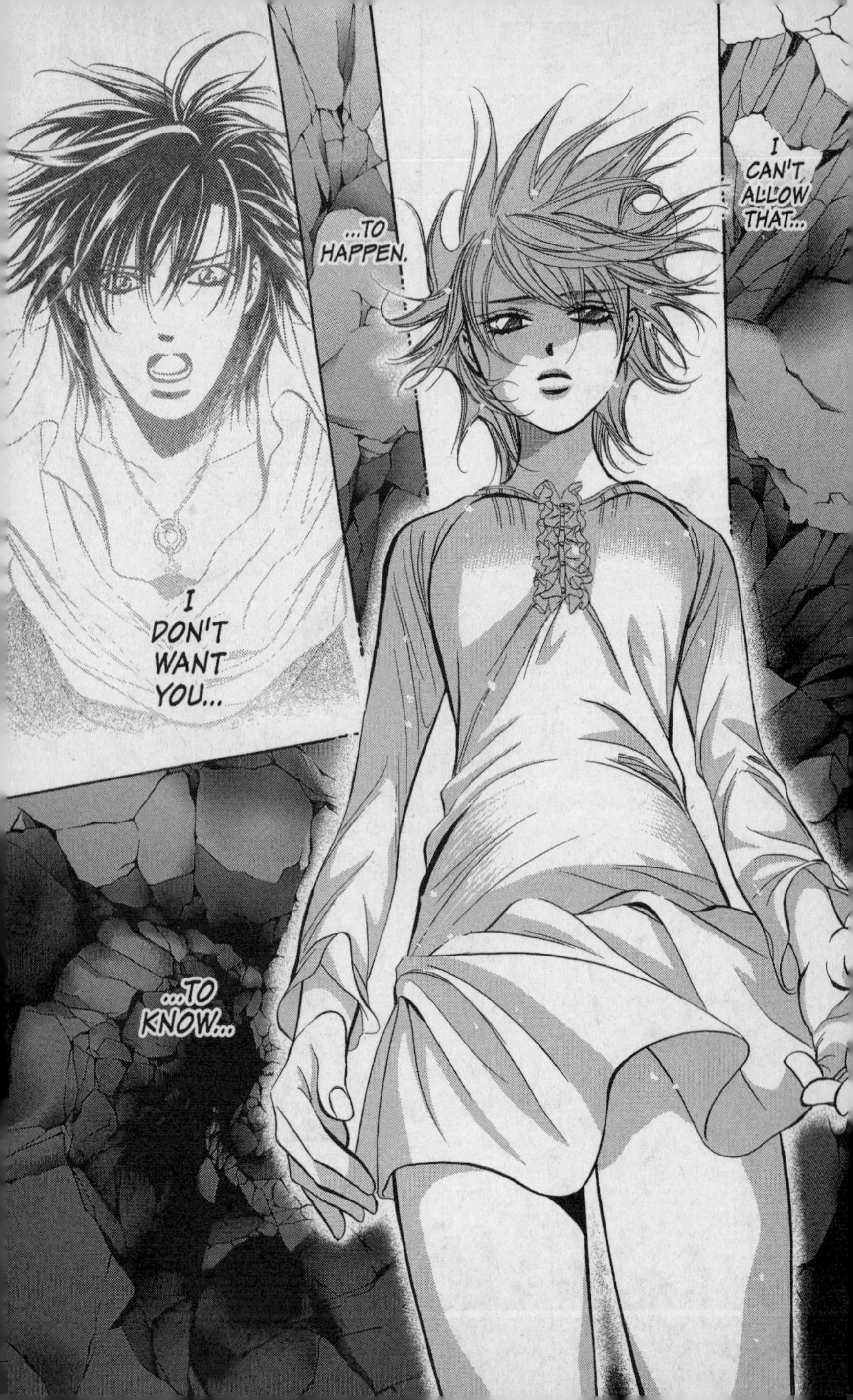
I CAN'T ALLOW THAT...
...TO HAPPEN.
I DON'T WANT YOU...
...TO KNOW...

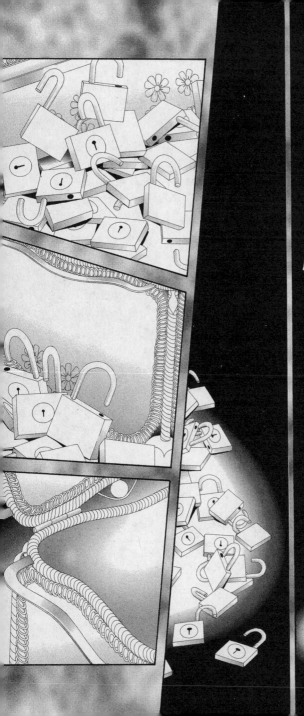

...TO
THIS
EMOTION
...

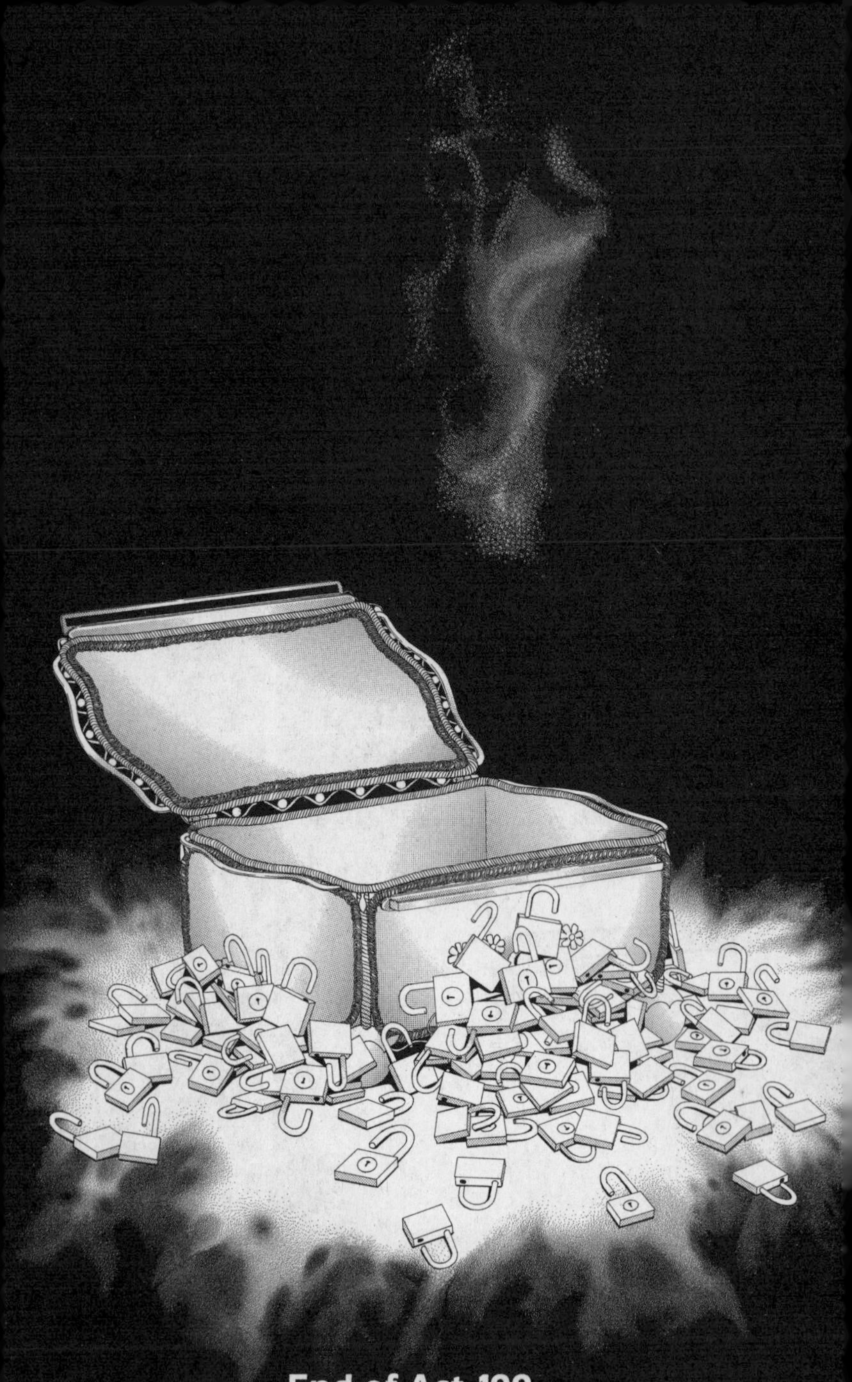

End of Act 199

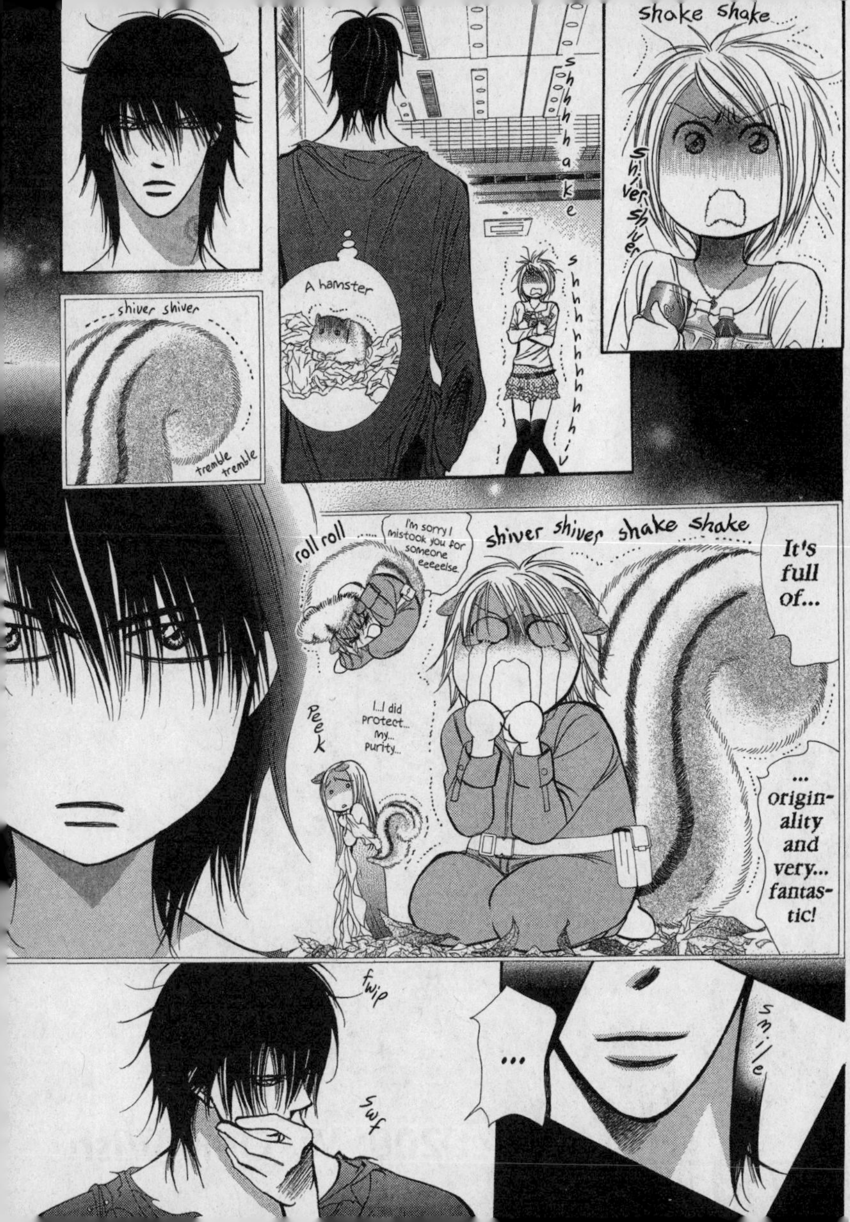
shake shake
shiver shiver
shhhhake
A hamster
shhhhhhhhhiv
shiver shiver
tremble tremble
It's full of...
... originality and very... fantastic!
shiver shiver shake shake
I'm sorry I mistook you for someone eeeeelse.
roll roll
I...I did protect... my... purity...
Peek
smile
...
fwip
swf

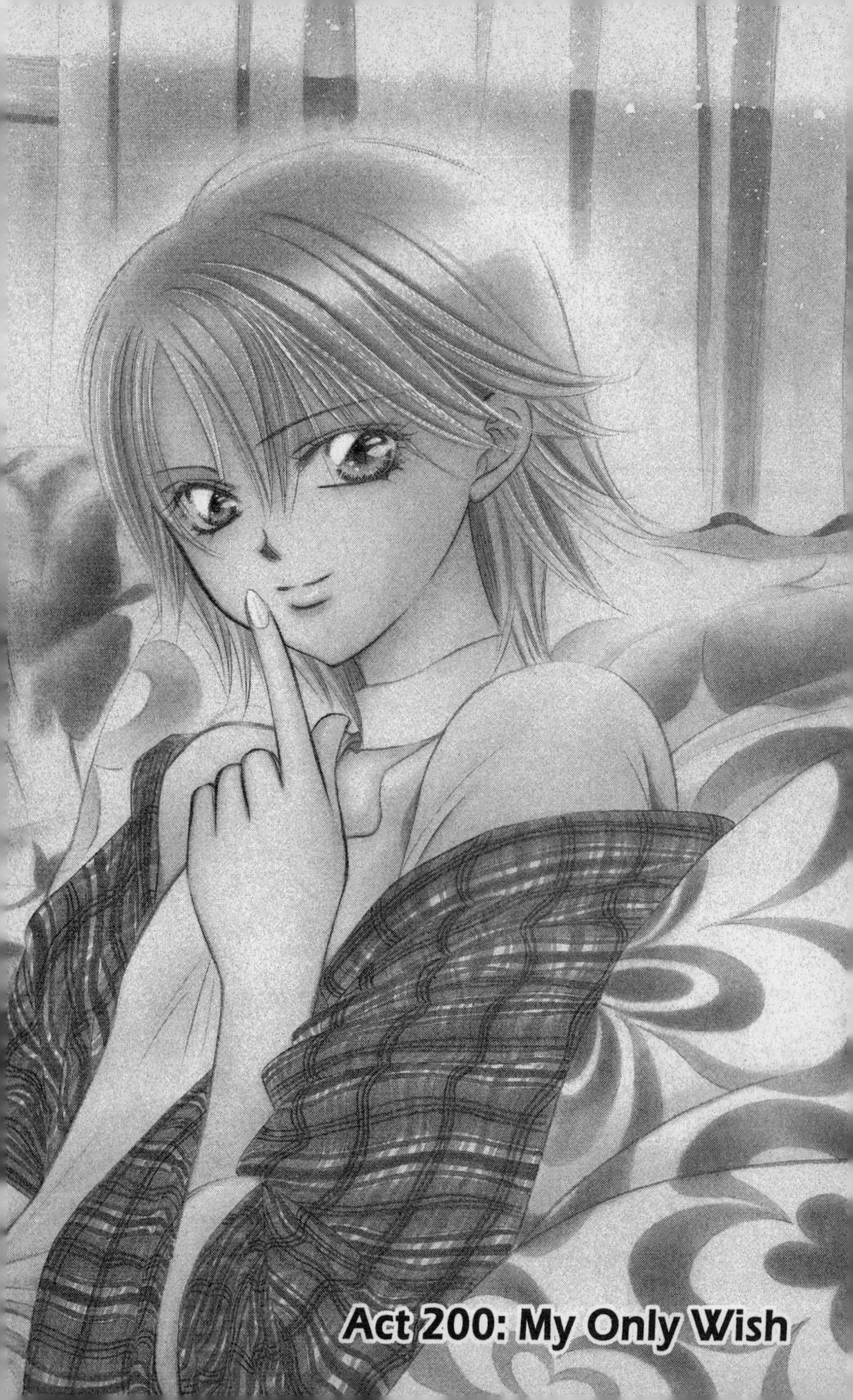

Act 200: My Only Wish

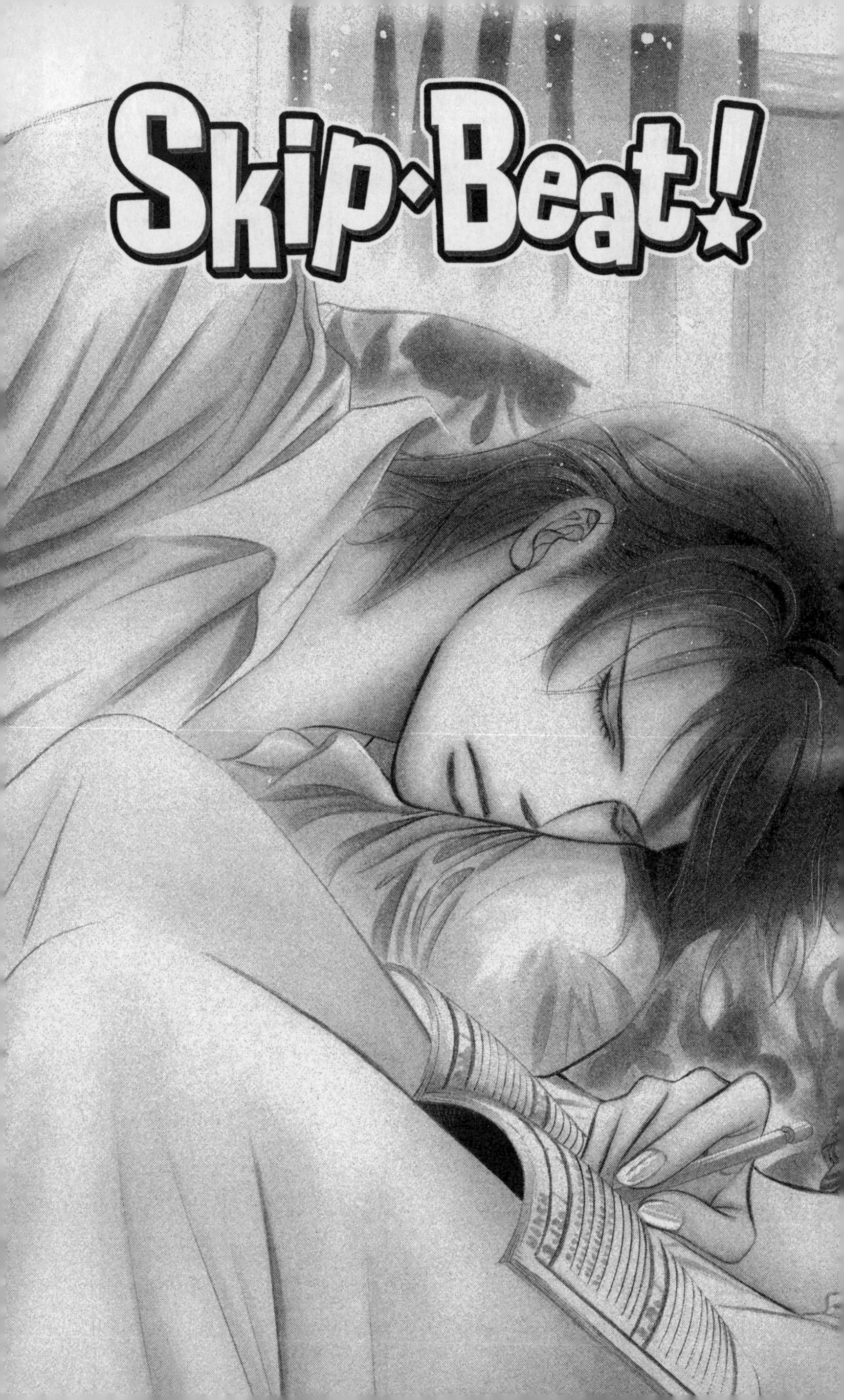
Skip·Beat!

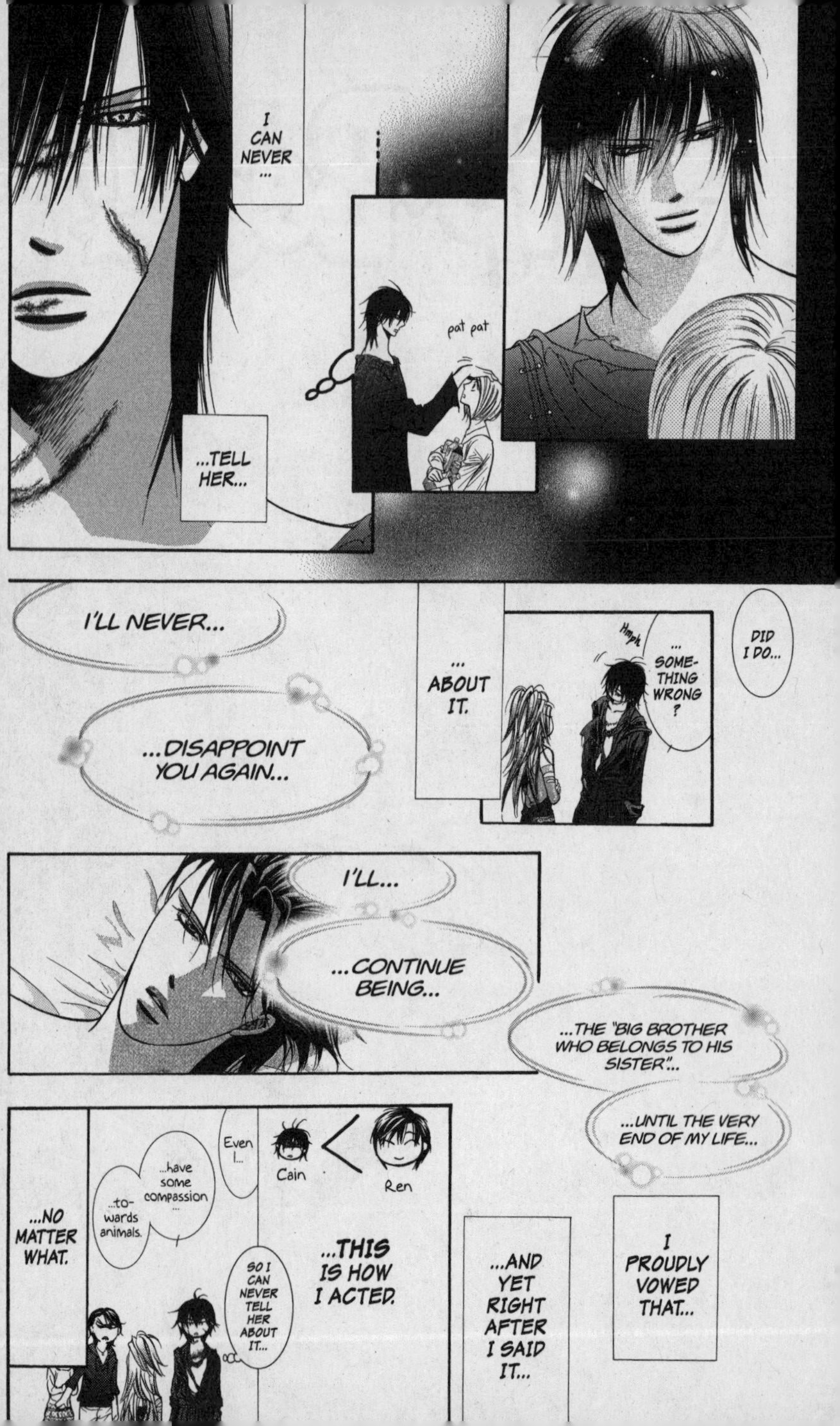

I CAN NEVER...
pat pat
...TELL HER...
DID I DO...
...SOMETHING WRONG?
Hmph
...ABOUT IT.
I'LL NEVER...
...DISAPPOINT YOU AGAIN...
I'LL...
...CONTINUE BEING...
...THE "BIG BROTHER WHO BELONGS TO HIS SISTER"...
...UNTIL THE VERY END OF MY LIFE...
I PROUDLY VOWED THAT...
...AND YET RIGHT AFTER I SAID IT...
...THIS IS HOW I ACTED.
Even I...
Cain
Ren
SO I CAN NEVER TELL HER ABOUT IT...
...have some compassion...
...to-wards animals.
...NO MATTER WHAT.

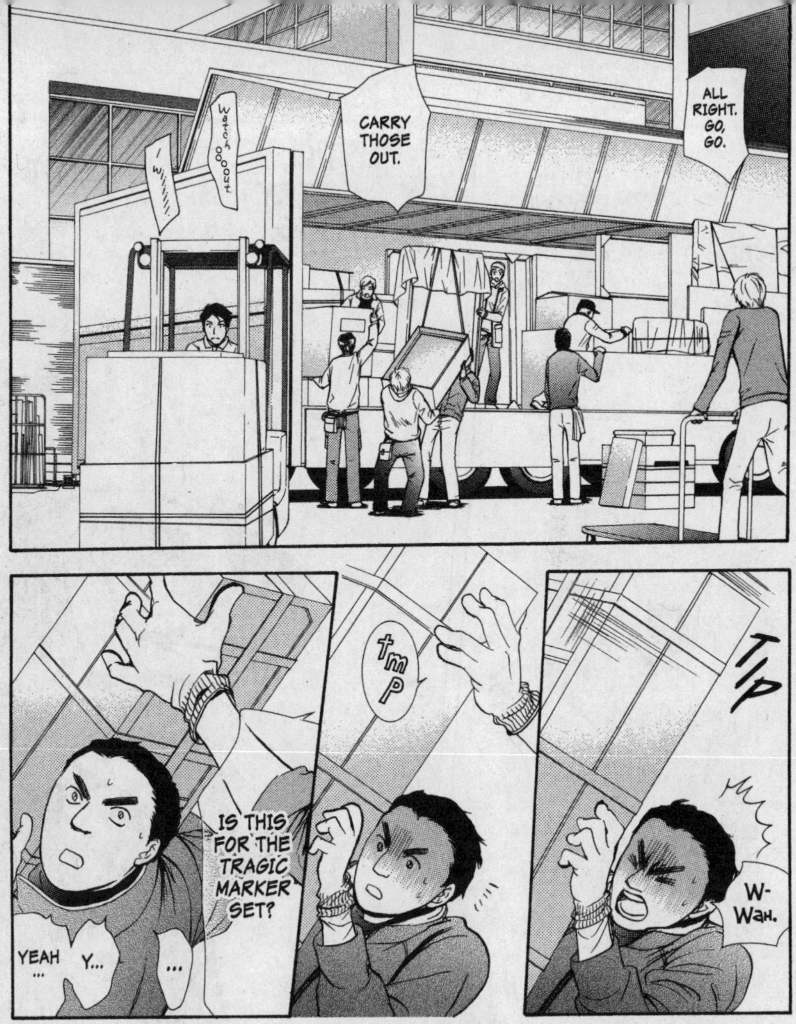
ALL RIGHT. GO, GO.
CARRY THOSE OUT.
Watch ooooout.
I wiiiiill.
TIP
W-WAH.
tmp
IS THIS FOR THE TRAGIC MARKER SET?
...
Y...
YEAH ...

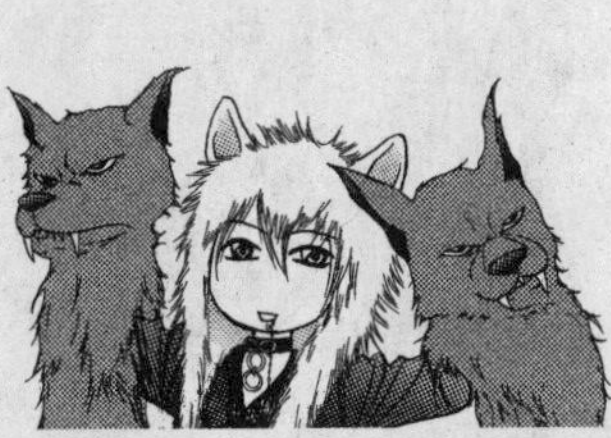

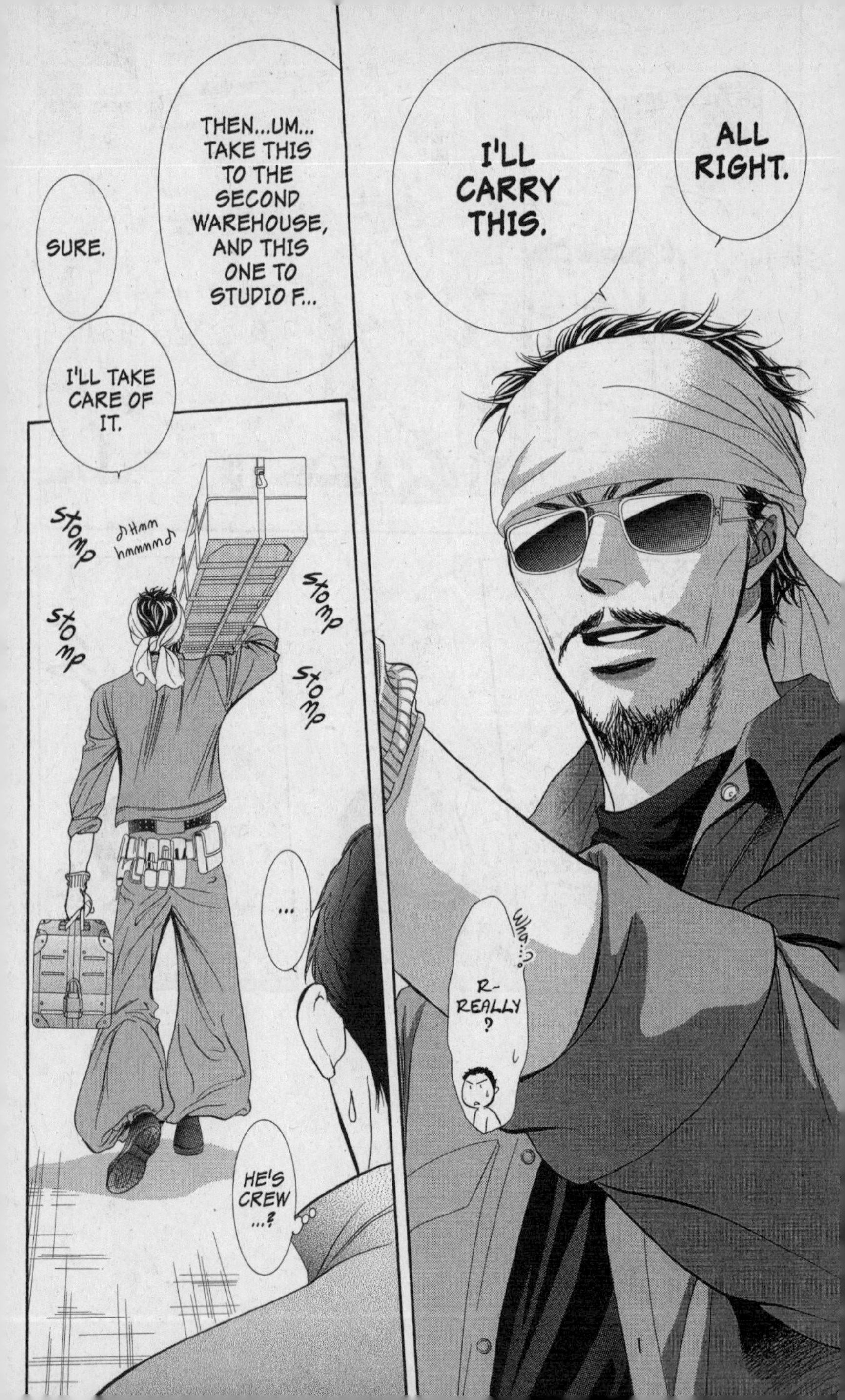
ALL RIGHT.
I'LL CARRY THIS.
Wha...?
R-REALLY?
THEN...UM... TAKE THIS TO THE SECOND WAREHOUSE, AND THIS ONE TO STUDIO F...
SURE.
I'LL TAKE CARE OF IT.
stomp
♪Hmm hmmmm♪
stomp
stomp
stomp
...
HE'S CREW ...?

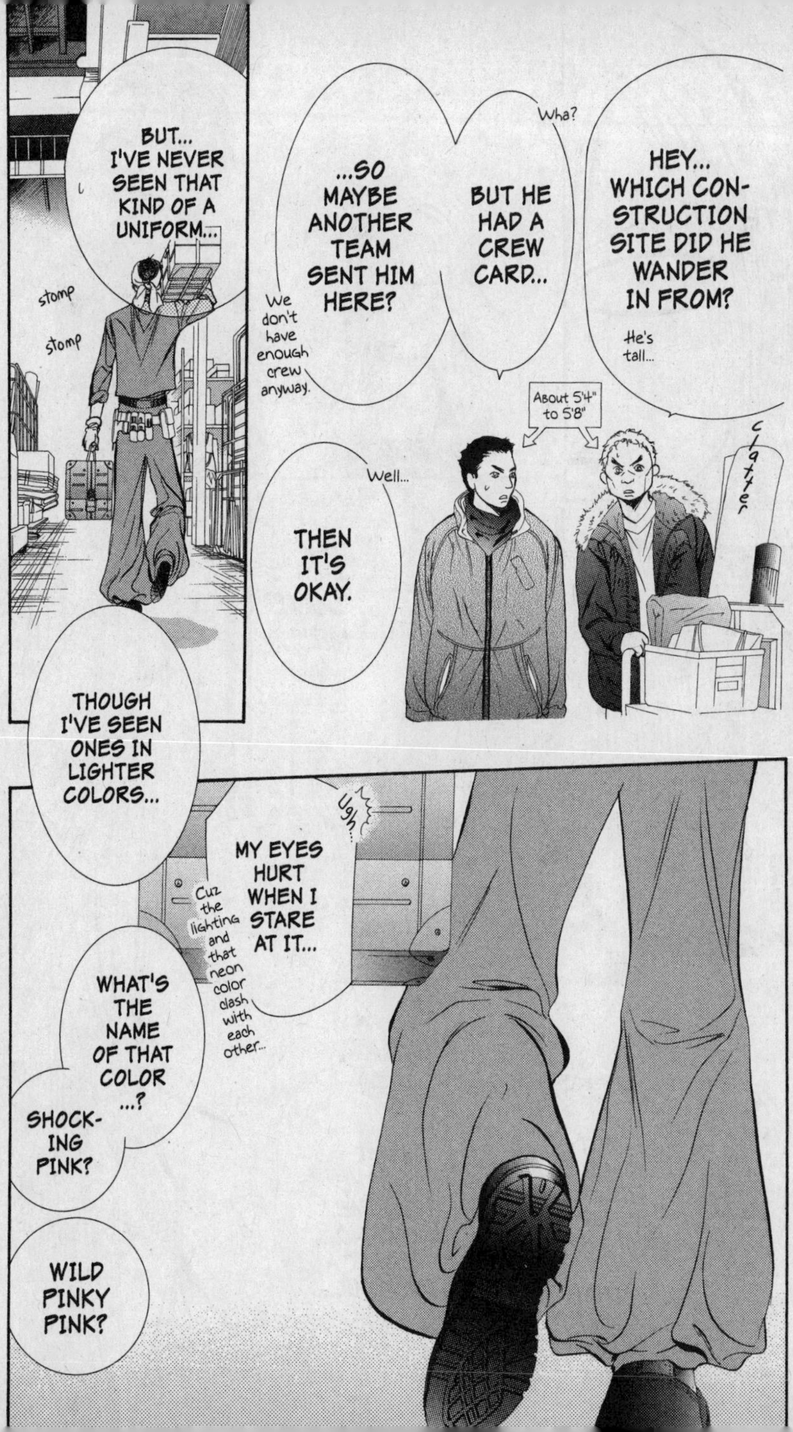
HEY... WHICH CON-STRUCTION SITE DID HE WANDER IN FROM?
He's tall...
Wha?
BUT HE HAD A CREW CARD...
...SO MAYBE ANOTHER TEAM SENT HIM HERE?
We don't have enough crew anyway.
About 5'4" to 5'8"
clatter
Well...
THEN IT'S OKAY.
BUT... I'VE NEVER SEEN THAT KIND OF A UNIFORM...
stomp
stomp
THOUGH I'VE SEEN ONES IN LIGHTER COLORS...
Ugh...
MY EYES HURT WHEN I STARE AT IT...
Cuz the lighting and that neon color clash with each other...
WHAT'S THE NAME OF THAT COLOR ...?
SHOCK-ING PINK?
WILD PINKY PINK?

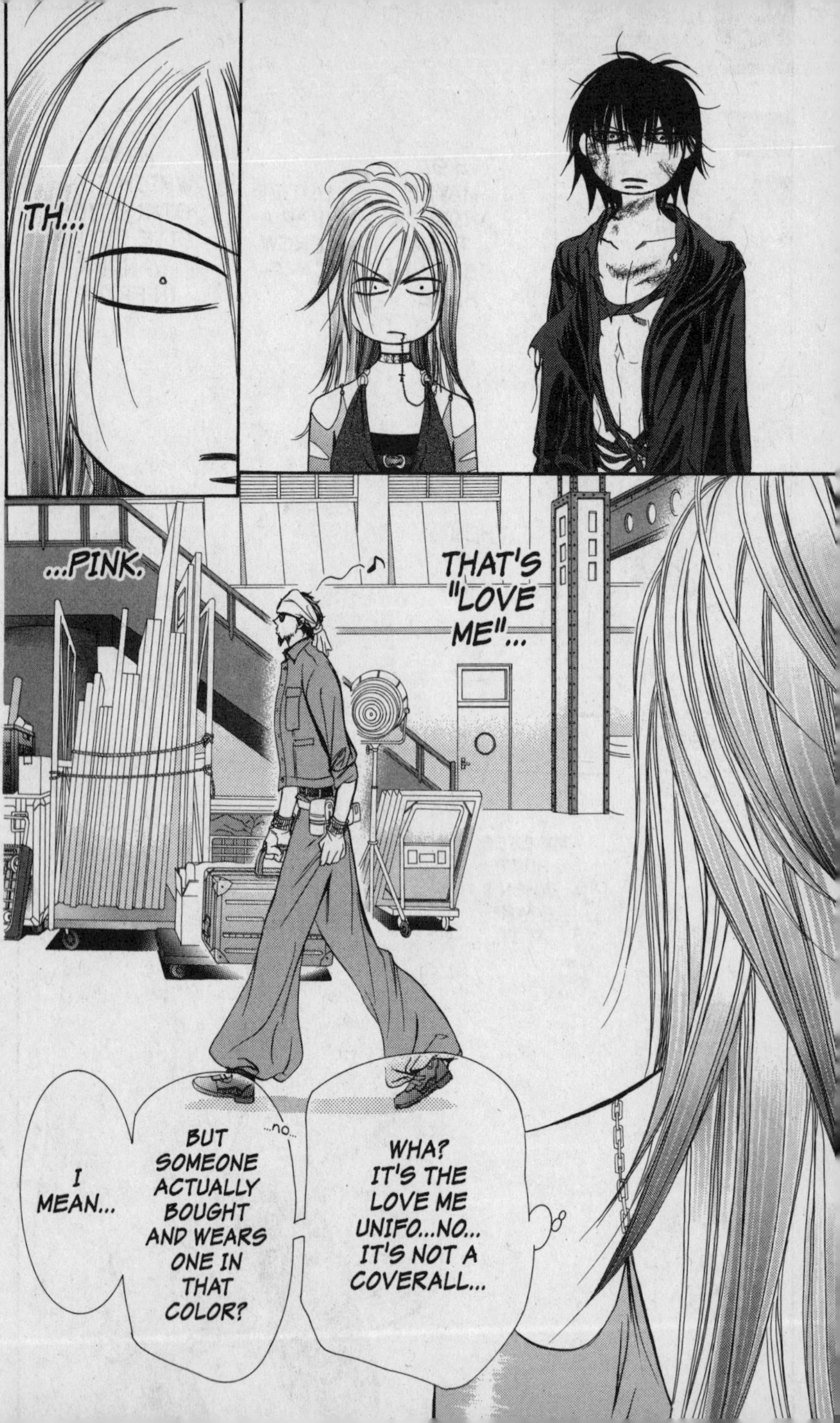
TH...
THAT'S "LOVE ME"...
...PINK.
WHA? IT'S THE LOVE ME UNIFO...NO... IT'S NOT A COVERALL...
...no...
BUT SOMEONE ACTUALLY BOUGHT AND WEARS ONE IN THAT COLOR?
I MEAN...

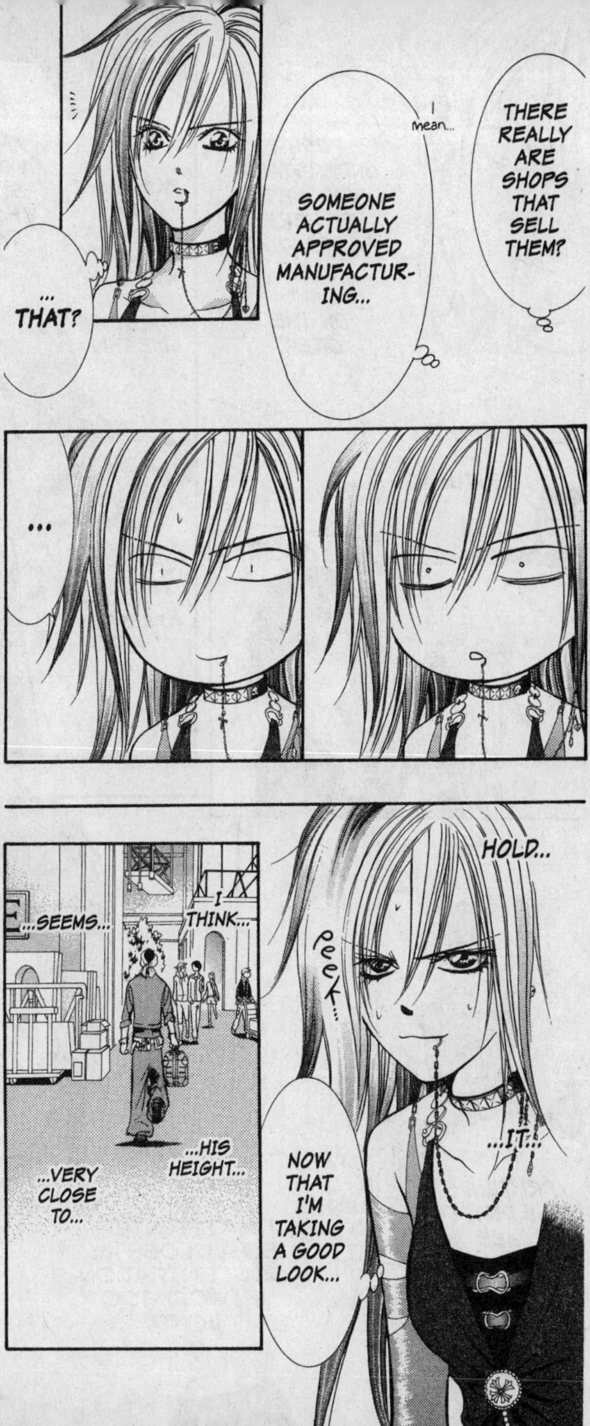
THERE REALLY ARE SHOPS THAT SELL THEM?
I mean...
SOMEONE ACTUALLY APPROVED MANUFACTURING...
...THAT?
...
HOLD...
Peek...
...IT...
NOW THAT I'M TAKING A GOOD LOOK...
I THINK...
...SEEMS...
...HIS HEIGHT...
...VERY CLOSE TO...
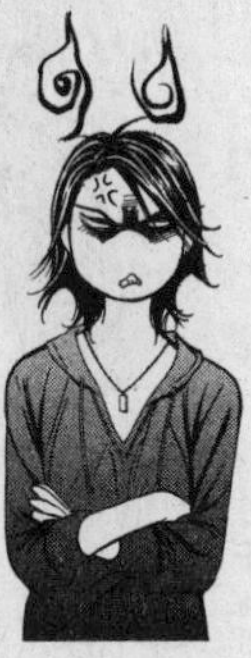

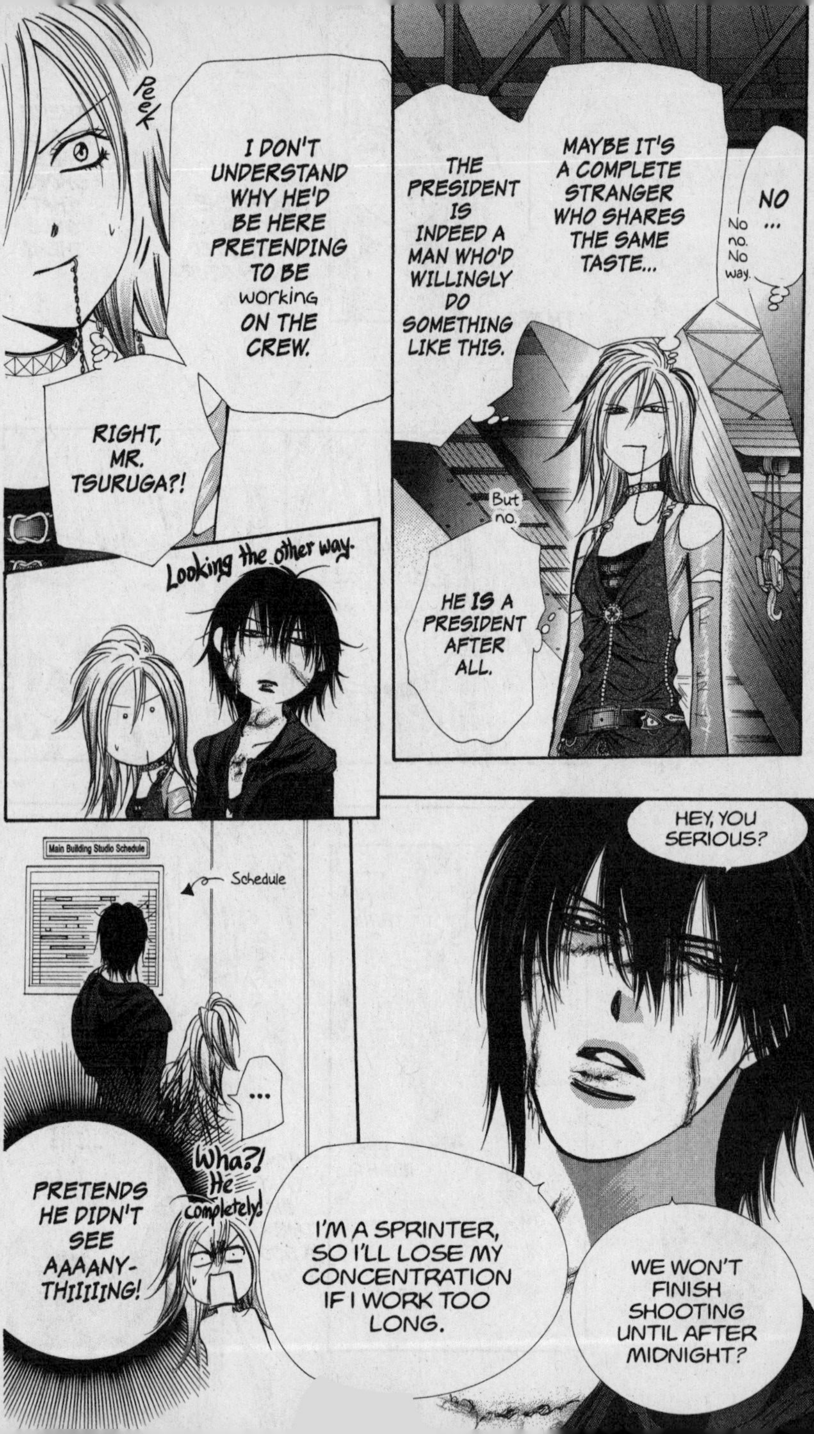

THE PRESIDENT IS INDEED A MAN WHO'D WILLINGLY DO SOMETHING LIKE THIS.
MAYBE IT'S A COMPLETE STRANGER WHO SHARES THE SAME TASTE...
NO ...
No no. No way.
But no.
HE IS A PRESIDENT AFTER ALL.
Peek
I DON'T UNDERSTAND WHY HE'D BE HERE PRETENDING TO BE working ON THE CREW.
RIGHT, MR. TSURUGA?!
Looking the other way.
HEY, YOU SERIOUS?
WE WON'T FINISH SHOOTING UNTIL AFTER MIDNIGHT?
I'M A SPRINTER, SO I'LL LOSE MY CONCENTRATION IF I WORK TOO LONG.
Main Building Studio Schedule
Schedule
...
Wha?! He completely!
PRETENDS HE DIDN'T SEE AAAANY-THIIIIING!

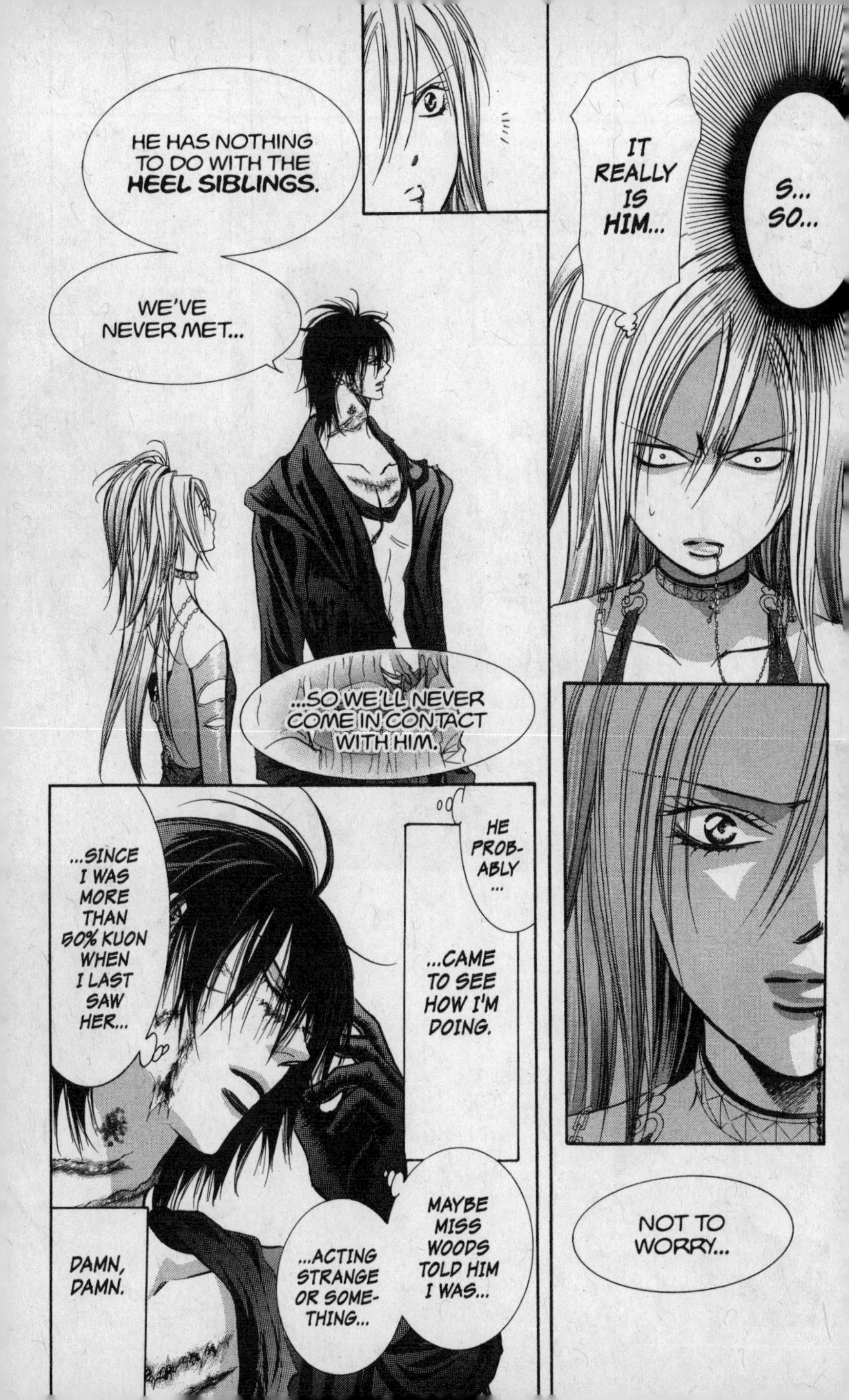
S... SO...
IT REALLY IS HIM...
NOT TO WORRY...
HE HAS NOTHING TO DO WITH THE **HEEL SIBLINGS.**
WE'VE NEVER MET...
...SO WE'LL NEVER COME IN CONTACT WITH HIM.
HE PROBABLY...
...CAME TO SEE HOW I'M DOING.
...SINCE I WAS MORE THAN 50% KUON WHEN I LAST SAW HER...
MAYBE MISS WOODS TOLD HIM I WAS...
...ACTING STRANGE OR SOMETHING...
DAMN, DAMN.

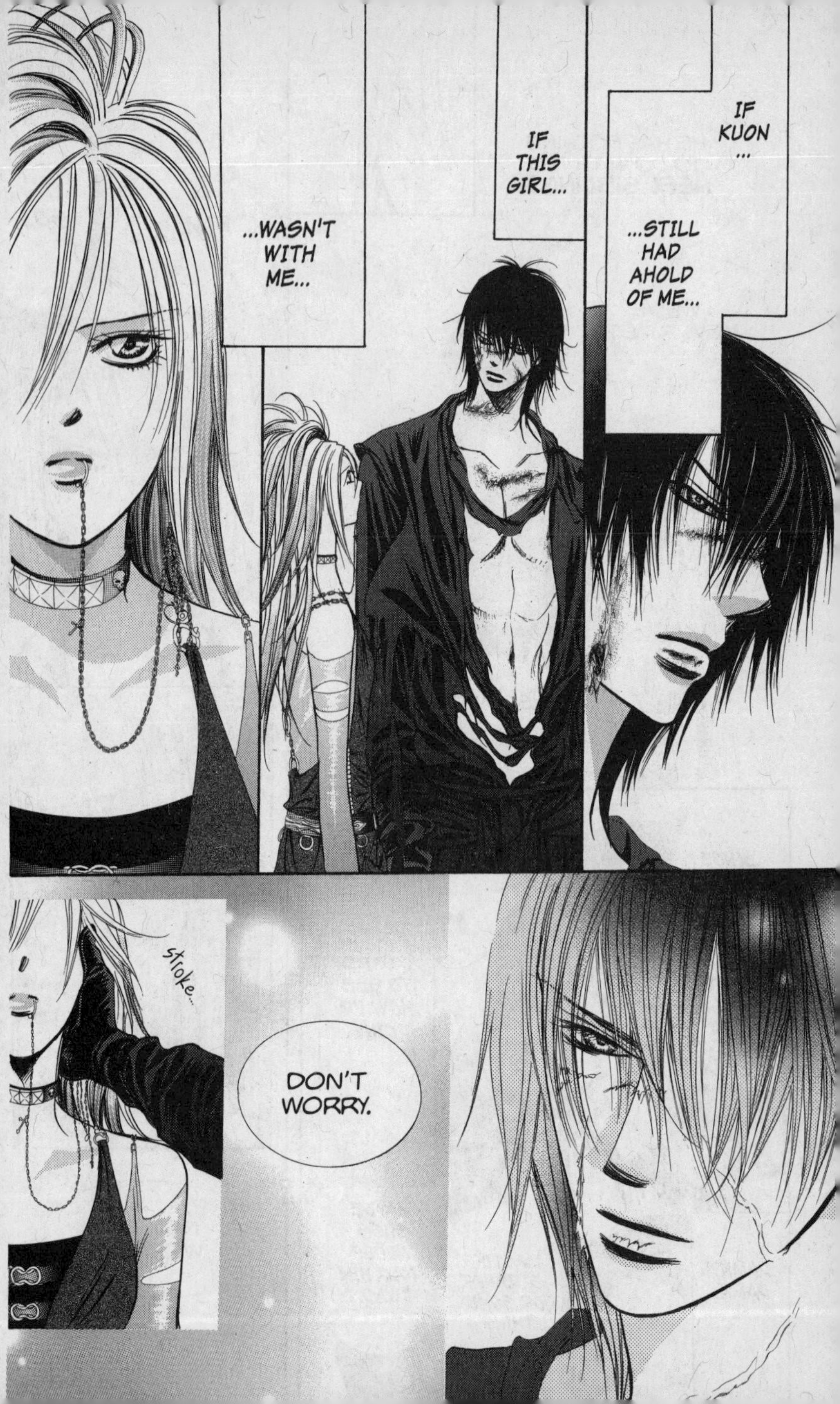
IF KUON ...
...STILL HAD AHOLD OF ME...
IF THIS GIRL...
...WASN'T WITH ME...
DON'T WORRY.
stroke...

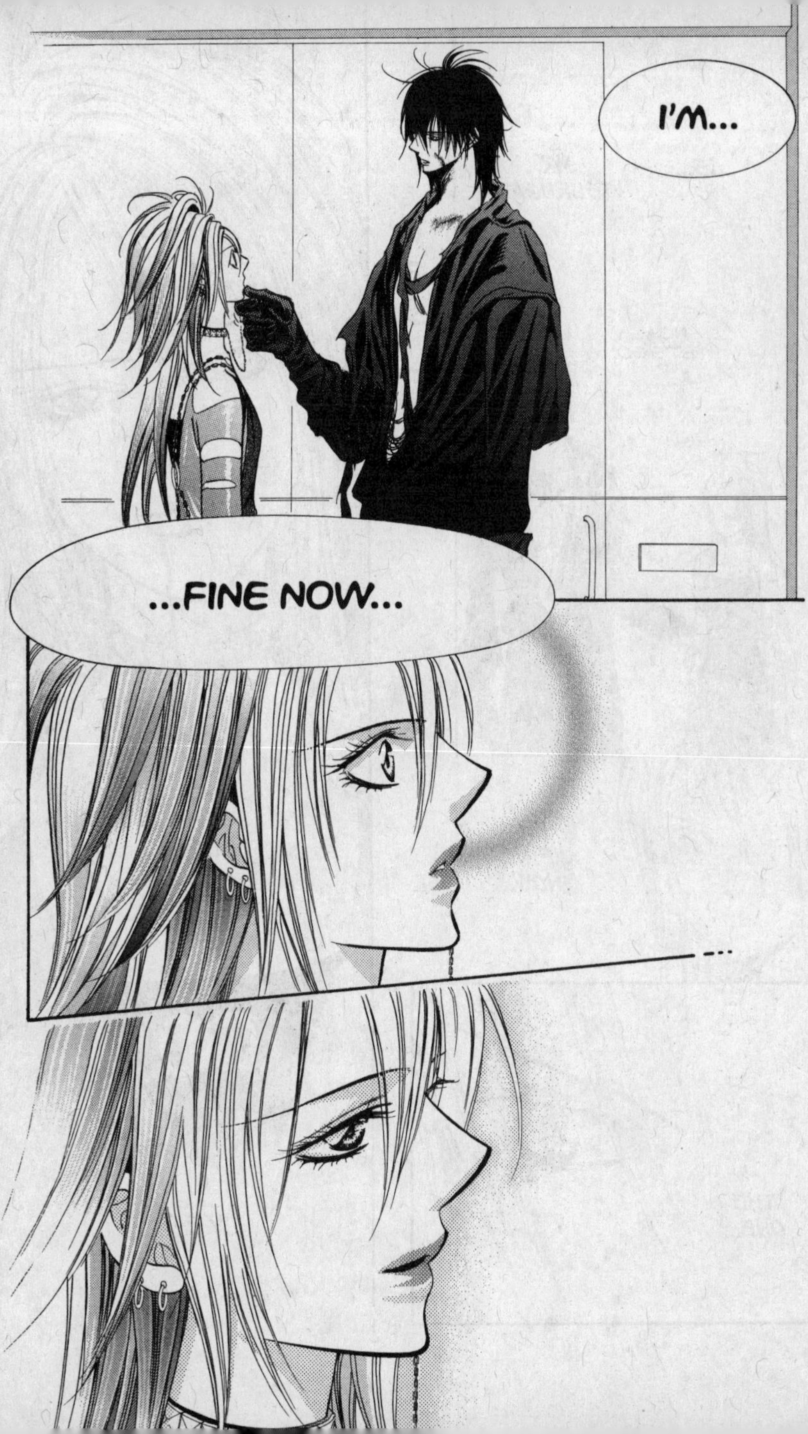
I'M...
...FINE NOW...
...

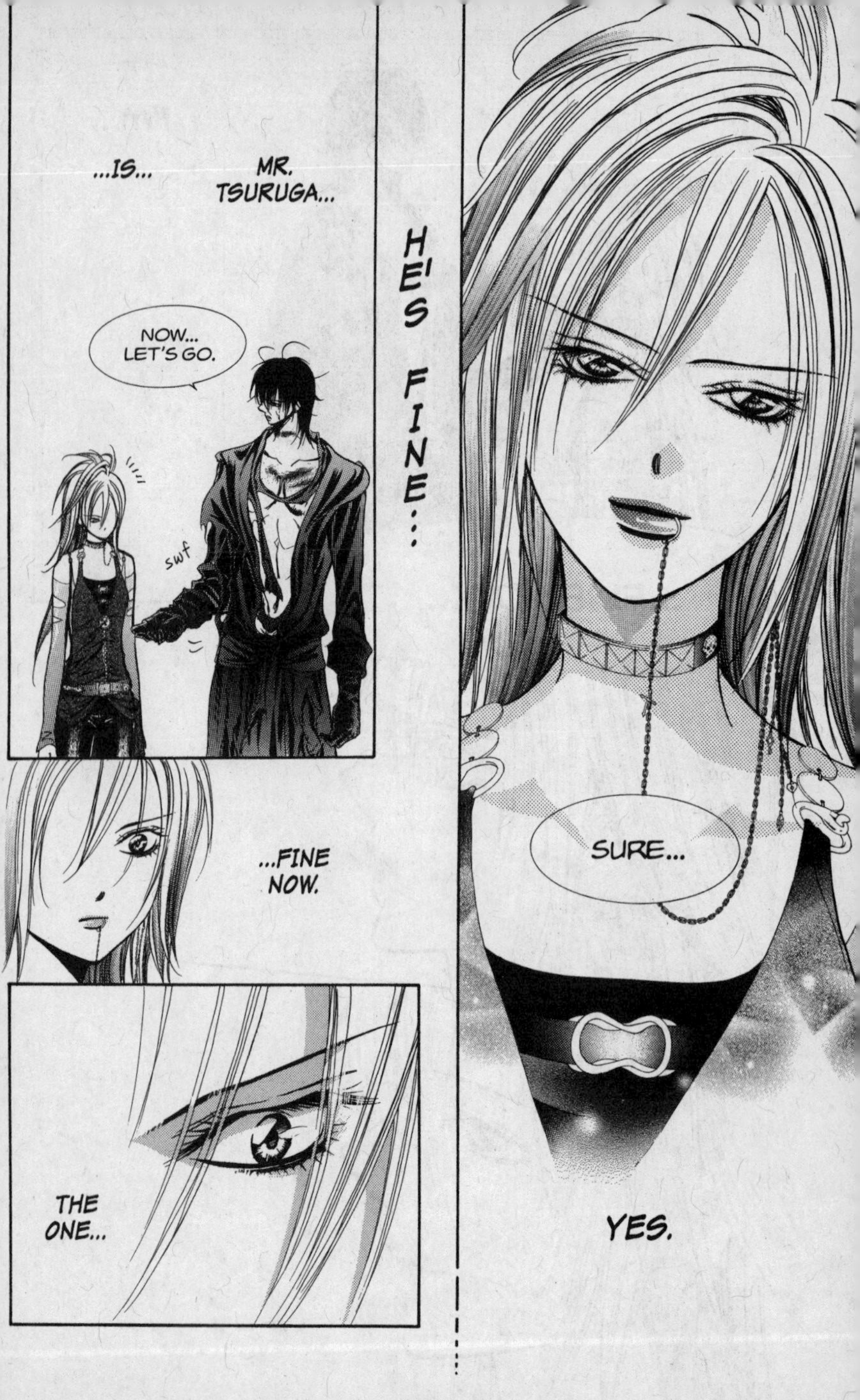
HE'S FINE...
SURE...
YES.
MR. TSURUGA...
...IS...
NOW... LET'S GO.
swf
...FINE NOW.
THE ONE...

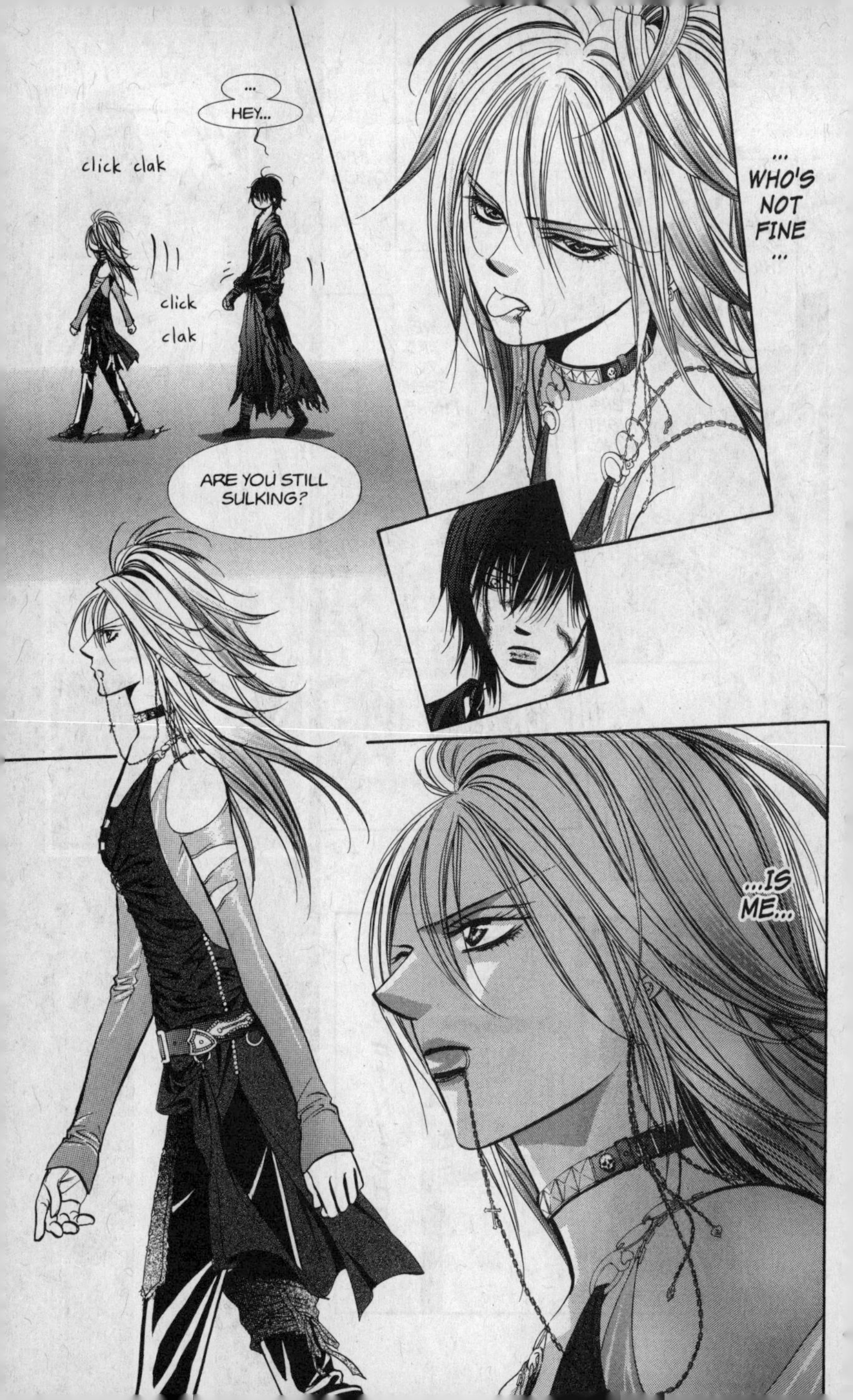
...
HEY...
click clak
click
clak
ARE YOU STILL SULKING?
... WHO'S NOT FINE ...
...IS ME...

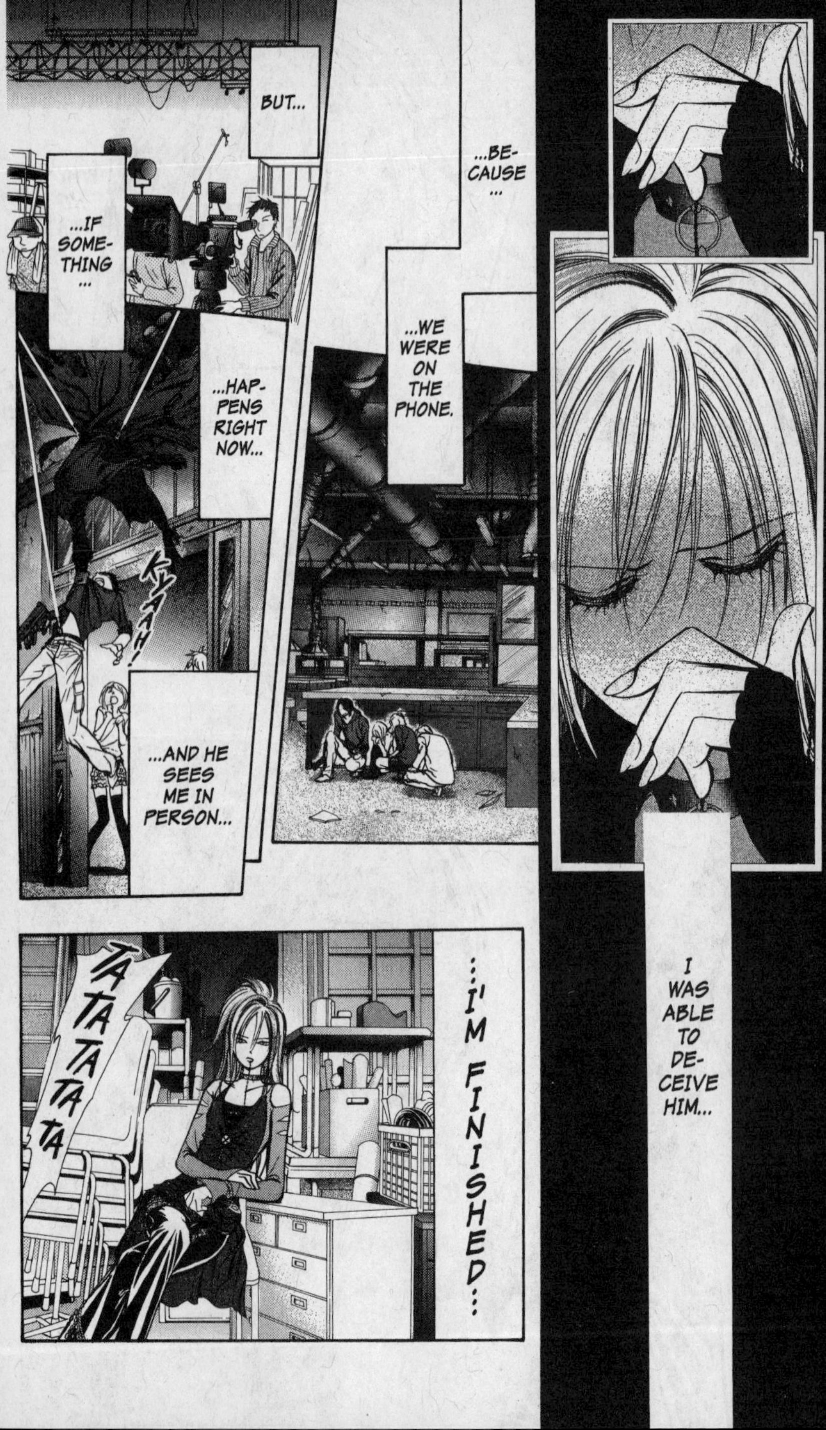
I WAS ABLE TO DECEIVE HIM...
...BE-CAUSE...
...WE WERE ON THE PHONE.
BUT...
...IF SOME-THING...
...HAP-PENS RIGHT NOW...
KYAAAH!
...AND HE SEES ME IN PERSON...
...I'M FINISHED...
TA TA TA TA TA

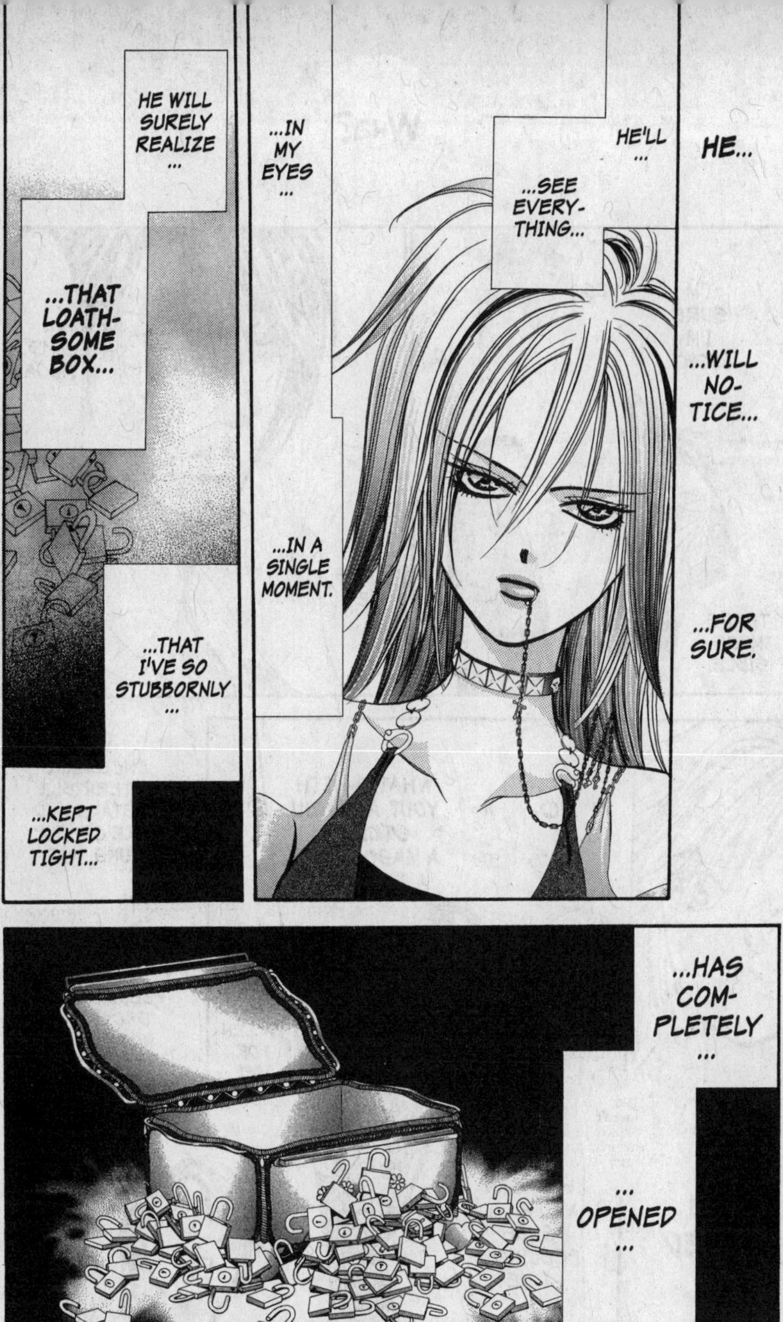

HE...
...WILL NOTICE...
...FOR SURE.
HE'LL...
...SEE EVERYTHING...
...IN MY EYES...
...IN A SINGLE MOMENT.
HE WILL SURELY REALIZE...
...THAT LOATHSOME BOX...
...THAT I'VE SO STUBBORNLY...
...KEPT LOCKED TIGHT...
...HAS COMPLETELY...
...OPENED...

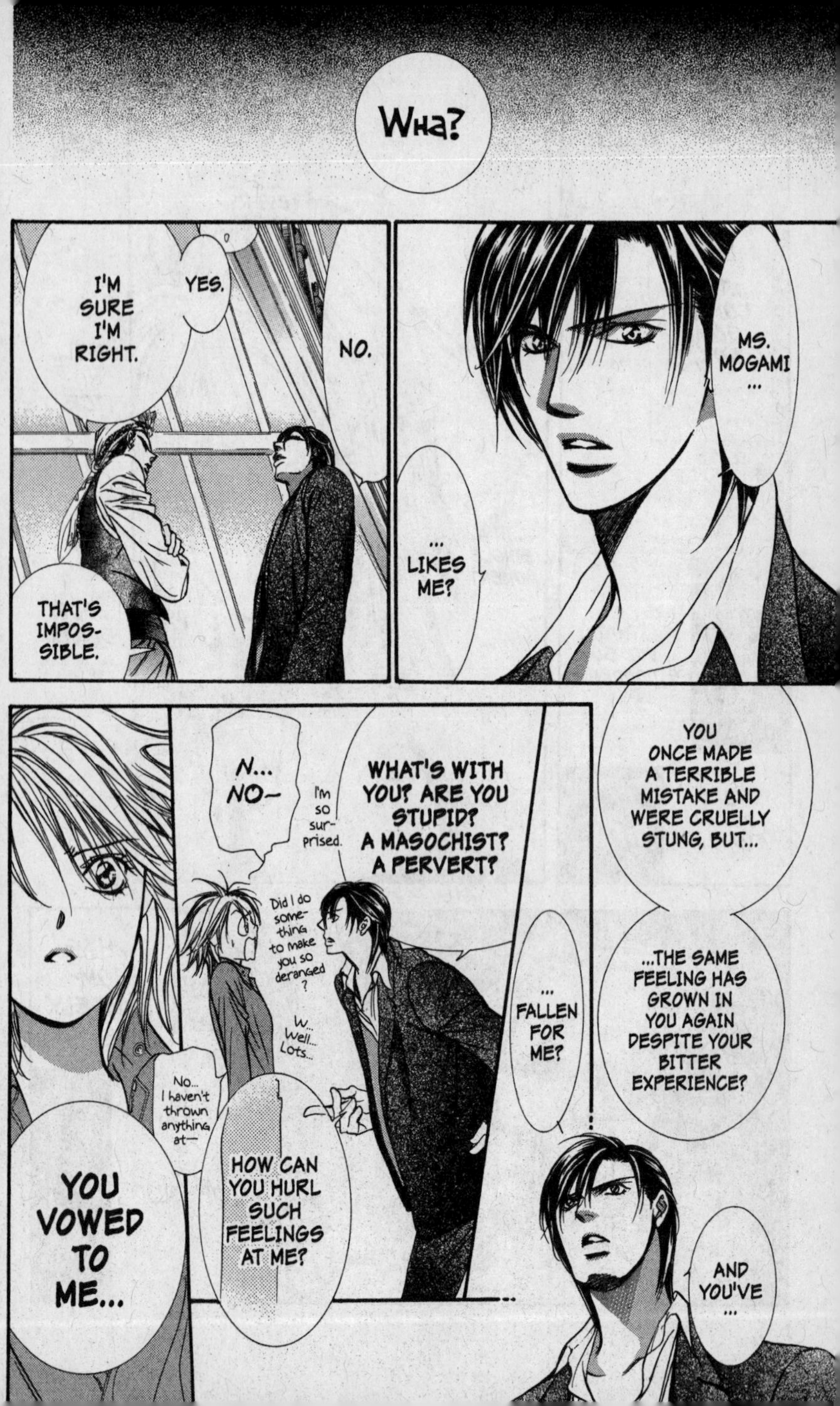
WHA?
MS. MOGAMI ...
... LIKES ME?
NO.
YES.
I'M SURE I'M RIGHT.
THAT'S IMPOS-SIBLE.
YOU ONCE MADE A TERRIBLE MISTAKE AND WERE CRUELLY STUNG, BUT...
...THE SAME FEELING HAS GROWN IN YOU AGAIN DESPITE YOUR BITTER EXPERIENCE?
AND YOU'VE ...
... FALLEN FOR ME?
WHAT'S WITH YOU? ARE YOU STUPID? A MASOCHIST? A PERVERT?
N... NO—
I'm so sur-prised.
Did I do some-thing to make you so deranged?
W... Well... Lots...
HOW CAN YOU HURL SUCH FEELINGS AT ME?
No... I haven't thrown anything at—
YOU VOWED TO ME...

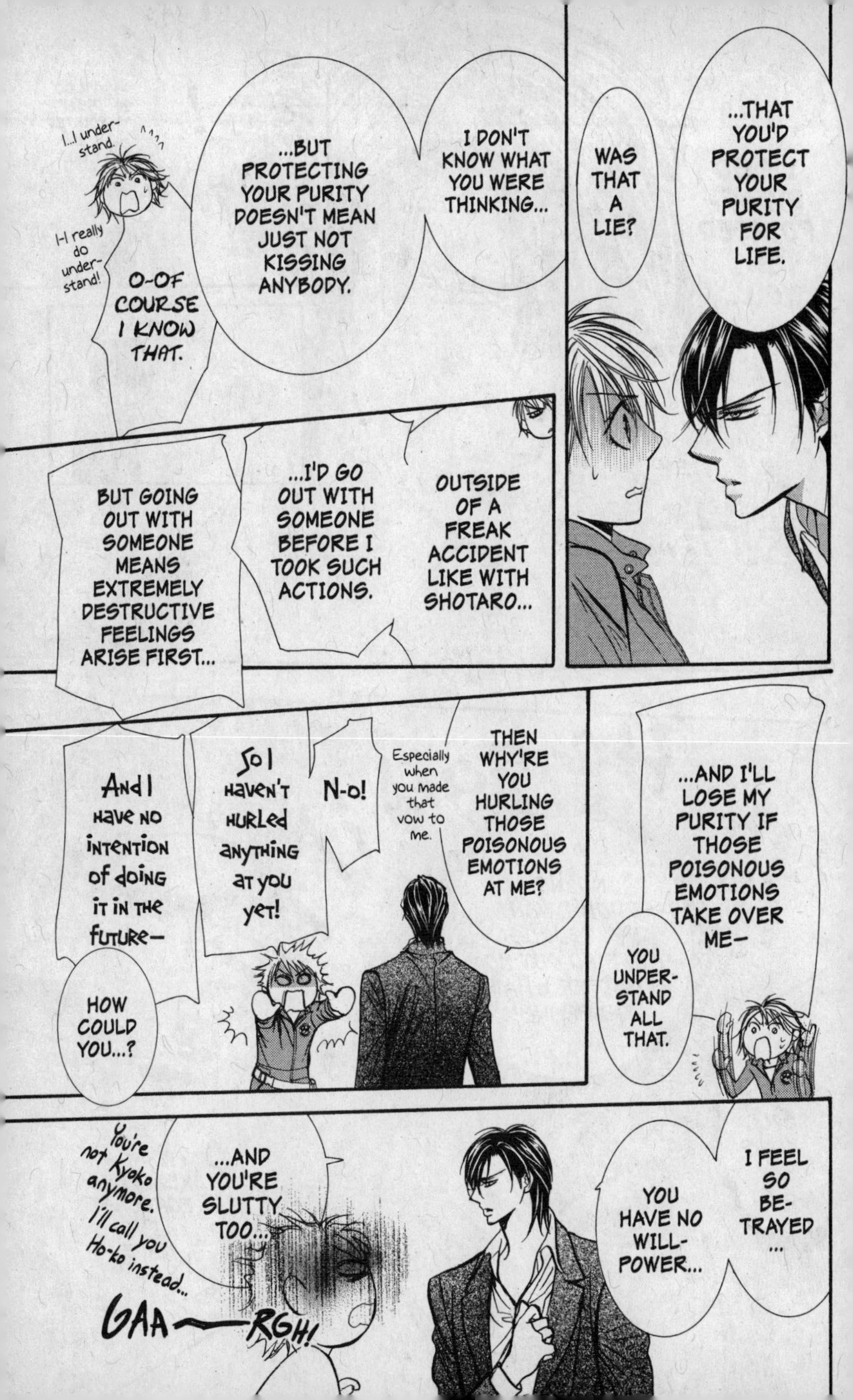
...THAT YOU'D PROTECT YOUR PURITY FOR LIFE.
WAS THAT A LIE?
I DON'T KNOW WHAT YOU WERE THINKING...
...BUT PROTECTING YOUR PURITY DOESN'T MEAN JUST NOT KISSING ANYBODY.
O-OF COURSE I KNOW THAT.
I...I under-stand.
I-I really do under-stand!
OUTSIDE OF A FREAK ACCIDENT LIKE WITH SHOTARO...
...I'D GO OUT WITH SOMEONE BEFORE I TOOK SUCH ACTIONS.
BUT GOING OUT WITH SOMEONE MEANS EXTREMELY DESTRUCTIVE FEELINGS ARISE FIRST...
...AND I'LL LOSE MY PURITY IF THOSE POISONOUS EMOTIONS TAKE OVER ME—
YOU UNDER-STAND ALL THAT.
THEN WHY'RE YOU HURLING THOSE POISONOUS EMOTIONS AT ME?
Especially when you made that vow to me.
N-o!
So I haven't hurled anything at you yet!
And I have no intention of doing it in the future—
HOW COULD YOU...?
I FEEL SO BE-TRAYED...
YOU HAVE NO WILL-POWER...
...AND YOU'RE SLUTTY TOO...
You're not Kyoko anymore. I'll call you Ho-ko instead...
GAA—RGH!

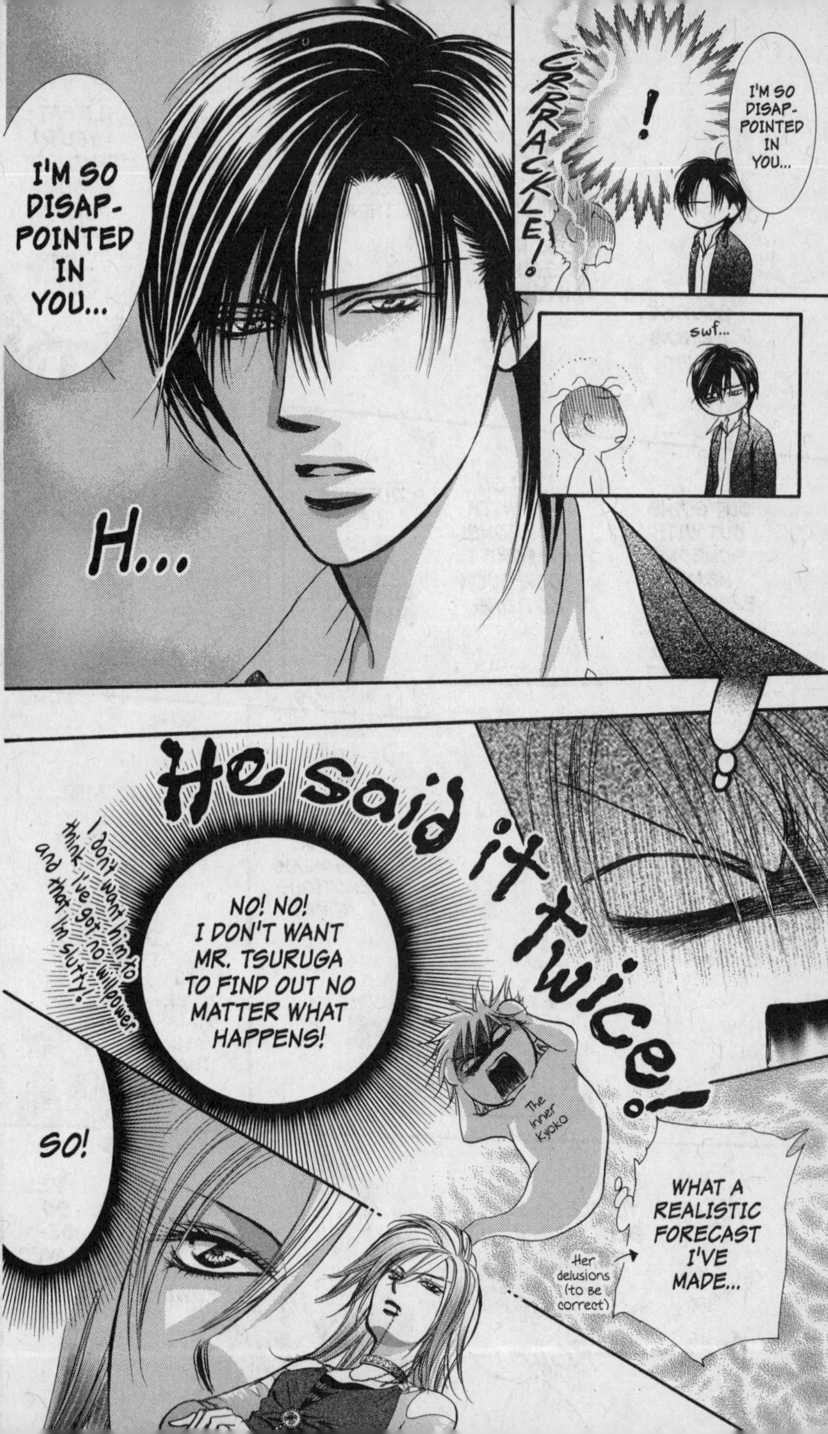
CRRRACKLE!
!
I'M SO DISAP-POINTED IN YOU...
swf...
I'M SO DISAP-POINTED IN YOU...
H...
He said it twice!
NO! NO! I DON'T WANT MR. TSURUGA TO FIND OUT NO MATTER WHAT HAPPENS!
I don't want him to think I've got no willpower and that I'm slutty!
The inner Kyoko
WHAT A REALISTIC FORECAST I'VE MADE...
Her delusions (to be correct)
SO!

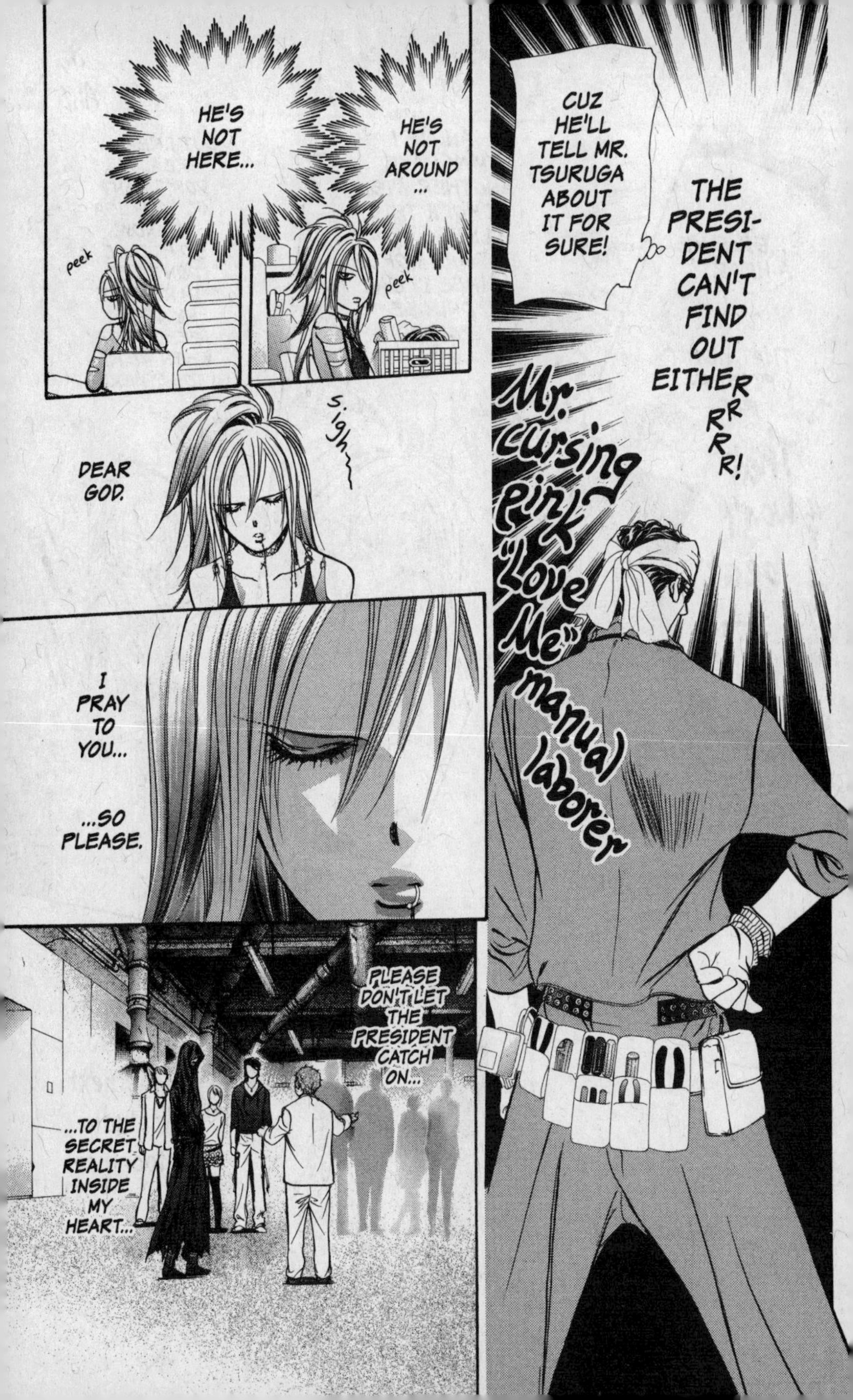
THE PRESIDENT CAN'T FIND OUT EITHERRRRR!
CUZ HE'LL TELL MR. TSURUGA ABOUT IT FOR SURE!
Mr. Cursing Pink "Love Me" manual laborer
HE'S NOT AROUND...
peek
HE'S NOT HERE...
peek
sigh
DEAR GOD.
I PRAY TO YOU...
...SO PLEASE.
PLEASE DON'T LET THE PRESIDENT CATCH ON...
...TO THE SECRET REALITY INSIDE MY HEART...

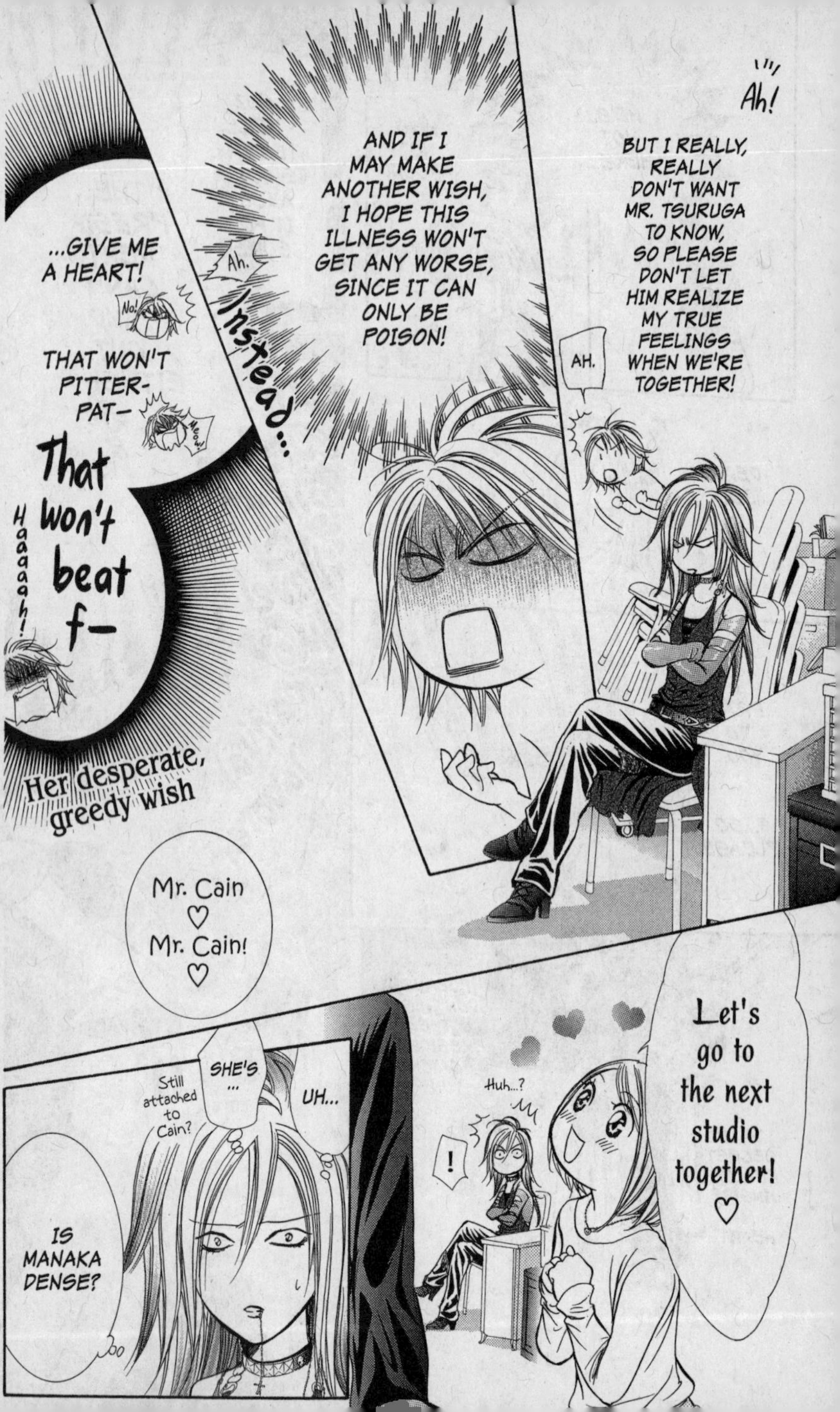
Ah!
BUT I REALLY, REALLY DON'T WANT MR. TSURUGA TO KNOW, SO PLEASE DON'T LET HIM REALIZE MY TRUE FEELINGS WHEN WE'RE TOGETHER!
AH.
AND IF I MAY MAKE ANOTHER WISH, I HOPE THIS ILLNESS WON'T GET ANY WORSE, SINCE IT CAN ONLY BE POISON!
Ah.
Instead...
...GIVE ME A HEART!
No!
THAT WON'T PITTER-PAT—
Meow!
That won't beat f—
Haaaaah!
Her desperate, greedy wish
Mr. Cain ♡ Mr. Cain! ♡
Let's go to the next studio together! ♡
Huh...?
!
SHE'S...
UH...
Still attached to Cain?
IS MANAKA DENSE?

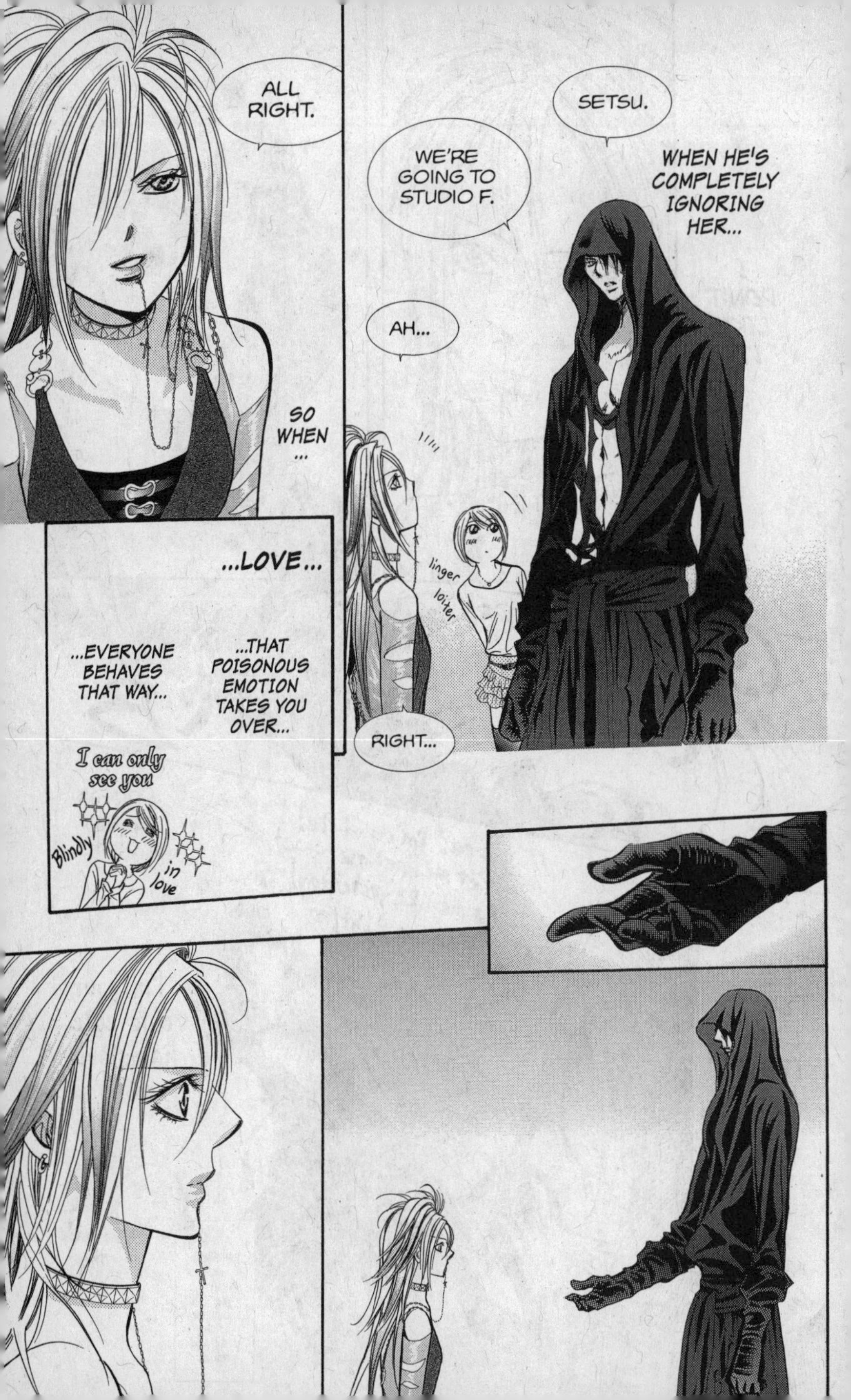
SETSU.
WE'RE GOING TO STUDIO F.
WHEN HE'S COMPLETELY IGNORING HER...
AH...
linger
loiter
RIGHT...
ALL RIGHT.
SO WHEN ...
...LOVE...
...THAT POISONOUS EMOTION TAKES YOU OVER...
...EVERYONE BEHAVES THAT WAY...
I can only see you
Blindly
in love

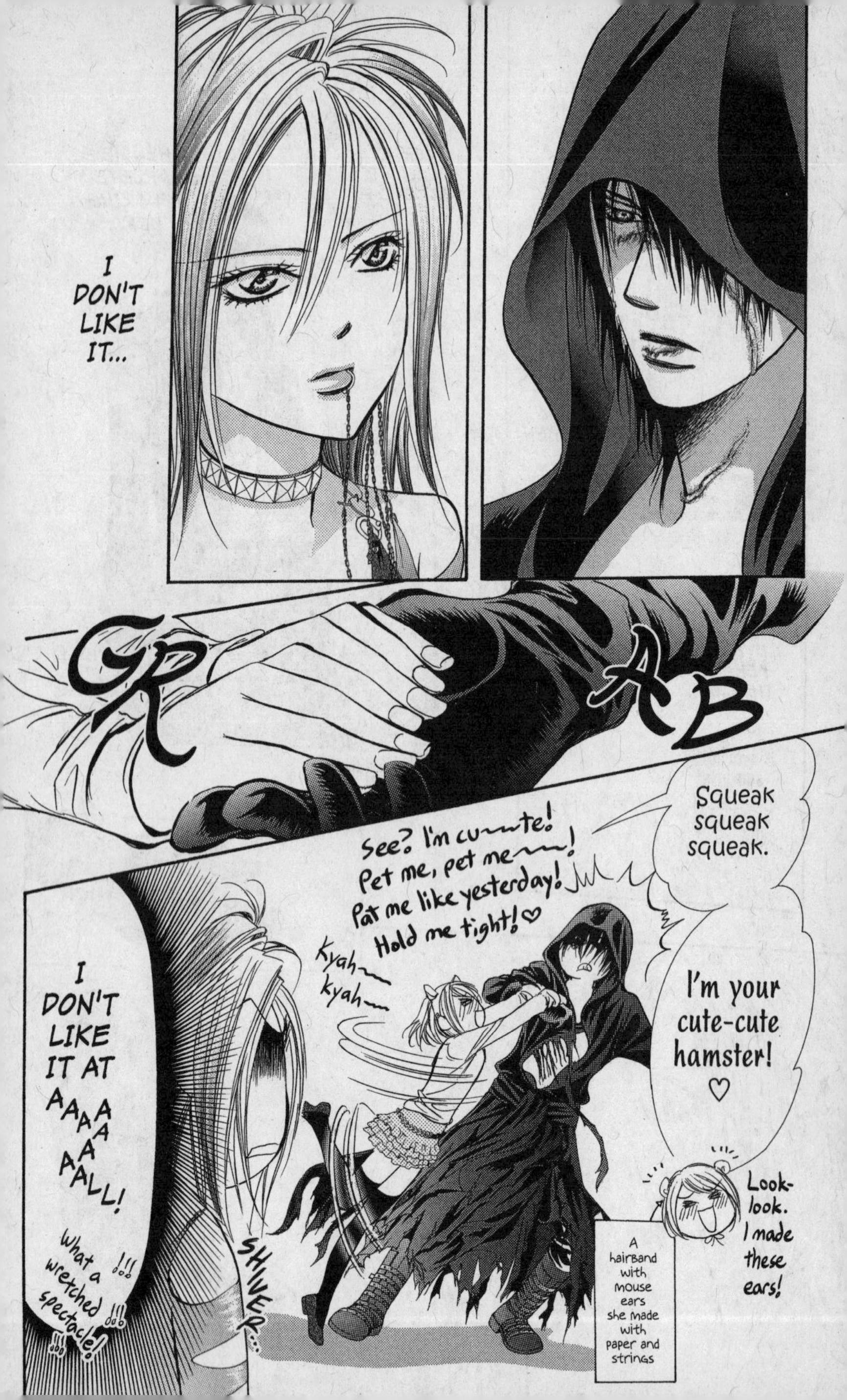
I DON'T LIKE IT...
GRAB
Squeak squeak squeak.
See? I'm cu~te! Pet me, pet me~! Pat me like yesterday! Hold me tight! ♡
I'm your cute-cute hamster! ♡
Kyah~ kyah~
Look-look. I made these ears!
A hairband with mouse ears she made with paper and strings
SHIVER...
I DON'T LIKE IT AT AAAAAALL!
What a wretched spectacle!!!

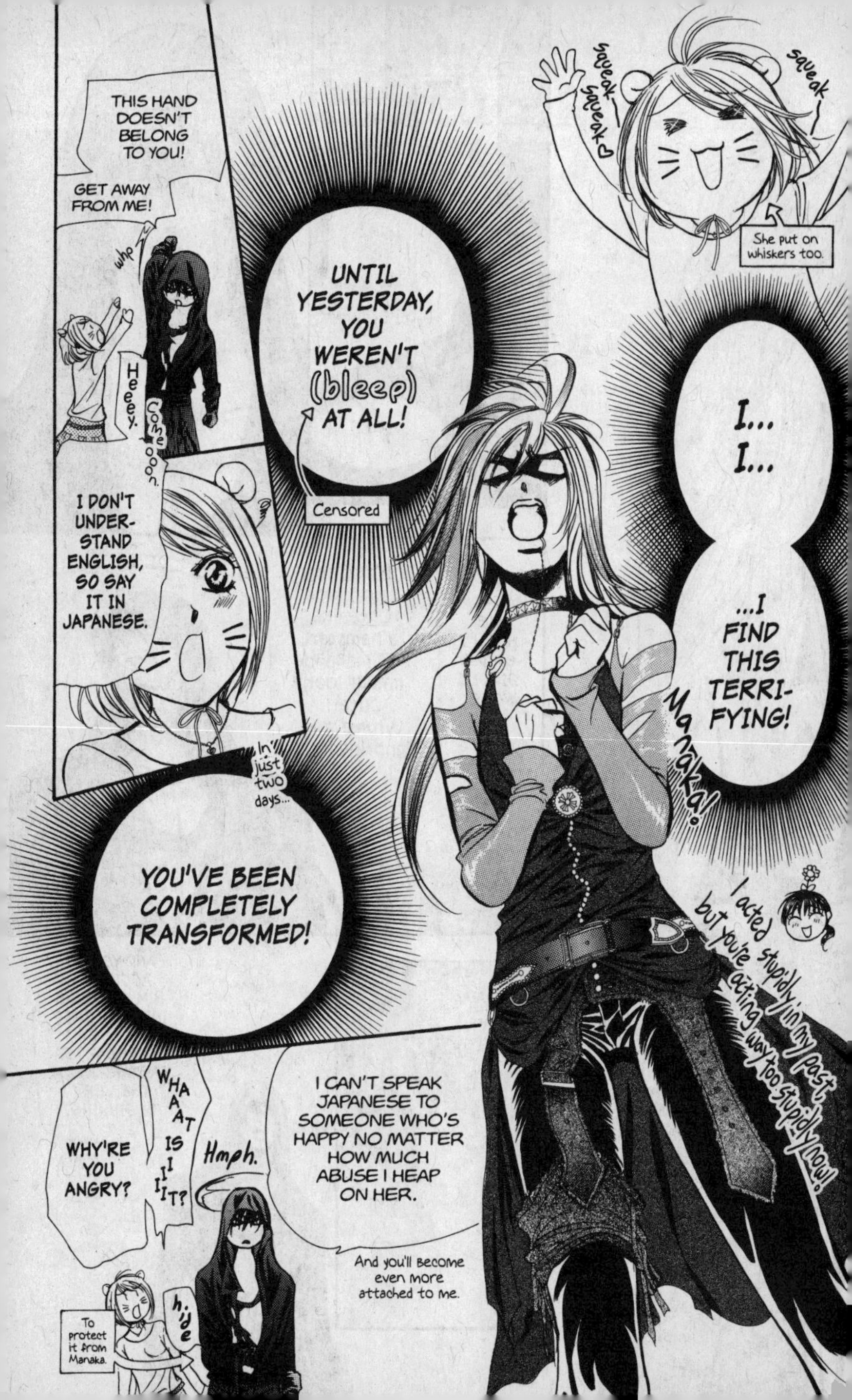
squeak squeak squeak♡
squeak
She put on whiskers too.
I... I...
...I FIND THIS TERRIFYING!
Manaka!
I acted stupidly in my past, but you're acting way too stupidly now!
UNTIL YESTERDAY, YOU WEREN'T (bleep) AT ALL!
Censored
THIS HAND DOESN'T BELONG TO YOU!
GET AWAY FROM ME!
whp
Heeey.
Come ooon.
I DON'T UNDER-STAND ENGLISH, SO SAY IT IN JAPANESE.
In just two days...
YOU'VE BEEN COMPLETELY TRANSFORMED!
I CAN'T SPEAK JAPANESE TO SOMEONE WHO'S HAPPY NO MATTER HOW MUCH ABUSE I HEAP ON HER.
And you'll become even more attached to me.
Hmph.
WHAAAT IS IIIT?
WHY'RE YOU ANGRY?
hide
To protect it from Manaka.

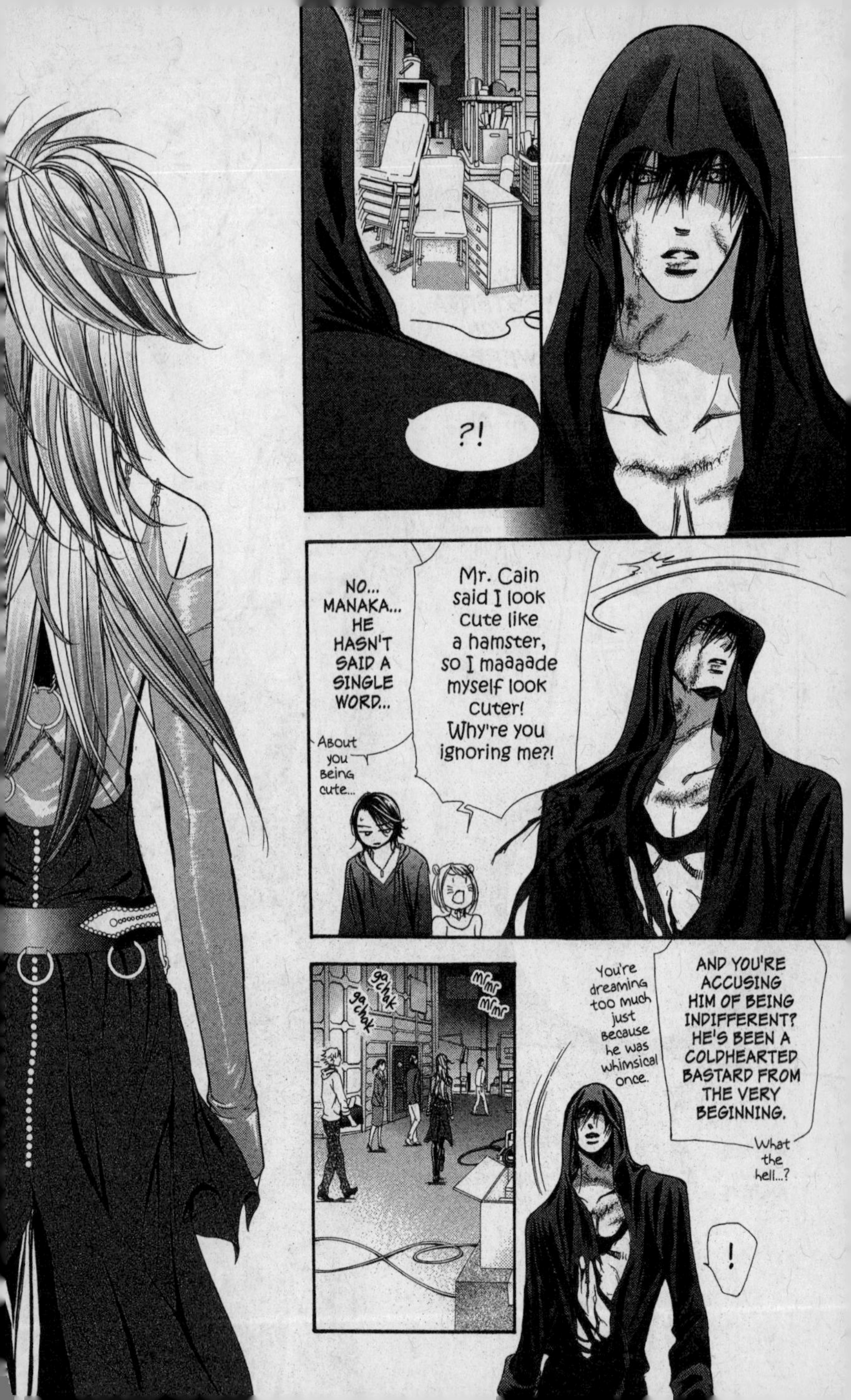
?!
Mr. Cain said I look cute like a hamster, so I maaaade myself look cuter! Why're you ignoring me?!
NO... MANAKA... HE HASN'T SAID A SINGLE WORD...
About you being cute...
AND YOU'RE ACCUSING HIM OF BEING INDIFFERENT? HE'S BEEN A COLDHEARTED BASTARD FROM THE VERY BEGINNING.
You're dreaming too much just because he was whimsical once.
What the hell...?
!
mrmr mrmr
gachak gachak

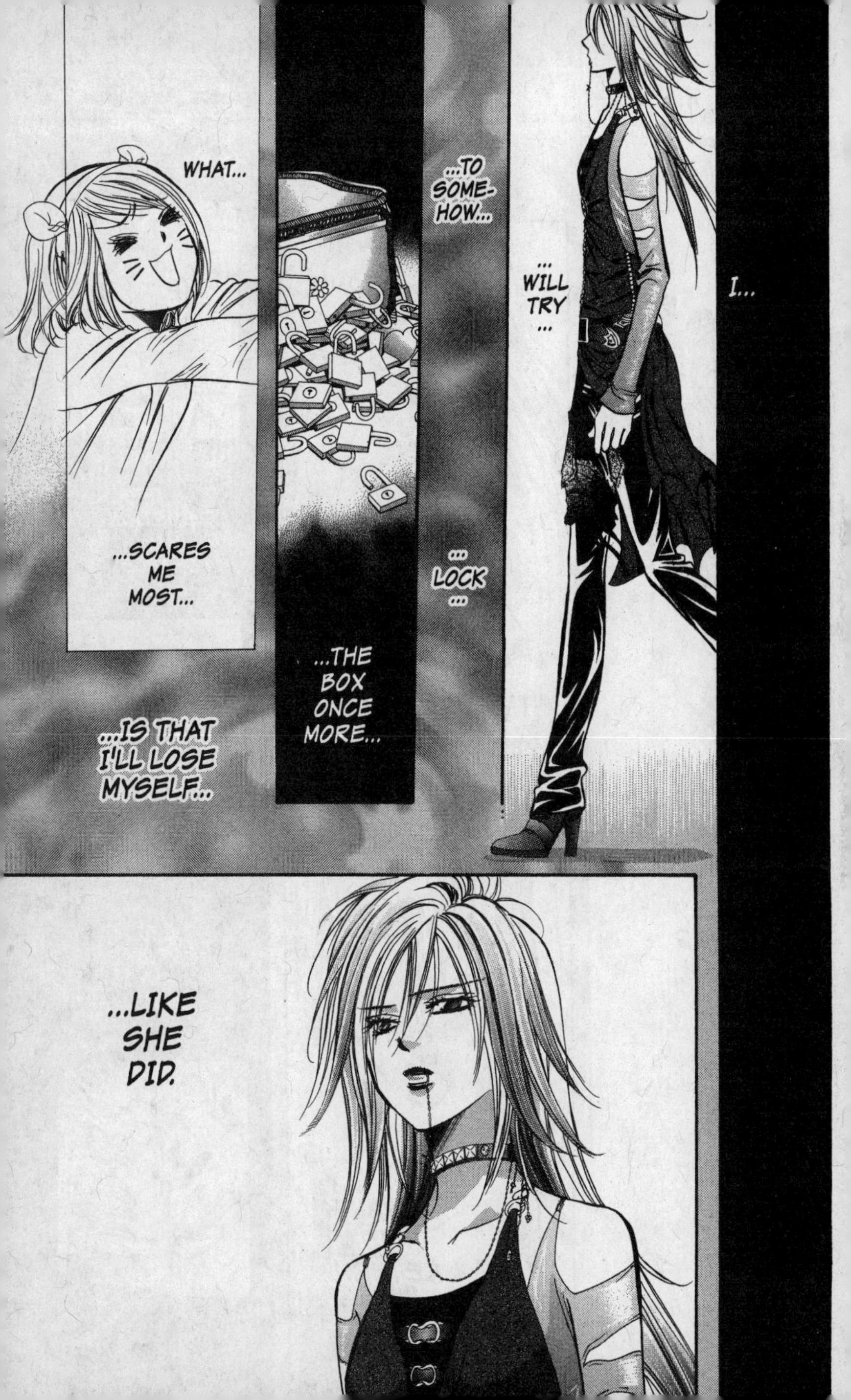
I...
...WILL TRY...
...TO SOMEHOW...
...LOCK...
...THE BOX ONCE MORE...
WHAT...
...SCARES ME MOST...
...IS THAT I'LL LOSE MYSELF...
...LIKE SHE DID.

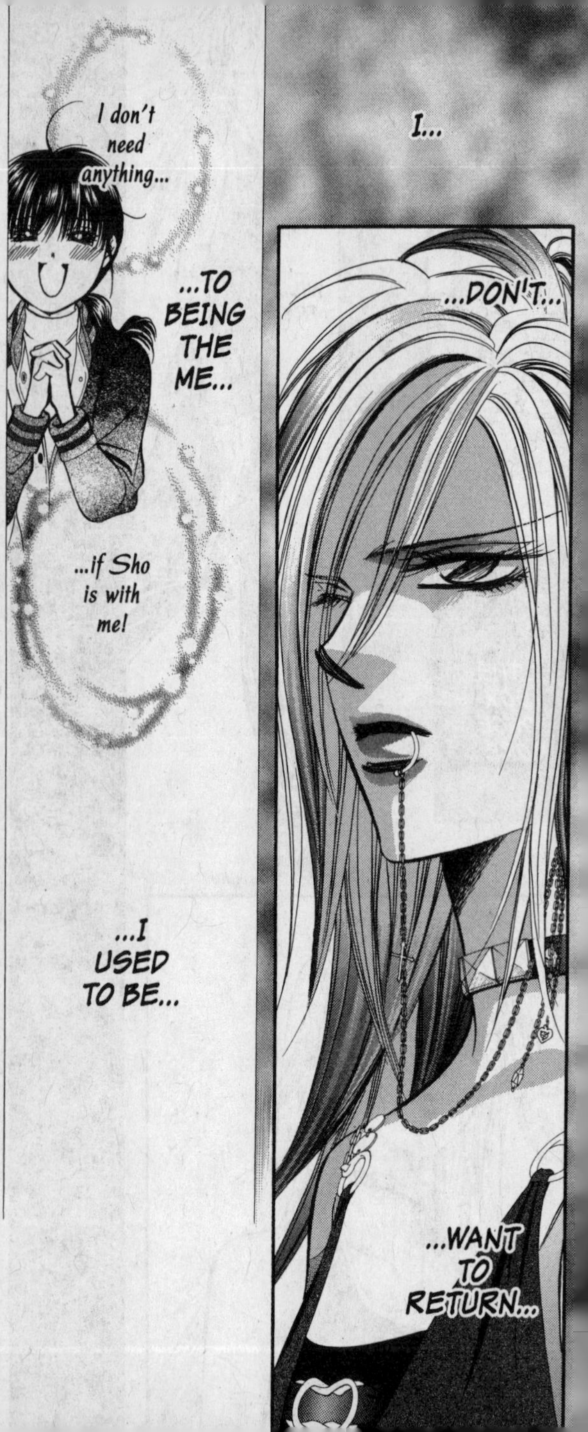
I...
...DON'T...
...WANT TO RETURN...
I don't need anything...
...TO BEING THE ME...
...if Sho is with me!
...I USED TO BE...

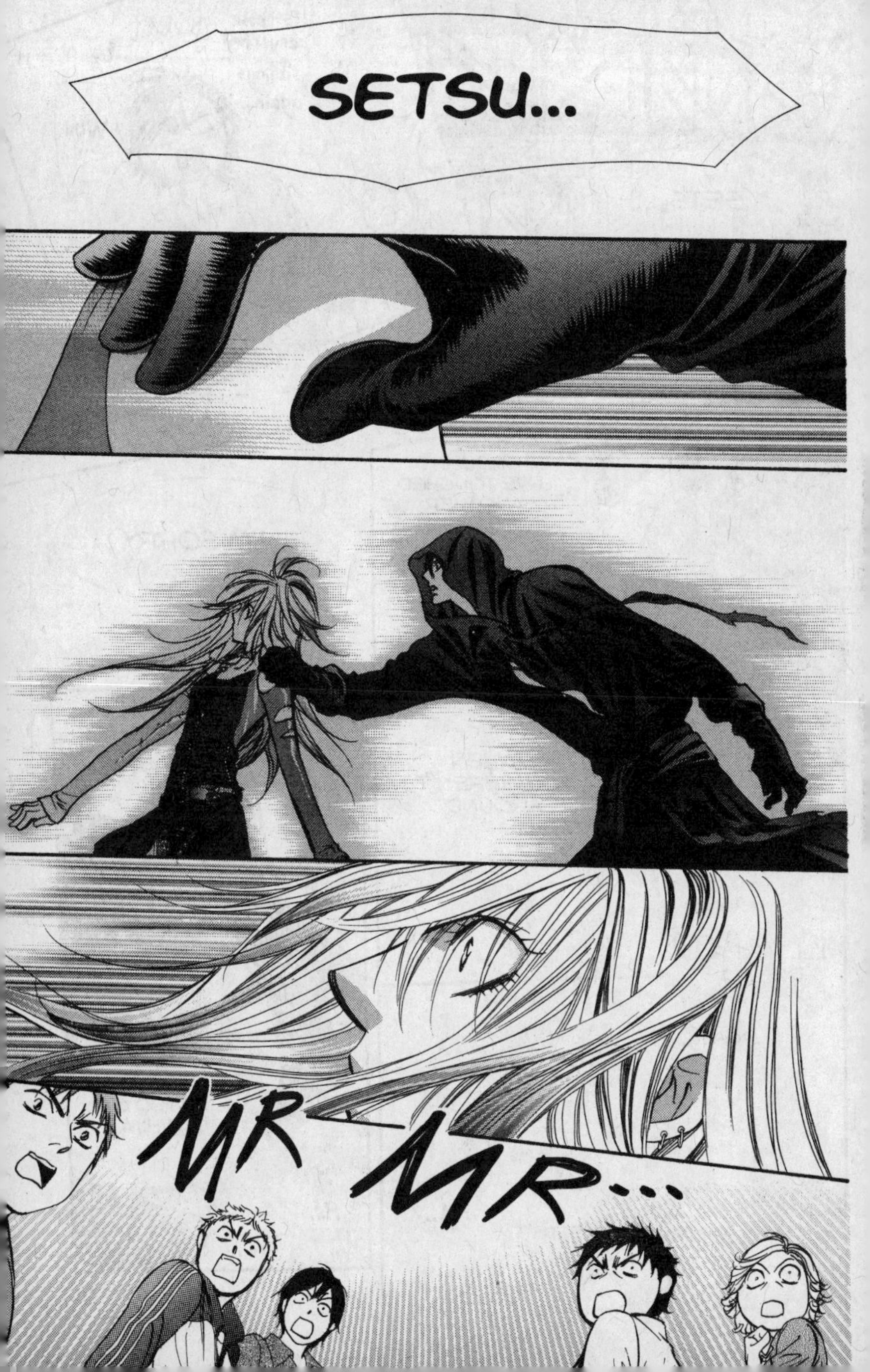
SETSU...
MR MR...

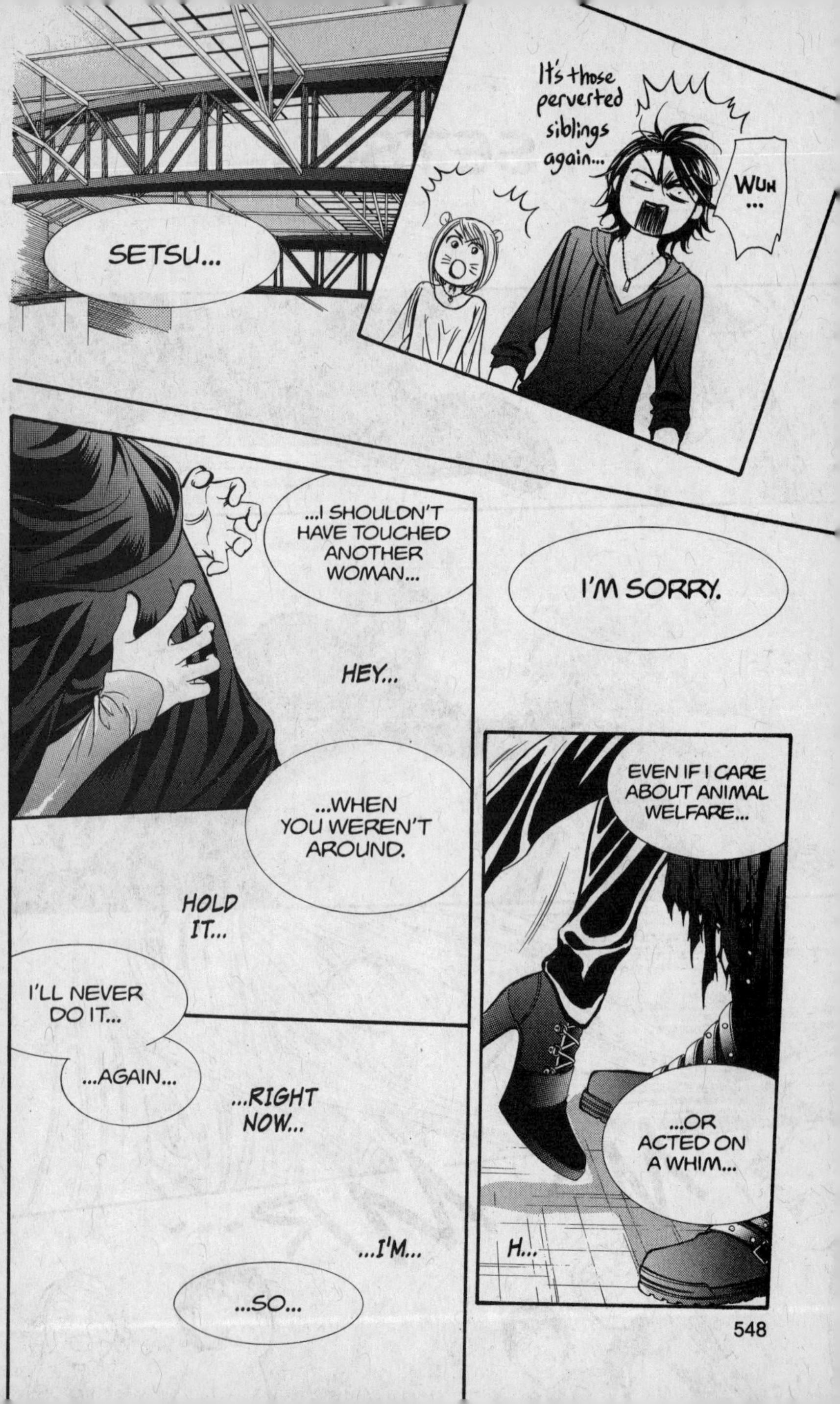

It's those perverted siblings again...
WUH...
SETSU...
I'M SORRY.
...I SHOULDN'T HAVE TOUCHED ANOTHER WOMAN...
HEY...
...WHEN YOU WEREN'T AROUND.
EVEN IF I CARE ABOUT ANIMAL WELFARE...
...OR ACTED ON A WHIM...
H...
HOLD IT...
I'LL NEVER DO IT...
...AGAIN...
...RIGHT NOW...
...I'M...
...SO...

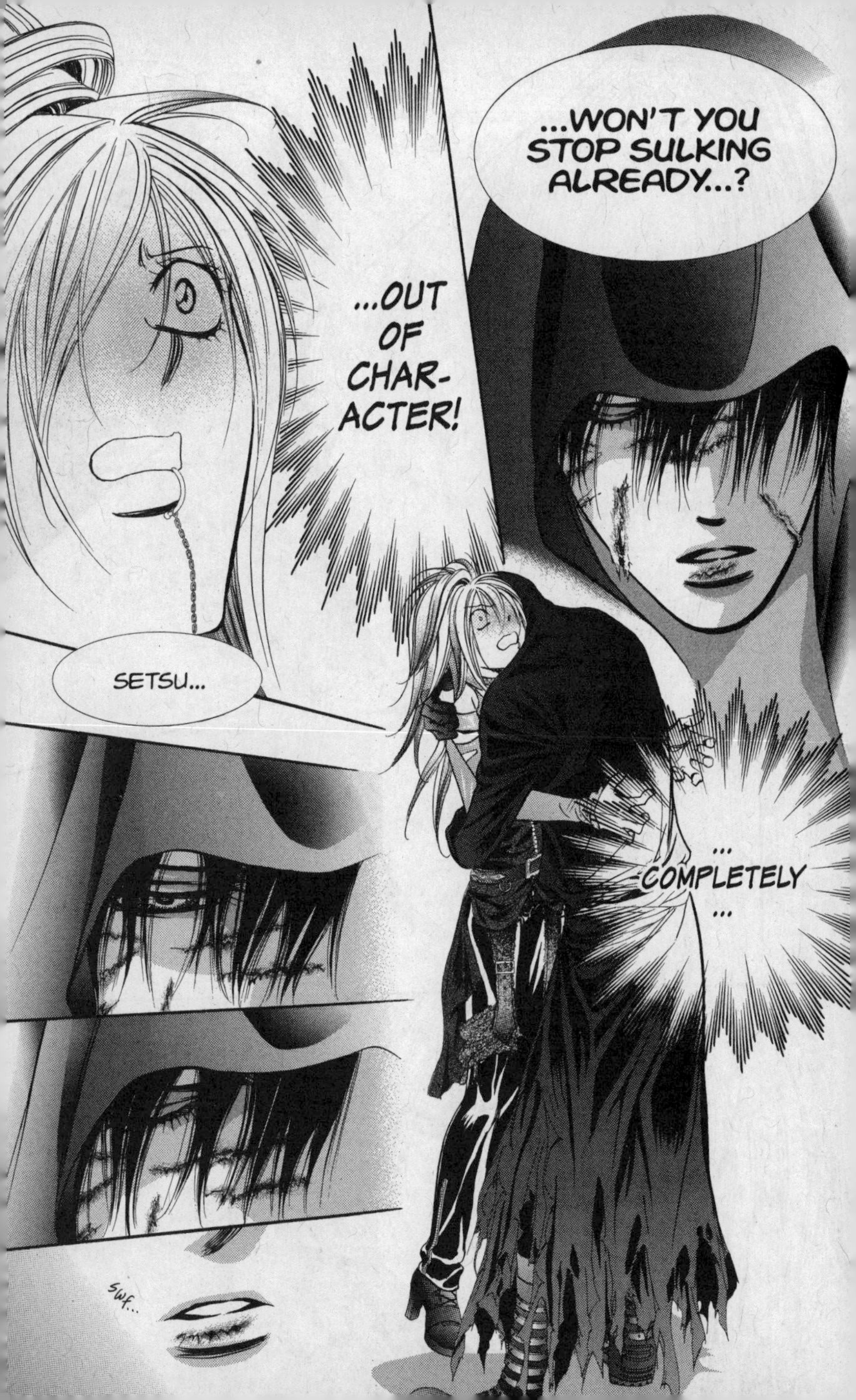
...WON'T YOU STOP SULKING ALREADY...?
...OUT OF CHAR-ACTER!
SETSU...
...COMPLETELY...
SWF...

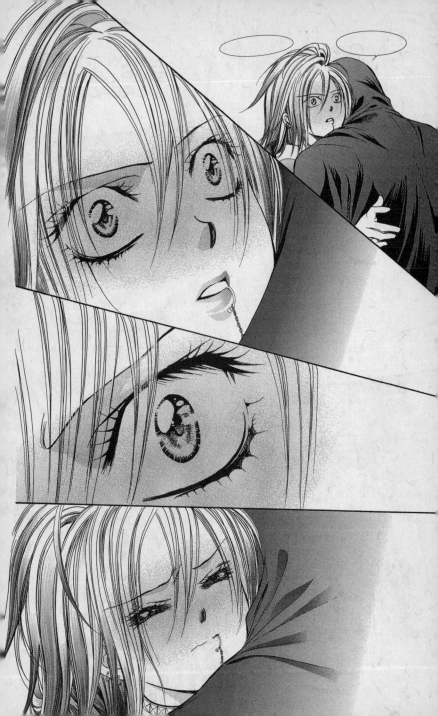

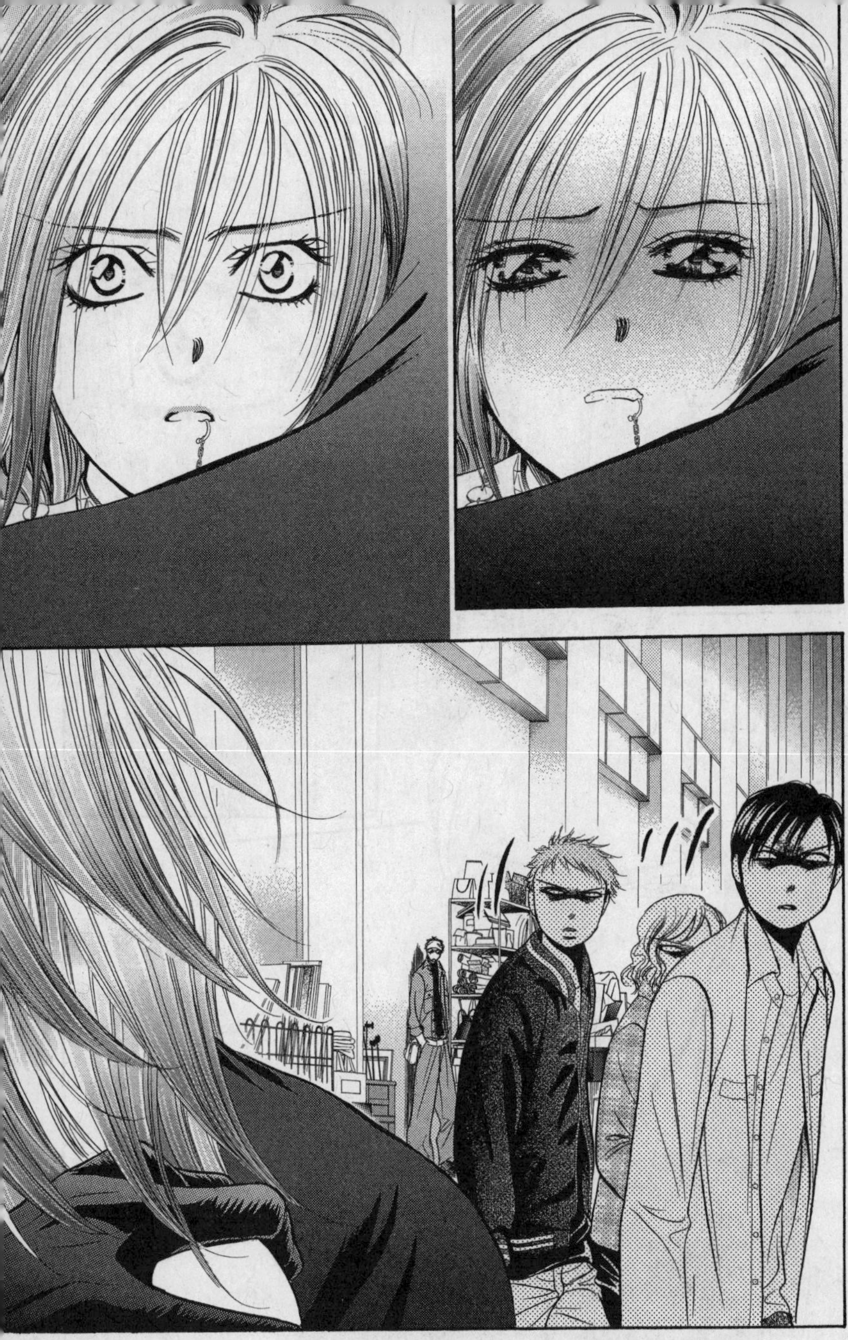

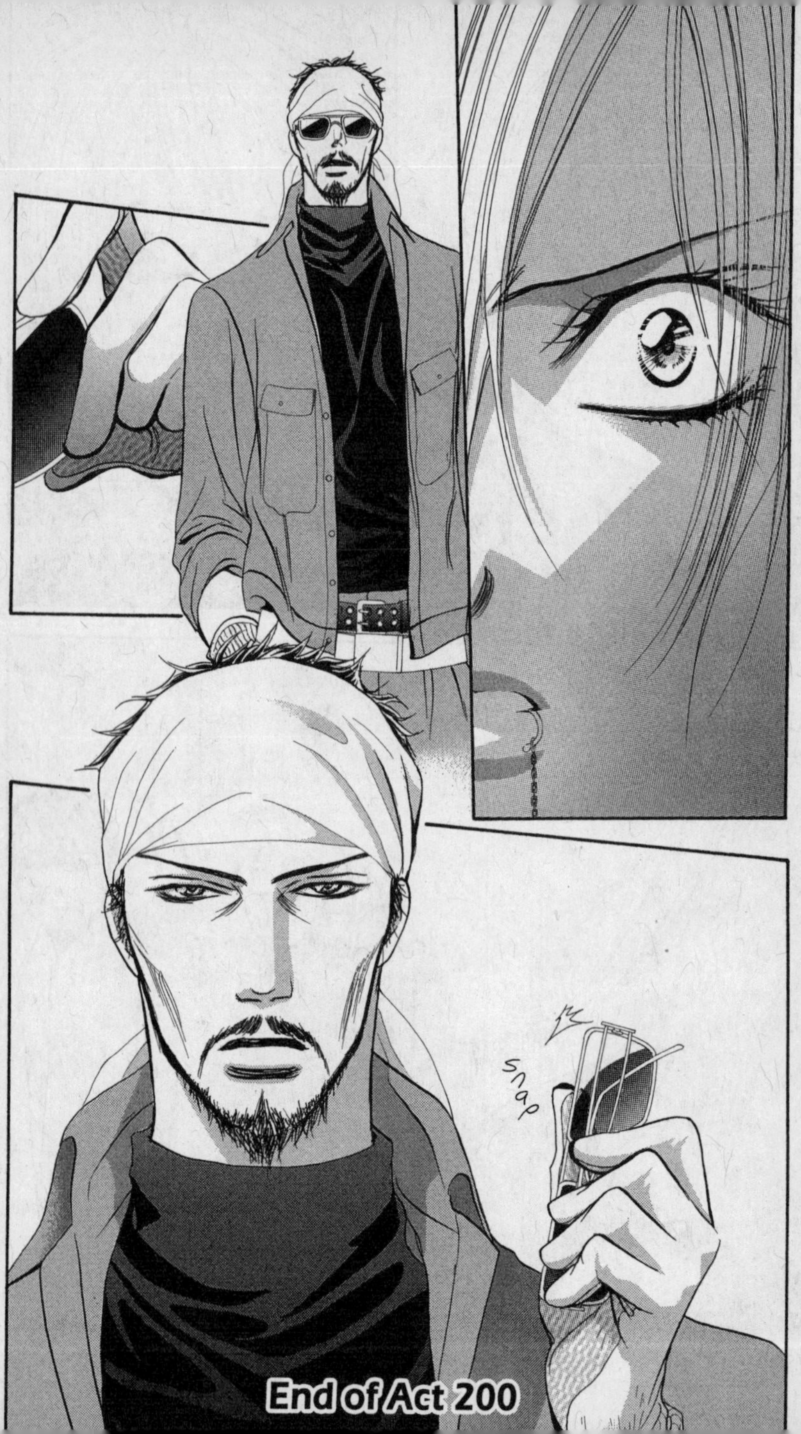
snap
End of Act 200

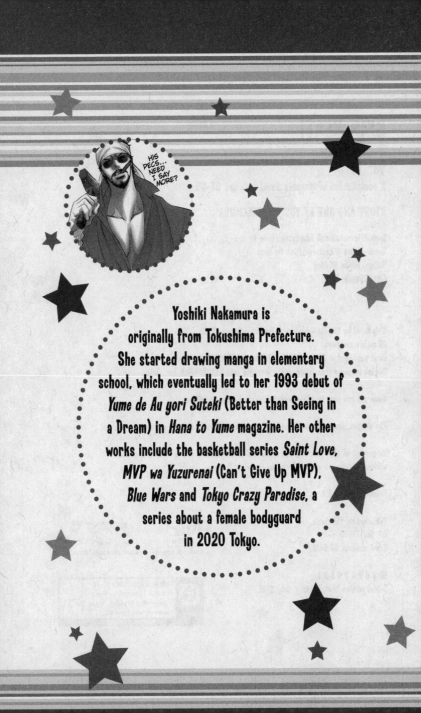

HIS PECS... NEED I SAY MORE?

Yoshiki Nakamura is originally from Tokushima Prefecture. She started drawing manga in elementary school, which eventually led to her 1993 debut of *Yume de Au yori Suteki* (Better than Seeing in a Dream) in *Hana to Yume* magazine. Her other works include the basketball series *Saint Love*, *MVP wa Yuzurenai* (Can't Give Up MVP), *Blue Wars* and *Tokyo Crazy Paradise*, a series about a female bodyguard in 2020 Tokyo.

SKIP-BEAT!

3-in-1 Edition

Vol. 11

A compilation of graphic novel volumes 31-33

STORY AND ART BY YOSHIKI NAKAMURA

English Translation & Adaptation/Tomo Kimura
Touch-up Art & Lettering/Sabrina Heep
Design/Yukiko Whitley
Editor/Pancha Diaz

First published in Japan in 2012, 2013 by HAKUSENSHA, Inc., Tokyo.
English language translation rights arranged with HAKUSENSHA, Inc., Tokyo.

Printed in the U.S.A.

Published by VIZ Media, LLC
P.O. Box 77010
San Francisco, CA 94107

www.viz.com
www.shojobeat.com

10 9 8 7 6 5 4 3 2 1
3-in-1 edition first printing, July 2015

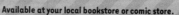
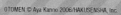

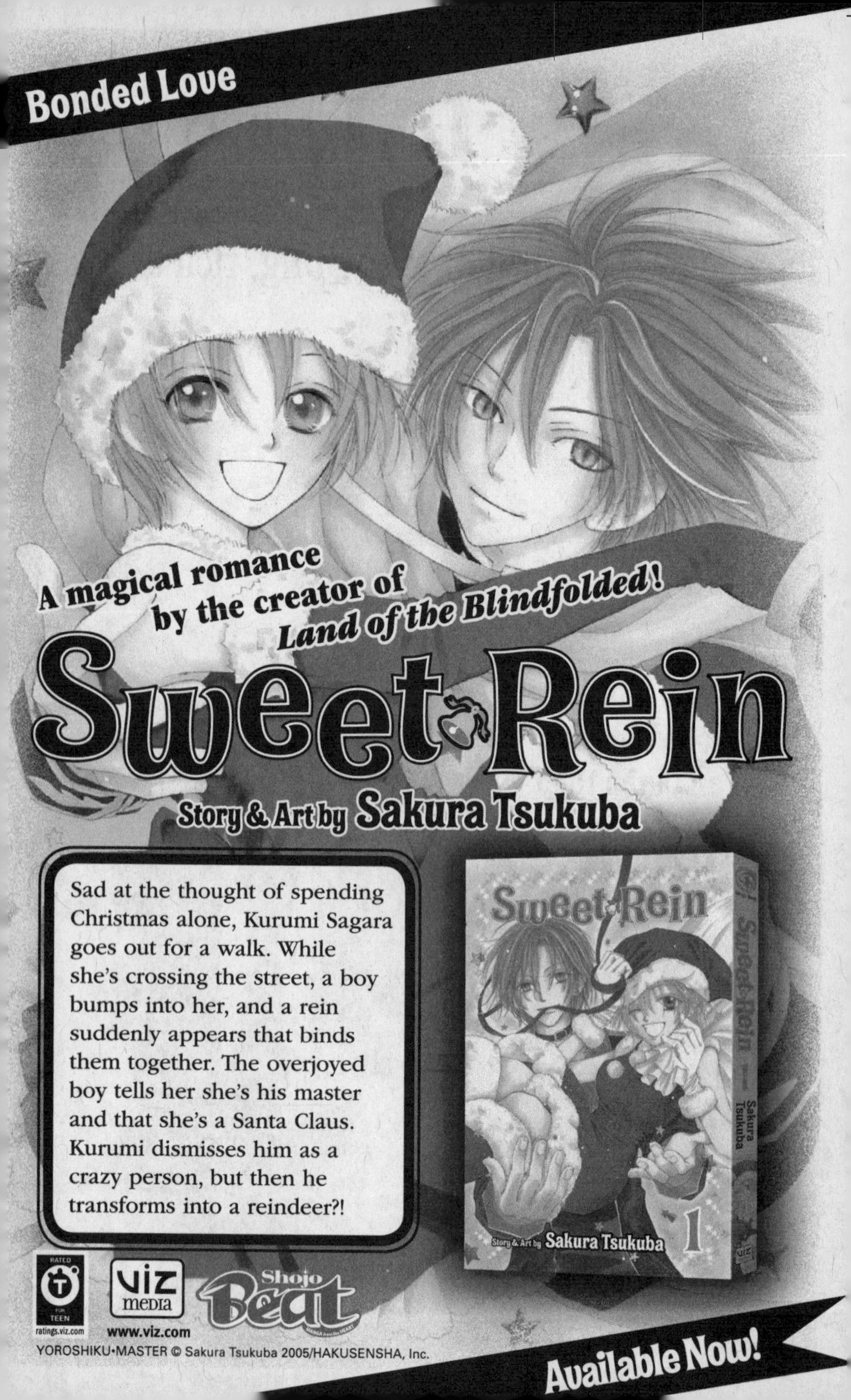
Bonded Love
A magical romance by the creator of Land of the Blindfolded!
Sweet Rein
Story & Art by Sakura Tsukuba
Sad at the thought of spending Christmas alone, Kurumi Sagara goes out for a walk. While she's crossing the street, a boy bumps into her, and a rein suddenly appears that binds them together. The overjoyed boy tells her she's his master and that she's a Santa Claus. Kurumi dismisses him as a crazy person, but then he transforms into a reindeer?!
Sweet Rein
Story & Art by Sakura Tsukuba
1
Sweet Rein 1 Sakura Tsukuba
RATED T FOR TEEN
ratings.viz.com
viz media
Shojo Beat
www.viz.com
YOROSHIKU•MASTER © Sakura Tsukuba 2005/HAKUSENSHA, Inc.
Available Now!

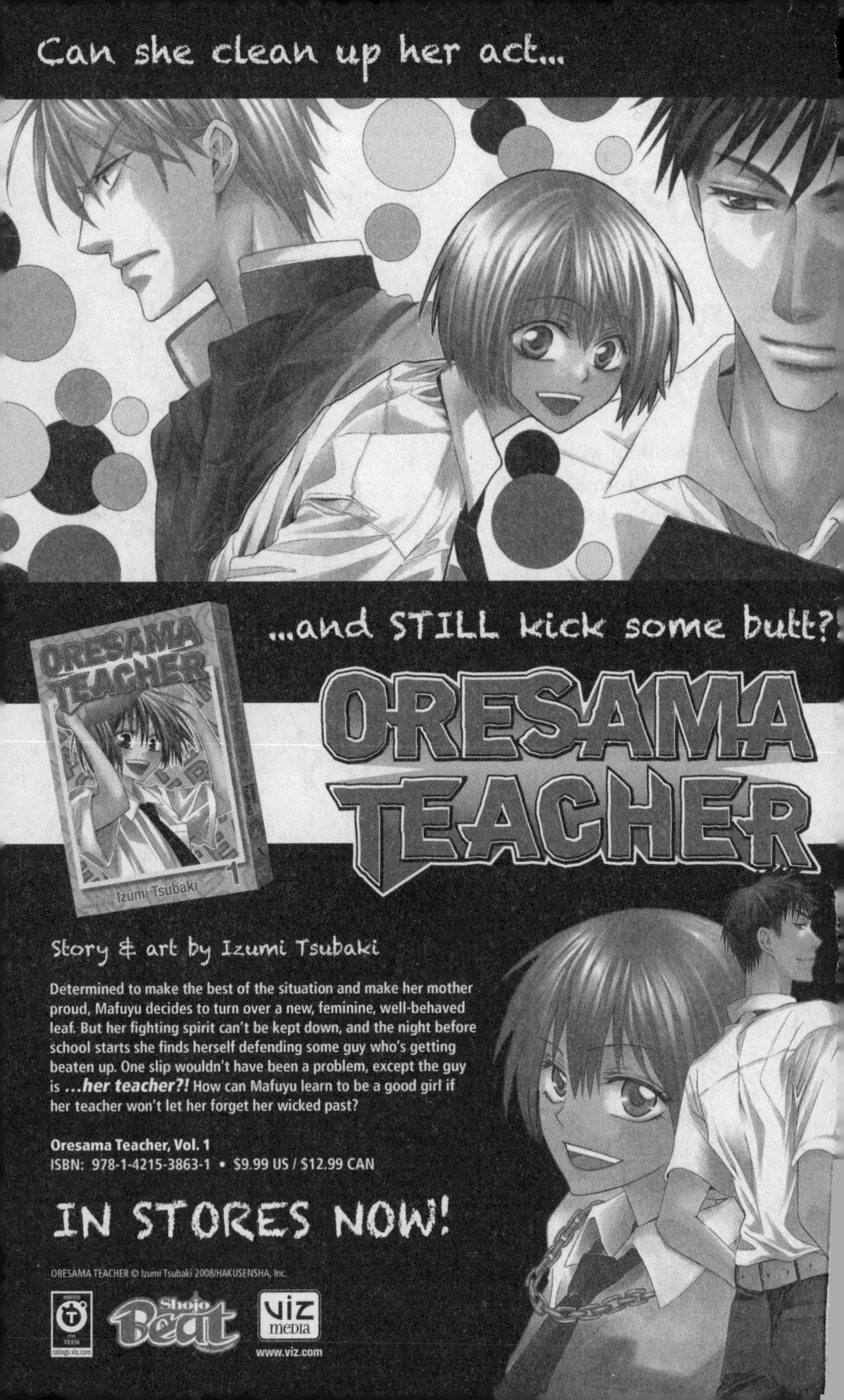

Can she clean up her act...
...and STILL kick some butt?
ORESAMA TEACHER
ORESAMA TEACHER
Izumi Tsubaki
1
Story & art by Izumi Tsubaki
Determined to make the best of the situation and make her mother proud, Mafuyu decides to turn over a new, feminine, well-behaved leaf. But her fighting spirit can't be kept down, and the night before school starts she finds herself defending some guy who's getting beaten up. One slip wouldn't have been a problem, except the guy is ...her teacher?! How can Mafuyu learn to be a good girl if her teacher won't let her forget her wicked past?
Oresama Teacher, Vol. 1
ISBN: 978-1-4215-3863-1 • $9.99 US / $12.99 CAN
IN STORES NOW!
ORESAMA TEACHER © Izumi Tsubaki 2008/HAKUSENSHA, Inc.
RATED T FOR TEEN
ratings.viz.com
Shojo Beat
VIZ media
www.viz.com

SURPRISE!

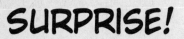

You may be reading the wrong way!

It's true: In keeping with the original Japanese comic format, this book reads from right to left—so action, sound effects, and word balloons are completely reversed. This preserves the orientation of the original artwork—plus, it's fun! Check out the diagram shown here to get the hang of things, and then turn to the other side of the book to get started!

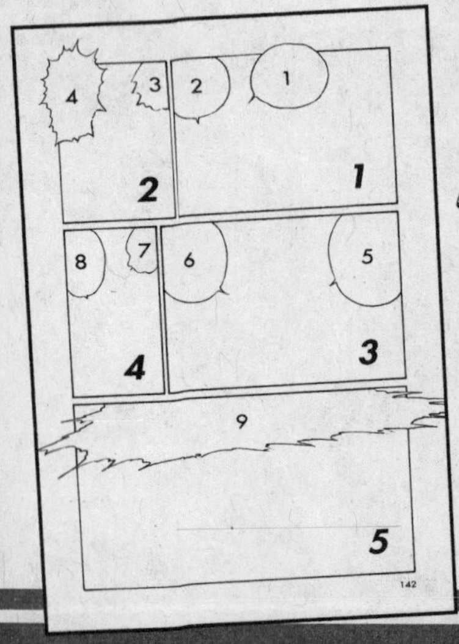
1
2
3
4
1
5
6
7
8
2
3
4
9
5
142

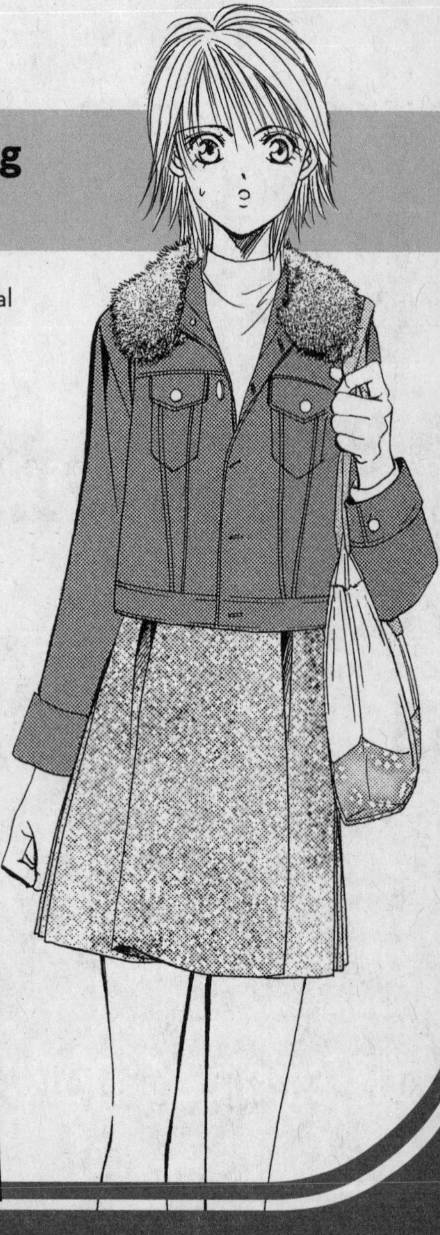